CONCISE EDITION

American HORIZONS

U.S. HISTORY IN A GLOBAL CONTEXT

Volume II | Since 1865

Michael Schaller
University of Arizona

Robert D. Schulzinger
University of Colorado, Boulder

John Bezís-Selfa
Wheaton College

Janette Thomas Greenwood
Clark University

Andrew Kirk
University of Nevada, Las Vegas

Sarah J. Purcell
Grinnell College

Aaron Sheehan-Dean
West Virginia University

New York Oxford
OXFORD UNIVERSITY PRESS

To all of our students.

The individual authors would also like to dedicate this book to the following people.

Michael Schaller: *to GS, N, G & D*

Robert D. Schulzinger: *to MES & EAS*

John Bezís-Selfa: *to PCZ & JBS*

Janette Thomas Greenwood: *to M, E & S*

Andrew Kirk: *to L, H & Q*

Sarah J. Purcell: *to H, E & M*

Aaron Sheehan-Dean: *to M, L & A*

Oxford University Press, Inc., publishes works that further Oxford University's objective of excellence in research, scholarship, and education.

Oxford New York
Auckland Cape Town Dar es Salaam Hong Kong Karachi
Kuala Lumpur Madrid Melbourne Mexico City Nairobi
New Delhi Shanghai Taipei Toronto

With offices in
Argentina Austria Brazil Chile Czech Republic France Greece
Guatemala Hungary Italy Japan Poland Portugal Singapore
South Korea Switzerland Thailand Turkey Ukraine Vietnam

For titles covered by Section 112 of the US Higher Education Opportunity Act, please visit www.oup.com/us/he for the latest information about pricing and alternate formats.

Published by Oxford University Press, Inc.
198 Madison Avenue, New York, New York 10016
http://www.oup.com

Oxford is a registered trademark of Oxford University Press

Library of Congress Cataloging-in-Publication Data

American horizons : U.S. history in a global context / Michael Schaller . . . [et al.].
    p. cm.
    Includes index.
    ISBN 978-0-19-973991-2 (volume 2: alk. paper)   1. United States—History.   I. Schaller,
Michael, 1947-
    E178.A5527 2013
    973—dc23

                                    2011049693

Printing number: 9 8 7 6 5 4 3 2

Printed in the United States of America
on acid-free paper

Brief Contents

Maps   *xvi*

Preface   *xviii*

About the Authors   *xxxv*

CHAPTER 15   Reconstructing America, 1865–1877   *562*

CHAPTER 16   Forging a Transcontinental Nation, 1877–1900   *600*

CHAPTER 17   A New Industrial and Labor Order, 1877–1900   *640*

CHAPTER 18   Cities, Immigrants, Culture, and Politics, 1877–1900   *680*

CHAPTER 19   The United States Expands Its Reach, 1892–1912   *722*

CHAPTER 20   An Age of Progressive Reform, 1890–1920   *758*

CHAPTER 21   America and the Great War, 1914–1920   *798*

CHAPTER 22   A New Era, 1920–1930   *840*

CHAPTER 23   A New Deal for Americans, 1931–1939   *878*

CHAPTER 24   Arsenal of Democracy: The World at War, 1931–1945   *920*

CHAPTER 25   Prosperity and Liberty Under the Shadow of the Bomb, 1945–1952   *966*

CHAPTER 26   The Dynamic 1950s   *1004*

CHAPTER 27   The Optimism and the Anguish of the 1960s   *1050*

CHAPTER 28   The Vietnam Era, 1961–1975   *1088*

CHAPTER 29   Conservatism Resurgent, 1974–1989   *1126*

CHAPTER 30   After the Cold War, 1988–2000   *1168*

CHAPTER 31   21st-Century Dangers and Promises, 2000–Present   *1208*

APPENDIX A: Historical Documents   *A-1*

APPENDIX B: Historical Facts and Data   *B-1*

Glossary   *G-1*

Credits   *C-1*

Index   *I-1*

Contents

Maps · xvi

Preface · xviii

Supplements · xxvi

Acknowledgements · xxxi

About the Authors · xxxv

CHAPTER **15**

Reconstructing America, 1865–1877 · 562

The Year of Jubilee, 1865 · 566

African American Families · 567

Southern Whites and the Problem of Defeat · 569

Emancipation in Comparative Perspective · 571

Shaping Reconstruction, 1865–1868 · 572

Andrew Johnson's Reconstruction · 572

The Fight over Reconstruction · 574

The Civil War Amendments and American Citizenship · 575

Congressional Reconstruction · 577

Reconstruction in the South, 1866–1876 · 580

African American Life in the Postwar South · 580

Republican Governments in the Postwar South · 583

Global Passages: Reconstruction Abroad · 584

Cotton, Merchants, and the Lien · 586

The End of Reconstruction, 1877 · 588

The Ku Klux Klan and Reconstruction Violence · 589

Northern Weariness and Northern Conservatism · 591

Legacies of Reconstruction · 594

CHAPTER **16**

Forging a Transcontinental Nation, 1877–1900 · 600

Meeting Ground of Many Peoples · 604

Changing Patterns of Migration · 604

Mexican Borders · 607

Chinese Exclusion · 609

Mapping the West · 611
The Federal Frontier · 612
Myth and History · 612
Promotion and Memory · 613
The Culture of Collective Violence · 614

Extractive Economies and Global Commodities · 616
Mining and Labor · 617
Business Travelers · 618
Railroads, Time, and Space · 619
Industrial Ranching · 621
Corporate Cowboys · 622

Clearing the Land and Cleansing the Wilderness · 623
Indian Conflict and Resistance · 625
Education for Assimilation · 625
The Destruction of the Buffalo · 628
The Dawes Act and Survival · 630
Tourism, Parks, and Forests · 631
Global Passages: Settler Societies and Indigenous Peoples · 632

CHAPTER 17
A New Industrial and Labor Order, 1877–1900 · 640

Global Webs of Industrial Capitalism · 644
The New Industrial Order · 645
U.S. Industrial Growth in Global Context · 647
Combinations and Concentrations of Wealth · 649
Markets and Consumerism · 651
Global Passage: Titled Americans · 652

Work and the Workplace · 655
Global Migrations · 655
Blue Collar and White Collar Workers · 656
Regimentation and Scientific Management · 658
Working Conditions and Wages · 659
Economic Convulsions and Hard Times · 660
Women and Children in the Workplace · 661

Workers Fight Back · 662
The Great Railroad Strike of 1877 · 663
Organizing Strategies and Labor Violence · 664
The Farmers Organize · 668
The Labor Movement in Global Context · 670

The New Industrial Order: Defense and Dissent • 671
  Defending the New Order • 671
  Critiquing the New Order • 673

CHAPTER **18**

Cities, Immigrants, Culture, and Politics, 1877–1900 • **680**

Urbanization • **684**
  The Growth of Cities • 685
  The Peopling of American Cities • 685
  Types of Cities • 687
  Cities Transformed and "Sorted Out" • 688

Global Migrations • **689**
  A Worldwide Migration • 690
  "America Fever" and the "New" Immigration • 692
  The "Immigrant Problem" • 693
  The Round-Trip to America • 694

Streets Paved with Gold? • **695**
  Global Passage: Immigrants Who Returned • **696**
  Surviving in "The Land of Bosses and Clocks" • 696
  Creating Community • 698
  Becoming American • 701

The Promise and Peril of City Life • **702**
  A World of Opportunity • 702
  A World of Crises • 705

Tackling Urban Problems • **707**
  City Missions and Charity Organizations • 708
  The Settlement House Movement • 709
  Creating Healthy Urban Environments • 710

Challenges to the Politics of Stalemate • **711**
  Key Issues • 712
  Ethnicity, Gender, and Political Culture • 713
  The Populist Challenge • 714
  The Election of 1896 • 716

CHAPTER **19**

The United States Expands Its Reach, 1892–1912 • **722**

The New Imperialism • **726**
  A Global Grab for Colonies • 728

Race, Empire, Bibles, and Businessmen • *728*
Precedent for American Empire • *730*
The Crises of the 1890s • *730*

The United States Flexes Its Muscles • 732
Latin America • *732*
Hawaii • *733*
The Cuban Crisis • *734*
"A Splendid Little War" • *736*

The Complications of Empire • 738
Cuba and Puerto Rico • *739*
The Philippines • *740*
The Debate Over Empire • *740*
The American-Philippine War • *742*
Global Passages: African Americans and International Affairs, 1898–1912 • **744**
China • *745*

The United States on the World Stage: Roosevelt and Taft • 747
Roosevelt's "Big Stick" • *747*
Taft's Dollar Diplomacy • *750*

CHAPTER 20
An Age of Progressive Reform, 1890–1920 • 758

Progressivism as a Global Movement • 762
Principles of Progressivism • *763*
The Global Exchange of Progressive Ideas • *763*

Urban Reform • 764
The "Good Government" Movement • *765*
The Housing Dilemma • *766*
Municipal Housekeeping • *766*
Segregation and the Racial Limits of Reform • *768*

Progressivism at the State and National Levels • 773
Electoral Reforms • *774*
Mediating the Labor Problem • *776*
Regulating Business: Trust Busting and Consumer Protection • *780*
Conservation vs. Preservation of Nature • *784*

Progressivism and World War I • 786
A Progressive War? • *786*
Uniting and Disuniting the Nation • *787*

Votes for Women • 788

Progressivism in International Context • 789

Global Passage: The International Women's Peace Movement • 790

CHAPTER 21

America and the Great War, 1914–1920 • 798

The Shock of War • 803

The Origins of Global Conflict • 803

A War of Attrition • 805

America's Response to War • 809

The U.S. Path to War, 1914–1917 • 811

Conflicting Visions of National Security • 811

U.S. Mediation, the Election of 1916, and Challenges to Neutrality • 812

Intervention in Latin America • 813

Decision for War • 815

America at War • 816

Mobilizing People and Ideas • 816

Controlling Dissent • 818

Mobilizing the Economy • 819

Women and African Americans in Wartime • 820

Over There • 822

Building an Army • 822

Joining the Fight • 823

Political and Military Complications • 824

Influenza Pandemic • 826

Making Peace Abroad and at Home • 827

Making Peace and Fighting Communism • 828

Global Passages: The Anticolonial Struggle in Paris • 830

Red Scare • 832

The Fight for the Treaty • 834

CHAPTER 22

A New Era, 1920–1930 • 840

A New Economy for a New Era • 845

Wireless America • 845

Car Culture • 847

Advertising for Mass Consumption • 849

Ethnic and Racial Divides • 850

   Immigration Restriction • 851

   The Ku Klux Klan • 853

   African American Renaissance and Repression • 854

   Black International Movements • 856

A National Culture • 857

   Popular Entertainment: Movies, Sports, and Celebrity • 858

   The New Skepticism • 859

   The New Woman of the 1920s • 859

   Religion and Society • 861

   Global Passages: Aimee Semple McPherson • 862

   Prohibition • 864

Post-World War I Politics and Foreign Policy • 865

   Government and Business in the 1920s • 865

   Coolidge Prosperity • 866

   The Election of 1928 • 867

   Independent Internationalism in the 1920s • 868

   The United States and Instability in the Western Hemisphere • 869

The Crash • 871

   The End of the Boom • 871

   The Great Depression • 872

CHAPTER 23

A New Deal for Americans, 1931–1939 • 878

The New Deal • 882

   Spiral of Decline, 1931–1933 • 882

   From Prosperity to Global Depression • 883

   Suffering in the Land • 884

   The Failure of the Old Deal • 885

   The Coming of the New Deal • 885

Reconstructing Capitalism • 888

   The Hundred Days • 889

   Voices of Protest • 893

The Second New Deal • 895

   Social Security • 898

   Labor Activism • 899

   The 1936 Election • 899

   Global Passages: Economic Intervention • 900

Society, Law, and Culture in the 1930s • 904
Popular Entertainment • 904
Women and the New Deal • 906
European Ethnics and the New Deal • 907
A New Deal for Blacks • 908
Hispanics and the New Deal • 909
The Indian New Deal • 909
Nature's New Deal • 910

The Twilight of Reform • 912
The New Deal and Judicial Change • 912
Recession • 913
Political Setbacks • 914

CHAPTER 24

Arsenal of Democracy: The World at War, 1931–1945 • 920

The Long Fuse • 925
Isolationist Impulse • 925
Disengagement from Europe • 926
Disengagement in Asia • 927
Appeasement • 928
America at the Brink of War, 1939–1941 • 929
Day of Infamy • 932

A Grand Alliance • 934
War in the Pacific • 935
The War in Europe • 939
The Holocaust • 940

Battle for Production • 942
War Economy • 942
A Government-Sponsored Industrial Revolution • 945
Mass-Produced Weapons • 945
Organized Labor and the War • 946
The Draft • 947
Global Passages: The Bretton Woods System, 1944–1971 • 948

On the Move: Wartime Mobility • 949
Wartime Women • 950
Mexican Migrants, Mexican Americans, and American Indians in Wartime • 950
African Americans in Wartime • 952
Japanese American Internment • 953

Wartime Politics and Postwar Issues • 955

Right Turn • 955

The 1944 Election and the Threshold of Victory • 956

Allied Mistrust and Postwar Planning • 957

CHAPTER 25

Prosperity and Liberty Under the Shadow of the Bomb, 1945–1952 • 966

The Cold War • 970

The Roots of Conflict • 971

Managing Postwar Europe in Potsdam • 971

The Defeat of Japan • 973

Dividing the Postwar Globe • 973

A Policy for Containment • 976

The Red Scare • 977

War in Korea • 978

Domestic Containment • 981

The Color of Difference Is Red • 982

Hollywood and the Pumpkin Papers • 982

A New Affluence • 983

The Fair Deal • 983

The GI Bill • 984

Working Women • 985

Postwar Migrations • 987

Military-Industrial West and South • 988

Hispanics Move North • 990

Mobile Leisure • 992

Laying the Foundations for Civil Rights • 993

First Steps • 993

Jack Roosevelt Robinson • 994

The Influence of African American Veterans • 995

Global Passages: Rebuilding the World • **996**

Black Migration and the Nationalization of Race • 998

CHAPTER 26

The Dynamic 1950s • 1004

The Eisenhower Era • 1008

The End of the Korean War • 1010

The New Look • 1010

The Rise of the Developing World · 1012
Hungary and the Suez, 1956 · 1014
France's Vietnam War · 1015
McCarthyism and the Red Scare · 1016

A Dynamic Decade · **1018**
The Baby Boom · 1019
Suburban Migrations—Urban Decline · 1020
Consumer Nation · 1024
Corporate Order and Industrial Labor · 1025

The Future is Now · **1026**
Auto Mania · 1027
Oil Culture · 1028
Television · 1028

Conformity and Rebellion · **1030**
Old Time Religion · 1032
Women in the 1950s · 1033
Organization Men · 1035
Teens, Rebels, and Beats · 1036

Laying the Foundation for Civil Rights · **1038**
Brown and the Legal Assault · 1039
Showdown in Little Rock · 1040
Boots on the Ground · 1040
MLK and the Philosophy of Nonviolence · 1041
**Global Passages: Cold War Media—The USIA and the Globalization of
American Culture** · **1042**

CHAPTER **27**

The Optimism and the Anguish of the 1960s · 1050

The New Frontier · **1055**
JFK's New Frontier · 1055
The Challenge of Racial Justice · 1056
Cold War Tensions · 1058
Kennedy Assassination · 1060

The Great Society · **1061**
Civil Rights Laws · 1061
Great Society Programs · 1063
The Supreme Court and Rights and Liberties · 1065
The United States and the World Beyond Vietnam · 1066

A Robust Economy • 1068

   Technological Change, Science, and Space Exploration • 1068

   The Rise of the Sunbelt • 1070

Race, Gender, Youth, and the Challenge to the Establishment • 1071

   Urban Uprisings and Black Power • 1072

   Latinos and Indians Struggle for Rights • 1075

   The New Feminism • 1077

   The New Environmentalism • 1079

   Youth and the Counterculture • 1079

   Global Passages: The British Rock Invasion of the 1960s • 1080

CHAPTER 28

The Vietnam Era, 1961–1975 • 1088

Background to a War, 1945–1963 • 1092

   Vietnam and the Cold War • 1093

   American Commitments to South Vietnam • 1095

   The 1963 Turning Point • 1096

An American War, 1964–1967 • 1097

   Decisions for Escalation, 1964–1965 • 1097

   Ground and Air War, 1966–1967 • 1100

   The War at Home • 1102

1968: Turmoil and Turning Points • 1104

   The Tet Offensive • 1104

   The Agony of 1968 • 1105

   Global Passages: The Growth of the Global Antiwar Movement • 1106

Nixon and the World • 1110

   From Vietnamization to Paris • 1111

   The End of the Vietnam War • 1112

   Reduction of Cold War Tensions • 1113

Domestic Policy and the Abuse of Power • 1116

   Curtailing the Great Society • 1116

   Watergate • 1118

CHAPTER 29

Conservatism Resurgent, 1974–1989 • 1126

Backlash • 1130

   An Accidental President • 1131

   The Politics of Limits and Malaise • 1133

A Dangerous World, 1974–1980 • *1136*

America Held Hostage • *1138*

The Rising Tide on the Right • 1141

Economic Limits • *1141*

The Religious Right and Neoconservatism • *1143*

The Collapse of the Political Center • *1145*

It's Morning Again in America • 1146

The Rise of Reagan • *1147*

Global Passages: The Changing Face of America • **1148**

A New Administration • *1150*

Economic Realities • *1150*

Conservative Justice • *1152*

Sexuality, Families, and Health • *1153*

Challenging the "Evil Empire" • 1155

A New Arms Race • *1155*

Interventions • *1157*

Iran Contra • *1158*

Cold War Thaw • *1161*

CHAPTER 30

After the Cold War, 1988–2000 • 1168

George H. W. Bush and the End of the Cold War • 1172

The Election of 1988 • *1173*

The Bush Presidency at Home • *1174*

The New World Order • *1176*

The Election of 1992 • *1181*

The Good Times • 1182

Innovation and New Technology • *1183*

Work, Science, and Discontent • *1186*

Migrants • *1188*

Global Passages: America's Global Cities • **1190**

Bill Clinton and the New Democrats • 1192

An Awkward Start • *1192*

Clinton's Recovery • *1194*

Clinton's Second Term • *1196*

A Post-Cold War Foreign Policy • 1197

Intervention and Mediation • *1197*

International Terrorism • *1199*

The Disputed Election of 2000 · 1200

Bush Versus Gore · 1200
The Election in Florida and a Supreme Court Decision · 1201

CHAPTER **31**

21st-Century Dangers and Promises, 2000–Present · 1208

The Age of Sacred Terror · 1212

The United States and Terrorism Before September 11, 2001 · 1212
September 11 and Al Qaeda · 1213
The Iraq War · 1215

Conservatism in the Bush Years · 1220

Culture Wars · 1221
Justice in the 21st Century · 1224
Compassionate Conservatism · 1225
Hurricane Katrina · 1226
Immigration · 1227
The Election of 2006 · 1229

Economic Turmoil · 1231

The Dot-Com Bust and the Middle-Class Squeeze · 1231
Global Passages: Globalization on Trial · 1232
Collapse · 1234

The Obama Years · 1237

The Election of 2008 · 1238
The Obama Presidency · 1240

Appendix A: Historical Documents · A-1
Appendix B: Historical Facts and Data · B-1
Glossary · G-1
Credits · C-1
Index · I-1

Maps

15.1   Black Population of the United States, 1880 • *568*

15.2   Military Districts Established by the Reconstruction Acts, 1867 • *578*

15.3   1876 Presidential Election, by State • *593*

16.1   Technology, Time, and Space • *606*

16.2   Borderlands • *608*

16.3   Climate and Consolidation • *610*

16.4   Indian Battles and Rail Road Lines • *624*

17.1   Rich in Resources • *646*

17.2   Commercial Empire • *654*

18.1   Global Migration, 1840–1900 • *691*

18.2   Ethnic Enclaves • *700*

18.3   The Election of 1896 • *717*

19.1   World Colonial Empires, 1900 • *729*

19.2   The United States in Latin America, 1898–1934 • *752*

20.1   Conserving for the Future • *785*

20.2   Woman Suffrage Around the World • *792*

21.1   European Political Boundaries Before World War I • *804*

21.2   Battles of World War I • *808*

21.3   America Joins World War I, 1917–1918 • *825*

21.4   European Political Boundaries After WWI • *829*

22.1   The Reach of Radio by 1939 • *846*

22.2   Automobile Roads, 1907 and 1920 • *848*

22.3   Presidential Election of 1928 • *868*

23.1   The Dimensions of the Dust Bowl in the 1930s • *911*

24.1   Map of the European Theater of War (WWII) • *935*

24.2   Map of the Pacific Theater of War (WWII) • *936*

25.1   Dividing Postwar Europe • *974*

25.2   The Election of 1948 • *977*

25.3   The Deceptive Complexity of Proxy War • *979*

25.4   Modern Military West • *989*

26.1   The Postwar World • *1013*

26.2   Defense and Mobility • *1022*

27.1   Freedom Riders • *1057*

27.2   The Bay of Pigs • *1059*

27.3   Manufacturing • *1069*

28.1   Divided Vietnam • *1094*

28.2   Ho Chi Minh Trail • *1100*

29.1   Reagan Era Military Interventions • *1156*

30.1   After the Fall: Russia and Eastern Europe Since 1991 • *1178*

30.2   War in the Persian Gulf, 1991–1992 • *1179*

31.1   War in Iraq Since 2003 • *1216*

31.2   War in Afghanistan Since 2003 • *1217*

31.3   2008 Election: Obama's Victory • *1239*

Preface

American Horizons is a new text for the course in American history.

For more than 400 years, North America has been part of a global network centered upon the exchange of peoples, goods, and ideas. Human migrations—sometimes freely, sometimes forced—have continued over the centuries, along with the evolution of commerce in commodities as varied as tobacco, sugar, and computer chips. Europeans and Africans came or were brought to the continent, where they met, traded with, fought among, and intermarried with native peoples. Some of these migrants stayed, while others returned to their home countries. Still others came and went periodically. This initial circulation of people across the oceans foreshadowed the continuous movement of people, goods, and ideas that made the United States. These are the forces that have shaped American history, both dividing and unifying the nation. American "horizons" truly stretch beyond our nation's borders, embracing the trading networks established during and after the colonial era to the digital social networks connecting people globally today.

American Horizons tells the story of the United States by exploring this exchange on a global scale and placing it at the center of that story. By doing so, we provide a different perspective on the history of the United States, one that we hope broadens the horizons of those who read our work and are ever mindful of the global forces that increasingly and profoundly shape our lives. At the same time, *American Horizons* considers those ways in which U.S. influence reshaped the lives and experiences of people of other nations.

U.S. history is increasingly perceived, interpreted, and taught as part of a global historical experience. The mutual influence of change—of global forces entering the U.S. and of American ideas, goods, and people moving out through the world—has been a consistent feature since the 16th century. While most Americans today are aware that their influence is felt abroad and are increasingly aware of the influence of events abroad on their own lives, they tend to think of these as recent developments. In fact, those earliest exchanges of beliefs and products some 500 years ago established a pattern of interaction that continues today.

We have written a narrative that encourages readers to consider the variety of pressures that spurred historical change. Some of these pressures arose within America and some came from outside its borders. In the 1820s, the global market for whale oil shaped labor conditions throughout New England. At the same time, the American political system was transformed by the unique inheritance of the American Revolution and the relative abundance of land in North America. In the 1940s and 1950s, the federal government designed a unique set of policies to help World War II veterans readjust to civilian life, while the Civil Rights Movement unfolded within a global context of decolonization in Africa and Asia. Topics such as these help us ask the reader to consider the relationship between local and global forces that shaped American history.

This book was conceived as an opportunity to present the nation's history as more than a mere sequence of events for the student to memorize. The approach of *American Horizons* reflects this. Although adhering to the familiar chronological organization of this course, our narrative style and structure provide the flexibility of shifting emphasis from time to time to the global aspects of American history. While the story of the United States is always at the center of the story, that story is told through the movement of people, goods, and ideas into, within, or out of the United States.

What qualities make the United States unique? What accounts for the diversity of dialect and lifestyle across this country? How did the United States become a major player on the world stage of nations? History includes many storylines that contribute to this narrative. *American Horizons* is the story of where this nation came from and how it has been shaped by its own set of shared values as well as its interaction with the rest of the world. It recognizes that many of the significant events in American history had causes and consequences connected to developments elsewhere and presents those events accordingly. *American Horizons* depicts this intersection of storylines from many nations that influenced, and were influenced by, the United States of America.

As readers engage the text, we encourage them to think explicitly about what makes history. What matters? What forces or events shaped how people lived their lives?

About the Concise Edition

In addition to the comprehensive edition of *American Horizons*, we are delighted to offer this concise edition for those instructors who need to teach the course in a short term, assign readings in addition to the textbook, or prefer a more economical option for their students without sacrificing the primary advantages of the full edition. To meet this goal, the concise edition was designed with 10 percent fewer words and photographs. This was achieved without sacrificing any tables, maps, or figures, all of which are critical to the realization of *American Horizons*.

A GUIDED TOUR OF
AMERICAN HORIZONS

American Horizons is distinguised by three elements: a global theme, innovative scholarship, and features that encourage active learning.

CHAPTER INTRODUCTIONS

Each chapter of *American Horizons* begins with a compelling story at the core of each chapter theme.

GLOBAL THEME

American Horizons seamlessly incorporates connections to global history throughout the text, including discussion rarely found in other books.

The layout of homes changed to accommodate the purchasing power of the rising middle class. "Parlors" started to appear—private but comfortable rooms in which families could display the furniture, carpets, and chandeliers that signaled their station.

GLOBAL PASSAGES

"Global Passages" boxes feature a unique story connecting America to the world.

INNOVATIVE SCHOLARSHIP

American Horizons is informed by the most current scholarship available. The text offers multiple perspectives and viewpoints on America's past that broaden the student's understand of America's unique place in history.

The Story of American Indians

The Colonial European Empires

The Impact and Contributions of Hispanics and Mexican Americans

The Story of Immigration and Migration

Women in American History

LEARNING FEATURES

American Horizons offers vivid features to help students read, comprehend, and analyze key information, often using innovative visual aids.

America in the World

Found in each chapter, this is a visual guide to key interactions between America and the world.

Maps and Infographics

A rich graphics program explores essential
themes in new ways.

Path of the United States Exploring Expedition, 1838–1842 Navy Lieutenant Charles Wilkes led the first American circumnavigation of the globe. His flotilla included scientists who sought to map and identify places and products of interest to American traders and politicians.

Rich in Resources An abundance of agricultural products and raw materials from the South and West, manufactured largely in the northeast and upper Midwest, helped make the United States the world's leading industrial power by 1900.

Commercial Empire By 1900, Singer Sewing Machine Company, the nation's first and largest international company, established a vast global commercial empire, selling its products in over a thousand retail shops around the world.

Indian Removals, 1830s This map shows the routes along which Indians were driven by the U.S. army during the forced relocations of the 1830s. Jackson's policies moved the last large Indian communities living east of the Mississippi River into the frontier regions of the Oklahoma Territory.

Timeline in Every Chapter

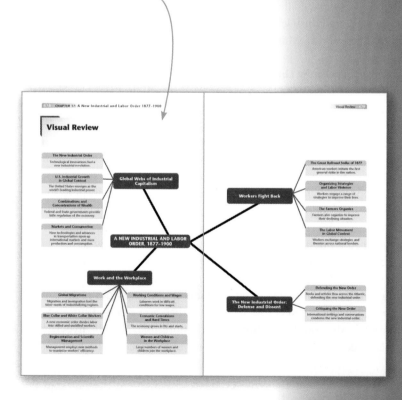

Visual Review

At the conclusion of each chapter, this feature provides a post-reading summary to help students make links to key themes or events within a chapter.

SUPPLEMENTS

FOR STUDENTS

Oxford University Press offers a complete and authoritative package of supplementary materials for the student, including print and new media resources designed for chapter review, primary source reading, essay writing, test-preparation, and further research.

Student Companion Website at www.oup.com/us/americanhorizons

The open-access Online Study Center designed specifically for *American Horizons* helps students to review what they have learned from the textbook as well as explore other resources online. Note-taking guides help students focus their attention in class, while interactive practice quizzes allow them to assess their knowledge of a topic before a test.

- **Online Study Guide**, including
  - Note-taking outlines
  - Multiple-choice and identification quizzes, (two quizzes per chapter, thirty question quizzes—*different* from those found in the Instructor's Manual/Testbank)
- **Primary Source Companion & Research Guide**, a brief online Research Primer, with a library of annotated links to primary & secondary sources in U.S. history.
- **Interactive Flashcards**, using key terms and people listed at the end of each chapter, these multimedia cards help students remember who's who and what's what.

American National Biography Online   www.anb.org

Students who purchase a **new** copy of *American Horizons* will find an access code for a six-month (Volumes 1 or 2) or a one-year **free subscription** to this powerful online resource published by Oxford University Press.

American National Biography online offers **portraits of more than 17,400 women and men**—from all eras and walks of life—whose lives have shaped the nation. More than a decade in preparation, the *American National Biography* is the first biographical resource of this scope to be published in more than sixty years. Originally published in 24 volumes in 1999, the *American National Biography* won instant acclaim as the new authority in American biographies. **Winner of the American Library Association's Dartmouth Medal** as the best reference work of the year, the *ANB* now serves readers in thousands of school, public, and academic libraries around the world. The publication of the online edition makes the *ANB* even more useful as a dynamic source of information—updated semiannually, with hundreds of new entries each year and revisions of previously published entries to enhance their accuracy and currency. The *ANB Online* features **thousands of illustrations**, more than **80,000 hyperlinked cross-references**, links to select web sites, and powerful search capabilities.

ANB Online is also a great teaching resource, since it can be actively incorporated into classroom lessons. To assist teachers in fully utilizing ANB Online, we have prepared a Teacher's Guide to Using ANB Online. Developed with the participation of librarians and teachers, the Teacher's Guide offers six lessons that highlight the importance and value of studying biography as an end in itself and as a starting point for doing further research into the lives of those who shaped the American experience.

Writing History: A Guide for Students Third edition, by William Kelleher Storey, Associate Professor at Millsaps College.

Bringing together practical methods from both history and composition, *Writing History* provides a wealth of tips and advice to help students research and write essays for history classes. The book covers all aspects of writing about history, including **finding topics** and **researching** them, **interpreting source materials**, **drawing inferences from sources**, and **constructing arguments**. It concludes with three chapters that discuss writing effective sentences, using precise wording, and revising. Using numerous examples from the works of cultural, political, and social historians, *Writing History* serves as an ideal supplement to history courses that require students to conduct research. The third edition includes expanded sections on **peer editing** and **topic selection**, as well as new sections on searching and using the Internet. *Writing History* can be packaged for free with   *American Horizons*. Contact your Oxford University Press Sales Representative for more information.

The Information-Literate Historian: A Guide to Research for History Students by Jenny Presnell, Information Services Library and History, American Studies, and Women's Studies Bibliographer, Miami University of Ohio.

This is the only book specifically designed to teach today's history student how to most successfully select and use sources—primary, secondary, and electronic—to carry out and present their research. Written by a college librarian, *The Information-Literate Historian* is an indispensable reference for historians, students, and other readers doing history research. *The Information-Literate Historian* can be packaged for free with *American Horizons*. Contact your Oxford University Press Sales Representative for more information.

Primary Source Documents

Our Documents: 100 Milestone Documents from the National Archives brings documents to life, including facsimiles side-by-side with transcripts for students to explore; explanations and a forward provided by Michael Beschloss. This primary source book can be **packaged for free** with *American Horizons*. Among the documents it contains are: Declaration of Independence; U.S. Constitution; Bill of Rights; Louisiana Purchase Treaty; Missouri Compromise; The Dred Scott decision; Emancipation Proclamation; Gettysburg Address; Fourteenth Amendment to the U.S. Constitution; Thomas Edison's light bulb patent; Sherman Anti-Trust Act; Executive order for the Japanese relocation during wartime; Manhattan Project notebook;

Press release announcing U.S. recognition of Israel; President John F. Kennedy's inaugural address, as well as many more.

Other primary source books that can be packaged with *American Horizons* include Chafe's *History of Our Time* and Bloom's *Takin' It to the Streets*, as well as *The Boisterous Sea of Liberty: A Documentary History of America from Discovery through the Civil War*; and *Documenting American Violence: A Sourcebook*.

FOR INSTRUCTORS

For decades, American history professors have turned to Oxford University Press as the leading source for high quality readings and reference materials. Now, when you adopt *American Horizons*, the Press will partner with you and make available its best supplemental materials and resources for your classroom. Listed here are several series of high interest, but you will want to talk with your Sales Representative to learn more about what can be made available, and about what would suit your course best.

Instructor's Manual & Testbank. This useful guide contains useful teaching tools for experienced and first-time teachers alike. It can be made available to adopters upon request, and is also available electronically on the Instructor's Recourse CD. This extensive manual and testbank contains:

- **Sample Syllabi**
- **Chapter Outlines**
- **In-Class Discussion Questions**
- **Lecture Ideas**
- **Oxford's Further Reading List**
- **Quizzes** (two per chapter, one per half of the chapter, content divided somewhat evenly down the middle of the chapter: twenty-five multiple choice questions each)
- **Tests** (two per chapter, each covering the entire chapter contents: each offering ten identification/matching; ten multiple-choice; five short-answer, two essay)

Instructor's Resource CD. This handy CD-ROM contains everything you need in an electronic format—the Instructor's Manual (PDF), PowerPoint Slides (fully customizable), Image Library with PDF versions of *all* 120 maps from the textbook, and a Computerized Testbank.

A complete **Course Management cartridge** is also available to qualified adopters. Instructor's resources are also available for download directly to your computer through a secure connection via the instructor's side of the companion website. Contact your Oxford University Press Sales Representative for more information.

OTHER OXFORD TITLES OF INTEREST FOR THE U.S. HISTORY CLASSROOM

Oxford University Press publishes a vast array of titles in American history. Listed below is just a small selection of books that pair particularly well with *American*

Horizons. Any of the books in these series can be packaged with *American Horizons* at a significant discount to students. Please contact your Oxford University Press Sales Representative for specific pricing information, or for additional packaging suggestions. Please visit www.oup.com/us for a full listing of Oxford titles.

NEW NARRATIVES IN AMERICAN HISTORY

At Oxford University Press, we believe that good history begins with a good story. Each volume in this series features a compelling tale that draws on a sustained narrative to illuminate a greater historical theme or controversy. Then, in a thoughtful Afterword, the authors place their narratives within larger historical contexts, discuss their sources and narrative strategies, and describe their personal involvement with the work. Intensely personal and highly relevant, these succinct texts are innovative teaching tools that provide a springboard for incisive class discussion as they immerse students in a particular historical moment.

> *Escaping Salem: The Other Witch Hunt of 1692*, by Richard Godbeer
> *Sleuthing the Alamo: Davy Crockett's Last Stand and Other Mysteries of the Texas Revolution*, by James E. Crisp
> *In Search of the Promised Land: A Slave Family in the Old South*, by John Hope Franklin and Loren Schweninger
> *The Making of a Confederate: Walter Lenoir's Civil War*, by William L. Barney
> *"They Say": Ida B. Wells and the Reconstruction of Race*, by James West Davidson
> *Wild Men: Ishi and Kroeber in the Wilderness of Modern America*, by Douglas Cazaux Sackman
> *The Gentle Subversive: Rachel Carson, Silent Spring, and the Rise of the Environmental Movement*, by Mark Hamilton Lytle
> *"To Everything There is a Season": Pete Seeger and the Power of Song*, by Allan Winkler

PAGES FROM HISTORY

Textbooks may interpret and recall history, but these books **are** history. Each title, compiled and edited by a prominent historian, is a collection of primary sources relating to a particular topic of historical significance. Documentary evidence includes news articles, government documents, memoirs, letters, diaries, fiction, photographs, advertisements, posters, and political cartoons. Headnotes, extended captions, sidebars, and introductory essays provide the essential context that frames the documents. All the books are amply illustrated and each includes a documentary picture essay, chronology, further reading, source notes, and index.

> *Encounters in the New World* (Jill Lepore)
> *Colonial America* (Edward G. Gray)
> *The American Revolution* (Stephen C. Bullock)
> *The Bill of Rights* (John J. Patrick)
> *The Struggle Against Slavery* (David Waldstreicher)
> *The Civil War* (Rachel Filene Seidman)
> *The Gilded Age* (Janette Thomas Greenwood)

The Industrial Revolution (Laura Levine Frader)
Imperialism (Bonnie G. Smith)
World War I (Frans Coetzee and Marilyn Shevin-Coetzee)
The Depression and the New Deal (Robert McElvaine)
World War II (James H. Madison)
The Cold War (Allan M. Winkler)
The Vietnam War (Marilyn B. Young)

PIVOTAL MOMENTS IN AMERICAN HISTORY

Oxford's Pivotal Moments in American History Series explores the turning points that forever changed the course of American history. Each book is written by an expert on the subject and provides a fascinating narrative on a significant instance that stands out in our nation's past. For anyone interested in discovering which important junctures in U.S. history shaped our thoughts, actions, and ideals, these books are the definitive resources.

The Scratch of a Pen: 1763 and the Transformation of North America (Colin Calloway)
As if an Enemy's Country: The British Occupation of Boston and the Origins of the Revolution (Richard Archer)
Washington's Crossing (David Hackett Fischer)
James Madison and the Struggle for the Bill of Rights (Richard Labunski)
Adams vs. Jefferson: The Tumultuous Election of 1800 (John Ferling)
The Birth of Modern Politics: Andrew Jackson, John Quincy Adams, and the Election of 1828 (Lynn Parsons)
Storm over Texas: The Annexation Controversy and the Road to Civil War (Joel H. Silbey)
Crossroads of Freedom: Antietam (James M. McPherson)
The Last Indian War: The Nez Perce Story (Elliot West)
Seneca Falls and the Origins of the Women's Rights Movement (Sally McMillen)
Rainbow's End: The Crash of 1929 (Maury Klein)
Brown v. Board of Education *and the Civil Rights Movement* (Michael J. Klarman)
The Bay of Pigs (Howard Jones)
Freedom Riders: 1961 and the Struggle for Racial Justice (Raymond Arsenault)

VIEWPOINTS ON AMERICAN CULTURE

Oxford's Viewpoints on American Culture Series offers timely reflections for twenty-first century readers. The series targets topics where debates have flourished and brings together the voices of established and emerging writers to share their own points of view in compact and compelling format.

Votes for Women: The Struggle for Suffrage Revisited (Jean H. Baker)
Long Time Gone: Sixties America Then and Now (Alexander Bloom)
Living in the Eighties (Edited by Gil Troy and Vincent J. Cannato)
Race on Trial: Law and Justice in American History (Annette Gordon-Reed)
Sifters: Native American Women's Lives (Theda Perdue)
Latina Legacies: Identity, Biography, and Community (Vicki L. Ruiz)

OXFORD WORLD'S CLASSICS

For over 100 years, Oxford World's Classics has made available a broad spectrum of literature from around the globe. With well over 600 titles available and a continuously growing list, this is the finest and most comprehensive classics series in print. Any volume in the series can be **packaged for free** with *American Horizons*. Relevant titles include Benjamin Franklin's *Autobiography and Other Writings*, J. Hector St. John de Crèvecœur's *Letters from an American Farmer*, Booker T. Washington's *Up from Slavery*, and many others. **For a complete listing of Oxford World's Classics, please visit www.oup.com/us/owc.**

ACKNOWLEDGMENTS

A book as detailed as this draws upon the talents and support of many individuals. Our first thanks must certainly go to our families for their support and patience during the development of this textbook. We would also like to acknowledge the team at Oxford University Press for their support in making this book a reality. Thanks go first to our editor, Brian Wheel, who encouraged and challenged us at every step of the process. Oxford publisher John Challice supported the project at an early stage and spurred us to think broadly about how we envisioned it. We appreciate the able assistance of development editors Thom Holmes and Danielle Christensen. Editorial assistant Sarah Ellerton was especially helpful in wrangling the photo, map, and figure program for the book. Taylor Pilkington picked up late in the process and helped shepherd the project through to completion. Editorial assistants Laura Lancaster and Danniel Schoonebeek helped us organize and manage the project in the early stages. We thank the Oxford production team, led by managing editor Lisa Grzan, for their encouragement and help in generating this book and shaping its final form. Senior production editor David Bradley deserves special recognition for his work in coordinating the work of all the authors and for assembling the many maps, images, and graphics in the volumes. The production team also included copyeditor Deanna Hegle and proofreader Heather Dubnick. The interior and cover design were created by art director Michele Laseau and designers Binbin Li and Pam Poll, based on a plan originally conceived by Paula Schlosser. The compelling photographs were researched by Mary Rose Maclachlan and Derek Capitaine. The innovative map program was created by International Mapping through the efforts of Alex Tait, Dan Przywara, Vickie Taylor, and Kim Clark, with the consultative help of Erik Steiner, director of the Spatial History Lab at Stanford University. We also benefited enormously from the advice of all the outside readers on the manuscript. We thank them all.

THE DEVELOPMENT STORY

The seven co-authors of this book specialize in a variety of time periods and methodologies. Based on our research and teaching, we all share the idea that the nation's history can best be understood by examining how, from the colonial era forward, the American experience reflected the interaction of many nations, peoples, and events. We present this idea in a format that integrates traditional narrative history with the enhanced perspective of five centuries of global interaction.

MANUSCRIPT REVIEWERS

We have greatly benefited from the perceptive comments and suggestion of the many talented scholars and instructors who reviewed the manuscript of *American Horizons*. Their insight and suggestions contributed immensely to the published work.

Stanley Arnold
Northern Illinois University

Shelby M. Balik
Metropolitan State College of Denver
University of Colorado

Eirlys M. Barker
Thomas Nelson Community College

Toby Bates
University of Mississippi

Carol Bender
Saddleback College

Wendy Benningfield
Campbellsville University

Katherine Benton-Cohen
Georgetown University

Angela Boswell
Henderson State University

Robert Bouwman
North Georgia College & State University

Jessica Brannon-Wranosky
Texas A&M University–Commerce

Blanche Brick
Blinn College

Howard Brick
University of Michigan

Margaret M. Caffrey
University of Memphis

Jacqueline B. Carr
University of Vermont

Dominic Carrillo
Grossmont College

Brian Casserly
Bellevue College

Cheryll Ann Cody
Houston Community College–
Southwest College

Elizabeth Collins
Triton College

Edward M. Cook, Jr.
University of Chicago

Cynthia Gardner Counsil
Florida State College–Jacksonville

C. David Dalton
College of the Ozarks

David Dzurec
University of Scranton

Brian J. Els
University of Portland

Kevin Eoff
Palo Verde College

Richard M. Filipink
Western Illinois University

Joshua Fulton
Moraine Valley Community College

David Garvin
Highland Community College

Glen Gendzel
San José State University

Tiffany Gill
University of Texas–Austin

Aram Goudsouzian
University of Memphis

Larry Gragg
Missouri University of Science and
Technology

Jean W. Griffith
Fort Scott Community College
Labette Community College

Mark Grimsley
Ohio State University

Elisa M. Guernsey
Monroe Community College

Aaron Gulyas
Mott Community College

Michael R. Hall
Armstrong Atlantic State University

David E. Hamilton
University of Kentucky

Peggy J. Hardman
Eastern New Mexico University

Kristin Hargrove
Grossmont College

Claudrena N. Harold
University of Virginia

Edward Hashima
American River College

Robin Henry
Wichita State University

John Herron
University of Missouri–Kansas City

L. Edward Hicks
Faulkner University

Matt Hinckley
Richland College

D. Sandy Hoover
East Texas Baptist University

Jerry Hopkins
East Texas Baptist University

Kelly Hopkins
University of Houston

Kenneth W. Howell
Prairie View A&M University

Raymond Pierre Hylton
Virginia Union University

Bryan M. Jack
Winston-Salem State University

Brenda Jackson-Abernathy
Belmont University

Volker Janssen
California State University–Fullerton

Lawrence W. Kennedy
University of Scranton

William Kerrigan
Muskingum University

Andrew E. Kersten
University of Wisconsin

Todd Kerstetter
TCU

Patricia Knol
Triton College

Jeffrey Kosiorek
Hendrix College

Peter Kuryla
Belmont University

Peggy Lambert
Lone Star College–Kingwood

Alan Lehmann
Blinn College

Carolyn Herbst Lewis
Louisiana State University

Christopher J. Mauceri
Farmingdale State College of New York

Derrick McKisick
Fairfield University

Marian Mollin
Virginia Tech

Linda Mollno
Cal Poly Pomona

Michelle Morgan
Missouri State University

Susan Rhoades Neel
Utah State University

Caryn E. Neumann
Miami University

Jeffrey Nichols
Westminster College

Christopher H. Owen
Northeastern State University

Jeffrey Pilz
North Iowa Area Community College

Amy M. Porter
Georgia Southwestern State University

William E. Price
Kennesaw State University

Emily Rader
El Camino College

Matthew Redinger
Montana State University–Billings

Yolanda Romero
North Lake College

Jessica Roney
Ohio University

Walter L. Sargent
University of Maine–Farmington

Robert Francis Saxe
Rhodes College

Jerry G. Sheppard
Mount Olive College

Robert Sherwood
Georgia Military College

Terry L. Shoptaugh
Minnesota State University–Moorhead

Jason H. Silverman
Winthrop University

Nico Slate
Carnegie Mellon University

Jodie Steeley
Merced Community College

Jennifer A. Stollman
Fort Lewis College

James S. Taw
Valdosta State University

Connie Brown Thomason
Louisiana Delta Community College

Kurt Troutman
Muskegon Community College

Stanley J. Underdal
San José State University

David Voelker
University of Wisconsin–Green Bay

Charles Waite
University of Texas–Pan American

R. Stuart Wallace
NHTI—Concord's Community College
University of New Hampshire–Manchester

Pamela West
Jefferson State Community College

William Benton Whisenhunt
College of DuPage

Louis Williams
St. Louis Community College–Forest Park

Scott M. Williams
Weatherford College

Mary Montgomery Wolf
University of Georgia

Bill Wood
University of Arkansas Community College–Batesville

Melyssa Wrisley
Broome Community College

Charles Young
Umpqua Community College

Nancy L. Zens
Central Oregon Community College

About the Authors

Michael Schaller (Ph.D., University of Michigan, 1974) is Regents Professor of History at the University of Arizona where he has taught since 1974. His areas of specialization include U.S. international and East Asian relations and the resurgence of conservatism in late-20th-century America. Among his publications are *Altered States: The United States and Japan Since the Occupation* (Oxford University Press, 1997), *The U.S. and China into the 21st Century* (Oxford University Press, 2002), *Right Turn: American Life in the Reagan-Bush Era* (Oxford University Press,, 2007), and *Ronald Reagan* (Oxford University Press, 2011).

Robert D. Schulzinger is College of Arts and Sciences Professor of Distinction of History and International Affairs at the University of Colorado–Boulder. He specializes in 20th-century U.S. history and U.S. diplomatic history. Books include *A Time for War: The United States and Vietnam, 1941–1975* (Oxford University Press, 1997), *U.S. Diplomacy Since 1900* (Oxford University Press, 2002), and *Present Tense* (Houghton Mifflin, 2004).

John Bezís-Selfa is Associate Professor of History at Wheaton College (Ph.D. at the University of Pennsylvania). He specializes in the history of the early Americas and teaches U.S., Latin American, and Latino/a history. Books include *Forging America: Ironworkers, Adventurers, and the Industrious Revolution* (Cornell University Press, 2004).

Janette Thomas Greenwood is Professor of History at Clark University (Ph.D. at the University of Virginia), and specializes in African-American history and history of the U.S. South. Books include *The Gilded Age: A History in Documents* (Oxford University Press, 2000), *Bittersweet Legacy: The Black and White "Better Classes" in Charlotte, 1850–1910* (University of North Carolina Press, 1994), and *First Fruits of Freedom: The Migration of Former Slaves and Their Search for Equality in Worcester, Massachusetts, 1862–1900* (University of North Carolina Press, 2010).

Andrew Kirk is Professor of History at University of Nevada, Las Vegas (Ph.D. at the University of New Mexico), and specializes in the history of the U.S. West and environmental history. Books include *Collecting Nature: The American Environmental Movement and the Conservation Library* (University of Kansas Press, 2001), and *Counterculture Green: The Whole Earth Catalog and American Environmentalism* (University Press of Kansas, 2007).

Sarah J. Purcell is Associate Professor of History at Grinnell College (Ph.D. at Brown University), and specializes in the Early National period, Antebellum U.S., popular culture, politics, gender, and military history. She also directs the Rosenfield Program in Public Affairs, International Relations, and Human Rights. Books include *Sealed with Blood: War, Sacrifice, and Memory in Revolutionary America* (University of Pennsylvania Press, 2002), *The Early National Period* (Facts on File, 2004), and *The Encyclopedia of Battles in North America, 1517–1916* (Facts on File, 2000).

Aaron Sheehan-Dean is the Eberly Professor of Civil War Studies at West Virginia University (Ph.D. at the University of Virginia), and specializes in Antebellum U.S. and the U.S. Civil War. Books include *Why Confederates Fought: Family and Nation in Civil War Virginia* (The University of North Carolina Press, 2007), *The View from the Ground: Experiences of Civil War Soldiers* (The University Press of Kentucky, 2006), and *Concise Historical Atlas of the U.S. Civil War* (Oxford University Press, 2008).

Reconstructing America

C ato, Patience, Peggy, Jane, Porter, and Stepney were among many enslaved black Southerners who lived on plantations in Liberty County, Georgia. In early 1865, they watched as the first wave of "Bummers," or deserters from Sherman's Union army, came through the county. The Union deserters raided plantation houses and slave cabins alike, taking everything edible (and much that was not) and shooting animals they could not carry away. One Confederate described the raiders as "lost in the world of eternal woe. Their throats were open sepulchers, their mouths filled with curs-ing and bitterness and lies." Despite the hard-ship that ensued, enslaved people living in the region did nothing to obstruct the Union Army. Cato and Stepney, who both worked as drivers organizing and managing slave labor under the eye of a white overseer, effectively supported the Union by their inaction. Their stature in the com-munity surely influenced others. They behaved, in the bitter but accurate words of a local slave-holder, as though they "now believe themselves perfectly free." In Liberty County, and through-out the rural South, whites and blacks shared a world based in the hierarchy of slavery and racial dominance, and organized around the produc-tion schedules of staple crops. As Cato and the others observed the Yankee conquest of Georgia they saw the dawning of a new era and began to work out what freedom meant. A wide range of choices, opportunities, and perils awaited black Southerners across the region.

Cato and his wife Jane, who lived on a nearby plantation, bided their time through the collapse of the Confed-eracy. Cato's long expe-rience working the land and managing workers

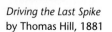

Driving the Last Spike
by Thomas Hill, 1881

CHAPTER OUTLINE

THE YEAR OF JUBILEE, 1865
> African American Families
> Southern Whites and the Problem of Defeat
> Emancipation in Comparative Perspective

SHAPING RECONSTRUCTION, 1865–1868
> Andrew Johnson's Reconstruction
> The Fight over Reconstruction
> The Civil War Amendments and American Citizenship
> Congressional Reconstruction

RECONSTRUCTION IN THE SOUTH, 1866–1876
> African American Life in the Postwar South
> Republican Governments in the Postwar South
> Cotton, Merchants, and the Lien

continued on page 567

America in the World

The Colfax Massacre showed that racially motivated violence remained a serious issue during Reconstruction (1873).

The Force Act was passed to crack down on Ku Klux Klan actions to keep Blacks from voting (1865–1871).

U.S. event that influenced the world

International event that influenced the United States

Event with multinational influence

Conflict

The Fourteenth Amendment established citizenship rights and due process (1867).

Although rarely enforced, the Civil Rights Act was intended to eliminate segregation by race in public spaces (1875).

The Fifteenth Amendment prohibited voting discrimination based on race or servitude (1870).

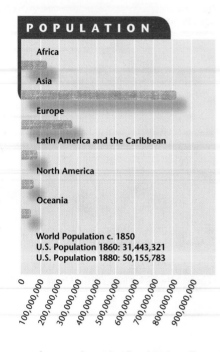

POPULATION

Africa

Asia

Europe

Latin America and the Caribbean

North America

Oceania

World Population c. 1850
U.S. Population 1860: 31,443,321
U.S. Population 1880: 50,155,783

0
100,000,000
200,000,000
300,000,000
400,000,000
500,000,000
600,000,000
700,000,000
800,000,000
900,000,000

led him to reject the authority of a new overseer hired in late summer 1865. Cato's former owner denounced him as "a most insolent, indolent, and dishonest man." In response, Cato and his wife exercised their freedom in most fundamental sense—they left Liberty County altogether, moving to nearby Savannah. No longer able to control her former slaves, Cato's ex-owner lashed out by asserting that black people would not last: "with their emancipation must come their extermination."

Despite the rising anger among whites, many freedmen and freedwomen remained in Liberty and set about making contracts for their work. Porter and Patience stayed in the area and, in spite of the fluctuating labor and pay agreements with area planters, managed to buy their own farm outright. Patience's brother Stepney resided on Arcadia, a coastal plantation that supported two lucrative crops: rice and sea island cotton. He began to manage much of the former plantation land at Arcadia and helped coordinate the rental and purchase of land by freed people. The close family networks established among the Gullah people, as the black Southerners in this region were known, undoubtedly aided many in their transition to freedom.

Unfortunately, few freed people experienced the success they did. Peggy, who had lived on the same plantation as Cato, moved to Savannah but contracted smallpox and died. Some freed people began to labor for wages on the plantations that they had once farmed as slaves, but this rarely brought them the financial independence they desired. Others rented land or farmed on shares, splitting the proceeds from the yearly crop with the landlord. This latter sharecropper system, adopted widely across the South, trapped tenant farmers in cycles of debt and prevented the southern agricultural sector from diversifying as the world cotton market collapsed. In Liberty County, as elsewhere in the South, the reintegration of the southern economy into the larger global market reflected the efforts Southerners and Northerners made to reconstruct the nation. But Southerners' failure to build a sustainable and humane economy or a just social and political system in the postwar South reinforced the larger failure of the nation in Reconstruction.

THE YEAR OF JUBILEE, 1865

The dramatic changes underway in the South and the nation produced surprising outcomes. At the end of the Civil War, white Southerners were defeated and resentful, while black Southerners celebrated Jubilee, their deliverance from bondage. Northerners likewise celebrated, because they had preserved the Union and extinguished slavery in the United States. But great questions remained: what role would recently freed slaves play in American life? What rights would they possess? What obligations did the federal government have to ensure a meaningful freedom? For Washington, the first order of business was reestablishing loyal governments in the South and bringing the region back into a normal relationship with the nation. No precedents guided this process and grand constitutional questions about the nature of the Union and the meaning of republican government

CHAPTER OUTLINE

continued from page 563

THE END OF RECONSTRUCTION, 1877
> The Ku Klux Klan and Reconstruction Violence
> Northern Weariness and Northern Conservatism
> Legacies of Reconstruction

acquired immediate political weight. Republicans and Democrats, Northerners and Southerners, and blacks and whites, divided over the answers to these questions. The wartime task of reunion gave way to the postwar task of reconstruction, which entailed the reorganization of the southern political system and the rebuilding of shattered public and private institutions.

African American Families

Of the nearly four million enslaved people in the South before the Civil War, approximately 500,000 fled to freedom during the war and the rest claimed their freedom at the war's conclusion. The most important task confronting freed people was reestablishing families broken by slavery. White Southerners wanted to restore what they considered normal labor relations, but most black Southerners' desire to locate displaced family members outweighed even the desire for a steady wage. According

After four long years, Northerners celebrated Union victory in the Civil War and the end of slavery. But the war's conclusion only began the struggle to define what freedom would mean in practice.

to many enslaved people, the central crime of slavery was the destruction of black families. Through the late spring and summer of 1865, as white southern soldiers headed home in defeat, black Southerners took to the road, following letters, reports, and rumors to track the exodus of children, parents, siblings, and loved ones as a result of slave sales. This movement added to the uncertainty of the postwar period and alarmed whites who expected blacks to stay and continue the work they had done before emancipation.

The next question that confronted freed people was what work they would do. Across the South, black Southerners faced several choices: wage labor, renting land to farm themselves, sharecropping, or some combination of the three. But the question of where that work happened often took precedence. "If I stay here, I'll never know I'm free," explained one freedwoman as she left the plantation on which she had labored as a slave. Many thousands made the same choice, leaving behind farms and plantations on which they had been raised in favor of a new, if uncertain, life somewhere else. Often, they moved to cities, most overcrowded from the influx of refugees during the war. Memphis and Nashville both grew by more than a third between 1860 and 1870, while Atlanta's population more than doubled.

In rural areas, labor contracts and work were the most pressing priorities. Very few enslaved people owned any real estate before the war, which required them to work for wages. The main challenge was working out fair and enforceable contracts

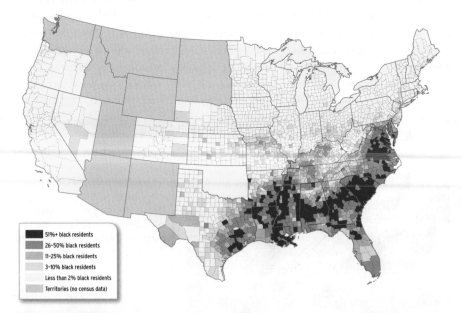

51%+ black residents
26–50% black residents
11–25% black residents
3–10% black residents
Less than 2% black residents
Territories (no census data)

▲ **Map 15.1**

Black Population of the United States, 1880 Despite the opportunities for movement created by emancipation, few former slaves had the resources to make a full relocation out of the region. As a result, black Americans continued to live predominately in the South until the second and third decades of the 20th century.

with former masters or other whites. The Bureau of Refugees, Freedmen, and Abandoned Land (usually called the **Freedmen's Bureau**), established within the Army in early 1865, helped adjudicate labor disputes in the summer and fall of 1865. Led by former Union general **Oliver Otis Howard**, the Bureau also distributed food rations to blacks and whites during the hard winter that followed and initiated the building of schools, hospitals, and other communal institutions. Despite this important work, elite Southerners resented the intrusion of the federal government and joined with northern Democrats to denounce the Bureau as an unnecessary federal imposition on states' rights. Because slaves had labored without incentive, whites did not expect them to understand paid work. In fact, most African Americans adjusted quickly, even when they could not rely on landowners to fairly fulfill the terms of labor contracts. One man, who had relocated to Ohio at the war's end, responded to a request from his former master to return to Tennessee, by asking "you to send us our wages for the time we served you." "Here I draw my wages every Saturday night," wrote Jourdan Anderson, "but in Tennessee there was never any pay day for the negroes any more than for the horses and the cows."

Southern Whites and the Problem of Defeat

The spring and summer of 1865 exhilarated and bewildered Americans throughout the country. The most shocking event was the assassination of **Abraham Lincoln**. After celebrating the official surrender of Lee's Army of Northern Virginia on April 12, 1865, Lincoln attended a play on the evening of the 14th, Good Friday. **John Wilkes Booth**, a member of America's most famous acting family, organized a conspiracy to kill Lincoln and several cabinet members. Booth shot Lincoln in his box at Ford's Theater while a conspirator stabbed Secretary of State **William Seward** in his home. Lincoln, unconscious but still alive, was taken to a house across the street from the theater, where doctors tried to save him. Cabinet members, generals, and other officials visited the room where he lay before Lincoln died just after dawn. Secretary of War **Edwin Stanton** summarized the grim morning and its effect on America's memory of Lincoln: "now he belongs to the ages." Booth escaped into Maryland before being killed by U.S. troops. Grief and anger flooded across the North, with many citizens blaming the conspiracy on **Jefferson Davis**, who fled south after evacuating Richmond in early April. Despite the controversies he stoked as president, Lincoln earned the deep appreciation of Northerners by steering the country through the crisis of disunion. Walt Whitman, who had seen Lincoln on his melancholy early morning walks around Washington, spoke for many when he lamented:

> O the bleeding drops of red,
> Where on the deck my Captain lies,
> Fallen cold and dead.

Some Southerners, **Robert E. Lee** among them, recognized Lincoln's turn toward generosity late in the war and regarded his murder as damaging to their interest.

Others, however, could not help but exalt this final turn of events. "Hurrah! Old Abe Lincoln has been assassinated!" a South Carolina woman wrote in her diary. "Our hated enemy has met the just reward of his life." Northerners could not comprehend such an attitude. For them, the restoration of the Union brought relief and confirmation of God's favor over their society. Even as Southerners struggled to reconcile their religious understanding of defeat—many believed it was another test offered by God for his chosen people—they resisted the political consequences of Union victory. A number of high-ranking Confederate military officers fled to South America, fearful of punishment they might receive from the Union government. **Edward Porter Alexander**, Lee's chief of artillery, laid his plans on the retreat to Appomattox: "I had made up my mind that if ever a white flag was raised I would take to the bushes. And, somehow, I would manage to get out of the country & go to Brazil. Brazil was just going to war with Paraguay & I could doubtless get a place in their artillery. . . ." Several thousand white Southerners relocated to Brazil, where they created an expatriate community in one of the last two major slave societies remaining in the western hemisphere. More than 10,000 Confederates exiled themselves after the war. This exodus carried men, and sometimes their families, around the world. Many ended up serving as military advisors to foreign governments, including Britain, France, Germany, and several employed by the Khedive of Egypt.

Even as white Southerners lamented the war's outcome, they sought the easiest path toward readmission to the Union in hopes of restoring some measure of normality in the South and because it might allow them to retain authority over the freed people. So, despite their vigorous pursuit of independence and their wartime insistence that the Confederacy was a separate nation, many Southerners assumed that they could quickly and easily resume their old position within the United States. Northern Democrats largely agreed. They had long believed that Southerners could not leave the Union and so restoration of rights, especially property rights for southern whites, would be a simple matter of affirming their future loyalty. Republicans resisted these easy terms but fought amongst themselves about the proper way to rebuild the nation's political system.

White Southerners also grappled with restoring order in their communities and explaining defeat to themselves. This proved particularly challenging for southern men. In the prewar era, white men had claimed authority by promising to protect and care for members of southern society they viewed as inferior to them, including women, children, and black people. Confederate defeat revealed the failure of **paternalism**. Southern women, in particular, had been forced to assume new burdens and responsibilities during the war. On Virginia plantations the economic consequences of defeat and emancipation forced men and women to share tasks and roles that were distinct before the war. By the 1870s, local agricultural organizations were encouraging men and women to cooperate in running their households and their farms. The **Farmers' Alliance**, a national version of these local bodies, maintained this policy. In their journal, distributed to hundreds of thousands of farming households across the country, the Alliance advised that "It is not too much to say that there is no other occupation in which men and women are engaged, whose work and cares and responsibilities fall with such nearly equal weight on the husband and wife, as do those of farming." The ethic of mutuality that developed in some rural communities around the South came more from necessity than ideology, but it still challenged one of the core aspects of prewar gender relations. In other places, the effects of the war compelled some women to reaffirm the hierarchy rather than press forward with changes. To do this, white women relinquished their wartime responsibilities and advocated traditional gender relationships. As one editorial in a Georgia newspaper noted, "a married man falling into misfortunes is more apt to retrieve his situation in the world than a single one, chiefly because . . . although abroad may be darkness and humiliation, yet there is still a little world of love at home of which he is monarch."

Emancipation in Comparative Perspective

Americans followed neither an inevitable nor an entirely distinct path after emancipation. Both Jamaica and South Africa experienced similarly sudden and disruptive emancipation moments in the mid-19th century. Although both places functioned as British colonies when they freed their slaves, in all three societies, whites followed emancipation by vigorously pursuing racial supremacy. This pursuit took different forms. In Jamaica, white elites used the emerging scientific consensus behind racial hierarchy to abdicate local control to London. As a consequence, white property holders on the island were protected at the expense of black workers. In South Africa, local whites achieved greater autonomy from the colonial office, and although they allowed black voting, whites retained economic and social power. Unlike Jamaica, which had a society sharply divided between a small number of white elites and a high number of landless blacks, South Africa possessed a sizeable rural white population. Like its southern counterpart in the United States, rural whites joined with elites to resist emancipation and, when resistance proved futile, work to establish white supremacy.

A pivotal moment in Jamaican emancipation came 30 years after the start of the process. In the fall of 1865, as Americans were struggling to devise the rules and goals of their own post-emancipation Reconstruction, word spread through the hemisphere of a rebellion of black farm workers in Jamaica. The **Morant Bay Rebellion** stemmed from inequities in post-emancipation Jamaica. The black laboring class continued to be denied access to land or political power, a consequence of policies designed by white leaders that restricted blacks to working as agricultural laborers. The rebellion consumed the eastern half of the island and left hundreds of black laborers dead and hundreds more beaten by state militia forces. American newspapers tracked the event and filtered it through the perspectives of the ongoing struggle over the role of the freedmen in American life. A southern paper described "terrible massacres of the whites" by bands of deranged blacks. In contrast, American abolitionists used the event as an object lesson in why full equality and political rights were necessary for all Southerners. According to Senator **Charles Sumner**, the freedmen of the South "were not unlike the freedmen of San Domingo or Jamaica . . . and have the same sense of wrong."

The United States avoided a Morant Bay Rebellion, though it did not grant freed people the degree of freedom Sumner recommended. A key distinction between the three experiments in Reconstruction proved to be the nature of political change in each society. In Jamaica, a mulatto elite, composed mostly of the descendents of slaveholders and their slaves, entered into the political system, but they mostly sided with the white elite. When legislators granted blacks the right to vote in South Africa, they also enacted a property restriction that ensured white domination. In contrast, black southern men received the vote without restriction. This helped make American Reconstruction the most radical of those slave societies that experienced emancipation in the 19th century.

STUDY QUESTIONS FOR THE YEAR OF JUBILEE, 1865

1. How did white and black Southerners respond to the end of the Civil War?
2. What did each group want for the postwar world?

SHAPING RECONSTRUCTION, 1865–1868

In 1865, a small group of Republican congressmen and senators had high hopes for a vigorous Reconstruction plan. Some were former abolitionists, and others had emerged during the war as advocates for a transformed South. These men—and a substantially more diverse body of black and white male and female reformers who urged them on—foresaw not just the expansion of free labor but a redistribution of southern wealth and an egalitarian political order that included black male suffrage. Between 1865 and 1866, this group—known as the "radical Republicans"—went from the margins to the center of the political debate, and they did so largely because Northerners perceived President Andrew Johnson as currying favor with an unrepentant South. The fight that erupted between Johnson and his own party in Congress opened strange new rifts in American politics and propelled Republicans toward a surprising and dramatic shift in Reconstruction. In a series of clashes with Johnson, Congressional Republicans adopted increasingly radical measures meant to secure the fruits of Union victory in the war and protect the rights of the freed people. The different phases of Reconstruction that followed illuminate the unpredictability of events after the war and the importance of partisan and sectional alignments in American politics.

Andrew Johnson's Reconstruction

As the uncertainty of spring gave way to summer, southern whites confidently assumed they would be allowed to continue with "self-reconstruction." Under this theory, white Southerners reaffirmed their loyalty to the United States through existing political systems. With Congress out of session, Andrew Johnson, the Tennessee Unionist who had become president after Lincoln's assassination, set the terms. Despite radicals' hopes that Johnson would impose strict conditions on the reentry of southern states, he set the bar low. Southerners needed to repudiate secession and state debts incurred during the war and confirm emancipation by ratifying the **Thirteenth Amendment**, which outlawed slavery in the United States. Johnson also extended amnesty to most of the high-ranking military and civilian officials of the Confederacy. Before the war, Johnson was a bitter enemy of the plantation elite, championing the cause of the white artisans and nonslaveholding farmers of East Tennessee. But in his efforts to keep pace with the shifting political alignments of the postwar era, Johnson became a staunch defender of white supremacy and recast himself as the defender of embattled white elites.

In fall 1865, southern states held new state elections. In the Upper South, a significant number of former Whigs and Unionists won, but voters in the Lower South largely reelected Democratic Party elites who led the region during the war. **Alexander Stephens**, the former vice president of the Confederacy, was elected U.S. senator from Georgia. Most Northerners, and even some Democrats, reacted with shock and anger. Did the South really imagine it could send the very men who had led a bloody rebellion against the United States to serve in Congress? Andrew Johnson, while frustrated that the election of openly disloyal men would prejudice the North against the region, accepted the results as a product of the democratic process. Radical Republicans grew increasingly uneasy with Johnson's leniency.

Forced to accept emancipation, reconstituted state governments across the region adopted a series of laws known collectively as the "**black codes**"in the fall of 1865, which proscribed both the extent and the limits of freedom for black residents in the region. The rights granted to freed people included the right to marry, to own property, and to participate in the judicial process, through suing and being sued and giving testimony in court cases, but the legislators paid much more attention to restrictions on black freedom. The most nefarious of these were the "apprenticeship" laws, which gave county courts the authority to take children away from parents if those parents were not capable of providing for them. Black Southerners and many Northerners perceived this as a blatant attempt to reimpose slavery. The codes also focused not just on ex-slaves but on "all freedpeople, free negroes, and mulattoes," effectively creating a new legal designation in southern law that singled out black people where previously status (free or slave) had been the key distinction among residents.

For Northerners, the second half of 1865 proved nearly as disorienting as the first half. Just as they experienced the elation of victory and anguish over Lincoln's assassination, Northerners moved from supporting Johnson's initial measures to reconstruct the South quickly to anger at Johnson's capitulation to Southern arrogance. Carl Schurz, a prominent Civil War general and radical Republican, had been sent on a tour of the South by Johnson in late 1865 to assess the situation, but his findings undercut support for Johnson's policies. White Southerners did not think of themselves as Americans and did not trust black Southerners to work in a new free labor economy. Schurz concluded that "it is not only the political machinery of the States and their constitutional relations to the general government, but the whole organism of southern society that must be reconstructed, or rather constructed anew, so as to bring it into harmony with the rest of American society." As Congress reconvened in December 1865, its members weighed the merits and methods of reconstructing the

South. After much debate, Congress slowed down the process of Reconstruction by refusing to seat the delegations recently elected from southern states.

The Fight over Reconstruction

The desire to punish the South for its refusal to accept the verdict of war manifested itself in the first session of the 39th Congress. These were the men elected in fall 1864, at the moment of the Union's triumph at Atlanta, Mobile Bay, and the Shenandoah Valley. They came into office on Lincoln's coattails, and they were overwhelmingly Republican. They held more than a 2-to-1 advantage in the House of Representatives and a 3-to-1 advantage in the Senate. Further, as Johnson alienated himself from moderate Republicans the balance of power in the party shifted toward the radicals. So it was with relative ease that Republicans overcame Democratic objections and refused to seat the delegations sent to Washington by the former Confederate states. Doing so amounted to a public challenge to Johnson's leadership and signaled a clear desire to slow down Reconstruction. Although Republicans would never have a free hand from their constituents, who worried about Reconstruction's costs and duration, a majority of Northerners and many southern unionists wanted to reevaluate the purpose and direction of Reconstruction policy in late 1865 and early 1866.

Republican congressmen worried about the economic state of the former Confederacy. Union and Confederate forces alike had destroyed huge swathes of the southern landscape, tearing down fence rails for firewood and tearing up railroads to weaken the Confederates' ability to fight. Most economically damaging of all was emancipation, which represented a capital loss of at least $3 billion for white Southerners. By one estimate, slave property comprised 60 percent of the wealth of the Deep South cotton states. The results on the Civil War in per capita terms were striking: the average total wealth of all southern farm operators dropped from $22,819 in 1860 to $3,168 a decade later. Freed people thus entered the labor market during a period of severe contraction, with most farmers possessing little cash with which to pay workers.

Because of the immediate necessity for freed people to sign a contract of some sort and begin earning money, they were in a poor position to negotiate with landowners. Agents of the Freedmen's Bureau served as the only check on exploitative labor agreements. In southwest Georgia, the bureau received a complaint from **Felix Massey**, a former slave who stated that "Sidney Burden had ambushed him along a country road, attempted to gouge out his eyes, and then fired a pistol his way 'contrary to the laws of the United States.'" Freedmen's Bureau agents settled labor disputes when they arose, but the Bureau never fielded more than 900 agents in the whole South, which rarely amounted to more than one per county. Despite the importance of their work, Johnson and Congressional Democrats denounced the Freedmen's Bureau as an unwarranted extension of federal power. White Southerners were much less subtle in their critique. **Josiah Nott**, an Alabamian and prominent prewar doctor, fumed against the reorganization of Mobile's public space to accommodate African Americans. "See how the damd Military, the nigger troops, the Freemen's Bureau spit upon us and rub it in." Republicans remained committed to a limited government, and many were concerned about the constitutional issues raised by the Bureau, but most regarded the work as too important to abandon. In 1866, Congress approved a one-year renewal of the Bureau. Johnson vetoed the bill and, in a sign of growing Republican solidarity, Congress overrode his veto.

Partisan politics played a large role in shaping the nature of Reconstruction. The Republican Party was only a decade old and had yet to establish any presence in the southern United States, which it needed if it was to remain a viable entity. Republicans sought to build a coalition of "loyal" voters—drawing on former Unionists in the South and African Americans if they were enfranchised, along with their core base in the North. A key component of their rhetoric in the period focused on the "Bloody Shirt," a patriotic appeal to reward Republicans for steering the country through the Civil War. They condemned Democrats as traitors who abetted the Confederacy. Republicans benefited from the rise of the veteran as an American icon during this period. In previous wars, veterans had been honored, but only after the Civil War was military service promoted as the purest expression of civic pride. Veterans themselves played a key role in promulgating this idea.

Fresh from his defeat over the renewal of the Freedmen's Bureau, Johnson picked another fight with Congress, this time over the 1866 Civil Rights Act. The first instance of federal law designed expressly to protect the rights of citizens, rather than prohibiting the actions of government, the bill was authored by moderate Republican **Lyman Trumball** of Illinois and was intended as a middle ground between radicals who wanted strong intervention in southern states to ensure racial equality and conservatives who feared the centralizing nature of such action. The bill established a common national citizenship for all people born in the United States and promised the "full and equal benefit of all laws and proceedings for the security of person and property." Although as one northern senator noted, "this species of legislation is absolutely revolutionary," because the bill did not spell out the rights that citizens enjoyed, it concealed continuing differences among Republicans. Johnson refused to accept even this moderate measure and he vetoed the bill. Johnson's explanation, as with his earlier veto of the Freedmen's Bureau, conveyed his refusal to accept the "centralization" of power initiated by the bill. Johnson also made white supremacy an important part of his veto, arguing that by granting black Americans equal access to the law, it denied rights to whites. To Johnson's horror, the bill seemed to grant "a perfect equality of the white and colored races . . . to be fixed by Federal law in every State of the Union." Congress again overrode Johnson and enacted the legislation. Johnson's opposition to these two central measures and his intemperate veto messages isolated him politically and pushed the sizeable body of moderate Republicans closer to the radicals.

The Civil War Amendments and American Citizenship

After the Civil Rights bill passed, Republicans began debating a broader protection of individual rights. As they discussed what would become the **Fourteenth Amendment,** Republicans again quarreled among themselves about the propriety of creating federal safeguards for individual rights. And again, moderates won the day, this time crafting a broad guarantee of national citizenship and equality before the law, but offering no specific protection of freed people's political rights. The second section of the amendment punished states that denied the vote to black men by reducing their representation in Congress. Under the prewar constitution, enslaved people counted as three-fifths of a free person for the purposes of apportionment; under the Fourteenth Amendment, if not enfranchised, they would effectively count as zero-fifths. This feature might compel southern states to enfranchise black men, but it put little pressure on Northern states to do the same because ignoring their small black populations did not substantially reduce northern representation in Congress. The amendment also repudiated the debt accumulated by the Confederate and Southern state governments, leaving the millions of dollars issued during the war in bonds and currency worthless.

In post-emancipation Jamaica, the British had pursued a similarly bold plan for full civil equality, although it imposed through the policies of the colonial secretary, Lord Glenelg, rather than through a constitution. In 1837, Glenelg explained that the "great cardinal principle of the law for the abolition of slavery is, that the apprenticeship of the emancipated slaves is to be immediately succeeded by personal freedom, in the full and unlimited sense of the term in which it is used in reference to the other subjects of the British Crown." Glenelg's policies held for a decade, but by the late 1840s, the government imposed restrictions on the right to vote and eventually suspended Jamaican self-government entirely. In Jamaica and the United States, the central governments issued broad grants of civil equality to recently freed slaves only to back away from these to give landholders more control over their labor force and to prevent black people from entering the political system.

During the debate over the Fourteenth Amendment, the moderate Republican senator from Maine **William Pitt Fessenden** inserted two words into the first section. His change, adopted without a vote, granted citizenship to "naturalized" residents alongside African Americans. This change extended America's protection of its foreign-born citizens around the globe. It proved particularly important for Irish Americans who had emigrated to the United States but who continued to participate in the effort to free Ireland from British rule. By declaring all naturalized residents of the United States citizens, the Fourteenth Amendment brought under the protection of the constitution immigrants who had persevered through the 1850s when nativist sentiment drove the creation of laws that denied them the vote or otherwise singled them out as second-class citizens. For the Fenians, U.S. citizenship also provided a crucial level of protection against arbitrary British imprisonment or conscription. Even as the amendment expanded rights for some, it contracted rights for others. For the first time, constitutional language restricted voting specifically to "males." Article I of the constitution refers only to "people" in sections on voting, but the Fourteenth Amendment set the minimum requirements as "male inhabitants" at least 21 years of age.

The issue of black voting lurked just beneath the surface of the disputes among Southerners, Johnson, and Congressional Republicans. Radicals and even some moderates had long believed in the wisdom and justice of the measure. In 1864, as loyal representatives of Louisiana considered a new state constitution, Abraham Lincoln had suggested voting privileges for the men of color, "especially the intelligent and former soldiers." A partisan imperative was at work as well. Republicans knew that the end of slavery also meant the end of the three-fifths principle in the constitution, where five enslaved people were counted as three free people for the purposes of enumeration. The result of emancipation would be a substantial gain for the South in terms of representation in the House of Representatives and the Electoral College. Enfranchising black men would give Republicans the means to defend themselves and also ensure that the party could build a base of support in the South. Participants in the struggle to adapt political and civil frameworks in a post-emancipation world understood their effort in a global context. Henry Turner, a leading black minister, equated emancipation and the postwar amendments with "the almost instantaneous liberation of the Russian serfs, and their immediate investiture with citizens' immunities."

Shortly after passage of the Fourteenth Amendment, Republicans began work on the **Fifteenth Amendment**. Ratified in 1870, the amendment issued a blanket prohibition against denying the right to vote on the basis of race. The amendment's failure to enfranchise women incensed women's suffrage advocates who had been working since the 1830s to win women the right to vote. Leading suffrage activists, like **Susan B. Anthony** and Elizabeth Cady Stanton, had essentially paused their work on this project during the war to help further emancipation. Congress's failure to consider women's suffrage created deep bitterness and led to tensions within the movement along racial lines. Elizabeth Cady Stanton railed, "think of Patrick and Sambo and Hans and Ung Tung who do not know the difference between a Monarchy and a Republic, who never read the Declaration of Independence . . . making laws for Lydia Maria Child, Lucretia Mott, or Fanny Kemble." Stanton's angry comparison of immigrants with the leaders of the women's rights movement underscored the personal nature of the issue.

The fighting between the radicals and the president had long-term significance. It empowered Congress to act decisively when the president would not. Georges Clemenceau, the future prime minister of France, came to the United States in 1865 as a journalist. He followed Washington politics carefully and succinctly summarized the status of affairs in September 1867: "The war between the President and Congress goes on, complicated from time to time by some unexpected turn. Contrary to all that has happened, is happening, and will happen in certain countries, the legislative power here has the upper hand." Clemenceau, an ardent liberal who had come to the United States to study the course of democracy after the war, approved. "Congress may, when it pleases, take the President by the ear and lead him down from his high seat, and he can do nothing about it except to struggle and shout . . . At each session they add a shackle to his bonds, tighten the bit in a different place, file a claw or tooth, and then when he is well bound up, fastened, and caught in an inextricable net of laws and decrees, more or less contradicting each other, they tie him to the stake of the Constitution and take a good look at him."

Congressional Reconstruction

Thaddeus Stevens, a Pennsylvania Republican, played a key role in the conflict with Johnson and the creation of federal protections for individual rights. Stevens helped lead the radical Republicans in Congress and served as perhaps the ablest and most dedicated white proponent of meaningful freedom for African Americans. Like other radicals, Stevens regarded the southern states as having actually left the Union. He believed that southern states could now be subjected to specific terms before they were granted reentry into the Union. For Stevens, the most important change—one compelled by humanity and justice as well as political necessity—was to diminish the clout of the white elites in southern life and elevate the freed people. Stevens believed that this could only be accomplished if the government broke up the great landholdings of the prewar era and distributed the land to former slaves, but President Johnson killed a brief experiment with resettlement undertaken by General **William T. Sherman** in early 1865. Despite Stevens' urging, Republicans could not bring themselves to advocate the redistribution of property.

For Stevens, the Southern reaction to the Fourteenth Amendment proved the necessity of radically reordering southern politics. After quick passage by Congress, white Southerners overwhelmingly rejected the measure. The boldness of the Southern refusal to consider the Fourteenth Amendment and the increasingly violent racial politics of the region—whites killed dozens of African Americans in Memphis and New Orleans during riots in the summer of 1866—pushed Congress to seize control of Reconstruction completely. In March 1867, Congress passed the first of a series of Reconstruction Acts. Dramatic in their scope, the legislation consolidated the 10

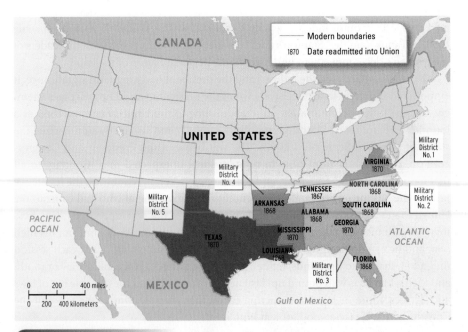

▲ **Map 15.2**

Military Districts Established by the Reconstruction Acts, 1867 One of the most radical pieces of legislation passed by the Reconstruction Congresses, these acts divided the South into five districts commanded by a military governor (usually a former Union army general). States had to revise their own constitutions to provide for universal manhood suffrage and ratify the Fourteenth Amendment before being returned to state status.

remaining ex-Confederate states into five military districts with former Union generals acting as military governors. Additionally, to return to the Union, states had to ratify the Fourteenth Amendment and revise their constitutions to provide for black male voting.

The legislative changes of 1867 signaled the decisive shift of power within Washington to Capitol Hill. Angry Republicans hamstrung Johnson with laws of bewilderingly intricacy in the hopes of creating a pretext for impeaching him. The "Tenure of Office" act, for example, restricted the president's ability to remove appointees that required Senate approval for their positions. After clashing with Congress over the constitutionality of this law in mid-1867, the House of Representatives impeached Johnson. The first U.S. president to ever be impeached, Johnson remained in office because the Senate failed to convict him by one vote. However, politically he was powerless. By the end of the year, Republicans turned with relief to selecting Johnson's successor, choosing the enormously popular Union general **Ulysses S. Grant**. Grant won election easily in 1868, running on a platform of sectional reconciliation under the slogan "Let Us Have Peace."

The first charge to the military governors now administering the southern states was to hold elections to select delegates for state constitutional conventions. Black

The impeachment of Andrew Johnson and his subsequent trial in the Senate (pictured here) established the clear dominance of Congress over the process and politics of Reconstruction.

men participated in the election and helped produce a strong Republican victory, including the election of a majority of black delegates in South Carolina and Louisiana. In other southern states, black delegates comprised only a small percent of the delegates, but even that small number invalidated the entire process for most white Southerners. The victories in the South confirmed that the Republican Party would stay competitive in the region as long as they could maintain the full support of the African American community.

STUDY QUESTIONS FOR SHAPING RECONSTRUCTION, 1865–1868

1. Why did Republicans endorse a more radical Reconstruction policy than Andrew Johnson?
2. How did the changes made by Congress reshape the relationship between state and federal power?

RECONSTRUCTION IN THE SOUTH, 1866–1876

Even as congress and the president fashioned and refashioned Reconstruction in Washington, black and white Southerners shaped the postwar world on the ground. They disputed the terms of work, housing, property, politics, and social relationships. For black Southerners, the first order of business was to create autonomous lives. True emancipation required not just free individuals but communities dedicated to uplifting and supporting its members. Politically, Reconstruction entailed creating Republican governments that would implement the policies articulated by Congress. Politics monopolized the public's attention but the success of Reconstruction, and the ability of African Americans to make their freedom real, hinged on rebuilding the southern economy.

African American Life in the Postwar South

The efforts that black Southerners made to reconstitute their families in the wake of emancipation laid the foundation for their postwar communities. The neighborhoods that defined the life of enslaved men and women in the plantation districts became the basis for new free communities. Churches occupied the heart of these new communities. In some cases, they were new congregations; in others, they were biracial parishes from before the war that split into separate white and black churches after the war. By 1866, 62 percent of black Methodists had left their prewar churches. But more people came to the independent black churches after the war, and those who did joined a community that played a key role in reconstructing the South.

Another key change came with the Freedmen's Bureau and their drive to build schools. Before the Civil War, no southern state maintained a public education system. Northerners viewed education as essential to both political and economic progress. Many Northerners believed that secession resulted from an undereducated white population. African Americans, in particular, viewed education as essential. Beginning in contraband camps during the war, freed people sought out **literacy**. Denied to them as slaves, literacy and higher education promised a life beyond the fields and satisfied many people's desire to read the Bible themselves. People of all ages lined up at churches and schools, where instruction was available throughout the day and usually well into the evening. Despite complaints from white Southerners about the cost, public education proved one of the lasting accomplishments of Reconstruction-era governments.

The eagerness with which black Americans embraced their new lives as full citizens of the United States manifested itself in public celebrations of Emancipation Day and the Fourth of July. The first of these events began during the war itself, in Union-occupied territory on the Sea Islands of South Carolina, where Union general **Thomas Wentworth Higginson** listened to a crowd of freed people spontaneously burst into the national anthem when the flag was raised. "I never saw anything so electric; it made all other words cheap . . . it seemed the choked voice of a race at last unloosed." Such celebrations formed the bedrock of an emerging black culture. The most enduring of these events, "Juneteenth," began in Texas as a commemoration of the war's end and evolved into a celebration of African American freedom that continues to be marked today.

The parades and festivals that accompanied these events provided an opportunity for community leaders—teachers, ministers, and politicians—to speak on themes both historical and contemporary. The messages they broadcast varied by place,

The act of voting signaled a bedrock equality between white and black men that few on either side could have imagined at the beginning of the Civil War in 1861.

gender, class position, and political ideology. Some emphasized cooperation with whites while others preached self-help. **Martin Delaney**, the highest-ranking black officer during the Civil War, told a South Carolina audience in 1865, "I tell you slavery is over, and shall never return again. We have now 200,000 of our men well drilled in arms and used to War fare and I tell you it is with you and them that slavery shall not come back again, if you are determined it will not return again." Some spoke through the language of religion and salvation, while others used the secular language of rights and law. Regardless of their differences, all of the speakers emphasized that black people would remain a permanent and progressive force for change and democracy within America. Rather than distancing themselves from the past, southern African Americans proudly remembered the perseverance of their ancestors through generations of slavery.

The festivals through which black Americans celebrated emancipation and Union victory also provided an opportunity for political organization. The Union League emerged as the most important institutional support for black politics. Started during the war as an adjunct to the Republican Party in the North, Union Leagues became social and political centers in many of the North's largest cities. After the war, the Leagues transformed into a grass-roots movement that helped black Southerners organize themselves politically. Albion Tourgee, a northern lawyer who lived in North Carolina during Reconstruction, wrote a famous novel, *A Fool's Errand*, that chronicled his experiences with Reconstruction. He described the Union Leagues as intended to "[cultivate] . . . an unbounded devotion for the flag in the hearts of the embryonic citizens, and [keep] alive the fire of patriotism in the hearts of the old Union element." The "fool" who comes south in the novel failed to appreciate the depth of hostility manifested by white Southerners against both their black neighbors and Northerners who came south. Inculcating love of the old flag was bad enough, but throughout the southern states, Republicans organized local Union Leagues that helped educate and mobilize voters.

Even though the Civil War ended the split in the U.S. economy between free and slave labor, it did not equalize wages between the two sections or between the races. The South replaced slavery with a low-wage free labor system and within that, African Americans consistently received lower pay for equivalent work done by white workers. The majority of black Southerners remained agricultural workers, but very few worked their own land. Instead, Southerners expanded a little-used prewar practice called sharecropping, in which landless workers signed contracts to take up residence and farm plots of land, often on property belonging to former slaveholders. In exchange for leasing land, property owners claimed 50 percent or more of the profits at harvest time. When sharecropping first came into use it met the needs of property owners who needed labor to farm the land but had no money with which to pay wages and workers who wanted more autonomy. **Sharecroppers** set their own schedules and supervised themselves in the field, but crucially it was usually landowners who chose the crop.

All across the Deep South and much of Arkansas, Tennessee, and North Carolina, that choice was cotton. Merchants, among the few actors in the postwar southern economic system with access to credit, insisted on receiving cotton. The changes in the

The political opportunities African Americans experienced during Reconstruction were not matched by economic opportunities. Across much of the Deep South, the only work available to black men and women continued to be agricultural labor in cotton fields.

global cotton market, however, produced price fluctuations and great uncertainty for growers. Adding to the structural problems, white landowners exploited their laborers and merchants squeezed them on prices for goods and supplies. Egypt and India entered the global cotton market during the Civil War, adding competition and uncertainty for U.S. producers. As a result, sharecropping quickly trapped farmers in cycles of debt. The results ensured overuse and poor treatment of southern lands, a stunted regional economy, and little progress for African American farmers. As Georges Clemenceau, who toured the country in the late 1860s, observed, "The real misfortune of the negro race is in owning no land of its own. There cannot be real emancipation for men who do not possess at least a small portion of the soil."

Republican Governments in the Postwar South

The Republican state governments established after the round of constitutional conventions in 1867–1868 were fragile and awkward alliances between groups with widely divergent interests. Black Southerners represented by far the largest component of the party. They wanted to receive a genuinely fair opportunity to perform work, buy land, gain an education, and live autonomous lives. White northern Republicans, labeled "carpetbaggers" by conservatives because they assumed Northerners were only coming South to make quick money, focused on economic development. As the national party shifted to support black voting, its southern wing did so as well, though this was never a priority for the leaders who represented the region in Congress and

GLOBAL PASSAGES

Reconstruction Abroad

As Clemenceau's presence demonstrated, emancipation was of interest to people around the globe. Before the Civil War, American abolitionists focused on the Caribbean, where the Haitian Revolution and British abolition formed two different alternatives to ponder as they sought to destroy slavery. Despite their opposition to the practice of slaveholding, only a few black radicals advocated anything like the Haitian Revolution. The vast majority of antislavery activists sought to emulate British emancipation, a legalistic event that left property and lives intact. As more time elapsed from their transition to free labor, American slaveholders also had more material with which to evaluate the effects of emancipation. According to one observer in 1860, "In St. Domingo, the French have been destroyed by the blacks; in Jamaica, the English are being fully absorbed by them." American slaveholders initiated secession and civil war to avoid the fate of either of these Caribbean neighbors.

For decades before the Civil War, hemispheric emancipation experiments had been discussed, written about, and pondered, but the shock and force of U.S. emancipation spread through the region with remarkable speed. Alongside the United States, in 1860 only Brazil and Cuba remained major slave powers in the western hemisphere. During the war, the absence of the South from the global cotton market proved a boon to Brazilian growers even as it weakened the Brazilian coffee industry, which relied on sales to the United States. In Brazil, this dynamic produced strong incentives for coffee growers to scale back slave purchases at the same time that southern Brazilian cotton growers increased them. This worried Brazilians who already knew, from the U.S. experience, that a regionally bifurcated slave economy could produce disaster. As one Brazilian senator noted in 1862, "was it not the case, that when some years ago in the United States the Northern states abolished

state houses. Native white Southerners proved the most troublesome part of the coalition. They had to brave the scorn of fellow whites when they joined the party. Usually prewar Whigs or wartime Unionists, white Southerners rarely came to the party with any interest in black voting or civil rights. Democrats eagerly exploited the conflicting interests in the Republican Party.

In those states with well-established free black communities before the Civil War, black voters demonstrated a greater diversity of political opinion. Charleston, Savannah, and New Orleans all included independent, educated, and prosperous communities of free people of color, many of whom carried into the postwar world conservative values on economics and community leadership. The split within black communities can be seen clearly in the case of Mobile, Alabama. After the Union navy captured the

slavery, and it remained in the Southern States, the industrial interests of the Southern States became entirely opposed to those of the Northern States? Was it not after the creation and growth of this diversity of interests that the explosion took place which has not yet terminated?"

The surprising end of the U.S. Civil War, with full, immediate, and uncompensated emancipation, worried Brazilian slaveholders much more than the problem of regional balance. Brazil, independent of Portugal since 1822, aspired to join the first rank of new world nations. Many of its leading politicians soon realized that doing so against the tide of global opinion that ranked slavery as a relic of the barbarous past would prove difficult if not impossible. The leading British diplomat in Brazil noted that after 1865, he detected "a rapidly growing feeling among the leading men of the necessity of the abolition of slavery." By 1871, Brazil had adopted a law freeing the children of enslaved mothers, the first step on a path to full abolition that concluded in 1888. In Cuba, which remained under the control of the Spanish empire, similar fears about the future of slavery manifested themselves as soon as the war concluded. In 1865, a conservative Spanish politician concluded, "the war in the United States is finished, and being finished, slavery on the whole American continent can be taken as finished." Like the Brazilians, the Spanish in Cuba implemented a much slower and more cautious emancipation policy. In the latter case, violent independence movements intersected with emancipation to complicate the situation still more. But Brazilians and Cubans saw clearly in 1865 that slavery's end in the United States shifted global opinion against the practice and left them intellectually and politically isolated. The interconnectedness of the American economies that had done so much to enrich Brazil and Cuba in the first two-thirds of the century proved a central part of their undoing in the last third.

- • How did Americans respond to British and French emancipation in the Caribbean?

- • How did U.S. emancipation affect other slave regimes in the hemisphere?

port city in August 1864, enslaved people flooded into it seeking freedom. After the initial flush of enthusiasm in the late 1860s, a deep division opened within the black community. On one hand, well-educated, middle-class blacks pursued a moderate politics focused mostly on economic recovery and the protection of property. To achieve these goals, they advocated cooperation with white Southerners who would work with the Republicans. A larger group, mostly freed people, pushed more aggressively for the protection of civil rights and education and they did so without white allies. Over the next several years, these groups competed to court black voters and even attracted the interest of white Southerners who saw a chance to dilute Republican strength.

In many places, white conservatives had initially boycotted elections that resulted from the constitutional conventions of 1867–1868. Hoping to undermine the

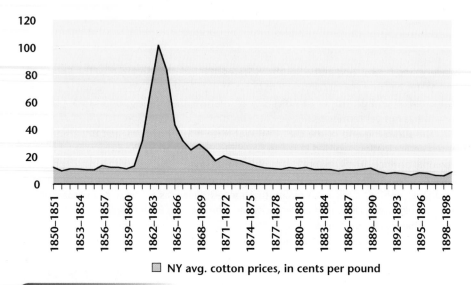

▲ **Figure 15.1**

U.S. cotton prices, 1850–1900 The stable and lucrative cotton market changed significantly because of the Civil War. Responding to the Confederate embargo on cotton sales, England and France turned to new suppliers in Asia and the Middle East, which drove prices down for the remainder of the century.

legitimacy of these new governments, they succeeded only in hastening Republican dominance. In other states, some conservatives made alliances with Republicans to create coalition governments. But the 1872 national elections, in which Ulysses S. Grant was reelected despite substantial opposition within his own party, revealed a weakness that Democrats longed to exploit. Beginning in 1873, white conservatives returned to the political system and used charges of corruption and profligacy to defeat the Republicans. Both charges contained some merit—Republican legislators in the South, like those of both parties in state governments all across the country, were susceptible to the bribes and favors of the rich and well connected. The wide scale of corruption within Grant's administration had even threatened his reelection. Also, the policies that Republicans implemented—especially public education—required new taxes. Before the war, slaveholders and large property owners shouldered most of the tax burden, but with no slave property to tax, postwar state governments imposed property taxes on a much broader range of people. Even though the children of white property owners benefited from public education, they condemned the taxes required to pay for them. Democrats capitalized on these legitimate policy disputes and campaigned vigorously on the platform of white supremacy to retake state governments.

Cotton, Merchants, and the Lien

In 1865, the southern United States was part of a region, extending south through Central America and the Caribbean and into northeastern Brazil, where plantation agriculture predominated. In the United States, cotton predominated; in the Caribbean,

Despite the numerous obstacles to cotton production, southern river and ocean ports looked much as they had before the Civil War, with bales of cotton stacked and ready for transport, only now into an increasingly competitive global market.

sugar; and in Brazil, coffee. This style of agriculture required huge plots of land, a large labor force, and high volumes of capital and credit. The plantation system changed but did not disappear after the Civil War. The major change entailed the use of tenant labor or sharecropping in place of the gang labor used under slavery, but land continued to be owned in large allotments and management functioned as it had before the war. Even though many sharecroppers worked with some autonomy, landowners determined crop choices, fertilizer use, and harvest dates.

Even with the scattered residential pattern typical of the postwar era and the substantial effort made by sharecroppers to claim ownership of the crop, landowning planters continued to dominate southern agriculture. They did so partly through the effective control of the **crop lien**, which represented farm workers' claim to ownership of the crops they raised. In Georgia, North Carolina, and Tennessee, the state supreme courts all ruled that the portion of crops given to a sharecropper constituted a wage. This removed from the sharecroppers any legal claim over the crops that they planted, raised, and harvested.

One of the few groups of workers to exercise some control over labor conditions and wages were sugar workers. Sugar's value had spurred Europeans' initial effort to import large numbers of Africans to the New World. Sugar growing and especially the process of harvesting earned an infamous reputation as the most deadly agricultural work in the Americas. It also required significant skill. Because the sugar cane had to be harvested at exactly the right moment and quickly processed, those workers with knowledge of the crop possessed more leverage to negotiate better terms with their employers. In the decade after emancipation, sugar workers—mostly in Louisiana's southern parishes—used politics and collective action to halt wage cuts and pursued the right to produce garden plots. Even after the Democrats regained power in the states, black sugar workers stayed their ground. Several large strikes in the early 1880s, some with white and black workers cooperating, laid the ground for the broader organization of workers under the **Knights of Labor** at the end of the decade. In the other major sugar-producing country in the hemisphere—Cuba—the post-emancipation story evolved differently. By the 1880s, when Cuba's emancipation took full effect, sugar work was not done exclusively by people of African descent. Black Cubans, mixed-race Cubans, and more recent Spanish immigrants all labored together, and their solidarity as workers undercut the use of racism that had been so effective in Louisiana. The comparatively stronger and more diverse community of Cuban sugar workers revealed another route that emancipation could take in the Americas.

Because sharecropping allowed white property owners to make their money from land, and related merchant work, they had no incentive to pursue industrial development. Between 1860 and 1880, the number of manufacturing establishments in the South increased from 30,000 to 50,000 and from 1880 to 1900 they grew from 50,000 to nearly 120,000, although this was still significantly lower than the northern total from 1860. The failure to build factories in the Reconstruction-era South was not for lack of trying. The Republicans who assumed power in southern states in the late 1860s and 1870s set economic development as their number one goal. The most important vital element of this plan was the railroad. Northern Republicans especially had a mystical faith in the railroad's ability to spur development of all sorts. As a Tennessee Republican asserted, "A free and living Republic [will] spring up in the track of the railroad as inevitably, as surely as grass and flowers follow in the spring." Unfortunately, southern states and southern investors could not meet the capital demands of new railroad construction. Northern and foreign investors found more lucrative and less risky places to put their money and despite significant public attention, few new lines were built. Further, frequent charges of corruption surrounding railroads weakened Republicans at the polls. Other Republican policies did more to earn the support of their constituents, most importantly Republican efforts to give sharecroppers and tenant farmers control over crop liens.

STUDY QUESTIONS FOR RECONSTRUCTION IN THE SOUTH, 1866–1876

1. What was the experience of Reconstruction like for freed people in the South?
2. How did they protect their interests? How did whites seek to subvert those interests?

THE END OF RECONSTRUCTION, 1877

For most of the 100 years following the end of Reconstruction, historians described the period as its contemporary white critics did—as the unconscionable elevation of blacks to positions of power from which they deprived whites of their rights and bankrupted southern states. Sympathetic to southern whites and grounded in openly racist assumptions about the moral and intellectual inferiority of black people, these historians promoted a factually inaccurate and deeply compromised view of the era as one that attempted too much and failed. Thanks to a fundamentally different attitude about the meaning of race and a generation of research, historians today hold a nearly opposite view. They regard Congressional Reconstruction as well intentioned and appropriate to the situation. In their view, Reconstruction failed because the federal government did not persevere against southern white resistance. The demise of Reconstruction—defined as the end of Republican governments in the region—came because of forces both internal and external to the South. The changes in how historians have accounted for that end and the meanings they have attached to it reveal how long it took America to outgrow the racial and political values of the era.

The Ku Klux Klan and Reconstruction Violence

The bitterest and most violent opponents of Reconstruction, and black freedom more generally, emerged at the very start of the era. In late 1865, a small group of men gathered in Pulaski, Tennessee, and organized the **Ku Klux Klan**. Membership in the group spread by word of mouth across the state and soon through the region. Within a year, Klan members made denying African Americans any legitimate role in the public

The Ku Klux Klan, a terrorist group bent on reestablishing white supremacy after the end of slavery, came to dominate many regions of the South. They pursued black leaders of all stripes—politicians, ministers, businessmen, and teachers—and their white allies with brutal violence.

sphere their principle goal. As a white newspaper enthusiastically reported about the Memphis chapter in 1868, "it is rapidly organizing wherever the insolent negro, the malignant white traitor to his race and the infamous squatter are plotting to make the South utterly unfit for the residence of the decent white man. It will arrest the progress of that secret negro conspiracy which has for its object the establishment of negro domination." They also targeted white Republicans—especially native white Southerners who cooperated with the party—for their efforts to build an interracial democracy in the South. Klan members whipped, beat, burnt, and killed all manner of community leaders through the South. They targeted ministers, teachers, political leaders, and successful businessmen or farmers. The high point of Klan-related violence came in response to the Reconstruction Acts and to the prominent role played by Africans Americans in the reorganization of southern life between 1868 and 1871.

Klan violence grew so public and so extreme that Congress finally took action. In 1870–1871, Republicans passed a series of laws, collectively known as the Force Acts, designed to impede the operation of the Ku Klux Klan. They did this by punishing as a federal crime any attempt to obstruct a person in the practice of a designated civil right. One of the Klan's most effective weapons was intimidation of black voters. The Enforcement Acts targeted this practice directly by designating as conspiracies any attempts to coerce black men at the polls or deny them access to the vote. Congress created the Department of Justice and tasked it with bringing cases against those men who used violence to enforce white supremacy. On a few occasions, President Grant sent the army itself into southern districts to disrupt and capture Klan cells. Finally, during 1871, Congress held hearings at which the testimony of both victims and alleged members of the Klan told their stories to a national audience. Although the Justice Department was underfunded and less energetic in their prosecutions than southern Republicans wished, they initiated thousands of prosecutions and secured hundreds of convictions across the South, driving the Klan underground.

Even with their success against the Klan, Northerners did not eradicate violence in southern life. Klan members became, in effect, an arm of the Democratic Party. In Louisiana, the Knights of the White Camellia and the White League superseded the Klan. Mississippi saw the creation of "rifle clubs." Regardless of the terminology, after 1871, southern whites reorganized their attack on Republican governments in the states. Louisiana saw a particularly bitter struggle. White conservatives in the state opposed the election of **Henry Warmoth**, a northern lawyer and Civil War officer who operated mostly as a party of one, appointing men loyal to him alone and throwing the state into chaos. He was succeeded by **William Kellogg**, a radical Republican even more noxious to Louisiana Democrats.

All across Louisiana in 1873, conservatives began organizing themselves and turning legally elected Republican officeholders out of office. Sometimes, they simply intimidated the local sheriffs, judges, and tax assessors who comprised the body of local government in the state. Others times, they committed violence against officeholders or the families. The most notorious episode involved an attack on the northern parish town of Colfax. Residents of the town learned of the plan in advance, and perhaps 200 black men from the area converged on the courthouse on the morning

THE LOUISIANA MURDERS—GATHERING THE DEAD AND WOUNDED.—[See Page 396.]

The Colfax Massacre embodied the ultimately successful strategy used in Louisiana, Mississippi, and South Carolina to drive the last Republicans from the region. The failure of local, state, and federal authorities to find any justice for the victims stands as one of the worst tragedies of Reconstruction.

of Easter Sunday, 1873. Armed with a variety of weapons, they came to protect the men they had elected. A white militia composed of several hundred men organized in neighboring Montgomery rode into town and drove the defenders back into the courthouse, which they set afire. The attackers shot men as they escaped and captured more, executing 37 that evening. By nightfall, they had killed around 150 defenders in the worst racial massacre in U.S. history. The lesson to Republicans around the state was clear—white Democrats would stop at nothing to purge them from office. Whites in other southern states observed the success of Louisiana conservatives, and many adopted the same strategy.

Northern Weariness and Northern Conservatism

Governor Kellogg's metropolitan police force helped keep order in New Orleans, but without the support of the federal government, he could do little to protect fellow Republicans in outlying parishes. In a few isolated instances, President Grant sent U.S. troops back into the South to help quell disorder. Interventions like these exposed

Grant to the charge that his administration had failed to secure the peace he promised in 1868. It opened Republicans to criticism from fiscal conservatives about the continuing expense of Reconstruction and, more cynically, to those who felt that black Southerners needed to defend themselves from whites or suffer the consequences. The violence in Mississippi in 1875 drove the governor, a young white Northerner named Adelbert Ames, to request federal troops. Grant had responded positively in 1874, sending a small contingent of troops to Vicksburg. The situation deteriorated even more the following year. Ames's telegram to the White House explained the dire situation: "I am in great danger of losing my life. Not only that, all the leading Republicans, who have not run away, in danger . . . The [White] league here have adopted a new policy, which is to kill the leaders and spare the colored people, unless they 'rise'." This time Grant worried more about weakening Republicans at the polls in the North than with defending Republicans in the South. "The whole public are tired out with these annual autumnal outbreaks in the South . . . [and] are ready now to condemn any interference on the part of the Government," he told his attorney general. Grant, who had conquered Vicksburg, Mississippi, for the Union in 1863, sent no troops this time.

Federal courts likewise reflected northern impatience with the duration and expense of Reconstruction in their increasing reluctance to support black or Republican plaintiffs. The most important of these cases revolved around the defendants arrested for leading the Colfax Massacre. Unable to secure justice in local courts, federal prosecutors sought a conviction on charges of violating the civil rights of the murdered officeholders. In *Cruikshank v. U.S.*, the Supreme Court ruled that the Fourteenth Amendment only protected citizens against official state actions not private violence. Because the massacre's ringleader, William Cruikshank, operated without state sanction, the amendment offered no protection. Cruikshank went free, and in the process the court dramatically narrowed the scope of protection offered by the Fourteenth Amendment. The *Cruikshank* case was decided in 1876, the same year that a new Republican won the presidency. Rutherford B. Hayes secured the office after the contested election of 1876, when Republicans and Democrats clashed over the returns from Louisiana, Florida, and South Carolina. Both sides agreed to count the presidential ballots for Hayes, but gave Democrats control at the state level. This ended the last three Republican state governments in the South and initiated an era of Democratic dominance that lasted for most of the next century. Shortly after his inauguration, Hayes recalled the last few thousand U.S. troops out of the South, officially ending the period of Reconstruction.

Northerners' fatigue with Reconstruction also resulted from their preoccupation with the rapid changes happening in their own region. The wave of city building in the 1840s and 1850s that had developed during the technological boom of that era (telegraph, canals, and railroads) increased after the war. Immigrants continued to pour into northern cities, where their rapid incorporation changed the political contours of the region. Legislation passed by the dynamic wartime Congress also began to bear fruit. The most important of these was the **Homestead Act**, which allowed families to claim 160 acres of land if they improved it over five years of residence. The bill opened the western United States to white settlement. Accompanying settlers in the

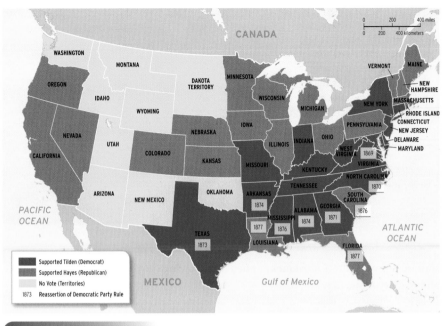

▲ Map 15.3

1876 Presidential Election, by State Although the Republican presidential candidate, Rutherford B. Hayes, was credited with the electoral votes of Louisiana, South Carolina, and Florida, these states all elected Democratic governors and legislatures. This ended the presence of statewide Republican rule in the South and marked the end of political Reconstruction.

movement west was the nation's first Transcontinental Railroad, which had also been authorized by the 37th Congress. Congressmen, land developers, and businessmen regarded the railroad line, which reduced travel time between the Atlantic and Pacific coasts from months to days, as the nation's most important economic development measure.

As the Union Pacific laid track, Indian communities of the West resisted. During the Civil War, the U.S. Army had largely ceded the region back to Indian control. Indians exploited the opportunity of a distracted United States and undermanned forts to reestablish their historic position. With the coming of peace in 1865, a newly expanded, trained, and disciplined U.S. Army moved west. The Sioux, in particular, had challenged U.S. authority during the war, culminating in a wide-scale uprising in Minnesota that was violently suppressed by the army. Military tribunals had originally sentenced 303 men to death for crimes against settlers during the Minnesota conflicts, but Lincoln commuted the death sentences for 264 prisoners and allowed the execution of 39 others. After the war, western Indians faced an emboldened army without the aid of a sympathetic executive. The shift away from Indian's hunting and low-impact farming practices to the more intensive style of American agriculture caused significant change throughout the Great Plains and the West and within a few decades

By settling the long-standing political conflicts over the future of slavery, the Civil War set in motion massive white migration into the western states and territories. This process brought white Americans into more intimate contact, both benign and malignant, with native peoples all across the western landscape.

spurred a preservation movement aimed at balancing the development of the region and conserving its natural beauty.

Legacies of Reconstruction

Before **John Muir**, one of the most important environmental activists of the era, gained fame as a protector and champion of the American West, he toured the South during Reconstruction. Leaving his home in Indianapolis in early 1867, Muir walked south to Florida, observing flora, fauna, and the human wildlife along the way. In addition to wry observations about the "long-haired ex-guerillas" of the Tennessee and North Carolina mountains, Muir chronicled the attitudes of the white and black citizens with whom he interacted on his trip. In Georgia, he observed, "the traces of war

TIMELINE 1865–1888

1865

January 31 Congress proposes the 13th Amendment

March 3 Congress establishes the Bureau of Refugees, Freedmen, and Abandoned Lands

April 9 Robert E. Lee's Army surrenders to Ulysses S. Grant at Appomattox, VA

April 14 Abraham Lincoln assassinated by John Wilkes Booth

April 26 Joseph Johnston's Army surrenders to William T. Sherman at Durham, NC

October Morant Bay Rebellion in Jamaica

December 6 Ratification of the 13th Amendment abolishes slavery in the United States

Southern state legislatures pass "Black Codes"

Ku Klux Klan organized in Pulaski, TN

1866

February 19 President Andrew Johnson vetoes the Freedmen's Bureau reauthorization bill

March 27 President Andrew Johnson vetoes the 1866 Civil Rights Act

May 1 Memphis race riot

June 13 Congress proposes the 14th Amendment

July 16 Congress overrides Johnson's veto of the Freedmen's Bureau Act and the Civil Rights Act

July 30 New Orleans race riot

1867

March Congress passes Reconstruction Acts

Southern state constitutional conventions begin across the South with mixed race delegates

1868

February 24 House of Representatives votes to impeach Andrew Johnson

April 9 Senate votes not to convict Andrew Johnson

June 9 Ratification of 14th Amendment establishes citizenship rights and due process for citizens

November 3 Republican Ulysses S. Grant elected president

1869

February 26 Congress proposes the 15th Amendment

are not only apparent on the broken fields, burnt fences, mills, and woods ruthlessly slaughtered, but also on the countenances of the people. A few years after a forest has been burned, another generation of bright and happy trees arises . . . So with the people of this war-field. Happy, unscarred, and unclouded youth is growing up around the aged, half-consumed, and fallen parents." The sadness that Muir observed in 1867 had changed to anger a decade later. Southern whites ended Reconstruction embittered against African Americans for the efforts they had made to claim civil rights, contemptuous of the federal government for assistance—however meager—they had given that effort, and deeply suspicious of the open, bipartisan politics that flourished briefly in the 1870s. All three of these attitudes weakened the South over time and encouraged whites to regard the most important political and social goal for their communities as the violent protection of white supremacy.

The unwillingness of federal authorities to enforce the civil rights laws and especially the Fourteenth and Fifteenth Amendments left southern African Americans isolated, but blacks were never solely victims. From the earliest days of North American slavery, they had resisted the institution, and their actions during and after Reconstruction reveal a similar refusal to be defined by white actions. In early 1866, a group of "colored citizens" in Florida complained to then Secretary of War Grant that "the Civil authoritys here are taking from the Colord People all the fire arms that they find in their Persesion, including Dubble barrel Shot Guns, Pistols of any kind." Without the means of self-defense they would be reliant on the government for their protection. Years before, Frederick Douglass had observed of black Americans, "It is enough to say, that if a knowledge of the use of arms is desirable in any people, it is desirable in us." As the Florida men who petitioned Ulysses Grant made clear, it remained desirable, sadly, imperative, after the war as well. Perhaps anticipating the day when Northerners would abandon the effort, they closed by noting that "if Congress Do not Stand Squarely up for us, and Make Laws that Will Protect us, over the heads of the States,

1870	Klan Hearings to assess and publicize violence against freed people and their white allies in the South	U.S. House of Representatives	U.S. troops from the South
February 3 Ratification of the 15th Amendment prohibits discrimination in voting on the basis of race or previous condition of servitude		**1875**	Democrats seize control of last three southern states (Florida, South Carolina, and Florida) still governed by Republicans
		March 1 Congress passes 1875 Civil Rights Act	
	1872	**1876**	
May 31 U.S. Congress passes "Force Act" giving it the power to crack down on the Ku Klux Klan (followed by complementary legislation later in 1870 and 1871)	**November 29** Republican Ulysses S. Grant reelected president	**March 27** Supreme Court issues *U.S. v. Cruikshank* verdict, which restricted meaning of 14th Amendment to protection against actions taken by state actors	**1879**
			Albion Tourgee publishes *A Fool's Errand*
	1873		
	April 13 Colfax Massacre in northern Louisiana kills approximately 150 people		**1886**
			Cuba abolishes slavery
1871	**1874**	**1877**	**1888**
Brazil passes gradual emancipation law	**November** Democrats gain control of	**March 4** Rutherford B. Hayes inaugurated president; recalls last	Brazil abolishes slavery
Congress holds Ku Klux			

We are Nothing More than Searfs." Congress did not stand up "squarely," but southern African Americans forged ahead on their own. They pursued an egalitarian politics through the Republican Party, and many protected and used that vote until the end of the century. They also built communities, churches, schools, and businesses. These institutions and the networks of support and self-improvement that developed among them sustained black Southerners until another struggle against Southern violence produced America's Second Reconstruction—the Civil Rights Movement of the 1950s and 1960s—and the nation finally stood square.

STUDY QUESTIONS FOR THE END OF RECONSTRUCTION, 1877

1. Why did Reconstruction end in 1877?
2. What explains the northern willingness to abandon the policies they initiated in 1867?

Summary

- In common with Brazil and Cuba, the two other major slave societies in the hemisphere, the American South struggled to reorganize its labor and landholding systems in the wake of emancipation.
- Unlike in those two nations, in America, blacks gained the vote and helped build new systems of public education over the opposition of southern whites and their allies in Washington.
- Southerners desperately needed money to rebuild and modernize the region's infrastructure, but stripped of capital by war and relying primarily on agricultural enterprises, Southerners had little success attracting American or European funds.
- Conservative southern whites used both voting and violence, the latter formalized in the Ku Klux Klan and white militias, to defeat the Republican governments that represented such a sharp break with the region's past and end Reconstruction.
- Northerners, eager to develop the West and extend American influence within the Caribbean and across the oceans and weary of the expense and trouble of the South, consented to a return to Democratic rule, but the community building and education already enacted by African Americans created the networks that sustained them through the years of Jim Crow.

Key Terms and People

Alexander, Edward Porter *570*
Anthony, Susan B. *577*
black codes *537*
Booth, John Wilkes *569*

crop lien *587*
Davis, Jefferson *569*
Delaney, Martin *582*
Farmers' Alliance *570*

Fessenden, William Pitt *576*
Fifteenth Amendment *577*
Fourteenth Amendment *575*
Freedmen's Bureau *569*
Grant, Ulysses S. *579*
Higginson, Thomas Wentworth *581*
Homestead Act *592*
Howard, Oliver Otis *569*
Kellogg, William *590*
Knights of Labor *588*
Ku Klux Klan *589*
Lee, Robert E. *569*
Lincoln, Abraham *569*
literacy *581*
Massey, Felix *574*

Morant Bay Rebellion *571*
Muir, John *594*
Nott, Josiah *574*
paternalism *570*
Seward, William *569*
sharecroppers *582*
Sherman, William T. *578*
Stanton, Edwin *569*
Stephens, Alexander *573*
Stevens, Thaddeus *577*
Sumner, Charles *571*
Thirteenth Amendment *573*
Trumball, Lyman *575*
Warmoth, Henry *590*

Reviewing Chapter 15

1. How did the United States experience of emancipation and nation building compare to other countries in the mid-19th century?
2. Was the Civil War and Reconstruction a "watershed" in American life? Explain what changed and what remained consistent.

Further Reading

Blight, David W. *Race and Reunion: The Civil War in American Memory*. Cambridge: Belknap Press, 2001. The fullest account of changes in the memory of the Civil War, especially the willingness of white Northerners to marginalize the history of slavery and emancipation in the conflict.

Foner, Eric. *Reconstruction: America's Unfinished Revolution, 1863–1877*. New York: Harper and Row, 1988. A comprehensive history of Reconstruction with particular attention to labor and emancipation in the South.

Litwack, Leon F. *Been in the Storm So Long: The Aftermath of Slavery*. New York: Vintage, 1980. A vivid chronicle of the experience of emancipation for black Southerners.

Perman, Michel. *The Road to Redemption: Southern Politics, 1869–1879*. Chapel Hill: University of North Carolina Press, 1984. The clearest analysis of the national- and state-level politics that produced the end of Reconstruction.

Ransom, Roger L. and Richard Sutch. *One Kind of Freedom: The Economic Consequences of Emancipation*. Cambridge, UK: Cambridge University Press, 1977. A comprehensive economic analysis of the effects of the Civil War on the South.

Silber, Nina. *The Romance of Reunion: Northerners and the South, 1865–1900*. Chapel Hill: University of North Carolina Press, 1993. An elegant study that emphasizes the cultural dimensions of the northern shift toward reconciliation after the Civil War.

Visual Review

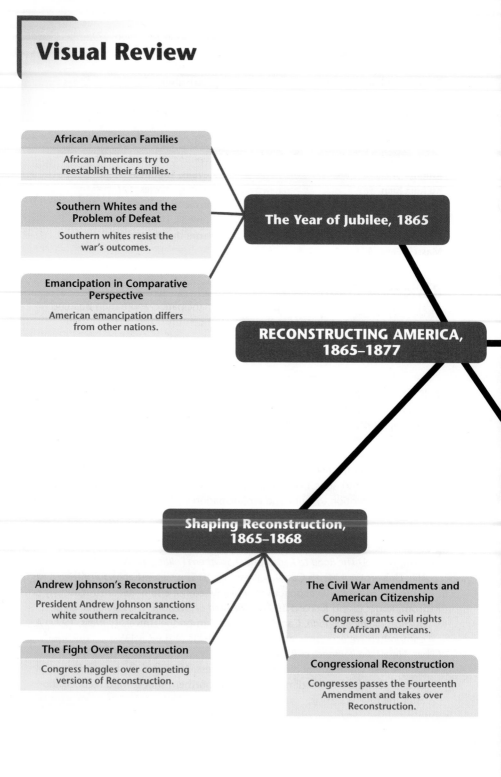

African American Families

African Americans try to reestablish their families.

Southern Whites and the Problem of Defeat

Southern whites resist the war's outcomes.

Emancipation in Comparative Perspective

American emancipation differs from other nations.

The Year of Jubilee, 1865

RECONSTRUCTING AMERICA, 1865–1877

Shaping Reconstruction, 1865–1868

Andrew Johnson's Reconstruction

President Andrew Johnson sanctions white southern recalcitrance.

The Fight Over Reconstruction

Congress haggles over competing versions of Reconstruction.

The Civil War Amendments and American Citizenship

Congress grants civil rights for African Americans.

Congressional Reconstruction

Congresses passes the Fourteenth Amendment and takes over Reconstruction.

Reconstruction in the South, 1866–1876

African American Life in the Postwar South

African Americans begin to build new communities.

Republican Governments in the Postwar South

Republican governments create awkward alliances.

Cotton, Merchants, and the Lien

White landowners and black workers struggle over terms of labor.

The End of Reconstruction, 1877

The Ku Klux Klan and Reconstruction Violence

African Americans experience violent opposition to their new freedoms.

Northern Weariness and Northern Conservatism

The North grows impatient with the duration and expense of Reconstruction.

Legacies of Reconstruction

African Americans are isolated from society and white Southerners violently protect white supremacy.

Forging a Transcontinental Nation

1877–1900

On the unusually cool morning of September 8, 1900, residents of Galveston flocked to beaches to watch the strangely violent surf. The booming city on Texas's Gulf Coast islands had experienced three decades of rapid growth after the Civil War. With a huge deep-water port and a unique location at the crossroads of the new West and the old South, Galveston was known as both the "Wall Street of the West" and the "Ellis Island of the West," and was poised to rival San Francisco and New Orleans in importance. Railroads, telegraphs, shipping lanes, cotton trading, and financial transactions from around the world crisscrossed in a complex network that made the "Queen City of the Gulf" a showpiece of the industrial age.

By the next day, however, a hurricane had left the city in ruins and 8,000 citizens dead in the worst natural disaster in American history. Suddenly, beliefs about the ability of new industry to triumph over nature had been shattered—along with the city.

The story of Galveston's spectacular rise and fall captures many critical issues involved in forging a transcontinental nation between the end of Reconstruction and the turn of the 19th century. Powered by the globalization of markets, international political and ethnic tensions, emerging economic opportunities, and advertisement by government and industry, Galveston was a gateway for the world's people, goods, and ideas streaming in and out of the American West.

In the conquest of the West modern Americans faced vexing questions about industrialization and independence; the ethics of empire; the relationship between Indians, immigrants, and American settlers; the expansion of the federal government; and the conflict between labor and capital, and environmental destruction and preservation.

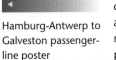

Hamburg-Antwerp to Galveston passenger-line poster

CHAPTER OUTLINE

MEETING GROUND OF MANY PEOPLES
> Changing Patterns of Migration
> Mexican Borders
> Chinese Exclusion

MAPPING THE WEST
> The Federal Frontier
> Myth and History
> Promotion and Memory
> The Culture of Collective Violence

EXTRACTIVE ECONOMIES AND GLOBAL COMMODITIES
> Mining and Labor
> Business Travelers
> Railroads, Time, and Space
> Industrial Ranching
> Corporate Cowboys

continued on page 605

America in the World

Congress repealed the Fort Laramie Treaty, taking the Black Hills from the Lakota (1880).

The first Transcontinental Railroad completed, cutting coast to coast travel time by weeks (1869).

The Indian Appropriations Act voided earlier treaties and made it easier for the government to seize Indian land (1871).

U.S. event that influenced the world

International event that influenced the United States

Event with multinational influence

Conflict

The Chinese Exclusion Act was an early anti-immigration law (1882).

Buffalo Bill Cody staged his Wild West Shows and played to Queen Victoria (1883–1887).

MEETING GROUND OF MANY PEOPLES

Boxer **Jack Johnson**, nicknamed the "Galveston Giant," became the first black heavyweight champion of the world. Born on March 31, 1878, on Galveston Island, Johnson was one of the most famous men of his time. Raised in one of Galveston's toughest neighborhoods, Johnson was witness to and a product of the whirlwind of cultural change and racial conflict of his age.

Racial prejudice governed the social structure of Johnson's birthplace, but Galveston's vibrant African American community wielded influence through the Negro Longshoremen's Association. Its members interacted with Jews from Poland, German Lutherans, Catholic Italians, and the thousands of other immigrants from around the world that flowed through the island. Accustomed to multicultural life, Johnson flaunted racial conventions with open relationships with white women, and triggered national race riots when he won the "fight of the century" in 1908 against the white heavyweight champion of the world Tommy Burns. Johnson's tumultuous career, like Galveston's history, mirrored the contest of old racial ideals and new multicultural realities that characterized the American West between 1877 and 1900. Prewar racial hierarchies of black and white grew complicated during the settling of the West. Foreshadowing America's multicultural future, Indians, Europeans, Hispanics, Asians, Mormons, and African Americans in the West competed and cooperated with one another. Poverty, restricted access to land, and a global population boom pushed immigrants from across the globe out of their native countries. Between 1877 and 1900 millions of immigrants from Europe, Asia, and Latin America joined migrant Americans from the Eastern and Southern United States and moved into the West, where they encountered Indians struggling to maintain autonomy against the latest tide of settlers. The West lured migrants and immigrants because they perceived the region to be a "virgin land" full of possibilities, mostly empty of people and restrictions.

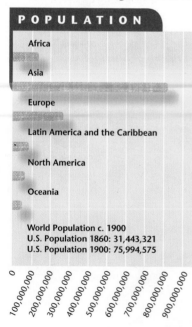

POPULATION

Africa

Asia

Europe

Latin America and the Caribbean

North America

Oceania

World Population c. 1900
U.S. Population 1860: 31,443,321
U.S. Population 1900: 75,994,575

0
100,000,000
200,000,000
300,000,000
400,000,000
500,000,000
600,000,000
700,000,000
800,000,000
900,000,000

Changing Patterns of Migration

The 1890 census indicated the western frontier "closed." Census data showed that all of the land west of the Mississippi was "settled," presumably ending centuries of conquest. Historian Frederick Jackson Turner publicized the census data, famously describing the settlement of the West as a "frontier process" where immigrants became Americans by confronting and conquering a "virgin land." For those like future president Theodore Roosevelt, who viewed the process of western settlement as the experience that made America exceptional and superior to other nations, the notion of a closed frontier caused great anxiety. Where next, Roosevelt and others wondered, would Americans find space to recreate themselves through the conquest of new lands.

Despite the census evidence, people could still find plenty of open western spaces in the post-Civil War decades. Significant sections of the West remained virtually empty well into the 20th century. Between 1877 and 1900, millions of people from all points of the globe and every region of the United States moved into the West. Within the West internal migrations reshaped the region's character, depopulating some areas and resettling others. But, many of those who sought frontier opportunity in the West ended up in cities.

CHAPTER OUTLINE

continued from page 601

CLEARING THE LAND AND CLEANSING THE WILDERNESS
> Indian Conflict and Resistance
> Education for Assimilation
> The Destruction of the Buffalo
> The Dawes Act and Survival
> Tourism, Parks, and Forests

"The Heart of the Continent," 1882, booster brochure of the idealized West, captures the utopian vision that drew millions to the region. Look closely and you will notice all the icons of settlement. The book told potential settlers they would find "an empire grander in its resources than any emperor or czar . . . ever swayed over."

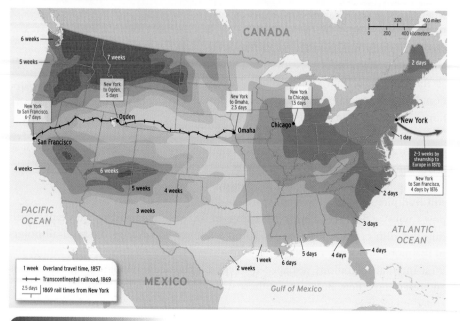

▲ Map 16.1

Technology, Time, and Space This map shows travel times between the 1850s and 1870s. Before the 1840s sailing ships took an average of five to six weeks across the Atlantic. Overland or around Cape Horn could take months or even years. By the 1870s the same distances could be covered in a week.

By 1890 the vast majority of western migrants had settled in cities like Denver (133,000), San Francisco (380,000), Los Angeles (124,000), Salt Lake City (53,000), and hundreds of towns scattered like islands in an ocean of sparsely inhabited land. Contrary to popular perception, the West was the most urban region in America and remains so today. The lure of open land, farming, and remote mines scattered people throughout the West, but environmental and economic forces drew them together again in cities.

After the Civil War, migration patterns changed for several reasons. Railroads made foreign and internal immigration far easier. Likewise, internal migration increased with rapidly expanding regional railway networks. Economic downturns, environmental disasters, and an influx of new immigrants, who lowered wages and often raised prejudices in other regions, pushed internal and foreign migrants to the West. In 1877, tens of thousands of African American "Exodusters," fleeing rising racial violence at the end of military reconstruction, migrated from the South to the West founding new towns and joining other workers and entrepreneurs hoping for a new start. All were pulled by the lure of new opportunities and moved frequently to take advantage of emerging markets and employment.

Women moved with their families and on their own and contributed a disproportionate amount of the daily labor required to establish businesses, homes, towns and communities across the West. Women's diaries of migrations reveal much of what historians know of daily life and the history of settlement. European and Euro-American women responsible for inhabiting a little understood region faced environmental challenges that Indian women had known for thousands of years.

Mobility was a key characteristic of the global economy in the 19th century. The American frontier experience was not unique. So called "Settler societies" in South America, Australia, and Canada also depended on significant internal and external migrations to solidify control of vast territories and negotiate with or displace indigenous peoples ahead of state-sponsored efforts. No destination, however, compared to the United States in the astounding diversity of immigrants pouring into a region already remarkably multicultural. There were many melting pots around the globe, but these melted two or three predominant immigrant groups. In the United States, and in the West in particular, immigrants from virtually everywhere lived together with thousands of Native Americans, freed slaves, Hispanics of many origins, Asians, and Euro-Americans of all types.

Mexican Borders

Much of what Americans think of as the "West" was long the Spanish and then the Mexican North. This "Far North" was a vast region only loosely controlled by distant Mexico City. Violent wars with powerful Indian tribes strained Mexico's control of northern provinces and paved the way for U.S. seizure of vast Mexican territories after the U.S.-Mexican War (1846–1848). Politics, economics, and an unstoppable tide of migrants conspired against Hispanic control in much of what became the American West. The U.S. Southwest and the Mexican North were seamlessly linked by nature and divided only by politics. These regions shared a contiguous desert ecosystem that stretched through what are now Arizona and California and north into Utah and Nevada. Spaniards, Indians, and Anglos in search of mineral wealth and rangelands moved throughout the region and fought for control of its resources for centuries.

While groups like the Texas Rangers systematically terrorized Mexicans after the Mexican War, U.S. and Mexican entrepreneurs shared a desire to capitalize on the movement of labor, capital, and commodities across political borders. Gold brought prospectors and investors to the Arizona territories in the 1860s, but the discovery of rich copper deposits 75 miles north of the Mexican border transformed the economy of the region. American brothers Jim and Robert Metcalfe found the copper in 1870 while traveling as Army scouts searching for Apache resistance leaders Vitorio and Geronimo.

News of the Arizona discoveries brought entrepreneurs from across the globe. One of them, an Eastern European Jew named Henry Lesinsky, exemplified the remarkable mobility of the region and the age. He immigrated to England as a boy, left to prospect for gold in Australia, and then traveled to mines of California, Nevada, and New Mexico, and finally to the Arizona territory. Lesinsky made little from gold or silver but a fortune selling supplies to U.S. troops fighting Indians. He used the funds to buy out the Metcalfe's copper claims and founded the Longfellow Copper Mining Company in 1873. Using a combination of Australian mining techniques,

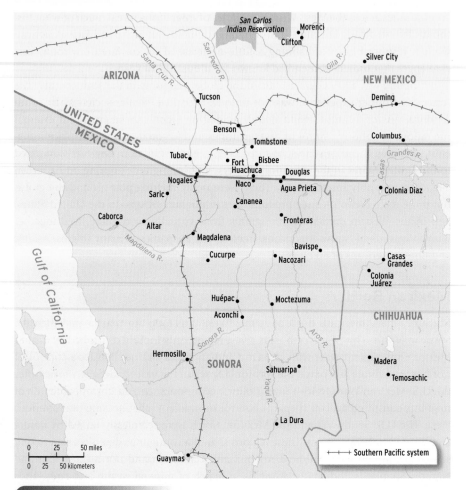

▲ **Map 16.2**

Borderlands This map of the "Copper Borderlands" shows how economy and ecology were sometimes more important than national borders in developing regions. The remarkable movement of people, goods, and ideas throughout this contested zone shaped the national histories that followed.

Detroit financing, Baltimore smelting, and Mexican labor, Lesinsky created the transnational model for the "copper borderlands."

By the 1890s the majority of Arizona copper was controlled by the powerful Phelps Dodge Company centered in Bisbee. American companies like Phelps Dodge and William Cornell Greene's Cananea, Mexico, copper mining empire linked the United States and Mexico through the exchange of metal, labor, and capital. As the United States expanded its communication system with millions of feet of copper wire, the mineral networks gained importance. American and Mexican businessmen negotiated mutually beneficial trans-border relations ahead of official diplomacy and national policy.

On the fuzzy U.S. Mexican borderlands of the late 19th century, Mexicans moved back and forth across *La Linea* with relative freedom. Migrant laborers moved north to the "West" along centuries-old migration corridors. The El Camino Real corridor running south to north linked Mexico City to Zacatecas, Durango, Chihuahua, El Paso, Albuquerque, and Santa Fe. The web of trails that comprised the Sonoran corridor funneled workers throughout the copper and cotton corridors and linked copper labor routes to the seasonal cotton fields stretching from Yuma, Arizona, to California's San Joaquin Valley near Los Angeles. By 1900 Mexicans made up 60 percent of all copper and seasonal farm workers. Mexicans who worked in the United States received less pay than Anglo workers, were barred from union participation, faced prejudice and segregation, and were "sent packing"— sometimes at the point of a gun—during economic downturns. Despite these hardships Mexican laborers in the late 19th century fared better than Chinese.

Chinese Exclusion

Although the Chinese are remembered primarily in American history for their role in building the Transcontinental Railroad, their importance in the West extended far beyond that single event. Chinese immigrants who came to work on the railroads, mines, and fields were part of a global Chinese diaspora and the "coolie trade" that sold contract Chinese laborers and Chinese women as indentured laborers and sex workers who lived little better than slaves. From the 1840s to the 1870s Chinese immigrants, free or contracted, moved to Australia, Southeast Asia, Peru, Cuba, and California. Those who migrated left sparse opportunities, a rigid class system, and grinding poverty in 19th century south China. No immigrant group faced more persistent racism and violence than the Chinese. Businesses sought out Chinese workers for their cheap and exploitable labor with the assumption that they would eventually return to China. They usually migrated as individuals and were overwhelmingly male in the first waves but were later joined by women and entire families, and during all phases of immigration quickly developed community-building strategies to combat, racism, and segregation. The Chinese managed to build successful enclaves wherever they went. Anchored by temples like the Bok Kai Temple of Marysville, California, or woven into "instant cities" like Denver and San Francisco, "China towns" became a lasting characteristic of the western urban landscape.

Legendary hard workers, the Chinese laborers were also "stickers." "If you can get them this year," wrote one observer, "you can get them next year . . . they become attached to your place and they stay with you." The Chinese proved indispensable to western development. In California they comprised half of all agricultural workers. In urban areas and on ranches Chinese men occupied up to 90 percent of service industry jobs like laundry and food preparation. During the heyday of western expansion the Chinese were tolerated and sometimes given grudging respect.

Starting in 1870, however, anti-Chinese sentiments increased as the western economy gained importance. In a pattern that repeated throughout the 20th century, communities and industries built by the cheapest foreign labor turned against these

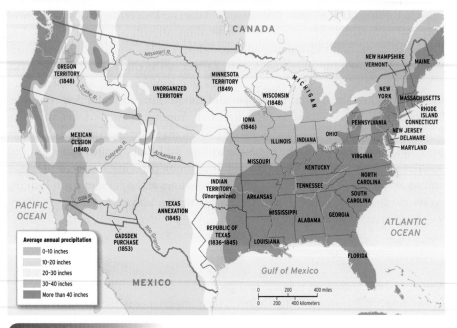

▲ **Map 16.3**

Climate and Consolidation This map shows the territorial acquisitions that established the modern U.S. West and set the borders for the nation as we now know it. The majority of this rugged terrain beyond the 100th meridian was arid and inhabited by Indian and Hispanic residents complicating perceptions of the area as "free" and forcing new inhabitants to learn how to modify their environmental expectations.

workers once they achieved community and economic stability. The Australians blazed the racist path that Americans followed by enacting Chinese exclusion acts as early as the 1850s. Urged by white labor organizers, anti-Chinese leagues, and community leaders, western states passed laws limiting Chinese opportunities and rights through the 1870s. State laws and political enthusiasm prompted the U.S. Congress to pass the **Chinese Exclusion Act** in 1882. The act, which nominally suspended immigration, was renewed and tightened over the years until harsh immigration restrictions enacted in the early 1920s ended virtually all Asian immigration to the United States.

STUDY QUESTIONS FOR MEETING GROUND OF MANY PEOPLES

1. For what reasons did the West become the most multicultural region of the United States?
2. For what reasons did white westerners and white Americans exclude and discriminate against the Chinese immigrants?

MAPPING THE WEST

The vast arid region between the Front Range of the Rocky Mountains in Colorado and the Sierra Nevada in California was the last portion of the contiguous United States to be explored and resettled. This immense landscape became the focus of federal attention in 1853–1854 when teams of surveyors were dispatched throughout the region in search of routes for the Transcontinental Railroad.

Prior to 1865 the U.S. Army conducted most expeditions, and private investors funded geologic investigations in hopes of discovering mineral wealth. Other explorers, such as John C. Frémont, guided pioneers along the Oregon Trail and crossed the Rockies and the expanse of the Great Basin to the Sierra Nevada several times; however, like the army before them, they gave little attention to formal surveying or mapping. It took the concerted effort of the federal government and a handful of ambitious individuals to organize and fund a general survey of the West. In four major expeditions between 1867 and 1879, a host of plant, animal, and mineral scientists, topographers, journalists, photographers, and artists chronicled the region. These surveys established the foundational knowledge for the organized settlement of the West. They also, however, raised serious questions about the environmental realities and the extensive inhabitation of the region. Many supporters thought these final systematic surveys of the West might usher in an era of logical progress as the vast region was settled in the new century. Those who experienced the region found a place full of cultural, environmental, and economic complexity with no clear defined path of progress.

Starting in 1869, one-armed Civil War veteran and geology professor **John Wesley Powell** led a series of critically important surveys of the Colorado River system. Powell's expedition was self-funded with only a few instruments and permission to borrow food from military posts along the way. Setting out at Green River, Wyoming, in four wooden boats, Powell followed the Colorado River through the Flaming Gorge, Desolation, Marble, and Grand Canyons. In a second expedition in 1872 Powell explored the expansive Colorado Plateau.

Powell was the first scientist to understand the critical importance of the Colorado River for the Southwest. His popular 1875 account of his one-armed adventures, *The Exploration of the Colorado River*, and extensive coverage of his travels by the press in the East established the scientist explorer as a popular hero. He followed these works with an insightful 1878 *Report on the Lands of the Arid Region*, which advocated the necessity of settlement based on his scientific findings about regional environments. Powell, warning that traditional settlement and agricultural practices would fail in the arid West, recommended a realistic approach in evaluating the potential for the region.

The surveys established the rough boundaries of the West and created the maps and marked the trails that millions of settlers used to travel to the region. They did not, however, convey the complex cultural landscape or environmental challenges these newcomers faced. Along with the maps and popular myths, a series of foundational federal land acts pulled often-unprepared migrants into the West where the rush for riches dimmed cautious voices like that of John Wesley Powell.

The Federal Frontier

The **Homestead Act of 1862**, passed during the Civil War by a Congress free of southern opposition, reflected the ideals and goals of a Republican United States. In keeping with the Jeffersonian vision of a nation of small farmers, the federal government sought to extend the system of individual land ownership west. The Homestead Act, expanding the basic system of settlement established by the Ordinance of 1785, provided a means for privatizing expansive western public lands. Before the Civil War homesteading west of the Mississippi River had proved problematic for individual families, as cheap lands intended for individuals quickly evolved into a commercialized system of land speculation.

The Homestead Act provided title to 160-acre parcels for individuals who made "improvements" to the land over a period of five years. Settlers had the option to purchase the land for $1.25 per acre after the first six months of residency, and some opted to pay up front to secure mortgages to fund improvements. This option encouraged speculation by allowing homesteaded land to be brought into the commercial market a quarter section (one quarter of a square mile) at a time at a higher resale value. Rather than improving the land, homesteaders often sold out to other individuals or commercial farms that grew grain crops over vast acreages.

For those homesteading west of Dodge City, Kansas, on the 100th meridian (the geographic line of aridity where annual rainfalls drop below 8 inches per year), 160 acres required expensive irrigation works for farming or other dry-land farming techniques. These parcels were also far too small for ranching. In addition, five years was too long to develop the land without the benefit of ownership and access to loans. Congress addressed these problems in 1877 with the **Desert Lands Act**. The act, applicable in eleven western states, allowed for homesteading on 640-acre parcels of arid land at 25 cents per acre and provided title within three years for a dollar an acre for settled, irrigated, land. However, there was no official definition of how much land and water constituted irrigated cultivation. For much of the desert West, agriculture required massive federal support that came with the creation of the Reclamation Service in 1902. The renamed Bureau of Reclamation (BOR) eventually funded extensive irrigation projects in 16 western states. The simple act of providing land and water to farmers and ranchers enormously expanded the growth and reach of the federal government.

Myth and History

It is hard to overestimate the power of perception in the creation of the West as both a geographical region and an ideal with lasting global appeal. In 1895 future president Woodrow Wilson wrote, "The West has been the great word of our history. The

Westerner has been the type and master of our American life." The "great word" was always more myth than truth, not entirely false but a powerful idea with enough fact to motivate millions to move great distances and suffer enormous hardship. The mythic version of the western story is still celebrated in literature, on film, and on TV. But the myth had a dark side. It justified the mistreatment of Indians and their ancestral environment and contributed to class and racial conflict that characterized the post-Civil War West.

At the heart of the mythic story of the West was a question: was the West the land of unlimited opportunity or a paradise lost? Promoters and "boosters" lured settlers, workers, and investors to the region by steadfastly portraying the West as a paradise to be tamed and civilized. Western boosters were masters of public relations and emerging techniques of advertising. Using all of the new mass media at their disposal—dime novels, traveling shows, posters, pamphlets, newspapers, graphic art, and photography—they promoted places that did not yet exist and invented simple solutions to complex cultural and environmental dilemmas. Boosters dismissed the lack of water in much of the region with claims like, "The rain follows the plow." The faith that ingenuity, technology, and hard work could transform even the weather was widespread and pushed global migrations to the West.

Claims of rain following civilization gave false hope to homesteaders on the Great Plains and Southwest where wet years regularly gave way to protracted droughts. "God speed the plow," wrote amateur scientist Charles Dana Wilber in 1870, "By this wonderful provision . . . the clouds are dispensing copious rains." Federal surveyor Ferdinand V. Hayden, a leading proponent of optimistic climate theory, supported the anecdotal observations of boosters like Wilber. Hayden's credentials legitimized agricultural settlement across the semi-arid U.S. plains he had surveyed. Circulating throughout Europe, these ideas inspired migrations even to the deserts of southern Australia, where immigrants—assuming that their labor would alter the climate of the region—built elaborate farming and ranching outposts. Global droughts throughout the late 1880s demonstrated how quickly fertile soil once stripped of its native cover and tilled could burn and blow away along with the hopes of settlers.

Promotion and Memory

While boosters and promoters made wild claims for the West, early settlers generated widely circulated literature of reminiscences, memoirs, and fictionalized accounts of the frontier process. As individuals or collectively through "pioneer societies," settlers lamented the passing of a grand age even as they exaggerated the savagery of the land and peoples they thought they had conquered. Settlers, together with an influential group of "artists, authors, dreamers, and deceivers," created such a powerful, persuasive mythology that even savvy observers had trouble discerning truth from fiction.

No single person blended history and myth better than **William "Buffalo Bill" Cody**. He was literally a legend in his own time, a man simultaneously a real person and a fictional character of international fame. Cody's heavily embellished life story of migration as a youth from LeClaire, Iowa, to the West, over the plains and through

Buffalo Bill's Wild West Company's Presentation to their Chief on his Birthday at Olympia, London, February 26, 1903. Cody and his troop traveled the world introducing Indian resistance leaders like Sitting Bull to queens and kaisers, along with hoards of commoners from Paris to Poland. Global perceptions of the United States and U.S. West were shaped as much by these cultural ambassadors as any other source.

the Rockies, encompassed all of the experiences global audiences recognized as part of western frontier life: buffalo hunting, Indian fighting, bronco busting, gunslinging, and military scouting. In the 1880s Cody's "Wild West" shows featured real-life Westerners recreating idealized versions of the actual history unfolding in the region at the same time. Cody traveled the world introducing Indian resistance leaders like Sitting Bull to queens and the young German Kaiser Wilhelm, along with hoards of commoners from Paris to Poland. Annie Oakley shot the tip of a cigarette out of Wilhelm's mouth, and she offered "to do it again" during World War I.

Such globetrotting shows provided one of many powerful nodes of transnational cultural exchange linking the frontier West to the world. Even as millions of immigrants crossed oceans from all directions to reach an actual place they knew as "West," Cody and other Americans—taking the mythic West out to the world—left an indelible impression of a particular facet of American identity that celebrated individual violence and heroic conquest. The reality of violence and valor in the region, however, was far more complex.

The Culture of Collective Violence

Dime novels, Wild West shows, and the 20th-century movies yet to come told stories of righteous individual violence. The "western" genre in all its forms had two basic narratives: the gunfight in the street between a good man and an outlaw, and brave pioneers versus murderous Indians. Foreign authors such as German Karl May, who never traveled to the West, sold millions of stories of individual violence that circled the globe. Buffalo Bill raised the appetite for them by reenacting an idealized version of regional violence. Figures like the violent young criminal Billy the Kid gained international fame for exploits that bore little resemblance to their decidedly unromantic lives. Thousands died bloody deaths in the violent West, but rarely were they lone figures dueling heroically in the streets. Individual violence was most often criminal or reckless with cheap alcohol as the fuel.

Collective violence was disturbingly premeditated and often carried out by otherwise upstanding community members or soldiers. The myth of individual violence conceals a more disturbing reality of group violence involving regular citizens and whole communities. Horrific organized violence against Indians, such as the profoundly disturbing Sand Creek and Wounded Knee massacres, was much more brutal and common than were gunfights. The idea that military action or group vigilantism provided a necessary corrective to the disorder of the frontier justified much of the violence in the West well into the 20th century. Prominent community and religious leaders joined "vigilance leagues" in San Francisco and Denver. Western papers wrote favorably about vigilante lynching mobs that "saved county money" and time by executing criminals without delay or due process. Western corporations hired thugs to

This disturbing image by G. Trager of a mass grave filled with 146 frozen bodies at Wounded Knee captured the shocking banality of violence in 19th-century America. The men in the grave and lining the pit don't appear celebratory or remorseful as they look at the Indians they killed. Photographs of the aftermath of battle challenged popular perceptions of the romantic character of violence in the contested West.

break strikes, remove unwanted workers, or impose order by threatening violence in company camps and towns.

Racial and ethnic violence were common in the 19th-century United States. Few non-Indian groups, however, suffered like the Chinese in the West. Throughout the 1870s and 1880s Chinese immigrants were beaten and murdered with shocking regularity and with little consequence for the perpetrators. Like blacks in the South, individuals and small groups of Chinese workers faced violence and lynching from rival white workers and ethnic groups. In 1880 violence reached a new level when an enraged mob of 3,000, yelling, "Stamp out the yellow plague," stormed into Denver's "Hop Alley," a Chinese enclave. The mob lynched one man in the street, injured hundreds, and burned or dismantled Chinese businesses and homes. Five years later race riots left 51 Chinese miners dead in Rock Springs, Wyoming. Viewing the survivors of the riots, Chinese Consul Huage Sih Chuen lamented, "words fail to give an idea of their sufferings, and their appearance is a sad one to human eyes to witness."

STUDY QUESTIONS FOR MAPPING THE WEST

1. **Why did government-sponsored surveys and land acts encourage migration to the West?**
2. **How does the history of collective western violence differ from the myth of the gunfight in the street?**

EXTRACTIVE ECONOMIES AND GLOBAL COMMODITIES

Out of the jostling coach window the arid landscape speeds by. Dusty frontier passengers listen for the crack of the driver's whip as he struggles to escape from the outlaws close behind. As the coach rounds a corner startled kangaroos scurry away. The early 1960s Australian TV show *Whiplash* popularized the story of American businessman and stage travel pioneer Freeman Cobb. Cobb was one of thousands of Americans who moved through the frontiers of the West and on to other developing regions as part of a global exchange of expertise and experience. Most of these multinational business pioneers worked in the extractive economy. Converting natural resources into commodities was the primary economic engine of the American West. Individuals led the way, but by the 1890s corporations had consolidated many of the industries across the region. The incorporation of the extractive economy of the West created economies and workscapes in stark contrast to the popular individualistic stories of the region circulating throughout the world.

Between 1877 and 1900 the dramatic expansion of railroad, communication, and financial networks throughout the American West enabled phenomenal growth in industrial ranching, farming, mining, and timber production. The Great Plains became the "bread basket of the world," the great forests of the Rockies and the Pacific Northwest yielded tremendous quantities of lumber, mines blasted deep into the Sierras and Rockies produced precious metals by the ton. The cattle ranches of the West became massive after the invention of the refrigerated railcar made it possible to turn Texas cows into New York steaks. The promise of quick wealth drew eastern U.S. and foreign investors. With the support of several administrations of the federal government that encouraged and funded this economic explosion, the once peripheral West became an important hub of American and global economic activity.

Mining and Labor

The mineral rushes of the mid-1800s pulled migrants to the West from all parts of the United States and the globe and generated staggering wealth. The Comstock Lode in Nevada alone produced $96 million dollars in silver—more than the combined total from all previous recorded American mining.

Legends spread around the world of instant riches from gold found lying on the ground. A handful of early arriving individuals in California did get rich with little effort. But western mining quickly became a game for serious international capitalists and a new class of engineers working in a complicated web of global exchange, although not before mining created the most diverse collection of nationalities in modern history. In western mining camps, conversations could be heard in English, Chinese, French, Spanish, German, Italian, Hawaiian, and many American Indian dialects. Following the Civil War industrialized mining turned individualistic prospectors and others into laborers who formed powerful unions like the Western Federation of Miners (WFM; 1893) and later the Industrial Workers of the World (IWW) or "Wobblies." Still, the get-rich-quick myth persisted long after industrialization and fueled migration into the 20th century.

After the 1870s the struggle for gold, silver, coal, and copper transformed into a fight between labor and capital complicated by race and ethnic strife. Industrial mining was terribly dangerous. Mines like the Comstock in Virginia City, Nevada, dug to unprecedented depths, made collapses and other forms of industrial accidents commonplace. Coal miners in Colorado faced these dangers along with deadly coal dust that killed slowly through disease or swiftly through explosion. Crushed, suffocated, dismembered, and diseased miners had good reason to act collectively. But ethnic tensions often stifled western labor organization. The universal appeal of mineral wealth was not matched by a uniformity of interests among competing ethic groups in mining towns. The cemetery of tiny Ely, Nevada, tells the tale of enclaves and segregation that often characterized western mining camps. Ely's grave yard was neatly divided into a grid of ethnicity and race, with Anglos placed in the choicest ground near the street followed by Cornish and Irish, Poles and Russians, Mexicans, and, finally, the Chinese in the barren backwash.

When miners did successfully organize, owners responded with violence. The gunning down of seven strikers in Coeur d'Alene, Idaho, led to the founding of the WFM. An angry young silver miner, "Big" Bill Haywood, joined in response, and

The underground working world of the Comstock Lode in Gold Hill, Nevada, "Sectional views of the Belcher Mine." Illustrations like this were designed to show the success of the companies that controlled the mines at conquering nature and engineering challenges. If you look closely they also reveal something of the working conditions of the miners.

went on to a storied career as an IWW leader loved by working men and hated by the corporations. He battled the federal government, was imprisoned during World War I, and would later die in exile. He was buried in the Kremlin.

Known as the land of individualism, the West was in fact the site of many of the most important battles between collective labor and consolidating corporate capital.

Business Travelers

Mine owners imported labor and investment for their enterprises as they exported minerals and wealth to investors. Woven into this dynamic economic transfer was a transnational exchange of culture and expertise. The mineral rushes created powerful and easily transferable business models. American businessmen like Freeman Cobb, for example, used experience with Wells Fargo to create successful stagecoach companies in Australia and South Africa.

Businessmen trained in the boom and bust economies of the West excelled at grand schemes in extractive industries, complex irrigation systems, and transportation networks. Americans like Cobb, who had traveled across America from Maine to

California, kept moving west to the Australian gold fields or south to Peru where they helped build vast railroad networks over difficult terrain. Or, like young future President **Herbert Hoover**, who combined talents in engineering with business, they became ambassadors of American culture who blended frontier knowledge with technical prowess. Though never as numerous as their British counterparts, American businessmen abroad nonetheless built connections that created significant global networks that sometimes ran ahead of federal foreign policy. American business and engineering skills combined with the globally appealing mythology and iconography of the West created a potent brew of reciprocal relationships and cultural exchange.

Railroads, Time, and Space

When the 1900 storm slammed into Galveston, 40 percent of Westerners lived in urban centers linked to the world through vast transportation and communication networks of railroads, steamships, undersea telegraph cables, and overland telephone lines. The first warning of the storm came via telegraph under the Gulf of Mexico from Cuba while the last train out carried newly arrived Norwegian and German immigrants toward the Oklahoma and Dakota territories. Galveston's growth between 1877 and 1900 showed how fast the United States had become dependent on new technologies that linked remote urban outposts to the rest of the nation and the world. The web of steel rails and copper wires that spread in all directions from border cities like Galveston made possible the phenomenal growth of the West and permanently bound the region to the nation and the world economy.

Generous federal land grants and subsidies pushed the completion of the Transcontinental Railroad. When finished, it opened the Great Plains and connected the Pacific to Atlantic and Gulf ports spurring rapid global exchange. In 1869 the driving of the golden spike linking the last rail from east to west ended the first phase of western railroad development. Between 1869 and 1900 regional railroad entrepreneurs like "Empire Builder" James J. Hill stepped in when the "Robber Barons" of the Transcontinental epoch moved on to greener pastures. A Canadian, Hill migrated to St. Paul, Minnesota, and saw opportunity for transportation development across the northern borderlands. Hill first linked the expansive Canadian prairie with the Great Plains and distant markets with lines between St. Paul and Winnipeg, Canada. Throughout the 1880s Hill connected his Great Northern Railway lines east to Chicago and finally in 1893 west to Seattle and the Pacific.

Regional rail development in the 1880s and 1890s used 25 percent of U.S. annual timber production and spawned the massive or "bonanza" wheat farms of the Dakotas and the fruit and vegetable economies of Arizona and California. Western coal mining grew from regional rail demands for cheaper energy. A combination of federal land grants and savvy land deals with boosters and politicians gave the railroads massive checkerboard tracts of land to sell to cash-poor migrants.

Although land was cheap, transportation costs were not. Farmers and ranchers who bought land from the railroads or acquired homesteads depended on the railroad for access to the world markets that dictated the values of their crops and animals. The railroads even set the farmers' clocks when they established "time zones" in the 1880s. The large distances traversed by U.S. and Canadian railroads especially necessitated a closely regulated system of time to replace the confusion of the solar time that shaped the lives of humans for millennia. Railroad land grants continue to this day to shape life and economies in the West, where companies like the Southern Pacific maintain large landholdings and control critical transportation corridors.

Farmers suffered more than any other group from the unpredictability of international commodities markets. Migrant families who rode Jefferson's yeoman dream of self-sufficiency and independence into the heartlands opened by the rails often found themselves at the mercy of powerful distant forces. Many migrants were Russian-Germans driven across the globe by new immigration restrictions imposed by Czar Alexander II that forced them out of Russia. Railroad owners sent American agents loaded with German-language brochures to the steppes of Russia to sell the promise of Kansas and Nebraska to the persecuted Germans. Whole German villages arrived in Galveston bound for Oklahoma and the Plains.

During the 1880s, when unusually high rainfalls produced bumper crops across the Plains, the population of Kansas and Nebraska increased by 43 percent and 134 percent, respectively. The Dakotas increased their population by 278 percent. These

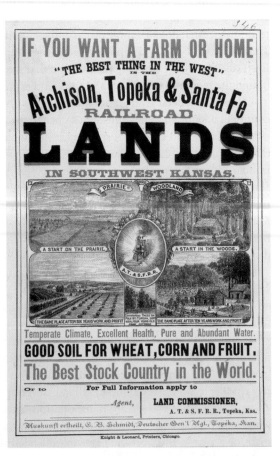

ATSF Railroad handbill advertising "climate, health and water" in land in the West. Handbills like this were widely distributed throughout Europe. Even for those who could not read English the message was clear.

population increases and development helped seven territories become states in the 1880s and 1890s. The possibilities seemed limitless: for a time production soared and consistent rain seemed to confirm booster claims. Dry years and wildly fluctuating international commodities markets in the late 1880s and throughout the 1890s, however, demonstrated the elusiveness of long-term success. Time revealed that devastating bust cycles were a normal part of western agriculture—if not the economy in general. Droughts in the 1890s baked crops year after year and sparked a long series of agricultural depressions that fueled political unrest.

During the heyday of the 1880s, rail competition drove down transportation costs in most parts of the West. Farmers both benefited and suffered from greater access to national and international markets facilitated by powerful railroad corporations. Through lean times farmers borrowed heavily to finance future crops and pay shipping. When the fickle environment cooperated, farmers used new technologies like the McCormick Harvesting Machine to produce massive yields that drove down prices of staples like wheat. Unlike industrial capitalists, individual farmers rarely benefited from economies of scale. The harder they worked, and more efficient they were, the less they profited.

The Populist Movement rose out of the ashes of the arid conditions of the 1890s when farm economies collapsed. Geographically dispersed farmers seeking collective organization faced significant challenges. Farmers united first through social organizations like the Grange and then political Alliances that linked South and West. Encouraged by fiery leaders like **Mary Elizabeth Lease** to "raise less corn and more hell," farmers formalized their Populist Party at an 1892 convention in Omaha, Nebraska. Lease was representative of the Populists. Born to Irish immigrant parents in Pennsylvania, she moved to Kansas in 1870 to teach, met her husband, and started a family. The couple lost everything in the crash of 1873. They moved to Texas where Lease joined prohibition and women suffrage groups. A move back to Kansas followed where she gave her energy and powerful voice to the growing Populist Party. Lease became one of the movement's most effective speakers. Critic **William Allen White** thought a women's place was in the home and labeled her a "harpie" in his famous essay, "What's the Matter with Kansas?" Undeterred, "Yellin' Mary Ellen" became a legendary stump speaker before moving to New York to work as a lawyer and lecturer.

The Populist Party "Omaha Platform" advocated socialization of the nation's railroads and other farsighted reforms aimed at empowering family farmers in the industrial age. In the long run, agribusiness, industrial ranching, and federal subsidies provided the only consistently successful method for reaping the riches of the Plains.

Industrial Ranching

It was the Spanish who brought cattle to the New World. As early as 1500 Spanish *vaqueros* (cowboys) tended large herds in the Caribbean with the help of African slaves who contributed knowledge and lasting terminology to the bovine industry. The word *dogie*, cowboy slang for a motherless calf, derives from the Bambara language brought to North America by West African slaves. As Spain's empire spread across the Caribbean and into North and South America, cattle played a central economic role. Some Indian tribes, like the Seminole and Choctaw of the Southeast, adopted cattle raising, and the "Five Civilized Tribes" brought their herds on the Trail of Tears from the Southeast to the Oklahoma territory.

Throughout the 1800s the Texas Gulf coast served as a laboratory for an expanding global cattle industry. The techniques of the cowboy, the business of cattle raising for market, and the transportation of cattle across land and sea were developed in the culturally and politically contested Gulf coast. Galveston became a critical distribution point. The long sandy island was perfect for ranging cattle before shipping them to points south and east by steamer. Galveston also served as an entry point for cattle shipped in and driven northeast and west overland to the grazing lands of Texas and the Great Plains. In ports like Galveston, black and Hispanic cowboys shared their expertise from Africa, South America, and the Caribbean with white cattle workers and European immigrants who took the knowledge into the expanding markets of the West. Wherever they went, cattle changed ecosystems and transformed cultures.

Between 1866 and 1884 ranchers shipped over five million Texas cattle north to slaughter houses. This style of ranching influenced the industry's development in Arizona and Colorado, and throughout the northern Great Plains into Canada. As the industry expanded, eastern and foreign speculators in land and livestock invested millions of dollars in creating a system of absentee ownership that birthed the "beef bonanza" of the 1880s. But, like bonanza farmers, ranchers went bust at the height of production during a cycle of drought and extreme winters. Ecological devastation caused by overgrazing, brutal winters, and encroachment of farms and barbed wire fencing invented in 1868 ended the "open range era."

Corporate Cowboys

Not everyone went bust, however. In 1858 San Francisco businessmen Henry Miller and Charles Lux, immigrants from southwestern Germany, formed Miller & Lux, a corporation that employed vertical integration—overseeing the cattle from birth to butcher shop—to the industry. Born into a family of butchers, both men had immigrated to the United States in the 1840s and eventually arrived in San Francisco in the early 1850s following the gold rush. Similar to other industrial firms of the late 19th century, the Miller & Lux corporation reduced investment risks, developed a segmented system of labor, and integrated all aspects of production into a tightly controlled business model. They employed a vast pool of low-wage immigrant workers divided by trade and race. Given their unique understanding of the California landscape and superior equestrian skills, Mexican *vaqueros* formed the backbone of the skilled labor force as they conducted roundups, brandings, pasturing, and culling of cattle herds. Chinese workers provided domestic labor services, especially as cooks, and southeastern Europeans, constructing irrigation works and haying, provided field labor. The company contracted with the Southern Pacific Railroad to provide transportation at a low rate and in exchange gave the railroad a transportation monopoly on their product. This corporate model of ranching allowed control over every aspect of beef production, manipulation of the environment to increase production, and formed the model for modern agribusiness in California's Central Valley.

The best known character of the western story, the cowboy, was on the stage for only a short time and looked little like the image popularized by literature and later movies. A more unlikely hero than the cowboy is hard to imagine. Cowboys were laborers who worked long and hard and earned little. They spent their days and nights in filthy primitive conditions with dangerously unpredictable animals and often died unromantically on the job. Most cowboys were white laborers from Texas or Louisiana, but at least a third were African American, Mexican, and Indian. Cattle drives featured a potent brew of racial prejudice and rivalry that contributed to difficult working conditions. The cowboy period of long summer cattle drives on the open range lasted less than 20 years before the onslaught of migrants, barbed wire, cities, and government regulation and systematic distribution of land.

STUDY QUESTIONS FOR EXTRACTIVE ECONOMIES AND GLOBAL COMMODITIES

1. What global trends shaped the development of the extractive economy of the West?
2. How did the myth of the cowboy contrast with the life of cattle workers?

CLEARING THE LAND AND CLEANSING THE WILDERNESS

After a five-day fight, the exhausted Indians agreed to surrender. There were only 430 left after a remarkable 1,500 mile running battle throughout Montana. The leader of the remaining Nez Perce, Chief Joseph, captured the tragic spirit of the moment. "I am tired of fighting," he told his captors. "It is cold and we have no blankets. The little children are freezing to death. I want to have time to look for my children . . . maybe I shall find them among the dead. I will fight no more forever."

Continental empire building in the West between 1877 and 1900 was more than the adventures of cowboy heroes in dime novels or a convenient final act for Wild West Shows. Dreams of material wealth and the lure of "free" land pulled millions of immigrants from across the globe to the region. Environmental challenges demonstrated the perils of hasty government policies and dashed many settlers' dreams. In the years to come the shocking environmental consequences of the extractive economy spurred a conservation movement and led to the creation of the world's first national park. During the same period, new efforts to refashion Indian policy resulted in the greatest injustices of the age.

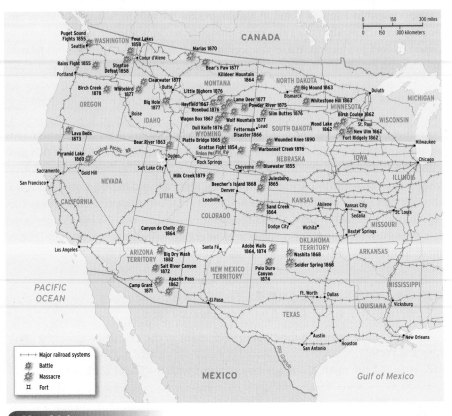

▲ **Map 16.4**

Indian Battles and Railroad Lines Conflict between Indians and emigrants preceded the advance of the railroads but this new technology accelerated conflict, facilitated military and commodity transport, and helped hasten the near extinction of the buffalo.

Changing perceptions of "the Great American Desert" of the Plains and Southwest combined with the Homestead and Desert Lands Acts to make Indian lands, once thought worthless, appealing. For Indians, dire consequences followed the ever-rising tide of people flowing into and through their lands.

The "Indian Wars," well underway by the close of reconstruction, expanded as the military moved out of the South and reinforcements moved quickly into the West. The military in the West was small and ethnically diverse—in essence, a police force enforcing ethnic apartheid in the region. These wars rarely involved large battles but featured protracted guerilla warfare as Indians fought with and against U.S. troops and rival tribes. In June 1876 the Battle of Little Big Horn, where Custer and the 7th Cavalry fell to Oglala Sioux leader Crazy Horse and Sitting Bull of the Hunkpapa Sioux, was a rare victory for Indians pressured by accelerating U.S. expansion. In the decisive year of 1877 following Custer's instantly mythologized "last stand," Crazy Horse surrendered and was executed at Fort Robinson, Nebraska. Later that same year, after an epic 1,500 mile journey, Nez Perce resistance leader Chief Joseph surrendered to General Oliver

Howard. Finally, Congress, repealing the Fort Laramie Treaty, took the Black Hills from the Lakota and opened the region for gold seekers and land speculators. This quick series of military actions set the stage for a civilian invasion of Indian lands and a century-long reconsideration of best use of this newly secured territory.

Indian Conflict and Resistance

In the 1880s and 1890s military action and federal legislation in tandem with cultural and economic forces erased established Indian territorial lines drawn under the Fort Laramie Treaty, and thus drastically reduced the amount of Indian-controlled land and isolated them against their will on small scattered reservations.

The visible boundaries of Indian lands could still be mapped in the late 1870s, but they remained contested regions. The lines on maps only provided an illusion of geographic organization during a time of shifting borders, tribal movements and alliances, and disastrous government policies. In 1869 newly elected President Ulysses S. Grant, concerned by public criticism of the corrupt Department of Indian Affairs, met with a coalition of Christian leaders who urged him to adopt a peaceful Indian policy based on Christianity. Weary of war the president replied, "Gentlemen, your advice is good. Let us have peace."

The landmark Indian Appropriations Act of April 10, 1869, authorized the president to appoint a commission to "exercise joint control with the Secretary of the Interior" over Indian appropriations. Grant chose a personal friend, General Ely Samuel Parker, a Tonowanda-Seneca member, as the first chair of the Board of Indian Commissioners. Under Parker's leadership the Board initiated what became known as the "**Peace Policy**." Between 1869 and 1876, however, competing goals made peace impossible to achieve. The Indian commissioners and leaders of various Christian denominations provided Indians with food and clothing in exchange for promises to abandon cultural traditions and to assimilate into American society. Simultaneously, Indians were pushed, often under direct military threat, to move to increasingly smaller reservations on land considered unsuitable for migrant settlement or industry. By the 1880s the U.S. government acknowledged that the only Indian territory left was that on rapidly shrinking reservations. At the same time, and with strong public support, the U.S. military waged constant war with the same people that Indian Commissioners and the U.S. Department of the Interior were working to assimilate. General Philip Sheridan infamously captured the contradictions of the Peace Policy when he remarked, after an introduction to a Comanche Chief, "the only good Indians I ever saw were dead." More insightfully he also said "a reservation is a piece of land occupied by Indians and surrounded by thieves."

Education for Assimilation

Of the disputes that defined the Peace Policy era, none was—and remains—more controversial than Indian education. The idea was simple. Take children away from their "ignorant" parents and "backward" communities and train them to be Americans who cherish individualism and republicanism over tribal life. Reformers,

Both of these photographs of Chiracahua Apaches on arrival at the Carlisle Indian School and after "training," captured in 1886, are obviously carefully composed images. What is the message they are meant to convey?

convinced that "the time for fighting was passed," called for an "army of Christian school teachers" to lead Indian children from "barbarism" toward civilization and salvation.

In 1870 Congress supported assimilation with a $100,000 appropriation to establish federal industrial schools mainly on existing reservations. These early efforts often failed because of Indian parents resented efforts to dismantle their cultures through their children, and because students simply ran away. Administrators, replacing reservation-based day schools with remote boarding schools, separated children from their parents. Industrial education for Indians drew support from the notions of **Social Darwinism** and from the efforts of pragmatic reformers in the American South such as Samuel Armstrong, founder of the Hampton Institute in Virginia. Armstrong had advocated the development of trade skills as a mechanism for gradual assimilation of freed slaves. In 1879, 84 Lakota children became the first students at the Carlisle, Pennsylvania, Indian Training School. Their education there marked the beginning of a generation-long effort to assimilate Indian children coercively in 81 schools from Carlisle to Riverside, California. Carlisle School founder **Richard Henry Pratt** studied the Hampton model as he developed his ideas for an Indian school system.

The story of Indian education is complicated. Students sometimes went willingly to the boarding schools for personal reasons or as an escape from the humiliation and privation of the reservation. Other students were lured with vague promises of exciting trips. Some parents willingly signed over their children hoping that education promised them a better life. Others signed without realizing their children would be sent far away for extended periods. The Indian children bore the most painful burden as they left their families for the military-like routines of boarding school. Many years later **Plenty Kill**, a Lakota Sioux, remembered a "sad scene" as Indian children said goodbye to their parents. Separation from their parents was the first step in a process that isolated Indian children from their culture and traditions. At the schools teachers gave children new names and clothes: uniforms for boys and long dresses for girls. The setting, lifestyle, and the curriculum were designed to teach Indian children to conform to the ways the white world. At Carlisle Pratt told arriving students and visitors that he would "kill the Indian to save the man."

By 1900 the U.S. government had spent $2,936,080 on Indian boarding schools. Between 1877 and 1900 enrollment increased from 3,598 to 21,568 students, or 50 percent of school-age Indian children. Despite these numbers, the assimilation-through-education experiment failed to destroy Indian culture. Indian schools created a generation of students who returned home as agents of cultural change with valuable knowledge of the workings of the white world and a new awareness of collective Indian identity that fostered a more united Indian civil rights front. Others, "too white to be red, too red to be white," left the schools with no real cultural identity and little chance for success in either world. The United States was not alone in these efforts. Canadians used similar education programs to assimilate their "First Nations," and Australian officials attempted assimilation through education before resorting to more violent measures.

The Destruction of the Buffalo

Alongside government policies for war or peace, and education or removal, a contest over animals and land use shaped the destruction of traditional tribal life. Economic and environmental forces, linked with changing perceptions of the natural world, undermined the ability of Indians to live on lands that had supported them for thousands of years.

On the plains of the 1870s open-range cattle drives, an expanding web of rail lines, hunting, environmental factors, and politics contributed to a rapid decline of the once vast herds of American buffalo. For the Plains Indians, buffalo provided food and shelter, dictated tribal migration patterns, was a vital trade commodity, shaped diplomatic relations between tribes, and played a central role in Indian culture and religion. For millennia more than 24 million buffalo had migrated seasonally throughout the plains and valleys west of the Missouri River. In the 1840s the ability to use horses and steel to harvest the buffalo helped the Comanche forge an unprecedented empire covering six U.S. states and several Mexican *estados* in the 1840s. Between the 1830s and 1870s, however, the herds that had moved "over the land like the shadows of scudding clouds," began a dramatic decline toward near extinction.

Mountain of buffalo skulls, 1880. This iconic image of slaughter helps convey some sense of the scale of the Buffalo hunts that nearly wiped out the species.

The decline of buffalo began before the Civil War when Indians and whites observed significant declines in numbers, especially on the Northern Plains. Observers also noted starvation and new migration patterns among Indian peoples of the upper plains. The Lakota, Cheyenne, Kiowa, and Arapahoe suffered greatly from declining buffalo populations in the 1840s and 1850s. The demise of the buffalo herds in the decades before the Civil War was universally attributed to the activities of migrants who hunted the animals for food and sport and forced buffalo from the grazing grounds of their cattle. General William Tecumseh Sherman echoed common perceptions that in the contest for grass, cattle beat buffalo and cowboys beat Indians. For him, replacing, "the wild buffaloes by more numerous herds of tame cattle, and by substituting for the useless Indians the intelligent owners of productive farms and cattle ranches" was a logical and desirable frontier process. Cattle drives and ranching, overland migration, and depletion of resources contributed to the decline of the buffalo, but hunting and a short-lived but expansive market for buffalo hides was even more significant.

The decimation of the great buffalo herds began with Indians caught in a convergence of ecological, political, and economic change. In the decades before the Civil War some Plains tribes resolved old tensions and forged new alliances to cope with migrant encroachment on tribal lands. Indians were not simply caught up in global changes in land use facilitated by the industrial revolution; they were also, as they had always been, agents of environmental change. Between 1840 and 1870, facing increasing waves of migration and infiltration of their hunting grounds, Indians participated in the growing hide trade while maintaining traditional hunting practices. The interplay of migrant intrusion, tempting market forces, U.S. Army aggression, and new Indian alliances that freed time and resources for hunting contributed to the buffalo's decline.

For buffalo-hunting Indians, the true crisis came in the 1860s and 1870s when the completion of the Transcontinental Railroad enabled mass hunting and an international hide trade. Mechanizing industries used leather hides for machine belts. High demand caused shortages. Factory owners imported tanned hides from South America but longed for a cheaper substitute. Entrepreneurs, developing new methods for tanning buffalo hides, created a better product at less cost. Buffalo hunters then followed the rails, and new train lines carried the hides to the factories of the East.

Legendary hunters like Buffalo Bill were credited with killing a thousand animals a day. Though the numbers were often exaggerated, between 1865 and 1883 hide hunters did kill vast numbers of buffalo and pushed the already declining buffalo population to the edge of extinction. Hunters, killing from slowly moving trains with high-powered rifles, skinned the animals and left their huge bodies to rot. Military leaders, understanding that the destruction of the buffalo crippled the Indians who depended on them, encouraged the slaughter. "If I could learn that every Buffalo in the northern herd were killed," General Sheridan proclaimed in 1881, "I would be glad." Sheridan almost got his wish. Migrants passing over trails in the 1880s remarked on the vast fields of bleached bones, piles of skulls, and displays of heads and hides—grisly evidence of the systematic slaughter of a species. Congress belatedly commemorated the iconic herds by coining a "buffalo nickel" in 1913, with an image of an American Indian on the reverse. Millions of these tiny tributes changed hands until the 1960s.

The Dawes Act and Survival

In 1887 Congress passed the Dawes or **General Allotment Act**, yet another new phase in federal Indian policy. The Dawes Act, dividing reservation land into individual parcels, turned tribal land into individual pieces of property. Reformers hoped that the act would protect Indians against fraud and land grabbers better than the reservation system had and would enable Indians, too, to enjoy the Jeffersonian yeoman dream that drew so many migrants to the West. For supporters like Teddy Roosevelt, the Dawes Act served as a "mighty pulverizing engine to break up the tribal mass," to the benefit of the individual Indian. The act also granted Indians U.S. citizenship and offered Indians greater protections from U.S. courts.

Like all of the Indian policies of the 19th century, allotment was the product of reformer's hopes and Indian haters' prejudice. Regardless of motive, the results for the tribes were disastrous. Like Indian education, allotment sought to assimilate Indians into broader society through direct intervention in daily tribal life and culture. The reservation system was hated by most Indians, but allotment proved much more insidious. Between the passage of the act in 1887 and its repeal in 1934, American Indians lost two-thirds of their remaining lands, or more than 90 million acres. The division of the reservations into thousands of individual holdings made large-scale fraud and legal sales of tribal lands not harder, but easier, and the solid blocks of reservation became a mind-boggling checkerboard of vulnerable dispersed lands. Allotment created a complicated map that has vexed courts and putative Indian landowners to the present. Contrary to the optimistic hopes of reformers, sustainable Indian farming and self-sufficiency declined after 1887. Indian farmers and ranchers faced the same unforgiving environmental challenges as did all residents of the region.

Disillusioned by the confluence of failed government policies, ecological catastrophe, cultural collapse, and the erosion of tribal sovereignty, some Indians turned to the Ghost Dance religion led by the Paiute prophet Wovoka. The divestment of Indian lands through allotment fueled the movement. Ghost dancers wore distinctive white costumes, and the mystery surrounding the religion and the dancers' beliefs about achieving a death-like state of grace gave the movement its popular name. Although Wovoka envisioned a peaceful coexistence of Indians and whites, Lakota Ghost Dance followers, such as Sitting Bull and Kicking Bear, rejected that vision and insisted instead that violence remained the only option for Indians. Some Sioux Ghost Dancers believed that if they united in violent uprising they would spark an apocalypse that would raise the dead and restore the land and animals. The number of Ghost Dancers was small, but enough participated to raise concern with the Office of Indian Affairs, which outlawed the religion in 1890, and with the military, which strengthened positions on the northern plains.

On December 15, 1890, soldiers killed Sitting Bull during a raid on his Standing Rock cabin. Troops with the U.S. 7th Cavalry then followed Minneconjou Ghost

Dancers and their leader Big Foot, to Wounded Knee, South Dakota, where they met up with Chiefs Short Bull and Kicking Bear. On the morning of December 28, soldiers surrounded the dancers. After a brief confrontation with a medicine man named Yellow Bird, a shot rang out and the soldiers—opening fire with light artillery—killed between 150 and 300 Indian men, women, and children.

In 1893, only two years after the killing of the Lakota Ghost Dancers and their families, the U.S. government attempted to rewrite the tragic history of Indians into a story of success. At the World Columbian Exposition in Chicago, commemorating the 400th anniversary of Columbus's arrival in the Western Hemisphere, the fair celebrated "A Century of Progress." Half of the U.S. government buildings featured American Indian exhibits with a special emphasis on federal Indian education and assimilation programs. Near the government pavilion a Smithsonian Institution exhibit presented careful reconstructions of traditional Indian cultures. Representatives of the Pueblos, Navajo, Sioux, Apache, and Nez Perce traveled to Chicago to participate in the Smithsonian exhibits. Chicago fairgoers saw in these exhibits the ambivalence toward Indians that had characterized the period. Indians were feared and revered; their passing to a new stage of history was hailed and lamented. Indians displayed themselves as culturally viable members of tribes with a past and future next to exhibits that portrayed them as something akin to natural artifacts.

Tourism, Parks, and Forests

The perceived closing of the frontier and unprecedented conquest of the environment between 1877 and 1900 caused anxiety about the depletion of resources and destruction of natural wonders. As Americans saw their manifest destiny of a transcontinental empire achieved, frontier nostalgia shaped culture and policy. The need to protect what remained of the frontier gained national attention as early as the 1870s. Eastern and European travelers, lured to the exotic Wild West by writers such as Mark Twain and artists such as Thomas Moran and Albert Bierstadt, found natural wonders but also graphic evidence of human impact. Even from train windows tourists viewed mountains of buffalo skeletons, denuded forests, toxic mining waste and blasted landscapes, and trails of discarded possessions.

In the mid-19th century, publicity about the "discovery" of the Yosemite Valley and several nearby groves of giant Sequoia trees prompted the first western tourist rush. Early entrepreneurs, spurring demand for private enterprises to transport, house, and guide tourists through the area for profit, promoted Yosemite. Recognizing the area's unique scenery and tourism potential, Congress reserved the land for public use. Yellowstone in the northwest corner of the Wyoming territory became America's first official "National Park" on March 1, 1872, when President Ulysses S. Grant signed an act designating over 2.2 million acres of geological wonders as a "pleasuring ground for the benefit and enjoyment of the people."

The presence of Indians in both parks complicated the global image of Yellowstone and Yosemite as icons of western nature. The Nez Perce and other northern tribes had moved through and lived in the Yellowstone region for centuries. In the

GLOBAL PASSAGES

Settler Societies and Indigenous Peoples

The experience of Indians in the United States was not exceptional. There were parallel developments in Australia regarding the fate and welfare of its native peoples, known as Aboriginals. In the geographically isolated American West and in Australia, for example, expansion into lands occupied by indigenous peoples shared key characteristics. In both, occupation by newcomers required conquest and dependence on extractive export economies. There was an explicit desire by state authorities to dominate Indian and Aboriginal peoples and redistribute their lands to leading edge entrepreneurs, capitalists, and migrating settlers. In both, virgin soil epidemics—before the onslaught of significant waves of settlers—did much of the early damage to lives of the indigenous peoples as they disrupted cultural patterns and caused strife among the tribes. And, in Australia under British rule and in the West during the 19th century, distant governments and their local representatives used questionable diplomacy or outright military force to undermine Indian and Aboriginal peoples' ability to survive. American Indian policy was brutally pragmatic but always hotly debated with significant voices of dissent. The British in Australia were even less idealistic than Americans in their dealings with indigenous tribes. After limited efforts to negotiate with the widely dispersed Aboriginal tribes, the British simply gave up and declared the area *Terra Nullius*, or empty land.

Both of these strikingly similar arid ecosystems offered few real opportunities for unsupported individuals to thrive with or without indigenous peoples. Successful ranches, measured by the square mile, operated on corporate models supported by elaborate government-funded irrigation and transportation projects along with direct subsidies. Even large industrial endeavors such as mining required state military support to open and secure lands occupied by Indians or Aboriginals. The transfer and destruction of species also played a central role in the settler societies of the West and Australia. Species removal and addition undermined the ability of the indigenous peoples to live in traditional ways. Cattle and sheep in Australia and

1870s battles between Nez Perce Chief Joseph and General Sherman brought attention to the region. Following the well-publicized battles, park administrators launched a campaign to control and then systematically remove Indians from Yellowstone. Beyond military concerns, officials worried that fears of Indian attack might affect the growing tourist trade. Moreover, the perception of Yellowstone as pristine wilderness left no place for Indians. By 1900 the government removed Indians not only from the park but also from the history of the place. Advocates for preservation also failed to recognize the importance of these places for local economies. Generations of working

New Zealand transformed environments and economies just as replacement of the buffalo with cattle altered the American West. In Australia devastation of crops and entire regions by plagues of European wild rabbits and exotic species undermined thousands of years of careful land practices by the Aboriginal people.

Dislocation of one group of indigenous people was sometimes spurred by the migration of other groups that had been pushed out of traditional homelands by circumstance or force. Poland offers one interesting example. During the years between the end of the Civil War and the start of World War I, a multitude of immigrants made their way from Poland to the United States. Nineteenth-century Poland was a country defined by contested internal and external borderland regions, transnational cultural exchange, and rapidly shifting patterns of migration. As in the West, internal ethnic struggles tied to national politics and external economic and political pressures drove the movement of people.

Situated in the "heart of Europe," Poland weathered many centuries of territorial struggles, international tensions over conflicting claims of regional control, and profound conflict over the rights of Jews in particular. Polish Jews maintained their own language and culture within the shifting Polish state. Like Indians and Aboriginals they negotiated a tenuous autonomy with governments divided over their place in Poland's future and with a Christian population that mostly feared and hated them. Between the 1850s and 1914 the Polish state worked to assimilate Jews with the hope that they might abandon the cultural and linguistic traditions that made them distinct and placed them in the way of evolving notions of Polish national *spoleczenstwo* (society) and progress. These pressures caused Polish Jews to struggle to maintain their identity in their traditional homeland and forced many to choose migration across the Atlantic to new frontiers like the American West.

- How does the Aboriginal experience with the British enrich our understanding of American Indian history?

- Given the similarities between global settler societies and indigenous experiences, does the American frontier process seem exceptional?

class ranchers, timbermen, farmers, and miners asked tough questions about who should decide the best use of natural places.

In the spectacular Yosemite Valley of California's Sierras, the Ahwahneechee tribe lived for centuries before the first expeditions "discovered" this icon of exceptional American nature. The first white visitors closely linked the Ahwaneechee and their village culture with the astounding geological wonders of the "Incomparable Valley." With no significant military conflict with the Indians of the Sierra, military leaders and later the National Park Service "naturalized" the Indians and incorporated them

Thomas Moran's *The Grand Canyon of the Yellowstone* (1872, oil on canvas), so inspired viewers that it helped encouraged the creation of the first National Park.

into the park. Brochures described the Ahwaneechee to tourists as quaint natural features to be admired along with bears and waterfalls. As the national parks evolved in the 20th century, Indians were removed or displayed according to the demands of the western tourist industry.

While the government worked out environmental policies in the parks and forests, a wave of grass-roots environmental concern ignited a popular preservation

TIMELINE 1868–1900

1868

April 29 Treaty of Fort Laramie creates Great Sioux Reservation in Black Hills

1869

May 10 Transcontinental Railroad Central Pacific and Union Pacific lines meet in Utah

April 10 Indian Appropriations Act Signed "Peace Policy" begins

May 24 John Wesley Powell launched first in a series of surveys of the Colorado River

1870

May Buffalo hunters move onto plains initiating a decade of extermination

1872

March 1 Yellowstone becomes designated America's first National Park

1874

August 5 Custer expedition discovers gold in the Black Hills of Dakota

1875

J.W. Powell publishes *The Exploration of the Colorado River*

1876

June 25 and 26 Battle of Little Big Horn

September Congress repeals Fort Laramie Treaty taking the Black Hills from the Lakota

1877

September 5 Crazy Horse killed after surrendering at Ft. Robinson, NE

March 3 Desert Land Act allowing for purchases of up to 640 acres in arid regions

October 5 Nez Perce resistance leader, Chief Joseph, surrenders

1878

March 31 Boxer, Jack Johnson, born to two former slaves in Galveston, TX

J. W. Powell's *Report on the Lands of the Arid Region* published

40,000 Exodusters migrate to Kansas

1879

March 3 Congress creates United States Geological Survey

October 84 Lakota children enrolled at the Carlisle, PA, Indian Training School

1880

October 31 "Hop Alley" violence against Chinese

November 17 Chinese Exclusion Treaty restricts Chinese immigration and citizenship

1882

May 6 Chinese Exclusion Act halts Chinese immigration

movement. Naturalist **John Muir** formalized the movement with the founding of the Sierra Club in 1892. The Sierra Club was an example of growing national concern for the intrinsic value of nature. Inspired by transcendentalist authors like Walt Whitman and Henry David Thoreau, preservationists advocated the permanent protection of wilderness for its own sake. Their efforts bolstered the utilitarian arguments for conservation expressed by concerned observers such as Theodore Roosevelt and scientists like **Gifford Pinchot**. Roosevelt and other conservationists worried about the wanton waste of resources and especially forests intentionally burned to destroy Indian refuges or to further the charcoal trade and construction of mines. Industrial timber harvesting, which was reducing American forests at unprecedented rates, created support for government regulation of this vital resource. Amendment 24 of the General Appropriations Act of 1891 gave the U.S. president authority to remove forested lands from the public domain and protect them from exploitation. This law brought millions of acres under federal protection during the 1890s and early 20th century.

Gifford Pinchot traveled to France and Germany to learn the techniques of scientific forestry. He returned with a vision for the "wise use" of natural resources for "the greatest good to the greatest number for the longest time." America's first professionally trained forester, Pinchot enforced the Appropriations Act first as a member of the National Forest Commission and then as head of the U.S. Division of Forestry. In the early 1900s he worked with Theodore Roosevelt to dramatically expand the land management role of the federal government. In the space of only three decades the West had developed to the extent that many believed government protection was the only way to avoid wholesale destruction of the region. The collective realization that the seemingly unlimited resources of the West were finite marked a critical juncture in American history.

1883

Summer American Buffalo near extinction after last mass hunt on Northern Plains

Buffalo Bill stages his first Wild West Show

1884

February Roosevelt moves to his Dakota cattle ranch

1885

September 2 51 Chinese miners killed during race riots in Rock Springs, WY

1887

February 8 Dawes/ General Allotment Act breaks up Indian reservations

June 25 Buffalo Bill's Wild West Show plays to Queen Victoria in London

1888

March 11–14 Blizzards and cold decimate cattle herds across the Great Plains

1890

December 15 Sitting Bull killed

December 28 Lakota Ghost Dancers murdered at Wounded Knee, SD

June 2 Census data suggests that frontier is "closed"

1891

March 3 Forest Reserve Act gave President authority to remove forested lands from the public domain and protect them from exploitation

1892

May 28 Sierra Club founded with John Muir as first president

1893

May Western Federation of Miners (WFM)

May 1 The World Columbian Exposition opens in Chicago

1900

September 8 Storm destroys Galveston, TX, killing 8,000

STUDY QUESTIONS FOR CLEARING THE LAND AND CLEANSING THE WILDERNESS

1. How did environmental factors contribute to U.S.-Indian policy?
2. What did Indian reformers intend to accomplish through their policies? To what degree did they succeed? How did Indians respond?

Summary

- With the end of the Civil War and completion of the Transcontinental Railroad, American attention turns to the West.
- The federal government creates new agencies and sponsors surveys that complete the map of the West and highlight new opportunities but raise new concerns.
- The Homestead Act and land grants to railroads spark a new wave of migration.
- Ideas of American exceptionalism shape government policies and create a powerful myth of the American West in the entire world.
- Indians struggle to retain tribal lands and cultural autonomy in the face of immigrant onslaught, military action, and misguided U.S. reform policies.
- The near extinction of the American buffalo undermines Indian economies and demonstrates extent of environmental impact of settlement.
- New technologies collapse time and space and enable the industrialization of the western extractive economy.
- A highly mobile multicultural workforce labors in a rapidly changing regional economy and is linked to ups and downs of world markets.
- Ethnic and class tensions fuel culture of violence.
- The speed and extent of land use in the West inspire grass-roots and federal environmental preservation efforts.

Key Terms and People

Chinese Exclusion Act 610
Cody, William "Buffalo Bill" 613
Desert Lands Act 612
General Allotment Act 630
Haywood, "Big" Bill 617
Homestead Act of 1862 612
Hoover, Herbert 619
Johnson, Jack 604
Lease, Mary Elizabeth 621

Muir, John 635
Peace Policy 625
Pinchot, Gifford 635
Plenty Kill 627
Powell, John Wesley 611
Pratt, Richard Henry 627
Social Darwinism 627
White, William Allen 621

Reviewing Chapter 16

1. Where was the West? West of Where? When was the West? Did this region have a beginning and an end in time and space?
2. What role did misperceptions about regional environment and culture play in the conflicts that characterized the history of the nation as it moved to consolidate modern borders?
3. What role did the federal government play in the consolidation of the American West?

Further Reading

DeLay, Brian. *War of a Thousand Deserts: Indian Raids and the U.S.-Mexican War.* New Haven: Yale University Press, 2008. Remarkable new perspective on the role of Indian Nations and the Mexican War and the creation of the transnational borderlands.

Hine, Robert, and John Mack Faragher. *The American West: A New Interpretive History.* New Haven: Yale University Press, 2000. Depth and detail on the range of issues covered in this chapter.

Igler, David. *Industrial Cowboys: Miller & Lux and the Transformation of the Far West, 1850–1920.* Berkeley: University of California Press, 2001. Insightful analysis of western industry.

Isenberg, Andrew C. *The Destruction of the Bison: An Environmental History, 1750–1920.* Cambridge: Cambridge University Press, 2000. A riveting account of the near extinction of the bellwether species of the American West.

Truett, Samuel. *Fugitive Landscapes: The Forgotten History of the U.S.-Mexico Borderlands.* New Haven: Yale University Press, 2006. Fascinating account of the complicated environment, cultural, and economic relations of the transnational borderlands.

Warren, Louis S. *Buffalo Bill's America: William Cody and the Wild West Show.* New York: Vintage, 2005. The embodiment of the myth of the West placed in context and captured in great detail.

Visual Review

Mining and Labor

Mineral rushes pull migrants to the West and generate enormous wealth.

Business Travelers

Mine owners import labor and export minerals.

Changing Patterns of Migration

Migration west continues, boosting and diversifying the economy.

Mexican Borders

Mexicans and Americans flow across the national borders.

Chinese Exclusion

The Chinese face intense discrimination and labor exploitation.

Meeting Ground of Many Peoples

FORGING A TRANSCONTINENTAL NATION, 1877–1900

Mapping the West

The Federal Frontier

The federal government promotes western land ownership and development.

Myth and History

Boosters promote the west as a land of promise and opportunity shaping national identity.

Promotion and Memory

Early settlers generate accounts of the frontier sometimes at odds with reality.

The Culture of Collective Violence

Westerners embrace the idea of vigilantism and organized violence against Indians.

Railroads Time and Space

Vast transportation and communication networks connect the West to the national and world economy.

Industrial Ranching

The West builds an expanding global cattle industry.

Corporate Cowboys

Cowboys develop as cultural icons and actual laborers.

Extractive Economies and Global Commodities

Indian Conflict and Resistance

Indians resist military action taken by the U.S. government to control their land.

Education for Assimilation

The U.S. government enacts policies to educate Indians.

The Destruction of the Buffalo

Government policies over animal and land use impacts Indian life.

The Dawes Act and Survival

The U.S. government divides reservations in a misguided effort to protect Indians through assimilation.

Tourism, Parks, and Forests

Congress creates policies to reserve and preserve public lands.

Clearing the Land and Cleansing the Wilderness

A New Industrial and Labor Order

1877–1900

In 1903 Englishman Arthur Shadwell traveled to Pittsburgh, the U.S. iron and steel center. Although familiar with Europe's industrialization, Shadwell was shocked by what he encountered. "Grime and squalor unspeakable, unlimited hours of work, ferocious contests between labour and capital, the fiercest commercial scrambling for the money literally sweated out of the people, the utter absorption . . . of getting and grabbing. . . ." All of these traits, Shadwell noted, had once defined Great Britain as it spearheaded industrialization. Now the United States found itself "Europeanized" to the extreme. Pittsburgh, he believed, was worse than any of its European counterparts. Even the filthy English industrial city of Sheffield seemed like "a pleasure resort" in comparison.

Homestead, located outside of Pittsburgh, was especially horrific. "If Pittsburgh is hell with the lid off," Shadwell exclaimed, "Homestead is hell with the hatches on." The site of magnate **Andrew Carnegie**'s massive steel works, Homestead "is nothing but unrelieved gloom and grind," where "men sweat out the furnaces and rolling mills twelve hours a day for seven days a week" and live in "rows of wretched hovels where they eat and sleep, having neither time nor energy for anything else." Attempts by workers to unionize to better their condition had "been put down with an iron hand dipped in blood."

To Shadwell, the Pittsburgh-area steel mills signified the ruthless drive of America's industrialists, their "unswerving devotion to money making relentlessly pursued." Accumulating unprecedented riches, they had "fattened on other men's brains and sweat." Carnegie's multimillion dollar fortune, he asserted, "carries a taint to it."

As Shadwell observed, the United States changed dramatically in the last quarter of the 19th century. The

Sears Catalog
Cover, 1899

CHAPTER OUTLINE

GLOBAL WEBS OF INDUSTRIAL CAPITALISM
> The New Industrial Order
> U.S. Industrial Growth in Global Context
> Combinations and Concentrations of Wealth
> Markets and Consumerism

WORK AND THE WORKPLACE
> Global Migrations
> Blue Collar and White Collar Workers
> Regimentation and Scientific Management
> Working Conditions and Wages
> Economic Convulsions and Hard Times
> Women and Children in the Workplace

continued on page 645

America in the World

U.S. Steel became the world's first billion-dollar industry, and United States emerges as the world's leading industrial power (1901).

Panics of 1873 and 1893 help trigger worldwide economic depressions.

 U.S. event that influenced the world

International event that influenced the United States

Event with multinational influence

Conflict

American heiress Jennie Jerome married into the British upper classes, representing the emerging trans-continental mobility of elite American women (1874).

The Paris Commune generated fears of communism in the United States (1871).

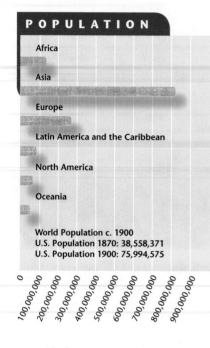

POPULATION

Africa

Asia

Europe

Latin America and the Caribbean

North America

Oceania

World Population c. 1900
U.S. Population 1870: 38,558,371
U.S. Population 1900: 75,994,575

0
100,000,000
200,000,000
300,000,000
400,000,000
500,000,000
600,000,000
700,000,000
800,000,000
900,000,000

growth of industrial capitalism transformed the landscape, changed business organization, transformed work and the workplace, and spurred migration and immigration worldwide while producing a flood of cheap, mass-produced consumer goods. The new order generated both unprecedented wealth and poverty.

Since 1873, when writers Mark Twain and Charles Dudley Warner dubbed this era the Gilded Age, the name has stuck because it is especially fitting. The United States seemed to be gilded, covered with the gold generated for millionaire industrialists like Carnegie. But that gold covering often proved to be a thin veneer, masking a world of greed, exploitation, and poverty.

The new economic order gave Americans both hope and anxiety. Wages increased and Americans had access to more and cheaper goods than at any time in human history. But troubling questions remained. Had the United States, as Shadwell argued, become Europe, with democracy and opportunity in decline, with a powerful industrial aristocracy ruling over a permanent working class?

GLOBAL WEBS OF INDUSTRIAL CAPITALISM

With its origins in England in the early 19th century, industrial capitalism transformed the economies of Northern Europe and then the United States, tightly knitting together first a North Atlantic and then a global economy. Profits derived from commercial capitalism earlier in the century provided the basis for industrial capitalism. Industrial capitalism, the private investment of massive amounts of money in machinery, technology, and massive and complex factories and processing plants, represented a striking new phase of economic development that required new organizational models. The United States entered this new phase of economic development later than many European nations. But by 1900 the nation emerged as the world's industrial leader. The new industrial order spun webs across the continent, across the Atlantic, and around the world over which money, technology, people, and goods flowed. American products, from Heinz pickles to Singer Sewing Machines, became household names around the world.

"Big business," as Americans referred to these new enterprises, generated unprecedented wealth for those who emerged victorious in the fierce competition that marked the era. In addition, industry produced more and cheaper consumer goods available to more people in more places than ever before in history. At the same time, "big business" spawned fears among many Americans. The unchecked power of industrialists, largely unfettered by regulatory laws, frightened them as they ruthlessly crushed competition, created monopolies, and wielded excessive influence over government. Moreover, extreme concentrations of wealth in the hands of a few seemed to create an aristocracy in the democratic United States. Was "big business," as industrialists argued, the natural evolution of the economic order that benefited all, or was it instead a new form of tyranny that undermined American ideals?

The New Industrial Order

CHAPTER OUTLINE

continued from page 641

WORKERS FIGHT BACK
> The Great Railroad Strike of 1877
> Organizing Strategies and Labor Violence
> The Farmers Organize
> The Labor Movement in Global Context

THE NEW INDUSTRIAL ORDER: DEFENSE AND DISSENT
> Defending the New Order
> Critiquing the New Order

Industrialization was not new in the United States in the late 19th century. What was new was the size, scale, nature, and function of this second Industrial Revolution. In the first Industrial Revolution, in the early 19th century, manufacturing tended to be small in scale and owned by one or two people or a few partners, who pooled their capital to start their enterprise. Early industries maintained a personal tone; owners knew their workers and oversaw shop floors. In addition, early shops and mills tended to be limited to areas that had access to wood or waterpower to drive machines. Although manufactured goods flowed across the Atlantic earlier in the century, many products tended to be distributed locally or regionally, limited by rudimentary transportation networks.

Technological innovations, powered by fossil fuels, made the new industrial order, industrial capitalism, possible in both the United States and Northern Europe. Coal

Carnegie Steel's Homestead Works, located outside of Pittsburgh along the Monongahela River, was the site of both technological innovation and labor strife. The Homestead Works produced 200 million tons of steel in its 105-year history and helped make Pennsylvania the steel capital of the world.

fueled steam engines and machines that were both bigger and faster than those in the first Industrial Revolution. It energized electricity grids that powered manufacturing as well as the railroads that carried these products to new markets. Coal also provided a crucial ingredient for one of the most important new products of this era, steel. Like those in Northern Europe, nearly all of the manufacturing regions of the United States sat atop or near rich coal deposits, most notably the northeast, with New York and Philadelphia the nation's leading manufacturing cities, and along the Great Lakes.

Innovative technologies spawned new manufacturing processes and products. Complex technical industries, such as steel, chemicals, petroleum, and pharmaceuticals, developed new production techniques. Huge factories running around the clock allowed manufacturers to produce larger volumes of their product at a lower cost, known as economies of scale. Not only could novel and larger amounts of products be manufactured in more places, these goods also could reach new markets due to the network of railroads that laced the nation.

Pioneered by the railroads, the **modern corporation** differed from corporations established earlier in the century in size, scale, and organization. First, modern businesses required massive infusion of capital, more than one investor or several partners—sufficient for early corporations—could provide. To finance the massive job of building a railroad, railroad corporations sold shares to investors. Second, modern

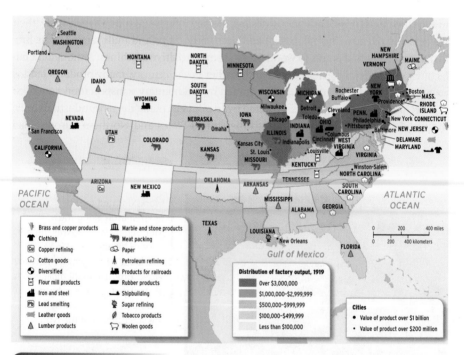

▲ Map 17.1

Rich in Resources An abundance of agricultural products and raw materials from the South and West, manufactured largely in the Northeast and upper Midwest, helped make the United States the world's leading industrial power by 1900.

corporations required new forms of management. Railroads found themselves faced with the vast challenge of administering and coordinating a complex, technologically advanced enterprise, involving the movement of cars over hundreds of miles. A board of directors, representing stockholders, provided joint, general control of the company. A layer of managers, with specialized skills, oversaw daily operations. Railroads organized departments, with clear lines of authority and communication, manned with specialists in engineering, scheduling, and finance, to name a few, creating an elaborate bureaucracy.

Modern corporations—for example, those dealing in steel, oil, meat packing, and chemical processing—replicated the railroads' model, as their businesses also required vast amounts of money to build factories and processing plants; purchase expensive machinery; set up warehouses, offices, and distribution centers; and establish complex management systems. Unlike pre-Civil War business and industry, large, modern business enterprises separated ownership from management. Businesses needed to operate steadily and efficiently to make a profit and required elaborate, carefully coordinated administrative networks made up of departments with specialized functions.

The money invested in Gilded Age corporations far surpassed that ventured in antebellum businesses. Before the Civil War, cotton textile mills were the nation's largest industry. Only a few, however, represented over $1 million of capital and employed more than 500 workers; not a single American company was worth more than $10 million. By 1904, over 300 companies in the United States were valued at $10 million. In 1901, U.S. Steel became the world's first billion dollar company, employing over 100,000 workers.

Industrial capitalism—or big business—was massive and impersonal in its scale, reach, and impact. But even as ownership in large business enterprises multiplied through stockholding and the new economic order grew impersonal, the public still identified individual businessmen with the specific big businesses they helped establish. Andrew Carnegie epitomized big steel; **John D. Rockefeller**, big oil; and **Cornelius Vanderbilt**, the railroads.

Big business generated wealth on an unprecedented scale. In 1860, approximately 300 Americans were millionaires. Roughly 40 years later that number had risen to around 4,500, with many multimillionaires. In the 1870s, the richest Americans were railroad men, such as Cornelius Vanderbilt, who topped the list with an estimated wealth of $100 million. By 1896, oil man Rockefeller and steel king Carnegie were the richest Americans, amassing fortunes of $200–300 million. Measuring wealth as a percentage of the economy, John D. Rockefeller remains to this day the richest individual in American history, outstripping even contemporary business entrepreneurs, such as Microsoft's Bill Gates.

U.S. Industrial Growth in Global Context

The new industrial order was well underway in Europe by the time the American economy began its transition during the Civil War. In 1870, Great Britain was the world's premier industrial power, followed by Germany. But by 1900, the United

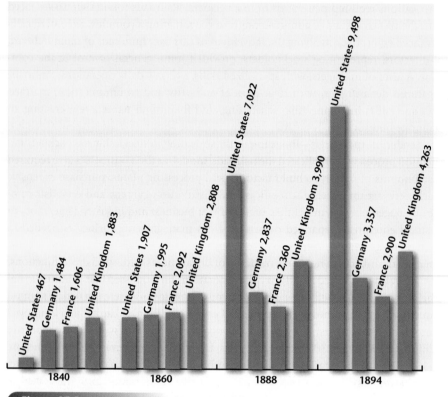

▲ **Figure 17.1**

Manufacturing Values, Europe and the United States, 1840–1894 (in millions of dollars) Manufacturing exploded in the United States in the last half of the 19th century. Innovations in industrial organization, technology, and transportation, as well as an abundance of raw materials and cheap labor, all propelled the United States past European rivals.

States emerged as the globe's leading industrial nation. By that point, the nation produced over 30 percent of the world's manufacturing output.

A number of factors account for this rise. The United States was blessed with an abundance of natural resources. Cotton from southern states, coal from Pennsylvania, and iron ore from Minnesota's Mesabi Range provided the raw materials necessary for rapid industrial growth. The United States also greatly benefited from Great Britain's industrial head start as British investors poured their surplus wealth into the United States, providing a large percentage of the money needed to help capitalize large-scale industry, particularly railroads. Moreover, the nation's dramatic population growth, through both natural increase and immigration, greatly aided industrial development. As the nation exploded from 31 million people in 1860 to 76 million in 1900, this population supplied labor for rapidly expanding industries as well as a healthy market of consumers to purchase the many goods mass produced by American industry.

Fierce competition characterized the new industrial order. Businesses failed at an alarming rate in the late 19th century; some observers estimated that 95 percent of businesses failed in the 1870s and 1880s. Cheap production, businessmen soon learned, depended on a company's ability to control every aspect of manufacturing as well as the distribution of goods, and they crafted new organizational structures that would be hallmarks of "big business." Vertical integration cut costs and guaranteed a regular flow of raw materials for production. Carnegie Steel, for example, owned, in addition to its massive steel mills, the mines that produced the raw materials needed for steel production—coal, coke, and iron ore—as well as the railroads and steamships to transport raw materials to steel mills. Carnegie also set up sales offices to distribute steel efficiently and thus controlled both the production and distribution processes.

Horizontal integration aimed to tame the destructive elements of vigorous competition. The early oil industry, for example, was especially competitive and unstable as oilmen engaged in cutthroat competition. John D. Rockefeller and Standard Oil were notorious for eliminating competitors through secret deals with railroads that penalized rival oil companies, and outright intimidation. To guarantee profits, oilmen first created cartels in which they agreed informally to fix prices and set quotas for production, and thus to share massive profits. But these informal agreements often broke down—and the American public vigorously protested price-fixing.

Seeking a way to centralize control through consolidation, Rockefeller devised the trust. Stockholders in individual oil corporations turned their stock over to a small group of trustees, including Rockefeller himself, who ran the various parts of Standard Oil as one company. In return, the stockholders received profits from the combination but had no direct control over the decisions of the trustees. Standard Oil soon had a monopoly of the oil industry, as a single company that controlled more than 90 percent of oil refining in the United States by the 1880s. By 1904, its profits reached a whopping $57 million. The first and most notorious trust, Standard Oil served as a model as trusts in beef, tobacco, and sugar soon followed.

Although the trust was a specific type of business organization, to the American public the term "trust" became synonymous with any large business combination. To men like Rockefeller, the trust represented the pinnacle of modern business enterprise. But to average Americans it meant the demise of small, independent businesses that could no longer compete, and higher prices for the consumer. In addition, many feared that trusts placed far too much power in the hands of a few individuals who would inevitably abuse their power.

Combinations and Concentrations of Wealth

Concentrations of wealth in the Gilded Age reflected the growth of combinations, trusts, and monopolies. A study in 1890 concluded that more than half of the nation's wealth was in the hands of just 17 percent of America's families, down from 29 percent in 1860. In the late 1880s an American economist warned that by his calculations, the United States suffered greater inequality than England; the United States, he argued, had developed its own aristocracy.

Public outcry over concentrations of wealth, combinations, and monopolies forced Congress to pass the **Sherman Antitrust Act** in 1890. **Henry Demarest Lloyd's** 1881 investigation of Rockefeller's Standard Oil, "The Story of a Great Monopoly," spawned subsequent articles in the popular press that fanned the flames of public outrage. Lloyd's description of Standard Oil's methods—which included fraud, intimidation, and the purchase of political influence, all at the expense of the consumer—supported his bold claim that "America has the proud satisfaction of having furnished the world with the greatest, wisest, and meanest monopoly known to history." Lloyd famously noted that Standard not only controlled two U.S. senators but the company had also "done everything with the Pennsylvania legislature except to refine it."

The Sherman Antitrust Act aimed at dismantling "combination in the form of trust or otherwise" that restrained trade. But the law was broadly drafted and many key concepts were left undefined, such as "fair competition" and "monopoly," leaving it up to the courts to interpret the law's meaning. In 1895, the Supreme Court decided the case of *U.S. v. E.C. Knight Co.* that centered on the American Sugar Refining Company, which controlled 98 percent of sugar refining in the United States. In an 8-to-1 decision, the court declared that the federal government could only regulate monopolies involved in interstate commerce. Because the company's refining took place in only one state, the

"King" John D. Rockefeller astride his Standard Oil monopoly. To his critics, Rockefeller epitomized the evils of big business. But Rockefeller saw himself as an agent of progress, working within the bounds of capitalism. "The day of combination is here to stay," he explained. "Individualism is gone, never to return."

federal government had no right to break up the company. As a result of the decision, Standard Oil, the chief target of antitrust legislation, remained intact until 1911.

The Sherman Antitrust Act also spun off several significant unintended consequences. Rather than dismantling unfair combinations, business interests used the legislation to attack unions. Labor unions were the victims of 12 of the first 13 convictions under the law, as courts agreed with business that unions constituted a monopoly when their members struck and stopped interstate trade. In addition, the courts ruled that although collusion was illegal, business combinations were not. The years 1895 to 1905 saw the largest number of business mergers in U.S. history. Approximately 300 firms disappeared, as tire companies such as Goodyear, oil companies such as Texaco, and food companies such as United Fruit all absorbed smaller competitors.

Federal and state government provided little regulation for the burgeoning new economic order. **Laissez-faire** (hands-off) **economics** was gospel to businessmen and the politicians they supported. This economic doctrine insisted that government not interfere with business or the market. Businesses should compete "naturally," unimpeded by government regulation; as a result, society as a whole would benefit. Men like Carnegie and Rockefeller believed that trusts and large, consolidated enterprises represented the natural evolution of business. In addition, their success as "captains of industry," they argued, came as a result of their "fitness"—their ability to adapt to the new economic order. As men who had risen from humble origins, they made no apologies for the massive fortunes they accumulated. Carnegie, for example, had immigrated to the United States from Scotland at the age of 13 and worked in a textile factory before climbing up the corporate ladder to become one of the world's richest men. Many business leaders of the era subscribed to the theory of Social Darwinism, popularized by British social theorist **Herbert Spencer**. Spencer posited that Charles Darwin's theory of evolution could be applied to human society. Society evolved— and inevitably improved—through competition, with "survival of the fittest." This theory also supported laissez-faire economics.

Despite their devotion to theories about nonregulation and the "self-made" man, American businessmen greatly benefited from governmental aid. Federal support for railroads, protective tariff legislation, a favorable legal climate, and the intervention of state and federal authorities to crush labor movements all fostered the nation's exceptional business growth and unprecedented profits.

Markets and Consumerism

Cheap, reliable transportation, swift communication systems, and technological advances made national and international markets possible, fueling the industrial growth of the United States. With the nation's extensive railway system, manufactured goods could now be shipped to previously isolated parts of the country. The telegraph, and later the telephone, made it possible to coordinate shipments through instant communication. Inventions such as the refrigerated railroad car, pioneered by Gustavus Swift, made it possible to ship dressed beef from Chicago's stockyards to eastern cities and across the Atlantic.

GLOBAL PASSAGES

Titled Americans

In 1874, after a whirlwind romance, the beautiful Jennie Jerome, 19-year-old daughter of a wealthy New York stock speculator, married Lord Randolph Churchill. The Jerome-Randolph marriage was the first of well over a hundred such marriages that took place between 1874 and 1914, which matched the daughters of Gilded Age America's newly rich with titled European aristocrats, mostly from England. Highly publicized and criticized on both sides of the Atlantic as "titles for money," these transatlantic marriages represented another dimension of capital and culture transfers through webs of industrial capitalism.

As the financial capital of the world, London was the center of a lively marriage market for young, wealthy American women. The growing ease of transatlantic travel helped create an international "high society" in London, and many wealthy American daughters spent the social season there. Patrons, such as Jennie Jerome Churchill, who had successfully negotiated entry into the aristocracy, not only provided them fashion and etiquette advice but also hosted social events where they could meet eligible aristocrats.

For wealthy Gilded Age families, a titled marriage secured their elite status, setting them apart from growing numbers of millionaire families. Even though many of the newly rich mimicked the style of European aristocracy in their dress, in clubs, and in elaborate estates, a title in the family gave them a claim to genuine aristocracy. For British aristocrats, marriage to an American "heiress," as the press referred to them, also had obvious benefits. Such marriages infused American capital into the cash-strapped and declining aristocracy, hurt by falling land prices and agricultural rents.

The press on both sides of the Atlantic characterized these marriages as tawdry affairs. The British press condemned the "invasion" of society by "vulgar" and "pushy" American women "buying titles" and "watering down" the aristocracy.

Mass production spawned a revolution in consumer items. The American public and the world had access to a flood of cheap, affordable items that were unthinkable just years before. Andrew Carnegie cited "the cheapening of articles" as one of the greatest advances in human history. Even "the poor enjoy what the rich could not before afford," he explained.

Mail-order catalogs provide one indication of the consumer items available to average Americans in this era. In 1872, **Aaron Montgomery Ward** founded the nation's first mail-order house, as railroads opened up new markets in rural America and factories produced cheap goods in massive quantities. His catalogs featured tens

By contrast, the American press censured aristocrats as cynical fortune hunters and denounced the transfer of millions of American dollars to shore up the crumbling British aristocracy.

Several highly publicized and disastrous marriages cemented these images in the public mind. The 1895 marriage of Consuelo Vanderbilt, of the Vanderbilt railroad fortune, to the Duke of Marlborough, Lord Randolph Churchill's nephew, was one of the most notorious. After intense negotiation with the Duke's attorney, the Vanderbilts agreed to a dowry estimated to be as much as $10 million. The American press noted that the family "could not afford to pay their workers a few cents more in wages a day" but "could afford to pay millions of dollars for matrimonial alliances with foreign titles." The demise of the Vanderbilt-Marlborough marriage in less than 10 years only underscored the contempt of the public for titled marriages.

Despite these popular views, recent research suggests that titled marriages were more complex than the stereotypes they generated. American "heiresses" were often more than mere vehicles of status. Some went abroad not to husband shop but to seek independence and new experiences. Few came from super-rich families and only a few had fortunes that far exceeded those of their husbands. In addition, not all marriages secured social status for young women or wealth for their husbands; some were simply love matches.

At least one titled marriage had significant consequences for world history. Jennie Jerome's marriage to Lord Randolph Churchill produced a son, Winston, the future prime minister of Great Britain. Lady Churchill played a crucial role in grooming her son for politics and promoting his career. His American heritage accounts in part for his affection for the United States and the strength of the British-American alliance in World War II.

- How were titled marriages a product of the new industrial order?

- What do these marriages suggest about the competition among America's newly rich in the Gilded Age?

of thousands of items, including farm equipment, Singer sewing machines, straight-edged razors, and gospel hymn books. Sears, Roebuck, and Company soon competed with Ward for the rural market, labeling its catalog "The Farmer's Friend." By 1900, Sears processed 10,000 orders a day in its Chicago headquarters. While offering a universe of goods to rural and small-town Americans, the mail-order firms deeply damaged the sales of small-town merchants who fought back against these big businesses by sponsoring bonfires of mail-order catalogs. To country merchants, Ward and Sears represented the evils of big business. But to their customers, the mail-order houses offered a huge assortment of affordable goods previously unavailable to them.

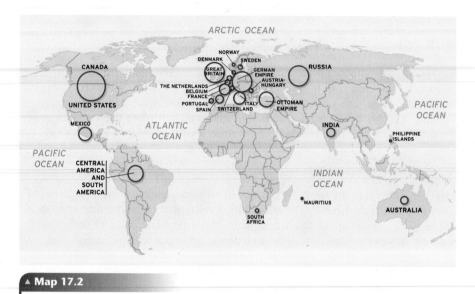

▲ **Map 17.2**

Commercial Empire By 1906, Singer Sewing Machine Company, the nation's first and largest international company, established a vast global commercial empire, selling its products in over a thousand retail shops around the world.

After successfully integrating and exploiting the national market, American firms marketed their goods abroad. Long before creating a political empire, Americans built a global commercial empire. Aided by technological innovations such as advances in steamship design and refrigeration and by a decline in transportation costs, American businesses first established international markets in Canada and Europe. They then extended webs of trade into Mexico, South America, and Asia, particularly India, Japan, and China. A plethora of products—from Singer sewing machines, to McCormick farm equipment, to Heinz pickles—became household names all over the world.

American companies followed the general pattern established by Singer: first selling their products abroad through international sales and distribution systems and then establishing factories abroad, from Europe to Asia, where they could take advantage of raw materials and cheap labor (Map 17.1). By the late 19th century, many American companies developed into full-fledged multinational corporations, including Kodak and Heinz.

STUDY QUESTIONS FOR GLOBAL WEBS OF INDUSTRIAL CAPITALISM

1. What was new about the new industrial order of the Gilded Age? What was old?
2. What were the key factors that made the new industrial order possible?
3. What steps did American businesses take to create global markets?

WORK AND THE WORKPLACE

The nation's startling industrial growth came about as the result of people laboring longer and harder than ever before, often in dangerous conditions. Although laborers worked in lethal environments everywhere in the industrial world, in the United States, as Europeans often remarked, work seemed especially ruthless. A Finnish laborer, writing home from Michigan, simply summarized the plight of the American worker: "Everyone works like hell."

Industrial capitalism transformed the nature of work and the workplace. As early as 1870, for the first time in its history, a majority of U.S. laborers worked for someone else, marking the end of the era of the independent, self-employed American. Millions of Americans, like their counterparts in Europe, left the countryside to work in burgeoning industries. Industrial laborers worked long and grueling hours in dangerous mills and factories at increasingly subdivided and mechanized tasks, making it possible for even small children to work repetitive, unskilled jobs.

Even before the Civil War, some workers labeled wage work "wage slavery," and condemnations continued as wage labor expanded in the new industrial order. As a critic wrote in 1871, "To put a man to wages, is to put him in the position of a dependent." Once viewed as a step on the ladder to independent land ownership, wage labor was now a permanent condition for a growing number of Americans, and a frightening prospect for many. A labor newspaper in 1876 exclaimed, "There was a time when the United States was once the land of promise for the workingman" but now, "We are in an *old country.*" Was individual independence, one of the nation's most valued ideals, a thing of the past? Had the new economic order "Europeanized" the United States, as Arthur Shadwell and others argued?

Global Migrations

A large pool of cheap, mobile labor made the new industrial order possible. Tens of millions of men, women, and children left the countryside to work in the industrializing regions on both sides of the Atlantic. Migration reached unprecedented levels in the late 19th century. As railroads and steamships provided cheap transportation, European migrants—facing overpopulation, a scarcity of land, political unrest, and stiff competition from mechanized American agriculture—extended traditional seasonal sojourns in European industry by crossing the ocean to work for higher wages in American industry. Similarly, rural Chinese and Japanese workers crossed the Pacific to labor in mining and railroad construction on the west coast and later worked in other industries, such as salmon canneries. To the north French Canadians boarded railroad cars in Quebec and headed south to toil in New England's textile mills. And from the south Mexicans crossed the border to help construct and maintain railroads in the southwest.

Rural Americans were also part of the global migration from farm to factory. The southern textile industry, concentrated largely in the Piedmont of Virginia, North and

South Carolina, and Georgia, drew its labor force from white families. Overpopulation and declining cotton prices, coupled with the crop lien system, forced them from their land into the region's burgeoning textile mills.

Southern textiles, like many other businesses and industries in Gilded Age America, enforced a color bar, hiring only whites. Most African Americans families remained tied to the land in the South, although some black men did find work in Southern coal mines and the lumber industry. Likewise, many Chinese and Japanese workers in the west and Mexican workers in the Southwest found themselves largely relegated to agricultural laborer.

Blue Collar and White Collar Workers

The new economic order divided labor into those who worked with their hands and those who worked with their heads. Manual wage workers, later known as "blue collar" workers for the blue work shirts they wore, provided the economy's foundation. Between 1870 and 1910, their numbers increased by over 300 percent as the overall population grew by 130 percent. Mechanization of production required mostly unskilled workers and only a few skilled workers. To maximize production and efficiency,

Russian steel workers, Homestead, Pennsylvania, 1908. Roughly two-thirds of steelworkers were foreign born. The 12-hour shift contributed to an exceedingly large number of deaths and injuries among them. As one investigator wrote, "It is a rare man who can keep his mental faculties keenly alert and centered on one object for twelve consecutive hours."

workers became, in the words of one late 19th-century commentator, "mechanical-ized," as they tended machines or executed simple, mind-numbing repetitive tasks. A clergyman, testifying before Congress, noted that the typical worker "makes nothing. He sees no complete product of his skill growing into finished shape in his hands." For example, divisions of labor in the ready-made clothing industry eliminated tradi-tional tailoring skills. Sewing machine operators did not fabricate an entire garment but focused only on stitching one part of a garment, such as sleeves, buttonholes, lapels, or pockets.

Although skilled workers did not disappear entirely, they were significantly re-duced in number and removed from the production process. Mechanization required only a few skilled workers to fix machinery or make tools for machines operated by unskilled workers. As work increasingly became "deskilled," these workers lost the most ground. Their fight to maintain their positions would lead to some of the bitter-est labor struggles of the era.

While skilled workers saw opportunities decline, "white collar" work expanded, as large business enterprises required specialized experts. "White collar" workers—dubbed as such for the formal white shirts they wore—were known as "brainworkers." Finance experts, accountants, advertising agents, managers, as well as engineers and attorneys, filled the ranks of white collar workers. Marketing also required salesmen. "Drummers," as they were known, traveled extensively on the nation's railway system, selling their goods in small towns and country stores. Unlike blue collar workers, who labored for hourly wages or were paid by the piece, most white collar workers were salaried specialists. These workers provided the core of a burgeoning middle class, rooted in urban industrial America. Although they did not own the businesses that they managed, white collar workers usually identified with the owners who employed them, not with the workers that they managed. This identification had long-term con-sequences for the labor movement as white collar workers provided popular support for antiunion efforts.

Although white collar workers were almost exclusively white males, the devel-opment of the modern office provided new opportunities for women as typists, ste-nographers, filing clerks, and, with the expansion of telephone service, switchboard operators. By 1900, more than 250,000 women labored in these jobs. The number of female stenographers and typists jumped from 4.5 percent of the total to 77 percent by 1900. Women office workers were especially attractive to employers, as they did the same work as male clerical workers for less pay and young women were drawn to cleaner and less taxing work. They still worked long hours, had to spend much of their income for proper office apparel, and frequently had to deal with harassment from male coworkers. These jobs, however, were generally reserved only for white, single, and native-born American women. Moreover, while male "clerks" used office work as a way to learn the business and as a first step up the corporate ladder, no such oppor-tunities existed for female "secretaries," who, according to prevailing belief, did not have the natural abilities to compete in the cutthroat world of business.

The division between blue collar and white collar workers, when compared to Eu-rope, seemed especially extreme. In Europe, smaller scale, family-owned businesses,

The modern office reflected the rise of modern business enterprises and the need for specialized white collar workers to manage them. In 1870, there were approximately 80,000 clerical workers; by 1920 there were 3 million.

with a more familial concern for employees, persisted longer than in the United States. In the hierarchical, corporate structure of American industry, managers grew detached from the needs of workers. Constant oversight and severe discipline from managers bent on maximizing production served as a major source of tension between managers and workers.

Regimentation and Scientific Management

Managers set firm rules and regulations, sometimes locking factory gates to keep workers on site. They also fined workers for tardiness, flawed work, and even talking on the job. Seeking an uninterrupted flow of production and maximum efficiency from workers, managers instituted time studies. **Frederick Winslow Taylor**, who pioneered "scientific management," or "Taylorism," as it was popularly known, argued that there was one best way to accomplish even the most mundane factory task. Armed with stopwatches, and later moving-picture cameras, Taylor's disciples instituted their methods in American factories in the early 20th century by studying every movement of a worker's task to eliminate "false moves" and to "drive the worker into a stride that would be as mechanical as the machine he tends." No job was too lowly for Taylor's efficiency experts. Taylor bragged that he had tripled Bethlehem Steel's coal yard production by determining the most efficient way to shovel coal. A well-run factory, Taylor insisted, required every worker "to become one of a train of gear wheels."

Piecework also contributed to the pressured, regimented atmosphere of the American workplace. Employers believed they could get more out of workers by paying them by the completed "piece" of a product, rather than an hourly wage. A variety of mills and factories instituted piecework, as did sweatshops, housed in crowded tenements and apartments, where entire families could be found completing products such as garments or artificial flowers. An investigator in 1913 described a scene in a New York City tenement where a grandmother, mother, and two tiny children labored making artificial flowers for 10 cents a gross (144 flowers), "and if they work steadily, from eight or nine in the morning to seven or eight at night, they may make twelve gross, $1.20."

Not surprisingly, laborers resented pressure to increase production, the intrusion of efficiency experts, and the discipline of ever-watchful managers. Workers at the Watertown Arsenal in Massachusetts, for example, walked out in support of a molder who refused to work under a manager's stopwatch. Workers often simply left jobs they did not like. Turnover was extremely high, especially in textile factories, steel mills, and clothing and machine shops, where most workers changed jobs every three years.

European visitors marveled at the regimentation of the American workplace. A French traveler to the United States noted, "Work in the American shops is altogether different from what it is in France. Nobody talks, nobody sings, the most rigorous silence reigns."

Yet laborers found ways to endure life on the shop floor. Many immigrant workers continued to take the day off for traditional religious holidays not in the American calendar. Others gave themselves a two-day weekend by skipping work on Mondays, observing what came to be known as "Blue Mondays." Cigar makers broke the monotony of the shop floor by appointing one person to read aloud to fellow workers.

Workers also found relief outside the shop walls, creating a vibrant culture of mutual support that helped sustain them in the grueling industrial world. For working men, social life centered on the saloon. In addition to being a place to fraternize and drink with fellow workers, saloons provided cheap food and entertainment, such as sing-alongs and boxing matches. Bartenders cashed paychecks, floated loans, and offered their facilities for union meetings. While male workers gathered in saloons, women workers socialized in their homes and neighborhoods, as they attended to housekeeping and children, often sharing what little they had. Churches and ethnic organizations provided additional opportunities to socialize and leave the rigors of work behind, with weddings and festivals offering welcome relief.

Working Conditions and Wages

Long hours and a demanding pace took its toll on American workers. With little interference from state and federal government, employers worked their laborers relentlessly. The industry standard was a 10-hour day for six days a week, although workers in some industries, such as steel, regularly worked 12-hour shifts. A Pennsylvania steelworker summarized the unyielding repetition of his life: "A man works, comes home, eats, and goes to bed, gets up, eats, and goes to work."

Without safety regulations enforced by state or federal government, American industry was a cauldron of fatigue, illness, death, and injury. A mule spinner in a Fall River, Massachusetts, textile mill estimated that he walked as many as 30 miles a day to tend his machines. Exhausted and working among dangerous machines, textile workers regularly lost fingers. Those who did not suffer injury died years later from "brown lung" from inhaling fibers in the factory air. Similarly coal miners expired from "black lung" after years of breathing in coal dust. American railroaders and coal miners died at three times the rate of their European counterparts, who enjoyed some government safety regulations of the workplace. By one estimate, 25 percent of immigrant men working the Pennsylvania steel industry's most dangerous jobs were killed or seriously disabled. Death or injury spelled disaster for working families. With no "safety net"— unemployment, workmen's compensation, or health benefits—and with little legal recourse against powerful corporations, working families regularly found themselves homeless and hungry overnight.

Economic Convulsions and Hard Times

In addition to the ever-present threat of injury or death, working families were especially vulnerable to economic cycles of boom and bust. Although the economy grew enormously overall in the last quarter of the 19th century, it did so by fits and starts. Work hours fluctuated from feast to famine, from overtime hours to sudden unemployment. Two severe and prolonged economic depressions, only 20 years apart, from 1873–1878 and from 1893–1897, affected the United States and all industrialized nations worldwide. Unregulated markets and rampant speculation in complicated, often incomprehensible financial instruments led to these upheavals, leaving millions without work. Those who managed to keep their jobs faced both shortened hours and wage cuts.

The Wall Street crash of 1873, precipitated by the failure of Jay Cooke and Company, the nation's largest investment bank, resulted in tens of thousands of business failures—6,000 alone in 1874. An article in *Harper's Weekly* in the winter of 1873 reported hundreds of deaths by starvation and 3,000 babies abandoned on doorsteps. In 1893, another Wall Street panic helped spawn a second lengthy worldwide depression even more severe than the depression of the 1870s. The winter of 1893–1894 was especially harsh, with widespread suffering. In February 1894, the *New York Times* reported the story of 12 Italian families in the city, 50 people "in a starving condition" ready to be evicted from their home where they lived without any food or heat. Families wandered about seeking food and shelter while single men "tramped" across the country, desperately seeking work.

Even in the best of times, a factory worker's wages purchased a living that straddled the poverty line. Although real wages—that is, wages adjusted for inflation— increased between 1860 and 1900, and were high compared to those of Europe, many families could not rely on one income alone and had to supplement the family income through the wages of mothers and children. Carrol D, Wright, Chief of the Bureau of Labor Statistics in Massachusetts, noted in 1882, "A family of workers can live well, but the man with a family to support, unless his wife works also, has a small chance of living properly."

Women and Children in the Workplace

The number of women in the workplace exploded between 1870 and 1910. In 1870, 1.5 million women worked for wages, the majority in domestic service jobs. By 1910, their numbers more than quadrupled and fewer than 40 percent were in domestic service. Women employed in industry concentrated in textile and garment production. Young, single women made up the bulk of the female labor force in the garment trades. Married women often took in piecework into their homes.

While the new economic order provided new opportunities for women, the workplace was often a site of sexual harassment and discrimination. Employers also paid women much less—half or less—than men for the same work. In addition, black and Latina women found themselves barred from many jobs open to white women, and instead toiled as domestic servants and laundresses.

Child labor also fueled the new economic order. In 1870, 750,000 children under the age of 15 worked in nonfarm and nonfamily businesses. Twenty years later, that figure doubled, to 1.5 million, with 18 percent of children between the ages of 10 and 15 employed in nonagricultural work. In depression years, the number of children spiked. Few child labor laws existed, and when they did they were rarely strictly enforced. Moreover, the parents of working children, who depended on their income, often opposed such laws; children had long labored on family farms, so labor in a factory or mill did not necessarily seem cruel or unusual.

But industrial labor involved dangers nonexistent on the farm. Children were especially vulnerable to exploitation and injury, as they worked long hours in hazardous conditions. Employers in some industries, such as textiles, sought out child laborers as they could pay them less and could more easily control them. Even children could run dangerous machines or engage in a simple, repetitive task on an assembly line. Small children filled the ranks of southern textile mills where they worked long shifts, their small hands especially adept at changing bobbins on weaving machines. Superintendents threw cold water in the faces of sleepy children to keep them awake; but exhausted, inattentive children regularly lost fingers and limbs in machines.

British writer **H.G. Wells** was horrified by American child labor. Traveling in New York in the late 19th century, he observed children selling newspapers and blacking boots, then saw them collapsed on the subway from exhaustion. He learned of children as young as five working all night in Southern textile mills. Wells noted that England's industrial history was "black with the blood of tortured and murdered children," yet England was far ahead of the United States in factory legislation, passing protective laws for women and children in the 1840s. Wells blamed the American emphasis on "liberty of property and the subordination of the state to business." Although some Gilded Age reformers protested child labor, few major improvements

Investigative photographer Lewis Hine took this photo of child laborers at a cotton mill in Macon, Georgia, in 1908. His caption: "Some boys and girls were so small they had to climb up on to the spinning frame to mend broken threads and to put back the empty bobbins."

occurred until the 1910s, when nearly every state passed minimum age and maximum hour legislation.

STUDY QUESTIONS FOR WORK AND THE WORKPLACE

1. How did work and the workplace change in the late 19th century?
2. What role did women and children play in the explosive economic growth of the United States in the late 19th century?

WORKERS FIGHT BACK

With worsening working conditions, along with the severe economic convulsions of the Gilded Age, workers began to organize collectively into labor unions to fight for a living wage, shorter hours, and better working conditions and to offset the power of employers. They framed their battle as a fight for American values against what they viewed as the encroaching Europeanization of their country. "America," explained a union newspaper in 1874, was once "the star" on which the world's workers "gazed" and dreamed of being "their own rulers." But "these dreams have not been realized" and American workers "suddenly find capital as rigid as an absolute monarchy."

Workers crafted a range of strategies for collective action in an attempt to offset the enormous power of industrialists. While some labor unions tried to organize all workers, others attempted to maximize their power by allowing only white, skilled workers to join. Still others insisted that workers would have more clout by organizing along industrial lines, in which strikes would bring entire industries to a standstill.

Conflict between workers and employees exploded. Between 1881 and 1905, 37,000 strikes, involving seven million workers, took place; many of these were violent. Even farmers, squeezed by banks, railroads, and "middlemen," organized collectively to try to better their condition. Labor conflict raised many questions and fears among Americans. Did the nation again verge on civil war, this time based on class? What was the best strategy for workers to seek justice and regain the dignity of their labor? Did labor unions threaten the public good or enhance it?

The Great Railroad Strike of 1877

In July 1877, in the midst of economic depression, American workers initiated the first and largest general strike in the nation's history. The Great Railroad Strike of 1877 set the stage for subsequent conflicts between labor and capital in the late 19th century.

Reeling from the depression of the 1870s, major railroads, including the Pennsylvania Railroad and the Baltimore & Ohio, cut wages significantly while severely reducing hours of work. Angry brakemen and firemen refused to work. Other railroad workers protested by obstructing the movement of freight trains near Baltimore and West Virginia, but they allowed passenger traffic to pass.

Violent strikes soon broke out in towns along the rails, from Baltimore to Pittsburgh. In addition, sympathetic strikes erupted spontaneously as railroad workers stopped trains as far away as San Francisco; other workers, in solidarity, brought factories, foundries, and building construction to a standstill.

At the request of railroad officials, governors in Maryland, Pennsylvania, and West Virginia sent out their state militias to try to break the strike. In Baltimore, armed militias confronted angry mobs of rock-throwing workers. Even wives and mothers of railroad workers joined in the strike. Firing into the crowd, the militia killed 10 people, inciting even greater violence. Roughly 14,000 protesters filled the streets of the city, sending a locomotive crashing into freight cars and cutting fire hoses. In Pittsburgh, where local militia sympathized with the striking workers, the governor had to call in troops from Philadelphia. They, too, fired into a crowd, killing 20 people including women and children. Soon the mob forced the militia to retreat to a roundhouse and then destroyed 39 buildings, 104 engines, 46 passenger cars, and over 1,200 freight cars. More than a hundred people died nationwide.

One newspaper headline labeled the railroad strike "The Lexington of the Labor Conflict." A Massachusetts clergyman called the strikers "the lineal descendents of Samuel Adams, John Hancock, and the Massachusetts yeomen" who revolted against the king a hundred years previously, "only now the kings are money kings." Like the Minutemen before them, workers saw the strike as the first shot against tyranny in defense of their liberty.

But the strike struck terror in the hearts of many middle-class Americans who saw it as a harbinger of social revolution already begun in Europe. In 1871, radical workers, and those sympathetic to their cause, declared themselves the governing body of the city of Paris. Ruling the city for two months, the Paris Commune sparked a bloody municipal civil war that left at least 25,000 insurgents and 1,000 troops dead, before government authorities suppressed the revolution. The Paris Commune received more newspaper coverage in the United States than any other event that occurred on foreign soil up to that time. Newspapers reported anarchy and bloody slaughter in the streets of the French capital. Fear that a "communist" revolution would spread to the United States

HARPER'S WEEKLY.
JOURNAL OF CIVILIZATION

Vol. XXI.—No. 1076.]   NEW YORK, SATURDAY, AUGUST 11, 1877.   [WITH A SUPPLEMENT. PRICE TEN CENTS.

THE GREAT STRIKE—THE SIXTH MARYLAND REGIMENT FIGHTING ITS WAY THROUGH BALTIMORE—From a Photograph by D. Bendann—[See Page 636.]

Harper's Weekly, a popular news magazine, depicts violence in Baltimore during the Great Railroad Strike of 1877. A Maryland National Guard regiment, called out by the governor at the request of the B&O Railroad president to put down the strike, fires on a crowd of pro-strike demonstrators, killing 10.

gripped many Americans, and the Railroad Strike of 1877 confirmed their suspicions that the communist movement had migrated successfully to the United States.

By the end of July, the strike had been broken, largely through the intervention of state and federal authority on behalf of the railroads. In addition to militia units sent out by governors, President **Rutherford B. Hayes** sent federal troops to help break the strike, an important precedent followed by later presidents. Workers found themselves not only fighting against the immense power of large corporations, but also state and federal authority siding with business. Notably, the Great Railroad Strike of 1877 hastened the growth of National Guard (state militia) units. Between 1877 and 1903, the National Guard and federal troops intervened over 500 times to suppress labor disputes.

Fears of communism, socialism, and **anarchism**, all of which aimed to dismantle the capitalist system, placed the judicial system overwhelmingly on the side of employers. In the name of social order and individual rights, courts condemned labor activity. As one judge explained, strikes were "a serious evil, destructive to property, destructive to individual rights . . ., tending to the disruption of society, and the obliteration of legal and natural rights." While judges rarely outlawed strikes, they frequently invoked injunctions to restrict strike activity. Although socialists, anarchists, and communists made up only a small percentage of the American labor movement, unions would subsequently be branded as threatening, revolutionary, and "un-American" organizations, bent on fomenting class warfare.

Organizing Strategies and Labor Violence

American workers engaged in a range of strategies to better their lot. These included forming one big union of all workers, creating exclusive craft unions, and building industry-wide unions. Some unions, such as the **Knights of Labor**, offered an alternative to capitalism while others, such as the American Federation of Labor, embraced the economic order, and simply sought "more of the pie."

In the wake of the Railroad Strike of 1877, the Knights of Labor emerged as the largest union. Founded in 1869 in Baltimore, originally as a secret organization, the Knights aimed to organize all laboring people into one large, national union. The union offered membership to "the producing masses," regardless of race, gender, or national origin, excluding only "social parasites"—lawyers, bankers, and liquor salesmen. At the height of its influence, in 1886, the Knights claimed a membership of more than 700,000, that included blacks and Mexicans, with about a tenth of the membership made up of women.

The Knights of Labor articulated a scathing critique of industrial capitalism, informed by the Declaration of Independence and the Bible. The union offered an uplifting alternative to capitalism. The Knights demanded "to the toilers a proper share of the wealth that they create." They condemned monopolies and concentrations of power in the hands of the few. Declaring that "an injury to one is the concern of all," they also opposed wage labor. They demanded an eight-hour day, condemned child labor, and emphasized worker education and cooperative institutions.

Both the organization and philosophy of the Knights, however, weakened its effectiveness. The Knights included both skilled and unskilled workers. But unskilled workers were easily replaced and had little leverage in strikes. Although the Knights hoped to achieve their goals within the existing system through collective bargaining with employers, leader **Terrence V. Powderly** discouraged strikes. Even so, the Knights of Labor won several strikes in the mid-1880s. Women textile workers and hat makers engaged in several successful strikes in 1884, leading Powderly to label them "the best men in the Order." The future of the organization seemed bright.

Then, in May 1886, socialist and anarchist leaders organized a meeting in Chicago's Haymarket Square to protest the deaths of four strikers killed at the city's International Harvester plant. When police arrived, someone threw a bomb, the police fired into the crowd, and chaos ensued. When the smoke cleared, 10 people lay dead—6 of them policemen—and 50 people were wounded. Although authorities never established the identity of the bomb thrower, 8 anarchist leaders, 7 of whom were foreign-born, were arrested, tried, and convicted; 7 were sentenced to death, despite the lack of evidence linking them to the crime. One of them belonged to the Knights of Labor.

A surge of hysteria against the labor movement, fueled by the perceived infiltration of foreign radicals, swept the country. Union leaders disavowed any connection to the violence at Haymarket, but the incident badly injured the Knights' reputation. Membership dropped by 20 percent in the following four years. Haymarket convinced many middle-class Americans that the labor movement was bent on destroying the capitalist order.

Even before Haymarket, the Knights of Labor came under attack from fellow workers. Craft unions, made up of skilled workers only, such as cigar makers and iron puddlers, argued that joining forces with unskilled laborers diluted their bargaining power. As highly skilled, hard-to-replace workers, they would have much more clout in negotiations. In 1886, craft unions organized the **American Federation of Labor** (AFL). Headed by **Samuel Gompers**, the AFL embodied "bread and

Women delegates to the Knights of Labor's national convention in 1886. The Knights welcomed women, who made up about 10 percent of the membership. Several held high positions, including Elizabeth Rodgers, depicted here holding her two-week-old baby. Rodgers was head of the Chicago Knight's assembly and a mother of 12.

butter" unionism. Embracing capitalism and rejecting the long-range, utopian goals of the Knights of Labor, the AFL focused on short-term, concrete aims, such as the eight-hour day and better wages. As Gompers remarked, "We have no ultimate ends. We are going from day to day. We are fighting only for immediate objects—objects that can be realized in a few years." Unlike the Knights, the AFL did not hesitate to strike to achieve its goals. Moreover, unlike the Knights, the AFL excluded women, blacks, and some immigrants—all of whom the AFL viewed as "cheap" competition that lowered wages.

Under Gompers's leadership the AFL made considerable gains. By the turn of the century, the AFL boasted about half a million members. Yet, because of its exclusive policies, the AFL represented only a fraction of American workers and undercut worker solidarity by driving a wedge between ethnicities. In 1903, for example, the Japanese-Mexican Labor Association (JMLA) conducted a successful strike in Oxnard, California, to increase the wages of beet thinners. Subsequently, the JMLA petitioned the AFL to charter their organization. Gompers refused unless the union kicked out its Chinese and Japanese workers. The JMLA refused to do so, citing them as "brothers." Without the support of the AFL, the JMLA collapsed after several years.

One of the most infamous labor conflicts of the era centered on the fight of a craft union at a Carnegie-owned steel mill in Homestead, Pennsylvania. The Homestead Lockout in 1892 epitomized the power of big business to crush the burgeoning labor movement. The Lockout pitted one of the nation's premier industrialists, Andrew Carnegie, against one of the country's most successful craft unions, the Amalgamated Association of Iron and Steel Workers. Carnegie viewed the powerful union as an obstacle to maximizing his profits, and—given increased mechanization—he no longer relied on skilled ironworkers and steelworkers. Wishing to crush the union once and for all, he and his right-hand man, **Henry Clay Frick**, offered to union workers a new contract that would cut their pay by as much as 26 percent. As Carnegie and Frick anticipated, the union rejected the offer outright.

Expecting a violent showdown, Carnegie left the country for his castle in Scotland and put Frick in charge. On June 10, 1892, Frick locked out the steelworkers and placed three miles of barbed wire fencing around the Homestead works. A private army of 300 Pinkerton detectives, hired to defend the steelworks, approached by river barge. Infuriated Homestead workers attacked the barge with cannon shot and a raft burning with oil-soaked wood. Soon both sides exchanged gunfire and seven workers and three Pinkertons lay dead.

At the request of Frick, Pennsylvania's governor sent 8,500 National Guardsmen to restore order and end worker resistance. Even though his carefully constructed image as a generous philanthropist suffered, he succeeded in crushing the union and even managed to extend the standard 12-hour shift. Another 40 years would pass before steelworkers again organized into an effective union.

Other American workers organized along industrial lines. **Eugene V. Debs**, a veteran activist in the craft union, the Brotherhood of Locomotive Firemen, believed that railway workers could increase their power by organizing one industry-wide union. In 1893, he founded the **American Railway Union** (ARU). The depression of the 1890s deeply hurt railway workers, as they once again experienced severe wage cuts and reductions in their work week. When the Great Northern Railroad instituted a series of wage cuts in April 1893, the ARU, with an 18-day strike, successfully had wages restored.

The next year, in 1894, Pullman Palace Car workers called a strike. In response to the Railroad Strike of 1877, **George Pullman** had built a model factory town outside of Chicago, where his workers manufactured fancy railroad sleeping cars. Pullman hoped that his model town would curb the worst excesses of the new industrial order; however, he wielded total control in his clean and orderly town.

As the depression set in, Pullman cut wages by 28 percent but did not cut rents on the houses where he forced his workers to live or the price of groceries in his company store. When Pullman refused to negotiate with his workers, they called a strike in May 1894. The ARU, at the request of the Pullman workers, supported the **Pullman Strike** and refused to move any trains that included Pullman cars. The boycott was so effective, with the union's 150,000 members participating, that train service to Chicago came to a standstill by June and rail service from the west coast to the Midwest slowed to a crawl.

Railroad owners soon countered with their own strategy to crush the powerful ARU. They ordered that all Pullman cars be coupled to U.S. mail trains. As the owners knew, interference with the mails justified federal intervention. The Attorney General, a former railroad officer, soon issued an injunction ordering strikers to move the mail trains. President **Grover Cleveland** sent federal troops to Chicago to enforce the passage of the trains. The strike and boycott soon collapsed, the ARU was demolished, and its members were blacklisted. Authorities used the Sherman Antitrust Act to arrest Debs for conspiring to interfere with interstate commerce and obstructing the mails. Although these charges were eventually dropped, Debs spent six months in jail on contempt charges, for ignoring court injunctions aimed at smothering the strike. After Pullman, Debs shifted his focus away from unionism. Convinced that workers would never make any significant progress in the capitalist system, Debs advocated a political solution to the plight of workers, as a leader and presidential candidate of the Socialist Party of America.

The United Mine Workers (UMW), founded in 1890 as an industrial union like the ARU, opened its membership to all mine workers, skilled or unskilled, regardless of ethnicity. The UMW fought against especially dangerous and exploitive working conditions. With a surplus of immigrant labor, coal companies kept wages to a bare minimum. Even by Gilded Age standards, working hours were especially inhumane and dangerous, with 14-hour days in boom times. Many miners had to live in company housing and received pay in company "scrip" to purchase their food and supplies from company-owned stores.

Unions such as the UMW fought a particularly difficult battle against the powerful mine owners and the state governments that supported them. In addition to National Guard units, called out by governors to break strikes, mine owners employed spies to infiltrate labor unions and regularly employed Pinkertons and the Pennsylvania Coal and Iron Police, a force established by the state legislature assembly and paid for by mine owners and known for their strong-arm tactics. Mine owners also regularly blacklisted union members, making it impossible for them to find mining jobs, and evicted union members and their families from company housing.

In addition to the power of the state, miners found it difficult to overcome ethnic divisions, a problem endemic in the nation's labor movement. Recently arrived immigrant miners, desperate for work, generally refused to join the UMW. A ready available pool of nonunion miners made it difficult for the UMW to make much headway.

The UMW organized numerous strikes in the 1890s. When the depression of the 1890s resulted in wage cuts, two- or three-day work weeks, and a glut of coal on the market, 200,000 miners struck in eight states. But nonunion miners continued to mine coal, ultimately wrecking the strike. In 1897, a UMW organizing campaign in the anthracite fields of Pennsylvania left 24 unarmed miners dead, killed by local deputies. Not until 1903, when a massive coal strike threatened the nation's fuel supply and President **Theodore Roosevelt** became the first America president to intervene on the side of labor, would coal miners achieve a major victory.

The Farmers Organize

The nation's industrial workers were not the only laborers who sought relief in collective action. Farmers also found themselves in the grip of global economic forces beyond their control and experienced an erosion of their cherished independence. Even before the deep depression of the 1890s, many of America's farmers faced hard times. Southern farmers found themselves entangled in the crop lien system as cotton prices plummeted on the world market beginning in the 1870s and as Southern cotton competed with cotton grown in Egypt and India. By 1890 it cost more to grow cotton than the crop could fetch on the market. Western farmers, like their southern counterparts, suffered from declining prices for their crops, particularly wheat and corn. Technological advancements, such as the mechanical reaper and combine and steam-powered thresher, significantly increased production, which drove prices down. By the end of the 1880s, a bushel of wheat plummeted from $1.19 to 49 cents. To make matters worse, as crop prices dropped, railroads, which continued to consolidate and take advantage of their transportation monopoly, sharply increased their freight rates.

Farmers in the South and West found their relentless toil repaid with poverty and the loss of their farms and independence. As one farmer wrote, "Each year the plunge into debt is deeper; each year the burden is heavier. . . . Cares are many, smiles are few, and the comforts of life are scantier. . . . Humiliation and dependence bow the head of the proud spirit." Frustrated farmers focused their anger on railroads, which charged exorbitant prices; bankers, who charged high interest rates in a tight credit market; and "middlemen," who profited handsomely by selling farmers' products.

Like industrial laborers, farmers hoped to seize the inordinate power wielded by the few and restore it to "the people" by organizing collectively. Building on the foundations laid by agricultural organizations such as the Grange, the Farmers' Alliance spread rapidly from the cotton belt to the western prairies. Started in Texas in 1876, the Alliance stressed that the only way for embattled farmers to challenge successfully the power of merchants and monopolies was to unite and work together. The Alliance sponsored traveling lecturers, who used powerful evangelical language to condemn economic evildoers and to recruit farmers and their families into their organization. Alliance members met regularly in their local organizations, where they pledged their mutual support, listened to lectures on a variety of subjects including scientific agriculture, and organized a range of collective activities.

The Alliance established cooperative stores, buying and cheap transportation clubs, and warehouses for wheat, corn, tobacco, and cotton. Mining a deep seam of bitterness toward the new economic order, the Alliance claimed 1.5 million members by 1890, about a quarter of whom were women, and who were treated as equals in the organization, even serving as lecturers and officers. As one of them explained, women "are the chief sufferers whenever poverty or misfortune overtakes the family," and farm women enthusiastically embraced the organization.

African American farmers faced the same problems as their white counterparts, but the Southern Farmers' Alliance barred them from membership. They formed their own parallel organization, the Colored Farmers' Alliance, which spread across the South in the late 1880s. Claiming a million members by 1890, the black organization also stressed education and cooperation. In addition to race, self-interest separated the two organizations. Unlike the white Alliance, made up largely of middling, propertied farmers, many members of the Colored Alliance were tenants and sharecroppers, whose interests were at odds with landowners.

Technically nonpartisan, the Alliance soon realized its political power; in 1890 in the West, some Alliance members created their own independent third party, the People's (Populist) Party. In the South, that same year, the Alliance, while not committing to a third party, helped elect four governors and 19 of 27 congressmen who agreed to endorse the Alliance agenda. Encouraged by their success, and frustrated by the unwillingness of Republicans or Democrats to enact any significant reform, farmers in 1892 created a national People's Party, its agenda summarized by the slogan, "equal rights to all, special privilege to none." As unprecedented economic disaster rocked the nation beginning in 1893, the Populists seemed poised to make an impact nationally, offering an alternative party with a clearly articulated reform agenda.

The Labor Movement in Global Context

American workers did not fight their battle for justice alone. They drew inspiration and ideas from their compatriots in other parts of the world. Moreover, as workers fluidly crossed national borders to seek employment, they carried ideas and experiences about collective action. Although the American labor movement generally was more conservative than that of Europe, some American laborers framed their struggles transnationally, stressing the common plight of workers in all industrial societies, regardless of nationality or ethnicity.

Crossing and recrossing oceans and borders, immigrants carried labor theories, strategies, and experiences with them. Miners from the British Isles, for example, carried strong union traditions to the coal fields of Pennsylvania where they played a crucial role in founding the United Mine Workers. They even modeled their strikes in the United States on successful strikes abroad. Their 1893 eight-state strike followed the example of British miners several years before. Conversely, immigrants who returned to their home countries from the United States took their experiences as union members back to their home countries. Schooled in the American labor movement, returning immigrants from countries as diverse as Norway, Italy, and Hungary emerged as labor leaders in their home countries. In addition, social and economic theories such as socialism, communism, and anarchism traveled through conduits of immigration.

American labor organizations provided models for unionization in other parts of the world. Workers in Britain, Australia, Belgium, Canada, France, and New Zealand, for example, all replicated the Knights of Labor's organizational structure. As early as the 1860s, some U.S.-based craft unions, including those for printers and cigar makers, were international organizations.

In addition, some labor activists forged bonds with workers in other industrialized nations as they shared common struggles. European and American labor leaders not only carefully studied political developments on both sides of the Atlantic, they also, at times, encouraged worker solidarity across national borders. In the 1880s, when American window glass workers found their jobs threatened by the importation of French, English, and Belgian glass workers, they sent a delegation to these countries and managed to halt further incursions of foreign workers by convincing them of the injury they caused fellow workers in the United States.

Despite the many links among the world's industrial workers, European labor movements fared much better than those in the United States. Comparatively speaking, American labor made relatively few gains and was generally far more conservative. A comparison of U.S. and French workers in this era is especially revealing. Workers in France did not have to deal with the cheap and abundant pool of unskilled labor—largely a result of immigration—that hampered collective action in the United States. Strikes in France tended to be much more successful, as labor could not easily be replaced. As in the United States, the national government regularly intervened in labor disputes in France; but unlike the United States, the French government generally sided with workers over employers. As a result French workers usually won at least some of their demands.

In the United States, state and federal government, with the support of the public, repressed labor activism and instead emphasized individualism and the defense of property as the revolutionary heritage. By contrast, drawing on the tradition of the French Revolution to support the rights of workers against the "aristocratic" tyranny of employers, the French public pressured government officials to aid workers. Finally, ethnic divisions, only minimally present in France, drove a wedge in worker solidarity in the United States. Samuel Gompers summarized the trials of American labor and the powerful opposition it faced: "Against us we find arrayed a host guarded by special privilege, buttressed by legalized trusts, fed by streams of legalized monopolies, picketed by gangs of legalized Pinkertons, and having in reserve thousands of embryo employers, who, under the name militia, are organized, uniformed, and armed for the sole purpose of holding the discontented in bondage."

STUDY QUESTIONS FOR WORKERS FIGHT BACK

1. Compare and contrast the strategies of workers in forming labor unions and the strengths and weaknesses of each approach.
2. What factors accounted for the lack of progress in the American labor movement of the late 1800s?

THE NEW INDUSTRIAL ORDER: DEFENSE AND DISSENT

The new economic order produced a great deal of anxiety about opportunity and success. Everywhere Americans looked, they saw progress in technological innovations, comforts, and goods unthinkable only a few decades before. But progress also brought misery, overt conflict, and a noticeably tightening and unbalanced social and economic order.

Gilded Age Americans engaged with their counterparts in Europe in passionate discussions about their world. Just as workers shared ideas across national borders, so, too, did businessmen, politicians, and reformers. Some writers dispensed advice about how to succeed in the new harshly competitive economic order while others debated pressing issues. Could they ameliorate the hostile and often violent labor conflict that threatened to tear the country apart? Were industrial capitalism and its many consequences products of the natural evolution of human progress or were they unnatural and retrograde, dividing people into warring factions? Might there be more humane alternatives?

Defending the New Order

The new economic order, with its cutthroat competition and its spasmodic growth, spawned a new genre of literature to alleviate the anxieties of middle-class Americans:

the success manual. These guidebooks, the forerunners of motivational and self-help literature popular today, were aimed at young men just embarking on their careers. Acknowledging a loss of faith in the American Dream, success manuals posited a relentlessly upbeat, confident message to encourage readers that success was still possible for those who worked hard. The *Royal Path of Life; or, Aims and Aids to Success and Happiness*, first published in 1877, was the most popular of scores of success manuals published in the late 19th century and sold an extraordinary 800,000 copies. The guide reassured readers that "Life is not mean—it is good," and emphasized that young men could still shape their lives through self-reliance, hard work, honesty, loyalty, frugality, and good character. Traditional values, the manuals insisted, still provided the key to success.

Horatio Alger's popular stories for boys also stressed the importance of individual effort and upright morals for success. But Alger included the crucial element of luck. Alger's main characters, typically plucky, self-reliant newsboys or shoeshine boys, worked in the urban jungle of New York. His heroes took control of their lives, just as the success manuals suggested, by saving their money and educating themselves. Their big breaks, however, came through lucky circumstances. Alger's stories promised upward mobility to those who worked hard, yet his emphasis on luck recognized the limits of diligence and character alone. Even so, his books, with titles such as *Risen from the Ranks*, reassured middle-class boys and their parents that the American Dream was still alive and well. Alger's books sold millions of copies around the world, providing assurance to generations of boys and men worldwide.

One of the best known defenses of the new economic order came from the pen of steel magnate Andrew Carnegie. In 1889 Carnegie published a widely disseminated essay popularly known as "The Gospel of Wealth." Carnegie argued that the benefits of industrialization clearly outweighed the problems it created. He acknowledged the "price which society pays for the law of competition," in brutal conflicts between workers and employees and the gap between rich and poor. But "the advantages," he insisted, "are greater still," in the cheap goods and comforts available to all. A disciple of Social Darwinism, Carnegie asserted that the competitive industrial order ensured "the survival of the fittest in every department" and was "essential for the future progress of the race."

Carnegie justified his massive fortune by becoming a public benefactor. No man, he claimed, should die rich. The wealthy were obligated to benefit society through philanthropy. Rejecting outright charitable contributions, Carnegie preferred to provide "the ladders upon which the aspiring can rise," such as parks, art museums, and libraries—institutions that "help those who help themselves." In this way, the rich returned their "surplus wealth" to the less fortunate and aided them permanently. Practicing what he preached, Carnegie gave away over $350 million by the time of his death in 1919. He funded more than 2,800 free libraries around the world and made generous financial gifts to colleges and universities, established a pension fund for college professors and steelworkers, and created an institution for international peace. Through his foundation oil man John D. Rockefeller gave away even more money than Carnegie, established the University of Chicago, and funded medical research.

The "Gospel of Wealth" sparked debate both nationally and internationally. Carnegie's ideas were discussed broadly in newspapers, journals, and magazines. Moreover, Carnegie preached his "gospel" in hundreds of speeches on both sides of the Atlantic.

Generous philanthropy, however, did not convince critics on either side of the Atlantic of the benefits of industrial capitalism. A prominent British minister contended that a truly Christian society would not have millionaires at all, as "millionaires at one end of the scale involve paupers at the other end." Similarly an American clergyman bluntly stated that the real problem that afflicted society was the distribution—not the redistribution—of wealth and that it was wrong "to make charity do the work of justice."

After the heartless Homestead Lockout in 1892, Carnegie's philanthropy came under especially withering attack. A St. Louis paper concluded, "Ten thousand 'Carnegie Public Libraries' would not compensate the country for the direct and indirect evils resulting from the Homestead lockout." In addition, thousands of Pittsburgh workers protested accepting Carnegie's gift of a public library and art museum to the city.

Critiquing the New Order

Henry Demarest Lloyd questioned Carnegie's claims regarding progress and the benefits bestowed by industrial capitalism. Instead, the new order created a society at

Horatio Alger wrote a hundred novels between 1867 and 1899. His writing had such a great impact on American culture that the "Horatio Alger story" is still used to refer to a "self-made" individual who has risen from "rags to riches."

war with itself and threatened to destroy American democracy. Lloyd's *Wealth Against Commonwealth* (1894) was a massive exposé of Rockefeller's Standard Oil Company.

Lloyd argued that the new economic order "has killed competition." Even more frightening, "corporations are grown greater than the State." The "winners" sitting atop the economic order now had "the powers of life and death" and "wield them over us by the same 'self-interest' with which they took them from us." Lloyd argued for the importance of the common good over the individualism so highly touted in the Gilded Age.

Poverty, not wealth, was "the striking feature" of the age. The riches of the nation's millionaires came through "appropriating the property of others." The "cheapness" of goods, so highly touted by Carnegie, resulted in "fortunes for a few, monstrous luxury for them and proportionate deprivation for the people." Lloyd called for a return to the Golden Rule, to "Love thy neighbor as thyself." He appealed to workers and farmers to spearhead a spiritual rebirth that would usher in a new, cooperative social order.

As people sought answers in the midst of the depression, Lloyd's book went through four printings in 1894 alone. People around the world debated his ideas. In Great Britain, Lloyd's passionate treatise incited discussion in business, legal, and labor circles and led to condemnation of American trusts. In Canada, Lloyd's tome inspired Canadian oil companies to develop European markets to ward off Standard Oil. In the United States, economically conservative journals such as *The Nation* condemned the book as "five hundred pages of the wildest rant." Rockefeller himself commented that he "paid no more attention to all this nonsense than an elephant might be expected to pay to a tiny mosquito." Nevertheless, Lloyd's attack on the excesses of unregulated capitalism deeply influenced future Americans, such as **Louis Brandeis**, who would play a part in dismantling some large trusts in the first decades of the 20th century, including Standard Oil in 1911.

Lloyd's writings also launched a new genre of reporting, investigative journalism. Derided by critics as "**muckraking**," his style of journalism inspired a whole generation of journalists to investigate nearly every dimension of the new economic order.

TIMELINE 1868–1901

1868

May Horatio Alger publishes *Ragged Dick; or, Street Life in New York*

1869

December Knights of Labor founded in Baltimore

1871

March Paris Commune generates massive newspaper coverage and generates fears of a communist revolution in the United States

1872

August Aaron Montgomery Ward pioneers the

nation's first mail order catalog

1873

September Stock market panic sets off economic depression that lasts until 1878

1874

April Jennie Jerome marries Lord Randolph Churchill, the first of scores of transatlantic Gilded Age marriages of wealthy American heiresses to European aristocrats

1876

May *Royal Path of Life; or,*

Aims and Aids to Success and Happiness, a popular Gilded Age success manual is published

1877

September Farmers' Alliance founded in Lampasas, TX

July Great Railroad Strike disrupts rail service nationally and sparks a nationwide general strike

1881

March Henry Demarest Lloyd publishes "The Story of a Great Monopoly," an

investigative exposé of Standard Oil

1886

May 4 Bombing in Chicago's Haymarket Square

December 8 Craft unions organize the American Federation of Labor under the leadership of Samuel Gompers

1888

January Edward Bellamy publishes *Looking Backward: 2000–1887*, a utopian novel that presents a cooperative, Christian socialist

Believing that exposing facts could rouse the American public to demand change, "muckraking" helped bring about major reforms in the late 19th and early 20th centuries (see Chapters 18 and 20).

Published in 1888, **Edward Bellamy**'s *Looking Backward* provided a fictional critique of the new industrial order. Like *Wealth Against Commonwealth,* this utopian novel advocated for a cooperative rather than a competitive society. Bostonian Julian West, put into deep sleep by a hypnotist in 1887, awakens 113 years later, in the year 2000, to a world that he no longer recognizes. Much to his shock, poverty, disease, violent labor struggles, and rampant individualism no longer exist. Instead, a perfect world unfolds before him, where the conflicts and problems of the late 19th century have dissolved before a cooperative, secure, society of plenty. Dr. Leete, West's guide in the strange new world, explains that this utopian society evolved naturally and nonviolently. Business consolidations led to one big trust, as the people took it over "in the common interest for common profit." This "nationalism," as Bellamy called it, saw individualism and selfishness give way to concern for the common good. All people labored in the national industrial army and women were treated equally to men. No job was menial, and labor once again recaptured its inherent dignity.

Looking Backward was an instant national and international bestseller, surpassed in the 19th century only by *Uncle Tom's Cabin* in its influence. The book sold half a million copies in the United States alone; both the Knights of Labor and the Farmers' Alliance provided their members with copies. *Looking Backward* was translated into every major European language as well as Chinese and Hindi. The novel found especially fertile ground in nations buffeted by massive industrialization. In Russia, the novel was tremendously popular in socialist, labor, and student circles. A German commentator remarked that "one could hear nothing else but Bellamy." In Britain, the book sold 100,000 copies by 1890 and sparked widespread debate. Members of the middle class found it particularly attractive as it promised a peaceful transition to a just future, through evolution rather than violence.

alternative to industrial capitalism	dismantling monopolies inadvertently sets off a flurry of corporate mergers	economic depression that lasts until 1897	attack on Standard Oil and unbridled capitalism
1889		**June 20** Eugene V. Debs organizes the American Railway Union, an industrial union	**1895**
June Andrew Carnegie publishes his influential and controversial essay, known as "The Gospel of Wealth," which justifies industrial capitalism's benefits for society, partly through the philanthropy of its wealthiest members	**1892**		**January 21** In *U.S. v. E.C. Knight Co,* the U.S. Supreme Court rules that the federal government can only regulate monopolies involved in interstate commerce
	June 28 Homestead Lockout begins, resulting in violence and the crushing of the Amalgamated Association of Iron and Steel Workers	**1894**	
		May 11 The Pullman Strike, led by the American Railway Union, begins, paralyzing rail service, and ends in August with President Cleveland's use of federal troops	
1890	**July** The National People's (Populist) Party founded in Omaha, NE		**1901**
January 22 United Mine Workers organized as an industrial union	**1893**	**September** Henry Demarest Lloyd publishes *Wealth Against Commonwealth,* an	**February 25** U.S. Steel becomes the world's first billion-dollar industry
July 2 Sherman Antitrust Law aimed at	**March** Wall Street panic precipitates an		

Looking Backward also stimulated the creation of Nationalist Clubs, also known as "Bellamy Clubs," to implement Bellamy's ideas. The first club was founded in 1888, immediately after the publication of the book; additional clubs mushroomed around the world. By 1892, Bellamy claimed that 150 clubs had spontaneously organized. When another major crisis of capitalism occurred in the 1930s, with the worldwide Great Depression, Bellamy Clubs once again emerged, in Asia and Africa.

STUDY QUESTIONS FOR THE NEW INDUSTRIAL ORDER: DEFENSE AND DISSENT

1. What do success manuals, Lloyd's "muckraking," and Bellamy's utopian novel suggest about the concerns and anxieties of Americans and their European counterparts regarding the new industrial order?
2. Who do you think makes the most convincing arguments: defenders of the new industrial order or those who criticized it?

Summary

- In the last quarter of the 19th century, a new industrial order linked the United States to a global economy and the creation of networks through which money, technology, labor, goods, and ideas flowed. By 1900, the nation emerged as the world's industrial leader.
- The new industrial order changed the nature of work and the workplace. Mechanization and specialization greatly reduced the need for skilled labor. "White collar" managers and employers emphasized productivity and profits at the expense of "blue collar" workers, and workers regularly faced unemployment and underemployment during economic downturns.
- The Gilded Age was a battlefield of industrial warfare, of bloody strikes and lockouts that pitted worker against employer.
- American workers forged ties and drew inspiration from fellow workers abroad. But in the Gilded Age, American workers made little headway, especially compared to their French counterparts.
- The new industrial order, with both its promise and its problems, sparked international conversations that both defended and attacked it.

Key Terms and People

Alger, Horatio 672

American Federation of Labor (AFL) 665

American Railway Union (ARU) 667

anarchism 664

Bellamy, Edward 675

Brandeis, Louis 674

Carnegie, Andrew 641

Cleveland, Grover 667

Debs, Eugene V. 667

Frick, Henry Clay 666

Gompers, Samuel 665

Hayes, Rutherford B. 664

Knights of Labor 664

laissez-faire economics *651*

Lloyd, Henry Demarest *650*

modern corporation *646*

muckraking *674*

Powderly, Terrence V. *665*

Pullman, George *667*

Pullman Strike *667*

Rockefeller, John D. *647*

Roosevelt, Theodore *668*

Sherman Antitrust Act *650*

Spencer, Herbert *651*

Taylor, Frederick Winslow *658*

Vanderbilt, Cornelius *647*

Ward, Aaron Montgomery *652*

Wells, H.G. *661*

Reviewing Chapter 17

1. Did the benefits of industrial capitalism, as Andrew Carnegie asserted, outweigh the negative consequences? Use examples from the chapter to support your argument.
2. Discuss ways that the relationship between workers and employers changed in the Gilded Age.

Further Reading

Domosh, Mona. *American Commodities in an Age of Empire.* New York: Routledge, 2006. Explores the commercial empire established before political empire in the late 19th century with a focus on the nation's five largest international companies, including Singer Manufacturing and H.J. Heinz Company.

Montgomery, Maureen. *Gilded Prostitution: Status, Money, and Transatlantic Marriages, 1870–1914.* New York: Routledge, 1989. Examines the phenomenon of wealthy young American women who married European aristocrats and the response to these marriages in the United States and Europe.

Nasaw, David. *Andrew Carnegie.* New York: Penguin, 2007. A comprehensive look at the life and times of Andrew Carnegie and his rise from impoverished immigrant to one of the world's richest and most powerful men.

Rodgers, Daniel T. *The Work Ethic in Industrial America, 1850–1920.* Chicago: University of Chicago Press, 1978. A classic study of the changing nature of work and the response of laborers to the new industrial order.

Trachtenberg, Alan. *The Incorporation of America: Culture and Society in the Gilded Age.* New York: Hill and Wang, 2007. A comprehensive examination of the impact of industrial capitalism on American culture.

Visual Review

The New Industrial Order

Technological innovations fuel a new industrial revolution.

U.S. Industrial Growth in Global Context

The United States emerges as the world's leading industrial power.

Combinations and Concentrations of Wealth

Federal and State governments provide little regulation of the economy.

Markets and Consumerism

New technologies and advances in transportation open up international markets and mass production and consumption.

Global Webs of Industrial Capitalism

A NEW INDUSTRIAL AND LABOR ORDER, 1877–1900

Work and the Workplace

Global Migrations

Migration and immigration fuel the labor needs of industrializing regions.

Working Conditions and Wages

Laborers work in difficult conditions for low wages.

Blue Collar and White Collar Workers

A new economic order divides labor into skilled and unskilled workers.

Economic Convulsions and Hard Times

The economy grows in fits and starts.

Regimentation and Scientific Management

Management employs new methods to maximize workers' efficiency.

Women and Children in the Workplace

Large numbers of women and children join the workplace.

Workers Fight Back

The Great Railroad Strike of 1877

American workers initiate the first general strike in the nation.

Organizing Strategies and Labor Violence

Workers engage a range of strategies to improve their lives.

The Farmers Organize

Farmers also organize to improve their declining situation.

The Labor Movement in Global Context

Workers exchange strategies and theories across national borders.

The New Industrial Order: Defense and Dissent

Defending the New Order

Books and articles flow across the Atlantic, defending the new industrial order.

Critiquing the New Order

International writings and conversations condemn the new industrial order.

PROSPER TY
AT
HOME,
PRESTIG
ABROAD
COMMERCE.
CIVILIZATIO
NORTHWESTERN LITHO CO. MILWAUKEE.

18

Cities, Immigrants, Culture, and Politics

1877–1900

I n March 1880 the arrival in New York of Englishman George Scott Railton and seven women associates "created quite a sensation," the *New York Times* reported. The small band, explained the newspaper, constituted "the advance guard of 'The Salvation Army.'" Organized in London 15 years earlier by William Booth, "The Hallelujah Seven" immediately revealed their grand plans for the United States. Marching down the gangplank, holding the Army's flag aloft, they planted their banner in American soil, claimed the nation for God and The Army, and sang a hymn: "With a sorrow of sin, let repentance begin."

Hoping to save the souls of the "unchurched" and eliminate the many "temptations" offered by rapidly expanding Gilded Age cities, the Salvation Army implemented a military approach to bring urbanites under the influence of Protestant Christianity. The Army established "corps" (missions) staffed with "officers" (clergy) assigned military ranks. They wore smart dark blue uniforms trimmed in yellow, their hats encircled with a scarlet ribbon. To publicize their work, they marched through the streets, bearing colorful flags, accompanied by their band featuring brass, drums, and tambourines. "They will preach in the streets to anyone who will listen to them," exclaimed the *Times*. The Army sought souls in barrooms, on street corners, and in brothels, and made their first American convert in a saloon hall: a well-known drunk, "Ash-Barrel Jimmy," who earned his nickname after police found him inebriated and frozen—head-first—in a barrel. The *New York World* labeled the Army "A Peculiar People amid Queer Surroundings."

"Prosperity at Home, Prestige Abroad," William McKinley campaign poster, 1896

CHAPTER OUTLINE

URBANIZATION
> The Growth of Cities
> The Peopling of American Cities
> Types of Cities
> Cities Transformed and "Sorted Out"

GLOBAL MIGRATIONS
> A Worldwide Migration
> "America Fever" and the "New" Immigration
> The "Immigrant Problem"
> The Round-Trip to America

STREETS PAVED WITH GOLD?
> Surviving in "The Land of Bosses and Clocks"
> Creating Community
> Becoming American

THE PROMISE AND PERIL OF CITY LIFE
> A World of Opportunity
> A World of Crises

continued on page 685

America in the World

London's Toynbee Hall inspires Jane Addams to open Hull House in Chicago, the nation's first settlement house (1889).

Baseball's National League formed and spread enthusiasm for American sports around the world (1876).

U.S. event that influenced the world

International event that influenced the United States

Event with multinational influence

Conflict

The Women's Christian Temperance Union was founded and spreads around the world (1874).

The Salvation Army arrived in New York City from London and ministers to the urban poor, spreading rapidly to cities across the United States (1880).

"American Fever" begins to spread around the world, bringing 13 million immigrants to the United States by 1914 (1870).

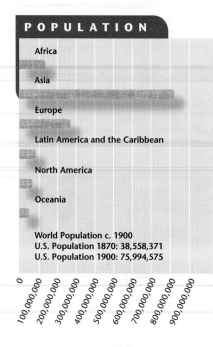

POPULATION

Africa

Asia

Europe

Latin America and the Caribbean

North America

Oceania

World Population c. 1900
U.S. Population 1870: 38,558,371
U.S. Population 1900: 75,994,575

0
100,000,000
200,000,000
300,000,000
400,000,000
500,000,000
600,000,000
700,000,000
800,000,000
900,000,000

Although viewed by some as eccentric, the organization spread rapidly to cities around the country, where it is still a presence today. Within a decade of its arrival, The Salvation Army spread to 43 states. The Army not only fed souls spiritually, it also fed hungry bodies. Thousands of "soldiers"—almost all native-born Protestant men and women—opened soup kitchens and established day nurseries, orphanages, "rescue homes" for prostitutes, and secondhand stores.

The Salvation Army was just one of many approaches to the social problems created by urbanization. London, New York, and other rapidly growing cities faced similar crises and reformers shared ideas and methods for social reform across the Atlantic. Protestant organizations, such as the Salvation Army, especially worried about the lack of moral influence in impersonal cities where temptations, such as saloons, seemed to blossom at every corner. In addition, they hoped to bring immigrants, most of whom embraced the "alien" Roman Catholic and Jewish faiths, under their influence.

Despite their many good works, the Salvation Army often faced resistance. Street toughs regularly attacked the "Hallelujah Lads and Lasses," pelting them with rotten eggs, rocks, and even dead cats. Roman Catholics especially resented their attempts to convert them to Protestantism. In the end, the Salvation Army made few converts among immigrants.

The story of the Salvation Army reflects the anxieties about urbanization and immigration experienced by many Americans, and responses to those concerns. Would the rapid shift from an agrarian to an urban-industrial nation change the character of the United States? Could the nation remain both united and ethnically diverse?

URBANIZATION

Urbanization, a consequence of the industrialization and the massive internal and global migrations that fueled the new economic order, largely defined the United States and other industrializing nations of the world in the late 19th century. As early as 1867, New York journalist Horace Greeley noted, "We cannot all live in cities yet nearly all seem determined to do so." The Gilded Age proved to be the pivotal period for the transition from rural to urban society, a trend that continued into the 20th century. Cities grew both horizontally, sprawling across the landscape, and vertically as new, taller buildings seemed to pierce the sky. They became increasingly segregated and fragmented by class, race, and ethnicity. The rapid growth of cities reconfigured and transformed the landscape and culture in troubling ways to contemporary observers. While cities embodied late 19th-century notions of progress and modernity, at the same time their growing dominance challenged the traditional Jeffersonian vision of the nation as a land of rooted, rural peoples and raised a disturbing question about the nation's future: Did impersonal, highly diverse cities represent the decline or advance of the republic?

The Growth of Cities

While cities throughout the industrializing world grew during the course of the 1800s, urbanization accelerated rapidly in the last 30 years of the century. At the midpoint of the 19th century, only two cities claimed a population of over a million people—London and Paris. By the turn of the 20th century, New York, Chicago, and Philadelphia in the United States—along with Berlin, Tokyo, St. Petersburg and Moscow, Buenos Aries, and Osaka—had reached, or were fast approaching, that mark. In addition to the growth of massive metropolitan areas around the world, towns and cities of all sizes, from industrial cities to trading centers and county seats, also expanded. But the "great cities," as they were called—those with a population of over 100,000—most often captured both the imagination of the public and stoked its fears.

Just as Great Britain pioneered industrial capitalism, it led the way in urbanization. As early as 1800, London claimed a million people; by 1890, three of four people in England lived in an urban area. By contrast, on the eve of the Civil War, only 1 in 5 Americans, roughly 6.2 million, lived in an urban area. By 1900, 30 million Americans, or two of every five, dwelled in cities, even though the South and parts of the West remained largely rural. By 1880, New York became the first American city to reach a million inhabitants, followed by Chicago and Philadelphia in 1890.

But as rapidly as urbanization occurred in the United States, cities in other parts of the world matched or outstripped it. Berlin, for example, grew roughly as fast as New York, and reached a million people by the turn of the century. Migrants from the countryside—internally and internationally—flowed into cities and were the key factor in explosive urban growth.

The Peopling of American Cities

Outlook, a popular magazine of the era, pointed out that towns and cities attracted both the rich and poor seeking more opportunity: "The towns are being recruited by those too poor to be able to live in the country, as well as by those too rich to be willing to live there." Overpopulation of the countryside, coupled with agricultural mechanization, in which machines replaced farm labor, forced rural peoples to look

CHAPTER OUTLINE

continued from page 681

TACKLING URBAN PROBLEMS
> City Missions and Charity Organizations
> The Settlement House Movement
> Creating Healthy Urban Environments

CHALLENGES TO THE POLITICS OF STALEMATE
> Key Issues
> Ethnicity, Gender, and Political Culture
> The Populist Challenge
> The Election of 1896

Table 18.1 Five Largest U.S. Cities: 1860 and 1900 Not only did the nation's five largest cities grow at a phenomenal rate between 1860 and 1900 (New York absorbed Brooklyn in 1898), they also reflected a geographical shift. In 1860, all five were located on the east coast; by 1900, Chicago and St. Louis cracked the list.

Rank	City	Population
	1860	
1	New York, NY	813,669
2	Philadelphia, PA	565, 529
3	Brooklyn, NY	266,661
4	Baltimore, MD	212,418
5	Boston, MA	177,840
	1900	
1	New York, NY	3,347,202
2	Chicago, IL	1,698,575
3	Philadelphia, PA	1,293,697
4	St. Louis, MO	575,238
5	Boston, MA	560,892

to cities for work. Worldwide economic depressions also deeply hurt farmers, who lost their farms when they could not pay creditors. For those better off, especially for ambitious young men, towns and cities in the industrial age seemed to offer unlimited business prospects and the chance to enjoy modern technology and a whole range of cheap leisure activities.

In the United States, African Americans continued to flow into cities. Approximately 341,000 blacks migrated from the South to the North between 1870 and 1900, a small migration compared to what would follow in the 20th century. But many more blacks migrated from the countryside to Southern towns and cities where, like their white counterparts, they also sought new opportunities. A small black middle class, made of businesspeople and professionals, developed in these cities as well. Atlanta's Auburn Avenue, for example, featured black-owned businesses, such as pharmacies and banks, and the offices of doctors, dentists, and lawyers. Even menial service jobs designated for blacks in cities, such as domestic labor, provided more opportunity and freedom than sharecropping.

But more than internal migrants from the countryside, immigrants from around the world expanded the size of towns and cities in the Gilded Age. Most of the 11 million immigrants who arrived in the United States between 1870 and 1900 settled in cities, where they were most likely to find employment. The great majority were Europeans, but Chinese, until their exclusion in 1882, Japanese, French Canadian, and Mexican migrants were also lured to the United States in hopes of jobs and a better future. By 1900, 60 percent of those who dwelled in the nation's 12 largest urban centers were either foreign born or had parents who were born abroad.

Types of Cities

Reflecting the massive economic transformations of the era, the industrial metropolis emerged as the typical city in this period. The three largest American cities in 1900, New York, Chicago, and Philadelphia, all featured diversified industry, business districts, and residential neighborhoods increasingly segregated by class, race, and ethnicity. Chicago, even more than its older, east coast counterparts, epitomized the new metropolis. With a population of roughly 4,000 when it was chartered as a city in 1837, this sleepy, dusty trading town on the shores of Lake Michigan boasted 100,000 residents by 1860. And in just 10 years, from 1880 to 1890, Chicago doubled its population to a million people, making it the nation's second-largest city. Ideally situated on the edge of the country's industrial and manufacturing belt to the east and rich farmlands to the west, Chicago emerged as a rail hub and teemed with products from Western farms and forests. Enterprising citizens constructed grain elevators, manufacturing plants and slaughterhouses, establishing a massive empire of trade both nationally and internationally. But market and credit networks kept cities such as Chicago inextricably linked to the countryside.

While the industrial metropolis cast a huge shadow, it was not the only type of city that grew at a remarkable rate. Just as railroads powered the growth of the nation's metropolises, they also fueled the expansion of smaller cities. Reflecting larger economic trends, these second-tier cities specialized in manufacturing or processing particular products for regional, national, and international markets. Denver specialized in slaughtering and packing western beef. Portland, Oregon, featured the lumbering industry and foundries while Tampa, Florida, manufactured cigars. One-industry mill towns, another type of small city, also mushroomed. Johnstown, Pennsylvania, produced iron and steel; and Winston-Salem, North Carolina, made cigarettes.

Following patterns of industrialization, urbanization developed unevenly in the United States and occurred most intensely in the Northeast and the manufacturing belt that extended from Pittsburgh, through the upper Midwest, to Chicago. By 1910, the Northeast contained 70 percent of the nation's urban population.

Despite inspiring images of wide, open prairies, the west also experienced rapid urbanization in the late 19th century, second only to the Northeast and upper Midwest manufacturing belt. The Transcontinental Railroad and its numerous branch and trunk feeders sparked urbanization in the West. In 1900, in the far West, San Francisco remained the region's largest city. But by 1910, Los Angeles had over 250,000 inhabitants and Seattle, Portland, and Denver over 200,000. Over half of Westerners lived in cities by that time.

Only the South remained largely rural, although it, too, experienced urban growth. In 1900, only about 17 percent of Southerners lived in a town or city, and the region contained only 11 percent of the nation's urban population. The inland cities of Atlanta, Charlotte, and Nashville emerged as quintessential New South cities.

Small, modest railroad towns at the time of the Civil War, these cities exploded in the late 19th and early 20th centuries as trading centers with some industry. They attracted relatively few immigrants, but drew many white migrants from the countryside, many of whom worked in textile mills. Atlanta, for example, grew from less than 10,000 people to 155,000 between 1860 and 1900. But New South cities remained relatively small. New Orleans remained the region's largest city in the Gilded Age, but only the 12th largest city in the nation.

Cities Transformed and "Sorted Out"

The late 19th-century city differed dramatically from earlier urban centers in its spatial patterns, sprawl, and vertical growth. Earlier in the century, most cities were compact "walking cities." Urbanites lived within walking distance of jobs, stores, and businesses, all located in the city core; city limits extended only as far as people could travel on foot, rarely beyond two miles. Businesses, homes, and factories all shared space in these densely populated areas, and people of all classes, races, and ethnicities lived and worked in close quarters.

Transportation innovations, especially the streetcar, transformed American cities. First implemented in Richmond, Virginia, in 1888, the electric streetcar made it possible to work and shop in the center city while living on its fringes, in suburbs miles from congestion and grime. Electric-powered subways, first introduced in Boston in 1897, provided another source of cheap urban transportation, as did elevated streetcars and cable cars. Gilded Age cities began to sort out by class, race, ethnicity, and land use. Wealthier white residents separated themselves from poorer urban dwellers, especially immigrants and people of color, abandoning the city center, once the most desirable place to live because of its proximity to jobs and services. They flocked to quiet, clean, and new residential developments in suburbs, residential developments outside of city limits, easily accessible by streetcars.

Suburbanization, along with urbanization, was an important characteristic of Gilded Age America. To those well off enough to afford them, suburbs, with their quiet, tree-lined residential enclaves, offered escape from urban squalor and an easy commute to work by streetcar. Moreover, suburbs offered the privacy of single-family homes, difficult to come by in cities because of rising real estate prices and housing demands. In addition, some exclusive suburbs guaranteed that residents would live only among people like themselves, forbidding the sale of property to blacks, Roman Catholics, and Jews.

Central cities also reflected the sorting out process. Specialized districts emerged devoted to banking and finance, shopping, transportation, distribution, and entertainment, often in close proximity.

Cities also grew vertically. The new industrial order required office space to house the armies of white collar workers needed to run increasingly complex businesses. Congested and densely packed, many cities had only one way to go—and that was up. Technological innovations, especially structural steel frameworks, light masonry walls, and plate glass windows, made skyscrapers possible for the first time. Chicago boasted the nation's first skyscraper, the 10-story Home Insurance Building, erected in 1885. The electric elevator made even taller buildings practical, and by 1913 New York's Woolworth Building topped 55 stories.

The demand for urban space transformed housing as well. Multifamily housing replaced the single-family home. Both tenements for the poor and apartments for the middle class and well to do, common in Europe but new to American cities, shot skyward in great cities. In New England mill towns, multifamily triple deckers dotted the urban landscape.

STUDY QUESTIONS FOR URBANIZATION

1. What factors account for rapid urbanization globally in the late 19th century?
2. How did technological innovations transform America's cities?

GLOBAL MIGRATIONS

No single group contributed to America's urbanization more than immigrants. "Once a person from this area, man or woman, has been seized by this epidemic American fever," reported a Swedish physician in the late 19th century, "there is nothing one can do about it." Between 1870 and 1900, "America fever" swept the globe as over 11 million immigrants arrived in the United States, more than in the previous 250 years. This tide of immigrants would continue until the outbreak of World War I in 1914; in those 14 years an additional 13 million immigrants entered the country.

While the United States attracted the greatest portion of migrants and immigrants, the last quarter of the 19th century and the first years of the 20th witnessed a massive movement of the world's peoples. A consequence of industrial capitalism, this global migration spurred urbanization not only in the United States but also in other industrial nations. Technological advances, especially steamships, made long-distance migration much easier and cheaper. Contrary to popular conceptions, many migrants regularly crossed and re-crossed the Atlantic. About one-third of immigrants to the United States returned permanently to their countries of origin.

While the United States had always been a nation of immigrants, the volume and origin of these migrants, referred to as "new" immigrants—as most originated in southern and eastern Europe, previously unrepresented in U.S. immigration—created new fears and anxieties among some native-born Americans. Anti-immigrant sentiment exploded, and Americans debated whether immigration should be restricted. Growing numbers of native-born Americans questioned whether these "new" immigrants could ever be good Americans. Were they as a congressman argued, "the ignorant, the pauper, and the vicious class . . . utterly unable to discharge the duties of American citizenship"? Or did they have the right, as another congressman contended, to enjoy "'the land of the free' where the outcast of every nation . . . could breathe our free air?"

A Worldwide Migration

Cities around the world attracted a hodgepodge of migrating people. Many were rural peoples unable to sustain themselves in an overpopulated countryside or to compete with mechanized agriculture and cheap, imported grains from the American Midwest. Political unrest, ethnic conflict, and religious persecution persuaded others to look abroad. Uprooted rural people went to where the jobs were: largely to industrializing cities in Europe and North and South America, Australia, and New Zealand. Whereas the United States attracted the largest numbers of immigrants, Argentina had the largest *proportion* of immigrants (Map 18.1).

Transoceanic migration extended internal European migration trends. European laborers had traditionally migrated to work in seasonal harvests and then they migrated for work in the continent's burgeoning industries. Advances in transportation made migration across the ocean seem like a natural next step. These improvements, as an Irish immigrant explained, "brought America so near to this country, that it was just around the corner." In the late 19th century, steamships could cross the Atlantic in two weeks or less, compared with sailing ships that took as long as 42 days. Fare wars among steamship lines also drove prices down, making it possible to cross in steerage for as little as $10. The poorest immigrants managed to raise fare money by selling personal possessions or receiving a ticket from someone who had already migrated.

Out-migration did not just flow westward across the Atlantic from Europe. Smaller numbers of migrants from Asia, mostly from China and Japan, streamed eastward, across the Pacific. Before the Civil War, worsening economic conditions drove Chinese, mostly men from southeastern China, to "Gold Mountain," to work in mines and building railroads on the west coast. They later dug the irrigation canals, dikes, and ditches that provided the foundation for California's agricultural empire. Others worked in low-paying industrial jobs. Beginning in the mid-1880s, Japanese

In 1892 the federal government opened Ellis Island, in New York harbor, as the first federal immigration center. When it closed in 1954, 12 million immigrants had entered the United States through Ellis Island, roughly four of five European immigrants. Approximately 40 percent of present-day Americans have an ancestor who passed through Ellis Island.

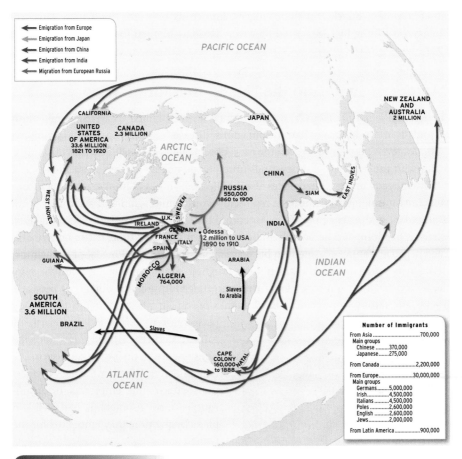

Emigration from Europe
Emigration from Japan
Emigration from China
Emigration from India
Migration from European Russia

PACIFIC OCEAN

NEW ZEALAND
AND
AUSTRALIA
2 MILLION

CALIFORNIA

JAPAN

UNITED
STATES
OF AMERICA
33.6 MILLION
1821 TO 1920

CANADA
2.3 MILLION

ARCTIC
OCEAN

CHINA

WEST INDIES

RUSSIA
550,000
1860 to 1900

SIAM

EAST INDIES

IRELAND
U.K.
SWEDEN
GERMANY
FRANCE
ITALY
SPAIN

Odessa
2 million to USA
1890 to 1910

INDIA

GUIANA

MOROCCO

ALGERIA
764,000

ARABIA

Slaves
to Arabia

INDIAN
OCEAN

SOUTH
AMERICA
3.6 MILLION

BRAZIL

Slaves

ATLANTIC
OCEAN

CAPE
COLONY
160,000
to 1888

NATAL

Number of Immigrants

From Asia 700,000
Main groups
    Chinese 370,000
    Japanese.......275,000

From Canada 2,200,000

From Europe.....................30,000,000
Main groups
    Germans.........5,000,000
    Irish..............4,500,000
    Italians 4,500,000
    Poles 2,600,000
    English 2,600,000
    Jews.............2,000,000

From Latin America.................900,000

▲ **Map 18.1**

Global Migration, 1840–1900 Global migrations accelerated in the late 19th and early 20th centuries with the rise of industrial capitalism. The United States attracted six times more migrants than Argentina, the second-favored destination, and also drew peoples from many more places around the world.

immigrants also turned eastward, victimized by rising taxes used to fuel Japan's industrial and military development. Several hundred thousand Japanese arrived in Hawaii and the United States where they largely worked as agricultural laborers. Mexicans turned to the north, mainly as agricultural laborers, lured by the promise of wages unavailable in Mexico, and regularly crossed the border seasonally. French Canadians from Quebec, faced with an overpopulated countryside and diminishing access to land, headed south, boarding trains for the relatively high wages offered by the textile mills of New England.

Economic reasons were not the only motivation for migration. Religious persecution catalyzed the movement of eastern Europeans Jews to the United States. Forced to live in the Pale of Settlement in the Russian empire, under severe restrictions, Jews suffered violent attacks on their villages, known as pogroms, with increasing frequency, beginning in 1881, when they were wrongly blamed for the assassination of Czar Alexander II.

"America Fever" and the "New" Immigration

"Emigration is spontaneous," an Italian landowner explained to a U.S. immigration commission. "It becomes like a contagious disease." Steamship agents promoted "America fever," appearing in even the most obscure villages to sell tickets to the United States with the promise of a new and more prosperous life. Letters from friends and relatives already in the United States also extolled the virtues of immigration: As a Congressional immigration committee reported, "word comes again and again that 'work is abundant and wages princely in America.'" Letters also stressed the social equality, religious freedom, and democracy to be enjoyed. At the same time, letters honestly related negative features of American life, particularly the backbreaking labor facing most newcomers, often insisting that only the toughest should immigrate, warning away those "too weak for America." Employers encouraged immigrant workers to persuade friends and family to migrate to fill the ranks of industry. Responding to the bloody persecution of European Jews, Jewish organizations in the United States aided the immigration of their coreligionists to the United States. Whether through connections with friends, employers, or organizations, most immigrants had well-laid plans by the time they embarked for the United States.

America fever brought immigrants from new parts of Europe, from places previously unrepresented in earlier migrations. For the first time, southern and eastern Europeans arrived in large numbers. While northern and western Europeans still dominated from 1870 to 1900, making up roughly two-thirds of immigrants, a flood of southern and eastern Europeans—Italians, Greeks, Poles, Hungarians, Slavs, and Russian Jews—accounted for the other third. Between 1900 and 1914, these immigrants surpassed those from northern and western Europe. Men made up a large majority of immigrants nearly 70 percent of the immigration population between 1880 and 1910.

This 1888 poster invites immigrants to the Dakota Territory, touting the advantages of the "New World" compared to the "Old World."

The origins and massive numbers of these migrants led Americans to refer to the "new" immigration. Native-born Americans tended to use this designation as a negative label, unfavorably contrasting "new" immigrants with "old" immigrants, from the British Isles and northern Europe. "New" immigrants seemed especially foreign; their cultures, languages, and religions seemed too different for them ever to become "true Americans." Most were Roman Catholic or Jewish, making them especially problematic to Protestant Americans, who believed that they were unfit for self-government. Roman Catholics, they argued, could never be loyal Americans because of their primary allegiance to the Pope. Jews seemed especially threatening to Americans who thought of their country as a Christian nation. Asian immigrants, especially the Chinese, seemed even more different, and incapable of assimilating.

The "Immigrant Problem"

The vast numbers of "new" immigrants and their especially "foreign" origins created a backlash against them. **Nativism**, opposition to immigrants and immigration, spiked in the late 19th century. In union halls, colleges and universities, on the floor of Congress, and in the popular press, native-born Americans discussed the "immigrant problem." Native-born workers claimed that desperate immigrants would work for very little and drove down their wages. Social Darwinists depicted immigrants, in the words of Francis A. Walker, head of the Bureau of the Census, as "beaten men from beaten races, representing the worst failures in the struggle for existence." Popular racial theories not only asserted the superiority of white-skinned peoples over blacks and Asians, but also established a hierarchy of European peoples, with the "Nordic" peoples of northern Europe the "natural" superiors to the darker, "Mediterranean" peoples of southern and eastern Europe. Others claimed that the infusion of "inferior racial stock" would "mongrelize" the American nation.

In 1887, nativists formed the **American Protective Association** (APA). At its peak in the mid-1890s, the organization boasted half a million members. Advocating strict immigration laws, the APA, like anti-immigrant groups before the Civil War, spread wild conspiracy theories about Roman Catholics. They blamed the economic collapse of the 1890s on the pope and claimed that he sent immigrant laborers to overthrow the U.S. government. APA members promised never to employ Roman Catholics "in any capacity" and pledged to keep them from holding any public office.

Other, less conspiratorial groups also argued for immigration restriction. The Immigration Restriction League, founded in Boston in 1894, promoted legislation to filter out "inferior" peoples flowing into the country. During the depression of the 1890s, Congress debated the Immigration Restriction Bill, which would allow only those literate in their own language to immigrate. A Massachusetts congressman condemned the "masses of men who either fester in the slums of our great cities or make predatory incursions into industrial centres, where they work for wages upon which American workingmen cannot live." But others defended immigrants and their invaluable contributions, pointing out that many filled jobs that native-born Americans would not take. While Congress passed the bill in 1897, President **Grover Cleveland** vetoed it, labeling it "illiberal, narrow, and un-American."

In the 1880s, Chinese immigrants were not as fortunate. Although small in number, the Chinese, more than any other immigrant group in this era, became a target of bigotry and violence. Many native-born Americans viewed the Chinese as people so culturally different that they could never be Americans, and placed them in the same inferior racial category as Indians and blacks. Moreover, as many were sojourners planning on returning to China, they maintained their language, dress, and hairstyles, and were easily identifiable. A magazine article summed up the stereotypes regarding "John Chinaman": he lived in "squalor and filth," he "gambles incessantly" and "smokes opium," and was guilty of "degrading white labor to a bestial scale."

Located almost exclusively on the west coast, the Chinese had suffered economic and legal discrimination for years when the severe economic depression of the 1870s kindled a blaze of anti-Chinese sentiment. Shouting the slogan, "The Chinese Must Go," California's Workingman's Party demanded an end to Chinese immigration, blaming them for their unemployment and low wages. By 1882, anti-Chinese sentiment grew so great that Congress passed the Chinese Exclusion Act. The law barred the immigration of Chinese laborers and made it extremely difficult for nonlaborers to enter the country, all but ended Chinese immigration. The first such law in U.S. history, it remained in effect until 1943.

Anti-Chinese sentiment reached far beyond the borders of the United States. Canada, which attracted Chinese laborers to complete the Canadian Pacific Railroad, first limited Chinese immigration in 1885. The Canadian government later passed a Chinese exclusion act, in effect from 1923–1947. From 1901 to 1957, Australia targeted Asian migration in general by requiring a test in which immigrants had to write 50 words in a European language.

Another less radical approach to the "immigrant problem," was the attempt to "Americanize" immigrants. A congressman explained in the1895 debate over immigration restriction, "The newcomers will not change us, but we will change them." Public education served as a key instrument in this process. In 1906 an educator proclaimed the public schools "the sluiceways into Americanism. When the stream of alien children flows through them, it will issue into the reservoirs of national life with the Old World taints filtered out." This definition of "Americanism" had no appreciation for cultural diversity or complex identities; instead to be an American meant throwing off all of the "inferior" ways of the Old World—language, appearance, culture, and values—for "superior" American ways. Americanization efforts could create tensions and misunderstandings in families, as parents often insisted on maintaining their traditional culture and values.

The Round-Trip to America

Despite the rise of nativism, immigrants continued to pour into the United States. With the relative ease of the transatlantic crossing, many immigrants—mostly young men—thought of their sojourn as temporary. They planned to work for the relatively high wages offered in America and then return home. Approximately a quarter to a third of immigrants who arrived between 1880 and 1930 did just that. Some ethnic groups had very high rates of return: nearly 9 of 10 Bulgarians, Serbs, and Montenegrans returned to their homelands, while 6 of 10 Southern Italians remigrated, as did almost half of all Greek immigrants. Some, known as "birds of passage," crossed and re-crossed the Atlantic numerous times, including Italian stonemasons.

Others returned home, not as part of a master plan, but because the United States turned out not to be the "golden door" to a better life. Illness or injury sent some home broken and dispirited. Others simply succumbed to homesickness. Still others became disillusioned with the United States, especially the relentless hours of work in dangerous industrial jobs. Some, from Polish Catholics to Swedish Lutherans to observant Jews, cited the nation's "godlessness." A Hungarian folksong summed up the feelings of many returnees:

> I boarded the ship on Tuesday morning
> Going back to Hungary.
> God bless America forever,
> Just let me get away.

The transitory nature of this immigration had significant ramifications. Those who planned to return had little interest in joining unions, as strikes and union dues defeated their goal of accumulating money as quickly as possible and returning home. In addition, they also made little effort to assimilate. They did not learn English, attend schools, or become American citizens. Temporary immigrants were often criticized especially by labor unions and native-born Americans who were insulted that not all immigrants embraced their nation and way of life.

STUDY QUESTIONS FOR GLOBAL MIGRATIONS

1. What factors account for the massive global migrations of the late 19th and early 20th century?
2. What explains the rise of nativist sentiment during the Gilded Age? What policies did nativists advocate to restrict immigration?

STREETS PAVED WITH GOLD?

Evidence of the promise of America—migrants returning with money, glowing letters from friends and relatives—filled immigrants with great expectations. The image of America as a land of "gold" cut across nearly all ethnic groups and nationalities. But many immigrants found the harshness of American life shocking. An Italian immigrant recalled, "We thought the streets were paved with gold. When we got here we saw that they weren't paved at all. Then they told us that we were expected to pave them."

Immigrants filled the ranks of unskilled labor in industrial, urban America. As a minister noted in 1887, "Not every foreigner is a working man but in the cities, at

GLOBAL PASSAGES

Immigrants Who Returned

In 1911, as part of a massive Congressional study, investigators from the Bureau of Immigration traveled to Europe to study the phenomenon of return migration. Returned immigrants, they found, played major roles as "great promoters" of immigration to the United States. In Italy, the investigators found countless examples of successful "Americanos": many had managed to purchase land, even small estates. "Americanos," they found, "live better and have cleaner houses." Many "build a nice cottage" of brick—in an American-style, noticeably devoid of "the pigs, donkey, or chickens" that inhabited the houses of Italian peasants. They also "dress well," and had adopted new standards of cleanliness. In addition, as the mayor of a small Italian town pointed out, "those who have been to America do not work as willingly now as before." One villager told the American investigators, "The Americans have brought here the paradise."

"Americanos" in Italy, "Amerikanty" in Poland, and "Ok Boys," as they were dubbed in Greece—for their use of that ubiquitous American affirmation—carried money, new ideas, and American culture back to their homelands. Wages earned in mills, mines, and factories made it possible for many to fulfill the dream of landownership. Dramatic increases in landholding occurred in Italy, for example, as a result of return migration, engendering social changes in that country. Others purchased businesses or opened shops. American-style houses mushroomed across the European countryside. Their brick or shingle facades, tile roofs, and painted interiors stood in sharp contrast to simple peasant huts. They dressed like Americans, "peacocks," in the view of one Swede, and they incorporated American words into

least, it may almost be said that every workingman is a foreigner." While American wages outstripped those in Europe or Asia, economic cycles of boom and bust, as well as industrial accidents and sickness, made immigrant laborers especially vulnerable to economic disaster. With few safety nets, immigrants devised their own strategies and supportive communities to cope with the uncertainties of American life and the radical changes they faced in urban America. Immigrants also faced other perplexing challenges. How much of the old world should they maintain? How much of the new world should they embrace?

Surviving in "The Land of Bosses and Clocks"

Immigrants provided the labor for the nation's exploding industrial growth. The mechanization of industry made it relatively simple to move into an unskilled industrial

their native languages—"bodi" for buddy in Hungarian, "giobba" for job in Italian. Returnees even introduced American-style pies and cakes, which they insisted on eating on separate plates—American style—rather than in communal bowls used by European peasants. Some also brought back new technologies, introducing new implements to farmers and phonographs to delighted villagers. And they formed their own social clubs, such as the "United States Club" in Denmark and the "George Washington Greek-American Association" in Greece.

But perhaps most importantly, they carried back new ideas. Immersed in American democracy, those who returned seemed far less deferential to authority and their social superiors. In addition, some transplanted reform movements to their own countries, becoming temperance organizers, educational reformers, and politicians. Three American sojourners even emerged as their nation's leaders: Johan Nygaardsvold, once a construction worker in the United States and active in radical labor politics, became prime minister of Norway in 1935. Oskari Tokoi toiled in mines in the western United States for a decade in the 1890s. When he returned to Finland, he spread the labor union ideas he had learned in America. In 1917, he became that nation's prime minister. Latvia's Karlis Ulmanis labored for eight years in the United States and ultimately served seven times as prime minister.

The bonds between the United States and those who returned remained strong for many years. American troops fighting in Italy in World War II often found themselves greeted affectionately by villagers bearing snapshots and other souvenirs attesting to their time in the United States.

- In what ways did return migrants impact the cultures of their home countries?

- What did they carry back with them from the United States?

job. Through chain migration, in which immigrants helped bring family and friends to the United States, specific ethnic groups soon concentrated in particular jobs and industries. Eastern Europeans—Poles, Hungarians, and Slavic peoples—labored in the mining districts and steel mills of Pennsylvania as well as the stockyards of Chicago. Eastern European Jews, many of whom were already skilled in the needle trades, flowed into the expanding ready-made garment industry in New York, established by German Jews. Italian men wielded the shovel, dominating municipal works crews in New York, Chicago, and San Francisco, paving streets and digging sewer and water lines; Italian women toiled in the garment industry.

Labor demands came as a shock. While some had experience working in European industry, most came from rural backgrounds. To them America seemed like nothing but "The Land of Bosses and Clocks." A Polish immigrant explained in a letter home that in America one had to "sweat more during the day than during a whole week in Poland." A sweatshop garment worker recalled, "We were like slaves. You couldn't pick your head up. You couldn't talk."

Channeled into the most dangerous and demanding jobs, immigrant laborers suffered death and injury at much higher rates than their native-born counterparts. Language barriers contributed to being hurt on the job, as immigrants, working among hazardous machines, did not always understand directions. Overworked and exhausted, they also succumbed to diseases such as tuberculosis and typhoid fever.

Even though real wages earned by American laborers increased significantly in the late 19th century—as much as by 50 percent by some estimates—workers, especially immigrants, faced particular challenges maintaining a minimal standard of living. Immigrants generally toiled in the lowest paying jobs. As the most recently hired, they were often the first fired, making them especially vulnerable to layoffs when the economy slowed. Depressions and economic downturns often resulted in a flurry of return migration.

Immigrants who remained embraced a number of strategies to make ends meet. As most immigrant men did not make enough money to support an entire family, their wives and children pitched in. Before 1900, foreign-born women made up over half of wage-earning women in the U.S. workforce. Earning only one-half to two-thirds of the wages paid to men, they usually left paid employment outside the home after they married or had their first child. But even then they found ways to combine marriage, motherhood, and paid labor. Taking in boarders—cooking, washing, and providing beds for the many single, male laborers working in American cities—was an especially common way to supplement the family income. But boarders meant even more backbreaking work for already overburdened women. Some women took in "home work," most commonly finishing garments for which they were paid by the piece, to help support their families. Home work allowed women to stay home and care for their children while earning money. Children even participated in the work, performing simple tasks, such as pulling out basting threads in pieces of clothing.

Sending children to work rather than school had long-term consequences. Italian immigrants, largely unskilled, peasants, worked in the lowest paying jobs. As a result, many found the employment of their children crucial to keeping their families afloat. As one historian has noted, "The peasant shovel was passed from one generation to the next." As late as 1914, 90 percent of Italian girls and 99 percent of Italian boys in New York City left school at the age of 14 to work. By contrast, eastern European Jews, the most literate and skilled of the "new" immigrant groups, generally found employment in higher paying, skilled positions, such as tailoring, in the garment industry. More economically secure, and valuing education, many managed to send their children to school, allowing a relatively large percentage of the next generation to enter managerial and professional occupations.

Creating Community

Immigrants created their own ethnic communities in America's urban and industrial centers that helped cushion their adjustment. They clustered not only by ethnicity or nationality but also by region or village. Whether forming a "Little Italy,"

New York's Lower East Side, like many immigrant neighborhoods was, as social reformer Mary Simkhovitch noted, "not a melting pot but a boiling kettle."

a "Chinatown," "el Barrio," or a "Hunky (Hungarian) Town," immigrants recreated familiar surroundings in a new setting, mixing old and new, tradition and adaptation. Eastern European Jews, for example, constructed a Jewish world on the Lower East Side, complete with newspapers and theater in their own language, Yiddish, a German dialect with numerous Hebrew words. Immigrant family life played out in tenement hallways, stoops, sidewalks, and even the streets, where children played and parents socialized. Notably, immigrant enclaves were seldom exclusive and immigrants rarely remained isolated. Even the largely Jewish Lower East Side included Italians, Poles, and other ethnicities.

In their communities, immigrants created informal networks as well as formal organizations to provide support. Despite their own hardships, immigrant families opened their homes to newly arrived family members and friends, providing them with a foothold in America. Immigrant women shared meager resources, and provided each other with food and rent money when unemployment inevitably occurred. Self-help organizations also aided immigrants to adjust to the United States on their own terms. Mutual aid societies, whose members paid small monthly dues, provided a range of services, including credit and sickness and death benefits. Jews organized *landsmanshaftn,* mutual aid societies consisting of people from the same town of origin. Mexican workers in the southwest, most of whom worked in agriculture, mining, or as railroad laborers—and were, in most cases, barred from unions—formed mutual aid groups. The Alianza Hispano Americana started in Tucson, Arizona, in 1894. These societies also organized social events, such as picnics, dances, and concerts.

▶ **Map 18.2**

Ethnic Enclaves By 1900, Chicago, like most major U.S. cities, was made up of a wide range of ethnic groups. As older immigrant groups, such as the Germans and Irish, moved out of industrial areas on the South Side to neighborhoods with better housing, "new" immigrants, from southern and eastern Europe, moved into areas they abandoned. A small group of Southern black migrants also settled on the South Side, forerunners of the massive black migration that would begin with World War I.

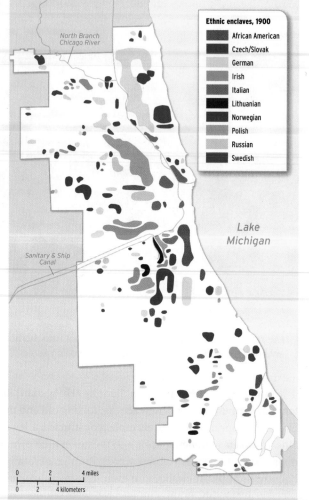

Ethnic enclaves, 1900

- African American
- Czech/Slovak
- German
- Irish
- Italian
- Lithuanian
- Norwegian
- Polish
- Russian
- Swedish

North Branch Chicago River

Sanitary & Ship Canal

Lake Michigan

0   2   4 miles
0   2   4 kilometers

Mutual aid societies often provided the nucleus for churches and synagogues. Although most of the "new" immigrants were Roman Catholic, they resisted joining parishes previously established by Irish and German immigrants. Instead, despite their poverty, they insisted on building their own separate ethnic parishes, with their own priests who spoke their language. Ethnic churches often established parochial schools, organized clubs, and sponsored festivals. Similarly, many religious eastern European Jews rejected Reformed Judaism pioneered by German Jews earlier in the century, which they viewed as too liberal, and instead established Orthodox congregations. Churches and synagogues played an especially important role in providing spiritual, social, and economic sustenance as well as preserving traditional culture.

The immigrant church and synagogue provide valuable insights into the complex ways that religious establishments both aided immigrants in assimilating to American life and maintained tradition. Many offered English classes, taught immigrants about American customs, and encouraged them to seek citizenship and to put down roots. At the same time, religious institutions maintained traditions and ties to the Old World, especially in preserving language.

Ties between the old and new worlds helped create transnational identities, especially among those groups with deep migration traditions, such as Italians, Poles, and Jews, who regularly moved across national borders. Rather than embracing a single identity, they maintained complex attachments and loyalties to more than one nation and culture. Moreover, many immigrants also retained translocal ties that connected immigrants from a village or region in one nation with those in another nation.

Becoming American

Not all immigrants wished to retain ties with the Old World. Young people, especially young women, eagerly embraced all things American, throwing off what they viewed as the stifling yoke of Old World ways for the modern freedoms of America. Mary Antin, who fled Russia with her family during the pogroms, happily fled "the cage of my provincialism," as she put it. With her sisters, she immediately shed her "hateful European costumes" for "real American machine-made garments," and changed her name from Maryashe to Mary. Antin leapt at the opportunity to take advantage of America's free public school education and pursued a successful career as a teacher and writer.

Some young working women also rebelled against traditional parental authority and control. They resented the expectation that they turn over their pay packet to their parents. Instead, they asserted their independence, keeping money for themselves to spend on stylish clothing and to socialize far from the view of their parents. Candy stores, soda shops, dance halls, amusement parks, and department stores drew young people out of their neighborhoods, where they mingled and became more "American." Many also rejected the tradition of arranged marriages, embracing more American notions of romantic love. Tensions often flared between immigrant parents who wished to maintain Old World ways and children who assimilated American values.

Despite the pressures and tensions faced by immigrants, the United States proved to be a "promised land" for many of them. The streets may not have been paved with gold, but immigrants nonetheless found jobs with wages higher than those in Europe and other opportunities, unthinkable in many parts of the world, such as free public education, and political and religious freedom. Free education, as immigrant Mary Antin wrote, was "the one thing" her father was able to promise her in America, comprising "the chief hope for us children, the essence of American opportunity."

STUDY QUESTIONS FOR STREETS PAVED WITH GOLD?

1. **What factors account for the unprecedented volume of immigration to the United States, beginning in the Gilded Age?**
2. **What specific challenges did immigrants face? How did they respond to these challenges?**

THE PROMISE AND PERIL OF CITY LIFE

Traveling to Chicago at the turn of the 20th century, British writer **H.G. Wells** marveled at the "creative forces at work." "Men are makers," he contended, "American men, I think, more than most." American cities were full of technological and cultural innovations—electric streetcars, skyscrapers, department stores, and new forms of entertainment. At the same time, Welles noted the "reek" of Chicago's stockyards along with "vast chimneys, huge blackened grain elevators, flame-crowned furnaces and gauntly ugly and filthy factory buildings, monstrous mounds of refuse, desolate, empty lots littered with rusty cans, old iron, indescribable rubbish." He summed up the city in one word: "Undisciplined." The word described most late 19th-century cities, teeming with people, filth, and industrial waste.

Diversity was another hallmark of the American city. Compared to their European counterparts, cities in the United States attracted a much broader range of people, a mix of humanity described by one observer as "a queer conglomerate mass of heterogeneous elements."

It is little wonder that concerned citizens in both the United States and Europe viewed cities as the primary social problem of the age. Above all cities were studies in contrasts—beauty and ugliness, wealth and poverty, innovation and decay, promise and peril. Did the city embody the promise of American life or was it, as minister Josiah Strong argued, a rogue's gallery of "roughs, gamblers, thieves, robbers, lawless and desperate men of all ages"?

A World of Opportunity

Cities teemed with opportunity and energy, offering a universe of activities unimaginable to rural dwellers in the United States or Europe—from new consumer opportunities to novel forms of entertainment. Department stores sprung up in late 19th-century cities. Some, such as Macy's, remain household names even today. Mass production, technological and transportation advances, and exploding urban growth made department stores possible. Designed as "palaces of merchandise," these stores provided the convenience of doing all of one's shopping under one roof. Featuring an abundance of items, goods were organized into "departments"—such as home furnishings, stationary, toys, clothing—for easy shopping, and provided a ready outlet of manufactured goods, shipped by railroad, to the burgeoning city. The development of plate-glass windows allowed merchants to entice passersby with attractive displays of their merchandise and a new leisure activity—"window shopping"—was born.

As working hours decreased and real wages increased, working class people had both more time and money to enjoy new forms of entertainment. Appealing to both rich and poor, native and immigrant, these entertainments helped bind fragmented cities together, offering common ground and experiences for diverse urbanites.

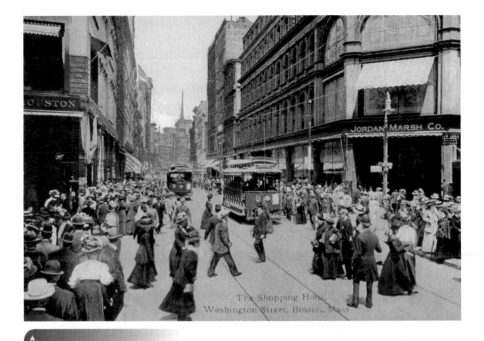

The Jordan Marsh department store anchors Boston's main shopping district, Washington Street, in this 1910 postcard depicting the hustle and bustle of "Shopping Hour."

Palatial theaters, which created a fantasy world with grand lobbies, paintings, and luxurious surroundings, offered vaudeville shows affordable to all. Usually nine-act bills, these variety shows featured comedy routines, music, gymnastics, and animal acts. Sentimental songs, many about the longing for family and friends left behind, provided an emotional outlet for homesick immigrants. Comedy sketches featured stock characters, such as the "hayseed" visitor to the city and ethnic characters that played on contemporary ethnic stereotypes. As the audience laughed with and at each other, humor helped ease ethnic tensions and ultimately created a sense of belonging.

Amusement parks, like New York's Coney Island were also a product of the Gilded Age city and sprung up across the country, often at the end of streetcars lines. Fare to Coney Island was a nickel, and those who could not afford to spend more for park rides could still enjoy the festive atmosphere or while away their time at the beach. Amusement parks provided a much-needed outlet for urban dwellers—offering fantasy, thrills, and fun—and were especially attractive to young, single, working people who relished the freedom and escape from nosy parents and chaperones.

Spectator sports also flourished, becoming a fundamental element of American culture. While boxing and horseracing enjoyed widespread popularity, professional baseball emerged as the national pastime. Railroad networks enabled teams from around the nation to compete with each other, and the telegraph instantaneously reported scores, published in increasingly prominent sports sections of city newspapers.

WAGNER, PITTSBURG

First packaged in cigarette packs in the late 1880s, baseball cards reflected the surging popularity of the "National Game." Baseball cards allowed young fans, who might never be able to attend a major league game, to see what their heroes looked like.

Professional teams built large ball parks in cities where crowds became so great that brick and steel facilities soon replaced rickety wooden structures. Baseball helped to create a sense of community in diverse and fragmented cities as hordes of fanatical followers, rich and poor, native-born and immigrant, men and women, cheered on their hometown teams.

Some of the greatest players in the history of the game were born into immigrant families. The national pastime provided them an escape from industrial employment. The Pittsburgh Pirates' **Honus Wagner**, the son of German immigrants, toiled in Pittsburgh-area's steel mills before beginning his professional career in 1897. **Napoleon "Nap" Lajoie**, the youngest son of French-Canadian immigrants, labored in Woonsocket, Rhode Island's, textile mills, before signing with the Philadelphia Phillies in 1896. "The National Game" was not immune from racial prejudice. When some white players, most famously the Chicago White Stockings' "Cap" Anson, refused to compete with blacks, team owners concurred, effecting a "gentleman's agreement" that barred blacks from major league baseball until 1947. During that time, teams were strictly segregated by race. Beginning in the 1880s, African Americans formed their own separate professional leagues, with teams in major cities, such as the Cuban Giants (New York) and the St. Louis Black Stockings.

Participatory sports also flourished. Beginning in the 1890s, towns and cities seemed to explode with physical activity. Bicycling became a national craze. Men and women joined hiking and camping clubs. The sports and recreation craze was part of a larger reaction to the regimentation of urban-industrial society. Americans had learned to conform to the discipline of the time clock and to working indoors, whether in an office or factory, but many bridled at the costs. Middle-class Americans, especially, felt constrained by their dull daily routines and strict notions of respectability.

Middle-class men especially worried that city life and white collar office work had made them "soft" and unmanly and soon vaunted a masculinity that stressed physical prowess and vigorous activity that became known as "strenuosity." Among the most forceful evangelists for the strenuous life was Theodore Roosevelt, who linked the nation's progress and international prominence to physical prowess. Sickly as a child, Roosevelt took up boxing, wrestling, and horseback riding, spent time on the Dakota frontier, and fashioned himself into a living example of vital manhood, as a reform politician, war hero, and president. Men popularized the new and controversial sport of football, created on college campuses, playing in a violent, "manly" style, without helmets or pads.

Middle-class women embraced an even more radical ideal: "the New Woman." Breaking away from the restrictive ideal of the fragile homebody, the new woman discarded her confining corset, took up bicycling, tennis, and the newly invented game, basketball, first played in 1891 at the YMCA in Springfield, Massachusetts. She regularly participated in vigorous physical activity beside her male counterparts. Outdoor clubs, such as the Sierra Club, attracted large numbers of women who hiked, camped, and climbed mountains. Vigorous physical activity among women drew criticism from numerous physicians who feared that such "unnatural" activity would damage their reproductive organs.

A World of Crises

While cities embodied opportunity and energy, they roiled with crises. Not only were cities disorderly and dirty, they were also dangerous and violent. Most lacked adequate police protection and crime rates soared. Ease of access to saloons, gambling dens, and prostitution coupled with the anonymity of city life, many believed, led to moral decline. Social bonds seemed to fragment, as men and women left the countryside and close-knit villages to live among strangers, many of whom came from faraway places and spoke foreign languages.

Cities struggled to house the flood of new arrivals. Indeed, the housing shortage emerged as one of the greatest urban crises. Although tenements mushroomed and could house from 16 to 24 families, and single-family homes were subdivided, there were simply not enough rooms to go around. Population densities in major cities reached alarming proportions, creating health and safety hazards. Landlords did little to maintain property, and inner-city housing deteriorated into slums. Untouched by the technological advances enjoyed by the middle class, the poor crowded in tenements without indoor plumbing, running water, or electric lights.

Overcrowded cities offered few social services to the poor immigrants who desperately needed them. This void was often filled by political machines, headed by "bosses" who traded goods and services for votes. Highly disciplined, political machines curried loyal voters by distributing everything from jobs to Christmas turkeys. Journalist **William L. Riordon** explained the role of the "ward boss," in charge of getting out the vote for the machine: "Everybody in the district knows him, and nearly everybody goes to him for assistance of one sort or another, especially in the poor tenements."

But political machines often seemed more interested in lining their pockets than improving the lives of those who elected them. As a result, many cities were

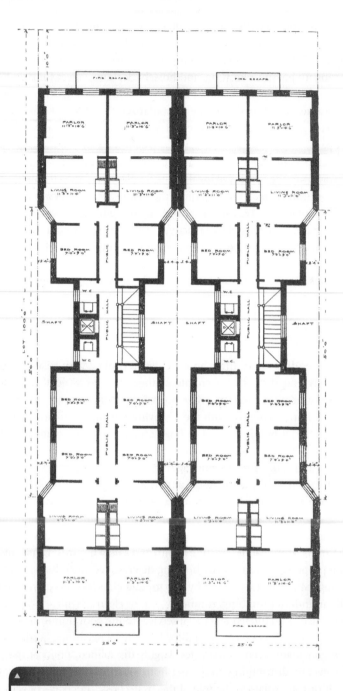

Introduced in 1879 as a housing reform, the dumb-bell tenement offered courtyards and more ventilation than tenements built side by side. Dumb-bell tenements sprung up across the urban landscape as cheap, multifamily housing. But occupants still had to endure dark, tiny rooms and ventilation remained inadequate.

badly governed. Contracts for urban services, from streetcars to garbage disposal, often went to those willing to provide the largest kickback. Bosses cemented loyalty by dispensing secure and well-paying political jobs, filling city positions with incompetent and corrupt supporters. Patronage was the lifeblood of Gilded Age politics. One Chicago alderman bragged that he dispensed 2,000 jobs to loyalists in his ward alone. To numerous concerned citizens, the political machine epitomized the chief obstacle to creating livable cities. New York City's infamous Tammany Hall, the Democratic political machine established before the Civil War and headed by William M. "Boss" Tweed, epitomized political corruption. Tweed and his cronies stole between $50 million and $200 million dollars from New York City taxpayers, through kickbacks and other schemes.

Primitive municipal services, such as impure water supplies and lack of sewage systems, made cities cauldrons of disease. For years, Chicago's sewage system consisted of simply dumping waste into Lake Michigan even though the lake doubled as the source of the city's drinking water. While both water and sewage treatment facilities improved overall, cities remained polluted, hazardous environments.

STUDY QUESTIONS FOR THE PROMISE AND PERIL OF CITY LIFE

1. What new entertainments emerged in cities? In what ways did these new pastimes unite diverse urban dwellers? How did they divide city residents?
2. What were the chief problems urban dwellers faced?

TACKLING URBAN PROBLEMS

As cities expanded, concerned citizens around the world shared their ideas about how to attack unprecedented poverty, slums, disease, and social fragmentation. Transatlantic conversations and experiences would, by the turn of the 20th century, gel into progressive politics and social reform movements in both the United States and around the world. As our opening story of the Salvation Army indicates, people, ideas, and strategies flowed back and forth across the Atlantic in the late 19th century as reformers set about attacking the problems generated by the rise of the city internationally.

Reformers struggled to find solutions to the overwhelming problems faced by urban dwellers. Some reformers focused on trying to dilute what they considered the "foreign" influence of Roman Catholicism by saving souls and redeeming cities through Protestant moral instruction. Others sought to bridge the widening chasm between rich and poor, native born and immigrant, and still others stressed creating healthy environments. Whatever their approach, all reformers struggled with much larger questions: What was the best way to eliminate poverty and human misery? Could reforms forge a strong, united America from the diverse, foreign, and impersonal elements of city life?

City Missions and Charity Organizations

Minister Josiah Strong articulated a call to arms against the evils of the city in several widely circulated books in which he labeled the city "a serious menace to our civilization," to which Protestant Christians needed to bring salvation. Protestant ministers, journalists, and politicians around the nation repeated his rallying cry, which served as the cornerstone of the **Social Gospel** movement. Broad, multidimensional, and international, the Social Gospel insisted that Christian principles be applied to social problems. Reformers dove into the heart of America's cities with the goal of not only alleviating social problems but also saving society's soul.

The Salvation Army was only one of a number of Protestant organizations that attacked "the devil" in America's cities and aimed to blunt the influence of Roman Catholicism by creating city missions. Scores of Protestant reformers established numerous organizations and institutions to save the soul of the city and ultimately the nation. Along with city missions, which like those of the Salvation Army, featured lively preaching and music to save souls, they established homes to reform prostitutes, and shelters for street children. Business interests, fearful of potential revolution among the impoverished, contributed generous financial support.

While providing much-needed aid to the impoverished, city missions generally failed to convert immigrants to Protestantism. Neither the Salvation Army nor denominational missions managed to blunt the influence of "Romanism." After several decades of mission work, the American Home Missionary Society reported little progress: "The hostile forces that threaten the future of America" remained "intrenched behind miles of tenement blocks."

Just as the city mission movement gained inspiration from abroad, through the Salvation Army, so did the charity organization movement. Another approach to the problems of city life, this movement attacked social ills by emphasizing the moral rehabilitation of the poor, rather than their conversion to a particular sect. England again provided the model, having established the London Society for Organized Charitable Relief and Mendicity in 1869. A veteran of London's charitable work, Anglican clergyman **S. Humphreys Gurteen** founded the nation's first organized charity in Buffalo in 1877. Horrified by the violence of the Great Railroad Strike, Gurteen transplanted this new approach in the United States. By the 1890s, charity organizations mushroomed in American cities.

But charity organizations worked under several assumptions that blunted their effectiveness. Disregarding the harsh consequences of industrial capitalism, these groups viewed poverty as moral failure: The poor, they believed, bore responsibility for their condition; character defects, they believed, drove people into poverty. Fearful of creating dependency, charity organizations aided only those who they deemed worthy of their help. As a result, charity workers, usually middle-class women, regularly investigated families to discern their worthiness. "Friendly visitors," as they called themselves, also met with their charges to uplift them by modeling moral behavior. Not surprisingly, invasions of privacy and condescension did little to build the "neighborly" bonds that visitors hoped to create.

The Settlement House Movement

An alternative and far more sympathetic approach to solving the problems of poor city dwellers also originated in England: the Settlement House Movement. In 1884, social reformer **Samuel Barnett** established Toynbee Hall amidst the slums of London's East End. The settlement house aimed to create a place where both well-to-do and working classes could live together, bridging the gap between rich and poor to connect fragmented social classes into a unified community. The more fortunate could offer guidance and educational programs to the less fortunate.

After witnessing the "hideous human suffering" of London's poor on a tour of Europe in the early 1880s, Illinois native **Jane Addams** returned to London and worked at Toynbee Hall. Inspired by her stay, Addams returned to the United States and with her friend **Ellen Starr** purchased a dilapidated mansion in a run-down section of Chicago. There, in 1889, they established Hull House, one of the nation's first settlement houses. By 1900, the number of settlement houses in U.S. cities reached approximately 100.

At first Addams and her fellow settlement workers suffered from the same sense of superiority that infected charity workers: they would uplift immigrants through their example. But immigrant women soon made it clear that they needed much more practical assistance, particularly a kindergarten and nursery school for their children. Rather than condemn immigrant culture as alien and something to be eliminated, Addams and her fellow workers encouraged pride in traditional culture while smoothing the transition to American life. Hull House eventually offered a variety of programs, including sewing and cooking classes, clubs for children, and lectures by university professors.

Hull House and the settlement house movement represented another dimension of the Social Gospel. To live among the poor and share their lives, Addams asserted, expressed "the spirit of Christ" and represented a

▲ Jane Addams (1860–1935) summarized the purpose of the settlement house: "to aid in the solution of the social and industrial problems . . . engendered by the modern conditions of life in a great city. It is the attempt to relieve, at the same time, the overaccumulation at one end of society and the destitution at the other."

"renaissance in Christianity." Moreover the settlement house provided another anti-dote to the problem of urban fragmentation as well as a means to instill democracy among immigrants.

The settlement house not only shaped the lives of its neighbors, it also trans-formed the lives of Addams and the many single, educated, middle-class women who worked with her. A college graduate, Addams had struggled against a feeling of "use-lessness" and "futility" to find a place in Gilded Age society and meaningful work. She, and many women like her, found it in the settlement house movement.

Creating Healthy Urban Environments

Living among the poor, settlement house workers and other reformers began to see the negative effects of a destructive environment. Rather than blaming the poor for their own problems, they concluded that the environment in which people lived shaped their lives. Poverty and its consequences were not moral failures but social ones.

Journalist **Jacob Riis** played a key role in an environmental approach to social reform. An immigrant himself, Riis empathized with the city's poor in ways that few others did. He explored and wrote about the underside of New York City: a world of saloons, gambling dens, brothels, overcrowded and filthy tenements, and swarms of street children. He soon began snapping photographs to document the lives of the "other half," a side of the city rarely glimpsed by the more fortunate, capturing startling images of street urchins and sweatshop workers. In 1890, Riis published his

Street Arabs in Sleeping Quarters, c.1880. This photograph, taken by reformer Jacob Riis and included in *How the Other Half Lives*, shows children sleeping on a steam grate for warmth. Images like these shocked Riis's middle-class audience and proved to be a powerful weapon for social reform.

findings in *How the Other Half Lives: Studies Among the Tenements of New York,* which proved to be a powerful weapon for social reform. Through his efforts some of New York's worst tenements were destroyed and child labor laws more effectively enforced.

Other reformers targeted the saloon as the source of society's ills. With roots in the antebellum era, the movement to curb and end alcohol consumption gained considerable momentum with the increase in immigration and the arrival of large numbers of Roman Catholics. "Rum and Romanism" had long been linked in the minds of American Protestants. In addition, alcohol consumption, high throughout the 19th century, spiked in the Gilded Age. "Antis" argued that alcohol was the root cause of many social problems, such as poverty, domestic violence, and crime.

Middle-class women played a leading role in the fight against the saloon, embracing the cause as a defense of the home. They boldly entered saloons—all-male bastions—dropped to their knees, and prayed for the souls of offending drinkers, trying to persuade them to give up "demon rum." But they soon turned from moral suasion to politics to make real change. Unable to vote, prohibitionist women nevertheless did what they could to influence local elections to ban liquor licenses.

Political involvement in temperance and prohibitionist organizations also led many women to fight for the right to vote, to extend their moral authority into the political arena. Under the leadership of **Frances Willard**, the **Women's Christian Temperance Union** (WCTU), formed in 1874, one of the nation's largest women's organizations, began to advocate for suffrage by 1879. As Willard explained, "the mothers and daughters of America" had a right to voice their opinion on whether "the door of the rum shop is opened or shut beside their homes."

Like many reforms of the era, temperance and prohibition was an international movement. In 1884, Willard initiated a campaign to ban drinking around the world and dispatched WCTU missionaries who collected a million names, representing 50 countries, on petitions calling for an end to the saloon. In 1891, the WCTU convened a world conference in Boston with delegates from around the globe.

STUDY QUESTIONS FOR TACKLING URBAN PROBLEMS

1. Describe the different approaches reformers took to address urban problems. Where did they agree? Disagree?
2. What were the main obstacles to urban reform?

CHALLENGES TO THE POLITICS OF STALEMATE

Social and economic crises in the late 19th century cried out for political solutions. But after closely observing American politics, British writer Lord James Bryce concluded that neither the Republican nor Democratic party "has anything definite to say" on the issues of the day; "neither party has any principles, any distinctive tenets. . . . All has been lost, except office or the hope of it."

Had Bryce queried Gilded Age voters, they would have violently disagreed with his assessment. They were obsessed with politics. Not only did the two major parties, as they had before the Civil War, continue to distinguish themselves in terms of economic policy and the role of government, they garnered enough rabid support to foster the highest voter turnout in the nation's history.

At the same time, national politics in the late 19th century, as Bryce suggested, accomplished little of substance. Because the parties were so evenly matched, neither party risked upsetting the precarious balance with innovative or controversial legislation, despite the multitude of challenges that the nation faced. Holding on to office, not reform, remained the main focus of politicians.

But by the 1890s, the **People's (Populist) Party**, largely made up of farmers, formed one of the largest third-party movements in American history and challenged the politics of stalemate. Populists helped set the stage for the decisive presidential election of 1896, which in many ways embodied the conflict between older rural America and the rapidly urbanizing nation. The nation stood at a crossroads: would it embrace its traditional rural roots or a modern, urban, industrial future?

Key Issues

Tariffs may hardly seem like the subject of passionate partisan politics, but to Gilded Age voters, the tariff was central to national political debate and concretely defined party differences. Republicans supported the protective tariff—a tax on imported goods—to promote American industry and agriculture. Placing a tariff on British steel, for example, increased its cost, making it more likely that American builders would purchase American-made steel, helping guarantee the expansion of the industry and its labor force. By contrast, Democrats insisted that the protective tariff ultimately raised prices and hurt consumers. Republicans continued to embrace the nationalist vision of the Civil War, and advocated using the power of the federal government to promote economic growth, whereas Democrats remained committed to limited government and states' rights.

The currency issue also loomed large in Gilded Age politics. Beginning in 1873, the little-noticed **Coinage Act** made gold the nation's monetary standard. Before this time, both gold and silver had been part of the money supply. But the population exploded in the late 19th century as the money supply remained the same, increasing the value of the dollar, and tightening the amount of money available for credit. For those in debt, especially farmers who regularly relied on credit to plant their crops, the monetary situation created a crisis. Some Democrats, and later Populists (see below) saw a massive conspiracy in the Coinage Act, and began to advocate the coinage of silver to put more money into circulation, make more credit available, and create inflation, which would increase the price that farmers got for their agricultural products. Republicans, however, insisted on maintaining "sound money," backed with gold.

A third issue also emerged in the national political arena: civil service reform. While political patronage was nothing new, it reached unprecedented levels of corruption in the late 19th century, adding to the ineffectiveness of government. Reformers in both parties began to call for replacing incompetent party hacks with a professional work-force who would do the work of government. After crazed office seeker Charles Guiteau assassinated President **James Garfield** in 1881, Congress finally took action, passing the **Pendleton Civil Service Act** in 1883. The act established the modern civil service and initiated an examination for a classified list of federal jobs. The Pendleton Act elimi-nated some incompetence and corruption, but it barely made a dent in federal patron-age as more jobs kept being added. In 1900, the federal government still offered the same number of patronage jobs as it had in 1883, the year the law was passed.

Ethnicity, Gender, and Political Culture

The Republican and Democratic parties generally drew their followers from different ethnic and religious backgrounds. Republicans tended to be Protestant and native born, although the party also attracted evangelical German and Scandinavian immi-grants. Before disfranchisement in the South, beginning in 1890, African American vot-ers remained loyal Republicans. Advocating the use of government to compel "moral" behavior, Republicans often supported temperance and prohibition. Democrats, on the other hand, rejected the coercive use of government, placing more emphasis on individual freedom. Democrats, through their Irish-dominated city machines, contin-ued to draw Roman Catholic immigrants to their party. In addition, the Democratic Party retained its stronghold in the white South as the party of white supremacy.

Political parties fomented enthusiasm and loyalty through elaborate rituals and social events. Political participation provided a way for men to demonstrate their masculinity and the male ideals of loyalty, courage, and independence. Election cam-paigns were characterized as "wars" and "battles" with voters as foot soldiers loyally supporting their party's candidate. Above all party politics remained a male domain—even as some women began to demand the right to vote—and political participation a way to prove one's masculinity.

Political parties bonded men of different classes and ethnicities. Political ma-chines also aided immigrant males by incorporating them into the political system. They inculcated party loyalty along with civic education, and male bonding through rituals, such as partisan parades and speeches. Party loyalties and effective party orga-nizations help account for massive voter turnout in this era. In 1896, for example, 80 percent of the eligible male electorate voted in the presidential election. Similar high rates occurred in state and local elections.

For most of the late 19th century, voters were almost evenly split between the two parties. Between 1875 and 1897, Republican presidents dominated, but elections were close with Democratic presidential candidates receiving the popular vote in four of five elections. Congress remained almost evenly divided with Democrats generally controlling the House and Republicans the Senate. With such a precarious balance, party leaders refused to risk alienating any of their voters, and this conservative ap-proach snuffed out the passage of ground-breaking legislation.

The Depression of the 1890s ultimately dismantled the politics of stalemate. Soon after President Grover Cleveland, a Democrat, began his second term in 1893, economic panic, fueled by rampant speculation and unregulated markets, plunged the nation into a four year depression. Although the crisis had deep and complex roots, Cleveland and the Democrats bore the blame. In 1894, the Democrats lost 113 seats in Congress as the Republicans gained 117, the largest transfer of power in Congressional history to this day. Two years later, in 1896, the voters elected **William McKinley** president, ushering in an era of Republican dominance that, with the exception of Woodrow Wilson's two terms, would not be substantially broken until Franklin D. Roosevelt's election in 1932.

The Populist Challenge

To capture the presidency in 1896, McKinley had to fight off one of the largest democratic movements in U.S. history. The presidential election of 1896 saw the zenith of a major third-party movement, the People's (Populist) Party. Many Americans criticized the injustices and corruption of Gilded Age America. But the most thorough program for reform came not from cities but from the countryside, not from labor radicals or middle-class reformers but from farmers, often considered to be among the most conservative Americans.

Once the backbone of the nation, farmers found themselves in the midst of decline, unable to reap the economic abundance enjoyed by many in the Gilded Age. They felt exploited by bankers, who charged them high interest rates on the money they borrowed every year to plant their crops; by railroads, who set exorbitant freight rates to carry their goods to market; and by "middlemen" who reaped large profits from the crops that they marketed, while farmers fell deeper into debt and poverty, with many losing their land in foreclosure. They demanded that federal and state government intervene to ensure "equal rights to all, special privileges to none."

TIMELINE 1873–1901

1873

February 12 Congress passes the Coinage Act, establishing the gold standard for currency

1874

November 20 The Women's Christian Temperance Union (WCTU) founded

1876

February 2 Baseball's National League formed, the sport's first "major league"

1877

December Clergyman S. Humphreys Gurteen founds the nation's first organized charity in Buffalo, NY

1879

October Frances Willard elected president of the Women's Christian Temperance Union, and leads organization to fight for woman suffrage

1880

New York City becomes first American city to reach a population of one million

March 10 The Salvation Army arrives in New York City and soon establishes city missions throughout the United States

1881

March 13 The assassination of Russian Czar Alexander II sets off pogroms aimed at Jewish settlements,

spurring immigration to the United States

September 19 President James A. Garfield, shot in July by frustrated office seeker, Charles Guiteau, dies

1882

May 6 United States enacts the Chinese Exclusion Act

1883

January 16 Congress passes the Pendleton Civil Service Act

1884

December 24 Social reformer Samuel Barnett establishes the first settlement house, Toynbee Hall, in the slums of London's East End

1885

July 20 Canada restricts Chinese immigration by requiring a $50 head tax

Fall The nation's first skyscraper, 10-story Home Insurance Building, completed in Chicago

Fall Congregational minister Josiah Strong publishes *Our Country: Its Possible Future and Its Present Crisis*

1887

March 13 The anti-immigrant American Protective Association founded

1888

February 2 The nation's first electric streetcar is

The **Farmers' Alliance** provided the foundation for what would become the Populist Party. Quickly attracting an enthusiastic following of farm men and women in the South and West eager to halt their worsening economic condition, the nonpartisan organization soon realized its political clout. By the 1890s Alliance men dominated eight state legislatures and helped elect four governors and numerous congressmen. "Farmers' legislatures" passed numerous reforms, including legislation aimed at regulating railroads more stringently.

Frustrated with the unresponsiveness of the two major parties, which remained indifferent to their pressing needs, some Alliance members decided to form a third party, the People's (Populist) Party. First appearing in the West in 1890, a national Populist Party burst onto the national political stage two years later. In 1892, the Populists devised a national platform in Omaha and nominated their first presidential candidate, **James B. Weaver** of Iowa.

The party's Omaha Platform provided an eloquent and powerful critique of Gilded Age America. "[W]e meet in the midst of a nation brought to the verge of moral, political, and material ruin," the platform's preamble explained, a nation tainted by corruption at every level. The United States had been reduced to "two great classes—tramps and millionaires." The Omaha Platform laid out a series of solutions that included government ownership of railroads, telegraph and telephone systems; and the free and unlimited coinage of silver, which, they believed would expand credit and increase the price of their crops. They also proposed subtreasuries to store crops and advance loans to farmers so that they could wait for optimal market conditions to sell their crops. In addition, Populists endorsed the direct election of senators, a graduated income tax, and protection of labor unions.

Dismissed as "cranks" and wild-eyed crazies by newspapers such as the *New York Times*, the Populist Party was blessed with colorful, passionate, plain-speaking

---

introduced in Richmond, Virginia

October A team of National League All-Stars departs on a six-month world tour to introduce baseball, and expand American influence, around the world.

1889

September 18 Jane Addams and Ellen Starr open the doors of Hull House, the nation's first settlement house, in Chicago

1890

Chicago and Philadelphia reach the 1 million population mark

Jacob Riis publishes *How the Other Half Lives: Studies Among the Tenements of New York*

1891

December Basketball, invented by Dr. James Naismith in Springfield, Massachusetts, first played

November WCTU holds international conference, with delegates from around the world, in Boston

1892

July People's (Populist) Party holds its first national convention in Omaha, NE

November Democrat Grover Cleveland defeats Republican incumbent Benjamin Harrison and Populist James B. Weaver for the presidency

1894

May Immigration Restriction League is founded in Boston

1897

March Immigration Restriction Bill passed by Congress is vetoed by President Grover Cleveland

November Republican William McKinley defeats Democratic and Populist candidate

William Jennings Bryan for President

September 1 The first subway in the United States opens in Boston

1901

January 28 Professional baseball's American League organized

December 25 Australia curbs Asian immigration by requiring European language literacy test

leaders, such as Kansan **Mary Elizabeth Lease**, who demanded that farmers "raise less corn and more hell." Despite widespread criticism in the press, dominated by the two major parties, the Populists still garnered a million popular votes and 22 electoral votes for their presidential candidate. Democrat Grover Cleveland emerged as the victor in the election, defeating incumbent Republican Benjamin Harrison for the presidency.

Between 1893 and 1896, as the nation plunged into economic depression, the People's party continued to make gains especially in state legislatures where they instituted a number of significant reforms, including rewriting state election laws to make voting more democratic; setting limits on interest rates; and increasing funding for schools, state institutions, and prisons.

The Election of 1896

Massive unemployment, bank failures, and countless mortgage foreclosures set the stage for the crucial presidential election of 1896. The Populists seemed well positioned to attract the votes of desperate and frustrated Americans. The Democratic Party nominated **William Jennings Bryan** of Nebraska for the presidency. Sympathetic to the plight of farmers, Bryan won the nomination after he electrified the party convention with a speech that became known as "The Cross of Gold Speech." Bryan advocated the free coinage of silver and condemned the gold standard: "You shall not press down upon the brow of labor this crown of thorns, you shall not crucify mankind upon a cross of gold." His speech also stressed the central role of the nation's farmers to the rapidly urbanizing nation. "Burn down your cities and leave our farms," he cried, "and your cities will spring up again as if by magic; but destroy our farms and the grass will grow in the streets of every city in the country." The Populists decided to cast their lot with Democrat Bryan and endorsed his candidacy. At the same time, they nominated their own vice-presidential candidate, Tom Watson of Georgia.

The 1896 election, in the words of Kansas journalist William Allen White, "took the form of religious frenzy." The future of the nation seemed to hang in the balance, with Democrat/Populist Bryan representing an older, rural America and McKinley the emerging urban, industrial nation. Bryan crisscrossed the country in the first truly modern presidential campaign, taking his message to the people by logging 18,000 miles by train, and giving 600 speeches—sometimes as many as 20 a day—filled with religious imagery and evangelical zeal. By contrast, Republican candidate William McKinley, dubbed by his party as "the Advance Agent of Prosperity," remained rooted to his Canton, Ohio, home where he conducted a "front porch campaign" in which he spoke with various visiting delegations. McKinley promised the American worker "a full dinner pail," through economic stability and prosperity and labeled Bryan's silverite schemes an economic disaster. Backed by big business—banks, businessmen, and industrialists—McKinley and the Republicans

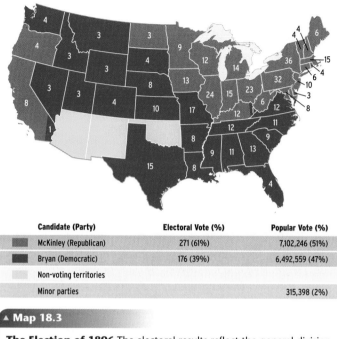

Candidate (Party)	Electoral Vote (%)	Popular Vote (%)
McKinley (Republican)	271 (61%)	7,102,246 (51%)
Bryan (Democratic)	176 (39%)	6,492,559 (47%)
Non-voting territories		
Minor parties		315,398 (2%)

▲ **Map 18.3**

The Election of 1896 The electoral results reflect the general division between industrial/urban America, carried by McKinley, along with several key agricultural states, and rural America, which supported Bryan.

spent as much as $7 million on the campaign, with at least $250,000 contributed by **John D. Rockefeller**'s Standard Oil Company.

McKinley handily defeated Bryan in the most decisive presidential election since 1872, a clear sign of the end of political deadlock. While McKinley polled only half a million votes more than Bryan (7 million to 6.5 million), he swamped Bryan in the electoral college, 271 to 176 (Map 18.3). The Populist party managed to survive Bryan's crushing defeat but only as a shadow of its former self. Despite its ultimate demise, many reforms the party advocated—and critics rejected as too radical in the 1890s—were taken up by progressive reformers in the early 20th century. The fundamental Populist demand that the federal government intervene on behalf of the people to offset powerful corporate interests would be echoed by progressives within the next 10 years. In addition, specific reforms advocated by the Populists, such as the graduated income tax and direct election of senators, would be enacted within the next 20 years. But the defeat and the demise of the farmer's party, despite the party's innovative and progressive reforms, symbolized, in a powerful way, the ultimate eclipse of the countryside by urban, industrial America.

STUDY QUESTIONS FOR CHALLENGES TO THE POLITICS OF STALEMATE

1. What were the chief differences between Democrats, Republicans, and Populists?
2. What does the story of the People's Party suggest about the difficulties that third parties face in mounting a challenge to the two-party system?

Summary

- Urbanization was a hallmark of the late 19th century, in both the United States and other industrializing nations. A consequence of massive internal and global migrations, the rapid growth of cities reconfigured the landscape and reshaped society and culture. Cities grew both horizontally and vertically and became increasingly segregated and fragmented by class, race, and ethnicity.

- Immigration, a global phenomenon, greatly contributed to America's urbanization. Between 1870 and 1900, "America fever" brought approximately 11 million immigrants to the United States and an additional 13 million entered the country between 1900 and 1914. About one-third of immigrants to the United States returned permanently to their countries of origin. The "new" immigrants faced severe challenges not only in the re-emergence of nativism, but also in their adjustment to the harsh demands of the industrial order. Building strong communities, with churches and mutual aid societies as cornerstones, helped immigrants adjust to life in the United States.

- The nation's Gilded Age cities were studies in contrasts, encompassing great wealth and extreme poverty, decay and innovation, ugliness and beauty. Rapid urbanization spawned a multitude of crises, which included inadequate housing, primitive municipal services, and corrupt city government. At the same time, cities teemed with opportunity, offering new forms of culture, entertainment, and consumer activities. Social reformers, most of whom were native-born Protestants, were part of a transatlantic community of urban reformers, who shared a variety of ideas and strategies in attacking the problems of the city.

- For most of the Gilded Age, national politics was gridlocked, with the two major parties, Democrats and Republicans, evenly matched. Despite the many problems facing the nation, the parties feared upsetting the precarious balance, so little was accomplished on the national level. But party politics nevertheless engendered the rabid support of male voters, and Gilded Age elections saw the highest voter turnout in the nation's history. The Depression of the 1890s helped break the Gilded Age stalemate and by 1896, the People's (Populist) Party mounted a major challenge to the two-party system.

Key Terms and People

Addams, Jane *709*

American Protective Association
(APA) *693*

Barnett, Samuel *709*

Bryan, William Jennings *716*

Cleveland, Grover *694*

Coinage Act *712*

Farmers' Alliance *715*

Garfield, James *713*

Gurteen, S. Humphreys *708*

Immigration Restriction League *693*

Lajoie, Napoleon "Nap" *704*

Lease, Mary Elizabeth *716*

McKinley, William *714*

nativism *693*

Pendleton Civil Service Act *713*

People's (Populist) Party *712*

Riis, Jacob *710*

Riordon, William L. *705*

Rockefeller, John D. *716*

Social Gospel *708*

Starr, Ellen *709*

tariff *712*

Wagner, Honus *704*

Weaver, James B. *715*

Wells, H.G. *702*

White, William Allen *716*

Willard, Frances *711*

Women's Christian Temperance
Union (WCTU) *711*

Reviewing Chapter 18

1. How did immigrants, urban reformers, and Populists address the challenges posed by urbanization and immigration?
2. Which approaches were most successful in your opinion? Why?

Further Reading

Barth, Gunther Paul. *City People: The Rise of Modern City Culture in Nineteenth-Century America.* New York: Oxford University Press, 1980. An exploration of the new culture that emerge in American cities and how urban culture transformed the countryside as well.

Gabaccia, Donna, *Immigration and American Diversity: A Social and Cultural History.* Malden, Mass: Blackwell Publishers, Inc., 2002. A valuable, fresh overview of immigration that explores issues such as individual identities, ethnic group formations, and interactions between immigrants and the native-born.

McMath, Robert C., Jr. *American Populism: A Social History, 1877–1898.* New York: Hill and Wang, 1993. An easy-to-read, accessible volume on the often complex story of the Farmers' Alliance and the Populist Party.

Warner, Sam Bass, Jr. *The Urban Wilderness: A History of the American City.* Berkeley: University of California Press, 1995. This classic work places the Gilded Age city within the larger context of urban development.

Wyman, Mark. *Round-Trip to America: The Immigrants Return to Europe, 1880–1930.* Ithaca, NY: Cornell University Press, 1996. Explores the return-migration of "new" immigrants and the many consequences of their temporary stay in the United States, including the ideas and goods that they took back with them to Europe.

Visual Review

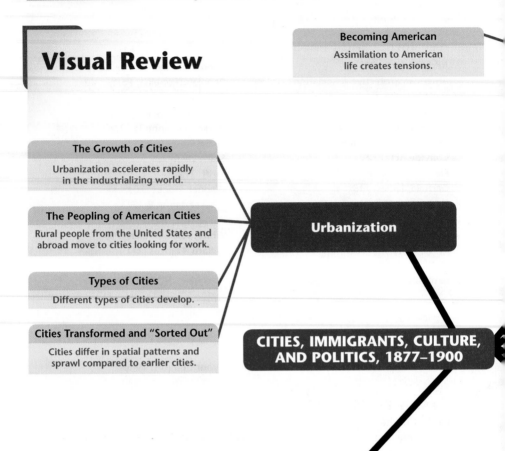

Becoming American

Assimilation to American life creates tensions.

The Growth of Cities

Urbanization accelerates rapidly in the industrializing world.

The Peopling of American Cities

Rural people from the United States and abroad move to cities looking for work.

Types of Cities

Different types of cities develop.

Cities Transformed and "Sorted Out"

Cities differ in spatial patterns and sprawl compared to earlier cities.

Urbanization

CITIES, IMMIGRANTS, CULTURE, AND POLITICS, 1877–1900

Global Migrations

A Worldwide Migration

Cities around the world attract numerous migrating people.

"America Fever" and the "New" Immigration

Numerous immigrants from southern and eastern Europe come to the United States for the first time.

The "Immigrant Problem"

Nativism increases with the new wave of immigration.

The Round-Trip to America

Many immigrants come to America for work and then return home.

Streets Paved with Gold?

Surviving in "The Land of Bosses and Clocks"

European immigrants work in dangerous and demanding jobs and create strategies for survival.

Creating Community

Immigrants create their own ethnic communities and support systems.

The Promise and Peril of City Life

A World of Opportunity

Cities offer new opportunities for goods and leisure.

A World of Crises

Cities are dirty, crime ridden, and corrupt.

Tackling Urban Problems

City Missions and Charity Organizations

Organizations form to aid the impoverished.

The Settlement House Movement

Settlement houses are created to aid immigrants and address urban ills.

Creating Healthy Urban Environments

Reformers stress healthy environments to solve social problems.

Challenges to the Politics of Stalemate

Key Issues

Key issues shape the political debate: tariffs, currency, and civil service reform.

The Populist Challenge

Farmers build a third party to challenge corruption and political stalemate.

Ethnicity, Gender, and Political Culture

Political parties differ by class and ethnicity and promote masculine ideals.

The Election of 1896

William McKinley defeats William Jennings Bryan, resulting in the demise of the Populists.

19

The United States Expands Its Reach

1892–1912

I n 1904, roughly 20 million people visited the St. Louis World's Fair commemorating the centennial of the Louisiana Purchase. Showcasing progress in the United States and abroad, the fair featured the latest technology and carnival rides, and visitors feasted on ice cream cones—first introduced there. But the most popular question asked of fair guides, reported the *New York Times*, was "Which way to the Philippines?"

The federal government, with the aid of a team of anthropologists, spent $1 million to construct a "Philippines Reservation" at the fair. A living exhibit, the reservation featured 1,200 Filipinos living in native "villages." The United States had taken possession of the Philippines in the Spanish-American-Philippine War of 1898; after heated debate, American leaders decided to make the islands a colony. Occupation of the Philippines triggered a bloody war for independence, which, for the most part, the United States had suppressed by the time of the fair. But the brutal war only strengthened criticism of colonization. The exhibit, officials believed, offered an excellent opportunity to introduce the Filipino people to the public and help make the case for empire.

Reflecting the racialist thinking of the era, the exhibit showcased a range of Filipinos. Anthropologists arranged them from the most "primitive"—the dark-skinned "negritos"—to the most "advanced"—the Filipino constables who kept order at the exhibit, those "uplifted" by American tutelage. But the "wild savages" attracted the most attention. The Negritos demonstrated their skills with bows and poisoned arrows. The Igorots, another "primitive" group,

Encouraging the Child by Udo Keppler, 1901

CHAPTER OUTLINE

THE NEW IMPERIALISM
> A Global Grab for Colonies
> Race, Empire, Bibles, and Businessmen
> Precedent for American Empire
> The Crises of the 1890s

THE UNITED STATES FLEXES ITS MUSCLES
> Latin America
> Hawaii
> The Cuban Crisis
> "A Splendid Little War"

THE COMPLICATIONS OF EMPIRE
> Cuba and Puerto Rico
> The Philippines
> The Debate Over Empire
> The American-Philippine War
> China

THE UNITED STATES ON THE WORLD STAGE: ROOSEVELT AND TAFT
> Roosevelt's "Big Stick"
> Taft's Dollar Diplomacy

America in the World

The United States annexed the Republic of Hawaii (1898).

The United States built the Panama Canal, a major trade channel affecting world economies (1903–1914).

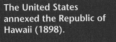 U.S. event that influenced the world

International event that influenced the United States

Event with multinational influence

Conflict

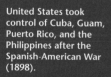

USS *Maine* exploded in Havana harbor; McKinley declared war on Spain (1898).

United States took control of Cuba, Guam, Puerto Rico, and the Philippines after the Spanish-American War (1898).

United States fights bloody war to suppress Philippine independence movement (1899–1902).

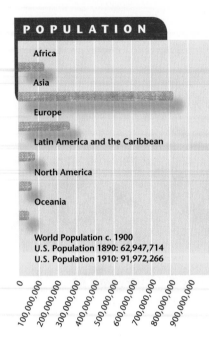

POPULATION

Africa

Asia

Europe

Latin America and the Caribbean

North America

Oceania

World Population c. 1900
U.S. Population 1890: 62,947,714
U.S. Population 1910: 91,972,266

0   100,000,000   200,000,000   300,000,000   400,000,000   500,000,000   600,000,000   700,000,000   800,000,000   900,000,000

excited the crowds with "war dances to the beat of the tom-tom." The exhibit asserted that the Igorots, like American Indians, could be civilized with education.

The Filipino exhibit did more than entertain and titillate the millions who visited it. (Their lack of clothing, for example, created a great deal of controversy). The federal government hoped that it would convince the public that keeping the islands rather than granting them their independence was the best choice. The "uncivilized" inhabitants, the exhibits architects claimed, offered proof that the Filipinos were simply incapable of self-rule; they needed the United States to educate, guide, and protect them.

The Philippines Exhibit reflected the new role of the United States as an imperial power and the conflicts over that role. Only a few years earlier the nation had stood at a crossroads. Should the United States take the path to empire, like other world powers? Or should it remain a true republic, unencumbered by colonies? By 1898, driven by the same commercial interests and quests for influence that drove other world powers into a scramble for colonies, the United States chose empire. But not all Americans felt comfortable with this new role. The exhibit raised troubling questions about colonization. Could the United States, which had fought for independence as a colony of Great Britain, be a colonial power itself without compromising its fundamental ideals? Moreover, had the nation, by stepping out so boldly on the world stage, committed itself to a future of global entanglements and wars, from which there would be no turning back?

THE NEW IMPERIALISM

In the last quarter of the 19th century, industrial capitalism spawned a new race for empire. For most of the century, through the 1870s, old European empires, established much earlier in the "new world," declined or disappeared. Revolutions had divested Great Britain, France, Portugal, and Spain of most or all of their colonies in the Americas. But in the last quarter of the 19th century industrial nations faced global economic depressions; the first occurred in the 1870s, and a second, even more severe depression, in the 1890s. Business leaders blamed overproduction for these economic convulsions. Industrial capitalism had produced a glut of goods that simply could not be absorbed in established markets. Finding new consumers in the world's untapped markets, they believed, would solve the problem. Colonies also bestowed prestige on

Living exhibits, such as the Philippine Reservation at the 1904 St. Louis World's Fair, helped popularize anthropological theories of racial hierarchy as well as justify imperialism.

imperial powers as well as access to raw materials. Africa, Asia, and the islands of the Pacific were the most sought-after prizes in the competition for colonies.

Racialist theories, propped up by new allegedly scientific claims of white intellectual and moral superiority over darker skinned peoples, provided ideological justification for colonization. Colonists also presented themselves as aiding and "uplifting" the uncivilized. Missionaries, intent in spreading the Christian Gospel abroad, often laid the groundwork for expansion, and businessmen and political leaders soon followed in their footsteps.

The United States, unlike European powers, did not have a long tradition of empire building. After all, the nation had been established by repudiating Great Britain's colonial claims. In the 19th century the political extension of the United States beyond its continental boundaries represented a new departure. But in many ways colonization abroad continued the federal government's policies of westward expansion within the continental United States and its conquest of indigenous peoples. Even as many Americans remained uneasy about the nation's scramble for empire abroad, a combination of crises in the 1890s—economic, social, political, and cultural—thrust the nation into the global scramble for empire.

A Global Grab for Colonies

Creating new consumers did not necessarily lead to colonization. The world's strongest industrial powers, particularly Great Britain and the United States, generally preferred "open door" policies. In other words, they asked only for unhindered access to markets where, they confidently believed, they could compete successfully against economic rivals. But weaker industrial nations preferred the security of colonies. Once nations began to stake colonial claims in less developed parts of the world, international rivalries soon pushed all industrialized nations into a scramble for empire. By 1899, even the United States, which had pursued a commercial empire with great success, followed its European rivals in creating formal colonies.

The untapped markets of Africa, Asia, and the Pacific, as well as their natural resources, loomed large in the eyes of expansionists. Factories required rubber, vegetable oils, and minerals such as copper. Beginning in the 1870s, and accelerating in the 1880s, European powers ruthlessly carved up most of Africa into colonies. In 1884–1885 they met in Berlin—without the presence of a single African nation—primarily to deal with rival claims in the Congo and Niger basins, but ultimately to divide much of the continent among themselves. Their actions set off decades of bloody wars to gain control of territories on the continent. Although not seeking land, U.S. representatives succeeded in getting a pledge from European powers for an "open door" to market goods in the Belgian Congo.

Imperialists found Asia even more alluring than Africa. European powers partitioned Southeast Asia, as they had Africa in the 1880s, with France acquiring Indochina (present-day Vietnam, Cambodia, and Laos) and Britain annexing Burma (present-day Myanmar). China, a weak nation at the time with 300 million people and potential consumers, would be the site of numerous conflicts among the rival world powers. European powers and Japan "carved the Chinese melon" into territorial slices of domination as the United States demanded fair access to the China market. In the 1880s and 1890s many Pacific islands found themselves annexed by Britain, Germany, and the United States, while Japan claimed parts of China, Russia, and Korea. Between 1876 and 1915 the world's powers, imposing colonialism around the globe, claimed roughly 25 percent of the world's lands and peoples (Map 19.1).

Race, Empire, Bibles, and Businessmen

As the Philippine Reservation at the St. Louis World's Fair reflected, notions of race provided justification for colonization. Social Darwinism, the theory that applied "survival of the fittest" to both individuals and nations, offered a powerful rationale for empire. The new discipline of anthropology also ranked the world's peoples in a hierarchy, from the uncivilized to the civilized, according to their stage of development.

New scientific theories found reinforcement in a growing faith in Anglo-Saxonism. As the United States and Great Britain emerged as the world's leading industrial powers, many began to believe that the English-speaking nations shared common racial characteristics that accounted for their preeminent world standing. Anglo-Saxons,

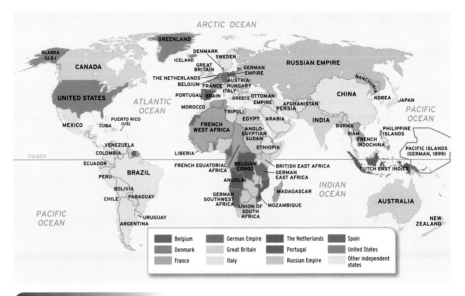

▲ **Map 19.1**

World Colonial Empires, 1900 A handful of world powers divided much of the globe among themselves. Between 1876 and 1915, Great Britain added 4 million square miles of land to its empire, Germany more than 1 million, and Belgium and Italy 1 million square miles each. The United States added 100,000 square miles, mostly from Spain in 1898.

they believed, possessed superior intelligence, were industrious, and had a special talent for spreading freedom and their advanced culture around the world. At the top of the racial and cultural hierarchy, Anglo-Saxons bore the responsibility, they believed, to "take up the white man's burden"—as the British poet **Rudyard Kipling** famously put it, to enlighten those who stood in darkness, to uplift "savage" and "backward" peoples who would gratefully submit to their leadership.

Congregational minister **Josiah Strong** emerged as the leading spokesman for Anglo-Saxonism in the United States and challenged Americans to take the lead in fulfilling their God-ordained mission to civilize and Christianize the world. He challenged them to "move down upon Mexico, down upon Central and South America, out upon the islands of the sea, over Africa and beyond." Notably, economic benefits were sure to follow: "Commerce follows the missionary."

Strong had plenty of proof for this assertion. Missionaries, along with traders and businessmen, served as the advance guard of Western influence throughout the world. They established informal empire, by both cultural infiltration and economic control. Intent on converting "heathen" peoples to Christianity in Africa, Asia, and the Middle East, both Protestant and Roman Catholic missions proliferated. Missionaries expected native culture and traditions to yield to their "superior" civilized ways, propagating cultural imperialism as a prelude to political domination. American missionaries zealously worked to create Christian nations wherever they went. In Hawaii, for example, New England missionaries arrived in 1820, following in the wake of whalers who frequented the islands for supplies on long voyages across the Pacific. There they established out-posts of New England culture and society and worked zealously to stamp out native culture. With their grasp of local knowledge and native languages, missionaries proved themselves invaluable to governments seeking influence in far-off lands.

Missionary activity also extended beyond political and social transformation to engagement in business and trade. In Hawaii, missionaries quickly evolved into busi-nessmen, purchasing vast tracts of land from natives and establishing the islands' lucrative sugar industry. By the 1850s Americans owned 75 percent of businesses on the islands.

Precedent for American Empire

Through much of the 19th century, policymakers laid the groundwork for empire abroad, with expansion across the continent and the conquest of native peoples. Be-ginning with the Louisiana Purchase in 1803, the United States added to its contigu-ous territory through both peaceful annexation and war. In the modern, progress-filled years of late 19th century, Indians at home and then natives in other lands seemed like a relic of the past, the "primitive" losers in the struggle for survival, who "naturally" yielded before a "superior" civilization. **Theodore Roosevelt**, historian and future president, who would play a key role in establishing the United States as an impe-rial world power, wrote extensively about westward expansion and viewed the clash between "savagery" and "civilization" as inevitable and necessary.

Treatment of Indians provided important precedents for empire building. Not only did the United States acquire by force lands that had belonged to Indians, it also rejected the right of native peoples to rule themselves and imposed direct rule on them. In addition, the Supreme Court ruled in 1884 that Indians born on reservations were not citizens but instead "nationals" who owed allegiance to the United States but had none of the privileges of citizenship—a status that lasted until 1924. These legal concepts were later applied to colonized peoples in both Puerto Rico until 1917 and the Philippines.

The Crises of the 1890s

A combination of crises in the 1890s thrust the nation into the global scramble for empire. Even as the United States extended its global economic reach into foreign markets, economic convulsions pointed to the need for new markets. Despite massive economic growth and industrial production, the depressions of the 1870s and 1890s convinced many Americans that overproduction of goods was the source of economic turmoil. Both domestic markets and current foreign markets could no longer absorb the massive output of American industry and agriculture. New markets would secure America's position as the world's greatest industrial power and would guarantee peace domestically. The social turbulence spawned by the depression of 1893–1897—massive unemployment, farm foreclosures, and labor strife—convinced Democrats,

Republicans, and Populists alike that new markets would provide the antidote to the nation's domestic problems.

In 1893, as the stock market plunged, a young history professor, **Frederick Jackson Turner**, added to growing anxiety with a highly influential essay entitled "The Significance of the Frontier in American History." Turner explained that according to the 1890 census the frontier had disappeared with the complete settlement of the West. The "closing" of the frontier had, he argued, many serious consequences. Most importantly, because "economic power secures political power," free land in the West had been essential to maintaining American freedom and opportunity. The inability of its people to expand into free lands threatened the very future of the republic.

Support for expansion also came from military experts, anxious about international prestige and defense. As European powers and Japan competed for global influence, some argued that the United States could not stand idly by. If it failed to contend for empire, many believed, the nation would be left behind as a second-rate power and inevitably decline in a world where only the strongest survived. Moreover, at the very least, simple self-defense required a vigorous foreign policy. If not checked, foreign powers might even dominate in the western hemisphere. Although, since the declaration of the Monroe Doctrine in 1823, the United States had managed to reduce foreign influence in the Americas, Great Britain—with its Caribbean possessions, with Canada as part of its commonwealth, and with its domination of South American trade—remained a major player.

To prepare for the nation's new global role, Congress authorized the modernization of the U.S. Navy, a fleet in disrepair since the Civil War. Captain **Alfred Thayer Mahan**, director of the Naval War College, emerged as the leading proponent of a "New Navy." He contended that history proved that a powerful navy provided the key to attain national greatness and international power. To control the oceans was to control the world. Colonies played a crucial role in Mahan's theory, to provide strategic military bases and coaling stations for far-flung global conflicts that were sure to come.

Other Americans in the 1880s and 1890s, like Mahan, advocated for a muscular foreign policy; they viewed war as an antidote to what they deemed the crisis of "overcivilization." According to contemporary observers, American men—middle-class men, specifically—had grown soft and flabby. They spent too much time working indoors, with little physical activity. Whereas their fathers had fought in the Civil War, they slaved away in their offices pursuing money instead of greatness on the battlefield. Many worried that the current generation was not tough enough, their "manly" spirit dissipated by their soft white-collar world. Theodore Roosevelt, one of the leading disciples of the cult of strenuosity, challenged the nation in the 1890s to "boldly face the life of strife. . . . Oversentimentality, oversoftness . . ., and mushiness are the great danger of this age and this people." Despite a resurgence in physical activities in the 1890s—especially rough sports such as boxing and football—many young men longed for the ultimate test: to fight in a war to prove their manhood and to reinvigorate the nation.

STUDY QUESTIONS FOR THE NEW IMPERIALISM

1. What general factors account for the global grab for empire in the late 19th century?
2. What specific factors pushed the United States into the scramble for colonies?

THE UNITED STATES FLEXES ITS MUSCLES

The United States had no overarching, long-range plan to create a political empire. Instead, policy makers initially emphasized commercial growth. In the 1880s Secretary of State **James G. Blaine** explained, "Our great demand is expansion." He noted, however, that this did not mean "annexation of territory" but rather "annexation of trade." But a decade of aggressive foreign policy intent on expanding and protecting the nation's global commercial empire, coupled with the crises of the 1890s, paved the way for the establishment of a political empire.

First asserting dominance in the western hemisphere, U.S. policy makers soon defined the nation's strategic interests broadly and forcefully in the Pacific and Asia as well. The three-month-long Spanish-American-Philippine War in 1898 paid huge dividends to the United States. Entered into with limited aims—ostensibly to aid Cuban independence and defend American business interests there—the war resulted in control of Cuba, Puerto Rico, Guam, and the Philippines. Although a latecomer, the United States—with its modern navy playing a key role—now joined its European and Japanese rivals as participants in the New Imperialism.

The nation's new and aggressive foreign policy raised many questions that Americans continue to struggle with to this day. What is the role of the United States in the world? What are "American interests"? When, if ever, do American interests justify intervention in foreign countries and wars abroad?

Latin America

The United States had long kept a watchful eye on foreign influence in the western hemisphere. The Monroe Doctrine had stood as the foundation of American foreign policy since 1823. Beginning in the 1880s the United States embarked on a more expansive foreign policy in Latin America, to protect markets and American investments there. Secretary of State **James G. Blaine**, who served under Republican Presidents **James Garfield** (1881) and **Benjamin Harrison** (1889–1893), was the chief architect of this new policy, which would last well into the 20th century. Blaine asserted that the United States must maintain stability in Latin America to guarantee healthy trade and to secure its markets. In 1890 Blaine played a key role in Congress's passage of the first major reciprocal tariff. This legislation allowed certain goods from Latin America, such as sugar, coffee, and hides, to enter the country with no tariff as long as Latin American countries allowed the free passage of U.S. goods in turn. Trade with Cuba and Brazil exploded as a result.

Subsequent administrations embraced Blaine's policy. Interference in the internal affairs of Latin American countries and even military intervention soon resulted. In 1893, for example, when Brazilian monarchists, encouraged by the British, threatened to revolt against the recently established, pro-American republican regime, President **Grover Cleveland** helped quash the revolution at the behest of U.S. business interests there.

Venezuela emerged as a trouble spot a few years later, in 1895–1896. A long-disputed border between Venezuela and British Guiana catalyzed American intervention when Great Britain reasserted its claims to territory that included the gateway to trade for much of the continent. Citing the Monroe Doctrine, President Cleveland insisted that the British arbitrate the disputed land claim. When Great Britain ignored his request, an angry Cleveland explained that not only would the United States enforce the Monroe Doctrine in the dispute, but it would also "resist by every means in its power" Britain's Venezuelan claims. Great Britain, caving in to U.S. demands, ultimately lost its territorial claims, as arbiters sided with Venezuela, and the United States reinforced its dominance in the western hemisphere.

Hawaii

The United States also engaged in muscular foreign policy in the Pacific, protecting business interests established earlier by American missionaries and traders. In 1875 the American-dominated government of Hawaii had established a reciprocity agreement with the United States that allowed Hawaiian sugar to enter the United States duty free; this resulted in the tripling of sugar production in 10 years. But the **McKinley Tariff**, passed by Congress in 1890, ended Hawaii's favored status and threatened the sugar industry there. Immediately, Americans in Hawaii began to pursue annexation to the United States as a solution to their export problems.

As the Hawaiian economy nearly collapsed, **Queen Liliuokalani** threatened American domination when she ascended to the throne upon her brother's death in 1891. Four years earlier, Americans in Hawaii had implemented a new constitution, referred to by native Hawaiians as "the bayonet constitution," that limited the political power of natives and their monarchy. In 1893 the queen, intent on returning control of the islands to her people, now a minority in their own country, drew up another constitution that restored the power of the monarchy and returned political rights to native Hawaiians. But American missionary-planter interests, headed by **Sanford B. Dole**, organized a coup and overthrew the queen. At their request, the U.S. government dispatched marines to prevent the queen and her supporters from fighting back.

American residents established a provisional government and requested annexation to the United States. But after a thorough investigation President Grover Cleveland rejected their proposal. Hawaii "was taken possession of by the U.S. forces without the consent or wish of the government of the islands." In the meantime the

The last monarch to reign over Hawaii, Queen Liliukalani (1838–1917) was deposed by American-planter interests in 1893 and imprisoned for a year after she was accused of attempting to restore the monarchy in 1895.

provisional government established the Republic of Hawaii on July 4, 1894, with coup-leader Dole as president. Passing a tariff bill granting the islands favored treatment in selling sugar in the United States, Congress then restored prosperity to the sugar planters there.

The Cuban Crisis

Cubans had long chafed under Spanish rule and had instigated numerous unsuccessful rebellions, launched yet another revolution against Spain in the 1890s. In 1894 U.S. tariff agreements granting Hawaiian sugar favored status plunged Cubans into an economic crisis, as their once-prosperous sugar trade vanished. Economic collapse and unemployment only served to remind Cubans of their lack of political power. In February 1895 Cuban insurgents took advantage of widespread discontent and began to fight against Spanish authorities. By 1896 revolutionaries, under the banner of *Cuba Libre*, took their fight to the countryside; torching sugar fields, they vowed that there would be no peace, production, or protection of property until Spain granted independence.

Intent on holding on to the last jewel in its once-expansive necklace of colonies, Spain attempted to crush the rebellion with an iron fist. General Valeriano Weyler, formulated a new policy, *reconcentración*, ordering the rural population to move to designated, fortified areas under Spanish control. Spanish soldiers also burned villages, food supplies, and peasant fields; slaughtered animals; and destroyed any resource that could aid the insurgents. Weyler's policies created hundreds of thousands of refugees, and tens of thousands of sick and hungry Cubans perished.

Negative depictions of the Spanish in the American press stirred anti-Spanish sentiment among the American public, and helped galvanize support for war against Spain in Cuba.

Developments in Cuba quickly captured the attention of Americans. The rebellion and the scorched-earth tactics of both sides threatened American investments, estimated at $50 million. As early as1882 E. Atkins & Company of Boston emerged as the largest landowner on the islands. Many also feared that Cuba might easily be plucked from Spain by a much more powerful European rival. Major newspapers, especially those owned by **William Randolph Hearst** and **Joseph Pulitzer**, competed for readers by publishing sensational front-page stories that described atrocities in Cuba. "Yellow journalism," as it was dubbed, provoked widespread public support for the Cuban rebels. Vivid, often fabricated stories portrayed the brutal policies of "Butcher" Weyler. Newspapers cried out for American military intervention on behalf of the insurgents in their fight for freedom.

Despite wide-ranging concerns, neither the Democratic Cleveland administration nor the subsequent Republican administration of **William McKinley** acted hastily. McKinley instead sought a diplomatic solution. In 1897, his first year in office, he demanded that Spain implement reforms to end the Cuban revolt. Spain complied by removing General Weyler, declaring amnesty to insurgents, and establishing a liberal government that granted Cuba partial independence. But half-way measures only angered Spanish loyalists and those seeking independence. When riots by Spanish loyalists tore through Havana in late 1897, President McKinley ordered the battleship **USS Maine** to Havana harbor to protect American citizens and property there.

In February 1898 two events pushed the nation to the brink of war with Spain. Early in the month the *New York Journal* published an intercepted, private letter, written by Spain's minister in Washington, **Enrique du Puy de Lôme**. The letter insulted McKinley by calling him a "weak bidder for the admiration of the crowd." As an outraged American public cried out for revenge, the drumbeat for war grew steadier and louder. Then, on February 15, the *Maine* blew up in Havana harbor, killing 260 of the

276 American sailors aboard the ship. Most Americans immediately concluded, as did Assistant Secretary of the Navy Theodore Roosevelt, that the explosion was "an act of dirty treachery on the part of the Spanish." A hastily convened Naval Board of Inquiry conducted an investigation and concluded that a detonated mine had destroyed the ship. The public clamored even more loudly for war, declaring, "Remember the Maine! To hell with Spain!"

On April 11, 1898, after attempting a final diplomatic solution, McKinley asked Congress for a declaration of war against Spain, which it passed unanimously. The Cuban crisis, he explained, "threatened Cuban lives, U.S. property, and tranquility in the U.S. itself." In addition, American intervention was a defense of "human rights." To placate those who worried that the United States might try to colonize Cuba—and to protect the beet-sugar industry of his own state from competition with cheap Cuban sugar—Senator **Henry Teller** of Colorado added an amendment to the war declaration. The Teller Amendment stated that the United States would not colonize Cuba.

"A Splendid Little War"

The nation embarked on its war with Spain in a near-holiday spirit. As men eagerly embraced the chance to fight, women organized relief organizations to support the troops. But logistical problems plagued the campaign. Many soldiers, for example, never received proper equipment or training; they lacked even the most basic necessities, such as tents and mess kits. In addition, the government issued standard wool uniforms unsuitable for a summer war in a tropical climate.

As soldiers gathered in Tampa, Florida, to embark for Cuba, Commodore **George Dewey** scored the first American victory of the war on the other side of the globe. In February 1898, 10 days after the *Maine* explosion, Assistant Secretary of the Navy Theodore Roosevelt ordered Dewey to engage the Spanish in their Pacific colony, the Philippines, should war break. On May 1, Dewey defeated the Spanish fleet in Manila Bay, without losing a single man. The Philippines had hardly figured into the discussion leading up to the war, but with the China market endangered in 1898, the United States immediately expanded its war against Spain to include the strategically located Philippines. By late June, the first American ground troops arrived in Manila.

In mid-June, U.S. troops finally left for Cuba, landing in Daiquirí on June 22. Despite more logistical problems for the Americans, it soon became clear that the Spanish could not compete. The antiquated Spanish navy, with its wooden ships, proved to be an easy foe for the modern, steel ships of the U.S. Navy. In Santiago harbor, just prior to the landing of troops at Daiquirí, 12 American ships destroyed the entire Spanish squadron with the loss of a single American life.

On July 1, 1898, the U.S. Army defeated the Spanish in the war's biggest land battle, at San Juan Hill. Colonel Theodore Roosevelt and his First Volunteer Cavalry Regiment, known as the "**Rough Riders**," became national heroes for their daring exploits during the battle. The son of a patrician New York family, Roosevelt resigned his post as Assistant Secretary of the Navy when the United States declared war and organized his own regiment. The Rough Riders were a motley mix of cowboys, Native

Americans, Mexican Americans, several New York City policemen, and Ivy League athletes. The only Rough Rider on horseback, Roosevelt led a risky charge up Kettle Hill, part of the battle for nearby San Juan Hill. With the support of several African American cavalry units, he and his troops emerged victorious, their exploits widely reported by the American press. Roosevelt called the battle "the great day of my life." Although Roosevelt initially acknowledged the valor of the black soldiers, he later discounted their contribution, and they never received the same publicity as the Rough Riders.

On August 12, 1898, the Spanish signed a protocol of peace ending the war after only three months. Within that short time U.S. war aims had expanded considerably. American troops had not only defeated the Spanish in Cuba and Manila Bay but they had also seized Guam and Puerto Rico. In July 1898, just as the war heated up, Congress approved the annexation of Hawaii. On August 14, two days after Spain agreed to end the war—but before word of the war's end reached the Philippines—American troops, with the aid of Filipino rebels, captured the city of Manila. In a matter of weeks the United States had substantially extended its influence and power in the Pacific and Asia.

Long seeking military glory, Colonel Theodore Roosevelt called the Battle of San Juan Hill "the great day of my life." Reports of his heroism greatly accelerated his political career, first as governor of New York, then as vice president, and finally as president from 1901–1909.

In Cuba, U.S. war aims changed from a war of liberation into a war of conquest. Despite its high-toned language on behalf of Cuban independence, the American war declaration did not recognize the rebels or their provisional government and refused to allow the rebels to take an active part in the war against Spain. Military leaders, as well as journalists, depicted them in negative, racial stereotypes. They seemed surprised that many Cubans were dark skinned. One officer described them as "lazy," "cowardly," "dirty," and "childlike," clearly incapable of self-government.

Although Secretary of State **John Hay** called it a "splendid little war," the Spanish-American War exacted a toll, much of it unnecessary, on those who fought it. In addition to lacking basic equipment and proper tropical uniforms, soldiers suffered from

"Hurrah for the Fourth of July." Published in the midst of the Spanish-American-Philippine War, in July 1898, this cartoon depicts Hawaii, Cuba, and the Philippines as racialized children on their way to inclusion in the United States.

HURRAH FOR THE FOURTH OF JULY
We're Coming In on Independence Day Celebrations, Too.

filth and disease. **Clara Barton** and the Red Cross found it nearly impossible to get vital medical supplies and equipment unloaded from ships in Cuba. Soldiers also subsisted on rancid canned beef, full of gristle and maggots, sold to the army by the Chicago meatpacking giant Armour and Company. Many more American soldiers died of food poisoning and disease than Spanish bullets; in fact, sickness and disease accounted for approximately 2,500 of 2,900 total deaths.

The Treaty of Paris, signed in December 1898, officially ended the war with Spain, pending Senate ratification. Spain ceded Cuba and Puerto Rico in the Caribbean and Guam and the Philippines, for an additional $20 million, in the Pacific. The war proved to be a stunning debut for the nation as a world power.

STUDY QUESTIONS FOR THE UNITED STATES FLEXES ITS MUSCLES

1. What factors and events led the United States to declare war on Spain in April 1898?
2. How did U.S. war aims change over the course of the Spanish-American War?

THE COMPLICATIONS OF EMPIRE

Americans generally basked in the glow of their victory over Spain. A nation hungry for heroes embraced naval hero Commodore Dewey, who even appeared in soap ads, and the press published numerous stories about the feats of Theodore Roosevelt and the Rough Riders. Americans also celebrated the national reconciliation evident in the

Spanish-American-Philippine War. The war provided the first opportunity since the Civil War for Northerners and Southerners to fight as a united nation against a common foe.

But celebration of the war soon gave way to pressing questions. What should the United States do with the territories it had won in the war? The Teller Amendment prohibited the United States from colonizing Cuba; but should the United States maintain control through other means? And what about the other acquired territories—especially Puerto Rico and the Philippines—where the United States was not bound by any prewar legislation?

The Philippines soon emerged as the focal point for a heated and divisive national debate. The nation seemed poised at a crossroads, with the final choice entailing massive consequences. Should the islands be given their independence? Or should they be colonized in an attempt to secure American interests in the Pacific? Could a republic like the United States be a colonial power without undermining its most cherished values, such as self-determination? Or were colonies an inevitable outgrowth of international greatness?

Choosing the road to empire, the United States would soon learn the high cost of that decision as it fought a protracted, bloody war to subdue Philippine independence. Moreover, the nation's presence in Asia guaranteed its involvement in future Pacific wars.

Cuba and Puerto Rico

Just as the United States did not allow Cuban rebels to take part in the war with Spain, they did not allow Cubans a role in negotiating the peace treaty or in determining their postwar fate. Although the Teller Amendment forbade the United States from annexing Cuba, McKinley and Congress did not hesitate to take formal control of the island. They instituted military occupation in January 1899, as General **Leonard Wood** assumed the position of military governor. Wood explained that the United States required a stable Cuba as stability engendered "business confidence." At the same time, claiming that the Cubans were incapable of self-government, the United States did what it could to discredit Cuba's independence movement. But the Cuban independence movement remained strong.

Unable to colonize Cuba, and soon weary of maintaining military occupation, the United States seized on another form of control, the **Platt Amendment**. Passed by Congress in 1901 as an appendix to a new Cuban constitution, the Platt Amendment gave the United States broad authority to intervene to preserve Cuban independence and required Cuba to sell or lease land for U.S. naval stations and coaling bases. Outraged delegates to Cuba's constitutional convention opposed the amendment but under intense pressure passed it, 15 to 11. Governor Wood confessed privately, "There is, of course, little or no independence left Cuba under the Platt Amendment." Within five years, in 1906, the United States sent troops to Cuba to maintain order and the Platt Amendment served as the basis of U.S.-Cuba relations until 1934.

Unlike Cuba, Puerto Rico had no protection from annexation. U.S. forces had invaded the island in July 1898, and for the next 18 months they ruled there. In 1900 Congress passed the Foraker Act, defining Puerto Rico as an "unincorporated territory" under Congressional control, and a U.S. civilian government replaced military rule. Notably, annexation did not grant citizenship or even civil rights. In a series of cases known as the **Insular Cases**, the Supreme Court ruled that the Constitution did not follow the flag; that is, American rights and liberties did not extend to all lands under U.S. control. Puerto Ricans strongly protested their new status as subjects of the United States. A Puerto Rican newspaper angrily denounced the ambiguous status of Puerto Ricans: "We are and we are not a foreign country. We are and we are not citizens of the United States. . . . The Constitution . . . applies to us and does not apply to us." While initially limiting the rights of Puerto Ricans, the United States acted swiftly to tie the island to the mainland's economy by passing legislation that facilitated Puerto Rican exports to the mainland. In 1917 the Jones-Shafroth Act granted citizenship—but not full political rights—to Puerto Ricans. To this day Puerto Ricans cannot vote for president and have no representation in Congress.

The Philippines

The colonization of the Philippines became one of the most troubling and divisive legacies of the Spanish-American War. After Dewey's defeat of the Spanish fleet in Manila Bay in May 1898, McKinley seemed interested in American control only of Manila Bay, as a strategic base for commerce and naval operations, rather than of all of the Philippine islands. Governing the islands posed numerous difficulties. The Philippines, on the other side of the globe, consisted of hundreds of islands extending over 115,000 square miles. Moreover, Filipinos intent on self-government had fought against Spain for independence and had even aided the United States in defeating Spain in hopes of gaining their autonomy.

McKinley's intentions soon became clear: the United States planned to colonize the islands. In December 1898 McKinley articulated a policy of "benevolent assimilation" for the Philippines. The Americans came, the president explained, "not as invaders or conquerors but as friends, to protect the natives in their homes, their employments, and in their personal and religious rights."

McKinley rationalized this choice through a series of considerations. He was convinced that the Filipinos were incapable of self-government. In addition, he feared that if the United States did not control the Philippines, another imperial power would step in and help themselves to the islands. The Philippines also seemed especially crucial as a foothold in Asia, to expand America's influence, its naval power, and its global standing.

The Debate Over Empire

The colonization of the Philippines sparked bitter debate across the nation. Although a poll found that the overwhelming majority favored empire, with westerners most supportive, critics swiftly organized. In November 1898 in Boston, concerned Americans formed the **Anti-Imperial League**, which soon boasted 25,000 members. The League included a wide range of some of the nation's most prominent citizens, including reformer Jane Addams, former President Grover Cleveland, labor leader Samuel Gompers, presidential hopeful and former Congressman William Jennings Bryan, African American intellectual **W.E.B. Du Bois**, and steel magnate Andrew Carnegie.

Anti-imperialists rejected colonization as un-American, inconsistent with the nation's ideals. A republic, they argued, could not be an empire. As Senator **George Frisbie Hoar** of Massachusetts summarized, "The danger is that we are to be transformed from a republic founded on the Declaration of Independence . . . into a vulgar, commonplace empire founded upon physical force, controlling subject races and vassal states."

Imperialists denigrated such talk as old fashioned. "America," exclaimed Senator **Albert Beveridge** of Indiana, a leading voice for colonization, "is the young man of the nations. We are engaged in our great rivalry with other powers of the world. And this is the destiny of every nation that achieves its manhood." Moreover, he argued, the creation of empire abroad simply continued the march of the flag across "unexplored lands and savage wildernesses." In its triumphal march beyond American borders, the nation continued to fulfill its destiny. The United States must "accept the gift of events," new markets and trade and the opportunity to provide benevolent rule for people incapable of ruling themselves. If the United States did not act, a foreign foe would surely rule the Philippines.

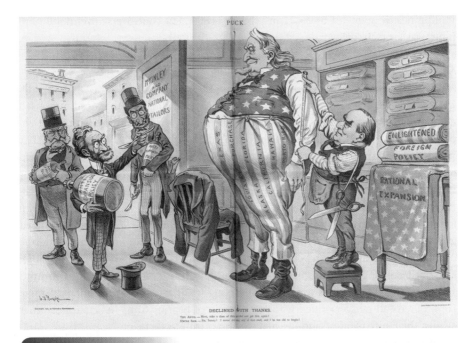

This pro-imperialist cartoon depicts a newly enlarged Uncle Sam rejecting antiexpansionist tonic from Carl Schurz, former U.S. senator and vice president of the Anti-Imperialist League, and two fellow anti-imperialists. President McKinley, Uncle Sam's tailor, measures him for a new suit of clothes to fit his new size.

Anti-imperialists rejected governing the Filipinos without their consent; impe-rialists countered that the United States had long governed Native Americans with-out their approval. Antis cited George Washington, the victor over the British empire, as their symbol; champions of empire claimed Jefferson as "the first Imperialist of the Republic," his Louisiana Purchase the U.S. precedent for annexation of "savage" populations. Anti-imperialists insisted that governing and defending a colony 7,000 miles from California would drain the nation economically; imperialists responded with visions of American riches derived from new Asian markets.

The issue of race figured prominently on both sides of the debate. Some Ameri-cans, especially southern senators in the midst of disfranchising black voters, feared the addition of more people of color to the United States. Imperialists assured them that they could be annexed—as Indians had been—without granting them voting rights. At the same time, African Americans criticized the United States for allegedly expanding democracy to the Philippines while denying it to blacks at home. Black leader **Booker T. Washington** endorsed self-governance for the Philippines, remark-ing, "Until our nation has settled the Negro and Indian problems I do not believe that we have a right to assume more social problems." But imperialists argued that Anglo-Saxons, as racial superiors, bore a responsibility to govern and ultimately "uplift" their inferiors and to bestow on them the glories of democracy.

After intense debate, the Senate ratified the peace treaty and the annexation of the Philippines by a vote of 57 to 27 in February 1899. But controversy over the Philip-pines was far from over.

The American-Philippine War

Even as the Senate ratified the peace treaty with Spain, the United States found itself entangled in an ugly war of repression against Filipinos demanding their indepen-dence. Led by **Emilio Aguinaldo**, freedom fighters had aided U.S. troops when they invaded the islands, viewing them as allies against colonialism. When the United States, in turn, colonized the Philippines, Aguinaldo led his warriors against the new imperialists. After fighting a conventional war, in November 1899 Aguinaldo orga-nized a guerilla campaign against U.S. occupiers. American soldiers could not tell friend from foe and a bloody, brutal war of attrition ensued. Atrocities abounded as frustrations mounted, yet the powerful United States was unable to subdue the outnumbered, outgunned rebels. In the most notorious incident of the war, Brigadier General Jacob H. Smith, in retaliation for an ambush of American troops in April 1900, ordered his soldiers to make "a howling wilderness" of the island of Samar. He ordered "all persons killed who are capable of bearing arms in actual hostilities against the United States" and insisted that no prisoners be taken.

Devolving into a race war, the American-Philippine conflict fueled the brutal treatment of Filipinos—civilians and guerilla fighters alike. White soldiers regularly referred to Filipinos as "gugus" and "niggers." Moreover, soldiers and officers—along with journalists and politicians—continually compared the Filipinos to Native

Emilio Aguinaldo (1869–1964) declared Philippine independence from Spain in June 1898, and in January 1899, a Filipino constitutional convention declared him provisional president of the Philippines. When the United States refused to recognize Philippine independence, he led a war against the United States and was captured in March 1901.

Americans; in their view the war against Aguinaldo was just another Indian war, with "civilized" forces subduing "savages."

The treatment of Filipinos deeply angered many African American soldiers. Some identified with the Filipinos as fellow people of color victimized by white supremacists. Although some black soldiers defended the war, others helped publicize the atrocities, despite the U.S. government's efforts to censor negative news from the islands. They dispatched numerous letters home published in the black press. Some even deserted and joined forces with Aguinaldo and fought against the United States.

After declaring victory several times, the United States finally suppressed the insurgents—for the most part—after three years, in 1902. But rebellion against occupation continued to erupt for many years afterward and U.S. domination came at a steep price. The United States spent $400 million to stifle the revolt and more than 126,000 American soldiers fought against the Filipino rebels. Roughly 4,200 Americans and 18,000 Filipinos died in battle; at least 250,000 Filipinos succumbed to gunfire, disease, and starvation.

In 1901 **William Howard Taft** became the first governor-general of the Philippines, to aid "our little brown brothers," as he called to them, in establishing a civilian government. The United States worked to win the hearts and minds of the Filipino people by investing in a massive public works program that built roads, bridges, and schools—a program that stressed the same manual training programs offered to Indians and blacks in the United States. At the same time, the United States began transferring some authority to Filipinos who supported their regime.

An Atlantic power before the war, the United States, with the conquest of the Philippines, was now a Pacific power, too, with naval bases and coaling stations to

African Americans and International Affairs, 1898–1912

African Americans voiced mixed opinions regarding the United States's expanding role in world affairs. Empire building occurred just as they watched their own rights violated with the rise of segregation laws, the abridgement of voting rights, and a spike in lynching. As a result, they viewed American imperialism through the lens of their own deteriorating position. Victimized at home, they increasingly identified with people of color around the world who also suffered at the hands of white supremacy. Black Americans, especially soldiers, struggled with the irony of taking up "the white man's burden."

Many African Americans supported U.S. military intervention to liberate Cuba from Spanish rule. They identified the Cuban struggle as the fight of people of color against white European domination. Some, even hoping to emigrate to a free Cuba, looked longingly to the country as a racial utopia, as a possible haven from American racism. When Congress declared war on Spain in April 1898, however, some called it a "white man's war," and questioned whether African Americans should fight for a government that refused to defend the rights of its own black citizens. The black newspaper the *Washington Bee* declared, "The Negro has no reason to fight for Cuba's independence. He is opposed at home. He is as much in need of independence as Cuba is." Despite this sentiment, more than 10,000 black men volunteered for military service in the Spanish-American War. In addition, four black regiments of regular soldiers serving in the West, "Buffalo Soldiers," were among the first to be mobilized to invade Cuba. Many African Americans undoubtedly agreed with the Reverend H. H. Proctor of Atlanta, who insisted in a sermon that "righteous war" provided "splendid opportunities" to remind the nation that "we are a real part of this country."

But black soldiers, serving in segregated units, usually under the command of white officers, suffered humiliation and violence at the hands of white soldiers and

extend both its military and commercial influence. At the same time, however, the acquisition of the Philippines created new vulnerabilities. The islands proved to be difficult and expensive to defend, especially against Japan, the emerging power in Asia. Should the Japanese choose to expand southward, the United States would find itself at war. Less than four decades later, in December 1941, only days after the attack on Pearl Harbor, the Japanese invaded the Philippines and held the islands for most of World War II. The Philippines remained an American colony until 1946.

civilians. In June 1898, as they waited to embark for Cuba, fights broke out between white and black soldiers in Tampa when black soldiers rescued a two-year-
old black child being used by soldiers for target practice. Black soldiers also came
under regular attack from white civilians, who resented the presence of black men
in uniform. In Cuba black soldiers, despite their bravery, never received the credit
they deserved—most notably, their role in the success of the Rough Rider's charge
at the Battle of San Juan Hill; in fact, Theodore Roosevelt questioned their bravery.

The Cuban war soured many African Americans on empire even before the
United States colonized and subdued the Philippines. In the aftermath of the war
with Spain, many African Americans loudly protested imperialism. Several prominent civil rights activists, including W.E.B. Du Bois and Ida B. Wells, joined the
Anti-Imperial League, while others organized separate black anti-imperialist organizations. Black protest grew so loud that the War Department questioned whether it
should even send black troops to the Philippines to quash the independence movement there. Black soldiers, feared one war department official, might not shoot at
their "colored Filipino cousins." Effective fighters against the rebels, black troops
generally refused to treat the civilian population, which some called "our kinsmen"
and "our brothers," with the brutality commonly displayed by white soldiers. Although nearly all did their duty as soldiers, some, responding to Aguinaldo's pleas
to switch sides, actually deserted.

Global imperialism, whether in the Philippines, Africa, or other parts of the
world, prompted W.E.B. Du Bois in 1903 to pen a powerful essay that began with
an eloquent and profound statement: "The problem of the twentieth century is the
problem of the color-line,—the relation of the darker to the lighter races of men in
Asia and Africa, in America and the islands of the sea." America's race problem, as
he pointed out—and his fellow African Americans had come to see—was merely a
phase of a much larger global problem.

- What factors account for the identification of African Americans with Cubans and
  Filipinos?

- What factors inhibited this identification?

China

The ratification of the peace treaty with Spain in February 1898 allowed McKinley to
address land grabs in China that threatened to close access to the vast China market,
with hundreds of millions of potential consumers for American goods. Just recovering from the devastating depression of the 1890s, the United States acted forcefully to
blunt any limitations to the lucrative China market.

In 1899 Secretary of State John Hay articulated American policy by penning the first "Open Door" notes addressed to the world's powers. The notes requested that they open up areas claimed by each power—its "sphere of interest"—to other nations, such as the United States, to allow them to compete fairly for Chinese trade. He also requested that world powers respect the integrity of China and allow the Chinese themselves to raise and collect tariffs within these spheres of interest.

Hay's Open Door notes initially prompted only minimal response. Great Britain and Japan affirmed the policy. The remaining powers—France, Germany, and Russia—evaded a firm commitment to the **Open Door Policy**; they simply refused to ensure its implementation. Nevertheless, Hay made the claim that the world's powers had consented to the Open Door in China. Hay had successfully, through diplomatic means, achieved tacit agreement for the United States to market its goods to all of China.

But after years of being invaded and picked apart by foreign powers, the Chinese fought back. In 1900 a secret organization, "The Righteous and Harmonious Fist"—dubbed the "Boxers" by foreigners for their boxing rituals—began a violent attack to eradicate "foreign devils" and their influences in China. Their expulsion, they believed, would revitalize their downtrodden nation and usher in a new, glorious age. Encouraged by the **Empress Dowager Cixi**, the Boxers especially targeted Christians—both foreign and Chinese converts—who undermined Chinese traditions. The Boxers killed suspected Chinese Christians on sight and forced missionaries to flee for protection as Boxers destroyed their churches and residences.

After the Boxers successfully attacked foreign ministries, even killing the German minister, and cut off all communications between Beijing and the outside world, foreign powers mobilized quickly, and sent an international force to suppress the rebellion. President McKinley ordered 50,000 American troops from Manila, fearing that the Boxer Rebellion would be used by other powers to shut the open door. By August 1900 the international army captured Beijing, released besieged foreigners there, and smothered the Boxer Rebellion.

Although many Americans praised the McKinley administration as China's saviors, anti-imperialists viewed the Boxer Rebellion as another symptom of wrongheaded policies. In a speech in late 1900 Mark Twain pointed out the hypocrisy that the United States invaded China while barring Chinese immigration to the United States: "We do not allow Chinamen to come here, and I say in all seriousness that it would be a graceful thing to let China decide who shall go there."

STUDY QUESTIONS FOR THE COMPLICATIONS OF EMPIRE

1. In what ways did colonization and America's entry onto the world stage represent a continuation of past policies? In what ways did it represent a break from the past?
2. What were the key arguments made by imperialists and anti-imperialists for and against empire? Which side, in your opinion, made the most convincing case? Why?

THE UNITED STATES ON THE WORLD STAGE: ROOSEVELT AND TAFT

Secretary of State John Hay's approach to expanding American power in China set the course for subsequent foreign policy in the 20th century. Policy makers emphasized diplomacy that established unrestricted trade rather than territorial expansion. The United States had joined the club of political imperialists, but the price had been steep. In the first decades of the 20th century, the United States focused on expanding its commercial empire instead of adding to its territorial empire.

Whether Roosevelt's "Big Stick" or Taft's "Dollar Diplomacy," presidential power to define foreign policy expanded considerably, at the expense of Congress. Roosevelt, especially, helped define the modern presidency by often acting quickly and independently on matters of foreign relations. Although they were a study of contrasts in appearance, personality, and style, neither Roosevelt nor Taft hesitated to commit American troops to Latin America in defense of American interests and domination there. During their presidencies, from 1901 to 1913, the United States intervened 12 times in Latin America—in Honduras, the Dominican Republic, Cuba, Nicaragua, and Panama.

The United States established itself as the "policeman" of Latin America. This role secured American domination of its neighbors but led to strained relations. With its colonization of the Philippines as its foothold in Asia, the United States also continued to expand there commercially and to defend any infringement of its trade.

Thus, both Roosevelt and Taft expanded the nation's role and influence on the world stage between 1901 and 1912 and set the course for the leading role the United States would play in world affairs for the rest of the century.

Roosevelt's "Big Stick"

The assassination of William McKinley at the World's Fair in Buffalo, New York, in September 1901, less than a year into his second term, thrust Theodore Roosevelt into the presidency. McKinley had selected the hero of San Juan Hill as his running mate in 1900, and Roosevelt, at the age of 42, became the youngest man ever to hold the office. Less than two weeks before McKinley's death, Roosevelt addressed an audience at the Minnesota State Fair. He exclaimed, "There is a homely adage that runs 'speak softly and carry a big stick; you will go far.'" Roosevelt's "homely adage" encapsulated his foreign policy. The young president did not hesitate to use a big stick to expand American influence and maintain order, essential to trade, especially in Latin America. Roosevelt also enhanced presidential power in foreign policy, using the "big stick" of the presidency to act swiftly and decisively, often without congressional approval. Few presidents—before or since—relished the role of president as much as Roosevelt, and he stamped his foreign policy with his exuberant and irrepressible personality as he boldly led the United States onto the world stage and guaranteed its place as a world power.

The completion of an isthmian canal connecting the Atlantic and Pacific in central America had been discussed for decades by both Americans and Europeans, and it had been attempted unsuccessfully in the 1880s by France. The colonization of the Philippines and the massive expansion of the China trade made a canal even more crucial so that ships and goods could be moved quickly from the Atlantic to the Pacific. Roosevelt made completion of a canal his highest priority. But the United States remained entangled in the 1850 treaty with Great Britain, the Clayton-Bulwer Treaty, which guaranteed that neither nation could build a canal without an equal partnership with the other. After providing aid to Britain in the Boer War in South Africa, Secretary of State Hay negotiated the release of the American commitment to British partnership.

The United States considered a number of sites for an isthmian canal. Panama, a province of Colombia, had obvious advantages. Shorter than a Nicaraguan route, the Panama site also featured the partly completed canal constructed by the French. In June 1902 Congress authorized the president to pay $40 million to the French company that owned the construction rights to the canal and to purchase a six-mile-wide strip, a canal zone, for the United States. In return, Colombia would receive a $10 million payment and $250,000 annually for six years.

When Colombia rejected the proposal, an angry Roosevelt encouraged the Panamanians to revolt against Colombia. When the province rebelled, the president immediately recognized the new nation of Panama and ordered U.S. warships to prevent Colombian forces from landing in Panama to suppress the revolution. Then, in 1903, the Roosevelt administration signed a treaty with a self-proclaimed representative of Panama—Frenchman Philippe Bunau-Varilla, who had not been in Panama for years but served as a director of the French canal company—granting the United States a

To the delight of the public, President Roosevelt traveled to Panama in 1906—the first executive to leave the country while in office—mounted a steam engine, and had himself photographed in stereoview digging the canal.

10-mile-wide canal zone, which cut the new nation in half. Panama would receive $10 million initially and $250,000 per year. In addition, the United States promised to guarantee Panama's independence. Panamanians, outraged to be subject to a treaty not signed by a Panamanian, bitterly protested.

Roosevelt's heavy-handed tactics in Panama sparked more criticism than any other act of his presidency. The *New York Times*, for example, labeled his actions, "an act of sordid conquest." Mark Twain noted that Roosevelt willingly "kicked the Constitution into the backyard whenever it gets in the way." But Americans generally supported the president: the United States needed a canal and, with a "big stick," Roosevelt had secured one. He cited it as his greatest achievement as president. The largest construction project in world history, the **Panama Canal** was completed in 1914. The canal reduced the distance from New York to San Francisco from over 13,000 miles to 5,300 miles. But the canal poisoned U.S. relations with Latin America, whose nations viewed the United States as an unscrupulous bully. The canal remained under American control until December 1999, when the Torrijos-Carter Treaty, signed by President Jimmy Carter in 1977, gave control of the canal to Panama.

Roosevelt acted decisively in other ways to assure American influence in the western hemisphere. In December 1904 the president declared an addition to the Monroe Doctrine, known as the **Roosevelt Corollary**: the nation's right to intervene in the internal affairs of Latin American nations to ensure order and to suppress European influence. The "international police power" of the United States, he promised, would be used sparingly, only as a last resort. Not only did the Roosevelt Corollary define the United States as the "policeman" to keep order in Latin America, it also subverted an original intent of the Monroe Doctrine, which supported independence movements in Latin America by forbidding European (and even U.S.) intervention. The Roosevelt Corollary ensured not only that the United States firmly controlled markets in Latin America but that it would also use its power to quell revolutions, readily defined as "instability."

Roosevelt also worked to maintain the Open Door Policy and access to the vast China market, which both Russia and Japan threatened. In 1904, when Russia claimed Manchuria and Korea, the U.S. backed Japan's surprise attack on Russia's Pacific fleet at Port Arthur, in China, an action sparking the **Russo-Japanese War**. Japan seemed more sympathetic than Russia to American goals in China. Roosevelt intervened to broker a peace agreement. Holding secret meetings in Portsmouth, New Hampshire, Roosevelt and representatives from the two nations crafted a peace treaty, signed in September 1905. Both nations agreed to maintain the Open Door and each gave up claims to Manchuria. Japan, which had for all intents and purposes defeated Russia in the war, gained some key Chinese ports that had belonged to Russia and, more notably, Korea. As part of a secret deal, Japan promised to refrain from any interference in the Philippines given the United States' recognition of Japan's claims to Korea. Roosevelt's efforts earned him the Nobel Peace Prize in 1906.

American-Japanese relations, however, soon grew tense when anti-Japanese hysteria broke out in California in 1906. Like the Chinese before them, Japanese immigrants found themselves the targets of anti-Asian discrimination. In 10 years, between

1890 and 1900, the soaring Japanese immigrant population—from 2,000 to 24,000—created a backlash. In addition to segregating schools to keep Japanese children from "contaminating" native-born children, California's legislature threatened to pass an Asian exclusion bill. Anti-Japanese riots also broke out. Outraged Japanese officials demanded that Roosevelt calm the crisis; relations soured so much that war seemed a real possibility. In 1907, the president and Japanese officials reached a "**gentlemen's agreement**": Roosevelt promised to end the anti-Asian hysteria in California and the Japanese promised to ban the immigration of adult male laborers to the United States.

The crisis demonstrated Japan's growing power. In 1907, to make a show of American power to the Japanese, and to show that the "gentlemen's agreement" did not consist of capitulation, Roosevelt dispatched the "Great White Fleet," made up of the navy's 16 battleships, on a world tour, with a special stop in Japan. Seemingly impressed with U.S. naval power, the Japanese nevertheless continued to act aggressively in Manchuria; they made a secret agreement with the Chinese guaranteeing the sole rights to develop a railroad there and thus subverting an American company's plans.

Taft's Dollar Diplomacy

By 1908 Theodore Roosevelt had served seven highly eventful years as president, completing McKinley's unfinished term and being elected in his own right in 1904. Although just 50 years old, and still vigorous, Roosevelt chose not to seek reelection. Not only had he made a pledge in the 1904 election not to run again, he also had alienated conservatives in the Republican Party who viewed with alarm his domestic

TIMELINE 1890–1914

1890

May Congress authorizes the construction of three modern battleships

October 1 The McKinley Tariff goes into effect

1891

January 29 Queen Liliukalani ascends to the throne of the Hawaiian monarchy

1893

January 17 Sanford B. Dole leads successful coup in Hawaii deposing Queen Liliukalani

December 18 The Cleveland Administration refuses to annex Hawaii

1894

July 4 Republic of Hawaii founded with Sanford Dole as president

1895

February Cuban insurgents begin revolt against Spanish rule

July Crisis erupts between United States and Great Britain over disputed Venezuelan boundary

1896

February General Valieriano Weyler implements reconcentration policy in an attempt to crush Cuban revolution

1898

January 25 USS *Maine* arrives in Havana harbor

February 9 The De Lôme letter published in the *New York Journal*

February 15 USS *Maine* explodes in Havana harbor, killing 260 American sailors

March European powers and Japan threaten the U.S. "open door" in China

April 11 McKinley asks Congress to declare war on Spain

May 1 Commodore Dewey defeats the Spanish fleet in Manila Bay

July 1 Battle of San Juan Hill

July 8 United States annexes Hawaii

July 25 United States begins military occupation of Puerto Rico

August 12 Spanish-American War ends and peace negotiations begin

November 19 Anti-Imperial League founded in Boston

December 10 Treaty of Paris, officially ending Spanish-American War, signed

1899

January 1 United States establishes military government in Cuba

February 6 Treaty of Paris ratified by U.S. Senate

September 6 Secretary of State John Hay issues first "open door notes"

November Aguinaldo implements guerilla war against the United States

November 2 Boxer Rebellion breaks out

1900

July 3 Secretary of State Hay issues second set of "open door notes"

August 14 International military force, including U.S. troops, arrives in Beijing to crush Boxer Rebellion

reforms, especially his attempts to limit corporate power, and he feared he might not receive the nomination.

Roosevelt handpicked the rotund William Howard Taft as his successor, and Taft won the presidency in 1908. He hoped to replace Roosevelt's "big stick" with American dollars. "Dollar Diplomacy" aimed to use America's growing wealth, instead of military force, to create order and stability throughout the world. Corporate investment to aid the economic growth of less developed countries would enrich the United States, Taft believed, while extending and ensuring its influence globally. "Modern diplomacy is commercial," Taft succinctly explained. But Taft's foreign policy, which proved to be as clumsy as Roosevelt's was deft, led to a number of setbacks.

Taft brought impressive foreign policy experience to the presidency, with special expertise in Asia. Not only had he served as Roosevelt's secretary of war, he had experience negotiating with the Japanese and had served as the first governor general of the Philippines. But Taft made the mistake of choosing as his secretary of state Pittsburgh corporate lawyer Philander C. Knox, who blundered his way through the next four years.

In China Knox tried to break an agreement that recognized Russia's dominance of northern Manchuria and Japan's dominance of the south. Each had established railroad interests there, but Knox believed that whoever controlled the railroad would control access to the massive China market. In 1910 he proposed that all major powers pool their resources, buy the Russian and Japanese railroads, and then operate them, based on the Open Door Policy. Knox's scheme backfired badly when the former enemies, Japan and Russia, signed a friendship agreement to fend off Knox's plan. Japan

May 1 Foraker Act defines Puerto Rico as an "unincorporated territory" under Congressional control	**July** Filipino war for independence ends	**December 6** Roosevelt Corollary announced	**1908**
	1903	**1905**	**November** William Howard Taft elected to Presidency
1901	**November 18** Hay-Bunau-Varilla Treaty signed, granting United States rights to build an isthmian canal in Panama	**September 5** Peace treaty negotiated by Roosevelt ends Russo-Japanese War	**1914**
March 23 Aguinaldo captured by U.S. forces			**August 15** Panama Canal opens
February 27 Cuba approves constitution ceding much authority to United States	**1904**	**1907**	
September 14 President McKinley dies after shooting and Vice President Roosevelt ascends to presidency	**February 10** Russo-Japanese War breaks out	**March 14** Roosevelt negotiates a "gentlemen's agreement" with Japan regarding immigration	
	June 18, 1904 "Philippines Reservation" opens at World's Fair in St. Louis	**December 1907** Roosevelt dispatches the "Great White Fleet" around the world	
1902	**November** Theodore Roosevelt wins presidential election		
June 19 Congress passes Spooner Amendment			

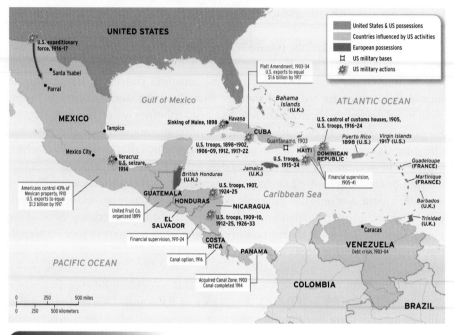

Map 19.2

The United States in Latin America, 1898–1934 The growth of U.S. economic investment and military presence to defend those interests helped define the United States' relations with Latin America.

also formally annexed Korea and closed the open door in Manchuria by replacing American-made goods with those made in Japan. A failed railroad scheme, in which a crumbling Chinese government purchased worthless American railroad stock, helped cause the collapse of the regime and bring about a revolution in China in 1911. An alarmed Theodore Roosevelt, watching his carefully crafted policies unravel in China, condemned Knox's "bumbling."

In Latin America, where the United States dominated and did not have to compete with other world powers, dollar diplomacy achieved more success. In several Latin American countries U.S. corporations already controlled the government and economy; thus, military intervention was unnecessary. The Boston-based **United Fruit Company**, for example, controlled not only the banana market but also the railway system, shipping, banking, and the governments of Honduras and Costa Rica. With the tentacles of "The Octopus," as Latin Americans referred to the company, encircling nearly every dimension of the economy and politics in the two countries, the United States did not need to intervene; American business had established the stability for investment and profit that it sought. But in less stable countries such as Haiti, American bank loans helped pull that nation from the brink of domestic turmoil in 1910.

Other parts of Latin America remained more volatile, and the Taft administration did not hesitate to send troops, under the Roosevelt Corollary, to defend American interests. When rumors spread in 1910 that Nicaragua's dictator planned to make an agreement with Europeans for a second isthmian canal, the United States sent marines to help rebels depose the regime. American investors soon swooped in to purchase Nicaraguan banks and railroads. When in 1912 President Adolfo Diaz offered his country as a U.S. protectorate in exchange for more loans, his angry constituents rose up against him. Taft again ordered marines to Nicaragua to protect the pro-American president against his own people. They remained in that country continuously, except for a brief time in 1925, until 1933.

STUDY QUESTIONS FOR THE UNITED STATES ON THE WORLD STAGE: ROOSEVELT AND TAFT

1. Provide examples of the ways in which Roosevelt's foreign policy was reflected in the phrase, "Speak softly and carry a big stick—and you will go far."
2. Provide examples from Taft's presidency for his statement, "Modern diplomacy is commercial." Is this statement still true today? Why? Why not?

Summary

- In the last quarter of the 19th century, the world's industrial powers embarked on a scramble for colonies, often called the New Imperialism.
- A combination of crises in the 1890s—economic, social, political, and cultural—thrust the United States into the global scramble for empire.
- Social Darwinism, the new discipline of anthropology, and Anglo-Saxonism all justified the colonization of people deemed racially inferior.
- In 1898, after defeating Spain in a brief war under the leadership of President William McKinley, the United States possessed Cuba, Puerto Rico, Guam, and the Philippines and established a global empire.
- Succeeding McKinley after his assassination, Theodore Roosevelt used a "big stick" to expand American influence and maintain order, essential to American trade, especially in Latin America.
- William Howard Taft, elected in 1908, replaced Roosevelt's "big stick" with "dollar diplomacy," emphasizing American investment to establish influence and stability, especially in Latin America.

Key Terms and People

Aguinaldo, Emilio *742*

Anti-Imperial League *740*

Barton, Clara *738*

Beveridge, Albert *741*

Blaine, James G. *732*

Cixi, Empress Dowager *746*

Cleveland, Grover *733*

Dewey, George *736*

Dole, Sanford B. *733*

Du Bois, W.E.B. *741*

Du Puy de Lôme, Enrique *735*

Garfield, James *732*

gentlemen's agreement *750*

Harrison, Benjamin *732*

Hay, John *737*

Hearst, William Randolph *735*

Hoar, George Frisbie *741*

Insular Cases *740*

Kipling, Rudyard *729*

Liliuokalani (queen) *733*

Mahan, Alfred Thayer *731*

Maine (battleship) *735*

McKinley Tariff *733*

McKinley, William *735*

Open Door Policy *746*

Panama Canal *749*

Platt Amendment *739*

Pulitzer, Joseph *735*

Roosevelt Corollary *749*

Roosevelt, Theodore *730*

Rough Riders *736*

Russo-Japanese War *749*

Smith, Jacob H. *742*

Strong, Josiah *729*

Taft, William Howard *743*

Teller, Henry *736*

Turner, Frederick Jackson *731*

United Fruit Company *752*

Washington, Booker T. *742*

Wood, Leonard *739*

Reviewing Chapter 19

1. 1. What assumptions did the foreign policies of Presidents McKinley, Roosevelt, and Taft share? Where did their foreign policies diverge? Were their foreign policies more similar than different? Defend your answer.
2. What did the United States gain by expanding political and commercial empire? What were the costs of empire? Did gains outweigh costs? Explain.

Further Reading

Hunt, Michael H. *Ideology and U.S. Foreign Policy*. New Haven: Yale University Press, 1987. An excellent discussion of the influence of racial ideology on foreign policy.

Hoganson, Kristin L. *Fighting for American Manhood: How Gender Politics Provoked the Spanish-American and Philippine-American Wars*. New Haven: Yale University Press, 1998. Examines U.S. foreign policy in the late nineteenth century through the lens of gender and shows how debates and decisions were shaped by notions of manliness.

Kramer, Paul A. *The Blood of Government: Race, Empire, the United States, and the Philippines*. Chapel Hill: The University of North Carolina Press, 2006. A transnational history of race and empire that explores the connection between race-making and war in the Philippine-American War.

Lafeber, Walter. *The American Age: United States Foreign Policy at Home and Abroad since 1750*. New York: W. W. Norton & Company, 1989. A sweeping look at American foreign policy with especially helpful chapters on the foundations of American "superpowerdom" and the "turning point" of McKinley's presidency.

Musicant, Ivan. *Empire By Default: The Spanish-American War and the Dawn of the American Century*. New York: Henry Holt and Company, 1998. A thorough overview of the Spanish American War.

Rydell, Robert W. *All the World's A Fair: Visions of Empire at American International Expositions, 1876–1916*. Chicago: University of Chicago Press, 1987. An engaging look at international expositions in the age of empire, including the 1904 St. Louis World's Fair and the Philippines Reservation.

Visual Review

A Global Grab for Colonies

The major powers look to untapped markets in African, Asia, and the Pacific.

Race, Empire, Bibles, and Businessmen

Racial theories provide justification for colonization and businessmen and missionaries lead the way.

Precedent for American Empire

Imperial policies build on previous policies of Western expansion.

The Crises of the 1890s

Economic depression, the "closing" of the frontier, and a crisis in masculinity prompts the United States to expand abroad.

The New Imperialism

THE UNITED STATES EXPANDS ITS REACH, 1892–1912

The United States Flexes its Muscles

Latin America

The U.S. embarks on a more expansive foreign policy in Latin America, to protect markets and American investments there.

Hawaii

The United States asserts its interests in the Pacific, particularly in Hawaii.

The Cuban Crisis

United States declares war on Spain in the name of Cuban independence.

"A Splendid Little War"

The United States defeats Spain in a 90-day war, garnering new territories.

The Complications of Empire

Cuba and Puerto Rico

The United States imposes control on Cuba and Puerto Rico.

The Philippines

President McKinley announces plans to colonize the Philippines.

The Debate Over Empire

Americans debate the benefits and liabilities of empire.

The American-Philippine War

The United States crushes Filipino demands for independence in a bloody war of attrition.

China

The United States seeks open access to China's markets and intervenes in the Boxer Rebellion.

The United States on the World Stage: Roosevelt and Taft

Roosevelt's "Big Stick"

Theodore "Teddy" Roosevelt becomes president and works aggressively to ensure U.S. interests abroad.

Taft's Dollar Diplomacy

William H. Taft aims to use America's wealth to create order and stability.

An Age of Progressive Reform

1890–1920

I n June 1900 social reformer Jane Addams, accompanied by friend and fellow reformer Julia Lathrop, crossed the Atlantic to attend the mammoth Paris Exposition. Addams had been appointed as a juror for the "Social Economics Exhibit" at the international world's fair. The exhibit especially attracted the two reformers, as it provided a chance to learn how other countries addressed major problems facing the rapidly industrializing and urbanizing world. Addams and Lathrop, both of whom had witnessed firsthand the disastrous 1894 Pullman strike, were, as Addams explained, "enormously interested" in how other nations approached the problem of workers' housing.

Addams and Lathrop also took part in the meeting of the International Council of Women (ICW), one of many international conferences held at the Exposition. The conference stressed the special responsibility of women to protect, educate, and elevate society. In addition, the two women attended the convention of a "dissenting group of radical feminists," which had broken with the more moderate ICW. They witnessed a lively debate among French "militant suffragists," according to Addams, who attacked the sexism of their country's legal system with such explicitness that the shocked American delegation—except for Addams and Lathrop—marched out "in a huff."

The experiences of the two women in Paris point to several key dimensions of progressivism, a movement that flowered from the 1890s through World War I. Men and women in industrializing and urbanizing societies around the world, usually from the middle class, attacked a wide range of social and economic problems with

Protest against child labor, 1906

CHAPTER OUTLINE

PROGRESSIVISM AS A GLOBAL MOVEMENT
> Principles of Progressivism
> The Global Exchange of Progressive Ideas

URBAN REFORM
> The "Good Government" Movement
> The Housing Dilemma
> Municipal Housekeeping
> Segregation and the Racial Limits of Reform

PROGRESSIVISM AT THE STATE AND NATIONAL LEVELS
> Electoral Reforms
> Mediating the Labor Problem
> Regulating Business: Trust Busting and Consumer Protection
> Conservation vs. Preservation of Nature

continued on page 763

America in the World

American progressives learn from and share ideas with their counterparts in other parts of the world to solve social problems (1890–1920).

The 18th Amendment outlawed the manufacture and sale of alcohol in the United States (1920).

⊛ U.S. event that influenced the world

✦✶✦ International event that influenced the United States

◎ Event with multinational influence

✪ Conflict

President Wilson declared war on the Central Powers in Europe, engaging the United States in World War I (1917).

The National Association for the Advancement of Colored People established to fight for civil rights (1909).

The 19th Amendment granted voting rights to women (1920).

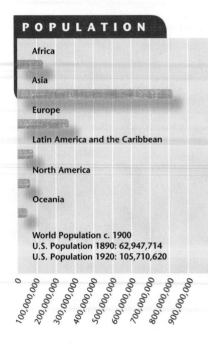

POPULATION

Africa

Asia

Europe

Latin America and the Caribbean

North America

Oceania

World Population c. 1900
U.S. Population 1890: 62,947,714
U.S. Population 1920: 105,710,620

0
100,000,000
200,000,000
300,000,000
400,000,000
500,000,000
600,000,000
700,000,000
800,000,000
900,000,000

the tools of rationality, organization, and science and they shared their ideas across national boundaries. Women like Addams and Lathrop played an especially important role in progressivism, and their defense of the household and children propelled women into the public arena. Although progressives around the world shared their ideas for a better world, progressivism in the United States contained distinctive features. As Addams suggested in the American response to radical French feminists, progressive reform in the United States tended to be more conservative and more moralistic than its European counterpart. American society and government often limited the changes that they and other progressives sought.

Progressives and their many reforms prompted questions that Americans still struggle with today: Do state and federal governments have a role in intervening on behalf of the public good? Are there limits to their power? How is the public good defined?

PROGRESSIVISM AS A GLOBAL MOVEMENT

In industrial societies around the world, in the late 19th and early 20th centuries, concerned citizens grappled with what they called "The Social Problem," a term that encompassed all of the plights of the urban-industrial city—labor conflicts, unprecedented poverty, slums, disease, social fragmentation, and ineffective city government. Worldwide economic depressions had left millions unemployed and hungry. Industrial warfare raged and intensified between workers and employers. Cities around the globe burst at the seams and degenerated into cauldrons of disease and despair. The world seemed to be spinning out of control.

These crises bound together a diverse international group of reformers known as progressives. Mostly educated members of the middle class, they engaged in a broad range of reforms. As progressive William A. White recalled, "We and all the world in those days were deeply stirred. Our sympathies were responding excitedly to a sense of injustice that had become part of the new glittering, gaudy machine age."

Progressive solutions and models of social reform crossed back and forth across the Atlantic and encompassed Latin America, Japan, China, Australia, and New Zealand as progressives established international networks and organizations. American progressives eagerly embraced ideas from abroad and adapted and modified them to fit the specific and needs of their own country.

Principles of Progressivism

CHAPTER OUTLINE

continued from page 759

PROGRESSIVISM AND WORLD WAR I
> A Progressive War?
> Uniting and Disuniting the Nation
> Votes for Women
> Progressivism in International Context

Although social reformers had long attempted to deal with the problems of industrializing, urbanizing society, progressives attacked them in new and varied ways. Although never a unified movement, progressive reform coalesced around several common principles. Rejecting unregulated markets and cutthroat individualism, but also fearing an all-powerful state, progressives sought a middle way, to conserve capitalism while eliminating its excesses. They sought reform, not revolution. They demanded state intervention to offset the power of corporations and fought against monopolies to protect what they deemed the "public interest." As Theodore Roosevelt, who in many ways embodied progressivism, proclaimed in 1912, "This new movement . . . proposes to put at the service of all our people the collective power of the people, through their Government agencies."

Progressives also sought to connect diverse peoples and interests, knitting a fragmented society into an organic whole. Progressives sought to build bridges between the rich and poor, native born and immigrant, and foster a sense of common purpose in their increasingly anonymous, segmented world. They were optimistic and energetic, with a deep faith in the malleability of human nature. Progressives denounced the cult of individualism for social connection and cooperation.

Progressives also believed in applying the tools of the modern corporation to social problems. Emphasizing efficiency and specialization, they gathered and analyzed information and called on experts to fashion rational solutions. Journalist **Walter Lippmann** summed up this aggressive, novel approach in 1914: "We can no longer treat life as something that has trickled down to us. We have to deal with it deliberately, devise its social organization, alter its tools, formulate its method, educate and control it."

The Global Exchange of Progressive Ideas

As soldiers in a global war against social ills, progressives shared ideas and practices across national boundaries. American progressives eagerly sought advice from their counterparts around the world, hoping to jumpstart reform in the United States. Not only did they fear social revolution, they were also concerned that the United States lagged behind the rest of the industrial world in solving its problems.

Progressives around the world connected with each other through a variety of networks. Some, like muckraker **Henry Demarest Lloyd**, embarked on a worldwide tour to collect "all the good ideas of Europe and Australasia." Other progressives studied abroad at European universities where they witnessed governments intervening to provide social services for their citizens and to create more livable cities.

Religion provided another vital link. Advocates of the Social Gospel connected with their European counterparts, especially in England, and shared ideas about implementing Christian social justice. Jane Addams, for example, took her original inspiration for her Chicago settlement house, Hull House, from London's Toynbee Hall. Settlement houses served as incubators for numerous progressive reformers. Roman Catholic social reformers in the United States, Europe, and Latin America drew inspiration from Pope Leo XIII's 1891 encyclical, **Rerum novarum** (Of New Things). Although rejecting socialism, the pope condemned the exploitation of laborers and supported state intervention to promote social justice.

Progressives around the world also formed international organizations on nearly every issue, from unemployment to child labor. Progressive journals and magazines such as *Outlook* and *McClure's Magazine*, circulating around the world, provided a valuable forum for progressive ideas. Progressives even organized study trips abroad, in which they participated in packaged tours to model sites of reform.

Although American progressives looked for guidance abroad, they adjusted their agenda and strategies to the particular context of the United States. American progressives tended to be young and armed with a righteous moralism that easily bled into social control and gave their reforms a unique flavor. Reflecting the crusading spirit of American progressives, Theodore Roosevelt announced, "We stand at Armageddon, and we battle for the Lord."

STUDY QUESTIONS FOR PROGRESSIVISM AS A GLOBAL MOVEMENT

1. What common concerns and problems did progressives around the world share? How did they share information and possible solutions?
2. Compared to earlier Gilded Age efforts at reform, what was new about the progressive approach?

URBAN REFORM

It is not surprising that urban ills became the first targets of progressive reform. As reformer Frederick C. Howe explained, "The challenge of the city has become one of decent human existence." Progressives first addressed the problems that impacted their daily lives directly. Every day middle-class urban dwellers faced a wide range of problems that they simply could not avoid. Filth, pollution, unclean water, and lack of sanitary sewage systems spawned disease and misery that knew no neighborhood boundaries. The stench of uncollected garbage wafted from city streets. Contracts for city services often went to those who offered the largest bribes or kickbacks to city officials. Even getting to work on the streetcar became a daily challenge as privately owned streetcar companies established monopolies of confusing and highly inefficient systems. Inadequate housing increased the misery of poorer urbanites living in crowded tenements.

Middle-class residents also worried about the moral climate of their cities and were horrified by the proliferation of saloons and houses of prostitution. Progressive women played an especially crucial role as "municipal housekeepers," working to clean up cities—physically and morally—and protecting and defending children and their right to a healthy childhood.

But progressive reform could feel like control to those people it wished to help. White, middle-class progressives often proved blind to the rights of minorities and the working classes, and progressives divided by race, region, and gender. In many ways, urban reform embodied fundamental tensions in progressivism: How far could reform in the "public interest" extend before it interfered with individual rights? Did the progressive "public good" benefit everyone or largely the middle class?

The "Good Government" Movement

With city governments often ruled by corrupt political bosses and machines and unresponsive to urban problems, progressives rallied for "good government"—honest, efficient government that would work for the good of all citizens. Investigative reporters such as **Lincoln Steffens** documented the deep corruption at the core of city governments and confirmed what most city dwellers already knew. In 1904, Steffens published *The Shame of the Cities*, focusing on corruption in six major cities. Steffens insisted that the fault lay not with crooked politicians, "any one class," or the "ignorant foreign immigrant." Instead, "The misgovernment of the American people is misgovernment by the American people." To get good government, Steffens argued, Americans needed to demand it.

Progressives initiated "good government" movements in nearly every city across the country. Spanning both major parties, urban reformers formed national organizations such as the **National Municipal League**. They organized reform tickets that managed to oust some of the nation's most prominent political machines, including New York's Tammany Hall in 1901. Using the corporation as their model, they established new, efficient, and honest forms of municipal government.

The disastrous Galveston hurricane of 1900 sparked a new model of city governance. To respond quickly and efficiently to the storm's destruction, Galveston replaced its government with a special commission of expert managers who took charge of various city departments. This system was so effective that it evolved into the city manager system in which a nonpartisan expert administered city services, aided by career civil servants. Progressives also revised city charters to eliminate the old ward system of voting whereby each ward elected a representative to city council, a system fundamental to perpetuating political machines. They replaced this system with "at large" elections.

"Good government" also entailed more efficient and effective municipal services. In the late 19th century, political machines awarded contracts for an array of services and utilities, such as water, garbage collection, streetcars, gas, and telephone service. In many cities these services had become, in the words of one reformer, "private monopolies," charging "unjust rates" and even influencing elections to maintain their control. Impressed by the success of Glasgow, Scotland, in establishing municipal ownership of its streetcar system, progressives convinced city officials in Toledo, Ohio, for example, to purchase the jumble of privately owned transit lines and manage them as a singular efficient system. Following European examples, some cities took over established municipal water, gas, and electric companies. Although municipal ownership of public services was never as extensive as in Europe, many U.S. cities nevertheless benefited from this battle to improve city life.

The Housing Dilemma

Urban housing was another key concern of progressives. Cities sagged under the strain of too many people and not enough adequate housing. Working people, especially, found themselves crowded into unhealthy tenements and subdivided apartment buildings with little fresh air or sanitation. Tenement apartments, often doubling as workplaces, created hazardous environments. Some sections of American cities, such as New York's Lower East Side, were among the most overcrowded in the world. Not only did the squalor of working-class housing create serious public health issues, but progressives also viewed the right to decent housing as an issue of social justice.

To address this issue, **Florence Kelley**, a veteran of Hull House, formed the Committee of Congestion of Population in New York. Participating in international housing organizations and conferences, and drawing on examples from Europe, India, and Japan, the committee shared solutions to urban housing. But neither the committee nor national organizations such as the National Housing Association made much progress, especially when compared to their European counterparts. Clinging to traditional notions of property rights and unwilling to invest tax money for public housing, few city governments responded. Housing reformers learned the hard lesson that many Americans, and especially the courts, continued to view government intervention for the public good as a conflict with the Constitution's stress on limited federal government and protection of private property.

Municipal Housekeeping

Viewing the city as a home, progressive women spearheaded a number of urban reform movements. Protecting their homes had spurred women in the late 19th century to enter the political arena and advocate for temperance. Now, progressive era women—as "municipal housekeepers" emphasizing "public motherhood"—extended and broadened their concept of the home to urban society and the community at large.

Women's clubs and institutions established schools and libraries, affordable day care, and home economics courses for working mothers. When officials did little to address adulterated, bacteria-ridden milk that sickened children, women's organizations opened their own distribution centers offering pure milk. Women's clubs proliferated at such a great rate that clubwomen organized a national association, the General Federation of Women's Clubs in 1890, to coordinate their activities.

African American women created their own parallel national organization, the National Association of Colored Women in 1896. With the motto "Lifting As We Climb," the largely middle-class organization addressed the needs of black neighborhoods, generally ignored by white urban reformers and politicians, by establishing hospitals, orphanages, kindergartens, and day care facilities. Black women's clubs also attacked segregation and lynching and defended the respectability of black women, often popularly depicted as women with questionable morals.

Perhaps no reform effort illustrates "public motherhood" more than progressives' efforts to ensure a healthy childhood. Middle-class women were especially appalled by the contrast between the sheltered, nurtured lives of their own children and those of the working class and demanded a "right to childhood" for all. Florence Kelley and other settlement house workers in New York formed a child labor committee; armed with facts and statistics, they pushed for legislation and managed to get child labor laws passed in both New York and Illinois in the first years of the 20th century.

Then, taking their battle to the national level, they formed the National Child Labor Committee in 1904. They hired photographer Lewis Hine to document and publicize the horrors of child labor. But stiff resistance on the part of both employers and parents blunted reform. Working class parents, many of whom relied on their children's income to sustain their families, resented the reformers' intrusion in their lives. Although Congress passed the modest **Keating-Owen Child Labor Act** in 1916, banning interstate commerce in goods produced by child labor, the Supreme Court struck it down two years later as an unconstitutional expansion of government regulation of interstate commerce. Once again progressives found their reforms limited by older, traditional interpretations of the Constitution.

Progressives proved more effective in applying "public motherhood" to the nation's children at the grassroots level. Concerned about the unsupervised play of children in city streets as well as the allure of dance halls for working-class teenagers, reformers tried to create "healthy" and "uplifting" leisure environments. The playground movement, a uniquely American progressive reform led by the national Playground Association of America (1906), established over 1,500 playgrounds in over 260 cities in just three years. Boys' and Girls' Clubs and Boy Scouts and Girl Scouts also offered supervised, educational opportunities, teaching middle-class values to working-class children. To counter a dance craze that featured sexually suggestive dances, settlement houses and other organizations offered "respectable" folk dancing that required proper behavior.

But children and teens often rebelled at supervision. An 11-year-old boy in Worcester, Massachusetts, complained, "I can't go to the playgrounds now. They get on me nerves with so many men and women around telling you what to do." Similarly many young people rejected the tame dance scene as "slow" or simply refused to abide by the rules, "using vile language, smoking cigarettes, and shimmying while dancing." Progressive reforms, especially those aimed at working-class children and families, often engendered resentment as they viewed these reforms as intrusive.

The juvenile justice system also illustrates tensions created by progressive reform. Concerned that courts treated youthful offenders the same as adults, meting out harsh punishments and incarceration among hardened criminals, progressives succeeded in establishing a separate juvenile court system. It focused on rehabilitating "delinquents," as they referred to them, providing them with counseling and probation, and reform school rather than prison. But some reformers, as well as teachers and parents, used the juvenile courts as a means of social control, to remove problem teenagers from the streets and schools.

Public motherhood and municipal housekeeping, and concerns with social behavior and morality, also led progressives to attack the saloon, cigarettes, and prostitution. Between 1880 and 1900 saloons nearly doubled in number—Americans drank 1.2 billion gallons of beer and malt liquor in 1900, up from 590 million gallons in 1885. Although the bane of the middle class, the saloon served as a focal point for working-class and immigrant communities. But to antialcohol crusaders, the saloon was the devil's workshop. Women reformers especially viewed alcohol as a threat to the sanctity of the home. Men drank up paychecks and abused women and children in drunken rages.

Alcohol also sparked crime and led to other vices. Hatchet-brandishing **Carry A. Nation** smashed apart barrooms, which she called "murder mills." National organizations such as the **Woman's Christian Temperance Union** (WCTU), founded in 1874, took a less extreme approach, supporting local elections banning alcohol sales, fighting for state regulations for alcohol control, and sponsoring alcohol education in schools. The Anti-Saloon League, founded in 1895, sought a nationwide ban on drinking. Between 1906 and 1917, 21 states, mostly in the South and West, passed prohibition laws—despite formidable opposition from liquor interests. In 1919 the **Eighteenth Amendment** to the Constitution, barring the manufacture and sale of alcohol in the United States, was ratified. It remained in effect from 1920 to 1933.

Reformers also attacked cigarettes, mass produced for the first time in the 1880s, as a moral and health issue. "Coffin nails," they claimed, not only led to health problems, such as shortness of breath, but also led smokers down the path of moral decline. The National Anti-Cigarette League embarked on a public education campaign and helped to outlaw cigarette smoking in 16 states.

"Red light" districts in the nation's cities alarmed many middle-class residents. Not only was prostitution openly practiced, but knowledge of venereal diseases also had grown. Concerned about journalists' stories of "white slavery," where unsuspecting young women were lured into prostitution rings and held against their will, Congress passed the **Mann Act** in 1910, outlawing the transport of women across state lines "for immoral purposes."

Segregation and the Racial Limits of Reform

Although progressives often spoke of the importance of strengthening social bonds among urban society's diverse elements, racial segregation in the nation's cities was a product of the progressive era. Some reformers justified segregation as a modern solution to the "race problem," a way of eliminating conflict between the races and protecting blacks from further violence.

Segregation laws, known as **Jim Crow laws**, which legally separated people according to race, originated on southern railroads in the mid-1880s. Southern whites grew especially resentful of middle-class blacks who purchased tickets in first-class cars and traveled with them as equals. In addition, when black men sat near unaccompanied white women in the parlor-like cars, white men grew especially anxious regarding the "protection" of their women, as they viewed all black men as potential rapists. As a result, southern states passed legislation separating blacks and whites on railroad cars.

Homer Plessy, with the support of the Citizens' Committee to Test the Constitutionality of the Separate Car Law, challenged Louisiana's 1890 law, which forced blacks to sit in a separate "colored" section, all the way to the U.S. Supreme Court. Plessy's lawyer argued that the Louisiana law, by denying Plessy equal protection under the law, violated the Fourteenth Amendment of the Constitution. In *Plessy v. Ferguson* (1896), the court upheld segregation, ruling 7 to 1 that the law was "reasonable" as it was consistent with local custom and helped preserve "the public peace and good order." Segregation was constitutional as long as "separate but equal" facilities were provided.

The ruling constituted a massive setback for African Americans. Segregation by both legal statute and unwritten law soon spread to nearly every aspect of life in the South. Railroad waiting rooms, streetcars, public parks, movie theaters, employment, and even cemeteries were all segregated. Separate facilities were seldom, if ever, equal, and segregation provided a daily reminder to African Americans of their inferior status.

Southern progressives often justified segregation as an enlightened solution to the "race problem," a middle way between the extremes of race war—which they deemed a threat as blacks and whites interacted in modern cities—and the outright expulsion of blacks. Whites attacked blacks with a new ferocity in the late 19th century, conjuring up frightening images of the "black beast rapist" intent on ravishing white women to justify the lynching of thousands of black men. **Lynchings**, often public affairs in which black victims were often tortured and then hanged or shot, averaged over a hundred a year in the 1880s and 1890s.

Segregation, insisted Southern progressives, would protect blacks by reducing interracial contact. Alabama progressive Edgar Gardner Murphy, an Episcopal clergyman, insisted that the white South had an "obligation" to "improve" the black race and could do so only by establishing a protective wall behind which blacks would be safe and given the chance to "develop" on their own.

Northern white progressives did little to renounce Jim Crow in the South; in fact, they supported informal segregation in their own cities. Although 90 percent of African Americans still resided in the South in 1900, a black migration to the North was evident by the 20th century and accelerated during World War I with new employment opportunities. Even as most northern schools remained integrated, organizations in some northern cities, such as the YMCA, rejected black members, and hotels, restaurants, and department stores regularly refused service to blacks. Unable to purchase or rent homes in white residential areas, African Americans, regardless of class, found themselves relegated to black-only neighborhoods.

George Meadows, lynched in 1889 at Pratt Mines, Alabama. Antilynching laws were introduced in Congress in the first half of the 20th century, and several passed in the House. But Southerners quashed them in the Senate. In 2005, the U.S. Senate passed a resolution apologizing for failing to enact antilynching laws.

Even some of the most open-minded progressives, such as Jane Addams, never managed to bridge the racial divide. Although Hull House opened its arms to European immigrants, settlement house workers there made little effort to reach out to their black neighbors. One Hull House worker noted that when black women attended events at the settlement house, they "were not always received warmly," as "the settlement seemed unwilling to come to grips with the 'Negro problem' in its own environs." Like their Southern counterparts, many white northern progressives stressed the development of the black race through "self-help" organizations.

Segregation, however, did not improve race relations. Anti-black riots exploded in the nation's cities. In September 1906 a three-day riot erupted in Atlanta when a mob of armed white men, 10,000 strong and fueled by rumors of a black man's assault of a white woman, terrorized the city's blacks. They targeted black businesses, attacking, killing, and torturing black men and women in their path and leaving approximately 25 dead and dozens wounded. The *Atlanta Constitution* reported that "the sidewalks ran red with the blood of dead and dying negroes." Northern cities and towns, including New York and Springfield, Illinois, also experienced anti-black riots.

President Theodore Roosevelt added fuel to the fire of racial animosity by his treatment of black soldiers accused of participating in an incident in Brownsville, Texas. In August 1906 some black soldiers were accused of involvement in a disturbance in which a local white bartender was killed and a police official was injured.

When questioned by local officials, members of the black 25th Regiment insisted that they had been in their barracks and knew nothing about the event. Initially the soldiers' white commanders supported their claims. But pressured by the local white citizenry, who offered questionable evidence, the commanders withdrew their support. When the soldiers continued to deny any involvement, the government charged them with a conspiracy of silence. Roosevelt then discharged 167 black soldiers dishonorably—with no additional trial or due process. The men included Medal of Honor winners and many who had served honorably in both Cuba and the Philippines. Although Roosevelt later relented and agreed to allow the discharged soldiers to appeal, only 14 of them were allowed to rejoin the army.

Southern-born **Woodrow Wilson** continued the disheartening display of presidential prejudice after he became president in 1913. Wilson dismissed 15 of 17 black supervisors holding federal positions as well as many working in lower positions. He also refused African Americans ambassadorships to places in which they had traditionally been held, such as Haiti. Moreover, he allowed the segregation of federal offices in Washington. In 1915 Wilson watched D. W. Griffith's film, *The Birth of a Nation*, in the White House. The film depicted the Ku Klux Klan as the South's saviors after the Civil War, caricatured African Americans, and was vigorously denounced and protested by black civil rights organizations. By screening the film, Wilson seemed to endorse it.

Hostility toward blacks, evident at the highest levels of government, elicited a range of responses from black Americans. Some, like **Booker T. Washington**, rose to national prominence by advocating a strategy of economic development over political

In July 1905, a group of activists, including W.E.B. Du Bois (pictured at center) met in Buffalo to organize the Niagara Movement, which demanded equal rights for African Americans and rejected the accommodationist strategy of Booker T. Washington. The Niagara Movement was the forerunner of the NAACP, founded four years later.

engagement to dampen the fires of race hatred. At the Atlanta Exposition in 1895, Washington delivered an address that would make him famous: he argued that "agitation of questions of social equality is the extremest folly," and that African Americans prepare themselves for full-fledged citizenship and equality by finding a niche in the southern economy—through industrial education and enterprise—to earn the respect of white people who would ultimately reward them with political rights.

Other black leaders, such as W.E.B. Du Bois, criticized what he saw as Washington's accommodation to white supremacy, what he termed "the Atlanta Compromise." The "burden" for Jim Crow, lay not on "the Negro's shoulders," insisted Du Bois, but on "the nation. . . ." Blacks needed to fight for the equality they were guaranteed in the aftermath of the Civil War: "the hands of none of us are clean if we bend not our energies to righting these wrongs." To that end, and in part as a response to the Springfield Riot, Du Bois helped found the **National Association for the Advancement of Colored People** (NAACP) in 1909. The NAACP investigated and publicized lynching, condemned the segregation of federal offices, and organized protests against the movie *The Birth of a Nation*.

Ida B. Wells, black club woman and later a founding member of the NAACP, spearheaded the attack on lynching. In 1887 she became an editor and part owner of the *Free Speech*, a small Memphis newspaper. When a mob lynched three black grocers

As a young teacher, Ida B. Wells was thrown off a Jim Crow train when she refused to move from a first-class car, for which she had purchased a ticket. Wells initially won damages in court, but a higher court overturned the decision.

in 1892, Wells came to the realization that lynching had nothing to do with the alleged rape of white women. Instead, it was an "excuse to get rid of Negroes who were acquiring wealth and property and thus keep the race terrorized and 'keep the nigger down.'" For revealing this truth in her newspaper, Wells became the target of white violence, her newspaper offices and presses destroyed. She fled the South and settled in Chicago; threatened with death should she ever return to Memphis, she continued her crusade against lynching by conducting detailed investigations.

Wells then took her campaign abroad where she lectured and created international alliances. Wells's British lectures forced Memphis city leaders to condemn lynching when they began to worry that bad publicity might damage their cotton trade with Great Britain.

Despite the heroic efforts of Wells, Du Bois, and countless other black Americans, this period marked a low point of American race relations. In 1908, at one of the meetings of the Niagara Movement, a precursor to the NAACP, Du Bois noted this precipitous decline since Reconstruction: "Once we were told: Be worthy and fit and the ways are open. Today the avenues of advancement in the army, navy and civil service, and even in business and professional life, are continually closed to black applicants of proven fitness, simply on the bald excuse of race and color."

STUDY QUESTIONS FOR URBAN REFORM

1. In what ways did women shape progressivism?
2. On what grounds did white progressives justify segregation as a progressive reform?
3. In what ways and on what grounds did black progressives respond?

PROGRESSIVISM AT THE STATE AND NATIONAL LEVELS

Battles against urban ills at the local level led progressives to harness the power of state and federal governments to intervene on behalf of "the public good." Just as they worked to cleanse municipal government, they worked to purify corrupt state legislatures, often in the grip of business interests; elect progressive governors to enact statewide reform agendas; and place politics back into the hands of the people.

Successful on the state level, progressives also seized power nationally, most notably in the three successive progressive presidencies of Republicans Theodore Roosevelt (1901–1909) and William Howard Taft (1909–1913) and Democrat Woodrow Wilson (1913–1921). The Election of 1912 saw national progressivism at its height when three progressive candidates vied for the presidency. Incumbent Taft won the Republican nomination. Roosevelt, who chose not to run for a second term in 1908, reentered the presidential fray as the nominee of a new third party, the National

Progressive Party, or "Bull Moose" Party, made up largely of progressive Republicans angry at their party's turn to the right under Taft. With Roosevelt splitting the Republican vote, Wilson, progressive governor of New Jersey, handily won the election and became the first southern-born president since before the Civil War. Notably, Eugene V. Debs, nominee of the American Socialist Party, rounded out the field, as he garnered nearly a million votes.

Progressive presidents not only broadened the power of the executive, with the aid of progressive Congresses, they also used the power of the federal government to regulate big business by breaking up monopolies and demanding consumer protection. Conservation of natural resources emerged as another hallmark of progressivism at the national level.

Progressivism at the state and national levels, like that of urban reform, was full of tensions and conflicts. "Cleaning up" voting, in the name of democracy, actually reduced the voting population. Limiting working hours, outlawing child labor, and introducing workers' insurance conflicted with individual freedoms, and courts regularly struck down or softened labor reforms. Even progressives who shared a love for nature divided sharply over what best defined the public good.

Electoral Reforms

The state of Wisconsin came to epitomize progressive state politics. Earning the title the "laboratory of democracy," Wisconsin was led by Republican **Robert "Fighting Bob" La Follette**, elected governor in 1900. He instituted a wide range of innovations and reforms, known as "the Wisconsin Idea," which were replicated by other states around the nation. La Follette enlisted social scientists from the University of Wisconsin to help draft laws regarding civil service and public utilities, and to administer new state commissions on industrial relations and natural resources, among others. Wisconsin doubled the taxes on railroads, broke up monopolies, and protected the rights of small farmers. In addition, the state instituted the direct primary, which allowed voters, rather than party bosses, to choose candidates for office.

Wisconsin, and many other states, also established **the initiative, referendum, and recall**, first proposed by the Populists in the 1890s. The initiative and referendum, adopted originally in Oregon, made it possible for voters to place legislation directly before the electorate for a vote in general elections; the referendum allowed voters to repeal state legislation that they did not approve of. The recall gave voters the power to remove any public official who did not, in their view, act for the public good.

On the federal level, the **Seventeenth Amendment** to the Constitution constituted another significant electoral reform. Ratified in 1913, the amendment mandated the direct election of senators by popular vote, rather than by state legislators. Direct election not only brought government closer to the people, an aim of the progressives, it also helped block corporate influence in government.

In addition, progressives worked to refine the electorate, most notably through ballot reform. Previously, parties had controlled the voting process. They printed their own ballots, designated by color, allowing illiterate voters to participate and making it easy for political parties to bribe voters with liquor, food, and other gifts. To reform elections, and to limit the ballot to "qualified" voters, nearly every state adopted the secret, or Australian, ballot along with uniform printing.

When reforming voting, progressives often ignored the role and function of political machines and the corrupt bosses that they so despised. The reforms they enacted not only smothered the party loyalty and high voter turnout that marked the Gilded Age, they also destroyed the positive social services, from Christmas turkeys to jobs, which political machines provided to their constituents.

In the North, limiting the franchise to the most qualified voters, in the view of progressives, meant eliminating illiterate, uneducated, easily influenced immigrant voters. In the South, however, white Democrats took aim at black voters—educated or not. Although not always springing from the same progressive impulse as northern ballot reform, southern ballot reform coincided with progressive reform. Progressivism provided justification for disfranchisement and a return to unchallenged white supremacy, the aim of white southern Democrats since Reconstruction. Like their counterparts in the North, Southern whites claimed that their reforms would reduce fraud and guarantee that the "best" people would vote and win elections. Disfranchisement, southern progressives hoped, would also defuse the possibility of another Populist threat, which, in the 1890s, had, in some states, unseated the Democrats and enhanced the power of black Republicans. Disfranchisement would eliminate both the black vote and the vote of "unreliable" whites, cementing the rule of the Democratic Party.

In addition to adopting the secret ballot and the direct primary, every southern state, beginning with Mississippi in 1890 and ending with Georgia in 1908, added a disfranchisement amendment to its state constitution. The amendments effectively eliminated the black vote in the South and ensured white control; whites would never have to contest another election. Never mentioning race, to avoid outright violation of the Fourteenth and Fifteenth Amendments, southern states set up a set of requirements for voting. These included literacy tests, poll taxes, and "understanding clauses," that required the voter to interpret, for example, a section of the state's constitution to the satisfaction of the voting registrar.

Although technically "color blind," the new state voting laws included loopholes that allowed illiterate white voters to pass through while blocking even the most highly educated black voters. For example, the **grandfather clause**"allowed any voter who had voted before 1867, or had a father or grandfather who had voted, to be exempt from the literacy test or other restrictions. Only white voters qualified, since nearly all black voters and their ancestors had been slaves. Moreover, white Democratic legislatures guaranteed that the voting registrar, who determined who was qualified to vote, was always a member of their party and would reject black voters out of hand.

Despite the blatant violation of civil rights, federal courts upheld disfranchisement. Even Republican presidents, whose party consisted almost exclusively of black voters in the South, refused to intervene. In *Williams v. Mississippi* (1898) the Supreme Court ruled that Mississippi's suffrage requirements did not "on their face discriminate between the races."

Southern disfranchisement of black voters continued, with little change, especially in the Deep South, until the **Civil Rights Act of 1964**. Congressman **George H. White** of North Carolina, defeated in the 1900 election, was the last of 40 African Americans to serve in the House of Representatives since Reconstruction. In his last speech to Congress in 1901, he predicted that "phoenix-like" African Americans "will rise up some day and come again" to sit in Washington. But it would be another 27 years until Chicagoan Oscar DePriest once again broke into the all-white body and another 64 years until the Voting Rights Act of 1965 dismantled the last vestiges of disfranchisement.

While progressive-era voting reforms trimmed the electorate in the North, in the South they eliminated large segments of the voting population, not only excluding the black vote and but also seriously reducing white voter participation, as poorer southern whites refused to pay poll taxes; others simply lost interest in one-party politics. Election reform also drastically reduced interest and popular participation in politics (Figure 20.1). Notably, the progressives' reduction of the electorate sharply contrasts with election reforms taking place simultaneously in Europe where reformers aimed to expand voting rights to the propertyless and uneducated.

Mediating the Labor Problem

The industrial warfare of the Gilded Age, pitting workers against owners, often in violent confrontations, only increased by the turn of the 20th century. The United States led the world in strikes and lockouts, with more than 1,800 strikes and lockouts in

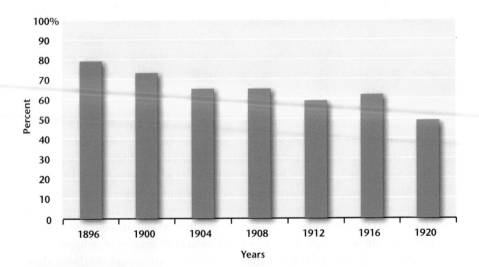

▲ **Figure 20.1**

Declining voter participation Progressive electoral reforms, which included voting restrictions and the demolition of political machines, resulted in declining voter participation and interest.

1900 and more than 3,000 the next year. Faced with a worsening crisis, progressives demanded federal intervention to try to halt the nation's industrial warfare.

In the fall of 1902, anthracite coal miners, under the banner of the United Mine Workers (UMW), organized a massive strike that threatened the welfare of the nation. The union made a series of demands that included an eight-hour day, a 20 percent increase in pay, and, most importantly, recognition of the UMW by the mine owners. The owners rejected the demands outright and miners went on strike as union chief John Mitchell vowed a fight to the finish.

The coal strike soon precipitated a panic. Americans depended on coal not only to run their factories and fuel their railroads, but also to heat their homes. Fearing what he privately called "a social war" should the strike continue much longer, President Roosevelt intervened on behalf of what he deemed the public interest. In October 1902, the president invited both union leaders and mine owners to the White House in hopes of mediating a settlement. But arrogant owners insulted the president, criticizing him for even negotiating with "the fomenters of this anarchy." By contrast, union head Mitchell deeply impressed Roosevelt, whose sympathies for the miners only grew as a result.

When Roosevelt threatened to seize the mines, the owners agreed to his request for arbitration. An independent presidential commission ultimately found in favor of most of the miners' demands, and the union won a 10 percent increase in wages and a nine-hour work day. Unlike Gilded Age presidents, who used federal troops to crush strikers, Roosevelt used the power of the state to mediate labor conflict, in the name of the public interest, and recognized the right of workers to organize.

Despite Roosevelt's example and the UMW's victory, employers still managed in many cases to undercut and even destroy unions. In 1914, in Ludlow, Colorado, in the midst of a massive UMW strike, local deputies and state militia, at the request of mine owners, attacked a camp of striking miners who had been evicted from company-owned housing. Drenching the miner's tents with kerosene and setting them on fire, they shot up the encampment with machine guns and killed 14 people, including 11 children. Soon labeled the **Ludlow Massacre**, the gruesome deaths of the victims sparked violent retaliation by the miners. President Wilson reluctantly sent federal troops to restore order and the strike came to an end.

While some companies simply refused to recognize unions, others created "welfare capitalism" to counter the growing power of labor unions. They offered new benefits, such as profit sharing, pension plans, baseball teams, and athletic facilities, to enhance worker loyalty and undermine the appeal of labor unions. The courts continued to defend the property rights of owners at the expense of workers' rights and rejected unions as a threat to the right to contract individually. The right to organize unions would not be guaranteed in law until the New Deal's Wagner Act in 1935. But progressives still managed to diminish the threat of class warfare, with strikes and lockouts declining in number between 1903 and 1914.

The progressive "middle way"—preserving capitalism through intervention and regulation—faced stiff challenges from a growing number of labor radicals. Rejecting capitalism outright, unlike the more moderate UMW, the Western Federation of

Miners (WFM) sought, in the words of its leader, to "overthrow the whole profit-making system." A massive and violent strike in Colorado in 1903, which resulted in the illegal arrest and deportation of WFM members, only fueled labor radicalism. In 1905 members of the WFM organized the Industrial Workers of the World (IWW), which aimed to create "one big union" of all industrial workers. Headed by charismatic, one-eyed **William D. "Big Bill" Haywood**, the Wobblies, as they were called, rejected the "class collaboration" of conservative Samuel Gompers and the **American Federation of Labor** and welcomed all workers. The most inclusive labor organization in the nation's history, the IWW welcomed immigrants, women, and minorities, including blacks, Mexican, Chinese, and Japanese, as well as the unemployed. The union rejected electoral politics as hopeless and demanded the overthrow of capitalism through class warfare. In addition to strikes, boycotts, and slowdowns, Wobblies also advocated industrial sabotage. By 1912 the IWW claimed 100,000 members. The Wobblies became such a threat that 20 states passed anti-syndicalism laws, making illegal any organization committed to the use of violence, crime, or sabotage.

The appeals of the radical left as well as the excessive power of corporations on the right compelled progressives to seek a middle way to guarantee justice for America's workers and its citizens in other crucial ways. Especially influenced by European notions that government was responsible for the welfare of its people, progressives hoped to curb the appeal of socialism by instituting reforms that guaranteed a decent life for all.

Worker's insurance was one such reform. At the turn of the 20th century, Americans remained the most vulnerable workers in the industrial world. Victimized by exorbitant industrial accident rates, workers in the United States had few resources to

The founding preamble of the IWW stated, "The working class and the employing class have nothing in common. There can be no peace so long as hunger and want are found among millions of working people and the few, who make up the employing class, have all the good things of life."

rely on when a family member was injured or died on the job. In Pittsburgh's steel mills, one out of four families of skilled workers received no compensation whatsoever. Few workers had the assets to challenge the deep-pocketed, powerful steel companies in court.

The plight of American workers had become an international embarrassment. President Roosevelt, in his 1908 annual message, found it "humiliating" that at international conferences the United States "should be singled out" for its lack of progress regarding employer liability law. Unions, however, originally rejected workers' compensation, fearing that they would lose their right to sue. But as courts continued to side with employers, unions supported workers' compensation. Employers, happy to dispense with expensive lawsuits and hoping to undermine the appeal of unions, also supported compensation legislation. In 1910 New York became the first state to enact a workers' compensation law and by 1913, 21 additional states did so. Notably, Americans modeled their legislation on Great Britain's 1897 law.

Compared with their European counterparts, however, progressives in the United States made little headway with other forms of social insurance. Whereas European countries, including Germany, France, and Great Britain, implemented various types of legislation guaranteeing a pension to elderly citizens, American progressives found little public support for this idea. Labor unions also opposed any additional programs that would result in deductions from workers' paychecks. Not until the crisis of the Great Depression would Americans implement old-age pensions through the Social Security Act of 1935.

Progressives found more success at the state and national levels in enacting legislation to improve working conditions. Influenced by international organizations and conferences, American progressive economists in 1905 established the American Association for Labor Legislation, which lobbied for legislation including workers' compensation and improved working conditions for women and children.

The National Consumers' League (NCL), founded in 1898, offered another strategy to improve the lives of workers. Modeled on a London organization, and replicated across Europe, the NCL used the clout of buying power to effect change. As NCL head Florence Kelley explained, "To live means to buy, to buy means to have power, to have power means to have responsibility." Appalled by the working conditions of store clerks in New York City, the NCL created lists of stores to be boycotted until they improved the lot of their employees. By 1904, the NCL claimed 64 leagues in 20 states and expanded the scope of their efforts to include child labor and sweatshops.

Reformers regularly faced conservative courts that regularly negated their efforts. The courts generally continued to privilege the right of an individual to contract freely regarding the number of hours worked. In 1898, in *Holden v. Hardy*, the Supreme Court upheld a Utah law that limited miners to an eight-hour day, citing the public interest in such a law, as miners' work was so dangerous. However, in 1905, in **Lochner v. New York**, the court struck down a New York law limiting the hours of male bakers because, in the court's opinion, the state had no right to regulate their hours and interfere with their right to contract as no health issues, they claimed, were at stake.

Progressives made more headway when they focused on women and children. But even then they saw only limited gains. In 1916 they managed to pass the first law regulating child labor, the Keating-Owen Child Labor Act, which banned interstate commerce in goods produced by child labor, but the Supreme Court struck down the law as unconstitutional two years later. In 1908, in *Muller v. Oregon*, the Supreme Court upheld an Oregon law limiting the work day of female laundry workers to 10 hours. Defending the law before the Supreme Court, attorney Louis Brandies marshaled a vast array of social scientific data, known as the Brandeis brief. The brief included a large appendix that cited legislation limiting women's labor in European countries. Brandeis argued that long hours of work damaged the health of women, and, in turn, harmed the future of the nation. The court agreed. In a unanimous decision, the justices concluded that "healthy mothers are essential to healthy offspring."

But, like many progressive reforms, *Muller* produced unintended consequences. Although a victory for working women, it nonetheless placed women in a separate, unequal, and inferior legal category. Moreover, some employers readily fired their female employees so that they would not be bound by the law.

A horrific tragedy in March 1911 made the plight of working women especially vivid. A raging fire swept through the Triangle Waist Company in New York's Lower East Side. Employing mostly young Jewish and Italian immigrant women, Triangle was a nonunion shop with atrocious working conditions. Unable to escape the fire— the employers had locked the doors as they feared their workers might steal—workers had access to only one flimsy fire escape that did not even reach street level. As a result, 146 of 500 employees died, burned alive or killed jumping to the street in desperation. The **Triangle fire** was the worst industrial accident in the nation's history.

The Triangle tragedy sparked both union organizing and workplace reforms. Blocked from membership by the powerful American Federation of Labor, women workers flocked to their own unions, such as the International Ladies Garment Workers' Union (ILGWU), which had begun organizing even before the fire and grew significantly in its wake. Their efforts were supported by the National Women's Trade Union League, founded by middle-class women reformers. The two groups demanded a state investigation of the fire, collected their own testimonies of fire victims, held rallies publicizing the unsafe conditions in factories, and successfully lobbied the New York state legislature for safer factories.

Regulating Business: Trust Busting and Consumer Protection

By 1900, to the concern of many citizens, nearly every aspect of the American economy was dominated by massive corporations. Americans purchased their meat from the "beef trust," sugar from the "sugar trust," and their fuel from Standard Oil. Nearly all progressives believed that big business was far too powerful and required regulation. But they disagreed on both the means and the end goals of regulation. Some, calling for the nationalization of corporations, claimed that public ownership was the only solution. Others, rejecting socialism as too extreme, called for various types of governmental regulation to keep capitalism intact. But interventionists also varied by degree. Some, demanding a complete breakup of big business, imagined a return to small, competitive businesses that would compete on a level playing field. Others insisted on only minimal regulation of the worst offenders.

President Theodore Roosevelt made attacks on trusts a hallmark of his presidency. "The executive," he boldly proclaimed, "is the steward of the public welfare." Happily using the "bully pulpit" of the presidency to attack big business, Roosevelt nonetheless did so in a decidedly selective and moderate fashion. He made it clear that he was not opposed to big business in principle. Roosevelt believed that large corporations were not only inevitable—part of the natural evolution of business—but they also benefited society through the abundant production of cheap goods and their ability to compete internationally and strengthen the American presence globally. There were, he insisted, both good trusts and bad trusts. Only bad trusts—those that engaged in unfair competition and practices such as price fixing and issuing watered stock—should be broken apart.

Carefully choosing several high-profile trusts to attack, Roosevelt soon gained a reputation as a "trust buster." In 1902 he took on Northern Securities, a planned railroad monopoly created principally by J. P. Morgan and John D. Rockefeller. At Roosevelt's request, the Justice Department successfully prosecuted the company by using the Sherman Antitrust Act; it charged the company with illegal restraint of trade and claimed that its practices led to higher and unfair freight charges for consumers. A few months later, the Justice Department successfully attacked the "beef trust," especially unpopular with the public given the "embalmed beef" scandal that had poisoned and killed more U.S. soldiers than Spanish bullets in the Spanish American War. The federal government charged the beef trust with price fixing and restraining competition. To the delight of Roosevelt and the public, the Supreme Court upheld both cases, and both trusts were dissolved.

In his second term, Roosevelt continued his selective prosecution of "bad trusts." Promising a "square deal" for the American people, Roosevelt responded to growing public outrage against Standard Oil. Probably the most hated company in the nation, Standard's reputation, and that of its head, John D. Rockefeller, grew even worse after muckraker **Ida Tarbell** published a massive exposé of the company, published in *McClure's Magazine*, from 1902–1904. The report depicted Standard as a cutthroat corporation with no concern for the public good and Rockefeller as unscrupulous and "money-mad."

Tarbell's efforts sparked hearings and investigations of Standard Oil at the state level and the company soon faced prosecution in eight states. In 1905 Roosevelt ordered a federal investigation that revealed a range of unfair and illegal practices, such as secret agreements and kickbacks from railroad companies and "monopolistic control" of the oil business. In 1906 the federal government began its successful prosecution of Standard Oil, and in 1911 the Supreme Court upheld a federal court's ruling charging the company with violating antitrust laws and ordered that the massive trust be dismantled.

Roosevelt's attacks on the trusts, however, hardly made a dent in the power of massive corporations. Despite upholding the dismantling of several key trusts,

This 1909 cartoon shows President Roosevelt slaying "bad trusts" while restraining "good trusts."

courts—remaining conservative in their interpretation of the Sherman Antitrust Act— pointed out that only "unreasonable" limits on interstate trade were illegal. Rather than shriveling up, Standard, for example, continued to flourish, and Rockefeller's wealth and power were undamaged and actually enhanced.

Despite Roosevelt's reputation as a trustbuster, his successor, Republican William Howard Taft, actually engaged in twice as many antitrust suits as Roosevelt. His administration successfully prosecuted U.S. Steel and the sugar trust. But the corpulent and lumbering president—the antithesis of the charismatic, athletic, and energetic Roosevelt—never managed to get credit for his accomplishments, as he was unable to maintain the positive relationship with the press and public cultivated by Roosevelt.

Although Taft admired Roosevelt, he was more conservative than his predecessor. During his presidency he aimed to reign in the expanding role of the federal government. Through a series of missteps, Taft managed to disillusion both the progressive and conservative "Old Guard" wings of the Republican party. His blunders led to Roosevelt's decision to run as the Progressive (Bull Moose) candidate in 1912, which split the party and guaranteed Taft's defeat by Wilson.

During the campaign Democratic progressive Woodrow Wilson rejected Roosevelt's distinction between "good" and "bad" trusts as well as his vision of an expansive federal government. The **"New Nationalism,"** Roosevelt's platform in 1912, advocated expansive government used for the public interest. By contrast, Wilson attacked all "bigness," whether in government or business, and advocated the **"New Freedom"** in hopes of restoring small business and fair competition enforced with only minimal government interference.

As president, however, Wilson did expand the power of the federal government and used it to regulate business. Wilson signed more reform legislation than Roosevelt and Taft combined. In 1913 he signed the Federal Reserve Act, to create a central banking system that significantly strengthened the country's financial system by overseeing the nation's monetary policy and providing supervision and regulation for the nation's banks. The next year, under Wilson's direction, Congress passed the Clayton Antitrust Act, meant to supplement and strengthen the Sherman Act of 1890 by outlawing a number of practices such as exclusive sales contacts, holding companies, and price discrimination. Moreover, the law outlawed the use of injunctions against labor unions and legalized peaceful strikes, pickets, and boycotts.

Hoping that his novel would inspire a Socialist revolution, author Upton Sinclair wistfully stated, "I aimed at the public's heart and by accident hit it in the stomach."

But, like the Sherman Act before it, the Clayton Antitrust Act also contained numerous loopholes. Subsequent court decisions also weakened its effectiveness. Notably, the Clayton Act was signed at the same time as another important regulatory act establishing the Federal Trade Commission (FTC), charged with overseeing and regulating business activity and halting unfair trade practices.

Another key reform, initiated by the Taft Administration and instituted under Wilson's, was the 1913 ratification of the **Sixteenth Amendment**, authorizing a federal income tax on both personal and corporate income. Before this time the United States had one of the lowest tax rates in the industrial world. Populists, socialists, and progressives had long called for a graduated income tax that would place a heavier tax burden on wealthy individuals and corporations. Before 1913, federal revenues derived from public lands and customs. After 1913 the federal income tax would provide the bulk of the monies that filled federal coffers.

Progressives also passed laws to protect consumers. In 1906, 28-year-old writer **Upton Sinclair** shocked the nation with his novel *The Jungle*. A plea for socialism, the novel told the story of the Lithuanian immigrant Rudkus family and their bitter experiences in Chicago as they are victimized by the heartless industrial and corrupt political order. But, rather than embracing socialism, readers instead focused on the roughly 12 pages out of over 300 that Sinclair devoted to the meatpacking industry. Based on his own investigation, Sinclair turned Americans' stomachs with vivid descriptions of rats being ground into meat, choleric hogs rendered into lard, and corrupt inspectors passing off tubercular beef to an unsuspecting public.

The Jungle sparked public pressure for action, and meat consumption dropped precipitously. Acting quickly, President Roosevelt called for an independent investigation to verify Sinclair's claims. Not only did they confirm them, investigators added new, disgusting stories of their own. In response, the **Meat Inspection Act** and **Pure Food and Drug Act** both passed Congress on the same day in 1906. The Meat Inspection Act required federal inspectors from the U.S. Department of Agriculture to inspect livestock in slaughterhouses and to guarantee sanitary standards. The Pure Food and Drug Act aimed at outlawing adulterated or mislabeled food and drugs and gave the federal government the right to seize illegal products and fine and jail those who manufactured and sold them.

Like many progressive reforms, these regulations were modest in scope and aimed at both preserving American business and protecting the public. The meatpacking industry, for example, embraced regulation to rebuild its reputation and sales. Large meatpackers also hoped that federal inspection requirements would eliminate smaller competitors.

Conservation vs. Preservation of Nature

Theodore Roosevelt, an avid outdoorsman, also spearheaded another significant progressive reform at the national level—conservation. By the turn of the 20th century, after decades of wasteful consumption of natural resources, Americans had grown acutely aware of the environmental crisis facing the nation. The country's once expansive forests had been seriously depleted, reduced by as much as 80 percent. Mining and oil companies extracted resources with abandon. Much of the nation's farmland had been exhausted and water rights increasingly fell into private hands, limiting access. The nation's natural resources, progressives such as Roosevelt argued, needed to be managed by experts and used efficiently for the public good.

Naturalist John Muir had already convinced many Americans, through his prolific writing, of the value of nature and the tragedy of its loss. Muir's writings generated massive public support for the establishment of national parks. In 1892 Muir and his supporters established the Sierra Club to preserve nature. In 1903 Muir invited the president to visit Yosemite Valley, in California. Roosevelt and Muir, hiking to the backcountry, shared a campfire and a night under a vivid blanket of stars.

But the two men had different visions regarding the natural environment. Preservationists such as Muir and the Sierra Club aimed to maintain nature intact. They wished to protect it from development to provide "fountains of life"—in Muir's words—to restore the parched modern soul. Roosevelt, on the other hand, while sharing Muir's love for the wilderness, concerned himself more with the wise use of natural resources. Conservationists like Roosevelt argued that natural resources could be used for economic development, but they should be carefully managed to guarantee their use for future generations.

In 1902 Roosevelt signed the Newlands Reclamation Act, which appropriated proceeds of public land sales in 16 western states to finance irrigation projects in those states. Roosevelt also quickly expanded the U.S. Forest Service and placed Gifford Pinchot at its head. Like Roosevelt, Pinchot embraced conservationism and played an important role in defining federal action. Roosevelt increased by fourfold, to 200 million acres, land placed into government reserves and developed under government supervision. At the same time, he helped preserve nature by creating five national parks (for example, Crater Lake National Park in Oregon) and by declaring the Grand Canyon a National Monument in 1908, one of 18 he helped establish, along with 150 national forests, 51 federal bird reservations, and 4 game preserves.

The most dramatic conflict between the two arms of environmentalism came to a head—after years of controversy—over Hetch Hetchy, an unspoiled, strikingly beautiful valley in Yosemite National Park. Conservationists led by Pinchot, along with the city of San Francisco, insisted that Hetch Hetchy would best serve the public through the creation of a reservoir to supply San Francisco's rapidly growing population. Preservationist John Muir and The Sierra Club helped make the threatened valley a national story by disseminating booklets and leaflets about the Hetch Hetchy

▲ **Map 20.1**

Conserving for the Future President Theodore Roosevelt, acting on progressive concerns for conserving and preserving the environment, greatly expanded protected public lands, including five National Parks and 150 National Forests. An estimated 230 million acres came under federal protection during Roosevelt's presidency.

showdown. The federal government was inundated with letters from the public pleading for the preservation of the valley. But in 1913 the conservationists won the battle when Congress approved legislation to dam up the valley, and President Wilson signed the bill into law.

For the defeated preservationists the outcome at Hetch Hetchy, as Muir put it, was a "dark damn-dam-damnation." But Hetch Hetchy helped inspire preservationists to expedite the passage of the **National Parks Act of 1916**, which provided a federal preservationist counterweight to the conservationist U.S. Forest Service. The act created the National Park Service and aimed, in part, to preserve national park lands and "leave them unimpaired for the enjoyment of future generations."

STUDY QUESTIONS FOR PROGRESSIVISM AT THE STATE AND NATIONAL LEVELS

1. What reforms did progressives enact at the state level?
2. In what ways did state reforms influence the federal government? How did federal reform impact states?

PROGRESSIVISM AND WORLD WAR I

American progressives responded with mixed sentiments to news of the outbreak of war in Europe in August 1914, and later to U.S. involvement in the war in 1917. Never united, progressives found themselves sharply divided by the war. Some progressives viewed it as a tragic setback, whereas others seized the war as a fortuitous moment to expand federal regulatory power and forge a stronger nation and world.

In many ways, World War I proved to be the death knell of progressivism. Boldly expanding federal power and the nation's global role, President Wilson and his supporters overreached, sowing seeds for a massive backlash in the postwar years. Progressivism's conservative opponents used the war to implement their own agenda and to help bring about the demise of progressivism. Although progressives in the United States overall did not have the same success as their European counterparts, they nevertheless initiated reforms that permanently changed the role of government in the lives of the nation's citizens.

A Progressive War?

For some progressives, World War I shattered their optimistic faith in human progress and the improvability of human nature. Some progressives had even suggested that humankind had outgrown war in its remarkable advancement. Both Jane Addams and Wisconsin's "Fighting Bob" La Follette boldly condemned American involvement in the European conflict. Addams predicted that the war "will set back progress for a generation." Braving vicious attacks on her patriotism, she boldly headed an international peace movement that tried to end the war. La Follette, who after successful terms as governor was elected Senator from Wisconsin, was only one of six senators who voted against the war declaration in April 1917.

Other progressives, however, saw the war as a golden moment, a chance to institute bold changes both abroad and at home. President Wilson, who framed the war as a war "to make the world safe for democracy," envisioned an America providing world leadership, molding a progressive world order that would dismantle empires and tyrannical governments and replace them with democratic institutions. He and other progressives also saw the war as an opportunity to broaden public power at home by expanding the scope of the federal government and diminishing the clout of private enterprise and creating a sense of common purpose among the American people. President Wilson summed up the hopeful sentiments of pro-war progressives when he declared in his war address to Congress, "This is our opportunity to demonstrate the efficiency of a great Democracy and we shall not fall short of it."

Uniting and Disuniting the Nation

When Congress declared war against the Central Powers in April 1917, the Wilson administration faced the paramount task of mobilizing the nation on an unprecedented scale. Massive mobilization required a major expansion of federal power and unprecedented intervention in business and labor. New federal agencies, taking charge of regulating nearly every aspect of the American economy, advanced the progressive agenda.

The federal government extended its unprecedented economic expansion into a war for the American mind. Fearing disloyalty, especially among "hyphenated Americans," those who had come to the United States in the late 19th and early 20th centuries, the Wilson administration embarked on a massive propaganda campaign to ensure the loyalty of all of the American people. German Americans became prime victims of patriotic hatred; labor radicals, especially socialists, also bore the brunt of the federal government's repression. A series of laws, including the **Alien Act**, the Alien Enemies Act, the **Espionage Act**, the **Sedition Act**, and the Selective Service Act allowed the federal government to fine, jail, and in some cases, even deport anyone who hindered the war effort.

Free speech was an early casualty of the war. Socialist Eugene V. Debs, who had garnered nearly a million votes for president in 1912, was slapped with a 10-year jail sentence for speaking out in opposition to the war. The federal government also conducted raids on IWW halls, using the war as a chance to rid the nation of the troublesome Wobblies once and for all. Hundreds of them were jailed, and one was lynched.

The war also heightened racial conflict. When the war halted European immigration, desperate Southern blacks seized the opportunity to migrate north and fill the ranks of northern industry. The "Great Migration," as it would be known, changed the face of northern cities as blacks, leaving the repression of the Jim Crow South behind for opportunity in the north, "voted with their feet." The massive influx of blacks and job competition led to some of the worst race riots in the nation's history. In East

St Louis in July 1917, angry white mobs, incited by a rumor that a white man had been killed by a black man, raged for a week, leaving at least several hundred blacks dead.

The end of the war in November 1918 did not bring about the end of conflict and repression. In 1919, 25 race riots ripped apart America's cities. At the same time "100 percent Americanism" soon became channeled into a "red scare" in which the federal government crushed what remained of the nation's radical organizations. Labor unions, intent on keeping the gains they had made during the war, called a series of strikes in some of the nation's most important industries, including textiles and steel.

Rather than unite Americans by forging the new, collective nation that many progressives hoped for, the war and its aftermath seemed only to divide the country. The war unleashed irrational and often uncontrollable hatred that was the antithesis of the rational and organic progressive vision of society. The American public had grown tired of remaking their nation, and the world and many progressives had become disillusioned, their faith in humanity shattered. The U.S. Senate, rejecting the **Treaty of Versailles** and Wilson's progressive vision to "make the world safe for democracy" in a new world order, reflected the general sentiments of a nation weary of crusades, both domestically and internationally.

Votes for Women

Despite the domestic calamities engendered by the Great War, woman suffrage, fought for by generations of women since the mid-19th century, received a major boost. In the 1910s a new generation of suffragists, headed by **Alice Paul**, reinvigorated the movement. In 1907 Paul, a settlement house worker, moved to England to study social work and met suffragists Christobel and Emmeline Pankhurst. Convinced that women would never get the vote with petitions or persuasion, the Pankhursts advocated direct action, which included civil disobedience and hunger strikes to publicize their cause. Paul became a disciple of the Pankhursts, participated in numerous protests, and even served jail time for her activities.

Paul returned to the United States in 1910 and immediately joined the **National American Woman Suffrage Association** (NAWSA), headed by Carrie Chapman Catt. She soon found herself at odds with Catt. While Catt and NAWSA endorsed Wilson for president in 1912 and considered him an ally in the struggle, Paul borrowed a page from her British mentors and insisted on pressuring Wilson directly, through dramatic protests.

In 1913 Paul organized a massive parade of women down Pennsylvania Avenue that coincided with Wilson's inauguration. The parade turned violent when male opponents assaulted suffragists. In 1916 Paul severed her ties with Catt and NAWSA and with like-minded suffragists formed the National Woman's Party (NWP). Organizing "silent sentinels," the NWP protested outside the White House and boldly continued their actions even after the United States entered World War I. Attacked by angry "patriots" in the heat of war, many of the demonstrators were arrested for "obstructing traffic," and sent to prison. They held hunger strikes. Authorities attempted to force feed them and even tried to get Paul declared insane. But newspaper reports publicizing the plight of the suffragists garnered public sympathy for their cause.

Risking arrest, suffragists bravely protested "Kaiser Wilson" outside of the White House during World War I and implored him to support the vote for women.

KAISER WILSON

HAVE YOU FORGOTTEN YOUR SYMPATHY WITH THE POOR GERMANS BECAUSE THEY WERE NOT SELF-GOVERNED?

20,000,000 AMERICAN WOMEN ARE NOT SELF-GOVERNED.

TAKE THE BEAM OUT OF YOUR OWN EYE.

Finally, in September 1918, Wilson linked the war effort and its aim to "make the world safe for democracy" to woman suffrage. The vote for women, he proclaimed "is vital to the winning of the war." While Alice Paul and her compatriots successfully pressured Wilson, others played a major role in supporting the war effort, a contribution that Wilson could not ignore. Over a million American women labored in war industries at home. Women also served as nurses and telephone operators for the American military and worked as volunteers in France for organizations such as the YMCA. In 1920 the states ratified the **Nineteenth Amendment** to the Constitution.

Progressivism in International Context

Compared to their European counterparts, progressives in the United States had only limited success. In housing, social insurance, and factory legislation progressives found their reforms curtailed by what one European called the "cast-iron constitution" of the United States: traditional legal concepts that emphasized individual and property rights at the expense of a powerful state intervening for the common good. Moreover, progressives seldom transcended class or race. They too often imposed their own middle-class values on those they aimed to help; white progressives not only remained aloof from the nation's race problems, they also often enhanced them. And, as moderates treading a middle way, they tended to exhibit caution, which limited the impact of their reforms. Intent on securing their own political power, they diminished

GLOBAL PASSAGES

The International Women's Peace Movement

In the midst of imperial wars, heightened nationalism, and international conflict, progressive women joined hands across international borders to try to end all wars. Demanding that conflicts be resolved by mediation, women presented an alternative global vision and worked internationally to implement it. Often ridiculed and dismissed by those in power, they nevertheless had an impact that continues to this day.

The International Council of Women (ICW) first brought women from around the world together for the cause of peace. In 1888, at a conference convened by American suffragists Elizabeth Cady Stanton and Susan B. Anthony, a group of international women established the ICW as a permanent body. By 1899 the organization made international peace its main focus, as "nothing touched a woman's heart so much as this."

The outbreak of war in Europe in 1914 instilled a new sense of urgency among internationalist women. Intent on keeping the United States out of the conflict, women activists appealed to their sisters around the world—who believed "that international disputes should be settled by pacific means and that women should have the vote"—to meet in April 1916 as an International Congress of Women. Despite the dangers inherent in meeting in the midst of war-torn Europe, women from both neutral nations and those at war convened in the Netherlands. The United States sent a delegation from the newly formed Women's Peace Party, headed by Jane Addams, and she was chosen to preside over the international meeting.

The congress, organized permanently as the International Committee of Women for Permanent Peace (ICWPP), passed a series of resolutions demanding mediation of the war, the vote for women, and the establishment of an international organization to peacefully resolve conflicts. In addition, the Congress sent representatives to both warring and neutral nations to seek an end to the war and presented a plan for negotiating peace. But President Wilson, crucial to the implementation of their plan, rejected it outright.

When the United States entered the war in April 1917, pacifist women continued to speak out. Addams was included in a War Department list of "dangerous, destructive, anarchistic" enemies of the state. But ridicule and intimidation did not thwart pacifist women. Even before the war ended, the ICWPP pledged to meet at the war's end to try to influence the terms of the treaty. The Treaty of Versailles represented, in their view, a disaster. While they were supportive of the League of

Jane Addams and fellow peace activists aboard the MS *Noordam* in 1915 en route to the International Congress of Women held in the Netherlands.

Nations, they feared that the treaty's heavy-handed reparations and war-guilt clause only set the stage for future conflict.

Although unable to shape the treaty or prevent a second bloody global war, the women's international peace movement continues to this day. In 1919 the ICWPP became the Women's International League for Peace and Freedom, and it is the oldest women's international peace organization in the world. With 37 national units, the organization remains true to the vision of its founders, as it works to end armed conflict and to institute social justice around the world.

In 1931 Jane Addams was awarded the Nobel Peace Prize for her labors in international peace, the first American woman to be so honored. Presenting her with the prize, Norwegian foreign minister Halvdan Koht stated, "Even when her views were at odds with public opinion, she never gave in, and in the end she regained the place of honor she had before in the hearts of her people."

• Why did peace become a "woman's issue" in the early 20th century?

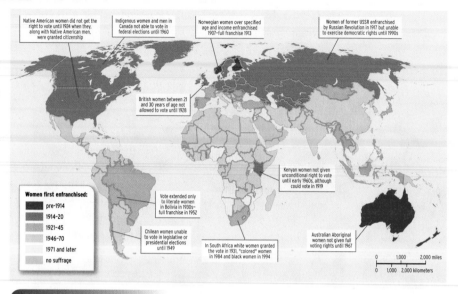

Native American women did not get the right to vote until 1924 when they, along with Native American men, were granted citizenship

Indigenous women and men in Canada not able to vote in federal elections until 1960

Norwegian women over specified age and income enfranchised 1907–full franchise 1913

Women of former USSR enfranchised by Russian Revolution in 1917 but unable to exercise democratic rights until 1990s

British women between 21 and 30 years of age not allowed to vote until 1928

Kenyan women not given unconditional right to vote until early 1960s, although could vote in 1919

Women first enfranchised:
- pre-1914
- 1914–20
- 1921–45
- 1946–70
- 1971 and later
- no suffrage

Vote extended only to literate women in Bolivia in 1930s– full franchise in 1952

Chilean women unable to vote in legislative or presidential elections until 1949

In South Africa white women granted the vote in 1931, "colored" women in 1984 and black women in 1994

Australian Aboriginal women not given full voting rights until 1967

0   1,000   2,000 miles
0   1,000 2,000 kilometers

▲ **Map 20.2**

Woman Suffrage Around the World Women around the world faced resistance to voting rights. In many places, race and education requirements continued to deny many women the right to vote.

TIMELINE 1888–1920

1888

March–April International Council of Women founded by women reformers from around the world

1890

March General Federation of Women's Clubs established to coordinate the activities of American women's clubs

November 1 Mississippi becomes the first Southern state to pass a disfranchisement amendment to its state constitution to eliminate the black vote

1895

December Anti-Saloon League of America founded

1896

May 18 In *Plessy v. Ferguson*, the U.S. Supreme Court upholds segregation as constitutional

July 21 Black clubwomen form the National

Association of Colored Women

1898

February 28 In *Holden v. Hardy*, the U.S. Supreme Court upholds a Utah law limiting the hours of miners

April 25 In *Williams v. Mississippi*, the U.S. Supreme Court rules that the Mississippi disfranchisement amendment does not violate the Constitution

1900

September 8 The disastrous Galveston hurricane sparks a new model of city government of expert managers running specialized offices

1901

February 25 U.S. Steel is formed, becoming the nation's first billion-dollar industry

1902

February 19 The Roosevelt Administration initiates

its first "trust busting" by prosecuting Northern Securities

June 17 Newlands Reclamation Act passed

October 3 President Roosevelt intervenes in the anthracite coal miners strike

November The first of Ida Tarbell's 19-part investigative report on Standard Oil is published

1904

March Lincoln Steffens publishes *The Shame of the Cities*

April 15 National Child Labor Committee organized to fight for child labor laws

1905

April 17 U.S. Supreme Court strikes down a New York law limiting working hours of bakers in *Lochner v. New York*

June–July Industrial Workers of the World founded

1906

January Upton Sinclair's *The Jungle* creates public outcry that leads to the passage of the Meat Inspection Act and the Pure Food and Drug Act

February David Graham Phillips publishes "The Treason of the Senate"

April Playground Association of America founded to establish playgrounds and supervised play for America's city children

August President Roosevelt discharges 167 black soldiers dishonorably after incident in Brownsville, Texas

September Race riot in Atlanta leaves 25 blacks dead and dozens wounded

November The Roosevelt Administration begins its successful prosecution of Standard Oil for its "monopolistic control" of the oil business

the power of those they deemed less worthy, especially immigrants, the working class, and African Americans. Yet they also managed to curb some of industrial capitalism's worst excesses while improving the lives of countless men, women, and children through their wide array of reforms.

Despite the shortcomings of their movement, progressives nevertheless bequeathed a valuable legacy to subsequent generations. Although Americans continue to debate about the primacy of individual rights versus the common good and the proper limits of governmental authority, progressives managed to fix permanently in the minds of Americans notions of social justice that insist on the state's responsibility for preserving at least minimal standards of living for its citizens and a rejection of unbridled, unregulated capitalism. In many ways, progressives set the agenda for liberalism in the 20th century, as they deeply influenced Franklin Roosevelt's New Deal and Lyndon Johnson's Great Society. Indeed, their ideas and concerns about the economy, social justice, and democracy remain relevant today.

STUDY QUESTIONS FOR PROGRESSIVISM AND WORLD WAR I

1. Why did the Great War deeply divide progressives so deeply?
2. How did progressive reforms during the war lead to the demise of the movement?

1908

January 11 President Roosevelt designates the Grand Canyon a national monument

February 24 In *Muller v. Oregon* the U.S. Supreme Court upholds an Oregon law limiting the hours of female laundry workers

August 14 Anti-black riot erupts in Springfield, Illinois

1909

February 12 The National Association for the Advancement of Colored People (NAACP) founded

1910

June 25 The Mann Act, outlawing the transport of women across state lines "for immoral purposes" passed by Congress

1911

March 25 A fire at New York's Triangle Waist Company kills 146 employees

1912

November Three progressive candidates—Republican Taft, Progressive Roosevelt, and Democrat Wilson—vie for the presidency, along with Socialist Eugene V. Debs, with Wilson winning the election

1913

February 3 The Sixteenth Amendment to the U.S. Constitution is ratified, authorizing a federal income tax

April 8 The Seventeenth Amendment to the U.S. Constitution, mandating the direct election of senators, is ratified

December 23 The Federal Reserve Act passed

December Congress approves the development of the Hetch Hetchy in Yosemite Valley as a reservoir to supply water to the city of San Francisco

1914

April 20 The "Ludlow Massacre" in the Colorado coal fields leaves 14 dead

September 26 The Federal Trade Commission is established

October 15 The Clayton Antitrust Act enacted

1916

April Women from around the world form the International Committee of Women for Permanent Peace (ICWPP)

June Suffragist Alice Paul founds the National Woman's Party

August 25 Congress creates the National Park Service

September 2 Keating-Owen Child Labor Act signed into law

1917

April At the request of President Wilson, Congress declares war on the Central Powers

1918

November 11 The Great War in Europe ends

1919

January 16 The Eighteenth Amendment, outlawing the manufacture and sale of alcohol in the United States, ratified

1920

August 18 The Nineteenth Amendment to the U.S. Constitution, granting suffrage to women, ratified

Summary

- Progressivism was a global movement of made up mostly of middle-class reformers intent on ameliorating the excesses of industrial capitalism. Never a unified movement—divided by nation, region, gender, and race—progressives sought a middle way, conserving capitalism while eliminating its excesses.
- Progressives around the world exchanged ideas across national borders through international conferences, journals, exhibitions, and study trips.
- Urban ills became the first target of progressives in the United States and abroad. In the United States, progressives mobilized "good government" campaigns, aimed at more honest and efficient city government and more livable cities. Women progressives fashioned themselves as "municipal housekeepers" who emphasized "public motherhood." White progressives also justified segregation as a social reform that they argued would eliminate racial conflict. African American progressives fought against segregation as well as lynching and disfranchisement.
- Progressives harnessed the power of state and national governments to institute a series of reforms, including electoral reforms, mediation of labor problems, protective labor legislation, trust busting, and consumer protection. Between 1901 and 1920 progressive presidents of both parties sat in the White House.
- Progressives divided over the nation's involvement in World War I. The Wilson administration used the war to advance a progressive agenda both at home and abroad. But the war engendered divisions at home and prompted a conservative backlash that helped end the progressive era.

Key Terms and People

Alien Act *787*

American Federation of Labor *778*

Civil Rights Act of 1964 *776*

Eighteenth Amendment *768*

Espionage Act *787*

grandfather clause *775*

Haywood, William D. "Big Bill" *778*

initiative, referendum, and recall *774*

Jim Crow laws *769*

Keating-Owen Child Labor Act *767*

Kelley, Florence *779*

La Follette, Robert "Fighting Bob" *774*

Lippmann, Walter *763*

Lloyd, Henry Demarest *763*

Lochner v. New York 779

Ludlow Massacre *777*

lynchings *769*

Mann Act *768*

Meat Inspection Act *784*

Muller v. Oregon 780

Nation, Carry A. *768*

National American Woman Suffrage Association (NAWSA) *788*

National Association for the Advancement of Colored People (NAACP) *772*

National Parks Act of 1916 *786*

National Municipal League *765*

New Freedom *782*

New Nationalism *782*

Nineteenth Amendment *789*

Paul, Alice *788*

Plessy v. Ferguson 769

Pure Food and Drug Act *784*

Rerum novarum 764

Sedition Act 787
Seventeenth Amendment 774
Sinclair, Upton 783
Sixteenth Amendment 783
Steffens, Lincoln 765
Tarbell, Ida 731
Treaty of Versailles 788
Triangle fire 780

Washington, Booker T. 771
Wells, Ida B. 772
White, George H. 776
Williams v. Mississippi 775
Wilson, Woodrow 771
Woman's Christian Temperance
    Union (WCTU) 768

Reviewing Chapter 20

1. Although progressives disliked much of what they inherited from the Gilded Age, their reforms have often been described as conservative, as an attempt to preserve many aspects of the Gilded Age. Does the evidence presented in this chapter support that interpretation? If so, why? If not, why not?

2. Some people have observed that Americans are living through a second Gilded Age. Are there similarities, in terms of problems and the solutions put forward by progressives, between today and the late 19th and early 20th centuries?

Further Reading

Chambers, John Whiteclay, II. *The Tyranny of Change: America in the Progressive Era, 1890–1920.* New Brunswick, New Jersey: Rutgers University Press, 2006. A thorough exploration of the progressive era that combines the story of well-known policymakers with the stories of activist working women and men and the many layers of reform—from grass-roots activism to federal policies.

McGerr, Michael. *A Fierce Discontent: The Rise and Fall of the Progressive Movement in America.* New York: Oxford University Press, 2003. An engaging overview of the progressive movement in the United States with an emphasis on the impulse of progressives to remake American society in their own image.

Perman, Michael. *Struggle for Mastery: Disfranchisement in the South, 1888–1908.* Chapel Hill: The University of North Carolina Press, 2000. An in-depth examination of the disfranchisement of black voters, and the reduction of the white electorate, that explores the specific circumstances of this development on all ten southern states.

Righter, Robert W. *The Battle Over Hetch Hetchy: America's Most Controversial Dam and the Birth of Modern Environmentalism.* New York: Oxford University Press, 2005. An in-depth examination of the battle over the Hetch Hetchy valley—whether to preserve it or to make it into a reservoir—that helped give birth to the modern environmental movement.

Rodgers, Daniel T. *Atlantic Crossings: Social Politics in a Progressive Age.* Cambridge: The Belknap Press of Harvard University Press, 2000. Explores many ways that progressives on both sides of the Atlantic shared ideas and methods to ameliorate social problems in the industrial world.

Visual Review

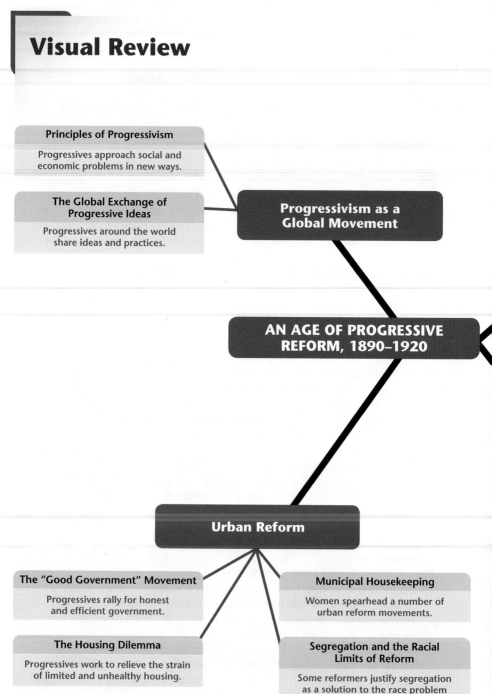

Principles of Progressivism

Progressives approach social and economic problems in new ways.

The Global Exchange of Progressive Ideas

Progressives around the world share ideas and practices.

Progressivism as a Global Movement

AN AGE OF PROGRESSIVE REFORM, 1890–1920

Urban Reform

The "Good Government" Movement

Progressives rally for honest and efficient government.

Municipal Housekeeping

Women spearhead a number of urban reform movements.

The Housing Dilemma

Progressives work to relieve the strain of limited and unhealthy housing.

Segregation and the Racial Limits of Reform

Some reformers justify segregation as a solution to the race problem and African Americans respond.

Electoral Reforms

States work on electoral reform, expanding more direct democracy while disenfranchising some voters.

Mediating the Labor Problem

Progressives seek federal intervention to solve the labor struggle.

Regulating Business: Trust Busting and Consumer Protection

Progressive try to regulate big business.

Conservation vs. Preservation of Nature

Environmentalists take two different approaches to the environment.

Progressivism at the State and National Levels

A Progressive War?

Progressives divide on the Great War.

Uniting and Disuniting the Nation

President Woodrow Wilson mobilizes the country for war, but the war divides Americans.

Votes for Women

Woman suffrage is approved.

Progressivism in International Context

U.S. progressives achieve only limited success.

Progressivism and World War I

JOIN T
ARMY AIR SERVIC
BE AN AMERICAN EAGL
CONSULT YOUR LOCAL DRAFT BOARD. READ THE ILLUST
BOOKLET AT ANY RECRUITING OFFICE, OR WRITE TO THE
SIGNAL OFFICER OF THE ARMY, WASHINGTON, D. C.

America and the Great War

1914–1920

I n 1913 John Reed, the adventurous son of a wealthy Oregon family, recent Harvard graduate, and aspiring journalist, persuaded the *Metropolitan Magazine* to send him to Mexico as its correspondent. For several months Reed rode on horseback along with Francisco "Pancho" Villa, a sometime bandit, sometime revolutionary who led an army of peasant insurgents in northern Mexico. He filed graphic accounts of a battalion of 2,000 dark, Indian-looking soldiers, many of them teenagers, "on dirty little tough horses, their serapes flying out behind, their mouths one wild yell." Too busy to cook meals between battles, the American joined the rebels in drinking cow's blood to fortify himself. The rebels might have "little discipline, but what spirit!" Reed quoted one of Villa's lieutenants as predicting, "when we win the revolution, [Mexico] will be governed by the" ordinary people, "not by the rich."

In 1914 Reed's dispatches appeared in a best-selling book, *Insurgent Mexico*, which became the basis of a popular silent film called "The Life of General Villa." Prominent Americans, including President Woodrow Wilson and former president Theodore Roosevelt, sought Reed's advice on how to respond to the Mexican revolution. Reed urged them to support Villa, the leader of what he called a "people's insurgency."

By 1915, however, Reed's romantic notions about war had dissolved in the carnage he witnessed on European battlefields. Reporting for the radical magazine *The Masses*, he described the sickening slaughter produced by the Great War of 1914–1918, or World War I. In place of dashing Mexican horsemen, industrial-scale warfare produced endless corpses with "holes torn in bodies with jagged pieces of melanite shells . . .

"Be an American Eagle" recruiting poster for the Army Air Service, 1917

CHAPTER OUTLINE

THE SHOCK OF WAR
> The Origins of Global Conflict
> A War of Attrition
> America's Response to War

THE U.S. PATH TO WAR, 1914–1917
> Conflicting Visions of National Security
> U.S. Mediation, the Election of 1916, and Challenges to Neutrality
> Intervention in Latin America
> Decision for War

AMERICA AT WAR
> Mobilizing People and Ideas
> Controlling Dissent
> Mobilizing the Economy
> Women and African Americans in Wartime

continued on page 803

America in the World

U.S. military invaded Mexico to capture Pancho Villa after his border attacks on the United States (1916).

Race riots erupted across the United States between blacks and whites (1917–1919).

U.S. event that influenced the world

International event that influenced the United States

Event with multinational influence

Conflict

Dept. of Justice Palmer Raids to deport leftist immigrants were largely thwarted by the Dept. of Labor as unjust (1919).

World War I changed the political landscape of Eastern Europe (1914–1920).

The United States occupied Central America and Haiti and forced regime changes (1914–1918).

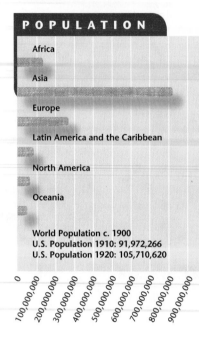

POPULATION

Africa

Asia

Europe

Latin America and the Caribbean

North America

Oceania

World Population c. 1900
U.S. Population 1910: 91,972,266
U.S. Population 1920: 105,710,620

0
100,000,000
200,000,000
300,000,000
400,000,000
500,000,000
600,000,000
700,000,000
800,000,000
900,000,000

sounds that make you deaf . . . gases that destroy eyesight . . . wounded men dying day by day and hour by hour within forty yards of 20,000 human beings who won't stop killing each other long enough to gather them up." The warring nations claimed they fought for a better world, but Reed attributed the slaughter to a "falling out among commercial rivals" as greedy capitalists struggled for bigger profits.

By the time the United States entered the war in April 1917, Reed's faith in democracy and capitalism evaporated completely. He traveled to Russia in time to experience the Bolshevik (Communist) Revolution of November 1917 that pulled Russia out of the war and created a radical new regime. His exuberant eyewitness account, published in 1919 as *Ten Days that Shook the World*, celebrated what he predicted would be the first of many revolutions destined to remake the world.

John Reed—muckraking journalist and American radical who reported on and participated in the Mexican and Russian revolutions.

THE SHOCK OF WAR

CHAPTER OUTLINE

continued from page 799

OVER THERE
> Building An Army
> Joining the Fight
> Political and Military
  Complications
> Influenza Pandemic

MAKING PEACE ABROAD AND AT HOME
> Making Peace and Fighting
  Communism
> Red Scare
> The Fight for the Treaty

During the Great War of 1914–1918 combatants harnessed technology and science, along with millions of factory workers and peasants, to fight on a scale never before seen. Generals launched offensives to kill troops and seize territory and to bleed the enemy into surrendering by crippling the economy and starving civilians. The war killed around 10 million soldiers, mostly in Europe but also in the Middle East, and Asia, and caused the death of about seven million civilians who perished from persecution, disease, or starvation. The war led to the overthrow of monarchies in Germany and Austria-Hungary, to the dissolution of the Ottoman Empire in the Middle East, and to the replacement of the Russian czar by a revolutionary Communist government. The United States and Japan emerged from the war as major world powers.

The United States joined the conflict during its final 19 months, from April 1917 through November 1918. American troops suffered 116,000 deaths (48,000 in combat, the rest from disease), or about 1.5 percent of the total military losses in the war. Yet, actions taken by the United States from the moment the war began affected the outcome of that horrific struggle. Events in Europe also affected America's economy, politics, and social system.

The Origins of Global Conflict

The 1914 outbreak of war in Europe surprised most Americans. During the preceding decade, numerous popular writers had predicted that the global movement of capital, goods, labor, and ideas made war unlikely. Money for investment circulated easily, funding everything from diamond mines in Africa to railroads in the Americas. Safe and inexpensive steamship travel allowed large numbers of people to move easily.

Leading American progressives such as the social reformer Jane Addams and the philosopher **William James** forged links to counterparts in Europe, Latin America, and Australia. They attended international meetings and formed alliance with groups promoting temperance, public health, women's suffrage, and the arbitration of disputes among nations. Their optimism found expression in a global best-selling book, *The Great Illusion*, written by the English journalist Norman Angell in 1910. Angell declared that "war has no longer the justification that it makes for the survival of the fittest." He dismissed as the "great illusion" any notion that war could benefit nations.

Real progress, and wealth creation, he stressed, depended on increasing the peaceful global exchange of goods, services, and people.

Despite such optimistic predictions, bitter national rivalries persisted. Major European powers along with Japan hoped to expand their holdings in Asia, Africa, and the Middle East. Since most of the world was already under the control of one or another empire, acquiring new colonies meant grabbing one from a rival. Although the United States had little interest in annexing additional land beyond what it acquired from defeating Spain in 1898, prominent Americans favored economic expansion, especially in Latin America.

Competition for trade and territory sparked an arms race between nations such as Great Britain and Germany, each of whom sought to build dominant land and sea forces. To preserve a precarious **balance of power** in Europe and other parts of

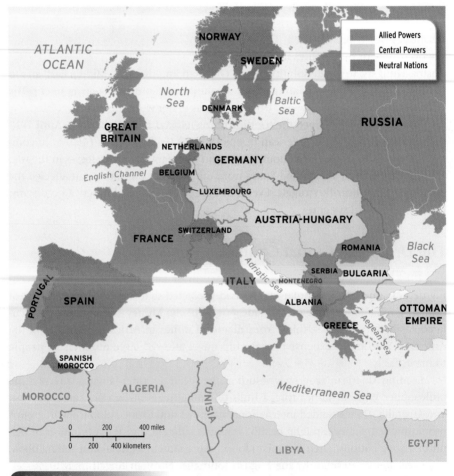

▲ **Map 21.1**

European Political Boundaries Before World War I The German, Austro-Hungarian, Czarist, and Ottoman monarchies dominated most of Europe and the Middle East.

the world, each of these nations forged alliances with other states. This complex alliance system culminated as Great Britain, France, Russia, Japan, and (after the war began) Italy became known as the Allies, and Germany, Austria-Hungary, and Ottoman Turkey became known as the **Central Powers**. As each coalition added a partner, the other felt more threatened. Strident nationalism—an extreme emphasis on national or ethnic identity—made the situation even more unstable. In the Balkans, various Slavic groups such as Serbs and Croats, along with local Muslims, contended for power as the Ottoman and Austro-Hungarian empires lost their grip over the region. Rival nationalism led to several small Balkan wars in the years leading up to the Great War. Some of the worst tension existed between independent Serbia and Austria-Hungary, which controlled Bosnia, a province with a large Serb minority.

In June 1914 a teenage Serb nationalist named Gavril Princip assassinated the Austrian heir to the throne, **Archduke Franz Ferdinand**, as he visited the city of Sarajevo in Bosnia. When Austria threatened retaliation against Serbia (which supported the terrorist group the Black Hand, to which Princip belonged), Russia pledged to defend its fellow Slavs in Serbia. Germany, which feared Russia's expanding reach in Europe as it industrialized, promptly backed its German-speaking ally, Austria-Hungary. France had already allied itself with Russia to balance the threat it saw from Germany. Concerned that German military and industrial might would overwhelm Europe and threaten its overseas empire, Great Britain supported France and Russia against the threat from Germany. By August these rival coalitions mobilized their forces and rushed troops and heavy weapons by train to forward positions.

Capitalists and factory workers along with conservative and socialist politicians in most of Europe enthusiastically supported their own national armies. Even the apostle of peace, Norman Angell, decided that fighting Germany was morally justified and called on his British compatriots to "crush the Hun."

A War of Attrition

In August 1914 German forces struck first, overrunning neutral Belgium to outflank French and British forces deployed in northern France. They seized much of eastern France, which they held for the next four years. To the east, German and Austrian armies inflicted major defeats on Russian and later Italian forces.

Although German armies won most of the initial battles, they failed to achieve the quick knockout blow that would enable Berlin to dictate peace terms. Instead, by the end of 1914, German, French, and British troops hunkered down in 400 miles of parallel trenches in eastern France stretching from Switzerland to the North Sea. The trenches, as deep as 12 feet and laid out in a zigzag pattern, were often water logged, polluted with sewage and corpses, and rat infested. Unable to dry their socks or feet for days on end, most soldiers suffered from trench foot, a chronic fungal infection. Millions of frontline troops lived in these hellholes for weeks or months at a time.

Although the bulk of troops on all sides was drawn from the ranks of workers and farmers, the British and French armies recruited heavily among their colonial subjects. About a million Indians and many West Indian regiments joined the British army during the war, fighting in Europe and especially in the Middle East and Africa. Canadian, New Zealand, and Australian soldiers fighting for Britain had some of the highest mortality rates. France recruited colonial soldiers as well as several hundred thousand Asian and Arab laborers for war work, including the arduous job of digging trenches.

Once the opposing armies settled in, battle followed battle with deadly repetition. In just a matter of hours, trains and motorized vehicles moved large numbers of soldiers and vast quantities of war supplies from factories to rear areas and on to the frontlines. Newly invented airplanes flew observation missions over the countryside. Offensives often began with one side's artillery pounding the trench line of the other for hours or even days. Some German artillery pieces, such as "big Bertha," could lob a shell that weighed about as much as a small car 20 miles. Specialized fuses allowed some shells to fragment, others to penetrate earthworks, and some to rip through barbed wire. Specialized combat engineers called Sappers sometimes dug long tunnels under opposing trench lines, packed them with explosives, and blew up the earth above to clear a path for attack. Many soldiers recalled being shelled as the "worst thing in the world." A "faraway moan" grew to a "scream and then a roar like a train followed by a ground shaking smash and a diabolical red light."

As artillery laid down a covering barrage, officers blowing whistles led their men "over the top" by the thousands to charge on foot across the few hundred yards of so called no man's land that separated the parallel trench lines. Advancing infantry often became entangled in barbed wire barriers. At this point, enemy artillery and machine guns, most of which survived the bombardment, mowed down the attackers.

Generals on both sides relied on 19th-century tactics to fight the 20th century's first major war. Factories produced vast quantities of rapid fire rifles, machine guns, and long-range artillery with highly explosive shells that made it extremely perilous for foot soldiers to cross defended ground. Chemists developed a new terror weapon, poison gas delivered in artillery shells, which the German army introduced in 1915, followed by the British and French. At first, gas stunned and immobilized troops. Soon, however, the use of gas masks—some specially fitted for horses—reduced the weapon's utility. Only about 3 percent of battlefield deaths were caused by gas. Nevertheless, gas blinded many soldiers or ravaged their lungs, often for life.

Those in command believed that if they simply fired more artillery shells and launched more infantry attacks, they would eventually achieve a breakthrough. The new technologies of death devalued individual courage and transformed war into industrial-scale slaughter. In massive engagements that lasted days and sometimes weeks or months, half a million men or more perished in battles that moved the opposing lines a few miles or less.

The epic battles of 1914–1917 were seared into European consciousness. At the first Battle of the Marne in September 1914, about 250,000 men fell in both the German and French armies. During the siege of the French fortress of Verdun that lasted from February to December 1916, the French and German casualties totaled nearly one million. Along the Somme battlefront between July and November of 1916, 58,000 British troops were lost on the first day of fighting, followed by over half a

Table 21.1 Deaths in World War I Although the numbers are approximate, between 8 and 10 million soldiers died during World War I, along with about 7 million civilians.

	Population (Millions)	Military (Millions)	Dead
Central Powers			
Austria-Hungary	52.0	7.8	1,200,000
Germany	67.0	11.0	1,800,000
Turkey		2.8	320,000
Bulgaria		1.2	90,000
Allies			
France	36.5	8.4	1,400,000
Britain	46.0	6.2	740,000
British Empire		2.7	170,000
Russia	164.0	12.0	1,700,000
Italy	37.0	5.6	460,000
United States	93.0	4.3	115,000

Estimated civilian war-related deaths: 6–10 million.

million Allied casualties and at least as many Germans. At the third battle of Ypres, in Belgium, in the summer and fall of 1917, over 300,000 British troops and 260,000 German soldiers became casualties. Things were as bad on the Eastern and Italian fronts. In the Battle of Tannenberg in present day Poland in August 1914, the Germans killed 30,000 Russians and captured about 100,000 more. Italian and Austrian troops fought an astounding 12 battles along the Isonzo River between 1915 and 1917, resulting in Italian losses of 300,000 and 200,000 Austrian casualties.

A quiet moment amidst the squalor of life in the trenches during World War I.

Soon, the ostensible causes of the struggle, such as Balkan rivalries, mattered less. Instead, leaders of the major warring nations anticipated a victory that would give them new territories and influence. Germany hoped to expand into Eastern Europe and parts of Russia, and to take some of Britain and France's overseas colonies. British, French, and Russian strategists savored the prospect of stripping territory from Germany, Austria-Hungary, and the Ottoman Empire, which had joined the Central Powers in 1915. Japan joined the Allies a few months after the war began mostly as an excuse to seize German colonies in the Pacific and on the China coast. Italy bargained for months with both sides before deciding to throw in its lot with the Allies in return for promised chunks of Austrian territory in the Alps and along the Adriatic coast.

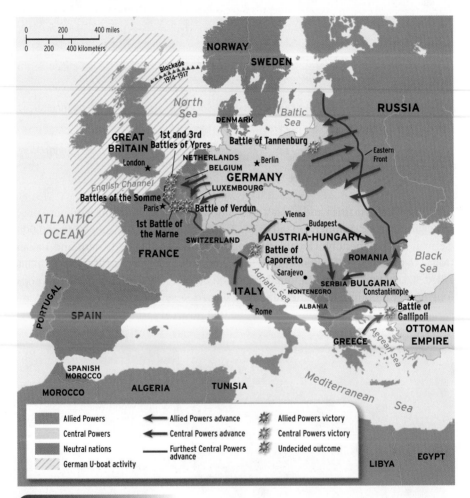

▲ **Map 21.2**

Battles of World War I The battle lines of World War I stretched from the English Channel to the steppes of Russia, and from the North Sea to the Italian Alps. Many of the most destructive battles between 1914 and 1917 were fought along a front that ran through eastern France to northern Italy.

America's Response to War

Most Americans interpreted the war in Europe and U.S. detachment as proof of their own good sense in contrast to other people's violent passions. President Woodrow Wilson reacted to the outbreak of fighting by issuing a neutrality declaration that called on Americans to stay neutral "in thought as well as in deed." Although Wilson admired Great Britain's democratic system, he considered all the warring nations partly at fault for their greed, competing alliances, and aggressive nationalism. He particularly detested Germany's militaristic stance and its effort to acquire new territories, which posed a threat to American interests in the Caribbean and Latin America.

Americans harbored a wide range of sentiment toward the warring powers. Most wealthy industrialists and bankers traced their heritage to the British Isles. Many elite families had married their daughters to the sons of English aristocrats in a bid to boost their own social standing. As a sign of solidarity and with government approval, major New York banks loaned nearly $2.5 billion (worth about $50 billion in 2011 dollars) to the British and French during the first two-and-one-half years of the war.

At the other end of the social spectrum, Irish, German, Polish, and Eastern European Jewish immigrants scoffed at the Allies' democratic credentials. For decades the Irish had fled hunger and oppressive British rule of their homeland. German immigrants who flocked to the United States in the 19th century often in a quest for greater freedom felt little kinship with **Kaiser Wilhelm**'s strutting militarism, but they resented Allied propaganda depicting their culture and homeland as brutal and savage. Jews who came in growing numbers to this country after the 1880s had fled anti-Semitic policies of Imperial Russia, which also ruled much of Poland.

Nevertheless, President Wilson, along with most business leaders, believed that American security and prosperity required maintaining close ties to the British and French. Since the Civil War the export of grain, cotton, and minerals to Western Europe, and British investments in the United States, had provided the capital to spur economic growth. If the war in Europe stopped exports, the United States would suffer immense harm. Factory owners and mill workers, prosperous farmers and tenant sharecroppers, would all be hurt if the war closed down the Atlantic sea lanes.

Appealing to both international law and self-interest, Wilson spoke for most Americans when he insisted that a neutral United States had the right to export nonmilitary goods to all the warring powers and to have its citizens safely travel on passenger ships including those owned by belligerent, or warring, nations. The country had no right to sell so-called contraband, items such as guns or munitions, to any of the belligerents. But the president believed it had every right to sell raw materials and nonmilitary products.

Britain's Royal Navy dominated the Atlantic Ocean from the time the war began. After eliminating German cargo ships, the Royal Navy imposed a blockade against all neutral shipping bound for German controlled ports in Europe. British warships either turned back or impounded cargo carried by neutral merchant ships, including U.S. vessels, attempting to deliver food or raw materials to Germany. This step made it impossible for Germany to import either food or raw materials—some of it bound for civilians as well as for war use—from neutrals like the United States, even while the Allies could do so. Germany retaliated by declaring the waters around Britain and France a war zone and threatened to attack with submarines any ship, Allied or neutral, in the area.

Wilson condemned British interference with U.S. merchant ships bound for German ports. But, since the blockade did not kill Americans or destroy their property, the violations of international law elicited diplomatic protests—not threats of violent retaliation. In contrast, Germany's seemingly indiscriminate use of submarines to attack merchant ships shocked most Americans. In May 1915, a U-boat torpedoed the huge British liner *Lusitania*, en route from New York to England, in the Irish Sea. At the time, it was not known that the doomed ship carried in its hold weapons purchased in the United States. The attack killed 1,200 of the 2,000 passengers and crew, including 128 Americans. Newspaper headlines and many public officials condemned this as a "terrorist attack."

Secretary of State William Jennings Bryan showed some sympathy for the German position. He argued that American civilians had no business traveling in a war zone and that selling any products to warring nations was provocative. President Wilson rejected Bryan's reasoning and threatened retaliation unless Germany pledged to stop submarine attacks on all civilian vessels and paid reparations for the sinking. When Germany failed to respond, Wilson sent a stiffer warning. Bryan resigned in protest against what he saw as the president's anti-German belligerence, but Wilson's pressure appeared to pay off.

In mid-1915, Germany possessed only about two dozen submarines, too few to stop all Atlantic shipping. Rather than risk war with the United States, the German government agreed to halt most U-boat attacks on merchant and passenger ships. But with an eye to the future, the German navy accelerated submarine construction.

Meanwhile, the continued fighting in Europe took a ghastly human and economic toll. To feed, equip, and move their armies, the Allies borrowed billions of dollars from American banks and used the funds to buy vital raw materials. In 1914, the value of goods that Britain and France bought from the United States totaled about $754 million. By 1916, the value had more than tripled, to $ 2.75 billion. With this influx of capital, the United States displaced Britain as the world's leading creditor nation, a rank it held until the 1980s. At the same time, because of the British blockade, Germany's transatlantic purchases dwindled from $345 million in 1914 to almost nothing by 1916. Even as U.S. loans flowed to the Allies, American banks loaned almost no money to Germany. Burgeoning trade deepened the connection between American business and political leaders and the Allies. It also enraged German leaders, who saw Wilson as a hypocrite for tacitly accepting the British naval blockade, which harmed civilians as well as soldiers, while condemning German naval warfare as piracy.

STUDY QUESTIONS FOR THE SHOCK OF WAR

1. **What were the main causes of the Great War?**
2. **What new technologies made the war so deadly?**
3. **How did U.S. economic policy and trade affect the war in Europe?**

THE U.S. PATH TO WAR, 1914–1917

Between August 1914 and the spring of 1917, the United States maneuvered to stay out of the European conflict even while it benefited from what it saw as the world's folly. Divided economic interests, ethnic loyalties, and partisan politics pulled at the fabric of American society. Strident nationalists criticized Wilson for not confronting Germany more forcefully or providing greater encouragement to the Allies. America must rearm, they cried, to avoid or win an eventual war. Progressive social reformers complained that military spending and growing intolerance toward immigrants and labor unions undercut the progress made in recent years toward creating a more just society and mitigating the untrammeled power of corporations. President Wilson tried to placate both camps while attempting to mediate an end to the slaughter across the Atlantic. Partly to demonstrate his determination to defend national interests, he sent military forces to intervene in internal disorders in both Haiti and Mexico.

Conflicting Visions of National Security

Former president and Republican presidential hopeful Theodore Roosevelt typified those who accused Wilson of endangering the nation by leaving it a weak and vulnerable target for Germany or other aggressors. Roosevelt issued calls for the federal government to boost military preparedness, drastically restrict new immigration, and implement compulsory "Americanization" programs to curb the influence of ethnic groups whose loyalty could not be counted on.

Roosevelt's allies, such as Massachusetts Senator Henry Cabot Lodge and General Leonard Wood, supported nongovernmental organizations such as the Immigration Restriction League, the **National Security League**, and the American Defense Society, which warned against foreign threats and advocated military training for young men along with efforts to enforce proper "social order" among working class and ethnic Americans. In 1915 wealthy donors responded to these calls by setting up a private program for training military officers in Plattsburgh, New York. It drew hundreds of undergraduates from elite colleges who later became army officers.

In 1914 a group of wealthy industrialists, including auto manufacturer **Henry Ford**, members of the chemical producing DuPont family, and railroad magnate E.F. Harriman, organized the National Americanization Committee to promote what they called the "civilian side of national defense." They pushed to "Americanize" Eastern and Southern European immigrants by teaching English to nonnative speakers; promoting Protestant social and religious values among these largely Catholic, Eastern Orthodox, and Jewish groups; and encouraging Prohibition. These industrialists championed "race consciousness," the notion that white Anglo-Saxons and "Nordics" (northern Europeans) had to defend themselves against inferior racial groups. Pro-defense, anti-immigrant advocates insisted that sympathy for Great Britain was patriotic, but pro-German sentiment was anti-American. Partly to refute charges of labor's disloyalty, and also to limit the ranks of the unskilled who competed for jobs, Samuel Gompers, head of the American Federation of Labor (AFL) and himself an immigrant, joined those calling for strict limits on immigration.

The upsurge in conservative and militaristic activities deeply troubled progressive reformers like the philosopher **John Dewey** and peace activist and social worker Jane Addams. They worried that Republican politicians like Roosevelt and Lodge would ride the issue of national security back into the White House. Unlike Roosevelt and his circle, they rejected the insinuation that immigrants were disloyal and praised the diverse origins and cultural pluralism of the American population. Some progressives reacted to the call for a military buildup by organizing the American Union Against Militarism, which opposed talk of a peacetime draft and calls to enter the war on the side of the Allies.

U.S. Mediation, the Election of 1916, and Challenges to Neutrality

What President Wilson called the "vast, gruesome contest of systematized destruction" in Europe during 1915 and 1916 prompted both private and official mediation efforts. In December 1915, Henry Ford, who fluctuated between issuing calls for preparedness and pacifism, chartered a vessel, dubbed the Peace Ship, which took him—along with 100 social reform advocates—on a voyage to Scandinavia and Holland. They appealed ineffectually for all warring nations to stop fighting and to submit their grievances to international arbitration.

Wilson also tried to stop the war. Early in 1916, he dispatched his confidant and adviser, Colonel **Edward M. House**, on a mission to London, Paris, and Berlin. House met first with British foreign secretary **Sir Edward Grey**, who urged the United States to join the war, perhaps as an "independent" force fighting alongside the Allies. Grey proposed that Wilson call for all sides to pull their forces back to the prewar boundaries as a prelude to peace talks. This, of course, favored the Allies, who had lost territory. Germany would have to evacuate its forces from France, Belgium, and Poland *before* a peace conference, an unlikely event.

For a time, Wilson considered endorsing the so-called House-Grey Memorandum. But, on reflection, he realized that Germany would surely reject the one-sided terms of the proposal. This stance would either drag the Americans into the conflict on the side of the Allies, something Wilson was not prepared to do, or expose the president as a bluffer. Instead, he issued a vague offer of American mediation that neither side accepted.

The grim news from Europe affected the presidential campaign of 1916. The Republicans rejected the divisive Theodore Roosevelt in favor of a unifying figure, former New York governor and current Supreme Court Justice **Charles Evans Hughes**. Hughes did not propose intervening in Europe but complained that Wilson had placed the nation at risk by not adequately preparing for the likelihood of war.

Wilson insisted that his record showed him to be strong on both defense and social reform. He backed up the claim by pressing Congress to pass the National

Defense Act of 1916, which doubled the size of the army to 200,000 men. Wilson created a new federal agency, the Council for National Defense, to coordinate the nation's response to the war in Europe. The Council drew on federal and state officials as well as private citizens to encourage public support for defense measures. Progressives, such as labor leader Samuel Gompers and the woman's rights crusader **Carrie Chapman Catt**, endorsed these actions.

To further bolster his standing among progressives in both parties before the November election, Wilson secured congressional approval of the Keating–Owen Act limiting child labor and the **Adamson Act** granting railroad workers an eight-hour work day. The **Tax Act of 1916** increased levies on the wealthy in accord with the just ratified Sixteenth Amendment, which permitted a graduated income tax. These legislative accomplishments—along with a snappy reelection slogan, "He Kept Us Out of War!"—helped Wilson win a narrow victory in November.

Intervention in Latin America

President Wilson also demonstrated his commitment to power by using military force in the Caribbean and Latin America. Several times he sent Marines and naval vessels to intervene in Nicaragua, Honduras, the Dominican Republic, and Cuba, where internal power struggles threatened American investments and the repayment of past loans. Wilson also feared that instability in these countries might create a pretext for German intervention.

Disorder in Haiti, the mostly black republic that shared the island of Hispaniola with the Dominican Republic, especially worried Americans. The United States had few commercial interests in Haiti, but Wilson worried that its chaotic political and economic problems might tempt Germany to seize a naval base that could threaten U.S control of the Panama Canal. When in 1915 Haitians resisted a U.S. plan to take over and stabilize the country's finances, Wilson dispatched 300 Marines to seize key locations. In addition to the perceived German threat, Wilson justified his action by labeling nonwhite countries as living in the "childhood of political development." In 1918, when Haitians rose up against the foreign presence, Wilson sent a larger force. About 2,000 Haitians died fighting the Americans.

The Mexican Revolution, which began in 1910 and continued for a decade, posed greater challenges to the United States. Fighting between various armed factions pushed hundreds of thousands of Mexicans into the American southwest. In 1911 a coalition of Mexicans overthrew the long-serving dictator, Porfirio Diaz, who had welcomed foreign investors into the mining, oil, railroad, and agricultural sectors. His successor, a reformer named **Francisco Madero**, rattled these investors by questioning the validity of foreign-owned mineral resources and the large landholdings of the Catholic Church. Just as Wilson took office in 1913, one of Diaz's former generals, **Victoriano Huerta**, seized power and, with what many Mexicans believed was the tacit approval of the U.S. ambassador, murdered Madero.

Wilson, in fact, supported the goals of moderate reform in Mexico and was stunned by Madero's murder. He denounced Huerta as a "butcher" and undertook

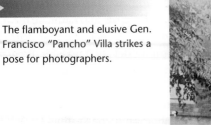

The flamboyant and elusive Gen. Francisco "Pancho" Villa strikes a pose for photographers.

various efforts to drive him out and bring to power moderate reformers who would stabilize the country and cooperate with the United States.

In April 1914, as part of the effort to force Huerta from power and to prevent a shipment of German weapons from reaching him, Wilson ordered naval forces to occupy the city of Veracruz on the Gulf of Mexico. The fighting there killed 126 Mexicans and 19 Americans. A few months later, after Huerta fled Mexico, the path to power opened for Venustiano Carranza, leader of the reformist Constitutionalist Party. Wilson found Carranza's talk of nationalizing foreign-owned land and mineral rights deeply disturbing.

As a counter to Carranza, Wilson backed another contender for power, General **Francisco "Pancho" Villa**. In spite of this assistance, Carranza's army defeated Villa and pushed his remaining forces north toward the U.S. border. After Wilson cut off aid to Villa, he retaliated in March 1916 by attacking the town of Columbus, New Mexico, and killing 19 Americans. Villa went on to raid several other border towns between Arizona and Texas.

Wilson, stung by critics who accused him of failing to defend American soil, dispatched nearly 12,000 troops under the command of General John J. "Black Jack" Pershing to subdue Villa. During the next nine months, Pershing futilely chased the "bandit general" deeper into Mexico. Eventually, American troops clashed with Mexican soldiers sent north by Carranza, who guessed that Pershing's hunt for Villa was actually a pretext to defend foreign oil leases against Mexican plans to nationalize them.

In July 1916, to avert a wider and unwanted war, Wilson and Carranza agreed to submit grievances to a joint commission. When it convened, Mexican officials demanded that foreign soldiers leave their country immediately. U.S. negotiators retorted that Pershing's troops would stay put until the government in Mexico City guaranteed the safety of foreign investments whose legality had been questioned by the recently drafted Mexican constitution.

Negotiations deadlocked in January 1917, at the same time as Germany decided to resume submarine attacks against American shipping. This new threat in the Atlantic overshadowed tensions with Mexico. Wilson soon withdrew U.S. troops and later extended full diplomatic recognition to Carranza's government. Nevertheless, U.S. relations with Mexico remained sour for the next 20 years.

Decision for War

By the end of 1916, the European conflict had become a total war. Nearly all able-bodied men had been drafted to replenish the ranks of the fallen; most industrial production went to the war effort; and military commanders overshadowed civilian leaders. In Germany, for example, the military high command, rather than the weak civilian government or even Kaiser Wilhelm, made all key decisions.

The German general staff feared that the British sea blockade would soon starve both troops and civilians, making it impossible to continue fighting. They hoped, however, that if the navy unleashed its now expanded submarine force of 120 U-boats against all merchant shipping in the Atlantic, they could starve Britain and France and initiate a win-the-war ground offensive before the United States became much of a military factor in Europe. On January 31, 1917, Germany informed the United States that it intended to order its U-boats to sink any American ships supplying the Allies.

German strategists hoped to incite war between Mexico and the United States and thereby limit America's ability to fight in Europe. In mid-January, as negotiations over the Pershing invasion became deadlocked, German undersecretary for foreign affairs **Arthur Zimmerman** cabled instructions to the German ambassador in Mexico City. He was to propose to Carranza that if Mexico joined Germany in a war against the United States, a victorious Germany would return to Mexico the lost territories of Texas, New Mexico, and Arizona.

Wisely, the Mexican government shunned this proposal. But British intelligence agents had intercepted the so-called Zimmerman Telegram and then passed it to American officials in late February 1917, just as German U-boats were poised to resume their attacks on all shipping. Evidence of Germany's deceit outraged Americans. In Wilson's mind, Germany had become more than an aggressor and violator of neutral rights. It now directly threatened the United States—as well as world peace and democracy. The United States could not prosper in a German-dominated world. Wilson ordered the arming of American merchant ships and awaited the inevitable U-boat attacks. In late March, German submarines sank five American ships, killing dozens of sailors and wounding many more.

On April 2, 1917, Wilson asked Congress to declare war against the German autocracy and militarism that had unleashed what he described as unprovoked attacks on American lives and property. The United States, he insisted, would not fight for territory or selfish gain. It desired only to create a "universal dominion of right" through a "concert of free peoples" to bring "peace and safety to all nations and make the world itself at last free." In short, Wilson promised to use American power to achieve a "world made safe for democracy." The United States would enter the war as an "associated power" rather than as a formal ally of Britain and France.

Most elected representatives, as well a large majority of Americans, agreed that Germany posed a real threat to the nation. The president's vision of using the war as a tool to improve the world also enjoyed wide support. A few members of Congress, however, questioned the president's judgment. Progressive Republican senators such as **Robert La Follette** of Wisconsin and **George Norris** of Nebraska condemned Wilson as a dupe of British imperialism and Wall Street financiers. War, they cautioned, would kill reform at home. In the House, the first woman elected to Congress, Republican **Jeanette Rankin** of Montana, opposed the war as immoral. But these dissenters were ridiculed as "treasonous" by large majorities of their colleagues. On April 6, 82 senators voted for war and just 6 against. In the House, the vote was 373 to 50.

STUDY QUESTIONS FOR THE U.S. PATH TO WAR, 1914–1917

1. **How did Wilson prepare the country for war?**
2. **Why did the United States intervene in the Mexican Revolution?**
3. **Why did Germany choose to risk war with the United States in 1917?**

AMERICA AT WAR

The decision to fight shaped domestic policies and the international role of the United States for decades. After April 1917, the nation raised an army of five million men in a year and dramatically increased military and financial assistance to the Allies Although American troops did not "win" the war, they played a critical role by bolstering the Allies and rebuffing the last German offensive. During the war the federal government assumed a major role in managing the economy, mobilized public opinion in support of the war, and began planning for an expanded role in the world community.

Mobilizing People and Ideas

The federal government worked hard to generate enthusiasm for the war. Wilson appointed the progressive journalist, George Creel, to head the Committee on Public Information (CPI), an agency tasked with promoting the war at home and abroad as a democratic crusade. Creel and his staff saw their task as "selling" the war to consumers and used innovative marketing methods to accomplish this. CPI provided newspapers and magazines with war information and distributed pamphlets, books, cartoons, posters, billboards, and even films directly to the public. The materials were presented in multiple languages and formats to appeal to recent immigrants and specific subgroups of Americans, such as workers, farmers, adolescents, and so forth. CPI also opened information bureaus in Latin America, Asia, Africa, and the Middle East to communicate directly to millions of people abroad.

Creel recruited thousands of Americans to serve as so-called 4 Minute Men, assigned to give short speeches in support of the war at public gatherings or between the reels of movies. CPI screened pro-war films in nearly all 12,000 American movie theaters. The first CPI movie, "Fit to Fight," warned soldiers and the public about the dangers of catching venereal disease from prostitutes. Later titles included "A Girl's a Man for A' That," encouraging women to take jobs in war industries; "The American Indian Gets in the War Game"; and "Pershing's Crusaders." Propaganda posters often portrayed German soldiers as fanged beasts or apes, assaulting women. Others portrayed scantily clad women beckoning boys to join the army and navy. Some depicted these new recruits as Christian knights galloping into battle.

Many leading Progressives such as educator and philosopher John Dewey, journalist **Walter Lippmann**, women's rights campaigner Carrie Chapman Catt, along with George Creel, became formal or informal employees of wartime federal agencies.

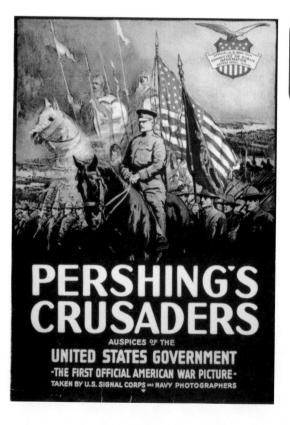

Recruiting poster for the U.S. Army announcing release of the first World War I morale film, "Pershing's Crusaders."

The nation's foremost African American intellectual, NAACP founder and editor of the *Crisis*, W.E.B. Du Bois, expressed hope that the war overseas for democracy would improve race relations at home. When Treasury Secretary William Gibbs McAdoo announced a series of "liberty loan" bond drives to raise money for the war, women's clubs and labor unions joined the sales effort, which raised about $16 billion of the $24 billion cost of the war. In addition to direct defense expenditures, the U.S. government—supplanting the role of private banks—loaned the Allies $11 billion, more than $200 billion in today's value.

Social scientists also helped the war effort. Psychologist Robert M. Yerkes persuaded the War Department that he could develop an intelligence test that sorted out the most gifted recruits from those mentally unfit for service. Commissioned as an army major, Yerkes created standardized "IQ" tests, dubbed Alpha for the literate and Beta for the illiterate. Alpha tests examined recruits in mathematics, language, analogies, the plays of Shakespeare, and the different engines that powered luxury limousines. Beta tests consisted of pictures, often missing an element that had to be filled in, like a tennis court without a net or a camel without a hump. The test results were interpreted as proof that native-born whites were smarter than African Americans or Eastern and Southern European immigrants, many of whom Yerkes classified as "morons." These flawed studies were cited to justify emergency wartime immigration restrictions and, after the war ended, became a basis to establish strict quotas against "undesirables."

Controlling Dissent

As the United States prepared to send millions of soldiers abroad to protect victims of German aggression, it began restricting many of those victims from entering this country. The war itself temporarily stopped most transatlantic immigration. But Congress quickly moved to begin the future exclusion of groups now dubbed "undesirables." By an overwhelming vote in 1917 it passed the **Literacy Act**, a law barring the entry of any persons unable to read in their own language on the grounds that this lack demonstrated their ignorance.

Other restrictive legislation included the Espionage Act of 1917 and the Trading with the Enemy and **Sedition Acts of 1918**. These laws expanded the definition of treason to prohibit most public and private utterances of words or ideas deemed interference with the war effort. The U.S. Post Office adopted a censorship program that banned delivery of letters, magazines, or newspapers that questioned the justice of the war and the draft or criticized America's allies. The Justice Department and local authorities accused organizations and individuals of subversion if they spoke against the war.

Federal or state authorities arrested over 2,000 war critics and sentenced 1,200 of them to prison. Among those convicted for criticizing the draft and the "capitalist" war that benefited "plutocrats" and killed workers were Socialist Party and labor union leader **Eugene Debs** and IWW leader **William D. "Big Bill" Haywood**. Sometimes unintentional critics suffered the government's wrath. For example, movie producer Robert Goldstein received a 10-year prison sentence for "attempting to cause insubordination in the armed forces" by releasing a film about the American Revolution called the "Spirit of '76" in which British Redcoats were depicted as the enemy.

Despite such incidents, one measure of the war's underlying popularity was the large voluntary network that assisted the Justice Department. This included 250,000 members of the **American Protective League** (APL), which had branches in most cities. APL "special agents" wearing official-looking badges opened mail, wire tapped telephone conversations, and conducted raids against newspapers and bookstores. APL members formed squads looking for slackers, young men who avoided the draft. In one raid in New York City in 1918, APL vigilantes rounded up 50,000 suspects.

German Americans and German culture were frequently targeted by vigilantes. Delicatessen owners were ordered to rename sauerkraut "liberty cabbage" and frankfurters "liberty sausages." Symphony orchestras were threatened with boycotts if they played the works of German composer Ludwig van Beethoven. Half of the states passed laws banning speaking German in public or over the telephone, and forbade teaching it in schools.

The Civil Liberties Bureau, a predecessor of the American Civil Liberties Union, challenged these repressive activities without much success. In 1919, after the war ended, the Supreme Court unanimously upheld the constitutionality of the Espionage Act in the case of *Schenck v. U.S.* Schenck had been convicted for distributing antidraft pamphlets and had challenged this as a violation of his free speech rights. Justice **Oliver Wendell Holmes, Jr.**, wrote that the Constitution did not protect the "clear and present danger" posed by "a man falsely shouting fire in a theater and causing a panic." In the related case of *Abrams v. U.S.*, the court ruled that in wartime no citizen had the blanket right to criticize the government or advocate a strike by munitions workers.

Mobilizing the Economy

Mobilizing the economy for war production proved more challenging than officials had anticipated. The War Department relied on outmoded procurement methods unsuited for modern war. Bottlenecks quickly developed in railroad transportation and shipping. Food, munitions, coal, and other vital supplies were often stuck at depots for weeks while ships waited idly for cargo. To remedy this holdup, the federal government created new regulatory agencies with broad powers over the economy. These included the War Industries Board, the Railroad Administration, the Food Administration, and the Fuel Administration. Many of those chosen to oversee regulatory boards were business executives hired by the government for nominal salaries and dubbed "dollar-a-year-men."

The Woman's Land Army worked with the Department of Labor to mobilize as farm hands over 20,000 young, single women, many of them enrolled in college and active in suffrage and other reform movements. Dubbed "farmerettes," they moved from cities to rural areas, where they plowed fields, drove farm equipment, and harvested crops on farms throughout the nation.

To mobilize workers in support of the war, Wilson created the National War Labor Policies Board. It drew membership primarily from the ranks of pro-war unions such as the AFL. The board discouraged strikes and pressed workers to forego some benefits in return for pledges of full employment at wages above peacetime levels. This and other groups affiliated with the AFL also established ties with European labor organizations in an effort to build international labor support for the war.

Some unions rejected patriotic appeals. The IWW led strikes in mining towns like Bisbee, Arizona, to demand higher wages. They complained that while large companies profited hugely from military contracts, workers received token increases. Local vigilantes, mine guards, and federal agents responded violently. During the summer of 1917, for example, over 1,000 striking IWW miners were rounded up, placed in railroad box cars, and abandoned in the New Mexico dessert.

Women and African Americans in Wartime

The war created special challenges and opportunities for women and African Americans. As five million men entered military service and most immigration ceased, paid employment opportunities expanded for women and minorities, who had usually been relegated to work in agriculture, service jobs, or as household domestics. However, politically active women had for decades created an array of local, state, and national organizations to promote suffrage. By 1917, 11 states, nearly all in the west, allowed women to vote. Wilson weakly favored women's suffrage but did not press Congress to pass a constitutional amendment, arguing that the right to vote was a state, not a federal, issue.

Women's organizations, including the National American Woman Suffrage Association (NAWSA), endorsed the war in the hope that their support would also build national support for voting rights. NAWSA leaders pointed out that millions of women had assumed new and vital roles in manufacturing, transportation, agriculture, and government bureaus. Nearly 25,000 women served as Army nurses in

Suffragists demonstrate in front of the White House in 1917, trying to shame President Wilson into supporting a woman's right to vote.

Europe. Thousands of others drove ambulances, staffed canteens for soldiers in the field, or worked as military clerks. More radical suffragists, such as National Women's Party founder **Alice Paul**, defied bans on demonstrations by staging vigils in front of the White House with signs ridiculing talk of a democratic war in a country that barred half its population from voting.

The political winds shifted in favor of suffrage when in 1917 New York State granted women the vote. Wilson in 1918 endorsed a suffrage amendment that Congress soon passed and sent on to the states for ratification. By August 1920 enough states ratified the **Nineteenth Amendment** to allow women to vote in that year's presidential election.

The wartime economic boom, the millions of men who entered military service, and the cessation of transatlantic immigration created labor shortages that pulled African Americans out of the rural South. Around a half million blacks quit agricultural work and domestic labor to seek jobs in southern and northern cities in a Diaspora that contemporaries called the **Great Migration**. Black-oriented newspapers such as the *Chicago Defender* called this an "Exodus" comparable to the ancient Hebrews fleeing slavery in Egypt.

The migrants headed for cities such as Atlanta, St. Louis, Chicago, Detroit, and New York. Some were specifically recruited by factory owners as strikebreakers, fueling white, working class hostility to the new arrivals. Racism, along with competition for scarce housing and better paying jobs, contributed to major outbreaks of violence during and just after the war. Race riots occurred in East St. Louis in 1917, in rural Arkansas in 1919, and in Chicago in 1919. In each of these incidents dozens of blacks were killed and thousands were left homeless. In the aftermath of the violence in East St. Louis, the NAACP organized a silent protest in which 8,000 black demonstrators in New York marched to the sound of muffled drums, carrying signs that resembled those of the Suffragists, asking "Mr. President, Why Not Make America Safe for Democracy?"

African American leaders and organizations such as W.E.B. Du Bois and the NAACP supported the war despite Wilson's dismissal of blacks as an "inferior race." They hoped that the struggle for democracy abroad would spur progress at home. Du Bois urged black Americans to set aside their "special grievances" and "close . . . ranks with . . . white fellow citizens." Wartime service, many black leaders hoped, would promote reforms giving the "American Negro . . . the right to vote and the right to work and the right to live without insult." A war for democracy, they believed, would also help people of color around the world. The war, he predicted, would help create an independent China, self-governing India and Egypt, and "an Africa for the Africans."

STUDY QUESTIONS FOR AMERICA AT WAR

1. How did the U.S. government "sell" the war to the public and was it successful?
2. What methods did the government use to boost war production?
3. What legal and informal means did the government use to silence war critics?

OVER THERE

The U.S. Army numbered about 200,000 men in April 1917. Over the next 19 months, it grew to over five million men. To achieve this extraordinary growth, the government encouraged volunteers and Congress passed a selective service (draft) law that required men aged 18 to 31 to register with local draft boards that determined who would be conscripted, or drafted, into service.

Under the command of General John J. Pershing, the **American Expeditionary Force** (AEF) trained, transported to France, and led into battle millions of men—dubbed doughboys—drawn from all walks of life. The AEF entered the war at a critical time, just as Germany launched a massive offensive to break the deadlock on the western front. Their arrival in France, along with the increased military aid to the Allies that accompanied them, blunted the German onslaught. Americans not only faced death on the battlefield but suffered the ravages of a little understood influenza pandemic that killed about as many of them as did enemy bullets.

Building an Army

To promote enlistment, the War Department distributed millions of posters and pamphlets encouraging voluntary service. These included an iconic image of Uncle Sam saying "I Want You," images of U-boat victims and children mutilated by German troops, and a poster of a winsome young woman dressed in a sailor's suit declaring "Gee!! I Wish I Were a Man—I'd Join the Navy."

For those not sufficiently motivated to enlist, there was the draft. About 24 million men registered, an overwhelming percentage of those required to, and about 10 percent of these were chosen by local boards to enter military service. The law permitted the 65,000 "conscientious objectors" who opposed war on religious grounds to perform noncombat work as medics or orderlies in hospitals. However, those who refused to do so because their beliefs did not permit any cooperation with the military were labeled "enemies of the republic" and given stiff prison sentences.

About 70 percent of the five million Americans in uniform were native-born whites. A fifth were foreign born, and nearly 10 percent were African Americans. All the nearly 400,000 blacks served in segregated units, mostly in labor battalions under white officers. Only 1,000 blacks received officer rank.

French civilian and military authorities, who had long relied on service by their own African colonial troops, resented efforts by American officers to enforce rigid segregation on foreign soil. U.S. officers insisted that the French military *not* treat black soldiers as equals, never praise them in front of white troops, and keep them away from white French women.

The War Department and voluntary groups such as the YMCA that worked closely with conscripts during their training and deployment often expressed more concern about the troops' moral health than about their fighting aptitude. In U.S. training camps and later in France, many young men frequented brothels during their time off. One YMCA leader remarked that defeating Germany might not be worth it if the effort destroyed the "moral health of the young men" doing the fighting. Congress enacted emergency measures to close brothels near army camps in the United States and to temporarily prohibit most alcohol production. Patriots condemned beer, in particular, as a German product unfit for real Americans. Such sentiment gave new momentum to standing calls to ban alcohol consumption, and in 1918 Congress passed the Eighteenth, or Prohibition, Amendment and sent it to the states for ratification, which took place in 1919.

Moral hazards multiplied when the doughboys reached France. AEF commander General Pershing, who himself had taken a French mistress, declared brothels off limits to U.S. troops and threatened to court martial soldiers infected with venereal disease because the affliction had debilitated so many of them. French officials considered the U.S. obsession with sex, alcohol, and segregation bizarre.

Many soldiers adopted what they considered a simpler way to limit exposure to sexually transmitted disease. At the suggestion of local prostitutes, they engaged in sex "the French Way," a euphemism for oral sex. Army and YMCA officials fretted deeply that returning soldiers might transmit this "degenerate idea" to American women. Ultimately, a combination of better hygiene and threats of court martial reduced infection rates.

With access to alcohol and women restricted, tobacco—especially cigarettes—became a common vice among soldiers. Before the war, most tobacco was either chewed or smoked in cigars. Sixteen states had previously outlawed cigarettes as a health threat. But in the trenches soldiers enjoyed the camaraderie of a quick smoke. General Pershing declared cigarettes as vital for the troops as bullets and issued an appeal for Americans to send "smokes" to the boys. Groups such as the YMCA, Red Cross, and Salvation Army, which had earlier denounced cigarettes as a moral and health danger, became the largest tobacco distributors in the world during the war. This development led one frustrated anticigarette crusader to publish a pamphlet titled *Kaiser Nicotine*, predicting, correctly, that over time tobacco would kill more soldiers than would German bullets.

Joining the Fight

General Pershing insisted that American troops deployed in Europe fight as freestanding units under U.S. command—not as replacements for badly depleted French and British ranks. Pershing made one major exception to this rule, granting the French request to have the 92nd Division of black troops fight alongside their soldiers. Elements of the 92nd Division spent more days in battle than any other American unit during the war. But when French officers presented these brave soldiers with medals, Pershing chastised them for "spoiling the Negroes."

Life in the trenches continued to be cold, wet, and terrifying. Food rations often failed to reach frontline soldiers and they frequently had to drink rainwater collected in shell holes, spreading dysentery. After German mustard gas attacks, many

African American "Doughboys" on patrol in France, 1918. Unlike most of their peers, this unit was armed for combat, not confined to service work.

men suffered temporary blindness. Nearly all those in the trenches were covered by lice. The term "basket case" entered the language in reference to soldiers who had lost limbs and were confined to a basket in a hospital.

By the end of the war about 100,000 American soldiers were admitted to field hospitals suffering from what doctors then called "shell shock." The symptoms, already common among British and French troops, included staring eyes or a frozen, terrified look; violent tremors; and cold and sometimes blue extremities. Some victims became blind, hysterical, or paralyzed. Doctors initially thought that high explosive shells rattling the brain caused the condition. The affliction probably resulted, however, from emotional strain caused by long periods in the trenches alternating with intense combat. In Vietnam and later wars, these symptoms are often called post-traumatic stress disorder, or PTSD. About half the victims returned to duty after a brief hospitalization, but many remained under care. Symptoms of shell shock sometimes reappeared months or even years later among those who had seemingly recovered.

Political and Military Complications

Around the time the Americans entered the war, events in Russia created new problems on the western front. Since the overthrow of Czar Nicholas in the spring of 1917, Russian armies had largely stopped fighting. In November the Bolsheviks, or Communists, led by **Vladimir Lenin**, seized power from the pro-Allied regime that briefly replaced the czar. In the spring of 1918, Lenin approved the Treaty of Brest

Litovsk with Germany and formally pulled Russia out of the war. This move allowed German commanders to transport hundreds of thousands of troops from Eastern to Western Europe. In March, the expanded German forces in the West launched a major offensive designed to overrun France before more American supplies and soldiers could arrive.

Unfortunately for Germany, a growing number of American troops joined the battle and blunted the German advance along the Marne River at Chateau Thierry. By the summer and fall of 1918, hundreds of thousands additional doughboys helped push back the Germans in the battles of Chateau Thierry and Bellau Woods in June and the 2nd Battle of the Marne in July and August. The intense fighting during the 10 months of combat in 1918 killed around 50,000 Americans and wounded many more. While these casualties shocked the American public, they were only a small fraction of the British, French, and German losses at this time. By October German generals ran out of troops, supplies, and time. To make matters worse, Germany's Austrian, Turkish, and Bulgarian allies quit fighting.

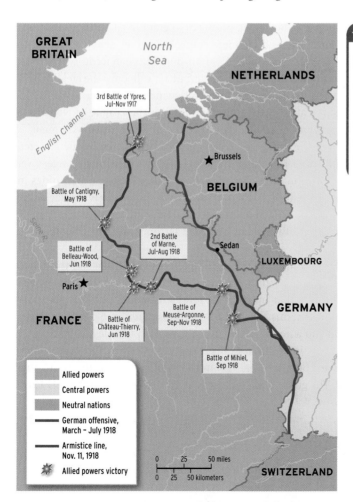

◀ **Map 21.3**

America Joins World War I, 1917–1918 U.S. armed forces entered European combat in large numbers during 1918. They played an important role in breaking the stalemate on the Western Front.

Although the German army still occupied Belgium, parts of France, Poland, and western Russia, they faced desperate odds. Within Germany hunger and war weariness sparked riots. Unless the fighting stopped quickly, the German high command feared an Allied push into Germany and the possible seizure of power by communists. To prevent this and to preserve the fiction that the army had not been defeated, German military leaders insisted that the country's previously ignored civilian politicians seek a U.S.-brokered cease-fire.

German moderates embraced the opportunity to end the war and create a democratic regime. In January 1918 Wilson had offered a peace plan, called Fourteen Points, which outlined how to end the war and reconstruct the world. Wilson called for an end to secret deals among nations and a push for "open diplomacy." He favored agreements among the victors and the vanquished to expand world trade, reduce armaments, permit self-rule for ethnic minorities in Eastern Europe, and assure the "impartial adjustment of all colonial claims." As an inducement to speed a German surrender, he promised to treat a democratic Germany fairly in the postwar settlement.

Wilson's call for self-determination and readjustment of colonial arrangements partly represented a response to Bolshevik promises to grant freedom to Asians, Africans, and Arabs under European and Japanese control. The president also hoped to preempt Allied plans to divide up German, Austrian, and Ottoman territory. The 14th point, which Wilson considered the most important of all, called for the creation of a new "association of nations" to ensure "political independence and territorial integrity to great and small states alike." This soon took form as the **League of Nations**, a world forum that Wilson intended to incorporate in the ultimate peace settlement.

When Wilson received German peace feelers in October–November he adopted a harsher tone. He might have reacted to the bitter realities of combat, anger over evidence that retreating German forces had destroyed farms, factories, and mines in Belgium and France, or simply have aligned his approach more closely to that of the British and French. In any case, Wilson rejected a cease fire until the Kaiser abdicated, and German troops agreed to evacuate all occupied territory and to surrender their heavy weapons.

Germany had to swallow another bitter pill. Following an armistice, the Allied food blockade would continue—victimizing mostly civilians—until Germany signed a final peace treaty, a process that might last months. Germany's democratic politicians deeply resented these terms but had few options. Early in November Kaiser Wilhelm fled to Holland and a new civilian government accepted the harsh armistice terms. Anxious to shift the pain of defeat to the shoulders of others, German military leaders promptly accused liberals, Socialists, and Jews of a "stab in the back" that betrayed the fatherland. The guns of war fell silent at 11:11 AM on November 11, 1918, but peace remained elusive.

Influenza Pandemic

During the last half of 1918 and into 1919, a global epidemic, or pandemic, ravaged the world. The "flu," an annual arrival, usually resembled a bad cold. Because the flu virus mutates quickly, however, immunity seldom carried over from one year to the next.

Scientists now understand that occasionally the virus mutates dramatically or "jumps species." Thus a swine or bird flu can evolve in ways that allow it to infect humans and cause a more severe illness. Something of this sort occurred in 1918–1919 when otherwise healthy soldiers in the trenches of the western front came down with a severe flu that killed its victims, sometimes in a few hours. Nearly half of all 116,000 U.S. military deaths in Europe resulted from the flu. The illness spread quickly in military barracks and was carried around the world by infected travelers on steamships. Unlike most diseases, which typically hit the very young and old the hardest, the 1918 variant struck healthy young adults most seriously, possibly by overstimulating immune systems to inflame air passages in the lungs.

The disease was first reported in March 1918 among soldiers based in Kansas. Troops carried it to Europe where it may have mutated further and spread quickly around the world. The virus proved even more virulent in its second appearance in the fall. In October alone, the flu killed 200,000 Americans.

In the United States, panicked officials tried to halt transmission of the disease by canceling public gatherings and closing theaters and schools. People on the street often wore gauze masks to keep from inhaling infectious particles—a vain endeavor since microscopic viruses easily passed through the cloth. Rumors quickly spread accusing German agents of engaging in "germ warfare." By mid-1919 the virus had struck down those most susceptible to it, and had possibly mutated into a less virulent strain. Ultimately, the pandemic killed about 600,000 Americans and at least 40 million people worldwide, with most of the deaths in China and India.

Early in the 21st century scientists utilized new techniques to recover DNA particles from the 1918 virus lodged in the remains of victims buried in the frozen tundra of Norway and Alaska. Among their findings was the disturbing fact that only subtle mutations distinguished the "killer flu" from the mundane variety. This finding made it all but certain that similar pandemics could and would again occur.

STUDY QUESTIONS FOR OVER THERE

1. What methods did the United States employ to quickly raise a mass army?
2. What impact did the arrival of U.S. troops in Europe have on the war?
3. How was the Fourteen Points intended as a plan to both end the war and shape the peace?

MAKING PEACE ABROAD AND AT HOME

President Wilson's popularity among Americans declined after the initial enthusiasm for war. The idealistic goals he proclaimed often seemed obscured by battlefield casualties and friction with coalition partners. The president blundered badly when he asked voters early in November 1918 to make the imminent congressional election a referendum on his leadership and plans for peace. Instead, a majority of voters blamed Democrats for a war they had grown weary of and a variety of accumulated economic grievances. After the armistice, Wilson had to deal with emboldened Republican critics that controlled Congress, Allied leaders bent on revenge, and a communist regime in Russia trying to spread revolution. These factors complicated the president's effort to win Senate approval for a treaty that included membership in a new League of Nations.

Making Peace and Fighting Communism

In November 1918, just before the armistice, Republicans won control of both the House and the Senate. Thus, any treaty negotiated by Wilson would have to gain substantial Republican backing in the Senate to be ratified by the required two-thirds vote. To reach this number, Wilson had to seek at least tacit support from Republican Henry Cabot Lodge, chairman of the Senate Foreign Relations Committee. Lodge, like Wilson, had a career as an academic author of historical and political treatises, but considered Wilson a sanctimonious idealist and second-rate scholar. Wilson dismissed Lodge as a vain, political hack.

Rather than reaching out to Lodge and other rivals, Wilson refused to name any prominent Republicans, or any senators at all, to the peace delegation he personally led to Europe in December 1918. In addition to the president, the American delegation consisted of Wilson's friend Edward House, Secretary of State Robert Lansing, **Henry White** (a career diplomat and the delegation's nominal Republican), and General Tasker Bliss. House had previously organized a group of experts, known as the Inquiry, to provide detailed position papers on a range of political, economic, and military issues. But Wilson had no more use for their advice than he had for that of his political rivals.

In December 1918, Wilson led a peace delegation to Europe. Before going to Paris, he visited London and Rome where adoring crowds responded to his calls for negotiating a "people's peace."

Thirty-two nations, not including Germany or communist Russia, attended the peace conference in Paris between January 18 and June 28, 1919. American, British, French, Italian, and Japanese delegates did most of the important work behind closed doors, isolated from public scrutiny and with little input from other nations. They concentrated on forging a new map of Europe and dividing the colonial territories of the defeated powers. But to their surprise and irritation, stateless and colonial peoples including Armenians, Africans, Jews, Arabs, Chinese, Koreans, Indians, and Egyptians tried hard to influence the outcome.

During the months-long deliberations in Paris, British Prime Minister Lloyd George, French Premier Georges Clemenceau, and Italian leader Vittorio Orlando concentrated on carving out spheres of interest in Europe and the Middle East. Lloyd George and Clemenceau insisted on weakening Germany by imposing strict limits on future German armaments, having France occupy some German territory along its border, and imposing a huge reparations bill designed to make Germany pay for wartime destruction. The British and French also insisted that Germany accept as part of the peace treaty a "war guilt clause" in which it assumed sole responsibility for the Great War.

▲ **Map 21.4**

European Political Boundaries After World War I The breakup of the German, Austro-Hungarian, Ottoman, and Russian empires gave rise to a dozen or more new nations in Eastern Europe and the Middle East.

Wilson had a difficult time resisting these harsh demands. Even though the tone and substance of many decisions made at the conference violated the spirit of his Fourteen Points, Wilson focused his energy on drafting plans for a League of Nations. Since he needed British and French support for this, he hesitated to break with them.

Although the president privately acknowledged that the peace treaty drafted in Paris was far from ideal, he believed that once the League began to function it could modify these imperfect territorial, economic, and political shortcomings. Above all else, Wilson insisted that future peace and prosperity required the United States and the world's major powers to accept Article 10 of the proposed league's covenant, or charter. This established a system of "collective security" that pledged all League

GLOBAL PASSAGES

The Anticolonial Struggle in Paris

Wilson's soaring wartime rhetoric about self-determination, the equality of nations, and liberty for "people of many races" had been translated into dozens of languages and spread world wide by the CPI. During the spring of 1919, the Indian National Congress, the Muslim League, Korean and Chinese nationalists, Zionists, several Pan-African groups (one organized by American black activist W.E.B. Du Bois), and even some Haitians and Dominicans presented appeals in Paris for independence.

Among these emissaries was Nguyen Tat Than, a Vietnamese living in France. Nguyen (pronounced "new win") tried to deliver to Wilson a petition seeking support for Vietnamese independence from France. Wilson's staff kept Nguyen and other supplicants far away from the president.

In fact, Wilson's support for self-determination was aimed mainly at European ethnic groups, like the Poles and Czechs, who also had many voting relatives in the United States. His call for adjusting colonial claims meant redistributing colonies in an orderly way, not granting rapid independence. In Paris, Wilson confided to aides that when he had spoken about self-determination, he had not anticipated mobilizing the many "nationalities which are coming to us day after day." Self-determination, Secretary of State Lansing added, was too "dangerous" an idea to put "into the minds of certain races." Wilson proposed that the League of Nations should designate most existing colonies as mandates that the "advanced powers" would administer on behalf of "backwards people" for varying periods of time. In effect, the darker the population, the longer the period of foreign control. This stance would assure colonial people eventual independence and, Wilson hoped, counter the appeal of the Bolsheviks, who called for swift decolonization.

members to safeguard the territory and independence of all other members. This system, he argued, would deter future aggression or quickly punish any transgressors.

Wilson had another reason for accommodating the wartime allies. Like the British, French, and Japanese, he feared the spread of revolution from Russia and wanted quick, cooperative action to stifle the Bolshevik regime. In mid-1918, following Lenin's peace deal with Germany that took Russia out of the war, the United States and the Allies had sent troops to northern Russia, ostensibly to keep war supplies stored there out of German hands. In fact, the foreign armies assisted the "Whites," as the anticommunists were known, in what became a brutal three-year civil war with the Bolsheviks. Wilson sent additional troops to Siberia, where they joined Japanese and European forces in a vain effort to hold the vast region against the Communists.

The Versailles Treaty created independent Poland, Czechoslovakia, Yugoslavia, Hungary, Finland, and the Baltic states of Latvia, Lithuania, and Estonia. These nations were expected to contain the communist regime in Russia—if it survived at all. But Great Britain and France refused to relinquish their existing empires. They consented, instead, to place the new territories they had seized from Ottoman Turkey and Germany, including Iraq, Palestine, Syria, Lebanon, Trans-Jordan, and Southwest Africa, under nominal supervision by the League of Nations. Japan also insisted on maintaining its grip over Shandong Province in China, formerly German dominated, and of Korea. Hoping to soothe Japan's anger over U.S. and British refusal to acknowledge Japanese racial equality, Wilson reluctantly agreed.

These rebuffs radicalized many of those who had hoped that Wilson would promote their independence efforts. In May 1919, students in Beijing denounced the decision in Paris to approve Japan's continued occupation of Shandong. Many of these protestors, including Mao Zedong, joined the new Chinese Communist Party. Nguyen Tat Than, better known to Americans during the Vietnam War as Ho Chi Minh, also abandoned faith in democratic reform and joined the new communist movement, which promised to support Asian freedom struggles. In Korea, nationalists staged a doomed uprising against Japanese rule. In April 1919 British troops in the Indian city of Amritsar shot and killed nearly 400 demonstrators demanding independence. This attack led moderate Indian and Egyptian nationalists, such as Mohandas Gandhi and Sa'd Zaghlul, to reject a policy of gradual self-rule. Instead, they demanded a quick and complete break with Great Britain.

• How had Wilson inspired hopes among colonial peoples?

• What did Wilson actually mean by self-determination?

• How did the deals made in Paris in 1919 push some nationalists into the communist camp?

Around the time of Germany's surrender in November 1918, communist groups inspired by the Bolsheviks briefly seized power in Berlin and other German cities and in Hungary. The concern with halting the spread of communism from Russia contributed to the decision at Paris to create a buffer of anticommunist states—Finland, Poland, Estonia, Latvia, and Lithuania—out of what had been the western fringe of czarist Russia.

The victors completed drafting the peace treaty in June, nearly eight months after the armistice, and presented it to Germany on a nonnegotiable basis. On June 28, 1919, with its ports still blockaded, with its economy in ruins, and amid threats of uprisings by left-wing revolutionaries or right-wing militarists, the German government accepted the harsh terms.

Red Scare

The political and economic climate in the United States had changed dramatically by the time the peace treaty came back to Washington for Senate ratification in the summer of 1919. The cancellation of most war contracts triggered a sharp recession. Economic uncertainty coincided with a growing fear of Bolshevism abroad and at home, especially the belief that communist agents—referred to as "Reds"—either caused or planned to take advantage of labor unrest to seize power. During 1919 major employers cut workers' wages and hours, prompting a nationwide wave of labor unrest.

In January 1919 unions in Seattle called a general strike that briefly shut down the city. During May and June several prominent government officials and financiers received bombs in the mail, apparently sent by an anarchist group. Several exploded, killing innocent bystanders rather than their intended targets. These, along with later bombings, convinced many Americans that labor activists and communists were little more than terrorists. In the fall Boston police officers went on strike, prompting Massachusetts Governor Calvin Coolidge to send in the National Guard as replacements. Coolidge became a national celebrity by declaring "there is no right to strike against the public safety by anybody, anywhere, anytime." In September over 300,000 steel workers walked out when the big mills tried to restore the 12-hour day, seven-day work week at reduced wages. Industry executives denounced the strikers as revolutionaries and hired many replacement workers, including 30,000 African Americans, as strikebreakers.

Attorney General **A. Mitchell Palmer** declared that these events taken together revealed that a "blaze of revolution" had engulfed the nation. By dousing the flames, he hoped to win the Democratic presidential nomination in November 1920 and

TIMELINE 1913–1920

1913

March Woodrow Wilson inaugurated president

1914

April U.S. Naval force occupies Mexican port of Veracruz after "insult" to flag

June Archduke Franz Ferdinand assassinated in Bosnia, sparking crisis among European rivals

August Panama Canal opens

August World War I begins in Europe as Allies confront Central Powers

August Wilson issues Neutrality Declaration but allows nonmilitary trade with warring nations

1915

May British passenger liner *Lusitania* sunk by German U-boat, killing over 100 Americans

July U.S. Marines occupy Haiti where they remain until 1934

1916

March Pancho Villa attacks several U.S. towns along Mexican border

March Gen. John J. Pershing leads punitive military expedition into Mexico ostensibly to catch Villa but leads to U.S.–Mexican confrontation

May U.S. Marines occupy Dominican Republic where they remain until 1924

November Wilson reelected president in close contest with slogan "he kept us out of war"

1917

January Zimmerman telegram sent by German government to Mexico proposing joint war against United States

February German navy resumes unrestricted submarine warfare against U.S. ships supplying Allies

March Russian Czar Nicholas overthrown by pro-Allied reformers

March U.S. Merchant ships sunk by U-boats with loss of American lives

April U.S. Congress declares war on Germany, endorsing Wilson's call to "Make the World Safe for Democracy"; federal agencies established to regulate agricultural and industrial production and transportation

May–July East St. Louis race riots

June Espionage Act passed restricting antiwar speech and activities

November Bolsheviks seize power in Russia

1918

January Wilson issues Fourteen Points peace plan directed at Germany, Allies, Bolsheviks, and colonial peoples

to succeed Wilson. Palmer appointed a young protégé, **J. Edgar Hoover**, to lead the intelligence division within the Justice Department to track radicals. In 1919 Hoover compiled lists of thousands of suspects, many of them immigrants, who belonged to groups like the IWW and the newly organized Communist Party. In December about 250 of these noncitizens were seized and deported to communist-ruled Russia. In January 1920, the Attorney General authorized a broader sweep. The so-called Palmer Raids occurred in 33 cities where federal agents without warrants broke into homes and meeting halls to arrest over 4,000 people on charges of subversion. About 600 of those seized were later deported.

The Attorney General overreached. In the spring of 1920 he claimed to have uncovered a "Red" plot to seize national power on May 1 and deployed troops to protect government buildings and officials. When the day passed peacefully, and Palmer could not show evidence that such a plot had actually existed, his credibility—and presidential hopes—dissolved. However, his young assistant, J. Edgar Hoover, survived the episode. Hoover stayed on after the Republican sweep in 1920 and in 1924 became director of the Justice Department's Bureau of Investigation (later renamed the Federal Bureau of Investigation, or FBI), a job he held for nearly 50 years.

An actual terror attack, about which he knew nothing, took place after Palmer's disgrace. On September 16, 1920, an anarchist group exploded a large bomb in front of the offices of J. P. Morgan Company on Wall Street in New York City. The explosion—the deadliest terror incident on American soil until the Oklahoma City bombing of 1995—killed 38 people and wounded 400 others. Like earlier attacks, the victims were mostly working people, not powerful bankers. The attack frightened ordinary Americans and contributed to a more conservative drift in national politics.

February–March Russia signs Brest-Litovsk Peace Treaty with Germany and quits war

March Influenza pandemic begins and kills tens of millions of people globally

March–November U.S. combat forces join fighting in France against Germany

July Allied intervention in Russia against Bolsheviks begins; foreign troops continue fighting in Russia through 1920

November Republicans win midterm congressional elections

November Armistice signed ending fighting in Europe; Allied blockade of Germany continues along with anticommunist effort in Russia

1919

January Paris Peace Conference begins with Germany and Bolsheviks excluded

January Eighteenth Amendment (Prohibition) ratified

July Chicago race riots

May–June Anarchist bombings in United States promote conservative backlash

June Peace treaty ending Great War signed at Versailles despite Wilson's misgivings

September Elaine, Arkansas, race riots

November Palmer Raids against radicals begin with roundup of several thousand immigrants

1920

March U.S. Senate rejects Versailles Treaty by failing to muster two-thirds vote

August Nineteenth Amendment ratified, giving women the right to vote

September Wall Street bombing kills dozens

November Republican Warren G. Harding elected president with pledge to restore "normalcy"

The Fight for the Treaty

Even before Wilson formally submitted the Versailles Treaty for ratification, 39 senators—more than the one-third needed to defeat it—signed a petition demanding that the League of Nations recognize that the Monroe Doctrine gave the United States preeminence in the Western Hemisphere. When the treaty reached the Senate in the summer of 1919, Senator Lodge bitterly criticized it. He argued that Article 10 of the League Covenant, the basis for collective security, unfairly restricted America's freedom of action and might oblige the country to engage in unwise military ventures without congressional approval. During extended public hearings, Lodge introduced many revisions of the text designed to protect Congress's power to make war and to control domestic issues with international ramifications, such as immigration, tariffs, and so forth.

To Wilson's surprise, many progressives voiced doubts about the treaty and League. Senator William Borah, an Idaho Republican, worried that if the United States joined the League, it would have to defend British and French colonies or join the Europeans in an anticommunist crusade. Other liberals complained that Wilson had deserted his own principles by imposing a harsh peace on Germany, by allowing Japan to control parts of China, and by ignoring his pledge to spread democracy. Imposing harsh penalties on Germany, they warned, would fuel a desire for revenge—a prediction partly confirmed by Hitler's later rise to power.

Wilson dismissed nearly all these criticisms by saying that he had been compelled to make compromises to assure British and French support for the League of Nations. Most of the problems that senators identified could be solved after the treaty had been ratified and once the League of Nations—with the United States as a member—began its work.

Wilson began a cross-country speaking tour in September 1919 to bolster popular support for Senate approval of the treaty without changes. He delivered three dozen speeches in three weeks, often to large and enthusiastic crowds. To reject the treaty and League, he warned, would bring on a new war and the "very existence of civilization would be in the balance." On September 26, at the end of a speech in Pueblo, Colorado, Wilson collapsed. Four days later he suffered a nearly fatal stroke that paralyzed his left side.

For several months, First Lady Edith Wilson hid the gravity of her husband's condition and acted as his surrogate. After partially recovering, Wilson became even more stubborn. He rejected any compromise with his opponents or supporters. The president even insisted that Senate Democrats prove their loyalty by voting against an amended treaty even if they agreed with the changes. As a result, three times between November 1919 and March 1920, the Senate voted down the treaty, with and without amendments. If Wilson had allowed Senate Democrats to vote in favor of the amended treaty, it would likely have passed.

The rejection of the Versailles Treaty and League membership signified a deep division among American leaders. Some, like Wilson, believed the Great War proved the United States must join formally with other nations in managing world trade and enforcing peace. Critics of the League argued that membership would needlessly entangle the United States in European conflicts and restrict America's freedom to act. Both sides of the debate actually agreed that the nation had global interests and could not isolate itself from world affairs. But they disagreed strongly over how the United States should exercise its power and defend its interests, collectively through the League of Nations or unilaterally by picking and choosing issues and nations with whom it would cooperate.

STUDY QUESTIONS FOR MAKING PEACE ABROAD AND AT HOME

1. What compromises did Wilson make in negotiating peace and why?
2. Why did many liberal and conservative Senators oppose the Versailles Treaty?
3. What events in Europe in 1919–1920 and at home created fear of domestic radicalism?

Summary

- The outbreak of war in 1914 shocked Americans, who tried to avoid involvement while they benefited from exporting raw materials to the warring nations.
- Expanding economic links to the Allies and growing fears of German militarism gradually moved the United States toward direct involvement.
- Once in the war the government used its new power to raise a mighty army, boost production, and stifle dissent.
- As large numbers of American troops joined the fighting early in 1918, they played a decisive role in defeating Germany.
- In 1918–1919, an influenza pandemic killed millions of people worldwide.
- Wilson personally negotiated the peace treaty, hoping to use it as a vehicle to create a League of Nations that would insure future peace and prosperity.
- Support for the treaty, and for liberal policies, was undermined by a wave of strikes, bombings, and fears of terrorism during 1919–1920.

Key Terms and People

Adamson Act 813
American Expeditionary Force
   (AEF) 822
American Protective League
   (APL) 819
balance of power 804
Catt, Carrie Chapman 813
Central Powers 805
Debs, Eugene 818
Dewey, John 812
Franz Ferdinand, Archduke 805
Ford, Henry 811
Great Migration 821
Grey, Sir Edward 812
Haywood, William D. "Big Bill" 818
Holmes, Oliver Wendell, Jr. 819
Hoover, J. Edgar 833
House, Edward M. 812
Huerta, Victoriano 813
Hughes, Charles Evans 812

James, William 803
La Follette, Robert 816
League of Nations 826
Lippmann, Walter 817
Literacy Act 818
Lusitania 810
Madero, Francisco 813
National Security League 811
Nineteenth Amendment 821
Norris, George 816
Palmer, A. Mitchell 832
Paul, Alice 821
Rankin, Jeanette 816
Sedition Act of 1918 000
Tax Act of 1916 813
Villa, Francisco "Pancho" 814
Lenin, Vladimir 824
White, Henry 828
Wilhelm, Kaiser 809
Zimmerman, Arthur 815

Reviewing Chapter 21

1. How did the war in Europe impact the United States early on?
2. What were President Wilson's major war aims?
3. How did the federal government suppress wartime dissent?
4. What international and domestic events complicated Wilson's efforts to control the peace settlement?
5. What unresolved problems from the war contributed to postwar instability?

Further Reading

Freeberg, Ernest. *Democracy's Prisoner: Eugene V. Debs, the Great War, and the Right to Dissent.* Cambridge, Mass.: Harvard University Press, 2008. Debs had several careers as a labor organizer, Socialist leader, and principled opponent of the war. His prosecution revealed the extent to which the Wilson administration went in stifling peaceful dissent.

Gardner, Lloyd. *Safe for Democracy: The Anglo-American Response to Revolution, 1913–1923.* New York: Oxford University Press, 1984. Amidst the carnage of the Great War, British and American leaders tried to control the social upheavals in Mexico, Russia, and Eastern Europe, and China.

Kennedy, David. *Over Here: The First World War and American Society.* New York: Oxford University Press, 1980. U.S. entry into the Great War set in motion economic, political, and social changes that had long term consequences in the lives of ordinary Americans.

Knock, Thomas. *To End All Wars: Woodrow Wilson and the Quest for a New World Order.* New York: Oxford University Press, 1992. The author explains how Wilson saw American participation in the Great War as a way to reshape global politics and impose a uniquely American reform agenda on the world.

MacMillan, Margaret. *Paris 1919: Six Months That Changed the World.* New York: Random House, 2002. The author examines the personalities and politics behind the long peace conference after the Great War and evaluates the successes and failures of the peacemakers.

Manela, Erez. *The Wilsonian Moment: Self-Determination and the International Origins of Anticolonial Nationalism.* New York: Oxford University Press, 2007. Wilson's call for self-determination following WWI aroused great hopes among colonial peoples. But the failure to implement this promise pushed many Asians, Africans, and Arabs in radical directions.

Visual Review

Mobilizing People and Ideas

Government builds enthusiasm for war.

Controlling Dissent

Congress passes laws that curb speech and redefine treason.

The Origins of Global Conflict

National rivalries lead to global war.

A War of Attrition

Old fashioned tactics and new technology lead to stalemate.

America's Response to War

Despite an official declaration of neutrality, the U.S. government establishes ties with the Allies.

The Shock of War

AMERICA AND THE GREAT WAR, 1914–1920

The U.S. Path to War, 1914–1917

Conflicting Visions of National Security

People and groups disagree on U.S. participation in war.

Intervention in Latin America

Wilson commits military power in the Caribbean and Latin America.

U.S. Mediation, the Election of 1916, and Challenges to Neutrality

The United States tries to mediate peace.

Decision for War

U.S. Congress declares war after naval attacks by Germany.

America at War

Mobilizing the Economy

The federal government creates new regulatory agencies to mobilize the economy.

Women and African Americans in Wartime

Women and African Americans face special challenges and opportunities during wartime.

Over There

Building an Army

The War Department promotes enlistment.

Joining the Fight

American troops encounter hardships and grueling trench warfare.

Political and Military Complications

The Czar's overthrow in Russia and events within Germany complicate the war effort.

Influenza Pandemic

A global pandemic ravages the world resulting in a huge loss of life.

Making Peace Abroad and at Home

Making Peace and Fighting Communism

Nations meet to conclude the peace treaty.

The Fight for the Treaty

The U.S. Senate fails to ratify the Versailles Treaty.

Red Scare

The United States is gripped by a growing fear of communism.

A New Era

O n August 26, 1926, a crowd of 100,000, most of them women, filled the streets of Manhattan near the Campbell Funeral Home to mourn actor Rudolph Valentino, who died at age 31 after a brief illness. Many in the crowd fainted; others tried to break into Campbell's. The raw emotion of that stifling summer day crystallized some of the most salient issues of the 1920s: The mass appeal of the movies, the creation of instantaneous celebrities, the uneven integration of new immigrants, and the fast-changing attitudes toward sexuality.

Valentino was born Rodolfo Alfonso Raffaello Piero Filiberto Guglielmi in Castellaneta, Italy. After his arrival in New York in 1913, he worked for a while as a taxi dancer (a man who danced with unescorted women for a fee), befriended members of New York's high society, and changed his name to Rudolph Valentino. In 1919 he went to Hollywood where he took bit parts as a gangster in silent films. His dark complexion, coal black eyes, and slicked-back hair stood in sharp contrast to America's fairer skinned, lighter haired standards of male beauty of the day.

Valentino's movie roles captured the spirit of changing gender roles in the 1920s. In 1921 he starred as Ahmed Ben Hassan in the silent film *The Sheik*. His character abducts Lady Diana Mayo, who resents his rough treatment at first but soon falls madly in love with him because of his kindness and dark good looks. Lady Diana is kidnapped by another sheik, rescued by Ben Hassan, and the two eventually marry. Along the way, the film reveals that Ben Hassan is actually half-European; a sexual relationship between a white European woman and an Arab would have been too shocking to U.S. audiences.

Village Quartet by Jacob Lawrence, 1954

CHAPTER OUTLINE

A NEW ECONOMY FOR A NEW ERA
> Wireless America
> Car Culture
> Advertising for Mass Consumption

ETHNIC AND RACIAL DIVIDES
> Immigration Restriction
> The Ku Klux Klan
> African American Renaissance and Repression
> Black International Movements

A NATIONAL CULTURE
> Popular Entertainment: Movies, Sports, and Celebrity
> The New Skepticism
> The New Woman of the 1920s
> Religion and Society
> Prohibition

continued on page 845

America in the World

African American jazz caused a sensation across the globe (1920s).

The Universal Negro Improvement Association inspired black pride and nationalism (1920).

The U.S. Border Patrol was formed to prevent illegal immigration across Mexican and Canadian borders (1924).

U.S. event that influenced the world

International event that influenced the United States

Event with multinational influence

Conflict

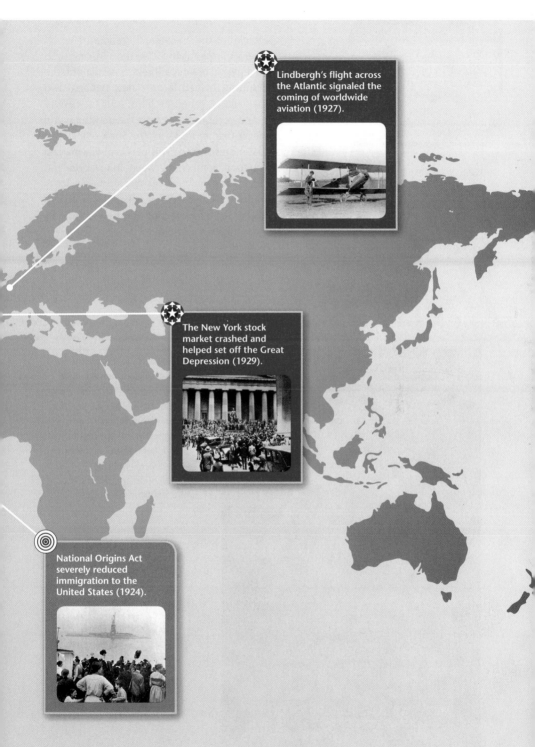

Lindbergh's flight across the Atlantic signaled the coming of worldwide aviation (1927).

The New York stock market crashed and helped set off the Great Depression (1929).

National Origins Act severely reduced immigration to the United States (1924).

POPULATION

Africa

Asia

Europe

Latin America and the Caribbean

North America

Oceania

World Population c. 1900
U.S. Population 1920: 105,710,620
U.S. Population 1930: 122,775,046

0
100,000,000
200,000,000
300,000,000
400,000,000
500,000,000
600,000,000
700,000,000
800,000,000
900,000,000

Valentino's funeral was one of the great spectacles of the "new era," President Herbert Hoover's phrase for the "Twenties."\The 1920s were a period in which the new media of radio and movies helped forge a new national and global culture. \American films, tourists, celebrities, and consumer products flooded the world as never before, and—as *The Sheik* reflected— sexual mores shifted. This new era was marked by cultural conflict, between innovation and tradition, between those who enthusiastically embraced change and social critics and religious leaders who decried the new culture as vulgar and even immoral.

The Sheik, a silent film released in 1921, made Italian immigrant Rudolph Valentino Hollywood's first male sex symbol. While male moviegoers were reported to walk out and laugh aloud at the film's love scenes, women were smitten with Valentino and the movie's erotic, exotic romance story.

A NEW ECONOMY FOR A NEW ERA

In the decade after World War I the spread of new technologies increased American engagement with the world. American business also became more international than ever before. People around the globe bought American products and watched American-made movies. At the same time, many Americans tried to isolate the country from the rest of the world. Hostility to outsiders led to harsh restrictions on immigration. Parts of the American and the world economy thrived, but the widening gap between rich and poor, and the unhealthy economic legacy of the war, eventually led to a long depression. Modern advertising encouraged demand for newly available goods, and Americans borrowed billions of dollars to buy modern marvels such as cars, radios, and electrical appliances. Many Americans reveled in this consumer culture and were proud that people around the globe sought to emulate it. Others, however, decried modern mass consumption as boorish and hollow.

CHAPTER OUTLINE

continued from page 841

POST-WORLD WAR I POLITICS AND FOREIGN POLICY
> Government and Business in the 1920s
> Coolidge Prosperity
> The Election of 1928
> Independent Internationalism in the 1920s
> The United States and Instability in the Western Hemisphere

THE CRASH
> The End of the Boom
> The Great Depression

Wireless America

Radio developed into one of the most popular modes of communications in the 1920s. By the end of World War I, the technology and the corporate structure were in place for a revolution in communication that would allow listeners easy access to information and entertainment created halfway around the world. Early radios were sold as kits assembled at home and often modified and improved by builders. These radios quickly captured the imagination of inventive Americans eager to tinker with the shoebox-sized contraptions.

Commercial radio broadcasting started on the night of November 2, 1920. A small audience of "wireless" enthusiasts in the Northeast tuned in to hear East Pittsburgh's new station KDKA broadcast the Warren Harding-James Cox presidential election returns. Two years later there were 500 radio stations around the country, with radios in three million American homes and President Harding's office. The hobby of the few had become a national obsession and a $60 million a year business. Radio broadcasts quickly spread worldwide. American companies battled each other over patent rights and engaged in a heated rivalry with British allies over who would control the airwaves. Woodrow Wilson deemed American supremacy in radio technology important enough to help convince General Electric (GE) to reassign patent

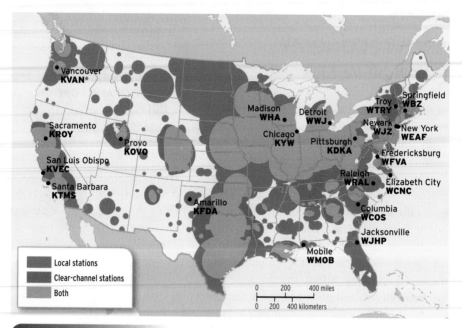

▲ **Map 22.1**

The Reach of Radio by 1939 Beginning with KDKA, and its first commercial radio broadcast in 1920, radio stations mushroomed around the country, with 550 in existence by 1923. By 1930, 60 percent of Americans had purchased radios and took advantage of the powerful clear channel stations that broadcasted news, music, and dramatic programs from cities hundreds of miles away.

rights and establish the Radio Corporation of America (RCA). The rapidly evolving technology spawned a powerful communications industry and RCA emerged as the dominant company. In 1926 it created the National Broadcasting Corporation (NBC), the first country-wide network of radio stations. The next year, another company, the Columbia Broadcasting System (CBS), starting broadcasting nationwide. GE and Westinghouse also built radio receivers, Western Electric sold transmitters, and AT&T reaped lucrative tolls from broadcast stations. By 1922 the radio was the most sought-after consumer product in the nation, and radio broadcasts were the most significant form of mass culture and profoundly altered patterns of daily life as families reorganized their habits to catch favorite shows.

Radio changed the way people thought and bought. As radios became increasingly elaborate and expensive, consumers often had to buy their sets on credit. For rural Americans the radio provided a vital link to the broader civic and cultural life of the nation.

Some traditionally minded critics disapproved of the open access of the airwaves, fearing that it fostered immorality. Like other popular media of the 1920s, radio openly expressed the sexual desires of the age. Songs like "Burning Kisses" and "Hot Lips" floated on the air, easily accessible to young people who gravitated to the new technology with a fervor that frightened many religious and community leaders. For African Americans, radio perpetuated old stereotypes through wildly popular shows like *Amos 'n' Andy* in which white actors portrayed black characters as good-natured, submissive fools.

Car Culture

Along with the radio, the growth of the automobile industry had a profound effect on American society in the 1920s. **Henry Ford** adopted mass production techniques with the introduction of the moving assembly line in 1903. This method, dubbed "Fordism," allowed Ford to manufacture his Model T quickly, efficiently, and cheaply in his Highland Park, Michigan, plant. With the Model T automobiles for the first time became affordable, versatile, and relatively reliable. Sales of Ford's "Tin Lizzie" soared. Car purchases from General Motors (GM) and the third of the "Big Three," Chrysler, multiplied as well. Vehicle registration more than doubled from 3 million in the early 1920s to 8.25 million by 1927.

Cars changed the ways Americans viewed consumption in fundamental ways. In the mid-1920s **Alfred P. Sloan**, chairman of GM, attacked Ford's dominant market position by introducing new models every year. Sloan's "planned obsolescence" boosted sales, luring consumers into purchasing new cars before their old ones wore out. GM also increased sales by offering installment purchasing and promoting the idea of a product ladder with different grades of cars pegged to different incomes. By 1927 two-thirds of car buyers used the installment plan, as they sometimes spent above their means to participate in the car craze. In late 1927 Ford responded to GM's innovations; their rollout of the more comfortable Model A to replace the Model T resulted in a frenzy of interest from the media and the public.

Cars revolutionized mobility. Farmers and their families could now easily travel to town to shop, eat, and enjoy other recreational opportunities. Urban families took leisurely Sunday drives through the countryside. Some grabbed food at the new drive-in restaurants. Cars served as "mobile bedrooms" for teens and young adults who wished to escape their parents' watchful eyes. Car owners embarked on long-distance vacations, on which they could stay at an auto camp or one of the new motels popping up along the highways.

Cars and better roads also facilitated the rapid growth of suburban communities on the outskirts of the nation's major cities. The population of Grosse Pointe, outside of Detroit, increased 724 percent throughout the 1920s; and the Los Angeles suburb of Beverly Hills swelled by 2,485 percent. Open spaces and comfortable homes attracted middle-class families to the new residential communities.

By the mid-1920s automobile manufacturing was the country's fastest growing industry and provided much of the decade's labor growth and prosperity. One out every five dollars spent by consumers went toward automobiles. By 1929, the industry employed almost 13 percent of all manufactures. The financial health of other industries, such as the petroleum, steel, glass, and rubber, relied on the auto industry.

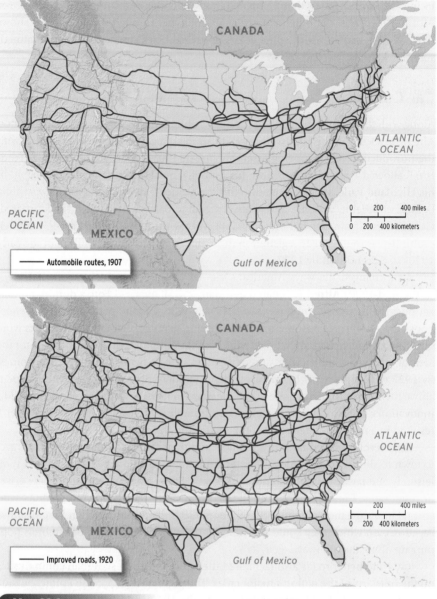

▲ **Map 22.2**

Automobile Roads, 1907 and 1920 Highway construction exploded in the first decades of the 20th century, with roadways lacing nearly every part of the nation.

Industrialists such as Henry Ford branched out globally. In an ultimately futile effort to find a cheap and stable source of natural rubber for tires, Ford carved a vast plantation—called Fordlandia—out of the Amazon rain forest in Brazil. Tire manufacturer Henry Firestone built more successful rubber plantations in Liberia. Automakers also sold their products abroad, modifying their cars for foreign tastes, establishing

La nuova Ford, guida interna a due porte è uno dei modelli più eleganti, in cui la linea allungata e bassa si accorda insuperabilmente col comfort e la massima comodità. Prezzo di vendita L. 22.400, franco Trieste, sdoganato, con 5 ruote gommate con pneus balloon.

Il nuovo coupé Ford è un esempio perfetto e caratteristico dell'eleganza e massimo comfort delle nuove carrozzerie Ford. Prezzo di vendita L. 22.400, franco Trieste sdoganato, con 5 ruote gommate con pneus balloon.

Henry Ford marketed his affordable and reliable cars not only to Americans but also to consumers around the world. This 1928 ad featured two types of Fords available in Italy.

subsidiaries, and building plants outside the United States. By 1928 American multinational firms in France and Germany outpaced production of domestic auto industries in those countries. By the mid-1930s, Ford and GM had assembly operations in nearly every major market worldwide. U.S. production plants popped up in Australia, Japan, and even in the communist Soviet Union.

Advertising for Mass Consumption

In the 1920s advertising took on new importance as mass consumption drove the American economy. American business, perfecting methods to make people believe that they needed new goods, created sophisticated campaigns. Ads aimed to show how a product could reshape a consumer's image and even enhance social standing. They frequently employed movie stars and other popular personalities to endorse mundane products. By gargling the same brand of mouthwash as movie idol Rudolph Valentino, consumers were promised a new status and even happiness as the result of a simple purchase. Cigarette makers encouraged women to "reach for a Lucky instead of a sweet." Ads also heightened demand for amazing new home appliances such as electric washers, stoves, refrigerators, and vacuum cleaners.

"Ad men" of the 1920s perfected methods that drew on insights from psychology to shift Americans away from traditional values of thrift toward borrowing and spending on nonessential personal items. Savvy "copy writers" used market research to understand the "mass mind" and the "typical consumer." Edward Bernays, a nephew of the newly popular psychoanalyst Sigmund Freud, pushed for explicitly sexual appeals in ads. Ads in magazines and newspapers, on roadside billboards, and on the radio raised awareness of personal health, hygiene, and appearance. Dramatic ads, warning

Lucky Strike's ad campaign, "Reach for a Lucky instead of a Sweet," introduced in the late 1920s, appealed to women who wished to stay thin.

Americans of the shame of bad breath and the dangers of bad manners, generated remarkable sales for products as different as mouthwash and self-improvement books. By 1927 American corporations spent more than $1.5 billion on advertising annually.

STUDY QUESTIONS FOR A NEW ECONOMY FOR A NEW ERA

1. What new goods became available to Americans in the 1920s?
2. What impact did these goods have on Americans' lives and U.S. engagement with the world?
3. How did modern advertising promote the desire for new goods?

ETHNIC AND RACIAL DIVIDES

Many of these rapid social and economic changes provoked resistance from some traditional-minded Americans. Some of them focused resentment on recent immigrants and people of color who they believed threatened harmony and order. New laws restricted immigration. Despite hardships, people of color and recent immigrants changed American culture, even as they adapted their own ways of life. They shared some of the decade's new, fragile prosperity. Internal migration continued for newcomers and African Americans, and increasingly more of American life took place in cities and suburbs rather than on farms and in small towns.

Immigration Restriction

The 1920s began with ominous signs that Americans were hardening their views about who could enter the United States. Immigration had stopped during World War I and "nativists" and "restrictionists," active since the late 19th century, now added new reasons for limiting immigration when the war ended: the dangerous political ideas that influenced immigrants, especially through the successful Russian revolution of 1917. In 1921, some Americans expanded their campaign to limit immigration.

An economic downturn and rising numbers of immigrants converged in 1920–1921, and long-simmering racial tensions and religious prejudices catalyzed legislative change. Debates during this time revealed a particular bias against "new immigrants" from areas in Eastern Europe hardest hit during the war. Immigration restrictionists especially condemned Polish Jews, who they believed came as communists.

Research in eugenics supported the nativism of the early 1920s. Eugenics fused racism with science to provide "evidence" of the inferiority of new immigrants for those eager to justify ethnic and racial immigration restrictions. Prominent researchers produced considerable literature on the importance of heredity over environment in shaping ability.

With the passage of the **Emergency Immigration Act of 1921** Congress created specific immigration limitations based on national origin. The law was a compromise between more liberal policy makers who sought to restrict immigration and those who favored suspending immigration altogether. The act banned all immigration from Asia, but it allowed free immigration from the Western Hemisphere, as the Southwest depended on Mexican and Central American labor. The law also imposed numerical quotas on immigration from Europe, with 357,000 immigration slots, 200,000 of them allocated to Western Europeans. Three years later immigration quotas became permanent under the **National Origins Act of 1924**, which limited immigration to only 120,000 Europeans per year—primarily from countries like England and Germany. The act drastically cut quotas for Eastern and Southern Europe. Notably, other countries followed the American model in restricting immigration on the basis of national origin. Australia banned immigration from Asia, and Germany barred entry from Poland. The National Origins Act enshrined in immigration policy an annual ceiling on legal immigration. It created the Border Patrol and required foreigners to carry passports and visas to enter the United States.

Fear of immigrants' political radicalism continued throughout the 1920s. In 1920, **Nicola Sacco** and **Bartolomeo Vanzetti**, two Italian immigrants with anarchist sympathies, were arrested for killing two payroll clerks in Massachusetts. They were convicted in 1924 and sentenced to death. After their trial Harvard Law School Professor Felix Frankfurter led a movement questioning the judge's fairness. In 1927, as the date of their execution approached, it was revealed that Judge Webster Thayer, who sentenced the men to death, had remarked, "Did you see what I did with those anarchistic bastards the other day? I guess that will hold them for a while! Let them go to the Supreme Court now and see what they can get out of them!" Nevertheless, the Court denied their appeal and Sacco and Vanzetti were put to death. The execution of the two political radicals convicted in a biased trial provoked demonstrations of outrage in the United States and around the world, including London, Paris, Tokyo, Buenos Aires, and Johannesburg.

The passage of the National Origins Act also incited global protests. After 1924 Japanese Americans rightly feared they would remain targets of persecution in years to come. The anti-Japanese sentiment of the Origins Act contributed to souring relations with Japan during the decades leading to World War II. Even more disturbingly, the United States denied approximately 300,000 potential Jewish immigrants entry in the 1920s and 1930s, among them Jews who might have escaped the horrors of the coming Holocaust.

The only groups of new immigrants to benefit from the 1924 restrictions were Mexicans and Latin Americans. Exempted from quotas, hundreds of thousands moved to the U.S. Southwest. During the early 1920s, approximately half a million Mexicans crossed the border. Many came to stay, rather than working as guest workers and returning home. With the support of both southwestern agribusiness and the Mexican government, approximately 800,000 Mexicans moved to the U.S. Southwest during the 1920s. By 1930, 1.4 million Mexicans resided in the United States.

Prior to 1920 the Mexican government, concerned with preserving the "cultural integrity" of Mexicans in the United States, established a network of consulates in the Southwest primarily to encourage return migration. Beginning in 1920 the consulates

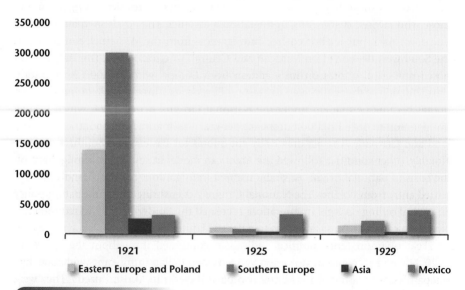

▲ **Figure 22.1**

The impact of immigration restrictions Immigration restrictions in the 1920s, which targeted specific ethnic groups, drastically diminished the number of immigrants, from 805,000 in 1921 to 280,000 in 1929.

recognized that most emigrants planned to stay; they focused their attention on aiding Mexican Americans by sponsoring patriotic celebrations, organizing educational conferences, and advocating bilingual programs. The consuls also sought to capture migrants' dollars and loyalties partly because the new revolutionary regime of Mexican President Alvaro Obregon (1920–1924) recognized that its political legitimacy rested on how well he protected "Mexico de afuera [Mexico abroad]."

Though welcomed for their labor, these new permanent residents faced racial discrimination and anti-immigrant hostility. Mexican American children were sometimes segregated into special schools. Mexican American workers faced abrupt firings, and, like African Americans in the South, they often found the legal system stacked against them. In cities like Los Angeles they nevertheless built vibrant and lasting communities that blended familiar traditions with the evolving culture of their new home. The result was a distinctive Mexican American identity. Most Mexican families settled in urban areas where their children attended school; they built Catholic churches, formed social and political associations, and avidly supported role models of American success like boxing sensation Bert Colima, "el Mexicano de Whittier."

Like all communities of new immigrants, Mexicans sometimes faced deep divisions between those born in Mexico and those born in the United States and tensions from intermarriage between Mexicans and Mexican Americans. Anglo hostility could at times mitigate such divisions and at other times widen them. During the 1920s fears of mass migration of Mexicans shaped popular perceptions, and by the end of the decade "illegal aliens" became popularly associated with "Mexicans."

The Ku Klux Klan

Racism merged with anti-immigrant sentiment in a revived Ku Klux Klan. The Klan of the Reconstruction Era resurfaced in the 1920s with a new anti-immigrant, anti-Catholic, anti-Jewish message. The appearance in 1915 of a blockbuster film about Reconstruction, *The Birth of a Nation*, directed by **D.W. Griffith**, helped spur the revival. The movie, a technical marvel of early cinema, depicted the Klan as a heroic organization saving civilization by rescuing white women from brutal, sex-crazed black men.

As one leader declared, the Klan opposed the "Jew, the [whiskey] Jug and the Jesuit." Depicting Jews as dangerous radicals with an inordinate influence in banking and business, the Klan insisted that Catholics also threatened the nation as the Pope planned to overrun the country, and it warned against the "rise of Catholic power." But the Klan also aimed its wrath more broadly to those whom they deemed immoral. Klansmen whipped or mutilated alleged bootleggers, adulterers, abortionists, and those guilty of "race mixing."

The ranks of the Klan swelled after 1920, more in the Midwest than in its original birthplace in the South. It even spawned imitators abroad. In Cuba, for example, a Ku Klux Klan Kubano arose to enforce segregation and "protect" white women. White women also joined, and formed the Women of the KKK (WKKK), in which they advocated for the protection of "Pure Womanhood" and "the sanctity of the American home."

Klan membership peaked in 1925 at about 5 million. That year 40,000 robed members paraded down Washington's Pennsylvania Avenue. Their visibility and tactics provoked an anti-Klan backlash. A coalition of Catholic and Jewish leaders and civil libertarians organized to oppose its activities. Klan membership hemorrhaged in the final years of the decade, shaken by scandal. The Grand Dragon of Indiana committed highly publicized sexual assaults; additional cases of assault, drunkenness, and financial fraud undermined the group's credibility. The passage of the 1924 quota bill, which ended most immigration from southern and eastern Europe, deprived the Klan of its major issue.

African American Renaissance and Repression

To escape the Jim Crow South, African Americans continued their massive migration from the southern countryside to northern cities. Continuing the flow of the half-million who migrated during World War I, one million blacks left the rural South in the 1920s.

Despite an atmosphere of repression, African Americans made some notable progress in the 1920s. Harlem, a largely black section of New York City, came to epitomize the vibrant black artistic and literary culture that flowered in the 1920s. A product of the ongoing migration of blacks, both from the South as well as from the West Indies, the **Harlem Renaissance** helped construct a new identity for black Americans:

This sheet music, "We Are All Loyal Klansmen," produced in 1923, reflects the widespread appeal of the Ku Klux Klan in the 1920s.

The New Negro who exuded self-confidence, bowed to no one, and confronted racism head on. Writers and artists of the Harlem Renaissance disagreed about the nature of art: should it be a weapon in the battle for civil rights? Or should artists be free to create as they pleased? This creative tension helped to produce a wide range of artistic creations, some of which are considered masterpieces of art and literature, and moved the black experience to the mainstream of American culture.

Thrill-seeking whites sought out Harlem, especially its nightclubs, which featured jazz. The product of black migration and the cross-fertilization of musical styles carried to the nation's cities, jazz captured the mood of the 1920s. "The music from the trumpet at the Negro's lips is honey mixed with liquid fire," wrote African American poet Langston Hughes about this new musical form. The Cotton Club, Harlem's most famous nightclub, catered to fascination with "exotic" and "authentic" black culture, as packaged by white club owners. But these clubs were segregated, for white customers only. Blacks in Harlem, as in nearly every American city, patronized their own jazz clubs, often small speakeasies and "chicken shacks." Jazz clubs also flourished in European cities such as Paris. African American soldiers first introduced jazz to France during World War I and "musical missionaries," returning in the 1920s, recreated America's jazz culture in Paris. Technological advances such as the phonograph and

The world-famous Cotton Club, opened in the heart of Harlem in 1923, featured some of the greatest jazz and blues artists of the day, including Duke Ellington and Cab Calloway, but allowed only white patrons.

radio also broadened jazz's appeal both nationally and internationally. Conservative white and black leaders, however, criticized jazz as decadent, an immoral music performed in sinful settings.

Even as black culture flowered in the United States and around the world in the 1920s, African Americans enjoyed a smaller share of the decade's prosperity. Fluctuations in wage work created depression conditions for many blacks before the **Great Depression** of the 1930s. Competing against white workers for industrial jobs, blacks usually found themselves relegated to the dirtiest, most dangerous, lowest-paid unskilled positions. But African Americans did find some new opportunities, most notably at the Ford Motor Company, which employed 5,000 black workers by 1923, compared to 50 in 1916. Although most black women remained mired in domestic service jobs, they also made some inroads in better paying jobs in food industries, commercial laundries, and the needle trades. In 1925, angered at exclusion from white unions, Pullman railway porters organized the Brotherhood of Sleeping Car Porters, which, headed by leader **A. Philip Randolph**, played an active role in asserting black civil rights.

But large-scale racial violence overshadowed advances. Two of the most brutal assaults of the era occurred in Oklahoma and Florida. In May 1921 a white mob of around 5,000 men attacked a prosperous African American neighborhood in Tulsa, Oklahoma. The mob gathered to lynch a black teenager accused of assaulting a white woman; they soon torched homes and businesses, burning alive some residents and shooting others. By the time the National Guard restored order, about 300 blacks were killed. The thriving, mostly black mill town of Rosewood, Florida, suffered a similar fate in January 1923. Hundreds of white men descended on Rosewood's 700 residents and, setting fire to homes and businesses, forced them to flee. Officially, six blacks died although the actual tally was probably much higher.

Black International Movements

Faced with ongoing oppression at home, some black Americans began to reach out internationally. Pan-Africanism aimed to unite peoples of African descent around the world to seek equal rights and cast off white supremacy and colonialism. Harlem, home not only to American-born blacks, but also to West Indians and Africans, provided fertile ground for Pan-Africanism. "The pulse of the Negro world has begun to beat in Harlem," writer Alain Locke declared in 1925. Pan-Africanism received a major boost with the 1919 Versailles Peace Conference and plans for decolonization. Political activist and author W.E.B. Du Bois organized the Second Pan-African Congress, held in Paris in 1921, which attracted delegates from 15 countries and demanded "the development of Africa for the Africans and not merely the profit of Europeans."

An alternative Pan-Africanism emerged under the leadership of **Marcus Garvey**, a Jamaican immigrant to New York. His **Universal Negro Improvement Association** (UNIA) became the largest black nationalist movement in history. The charismatic Garvey captured the imagination of the masses in the United States and abroad. The

UNIA, insisting on black separatism and calling for "Africa for Africans," claimed that 400 million people of African descent could free Africa from white imperialists and create their own nation. The UNIA also established black-owned and -operated businesses, most notably the short-lived Black Star shipping line. Garvey inspired his followers around the world to think of themselves as a nation with a proud past and a sparkling future. He even created a national anthem, a flag, and a diplomatic corps, claiming for himself the title "Provisional President of Africa." The UNIA drew members from all over the world, including Africa, the Caribbean, and Canada. UNIA membership far outstripped other black organizations, such as the NAACP.

Garvey's movement generated both fear and ridicule. Mass rallies and parades of UNIA members in crisp military uniforms frightened many white observers. Critics mocked Garvey's grandiose plans and Napoleonic attire. Garvey brought criticism on himself through questionable business and political tactics, such as meeting with the Imperial Wizard of the KKK as a fellow racial separatist. Black critics, especially Du Bois, found him both embarrassing and threatening and supported a "Garvey Must Go" campaign. Cooperating with the federal government, especially fearful of "negro agitation," these critics helped bring about Garvey's demise. He was convicted of mail fraud in 1923, imprisoned, and deported in 1927. Although Garveyism faded as a force in the United States, its appeal remained strong in Jamaica and throughout the Caribbean where it helped foster national independence movements from European colonial control.

STUDY QUESTIONS FOR ETHNIC AND RACIAL DIVIDES

1. What were the immediate origins of the National Origins Act?
2. What challenges did Mexican immigrants face in the 1920s?
3. How and why did New York City become the capital of a black Atlantic world during the 1920s?

A NATIONAL CULTURE

The Harlem Renaissance and Pan-Africanism reflected just one aspect of a broader cultural awakening. News traveled fast in the 1920s, and new means of communications hastened the spread of a national culture. Across the country people attended the same movies, read the same books, followed the same sports teams, and cheered the same instant heroes. The new technologies of radio and the movies helped spread American culture around the globe. Especially in Europe, Asia, and the Western Hemisphere, new media fortified people's ideas of the United States as a huge, rich land. The new culture may have been highly popular, but many Americans were dismayed by the new trends. Some religious people expressed disappointment and outrage at what they considered to be the immorality of the modern age.

Popular Entertainment: Movies, Sports, and Celebrity

As the celebrity of Rudolph Valentino suggests, interest in popular entertainment rose to unprecedented levels in the 1920s. By the end of the decade, movies were the fifth largest industry in the nation. Each week almost as many Americans attended movies as lived in the entire country. Movie theaters, occupying lavish spaces, offered prestige, glamour, and comfort to moviegoers, all at an affordable price. The 1927 film *The Jazz Singer* marked the greatest technological breakthrough of the decade as the first "talkie" with extended dialogue.

Many movies of the 1920s reflected the tensions of the "new era." As films provided a glimpse into the lives of the rich and famous, Hollywood soon began to shape national and international perceptions about fashion, morals, and success. The movies' portrayal of unheard of wealth and high fashion may have had an even greater impact on people's ideas of American life around the globe than it did in the Unites States. At home, at least, people could compare their own, rather ordinary lives, to the images on the screen. They enjoyed the fantasy, but they knew it was just that, an unrealistic depiction of life. Internationally, American movies offered a tantalizing glimpse of a rich land populated with beautiful people wrapped in finery.

Not everyone appreciated the effect cinema's popularity had on traditional values. Facing pressure from conservative groups, in 1921, the movie studios appointed Postmaster General Will Hays to censor their films. Hays prohibited risqué content on the screen and monitored appropriate behavior for actors and actresses off the screen.

An unparalleled interest in sports skyrocketed several athletes into superstardom during the 1920s. **Babe Ruth** of the New York Yankees established himself as a larger-than-life figure as fans flocked to professional baseball games. Hitting 60 home runs during the Yankees' dominant 1927 season, the "Sultan of Swat" set a record that would stand for over 30 years. His gregarious personality off the field likewise endeared him to fans. Professional football player Harold "Red" Grange, boxer Jack Dempsey, tennis player William Tilden, and golfer Bobby Jones likewise drew millions of fans.

Huge crowds turned out for college football games. To the dismay of those who worried that too much attention to athletics would sidetrack the academic mission of higher education, several universities, including Yale, Ohio State, and Stanford, began building stadiums that held 60,000 people or more. By the end of the decade, more fans attended college football games than professional baseball games.

The 1920s was also a decade of instant celebrity. No one symbolized the spirit of the new era better than the boyishly handsome 25-year-old **Charles Lindbergh**, who collected a $25,000 prize for being the first aviator to fly solo across the Atlantic Ocean in 1927. Radio reporters breathlessly announced every minute of his 33-hour flight from Long Island to Paris in May of that year. Millions turned out for a ticker tape parade down New York's Fifth Avenue in "The Lone Eagle's" honor upon his return. This outpouring of pride in American technical prowess and individual derring-do was the largest mass assembly since the New York victory parade had welcomed the doughboys home from the Great War in 1919. As a goodwill ambassador, "Lucky

Lindy," as he was called, promoted America aviation around the world. Lindbergh's reputation suffered a severe blow in the late 1930s when he sympathized with Nazi Germany and opposed American entry into World War II.

The New Skepticism

Despite the general prosperity of the 1920s, not all Americans considered the United States a happy home. Some lost faith in traditional American values and grew alienated after the experience of World War I. Many writers and artists fled to Europe, especially France, where they hoped to live a more authentic existence. Other intellectuals remained in the United States but wrote scathing critiques of what they saw as the emptiness of mainstream, middle-class American culture.

Many of the intellectuals who left for Europe in the 1920s, the so-called Lost Generation, had become disillusioned with the present-day society and its ideas of progress. In his 1929 book *A Farewell to Arms*, **Ernest Hemingway** wrote, "the war annihilated all reason, virtue, and human compassion." Additionally, Hemingway and those who joined him in Paris, most notably **F. Scott Fitzgerald**, found life in the United States stifling, puritanical, driven by big business, and full of hypocrisy. In Paris they directly challenged those values, enjoyed a less inhibited lifestyle, partied, and began writing some of the decade's most influential works.

Regardless of the critique of literary expatriates, the 1920s was also a time of great artistic creativity in the United States. In 1920 **Sinclair Lewis** began the charge by attacking small-town life in *Main Street*. His incisive criticism of the bigotry and shallowness of middle-class America struck a chord, and the novel became a national best seller. In 1922 Lewis followed with *Babbitt*, an even greater success that satirized business culture. F. Scott Fitzgerald also addressed the hollow, unfulfilling lifestyle of the rich in *The Great Gatsby* (1925).

The loudest voice of social criticism during the 1920s came from Baltimore-based journalist **H. L. Mencken**. In 1924 he launched the magazine *American Mercury*, the vehicle for Mencken's piercing attacks on rural life, popular culture, religion, democracy, politicians, and the "booboisie." Mencken coined the derogatory moniker "Monkey Trial" for the Scopes evolution trial in Dayton, Tennessee, in 1925. He was especially popular among college students who imitated his irreverence. One Harvard student remarked: "*The American Mercury* was our Bible, and Mencken our God."

The New Woman of the 1920s

Just as jazz signified the 1920s, the "flapper" symbolized the "new woman" of that decade. She wore short skirts, cultivated a boyish figure, rouged her cheeks, bobbed her hair, and turned down her flesh-colored stockings. She smoked cigarettes in public, drank alcohol, danced "the shimmy" in jazz clubs, and flirted openly with her male playmates. Her behavior, scandalous by her mother's standards, represented "feminism—new style," according to an observer. Often indifferent to the women's organizations and causes such as suffrage and equal rights that had helped bond her mother's generation, the flapper stressed her individuality and freedom. **Clara Bow**, who was known as the "It Girl," epitomized the flapper/new woman of the 1920s. "It" was a quality of magnetic personality and physical attraction as well as self-confidence. With boyishly tousled bobbed hair, big brown eyes, and heart-shaped mouth, she was the biggest Hollywood star of the era, and women in the United States and abroad copied her "jazz baby" style. The flapper became a Jazz Age female ideal replicated around the world—especially through movies and broadly circulated American magazines.

The pleasure-seeking flapper embodied a new understanding of female sexuality in the 1920s. As youth culture expanded, with more young men and women attending high schools and coed colleges and universities, young Americans developed new ways of dating and interacting. New theories of sexuality stressed female pleasure and condemned "inhibitions" as unhealthy. Birth control also became more accessible. Liberated from the supervision of parents and chaperones, young men and women exercised their sexual freedom, engaged in "petting parties," and enjoyed the privacy of automobile backseats. Despite her rebellious image, the new woman of the 1920s continued to embrace many traditional values. Marriage generally remained her end goal, the means to personal fulfillment.

Flapper fashions, featuring hemlines above the knees and rolled down hose, spread around the world, as young women displayed a new sense of freedom and sexuality, unknown to their mothers' generation.

As women contended to land a husband, advertisements accentuated female competition. Ads, for example, tried to convince women that they needed to purchase beauty products to vie successfully for a husband—and to keep him. Sales of cosmetics exploded in the 1920s. The "Miss America" beauty contest, first held in 1921, also embodied the competitive dimension of new womanhood, as young women contended to represent the American ideal of beauty.

Notions of marriage also changed significantly in the 1920s. "Companionate" marriage emphasized husband and wives as friends. In addition, romance and sexual pleasure were viewed as necessary ingredients for a successful marriage. For the first time, sex manuals—rejecting older notions that sex, for women, was a necessary evil to be endured—stressed female pleasure.

Despite her pervasive image, the flapper was not the only "new woman" in the 1920s. Movies and magazines also glamorized the modern "working girl." Secretarial work, once the province of young businessmen on their way up the corporate ladder, now became a respectable job for young, middle-class, white women. But this kind of work was viewed not as a career but only as a temporary phase before marriage and a return to the home.

For working-class women, the carefree flapper, the college coed, the glamorous "working girl," or even the contented housewife, rarely reflected their lives. Most working women in the 1920s remained in the occupations they had held previously: domestic service, agricultural labor, and certain manufacturing jobs. Yet even among women in remote parts of the country, the "flapper" made an impact. Southern mill girls, for example, bobbed their hair, listened to jazz on the radio, danced the shimmy, and saved their money for cosmetics and stylish dresses.

Religion and Society

Early in the 20th century, as the nation became more urban, industrial, and commercial, old religious patterns frayed. Especially after 1890 millions of Catholic, Eastern Orthodox, and Jewish immigrants from Eastern and Southern Europe brought new religious traditions to America. In the 1920s Protestants debated how to respond to the new industrial order with its extremes of wealth and poverty and to the waves of immigrants professing new faiths.

Broadly speaking, Protestant denominations split into two groups, often called "Modernists" and "Fundamentalists." Modernists, influenced by the Social Gospel movement of the late 19th century, as well as Darwin's theory of evolution and archaeological discoveries, believed Christianity should respond positively to new knowledge and social conditions. Fundamentalists, in contrast, interpreted the Bible literally and rejected the notion that traditional faith should enter a dialogue with science and popular culture. They saw the Bible as the only path to truth and a bulwark against a corrupt, mostly urban, world. Fundamentalists condemned alcohol, tobacco, Hollywood films, and much of popular culture as sinful and subversive of traditional values.

Sister Aimee Macpherson shared Fundamentalists' loathing of Charles Darwin's theory of evolution and even invited three-time Democratic presidential candidate

Aimee Semple McPherson

Fundamentalists achieved fame and large followings during the 1920s by employing new technologies, such as the radio and film. Aimee Semple McPherson or "Sister Aimee" became an international celebrity utilizing mass media to reach hundreds of thousands of faithful listeners. Her message combined appeals to the values of the Bible and conservative politics with an embrace of people of different ethnic and racial backgrounds. This mixture of tradition and modern media struck a chord with people inside and outside the United States who longed to reconcile their traditional ideas and practices with the convenience and speed of modern life.

Intending to be missionaries, Sister Aimee, who emigrated from Canada, and her Irish-born husband Robert began their religious career together in 1910 by traveling to China. Robert's death soon after arriving in Hong Kong left his young widow and her infant daughter adrift. After they returned to the United States, Sister Aimee worked with several church groups before striking out on her own as a Pentecostal minister.

Moving to Los Angeles at the end of World War I, Sister Aimee resolved to build what today would be called a "megachurch." She supervised the construction of the "Angelus Temple" with a capacity of over 5,000. Soon after the temple opened in 1923, McPherson broadcast sermons over her own radio station, KFSG, heard throughout the West and in parts of Canada and Mexico. She invited Francisco Olazabal, a popular Mexican evangelist, to preach in Spanish. She embraced new technology, used modern public relations, and proclaimed a more assertive professional role for women. Her temple sent missionaries abroad where they distributed pamphlets translated into the local language.

Within the temple, McPherson staged elaborate theatrical productions based on biblical themes. Sister Aimee stressed God's divine love and the good times ahead for those who accepted Christ. She presented Jesus as a real person whose love would solve all problems. Thousands of invalids claimed to have been cured by McPherson. She often invoked faith to justify her political agenda, which included demands for stricter enforcement of Prohibition and—despite her own foreign birth—tighter controls on immigration. Sister Aimee also opened soup kitchens for

and now antievolution crusader William Jennings Bryan to preach at the Angelus Temple. In the summer of 1925 a prosecutor in Tennessee indicted a high school science teacher, **John Scopes**, for violating a state law that barred teaching "any theory that denies the story of the divine creation of man as taught in the Bible and teaches instead that man has descended from a lower order of animals." The World Christian Fundamentals Association recruited Bryan as a special prosecutor. Bryan feared that

Evangelist Aimee Semple McPherson prepares to scatter pamphlets over San Diego from an airplane. McPherson embraced the latest technology in the 1920s to spread her message, including traveling around the country in her "gospel car," flying from city to city by airplane, and broadcasting sermons on the radio.

the poor and welcomed blacks and Latinos to her church, a novelty in Los Angeles. She retained a large following during the 1930s and continued to utilize the radio and film to reach the masses. Shortly before her death from a drug overdose in 1944, she expressed interest in a still experimental medium, television.

- How did Aimee Semple McPherson effectively incorporate new technologies to disseminate her message?

- Why was McPherson's message so appealing to people in the 1920s?

irreligion, symbolized by evolution, threatened the soul of America. In response, Clarence Darrow, America's most prominent trial lawyer, volunteered to head the defense team. An avowed agnostic, he represented the urbane, worldly, sophisticated type that infuriated Fundamentalists.

After the judge barred testimony from scientists, a frustrated Darrow called Bryan to testify as a biblical authority. Bryan defended the Bible's accounts of creation and miracles despite many apparent lapses and contradictions in the text. The jury took only nine minutes to convict Scopes who was fined $100. The state supreme court later overturned the conviction on a technicality.

Although Fundamentalists took heart in the initial verdict, the trial left Bryan a broken man who died soon after. The national press, led by H. L. Mencken, portrayed Bryan and his supporters as small-minded, ignorant "boobs." Urbanites and college students gleefully repeated Mencken's jibes, while rural Southerners deeply resented being the butt of jokes. Several European reporters covering the trial made it an international sensation.

Prohibition

Conflicts over the prohibition of alcohol became another flashpoint of the cultural divisions of the 1920s. The Eighteenth Amendment, passed in 1919, forbade the "manufacture, sale or transportation" of intoxicating liquors. Although Prohibition put neighborhood saloons out of business, illegal "speakeasies" flourished. Nevertheless, "drys" defended Prohibition for driving down the rate of alcohol consumption. "Wets" countered that Prohibition drove drinking underground and penalized workers unable to afford the high prices charged by speakeasies. Prohibition also, they argued, promoted the rise of organized crime and violent criminals such as Al Capone, who supplied booze to a thirsty public.

Despite the controversy, Prohibition grew into an international movement. Several Canadian provinces restricted the consumption of alcohol at roughly the same time as the United States, but cries for repeal arose more quickly there. The provinces of Ontario and Alberta, however, repealed their antiliquor laws in 1927.

Prohibition also changed U.S. relations with its neighbors. Tourists flocked to Cuba to patronize casinos and brothels owned by American gangsters and well-stocked with liquor. Mexico and Canada became sources for smuggled whiskey. The provinces of Ontario and Quebec became major sources of Canadian whiskey. Distilleries north of the border produced liquor that was smoother tasting and not as physically harmful as some of the deadly concoctions made by American bootleggers.

Americans remained sharply divided over Prohibition throughout the 1920s. Many Protestants supported what they called the "great social experiment," while most Catholics and Jews condemned it as an assault on their culture and personal liberty. Republicans, along with many Southern and Western Democrats, generally supported Prohibition. Drys often identified with the anti-immigrant, anti-Catholic, anti-Semitic views of groups like the Ku Klux Klan. Northern Democrats, exemplified by New York governor **Al Smith**, bitterly opposed both Prohibition and nativism.

By 1928 Prohibition had become an intensely partisan issue. The northern, urban wing of the Democratic Party, led by its presidential nominee Al Smith, supported repeal of the Eighteenth Amendment. Republican **Herbert Hoover** defended Prohibition as a "noble experiment" and won the presidential election. But in 1933 the new Democratic president, Franklin D. Roosevelt, mobilized Congress and the states to repeal Prohibition.

STUDY QUESTIONS FOR A NATIONAL CULTURE

1. How did new forms of mass entertainment help create a national culture?
2. How did women's lives change during the 1920s? How did their lives remain the same?
3. On what grounds did some authors and religious fundamentalists criticize American society in the 1920s? How and why did prominent authors and religious fundamentalists agree or disagree?

POST-WORLD WAR I POLITICS AND FOREIGN POLICY

In contrast to their embrace of new modes of cultural expression, Americans sought a return to placidity in politics. Republican presidential candidates won three consecutive elections in the 1920s with promises of reversing progressive reforms, promoting the interests of business, and advancing the fortunes of what Herbert Hoover called "rugged individualism." In the aftermath of the presidential election of 1920s, Americans turned their back on Woodrow Wilson's vision of a peaceful world with the United States leading the League of Nations. Although the United States did not join the League, it remained an active, albeit independent, world power throughout the 1920s. The promotion of international trade became a major government initiative. The United States also worked to stabilize the international economy in the wake of the destruction of the Great War. By slowly moving away from the interventionist policies and military occupations of the early 20th century, the United States also sought to improve relations with the people of the Western Hemisphere.

Government and Business in the 1920s

In the presidential election of 1920 Ohio Republican Senator **Warren G. Harding** faced a fellow Ohioan, Democratic Governor **James M. Cox**. Harding ran a "front porch campaign" in which celebrities visited his home in Marion, Ohio. Voters appreciated his promise of "less government in business and more business in government." He mocked Woodrow Wilson's plans for international reform, as he promised to return the country to "normalcy." Harding won easily. He captured 16.1 million votes (60.1 percent), and 404 electoral votes, while Cox gained only 9.1 million votes (34.1 percent), and 116 electoral votes. Socialist candidate Eugene Debs, imprisoned since 1919 for opposing the draft during the war, won 914,000 votes, 3.4 percent of the total.

Harding, a friendly, handsome man, enjoyed the company of his buddies over cards and whiskey, a practice he continued during Prohibition. He had little knowledge of or interest in the details of public policy. He began his administration with some surprises. He disappointed conservatives by commuting the sentence of socialist leader Debs. He appointed some talented cabinet secretaries, including **Henry A. Wallace** as secretary of agriculture and **Andrew Mellon**, of a prominent Pittsburgh banking family, as secretary of the treasury. **Charles Evans Hughes**, former Supreme Court justice, served as an active and accomplished secretary of state. Herbert Hoover, who had achieved international fame for organizing food relief in Europe during and after the Great War, was secretary of commerce.

The thievery and corruption of hundreds of Harding's other appointments, however, quickly overshadowed the achievements of more talented and ethical cabinet members. In the summer of 1923 Congress prepared to investigate corruption in high places. Harding sought relief by taking a trip to Alaska. He fell ill on the return voyage and died in San Francisco on August 2.

In 1924 congressional investigations and criminal indictments revealed the broad extent of corruption in the Harding administration. Attorney General Harry Daugherty was accused of taking bribes and offering protection to bootleggers. Interior Secretary Albert Fall, an old Senate friend of Harding's, accepted bribes of $400,000 for granting lucrative secret leases to private oil companies on government-owned land in California and Wyoming. The episode became known as the **Teapot Dome scandal**, after the Wyoming property. Fall was fined $100,000 and went to prison for one year.

Coolidge Prosperity

Harding's successor, **Calvin Coolidge**, had won his place on the 1920 Republican ticket by breaking the highly unpopular Boston police strike of 1919 when he was governor of Massachusetts. Coolidge, like Harding, relied upon Treasury Secretary Mellon and Commerce Secretary Hoover to promote the interests of large corporations and expand the economy. Mellon encouraged Congress to lower income taxes, especially for the rich, and balance the federal budget. Mellon and Hoover also advocated high tariffs to protect domestic manufacturers.

Hoover energetically promoted American business at home and abroad. The Commerce Department helped form trade associations, collected vast amounts of business data, and sponsored conferences of business leaders across the country. Hoover also assigned hundreds of Commercial Attaches to promote American products in countries as far away as Malaya and Iran. American money amounting to $12 billion—a combination of purchases of foreign goods, money sent to relatives abroad, tourism, direct investments in foreign firms, and overseas lending—also flowed overseas in the 1920s. American firms created local subsidiaries to market cars, electrical equipment, and processed food, and American oil companies sold their products to car owners around the globe.

As Democrats descended into disarray, Republican Coolidge sought election in his own right in 1924 on a platform of "Coolidge Prosperity." The southern wing of the Democratic Party supported former treasury secretary William Gibbs McAdoo, Woodrow Wilson's son-in-law. The Southerners, along with McAdoo and many

Midwestern Democrats, supported Prohibition and white supremacy. Many had ties to the Ku Klux Klan, which the convention refused to condemn. Northeastern delegates to the Democratic National Convention supported New York governor Alfred E. Smith, a Catholic son of Irish immigrants, who advocated the repeal of the Eighteenth Amendment. Deadlocked after an unprecedented 103 ballots, delegates settled on a compromise candidate, **John W. Davis**, a Wall Street lawyer.

The fall election was a three-way race among Coolidge, Davis, and Wisconsin Republican senator Robert La Follette, who ran as a candidate of a newly reconstituted Progressive Party. Coolidge easily won the election with 16 million votes (54 percent) and 382 electoral votes to Davis's 8.3 million votes (28 percent) and 136 electoral votes. La Follette tallied 4.8 million votes (16.6 percent), and 13 electoral votes, primarily from Democrats disillusioned with the chaos and conservative drift of their own party.

Coolidge prosperity continued though 1928, although wealth was spread unevenly. Urban laborers and farmers suffered through lean times. Unions had trouble recruiting members in the face of stiff opposition from industry and the courts. Prices for farm products fell throughout the decade. Deeply indebted farmers tried to recover by growing more crops and raising more animals, which only drove prices down further. In 1927 and 1928 Congress offered relief by passing the McNary-Haugen Acts. These laws required the government to support crop prices by buying basic farm commodities. Coolidge vetoed both bills as unwarranted government interference in the economy.

The Election of 1928

In 1928 Coolidge announced, "I do not choose to run" for president. The Republicans then nominated Commerce Secretary Herbert Hoover. His 1922 book *American Individualism* explained how the American economy should operate on business principles. Business leaders should foster "welfare capitalism," voluntary cooperation between business and labor. Hoover enhanced his status as a decisive leader by organizing relief for victims of the Great Mississippi Flood of 1927. Incessant rains in late 1926 caused the Mississippi River to flood parts of six states. Seven hundred thousand poor farmers, nearly half of them African Americans, fled to 154 hastily constructed relief camps. Taking charge of organizing the relief efforts in the camps, Hoover won praise for his effective action.

Hoover faced New York Governor Alfred E. Smith in the election. The Democrats' battles over the Klan and Prohibition were over, and Smith easily won the nomination, becoming the first Roman Catholic to run for president. Urban residents, immigrants, Jews, and Catholics shared Smith's opposition to Prohibition and enthusiastically supported his candidacy. But their backing was not enough to overcome widespread satisfaction with the country's prosperity and widespread anti-Catholic sentiment. Some charged that he would take orders from the Pope. Hoover won an overwhelming victory with 21.4 million votes (58 percent) and 444 electoral votes to Smith's 15 million votes (41 percent) and 87 electoral votes (Map 22.3).

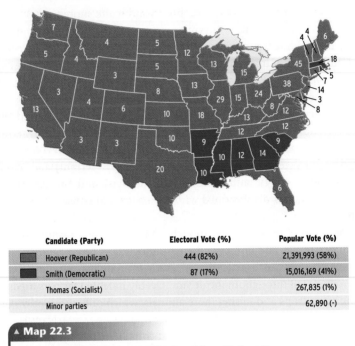

Candidate (Party)	Electoral Vote (%)	Popular Vote (%)
Hoover (Republican)	444 (82%)	21,391,993 (58%)
Smith (Democratic)	87 (17%)	15,016,169 (41%)
Thomas (Socialist)		267,835 (1%)
Minor parties		62,890 (-)

▲ **Map 22.3**

Presidential Election of 1928 Republican Herbert Hoover won a landslide victory over his Democratic opponent Al Smith, as voters continued to place their trust in Republican presidents who presided over the economic boom of the 1920s.

Independent Internationalism in the 1920s

Despite the Senate's rejection of the Versailles Treaty and League of Nations in 1919, government and business retained a keen interest in foreign affairs. Disarmament was one international reform that survived into the Republican era. A costly arms race among naval powers active in the Western Pacific threatened the peace and plans to balance the federal budget. In 1921 Secretary of State Charles Evans Hughes convened an international conference on naval disarmament to determine the future of East Asia. The three treaties culminating from the conference maintained the territorial status quo in East Asia and set limits on the size of the navies of the United States, Great Britain, Japan, France, and Italy.

A peace movement also gained strength in the 1920s. The Women's International League for Peace and Freedom founded by reformer Jane Addams pressed for disarmament and the end to all wars. Universities across the country introduced courses in international relations, many of which were devoted to explaining the causes of the Great War and exploring ways to avoid future armed conflicts. When the Columbia University professor of international law James T. Shotwell won an essay prize with a proposal to declare war illegal, Secretary of State Frank Kellogg (1925–1929) embraced the idea. In 1928 Kellogg proposed to French Foreign Minister Aristide Briand that the two nations agree to outlaw war instead of signing the formal alliance France had requested. In August 1928 the United States and France promised not to use war as an instrument of national policy, and they invited other nations to join them. Most countries worldwide signed the **Kellogg-Briand Pact**, although many officials remained skeptical of its effectiveness. Although the pact did not prevent the outbreak of war, Americans later opposed German, Italian, and Japanese aggression during World War II based on their violations of the Kellogg-Briand treaty.

American bankers cooperated with the Coolidge administration to minimize the hardships caused by the Great War. The Allies owed the United States approximately $10 billion in addition to interest for war loans. They delayed repaying the Americans until Germany paid its reparations of over $100 billion. But Germany considered the bill too high and refused to pay. France, a major recipient of reparations, responded by sending soldiers to occupy the Germany industrial territory of the Ruhr. As a result, Germany's economy collapsed in an unprecedented wave of inflation. In the summer of 1923 a loaf of German bread sold for one billion Marks. Coolidge appointed a commission, headed by Charles Dawes, to help restart German payments. The **Dawes Plan** provided a $110 million loan from private American banks to Germany. With German's currency stabilized, reparations and repayment of American war loans resumed. American firms invested heavily in Europe, fueling the continent's recovery from the war. It seemed as if cooperation between the American government and U.S. banks had returned prosperity to Europe. But the economic expansion rested on continued American loans and transatlantic trade. The Great Depression, which began in the fall of 1929 and dried up lending and international commerce, destroyed hopes for prosperity built on the partnership of government officials and private bankers.

The United States and Instability in the Western Hemisphere

Republican presidents of the 1920s backed away from justifications made earlier in the century for U.S. intervention in the Western Hemisphere to contain destabilizing nationalist revolutions. Still, the U.S. government remained committed to maintaining American preeminence in the Western Hemisphere and to promoting the interests of private U.S. business and investors.

Faced with growing hostility to military interventions, the United States gradually ended its occupations of countries in Central America and the Caribbean. In 1924, after the American Navy trained a local National Guard, the Coolidge administration withdrew the military from the Dominican Republic. But next door in Haiti, American Marines continued their occupation throughout the 1920s. American forces trained the Haitian National Guard and built roads, bridges, schools, and power stations. Cruelly mistreating the Haitians, they introduced racial segregation and favored the lighter skinned mulatto elite over the darker skinned majority. In 1919 Haitians resisted American efforts to press them into chain gangs, and the Marines began a counterinsurgency war that killed over 2,000 Haitians. Street protests erupted again in 1929, and in 1934 President Franklin D. Roosevelt finally withdrew the last of the American forces from Haiti.

The United States also moved haltingly to end the occupation of Nicaragua begun in 1910. The Progressive Party demanded the withdrawal of American troops during the election campaign of 1924, and the next year Coolidge withdrew them. In 1926, however, a civil war erupted between the Conservative party, which supported the Catholic Church, and the anti-clerical Liberal Party. The United States sent 5,000 marines back to Nicaragua, along with former secretary of war Henry Stimson who arranged a peace agreement among the factions. The marines supervised elections in 1928, 1930, and 1932. The Liberal Party then split into two factions. One, led by General **Cesar Augusto Sandino**, denounced Stimson's peace plan as an American attempt to impose Yankee control. Sandino led several thousand guerrillas in a guerrilla war against another Liberal Party general, **Anastasio Somoza**, the commander of the U.S.-trained National Guard. In January 1933 President Hoover removed the last of the U.S. Marines. Shortly thereafter, Somoza and his family began a 45-year-long dictatorship.

In Mexico, the United States reached an uneasy understanding with its new leaders. American mining and petroleum companies insisted that the Harding administration demand that Mexico compensate them for raw materials leases it had confiscated from American mining and petroleum companies. In 1923 Mexico agreed to acknowledge the right of exploration of American firms on land leased before Mexico adopted its 1917 constitution. But in 1925 Mexican President Plutarco Calles renounced the 1923 agreement, as it placed over half of Mexico's petroleum in the hands of U.S. firms. Coolidge named Dwight Morrow as the U.S. ambassador to Mexico. In 1928 Morrow negotiated a 10-year deal with Mexico, recognizing the ownership rights of U.S. oil companies to land acquired before 1917 and acknowledging their leases to oil fields acquired after 1917.

Latin American nations mounted pressure on the United States to renounce its policy of unilateral intervention in the Western Hemisphere. In 1930 the State Department adopted a memorandum on the Monroe Doctrine. The memorandum repudiated President Theodore Roosevelt's 1904 Corollary to the Monroe Doctrine. It stated that neither the Monroe Doctrine nor international law authorized unilateral military intervention in the Western Hemisphere. Although the United States did not end military interventions, after 1930 Washington regularly sought the agreement of other countries in the region before sending troops.

STUDY QUESTIONS FOR POST WORLD WAR I POLITICS AND FOREIGN POLICY

1. Why were Republican presidents and their policies popular in the 1920s?
2. What was "independent internationalism?"
3. How did the growing U.S. role in the global economy shape U.S. foreign policy in the 1920s?

THE CRASH

President Herbert Hoover took office in a buoyant mood on March 4, 1929. The world and the American economy seemed on a path toward permanent prosperity. He proclaimed that "we have reached a higher degree of comfort and security than ever existed before in the history of the world." Yet the prosperity of the 1920s was built on sand. Debts that never could be repaid piled up across the globe. The safety and even existence of banks in New York, London, and Paris, the major financial centers of the day, depended on dubious projects that they had financed. By the end of 1929 the world plunged downward into the Great Depression, the worst economic catastrophe of the modern era. The Depression spread to every corner of the country, wrecking lives and leaving people homeless, hungry, and desperate for work.

The End of the Boom

The 1920s seemed to be an era of limitless economic opportunities. One and a half million Americans invested in the stock market in the 1920s, and millions more invested indirectly as banks put their deposits into stocks. Prices soared in 1928. General Motors rose 75 points on the Stock Exchange in two months. RCA stock was at 85 at the beginning of 1928; at the end of the year it reached 420 and sold for $505 a share. Many people bought stock on "margin," putting down 10 percent of the purchase price and borrowing the rest from brokerage houses. Banks bought stock, and companies loaned banks money to buy more. When prices rose, people thought they were making money. However, if stock prices fell, borrowers could not pay off their loans with their stock. But few foresaw a stock market crash, and companies issued more and more shares to take advantage of ever-rising prices. Minimal government regulation allowed companies to issue shares with no underlying value; they were not required to certify the financial worthiness of investment holding companies or of banks that owned stock in major companies.

The Florida land boom and bust provided a foretaste of the catastrophe awaiting Wall Street. Cheap land, warm weather, and zealous promoters encouraged real estate developers to invest heavily in Florida in the early 1920s. Entrepreneurs promoted it as a vacation destination and to investors looking to get rich off its new popularity. Most investors simply intended to re-sell their property for a profit. Thousands of people paid increasingly outlandish sums for "fifty feet in paradise."

Speculation caught up with Florida by 1926. Investors discovered to their chagrin that much of the land they bought was unusable swampland or was permanently underwater. Many began pulling their money out of the state.

In addition to irresponsible speculation, income disparities and rampant use of credit also destabilized the economy. The income of the wealthiest 1 percent of Americans doubled, while the income of the bottom third rose only 6 percent. Income tax cuts returned money to the wealthy but did little for the middle class or the poor.

While rich Americans could keep on buying washing machines, refrigerators, radios, and cars, the bottom two-thirds found themselves stretched to the limit. By 1929 American factories, like farms, were guilty of overproduction. Manufacturers cut prices and then reduced their output. They laid off workers, who in turn cut back on their purchases. Borrowers stopped paying their consumer loans, leaving banks and stores with millions in bad debt.

Imbalances in international trade and finance intensified the economic strains of 1928 and 1929. High tariffs in the United States barred many European manufacturers from the American market. Europeans borrowed from American banks to pay reparations and war debts. They tried to expand their domestic markets and forgo imports. As American industry and agriculture found it harder and harder to sell abroad, surpluses of American goods and farm products increased.

The Great Depression

Wild speculation, inequities of wealth, massive consumer borrowing, lax government regulation, international trade barriers, and excessive international lending culminated in a perfect storm on Wall Street. Stock prices hit a peak in September 1929 and then drifted lower. On Thursday, October 24, prices fell sharply in the morning. At noon bankers met at the offices of J.P. Morgan and announced they would step in to buy shares, and prices stabilized. But on Monday, October 28, prices fell again, and then on "**Black Tuesday**," October 29, the bottom dropped out of the market. Everyone wanted out, as banks and brokerage houses demanded the sale of stock to pay off margin debt. By the end of the day, 16 million shares, three times the normal number, traded hands. All the gains of 1929 had been wiped out. By the end of the November stock prices fell to half of what they had been at their height.

TIMELINE 1920–1930

1920

January 1 The Eighteenth Amendment begins Prohibition

August The First International Convention of the Universal Negro Improvement Association

November 2 KDKA makes the first commercial radio broadcast

1921

October "*The Sheik*" is released, starring Rudolph Valentino

November The Washington Naval Conference begins;

the conference ends in February with treaties reducing naval arms and recognizing China's borders

1922

September Publication of Sinclair Lewis's *Babbitt*

September 21 Fordney-McCumber Tariff raises the duties on imports

1923

August 2 U.S. President Warren Harding dies; he is succeeded by Calvin Coolidge

November Inflation in Germany hits 1 million percent

1924

January First issue of *The American Mercury* edited by H. L. Mencken

January–May The Teapot Dome scandal reveals corruption at the top of the Harding administration

April Dawes Plan created to reduce Germany's reparation payments

May The National Origins Act sets immigration quotas

May Formation of the U.S. Border Patrol

November Calvin Coolidge is elected president

1925

April Publication of F. Scott Fitzgerald's novel *The Great Gatsby*

July Scopes trial in Dayton, TN, reveals a deep division between Christian fundamentalists and modernists over Charles Darwin's theory of evolution

August 8 40,000 Ku Klux Klansmen march in Washington

By 1930 people began to talk of a major economic depression. In 1929 the unemployment rate was a low 3.2 percent, but it shot up to 8.7 percent in 1930. Government policies made the Depression worse. Secretary of the Treasury Mellon thought the downward economic spiral would correct itself. "Liquidate labor, liquidate stocks, liquidate the farmers, liquidate real estate," he advised. "It will purge the rottenness out of the system."

The **Smoot-Hawley Tariff of 1930** made it even harder for international manufacturers to sell products in the United States. When other countries raised their tariffs in retaliation, the volume of international trade dropped from $2.9 billion in 1929 to $1.6 billion in 1931. The Federal Reserve made matters worse by raising interest rates and shrinking the money supply, devastating the nation's banks. More than 1,600 banks failed during 1930 alone and millions of homeowners lost their houses to foreclosure. Hoover tried to arrest the slide by encouraging voluntary actions to relieve the suffering. He insisted that "the fundamental business of the country . . . is on a sound and prosperous basis." But by 1931 few Americans believed the president, and there was a widespread fear that this economic downturn was worse than any previous one.

STUDY QUESTIONS FOR THE CRASH

1. What caused the Great Depression?
2. What made the early years of the Depression so severe?

August Withdrawal of U.S. Marines from Nicaragua

1926

March Release of the movie *A Social Celebrity*

August Funeral of Rudolph Valentino

November 15 National Broadcasting Company (NBC) launches the first major radio network

December U.S. Marines return to Nicaragua

1927

April The Great Mississippi Flood reveals deep discrimination against African Americans

May 21 Charles Lindbergh completes his flight across the Atlantic

June Release of the movie *Rolled Stockings*

August 23 Execution of Sacco and Vanzetti provokes international demonstrations

October Release of the movie *The Jazz Singer*, the first talking motion picture

December 2 Deportation of Marcus Garvey

1928

November Herbert Hoover is elected as president

1929

June The Young Plan further reduces Germany's reparation payments from the Great War

September Publication of Ernest Hemingway's novel *A Farewell to Arms*

October 29 Black Tuesday stock market crash on Wall Street

October–December Onset of the global Great Depression

December Street protests take place against Marines in Haiti

1930

March Renunciation of the Roosevelt Corollary to the Monroe Doctrine

June 17 Smoot-Hawley Tariff raises duties on imported manufactured goods

Summary

- Americans enjoyed unprecedented prosperity in the decade after World War I.
- The rapid social changes of the 1920s provoked resistance from Americans who believed that immigrants and people of color threatened harmony and order.
- New means of communications such as radio and the motion pictures hastened the spread of a national culture in the 1920s.
- The Republican presidents of the 1920s promised to reverse Progressive reforms and promote the interests of business.
- The United States remained an active, albeit independent, world power throughout the 1920s.
- By 1930 America and the world were plunging downward into the Great Depression, the worst economic catastrophe of the modern era.

Key Terms and People

Black Tuesday 872

Bow, Clara 860

Coolidge, Calvin 866

Cox, James M. 865

Davis, John W. 867

Dawes Plan 869

Emergency Immigration Act of 1921 851

Fitzgerald, F. Scott 859

Ford, Henry 847

Garvey, Marcus 856

Great Depression 856

Griffith, D.W. 853

Harding, Warren G. 865

Harlem Renaissance 854

Hemingway, Ernest 859

Hoover, Herbert 864

Hughes, Charles Evans 866

Kellogg-Briand Pact 869

Lewis, Sinclair 859

Lindbergh, Charles 858

Mellon, Andrew 866

Mencken, H. L. 859

National Origins Act of 1924 851

Randolph, A. Philip 856

Ruth, Babe 858

Sacco, Nicola 851

Sandino, Cesar Augusto 870

Scopes, John 862

Sloan, Alfred P. 847

Smith, Al 864

Smoot-Hawley Tariff of 1930 873

Somoza, Anastasio 870

Teapot Dome scandal 866

Universal Negro Improvement Association (UNIA) 856

Vanzetti, Bartolomeo 851

Wallace, Henry A. 866

Reviewing Chapter 22

1. In what ways was the decade of the 1920s a "new era" in U.S. history?
2. How did technological innovation shape life in the United States in the 1920s?
3. How did the U.S. role in the global economy change in the 1920s?

Further Reading

Brinkley, Douglas. *Wheels for the World: Henry Ford, His Company, and a Century of Progress*. New York: Penguin Books, 2003. A thorough exploration of the history of the Ford Motor Company from 1903 to 2003, that not only highlights founder Henry Ford and his many innovations but also his workers.

Cohen, Warren I. *Empire without Tears: American Foreign Relations, 1921–1933*. Philadelphia: Temple University Press, 1987. A study of foreign policy during the Harding, Coolidge, and Hoover administrations that explores the way Republican policymakers worked with business to ensure stability for U.S. economic interests.

Evans, Sara M. *Born for Liberty: A History of Women in America*. New York: Free Press Paperbacks, 1997. Both concise and comprehensive, this book examines the history of American women from the colonial period to the present, with a chapter devoted to women in the 1920s.

Hirsch, James S. *Riot and Remembrance: America's Worst Race Riot and Its Legacy*. New York: Mariner Books, 2003. An in-depth look at the 1921 Tulsa race riot that explores how authorities covered up the riot and the ways that victims and their descendants fought for justice.

Iriye, Akira. *The Cambridge History of American Foreign Relations, Vol. 3: The Globalizing of America, 1913–1945*. New York: Cambridge University Press, 1993. Explores the United States' emergence as global power with a discussion of the "Americanizing" of other nations.

Okrent, Daniel. *Last Call: The Rise and Fall of Prohibition*. New York: Scribner, 2010. A lively, engaging look at America's experiment with prohibition from 1920 to 1933 and its impact on nearly every aspect of society and culture.

Visual Review

Popular Entertainment: Movies, Sports, and Celebrity

Interest in popular entertainment rises to unprecedented levels.

The New Skepticism

Many intellectuals grow alienated from American values.

The New Woman of the 1920s

The flapper embodies a new female identity.

Wireless America

Radio revolutionizes communication.

Car Culture

Mass production techniques allow for the growth of the automobile industry and transforms leisure and consumption.

Advertising for Mass Consumption

Advertising incorporates new psychological theories and promotes mass consumption within American society.

A New Economy for a New Era

A NEW ERA, 1920–1930

Ethnic and Racial Divides

Immigration Restriction

Congress places restrictions on immigration based on national origin.

The Ku Klux Klan

Anti-immigrant sentiment revives the Ku Klux Klan.

African American Renaissance and Repression

African Americans build a vibrant culture constructing a new identity as racial violence erupts around the country.

Black International Movements

Pan-Africanism unites people of color around the world.

A National Culture

Religion and Society

Old religious patterns fray with Protestant denominations splitting into two groups.

Prohibition

Cultural divisions are exemplified by the prohibition of alcohol.

Post World War I Politics and Foreign Policy

Government and Business in the 1920s

The Harding administration is beset with corruption and scandal.

Coolidge Prosperity

Under President Calvin Coolidge, the U.S. economy grows while income disparities increase.

The Election of 1928

Republican Herbert Hoover is elected President over the first Roman Catholic to run for president, Democrat Al Smith.

Independent Internationalism in the 1920s

Government and business leaders maintain a keen interest in foreign affairs.

The United States and Instability in the Western Hemisphere

The United States maintains preeminence in the Western Hemisphere, while curtailing interventions.

The Crash

The End of the Boom

The economy crashes with little government regulation and intervention.

The Great Depression

Stock prices decline sharply, leading to economic depression.

A New Deal for Americans

On January 29, 1933, one of the nation's most respected journalists, Walter Lippmann, dined with President-elect **Franklin D. Roosevelt**. Lippmann had previously dismissed Roosevelt as an "amiable man . . . too eager to please" who lacked leadership qualities. But since the election in November 1932, he, like a growing number of Americans, considered Roosevelt the last hope to save a country in crisis. The situation is critical, Franklin," Lippmann warned. "You may have no alternative but to assume dictatorial power."

Lippmann and Roosevelt spoke of Germany, where Nazi Party leader **Adolf Hitler** was poised to become chancellor or prime minister, after his followers had won a plurality of seats in the Reichstag, the German parliament. German politicians, like their American counterparts, had bickered while the economy crashed. Hitler began his career as a fringe extremist blaming Jews and other scapegoats for Germany's problems in the 1920s. But he found a broader following when the global economic crisis hit Germany especially hard in 1931–1932, and he pledged to restore order and jobs, along with national pride, at any cost. Roosevelt, too, came to power pledging action to rescue the economy, a program he called the **New Deal**.

◄

Great Depression bread line, New York, winter 1932–1933

CHAPTER OUTLINE

THE NEW DEAL
> Spiral of Decline, 1931–1933
> From Prosperity to Global Depression
> Suffering in the Land
> The Failure of the Old Deal
> The Coming of the New Deal

RECONSTRUCTING CAPITALISM
> The Hundred Days
> Voices of Protest

THE SECOND NEW DEAL
> Social Security
> Labor Activism
> The 1936 Election

SOCIETY, LAW, AND CULTURE IN THE 1930s
> Popular Entertainment
> Women and the New Deal
> European Ethnics and the New Deal
> A New Deal for Blacks
> Hispanics and the New Deal
> The Indian New Deal
> Nature's New Deal

THE TWILIGHT OF REFORM
> The New Deal and Judicial Change
> Recession
> Political Setbacks

America in the World

U.S. unemployment hit 25% during the Great Depression (1932–1933).

U.S. event that influenced the world

International event that influenced the United States

Event with multinational influence

Conflict

Adolf Hitler was appointed German chancellor and established the Nazi party as the leading political force in Germany (1933).

The Second Sino-Japanese War resulted in the Japanese occupation of Chinese territory during World War II (1937–1945).

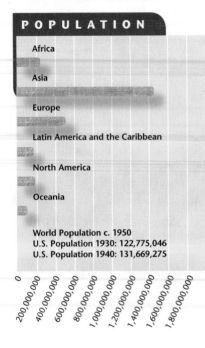

POPULATION

Africa

Asia

Europe

Latin America and the Caribbean

North America

Oceania

World Population c. 1950
U.S. Population 1930: 122,775,046
U.S. Population 1940: 131,669,275

0   200,000,000   400,000,000   600,000,000   800,000,000   1,000,000,000   1,200,000,000   1,400,000,000   1,600,000,000   1,800,000,000

THE NEW DEAL

During the long hiatus between the presidential election of November 1932 and the inauguration of March 1933, many voices demanded radical action. Kansas governor Republican Alfred M. Landon declared that the "hand of a dictator" was required to halt the nation's downward drift. Republican Senator David A. Reed of Pennsylvania remarked that "if this country ever needed a Mussolini," referring to the Italian fascist dictator, "it needs one now." On February 8, 1933, the lame-duck Senate approved a resolution urging Roosevelt to assume "unlimited power" when he took office. A Hollywood film released early in 1933, *Gabriel Over the White House*, portrayed a president who saved the country by declaring martial law, executing dissenters, and hiring millions of unemployed workers as an "army of construction."

In his inaugural speech on March 4, 1933, Roosevelt memorably declared that Americans had "nothing to fear but fear itself." But the audience reserved their loudest cheers for his assertion that he might need to assume "broad executive power to wage a war against the emergency, as great as the power that would be granted to me if we were . . . invaded by a foreign power." First Lady **Eleanor Roosevelt** told an interviewer she found the national mood "terrifying." Her husband's talk of wartime measures shook her deeply. She worried that in this country, as in Germany, if faith in democratic capitalism faded, people "would do anything—if only someone would tell them what to do."

Franklin D. Roosevelt never became a dictator, of course. In fact, he committed his 12 years as president to promoting democracy and economic justice. To accomplish these goals, he dramatically expanded the role played by the federal government in managing the economy and ameliorating human suffering. To an unprecedented degree, he made government more inclusive and attentive to the needs of small farmers, workers, women, and ethnic Americans. Most Americans welcomed changes in the size, role, and direction of federal policy, but others condemned the intrusion of a regulatory state, arguing that it eroded personal liberty and market freedom. This tension has continued for decades.

Spiral of Decline, 1931–1933

It took over three years after the stock market crash of October 1929 for the economy to hit rock bottom. Industrial production, employment, investment, and farm prices declined gradually. Meanwhile, most politicians, the heads of the Federal Reserve

System, economists, and business leaders predicted that after a couple of tough years the economy would recover. Downturns were simply part of a natural "business cycle" in which periodic panics drove out speculators and lowered wages and the price of goods in preparation for renewed growth. The Federal Reserve, the nation's central bank, shared the belief of bankers in Europe that the most important thing to do in any economic crisis was to maintain the gold standard that linked a nation's currency to its supply of gold and prevent inflation. Accordingly, the Federal Reserve raised interest rates and reduced the cash available to banks and other parts of the credit system. As one historian put it, "central bankers continued to kick the world economy while it was down until it lost consciousness." When in 1930–1931 President Hoover brought together business leaders to discuss ways to boost employment and stabilize tumbling prices, professional economists criticized this misguided "activism," which they said might delay recovery by undermining faith in the dollar's link to gold.

During 1931 the heads of some of the biggest corporations, such as U.S. Steel, the Ford Motor Company, and the New York Stock Exchange, buoyed by a brief economic uptick, declared the worst of the Depression already over. In December President Hoover assured Congress that the "fundamentals" of the economic system were sound. Soon after this, the economy collapsed and the capitalist system, at home and abroad, broke down almost completely.

From Prosperity to Global Depression

In 1929, President Hoover and the Republican Party took credit for eight years of economic growth that produced what they called a "new era." But by late 1932 Hoover's earlier prediction that poverty would soon be "banished" sounded absurd to most Americans. Gross annual domestic investment fell from $16 billion to $1 billion, stocks lost almost 90 percent of their value, and a fifth of the nation's 25,000 banks failed. Residential and business construction, steel production, and automobile output fell by one-half. At least 20 percent of workers, 12 million, were unemployed. The overall economy shrank by 33 percent.

About 40 percent of Americans still lived in rural areas and a quarter of the workforce held jobs related to agriculture, such as farming, food processing, building farm implements, and so forth. By 1932, prices for grain, cotton, dairy, and livestock had fallen to half their 1926 level, farm income had declined from $12 billion to $5.3 billion, and one million farms had been seized in foreclosures.

The United States did not lack raw materials, labor, or even capital. But investment and commerce had completely stalled. Instead of taking advantage of bargains as economic theorists predicted, nervous investors and banks stopped putting money into consumer industries such as automobiles and electric appliances because of declining demand. As unsold inventories mounted and investment funds dried up, factories laid off more workers, further driving down demand.

U.S. banks and investors ceased making foreign loans, and by 1933 international trade declined by two-thirds from its 1920s peak. In a futile effort to boost domestic sales by walling off imports, Congress in 1930 adopted the Smoot-Hawley Tariff that hiked duties on foreign goods. Most other countries enacted similar protectionist measures. These actions had the net effect of hurting just about everyone. As national income declined, Germany first reduced, then—under Hitler—simply ceased paying World War I reparations to Britain and France. Britain and France, in turn, stopped paying their war debts to Washington. When British economist John Maynard Keynes was asked if anything in history resembled this array of economic calamities, he replied "yes, it was called the Dark Ages, and it lasted 400 years."

Suffering in the Land

The scope of what was being called the Great Depression revealed the stark reality of poverty in America. By the winter of 1932–1933 around 15 million mostly white, urban males—25 percent of the workforce—were chronically unemployed. Businesses and local governments often fired married women workers to preserve jobs for male heads of households. Fifteen million was probably a low estimate of unemployment and did not count those working just a few hours per week or desperate farmers, sharecroppers, or tenants who worked outside the cash economy. Out of a total population of 126 million, close to half of all Americans lived a hand-to-mouth existence. Conditions were so bad that crowds routinely gathered at municipal dumps to rummage through garbage for food.

African Americans, who comprised about 10 percent of the population and lived mostly in the rural South, faced even more dire conditions. As cotton prices fell, landowners threw many families off the small plots they tilled. In the North, blacks worked mainly in the lower rungs of industry or in service and domestic jobs. Factory owners replaced many blacks with downwardly mobile white workers, while struggling, middle-class, white families fired black women who worked as cooks, cleaners, and nannies. About two-thirds of the black workforce in New York and Chicago, the centers of African American population in the North, had no jobs.

To get by, many families who owned homes or had apartments took in boarders. Younger people deferred marriage and lived with parents. Even so, by 1933, one-half of all home mortgages were in default. Birth rates decreased sharply and anecdotal evidence suggests that pregnant women had more frequent abortions during the 1930s. Rates of desertion by unemployed husbands climbed sharply. At least two million men and a quarter million boys under age 14 simply took off, riding freight trains and roaming the countryside as tramps or "hobos," dependent on odd jobs and handouts.

News stories highlighted odd proposals for dealing with the unemployed. A senior military officer proposed reducing surplus labor and poverty by killing the old and weak. Health reformer and antitobacco activist Bernarr McFadden suggested the "humane" alternative of somehow freezing the unemployed and thawing them out after prosperity returned. The Hoover administration sought to reduce surplus labor in the Southwest by deporting large numbers of Mexican nationals.

By law, most state and city governments had to balance their budgets. When local property taxes declined, cities and states fired municipal workers and reduced already meager social service budgets. One of the most generous urban welfare providers, the city of Philadelphia, provided a family of four $5.50 per week. New York offered

$2.39, the state of Mississippi about $1.50, and Detroit 60 cents. Private charities run by religious and voluntary groups like the Salvation Army and the Red Cross were equipped to assist individual hardship cases or emergency victims of floods or fires, not millions of long-term unemployed workers and their families.

The Failure of the Old Deal

Treasury Secretary Andrew Mellon assured President Hoover that the only way to restore economic growth was to "liquidate labor, liquidate stocks, liquidate the farmers, liquidate real estate . . . and purge the rottenness out of the system." Hoover made at least some attempts to stanch the economic hemorrhaging through limited government intervention. In 1932 Hoover persuaded Congress to create the **Reconstruction Finance Corporation** (RFC) to loan money to struggling banks, railroads, manufacturers, and mortgage companies. As a lender of last resort, the RFC tried to keep private companies afloat. Hoover instructed federal agencies to purchase unsold wheat and other farm products to sustain price levels.

Hoover rejected pleas that he spend federal funds to directly assist the unemployed. Decrying this as a "raid upon the treasury," the president insisted that the federal government had no obligation to unemployed individuals and that providing assistance would only create dependency, not jobs.

That June around 45,000 people, including 17,000 unemployed World War I veterans, trekked to Washington, DC. White and black veterans and their families camped together in fields and abandoned buildings they derisively called "Hoovervilles." The veterans demanded immediate payment of a $1,000 pension or "bonus" that Congress had approved in 1924 for distribution in 1945. "We were heroes in 1917," one despondent veteran remarked, "but now we are bums." Hoover pressured lawmakers to refuse early payment. As a consolation, Congress offered to give the Bonus Marchers of the so-called Bonus Expeditionary Force free bus and train tickets home. By late July around 15,000 demonstrators remained in the capital. On July 28 Hoover ordered police and the army, commanded by General **Douglas MacArthur**, to clear the city of "revolutionaries." Most Americans were appalled as tanks and cavalry rousted the protesters and burned their encampments, killing two veterans and a child.

The Coming of the New Deal

Franklin Delano Roosevelt was born in 1882 into a wealthy family in Hyde Park, New York, on an estate in the Hudson River Valley. He attended Groton Academy, Harvard College, and Columbia Law School and traveled abroad frequently. Like his distant cousin Theodore, he entered politics and won a seat in the New York legislature in 1910, running as a Democratic progressive.

In 1905 Roosevelt married his fifth cousin, Eleanor, with whom he had six children. Before her marriage Eleanor had attended a progressive school in England which introduced her to modern art, literature, and European socialist ideas. Later, she worked in a New York City settlement house and formed close friendships with women active in the labor and suffrage movements. In 1918 Eleanor discovered that Franklin was having an affair with her social secretary, Lucy Mercer. The couple stayed married but thereafter lived largely separate personal lives even though they remained political allies.

During the Great War, Roosevelt served as assistant secretary of the navy. In 1920 he ran as vice president on the unsuccessful Democratic ticket headed by Ohio governor James C. Cox. The next year Roosevelt suffered a crippling attack of polio. For the rest of his life he required help getting in or out of bed, dressing, or standing up. By wearing heavy steel braces, he could stand upright as long as he had someone or something to lean on. He could imitate walking for short distances by thrusting his hips forward while holding someone's arm. Roosevelt learned to use his upper body strength, exaggerated hand and head movements, and a broad smile to divert attention from his crippled lower body.

Coping with his disability transformed Roosevelt from a dilettante into someone who related to the everyday problems of ordinary people. During his long recovery in the 1920s he became closer to several of Eleanor's feminist and labor activist friends. Through them, Roosevelt gained greater insight into the lives of working people. **Frances Perkins**, a veteran of Jane Addams's Hull House who knew Roosevelt since 1911 and later as secretary of labor became the first female cabinet member, remarked that after polio "he was serious, not playing now . . . He had become conscious of other people, of weak people, of human frailty."

President Roosevelt charms reporters during an impromptu White House press conference in the mid-1930s.

Roosevelt reentered politics in 1928, running for governor of New York. Despite his victory, he feared that if the full extent of his paralysis became known, he would have difficulty winning elections or governing. To shape press coverage, as a presidential candidate and after election, he worked hard to woo journalists. During his first term in the White House, he held over 300 informal press conferences in which a hundred or more reporters crowded into his office for lively give-and-take. As a measure of their admiration, and not because of censorship, between 1929 and 1945 not a single journalist published an unflattering photograph or description of Roosevelt's physical limitations.

By 1932 Roosevelt was recognized as the nation's most prominent liberal Democrat. Unlike the passive Hoover, he recognized the Depression as the greatest crisis since the Civil War. The unemployed were not slackers, as Hoover implied, but victims of "complex and impersonal forces" over which individuals had no control. He called on states and the federal government to create work relief programs, unemployment insurance, and old age pensions. In addition to **Harry Hopkins**, a social worker who had headed a New York State agency that had hired the unemployed to work on public projects, and Eleanor Roosevelt, Roosevelt relied for ideas on three academic lawyers and economists from Columbia University, **Raymond Moley**, **Rexford Tugwell**, and **Adolph Berle**. They advocated increased regulation of business and greater government economic planning to salvage capitalism from its follies. Journalists called them the "brains trust."

After Roosevelt secured the Democratic presidential nomination in the summer of 1932, he spoke of rebuilding the economy from the bottom up by helping the "forgotten man." He pledged to use federal power to ensure a more equitable distribution of income and promised "bold experimentation" in pursuit of what he called a "New Deal" for Americans. As he later put it, "when Americans suffered, humanity came first." Hoover, in contrast, seemed immobile and campaigned on a pledge to stay the course. That meant no federal aid to the poor and reliance primarily on private enterprise, voluntary groups, and market forces to salvage the economy.

On November 8, 1932, Roosevelt trounced Hoover, winning nearly 58 percent of the popular vote or 22.8 million to 15.7 million. The challenger received 472 electoral votes to Hoover's 59, winning all but six states. Democrats took control of the House by a margin of 310 to 117 and the Senate by 60 to 35.

Roosevelt's landslide victory in November signaled hope, but no quick change. Nearly everything got worse between November 1932 and the inauguration in March 1933, including the weather. A drought that already afflicted the upper South spread west into Kansas, Colorado, Oklahoma, and Texas, carving out what would soon be known as the **Dust Bowl**.

Farmers not hurt by the drought faced shrinking markets and prices for their produce. In August 1932, a group of irate Iowa farmers formed the Farm Holiday Association and declared a 30-day ban on marketing agricultural products as a way to limit supply and drive up prices. As the movement spread through the Midwest and then to other regions, farmers set up roadblocks to prevent trucks from hauling grain and dairy products, sometimes overturning the vehicles and destroying their cargo.

Elsewhere, groups of farmers disrupted bank and sheriffs' auctions to block fore-closures and evictions. In many large cities, Unemployed Councils held rallies to de-mand work and often prevented evictions of families from apartments where the rent had not been paid.

Hoover, now a lame duck, spent the time from November through March calling on the president-elect to endorse his discredited economic policies. But Hoover had lost all credibility. What remained of the banking system virtually collapsed in January and February of 1933.

There were approximately 25,000 banks in the United States at the onset of the Depression. Many were small institutions with limited assets and could not survive the downturn without an infusion of cash from the Federal Reserve or the Treasury Department. About 5,000 small banks failed before the 1932 election, and another 5,500 went under by March 1933. Since deposits were not insured and ordinary Amer-icans had no idea which banks to trust, early in 1933 millions of small savers rushed to withdraw billions of dollars from their accounts. This escalating panic threatened to bring down even large, well-managed banks. When Hoover refused to intervene, most state governors imposed "bank holidays." They ordered banks to shut their doors to prevent mass withdrawals and inevitable collapse. By March 4, 32 states had suspended all banking activity, and the economy was paralyzed. Outgoing Secretary of the Treasury Ogden Mills told a banker friend planning a trip to the Bahamas, "don't buy a round trip ticket. When you return, there will be nothing worth returning to."

STUDY QUESTIONS FOR THE NEW DEAL

1. How did economic hardship affect ordinary American families in the early 1930s?
2. What did President Hoover do and not do in response to the economic calamity?
3. How did Roosevelt's personal and political background shape his view of the crisis as he assumed the presidency?

RECONSTRUCTING CAPITALISM

Like most of his advisers, Roosevelt came of age in the Progressive Era and saw gov-ernment as a positive force to mitigate the excesses and inequalities of the new in-dustrial order. New Dealers often disagreed among themselves on details of policy. Some favored balanced budgets, while others insisted that running deficits promoted growth. Some advocated central economic planning; others retained faith in free mar-kets. One group of New Dealers urged redistributing wealth to those at the bottom of the economic pyramid, while others insisted that government could help the poor most effectively by promoting overall growth. New Dealers generally sympathized with the efforts of workers to organize unions but hesitated to intervene on their behalf. Most New Dealers agreed that "underconsumption" by poorly paid workers and farmers along with selfish actions by financial institutions had caused the Depression. Recovery would require active federal regulation of capital markets, assistance to farmers and businesses, and increased government spending to boost production and consumption. Although many conservatives condemned them as radicals, despite their support of government intervention, neither the president nor his top advisers considered themselves socialists or enemies of capitalism.

Most bankers and traditional economists worried that New Deal policies would cause inflation and further economic ruin. Roosevelt's refusal to join a British-led effort in July 1933 aimed at restoring the international gold standard that linked most currency values to gold reserves especially worried them. Unless the dollar's link to gold was ironclad, they feared the government could manipulate the money supply and inhibit world trade. New Dealers countered that the gold standard had proven to be a straitjacket that made the Depression worse and that the United States had to concentrate on boosting employment and production levels at home rather than trying to export its way out of hardship.

The Hundred Days

In his inaugural speech on Saturday, March 4, 1933, Roosevelt condemned "unscrupulous money changers" who had "fled from their high seats in the temple of our civilization." But how could the remnants of the banking system be salvaged? Moments after taking the presidential oath, FDR invoked emergency powers to issue a proclamation closing all national banks effective Monday, March 6. He then called Congress into special session on Thursday, March 9.

In less than a day, the president persuaded Congress to pass an **Emergency Banking Relief Act**. This created a system to audit, loan funds to, and reopen banks under Treasury Department supervision. On the evening of March 12, Roosevelt explained the procedure to an anxious public in a 14-minute radio address, the first of three dozen **"fireside chats"** he delivered on policy issues over the next 12 years. Half of all American adults listened to the president as his aristocratic and reassuring voice described the causes of the banking crisis, the procedures to audit and reopen sound banks, and how regulators would safeguard future deposits. "Let us unite in banishing fear," he declared. "We have provided the machinery to restore our financial system; and it is up to you to support and make it work." The public was impressed that such an important person seemed to be speaking directly to them.

On the morning of Monday, March 13, a near economic miracle occurred. For the first time in months, ordinary Americans retrieved cash from under mattresses and began depositing it in newly reopened federally supervised banks.

In June Congress enacted the **Glass-Steagall Banking Act**, which established strict guidelines for banking operations and expanded the power of the Federal Reserve System. The law closed many small banks and forced several thousand others to merge with larger more stable institutions. It also separated risky commercial and investment banking from ordinary banking, a firewall that lasted until 1999. The new

Federal Deposit Insurance Corporation (FDIC) helped restore faith in banks by guaranteeing individual deposits for up to $5,000, an amount raised gradually over time.

The new administration also moved quickly to prevent the kind of wild speculation that led to stock market booms and busts. The **Securities Act of 1933** required companies selling stock to the public to register with a federal agency and provide accurate information on what was being sold. The subsequent **Securities Exchange Act of 1934** created a Securities Exchange Commission (SEC) to regulate stock markets and activities by brokers. This left the basic operation of capital markets in private hands but imposed rules and supervision over market operations.

Between March and June 1933, often dubbed the "**first Hundred Days**," Roosevelt prevailed on Congress to pass 14 major pieces of legislation, a record never duplicated and a testament to both presidential leadership and the country's desire for change. Congress enacted bills to raise agricultural prices, put the unemployed to work, regulate the stock market, reform banking practices, and assist home owners and farmers in paying mortgages. Telling aides he felt "it was a good time for a beer," Roosevelt convinced Congress to amend the Volstead Act to allow production of beer and wine while the states went through the long process of ratifying the 21st Amendment that repealed the 18th Amendment mandating prohibition.

To meet the challenge of youth unemployment, Congress created the Civilian Conservation Corps (CCC). Within a few months it enrolled 275,000 men, mostly in their 20s, in 1,300 labor camps. They received $ 30.00 per month plus room and board and

Table 23.1 Major Laws and Programs Passed in the First Hundred Days In just over the first three months of the Roosevelt administration in 1933, a period known as the "first Hundred Days," Congress passed a remarkable number of laws that stabilized and regulated the nation's faltering economic system.

Emergency Banking Act	March 9
Economy Act	March 15
Volstead Act modified to allow beer and wine	March 22
Civilian Conservation Corps	March 31
Agricultural Adjustment Act	May 12
Farm Mortgage Assistance	May 12
Federal Emergency Relief Act	May 12
Securities Act of 1933	May 27
Tennessee Valley Authority	May 18
Home Owners Loan Corporation	June 13
Public Works Administration	June 16
Railroad Coordination Act	June 16
National Industrial Recovery Act	June 16
Glass-Steagall Banking Act	June 16

had to send $22.00 home to their families. Because army officials organized the initial CCC efforts, critics worried it might resemble the Hitler Youth indoctrination camps established by the Nazis. In fact, they had little in common and did not delve into politics. In 1935, at its peak, 500,000 men worked on CCC projects; by the time the program ended in 1942, about 3 million men had served in the corps. In addition to conservation work, the CCC constructed the infrastructure of the national park system.

Other innovations included the Federal Emergency Relief Administration (FERA), the Public Works Administration (PWA), and the **Tennessee Valley Authority** (TVA). FERA, headed by Harry Hopkins, began with a $500 million appropriation to provide matching funds to states to hire the unemployed to work on public projects. PWA, managed by Interior Secretary Harold Ickes, spent over $3 billion in its first three years building large public works projects such as dams in the Pacific Northwest, highways, and public buildings.

TVA represented a vast experiment in regional planning. It built a network of dams and hydroelectric projects to control floods, generate power, and promote growth in a chronically poor area of the South. Cheap electricity generated by TVA dramatically improved life for millions of Southerners, and it still plays a major role in the region. Advocates hoped that TVA would become a model of planned regional development, but aside from some small demonstration projects it remained unique.

As one of the largest federal construction projects undertaken during the New Deal, the Grand Coulee Dam, seen here under construction in 1937, comprised part of the multidam effort to "tame" the Columbia River in the Pacific Northwest. Like the Tennessee Valley Authority in the Southeast, the river's power would be used to generate electricity for industry and to irrigate farms. The project's administrator hired folk singer Woodie Guthrie to compose several ballads, including "Roll on Columbia," that memorialized the effort.

Roosevelt tapped **Henry A. Wallace** as secretary of agriculture. An accomplished plant geneticist and editor of a major farm journal, Wallace possessed both practical and scientific skills. Critics later attacked him as a dangerous radical, but as secretary of agriculture (1933–1940), vice president (1941–1945), and secretary of commerce (1945–1946), Wallace played a major role in promoting science and technology to provide solutions to economic problems.

In 1933 the newly created **Agricultural Adjustment Administration** (AAA) and the related Commodity Credit Corporation provided credit, loans, and other subsidies to farmers. Financial incentives were offered to those who agreed to limit production of corn, wheat, cotton, tobacco, and livestock. Participating farmers who could not sell their crops above a certain price point could transfer them to the Commodity Credit Corporation, which held them as collateral for loans given to the farmers. The programs costs were paid by taxing food processors. Conservative critics of the program condemned it for interfering with the free market and for taxing nonfarmers to pay for it. Liberals complained that the crop support payments went disproportionately to large-scale farmers and did little or nothing to help tenants or sharecroppers. After the Supreme Court overturned the original AAA law in 1936, it was replaced by a modified program in 1938. Between 1933 and 1940, farm income doubled.

Early New Deal industrial policy had less success. The National Industrial Recovery Act created the **National Recovery Administration** (NRA), famous for its blue eagle logo. The NRA resembled World War I programs that brought together industry leaders and labor groups to boost production. NRA wrote "production codes" for each industry that encouraged cooperation among competing businesses to set stable prices and wages and bar cut-throat competition. Roosevelt hoped these measures would stabilize the economy and prompt private business to hire more workers. Neither occurred, and NRA failed to address the biggest impediment to recovery—the lack of new private investment funds and the large pool of unemployed workers who lacked the money to buy goods. In 1935 the Supreme Court declared the NRA an unconstitutional overreach of federal authority and it came to an unlamented end.

The New Deal's prewar achievements were substantial. Between 1933 and 1940, except for the recession of 1937–1938, the American economy grew on average 8–10 percent annually, a historically high rate. By the end of 1937, the Gross Domestic Product (GDP) recovered to its 1929 level. But growth varied from year to year, bypassed some key industries, and failed to solve the unemployment problem. Private sector employment did not reach the 1929 level until 1943. In the interim, government work relief projects gave jobs to many of the unemployed. Ultimately, it required the massive stimulus of wartime spending to spur full recovery.

The New Deal addressed both immediate problems and long-term needs. In an economy dominated by powerful business interests, New Dealers hoped to mitigate concentrated corporate power by creating what economists called "countervailing powers." For example, industrial labor unions could balance the influence of big business and promote workers' welfare. Electric power generated by government-built dams in the Tennessee Valley and Pacific Northwest and distributed by consumer-owned cooperatives would compete with private utilities and pressure them to improve service and reduce rates. New agencies to regulate banking and the stock market would empower private investors to take informed risks and small depositors to put their money in banks where it could be loaned out to promote economic expansion. Government-administered pensions funded by workers' and employers' contributions would provide the elderly a decent retirement and make them less dependent on the whims of their employers. Agricultural subsidies to farmers would provide a cash flow that made them less vulnerable to market blips or the power of large food processors.

Voices of Protest

Between 1933 and 1935 the New Deal saved democratic capitalism by stabilizing the banking system, regulating stock markets, protecting property owners, helping farmers, and providing emergency relief to the unemployed. Ironically, many of the Republican politicians and business executives who in 1933 had urged Roosevelt to assume dictatorial power now complained that he had—and used it against them. But some accused the New Deal of doing too little to assure social justice, assist labor unions, and redistribute wealth.

Several small fascist movements developed in the United States during the 1930s, but none gained national traction. The Communist Party, whose membership had increased from 9,000 to about 100,000, generally supported New Deal reforms. Roosevelt's most powerful critics often struck a populist tone that defied easy characterization.

In January 1934 Dr. **Frances Townsend**, health commissioner of Long Beach, California, founded a group named "Old Age Revolving Pensions Limited." It called on the federal government to impose a 2 percent income tax on all workers to finance monthly payments of $200 to everyone over age 60, as long as they spent all the money within 30 days. Townsend's group organized 4,500 local chapters with 2 million members and published a paper called the *Townsend National Weekly*.

Louisiana Democratic senator **Huey Long** announced the creation in 1934 of the "Share Our Wealth Society." Long blamed the Depression on a conspiracy by the rich. Under the banner "Every Man a King," he proposed to expand Townsend's ideas beyond the elderly by "soaking the rich" with taxes and giving every family a grant of $5,000 to buy a house and a guaranteed annual income of $2,500. Long's appeal spread quickly in the South and attracted a national following among the lower-middle class and small farmers. By 1935 Share Our Wealth Clubs claimed 27,000 chapters and 5 million members.

A Catholic priest from Royal Oak, Michigan, Father Charles Coughlin also attacked the New Deal as too conservative. Coughlin, a Canadian immigrant, broadcast radio sermons on social and political issues. Although initially a supporter of Roosevelt, declaring "the New Deal is Christ's Deal," by 1934 he accused the president of being a tool of powerful conspirators. Ordinary working people, he complained, benefited little from programs that bolstered bankers, brokers, and corporations. This was so, Coughlin charged, because "Franklin Double-Crossing Roosevelt" did the bidding

Father Charles Coughlin, the popular "Radio Priest" from Royal Oak, Michigan, attracted millions of listeners in the mid-1930s. Although he initially supported Roosevelt's New Deal, like fellow demagogue, Senator Huey Long, by 1935 he became a fierce critic. Coughlin's so-called Social Justice movement borrowed a theme from Adolf Hitler. He blamed Jews for the nation's economic woes and claimed they conspired to rule the world. Embarrassed church authorities silenced Coughlin in the late 1930s. He lived in obscurity until 1979.

of Wall Street, foreigners, and an "international conspiracy of Jewish bankers." His radio rants reached an estimated 30 million, mostly Catholic, listeners each week. Coughlin organized the "National Union for Social Justice," which demanded that the government guarantee "an annual wage system that is just and equitable" for all.

Townsend, Long, and Coughlin all highlighted real problems—the meagerness of aid to the poor, the insecurity of old age, and the maldistribution of wealth. But they offered only simplistic alternatives and demonized scapegoats. In September 1935 a Louisiana doctor, angered by Long's strong-arm tactics in Louisiana, shot and killed the senator. Several influential Catholic Democrats, including Joseph Kennedy, convinced the Church hierarchy that Coughlin had become an embarrassment. In 1936 his superiors ordered him to cease inflammatory broadcasts, although he resumed anti-Semitic diatribes in 1938. Townsend's political appeal waned quickly in 1935 with the passage of the **Social Security Act**.

In the mid-1930s a more traditional conservative coalition also attacked FDR and his program. Conservative Democrats, including two former presidential nominees, Al Smith and John W. Davis, joined business leaders such as **Alfred Sloan** of General Motors and Sewell Avery of Montgomery Ward to form the Liberty League. The League's 125,000 members accused Roosevelt of promoting class warfare and wrecking the economy. The group especially complained about First Lady Eleanor Roosevelt's activities, including her frequent visits to factories, mines, farms, and African American communities.

On the left side of the political spectrum, many industrial workers and union activists also grew frustrated with the slow improvement of wages and working conditions under the New Deal. During 1934 and 1935 industrial unions such as the United Mine Workers and United Automobile Workers broke away from the cautious **American Federation of Labor** (AFL) and created the more radical umbrella group, the **Congress of Industrial Organizations**, or CIO, led by John L. Lewis, head of the Mine Workers. Although Roosevelt sympathized with the goals of organized labor, at this point he still hoped that management–union cooperation—rather than labor militancy—would boost the economy.

During 1934 militant truck drivers in Minneapolis and longshoremen in San Francisco battled transportation companies that refused to recognize their unions. In September, 400,000 textile workers in mills throughout New England and the South went on strike in the biggest labor action since 1919. State governors called in the National Guard to break the strikes and keep factories open. These events prompted New York senator **Robert Wagner**, a pro-union politician, to introduce legislation to guarantee workers the right to organize and bargain collectively.

STUDY QUESTIONS FOR RECONSTRUCTING CAPITALISM

1. What did the New Deal do to stabilize the financial system in 1933?
2. What early New Deal Programs specifically helped workers and farmers?
3. What faults with the New Deal did critics on the Left and Right identify?

THE SECOND NEW DEAL

Despite the New Deal's early political victories, many liberals feared that in the face of conservative opposition Roosevelt had abandoned plans to restructure the economy or redistribute wealth. But on June 28, 1934, in a fireside chat, he renewed his promise to promote additional "social insurance" measures to improve living standards for ordinary people. Roosevelt warned that Republicans and others would attack his initiatives, labeling them as "fascism . . . or Communism . . . or Socialism."

Roosevelt then began an extended sea voyage, traveling through the Panama Canal and visiting several Latin American capitals to highlight his Good Neighbor Policy that treated hemispheric neighbors as equals. After a stop in Hawaii, he sailed back to the Pacific Northwest. From there he traveled by train back to the east coast, making side trips to visit many big federal construction projects underway, such as the dams being built along the Columbia and Missouri rivers.

The trip energized Roosevelt and generated much favorable publicity. In the Congressional elections of November 1934, Democrats not only held on to their large majorities, but liberal Democrats increased their numbers in both the House and Senate. FDR then launched a new burst of reforms, known as the second New Deal or second Hundred Days.

Table 23.2 Major Laws and Programs of the Second Hundred Days In a period of time during 1935 dubbed the "second Hundred Days," President Roosevelt proposed and Congress passed far reaching reform legislation, including Social Security, the National Labor Relations Act, and the vast Works Progress Administration employment program.

Emergency Relief Appropriation Act	April 8, 1935	Funds for work relief
Resettlement Administration	April 30, 1935	Aid to migrant farmers
Works Progress Administration	May 6, 1935	Mass hiring of unemployed
Rural Electrification Administration	May 11, 1935	Power to rural areas
National Labor Relations Act	July 7, 1935	Workers' right to unionize
Social Security Act	August 14, 1935	Pensions/social programs
Public Utilities Holding Company Act	August 26, 1935	Regulation of utilities

Early in 1935 Roosevelt introduced legislation to expand temporary work relief programs for the unemployed and to create a permanent economic security program for the aged and sick. Roosevelt opposed the notion of giving cash payments—known as the dole—to the unemployed. Instead, he proposed expanding government funded work relief for the jobless. Congress responded and passed a $5 billion Emergency Relief Appropriation Act in April, funding projects for both urban and rural Americans.

The new Resettlement Administration (RA) supervised rural relief activities. Its head, Rexford Tugwell, a member of the original Brains Trust, pushed for assistance to tenant farmers and sharecroppers—groups ignored by earlier farm aid programs. But

African American sharecroppers during the Great Depression.

opposition by rural Democrats and Republicans who opposed social engineering in the countryside limited RA efforts to construction of only 3 of a proposed 60 planned suburban towns—Greenbelt, Maryland; Greenhills, Ohio; and Greendale, Wisconsin. Only about 5,000 poor farm families were placed on better land. In 1937 the Farm Security Administration (FSA) replaced the RA. The new agency assisted about 20,000 tenant farmers to purchase their own land. It also constructed model housing camps for migratory farm workers. Many of the most famous photographs from the Depression era were taken by FSA photographers such as **Dorothea Lange**, Walker Evans, and **Arthur Rothstein**.

The Rural Electrification Administration (REA) benefited millions of Americans. Ninety percent of farms had no electricity in 1935. REA loaned money to locally owned nonprofit cooperatives to build rural power grids. One Arkansan from the Ozarks described the day in 1940 that the "lights came on." "I remember my mother smiling . . . when they came on full, tears started running down her cheeks. . . . It was a day of celebration. They had all kinds of parties—mountain people getting light for the first time." Within five years nearly half of all farms had electric power and by 1950, 90 percent were on the power grid. This advance created huge demand for home appliances and new farm equipment.

In 1935 FDR tasked Harry Hopkins to manage the largest of the new programs, the Works Progress Administration (WPA). Hopkins believed that work relief would prevent social unrest by giving the unemployed meaningful labor. The tools and raw materials used on WPA projects, along with the wages paid, would also stimulate the private economy. As an additional impetus to long-term growth, the projects would produce vital infrastructure, such as roads, bridges, libraries, airports, and schools.

Hopkins had a vision of inclusiveness. WPA reached out not only to laborers but to artists, sculptors, musicians, playwrights, novelists, dancers, and actors as well.

Table 23.3 Major WPA Construction Projects, 1935–1941 Between 1935 and 1941, the WPA revolutionized the national infrastructure, constructing parks, roads, dams, irrigation projects, airports, schools, and government buildings. It also employed artists, musicians, writers, and actors in a remarkable variety of public arts projects.

- 572,000 miles of rural roads; 67,000 miles of city streets; 31,000 miles of sidewalks
- 122,000 bridges and 1,000 tunnels
- 1,050 airfields and 4,000 airport buildings
- 500 water treatment plants and thousands of miles of sewer lines and water lines
- 3,300 sports stadiums; 5,000 athletic fields; 12,800 playgrounds
- 36,900 school buildings and 1,000 public library buildings
- 2,552 hospitals; 2,700 firehouses; 900 armories; 760 prison buildings
- 19,400 state and local government buildings
- 416 fish hatcheries; 7,000 miles of firebreaks

Between 1935 and 1942, about 8.5 million Americans worked for the WPA at some point. Thousands of WPA workers wrote letters expressing thanks. "Please continue the WPA program," a man from Michigan wrote the president. "It makes us feel like an American citizen to earn our own living." A girl from Illinois wrote "my father immediately got employed in the WPA. This was a godsend. This was the greatest thing. It meant food, you know. Survival, just survival."

Social Security

In 1935 the Roosevelt administration proposed a national plan for unemployment and disability insurance, aid to dependent children, and pensions for the elderly. Most western European nations had begun such programs decades earlier, but in the United States, only a few states even offered assistance to unemployed workers. Only one in seven private sector workers had any sort of pension.

The president assigned Labor Secretary Frances Perkins to supervise drafting the Social Security Act. She proposed a government administered system funded primarily by contributions—payroll taxes—from workers and employers, not general tax revenues. In this sense it represented an insurance program more than a welfare program.

Retirement pensions, normally paid beginning at age 65, would come from a fund into which workers and employers each contributed 1 percent of a salary, capped at $3,000. Each generation of younger workers contributing to the system financed the retirement benefits received by older workers, and they, in turn, would benefit the same way upon their reaching 65. Because they were based on the amount contributed, the value of pensions varied somewhat, but in practice the program returned more to lower income workers than to higher income ones; thus, it moderated the regressive terms of the 1 percent flat tax. Payments began at $15 per month in 1940, but over time benefit levels increased substantially.

The proposed act encountered fierce opposition from business owners, commercial farmers, and doctors, some of whom simply disliked paying taxes, while others denounced any government involvement in worker-employee relations. Republican politicians worried that those receiving pensions would all become loyal Democrats. Many business owners disliked having to contribute toward employee pensions. The American Medical Association complained so loudly about "socialized medicine" that the administration dropped plans to include a modest national health insurance plan within Social Security. To placate commercial farmers and wealthier Americans, the law exempted most agricultural and household domestic laborers. Many government workers, teachers, waitresses, and employees of nonprofit agencies were also denied coverage. These exemptions had the perverse effect of excluding from coverage one-half of all African American and women workers. The proposal as passed in 1935 included provisions to assist laid off and injured workers, surviving dependents of dead workers, and single mothers with young children. Over time, many more workers were covered by the law and payments rose from their meager early levels.

Labor Activism

Until the mid-1930s, Roosevelt had an uneasy relationship with labor unions. Craft unions representing trades such as carpenters, plumbers, and electricians dominated the largest labor organization, the **American Federation of Labor** (AFL). They largely ignored the plight of lower-paid industrial workers, excluded minority laborers, and often supported Republican candidates. This dynamic changed in 1935 when Congress passed and Roosevelt signed the National Labor Relations Act, or Wagner Act, named for its primary author, Senator Robert Wagner, Democrat of New York. The Wagner Act established the National Labor Relations Board (NLRB), empowered to protect the right of workers to form unions and to require employers to negotiate labor contracts with those unions. This gave a tremendous boost to steel, automobile, and mine workers whose past efforts to organize had been thwarted by violent company resistance.

During 1935 newly energized unions representing industrial workers formed the Congress of Industrial Organizations (CIO). Most CIO-affiliated unions accepted black and other minority workers and campaigned for Roosevelt's reelection in 1936. In December 1936 and continuing through 1937, the United Automobile Workers (UAW), led by brothers Walter and Victor Reuther, seized control of several General Motors and Ford plants in Flint and Detroit, Michigan, by staging "sit-down strikes." For weeks at a time workers occupied the auto plants while their wives and women supporters braved a gauntlet of company-hired thugs to bring food to the strikers.

This time Michigan governor **Frank Murphy** and Roosevelt refused to send police or troops to retake the factories. Instead, they called on GM and Ford to negotiate a deal with union officials. Over the next two years first automobile and then steel workers, through their unions, negotiated contracts with manufacturers.

Between 1930 and 1940 the proportion of factory workers in labor unions tripled, from under 8 to 23 percent. By 1945 a historically high 25 percent of nonfarm laborers were union members. Unionized blue collar workers enjoyed steadily rising levels of pay and benefits from the late 1930s through the mid-1970s. In spite of his initial wariness, Roosevelt became a champion of the Wagner Act and organized labor became a pillar of the Democratic Party.

The 1936 Election

The election of 1936 served as a national referendum on the New Deal. The Democrats found millions of new supporters among unionized workers, farmers who received crop support, ethnic voting blocs such as Catholics and Jews, and African Americans who had migrated north. Roosevelt skillfully dubbed his Republican opponents and corporate critics "economic royalists" that opposed the New Deal not because its policies had not worked but because they feared losing their grip on power. Democrats pointed out that among those who now complained that he had amassed too much power was Republican presidential nominee and Kansas governor Alfred Landon. In

GLOBAL PASSAGES

Economic Intervention

The Depression spread around the world nearly as quickly as the influenza pandemic of 1918–1919. By 1933 Canadian timber, Brazilian coffee beans, English textiles, German steel, Japanese silk, and U.S. automobiles found few buyers anywhere. Sparsely populated Canada, which had been the world's fastest growing economy, along with Australia, lost markets for their mineral and agricultural exports and experienced a nearly 40 percent drop in GNP, a 50 percent decline in exports, and an unemployment rate of about 27 percent. Industrialized Germany, like the United States, suffered nearly as much. The Depression pushed many countries—including Germany, Japan, Argentina, and Brazil—toward fascism or military dictatorship.

Argentina, Brazil, Colombia, and Mexico, unable to find new markets for their beef, wheat, coffee, and oil exports, imposed production controls on agriculture to sustain prices. Their government also made investments in domestic industry to reduce dependence on their traditional exports. As a result these countries ended the decade with growing economies.

Japan also mitigated economic hardship through government intervention. The government devalued its currency to make exports more competitive while also investing heavily in new factories, doubling production capacity by 1940. Much of the investment went to military-related sectors such as naval and aircraft construction.

The collapse of international trade and credit, along with the end of American loans, hit Germany especially hard. Hitler's promise to restore German pride, prosperity, stability, and work to the nation's 11 million unemployed earned the Nazis a plurality of parliamentary seats in 1933 and put Hitler in a position to seize dictatorial power.

1933 it was Landon who had urged the newly elected Roosevelt to take the power of a "dictator" to run the country.

Crossing the country Landon attacked Social Security along with most other New Deal programs as attacks on freedom by an incumbent who threatened the American way of life. Despite these claims, in November, Roosevelt won a resounding second-term victory by defeating Landon in every state except Maine and Vermont. Roosevelt received 60 percent of the popular vote to Landon's 36.5 percent, and 523 electoral votes to Landon's 8. Democrats increased their Congressional majorities and captured 26 of 33 races for governor.

Between 1933 and 1936, Germany and Fascist Italy pursued economic stimulus policies that resembled many New Deal recovery initiatives. These focused on large-scale public works projects to hire the unemployed. Germany, concentrating on highway construction, built autobahns, at the time the most advanced highway system in the world. By 1937 the number of unemployed Germans decreased from 11 million to less than 1 million, a much better record than that achieved by the New Deal. But as domestic growth reached a plateau, Hitler switched direction. In place of autobahns, he rapidly expanded the size of the military and invested heavily in armaments production. The German economic growth rate, like that of Japan, surpassed the U.S. rate during the 1930s.

The common element among the successful economic strategies pursued by the United States, Germany, Japan, and some other countries during the 1930s was adoption of ideas that resembled those formulated by the British economist John Maynard Keynes. Supporters of Keynesian theory relied on countercyclical deficit spending by government. This meant that during hard times, government spending would increase to boost demand for products and create jobs when the private sector failed to make needed investments. As the private sector recovered, government spending could be reduced and taxes would be collected to pay for public debt. Government employment could produce roads and schools or, as with Germany and Japan, tanks and fighter planes.

- What common economic problems afflicted most nations during the 1930s?

- What similarities—and differences—marked how other governments dealt with the Depression?

STUDY QUESTIONS FOR THE SECOND NEW DEAL

1. What major new programs were adopted during the "second New Deal" and how did they differ from earlier reforms?
2. How did Social Security create a national retirement system for many U.S. workers? Who was left out of it and why?
3. In what ways did the New Deal support industrial labor unions and how did this alter the power of industry?

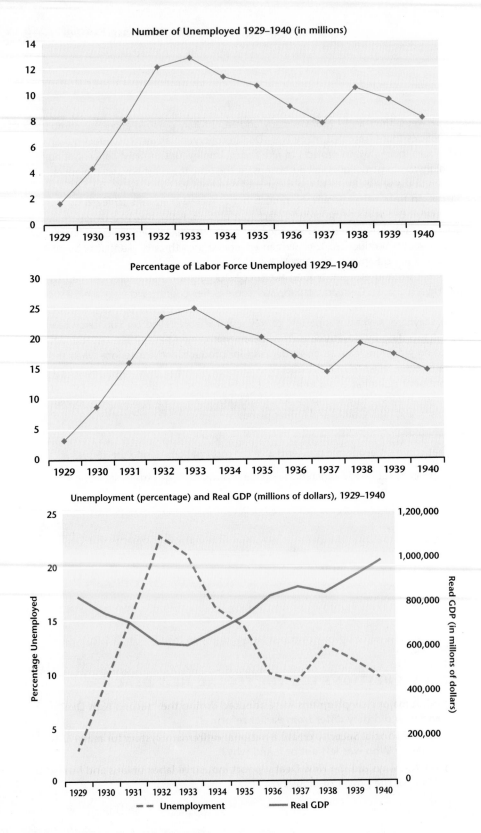

Number of Unemployed 1929–1940 (in millions)

Percentage of Labor Force Unemployed 1929–1940

Unemployment (percentage) and Real GDP (millions of dollars), 1929–1940

Percentage Unemployed

Read GDP (in millons of dollars)

- - - Unemployment ———— Real GDP

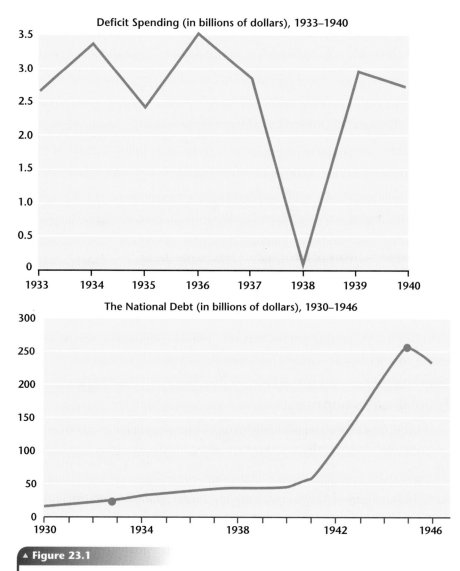

▲ Figure 23.1

National economic profile of the 1930s After the dismal economic decline between 1929 and early 1933, the nation's GDP improved dramatically during the first five years of the New Deal. The ranks of the unemployed shrank substantially. The economy nose-dived in 1937–1938 when President Roosevelt reduced federal spending, but recovered when he expanded job-creating programs. Overall levels of federal spending and debt were moderate during the New Deal, rising steeply when the United States entered World War II.

SOCIETY, LAW, AND CULTURE IN THE 1930S

Before 1933 most of those appointed to high posts or who served in the permanent bureaucracy were white, Anglo-Saxon men with a business background. Breaking with this tradition, the New Deal reached out to Catholics, Jews, African Americans, immigrants and their children, and women. The Roosevelt administration appointed individuals active in universities, labor unions, and social work, for example, to influential posts where they addressed the concerns of working class, ethnic, and minority Americans. Several of Roosevelt's closest advisers, such as Thomas Corcoran and James Farley, were Irish Catholics; Ben Cohen, Sam Rosenman, and **Felix Frankfurter** had Jewish immigrant backgrounds. Harry Hopkins was the first professionally trained social worker to serve as a presidential aide and became FDR's single most trusted adviser. Secretary of Labor Frances Perkins was the first female Cabinet member. In their daily lives millions of Americans found relief from the Depression in popular entertainment. The movies, radio, and fiction allowed them to enter a more carefree—or at least a different—life. Although most popular culture remained in the private sector, New Deal agencies funded major arts and cultural programs, such as the Federal Theatre Project and the painting of historic murals in public buildings, both to assist unemployed artists and to educate the public.

Popular Entertainment

Newspapers, magazines, and especially radio and movies informed and entertained the public. Inexpensive radio receivers were nearly ubiquitous, helped by New Deal construction of rural electrical grids. With the arrival of sound and color, movies became an even more popular escape. Trains still carried most long-distance travelers, but flying became more common with the introduction of the first modern passenger plane, the DC-3 in 1937.

Although overall crime rates did not rise during the Depression, high profile criminals, especially bank robbers, dominated newspaper headlines. John Dillinger, Baby Face Nelson, Bonnie and Clyde, Machine Gun Kelly, and Ma Barker gained celebrity status. Some gangsters achieved a kind of "Robin Hood" aura when they gave away some of the money they robbed from banks. At the same time, the public sought reassurance that the forces of law and order would prevail.

Roosevelt sensed that fighting a successful "war on crime" would enhance public faith in the New Deal's battle against economic hardship. He and Attorney General Homer S. Cummings designated J. Edgar Hoover, head of the Justice Department's small Bureau of Investigation (renamed the FBI in 1935), to lead the campaign. Hoover relished the chance to burnish his agency's image as the focal point of scientific crime fighting, but he faced a major public relations hurdle. Between 60 and 70 million movie tickets were sold each week, and crime films proved exceedingly popular. Many of the more than 50 gangster movies released in 1931–1932, such as

Little Caesar, The Public Enemy, and *Scarface,* depicted ruthless and violent men who gained wealth and power by breaking the law. But in 1934 Hoover's so-called G-men killed Dillinger, Nelson, and Floyd. Under government pressure, Hollywood studios adopted a production code that barred the sympathetic portrayal of gangsters. *G-Men,* released in 1935, followed by six FBI-centered films in 1936, featured Hoover's agents as symbols of rectitude who "always got their man." The illusory "crime wave" ended and Hoover secured his job as FBI director for the next 40 years.

Musicals such as *42nd Street* and *Babes in Arms* also found large audiences among a nation that savored an escape from hard times. Debonair dancers Fred Astaire and Ginger Rogers charmed movie audiences in films like *Top Hat, Flying Down to Rio, The Gay Divorcee,* and *Swing Time.* Comedy films starring the Marx Brothers, the Ritz Brothers, and W. C. Fields, along with cartoons produced by the Disney and Warner Brothers studios, also entertained film goers. Child star Shirley Temple, born in 1928, proved the biggest box office draw of the decade. Her dimpled cheeks, curly hair, and spunky innocence drew millions of adoring viewers old and young into theaters to watch films such as the *Littlest Rebel,* and *Curly Top.*

Americans spent much of their leisure time listening to the radio. Daytime melodramas—called soap operas because of their sponsorship—appealed to women working at home. Late afternoon programs targeted school-age children, dinnertime broadcasts provided highlights of the day's news, and evening shows played big band music and original comedy and drama. Ex-vaudevillians such as Jack Benny, Eddie Cantor, and George Burns and Gracie Allen had popular shows. Broadcasts of baseball games were also popular. The New York Yankees, with their colorful roster of Babe Ruth, Lou Gehrig, and Joe DiMaggio, seemed almost like a national team.

Amos 'n' Andy, a comedy in which white actors depicted two gullible African Americans scheming to strike it rich, was immensely popular. Nearly as many Americans tuned in several times a week to follow *The Goldbergs,* a comedy-drama set in a Bronx, New York, tenement. Actress Gertrude Berg played Mollie Goldberg, the matriarch of a Jewish family whose signature line was to lean out of her apartment window and call out "yoo-hoo" to neighbors with whom she gossiped. Berg, who pollsters reported was the woman most admired by Americans after Eleanor Roosevelt, wrote most of the scripts.

Black athletes also captured national attention. Both white and black Americans followed closely the remarkable achievements of runner Jesse Owens at the 1936 Olympics in Berlin. His four gold medals left Nazi officials fuming at his defeat of their "master race" of athletes. Black boxer Joe Louis, dubbed the Brown Bomber, also became a hero with his spectacular achievements in the ring after 1934 and his self-effacing personality. Louis's two fights against German Max Schmeling became proxy contests between the two nations. After Louis' disappointing loss to the German fighter in 1936, they fought a much anticipated rematch in 1938 dubbed "the fight of the century." Louis, who said he felt the "whole damned country was depending on me," knocked out Schmeling in the first round.

In this pretelevision age theater owners showed newsreels as well as cartoons before or between feature films. *The March of Time,* beginning in 1934, contained vivid footage of current events, natural disasters, and celebrity sightings. It also presented to a national audience highlights from popular sporting events such as college football, baseball, and boxing, and current fads, such as week-long Roller Derbies and marathon dance contests.

Newspapers remained the predominant form of journalism during the 1930s, but they faced great competition from magazines. *Reader's Digest* became the nation's most widely circulated periodical by 1938. News weeklies such as *Time* and *Newsweek* gained large readerships, and *Life* magazine won acclaim for its stunning photography. In the heartland readers particularly liked the *Saturday Evening Post*. Hard times pushed down overall book sales, but the literate public snapped up "tough guy" detective fiction by authors such as Raymond Chandler, Dashiell Hammett, and James Cain.

In 1934 the Treasury Department funded a one-year Public Works of Arts Project. This became a model for the much larger Federal Arts, Music, Dance, Theater and Writers Projects, all WPA programs created in 1935. The WPA employed thousands of struggling artists to paint murals in public buildings and teach art classes in public schools. Thirty-eight symphony orchestras performed free concerts nationwide. The Dance Project hired classical and modern ballet dancers to perform around the country. The Writers Project employed 10,000 people who traveled around the country recording regional music and folk stories, writing local histories and travel guides, and interviewing former slaves for a massive oral history.

The Federal Theater Project hired writers, directors, and actors to perform throughout the country. Productions included classics such as *Macbeth* and *The Mikado* as well as social dramas about the Depression and the threat of fascism such as *The Cradle Will Rock*, the *Living Newspaper*, and Sinclair Lewis's *It Can't Happen Here*. These plays, like many of the murals depicting workers and farmers, and photographs of the rural poor taken for the FSA, promoted a populist vision of culture that celebrated the "common man" and often depicted his, and her, difficult life. They also provoked a backlash. When conservative Democrats and Republicans in Congress gained influence during 1939, they denounced these arts programs as leftwing propaganda and cut off funds for the Federal Theater and other cultural projects.

Women and the New Deal

Women played a larger role in the Roosevelt administration than they had in any previous period, despite the fact that few New Deal programs specifically targeted women. Eleanor Roosevelt had no formal government job, but she transformed the traditional role of First Lady from hostess to social crusader. As a young woman Eleanor had worked at the Rivington Street Settlement House in New York City; she maintained a circle of feminist friends and social workers concerned with the well-being of working class women and their families. Through this network and her own travels she provided her husband with insights into a world he barely knew. Trade unionists, sharecroppers, and African Americans considered her their pipeline to the administration. Eleanor also arranged meetings between the president and labor activists who were her friends such as Molly Dewson and muckraking journalist Lorena Hickok. In 1937 she began writing a nationally syndicated newspaper column, "My Day."

On average, Eleanor Roosevelt traveled 200 days per year to inspect federal projects and the living conditions of ordinary Americans. Once she trudged across a half mile of mud to visit the shack of a tenant farmer. When she knocked on the door, the laborer opened it and with only a hint of surprise said "Oh, Mrs. Roosevelt, you've come to see me." In 1933, the *New Yorker* magazine published a cartoon depicting two weary coal miners glancing at the elevator cage hurtling down the shaft toward them. "Oh, migosh," one remarked, "here comes Mrs. Roosevelt to check on things." A few months later the First Lady, wearing a hard hat, descended into a West Virginia coal mine to inspect conditions.

Secretary of Labor Frances Perkins held the highest formal position among female New Dealers. Like Eleanor Roosevelt, she became politically active as a Progressive Era reformer promoting causes such as women's voting rights and industrial safety. As secretary of labor, Perkins pushed legislation to improve conditions for all workers, not just women. She played a key role in formulating the Social Security system. Most New Deal employment and relief programs adopted a traditional view of the male head of household as breadwinner who should be helped to support his family.

European Ethnics and the New Deal

The New Deal addressed only indirectly the social problems faced by ethnic Americans of European descent. New Deal administrators believed that general economic recovery as well as work relief programs would provide basic assistance to these groups. Harry Hopkins and Harold Ickes, both of whom abhorred racism and relished diversity, tried to ensure that WPA and PWA employed talented administrators and manual laborers of all backgrounds.

Because of hard economic times and lingering antiforeign sentiment, neither members of Congress nor the Roosevelt administration pushed to revise the restrictive National Origins Act of 1924. The prohibition was especially hard on Jewish refugees attempting to flee Nazi and other anti-Semitic campaigns in Europe during the 1930s.

In an era when prejudice lay close to the surface, as seen in Father Coughlin's popular radio rants, the president declined to confront the widespread hostility toward immigrants and left in place the barriers that restricted their entry.

The United States did permit some prominent European refugees, both Jews and Christians, to enter the country. As discussed in later chapters, dozens of accomplished physicists including Albert Einstein, Edward Teller, Enrico Fermi, and Leo Szilard found positions at leading American universities and played critical roles in developing the atomic bomb. When the acclaimed Italian orchestra conductor and fervent anti-fascist Arturo Toscanini fled to the United States in 1938, the NBC radio network created an orchestra for him to direct. The New School for Social Research in New York City became known as the "university in exile" when, beginning in 1933, it offered faculty positions for hundreds of academics fleeing Nazi persecution. Nearly a thousand Jewish and non-Jewish German film directors, screenwriters, cinematographers, and actors secured visas to work in Hollywood after the Nazis declared them disloyal and purged them from the film industry.

A New Deal for Blacks

African Americans, whether sharecroppers in the South or service workers in the North, suffered some of the worst ravages of the Depression. Some advisers close to the president, such as Eleanor Roosevelt and Interior Secretary Ickes, urged him to support civil rights and openly assist blacks. Roosevelt considered it more important to maintain good political relations with Southern Democrats in Congress, most of whom strongly opposed any kind of "outside" interference in the rigidly segregated world of the South.

Black community leaders wrote directly to Roosevelt and Harry Hopkins demanding that African Americans be included in federal work relief programs. A number of black officials created a "Federal Council on Negro Affairs." Educator Mary McLeod Bethune served as the informal head of the group. Eleanor Roosevelt arranged for periodic meetings between Bethune and the president.

WPA administrators in the South and Southwest agreed to hire blacks, Hispanics, and Native Americans but routinely paid them lower wages than whites received and assigned them menial tasks. By the late 1930s, most federal work relief programs allocated about 10 percent of their budget to minority employment. This matched the African American portion of the population, although blacks comprised about 20 percent of the poor. In 1939 about one-third of all black households received some income from WPA.

First Lady Eleanor Roosevelt meeting with Mary McLeod Bethune and other African Americans who comprised the informal "black cabinet."

Simple acts by New Dealers carried great symbolic weight. For example, when Eleanor Roosevelt attended a meeting in a segregated Alabama auditorium, she insisted on sitting in the "coloreds only" section. In 1939, after the Daughters of the American Revolution refused to allow black opera singer Marian Anderson to perform in its Washington, DC, concert hall, Eleanor Roosevelt resigned from the group and arranged for Anderson to perform on the steps of the Lincoln Memorial before a crowd of 75,000.

Roosevelt would not challenge segregation directly nor even endorse a federal antilynching law for fear of alienating Southern Democrats. But over time the New Deal record on race improved. Roosevelt appointed many federal judges who sympathized with minority aspirations. Among the eight judges FDR appointed to the Supreme Court between 1937 and 1944, several eventually played roles in the effort to dismantle the legal framework of segregation established after Reconstruction.

Although three-fourths of blacks still lived in the South and had no voting rights, New Deal policies paid a big political dividend to the Democratic Party in the North. In 1932 most northern blacks remained loyal to the party of Lincoln and voted for Hoover and his fellow Republicans. By 1936 blacks switched overwhelmingly in favor of Roosevelt and the Democratic Party.

Hispanics and the New Deal

The Depression decade proved especially hard on Mexican nationals and other Hispanics living in the West and Southwest. Under Hoover, border agents blocked new Mexican immigration and assisted state officials in deporting about 25,000 Mexican nationals and some Mexican Americans. After 1933 state and federal authorities rounded up and sometimes forcibly deported tens of thousands of additional Mexican nationals and Mexican Americans from California and the Rocky Mountain west. By 1935 nearly half a million Mexicans, about as many as had migrated to the United States during the 1920s, were sent back to their homeland.

Mexican nationals and those of Mexican descent who avoided deportation lived mainly in California, Texas, and other states in the Southwest. Many worked as migrant agricultural laborers on large commercial farms or on railroads. New Deal agricultural policies did little to help landless farm workers. Instead, federal crop support payments and subsidized irrigation projects helped large landowners. As in the South, commercial farmers often used the payments to mechanize their operations and reduce their need for migrant labor.

The Indian New Deal

Government policy toward American Indians changed dramatically during the 1930s. Since passage of the Dawes Act in 1887, about two-thirds of tribal lands had been sold off or confiscated; thus, many who lived on reservations became essentially landless. During the 1920s the notoriously corrupt Bureau of Indian Affairs (BIA) expanded its ban on native religious ceremonies and pressed families to send their children to distant boarding schools that discouraged traditional language and culture.

These policies outraged Interior Secretary Harold Ickes, who oversaw the BIA. He named **John Collier**, a social worker familiar with both immigrant communities and southwestern life, to head the BIA. In the 1920s, Collier had visited Taos, New Mexico, and became entranced by the culture of the nearby Pueblo tribe. He went on to lead the American Indian Defense Association and edit its magazine *American Indian Life*.

Collier persuaded the CCC to create an Indian division, convinced the Agriculture Department to fund projects on reservations and hire Indians as workers, and lobbied Congress to pass the Pueblo Relief Act in 1933, which compensated the tribe for past land seizures. Congress also approved the **Johnson-O'Malley Act of 1934** that encouraged states to provide better health care and education to Indian tribes. Collier increased the number of Indian BIA employees from a few hundred to over 4,000. He replaced many boarding schools with community day schools, lifted the ban on native religious ceremonies, and created an Indian Arts and Crafts Board to promote and market traditional handicrafts. In 1934, Congress replaced the Dawes Act with the **Indian Reorganization Act**. This action slowed the division of reservation land into small plots, encouraged tribal self-government, and established Indian-run corporations to control communal land and resources.

Many Western landowners objected to newly imposed limits on mining, grazing, and farming on or around reservations. Some Christian groups resented losing their religious monopoly and criticized Collier for allowing "heathen" worship. Some Indians complained that Collier's reverence for tradition was forcing them to "return to the blanket" and that he did not comprehend the diversity among various tribal groups. Before his departure in 1945, Collier only partly succeeded in persuading Indian tribes to reorganize themselves under a scheme of self-government.

Nature's New Deal

New Deal environmental policies pulled in sometimes contradictory directions. To assist commercial farming in the Pacific Northwest and California, federal agencies constructed irrigation canals and dams on the Colorado and Columbia Rivers. These heavily subsidized water projects boosted production on arid land otherwise unfit for large-scale agriculture. The massive TVA also relied on dam construction for flood control and power generation. Other New Deal projects undertaken by the CCC and WPA promoted reforestation and virtually created the infrastructure of the national park system.

Elsewhere, New Deal programs tried to ameliorate the consequences of overdevelopment. Decades of corn and wheat cultivation on the Great Plains, the destruction of native grasses, and prolonged drought created the Dust Bowl, a major ecological disaster. Beginning in the early 1930s and continuing for much of the decade, fierce windstorms blowing from west to east picked up dry topsoil and darkened the sky, sometimes for days. Oklahoma balladeer Woody Guthrie described these storms in haunting songs. In his 1939 novel *The Grapes of Wrath*, John Steinbeck immortalized the Joads, a mythical family of "Okies," poor farmers driven from Oklahoma by hard times and bad weather. Like the Joads, over two million people fled the plains states, many traveling Route 66 to California seeking work as migrant laborers.

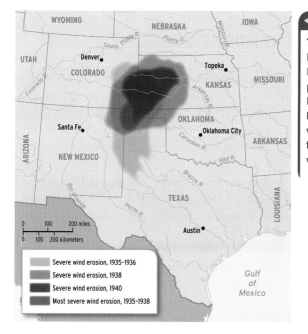

◄ Map 23.1

The Dimensions of the Dust Bowl in the 1930s The Dust Bowl of the mid-1930s affected parts of Colorado, Kansas, New Mexico, Texas, and Oklahoma. It's economic and social impact was even wider, as millions of farmers from this region sought work along the West Coast.

Roosevelt took a personal interest in solving these problems. Much of the early effort by the CCC was directed toward rural conservation projects in the West. Young volunteers planted over 200 million trees as part of a 3,600 mile, north-to-south system of windbreaks or "shelter belts" in the Midwest and Great Plains. Many experts scoffed at this idea, but over time the windbreaks worked as the president hoped. To protect the soil the Taylor Grazing Act of 1934 placed stricter limits on the number of livestock that could graze on public land in the West. Other programs pulled millions of acres of marginal land out of cultivation and replanted native grasses.

On a per capita basis, the West received more federal payments for development than any other region of the country during the 1930s. Much of the Western infrastructure built during the 1930s, such as dams, irrigation networks, electric grids, and roads, played a major role in speeding military production during World War II and regional growth afterward.

STUDY QUESTIONS FOR SOCIETY, LAW, AND CULTURE IN THE 1930S

1. How did New Deal reforms help or ignore problems faced by women and minorities during the Depression?
2. Did popular culture in the 1930s reflect social concerns or provide audiences with an escape from reality?
3. What impact did New Deal programs have on the American West?

THE TWILIGHT OF REFORM

Early in 1937, Congress convened with huge Democratic majorities, 331 to 89 in the House and 76 to 16 in the Senate. The New Deal seemed poised for another burst of social activism. Yet, by the end of 1938, hope for bold economic and social initiatives had faded. Roosevelt lost a fight to reorganize the Supreme Court, presided over a steep economic turndown, and failed in a bid to purge conservative Democrats from Congress.

Once the worst of the Depression crisis had abated, national politics reverted to its more conservative tradition. Southern Democrats, who feared that liberal New Dealers would promote racial reform, frequently joined forces with Northern Republicans, who opposed additional economic regulation, to block expansion of the welfare state. After 1938, this coalition, along with the gathering clouds of war in Europe and Asia, frustrated efforts by New Dealers to build on their previous accomplishments.

The New Deal and Judicial Change

Between 1934 and 1936, a five-vote conservative majority on the nine-member Supreme Court struck down as unconstitutional key pieces of New Deal legislation, including the NRA and AAA. The conservatives ruled that the interstate commerce clause of the Constitution granted Congress and the president very limited power to regulate the economy. It barred, they maintained, most federal efforts to set wage levels or regulate business.

Roosevelt complained that the Supreme Court's actions had created a "no-man's land where no government can function" or impose any meaningful regulation on business behavior. With the Court poised in 1937 to strike down such New Deal pillars as the Social Security and National Labor Relations acts, the president and his supporters expressed growing frustration.

Several of the most conservative Supreme Court justices were elderly men appointed decades earlier who saw themselves as guardians of property rights threatened by a president they hated. Roosevelt reciprocated their feelings and in 1937 proposed the Judiciary Reorganization Act. He asked Congress to "ease the burden" on elderly jurists—really to dilute the conservative bloc—by allowing him to appoint additional justices for each member of the high court over age 70.

The Constitution allowed Congress to adjust the size of the Supreme Court, and it had done so several times. But the number had settled at nine after the Civil War and had taken on an aura of inviolability. Roosevelt tried to push this change through Congress without much consultation, alienating members of both parties who complained about what they called the "court packing scheme." Their opposition forced the president to drop the plan at a substantial cost to his reputation.

Despite this failure, however, the Supreme Court soon swung around to support the New Deal. One conservative justice switched sides, joining the four liberals in voting to sustain key laws. Over the next few years the other conservative justices retired. By 1944, Roosevelt had the opportunity to appoint a total of eight Supreme Court justices, including Felix Frankfurter, Wiley Rutledge, Frank Murphy, **Hugo Black**, William O. Douglas, **Stanley F. Reed**, Robert H. Jackson, and **James F. Byrnes**.

This new majority supported the president's belief that the Constitution gave the federal government broad authority to regulate business, the economy, labor conditions, and the environment. In a series of rulings, the Supreme Court upheld minimum wage laws, workplace regulations, production limits on farmers, Social Security, and the government's right to require that businesses recognize labor unions.

Recession

Just as the judicial uncertainty hovering over the New Deal disappeared, new economic and political constraints stifled efforts at greater reform. Midway through 1937, a severe recession shook confidence in Roosevelt's leadership and prompted a conservative resurgence. Although many workers still sought jobs, the rate of unemployment had declined from 25 to about 14 percent. Roosevelt and Treasury Secretary Henry Morgenthau considered this drop evidence that the economic emergency had passed and the time had come to restore the principal of a balanced budget. At their urging, Congress reduced federal spending by about 10 percent in 1937–1938, eliminating funding for many WPA-related jobs programs.

This reduced consumer purchasing power and pushed the still fragile economy into a steep decline. Five years of steady stock price increases reversed and unemployment surged. Conservative economic advisers urged Roosevelt to make further cuts to balance the budget. New Deal liberals argued in favor of increased federal spending to stimulate economic growth.

Evidence in favor of additional deficit spending was provided by British economist John Maynard Keynes, who in 1936 published his landmark book, *The General Theory of Employment, Interest, and Money*. Keynes argued that deficit spending should be used as a normal tool to stimulate sluggish economic growth by boosting mass purchasing power. When private investment and orders for goods declined, Keynes asserted, the government should engage in "compensatory" or "countercyclical" spending to "prime the economic pump." This could take the form of building a playground, a post office, a dam, or a battleship. New orders for concrete and steel would boost output by heavy industry while at the end of the chain construction workers with money in their pockets would buy food, pay rent, and purchase clothes. Once recovery began, government could reduce its role, collect additional taxes, and restore a balanced budget.

Keynes and his American disciples considered the events of 1937 as proof that the private economy had only partially recovered from the trauma of the Depression and still required a big federal stimulus. Roosevelt dithered for months before taking action. In the spring of 1938 he abandoned his quest for an early balanced budget. He persuaded Congress to fund a $5 billion spending program to resume hiring the unemployed and increase mass purchasing power. This new spending, along with military orders placed in American factories from Great Britain and France in response to the German threat in Europe, restored economic growth.

In June 1938 Roosevelt won Congressional approval for what turned out to be the last major New Deal reform before World War II, the Fair Labor Standards Act. The law banned child labor, established a federal minimum wage starting at 40 cents per hour, and set the standard work week at 40 hours. But to secure the votes of Southern Democrats, Roosevelt agreed once again to exempt from coverage most agricultural and domestic workers, whose ranks included a high proportion of women, blacks, and Hispanics.

Political Setbacks

Frustrated by the continued opposition to his policies by conservative Democrats mostly from the South but a few in the North, Roosevelt tried to reshape the party in 1938. In that year's Democratic primary elections, he campaigned on behalf of insurgent liberals who ran against entrenched anti-New Deal Democrats. Despite his best effort, most of the old guard survived the challenge. Maintenance of the status quo was especially true in the South, where incumbents stoked fear among poor whites that Roosevelt supported reformer candidates as part of a scheme to empower blacks at their expense. When most of the old guard Southern Democrats returned to Congress in 1939, they became even more determined to block liberal reform.

The congressional election of 1938 brought more bad news for Roosevelt. Republicans picked up 81 additional House and 8 additional Senate seats. This revitalized GOP minority joined forces with southern Democrats to block most New Deal

TIMELINE 1932–1939

1932

January–July The Great Depression becomes more severe as businesses and banks fail and millions of workers lose jobs and savings

July President Hoover is discredited after he orders Bonus Army dispersed in Washington by police and troops; Democratic Party nominates Franklin D. Roosevelt as its candidate for president with promise of a "New Deal" for the American people

November Roosevelt elected president by a wide margin

November through March of 1933 Depression worsens in five months between the

election and Roosevelt's inauguration; thousands more banks fail and the unemployment rate rises to 25%, with another 25% working part-time for reduced wages

1933

January Adolf Hitler becomes the German chancellor and soon assumes dictatorial power

February–March Banking system virtually closes down throughout the United States, creating economic paralysis; many politicians urge Roosevelt to assume dictatorial powers

March Roosevelt inaugurated; proposes a series of government

initiatives to deal with economic crisis; he speaks directly to the public through his first "fireside chat" broadcasts over the radio

March–June "Hundred Days" of legislative reform enacted by Congress, including bank regulation, farm aid, and emergency relief appropriations for the unemployed; prohibition repealed by constitutional amendment

1934

April Indian Reorganization Act

June Securities Exchange Commission created regulating stock market

1935

Spring–Summer The 2nd Hundred Days of reform legislation begins

April WPA created to employ millions of jobless laborers and artists across the nation to work on federal projects

August Social Security Act passed creating old age pension system and programs to assist injured workers

1936

November Roosevelt reelected in a landslide and large Democratic majorities elected to Congress

December Automobile workers sit-down strikes begin in Michigan

proposals. Conservatives in both parties renewed demands to balance the federal budget, to curb the power of labor unions, and to spend less on the unemployed.

At the end of 1938 Roosevelt told an aide that it was sad but true that the global slide toward war would likely benefit the economy and bolster the Democratic Party. "Foreign orders for armaments . . . mean prosperity in this country and we can't elect Democrats unless we get prosperity." The president also recognized that to win broad support for a policy of resisting Germany and Japan, he needed to repair his strained relations with the business community as well as with conservatives in both parties. The outbreak of war in Europe in September 1939 pushed social reform further into the background as Roosevelt prepared the nation to confront the gathering threat from abroad.

The New Deal succeeded in many things and failed in others. Beyond its economic achievement it created a more inclusive nation. The New Deal accommodated demands for greater economic justice from industrial workers; it provided electric power, water, and price supports for millions of farm families; it gave new opportunity and hope to millions of African Americans and American Indians; and it opened a path to dignified retirement for the elderly and offered meaningful work to the unemployed. At the same time, resurgent conservatism in the late 1930s limited the scope of the New Deal and placed reform on hold until the United States entered World War II.

STUDY QUESTIONS FOR THE TWILIGHT OF REFORM

1. What issue led Roosevelt to clash with the Supreme Court in 1937?
2. Why did the economy suffer a setback in 1937–1938?
3. How did the New Deal lose political support after 1938?

demanding union recognition

February Keynes publishes *The General Theory of Employment, Interest and Money,* which describes how government spending can stimulate economic growth

1937

February Roosevelt proposes the Judicial Reorganization Act to enlarge the Supreme Court by adding liberal judges, but Congress rejects his plan

July Roosevelt agrees to reduce the federal deficit spending to balance the budget, triggering a steep recession and a surge in unemployment

July Japan invades China

1938

May Congress creates the House Committee on Un-American Activities to investigate left-wing influence in New Deal agencies

Spring–Summer Roosevelt resumes deficit spending on

federal projects and restores economic growth

June Congress enacts the Fair Labor Standards Act, the last major New Deal Reform before World War II

June–November Roosevelt fails in his effort to "purge" the mostly Southern conservative Democrats out of Congress by endorsing liberal opponents in party primaries

November Following midterm elections,

conservative Southern Democrats and an increased number of Northern Republicans in Congress join forces to block further New Deal reforms

1939

September War begins in Europe after Hitler's armies invade Poland

Summary

- The Depression grew steadily worse between 1929 and early 1933.
- Both the new urban poor and rural farmers received little help.
- The Hoover administration provided modest assistance to business but none directly to the unemployed.
- Franklin Roosevelt took an innovative approach to unemployment while he was governor of New York and brought this view to the presidency in 1933.
- The New Deal involved a series of regulatory reforms to stabilize the private economy and several programs to assist the unemployed and the rural poor.
- Critics on the right and on the left attacked the New Deal for doing either too much or too little.
- Roosevelt implemented additional radical social and economic reforms between 1935 and 1938.
- New Deal construction projects reshaped the American landscape.
- New Deal programs reached out to many groups previously ignored by government and built a political coalition that included organized labor, ethnic Americans, African Americans, and women.
- Throughout the 1930s, conservatives in Congress and on the Supreme Court opposed New Deal reforms and limited its scope.
- By 1938 a coalition of conservative Democrats and Republicans stymied further social and economic reform.
- Although the private economy did not fully recover until World War II, the New Deal helped preserve both capitalism and democracy in a world where both were endangered and developed infrastructure vital to both defense production during World War II and economic growth after 1945.

Key Terms and People

Agricultural Adjustment Administration (AAA) 892
American Federation of Labor (AFL) 899
Berle, Adolph 887
Black, Hugo 913
Byrnes, James F. 913
Collier, John 910
Congress of Industrial Organizations (CIO) 895
Dust Bowl 887
Emergency Banking Relief Act 889
fireside chats 889
first Hundred Days 890
Frankfurter, Felix 904
Glass-Steagall Banking Act 889
Hitler, Adolf 879
Hopkins, Harry 887

Indian Reorganization Act 910
Johnson-O'Malley Act of 1934 910
Lange, Dorothea 897
Long, Huey 893
MacArthur, Douglas 885
Moley, Raymond 887
Murphy, Frank 899
National Recovery Administration (NRA) 892
New Deal 879
Perkins, Frances 886
Reconstruction Finance Corporation (RFC) 885
Reed, Stanley F. 913
Roosevelt, Eleanor 882
Roosevelt, Franklin D. 879
Rothstein, Arthur 897
Securities Act of 1933 890

Securities Exchange Act of 1934 *890*
Sloan, Alfred *894*
Social Security Act *894*
Tennessee Valley Authority (TVA) *891*

Townsend, Frances *893*
Tugwell, Rexford *887*
Wagner, Robert *895*
Wallace, Henry A. *892*

Reviewing Chapter 23

1. How did the Depression worsen in the months after the 1932 election?
2. What were several early New Deal Recovery measures?
3. What major new reforms did the New Deal implement in 1935–1936?
4. What were some of the failures of the New Deal?
5. After 1938, what political barriers emerged to further reform?

Further Reading

Badger, Anthony. *The New Deal: The Depression Years, 1933–1940*. New York: MacMillan, 1989. Badger examines the dire economic conditions and social malaise that afflicted American workers and farmers as the Depression ravaged their lives.

Brinkley, Alan. *Voices of Protest: Huey Long, Father Coughlin, and the Great Depression*. New York: Knopf, 1982. Long and Coughlin were revered—and despised—by millions of Americans when they proposed radical solutions to the nation's distress.

Cohen, Lizabeth. *Making a New Deal: Industrial Workers in Chicago, 1919–1939*. New York: Cambridge University Press, 1990. Cohen explains how blue collar workers and their unions pressed for economic reform before the 1930s pushed the often cautious New Deal in more radical, pro-labor directios.

Downey, Kristin. *The Woman Behind the New Deal: The Life and Legacy of Frances Perkins*. New York: Nan A. Talese, 2009. As the first female Cabinet member, Secretary of Labor Frances Perkins shaped the nation's welfare policies and was the principal architect of the New Deal's best-known innovation, Social Security.

Kennedy, David. *Freedom from Fear: The American People in Depression and War, 1929–1945*. New York: Oxford University Press, 2001. A panoramic overview of the Depression and New Deal era that highlights the nearly unimaginably complex challenges faced by the Roosevelt administration at home and abroad.

Sitkoff, Harvard. *A New Deal for Blacks*. New York: Oxford University Press, 1978. Long oppressed by racial injustice, no group of Americans suffered more from the Depression than African Americans. New Deal reformers were among the first national leaders to attempt to ameliorate these wrongs.

Visual Review

Social Security

Congress creates a national plan for unemployment and disability insurance and pensions for the elderly.

Labor Activism

Congress passes legislation that empowers workers to form unions.

Spiral of Decline, 1931–1933

Industrial production, employment, investment, and farm prices decline gradually over the three years after the stock market crash.

From Prosperity to Global Depression

The national economy collapses.

Suffering in the Land

Poverty increases across the country.

The Failure of the Old Deal

The first attempts by Congress to fix the economy fail.

The Coming of the New Deal

Franklin D. Roosevelt is elected president to end the Great Depression.

The New Deal

A NEW DEAL FOR AMERICANS, 1931–1939

Reconstructing Capitalism

The Hundred Days

President Roosevelt ushers in a slate of economic reforms and measures.

Voices of Protest

Groups protest the expansion of the federal government.

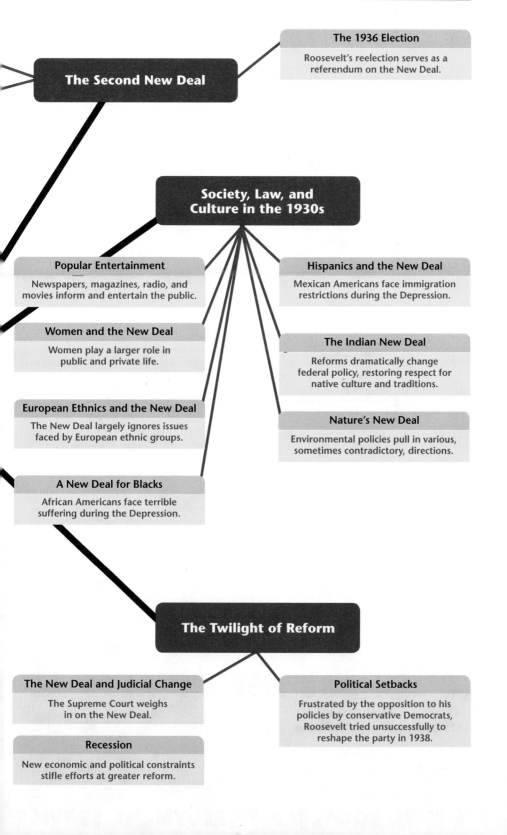

The Second New Deal

The 1936 Election

Roosevelt's reelection serves as a referendum on the New Deal.

Society, Law, and Culture in the 1930s

Popular Entertainment

Newspapers, magazines, radio, and movies inform and entertain the public.

Hispanics and the New Deal

Mexican Americans face immigration restrictions during the Depression.

Women and the New Deal

Women play a larger role in public and private life.

The Indian New Deal

Reforms dramatically change federal policy, restoring respect for native culture and traditions.

European Ethnics and the New Deal

The New Deal largely ignores issues faced by European ethnic groups.

Nature's New Deal

Environmental policies pull in various, sometimes contradictory, directions.

A New Deal for Blacks

African Americans face terrible suffering during the Depression.

The Twilight of Reform

The New Deal and Judicial Change

The Supreme Court weighs in on the New Deal.

Political Setbacks

Frustrated by the opposition to his policies by conservative Democrats, Roosevelt tried unsuccessfully to reshape the party in 1938.

Recession

New economic and political constraints stifle efforts at greater reform.

he more WOMEN at wor
the sooner we WIN
ZONE
X
TEMPORARY
0000
WOMEN ARE NEEDED ALSO AS:
FARM WORKERS
TYPISTS
SALESPEOPLE
WAITRESSES
BUS DRIVERS
TAXI DRIVERS
TIMEKEEPERS
ELEVATOR OPERATORS
MESSENGERS
LAUNDRESSES
TEACHERS
CONDUCTORS
—and in hundreds of other war jobs!
SEE YOUR LOCAL U.S. EMPLOYMENT SERVICE

Arsenal of Democracy: The World at War

1931–1945

Nazi führer (leader) Adolf Hitler believed German racial superiority assured victory over "mongrel" enemies like the United States and Soviet Union. The dictator's ideas came partly from reading the late-19th century novels of Karl May, a German writer of western adventure tales. American society, Hitler asserted, had taken a wrong turn after the North won the Civil War. The end of slavery and the plantation aristocracy, followed by mass migration from Eastern Europe, had created a "decadent" society, "half Judaized and the other half Negrified" that worshipped the dollar and corrupted everything it touched. As a morale booster, Hitler had copies of May's novels packed into soldiers' gear as they went off to battle.

The führer gloated over Japan's December 7, 1941, bold attack on the U.S. fleet in Pearl Harbor. This, along with the Wehrmacht's (German army) expected capture of Moscow, made victory in Europe certain. Roosevelt, he predicted, would have no choice but to focus on the Pacific. Having convinced himself that Germany could not lose, Hitler, along with his ally, Italian dictator **Benito Mussolini**, declared war on the United States.

German Foreign Minister Joachim von Ribbentrop had a gloomier view of the future. More knowledgeable than Hitler about Germany's newest enemy, he understood that unless victory came quickly things might go very badly. Ribbentrop told Hitler that Germany had at most "one year to cut off Russia from her American supplies . . . If we don't succeed and the munitions potential of the United States joins up with the manpower potential of the Russians," the war would be difficult to win.

"The more WOMEN at work the sooner we WIN!" U.S. Employment Service poster, 1943

CHAPTER OUTLINE

THE LONG FUSE
> Isolationist Impulse
> Disengagement from Europe
> Disengagement in Asia
> Appeasement
> America at the Brink of War, 1939–1941
> Day of Infamy

A GRAND ALLIANCE
> War in the Pacific
> The War in Europe
> The Holocaust

BATTLE FOR PRODUCTION
> War Economy
> A Government-Sponsored Industrial Revolution
> Mass-Produced Weapons
> Organized Labor and the War
> The Draft

continued on page 925

America in the World

The Bretton Woods Agreements regulated the monetary and economic recovery of Europe following World War II (1944).

American naval base at Pearl Harbor attacked, drawing United States into war with Japan (1941).

The Grand Alliance united the United States, Britain, and Soviets against Germany and Japan (1942).

★ U.S. event that influenced the world

★ International event that influenced the United States

◎ Event with multinational influence

✷ Conflict

World War II erupted in Europe (1939–945).

The D-Day landing marked the beginning of the Allied invasion of Europe to defeat Germany in World War II (1944).

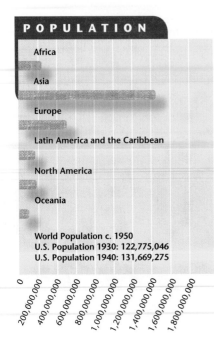

POPULATION

Africa

Asia

Europe

Latin America and the Caribbean

North America

Oceania

World Population c. 1950
U.S. Population 1930: 122,775,046
U.S. Population 1940: 131,669,275

0, 200,000,000, 400,000,000, 600,000,000, 800,000,000, 1,000,000,000, 1,200,000,000, 1,400,000,000, 1,600,000,000, 1,800,000,000

Soviet dictator and now U.S. ally **Josef Stalin** also recognized the critical importance of American industrial power. At his first face-to-face meeting with President Roosevelt in Tehran, Iran, late in 1943, Stalin declared, "The most important things in this war are machines . . . The United States . . . is a country of machines." He then offered a toast to the city of "Detroit," which "is winning the war."

World War II was the most destructive human-caused event of the 20th century. Around 60 million people, mostly civilians in Europe and Asia, perished in battles and fire-bombed cities, from war-caused famines and epidemics, or in industrial-scale death camps like those set up by the Nazis in Eastern Europe. When the killing stopped in 1945, the United States—which suffered about 400,000 military deaths—with just 6 percent of the world's population produced half of the world's goods. This relative level of economic power has never been

Table 24.1 Deaths in World War II As many as 50 to 60 million people died globally during World War II. At least as many civilians as soldiers perished, especially in Eastern Europe and China where German and Japanese armed forces killed large numbers of noncombatants and POWs.

	Military Dead and Missing	Civilian Dead	Jewish Holocaust Victims	Total Dead and Missing
United States	420,000	—	—	420,000
United Kingdom	370,000	60,000	—	430,00
France	250,000	270,000	90,000	610,000
Soviet Union	13,600,000	600,000	1,720,000	21,320,000
China	3,500,000	10,000,000	—	13,500,000
Germany	3,250,000	3,640,000	170,000	7,060,000
Italy	330,000	70,000	15,000	415,000
Japan	1,700,000	500,000	—	2,200,000
All other participants	1,180,000	4,690,000	3,998,000	9,868,000
Total	24,600,000	25,090,000	5,993,000	55,683,000

surpassed. It seemed, in the confident words of *Time-Life* magazine publisher **Henry Luce**, the beginning of the "first great American Century."

THE LONG FUSE

Several of the issues that sparked World War I—rival nationalism, competition for colonies, and security fears—continued to fester during the 1920s and 1930s. Many Germans felt betrayed by what they considered to be a harsh and unjust peace settlement at Versailles. Italy and Japan also resented the limited territories they had gained from victory. France remained terrified at the possibility of a revived Germany. A financially strapped Great Britain resolved to avoid a land war in Europe at almost any cost

CHAPTER OUTLINE

continued from page 921

ON THE MOVE: WARTIME MOBILITY
> Wartime Women
> Mexican Migrants, Mexican Americans, and American Indians in Wartime
> African Americans in Wartime
> Japanese American Internment

WARTIME POLITICS AND POSTWAR ISSUES
> Right Turn
> The 1944 Election and the Threshold of Victory
> Allied Mistrust and Postwar Planning

while preserving its empire. The Soviet Union, born from the ruins of czarist Russia, remained an international outcast that preached a doctrine of world revolution. Most Americans regretted the failure of the Great War to "make the world safe for democracy" and rued the fact that the lives lost and money spent had achieved so little.

The prosperity of the 1920s mitigated these tensions. As the Depression engulfed the world during the 1930s, old resentments surfaced. By the time of Roosevelt's inauguration in March 1933, dictators of the left and right ruled several major nations. Various forms of fascism—a political movement that linked militarists, big business, extreme nationalists, religious conservatives, and racial purists—dominated Italy and Germany, and they had footholds elsewhere in Europe and Latin America. In the Soviet Union Josef Stalin established a dictatorship under the banner of the Communist Party. In Japan power slipped away from the elected parliament and into the hands of the emperor and a coalition of military extremists and industrial tycoons who envisioned control of all Asia. Nazi dictator Adolf Hitler spoke of creating a "Greater Germany" in control of Central and Eastern Europe, while Italy's Benito Mussolini proclaimed a goal of rebuilding a "Roman Empire" in the Mediterranean and northern Africa.

Isolationist Impulse

Franklin Roosevelt, like most Americans, looked on events in Europe and Asia with a mix of detachment and disgust. He could scarcely believe that 15 years after Wilson's prediction of a "new world order" militarism again threatened peace. Americans, by and large, looked skeptically at any proposal to become militarily or politically involved abroad.

As the Depression took hold, most Americans turned increasingly inward. A prominent liberal Democrat, Pennsylvania governor George Earle, proclaimed in 1935, "if the world is to become a wilderness of waste, hatred, and bitterness, let us all the more earnestly protect and preserve our own oasis of liberty." Membership surged in antiwar groups such as the Women's International League for Peace and Freedom. Thousands of college students pledged not to fight in another war, while others mocked politicians by organizing a group called Veterans of Future Wars. Congressional probes issued reports blaming bankers and munitions manufacturers—so-called merchants of death—for duping Americans to fight in 1917.

Although Roosevelt had served as assistant secretary of the navy during World War I and had campaigned for membership in the League of Nations, by 1933 he opted not to challenge the isolationist or unilateralist tide that dominated public discourse. Shortly after becoming president in 1933 he refused to join an international effort to restore the gold standard among major industrial nations and cut the budget for the already tiny American Army of 140,000 men, a force about the size of Bulgaria's.

Early in his presidency, Roosevelt promoted a few noncontroversial foreign policy initiatives. These included a promise to act as a "good neighbor" and stop bullying Latin American nations. In December 1933 the United States informed a Pan-American Conference in Uruguay that it agreed that no nation, large or small, had the right to interfere militarily in the affairs of other hemispheric states. In 1938, when Mexico nationalized U.S.-owned oil wells, Roosevelt rebuffed demands from big petroleum companies to retaliate with force or harsh economic sanctions. The president also signed the Tydings-McDuffie Act in 1934, putting the Philippines on a 10-year path to independence, a first for any colonial power.

Roosevelt took a more controversial stand in November 1933 when he extended diplomatic recognition to the Soviet Union. Since the Russian Revolution in 1917 Washington had refused all dealings with the communist regime, a stance popular with political and religious conservatives. The president hoped that recognition would boost trade with the newly industrializing nation and might provide an incentive for Josef Stalin to resist German and Japanese expansion. But trade remained minimal, and disputes over payment of Russia's prerevolutionary debt and over Stalin's brutal collectivization of agriculture prevented significant cooperation before 1941.

Disengagement from Europe

In August 1935 Congress passed and FDR signed the first of five restrictive neutrality laws valid through 1939. These laws did not cause fascist aggression, but they reassured German, Italian, and Japanese leaders that the United States was unlikely to impede their actions.

The Neutrality Act of 1935 had stipulated that if a state of war exists between foreign nations, the U.S. government must impose an embargo on arms sales to the warring states and stop U.S. citizens from traveling on their ships. The law made no distinction between "aggressor" and "victim."

The impact of this policy was apparent in October 1935 when Mussolini ordered Italian troops to invade Ethiopia, one of only two independent nations in Africa.

The Italian army used airplanes, poison gas, and heavy artillery to kill thousands of Ethiopian civilians and its lightly armed soldiers. Many American were appalled by this brutality. Even though oil and other raw material sales were not covered by the embargo provisions of the neutrality law, Roosevelt requested that U.S. exporters impose a "moral embargo" restricting oil sales to Italy. Few companies complied. The British and French governments were eager to keep on good terms with Mussolini and permitted Italian military and supply ships to use the Suez Canal.

Congress expanded the scope of the Neutrality Act in February 1936. New provisions barred government or private loans and credits, as well as arms sales, to warring nations. Once again the law did not restrict sales of raw materials. A month later, in March 1936, when Hitler marched troops into the Rhineland, German territory along the French border that by treaty was supposed to remain demilitarized, Britain and France acquiesced.

Emboldened by their success, on November 1, 1936, Italy and Germany announced creation of an alliance they called the Rome-Berlin Axis. A few weeks later Japan and Germany signed the Anti-Comintern Pact, which Italy later joined. It pledged cooperation against communist threats instigated by the Soviet Union. In September 1940 the three nations signed the so-called Axis Alliance, a promise of cooperation that projected an image of a unified totalitarian front.

The outbreak of the Spanish Civil War in July 1936 prompted Hitler and Mussolini to rush military aid to General Francisco Franco, a Spanish fascist who led his troops in revolt against the leftist Spanish Republican government. Stalin, too, dispatched some military aid and advisers to assist the Republic. Roosevelt worked behind the scenes to impose economic sanctions against the Franco forces, but the governments of Great Britain and France refused to help.

The Spanish Civil War prompted Congress to pass a third Neutrality Law in January 1937. The new act extended the existing ban on loans and arms sales to warring states also covered factions in civil wars, as in Spain.

Several thousand French, British, and American men volunteered to fight for the Spanish Republic under the banner of the International Brigades, a group that included communist, antifascist, and pro-democratic activists. Ernest Hemingway, who reported from Spain, depicted their idealism in his 1940 novel *For Whom the Bell Tolls* in which Robert Jordan, an American college professor, dies heroically in defense of Spanish democracy. British writer George Orwell chronicled the complex politics of the war—in which socialists, communists, and anarchists fought each other as well as the fascists—in his 1938 account *Homage to Catalonia*. Franco's victory in 1939 further undermined the spirit of those who opposed fascism.

Disengagement in Asia

Japanese nationalists also nursed dreams of empire. In 1931 Japan's army had seized Manchuria and set up a puppet state called Manchukuo. Although this action violated treaty pledges Japan had signed with the United States a decade earlier, the Hoover administration responded with only a declaration by Secretary of State Henry Stimson that the United States would not recognize the legality of Japan's conquests. When the League of Nations condemned Japanese aggression, Tokyo, like Germany, quit the organization.

In mid-1937 the rival Chinese Communist and Chinese Nationalist parties formed an anti-Japanese United Front. Japan responded by invading China in July. China, Japanese officials boasted, would be incorporated into what they called the "Greater East Asia Co-Prosperity Sphere"—a euphemism for an empire that would eventually encroach on British, Dutch, French, and Americans colonies as well.

By the close of 1937 Japanese armies controlled most of coastal China but were frustrated by their inability to end resistance. China's large but poorly equipped forces fled inland, trading space for time. When Japanese troops captured the capital city of Nanking (Nanjing) in December 1937, they slaughtered between 200,000 and 400,000 civilians, an outrage soon known as the Rape of Nanking. Although such mass terror angered most Americans, a Chicago newspaper headline typified public sentiment: "We Sympathize, But It Is Not Our Concern."

In October 1937 Roosevelt had given a speech in Chicago proposing that democratic nations impose a "quarantine" on aggressor states. After being called a "warmonger" by many newspapers and Republican opponents, he dropped the idea.

Appeasement

Doubting their capacity to resist Hitler on their own, and with no prospect of U.S. support, the governments of Great Britain and France adopted a policy known as appeasement. Although this term later became an epithet hurled at politicians who favored diplomacy over threats, it initially implied compromising with rivals to deter war. European conservatives, who feared communism and the Soviet Union nearly as much as Nazi Germany, saw another benefit to appeasement. By accommodating Hitler's expansion into Eastern Europe, they hoped to turn him against the Soviet Union and spare themselves.

Appeasement not only failed a moral test, but, as Britain's future prime minister Winston Churchill noted, had a basic practical flaw: Hitler intended to go to war eventually to secure what he called *Lebensraum* or living space. He would settle for nothing less than a Greater Germany that would dominate Central Europe and annex most of Eastern Europe and Russia from which subhuman "races," such as the Jews, Poles, Slavs, and Gypsies, would be removed and eventually killed. He also coveted parts of Britain's and France's empires. As he told his inner circle, he intended eventually to strike both westward, to neutralize British and French power, and eastward to seize most of Eastern Europe and Russian territory that would become part of his "thousand year Reich."

Appeasement reached its peak during 1938. In March Hitler again defied the Versailles Treaty by annexing Austria, an action called *Der Anschluss* in German. In September he demanded that Czechoslovakia, a nation created in 1919 from the disbanded Austro-Hungarian Empire, turn over its Sudetenland region that had a large German-speaking population. Once stripped of this border province, the rest of the country would be defenseless. At a late-September conference in Munich, Germany,

British prime minister **Neville Chamberlain** and French leader Edouard Daladier again caved in to Hitler's demands, despite earlier pledges to defend the Czechs. Appeasement, Chamberlain claimed, had secured "peace in our time." Hitler got the territory he wanted but privately fumed about the British-French retreat, since he had hoped to make a show of smashing the Czech army while its patrons did nothing. A few months later the Nazis seized the remainder of Czechoslovakia.

A year later, Hitler targeted Germany's eastern neighbor, Poland. The British and French governments finally recognized the futility of appeasement and resolved to declare war on Germany if it attacked Poland. With reason, Soviet dictator Josef Stalin feared another round of appeasement in which Poland would be delivered to Germany as part of an Anglo-French plan to turn Hitler against the Soviet Union. To block this move Stalin secretly negotiated his own self-serving deal with Hitler. The German-Soviet Non-Aggression Pact signed in August 1939 provided for joint German-Soviet partition of Poland, Soviet delivery of raw materials to Germany, and a German pledge not to attack the Soviet Union.

Having neutralized the Soviet Union, Hitler attacked Poland on September 1, 1939. German forces quickly overpowered the courageous but outmatched Poles, who sent waves of cavalry in futile charges against *panzers*. Meanwhile, Soviet forces occupied the eastern portions of the country. Stunned by the cunning showed by both Hitler and Stalin, Great Britain and France declared war on Germany on September 3, 1939.

America at the Brink of War, 1939–1941

As required by law, Roosevelt responded to the European war by declaring American neutrality. But unlike Wilson in 1914, he did not ask Americans to remain neutral in their thoughts or passions. Roosevelt made clear he now believed the United States must do more to assist those who stood up to Axis aggression, and the public increasingly shared his view. But how to do so? The U.S. Army, with only 175,000 enlisted men in 1939, could not provide much help to anyone. Roosevelt hoped that the U.S. Navy could shelter the nation as it rebuilt its strength. Meanwhile he believed that the sale of weapons, especially planes, to Britain and France, would buy time. But that premise, too, remained uncertain. Roosevelt had to prod a reluctant Congress in November 1939 to permit arms sales to Britain and France, and then only if they paid cash and transported the weapons on their own ships.

After Poland's quick defeat, the ground war in Europe abated until the spring of 1940. In April Germany launched a series of rapid attacks in Western Europe, dubbed a Blitzkrieg or lightning war. France surrendered in June and WWI hero Marshal Philippe Petain formed a pro-German government, known as the Vichy regime, which administered the southern half of France. The French collapse stranded about 300,000 British troops who had been sent to help France, and some French forces loyal to General Charles de Gaulle, on the beaches at Dunkirk, caught between the advancing Germans and the English Channel. A heroic rescue effort by British fishing boats along with Royal Navy ships, as well as good luck, brought most of the troops—but little of their equipment—back safely to England.

After the fall of France, British resolve wavered. Key government officials, many of them advocates of the discredited appeasement policy, favored making peace with Hitler, leaving him in control of Europe if he allowed Britain to keep most of its empire. Only the ironclad determination of Britain's new Prime Minister, Winston Churchill, sustained morale and held peace advocates at bay during the summer of 1940. Churchill's description of the rescue at Dunkirk turned a near military disaster into a psychological victory. In his first and best remembered speech to the House of Commons, he grimly declared that he had nothing to offer but "blood, toil, tears, and sweat," but that no matter what Nazi Germany did, Britain, unlike France, would "never surrender."

This promise had an American as well as a British audience. Churchill sought to reassure Roosevelt and the American people that Britain could be counted on. Churchill and Roosevelt had barely known each other before the war, but they gradually formed a close personal bond through their exchange of frank and frequent messages. Roosevelt understood that if the Nazis conquered Britain and its colonies, they would dominate the Atlantic Ocean, the Mediterranean region, and the Middle East, making them nearly unbeatable.

During 1940, Congress acceded to Roosevelt's pleas to boost military spending and authorized a peacetime draft. In September Roosevelt used his executive power to transfer to the Royal Navy 50 World War I era U.S. destroyers in return for granting the United States naval base rights in the British West Indies. After the destroyer-base deal, Roosevelt pulled back temporarily from providing more assistance to Britain. He had decided to run for an unprecedented third term in November 1940 and feared his opponents would paint him as a war monger.

Anti-interventionist groups accused Roosevelt of planning to enter the war once reelected. Among his critics was aviation hero Charles Lindbergh, who admired Nazi accomplishments and played an active role in the America First Committee, founded in 1940 with the backing of several wealthy anti-New Deal corporate donors. Lindberg warned that British imperialists and a shadowy group of Jews were behind efforts to fight Germany.

During the summer and fall of 1940, Germany's Luftwaffe relentlessly bombed British cities, factories, and airfields in preparation for a cross-channel invasion. Americans closely followed the Battle of Britain in radio broadcasts on the CBS network, narrated by journalist **Edward R. Murrow**. Reporting from rooftops and air-raid shelters, with audible explosions in the background, he opened with the words "This . . . is London." These reports deepened popular support for the British people.

A secret technological breakthrough, along with heroic efforts by the Royal Air Force (RAF) and Royal Navy, sustained Britain. Mathematicians working at Bletchley Park, in rural England, constructed a primitive computer that deciphered coded messages sent on the German Enigma machine used to direct air and submarine attacks. Code named ULTRA, this project built on prewar research by Polish intelligence experts. British code-breakers often—but not always—learned from intercepts which cities or airfields the Germans targeted for attack. Later in the war they cracked German naval codes revealing where U-boats lurked in the Atlantic. Along with innovations such as radio detection and ranging (RADAR) and other new forms of electronic detection, ULTRA enabled the outnumbered RAF to concentrate on defending key targets.

In October 1940 the badly mauled Luftwaffe cut back its attacks and thus forced Hitler to postpone and then cancel the invasion of Britain. Germany now attempted to starve the British into submission by sending so-called wolf packs of U-boats to sink merchant ships carrying food and other supplies from the United States. Hitler turned his gaze eastward, redeploying German ground forces for a planned invasion of the Soviet Union he had contemplated for years.

In the run-up to the 1940 election Roosevelt blunted criticism about his military policies by appointing several prominent Republicans to powerful cabinet positions. He named the widely respected Wall Street lawyer **Henry L. Stimson**, who had served as President Hoover's secretary of state, as secretary of war. Republican newspaper publisher **Frank Knox** became the new secretary of the navy. Roosevelt's effort to sell a more robust defense policy got a boost when Republicans nominated as their presidential candidate **Wendell Willkie**, a moderate corporate executive who shared many of the president's concerns. Most Americans preferred Roosevelt to his little known challenger and he won reelection to an unprecedented third term in November.

Once reelected, Roosevelt acted more forcefully. When he learned in December that Britain had little cash left to purchase American weapons, he conceived a plan to provide vital assistance free of charge. In a Fireside Chat on December 29, 1940, he called for the United States to become the great "arsenal of Democracy." To keep Britain in their fight against Germany and China in their resistance of Japan, Roosevelt proposed "loaning," rather than selling them, weapons and raw materials.

In January 1941 Roosevelt submitted his so-called Lend-Lease proposal to Congress. He linked military aid to preservation of what he called the Four Essential Human Freedoms, or Four Freedoms—freedom of speech and of religion, freedom from fear and from want. Congress overwhelmingly passed Lend-Lease in March 1941. Secretary of War Stimson called it an "economic declaration of war" against the Axis powers. Initially funded at $7 billion, about as large as that year's entire federal budget, Lend-Lease eventually provided $50 billion in aid to Great Britain, China, and the Soviet Union.

During 1941 British and U.S. military planners informally agreed that their first priority should be the defeat of Germany, followed by Japan if it attacked in the Pacific. When Germany invaded the Soviet Union in June 1941, Roosevelt and Churchill realized that despite their past dislike of Stalin and his recent cooperation with Hitler, victory over Germany required that they assist the communist nation with Lend-Lease. If Hitler gained control of Russian oil, coal, steel, and grain, his well provisioned armies could be redirected against Britain and the Middle East.

During the final months of 1941 Roosevelt deployed U.S. warships to escort more than half way across the Atlantic British merchant ships carrying Lend-Lease supplies. German U-boats attacked and even sank several American vessels assisting the British in what amounted to an undeclared naval war.

In mid-August 1941, Roosevelt and Churchill held their first of several wartime meetings aboard ships off the coast of Newfoundland. Churchill came to request increased military aid, while Roosevelt pushed for a postwar plan that embodied the Four Freedoms. The **Atlantic Charter** issued by the two leaders on August 14 called for disarming defeated aggressors and establishing a "permanent system of general security." This new world order would include freedom of the seas, freedom from fear and want, the reduction of trade barriers, and the "right of all peoples to choose the form of government under which they will live." Churchill resented Roosevelt's swipe at colonialism but muffled his anger to win the promise of more aid. Like Wilson's Fourteen Points in World War I, the Atlantic Charter had no legal standing but represented a blueprint for spreading New Deal values globally.

Day of Infamy

Although Roosevelt and his military advisers considered Germany the greater threat to U.S. security, war came first with Japan. Since 1938 the United States had tried to restrain Japan by providing assistance to China and gradually imposing trade sanctions on Tokyo. Although the armies of Chinese leader Jiang Jieshi (Chiang Kai-shek) and the guerrilla forces of the small Chinese Communist Party won few battles, they tied down several million Japanese troops simply by not surrendering. To keep China fighting, the United States provided first economic assistance and then military aid. Although Japan imported valuable raw materials, including petroleum and scrap metal from the United States, the Roosevelt administration hesitated to cut off all trade with Japan, as this action might provoke an attack on resource-rich Southeast Asia.

But after German armies overran France and Holland in mid-1940, the Japanese began pressing for greater control of French Indochina and the Dutch East Indies and joined Germany and Italy in the Axis Alliance that pledged joint action if they were attacked. In July 1941 Japanese forces seized control of most of French Indochina. The United States responded by enlarging the size of the Pacific Fleet at Pearl Harbor in Hawaii and also sent several dozen new B-17 bombers to bases in the Philippines. Most significantly Roosevelt, embargoing all trade with Japan, halted the sale of petroleum on which the Japanese navy depended, as the country produced no oil of its own.

During the last months of 1941 Japanese and American diplomats discussed possible ways to avert war. Japanese negotiators insisted that the United States immediately resume oil sales and cease military aid to China; American officials countered with the demand that Japan withdraw its troops from China and Indochina and break its alliance with Nazi Germany before oil sales resumed.

Roosevelt rejected the idea of temporarily relaxing the oil embargo after reviewing secret messages exchanged between leaders in Tokyo, such as Prime Minister and General **Tojo Hideki**, and Japanese negotiators in Washington. U.S. Naval intelligence, in a remarkable operation codenamed MAGIC, had built a machine resembling that used by the Japanese for secret radio transmissions. They decrypted diplomatic communications, although it was not until later in the war that they broke military codes, which revealed that Japan's military leaders were unlikely to agree to or honor any compromises reached by civilian negotiators.

After talks broke off at the end of November, U.S. officials expected a Japanese attack within two weeks and sent warnings to commanders throughout the Pacific. Unfortunately, MAGIC did not reveal the exact timing or the target of Japan's battle fleets, and U.S. intelligence analysts guessed Japan would first strike at targets in Southeast Asia. Hawaii seemed far beyond the effective range of Japanese power.

Japanese admiral **Yamamoto Isoroku**, who had studied at Harvard 20 years earlier, planned the December attack on Pearl Harbor. He calculated that crippling the Pacific Fleet would delay for at least one year the ability of the United States to mount a counterattack. By then Japan should control China and resource-rich Southeast Asia. In a mirror image of Hitler's reasoning, Japanese strategists guessed that, with the expected Soviet defeat, Roosevelt would focus on the defense of the Atlantic, giving Japan a free hand in the Pacific.

Yamamoto, like German foreign minister Ribbentrop, recognized that provoking the United States entailed a terrific gamble. If Germany failed to defeat the Soviet Union, he warned his staff, the British and Americans would be able to fight in *both* Europe and the Pacific. U.S. supplies would keep China fighting and prevent redeployment of millions of Japanese troops to fight the Americans. In that case, Yamamoto conceded, Japanese forces would be able to "run wild" in the Pacific for a year or two but would then be overwhelmed by American military power.

Early on December 7, 1941—a date Roosevelt declared that would "live in infamy"—Japanese carrier-based aircraft mounted a surprise attack on ships and planes in Hawaii. Attacks in the Philippines and Southeast Asia began several hours later. The

A scene of devastation at Pearl Harbor Hawaii, shortly after the Japanese attack on the Pacific Fleet on December 7, 1941.

death of almost 2,400 sailors and soldiers at Pearl Harbor and nearby bases made it the deadliest single attack on American soil until September 11, 2001. The Japanese sank or damaged eight battleships and many other vessels and destroyed several hundred planes. By chance the Pacific Fleet's aircraft carriers were at sea on maneuvers and avoided destruction; they proved crucial for subsequent battles. Afraid to risk a second air strike after the successful first wave, Japanese commanders passed up the chance to destroy vital repair facilities and fuel storage tanks in Hawaii.

At Roosevelt's request Congress promptly declared war on Japan. Great Britain, whose Asian colonies had also been attacked, followed suit. On December 11, after deciding that with Japan as an ally in a two-front war "it was impossible" for Germany to lose, Hitler, followed by Mussolini, declared war on the United States.

America's new allies expressed relief that the United States had come into the war. Chinese leader Jiang Jieshi reportedly sang an opera aria to celebrate news of Japan's attack. Observing what he considered Japan's monumental folly in provoking a fight, Winston Churchill declared "So we had won after all . . .! Hitler's fate was sealed. Mussolini's fate was sealed. As for the Japanese, they would be ground to powder."

STUDY QUESTIONS FOR THE LONG FUSE

1. How did the Axis nations threaten world peace after 1931?
2. Why were most Americans "isolationists" during the 1930s?
3. Between 1939 and 1941, how did Roosevelt seek to help Great Britain and China? Why did he feel this was vital to U.S. security?

A GRAND ALLIANCE

During the first months after the Pearl Harbor attack, Americans heard nothing but bad news from the war front. Not only was there a string of U.S. defeats in the Pacific, but German submarines sank dozens of U.S. merchant ships within sight of ports stretching from Miami to New York. But Roosevelt calmed public fears by speaking frankly to Americans about the nation's heavy losses and the strategy he would pursue to defeat Germany, and then Japan. The struggle would be long and difficult, he explained, but by attacking America its enemies had sowed the seeds of their destruction.

On New Year's Day 1942 the United States, Great Britain, the Soviet Union, China, and two dozen smaller partners, issued a "Declaration of the United Nations," a pledge to fight for victory. The Soviet Union remained neutral in the war against Japan until August 1945, following Germany's surrender. The United States provided substantial military aid to this so-called Grand Alliance, recognizing that it would be a year or more before large numbers of American troops could engage the enemy. Meanwhile, Lend-Lease would help British, Chinese, and especially Soviet armies keep fighting.

As the U.S. military grew from a few hundred thousand to over 12 million, the command structure changed dramatically. Roosevelt encouraged the chiefs of the separate military services to meet jointly, later formalized by creation of the Joint Chiefs of Staff. Army chief of staff General George C. Marshall and Navy commander Admiral **Ernest J. King** assumed unparalleled authority over their respective services. The service chiefs and their large staffs moved into an immense new headquarters in Arlington, Virginia, the Pentagon, whose very name came to symbolize American power.

War in the Pacific

In the first six months of fighting, Japan's Imperial Army and Navy overran Burma, Hong Kong, Malaya, Singapore, the Philippines, the Dutch East Indies, and many Pacific islands and prepared to invade India and Australia. Asian peoples gazed in

▲ **Map 24.1**

Map of the European Theater of War (WWII) The European Theater of War stretched across the Atlantic, as far north as the Arctic Circle, as far east as the Ural Mountains, and south into North Africa. The heaviest fighting—that claimed tens of millions of lives—occurred in Eastern Europe and the Soviet Union.

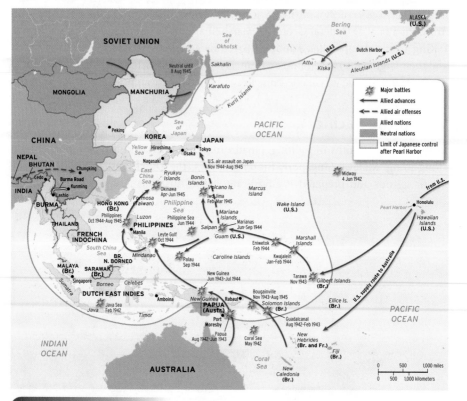

▲ **Map 24.2**

Map of the Pacific Theater of War (WWII) The war in the Asia-Pacific region was fought at sea, in jungles, and on countless islands. Most Japanese troops remained in China and Southeast Asia during the war. By early 1945, the United States began to bomb the Japanese home islands, attacks that culminated in the dropping of two atomic bombs in August 1945.

wonder as the Japanese rolled over British, Dutch, and American forces defending colonial outposts. These victories impressed nationalists, such as **Mao Zedong** in China, **Ho Chi Minh** in Vietnam, **Mohandas Gandhi** in India, and Sukarno in the East Indies. Like most Asians, they rejected Japanese claims to be liberators, but they were startled by how easily Japan had humbled the arrogant colonial rulers.

Other Asians responded differently to Japan's invasion. Many prominent Filipinos collaborated with the Japanese, as did some in Burma. Prominent Indian nationalists, led by Mohandas Gandhi, refused to support the war and were jailed because Churchill balked at promising independence. Some Indians joined a pro-Japanese army in Burma to fight the British.

On the Bataan Peninsula and the island fortress of Corregidor in the Philippines, U.S. and Filipino troops held out against Japanese invaders, under dire conditions, until May 1942. The Japanese forced many of the desperately ill 10,000 Americans and 60,000 Filipinos who surrendered to trek 80 miles to a prison camp. The so-called

Bataan Death March claimed the lives of over 600 Americans and 10,000 Filipinos and came to symbolize Japanese brutality toward surrendered Americans, even though most of its victims were Filipinos fighting for the United States.

Because it would take a year or more to gather the strength needed to counterattack Japan, Roosevelt approved a small, largely symbolic, raid against the Japanese home islands. On April 18, 1942, a handful of B-25 bombers under the command of Lieutenant Colonel **James H. Doolittle** flew off the deck of the aircraft carrier *Hornet* on a 650-mile one-way run. The planes dropped a few bombs on Tokyo and then flew off to crash land on the China coast where Chinese soldiers rescued most of the crewmen. Several others were captured and executed by the Japanese. Although the Doolittle raid did little physical damage, it cheered the American public and provoked the Japanese into a disastrous retaliatory strike.

In early May 1942 Australian troops blocked a Japanese effort to seize Port Morseby in New Guinea, intended as a jumping-off point for a Japanese invasion of Australia. Around the same time a joint U.S.– Australian naval force at the Battle of the Coral Sea turned back a Japanese naval force attempting to occupy other parts of New Guinea. Even though Japan enjoyed superior naval strength, in 1942 U.S. naval cryptographers deciphered a key Japanese naval code. This coup gave the outmatched U.S. Navy a critical edge in subsequent battles.

To eliminate the threat still posed by the U.S. Navy, Japanese strategists planned to draw the bulk of the navy's diminished Pacific Fleet into a decisive battle. They sent several aircraft carriers to attack Midway Island, at the far western end of the Hawaiian chain. The Americans were expected to defend Midway because losing it would place in jeopardy Hawaii and the entire U.S. position in the Pacific. The Japanese navy planned to destroy the Pacific Fleet when it approached Midway.

The strategy made good sense—except that U.S. intelligence had prior warning of the plan through decoded radio intercepts and had positioned its own aircraft carriers near Midway so their planes could pounce on the unsuspecting Japanese. On June 4, 1942, U.S. aircraft destroyed four of Japan's six large aircraft carriers, along with hundreds of planes and skilled pilots. The U.S. navy lost just one carrier, *Yorktown*. This one engagement shifted the balance of power in the Pacific dramatically in favor of the United States.

In mid-1942 American soldiers and marines began a prolonged fight to control Guadalcanal, part of the Solomon Islands near New Guinea, and Australia. The bloody, hand-to-hand combat and associated sea battles lasted from the summer of 1942 through February 1943, when Japanese ships evacuated their surviving troops. The intensity of combat, and its racial dimension, showed in one marine's diary entry: "I wish we were fighting Germans. They are human beings like us. But the Japanese are like animals."

During 1943, Roosevelt approved a two-pronged strategy against Japan. Admiral **Chester Nimitz** led a naval offensive in the Central Pacific to destroy enemy shipping and seize islands close enough to Japan to permit bombing by land-based aircraft. Simultaneously, Army general **Douglas MacArthur**, who had been sent to Australia to head the Southwest Pacific theater of war, was tasked with pushing the

Japanese out of New Guinea and the chain of Japanese-held islands leading to the Philippines.

With some exceptions, such as the struggles for Guadalcanal and New Guinea, most of the battles fought on Pacific islands from 1942 to 1944 were bloody but short. In attacks on islands such as Tarawa, U.S. naval gunfire pounded Japanese positions, followed by amphibious assaults by marine and army units. A high proportion of those storming ashore were killed and wounded. But, in comparison to the massive scale of fighting in Europe, North Africa, and China, these battles were relatively small, typically involving four or five thousand Japanese and twenty to thirty thousand Americans over the course of a week or two. The intensity and duration of fighting increased, however, when U.S. forces invaded the Philippines in October 1944. It took months of heavy combat to liberate the archipelago and some Japanese troops fought on until August 1945. The battles for Iwo Jima, February–March 1945, and Okinawa, April–June 1945, proved even more difficult.

The closer the Americans came to Japan the more fiercely the Japanese fought in what one historian has called a "war without mercy." As its military resources dwindled at the end of 1944, Japan unleashed kamikaze (suicide) planes loaded with explosives against U.S. ships and troops. The high casualties suffered in the fights for the Philippines, Iwo Jima, and Okinawa weighed heavily on the minds of U.S. planners as they prepared for a final assault on Japan and weighed the arguments for and against using the atomic bomb.

Tokyo after the U.S. firebombing of March 1945 that killed an estimated 100,000 civilians.

Roosevelt hoped that Chinese armies could do most of the fighting against the several million Japanese on the Asian mainland. But **Jiang Jieshi (Chiang Kai-shek)** rejected advice offered by General Joseph Stilwell, commander of the U.S. aid mission. Instead of reorganizing his army and using U.S. aid to fight the Japanese, Jiang hoarded supplies for a future showdown against his Chinese Communist rivals. By the close of 1944 Roosevelt lost faith in China as a wartime ally. Although he still hoped it would be a pro-American force in postwar Asia, the president turned to the Soviets for help in subduing Japan following Germany's defeat.

By early 1945 the U.S. Navy had severed Japan's economic links to Southeast Asia and China. The several million Japanese soldiers on the Asian mainland were cut off from home and supplies. That spring the Army Air Force, operating from newly captured bases on Saipan and other Pacific islands, began massive air raids on Japan. Eventually, as many as 1,000 giant B-29 bombers at a time dropped explosives and incendiary bombs that destroyed most of Japan's cities and factories and killed between 500,000 and 700,000 civilians. A single firebomb raid against Tokyo in March incinerated as many as 100,000 residents. Japan was beaten, but it remained unclear if its leaders were ready to surrender.

The War in Europe

In 1942, Roosevelt and Churchill promised Stalin they would soon open a Second Front in Western Europe to relieve pressure on the Soviets. But the competing needs of the global war made it difficult to keep the promise. Churchill was more reluctant than Roosevelt even to try. Recalling the slaughter of World War I, he feared high casualties from an early invasion of France. The British leader used this argument to justify the alternative offensives in North Africa and Italy during 1942–1943. Stalin considered the long-delayed Second Front a cynical ploy by Britain and the United States to fight Germany to the last Russian. Although this was not true, it had a corrosive effect on relations among the allies.

In November 1942, U.S. forces invaded North Africa with the goal of linking up with British troops in Egypt. At first, untested American troops were unsuccessful. But by May 1943, after months of desert combat, British and U.S. armies at last defeated German forces commanded by General Erwin Rommel, which earlier had nearly overrun the vital Suez Canal and jeopardized Allied access to Iraqi and Iranian oil.

After securing North Africa, Allied forces invaded the island of Sicily and then moved on to the Italian mainland. Churchill had pressed for the Italian campaign, insisting it would be a relatively easy fight that would weaken Germany without risking the heavy casualties of an early invasion of France. In fact, fighting in Italy proved long, difficult, and costly. Although Mussolini's government collapsed in 1943, the Wehrmacht remained entrenched in northern Italy until 1945, and the entire campaign had little effect on ultimate victory.

The Soviet Red Army, more than any single factor, assured Hitler's doom. In the first six months of fighting, June to December 1941, the Wehrmacht literally reached the gates of Moscow before winter weather and Soviet resistance stopped their advance. During the first two years of the war, the Red Army was in effect annihilated and rebuilt twice. In those 24 months alone, it lost nearly as many soldiers as the total number of Americans—12 million—who served in the U.S. armed forces and fighting on the Eastern Front killed 2 million German soldiers, nearly 10 times as many as died fighting the British and Americans during the entire war.

The scale of fighting on the Eastern Front dwarfed anything the Western Allies faced in North Africa, Italy, or France. Civilians were as likely to be killed as soldiers. In Leningrad, for example, one million residents perished during a 900-day siege. Ultimately, between 20 and 30 million Soviet citizens and soldiers died in what the government called the Great Patriotic War. One historian writing of these events explained Germany's defeat in this way: by not surrendering in 1940–1941, "Britain provided the time." Thereafter, "Russia supplied the blood" and "America the money and weapons."

The tide of battle turned early in 1943 when the Red Army defeated a large German force at Stalingrad, a city on the Volga River named after the Soviet leader. During the two years after Stalingrad, the Wehrmacht fought a slow but brutally effective retreat back across Russia and Eastern Europe toward Berlin. Although no one could predict when victory would come, Germany's fate seemed all but certain.

After nearly two years of delay, the D-Day invasion of France finally occurred on June 6, 1944. By then German forces were already in full retreat from Russia. The Anglo-American armies that invaded France under the command of General **Dwight D. Eisenhower** trapped the Wehrmacht in an unbreakable vice. German commanders and troops fought skillful rear-guard battles to slow both the Soviet and Anglo-American offensives; they even managed to launch large counterattacks, such as the **Battle of the Bulge** in Belgium, at the end of 1944, which temporarily stopped the Allied momentum. But the overwhelming power of the two-front Allied offensive drove steadily toward Berlin.

The Holocaust

Among the many horrors of war, none exceeded Nazi efforts to systematically murder whole categories of "inferior" people. In the late 1930s Nazi hostility toward Jews turned to violent persecution, and by 1942 Hitler sanctioned the mass extermination of "undesirables." German doctors had earlier assisted the Nazi regime in killing tens of thousands of fellow Germans who suffered from physical deformities and mental illness. Nazi ideologues then expanded the category of those to be eliminated, adding Jews, Gypsies, homosexuals, and then Poles and Soviet POWs. According to this plan, Germans would be resettled in Eastern Europe and western Russia once the Jews, Slavs, and other subhumans were cleared. The most systematic slaughter was visited upon the approximately 10 million Jews living in German-occupied Eastern Europe and the Soviet Union. Ultimately, about 6 million Jews were killed.

Special German military and police units, sometimes aided by local militias, began shooting and clubbing to death large numbers of Jews and many Slavs after the occupation of Poland in 1939. The process accelerated after June 1941 when the

Survivors of a Nazi concentration camp in Eastern Europe upon their liberation in the spring of 1945.

Wehrmacht invaded the western Soviet Union, home to around four million Jews. By the end of 1942 three or four million Jews and many Slavs had perished. With so many people to kill Hitler and his henchman devised a more systematic means of slaughter. Early in 1942 they approved a so-called Final Solution that envisioned concentrating all of Europe's surviving Jews and other undesirables in large-scale death camps and eliminating victims through the use of poison gas and other means. During the next three years about two million additional Jews deported from Western Europe, along with five million Poles and Soviet prisoners, died in these killing centers.

More than half the deaths of Jewish and Slavic civilians occurred before the time in 1944 when Allied aircraft possessed the range to reach extermination camps. Even when the possibility arose of bombing the rail lines that serviced death camps such as Auschwitz, British and American military strategists rejected the idea as a "diversion" from the central task of defeating the Wehrmacht and destroying war production. In addition, anti-Semitism remained common in the United States. Because leaders of Jewish-American organizations feared a backlash if they spoke out forcefully on behalf of European Jews, they lobbied quietly if at all.

During the war Congress maintained rigid immigration restrictions that barred entry for most European Jews. Lawmakers even rebuffed efforts to allow some Jewish children into the United States on an emergency basis or shelter those few Jews who escaped Nazi clutches. Ironically, dozens of Jewish scientists and some married to Jews who had fled Nazi persecution before the outbreak of war made vital, though secret, contributions to Allied victory through their work developing the atomic bomb. These notables included Albert Einstein, Hans Bethe, Enrico Fermi, Edward Teller, Leo Szilard, Eugene Wigner, and Lise Meitner, among others.

In 1944, President Roosevelt, who sympathized with the plight of those victimized by the Nazis but did not expend much political capital on their behalf, created a War Refugee Board to establish temporary havens in neutral countries or liberated territories overseas. These centers saved the lives of about 200,000 refugees. But during the entire war, fewer than 1,000 European Jews were permitted to enter the United States, and most of these were confined to a fenced-in camp in rural Oswego, New York.

STUDY QUESTIONS FOR A GRAND ALLIANCE

1. Why did the United States pursue a "Europe First" war strategy?
2. Why did U.S. strategists consider it vital to aid the Soviet Union?
3. How did U.S. officials and the public respond to the Holocaust?

BATTLE FOR PRODUCTION

Shortly after the Republicans scored big gains in the 1942 congressional election, Franklin Roosevelt told journalists that "Dr. New Deal," who had saved the country from the Depression, had been replaced by "Dr. Win-the-War."

The wartime Congress terminated several New Deal programs such as the WPA and CCC, but it left many others, including Social Security, farm price supports, and minimum wage laws, intact. Ultimately, the war acted as a catalyst for social and economic changes that enshrined the New Deal in American life. Unlike the outcome for any other country in the world, the war improved life for most Americans, ended unemployment, increased mobility, and laid a foundation for a postwar economic surge.

War Economy

Even though they were rigid dictatorships, neither Nazi Germany nor Imperial Japan developed cohesive military production policies. In Berlin and Tokyo, government agencies, the armed services, and private industrialists constantly bickered over which weapons to produce and how to distribute vital supplies. In their distinct ways, the United States, the Soviet Union, and Great Britain implemented much more successful policies to maximize military production. The Soviets, for example, packed up whole factories from European Russia and moved them east of the Ural Mountains, beyond the reach of German bombers.

Speaking to the nation in January 1942, Roosevelt set ambitious goals for war production (see Table 24.2 and Figure 24.1). Scoffing at advisors who wanted these goals kept secret, he boasted "I believe these figures will tell the enemy what they are up against" and erode their morale. During the next four years, the United States spent $300 billion on war production. The share of the GNP devoted to military spending rose from 2 to 42 percent, a historic high.

To mobilize industry, labor, capital, and public support for the war, FDR created agencies that resembled those used to fight the Depression. These were loosely supervised by the War Production Board (WPB). Most war orders went to large manufacturers, such as General Motors, Ford, General Electric, and U.S. Steel. One-half of all contracts went to the 33 largest corporations. Military contracts often contained a "cost-plus" clause in which the government agreed to pay the full cost of producing, say, a rifle, tank, or plane plus a guaranteed profit. At the end of the war, many of these manufacturers received valuable government-funded equipment in return for a token payment. Secretary of War Stimson believed this was the most sensible policy, because to fight a war in a capitalist country, "you have to let business make money out of the process or business won't work." By 1945 corporate profits had nearly doubled from the 1940 level.

Wartime spending boosted paid employment by 11 million workers. They included 3.5 million who came of age during the war and 7.5 million first-time adult workers, half of them women. With full employment families began saving money for the first time since the early 1930s. In fact, savings increased 10-fold during the war years, to $29 billion. Farm income also surged. The number of families with annual incomes below $2,000 fell by half, while those earning over $5,000 increased fourfold.

Before 1942 most working Americans made so little money they paid no federal income taxes at all, and the vast majority paid no more than a 4 percent tax. Only

Table 24.2 Military Production in the United States, 1942–1945 The surge in U.S. military production during WWII gave the allies at least a 3:1 advantage over their Axis enemies.

297,000 aircraft
193,000 artillery pieces
86,000 tanks
2.4 million military trucks and jeeps
1,200 combat vessels
8,800 total naval vessels
87,000 landing craft
3,300 merchant ships and tankers
14 million shoulder arms
5 million pounds of bombs
40 billion bullets

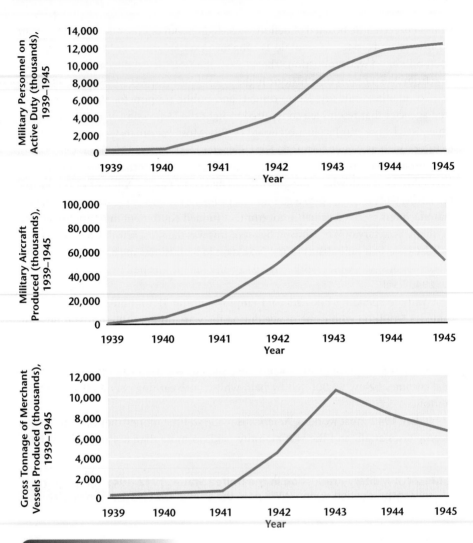

▲ **Figure 24.1**

The U.S. war economy, 1941–1945 Military production surged during WWII as the federal government invested heavily in factories and new technologies. This gave U.S. armed forces, and that of its major allies, a sizeable advantage over the Axis powers in terms of aircraft, ships, tanks, artillery, etc.

the very wealthy paid a significant amount. But by 1945 full employment and rising wages created a taxpaying base of 42 million Americans whose payments covered about half the $300 billion cost of the war. As a wartime measure that became permanent, the IRS introduced a payroll tax withholding system. Appealing both to patriotism and to a desire to earn a profit, celebrities promoted the sale of $50 billion in

Series E Bonds in small denominations to average citizens. Banks and large financial institutions purchased $150 billion in war bonds.

In 1943, to sort out disputes between civilian and military producers over how to allot raw materials, Roosevelt created a "super agency," the Office of War Mobilization (OWM). He chose as its powerful and effective director former Supreme Court justice **James F. Byrnes**, a man he called "my assistant president." Byrnes, who hoped to succeed Roosevelt, gloated that wartime priorities had helped conservative Democrats like him to push "the radical boys out of the way."

A Government-Sponsored Industrial Revolution

As part of the effort to spur production, the federal government boosted funding on scientific research from zero to about $1.5 billion annually. Money provided by the War Department's Office of Scientific Research and Development (OSRD) led to the construction of plants that produced synthetic rubber and fibers, advances in RADAR and SONAR, and the development of antibiotic drugs as well as computers, jet engines, and guided missiles. Academic laboratories at MIT and Cal Tech pioneered research into microwave electronics and rocket propulsion. Wartime research resulted in techniques to produce abundant quantities of formerly scarce penicillin as well as antimalarial drugs vital to troops fighting in the tropics.

OSRD also spent $2 billion developing the atomic bomb. The work took place in three new "atomic cities." Special facilities in Oak Ridge, Tennessee, and Hanford, Washington, processed uranium ore into fissionable bomb material. In remote Los Alamos, New Mexico, at the site of a former boarding school, nuclear physicists under the direction of **J. Robert Oppenheimer** designed and assembled the secret weapon. Nearly 150,000 people worked on some aspect of the so-called **Manhattan Project**. They ranged from the dozens of émigré nuclear physicists such as Enrico Fermi, Hans Bethe, and Edward Teller to Navajo and Hopi miners digging ore in the mesas of Arizona and New Mexico. In July 1945 their efforts culminated in the successful test of the atomic bomb in New Mexico. After the war Los Alamos became one of several federal laboratories that conducted both military and civilian research.

Mass-Produced Weapons

German and Japanese engineers excelled at designing advanced weapons, including tanks, jet aircraft, torpedoes, and giant battleships, like Japan's immense *Yamato*, which outclassed many weapons in the Allied arsenals.

But these weapons were so complex and costly that Germany and Japan could produce them only in limited numbers. Soviet factories mass produced the simple T-34 tank, dubbed "peasant proof" because of its ease of operation and effectiveness in battle. Swarms of agile T-34s overwhelmed the technically superior panzers. Lumbering American B-17 or B-24 bombers stood no chance against a jet-powered Messerschmitt, but German factories produced only a handful of these marvels compared to the tens of thousands of U.S. aircraft that dominated the skies over Europe by 1944.

The cargo vessel *Patrick Henry*, launched by the Kaiser shipyards in Richmond, California, at the end of 1941, had taken almost a year to build. By mid-1942, however, teams of male and female, black, white, and Hispanic workers cut construction time to four months. In 1943 they could complete one of these so-called Liberty Ships in seven weeks and by 1945 in just 17 days. American shipyards produced 2,700 of these vital cargo vessels.

The Ford Motor Company did for aircraft production what the Kaiser shipyards did for cargo vessels. A new plant at Willow Run outside Detroit, Ford workers assembled B-24 medium bombers. Rivets, aluminum, wiring, and engine parts started out at one end of the mile long production line and a plane emerged hourly at the other end. At Willow run 40,000 workers on three shifts produced 8,500 aircraft during the war.

Sybil Lewis, a black woman from rural Oklahoma, found her life transformed by war work. In 1942 she quit her job as a maid earning $3.50 per week and moved to Los Angeles where she found employment, along with thousands of other white and black women, as a riveter at Lockheed Aviation and earned $48 weekly. "When I got my first paycheck," Lewis recalled, "I'd never seen that much money before." After the war Lewis used her savings to attend college and get a job as a civil servant; she was the first in her family to enter the middle class.

Organized Labor and the War

Labor leaders, with the exception of the combative head of the United Mine Workers, John L. Lewis, issued a "no strike" pledge once the United States entered the war. The employment boom along with a government policy of encouraging union membership led to a steep increase in workers carrying union cards. By 1945, 15 million Americans belonged to labor unions, including one-third of all nonfarm workers—a historic high in percentage terms.

Union officials generally cooperated with management and federal agencies to boost production. The National War Labor Relations Board (NWLRB) and the Office of Price Administration (OPA) regulated both wages and prices to control inflation. With full employment and overtime pay, most workers earned about 27 percent more in real income at the end of the war than at the beginning.

To attract skilled workers without violating wage caps, many businesses provided generous medical and other benefits, including paid vacations and education assistance. The Kaiser Shipyards on the West Coast offered a prepaid medical insurance program that became Kaiser Permanente, a health maintenance organization. Blue Cross and Blue Shield medical insurance began before the war but expanded quickly when workers' fringe benefits began to cover health insurance. Job-based health benefits, however, had a down side: they reduced pressure by labor unions for a national health insurance system and left nonunion employees, the unemployed, and the elderly uncovered. As union membership declined later in the century, more and more workers were left without health insurance.

The Draft

The draft focused on American males aged 18–26, a cohort of 30 million men. The system relied on 6,500 local draft boards that had the power to grant exemptions, or deferments, based on marital status, job skills, and physical condition. During the war, two million farm laborers and nearly four million industrial workers received blanket exemption from military service. At first married men, especially those with children, were draft exempt, but they later became combat eligible. Ultimately, about 16 million men, or one in nine Americans, served in the military, and the armed services reached a peak size of 12 million.

Conscientious objectors (COs) were treated more fairly than in World War I, with some 25,000 assigned noncombat military duty including the dangerous job of battlefield medic. About 12,000 who refused any cooperation with the military served stateside, often as orderlies in mental hospitals.

Although women were draft exempt, about 350,000 volunteered for special units. Approximately 140,000 served as WACS (Women's Army Corps), 100,000 as WAVES (Women Accepted for Voluntary Emergency Naval Service), 13,000 as Coast Guard SPARS (after the Guard's motto, *semper paratus* or "always ready"), and 1,000 as WASPS (Women's Air Force Service Pilots), who flew planes in noncombat zones. About 75,000 female nurses also served in the military. In addition, 350,000 women volunteered to work for groups like the Red Cross and the United Service Organization (USO), which assisted troops.

African American pilots who were members of the famed Tuskegee Airmen during World War II.

GLOBAL PASSAGES

The Bretton Woods System, 1944–1971

In July 1944 the United States hosted 730 delegates from 44 nations who attended the blandly named "United Nations Monetary and Financial Conference" at a resort hotel in Bretton Woods, New Hampshire. The so-called **Bretton Woods agreements** that emerged from the conclave established a system for international trade and monetary values to promote postwar recovery. They also contributed to U.S. domination of the world economy for most of the next half century.

Harry Dexter White, an aide to Treasury Secretary Henry Morgenthau, conceived many of the ideas discussed by the delegates. He drafted the plan to create the International Bank for Reconstruction and Development (IBRD; later divided into the World Bank and the International Monetary Fund, or IMF). The new agencies made development loans to poor nations and provided funds to stabilize currencies and cover temporary trade imbalances. Participating nations established a mechanism to set fixed rates of exchange among the world's currencies to promote trade. Other provisions reduced global trade barriers and encouraged the free flow of investment capital. White hoped these rules would prevent the "beggar thy neighbor" protectionist economic policies that worsened the Depression and helped cause World War II. The Bretton Woods system established the dollar as a stable "reserve

Shared experiences of training and combat eroded many ethnic barriers among whites in the military. Wartime mixing encouraged more open housing and employment patterns in the postwar era. The black-white racial barrier proved harder to crack. Although the United States fought enemies engaged in exterminating "inferior races," it did so with a rigidly segregated army that relegated all-black units mostly to noncombat duty under the command of white officers. The Navy admitted blacks only as kitchen help while the Marines refused all black enlistees till late in the war. Black servicemen were startled when they witnessed German and Italian POWs who worked in southern towns being served in restaurants or admitted to movie theaters that barred blacks.

Army chief of staff General **George C. Marshall** rejected pleas to desegregate the army. The military, he asserted, was not a "sociological laboratory" and could not solve a "social problem that has perplexed the American people throughout the history of this nation."

The army eventually recruited a squadron of 1,000 combat pilots and 15,000 support personnel, known as the Tuskegee Airmen, from their training facility at the famous Alabama college. It also formed several black ground combat units. In 1940 the army had five black officers, but by 1945 the number rose to 7,000. In addition,

currency" that would be more flexible than the prewar gold standard. With its value set at the rate of $35 per ounce of gold, the dollar became the international medium of exchange. Most nations valued or "pegged" their own currencies in relation to the dollar. International transactions and prices for products like petroleum were denominated in dollars, giving an edge to American companies. These financial arrangements promoted rapid worldwide economic growth in the 25 years after World War II and made the United States the strongest economy in the world, in addition to the strongest military power. The system of dollar-gold convertibility lasted until 1971, when financial competition from European and Asian nations and the economic impact of the Vietnam War eroded the value of the dollar so badly that those holding dollar reserves dumped the paper currency in favor of gold or other assets. President Richard Nixon ended dollar-gold convertibility in favor of a system where world currency values fluctuated or "floated" in relation to one another.

In the late 1940s, evidence surfaced that during World War II Harry Dexter White passed classified information to the Soviet Union. Although White died before the charges could be verified, historians agree he probably did so. Whatever White's motives, the system of free trade and capital flows he nurtured at Bretton Woods contributed to U.S. prosperity, the ultimate triumph of capitalism, and the demise of communism.

• How did the trade and currency system set up at Bretton Woods repair the harm done by the Great Depression and set the stage for postwar recovery?

hundreds of thousands of black recruits learned to read in the army and picked up valuable job skills they utilized after the war.

STUDY QUESTIONS FOR BATTLE FOR PRODUCTION

1. What policies and incentives boosted wartime military production?
2. How did U.S. military production help assure Allied victory?
3. How did organized labor cooperate with business during the war?

ON THE MOVE: WARTIME MOBILITY

The war dramatically affected where Americans lived and worked. Sixteen million soldiers, sailors, and marines were deployed throughout the country and around the world. In addition, 15 million civilians, or one in eight Americans, relocated between 1941 and 1945. They included Midwestern farm hands heading to factory jobs in

Detroit and Chicago, black sharecroppers going north for war work, Mexican nationals recruited back into the Southwest after a decade of expulsion, Mexican Americans leaving the rural Southwest for cities like Los Angeles, women shifting from unpaid domestic work to paid employment, and 100,000 Japanese Americans, forcibly relocated from the West Coast to desert internment camps.

The warm, coastal states of the South, Southwest, and West Coast, later called the Sunbelt, grew rapidly during the 1940s. As one contemporary put it, "it was as if someone had tilted the country" so that "people, money, and soldiers all spilled west." The federal government invested $2 billion in developing western infrastructure such as roads and water projects and spent at least $30 billion purchasing products from the region. Two million war workers moved to California alone between 1942 and 1945, and the state grew 72 percent by the end of the decade.

Wartime Women

During the war, the number of women working for wages increased from 12 to about 19 million. Previously, women worked mostly in service jobs segregated along gender and racial lines. These included restaurant and secretarial work, domestic employment, and jobs in textile mills. In 1941 half of the women who worked were single. Only 15 percent of married women worked outside the home.

Wartime labor shortages changed public policy and attitudes toward women in the work force. The Office of War Information (OWI) released radio plays, films, and posters that encouraged women to join the industrial work force. Before the war 80 percent of the public told pollsters they disapproved of wives working outside the home. By 1942, 80 percent said they approved.

Even in many defense plants women continued to be assigned to gender-segregated tasks, to receive lower wages than men for similar work, and often to go without critical support services, such as day care for their children. Business and political leaders frequently disparaged complaints by women and urged them to think of factory work as a temporary status. They should keep their focus on the home and prepare to resume their lives as homemakers and mothers when the war ended.

After 1945 the number of women in industrial jobs, falling precipitously, returned to prewar levels. This drop resulted from the return of men to the workplace and ongoing gender discrimination, as well as rapidly rising marriage and pregnancy rates among American women. In fact, the so-called postwar "baby boom" actually began in 1944 and continued for the next 20 years.

Mexican Migrants, Mexican Americans, and American Indians in Wartime

Wartime labor shortages prompted federal officials to reverse the policy of expelling Mexican nationals. With so many Anglos entering the armed services or taking industrial jobs, farm managers in the Southwest had too few workers to harvest crops. In 1942, to redress this, the federal government signed a labor agreement with the Mexican government. Under the so-called **Bracero Program**, Spanish slang for "strong

The Bracero program recruited several million Mexican agricultural laborers to work on U.S. farms between the 1940s and 1960s.

arm," and formally known as the Emergency Farm Labor Program, U.S. authorities actively recruited Mexican farm and railroad workers.

By 1945 about 300,000 Braceros had entered the United States; they worked first in the Southwest and then throughout the country. The program, which continued until 1964, in total recruited an estimated four million Mexican laborers. Despite promises of fair treatment and payment of 30 cents per hour, some Braceros earned as little as 35 cents per day and many lived in terrible housing. On balance, however, the agreement provided a new measure of protection to migrant labor.

The two million or more Mexican Americans living mostly in the Southwest faced other strains during wartime. Schools, housing, and employment were often segregated. Social tensions flared in cities such as Los Angeles and Chicago, which experienced a rapid influx of Southern whites, blacks, and Mexican Americans. Some Mexican American youth gangs dressed in flamboyant clothes called zoot suits. Police and white servicemen frequently harassed them, sometimes cruising barrios in search of zoot suiters whom they attacked and humiliated by stripping off their clothes.

Racial violence exploded in Los Angeles in June 1943, when hundreds of marines and sailors on leave joined local police in attacking Latino youths as well as blacks and Filipinos. Military police had to restore order. When Eleanor Roosevelt attributed the riot to pervasive discrimination against Mexican Americans, the *Los Angeles Times* denounced her for promoting racial discord.

In spite of these difficulties, the war years also brought some important advances for Mexican Americans. Because they were classified by the army as "white," the half million or so Mexican Americans in uniform were not assigned to segregated units. Military service provided many young Mexican Americans with a sense of power and personal worth as well as new skills. Like white and black soldiers, they also benefited from the postwar GI Bill. After the war, many of these Latino veterans joined groups such as the League of United Latin American Citizens (LULAC) and the American GI Forum, both of which mounted campaigns against discrimination in the Southwest.

When the war began, most American Indians lived on reservations created in the late 19th century. Entering the military were about 25,000 Indians, including some 400 Navajo code talkers who participated in some of the bloodiest battles in the Pacific. These specially trained soldiers and marines provided vital assistance to their comrades by communicating battlefield information over the radio in the Navajo language. Many Indians who served in uniform continued their education or started businesses with benefits from the GI Bill passed in 1944. Rather than entering the military, an even larger number of Indians left the reservations for factory and service jobs in cities such as Los Angeles, Phoenix, Denver, and Chicago.

African Americans in Wartime

The war years held both new promises and old challenges for the nation's 12 million African Americans. In 1941, three-fourths of all African Americans still lived in the South under conditions of rigid segregation. Only one-fourth graduated high school while a third of the black population still worked as sharecroppers or tenant farmers. State laws and intimidation kept most people of color from voting.

On the threshold of war some black leaders envisioned military service and defense work as ways to break the stranglehold of poverty. In late 1940, **A. Philip Randolph**, head of the Brotherhood of Sleeping Car Porters, a union composed of mostly black railroad workers, met President Roosevelt and pressed him, without success, to desegregate the armed forces. A few months later, African American leaders complained to federal officials that even as war production expanded, skilled factory jobs were reserved for whites. Randolph made plans for a "march on Washington" to bring 100,000 African Americans to the capital on July 1, 1941.

On June 25, 1941, a week before the march, Roosevelt issued Executive Order 8802 that barred racial discrimination in defense industries or government employment, although it did not end segregation in the military. The president created a Fair Employment Practices Commission (FEPC) to investigate complaints and take remedial action. Over the next four years, the number of blacks working in defense plants nearly tripled, from 3 percent to 8 percent, totaling 600,000. The number of blacks in the federal civil service tripled, to 200,000. Nearly three-quarters of a million African Americans responded to these new employment opportunities by leaving the rural South for northern destinations such as Chicago, New York, and Detroit. Reflecting the surge in employment and the more tolerant politics of the North, membership in the NAACP grew ten-fold, to 500,000, during the war.

Most black political and social organizations supported the war but they also championed what they called a double victory, or Double V, campaign against fascism abroad and racism in America. As NAACP leader **Walter White** remarked during a fact-finding trip to the Pacific, African Americans soldiers knew the "real fight for democracy will begin when they reach San Francisco on their way home."

Black migration north and west sometimes provoked urban violence. For example, Detroit in 1942 and 1943, New York's Harlem in 1943, and Mobile, Alabama, in that same year experienced race riots. A fight among blacks and whites in a park sparked the 1943 Detroit violence. In Harlem the shooting of a black soldier by a white policeman led to rioting. Federal troops were required to stop the violence in Detroit. In all of these incidents a combination of the rapid expansion of black population from internal migration, blacks seeking homes in formerly all-white neighborhoods, and the opening of factory work previously reserved for whites sparked racial resentment.

Japanese American Internment

Japanese Americans were singled out for official persecution during wartime. Not only was Japan an enemy nation that inflicted a humiliating defeat at Pearl Harbor, but the United States had a decades-long legacy of anti-Asian agitation, especially in the West. The mere presence of ethnic Japanese aroused hysteria. The intensity of these feelings showed in popular songs during the war whose lyrics declared, "I'm gonna find me a fella who is yella and beat him Red, White, and Blue!"

Hawaii had the largest concentration of Japanese Americans, about 200,000, almost a fourth of the territory's population. They comprised such a vital part of the local economy that, aside from arresting a few ethnic Japanese who supported Tokyo's policies, authorities left the rest alone.

The 120,000 ethnic Japanese living on the West Coast were treated more harshly. Japan's rapid military victories in the Pacific inflamed public opinion and fueled exaggerated fear of an attack on California. For example, the organizers of the Rose Bowl football classic shifted the January 1942 game from Pasadena to North Carolina as a precaution against air attack.

Prominent journalists and public officials called for placing all ethnic Japanese "under guard." Representative Leland Ford of California insisted that Japanese Americans prove their loyalty by "submitting themselves to a concentration camp." General John DeWitt, head of the Western Defense Command, declared in a logic-defying statement that the total absence of sabotage on the West Coast constituted proof of a conspiracy among ethnic Japanese.

Bowing to pressure, on February 19, 1942, President Roosevelt issued Executive Order 9066, giving federal authorities power to exclude anyone it chose, whether ethnic Japanese or not or citizen or alien, from designated "military areas" within the United States. This became the legal basis for interning older Japanese, known as issei

Japanese families in California assembling for transport to relocation camps in desert locations early in 1942.

and who were barred from citizenship, and their American-born, citizen children, called nissei. Technically, the exclusion order also applied to the 800,000 German and Italian nationals living in the United States. Except for a few pro-fascist activists, however, they were generally left alone.

In May 1942, the new War Relocation Authority ordered 112,000 Japanese living along the West Coast to leave in a matter of days. Japanese Americans had to report to "assembly centers" such as the Santa Anna Race Track for transport to "relocation centers." One camp was located in Arkansas, and nine others in the arid West in places like Manzanar, California, and Gila Bend, Arizona. Nearly all Japanese complied, even though most had to abandon homes, farms, businesses, and personal property. Several U.S. allies, including Canada and Peru, also interned Japanese, placing some of them in American camps.

The relocation centers isolated and confined but did not kill the inhabitants. Nevertheless, the internees lived under armed guard, behind barbed wire, in crowded conditions, and with no legal recourse—since the Supreme Court declined to rule on the issue until 1944. In a ruling that year in a case brought against **Fred Korematsu**, the high court upheld the policy of forced relocation. Korematsu, a native-born citizen of Japanese ancestry, refused to leave a designated war zone on the West Coast. The Korematsu decision affirmed the government's right to exclude anyone it chose from designated areas on the basis of military necessity. Six of the nine justices denied that race was a factor because the government could, if it wished, exclude any group in addition to ethnic Japanese. In a powerful dissent, Justice **Frank Murphy** condemned the majority's reasoning as a "legalization of racism" based on prejudice and unproven fears.

Despite harsh treatment, about 35,000 Japanese Americans volunteered for military duty. Some served as translators and interpreters in the Pacific. Many fought in all-Japanese army units in Europe, such as the 442 Regimental Combat Team, achieving recognition for their bravery. By 1943 all Japanese young men were required to register for the draft. Those few who refused, either because they were pacifists or as a protest against internment, were convicted of draft evasion.

In mid-1944, with the Pacific war turning in its favor, the American government permitted about 25,000 internees to leave the camps on the condition that they move or attend college east of the Rockies. Shortly before Japan's surrender in the summer of 1945 all internees were allowed to return home. A few found that friends had protected their homes or businesses, but most lost the work and possessions of a lifetime. In 1948, acknowledging that "mistakes had been made," Congress offered token payments to wartime internees. A genuine apology and larger payment to survivors came only in 1988. By then the Justice Department had opened records showing that wartime officials knew that Japanese Americans posed no threat but claimed otherwise.

STUDY QUESTIONS FOR ON THE MOVE: WARTIME MOBILITY

1. What role did women play in the new wartime economy?
2. How did the war affect the lives of African Americans and Hispanics?
3. Why were Japanese Americans singled out for punishment?

WARTIME POLITICS AND POSTWAR ISSUES

In spite of events like Japanese internment, the United States remained a democracy during wartime. Politicians, journalists, religious groups, and ordinary citizens debated and voted on issues ranging from the conduct of the war to the future role of government in the economy. In a surprising wartime ruling in the case of *Barnette v. West Virginia*, the Supreme Court overturned state laws that compelled students to salute the flag as an unconstitutional limit on free speech. On some international issues, such as creating the United Nations Organization and the Bretton Woods system, Americans embraced the role of world leader. On others, such as helping victims of the Holocaust, the country shirked responsibility.

Right Turn

In November 1942, 22 million fewer people voted than had in the presidential race of 1940. The low turnout—caused partly by the influx of men into the military and millions of workers relocating—proved disastrous for the Democrats. Republicans gained 7 Senate seats (for a total of 43 out of 96), and 47 House seats (giving them 208 to the Democrats 222). Nearly half the remaining Democrats came from the party's conservative southern wing. Congress soon eliminated several New Deal agencies and rebuffed efforts by liberals to simplify voting by soldiers.

As the war progressed, fewer committed New Dealers remained in the president's inner circle. Those who did included Vice President Henry Wallace, Interior Secretary

Harold Ickes, advisor Harry Hopkins, and First Lady Eleanor Roosevelt. None worked harder than Eleanor Roosevelt to carry the torch for liberalism. The first lady visited American soldiers stationed around the world, toured defense plants and community centers, and spoke forcefully of the need to continue New Deal reforms.

Although constrained by the power of Congressional conservatism, President Roosevelt remained committed to expanding liberty and security for all Americans. On January 11, 1944, he broadcast his State of the Union speech that called for enacting a "**Second Bill of Rights** . . . an economic bill of rights" that would guarantee every citizen a job, a living wage, decent housing, adequate medical care, educational opportunity, and protection against unemployment in postwar America. Yet, except for a veterans' aid program, Congress balked.

In the summer of 1944 a coalition of liberal Democrats and conservative Republicans passed the Serviceman's Readjustment Act of 1944, or GI Bill of Rights. Initially conceived as a simple pension program, the GI Bill morphed into the last major piece of New Deal legislation. Under pressure from both veteran's groups and social liberals, Congress agreed to provide returning servicemen unemployment benefits, medical coverage, home mortgage guarantees, small business loans, hiring preferences for government jobs, and extremely generous education benefits. Since the law covered 16 million veterans and, indirectly, their spouses and families, it became after 1945 the biggest, longest running, and perhaps most successful New Deal social program.

Many soldiers shared the experience of Jack Short of Poughkeepsie, New York. Just 20 years old when his army unit landed in France in June 1944, he and his "band of brothers" fought their way into the heart of Nazi Germany. Short's unit liberated the Nordhausen concentration camp where they found the bodies of thousands of dead prisoners "stacked up like cordwood." In spite of this painful memory, Short felt the war transformed his life for the better. For generations his family had labored in factories, and none went beyond high school. But after the war ended Short used his GI Bill benefits. "It paid for 99 percent of your college expenses and gave you money to live on," he recalled. In 1950 Jack Short graduated from college and found a well-paying job in an innovative company, IBM.

The 1944 Election and the Threshold of Victory

Roosevelt won renomination for an extraordinary fourth term in 1944 but to do so had to appease conservative Democrats who disliked the liberal vice president, Henry Wallace. Roosevelt agreed to replace Wallace, whom he named as secretary of commerce, with Missouri senator Harry S. Truman. A political moderate, Truman had gained a measure of fame by investigating profiteering by military contractors.

Republicans nominated a moderate of their own for the presidency, New York Governor Thomas E. Dewey. He attacked the Democrats as "soft on communism" and beholden to labor unions, but endorsed many New Deal programs as well as Roosevelt's plans for the postwar world. In November 1944, with the war news from Europe and the Pacific mostly positive, Roosevelt won reelection, but by a much reduced margin. He received 25.6 million votes to Dewey's 22 million, and 432 electoral votes to Dewey's 94. Democrats picked up 20 House seats and retained their 56 to 38 majority in the Senate.

Allied Mistrust and Postwar Planning

In spite of overall wartime strategic cooperation, many points of tension had surfaced. For example, Stalin saw the delayed opening of the Second Front in Europe as proof that Roosevelt and Churchill hoped to see the Soviets weakened by prolonging the war on the Eastern Front. Many British and American officials worried that as the Red Army pursued the retreating Wehrmacht, Stalin would annex Polish and other territory and set up pro-Soviet states in Eastern Europe. Stalin had told Roosevelt and Churchill he intended to transfer some Polish territory to Soviet control, and they objected that this action would violate the principal of no territorial gains. They also worried that this would bring Soviet power closer to Western Europe. At the same time Roosevelt acknowledged that the Soviet Union had a legitimate interest in creating a security buffer in Eastern Europe, the route of two devastating German invasions since 1914.

The sad truth was that Stalin saw an independent Poland as a future threat to Soviet security and his regional control. This partly explained Stalin's decision in 1940 to have Soviet security troops massacre around 20,000 captured Polish officers and intellectuals, who were shot in the Katyn forest and elsewhere. In August and September 1944, when Polish resistance fighters in Warsaw rose up against the retreating Germans, Stalin ordered his armies to halt their offensive and thus allowed the Germans to kill 15,000 armed Poles along with 200,000 civilians who might have formed a counterweight to Soviet influence in liberated Poland.

Even Roosevelt and Churchill, the closest of allies, bitterly disagreed over the future of colonialism. The president argued that the native peoples in British, French, Dutch, and Belgian colonies that straddled Asia, the Middle East, and Africa would all demand freedom in coming decades. The Europeans would be wise to place their colonies on the path toward independence—as the United States had done with the Philippines. This action would assure future cooperation with former colonies and, Roosevelt predicted, undermine the appeal of revolutionary nationalism. Churchill fumed at the president's advice and balked at surrendering control of colonies as small as Hong Kong or as large as India.

Roosevelt recognized the likely difficulties of postwar cooperation, but he considered it vital to maintain good relations with his wartime allies. He also worked to build bipartisan support for internationalism. In the midst of the war, for example, Roosevelt designated his 1940 rival, Wendell Willkie, as his personal emissary on a global mission. Willkie, who recounted his travels in the best selling 1943 book *One World*, described how good relations with Britain, the Soviet Union, China, and the Middle East were vital to American security.

At several wartime summit conferences—starting with his meeting with Churchill in 1941 and continuing with gatherings at Casablanca, Cairo, Tehran, Quebec, and Yalta—Roosevelt stressed wartime cooperation as a prelude to postwar unity. He also outlined plans for what became the **United Nations Organization** (UN). Open to all nations, the UN would be dominated by what Roosevelt sometimes called the four policemen or sheriffs—the United States, the Soviet Union, Great Britain, and China—who would comprise the permanent membership of the UN Security Council. He expected each of the "great powers" to be predominant in its regional security zone, such as the United States in the Western Hemisphere. But all would cooperate to promote world trade, supervise decolonization, and rehabilitate Germany, Japan, and Italy as democratic societies. The UN was chartered at a conference of 50 nations in San Francisco in April 1945, shortly after Roosevelt's death.

All the Allies looked after their own interests even as they pursued the common goal of defeating the Axis. The British, French, and Dutch reclaimed their African, Middle Eastern, and Asian colonies as German and Japanese forces retreated. As Soviet forces pushed the Wehrmacht toward Berlin in 1944–1945, Stalin brutally imposed pro-Soviet regimes in most of Eastern Europe. Roosevelt continued to hope that at war's end America's predominant economic and military power would persuade or pressure the Allies into cooperating. As long as Germany fought on and Japan remained in the war, Roosevelt refused to risk a break with Stalin over the fate of Eastern Europe.

In February 1945, Roosevelt, Churchill, and Stalin met together at Yalta, a Soviet city on the Black Sea, to plan the final stage of the war and its aftermath. Stalin agreed to join the UN and to fight Japan soon after Germany's defeat. In return, the Soviets were promised reparations from Germany, special economic privileges in northeast China known as Manchuria, and a good deal of political control over Poland, Bulgaria, and Rumania. Critics soon labeled the Yalta accords a sellout by Roosevelt, who was too ill or naïve to resist Stalin. Roosevelt's health was failing and he perhaps trusted Stalin more than he should have. But ultimately Roosevelt's position counted

TIMELINE 1929–1945

1929

October U.S. Stock Market Crash sparks global depression

1931

September Japan Invades Manchuria

1932

November Roosevelt Elected

1933

January Adolf Hitler becomes German Chancellor

March Japan quits League of Nations

March Roosevelt inaugurated

September Germany quits League of Nations

1935

March German troops occupy Rhineland

August Congress pass first of several Neutrality Acts

October Italy Invades Ethiopia

1936

July Spanish Civil War begins

November–December Germany and Italy create "Axis" alliance and Germany and Japan sign Anti-Comintern Pact

1937

July Japan invades China

1938

March Germany annexes Austria

September Munich Agreement sacrifices Czechoslovakia

December United States begins economic aid to China

1939

May German-Italian alliance

August Nazi-Soviet Non-Aggression Pact signed

August Albert Einstein's warning to FDR about German atomic research spurs creation of U.S. atomic program

September Germany invades Poland; war in Europe begins; U.S. arms sales to British and French put on "cash and carry basis"

1940

May German Blitzkrieg in Western Europe

June France surrenders to Germany

Summer 1940 Start of yearlong Battle of Britain

September United States begins peacetime draft

September Germany-Japan-Italy sign Tripartite Pact (Axis Alliance)

September United States transfers warships to British Navy

November Roosevelt reelected to third term

1941

January FDR delivers "Four Freedoms Speech" and proposes Lend-Lease aid program

for little. Soviet forces already controlled or soon would control most of Eastern Europe; thus, they had a free hand to set up puppet regimes. Furthermore, misgivings about Stalin's intentions were outweighed by the insistence of nearly all American military planners that Roosevelt make whatever concessions were needed to guarantee Soviet military help in the final stages of defeating Germany and what looked to be a prolonged struggle to subdue Japan.

The wisdom of continuing to cooperate with the Soviet Union seemed confirmed by the immense human costs in the final stages of the war. During April and May 1945, the Soviet offensive that ultimately captured Berlin in the face of fierce resistance cost the Red Army hundreds of thousands of additional dead and injured soldiers. When Hitler killed himself inside his underground bunker at the end of April and when the remnants of the Nazi regime surrendered on May 8, most Americans saw the victory in Europe as a triumph of Allied cooperation.

Japanese troops and suicide pilots had inflicted heavy casualties on marines and soldiers who captured the islands of Iwo Jima and Okinawa during the first half of 1945. Japan's military leadership seemed determined to fight to the bitter end and had prepared the civilian population to join the army in resisting an Allied invasion set to begin near the end of 1945. Although casualty estimates were uncertain, no one doubted that large numbers of Americans as well Japanese would perish in the final battles. The American air campaign had already destroyed most of urban Japan and killed over a half-million civilians. The naval blockade threatened to starve a large portion of Japan's 70 million residents unless the war ended quickly.

American strategists were prepared to invade Japan, but they hoped that some other means to compel its surrender could be found. In the summer of 1945 two alternatives to an invasion seemed possible. Stalin had promised to join the war against

---

March Lend-Lease passed by Congress

June Germany invades Soviet Union

July United States embargoes oil sales to Japan

August Atlantic Charter issued by Roosevelt and Churchill

September–December Undeclared U.S.–German naval war in Atlantic

December Japan attacks Pearl Harbor

December Germany and Italy declare war on United States

1942

January United States and Allies issue Declaration

of United Nations and form Grand Alliance

April Internment of Japanese Americans; Doolittle raid on Japan

June U.S. Naval victory at Midway

November U.S. forces invade North Africa

1943

January Casablanca Conference

February German surrender at Stalingrad

May German and Italian troops surrender in North Africa

September Italy surrenders

November–December Conferences in Cairo and Tehran

1944

June D-Day landings in France

June GI Bill of Rights passed

July Bretton Woods Economic Conference

November Roosevelt reelected to fourth term

December Battle of the Bulge

1945

February Yalta Conference

February Battle of Iwo Jima begins

March Tokyo firebombed; battle for Okinawa begins

April Roosevelt dies, Harry Truman becomes president

April Hitler commits suicide

May Germany surrenders

June United Nations Charter signed

August Japan surrenders after atomic bombing and Soviet entry into war

Japan three months after Germany's defeat, around mid-August. This support would dash Japan's hope that the Soviet Union might mediate something short of an unconditional surrender. A Soviet attack would also result in the death or capture of several million Japanese troops now isolated in Manchuria and other parts of China. Japanese leaders also realized that if the Soviets entered the war, Stalin would demand an occupation zone like that in eastern Germany. Any or all these factors, American strategists hoped, might convince Japan to surrender.

If not, the United States had additional leverage. In mid-July 1945, at the same time as American, British, and Soviet leaders were meeting in the Berlin suburb of Potsdam to haggle over the future of Germany and Eastern Europe, scientists in New Mexico successfully detonated an atomic bomb. If used to destroy one or two Japanese cities, military planners believed, this new weapon might shock the Japanese into surrendering and thus make both Soviet help and an invasion unnecessary. The first two atomic bombs were transported to the island of Tinian in the Pacific early in August where specially trained B-29 bombing crews readied the weapons for use. As described in the next chapter, the bombs struck Japan on August 6 and 9, and the Soviet Union declared war on Japan on August 8. A week later, Japan surrendered.

The "Big Three" at the Yalta Summit Conference in February 1945. Prime Minister Winston Churchill, President Franklin D. Roosevelt, Premier Josef Stalin.

Four months earlier, on April 12, 1945, on the cusp of victory in Europe, while sitting for a portrait at his beloved retreat in Warm Springs, Georgia, the president died of a cerebral hemorrhage. His passing left a void in American life. Poet Carl Lamson captured the nation's sense of loss:

> I never saw him—
> But I knew him. Can you have forgotten
> How with his voice, he came into our house,
> The President of the United States,
> Calling us friends.

STUDY QUESTIONS FOR WARTIME POLITICS AND POSTWAR ISSUES

1. What conservative political trends emerged in American politics during the war?
2. What issues created mistrust between the United States and the Soviet Union as the war ended?
3. What was the importance of the GI Bill of Rights?

Summary

- The Great Depression destabilized the world and prompted German, Italian, and Japanese aggression.
- Disillusionment with the results of World War I convinced many Americans that the nation should avoid foreign conflict, whatever the cost.
- After Japan's attack on Pearl Harbor, the United States organized a global alliance to defeat the Axis powers and, Roosevelt hoped, to secure postwar peace.
- During 1943 the Soviet Red Army blunted and turned back the German armies, while U.S. Naval victories in the Pacific put Japan on the defensive.
- Tens of millions or more civilians died as a result of Nazi extermination policies in Eastern Europe, while Japanese troops inflicted horrible crimes on Chinese civilians.
- Wartime mobilization included raising a vast military and retooling the economy to produce weapons. American factories turned out remarkable numbers of ships, planes, tanks, rifles, etc., which went to U.S. and Allied troops.
- War production vanquished unemployment and brought broad prosperity to American workers, including large numbers of women and minorities who entered the industrial work force.
- Although business and conservative political interests regained influence, policies and programs adopted during the war years also enshrined New Deal values in American life.
- On the cusp of victory in the spring and summer of 1945, U.S. and Soviet leaders became increasingly suspicious of each other's postwar intentions.

Key Terms and People

Atlantic Charter *932*

Battle of the Bulge *940*

Bracero Program *950*

Bretton Woods agreements *948*

Byrnes, James F. *945*

Chamberlain, Neville *929*

Churchill, Winston *928*

Doolittle, James H. *937*

Eisenhower, Dwight D. *940*

Gandhi, Mohandas *936*

Ho Chi Minh *936*

Jiang Jieshi (Chiang Kai-shek) *939*

King, Ernest J. *935*

Knox, Frank *931*

Korematsu, Fred *954*

Luce, Henry *925*

MacArthur, Douglas *937*

Manhattan Project *945*

Mao Zedong *936*

Marshall, George C. *935*

Murrow, Edward R. *930*

Murphy, Frank *954*

Mussolini, Benito *921*

Nimitz, Chester *937*

Oppenheimer, J. Robert *945*

Randolph, A. Philip *952*

Second Bill of Rights *956*

Stalin, Josef *924*

Stimson, Henry L. *931*

Tojo Hideki *932*

United Nations Organization (UN) *957*

White, Walter *953*

Willkie, Wendell *931*

Yamamoto Isoroku *933*

Reviewing Chapter 24

1. During the 1930s, why did most Americans oppose foreign military intervention?
2. After the outbreak of war in Europe in 1939, how and why did Roosevelt aid the British?
3. Why did the U.S. emphasize the war against Germany rather than Japan?
4. What strains existed among the Allies during the war?
5. How did Roosevelt see the Grand Alliance as a basis for postwar cooperation?
6. How did defense spending transform the American economy?

Further Reading

Adams, Michael. *The Best War Ever: America and World War II.* Baltimore: Johns Hopkins University Press, 1994. The author demythologizes the war and highlights the many contradictions between American ideals, memory, and the realities of conflict.

Dallek, Robert. *Franklin D. Roosevelt and American Foreign Policy, 1932–1945.* New York: Oxford University Press, 1979. A comprehensive study of the diplomacy that led up to the outbreak of war and the ways in which Roosevelt tried to shape the postwar agenda.

Dower, John. *War Without Mercy: Race and Power in the Pacific War.* New York: Pantheon, 1993. The author shows that the ferocity of fighting in the Pacific reflected the racial hostility between Japan and the United States.

Overy, Richard. *Why the Allies Won.* London: Jonathan Cape, 1995. An incisive analysis of the material and political factors that assured an Allied victory over the Axis powers.

Roberts, Andrew. *The Storm of War: A New History of the Second World War.* New York: Harper Collins, 2011. A highly readable narrative history of the global conflict that examines both military and political elements.

Sherwin, Martin, *A World Destroyed: The Atomic Bomb and the Grand Alliance.* New York: Knopf, 1975. A fast-paced history of how the atomic bomb affected wartime strategy and postwar relations.

Snyder, Timothy, *Bloodlands: Eastern Europe Between Hitler and Stalin.* New York: Basic Books, 2010. A harrowing account of the vast scale of ethnic slaughter that occurred in the run-up to and during World War II.

Visual Review

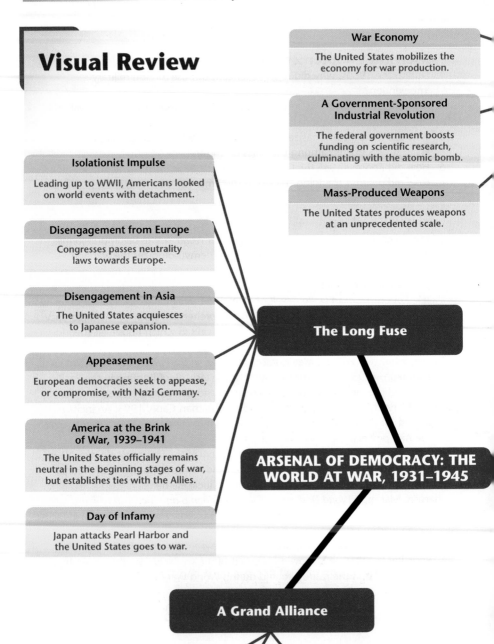

War Economy

The United States mobilizes the economy for war production.

A Government-Sponsored Industrial Revolution

The federal government boosts funding on scientific research, culminating with the atomic bomb.

Mass-Produced Weapons

The United States produces weapons at an unprecedented scale.

Isolationist Impulse

Leading up to WWII, Americans looked on world events with detachment.

Disengagement from Europe

Congresses passes neutrality laws towards Europe.

Disengagement in Asia

The United States acquiesces to Japanese expansion.

Appeasement

European democracies seek to appease, or compromise, with Nazi Germany.

America at the Brink of War, 1939–1941

The United States officially remains neutral in the beginning stages of war, but establishes ties with the Allies.

Day of Infamy

Japan attacks Pearl Harbor and the United States goes to war.

The Long Fuse

ARSENAL OF DEMOCRACY: THE WORLD AT WAR, 1931–1945

A Grand Alliance

War in the Pacific

Despite early Japanese victories in the Pacific, the Allies turn the tide and near victory.

The War in Europe

The Allies march toward victory over Germany.

The Holocaust

The Allies do little to stop Nazi genocide.

Battle for Production

Organized Labor and the War

Union leaders cooperate with management to boost production.

The Draft

Large numbers of American males are drafted into war.

On the Move: Wartime Mobility

Wartime Women

Labor shortages require women to join the labor force.

Mexican Migrants, Mexican Americans, and American Indians in Wartime

Mexican Americans and American Indians join the labor force.

African Americans in Wartime

African Americans make strides in U.S. society although they still face great challenges.

Japanese American Internment

Americans of Japanese descent are forced into detention camps.

Wartime Politics and Postwar Issues

Right Turn

Election results in 1942 and 1944 slow down New Deal initiatives.

The 1944 Election and the Threshold of Victory

Franklin D. Roosevelt is reelected for an unprecedented fourth term.

Allied Mistrust and Postwar Planning

The Allies disagree on postwar global policies.

Prosperity and Liberty Under the Shadow of the Bomb

1945–1952

O n the night of July 15, 1945, a group of 90 international scientists quietly boarded buses and headed out of the high desert town of Los Alamos, New Mexico, where they had spent the past two years working in total secrecy on the first atomic bomb. The men represented one of the greatest collections of scientific minds ever gathered in one place. They were "America's Athenian world," a melting pot of refugees from fascism and genocide.

The group included experts from many scientific areas, but all were pioneers in the new field of atomic physics. Many were Jews who had escaped Hitler's Europe in 1938 just as the last exits were closing, or refugees from fascist regimes in Italy and Hungary. Among the travelers that night were Nobel Prize winners such as Italy's Enrico Fermi, Denmark's Niels Bohr, and his son Aage Bohr. Nearly every seat held a genius like Hungarian Edward Teller or Austrian Jon von Neumann, a man that **Robert Oppenheimer**, the head of the **Manhattan Project**, called the "brightest person he ever met." Most of the scientists shared some doubts about the goal of the trip to the remote New Mexico desert. They knew that if their experiment, dubbed "Trinity," worked, they would change the course of history, and not all were sure it would be for the better.

The buses deposited the scientists 20 miles away from the test detonation point in a remote and desolate valley on the ancient Spanish *Camino Real,* locally known by the name explorer Oñate gave it in 1598, *Jornado del Muerto* (Journey

Thermonuclear detonation, Pacific Proving Grounds, 1967

CHAPTER OUTLINE

THE COLD WAR
> The Roots of Conflict
> Managing Postwar Europe in Potsdam
> The Defeat of Japan
> Dividing the Postwar Globe
> A Policy for Containment

THE RED SCARE
> War in Korea
> Domestic Containment
> The Color of Difference Is Red
> Hollywood and the Pumpkin Papers

A NEW AFFLUENCE
> The Fair Deal
> The GI Bill
> Working Women

POSTWAR MIGRATIONS
> Military-Industrial West and South
> Hispanics Move North
> Mobile Leisure

continued on page 971

America in the World

Truman created the National Security Council, Department of Defense, and Central Intelligence Agency to strengthen U.S. intelligence and defense (1947).

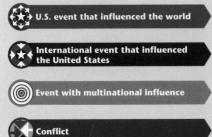

U.S. event that influenced the world

International event that influenced the United States

Event with multinational influence

Conflict

North Atlantic Treaty Organization formed a protective alliance of North American and European nations (1948).

The Korean War was a proxy war between Cold War foes (1950).

The Potsdam Conference established the postwar order and role of the Allies in defeated Axis nations (1945).

Hiroshima and Nagasaki were the first targets of the atomic bomb, leading to Japan's defeat and a deadly postwar buildup of nuclear weapons (1945).

POPULATION

Africa

Asia

Europe

Latin America and the Caribbean

North America

Oceania

World Population c. 1950
U.S. Population 1940: 131,669,275
U.S. Population 1950: 150,697,361

0
200,000,000
400,000,000
600,000,000
800,000,000
1,000,000,000
1,200,000,000
1,400,000,000
1,600,000,000
1,800,000,000

of Death). Crews constructed the atomic bomb in a commandeered ranch-house kitchen. In the predawn hours of the following day, Monday, July 16, 1945, observers received pieces of dark welder's glass to cover their eyes and sunscreen to protect their faces.

At 5:29 AM, exactly as planned, a flash 10 times brighter than the sun lit up the night of three states. An eerie multicolored plasma ball formed within a millionth of a second before launching a 38,000-foot cloud of radioactive debris into the atmosphere. At "ground zero" where the bomb had sat seconds before, a half-mile wide crater was covered by a sheet of grey-green glass called "trinitite"—formed when the heat of the blast melted the desert sands. Far above New Mexico radioactive isotopes floated into the atmosphere where they rained down on an area the size of Australia, showing up months later in straw grown in Maryland and in milk from cows outside of Chicago. Oppenheimer recalled the event by citing Hindu scripture: "Now I am become death, destroyer of worlds."

THE COLD WAR

Just one month later, on August 6, 1945, the use of the atomic bomb on Hiroshima and three days later on Nagasaki ended the brutal Pacific war. The first bomb, named "Little Boy," was carried to the Hiroshima by the B-29 Superfortress *Enola Gay*. The unescorted bomber flew alone over Japan to the target and obliterated an entire city with just the push of one button. Few events in modern history have generated as much controversy as the decision to use the atomic bomb on human targets.

Harry S. Truman, the man who made the decision to use those first two atomic weapons, was still a mystery to most Americans when he became president after the sudden death of Franklin Roosevelt, on April 12, 1945. Truman inherited the moral responsibility for the atomic bomb, the job of ending WWII, the management of a faltering alliance with the Soviet Union, and the drafting of American foreign and domestic policy in the dawning postwar world.

Thrust into power overnight, Truman faced some of the most vexing troubles of any 20th-century president. In an early press conference in which he asked the nation for their prayers, he said that he felt "as if the sun, moon, and the stars" had fallen on him. In the first weeks of his administration, with the war in Europe reaching its end, one of Truman's concerns was the growing rift between the United States and its wartime ally, the communist Soviet Union. In the coming months tensions grew in the global turmoil following the end of World War II. Strained relations led to a **Cold War** that defined domestic culture and U.S. relations with the world in the second half of the 20th century. Truman's decisions during the months and years following World War II spurred three generations of global competition with the Soviets and enormous consequences for peoples on every continent. How did wartime alliances so quickly dissolve into Cold War tensions?

CHAPTER OUTLINE

continued from page 967

LAYING THE FOUNDATIONS FOR CIVIL RIGHTS
> First Steps
> Jack Roosevelt Robinson
> The Influence of African American Veterans
> Black Migration and the Nationalization of Race

The Roots of Conflict

In April 1945 British and American troops closed in on Berlin from the West, while the Soviets slugged their way toward the city in the face of dogged resistance from the East. Hours after assuming the presidency, Truman learned that Stalin was pushing his troops to capture the city ahead of the Americans. With big shoes to fill on the world stage, Truman worked to understand the complicated relationship with the Soviets. FDR had left the Yalta Conference convinced that his hard won alliance with Stalin would help ensure that the Soviets live up to their agreements in Eastern Europe. In his first months in office Truman shared his predecessor's optimism. In his diaries he described Stalin as "honest" and "smart as hell."

Briefings with Roosevelt's top military advisers tempered Truman's optimism and raised his distrust of Stalin and the Soviets. They now cautioned Truman to avoid appeasing Stalin as he gained control of Eastern Europe. Truman sent top diplomat **W. Averell Harriman** to Moscow. Harriman's dispatches decried Stalin's "barbarian invasion of Europe." He warned the Soviets that Truman would not stand for communist expansion. Forced to formulate a foreign policy strategy in less than a week, Truman latched on to the strong anticommunist position of Harriman. The growing rivalry between the members of the Grand Alliance heated up as the final battle of the war in Europe took shape around Berlin.

By April 1945 the German army was reduced to young boys and old men and Berlin was in ruins. Still, the fight for the city remained brutal to the end. When the Soviets reached the city first, they symbolically hosted their red flag on the roof of the ruined Reichstag while Hitler lay dead of a self-inflicted gunshot in his underground bunker.

Mapping Postwar Europe in Potsdam

Germany formally surrendered on May 8, 1945. Even as the German guns finally fell silent, it was clear that the peace would be complicated and contested. While citizens and soldiers rejoiced, political and military leaders remained deeply concerned by news of deteriorating relations with Stalin. The Soviets occupied Berlin and controlled a vast territory stretching from the Black Sea in Romania to Poland's Baltic shores. They also controlled a large swath of eastern Germany past Berlin and up the Elbe River. The Allies had agreed at Yalta to partition Germany into occupation zones, but no formal mechanism existed for cooperation between the Soviets, the United States, and Great Britain. Tensions grew when the Soviets annexed a huge swath of eastern Poland, confirming the Poles' worst fears.

In Washington, only 11 days after taking office, Truman faced off with Soviet foreign minister **Vyachslav Molotov** and accused the Soviets of breaking their agreement to give Poland independence. Stalin responded by firmly maintaining they were only establishing a "security zone" in Poland and that Soviet interests in Eastern Europe were more important than good relations with America's new president.

The leaders of the Alliance met for the last time in Potsdam, a suburb of Berlin. On July 15 Truman and Secretary of State **James F. Byrnes** arrived at Potsdam without a clear understanding of the extent of Stalin's expansionist ambitions and with the war in Japan entering a pivotal moment. Still hoping for Soviet assistance in subduing the millions of Japanese troops on the Asian mainland, Truman tempered his position on Poland and agreed to the Soviet's occupation of eastern Europe.

The debate about Poland symbolized the brewing ideological Cold War to come. Two years earlier, at a critical meeting of the Alliance at Teheran, Iran, Roosevelt and

The utter devastation of Warsaw was one of the starkest monuments of WWII and harbinger of emerging Cold War tensions in the waning months of the war.

Churchill had secretly agreed to Stalin's demand that the allies accept Soviet control of Eastern Poland. Unaware of this agreement, Polish resistance leaders organized a massive uprising against the Germans in Warsaw with the assumption that the nearby Red Army would join the fight. In one of the bloodiest events of the war, German troops, crushing the uprising, slaughtered a quarter-million civilians, reducing Warsaw to ruins. The Soviets stayed away and allowed Warsaw to fall. Months later Truman agreed to let the Soviets formally redraw the map of Poland—a crushing blow to the Poles. From the perspective of Central Europe the battle lines of the coming Cold War were clear. The ideological battle between the emerging superpowers would be fought on other people's territory with profound and lasting consequences for those nations.

At Potsdam, Poland was only one piece of a global strategic puzzle. During this meeting, on July 16, 1945, Truman received coded word from New Mexico of the successful Trinity explosion. The news, he confided to advisers, was "a great load off my mind." Truman knew the atomic bomb would change the situation in the Pacific and mentioned the news of a "new weapon of great power" to Stalin. Stalin simply nodded, having known of the Manhattan Project through an elaborate espionage operation linking New Mexico to Moscow.

The Defeat of Japan

With some confidence about the stability of Europe, Truman prepared for the final assault on Japan. Fire bombings of Tokyo in March of 1945 killed more than 100,000 civilians while desperate fighting at Iwo Jima and Okinawa left tens of thousands of U.S. casualties. Truman had to choose between a full-scale invasion of the Japanese mainland with military estimates of death tolls in the millions or to use the atom bombs.

U.S. leaders feared the cost of a full-scale invasion of Japan, since the militarists in Tokyo seemed unwilling to surrender on any terms acceptable to the Allies. At Yalta and Potsdam, Stalin agreed to attack Japanese forces in Northeast Asia three months after Germany surrendered. Most of Japan's army was stationed on the Asian mainland. Although Soviet military help would greatly reduce America's burden and casualties, Truman feared that if the Red Army joined the war against Japan it would support communist forces in China. Given this potential problem, Truman chose to use the atomic bomb: its use could shock Japanese hardliners into surrender, avoid U.S. casualties, and end the war before the Soviets could move into Japan. Furthermore, the use of the bombs would provide a graphic example of U.S. power in the Soviet's backyard.

Dividing the Postwar Globe

The United States emerged from the cataclysmic war stronger and wealthier than before. Between 1940 and 1945, while U.S. enemies and allies alike endured massive physical and financial destruction, the U.S. gross national product (GDP) increased by over 170 percent. Aside from the attack on Pearl Harbor and a few Japanese incendiary bombs carried by balloon over the Pacific Northwest, the U.S. homeland

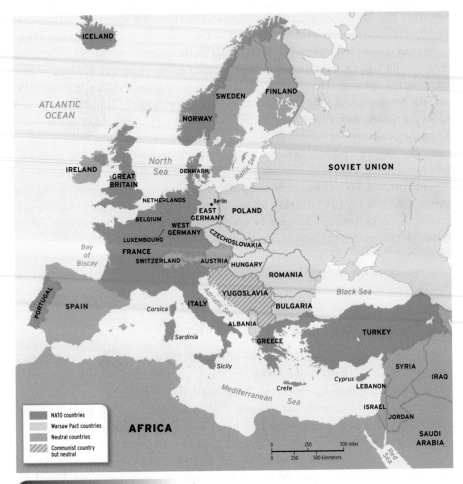

▲ Map 25.1

Dividing Postwar Europe This map shows the division of Europe into spheres of influence in the early years of the Cold War. By 1950 countries across a wide swath of the globe were divided by color on maps according to their relationship with NATO allies and Warsaw Pact signers. The developing world and neutral nations were shaded according to their importance to Cold War strategies on both sides.

remained unscathed. Its industrial complex had dramatically expanded, its navy and air force were unmatched, and its president and military leaders had sole possession of the atomic bomb. Meanwhile, the Soviet Union was devastated with entire cities leveled and an estimated 28 million citizens dead.

The war irreparably altered the colonial empires of European nations and enabled the rise of revolutionary nationalism in Asia, Africa, the Middle East, and Latin America. All over the world, in countries like India and French Indochina (soon to be known as Vietnam), crumbling colonial control fueled nationalist desires and demands for independence, modernization, and higher quality of life. Even before the war ended, boundaries shifted as diverse peoples searched for ideologies and leadership to enable a new phase of their history. U.S. policy makers pejoratively labeled these mostly nonwhite developing nations and contested regions the "Third World" in contrast to the presumed civility and superiority of the "First" and "Second" nations. The assumed lack of sophistication, cultural development, and national cohesiveness in former colonies prejudiced critical Cold War decision making in the coming years, often with disastrous results.

At the end of the war America had a clear military and economic advantage over the Soviets. To succeed in the growing Cold War, however, Truman needed another resource: an appealing ideology to counter communist promises that had gained popularity among those disillusioned by the democratic capitalist model. Many people in former colonies of Western powers viewed the capitalism of their colonizers as the cause of depression, war, and

What the atomic bomb can do to ships, or water, or land, and thereby to human beings, is told with clear implications for all of us by a brilliant young doctor whose job it was to watch for radioactive contamination during and after the Bikini tests.

David Bradley's best-seller *No Place to Hide* (1948) alerted the public about the coming atomic age. Having witnessed the first atomic tests after the war, radiation expert Bradley understood how difficult it would be to control the power of the atom.

fascism. In the coming decades the selling of American culture and ideology became an important weapon in the Cold War. Spreading American ideals through international marketing of everything from jeans and cars to music and movies provided the "soft power" behind hard-edged Cold War foreign policy.

There were very real reasons to fear the expansion of communism. By 1947 alarming statistics about the growing popularity of communism across Europe raised concerns that the Soviets would have the balance of power handed to them by nations reeling from the aftermath of war. Between 1935 and 1945, communist party membership increased from 17,000 to 70,000 in Greece, from 28,000 to 750,000 in Czechoslovakia, and from 5,000 to 1,700,000 in Italy. Much of this rapid growth stemmed from the key anti-Nazi role played by local communists during the war rather than from admiration for Stalin's policies. Still, there seemed to be evidence that communism was a powerful force in the postcolonial world.

A Policy for Containment

In 1946 Truman needed a clear policy to respond to both real and perceived changes in the global balance of power in the nuclear age. Inspiration for a critical foreign policy plan came from Soviet expert **George F. Kennan**. In 1946 he sent his analysis of the postwar Soviet Union from his post in Moscow to Washington in a widely circulated 8,000-word "Long Telegram." In July 1947 Kennan published an even longer version of his pessimistic assessment of the Soviets in the influential journal *Foreign Affairs*. Kennan argued that Soviet communism was "impervious to the logic of reason," inherently expansionist, and only controllable through "long-term, patient but firm and vigilant containment." Kennan's idea, **containment**, became the foundation of U.S. foreign policy for the next four decades.

Although Kennan's assessment was alarming, he assured policy makers that the Soviets did not want war. Instead, they hoped that economic desperation in Western Europe and Japan would drive these key regions into the Soviet camp. Kennan believed that if U.S. reconstruction programs stabilized Western Europe, Japan, and the Middle East and Third World, the Soviets would be contained and ultimately destroyed without actual war.

Faced with the need to garner support for massive funding efforts to fight communists across the globe, Truman stepped up his anticommunist rhetoric in a stark March 12, 1947, speech to Congress. Truman told Congress and the American people that "it must be the policy of the United States to support free peoples who are resisting attempted subjugation by armed minorities or by outside pressures." This bold new commitment to fight "communist tyranny" wherever it might appear became known as the Truman Doctrine.

Michigan Republican Senator Arthur Vandenberg advised Truman to "scare hell out of the American people," so they would understand the seriousness of the threat and thus win support from a GOP-led Congress. In several speeches Truman painted a dramatic picture of a world communist conspiracy that could only be contained through aggressive force. These warnings secured $400 million from Congress to fight communism in Greece and elsewhere while creating a high level of anxiety about communism in America. These fears fed a growing Red scare that challenged basic principles of democracy and individual liberty in the United States in the years to come.

At home the acceptance of the Truman Doctrine required a reorganization of the government in preparation for a protracted Cold War against communism. With the creation of the Department of Defense, the **National Security Act of 1947** consolidated the U.S. military command; a representative from each military branch would now advise a newly created secretary of defense and the president through the Joint Chiefs of Staff office. The Act also created a National Security Council to advise the president and the Central Intelligence Agency (CIA) to gather intelligence about hostile, mostly communist, activities throughout the world. After Truman's election in 1948, he appointed a new secretary of state, **Dean Acheson**, a strong supporter of a formal multinational alliance against the Soviet bloc.

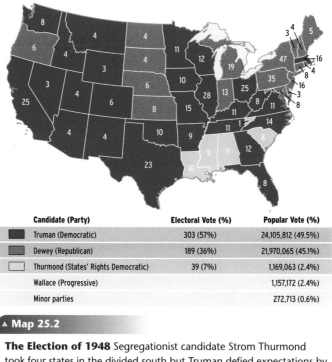

Candidate (Party)	Electoral Vote (%)	Popular Vote (%)
Truman (Democratic)	303 (57%)	24,105,812 (49.5%)
Dewey (Republican)	189 (36%)	21,970,065 (45.1%)
Thurmond (States' Rights Democratic)	39 (7%)	1,169,063 (2.4%)
Wallace (Progressive)		1,157,172 (2.4%)
Minor parties		272,713 (0.6%)

▲ **Map 25.2**

The Election of 1948 Segregationist candidate Strom Thurmond took four states in the divided south but Truman defied expectations by carrying the day with what remained of the Roosevelt coalition.

Working closely with European allies Acheson achieved his goal with the founding of the North Atlantic Treaty Organization (NATO). All of these foreign policy mechanisms demonstrated the military and diplomatic might of the United States. Of even greater lasting importance was the soft power side of the Truman Doctrine, the Marshall Plan to rebuild Germany and Japan as models of democracy and capitalism.

STUDY QUESTIONS FOR THE COLD WAR

1. What does the Warsaw Uprising tell us about the early Cold War?
2. In what ways did the policy of containment address U.S. fears of Soviet influence?

THE RED SCARE

At home, containment spawned a Red scare. Fear of communism led to restrictions of individual rights and the systematic persecution of diverse groups of American citizens. The decision to fight communism at all costs raised the crucial question:

Under what conditions are the sacrifice of civil liberties justified in a democratic society?

A series of disturbing events between 1948 and 1950 accomplished Harry Truman's goal to "scare the hell" out of the American public. First, the Soviets caused an international crisis when they blockaded Berlin in hopes of gaining control of the divided city and thwarting U.S. efforts to rebuild a powerful West Germany. Between June 1948 and May 1949, the Soviets, locking down all roads leading to the city, forced the first showdown of the Cold War. The United States responded with the most remarkable air supply effort in history. For almost a year U.S. transport planes carried food and coal into the city 24 hours a day. As they flew low over the city, U.S. pilots—earning the nickname "The Candy-Bombers"—took special pleasure in showering the children of Berlin with candy. The **Berlin Airlift** won the hearts of Berliners and humiliated the Soviets, who reopened the city on May 11, 1949. By then the United States had realized its goal of unifying the western zones of Germany into a pro-Western state in opposition to the Soviet controlled eastern zones. Policy makers had only a few months to enjoy the success in Berlin as the shocking news arrived on August 29, 1949, that the Soviets had successfully tested an atomic bomb. The Soviet's ability to catch up with American technology so rapidly revealed what U.S. leaders had suspected, that communist spies had successfully infiltrated the Manhattan Project. America's monopoly on atomic power was over.

In October 1949, only one month after the stunning news about the Soviet atomic bomb, China fell to the communists under the leadership of **Mao Zedong**. The formation of the communist People's Republic of China especially disheartened Americans because of their longstanding charitable and missionary aid to the nation and significant diplomatic efforts by General **George Marshall** to ensure that China would remain free. Marshall had spent most of 1946 in China arranging a coalition between the Chinese nationalists, led by **Chiang Kai-shek**, and his communist rivals, led by Mao. Despite Marshall's efforts, the coalition faltered. Chiang's incompetence contrasted with the Communists' rising popularity and superior organization. Full-scale civil war broke out in 1947 and by 1949 Mao led a unified China that allied itself with the Soviet Union. In the stridently anticommunist environment of Cold War America, the fall of any "third world" nation into the hands of communism became ammunition for domestic political rivalries. Republicans quickly blamed Truman for the "loss of China."

Americans worried that the new alliance between Stalin and Mao threatened to spread communism more widely in Asia. All of these events in 1949 raised U.S. fears and seemed to confirm the basic premise of the Truman Doctrine that communist revolutionaries threatened freedom around the globe. Any doubts about a world communist conspiracy faded with the news of a communist North Korean invasion of South Korea on June 25, 1950.

War in Korea

The North Korean attack turned the Cold War hot. In a limited "proxy" or "brush fire" war, distant rivals served as substitutes for the United States and Soviets, who stood behind or beside them. In Korea this stance was put to the test.

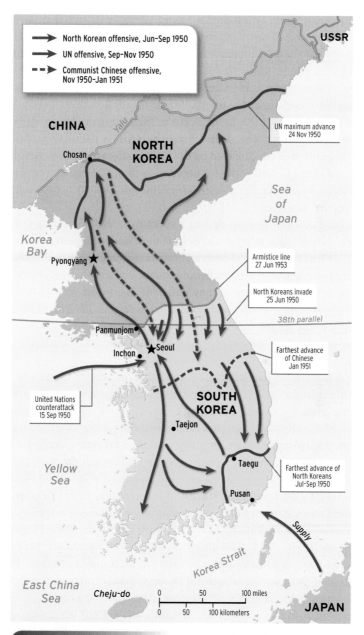

Map legend:
- North Korean offensive, Jun–Sep 1950
- UN offensive, Sep–Nov 1950
- Communist Chinese offensive, Nov 1950–Jan 1951

USSR

CHINA

NORTH KOREA

Chosan

Yalu

UN maximum advance 24 Nov 1950

Sea of Japan

Korea Bay

Pyongyang

Armistice line 27 Jun 1953

North Koreans invade 25 Jun 1950

38th parallel

Panmunjom

Inchon

Seoul

Farthest advance of Chinese Jan 1951

United Nations counterattack 15 Sep 1950

SOUTH KOREA

Taejon

Yellow Sea

Taegu

Farthest advance of North Koreans Jul–Sep 1950

Pusan

Supply

East China Sea

Cheju-do

Korea Strait

JAPAN

0   50   100 miles
0   50   100 kilometers

▲ Map 25.3

The Deceptive Complexity of Proxy War This map of the Korean conflict looks simple, but the war was vexingly complicated on every front. Maps like this appeared on the front pages of newspapers throughout WWII offering the public a means to gauge progress. The back and forth struggle in Korea, changing cast of key players, and ultimate stalemate indicated that the Cold War would be harder to map than previous conflicts.

At the close of World War II the Soviets and Americans agreed to the temporary North–South division of Korea, a Japanese colony since the early 20th century. The United States and the USSR agreed to divide Korea into occupation zones at the 38th parallel. Northern Korea had strategic importance for the Soviets, who considered the peninsula key to blocking future Japanese influence in the region and a counterweight to continued U.S. occupation of Japan. Between 1945 and 1950 the Soviets sponsored the creation in the north of the Democratic People's Republic of Korea under **Kim Il-sung**. The United States backed a separate government in the south, the Republic of Korea, headed by the conservative nationalist **Syngman Rhee**, who had lived in the United States for decades. Both of these new states experienced political insecurity and violence, with an estimated 100,000 people killed during constant internal struggles.

The rivalry between the North and the South intensified throughout the late 1940s. Both shared much in common despite their opposing political views. Repressive autocratic leaders controlled both sections of divided Korea, and both were willing to use violence against their own people and expend massive resources on military resources to prevent unification on any terms but their own. In a precedent-setting decision, the U.S. Joint Chiefs of Staff concluded as early as 1947 that Korea had little strategic value to the United States, but abandoning the unstable South Korean regime would almost certainly lead to war between the U.S.-supported South and the Soviet-supported North.

By 1950 U.S. leaders had growing concerns that communist China would join the fight as well. Under the logic of containment, this potential spread of communism was unacceptable, even if it meant supporting South Korea—a repressive malfunctioning government in a country known to few Americans with no significant strategic value.

On June 25, 1950, the Soviet-supplied North Korean army launched a large-scale invasion across the 38th parallel. The well-organized assault drove quickly through South Korea and into the capital city of Seoul, forcing the U.S.-backed government to flee. Stunned by the remarkable success of the invasion, Truman worried that this major communist incursion into a "free" state might allow communists in Asia to "swallow up one piece after another." Two days after the invasion the **United Nations Security Council**, with the Soviets absent so they could not veto the move, met and voted to authorize a U.S.-led coalition of forces to push the communists back across the 38th parallel. Truman named General **Douglas MacArthur**, Chief of the American occupation force in Japan, as U.S./UN theater commander in Korea.

From its onset the Korean War tested not only U.S. Cold War foreign policy but also the ability of the United Nations to create coalitions of supporters willing to fight for collective rather than national goals. During the conflict, 17 UN member nations from four continents sent troops to Korea, but U.S. troops far outnumbered all other nations combined. By the end of the war the United States sent over 500,000 troops; the British sent approximately 65,000 and other nations contributed as few as 400.

After North Korean forces pushed coalition troops to a small foothold in South Korea, MacArthur staged a dramatic counterattack at Inchon on the northwestern coast of South Korea on September 15, 1950. Pushing rapidly across the peninsula and liberated Seoul, U.S. and UN troops drove hundreds of thousands of North Korean troops north and won back the south in one sustained assault.

This surprisingly easy victory inspired both Truman and MacArthur to expand the war. Instead of simply restoring South Korea, the United States announced a new goal: destroying the North Korean regime and unifying the country under Syngman Rhee. In just a few weeks the coalition reached the Northern capital city of Pyongyang and seemed poised to retake the entire country. In the flush of apparent victory, both Truman and MacArthur ignored Chinese warnings that its forces would intervene to defend North Korea, especially if U.S. troops approached the Yalu River that separated Korea from China's industrial heartland in Manchuria. MacArthur's forceful personality convinced Truman that China was bluffing and that both the president and general would share in the glory of "rolling back" communism.

When a quarter million Chinese troops swarmed across the border and quickly pushed the United States all the way back to the 38th parallel, that assumption was dramatically proved wrong. With U.S. troops in retreat, MacArthur and Truman accused each other of incompetence and political posturing. In April, 1951, Truman fired MacArthur for insubordination. The 38th parallel was the focal point of three more years of protracted and bloody fighting with no decisive objective other than holding the line. The demilitarized zone (DMZ), or no-man's-land, splitting Korea at the 38th parallel, became a Cold War icon: a symbol of stalemate and a persistent reminder that proxy wars could lead to seemingly infinite conflict. Even before the Korean War, government and elected officials who believed that national security depended on a stronger military had ratcheted up anticommunist rhetoric to fan the flames of a long-simmering Red scare.

Domestic Containment

Fears of communism and Red scares were not new to the postwar era. During World War I, in the aftermath of the 1917 communist revolution in Russia, Americans worried about the global appeal of communism. Liberals and conservatives alike defined communism as the opposite of democracy and the economic collectivism of the new Soviet state as the antithesis of free market individualism. Political tensions in the 1930s energized American conservatives, who linked liberalism and communism and railed against the "creeping socialism" of New Deal social programs.

Systematic government efforts to enforce conformity in support of containment began before the end of World War II. Starting in 1944, the **House Committee on Un-American Activities** (HCUA) made the search for communists and conspiracies within the United States the centerpiece of a domestic containment. Between 1944 and 1946, the vehemently racist and anti-Semitic **John Rankin**, a Democratic Congressman from Mississippi, used the committee as a forum to attack liberal causes under the guise of fighting communists. From his seat on HCUA, Rankin railed against Jews and linked the "mongeralization" of the races with anti-Christian communism. Rankin's ravings enhanced a link in American culture between perceived cultural, racial, or religious differences and communism.

The Color of Difference Is Red

When John Rankin connected racial, religious, and cultural differences with communism, he opened a Pandora's box. Virtually any advocacy or protest could be linked to communism and encourage a pernicious climate of mutual suspicion. Although many Americans rejected this notion outright, the fear of communism caused significant numbers to acquiesce and agree to dramatic restrictions of civil liberties.

In 1946, responding to fears of communist infiltration of the U.S. government, Truman issued Executive Order 9835, which launched a Federal Employee Loyalty Program that by 1950 investigated over five million workers. Government employees were subjected to intense questioning about their behavior and beliefs. Membership in a long list of broadly defined "subversive" groups was grounds for dismissal. Proving one's loyalty in the face of often unfounded accusation was often extremely difficult.

In 1940, Congress passed the Smith Act, which made advocating the overthrow of the U.S. government a federal offense. The Act was widely interpreted as a tool for arresting suspected fascists and communists. That year, 11 members of the American Communist Party were arrested for discussing the overthrow of the government; they were prosecuted and convicted under the new act despite the lack of evidence suggesting they were plotting any action. The U.S. Supreme Court upheld the constitutionality of the act in 1951 in *Dennis v. United States*. The ruling demonstrated that there was consensus, across all three branches of the federal government, that communism was inherently subversive and that communists lurked in the United States itself.

Hollywood and the Pumpkin Papers

Starting in 1944 Hollywood became the focal point of a series of dramatic HCUA hearings when actors, directors, and writers were subpoenaed to appear before Congress. Friendly witnesses, such as future president Ronald Reagan and screen writer Ayn Rand, identified individuals they thought might be associated with communist activities. Most witnesses were horrified to be called to Washington, and many argued for protection of free speech under the First Amendment or chose to exercise their Fifth Amendment right to remain silent rather than "rat out" their friends and colleagues. Those who refused to cooperate were convicted of contempt of Congress and sentenced to a year in federal prison.

HCUA gained even more attention in 1948 when it investigated *Time* editor **Whittaker Chambers**. Chambers claimed that he had been part of an elaborate Soviet spy ring funneling U.S. secrets to the Soviets throughout the 1930s. He confided this story to a young Congressman from California named **Richard M. Nixon**. In August 1948 Chambers provided dramatic testimony to HCUA and named **Alger Hiss**, the head of the Carnegie Endowment for International Peace and former State Department official, as a collaborator and communist spy. Hiss sued Chambers for libel and the case became a national sensation. Chambers responded with a remarkable tale of secrets passed by Hiss during the 1930s, copies of which Chambers kept in a hollowed-out pumpkin on his Maryland farm. The FBI determined that the "Pumpkin

Papers," as they were dubbed, contained a variety of records, including some decade-old State Department documents retyped on a typewriter owned by the Hiss family. The United States tried Hiss, but the jury was unable to agree on a verdict. Charged a second time with perjury for lying about knowing Chambers, Hiss was convicted and sentenced to prison.

STUDY QUESTIONS FOR THE RED SCARE

1. Why was the Korean War called a "proxy" war?
2. Why would Americans tolerate the actions of HCUA?

A NEW AFFLUENCE

Cold War anxieties seemed at odds with rising domestic prosperity in the aftermath of World War II as programs like the GI Bill and Truman's **Fair Deal** created avenues to middle-class status for many Americans. The Cold War fostered a period of unprecedented economic growth in global capitalism. Military spending on new technologies led to advances in domestic production and consumer goods. These twin engines of economic growth created an extended period of domestic prosperity and more widely spread affluence than at any other time in American history.

This new prosperity depended on the globalization of the international economy. U.S. Cold War policies fostered free trade and the free flow of goods and capital among friendly nations. American business took advantage of these trends. The creation of powerful new multinational corporations resulted in an unprecedented global exchange of technologies and institutional practices. Further, philanthropic and international organizations became enormously influential during this period. Powerful and wealthy Non-Governmental Organizations (NGOs) supported American foreign relations and fostered the growth of global capitalism. Those Americans who supported the agenda of the New Deal saw the postwar boom as an opportunity to expand the scope and reach of social welfare programs.

The Fair Deal

On September 6, 1945, President Truman sent Congress an ambitious 21-point domestic agenda. He worked to secure the domestic goals of his predecessor while establishing a domestic program distinctly his own. Truman faced strong resistance to his domestic program from the first Republican majority in Congress since the Hoover administration. Despite their differences on domestic policy, however, the national security imperatives inherent in The Truman Doctrine fostered a level of consensus and cooperation rarely seen in the U.S. Congress.

Undeterred, Truman pressed his domestic agenda through speeches to Congress and to the people through national radio addresses. By 1946 the outlines of his

Fair Deal began to emerge. Truman offered some bold and controversial expansions of the New Deal. The 21-point program called for an increase in the minimum wage, comprehensive housing legislation for returning veterans, full employment and expanded unemployment benefits, permanent federal farm subsidies, expanded public works projects, and expanded environmental conservation programs. Most controversially, Truman proposed a comprehensive federal health insurance program and restructuring of Social Security programs.

Some of Truman's proposals were hard to oppose. With the memories of the ecological catastrophe of the Great Plains Dust Bowl still fresh, Truman's recommendations on the environment resulted in expanded conservation programs, new funding for the National Parks, and water reclamation projects in the West and South. Likewise, the return home of millions of soldiers caused a crisis in both employment and housing so severe there were fears that the nation might descend back into depression. Congress responded with the Veterans Emergency Housing Act and a series of reforms aiding the transition of soldiers to citizens.

The GI Bill

As the war wound down, concern for returning soldiers came from every quarter. Memories of inadequate treatment for veterans of World War I still resonated. In 1944 Congress passed the Servicemen's Readjustment Act, or GI Bill, with the support of liberals who saw it as a much-needed social welfare program and conservatives who considered it a patriotic vote of thanks. This enlightened legislation produced dramatic changes in American society. The GI Bill expanded access to higher education, enabled home ownership for a much wider segment of society, and helped create a climate of success for returning veterans.

Operating as comprehensive welfare program, the GI Bill provided returning veterans temporary unemployment assistance; government backed, low-interest loans to start businesses or buy homes; hiring preferences for civil service jobs; and extensive health services. The bill provided tuition and living stipends to all universities, colleges, and vocational schools.

The billions of dollars Congress authorized to fund the umbrella of support programs jump-started millions of veterans toward a higher standard of life. The impact on American higher education was equally dramatic. In the years following the war, over two million men and 64,000 women veterans found open doors at public and private colleges and universities.

Greater access to higher education during the 1940s and 1950s provided American industry with the best-educated, white-collar work force in the world. Another six million men used the GI Bill for technical and vocational training, building an army of highly trained workers for expanding American industries.

The programs of the GI Bill guaranteed a higher quality of life for many veterans while highlighting social and racial disparities for others. Educational and housing opportunities for blacks in the South remained severely restricted by legal segregation and existed in the North in more subtle ways. The desire for equal opportunity in education played a large role in directing civil rights efforts after the war, as African American vets watched their former comrades at arms prosper while they faced the same grinding poverty and inequality they had since the 1870s. For women of all backgrounds, the return of the soldiers raised questions about their role in peacetime.

Working Women

For the soldiers who benefited from education and preferential hiring policies, advantages often came at the expense of their wives, sisters, and mothers. In the years following the war, women were expected to move from their wartime identity as heroic "Rosie the Riveters" back to traditional roles as wives at home. Lower-income and minority women were forced back to the lower paying, limiting jobs they had held before the war. Many women resisted this trend, but employers, with support from the government, required most to leave lucrative jobs and abandon hard-earned skills.

During the war the percentage of married women and mothers entering the workforce had increased from 13.9 percent to 22.5 percent and 7.8 percent to 12.1 percent, respectively. Wartime polls showed that between 60 percent and 80 percent of these

This example of Soviet social realism captures the communist celebration of women workers. Compare this idealized view of working women with the following image of changing representations of U.S. working women.

women wanted to keep their jobs when the war ended. When the war ended, however, women workers faced pressure from a new wave of government propaganda encouraging them to hand their jobs back to men.

The systematic removal of women from the industrial workforce was more than a practical response to the return of male veterans; it became a Cold War imperative. Government Cold War propaganda stressed that American women could best fight the communist ideological menace by being homemakers. Comparisons between women's work in the Soviet Union and women's work in the United States became important points of differentiation for the two systems. The Soviets celebrated women workers as symbols of socialist equality. American politicians pointed to Soviet women workers as an example of the backward communist system that required all to slave away in service of the state. Images of well-dressed American housewives surrounded by new appliances became standard U.S. propaganda tools.

Globally, the United States and the USSR fought for the "hearts and minds" of Developing world women through competing organizations. The U.N.-supported International Council of Women (ICW) advocated for democracy and freedom for women and children. The Soviet-backed Women's International Democratic Federation (WIDF) supported nationalism and colonial independence and the fight against fascism and racial discrimination around the globe. In the international arena, the WIDF's pro-nationalist message had great appeal, while the ICW could point to the rising standard of living for women in America and U.S.-occupied Germany and Japan as evidence of the benefits of capitalism.

This image from the *New York Times Magazine*, June 1946, accompanied an article titled, "What's Become of Rosie the Riveter?" Unlike their Soviet counterparts, U.S. women were expected to leave the workforce after their exceptional wartime efforts. Government officials and industry leaders worked to convince American women that they could best support democracy and capitalism as mothers, housewives, and consumers.

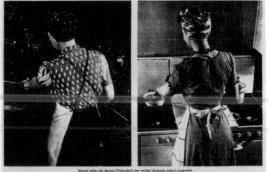

Sisters under the apron—Yesterday's war worker becomes today's housewife.

What's Become of Rosie the Riveter?

By FRIEDA S. MILLER,
Director, Women's Bureau, United States Department of Labor

STUDY QUESTIONS FOR A NEW AFFLUENCE

1. How did the GI Bill benefit the United States in the transition from World War II to Cold War?
2. Was the GI Bill an expansion of the social programs of the New Deal? Why or why not?

POSTWAR MIGRATIONS

In the searing heat of August anywhere in the South or Southwest temperatures reach dangerous levels. For centuries weather limited the design and scope of cities and settlements in these hottest regions of the nation. Following World War II the availability of millions of cheap window unit air conditioners enabled places like scorching Phoenix, Arizona, to attract businesses and people. Retirees and winter-weary migrants moved in record numbers from the North and the Midwest to the Sunbelt. Migrant workers moving north from Latin America through the United States ensured a supply of cheap labor. Libertarian-leaning western state governments allowed lax environmental standards, limited regulation, and low taxation for entrepreneurs and companies looking to build on the industrialization of the war.

Ongoing internal migrations of African Americans to the urban North played a major role in changing the demographic character of American cities and industries.

William Levitt became the Henry Ford of housing when he perfected mass production methods for suburban development. This image shows the best-known of the Levittowns, on Long Island, New York, May 14, 1954.

Renewed migrations of Mexicans north into the American Southwest built on long-established patterns but surpassed older trends in both numbers and reach. Across the country suburban growth fueled by these migrations and the GI Bill caused fundamental changes in American life. Finally, millions of Americans took to the road on seasonal migrations to National Parks, historic sites, and vacation spots. These leisure travelers elevated tourism to one of the most important sectors of the postwar economy.

The entire United States experienced significant demographic shifts during and after World War II, but the newly industrialized American West and South saw the greatest changes. Both regions benefited from the war mobilization that redistributed tens of millions of soldiers and support staff and billions of dollars to massive new military installations into these regions. In prewar 1939, the United States maintained a standing army of 200,000 men. By 1945 that number increased to 8,266,000 in the Army and 12,294,000 in the combined armed forces. This increase resulted in the most significant federally organized movement of people and resources in U.S. history. The U.S. Air Force (still part of the army during the war) alone required the construction of 500 new airfields and support facilities to build and service over 70,000 aircraft.

Military-Industrial West and South

Military leaders favored the South and West as locations for wartime mobilization for the regions' warm weather, clear skies, and wide-open spaces. Air bases were built in the desert Southwest where the climate was perfect for both training and storage, but the South got the lion's share of new air bases. Plentiful cheap labor and land combined with powerful southern politicians explain the clustering of air bases throughout the Southeast. The demographic and economic impact in areas surrounding military bases was immediate. Sleepy small towns such as Fayetteville in North Carolina and Killeen, Texas, saw their populations double or more in a matter of months from 50,000 to 100,000 in Fayetteville and 1,100 to almost 7,000 in Killeen.

Cold War imperatives ensured that the continued growth of the military industrial complex. Racial segregation ensured that white workers benefited from new federal opportunities in the South while black workers, including veterans, suffered from high rates of unemployment. White southern politicians used their new Cold War political influence to garner a large share of federal programs. At the same time, they maintained and even expanded the Jim Crow system to make sure that the South played by its own rules even as military and economic developments brought the region more closely into the fold of the nation.

For those working on America's new nuclear-industrial complex, the West afforded vast tracts of remote lands where large military bases could be hidden. Only one major atomic installation was built in the South, at Oak Ridge, Tennessee. The rest of America's atomic complex was scattered across the West in New Mexico, Washington, California, and Nevada. Los Alamos, New Mexico, hosted the international brain trust at the center of the Manhattan Project. White Sands, outside of Alamogordo, New Mexico, was used for the Trinity test. In Albuquerque a series of laboratories, eventually consolidated as Sandia National Labs, grew next to Kirtland Air Base. In

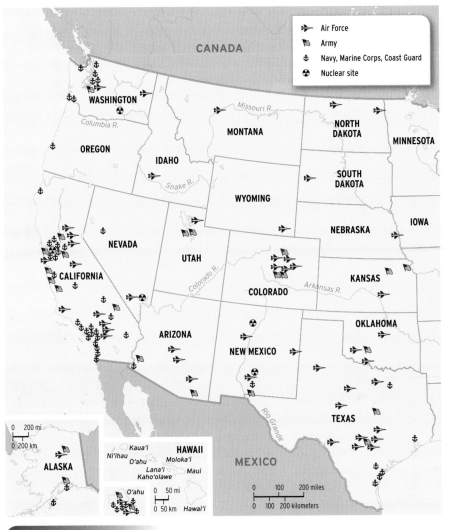

▲ **Map 25.4**

Modern Military West This map shows the extent of military development in the West during WWII and the Cold War. The West was transformed by the construction of the military industrial complex.

California both the California Institute of Technology and, starting in 1952, Lawrence Livermore National Laboratory became important centers of atomic research. Argonne, Brookhaven, and coalitions of eastern universities too came together in a system of national laboratories that formalized wartime relationships.

During World War II, Nellis Air Force base in Las Vegas, Nevada, used the largely unpopulated Mojave Desert as an extensive bombing range. The remoteness of the location, federal control of the lands under the Bureau of Land Management, and assumptions about the general worthlessness of desert lands made Nevada a logical choice for a continental nuclear testing facility. Starting in 1952, the Nevada Proving Ground, only 90 miles from Las Vegas, replaced remote Pacific Islands as the site where the United States perfected its nuclear arsenal. Dramatic nuclear tests became a regular feature of Las Vegas life, with mushroom clouds clearly visible from the city. On the other side of town, the Basic Magnesium facility employed 15,000 workers refining the "wonder metal" of modern aeronautics. Similarly extensive industrialization efforts like the Kaiser Ship Works in Long Beach, California, transformed the West from an extractive economy to a highly urbanized industrial powerhouse.

The military driven industrialization of the West dramatically expanded the political and cultural importance of the region. Between 1910 and 1950 migrations to the West led to significant congressional reapportionments resulting in a net gain of 28 new seats in Congress. California alone gained 19 new seats during this time. In the coming decades, California produced two presidents, completing the shift in the West from the frontier periphery to a vital center of American culture and politics.

Hispanics Move North

The ebb and flow of immigrants from Mexico and Latin America helped boost the health of the U.S. economy. During good times such as the 1920s Mexican immigration was loosely regulated and strongly encouraged by American industries that benefited from influxes of cheap labor. The crackdown on Mexican immigrants during the Depression years, however, resulted in a dramatic reduction of migration and a 60 percent decline in persons listing Mexico as their place of birth on the 1940 census.

World War II once again changed needs and attitudes. By 1942 U.S. war industries and the military absorbed a huge percentage of the workforce. Like African Americans and women of all backgrounds, Mexicans found closed doors suddenly open. Both in the military and wartime industry Mexican immigrants, like other U.S. minorities, saw an opportunity to prove their worth to a nation that had offered them only grudging respect during the best of times. A Mexican song of the war years, "*Soldado raso,*" captured the goal with lyrics proclaiming, "*les probaré que mi raza, sabe morir dondequiera*"—"I will prove my people know how to die anywhere."

In 1942 the United States and Mexico reached an agreement on a regulated worker immigration program to encourage Mexican workers to move north to jobs abandoned by the millions of American workers occupied by the war effort. The Emergency Farm Labor Supply or Bracero Program granted annual entry to hundreds of thousands of seasonal agricultural workers. Control of the border was generally loosened and hundreds of thousands of other Mexicans were lured north by growing opportunities in other areas of the greatly expanding U.S. economy. This shift in attitudes and policy led to a fourfold increase in the Mexican-born population of California alone and permanently transformed the demographic character of the Southwest.

Between 1940 and 1950 the U.S. Census recorded 450,000 Mexican-born resident aliens and 2.69 million Spanish-surnamed citizens. Census figures, however, never fully documented the extent of the flux of migration across the southern border

ALIEN LABORER'S IDENTIFICATION CARD

UNITED STATES DEPARTMENT OF JUSTICE
Immigration and Naturalization Service - I - 100D (12-7-55)

Identified only as "Mica from El Paso," this Bracero worker used his ID card to legally work in the southwest. During periods of economic prosperity political and industry leaders collaborated to facilitate mass migrations from Mexico and Latin America to meet labor demands. When labor markets tightened, these workers were no longer welcome.

and remain contested to this day. Many Bracero workers stayed beyond the season, moving throughout the West and in increasing numbers to the North to work in non-seasonal industrial jobs. Labor agents hired by American corporations operated ahead of or against official U.S. policy, pulling immigrants to the United States in large numbers unrepresented in census figures.

The return of millions of U.S. soldiers to civilian life once again drew attention to the Mexican migrant work force. Created in 1924, the U.S. Border Patrol facilitated the **Bracero Program** during the war. In the early 1950s, responding to concerns about the extent of illegal migration, the Patrol stepped up efforts to apprehend "wetbacks" (slang for illegal immigrants crossing into the United States over the Rio Grande River) and workers without proper documents. For Hispanic immigrants and their descendents, their indispensable work in wartime industry and their valiant service during the war were rewarded with widespread distrust and contempt.

As with all domestic issues during the period between 1945 and 1952, the Cold War affected immigration policies. Since the passage of the **National Origins Act of 1924**, strict quotas regulated the flow and character of U.S. immigration. In the aftermath of war, the need to admit displaced persons from Eastern Europe fleeing the aftermath of Nazi brutality or from the onset of Soviet control sparked debate about quotas. Truman argued for a less restrictive system able to cope with the global movement of peoples. In 1948 Congress passed a Displaced Persons Act that allowed about 100,000 (out of several million) refugees into the United States. There was also a gradual erosion of policies barring entry of Asian immigrants.

Organizations like the Daughters of the American Revolution, however, linked immigrants with the spread of communism and encouraged severe restrictions. Senator Pat McCarran of Nevada engineered such restrictions with his sponsorship of the Immigration and Naturalization Act that became law on December 24, 1952, over Truman's veto. The **McCarran Act** reinforced perceptions of immigrants as a source of radicalism during the Cold War and set the tone for a contentious debate about immigration in the coming decade. The new law retained all the worst features of the 1924 quota system and added new categories of "undesirables" barred from the United States.

Mobile Leisure

During World War II rationing severely restricted gasoline, rubber, metal, and all of the components needed for auto travel. Bald tires became a symbol of wartime sacrifice on the home front. As troops returned home to a revitalized economy, however, auto travel expanded drastically. (Chapter 26 will explore the huge impact of the Interstate Highway system launched by the Eisenhower administration.) Even before the dramatic expansion of the interstates, Americans took to the road in search of leisure, learning, and fun. For families who had endured almost two decades of hardship, the family vacation became the ultimate expression of freedom and affluence. Automakers rapidly retooled factories from military to domestic production and promoted ownership and travel. Along with the single-family home, car ownership marked a family's successful rise to the middle class, and personal mobility became a symbol of American freedom during the Cold War. Manufacturers promoted auto travel with catchy ad campaigns such as, "See the USA in your Chevrolet." Americans responded by purchasing cars in unprecedented numbers. Cold War patriotism inspired widespread interest in historic sites and boosted efforts to preserve America's heritage. The Gettysburg historic battlefield and other iconic historic sites sprouted "gateway" villages with miles of nearby motels catering to a new breed of "heritage tourist."

The GI Bill ensured that millions of Americans learned more about their history, and all forms of cultural resources benefited from an educated middle class with the time and the means to visits museums and cultural sites around the country. The rise of an outdoor industry provided new recreational opportunities while dramatically expanding the popularity of pursuits like hunting and fishing, skiing, and hiking. Starting in the late 1940s, newsstands from Manhattan to Los Angeles carried a wide array of magazines like *Field and Stream* and *Sports Outdoors* for the growing numbers of outdoor and "armchair" enthusiasts.

Businesses recognized the seemingly unlimited economic opportunities presented by an expanding middle class obsessed with travel and recreation. Companies like Ford capitalized on the popularity of outdoor recreation with advertising campaigns showing their vehicles loaded with camping gear and parked alongside a lake or in a mountain meadow. Cigarette companies eager to keep wartime smokers buying at home shifted from advertising that depicted dapper smokers in urban settings to ads showing rugged men and outdoorsy women enjoying a smoke around the campfire. Between the end of the war and the mid 1950s, wartime-boosted products and technologies moved into the general marketplace with far-reaching consequences for American culture and economy.

For those who could afford it, the vacation retreat to the slopes, the woods, or the beach provided a welcome distraction from Cold War anxiety. This relief was not shared equally. Carefully monitored visitor statistics in the National Parks showed that less than 1 percent of tourists were African American, and, even in the Southwest, the numbers for Hispanics were equally low. In the 1950s the world of recreational travel was almost exclusively white.

But after World War II many people of color were on the move in search of work, opportunity, and greater racial equality.

STUDY QUESTIONS FOR POSTWAR MIGRATIONS

1. What was the relationship between the Cold War and postwar immigration policies?
2. Why did the West and South gain importance after the war?

LAYING THE FOUNDATIONS FOR CIVIL RIGHTS

In the sweltering July heat of 1946, African American veteran George Dorsey, his wife Mae, brother-in-law Roger, and his wife Dorothy were tied to trees and executed by a mob in Monroe, Georgia. The bodies were dismembered by hundreds of bullets fired from the crowd. Dorsey was castrated. The lynching in Monroe was one of many across the South during that summer. Several of the most vicious murders were sparked by whites offended by the sight of a black man in uniform. Veteran status ensured that African American soldiers were heroes abroad, but those that returned to the South found their standing unchanged or worse. Veterans and minority workers who tasted freedom during the war and hoped for new access to freedom at home would energize the civil rights movement.

Between 1945 and 1952 African American civil rights advocates mounted challenges to racial discrimination and mobilized for a massive expansion of the movement in the coming decades. In the fight for equality, African Americans needed leadership, legal resources, strategic alliances with whites, and a unifying philosophy to propel their movement forward. Many of these core resources came together during and immediately after the war.

During the war the **National Association for the Advancement of Colored People** (NAACP) launched a widely publicized "Double V" campaign against the twin evils of fascism and racism; it was their hope that the racism of the Nazis would open American eyes to inequality at home. When Harry Truman became president, he brought an ambivalence about race not uncommon to politicians of his day. Despite personal uncertainties about racial equality, however, Truman made civil rights part of his domestic agenda at great political cost.

First Steps

In 1946 Truman established the President's Committee on Civil Rights and supported its controversial 1947 report, "To Secure These Rights." Truman's most significant civil rights achievement was the desegregation of the military. When leading Civil Rights leader and labor organizer **A. Philip Randolph** threatened to organize a boycott to protest segregation in the military, Truman responded quickly and courageously. On

July 26, 1948, Truman issued **Executive Order** 9981 declaring, "there shall be equality of treatment and opportunity for all persons in the armed services without regard to race, color, religion, or national origin." The military took almost six years to implement Truman's policy, but the desegregation of the military set a critical precedent; at least on paper, it erased one of the most glaringly contradictory policies of the leading nation of the "free world" during the Cold War.

At home and abroad American leaders reinforced the notion that the Cold War was a fight to protect the "free world." At the same time, during the 1940s and 1950s, the repressive and violent racism of the South and institutional racism throughout the nation contradicted U.S. foreign policy rhetoric. Conservative citizens' groups and politicians justified racism by equating civil rights with radical liberalism and communism. Despite these strident voices a slowly growing national consensus about the importance of civil rights in the fight against the world communist conspiracy emerged in the postwar years. For many white Americans pragmatic responses to racial inequality grew into genuine humanitarian concerns as they learned more about their fellow African American citizens from their war experiences and from the national media spotlight thrown on exceptional African American individuals.

Brooklyn Dodger Jackie Robinson poses in his batting stance, March 1953. Robinson's determined expression in this image reflected his grace under fire at the plate and as the spearhead of racial integration in Major League Baseball.

Jack Roosevelt Robinson

No one changed public opinion more significantly in the early postwar fight for civil rights than **Jack Roosevelt "Jackie" Robinson**. During his childhood Robinson's family moved from Georgia to southern California. A good student and gifted athlete, Robinson attended the University of California, Los Angeles, and starred in several sports. As an officer during World War II, Robinson refused to move to the back of a bus, and he gained notoriety by defending himself in a military Court Martial. Honorably discharged, Robinson resumed his athletic career. At the same time civil rights supporter and Brooklyn Dodgers owner Branch Rickey was looking for an opportunity to challenge segregation in professional baseball. In 1945 he offered Robinson a contract for the Dodgers' minor league team.

In April 1947, after an exemplary season, Rickey sent Robinson up to the major leagues. When Jackie Robinson walked on to the field wearing the Dodgers uniform, he took center stage in an early battle to win American hearts and minds in the battle against racism. In his first season he experienced constant racial slurs hurled from the stands, protests by opposing teams who threatened to boycott the Dodgers, and a steady stream of death threats. When the team traveled, Robinson, not allowed in segregated hotels, was forced to search for places to sleep on his own. Responding stoically, he played despite the controversy swirling around him, focusing on the game and demonstrating his remarkable talent and ability. His outstanding first season won him the National League Rookie of the Year award and legions of fans of all races who admired his excellence on the field and personal bravery in the face of racial hatred. Robinson scored two victories: one for baseball and another in the public relations campaign for civil rights.

Other black players soon followed Robinson into the major leagues. In the coming years African Americans used sports and entertainment to cross the color line and win the admiration of white fans who often became allies in the fight for equality.

The Influence of African American Veterans

America's critical role in World War II and Truman's strong assertion of American leadership in the postwar world ensured a much higher level of international scrutiny of American culture. The United Nations, headquartered in New York City, brought thousands of international diplomats and media representatives to the United States, where American life, warts and all, was plainly on view. Entrenched American racism, legal segregation in the South, and obscene levels of racial violence became international news.

The foreign policy implications of this new global attention were immediate and vexing. In an early 1946 exchange about Soviet denial of voting rights in Eastern Europe, a U.S. official faced quick questions from Soviet reporters about the complete denial of voting rights for blacks in the American South. Stumped, he was unable to respond. Over the next few years Soviet reporters and officials and representatives of Third World nations constantly questioned U.S. officials about racism. The inability of diplomats to respond to reasonable questions about American racial inequality was more than an embarrassment; it represented a serious threat to the very foundations of U.S. foreign policy during a vital period of global change.

Civil rights leaders were well aware of how the Cold War could aid their cause. The NAACP, growing dramatically during and after the war, increased its membership from 50,000 in 1940 to 450,000 by 1946. America's leading black intellectual, **W.E.B. Du Bois**, captured the NAACP philosophy at the dawn of the atomic age with his influential address to the United Nations, *An Appeal to the World* (1947). In *An Appeal*, Du Bois warned, "It is not Russia that threatens the United States so much as Mississippi." Du Bois's *Appeal* presented American racism and Cold War hypocrisy in rich detail and with eloquence and insight that could not be easily dismissed. His credentials as a long-time advocate of Pan-Africanism made his devastating critique all the more worrisome to U.S. officials concerned about nationalist movements in Africa and all the more welcome by Soviet propagandists. The harsh light of international

GLOBAL PASSAGES

Rebuilding the World

In June 1947 Truman's new Secretary of State, George C. Marshall, America's first five-star General and top ranking U.S. commander during WWII, gave a speech at Harvard University outlining what he called the **European Recovery Plan** (ERP). Popularly known as the **Marshall Plan**, this unprecedented proposal called for massive aid packages to help Western Europe—including West Germany—and Japan rapidly rebuild their devastated economies, restore industries and trade, and rejoin the free world. A military man willing to use force when needed, Marshall also understood the power of economics and believed that free markets created free people. The Marshall Plan dramatically expanded earlier efforts to use economic mechanisms like the International Monetary Fund (IMF) and the World Bank to stabilize the world capitalist economy that had malfunctioned so dramatically in the 1930s and had enabled the rise of totalitarian regimes in Germany, Italy, and Japan.

The United Nations was designed to provide for the type of global assistance Marshall proposed. But, under Marshall's plan, America stepped ahead of the UN and became the world's banker and policeman, a broker of strategic trade relations, and the CEO of the global capitalist economy. Like the occupations of Japan and Germany, the economic dependencies forged under the Marshall Plan and approved by the U.S. Congress in March 1948 had profound and lasting consequences for U.S. foreign policy and contributed to the rise of the postwar global economy. For example, the rebuilding of Western Europe required U.S. involvement in the development and protection of Middle Eastern oil reserves. However, although the reconstruction of Japan required U.S. involvement in Southeast Asia, former colonial

attention in the early years of the Cold War led to a series of judicial victories setting the stage for a major legal assault on segregation in the mid 1950s.

For African Americans the oppressive ironies of the Cold War South seemed unbearable. African Americans had served the United States with great distinction during World War II. They were treated as heroes in France and other liberated countries where, often for the first time in their lives, they were identified as Americans, not blacks. Southern African Americans fought for freedom during World War II knowing freedom at home only as an ideal never fully realized. Despite wartime civil rights efforts like the "Double V" campaign, veterans came home to a segregated Southern power structure more racist and conservative than when they left. Revelations of Nazi racism and the Holocaust drew global attention to the brutal realities of racial hatred in all its forms.

nations could supply natural resources to Japan and counterbalance growing communist economies in China and Korea.

Europe was the primary focus of the Marshall Plan as approved, but Japan also received massive aid and expertise to rebuild the country's industrial complex and promote strategic trade expansion. Japan remained occupied until April 1952. The rebuilding in Japan followed a different course, but one with the same goal, using economic redevelopment and open markets as a means of controlling the expansion of communism.

The aid to European countries was a strategic necessity but also a humanitarian imperative. With war-ravaged people starving and freezing to death because of diminished food and coal reserves in a Europe exacerbated by the worst winter in memory, it was easy to argue action was urgently necessary. The extent of the tragedy was well reported in the United States, as polls showed a majority of Americans supporting an extension of wartime food rationing to help the Europeans.

Fear of the appeal of communism to the desperate and destitute drove rebuilding efforts and justified the unprecedented expense. Marshall's brilliant plan never mentioned these political concerns and even offered assistance to the Soviets and their satellites. By presenting a positive economic solution in a time of urgent need, Marshall deftly took the moral high ground and left the Soviets no retort in the public relations arena of the Cold War. Over the next three years the United States appropriated over $15 billion in aid to Europe and Japan, an unprecedented transfer of wealth that aided one of the most remarkable economic recoveries in history. As a result, Germany and Japan became the two key bastions of American power during the Cold War. Further, America's liberal occupation policies created very positive images of Americans throughout the world. Marshall won the Nobel Prize in 1953 for his humanitarian efforts. The Marshall Plan crushed the hopes of Stalin to keep Germany and Japan weak and at the same time demonstrated the enormous economic might and global reach of the United States.

In the American South, however, black veterans discovered that civil rights activists were branded as subversives in the southern media, linked with communism, hounded by FBI and other federal officials, and even murdered by fellow Americans.

Stories of black veterans beaten, gunned down, or lynched after simply attempting to register to vote became international news. Veterans like Medgar and Charles Evers, who spoke out about the absurdity and moral perversion of racism in a country fighting for global freedom, faced coercion and violence from all levels of Southern authorities and the resurgent Ku Klux Klan. Medgar Evers repeatedly tried to register to vote only to be chased by a violent mob threatening death. But he refused to give in. Stories like these disturbed a growing number of white Americans while providing powerful ammunition to the Soviets and anti-American forces around the world.

Mrs. Medgar Evers with her children at Medgar Evers's grave in Arlington National cemetery, June 1964. Evers's murder at the hands of southern racists highlighted the violence and injustice of the segregated South.

Black Migration and the Nationalization of Race

The treatment of African Americans during World War II and the early Cold War demonstrated to the world the nature and extent of American racism. Within the United States a migration of African Americans during and after the war forced millions of Americans into closer contact with blacks and made it increasingly difficult to think of racism as a southern issue. Between 1946 and the 1960s, many African American Southerners, responding to disheartening postwar racism, fled the South for new opportunities in booming cities of the North and West.

Practical concerns also prompted migration. The perfection of a mechanical cotton picker in 1944 effectively ended the sharecropping system that had for so long locked a large percentage of southern blacks into a cycle of poverty and debt not unlike slavery. Out migrations toward wartime opportunities in places like the West also

TIMELINE 1945–1952

1945

March Tokyo fire bombings kill 100,000

March Tens of thousands of U.S. troops killed or wounded in brutal fighting on Iwo Jima and Okinawa

April 12 FDR dies; Harry S. Truman becomes president

April U.S. and Soviet Troops race toward Berlin

May 8 Germany formally surrenders

July 16 First atomic bomb successfully tested in New Mexico Desert

July 16–August 2 Potsdam Conference sets stage for Cold War

August 6 and 9 Hiroshima and Nagasaki are the first targets of atomic bomb

August 15 Victory in Japan Day (VJ Day)

1946

February 22 George F. Kennan's "Long Telegram" outlines new Soviet strategy

March 21 Truman signs Executive Order 9835 launching Federal Employee Loyalty Program

July 1 Dramatic demonstrations of new atomic bombs in the Bikini Atoll in Pacific

August 31 John Hersey's essay, "Hiroshima," is published by *The New Yorker*, raising nuclear fears

December 5 Truman establishes the President's Committee on Civil Rights

1947

March 12 Truman Doctrine explained in Congressional speech

April 15 Jackie Robinson desegregates Major League Baseball

June 5 George C. Marshal announces European Recovery Plan (Marshall Plan)

June 23 Taft-Hartley Act rolls back Wagner Act protections for unions

July George F. Kennan outlines Containment Policy

July 26 The National Security Act signed by President Truman creating National Security Council, Department of Defense, and Central Intelligence Agency undermined the system. Despite wartime movement and a major migration in the earlier part of the century, 77 percent of African Americans still lived in the South at the beginning of World War II; 49 percent of those lived in the rural South. By 1970, only half of America's African Americans lived in the South. The rest were concentrated in urban areas in the North and West.

In the 1940s the demographic character of cities and industries changed, and angry whites worried about the effect of race and cheap black labor on the character of their communities. Often they responded with violence. In the spring of 1943, race riots in Harlem killed 5 people, injured 400, and caused millions in damage. Similar riots in Detroit led to significant violence, creating lasting racial tensions in the city that came to represent the best and worst possibilities of the black migration. In many cases white Southern workers who had migrated north to work in war industry clashed with blacks who did the same. Across the nation white neighborhoods responded with racial covenants or "redlining" of cities creating a de facto system of segregation enforced by markets if not by law.

Between 1945 and 1952 progress in civil rights built a foundation for dramatic expansion of the movement that would occur in the 1950s and 1960s, when civil rights moved to the center of American politics and became part of a broader struggle to redefine American culture and values.

STUDY QUESTIONS FOR LAYING THE FOUNDATIONS FOR CIVIL RIGHTS

1. **What was the relationship between Cold War foreign policy and civil rights activism in America?**
2. **Why was baseball player Jackie Robinson's rise to national prominence important to early civil rights?**

September HCUA subpoenas 41 suspected American communists

October 23 W.E.B. Du Bois gives UN speech, *An Appeal to the World*, linking civil rights and Cold War politics

1948

January 27 Truman signs Smith Act

April 4 North Atlantic Treaty Organization (NATO) founded

July 26 Truman issues Executive Order 9981 desegregating U.S. military

August 3 Whittaker Chambers provides dramatic testimony to HCUA against Alger Hiss

August David Bradley's *No Place to Hide* raises nuclear concerns

1949

August 29 The Soviets successfully test atomic bomb ending U.S. monopoly

October 1 Mao Zedong announces communist People's Republic of China

1950

February 9 Joseph McCarthy announces list of communists in U.S. State Department

April 14 NSC-68 initiates a more confrontational Cold War strategy

June 25 North Korea invades South Korea, initiating the Korean War

September 15 MacArthur stages a dramatic counterattack at Inchon

November 26 Chinese forces enter Korea

1951

January 27 Nuclear testing begins at Nevada test site

June 4 *Dennis v. United States*

1952

April 11 Truman relieves MacArthur of command

December 24 McCarran Immigration and Naturalization Act restricts immigration

Summary

- Successful development of the atomic bomb shaped the military, diplomacy, and culture.
- Postwar geopolitics created tensions between United States and Soviet Union leading to Cold War.
- Cold War fears spawned a Red scare that forced Americans to grapple with issues of individual rights vs. conformity.
- Government programs like the GI Bill and Truman's Fair Deal provided new access to middle-class status for many Americans.
- Economic opportunity spurred mass migrations from within and to the United States.
- Civil rights advocates mounted challenges to racial discrimination in the early postwar years.

Key Terms and People

Acheson, Dean 976
Berlin Airlift 978
Bracero Program 990
Byrnes, James F. 972
Chiang Kai-shek 978
Chambers, Whittaker 982
Cold War 971
containment 976
Du Bois, W.E.B. 995
European Recovery Plan (ERP) 996
Executive Order 9981 994
Fair Deal 984
Harriman, W. Averell 971
Hiss, Alger 982
House Committee on Un-American
    Activities (HCUA) 981
Kennan, George F. 976
Kim Il-sung 980
MacArthur, Douglas 980

Manhattan Project 967
Mao Zedong 978
Marshall Plan 996
Marshall, George 978
McCarran Act 991
Molotov, Vyachslav 972
National Association for the
    Advancement of Colored People
    (NAACP) 993
National Origins Act of 1924 991
National Security Act of 1947 976
Nixon, Richard M. 982
Oppenheimer, Robert 967
Randolph, A. Philip 993
Rankin, John 981
Rhee, Syngman 980
Robinson, Jack Roosevelt "Jackie" 994
Truman, Harry S. 970
United Nations Security Council 980

Reviewing Chapter 25

1. Between 1945 and 1952, much of U.S. foreign policy involved discussions of the "Third World" (now known as the Developing Nations). What was this "Third World?" Why were these nations important during the very early years of the emerging Cold War?
2. The 1950s are often remembered as a time of great prosperity. What trends and programs contributed to the growth of affluence during the postwar years?
3. How did developing Cold War foreign policies contribute to rising concerns for civil liberties at home?

Further Reading

Borstelmann, Thomas. *The Cold War and the Color Line: American Race Relations in the Global Arena*. Cambridge, Mass.: Harvard University Press, 2001. Deeper context on the relationship between Cold War politics and civil rights.

Boyer, Paul. *By the Bomb's Early Light: American Thought and Culture at the Dawn of the Atomic Age*. New York: Pantheon Books, 1985. A wonderfully detailed study of Cold War popular culture.

Cohen, Lisabeth. *A Consumer's Republic: The Politics of Mass Consumption in Postwar America*. New York: Vintage, 2003. A detailed and compelling analysis of the transformative power of mass consumption.

Gutierrez, David G. *Walls and Mirrors: Mexican Americans, Mexican Immigrants, and the Politics of Ethnicity*. Berkeley: University of California Press, 1995. A different perspective on immigration and race.

Nash, Gerald D. *The American West in the Twentieth Century: A Short History of an Urban Oasis*. Albuquerque: University of New Mexico Press, 1977. A classic study of the West in the 20th century.

Rhodes, Richard. *The Making of the Atomic Bomb*. New York: Simon & Schuster, 1995. A Pulitzer Prize–winning account that proves that truth is stranger than fiction.

Visual Review

The Roots of Conflict

United States fears communist expansion after the end of the war.

Managing Postwar Europe in Potsdam

The Allies meet to determine the spheres of influence.

The Defeat of Japan

United States prepares the final assault of Japan.

Dividing the Postwar Globe

Despite military and economic advantages, U.S. leaders fear communist expansion in former colonies.

A Policy for Containment

U.S. leaders create a new strategy to challenge Soviet expansion.

Cold War

PROSPERITY AND LIBERTY UNDER THE SHADOW OF THE BOMB, 1945–1952

Red Scare

War in Korea

Cold War fears cause the United States to take action in Korea.

NSC-68—A Cold War Containment Policy

Truman adopts a strategy of military buildup and aggressive response to the Soviets.

Domestic Containment

The government makes efforts to contain communism at home.

The Color of Difference is Red

Significant numbers of Americans agree to restrictions of civil liberties.

Hollywood and the Pumpkin Papers

Hollywood is a target for anticommunist fears.

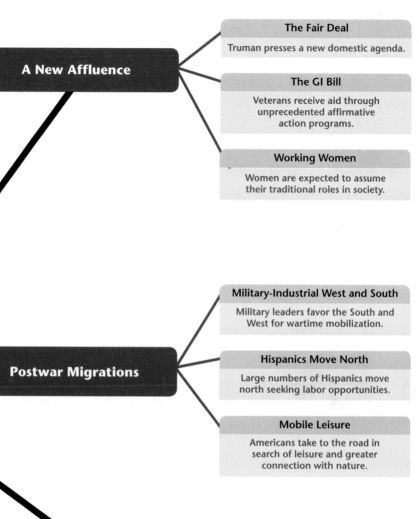

A New Affluence

The Fair Deal

Truman presses a new domestic agenda.

The GI Bill

Veterans receive aid through unprecedented affirmative action programs.

Working Women

Women are expected to assume their traditional roles in society.

Postwar Migrations

Military-Industrial West and South

Military leaders favor the South and West for wartime mobilization.

Hispanics Move North

Large numbers of Hispanics move north seeking labor opportunities.

Mobile Leisure

Americans take to the road in search of leisure and greater connection with nature.

Laying the Foundations for Civil Rights

First Steps

President Truman establishes a committee on civil rights.

Jack Roosevelt Robinson

Jackie Robinson changes attitudes by integrating Major League Baseball.

The Influence of African American Veterans

African American veterans point out the irony of racism in the United States during Cold War.

Black Migration and the Nationalization of Race

African American migration makes race a national issue.

The Dynamic 1950s

I n July 1959 Vice President Richard Nixon landed in Moscow after a record 11-hour transatlantic flight. Nixon traveled to the USSR to attend the first of a set of reciprocal state-sponsored cultural exhibitions. The American National Exhibition in Moscow resulted from a surprising comment from Soviet premier **Nikita Khrushchev** during an interview on the popular U.S. television news show *Face the Nation*. Khrushchev, who had come to power after Stalin's death, caught U.S. officials off guard by suggesting that the United States was responsible for restricting cultural relations between the two rivals.

When Khrushchev challenged American openness to dialogue, the Cold War entered a new phase focused on a global competition for quality of life and developing world hearts and minds. President Dwight Eisenhower worked during his two terms to ratchet down conflict with Soviet leaders and explore opportunities for cooperation. The Moscow exhibition seemed perfect both for demonstrating a new spirit of cooperation and for showing the superiority of the American way of life. During the 1950s many Americans enjoyed unprecedented affluence and the United States seemed to have the upper hand in the contest of exhibits.

As the centerpiece of their Moscow exhibit, U.S. officials decided to avoid propaganda about military technology and instead featured a model suburban home filled with modern appliances. Surrounded by an array of automobiles and consumer goods, the American dream

The Southdale Mall, Edina, Minnesota, 1957

CHAPTER OUTLINE

THE EISENHOWER ERA
> The End of the Korean War
> The New Look
> The Rise of the Developing World
> Hungary and the Suez, 1956
> France's Vietnam War
> McCarthyism and the Red Scare

A DYNAMIC DECADE
> The Baby Boom
> Suburban Migrations—Urban Decline
> Consumer Nation
> Corporate Order and Industrial Labor

THE FUTURE IS NOW
> Auto Mania
> Oil Culture
> Television

CONFORMITY AND REBELLION
> Old Time Religion
> Women in the 1950s
> Organization Men
> Teens, Rebels, and Beats

continued on page 1009

America in the World

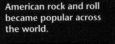

American rock and roll became popular across the world.

Jonas Salk introduced first polio vaccine to the public and it was used worldwide (1955).

⟨✦⟩ **U.S. event that influenced the world**

⟨✦⟩ **International event that influenced the United States**

◎ **Event with multinational influence**

◆ **Conflict**

Nixon and Khrushchev's "Kitchen Debate" contrasted American and Soviet values (1959).

Soviets launched Sputnik, beginning the space race (1957).

Geneva Conference divided Vietnam into North and South (1954).

The Suez Canal crisis strengthened the Soviet's presence in Egypt and ended Britain's role as a superpower (1956).

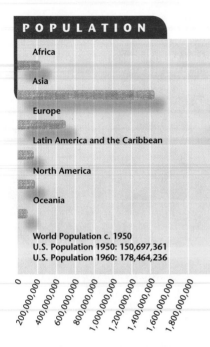

POPULATION

Africa

Asia

Europe

Latin America and the Caribbean

North America

Oceania

World Population c. 1950
U.S. Population 1950: 150,697,361
U.S. Population 1960: 178,464,236

0
200,000,000
400,000,000
600,000,000
800,000,000
1,000,000,000
1,200,000,000
1,400,000,000
1,600,000,000
1,800,000,000

home was intended to embody the benefits of a free market society.

The morning after his arrival in Moscow, Nixon toured the Tchaikovsky Street farmers market with Khrushchev—a crowd of Soviet officials and a multinational press corps filming their every move. The two politicians stopped often to debate the merits of their economic and political systems. Eventually they made their way to the National Exhibition for a private viewing before it opened to the eager Soviet public. Nixon stopped in the kitchen of the model home, where he passionately described the ideal of a suburban home headed by a male breadwinner and tended by a stay-at-home mom. Khrushchev scoffed at Nixon's pride in domestic women and their kitchens, as he compared them unfavorably to strong working Russian women.

The internationally publicized "kitchen debate" demonstrated the linking of American foreign policy and domestic culture during the 1950s. The Eisenhower administration celebrated Nixon's trip as a Cold War victory. To some extent Eisenhower was right. The opulence of the kitchen impressed the ordinary Russians who flocked to the exhibit in huge numbers. Both abroad and at home, however, Khrushchev's pointed questions about the ability of average Americans to attain the suburban dream resonated with critics who knew that race and class restricted 1950s affluence. Often dismissed as a nostalgic detour between the heroic 1940s and tumultuous 1960s, the 1950s was a dynamic decade characterized by both affluence and simmering discontent, a time when foreign policy and domestic life were more tightly linked than at any other period of American history.

THE EISENHOWER ERA

In 1952 Republicans nominated retired five-star U.S. Army General, Supreme Allied Commander during World War II, head of NATO, and president of Columbia University **Dwight D. Eisenhower** as their candidate for president. Eisenhower was a very popular choice with the American people. Few, however, knew much about his political views. Both the Democratic and Republican parties courted him as a potential candidate in 1948 before he revealed himself a Republican.

In 1952, when Eisenhower accepted the Republican nomination, the Korean War was stalled in bloody stalemate. Senator Joseph McCarthy still terrified the nation with his charges of communist conspiracies inside the government. The United States was on the verge of testing a hydrogen bomb, and an ailing and unpredictable Josef Stalin controlled the USSR. The U.S. economy, transitioning from war to peace with the help of government programs in areas such as education, transportation, and social services, created jobs and opportunities not seen for a generation. Still, global Cold War uncertainties and Red scare fears contributed to widespread support for a military hero as presidential candidate. To bolster his anticommunist credentials among right-wing Republicans, Eisenhower selected the 38-year-old Senator Richard M. Nixon of California as his vice-presidential running mate.

CHAPTER OUTLINE

continued from page 1005

LAYING THE FOUNDATION FOR CIVIL RIGHTS

> *Brown* and the Legal Assault
> Showdown in Little Rock
> Boots on the Ground
> MLK and the Philosophy of Nonviolence

Shortly after the nominating convention, Republicans revealed their campaign slogan as "K_1C_2." This was shorthand for Korea first, then Communism and Corruption. Republicans argued that the Democratic Truman administration had been lax in its prosecution of the Korean War, had dropped the ball on China, and had allowed subversives and corruption to run rampant in Washington and throughout the nation. Although Eisenhower stayed above the fray, he pledged to root out these evils. In the meantime, Nixon, attacking the Democratic nominee Adlai Stevenson, called him "Adlai the Appeaser" who earned his "Ph.D. from Dean Acheson's College of Cowardly Communist Containment."

Although effective in his political attacks, Nixon soon found himself in danger of costing Eisenhower the election and being removed from the ticket. On September 18, 1952, the *New York Post* reported that 60 Californians had set up a secret slush fund of $18,000 for Nixon during his tenure as senator. Nixon denied that he received any secret gifts and called the charge a "communist smear." In an emotional televised speech a somber Nixon defended the secret fund and made a public accounting of his rather modest finances admitting only one gift—to his daughters: a black and white cocker spaniel named Checkers. Claiming that his opponents would surely come after Checkers too, Nixon defiantly pledged to keep the dog.

The 1952 campaign was the first TV election. Eisenhower's decisive victory ensured that presidential campaigning would never be the same. "Ike" used the powerful new media more effectively than his opponent, and Nixon used it to save his political career. Eisenhower alone made 40 televised speeches. Stevenson, too, made TV speeches, but unlike Eisenhower's generally upbeat "sound bites," they were long, detailed, and intellectual presentations that stressed the nation's difficulties and lack of easy answers. Nixon's "Checkers Speech," drawing the largest viewing audience of any television broadcast to that date, demonstrated the critical new role of television in American politics. Liberals ridiculed Nixon for ignoring the key allegations against him, but he persuaded most viewers that he was an "ordinary" American.

Defining "ordinary" in Cold War America and a rapidly changing world was difficult. Ike was certainly not an average American. Globally recognized for his "tough as nails" brilliance during World War II, Eisenhower transitioned easily to civilian life where he enjoyed golf and captured in his personality the spirit of the times: an odd combination of razor's edge military brinksmanship and casual domestic affluence.

The End of the Korean War

On November 29, 1952, Eisenhower traveled to Korea, to fulfill a campaign pledge "to go to Korea" if elected. Voters assumed that the seasoned general, and leader of the D-Day invasion, had a plan for victory, when in fact he had no secret plan. Instead, the bloody stalemate dragged on for almost another three years. Determined to do something decisive, Eisenhower asked military advisors to study the use of atomic weapons in Korea, something Truman had considered. Advisors told both presidents that Korea had few targets appropriate for atomic attack, and use by the United States would only escalate the conflict and possibly undermine the impact of the bomb as the "ultimate weapon." Eisenhower privately accepted the argument against atomic warfare, but he leaked rumors of plans to escalate the war or even use atomic bombs in the hope of pressuring the Chinese Communists, whose troops made up the bulk of those fighting the Americans, to negotiate a settlement.

The atomic threats proved unnecessary after Stalin died on March 5, 1953, just weeks after Eisenhower took office. The absence of Stalin and the resulting confusion over his succession contributed to the Soviets' eagerness to see the Korean situation brought to a quick end. Further, the Chinese, weary of the costly war, were seeking better relations with the West. These factors, along with a Sino-American compromise over the return of prisoners, led to the end of the war, rather than did Eisenhower's atomic saber rattling.

On July 27, 1953, a ceasefire was finally achieved at Panmunjom, a village astride the North and South Korean divide. The agreement created a heavily fortified "demilitarized zone" (DMZ) or no-man's-land, splitting Korea at the 38th parallel, close to where the fighting began in 1950. The cost of this first proxy war was high. Ten million people, or one-tenth of the population of North and South Korea, had been killed, wounded, or declared missing. Another five million people had been dispossessed of their homes and uprooted. The inconclusive end to the war left troubling questions about the containment strategy in the complicated postcolonial world.

The New Look

Despite some relaxation of cold war tensions with the Korean armistice and Stalin's death, the "arms race" between the United States and the USSR expanded throughout the 1950s. Over the course of the decade, the competition between the two nations resulted in the production of enough atomic weapons to destroy the population of the world many times over. The successful U.S. detonation of the hydrogen bomb "Mike" in 1952 on the Eniwetok Islands in the South Pacific raised the stakes in the battle for technological supremacy.

Eisenhower inherited the arms race from President Harry Truman but brought his own philosophy on how to maintain technological dominance, cut military costs,

The B-52 Superfortress became a symbol of U.S. technological innovation and willingness to push the limits of military technology to command the Cold War.

and improve fighting efficiency. Working closely with his stridently anticommunist secretary of state **John Foster Dulles**, Eisenhower launched a military reorganization dubbed, "The New Look." The central philosophy of the New Look was Dulles's pronouncement of the doctrine of "massive retaliation" in January 1954. Simply put, massive retaliation meant that if the United States or its NATO and Japanese allies were attacked by the USSR, the United States would respond with enough nuclear strikes to completely destroy Soviet society. The plan was backed later by a "triad system" that kept some of the U.S. nuclear arsenal constantly on the move on trains, eternally patrolling aircraft, and eventually submarines, to ensure a rapid response to a Soviet first strike.

Under the New Look, the U.S. atomic arsenal increased from 1,000 to over 18,000 weapons. Additions to the military included the giant B-52 bomber capable of carrying nuclear payloads 7,000 miles from the United States to the heart of the USSR and the high-flying U2 spy plane. Eisenhower and Dulles believed the New Look had at least two advantages over Truman's containment policy: it would deter the Soviets from directly challenging U.S. interests and would be cost-effective, since atomic weapons ultimately cost less than a large conventional armed forces.

Critics of the new policy worried that the New Look committed the United States to an all-or-nothing response to Cold War threats. Others fretted about the expense of new military technologies and an endless arms race. Eisenhower sympathized, acknowledging, "Every rocket fired, signified, in a final sense, a theft from those who

▶ Hypothetical rendering of the hydrogen bomb "Mike" over the New York City skyline showed the enormous power of such weapons.

hunger." But the shift in policies and the Korean armistice enabled Eisenhower to reduce military spending from $52 to $36 billion during his first term and slash troop numbers in the Army and Navy.

Korea highlighted the need for new Cold War tools. The Eisenhower administration authorized the Central Intelligence Agency (CIA) to carry out covert military operations against unfriendly regimes. General James Doolittle had warned the president that a Cold War had "no rules" and that Americans "must learn to subvert, sabotage and destroy our enemies by more clever and sophisticated" means than in the past. Doolittle further cautioned that "accepted norms of human conduct" no longer applied. During his two terms, Eisenhower expanded the mission of the CIA far beyond intelligence gathering and analysis. He authorized it to conduct secret operations across the globe. The CIA conducted experiments with chemical weapons, tested LSD on unsuspecting U.S. citizens to see if the hallucinogenic drug could be used to dope the Soviets, plotted assassinations, and conducted elaborate surveillance of communists in allied and enemy states alike. During this time, the CIA played a critical role in America's efforts to win control of the Developing World.

The Rise of the Developing World

In the aftermath of World War II, the map of the globe changed dramatically with the collapse of the European colonial system. Former colonies across the globe sought and gained their independence from western European colonial powers. This trend, especially evident in Africa and Asia, figured heavily in U.S. foreign policy during the 1950s.

Decolonization coincided with the Cold War, and the United States and the USSR each sought to influence the politics of the newly independent nations. The U.S.

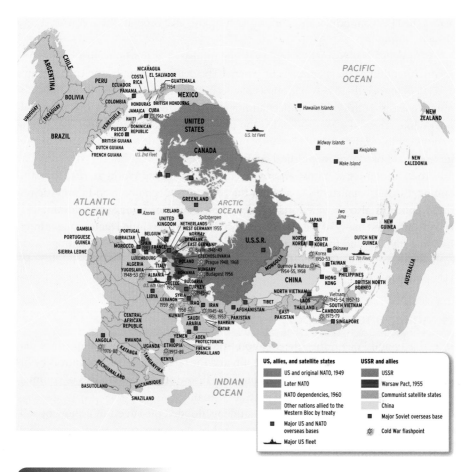

▲ **Map 26.1**

The Postwar World This map depicts the U.S. and Soviet spheres of influence during the Cold War. Debate over concept of "spheres of influence" dominated the final days of WWII. The Soviets occupied a massive swath of Eastern Europe by the time they reached Berlin, while the Americans and Allies controlled all of Western Europe and territories across the globe. The rapid remapping of the globe in the aftermath of war was supposed to be temporary but lasted for decades as Cold War conflict solidified the lines on the map.

policy of containment assumed, often correctly, that former colonial nations would gravitate toward communism or toward a neutral stance between the Cold War camps. As former wards of capitalist countries, many Developing World countries were wary of the intentions of the United States and its Cold War allies. Between 1945 and 1960, 37 nations gained independence, and a majority leaned toward or openly embraced communism. Most of these new nations were nonwhite, preindustrial, and poor. Further complicating the picture, many of these nations emerged with festering internal guerrilla insurgencies or outright civil war. During the 1950s alone, there were 28 prolonged insurgencies in the Developing World. Protests by Puerto Rican nationalists across the U.S. commonwealth and in Washington, DC, brought these concerns very close to home.

Nationalist leaders such as India's prime minister **Jawaharlal Nehru** stated, "We do not intend to be the playthings of others." The determination by the United States and USSR to treat these new nations as pawns in a fight between capitalism and communism led to profound misunderstandings about the power and extent of nationalism. While critics like Nehru derided the policies of containment, other developing nations exploited the Soviet-U.S. competition by playing one against the other to gain increased aid or to remove political enemies.

The Eisenhower administration viewed the Developing World as vital to maintaining a world balance of power with the Soviets. But economic and domestic political concerns also drove efforts to keep these countries from Soviet domination. Having inherited many of the world's postwar markets, the United States sought international stability and the protection of raw material sources. Vast Developing World oil reserves, in particular, elevated the strategic importance of emerging markets for U.S. policy makers.

Hungary and the Suez, 1956

In Hungary and Poland the Soviet Union brutally crushed nationalist uprisings that gained momentum after the death of Stalin and the relaxation of some controls by his successors. In the Middle East, Egypt sought to throw off the last vestiges of colonialism through the nationalization of the Suez Canal.

On October 23, 1956, Hungarian students flooded the streets in a show of solidarity with Polish protestors seeking removal of the Soviet-controlled government. Twelve days later, Soviet tanks rolled in and brutally crushed the demonstrations, ending the revolt. Despite having urged the uprising on Radio Free Europe, the Eisenhower administration backed away from a direct challenge to the Soviets within their East European sphere. The best the United States had to offer the fleeing Hungarian freedom fighters was "Displaced Persons" status—first applied as a precedent in the late 1940s to Jews escaping the Nazis.

While the eyes of the world were on Eastern Europe, Israel, and then France and Great Britain, launched an effort to retake the Suez Canal from the Egyptians. Nationalist Egyptian leader **Gamal Nasser**, who had recently deposed Egypt's decadent monarchy, sought to unify all Arabs under his banner by expropriating the canal from its British owners. Nasser saw the canal as a humiliating reminder of colonial control, a revenue source, and a potential instrument of power as half the world's oil supply passed through its waters. For the latter reason Israel, Great Britain, and France were unwilling to allow it to fall under Egyptian control. In addition, all had unstated reasons to risk war. Israel wanted to intimidate Nasser for launching raids from Gaza and to undermine his Pan-Arab appeal. Britain wanted to regain the canal, and France hoped to lessen the appeal of Algerian revolutionaries.

Having advised the British not to react militarily in Suez, Eisenhower was outraged when word reached him of the invasion. He had no love for Nasser but feared that any military action and occupation would only disrupt oil supplies, inflame Arab passions against Western nations, and possibly enable the Soviets to gain a foothold in the vital region.

As the fighting shut off traffic through the canal and strangled Western Europe's oil supply, Eisenhower refused to open American oil supplies to the British and instead of the aid the British expected, Eisenhower threatened additional oil sanctions if the involved nations did not remove all troops. Still, when the Soviets rattled their atomic sword at the British and French "aggressors," Eisenhower assured his Soviet counterpart that, should London and Paris be attacked, Moscow would be devastated "as surely as night follows day."

By early December French and British troops withdrew from the canal region and were replaced with UN peacekeepers. The last Israeli troops left the Sinai soon afterward. By publicly siding with Arab nationalists and against European colonizers, the United States gained considerable goodwill in the Arab world that served U.S. oil companies well. Eisenhower had carried the day but also committed the United States to a dramatically expanded role in Middle Eastern politics with far-reaching consequences.

France's Vietnam War

At the end of World War II, the small French colony of Vietnam epitomized the complexity of rapidly evolving postwar geopolitics. After the war the French regained control of colonial possessions in Southeast Asian "Indochina"—composed of Vietnam, Cambodia, and Laos. Vietnamese nationalists led by **Ho Chi Minh** had fought the Japanese in hope of winning U.S. backing for postwar independence. Instead, under Truman, Washington supported French efforts to reassert control. As a result, in 1946 Ho's followers, the Vietminh, launched a guerilla war against the French. In the southern part of the colony, where the Vietminh had less strength, the French created a puppet government led by a pliant playboy-emperor named Bao Dai. Bao then invited the French and Americans to help him fight the guerrillas.

The outbreak of the Korean War increased U.S. interest in Korea and the surrounding region. As a result, the Truman administration dispatched eight cargo planes of military supplies to French troops in Vietnam and thus began a pattern of direct military aid. When Truman left office in early 1953, the conflict ranked second only to Korea in terms of U.S. military aid. That year the United States covered 40 percent of French war costs. Shortly before Eisenhower's inauguration, outgoing Secretary of State Dean Acheson informed him that if the French situation in Vietnam deteriorated, the United States must be prepared to act decisively. Heeding Acheson's words, Eisenhower accepted the recommendations of the National Security Council "124/2" directive, which stated that the loss of any of the countries of Southeast Asia "would probably lead to relatively swift submission" by the remaining countries to Chinese Communist control. This concept soon became known as the Domino Theory and provided a rationale for American involvement.

In February 1954, the faltering French, with urging of the United States, agreed to enter into negotiations with the Vietminh in Geneva in April. In the meantime the French decided to strengthen their bargaining position by airdropping 12,000 troops into a valley in northwestern Vietnam called Dien Bien Phu. The troops were met, surrounded, and soundly defeated by 50,000 Vietminh forces. During the battle, as French defeat became certain, Eisenhower's advisers briefly considered the use of tactical nuclear weapons against the Vietminh positions.

On July 24, 1954, at the Geneva Conference, Vietnam was divided into North and South segments, with Ho Chi Minh in control of the North and Bao Dai's government in control of the South. In theory, popular elections were ultimately to decide the leadership of each government as well as to prepare for reunification. As with the "temporary" division of Korea, however, this division, too, became permanent. Eisenhower feared that communist control of the South would undermine the stability of noncommunist regimes throughout the region and would ultimately threaten Japan.

On February 12, 1955, Eisenhower deployed the first U.S. military advisors to the region to bolster the democratic South against the communist North. Between 1955 and 1960 billions of dollars of U.S. military and economic aid flowed to South Vietnam while U.S. military advisers trained South Vietnamese troops. Ho Chi Minh fumed at this division of Vietnam but could do little to oppose it. Until a rebellion erupted in the South in 1960, most Americans considered the result a successful case of anticommunist "nation building."

McCarthyism and the Red Scare

Red scares at home in part fueled the need to be tough on communists abroad. When Eisenhower took office in 1953, the Red scare was at its height. The House Committee on Un-American Activities (HCUA) hearings and the sensational Alger Hiss case had been eclipsed by the astonishing rise to power of an obscure junior Senator from Wisconsin named **Joseph McCarthy**. "Tail Gunner Joe" already had a sleazy reputation for his mean-spirited Senate campaign in 1946. As a struggling senator McCarthy capitalized on anticommunist hysteria to advance his career from the "worst senator" to one of the most powerful and feared men in America. McCarthy's rise began on February 9, 1950, when in a minor speech to a group of Republican women he made a startling claim about communist spies in the State Department. McCarthy said he had a secret list of 205 known communists working at the highest levels of U.S. government and whose names were known by President Truman and Secretary of State Acheson.

This stunning announcement, garnering extensive press coverage as McCarthy repeated the story over the coming weeks, launched him from obscurity and failure to America's leading communist hunter. In some ways McCarthy's charges were so outlandish it was impossible to disprove them. More responsible Republicans knew he peddled hot air, but they found him a useful wrecking ball to batter the Democrats. Between 1950 and 1954 McCarthy dominated a national communist witch-hunt so completely that his name became synonymous with a dark chapter in American civil liberties. Of course, there were spies on all sides during the Cold War. McCarthy, however, had little interest or ability to find them; instead, he sought headlines that would undermine Democrats. **McCarthyism** represented a sinister turn in government efforts to control communism within the United States. McCarthy's rise raised serious questions about the ability of the government to reconcile Cold War imperatives with American democratic traditions.

Although Eisenhower disliked McCarthy, he did not criticize the senator during his campaign in 1952. McCarthy's wild smears included Eisenhower's friend and political ally, retired general and former secretary of state **George Marshall**, whom McCarthy accused of perpetrating a "conspiracy so immense as to dwarf any previous such venture in the history of man." A series of sensational espionage cases aided McCarthy's rise to power. First, **Klaus Fuchs**, a theoretical physicist involved with the Manhattan Project, confessed to British Intelligence officers in January 1950 that he had spied for the Soviet Union. His confession drew much publicity in the United States and led to a 14-year prison sentence.

The furor over domestic communist conspiracies grew even stronger when, on March 6, 1951, **Julius** and **Ethel Rosenberg** went on trial for conspiring to provide the Soviet Union with U.S. atomic secrets. A jury convicted the couple of this charge and sentenced them to death. The Rosenbergs had two young sons, and the death sentence caused an international outcry for clemency for Ethel. Despite the protests and serious questions about Ethel's participation, on June 19, 1953, the Rosenbergs became the first American civilians executed for espionage.

Senator Joseph McCarthy fared much worse in the new media of TV, where he often appeared disheveled and far less convincing than when his words and tactics were interpreted in the print media.

In 1953–1954, when McCarthy launched an inquiry into alleged communist in-fluence in the army, it seemed apparent that his ultimate target was President Eisen-hower. McCarthy's power waned the next year after he launched a series of televised hearings on communists in the U.S. military. This bizarre investigation prompted Ike, who knew he was the real target, to encourage army leaders, behind the scenes, not to cooperate with McCarthy and to warn the senator to reconsider his attack. Un-deterred, McCarthy forged on. Twenty million people watched the Army-McCarthy hearings, as most got their first clear look at the tactics of the ranting rogue senator.

The hearings, along with a brave attack by TV journalist **Edward R. Murrow** on his show, *See It Now,* led to Senate disciplinary hearings; and in December 1954 the Senate publicly denounced McCarthy for "unbecoming conduct." Politicians from both parties celebrated the demise of the feared McCarthy, but his rise to power would not have been possible without the support of powerful cultural and political leaders. Before it faded, McCarthyism undermined basic constitutional principles, destroyed careers and lives, terrified millions of Americans, and gave ammunition to the Soviets and other adversaries who used the authoritarian McCarthy as an example of Ameri-can hypocrisy.

STUDY QUESTIONS FOR THE EISENHOWER ERA

1. What was the "Developing World"? Why did these nations gain signifi-cance during the Eisenhower administration?
2. Why did Americans tolerate McCarthy's tactics? How does one person gain so much power in a democracy?

A DYNAMIC DECADE

In his farewell address to the American people on January 17, 1961, a thoughtful President Eisenhower cautioned listeners to strive for balance and restraint in the "ever growing smaller" world of the future. Wary of overconfidence in the stability and equity of American affluence at home, he advised his fellow citizens to "avoid the impulse to live only for today, plundering for our own ease and convenience the pre-cious resources of tomorrow." Uneasy about the future of the technocratic Cold War globe he helped design, Ike left office with "a definite sense of disappointment." "As one who has witnessed the horror of war," and "as one who knows that another war could utterly destroy this civilization," the general knew the agony of war and dangers of militarization, and as a retiring president he had learned the complexity and fragil-ity of prosperity.

Those Americans who listened to Ike's final speech might have been surprised by the tone considering the remarkable statistics of the 1950s. During the decade, the United States led the world in economic growth. Fueled by the Cold War "mili-tary industrial complex," vastly increased consumer spending, a "baby boom," suburbanization, and government social programs like the GI Bill, the American economy grew to new heights.

Despite some short recessions in the 1950s, consumer spending remained strong throughout the decade and reached the $300 billion per year mark in 1959. Combined with a low unemployment average of 4 to 6 percent for the decade, the United States was becoming, in the words of economist John Kenneth Galbraith, an "affluent society."

The Baby Boom

Unprecedented population growth was the most dramatic sign of American affluence in the 1950s. After a decade of declining birthrates during the Great Depression, population growth escalated modestly during World War II before soaring upward in 1947. By 1958 a British tourist remarked while on vacation in the United States that "every other young housewife I see is pregnant." The tourist witnessed the apex of a demographic trend so significant it became known as the **baby boom**. This remarkable spike was part of a larger transnational trend that saw a dramatic increase in fertility rates in many Western European nations, including Britain and France. Because of devastating population losses during the war, the postwar population boom in the Soviet Union resulting in the "Sputnik Generation" was celebrated as an important victory by communist leaders. Australia and New Zealand also experienced population spikes during this period. Population growth became a measure of success and

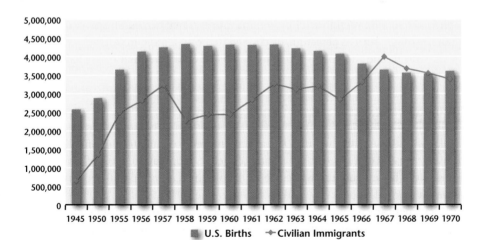

▲ **Figure 26.1**

Population boom Unprecedented population growth was the most dramatic sign of American affluence in the 1950s. After a decade of declining birthrates during the Great Depression, population growth escalated modestly during World War II before soaring upward in 1947, peaking in 1958. Despite Cold War restriction, foreign immigration increased during the 1950s from wartime and depression-era lows.

power during the Cold War. Likewise, population statistics were vital indicators of recovery in Germany and Japan, where sharp percentage declines from war casualties required dramatic birth rates just to achieve prewar population levels.

When the American baby boom began in 1946 it caught forecasters by surprise. American demographers predicted the trend was a temporary result of the end of the war and predicted a modest five million births by decade's end. Their estimate quickly proved far too low. In 1948 alone American mothers had a baby every eight seconds on average. By the year's end four million births almost matched the experts' prediction for the entire four-year period. By 1950 the total number of births surpassed nine million. By 1959 children under the age of 14 accounted for 50 million or approximately 30 percent of the nation's population.

There is no simple explanation for this dramatic birthrate increase. Affluence, health improvements, and an extended period of peace, interrupted only by the 1950–1953 Korean War, all contributed. Americans tended to marry at a younger age and extended their childbearing years. The federal government, through the GI Bill and FHA loans, shared some responsibility for helping to create an affluent and secure environment conducive to childbearing. Likewise, an emerging suburban culture celebrated by government leaders actively promoted a "procreation ethic." The mass media and popular culture honored and celebrated motherhood. Applied science, especially in medicine, led to massive public health campaigns to eliminate polio and other infectious diseases and to discourage dangerous behaviors such as smoking. During the 1950s public health groups such as the American Cancer Society, along with government researchers, used new statistical techniques to reveal and publicize the link between cigarettes and lung cancer. Scientists, including Dr. **Jonas Salk** who perfected the polio vaccine in 1954, became international heroes. The development of "miracle drugs" such as penicillin, discovered in the 1930s and mass-produced during World War II, and the polio vaccine made the American children of the baby boom the healthiest generation in history.

Suburban Migrations—Urban Decline

Millions of those with the financial capacity moved to dramatically expanding suburbs. By the end of the 1950s nearly half of the U.S. population, most of whom were white, lived in new suburbs, while people of color increasingly populated inner cities. America reached its peak as an urban nation in the early 1950s. In the early postwar period American cities remained dynamic places full of busy sidewalks, cafes, office buildings, and bustling neighborhoods, connected to downtowns. Urban railways ran full schedules, with cars often packed to capacity. By 1960 these urban railways had disappeared from all but the largest American cities. Former rail and mass-transit patrons embraced the automobile to ferry them to and from increasingly distant suburban homes. Eisenhower's 1956 **Interstate and Defense Highways Act**, the largest public works program in American history, facilitated the growth of suburbs and the complex of industries that sustained them.

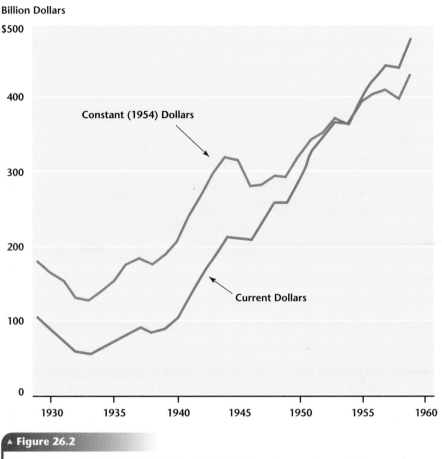

Billion Dollars

▲ **Figure 26.2**

Gross National Product (GNP) This critical indicator of economic growth increased steadily during WWII and dramatically during throughout the 1950s.

After 1956 wide concrete highways funneling people to and from suburbia bisected once vital neighborhoods and soared over other areas of town. Increasingly, as professionals and businesses left for the suburbs, decline of downtowns was evident in abandoned buildings, deteriorating neighborhoods, and increased crime. Perceptions of the inner city as crumbling, dangerous, and depressed only increased "white flight."

Those left behind were often minorities and working class whites with limited access to the jobs that fueled the affluent society. Blacks, Jews, and others were often explicitly denied the suburban dream by discriminatory loaning practices, redlining, and racist housing covenants in new neighborhoods. The U.S. Supreme Court outlawed racial covenants in *Shelly v. Kraemer* (1948), but they persisted in practice throughout the 1950s. Suburbs across the country used neighborhood and homeowner associations to restrict access on the basis of race, ethnicity, and religion.

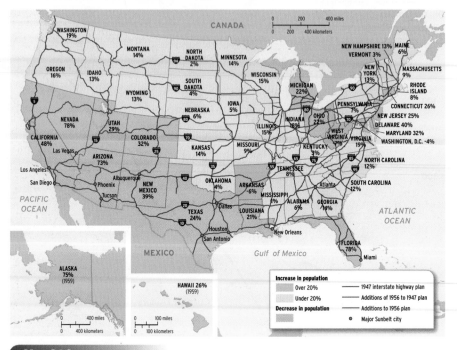

▲ **Map 26.2**

Defense and Mobility Regional population increases, particularly across the American West, were influenced by the growth of interstate highways that opened lightly populated areas to new development in the 1950s and 1960s. Across the nation, the construction of the interstate highway system enabled suburban growth, created markets for a new roadside economy and split cities obliterating centuries old patterns of urban development.

In the South, racial segregation, supported by law, remained entrenched. In the North racism could be overt, with posted signs informing blacks, Jews, or others they were unwelcome. Increasingly affluent Jewish Americans founded mainly Jewish suburbs in response to discrimination. Other communities across the United States were "sundown towns," where minorities were welcomed during daytime as workers but warned by posted signs: "N___'s! Don't Let the Sun Set on You In This Town!" Other communities used less obvious means to warn minorities of all backgrounds to look elsewhere. In whatever form, racism ensured that most suburbs outside the legally segregated South were completely white and not representative of the period's increasing racial diversity.

Suburbs grew because of demand and new technologies. The assembly-line "tract home" was the most significant innovation. Block after block of mass-produced homes, housing tracts, transformed enormous regions of rural landscape into seas of houses linked by highways to islands of new shopping and strip malls. Suburban housing pioneers, including **William Levitt**, builder of the prototypical modern tract suburb of Levittown on Long Island, New York, were hailed as heroes in the years after the war, when serious housing shortages left some returning war vets living with

This 1935 linoleum print illustrates the idea of the "sundown town" from the book, *Scottsboro Alabama*. Fifties versions of segregation like "redlining" might not be as blatant but had the same chilling effect.

parents or even in converted chicken coops. Using large tracts of farmland on the outskirts of big cities, Levitt built simple four-room homes complete with the latest kitchen appliances. The homes sold for $7,990 in 1947 (roughly $67,500 in 2000's dollars). Suburbs filled an urgent housing need and promised a level of comfort and modernity previously unknown to most city dwellers. Snapping up the houses as fast as Levitt could build them, enthusiastic buyers drew other developers, like California's **Henry J. Kaiser**, into the business. The federal government encouraged this trend with Federal Housing Administration (FHA) and Veterans Administration (VA) loans featuring modest down payments and reasonable interest rates.

Suburbs had long been a part of American life. By 1955, however, suburban planned communities accounted for 75 percent of all new housing starts. Five years later more Americans lived in suburbs than in cities and over one-fourth of the nation's housing stock was less than 10 years old. Suburban development was so dramatic during the 1950s that it prompted critics like historian Godfrey Hodgson to write about a "suburban-industrial complex" comparable in scope to the "military-industrial complex" of the Cold War.

Suburbs seemed to offer a more rural, or "natural," life than Americans could find in crowded cities. Suburban growth, bringing urban Americans into closer contact with the countryside and natural areas, helped build a new power base for environmental protection. Waves of suburbanites witnessed housing developments devour an area the size of Rhode Island every year. Suburbanites watched forests, meadows, and entire hillsides be cleared to accommodate the next wave of middle-class migrants. As suburbs encroached on open spaces previously used for recreation, some Americans began to support limits on growth and protection of at least some scenic lands.

Consumer Nation

Americans in the 1950s embraced consumption as a cornerstone of quality of life and an important weapon in the battle for hearts and minds during the Cold War. After nearly two decades of material sacrifice during depression and war, Americans emerged with an appetite for consumption not seen since the 1920s. As in the 1920s, sophisticated advertisements from savvy marketers peddled a wide variety of new technological wonders. During the 1950s more money was spent on advertising than on public education. Newly available credit cards, including the popular Diners Club, American Express, and Sears, made it easier for Americans to purchase and enjoy advertised products. By the end of the decade there were over 10 million Sears cards in American wallets, and millions of consumers began to rely on short-term credit to outfit their new homes.

Actively promoted by the U.S. government as a critical attribute of good citizenship, mass consumption represented more than just an economic trend. For the first time in American history political leaders, economists, and foreign policy experts recognized that consumption, not production, was the single most important contributor to America's economic health. Popular publications such as *Life* presented economic data suggesting the success of the postwar economy hinged on consumer purchase of new homes, appliances, and cars. Mass consumption was extolled as a virtue that would lift all Americans and provide universal employment and prosperity.

The Cold War figured prominently in both private and governmental encouragement of consumption. Nixon and Khrushchev's kitchen debate only reinforced a familiar association of consumption with patriotism. Mass consumption also represented American culture worldwide as American products traveled the globe. During World War II American products from cigarettes to sodas reached the far corners of the world. By 1950 the Coca-Cola Company had 60 bottling plants on six continents. Newly opened postwar trade routes even funneled American products behind the Iron Curtain. During Nixon's visit to the American National Exhibition in Moscow, he and Khrushchev paused at a Pepsi stand to debate geopolitics. Like the Japanese and Nazis during World War II, the Soviet government dismissed American products like soda as frivolous, but the two million Muscovites who attended the 1959 National Exhibition were as taken with dishwashers and sodas as were their American counterparts. People throughout the world came to know America through its material culture, exported by the millions of tons. Some embraced these material ambassadors and the culture they represented. Others viewed the tidal wave of American products in global markets with intensified anti-American animosity and felt these spearheads of American capitalism threatened the nature of their societies.

Corporate Order and Industrial Labor

Increasingly powerful American corporations fostered the 1950s culture of consumption. Large national corporations, seeing a repeat of pre-Depression business trends, consolidated production and distribution networks and perfected national and international marketing techniques. Most significantly, U.S. corporations began diversifying their holdings across the spectrum of the consumer economy to create conglomerates of dizzying size. Thus, corporations like General Electric produced hundreds of different products from light bulbs to televisions to military equipment. GE diversified its product lines while acquiring companies that made food, clothing, and products of all sorts. Through expansion and consolidation, GE became America's fourth largest company in the 1950s; with 136 factories in 28 states, it was the nation's third largest employer. As corporations became conglomerates, they spread their risk while increasing profits to record levels. The huge American corporations of the 1950s were also better able to take advantage of expanding global markets. U.S. exports, doubling during the decade, left the nation with a five billion dollar trade surplus in 1960.

Consumers were often unaware that these new giants gained political power as they forged a powerful new postwar business model. Those who worked for the corporations clearly understood the significance of the transformation of American business during this time. Giant corporations required a dramatically expanded workforce with a large managerial class and a tightly managed labor force. For millions of World War II vets, college educated with the help of the GI Bill, corporations offered lifetime employment and a ticket to the affluent society. Such companies, with bureaucracies as big as many nations, needed a seemingly endless supply of young executives to man thousands of offices around the nation and the globe. Unparalleled opportunities allowed a generation of men and some women (see below) to move into white-collar work. In return, these mostly male workers were expected to adhere to strict corporate codes of dress and behavior. Often moved from one state to another with short notice, they contributed to the transience of suburban life. Corporate life in the 1950s demanded a level of conformity that many men and their families came to resent even as they benefited from higher incomes.

Workers and labor unions prospered in the affluent society, but labor leaders had reason to wonder how long it might last. The culture of consensus during the 1950s, characterized by the fight against communism, economic growth, and wider-spread prosperity, appeared to ease relations between business and labor. Business leaders and Chambers of Commerce touted this perception but with a clear bias toward employers. Programs like Junior Achievement promoted the ideal of "free enterprise" among America youth, while free-market thinkers such as economists Friedrich von Hayek and Milton Friedman argued that universal employment and "people's capitalism" made unions obsolete.

Union membership remained steady through the decade. The nation's two largest unions, the **American Federation of Labor** and the **Congress of Industrial Organizations**, ended their long rivalry and united to form the AFL-CIO. However, by 1960, union workers comprised a smaller overall percentage of workers than in the 1950s. Moreover, high employment rates did not translate to economic equality. As the United States entered the 1960s, 5 percent of Americans controlled half the wealth of the nation. A close look at U.S. economic statistics revealed startling poverty rates in the "other America." For many elderly, minority, and rural Americans, the affluent society remained out of reach while American corporations, through conservative groups like the American Enterprise Association, actively worked to undermine the social safety net of the New Deal.

Even though blue-collar unionized workers did not gain any real control of the workplace during the prosperity of the 1950s, they did benefit materially through steady pay increases and significant expansions of job benefits, such as medical insurance, paid vacations, and retirement benefits. Big corporations provided these benefits in exchange for agreements like the "Treaty of Detroit" in 1955, when the powerful United Auto Workers (UAW) agreed to take labor radicalism off the table if the company expanded the benefits packages.

STUDY QUESTIONS FOR A DYNAMIC DECADE

1. By the end of the 1950s nearly half of the U.S. population lived in new suburbs. What factors contributed to this change?
2. In what ways was the 1950s consumer culture linked to Cold War politics? What impact did the goods and mass media that the United States exported have on the image of the United States internationally?

THE FUTURE IS NOW

With dramatic music blaring in the background, headlines flashed across the movie screen, "Cities Alerted for Final Stand Against Fantastic Invader" and "Nation Maps Fight Against Unknown Terror!" The scene shifts to the New Mexico Desert and the blinding flash of an atomic bomb before turning to the stern TV reporter who reveals that out of that explosion arose a mutant terror that threatened to destroy all humanity. In 1954 movie audiences gasped in terror at *Them!* They knew this was fiction, of course, but weirdly plausible fiction that resonated with very real concerns about the pace of technological developments and the power of science in the postwar world.

America has always been a nation obsessed with the future and with progress. The astonishing technological advances of the postwar period enhanced this tradition. Medical breakthroughs, nuclear science, labor-saving devices, and innovations in transportation and communication all created a sense of accelerating progress. Many of these advances, related to the Cold War, created a tension between fear that technology would run wild and the optimistic belief that technology was the cornerstone of an affluent future. Some Americans insisted that new technologies would usher in a period of unprecedented personal freedom and new standards of health and quality of life for everyone. Others worried about the pace of change. The wildly popular genre of science fiction exploited technological fears with films like *Them!* and *Godzilla* (1954), which showed mutants of technology turning on humanity.

Whether they feared it or celebrated it, Americans could not escape the reshaping of U.S. culture and geography by new and improved technologies. None was more important than the car. The rise of the corporation, the growth of suburbs, and 1950s consumer culture all depended on the automobile industry.

Auto Mania

By the 1950s the automobile had long been deemed by Americans as a necessity. Since the introduction of Ford's Model T in 1908, the automobile provided the average American with affordable individual transportation and occupied a central place in American culture and economy. The Great Depression and the wartime shortages that followed forced many Americans to give up the freedom of the family car. But in 1945, when scarcity began to fade, Americans lined up at dealerships to order the first new models in a generation. During the next decade, the American automobile industry matured, influenced policy, and became the critical link in the postwar consumer economy.

In 1955 the United States produced two-thirds of the world's supply of automobiles. Trends toward consolidation left the mature American automobile industry in the hands of three big producers. General Motors (GM), Ford, and Chrysler accounted for 94 percent of American automobile output. GM, under the dynamic leadership of Alfred P. Sloan, elevated the auto industry to unprecedented influence in American life. Between 1945 and 1955 GM's marketing strategies were so successful that "Sloanism" became a widely emulated business model. Sloan's philosophy was simple: use extensive marketing and constant design changes to convince Americans to buy new cars regardless of need. Sloan created a "ladder of consumption" with different brands of cars tailored to different income levels. The strategy was so successful that the family car became the most important marker of American success among all classes during the 1950s. No longer the stripped-down utilitarian transportation devised by Henry Ford, American cars now came loaded with push button transmissions, radios, powerful engines, and futuristic tailfins. Automakers used gadgets and "custom" features to encourage rapid obsolescence and generate demand for new models. Automakers also successfully convinced suburban Americans that they needed two cars to support their lifestyle.

The results were dramatic. During the 1950s auto production increased to eight million units annually and by 1960 there were over 70 million cars on the roads. In 1955, GM became the first U.S. company to make over $1 billion in single year. By 1960 it had become the world's largest corporation, surpassing in income the GNP of many nations.

The auto mania that transformed cities and enabled the suburban revolution grew from near total consensus by the American public. Everyone from corporate executives to union leaders celebrated the dramatic rise of the auto industry and supported federal programs to improve America's highway system. By 1956, when Eisenhower signed the Interstate Highway Act, the auto industry and web of connected ventures dominated the American economy. The expansion of the auto industry created demand for tires, gas, glass, steel, plastics, and electronics. Auto travel and tourism spawned a national building boom as motels, fast-food restaurants, drive-in movie theaters, and shopping malls sprang up to meet the desire of Americans to do everything in their cars.

Oil Culture

Cars accounted for the bulk of oil consumption in the United States after World War II, but from the farm to the factory and even in the suburban home oil was essential. New innovations such as petroleum-based plastics also contributed to skyrocketing oil demand during the 1950s. During the war chemists had perfected polyethylene, a versatile petroleum-based plastic used as insulation for radar and radio cables. After the war, DuPont researchers explored plastics for domestic use, and soon plastic was used to make millions of new products from milk jugs and food storage to televisions and satellite components. By 1960 virtually every product sold in the United States was affected by oil supplies and prices.

Millions of Americans worked to produce oil or oil-dependent products and materials. Providing jobs, goods, and fuel, the oil culture underwrote the decade's affluence. It also made the stability of the American oil supply a critical issue. If the second half of the 20th century marked the beginning of the "oil age," then national security and economic stability depended on plentiful supplies.

Prior to World War II the United States had relied primarily on its own oil reserves for cheap fuel. After the war U.S. companies took advantage of newly opened world markets in the Persian Gulf and Arabian Peninsula to secure external sources. The Eisenhower administration worked to keep prices low, oil-producing regions stable, and global sources flowing. Thus, areas of the world previously insignificant to the United States suddenly took on great importance. In the years that followed, this dependence on cheap sources of oil became problematic. The intensity of the Suez Canal crisis demonstrated the global web of connections and commitments forged by oil demand. Like the policies of containment, the oil culture of the 1950s permanently linked the United States to the rest of the world and made the isolationism of past decades impossible. In 1960, 7 of the nation's 10 largest corporations were either automobile or oil producers. Petroleum lubricated the culture, foreign policy, and economy of the 1950s.

Television

The meteoric rise of television in the 1950s as the preeminent source of information and entertainment was one of the most significant developments of the century. Television changed American culture, lifestyles, family dynamics, and economics, and broadcast American culture to most of the world.

Invented in 1928 by **Philo Farnsworth**, television remained an obscure technology through World War II. Wartime improvements in electronics and plastics made the rapid rise of television possible during the postwar period. Television became second only to the car as the most important appliance of affluence. By 1953 two-thirds of American households had television sets. At the end of the decade, 94 percent owned sets. Almost overnight television became the most popular entertainment medium.

Americans of the 1950s embraced television with open arms. By the end of the 1950s the average American watched approximately five hours of television each day. By the 1960s Americans spent nearly as much time on average watching TV as working. The federal government, through the Federal Communications Commission (FCC), gave television an important boost. In the early 1950s FCC streamlining of the license procedure helped local channels to air even in the smallest markets.

American corporations quickly adapted radio-marketing models to the new media. In the early years of TV, sponsors actually produced shows as vehicles for advertising. *Texaco Star Theater* and the *Goodyear TV Playhouse*, for example, built shows around their products with no clear line between content and advertisement. Cigarette companies like Philip Morris sponsored many popular shows including *I Love Lucy* and incorporated its products directly into the show as mass appeal drove prices down. Television was the ultimate mass medium, but marketers quickly realized the potential for "narrowcasting" to new audiences. Daytime shows sponsored by appliance and soap makers targeted housewives. Children's programming especially interested TV sponsors and advertisers. The most popular show of the decade, The *Howdy Doody Show*, was a prized advertising venue. Welch's juice sponsored *Howdy Doody*, and kids from the "peanut gallery" singing catchy Welch songs were woven into the show to great effect. *Howdy Doody* was also the first American TV show to go international, with popular offshoots broadcast in Cuba and Canada during the 1950s. By the end of the decade the three big television networks—NBC, CBS, and ABC—gained control of programming, but not before TV advertising became the most powerful force in the consumer economy.

Westerns proved the most popular genre in television's first decade; TV westerns focused on kids and teens and came with a strong dose of social values. *Hopalong Cassidy*, *The Lone Ranger*, *The Gene Autry Show*, *The Cisco Kid*, and *The Roy Rogers Show* all sought to instill a work ethic and belief in righteousness against great odds. Singing cowboys Gene Autry and Roy Rogers presented legions of fans in the United States and abroad with patriotic stories and God-fearing characters. In so doing they helped educate young baby boomers about morality and evil during the Cold War. Although these shows often painted a picture of cultural harmony out of sync with the realities of 1950s life, they were not completely without social awareness. Autry, in particular, featured positive commentary on Indians in the modern Southwest and even presented young viewers with early information on water conservation and sustainability.

The message of American exceptionalism and frontier heroism resonated with Cold War culture and made westerns popular with children and adults alike. In 1959 westerns accounted for 17½ hours of prime time network broadcasting weekly. The appeal of westerns and American TV was global.

By 1958 U.S. networks sold 15 million dollars' worth of American programming to other nations yearly. Many nations depended wholly on U.S. programs for their broadcasting needs. American networks also invested heavily in foreign networks. By

A Latin American version of the Howdy Doody show, *La Hora de Jaudi Dudi*, aired on CMQ-TV in Cuba in 1953 featuring Jaudi and his new sidekick, "Don Burro." Popular *Domingos Alegres* comics followed in 1954.

the early 1960s, for example, ABC owned a stake in 54 different stations in 24 nations. Not to be outdone, advertising firms joined the fight for international markets. The J. Walter Thompson Agency exported U.S. programming and marketing to Western Europe. Success in Europe led to cooperation between government and industry to use radio and TV broadcasting to fill the cultural void left in the vast areas of the globe vacated by the Japanese, Germans, and colonial powers after the war.

STUDY QUESTIONS FOR THE FUTURE IS NOW

1. **What challenges did unions face in the 1950s?**
2. **What was the significance of TV in the 1950s?**

CONFORMITY AND REBELLION

An estimated six thousand people spilled out of the "Canvas Cathedral" in Los Angeles. Billy Graham, the forceful young preacher with the wild sweeping mop of hair pointed to the audience and said, "You know there's a man in this audience tonight . . . who knows this is the decision he should make . . . *This* is your moment of decision."

Evangelist Billy Graham opens his eight-day Washington, DC, crusade in Griffith Stadium before an estimated crowd of 16,000 on June 19, 1960.

The preacher was reaching out to potential converts but could have been speaking for millions of 1950s Americans who felt alienated by the dominant trends and culture of their time and thought that it was truly a national "moment of decision."

The 1950s are often remembered as an age of consensus, conformity, and prosperity following the trials and tribulations of the Great Depression and World War II. Rising salaries, greater access to education, and high rates of employment all support this perception. Not all Americans, however, shared in the prosperity of the decade, and many who did were disturbed by the culture of conformity that came with prosperity during the Cold War. Although much of the popular culture of the time celebrated conformity, examples of growing discontent were easy to find. Writers such as Europeans Oswald Spengler, T. S. Eliot, and Aldous Huxley, and American conservative William F. Buckley railed against excessive materialism and "spiritual collapse." Cartoonists in *Mad Magazine* ridiculed politicians, the Cold War, and television. Frightening government civil defense programs spawned a bomb shelter industry

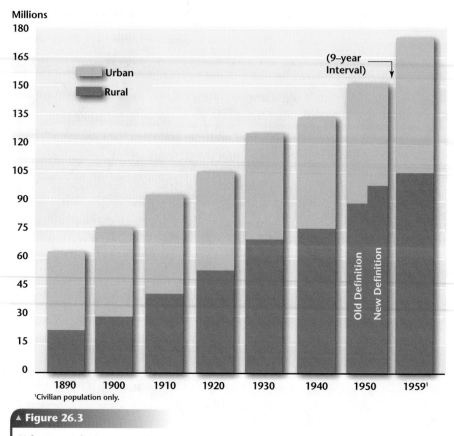

▲ Figure 26.3

Urban population growth Continuing trends of the 20th century, urban populations grew in proportion to rural. The growth of suburbs in the 1950s required a new definition of urban to account for the percentage of the population that was neither rural nor urban in the traditional sense.

as communities and individuals prepared for possible nuclear attack. In American schools children practiced "duck-and-cover" drills that caused deep anxiety about human helplessness in the face of new technologies of mass destruction.

Psychologists worried about rising rates of depression and clinical anxiety among suburbanites, corporate executives, and middle-class women, all beneficiaries of the postwar "good life." Suburban housewives, often overextended through domestic work and unrealistic expectations of domestic bliss, suffered high rates of depression. Likewise, parents and community leaders worried as never before about children rebelling and becoming juvenile delinquents.

Old Time Religion

Religion took on increased importance in public life during the 1950s, with American spirituality contrasted with what opponents characterized as godless communism. Politicians paid homage to their faith while religious leaders such as Cardinal Francis

Spellman, Norman Vincent Peale, Billy Graham, and Bishop Fulton Sheen became media stars and presidential advisors.

Billy Graham rose from obscurity to national prominence by explicitly linking the ideology of Containment with religious salvation. Graham began his rise to national prominence in the fall of 1949, when he launched a series of nightly revivals in his Los Angeles "Canvas Cathedral."

The 30-year-old Graham started his crusade after learning that the Soviets had the atomic bomb. In his fiery sermons he focused on world events and warned increasingly large audiences that nothing short of religious conversion could save America from nuclear apocalypse. Graham told his followers that communists had "declared war against Christ, against the Bible, and against all religion!" By the early 1950s Graham had appeared on the covers of *Time* and *Newsweek*, met the president, and toured the world meeting with political leaders. Through the medium of television the message of the "New Evangelical" movement spread widely. Graham, however, was only the most visible representative of a dynamic "plain folk" evangelical movement that linked politics and religion during the Cold War and laid the foundation for a new conservatism.

The warnings of Graham and others who linked religion and geopolitics fell on fertile ground. Religious participation surged during the 1950s. In 1950 alone membership in Protestant denominations increased by 4 percent, while the number of American Roman Catholics grew by 2 percent. This trend accelerated throughout the decade as church membership increased from 58 percent of the population in 1950 to 63 percent by 1959. Denominational change was equally dramatic. Evangelicals gained millions of converts during the 1950s, especially in the transient Southwest. Graham built his career in Los Angeles on the western revivalist tradition begun by radio pioneer Aimee Semple McPherson in the 1920s. By 1959 Americans invested $935 million annually in new church construction, much of it in Los Angeles and other rapidly growing western cities.

Religious fervor wedded to Cold War ideology served the goals of the federal government. Political leaders from both parties allied themselves with popular religious movements, and the line between church and state blurred. That religion was seen by many Americans as a weapon in the Cold War led Congress to pass an act making "In God We Trust" the nation's official motto and featuring it on all U.S. currency. During the 1950s the U.S. dollar replaced the British pound as the global currency of choice, and the message that the United States was a nation "under God" spread around the world.

Women in the 1950s

The linkage of religion and politics had special implications for American women. Social values appeared to veer off in contradictory directions in the 1950s. Even as a growing number of women attended college and worked outside the home, opinion leaders, popular TV shows, and advertisers began celebrating "traditional families" or "nuclear families" anchored by a working husband and homemaker wife.

The 1950s white suburban housewife and mother became a Cold War icon as powerful as Rosie the Riveter had been during World War II. Suburban culture and the changing nature of men's work forced many middle-class women to manage the family's needs while husbands were away at jobs, sometimes far from home. Advertisers, religious leaders, and politicians encouraged domestic consumption as the best means for suburban women to participate in public life and to fight communism.

Modern labor-saving appliances provided the centerpieces of suburban households in the 1950s. The newest percolator, range, or vacuum cleaner, advertisements assured, would shave time off of a housewife's busy daily routine. The purchase and use of appliances took on a major role for the 1950s housewife. While the husband often earned the income, the wife at least exercised authority over many household purchases. More than consumers, many suburban women became active dealers of appliances and household goods. Women sold the multicolored plastic Tupperware that filled 1950s cabinets and refrigerators door to door or through Tupperware parties in homes. Most of the female sales staff received their pay in Tupperware, not cash, while their male regional managers pocketed large cash commissions. Likewise, as masters of households women moved into real estate in increasing numbers and in effect transformed that industry. Thus, women of the 1950s often used their domestic status to open new career paths directly tied to the most significant economic trends of the day. At home or in new careers, middle-class women felt pressure to live up to

Both women and consumption are idealized in this Tupperware party advertisement, 1950. The elevation of food containers to art reflected pressure for women to create a distinctly American form of domesticity as a response to communism.

an idealized vision of patriotic femininity. TV moms such as *Father Knows Best*'s Jane Wyatt presented pictures of perfection, as they cooked breakfast in designer dresses and were always ready to tend to their family's needs. Despite all of the talk of motherhood and the home in the 1950s, many women, especially minority mothers, remained in the workplace, often at low-paying jobs, while others entered the workforce for the first time. In 1960 twice as many women held jobs outside the home as they did in 1940. Thirty-nine percent of women with children aged 6 to 17 held paying jobs at the end of 1959.

Professional women faced challenges gaining entrance to the best graduate schools and landing good jobs even with advanced degrees. Even the most accomplished women, such as scientist **Rachel Carson**, whose prize-winning books, *The Sea Around Us* and *Silent Spring* became environmental classics, faced prejudice. In Carson's case industry critics used the media to paint Carson as an "emotional women" who worried too much about plants and animals.

Many women found public outlets for their skills and opinions through volunteer societies such as the influential League of Women Voters. The LWV and other organizations, often at the request of the U.S. government, went beyond mere domestic activity to take on a role in international affairs. It also hosted foreign dignitaries visiting the United States and helped to shape the politics of the decade. Behind what writer **Betty Friedan** later named the "feminine mystique" of vacuous suburban domesticity, American women of the 1950s forged new opportunities for themselves while raising awareness of issues that were specific to women and those that reached far beyond the stereotypical suburban household.

Organization Men

1950s life was hardly ideal for males of the suburban castle—for the army of new corporate executives. Sociologist **David Reisman** uncovered widespread unhappiness in his study of corporate culture, *The Lonely Crowd* (1950). Reisman worried that Americans had lost what German sociologist Max Weber referred to as the Protestant Work Ethic: the moral drive to prosper through one's own individual hard work that had accounted for the greatness of America.

Journalist **William H. Whyte, Jr.**, published similar results in his widely read study *The Organization Man* (1956). Whyte discovered much anxiety among white-collar workers who were disengaged from their families and traditional social structures by rigid corporate work lives and long commutes. Whyte's contentions buttressed concerns on the part of religious leaders that increased affluence did not necessarily translate into universal happiness and social well-being. Novels like Sloan Wilson's 1955 bestseller *The Man in the Grey Flannel Suit*, which painted a disturbing picture of mind-numbing conformity in corporate America, helped popularized these concerns.

By the time these studies appeared, major demographic and social changes had transformed life for American men. In 1957 white-collar workers outnumbered blue-collar workers for the first time in American history. For critics these corporate strivers represented the apex of a conformist society. Directed to dress in uniform suits, they

The fear of communism and the cultural consequences of containment were explored in popular science fiction films like *Invasion of the Body Snatchers*, 1956.

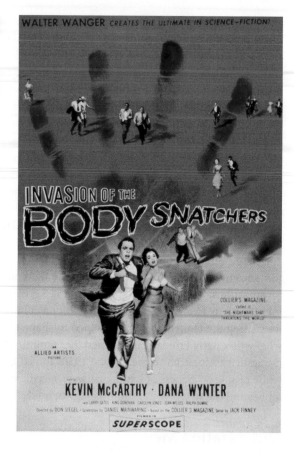

commuted on crowded trains or highways and worked long hours on bureaucratic tasks. To climb the company ladder they were expected to move often and to conform without question to corporate rules of behavior.

Teens, Rebels, and Beats

Middle-class affluence and extended education created a new category in American life in the 1950s, the teenager, who had money to spend and the power to influence popular culture. During the 1950s teenagers emerged as a distinct consumer group. By decade's end this influential demographic actively shaped American culture.

The word "teenager" first came into popular usage in the United States during World War II. In the 1940s many more adolescents than ever before found themselves grouped together in high schools. During and after the war many states passed mandatory school attendance statutes that resulted in a dramatic expansion of attendance and graduation figures. In 1930 only 50 percent of America's 14- to 17-year-olds attended high school; by 1950 this number had climbed to 73 percent. The percentage escalated throughout the 1950s as baby boomers entered their teens.

American businesses understood the potential buying power of this new group. As early as 1944, with the publication of *Seventeen Magazine*, ads aimed specifically at teens began to appear regularly. By the 1950s teens—driving sales of records and fashion—were the most sought-after market segment. By the 1960s, with an average income of $10 per week, teens contributed over $10 billion to the U.S. economy. Early teen advertisements and TV shows tended to portray teens as clean-cut, wholesome, middle class, and white. While marketers embraced these new consumers, cultural critics, parents, and law enforcement officials worried about the growing cultural influence of teenagers and their rebellious tendencies.

The high energy and open sexuality of rock 'n' roll fueled anxiety about a brewing youth rebellion. Rock 'n' roll emerged in the early 1950s as Chuck Berry, Fats Domino, Little Richard, and other black musicians mixed the musical traditions of gospel and rhythm and blues into a unique new form of distinctly American music. Black musicians, gaining popularity among white teens, launched a musical revolution with lasting social consequences.

By the mid-1950s young white men such as **Elvis Presley** and **Jerry Lee Lewis** repackaged the music emerging from the black community and made it acceptable for a much wider white audience. Elvis Presley's meteoric rise began at the humble Memphis Sun Records in 1955. By September of the next year he was signed to RCA's label and was selling records by the millions. Early media reactions to Elvis ranged from characterizations of him as "vulgar" and "suggestive" to racially coded claims that he was a purveyor of an "aborigines' mating dance." Parents, along with religious and political leaders, viewed the music and the reactions it caused as dangerously subversive. Despite concerted community and national efforts to ban the new music, teens embraced the rebellious and sexually charged rock 'n' roll with fanatical fervor. Fears of juvenile delinquency and racial mixing over the unsegregated radio airwaves fueled protest against the new music.

Popular films of the 1950s dramatized teenage troubles and contributed to popular anxieties about youth. Movies, especially *The Wild Ones* (1953), *Rebel Without a Cause* (1955), and *Blackboard Jungle* (1955), marked a stark departure from the patriotic offerings of the war years. Featuring Marlon Brando, James Dean, and Sidney Poitier as angry nonconformists, these films celebrated rebellion as well as contempt for parents and social institutions. Likewise, Leonard Bernstein's Broadway hit *West Side Story* (1957) celebrated ethnic diversity and youth rebellion. Mild by later standards, these productions, along with books like J. D. Salinger's hugely popular *Catcher in the Rye* (1951), frightened critics who rightly assumed that the buying power and sheer numbers of teenagers had led to the creation of an influential subculture.

Teenagers were not alone in using popular culture to express their discontent with Cold War culture. Much like the Lost Generation writers of the 1920s, Beatniks or Beat, slang for "down and out" writers such as Jack Kerouac, Allen Ginsberg, and William S. Burroughs, looked at postwar American society and did not like what they saw. Beats celebrated nonconformity and experimentation in their lives. Sexual experimentation, rootless travel, and anger permeated Kerouac's *On the Road* (1957) and Burroughs' *Naked Lunch* (1959). Even more disturbing was Alan Ginsberg's shocking "Howl," which gave poetic voice to the statistics of discontent compiled by sociologists Reisman and Whyte. Ginsberg's lament, "I saw the best minds of my generation destroyed," spoke to a growing number of alienated dissenters in a society obsessed with materialism and anticommunism. Photographer Robert Frank added visuals to the critique with his bleak 1959 portrait of the nation, *The Americans.*

Beat literature, 1950s films, and rock 'n' roll all revealed the diversity of American culture brewing beneath the conformity of the decade. The American culture of rebellion traveled the globe and circled back with new ideas from abroad. The 1950s critics helped link the Western world's postwar generation and bring in some new voices from the Developing World. This fusion of global concern established the foundation for the cultural revolutions of the 1960s. By calling into question America's traditional values, 1950s nonconformists had taken the first steps toward a critical collaboration between alienated progressive whites and black civil rights activists. Throughout the 1950s new advocates and old were asking the question, "what resources do we need to mobilize to achieve civil rights?"

STUDY QUESTIONS FOR CONFORMITY AND REBELLION

1. What was the relationship between foreign policy and mass culture during the 1950s?
2. Explain the changing status of men, women, and teens in the 1950s.

LAYING THE FOUNDATION FOR CIVIL RIGHTS

In 1959 jazz musician Miles Davis was rich and famous. His shows drew eager multiracial crowds to his New York City gigs, and his landmark contribution to modern musical history, *Kind of Blue,* topped the jazz charts. Leaving the upscale Birdland jazz club in August of that year, Davis was approached by two New York City police officers, who beat him severely with a blackjack after a brief and seemingly benign exchange of words. Covered with blood, Davis was arrested and thrown in jail. Pictures of the brutally beaten famous musician were in the news the next day. Though he was later acquitted of all charges, the incident demonstrated the racism that even the most successful African Americans living outside the South faced on a daily basis.

Davis was a smoky voiced iconoclast whose direct contributions to the civil rights movement included a few significant benefit concerts but little political advocacy or action. The scowling and quintessentially hip Davis couldn't have been more different from figures like the Reverend **Martin Luther King, Jr.** But there would not have been a successful civil rights movement without the diversity of opinion and action represented by Davis and King. Despite their obvious differences, King and Davis confronted the same question facing all civil rights advocates in the 1950s: Play slowly by the rules? Or, take a stand against the law now regardless of the consequences?

A civil rights revolution confronted all aspects of segregation and racism in the 1950s. The movement was not monolithic, and from the beginning fundamental tensions divided its proponents. The Cold War had added another layer of complexity to the basic fight for racial equality in the United States. The civil rights movement gained some support from federal officials aware that in the contest for the loyalty of the emerging nations of Africa, the Middle East, and Asia, "American apartheid" gave the Soviet Union a powerful Cold War propaganda tool.

By 1954 the civil rights movement divided over the best means to attack the pervasive racism that denied blacks access to the affluent society and basic human rights. Some activists felt that change should come rapidly through dramatic mass action. Others, including members of the NAACP, argued that gradual change brought about by strategic challenges to the legal system offered the best chance of long-term success.

Brown and the Legal Assault

The NAACP worked to mobilize the resources needed to launch an assault on *Plessy v. Ferguson* and the separate-but-equal doctrine of segregation. The legal fight required the NAACP to train talented black lawyers, raise money to fund cases, and build coalitions of progressive black and white researchers who could provide hard sociological data to undermine the premise of "separate but equal." The legal battle to overturn *Plessy* began in the 1930s when Charles Hamilton Houston, Dean of the Howard Law School, offered special classes, developed strategies, and trained a generation of talented lawyers.

The best known opportunity to test the method came when the Supreme Court agreed to hear the case of *Brown v. Board of Education* of *Topeka Kansas*. A compilation of multiple cases of educational discrimination, *Brown* was brought before the Supreme Court by NAACP Legal Defense Fund lawyer **Thurgood Marshall**. Marshall and NAACP colleagues George E.C. Hayes and James Nabrit, Jr., mounted a stunningly complete argument against segregation. Using sociological data, extensive research, and the Fourteenth amendment, they dismantled the basis of legal segregation. On May 17, 1954, Chief Justice Earl Warren's Court ruled unanimously that separate educational facilities for blacks and whites resulted in inherently unequal education. In his new role as Chief Justice, Warren was determined to use judicial power to help the powerless. The opinion of the Court, read by Warren, was decisive and powerful: "We conclude that, in the field of public education, the doctrine of 'separate but equal' has no place. Separate educational facilities are inherently unequal." This long-awaited decision set the precedent for the eventual desegregation of all public institutions, but the actual decision called for "all deliberate speed" only in the desegregation of schools.

The Warren Court's strongly worded unanimous opinion came at a moment of great concern regarding international attention to the American civil rights movement. By the early 1950s the inability of U.S. officials to respond to America's racial inequality was more than an embarrassment; it represented a serious threat to the very foundations of U.S. foreign policy during a vital period of global change. Warren was keenly aware of how segregation undermined the U.S. position in the Cold War just as African and Asian liberation movements were gaining traction. The NAACP and other civil rights organizations used the Cold War rhetoric of freedom and democracy for all as a powerful tool to motivate rapid action on long-festering issues like segregation.

The *Brown* decision opened the door, albeit slowly, for the nation's 11.5 million black children to receive an education equal to that of their white peers. The case helped move the nation further along the road to human rights than ever before. However, the battle against racism in schools was far from over.

Showdown in Little Rock

The first real test of the *Brown* ruling came in 1957 in Little Rock, Arkansas. That September, nine black students, armed with a federal court order, attempted to desegregate the city's Central High School. Governor Orval Faubus, responding by calling out the Arkansas National Guard to block their way, directly challenged the authority of the Federal Government.

On September 23, the situation escalated when the nine young students attempted to enter the school. Television cameras recorded the well-dressed students as they walked a gauntlet of abusive white students, parents, and community members, who spat and hurled obscenities at the "Little Rock Nine." School officials forced the children to withdraw from classes for their own safety. Governor Faubus promised to chain himself to the high school doors if the students returned, while the **Ku Klux Klan** made threats of violence against the Little Rock Nine and their supporters. Watching this dismal scene unfold on the Oval Office TV, President Eisenhower stepped in.

Eisenhower, who had spent his entire career in a segregated army, was ambivalent about civil rights but not about states' rights over federal authority. Ike's lukewarm response to the *Brown* decision had encouraged segregationists such as Faubus, who assumed the president would stay out of the fight. Faubus was wrong. Under pressure from a slowly changing tide of public opinion in the North and Cold War advisors who recognized the international public relations implications, Ike reluctantly sent federal troops to secure the students' safe passage into their school. Soldiers with the 101st Airborne escorted the children to class and stayed in Little Rock for the entire school year. This was the first time a Republican president sent federal troops into the South since Grant in 1874. Eisenhower followed the strong showing in Little Rock with support for a civil rights bill sent to Congress in 1957. The bill included controversial provisions for voting rights that even Eisenhower questioned. The Civil Rights Act of 1957 expanded voting rights on paper but once again failed to deal with the question of enforcement.

During the showdown at Little Rock television contributed to shifting the balance of power in the fight for civil rights. The glare of TV lights laid bare to the world the harsh tactics of the segregationist movement. Millions of white American viewers who watched the drama unfold converted to the cause of civil rights as they witnessed the calm dignity of the Little Rock Nine in the face of unfiltered racial hatred.

Boots on the Ground

During the long years of preparation for the legal assault on segregation, other civil rights activists mobilized to attack racism through direct protest. This movement gained momentum on December 1, 1955, after a humble protest by a tired seamstress and local NAACP member named Rosa Parks. On that evening Parks refused to give up her seat for a white passenger on a Montgomery bus as she traveled home from work. "My feet hurt," she recalled, and she was ready to learn, "once and for all what rights I had as a human and citizen." Local segregation laws and bus company policy required that when whites boarded a bus and needed seats any blacks on the bus must move to seats in the rear. After she refused to move, police arrested Parks.

The Montgomery Women's Political Council (WPC) seized on the arrest of the upstanding Parks as an example of racial injustice. Working with local NAACP leader **E.D. Nixon**, they launched a campaign against discriminatory practices on public transit. After securing legal representation for Parks, Nixon and the WPC assembled a critical coalition of local ministers to lead a boycott of the bus system.

To oversee the boycott, the ministers set up the **Montgomery Improvement Association** (MIA). They named 26-year-old minister Martin Luther King, Jr., as its head. King was chosen as the association's leader largely because he was new to town and an eloquent speaker. On the first night of the boycott King pushed his way through a tightly packed crowd in the Holt Street Baptist Church to address the gathered crowd. "We are here," he told the audience, because, "there comes a time when people get tired of being trampled over by the iron feet of oppression." In the months that followed, he became the face and strategist of the boycott. Most importantly he refined a philosophy of nonviolent protest for boycotters. The boycott lasted a year and sparked violence against King, Nixon, and other leaders, but it demonstrated the power of collective community action. During the 381 days of the boycott, Montgomery's protestors walked miles to work every day, were threatened with violence, and were arrested without cause. In the end the Supreme Court struck down the city's bus segregation.

The significance of the Montgomery boycotts spread well beyond Alabama. The boycott revealed that grassroots protest with thoughtful leadership could succeed. The victory in Montgomery provided national recognition for Martin Luther King, Jr., and it highlighted the role of religious leaders, women, and ordinary people in the coming fight for civil rights.

MLK and the Philosophy of Nonviolence

Leading a national Civil Rights Movement with global consequences was not what Martin Luther King, Jr., had in mind when he moved to Montgomery in 1955. The young minister summed up his feelings in a conversation with friends in early 1956: "If anybody had asked me a year ago to head this movement, I would have run a mile to get away from it." But, thanks largely to his role as leader of the successful boycott, King had emerged as the movement's public face.

King, along with NAACP associates **Bayard Rustin** and **Ralph Abernathy**, decided that they would lose an invaluable opportunity if they did not seize on the momentum generated by the bus boycott to work in changing the South and the nation. They scheduled a conference of black ministers and community activists for January 10 and 11, 1957, in Atlanta, Georgia. This meeting, called the "Southern Negro Leaders

GLOBAL PASSAGES

Cold War Media
The USIA and the Globalization of American Culture

During the 1950s multiple U.S. interests from soda companies, missionaries, corporations, filmmakers, and government agencies spread American culture across the globe to a greater extent than ever before. The spread of American culture abroad had accelerated with World War I propaganda programs; however, it gained urgency and extensive support after World War II and during the 1950s with the creation of the United States Information Agency (USIA) on August 1, 1953.

The USIA's roots lay in the World War I Committee on Public Information, the U.S. government's first concerted effort in distributing U.S. information abroad. Government-sponsored foreign information efforts faded during the 1920s but were revived by the Roosevelt administration in the years leading toward World War II. Gene Autry made a series of films distributed widely in Latin America and Europe and followed these with personal tours of Cuba and Great Britain, where crowds topping 250,000 greeted him. Press coverage referred to Autry as "Public Cowboy No. 1." During World War II Autry reached a global radio audience through his "The Sergeant Gene Autry Show" sponsored by Wrigley's gum. Autry's international appeal encouraged the creation of the Voice of America in February of 1942.

During the Eisenhower administration the USIA became a critical weapon in the competitive marketing of cultures during the Cold War. The USIA produced films, exported jazz music, and even distributed radios across Europe, the Middle East, and Africa so listeners could tune in to Voice of America and Radio Free Europe. Programming sponsored by the USIA reached an estimated audience of 30 million

Conference on Transportation and Nonviolent Integration," resulted in the Southern Christian Leadership Conference (SCLC). Electing King as their head, the SCLC quickly became one of the greatest forces for change in the Civil Rights Movement.

Although not universally supported by his follow activists, King proved such an effective spokesman that he was able to unify previously divided factions. As an expert in using the media, and TV in particular, King reached out to a much broader audience of supporters in America and abroad. A master orator with a doctorate in theology from Boston University, King was a deep thinker who crafted an effective and appealing ideology of peaceful mass resistance. Influenced by his readings of Henry David Thoreau's "Civil Disobedience" and Mahatma Gandhi's accounts of nonviolent protest in India, King strategically combined boycott and protest. After Montgomery, King

listeners in 80 countries. State Department officials carefully monitored international trends to target specific foreign audiences with American cultural products most likely to portray the United States as a force of progress and modernity in opposition to the backward Soviets. The CIA funded cultural programming and encouraged the conservative USIA to include controversial rock 'n' roll and jazz musicians in their programming. Thus audiences in Africa and the Eastern bloc heard artists including Buddy Guy and Elvis Presley not long after American listeners.

Direct efforts by foreign policy makers to use popular culture as a tool in the global Cold War had many unintended consequences. Foreign recipients recognized that many of the American performers were black and were suffering oppression at home. American civil rights activist Robert Williams worked with Cubans after the 1959 Cuban communist revolution to produce Radio Free Dixie; this broadcast encouraged black Southerners to take up arms against their white oppressors. Around the globe cultural exchange fostered by government officials resulted in artistic collaborations, new musical styles, and a global popular culture that did not necessarily serve the State Department goal of celebrating American exceptionalism. In other regions of the world, U.S. efforts to claim the mantle of progress and modernism created animosity among traditionalists and anticolonialists who rejected Western culture and values and came to see the United States as a threat to their belief systems.

- During the 1950s even U.S. allies complained of American cultural imperialism. Did efforts like the Voice of America and Radio Free Europe represent a form of imperialism?

- What were the unintended consequences of U.S. efforts to spread American popular culture abroad? Can you point to legacies of this effort in today's global politics?

preached about "militant nonviolence" and encouraged blacks and whites to confront racism everywhere. King warned segregationists, "We will soon wear you down by our capacity to suffer, and in winning our freedom we will so appeal to your heart and conscience that we will win you in the process."

The idea of massive resistance to segregation through militant nonviolence was ingenious and bold. It called on blacks of all ages to place their lives in danger and exercise a phenomenal level of willpower. King rightly concluded that if demonstrators refrained from violence, even in self-defense, the moral compass of world opinion would swing in their direction. In the age of television and worldwide media, recurring images of brutality used against groups and individuals peacefully demonstrating for their human rights gave protesters the high ground and forced political leaders to act. The "beauty of nonviolence," King said later, was that "It says you can struggle without hating. You can fight without war without violence." Through the waning years of the 1950s, King and a growing army of brave protestors perfected the method of nonviolent resistance. Across the South protesters as young as 10 and as old as 80 filled jails, stopped traffic, crippled businesses, and drew increasing numbers of reporters to the deep South to witness and publicize their fight.

At a time when the United States was engaging in a daily struggle to project images of equality, freedom, and Christian values, civil rights protesters drew attention to systematic racial oppression and discrimination. These activists knew that the world was watching. The impact of growing civil rights protest on global politics was not lost on national political leaders, who were aware that people of color made up the majority of newly independent Developing World nations critical to the Cold War balance of power.

The actions of African Americans fighting legal segregation in the South and whites awakening to the hypocrisy of American race relations inspired soul searching about inequality for all those seeking freedom. Just as the NAACP mobilized the black fight for equality in 1954–1955, over 1,000,000 Mexicans and Mexican Americans were deported from the U.S. by Operation Wetback. Under the direction of U.S. Immigration and Nationalization Service Director, General Joseph Swing, Operation Wetback raided Mexican American neighborhoods across the Southwest and Southeast, rounded up entire families, and deported parents and their native-born children who were American citizens. In some cases "Mexican-looking" American citizens were deported. In the United States and abroad critics accused the United States of "police-state" methods similar to those in communist nations. Latinos throughout the southern swath of the nation fought for their rights and won some early victories with cases like *Hernandez v. Texas* (1954).

TIMELINE 1950–1959

1950

January 24 Klaus Fuchs confesses to being a Soviet spy

February 9 Joseph McCarthy announces a list of communists in the U.S. State Department

June 25 North Korea invades South Korea, initiating the Korean War

November 26 Chinese forces enter Korea

1951

January 27 Nuclear testing begins at the Nevada Test Site

February 27 22nd Amendment to the U.S. Constitution is ratified

1952

July 18 *The New York Times* reports a questionable contribution to Richard Nixon's California campaign funds

November 1 United States detonates the first hydrogen bomb "Mike" on the Eniwetok Islands in the South Pacific

November 4 Dwight D. Eisenhower defeats Adlai Stevenson for the U.S. Presidency

November 29 President Eisenhower travels to Korea

1953

March 5 Death of Josef Stalin

March 26 Jonas Salk announces the first successful polio vaccine

June 19 Julius and Ethel Rosenberg are executed

July 27 Ceasefire achieved and a DMZ is created at Panmunjon, Korea

1954

March 9 Broadcast journalist Edward R. Murrow attacks Joseph McCarthy on the television show *See It Now*

May 7 French defeated at the Battle of Dien Bien Phu

April 7 President Eisenhower gives "Domino Theory" speech

April 22 to June 17 U.S. Army and the McCarthy Hearings

May 17 *Brown v. Board of Education* of Topeka Kansas decision

July 21 The Geneva Conference partitions Vietnam into North and South

October 31 The Algerian War for Independence begins

1955

February 12 U.S. President Eisenhower sends first military advisors to South Vietnam

April 12 The polio vaccine is introduced to the public

By the close of the 1950s the resources for an all-out multifront civil rights battle were in place. In the coming decade Americans would finally face the stain of racial inequality head-on and end a century of shameful denial and inaction.

STUDY QUESTIONS FOR LAYING THE FOUNDATION FOR CIVIL RIGHTS

1. What was the relationship between expressions of cultural dissent and civil rights activism?
2. What was the significance of the *Brown v. Board of Education* decision?

August 28 Emmett Till is murdered in Mississippi

December 1 Rosa Parks is arrested, marking the beginning of the Montgomery Bus Boycott

December 31 GM becomes the first U.S. company to make over $1 billion in a single year

1956

June 14 "Under God" is added to U.S. Pledge of Allegiance

November 6 Eisenhower is reelected President of the United States

June 29 The Federal Highway Act is enacted

July 26 Egypt nationalizes Suez Canal

July 30 Congress authorizes "In God We Trust" as the national motto

November 10 Hungary revolts against Soviet rule

October 24 Britain, France, and Israel launch military attacks against Egypt

December 20 The Montgomery Bus Boycott ends

December 22 Britain and France withdraw troops from Suez

1957

January 10 Southern Christian Leadership Conference (SCLC) founded

April 12 Allen Ginsberg's "Howl" is seized by U.S. Customs officials on grounds of obscenity

September 5 Jack Kerouac's *On The Road* is released

September 24 Little Rock's Central High School is desegregated

October 4 Soviets successfully launch Sputnik

1958

March 27 Nikita Khrushchev becomes the premier of the Soviet Union

1959

July 24 Nixon and Khrushchev's "Kitchen Debate"

August 21 Hawaii becomes the 50th state of the United States of America

Summary

- Cold War diplomacy shapes domestic life.
- American culture travels the globe.
- The Space Race intensifies the Cold War
- The United States leads the world in economic growth fueled by the "military industrial complex," vastly increased consumer spending, and the baby boom.
- American corporations consolidate production and distribution networks and perfect national and international marketing techniques.
- Applied science, especially in medicine, leads to massive public health campaigns to eliminate infectious diseases such as polio.
- Uneven economic prosperity and racial, gender, and generational tensions make the 1950s a time of affluence and anxiety.
- A civil rights revolution confronts all aspects of segregation in the 1950s, leading to critical legal victories and the rise of a widespread grassroots movement with dynamic leadership.

Key Terms and People

Abernathy, Ralph *1041*
American Federation of Labor *1026*
baby boom *1019*
Brown v. Board of Education of Topeka Kansas 1039
Carson, Rachel *1035*
Congress of Industrial Organizations *1026*
Eisenhower, Dwight D. *1008*
Farnsworth, Philo *1028*
Friedan, Betty *1035*
Fuchs, Klaus *1017*
Ho Chi Minh *1015*
Interstate and Defense Highways Act *1020*
Kaiser, Henry J. *1023*
Khrushchev, Nikita *1005*
King, Martin Luther, Jr. *1038*
Ku Klux Klan *1040*
Levitt, William *1022*

Lewis, Jerry Lee *1037*
Marshall, George *1017*
Marshall, Thurgood *1039*
McCarthy, Joseph *1016*
McCarthyism *1016*
Montgomery Improvement Association *1041*
Murrow, Edward R. *1018*
Nasser, Gamal *1014*
Nehru, Jawaharlal *1014*
Nixon, E.D. *1041*
Plessy v. Ferguson 1039
Presley, Elvis *1037*
Reisman, David *1035*
Rosenberg, Ethel *1017*
Rosenberg, Julius *1017*
Rustin, Bayard *1041*
Salk, Jonas *1020*
Whyte, William H., Jr. *1035*

Reviewing Chapter 26

1. What factors contributed to the massive demographic changes of the 1950s. How did the changes in the United States compare to the rest of the world?
2. Why did millions Americans leave cities for rapidly growing suburbs? What trends and policies supported this migration?
3. Some consider the 1950s to be the pivotal decade in the creation of an "oil culture" in the United States. What developments and policies elevated the importance of oil during this time? How did demand for oil redirect the flow of people, goods, and ideas during the period?

Further Reading

Dochuk, Darren. From Bible Belt to Sunbelt: Plain-Folk Religion, Grassroots Politics, and the Rise of Evangelical Conservatism. New York: W.W. Norton, 2011. The rise of one of the most influential post-war movements.

Freidan, Betty. The Feminine Mystique. New York: W.W. Norton, 1963. The book that helped spark a movement.

Harvey, Mark T. A Symbol of Wilderness: Echo Park and the American Conservation Movement. Albuquerque: University of New Mexico Press, 1994. The surprising 1950s origins of the wilderness movement.

McDougall, Walter. The Heavens and the Earth: A Political History of the Space Age. New York: Basic Books, 1985. Award winning account of the space race in Cold War context.

Rome, Adam. The Bulldozer in the Countryside: Suburban Sprawl and the Rise of American Environmentalism. Cambridge, U.K.: Cambridge University Press, 2001. The rise of suburbia creates environmental problems and inspires environmental protection.

Tyson, Timothy B. Radio Free Dixie: Robert F. Williams and the Roots of Black Power. Chapel Hill: University of North Carolina Press, 2001. Borderless nature of radio extends American civil rights into other nations.

Visual Review

The End of the Korean War

Events lead to a ceasefire and stalemate in Korea.

The New Look

Eisenhower plans new Cold War strategies.

The Rise of the Developing World

Newly independent nations are focus of Cold War strategies.

Hungary and the Suez, 1956

Conflicts in Europe and the Middle East have Cold War implications.

France's Vietnam War

The United States begins its support of South Vietnam.

McCarthyism and the Red Scare

Senator Joseph McCarthy searches for communist conspiracies in the United States.

The Eisenhower Era

THE DYNAMIC 1950S

A Dynamic Decade

The Baby Boom

Postwar spawns an unprecedented population growth.

Consumer Nation

American consumption increases dramatically.

Suburban Migrations—Urban Decline

Millions leave U.S. cities for the suburbs.

Corporate Order and Industrial Labor

Corporations forge a new model, while workers and unions prosper.

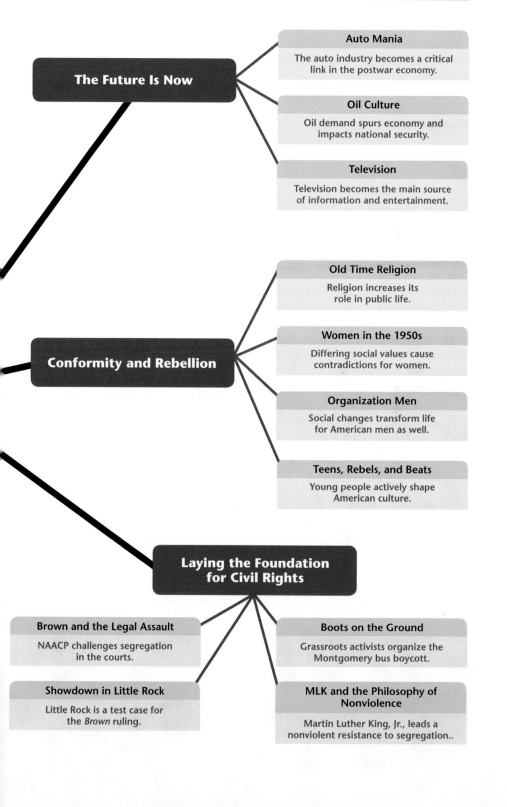

The Future Is Now

Auto Mania

The auto industry becomes a critical link in the postwar economy.

Oil Culture

Oil demand spurs economy and impacts national security.

Television

Television becomes the main source of information and entertainment.

Conformity and Rebellion

Old Time Religion

Religion increases its role in public life.

Women in the 1950s

Differing social values cause contradictions for women.

Organization Men

Social changes transform life for American men as well.

Teens, Rebels, and Beats

Young people actively shape American culture.

Laying the Foundation for Civil Rights

Brown and the Legal Assault

NAACP challenges segregation in the courts.

Boots on the Ground

Grassroots activists organize the Montgomery bus boycott.

Showdown in Little Rock

Little Rock is a test case for the *Brown* ruling.

MLK and the Philosophy of Nonviolence

Martin Luther King, Jr., leads a nonviolent resistance to segregation..

The Optimism and the Anguish of the 1960s

I n the fall of 1964 several activists, sitting at tables at the University of California at Berkeley, collected money for civil rights. Some of them had recently returned from registering African Americans to vote during the Mississippi Freedom Summer. The university administration barred political solicitations for any groups other than the officially recognized campus Democrats or Republicans. On October 1 campus police arrested Jack Weinberg, one of the activists. Before they could drive away, a jeering crowd surrounded the police car waiting to take Weinberg to jail. By nightfall more than 3,000 people had joined the crowd. After a 32-hour standoff police released Weinberg and dropped the charges.

The arrest sparked the beginning of Berkeley's Free Speech Movement. Speakers criticized the university for stifling their rights. They complained that their education prepared them for jobs they did not want in giant corporations while it prevented them from making society more just. They denounced the university's president, Clark Kerr, a liberal Democrat, for not supporting their cause.

The protests reached their climax on the night of December 3 when Kerr announced that he would continue the regents' ban on political solicitations. **Mario Savio**, a graduate student in philosophy, said "There's a time when the operation of the machine becomes so odious, makes you so sick at heart, that you can't take part . . . and you've got to put your bodies upon the gears and upon the wheels, upon the levers, upon all the apparatus, and you've got to make

◄ Black Panther Party rally, by Flip Schulke

CHAPTER OUTLINE

THE NEW FRONTIER
> JFK's New Frontier
> The Challenge of Racial Justice
> Cold War Tensions
> Kennedy Assassination

THE GREAT SOCIETY
> Civil Rights Laws
> Great Society Programs
> The Supreme Court and Rights and Liberties
> The United States and the World beyond Vietnam

A ROBUST ECONOMY
> Technological Change, Science, and Space Exploration
> The Rise of the Sunbelt

RACE, GENDER, YOUTH, AND THE CHALLENGE TO THE ESTABLISHMENT
> Urban Uprisings and Black Power
> Latinos and Indians Struggle for Rights
> The New Feminism
> The New Environmentalism
> Youth and the Counterculture

America in the World

John Glenn orbited the Earth, improving America's stature in the space race (1962).

The "Summer of Love" in San Francisco emanated youthful counterculture values across the globe (1967).

The Cuban Missile Crisis erupted, threatening nuclear war (1962).

U.S. event that influenced the world

International event that influenced the United States

Event with multinational influence

Conflict

The Soviets build the Berlin Wall, preventing East Germans from leaving their country (1961).

Rev. Martin Luther King, Jr., delivered his "I Have a Dream Speech," inspiring civil rights movements worldwide (1963).

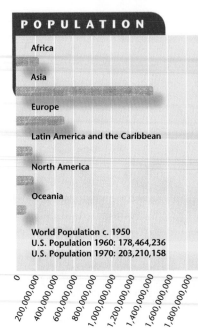

POPULATION

Africa

Asia

Europe

Latin America and the Caribbean

North America

Oceania

World Population c. 1950
U.S. Population 1960: 178,464,236
U.S. Population 1970: 203,210,158

0
200,000,000
400,000,000
600,000,000
800,000,000
1,000,000,000
1,200,000,000
1,400,000,000
1,600,000,000
1,800,000,000

it stop!" With that, 800 protesters marched into an administration building and sat down. The university charges brought against leaders of the sit-in prompted an even larger strike.

The Free Speech Movement ignited passions around the world. Students took up the cry that their universities were tied too closely to the government, the military, and large corporations. American activism inspired students in Europe, Latin America, and Asia to make their own demands for greater freedom of expression.

Some Americans were shocked at the students' disrespect for authority. In 1966 Republican **Ronald Reagan** defeated California's Democratic Governor Edmund G. "Pat" Brown. Reagan promised to "clean up the mess at Berkeley" and have the regents fire President Kerr.

Free Speech Movement protesters in front of Sproul Hall, University of California at Berkeley, Fall 1964. Protests at Berkeley galvanized politics in California. Ronald Reagan won the governorship with a promises to "clean up the mess at Berkeley."

THE NEW FRONTIER

The 1960s had started with widespread optimism. Many Americans believed that the prosperity of the 15 years after World War II could be widely shared, and they worked to remove the stain of racial discrimination. Most Americans followed their political leaders' call for greater efforts to contain Soviet communism in the Cold War. People in other countries saw a United States more deeply engaged in international affairs. The hopes of the early years of the decade became strained after the assassination of President **John F. Kennedy** in November 1963, a horrifying murder that shocked and saddened people around the globe. His successor, **Lyndon B. Johnson**, pursued an initially popular program of domestic social and economic reform. By 1966, however, Americans became deeply divided and angry with one another. Some, especially among the young and people of color, embraced change, although a sizeable number of them wanted even more. Others—mainly older, white Americans—believed that movements for social justice had turned violent and destructive. They feared that advances toward racial equality came at their expense.

JFK's New Frontier

The decade began with the election of 43-year-old Massachusetts Democratic Senator John F. Kennedy as the nation's first Roman Catholic president. Many Americans thrilled at his vibrant youth and his idealistic appeals to serve the public good. During the fall campaign of 1960, Kennedy challenged voters to explore and conquer a **New Frontier**. Although he offered few specifics, he inspired millions of Americans to believe they could improve their country. They expected to expand economic and social opportunities for those who missed the prosperity of the 1950s and, at the same time, wage the Cold War against the Soviet Union and its allies more energetically.

As president, Kennedy exuded youth, confidence, and fitness. The public thought they knew him better than almost any previous occupant of the White House, largely because he mastered the new medium of television. His quick wit and bright smile endeared him to White House reporters and millions of citizens who watched live broadcasts of his dazzling press conferences. Pictures of him with his beautiful and talented young wife, Jackie, and their two young children reinforced the view that he, like the nation he led, were ready to take on any challenge. Befriending movie stars and popular singers, the president suggested to a celebrity-struck public that he could move gracefully in the currents of popular culture. Few knew the full extent of Kennedy's chronic bad back, and Addison's disease, a serious adrenal disorder, left him in almost constant pain and sometimes even threatened his life. Fewer still, only his closest friends and a few reporters, knew at the time that he conducted a series of sexual affairs, both inside and out of the White House. Although the public's idealized image glossed over his troubled marriage and serious health problems, while he lived and in the years that followed many Americans viewed his administration "the age of "Camelot."

The Challenge of Racial Justice

The hopes inspired by Kennedy's call to conquer a new frontier represented one part of a more widespread sense that the time was ripe to remake the United States into a more just and more prosperous society. The African American struggle for civil rights inspired millions of Americans, black and white, to join a mass movement for racial equality. The grassroots movement originated in hundreds of African American churches and colleges across the South. Once it gained national visibility, the Kennedy administration responded by providing federal protection to embattled civil rights advocates and introducing far reaching civil rights legislation in Congress.

In February 1960 four black college students at North Carolina A & T State University demanded an end to segregation. These young men entered a Woolworth's in Greensboro, sat down on lunch counter stools reserved for whites, and asked to be served. Their request to be served in the same way as white customers were what started the "sit-in" movement that quickly spread throughout the South and eventually numbered 70,000 people in 150 different locations. Throughout the sit-ins, the protestors remained nonviolent. Encouraged by their involvement, sit-in veterans founded the Student Nonviolent Coordinating Committee (SNCC) in April 1960.

In 1961 SNCC joined the initiative of CORE (Congress of Racial Equality), another direct action civil rights group, to test court-ordered integration along interstate bus travel and in bus stations. The first "freedom ride" traveled from Washington, DC,

Freedom Riders being attacked in Birmingham, May 15, 1961. Dramatic images such as this achieved the goal of the freedom rides to use the media to undermine the credibility of southern segregationists who lived up to low expectations at every stop along the way.

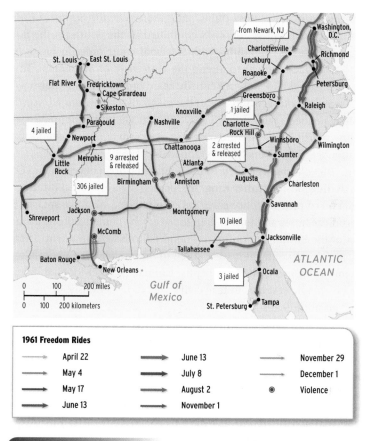

1961 Freedom Rides

→	April 22	→	June 13	→	November 29	
→	May 4	→	July 8	→	December 1	
→	May 17	→	August 2	◉	Violence	
→	June 13	→	November 1			

▲ **Map 27.1**

Freedom Riders This map details routes taken by Freedom Riders, 1961. All of the freedom riders knew that they were placing themselves in harm's way. The trip was punctuated by escalating violence as the buses moved deeper into the segregated South.

to Alabama, where mobs of angry whites attacked a small group of interracial activists and burned a bus. Local law enforcement rarely provided protection for the riders. The national and international media, however, gave the riders extensive, sympathetic coverage.

President Kennedy at first found the freedom riders too militant. He wanted racial justice to come about gradually. Although his brother, Attorney General **Robert F. Kennedy**, ordered U.S. Marshals to protect the riders when no other authorities would, he called for a "cooling off" period for the freedom rides and suggested that the racial tension at home would embarrass the president at his upcoming summit meeting with Soviet premier Nikita Khrushchev. But the freedom riders continued on to Mississippi, where they were arrested. Finally, in September 1962, the Interstate Commerce Commission enforced desegregation of bus facilities.

The challenge of integrating public education after the Supreme Court's 1954 decision in *Brown v. Board of Education* continued in the South. In the fall of 1962 Air Force veteran **James Meredith**—with a federal court order in hand—sought to become the first black student to attend the University of Mississippi. In response, thousands of whites rioted. Robert Kennedy again ordered federal marshals to shield Meredith. They were attacked and 160 of the marshals were wounded, several by gunfire. President Kennedy then ordered the National Guard to the university campus to defend the marshals and restore order. To the dismay of the white supremacists, Meredith attended the university and graduated in 1963.

In early 1963 civil rights leaders in the Southern Christian Leadership Conference (SCLC), including **Martin Luther King, Jr.**, focused their efforts on Birmingham, Alabama, a hotbed of racism. Police chief Bull Connor and his force sprayed protesters with powerful fire hoses and turned dogs loose on the demonstrators, including children. News of the Birmingham protests energized a wider movement. Energy turned to outrage when four young girls were killed in September after a bomb exploded in the basement of the Sixteenth Street Baptist Church, a center for civil rights organizing. Pushed by media coverage to take civil rights more seriously, Kennedy proposed civil rights legislation that summer.

The effort to gain national support for civil rights culminated with the March on Washington for Jobs and Freedom on August 28, 1963. Over 200,000 black and white demonstrators, more than double the number expected, marched from the Washington Monument to the Lincoln Memorial. There, they heard King deliver his "I Have a Dream" speech. Although Kennedy initially feared the march might turn violent and provoke an anti-civil rights backlash among whites, he soon supported it. The large turnout, peaceful demonstration, and positive media coverage gave his proposed civil rights bill even higher priority.

Cold War Tensions

Many advocates for civil rights saw the struggle for racial equality inside the United States as a way to win friends in the global Cold War competition with the Soviet Union. Kennedy devoted more attention toward winning the Cold War than to any other subject. During the 1960 campaign, Kennedy advocated more assertive U.S. actions in the Cold War; he charged that Eisenhower had allowed a "missile gap" to grow between the Americans' and the Soviets' arsenals. In his inaugural address he called on Americans to "pay any price, bear any burden, meet any hardship, support any friend, oppose any foe to assure the survival and success of liberty." In June 1961 Kennedy met in Vienna with Soviet Communist Party Chairman Nikita Khrushchev to discuss the Berlin question. The status of Germany had never been resolved after World War II and its division was a central question of the Cold War. The country remained split into two states, the pro-West Federal Republic of Germany (FRG) and the Soviet satellite Democratic Republic of Germany (DRG). Berlin, inside the DRG, was also divided into Western and Communist halves. Each week more than 4,000 people fled East Berlin for West Berlin in search of a better life in the West. At the summit he threatened to make a separate peace with the DRG, depriving the Western powers of their legal right to station military forces in Berlin, if the Western powers did not leave West Berlin by the end of the year.

Kennedy felt bullied by Khrushchev at Vienna. After he returned to the United States, the president went to great lengths to demonstrate his commitment to Berlin. He asked Congress for a $3.25 billion increase in the defense budget, recalled thousands of military reserves to active duty, and more than doubled draft calls. In August the Soviets responded by building a wall separating the two Berlins and preventing passage to the West. Later, in 1963, JFK went to Berlin to smooth things over, declaring to a receptive crowd, *"Ich bin ein Berliner"* ("I am a Berliner"). Actually, it meant in German "I am a doughnut"—but it endeared Kennedy to the Germans. The Berlin Wall remained standing for 26 years, a symbol of East–West tensions and of East German repression of its citizens.

Fostering legitimate governments and prosperous, growing economies, Kennedy advocated nation building. He created the Peace Corps, which sent thousands of idealistic young American volunteers to teach, give vaccinations, and build wells, schools, and hospitals throughout the Developing World. In Latin America, in particular, Kennedy hoped to counter the appeal of communism and **Fidel Castro**'s successful revolution in Cuba in 1959 by initiating in March 1961 the **Alliance for Progress**, a multibillion dollar aid program for Latin America.

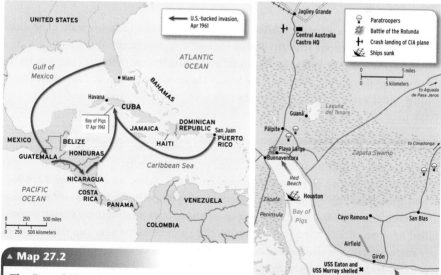

▲ **Map 27.2**

The Bay of Pigs This map shows the Bay of Pigs Invasion and training sites. JFK and other supporters were confident the invasion was well planned and supported sufficiently at home to succeed. Later critics pointed to the treacherous nature of the Bay and other miscalculations as insurmountable weaknesses.

Fidel Castro's revolution in Cuba had inspired interest in Latin America by offering an alternative approach to the political and economic promises of the United States. Castro had overthrown a pro-American government that allowed gambling, prostitution, and narcotics sales to flourish and held ties to organized crime and American business. Eager to see Castro removed from power, Kennedy approved a CIA plan in January 1961 initiated by the Eisenhower administration to train approximately 1,500 Cuban exiles to invade the Bay of Pigs in southern Cuba. When the raid began on April 17, Kennedy refused to approve any further assistance to the invaders, and the Cuban army quickly captured the U.S.-sponsored guerillas. After the **Bay of Pigs invasion** the CIA, through Operation MONGOOSE, continued attempting to overthrow or assassinate Castro. These unsuccessful efforts only managed to push Castro more firmly into the Soviet camp.

A little over a year after the Bay of Pigs fiasco, in October 1962, the installation of Soviet missiles in Cuba prompted the **Cuban missile crisis**, the most dramatic nuclear standoff of the Cold War. By early October Kennedy knew that the Soviets had built a missile base in Cuba, only 90 miles off the coast of Florida. Kennedy decided to initiate a blockade, or "quarantine," to stop future nuclear weapons from reaching Cuba and demanded that the Soviets withdraw the missiles already there. Anxiety rose across the nation as adults stocked up on groceries and school children went through air raid drills. On October 28, the Soviets, to Castro's dismay, pledged to remove the missiles in return for an American promise not to invade Cuba. The United States also secretly agreed to remove its own obsolete Jupiter missiles aimed at the Soviet Union from Turkey.

After the close call of the Cuban missile crisis, Kennedy and his team grew more willing to ease relations with the Soviet Union. The Americans and Soviets set up a "hot line" between the White House and the Kremlin in case of future emergencies. In August 1963 the United States and the Soviet Union signed a **Limited Test Ban Treaty** ending above ground atomic testing, but allowing continued testing underground.

Kennedy Assassination

How Kennedy would have responded to developments in the Cold War will forever remain unanswerable, as he was murdered in Dallas, Texas, on November 22, 1963. When the president's open motorcade passed the Texas Book Depository early that afternoon, Lee Harvey Oswald—firing three shots from the building's sixth floor—killed Kennedy. Police quickly apprehended Oswald. Over the next four days millions of Americans remained glued to their TVs, mourning and watching intently as newscasters provided new information. They also witnessed Oswald's own assassination by Dallas nightclub owner Jack Ruby on live television on November 24. The country united as it viewed Kennedy's emotional state funeral, at which Kennedy's three-year-old son, John, Jr., saluted his father's casket. People wept openly on streets around the world when they heard the news and saw the funeral on television. Many of Kennedy's backers, as well as those who had been lukewarm supporters or even critics, almost immediately romanticized his tenure in office. Later observers viewed his presidency as one full of promise tragically cut short.

STUDY QUESTIONS FOR THE NEW FRONTIER

1. How did the Kennedy administration promote a sense of optimism in the United States?
2. What events caused Cold War tensions to rise in the early 1960s?

THE GREAT SOCIETY

The early 1960s were years of enormous promise, temporarily dimmed, but not extinguished, by Kennedy's assassination. Optimism reflected the enduring appeal of political liberalism, the belief in using the power of the federal government to promote economic growth and social harmony. By the end of the 1960s, however, much of the hopefulness had soured, and many Americans became frustrated and angry with their leaders and most public institutions. Many rejected liberalism as a failed approach that raised false hopes.

From 1964 to 1966 President Lyndon B. Johnson pressed Congress to enact a series of social and economic reforms designed to promote what he called the **Great Society**. At first the public supported action to end racial discrimination, expand educational opportunities, end hunger and poverty, and make health care available for all. Public approval of the Great Society faded, however, as the war in Vietnam expanded, and many white Americans became angry and frightened by African American demands for civil rights.

Civil Rights Laws

On November 22, 1963, Johnson was sworn in as president aboard Air Force One, as Jacqueline Kennedy, her clothes stained with her husband's blood, stood by his side. In the days immediately following the assassination Johnson implored Kennedy's top aides to remain. They did so out of a sense of duty, but most left over the next 18 months, unable to overcome their grief and the sense that Johnson was an unworthy successor to their hero.

Almost immediately President Johnson expressed impatience with America's racial injustice. He told a grieving Congress the day before Thanksgiving that "We have talked long enough in this country about equal rights. We have talked for a hundred years or more." Johnson's addresses to Congress in 1963 and 1964 called on the country and lawmakers to enact Kennedy's unfinished agenda. He emphasized the need to eliminate the blight of poverty. He declared "unconditional war on poverty in America. . . . [and] we shall not rest until that war is won."

Johnson threw himself into the struggle to enact the Civil Rights law Kennedy had introduced in the summer of 1963. In the first six months of 1964, he pleaded with and badgered members of Congress to pass the law. He overcame the inclination of some Republican Senators to join with Southern Democrats to filibuster the bill when he told Everett Dirksen, the Republican Senate leader, that the party of Abraham Lincoln could not be seen as standing in the way of civil rights. In July Johnson signed the most sweeping Civil Rights law since Reconstruction, the Civil Rights Act of 1964. It outlawed segregation in restaurants, overnight accommodations, and transportation. It created a Fair Employment Practices Commission that could sue to guarantee equal opportunity in hiring and promotion in private firms with more than 99 workers. The law gave the Justice Department the power to file a suit when a person's civil rights were violated. The law also outlawed discrimination on the basis of sex as well as race.

Enactment of the Civil Rights Acts occurred as the presidential election campaign got underway. Johnson easily defeated the Republican candidate, Arizona senator **Barry Goldwater**. He campaigned, he said, to become "president of all the people." Johnson won 61.1 percent of the popular votes (43.1 million) and 486 electoral votes to Goldwater's 38.1 percent (27.2 million) and 52 electoral votes. The president carried every state with the exception of Goldwater's Arizona and five states in the Old Confederacy.

On election night it appeared as if Johnson and the Democrats had cemented a durable majority in favor of political liberalism and an active federal government. Despite the size of Johnson's victory, however, there were ominous signs for the future of the Democrats as the majority party, and portents of hope for Republicans. Goldwater's nomination represented the triumph of newly assertive conservatism. Unlike the Republican presidential nominees from 1940 to 1960 who had endorsed the idea of a federal government that would take responsibility for the country's economic and social well-being, Goldwater and his supporters considered the federal government an adversary of personal liberty.

After the election Johnson pressed forward with voting rights laws. In the spring of 1965 Martin Luther King, Jr., and the SNCC led demonstrations in Selma, Alabama, to demand the right to vote. Fifteen thousand voting age African Americans lived in Selma, but only 355 were registered voters. Would-be African American voters faced the prospect of losing their jobs or homes or even their lives if they applied to vote. Those brave enough to attempt registering faced hostile officials who rejected voter application forms if the would-be black registrant failed to cross a *t* or dot an *i*. Registrars asked black, but not white, applicants complicated questions like "what two rights does a person have after being indicted by a grand jury?" or "how many bubbles are there in a bar of soap?"

Over 3,000 demonstrators demanding the right to vote were arrested in January and February 1965. Sheriff's deputies knocked a woman to the ground and singed the skin of demonstrators with electric cattle prods. In response to the brutality, King and **John Lewis** of SNCC planned a 56-mile march from Selma to Birmingham. On Sunday, March 7, with television crews filming, 600 demonstrators assembled at the

Edmund Pettis Bridge at the edge of Selma, where they faced dozens of sheriff's deputies. Sheriff Jim Clark gave the demonstrators two minutes to disperse before ordering horse-mounted deputies into the crowd. They fired tear gas and swung bullwhips and rubber tubes wrapped with barbed wire at the demonstrators.

On March 15 Johnson addressed Congress on the need for voting rights. He recalled his days as a school teacher in rural Texas in 1928 where his poor, mostly Mexican American students often arrived without breakfast. "They knew even in their youth the pain of injustice. . . . Somehow you never forget what poverty and hatred can do when you see its scars in the hopeful face of a young child." He called on Americans to "overcome the crippling legacy of bigotry and injustice" and demand that Congress pass the Voting Rights Act.

In the summer of 1965 Congress responded to the widespread public revulsion at the displays of racism by enacting the Voting Rights Act. Under its terms, which outlawed literacy tests to vote, the Justice Department had the power directly to register voters in districts where discrimination existed. Justice Department officials also monitored the conduct of elections on polling days. The Voting Rights Act of 1965 succeeded in dramatically increasing African American voter participation. In fact, such supervision of the polls became a common international practice over the next decades. Independent election watchers representing international organizations, nongovernmental organizations, and the United States and other governments observed elections in countries new to electoral politics or with histories of voting rights abuses.

Passage of the Voting Rights Act also deepened the racial divide between the major parties. Newly registered African American voters overwhelmingly voted for Democratic Party candidates. In the Deep South white voters increasingly voted Republican rather than Democratic. From the 1980s to the early 21st century Southern states became the most heavily Republican region of the country.

Great Society Programs

In his first State of the Union address in January 1964, President Johnson declared "unconditional war on poverty." Later during the 1964 election campaign he painted a glorious vision of a Great Society where there was "abundance and liberty for all . . . an end to poverty and racial injustice . . . a place where every child can find knowledge to enrich his mind and to enlarge his talents." The Congress that convened in January 1965 had the largest Democratic Party majority since 1937. Over the next two years it enacted the most far reaching economic and social laws since the New Deal.

In 1948 President Harry Truman had proposed government-sponsored universal health insurance, similar to government-sponsored health plans that had been enacted in Western Europe. The medical profession strongly opposed Truman's plan, and it was never approved. By the 1960s elderly Americans were among the poorest people in the country, primarily because of their mounting health bills. In 1965 Congress passed **Medicare**, a health plan providing universal hospital insurance for Americans over 65. Medicare also included voluntary insurance to cover doctors' fees and nursing home charges. In 1966 Congress created **Medicaid**, a system in which the federal government provided states matching grants to pay for medical costs of poor people of all ages. Medicare helped reduce poverty among the elderly and both programs narrowed the gap in health care between the rich and the poor.

In 1965 and 1966 Congress enacted a wide array of programs designed directly to eliminate poverty. It created the Office of Economic Opportunity, headed by Sargent Shriver, the first Director of the Peace Corps, to supervise the War on Poverty. Congress also created Food Stamps to feed people whose income fell below the government-calculated poverty level. A later study concluded that Federal food programs had been "almost fully effective in reducing flagrant malnutrition." Congress created the Head Start program to provide preschool for children of poor families. The Job Corps, modeled on the Civilian Conservation Corps of the New Deal, employed 100,000 poor young men and women during its first eight years. Volunteers in Service to America (VISTA), patterned on the Peace Corps, recruited people to work in poverty-stricken areas in the United States. An ambitious **Model Cities** program was designed to encourage physical and economic revitalization of the nation's poorest urban areas; however, infighting among local and federal officials and lack of funds caused by the growing Vietnam War hampered its success. Congress created the cabinet Department of Transportation and Department of Housing and Urban Development to oversee programs to improve urban life.

In 1965 Congress ended the national quota system for immigration in place since the 1920s. After World War II advocates for refugees denounced the quota system for

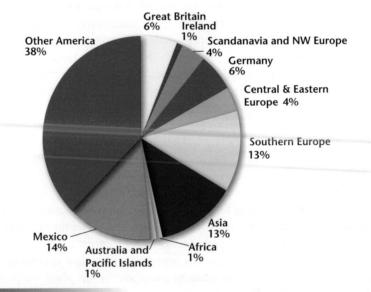

▲ **Figure 27.1**

1960s immigration Countries of origin of immigrants to United States after 1965. The 1965 immigration law reversed the harsh quota system that limited immigration for half a century. The law enabled a new wave of immigration from Asia and the Pacific Rim and Latin America.

denying Jews entry into the United States before the war—a stance that led to their eventual murder. Nevertheless, in 1952, in the midst of fears of communism, Congress passed over President Truman's veto an immigration law that retained the quotas and added restriction on the entry of political radicals. The 1965 immigration law replaced that system and allowed 170,000 immigrants from the Eastern Hemisphere and 120,000 from the Western Hemisphere to enter the United States each year. When Johnson signed the bill he said it ends "the harsh injustice of the national origins quota system" which was "a cruel and enduring wrong."

The 1965 law changed the source of U.S. immigration from Europe to Asia and the Western Hemisphere. A provision, little noticed at the time, permitted an unlimited number of visas for family unification. An immigration chain developed. An international student would earn an advanced degree in the United States, which entitled him or her to bring siblings, parents, spouse, and children. These, in turn, could ask that their relatives be granted visas. Before passage of the law, Europe and Canada contributed nearly half of the immigrants to the United States. By the late 1970s Europe and Canada accounted for 20 percent of legal immigrants, whereas Latin America and Asia made up 77 percent of immigrants.

Great Society reforms were popular at first, but enthusiasm faded in the last two years of Johnson's presidency. African American uprisings against police brutality, poverty, and continuing racial discrimination in major cities left dozens dead at the hands of police and National Guard units sent in by governors to quell the violence. Nearly all the dead were African Americans. The scenes of burning stores and sounds of gunshots and police sirens, played endlessly on television news, alarmed many whites. They expressed this "white backlash" by rejecting the Great Society and voting for Republican candidates who promised to restore law and order. Republicans replaced Democratic majorities in the congressional election of 1966. During the rest of his term, Johnson was able to persuade Congress to pass only one more major piece of social reform legislation. In 1968, after a Federal Commission on Civil Disorders reported that the United States was in danger of becoming two nations, one white and one black, separate and unequal, Congress passed a Fair Housing Law banning racial discrimination in public and private housing.

The Supreme Court and Rights and Liberties

The Supreme Court played a major role in expanding civil rights and liberties to people and groups formerly ignored or excluded from the protection of the Constitution. It broadly defined the rights of expression, defined the rights of criminal defendants, and it enhanced the right of privacy. The Court's 1960s decisions coincided with popular movements for greater personal freedom. The rulings also provoked significant resistance from many Americans who believed that they undermined the authority of police or religious institutions. Opposition to the Warren Court's expansion of rights and liberties became a significant element of a renewal of conservatism during the later 1960s.

In *New York Times v. Sullivan* (1964), the Court expanded the rights of news media to write about public officials or well-known public figures. The Court ruled against a public official who claimed that the *New York Times* had libeled him by printing false statements about him. The Court ruled that the false statements were trivial and only "recklessly false statements" made with "actual malice" violated libel laws. The Court also clarified the First Amendment's "establishment of a religion" clause with *Engel v. Vitale* (1962), which banned governments and local school boards from requiring prayers in public schools. Later in the decade it ruled that schools could not require devotional readings of the Bible.

Several decisions of the 1960s expanded the rights of criminal defendants. In *Mapp v. Ohio* (1961) the Court declared that state and local courts must exclude from trial evidence gathered outside the terms of a search warrant. In *Gideon v. Wainwright* (1963) it ruled that a defendant was entitled to a defense lawyer; if he or she could not afford one, the state would provide one. The most controversial criminal rights decision was *Miranda v. Arizona* (1966) which expanded the Fifth Amendment's prohibition on self-incrimination. The court held that someone arrested for a crime had to be clearly informed of the right to remain silent and to be represented by a lawyer. The Court also determined that the Constitution protected an inherent right to privacy; thus, in *Griswold v. Connecticut* (1965) the Court made ownership of contraceptives legal as a private matter.

Johnson appointed liberal justices committed to the Warren Court's expansion of civil rights and liberties. In the summer of 1967 he nominated **Thurgood Marshall**. When the Senate confirmed Marshall, he became the first African American Supreme Court Justice in U.S. history. Even at the time of Marshall's confirmation, however, a backlash against the Supreme Court was underway. Conservative legal scholars and political activists argued that recognition of rights for people formerly excluded from protection harmed the majority. For decades thereafter many presidential appointments to the Supreme Court ignited angry controversies, as conservatives sought to reverse the Court's expansion of rights and liberals tried to maintain them.

The United States and the World Beyond Vietnam

The rise and fall of the Great Society and growing controversies over the War in Vietnam absorbed most of President Lyndon Johnson's attention. Still, he tried with mixed success to continue the efforts of earlier administrations to project American power around the globe and to expand Kennedy's efforts to reduce tensions with the Soviet Union. As a result, the United States became involved in regional disputes in Latin America, the Middle East, and Europe.

In Latin America the Johnson administration minimized Kennedy's efforts to foster social reform. It supported military governments if they faced communist insurrections. In April 1965 the United States intervened militarily in the Dominican Republic to support a military government that had ousted a popularly elected president, Juan Bosch. The U.S. Embassy in Santo Domingo, the capital city, falsely claimed that 58 "identified and prominent Communist and Castroite leaders" were maneuvering to bring Bosch back from his temporary exile in Puerto Rico. Johnson ordered the marines to the Dominican Republic to put down Bosch's supporters and bolster the military government. He explained that "people outside the Dominican Republic are seeking to gain control."

The military intervention set off protests throughout Latin America and in the United States. Bosch complained that "this was a democratic revolution, crushed by the leading democracy in the world." In the United States liberals decried the military operation as a throwback to the bad old days of gunboat diplomacy of the late 19th and early 20th centuries. Combined with growing anxieties over the expanding U.S. role in fighting the Vietnam War, these misgivings undermined trust in Johnson's truthfulness.

American preoccupation with the Vietnam War contributed to the outbreak and bitter aftermath of the Six-Day War of June 1967 between Israel and the Arab states of Egypt, Syria, and Jordan. In the spring of 1967, Egyptian President Gamal Abdel Nasser insisted that the United Nations remove its forces from the Sinai Peninsula, which separated Israel and Egypt since Israel's attack on Egypt in 1956. After the UN force withdrew, Nasser closed the Strait of Tiran to ships bound for Israel. The Johnson administration urged Israel not to respond until the United States could organize an international naval force to open the straits. European nations, declining to join, believed that the United States, preoccupied in Vietnam, would not open the straits. The Israelis grew impatient with the delay and on June 5 launched a preemptive strike against Egypt. Jordan and Syria then entered the war against Israel. In six days Israel took the Sinai and Gaza Strip from Egypt, the West Bank of the Jordan River and East Jerusalem from Jordan, and the Golan Heights from Syria. The United Nations Security Council called for Israel to withdraw from captured territories in return for peace and security within recognized borders. It also called for a settlement of the Palestinian problem.

The aftermath of the war brought Soviet prime minister **Alexei Kosygin** to New York for a special session of the UN General Assembly. Kosygin then met with Johnson in Vienna in June 1967. Johnson pressed Kosygin for help in ending the Vietnam War, but the Soviet leader declined. He was competing with the People's Republic of China for the favor of the North Vietnamese. He did not wish to appear less committed to North Vietnam's war aims than were the Chinese.

Johnson and Kosygin agreed to intensify their efforts to end the competition in intercontinental ballistic missiles. In August 1968 the Johnson administration was preparing to announce that the president would visit Leningrad in September to confer on arms control. On August 20, however, the Soviet Union sent its armed forces into Prague, Czechoslovakia, to stop Czechoslovakia's efforts to loosen communist controls. *Pravda*, the newspaper of the Soviet Communist Party, justified the invasion and occupation of Czechoslovakia as an act of solidarity designed to prevent a friendly Communist state from falling "into the process of antisocialist degeneration." European and American newspapers called this reasoning the "Brezhnev Doctrine," after Soviet Communist Party chairman **Leonid Brezhnev**. Johnson canceled his visit to the Soviet Union, and the efforts to relax tensions with the Soviet Union once more failed.

STUDY QUESTIONS FOR THE GREAT SOCIETY

1. What factors led to the passage of the civil rights and voting rights laws?
2. Explain the rise and the subsequent decline of support for the Great Society.
3. In what ways did the Johnson administration continue and in what ways did it alter the foreign policies of the Kennedy administration?

A ROBUST ECONOMY

In the early and mid-1960s the economy of the United States boomed, technology advanced, and the quality of life for many Americans rose steadily. Between 1961 and 1965 average yearly economic growth exceeded 5 percent. Unemployment dropped to under 4 percent by 1966. By the end of the decade, however, the public's mood soured as economic growth fell to under 4 percent and inflation, tame since the late 1940s, exceeded 6 percent per year. Many Americans feared that the prosperity of the early part of the decade would not last. Their pessimism that their children's lives would not be better than their own intensified racial, regional, and class tensions.

Technological Change, Science, and Space Exploration

Technological innovations seemed to reinforce White's cheery forecast. Color television and other new electronics transformed home entertainment for the average American. By 1970, 96 percent of families had at least one TV at home. Satellites originally developed as part of the space program provided the infrastructure for telephone systems, television networks, military surveillance, and weather forecasting. By the end of the decade the integrated circuit microchip began to appear, although it would have its greatest impact on the personal computer revolution of a later period. And, in the later 1960s, government scientists developed an early version of the Internet, which promoted communications inside the defense department and among government research labs.

The American economy, growing every month from 1961 to 1969, enhanced the material well-being of many at home while sparking an economic nationalist backlash in other countries. The stock market also performed remarkably in the first half of the decade. American industrial exports surged. Chrysler, the third largest U.S. automaker, sold more cars in France than did all French car manufacturers combined. In 1967 French journalist Jean Jacques Servan-Schreiber published *The American Challenge*. Translated into many languages and widely read throughout Europe, *The American Challenge* predicted that Europe was becoming an economic and cultural satellite of the United States.

The 1950s marked a high point for American faith in science, and Americans continued to value scientific and technological advancement through the 1960s. Americans celebrated the discovery of pulsars, quarks, and quasars—even if they had little

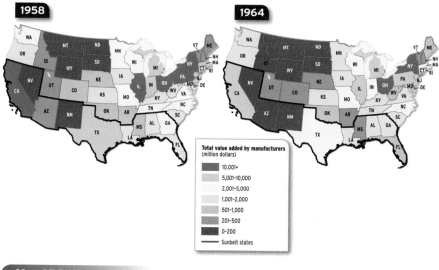

▲ **Map 27.3**

Manufacturing This map indicates the industrial and economic growth in the Sunbelt States during the 1960s.

practical impact on daily life and many did not really understand what they were. They were also encouraged by medical breakthroughs, such as the first successful heart transplant, improved vaccinations for children, and the possibility of new treatments for cancer, diabetes, and kidney disease.

Yet American confidence in science and technology began to waver over the course of the decade. Again, the Vietnam War played a critical role. Superior technology could not deliver victory on the battlefield, where the military unleashed the latest innovations. As had occurred after the use of the atomic bomb during World War II, some citizens expressed concern over the ways scientific knowledge and academic research were being used to bring death and destruction. Other skeptics thought that unquestioned reliance on scientific or technological solutions had created a dehumanized "technocracy" that failed to address serious social problems. Many also began to worry about the impact of science and technology on the environment. In the late 1960s the popular *Whole Earth Catalog*, for example, called for simpler living by promoting small scale "appropriate technologies" like solar water heaters. Consumer advocates and environmentalists collaborated in the coming years on product improvements and pragmatic efficiencies they hoped might lead toward a more sustainable economy.

One area where scientific and technological advancement enjoyed continued popularity was the "space race" between the United States and the Soviet Union. Americans saw the space race as a vital arena in the Cold War. Americans were still reeling from the embarrassment caused by *Sputnik*, the first successful satellite in space, launched by the Soviets in 1957. A nervous Congress responded in 1958 by creating the National Aeronautics and Space Administration (NASA) to coordinate U.S.

efforts. Despite NASA's Mercury program, which concentrated on sending an American astronaut into outer space, the Soviet Union once again beat the United States to the punch when cosmonaut Yuri Gagarin became the first person to reach outer space and the first to orbit the earth in April 1961. Only in February 1962 did the Americans match this feat when astronaut Alan B. Shepard became the first American in space and astronaut **John Glenn** successfully orbited the Earth.

Still, both *Sputnik* and Gagarin's successful trip raised the political stakes. Early in his presidency Kennedy addressed the competition for space supremacy by promising to land a man on the moon by the end of the decade. In May 1961 he told a joint session of Congress that it was "time for this nation to take a clearly leading role in space achievement, which in many ways may hold the key to our future on earth." The Apollo program, responsible for achieving Kennedy's goal, garnered a $20 billion budget and captured the public imagination. On July 20, 1969, in the midst of the tumultuous late 1960s, the nation rejoiced when the *Apollo 11* mission touched down on the moon.

The Rise of the Sunbelt

The space race also accelerated a shift in the nation's population and its political and economic strength from the North and East to the South and West, a region called the Sunbelt. During World War II, Western states had benefited from over $30 billion in defense contracts and more than $2 billion in federal investment. Heavy military

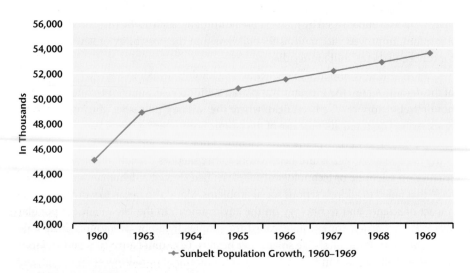

▲ **Figure 27.2**

Sunbelt population growth The Sunbelt states grew dramatically throughout the 1950s–1960s. WWII industrialized the West and sparked a mass migration to the Sunbelt states of the West and South. Generally low taxes, business friendly politics, and sunny weather attracted corporations, retirees, and workers shifting the economic and political balance of the nation. Growing opportunity and influence pulled millions of legal and illegal immigrants to these states, sparking another wave of debate about immigrants, labor, and the law.

spending continued in the West during the Cold War, and it expanded to the South, with its hospitable climate, through the construction of new military bases.

In addition to the new aerospace and defense jobs, related booms in computer and other high-tech firms, along with accompanying boosts in the service and banking industries, combined to make the Sunbelt the fastest growing section of the country. The West had 75 percent of the country's 30 most rapidly developing urban areas during the 1950s and 50 percent in the 1960s. The West, already the most urbanized part of the country, experienced a huge increase of urban residents.

Developers and local politicians attracted business to the Sunbelt by highlighting the cheap, nonunion labor, available land, low taxes, and minimal regulation in the region. Air-conditioned homes and numerous recreational options also attracted retirees from the North and Midwest to the Sunbelt. Workers moved to the Sunbelt to find new manufacturing or white-collar jobs. Development in the South and West came at significant cost to the natural environment. Hundreds of thousands of acres of farmland and forest disappeared as suburbs expanded outward and towns grew into major cities. The explosive population growth demanded new water projects for irrigation and electricity. Dams and reservoirs across the Sunbelt permanently flooded thousands of acres of virgin land, changed the source of ancient rivers, and endangered hundreds of plant and animal species.

STUDY QUESTIONS FOR A ROBUST ECONOMY

1. Why did the U.S. economy expand briskly in the 1960s?
2. Who benefited from the decade's legal precedents?
3. Why did the Sunbelt grow in the 1960s?

RACE, GENDER, YOUTH, AND THE CHALLENGE TO THE ESTABLISHMENT

American culture, social life, and politics underwent a radical transformation during the 1960s. Groups that traditionally had little power challenged traditional authorities and ways of ordering work, education, families, and private life. People of color insisted on civil rights. They also forged new ethnic and racial identities. A new feminist movement arose to demand economic and social equality and sexual freedom for women. Opposition to the war in Vietnam, which reached a crescendo during the climactic year 1968, profoundly influenced the course of other protest movements.

Many young people came to see themselves constrained by an uncaring society. Their exuberant flowering of racial, gender, sexual, and cultural protest—a **counterculture**—excited millions. The counterculture also provoked a fierce backlash from an equal if not larger number of Americans.

Urban Uprisings and Black Power

Advocates for civil rights for people of color altered tactics during the 1960s. In the beginning of the decade traditional civil rights organizations such as the **National Association for the Advancement of Colored People** (NAACP) and the National Urban League employed lawsuits, sit-ins, and mass demonstrations to highlight the moral injustices of segregation. By the middle of the decade the focus shifted from the struggle against legal segregation in the south to other forms of racial discrimination across the country. Many urban blacks outside the South felt that civil rights legislation failed to solve their most pressing problems. Young African Americans believed racial discrimination prevented them from fair access to jobs, housing, credit, transportation, education, and equal treatment from police. They thought that tradition civil rights organizations paid too much attention to ending legal segregation and too little to the crushing burden of poverty. More militant African American groups such as the Congress of Racial Equality, the Student Non-Violent Coordinating Committee, and the Nation of Islam rejected the style of traditional civil rights leaders as weak, accommodating, and unsuccessful. More militant, often younger African Americans advocated what they called Black Power—a combination of racial pride and forceful, even violent resistance to anti-black violence. This more militant assertion of rights and willingness to use "whatever means necessary" split the civil rights coalition. It also intensified the white backlash against political, social, and economic gains by African Americans.

The civil rights movement experienced a major turning point in 1965. On August 11, five days after Johnson signed the Voting Rights Act into law, violence broke out in the Watts neighborhood of Los Angeles. A crowd protesting the arrest of a young African American driver began to throw rocks and bottles at police in the streets of this poor, African American section of the city. For the next six days thousands of residents set fires, looted white-owned businesses, attacked white drivers, and fought the more than 15,000 police and National Guardsmen requested by California officials

Table 27.1 African American voter registration This chart shows 1960s changes in African American voter registration. No single issue sparked more intense civil rights activism and opposition than the simple effort to register African American voters. Segregationists feared the inevitable transformation of regional politics that would follow full democratic participation across the south. Grassroots civil rights activists put their lives on the line demanding this fundamental right.

	Black		White	
	Registered	**Voted**	**Registered**	**Voted**
1964	NA	58.5	NA	70.7
1966	60.2	41.7	71.7	57.0
1968	66.2	57.6	75.4	69.1

NA = not available

An army vehicle patrols 12th Street in Detroit, Michigan, during a race riot on July 25, 1967; 43 people died in race riots during the miserable summer of 1967. Images of military vehicles and combat troops in the streets of burning American cities demonstrated the fragility of the social coalitions that had so recently united in support of civil rights.

to restore order. The outburst resulted in 34 people dead, nearly all of them African American, over 1,000 injured, and more than 4,000 arrested. The shocking violence of Watts terrified and confused white Americans, but many African Americans understood the frustration and rage that was expressed there.

Rioting continued in major American cities throughout the rest of the 1960s. In 1966 the National Guard patrolled Cleveland, Chicago, Milwaukee, and other cities. In 1967 a particularly "long hot summer" resulted in 164 conflicts, including eight major riots. The most intense clashes occurred in Newark and Detroit, where 43 people died, most of them shot by police or National Guardsmen. Conservative and middle-class whites, often blaming the riots on outside agitators and undisciplined black youth looking for a thrill, wanted police to act forcefully against rioters. They turned against the urban social programs of the Great Society, which they thought rewarded rioters and threatened their suburbs.

By the mid-1960s some younger civil rights activists had grown frustrated with the nonviolent, integrationist approach of moderate leaders. Continued violence

Stokely giving Black Power speech, July 24, 1967. In dress and message Black Power advocates like Carmichael were completely different from MLK. They offered a powerful image to those activists ready to forcefully demand their rights while frightening some of the moderates who supported the earlier movement.

against blacks, extreme poverty, and the slow pace of change drove them to embrace more radical measures. In 1966 SNCC leader **Stokely Carmichael** announced, "We've been saying *freedom* for six years—and we ain't got nothin'. What we gonna start saying now is 'Black Power!'"

Carmichael and others turned to the black nationalist ideas of the minister **Malcolm X** for inspiration. After his release from prison in 1952 for petty larceny, Malcolm had joined the Nation of Islam, often referred to as the "Black Muslims." Malcolm promoted separatism because, he believed, white racism would never end. He also encouraged pride in African Americans' cultural heritage, supporting black businesses, and self-defense. Later, Malcolm left the Nation of Islam, embraced traditional Islam, moderated his anti-white stance slightly, and formed the Organization for Afro-American Unity. In early 1965 he was assassinated, however, by three Black Muslims angry that he had left their organization.

Although SNCC served as the early leading Black Power group, the **Black Panther Party** gained the most notoriety. Founded in Oakland in 1966 by Huey Newton and Bobby Seale, members of Black Panthers advocated black self-determination and armed self-defense against police brutality. Their shootouts with police—which resulted in several deaths on both sides—captured the close attention of the media and frightened many whites. Although they also developed health, education, and nutrition programs, their influence faded by the early 1970s.

The civil rights struggle and the Black Power movement had a worldwide impact. After Carmichael stepped down as the chairman of SNCC in 1967, he traveled widely

in Africa and married the South Africa singer Miriam Makeba, an outspoken opponent of apartheid, South Africa's policy of legal segregation. Carmichael eventually
settled in the West African country of Guinea, where he became an adviser to the nation's prime minister. He changed his name to Kwame Toure, in honor of two heroes
of African decolonization, Kwame Nkruma of Ghana and Sekou Toure of Guinea.
The black majority of South Africa took special notice of both the nonviolent and
the militant forms of the American civil rights movement. The brutality of apartheid
attracted the attention of American civil rights advocates. In June 1966 Robert F. Kennedy, now a senator from New York and growing ever more estranged from Lyndon
Johnson over the Vietnam War, visited South Africa and denounced apartheid. He
urged racially mixed audiences to follow the nonviolent approach of the protesters of
the early 1960s.

Latinos and Indians Struggle for Rights

The energy of the movement for civil rights for African Americans inspired members
of other traditionally excluded groups to demand equality. Latinos and Indians began
the decade with moderate tactics of strikes, boycotts, and demonstrations. Later in the
1960s each group developed its own versions of protest inspired by the militancy and
energy of the Black Power Movement.

The movement for rights for Mexican Americans burst into international prominence in 1965 when 5,000 members of the National Farm Workers Association

Cesar Chavez, the organizer and leader of the National Farm Workers Association, at a union
rally. Chavez successfully called for a nationwide boycott of nonunion picked grapes and
helped launch a civil rights movement; Delano, California, 1965 or 1966.

(NFWA) joined a *huelga*, or strike, against grape growers in Delano, California. **Cesar Chavez** and **Delores Huerta**, two charismatic leaders of the NFWA, led a nationwide boycott of the purchase of grapes to force the growers to recognize the union. The grape boycott spread across the Atlantic to the United Kingdom. The strike went on for five years until the growers signed a contract recognizing the NFWA as the pickers' representative. Chavez became an international leader for newly empowered Mexican Americans. His marches drew hundreds of sympathetic whites. Chavez, like Martin Luther King, Jr., used Christian imagery and nonviolent tactics. He saw himself as part of an international Catholic movement for social justice.

The NFWA's standard bore a stylized drawing of a black Aztec eagle, which became a symbol of Mexican American pride. Other Latinos advocated cultural nationalism similar to the Black Power movement. They found Chavez too committed to nonviolence and too eager to gain support from sympathetic white liberals. They described themselves as Chicanos appropriating what traditionally had been an ethnic slur used against them. In the late 1960s the Chicano movement grew across the Southwest and West.

Ethnic identity and militancy also spread among Puerto Ricans, both on the island and in the cities of the Northeast where hundreds of thousands of Puerto Ricans lived. Some militant young Puerto Ricans described themselves as *boricua*; this term of ethnic pride, too, had previously been hurled as a racial insult at Puerto Ricans. In the

Indian activists occupying Alcatraz, 1969. The abandoned prison off the coast of San Francisco was claimed by a coalition of Indian rights activists and student protestors in an effort to symbolically call attention to the occupation of Indian lands. They held the island for almost two years bringing new attention to another "century of dishonor" in U.S. Indian policy.

mid-1960s Puerto Rican activists in New York City created the Young Lords, patterned on the Black Panthers.

Indians were among the poorest Americans in 1960. About 200,000 Indians left reservations for cities after President Dwight Eisenhower ended "the status of Indians as wards of the government" in 1953. This policy of termination stopped federal aid to reservations but did not replace it with support for Indians who moved to cities. In June 1961 700 representatives from 64 different Indian nations met in Chicago to draft a Declaration of Indian Purpose. It stated that "we have the responsibility of preserving our precious heritage." The Declaration marked the beginning of the Red Power movement.

The **American Indian Movement** (AIM) formed in Minneapolis in 1968. The organization was inspired by the November 1969 occupation of Alcatraz Island in San Francisco Bay, when hundreds of young Indian activists demanded that the federal government turn over ownership of the land. In the 1970s AIM and other Indian advocacy groups staged several well-publicized protests. In November 1972 they took over the offices of the Bureau of Indian Affairs (BIA) in Washington, DC. In February 1973 AIM activists occupied the site of the 1890 Battle of Wounded Knee on the Pine Ridge Sioux Indian reservation of South Dakota. Richard Wilson, the president of the Oglala Sioux, denounced AIM as a band of "social misfits" and banned them from Pine Ridge. AIM, in turn, denounced Wilson and his tribal government as corrupt and vowed to stay at Wounded Knee until the federal government investigated what they called wholesale thievery and mismanagement at the BIA and in tribal councils. Federal marshals and AIM protesters faced off for 71 days. A gun battle in which two AIM activists were killed and a marshal was wounded ended the protest. Hundreds were arrested and both sides claimed victory. Although the government agreed to investigate claims of corruption, it did so only decades after the occupation at Wounded Knee.

The New Feminism

Women also demanded equality in both public and private life. Many middle-class white women believed their lives were constrained amid the prosperity of the post–World War II boom. In 1963 writer **Betty Friedan** gave voice to these concerns in her book *The Feminine Mystique*. She identified "the problem that has no name," and she described how educated, middle-class women felt isolated and useless in the "comfortable concentration camp" of the suburban house. She argued for meaningful work for educated women, at equal pay with men. In 1966 Friedan helped found the **National Organization for Women** (NOW), which advocated an end to laws that discriminated against women, opportunity to work at any job, and equal pay for equal work. Some women veterans of the civil rights movement came to see the situation of women as resembling that of blacks.

Changes in attitudes toward marriage and divorce enhanced the appeal of the new feminism. The family no longer seemed to be a safe haven from a heartless world of the 1960s. Divorce became more commonplace. Social workers and psychologists spoke out against violence by husbands against wives. Toward the end of the decade

Betty Friedan announcing a boycott of products insulting women in their advertisements, August 1970. In 1966 Friedan helped found the National Organization for Women (NOW) and became one of the most forceful advocates for meaningful work for educated women, at equal pay with men.

analysts began to discuss a hitherto taboo subject—sexual abuse of children by older males in homes.

In 1967 women's activists began calling opposition to women's rights "sexism," similar to racism, and described "male chauvinism" as a key element in blocking women's equality. They called for "women's liberation." NOW advocated the ratification of the Equal Rights Amendment (ERA) to the United States Constitution. First proposed in 1923, the ERA was a short declaration banning the denial or abridgment of rights on the basis of sex. Congress eventually adopted the ERA and sent it to the states for ratification, 35 states ratified the amendment, but it failed to achieve approval of the minimum of 38 state legislatures before a 1982 deadline. The new or Second Wave feminism inspired a global movement for women's rights. Large marches and rallies for gender equality occurred in cities such as Toronto, London, Berlin, Buenos Aires, Tokyo, and Sydney.

But feminism also encountered stiff opposition. Men who thought they might lose privileges, some middle class housewives who worried that they would lose legal protections, and some traditional Christians who believed that the Bible sanctioned male leadership in the home resisted the new feminism. Conservative activist **Phyllis Schlafly**, one of Barry Goldwater's earliest supporters for the presidency, organized a grass roots movement opposed to ratification of the ERA. Many African American women and Latinas considered the push for women's rights a white middle-class movement that did not understand the problems of domestic or farm workers raising children on their own.

Despite derision and the failure to ratify the ERA, women advanced in education and the workplace. In the 1970s and 1980s courts struck down numerous statutes and regulations that limited women's rights to property, employment, and reproductive choices. By 1990 women held about half the nation's jobs, and they had moved in large numbers into professions like law, medicine, dentistry, higher education teaching, and accounting. Despite these significant gains there were still inequities—for example, in the sciences. In most professions the wage gap between men and women narrowed. In 1970 women earned 59 cents for every dollar earned by men; by 2000 it was 76 cents for every dollar, leaving much room for improvement. Even as some women with postgraduate degrees moved into highly paid occupations, however, the poverty rate for single mothers increased in the decades after the 1960s and remains a serious issue.

The New Environmentalism

During the 1960s scholar activists exposed problems in the way citizens and corporations interacted with the natural environment. Scientist **Rachel Carson's** bestseller *Silent Spring* (1962) alerted readers to the harmful effect pesticides had on bird and other animal populations. Environmentalists focused on grassroots efforts and lobbying through long-established conservation groups such as the Sierra Club and new ones such as the Environmental Defense Fund, formed in 1967. Congress passed the Wilderness Act in 1964, the National Wildlife Refuge System of 1966, the National Wild and Scenic Rivers Act, and the National Trails Act, both in 1968. It also enacted laws aimed at limiting pollution, such as an amendment to the Clean Air Act and the Water Quality Act in 1965.

On April 22, 1970, 20 million supporters gathered in cities across the country for the first Earth Day. Even President Richard Nixon and major corporations supported the initiative. During the Nixon administration Congress created the Environmental Protection Agency (EPA) and Occupational Safety and Health Administration (OSHA) in 1970 to regulate and propose solutions, while environmental activists continued working both inside and outside of government channels. Increased awareness of environmental and behavioral threats to health affected government health programs. In January 1964 the U.S. Surgeon General confirmed the long suspected belief that smoking increased the risk of lung cancer and heart disease. Over the next generation the federal government gradually increased efforts to discourage tobacco use.

Youth and the Counterculture

During the 1960s young people played a larger role in the political, cultural, and social life of the United States than at any time before. Before 1965 a small minority of college students expressed their dissatisfaction with the political status quo, and with college administration. By the end of the decade student activism, deeply enmeshed in opposition to the war in Vietnam, rocked campuses across the country. Young people also profoundly influenced trends in popular culture. Many experimented with alternative lifestyles in the counterculture during the second half of the decade. Others simply wanted to have a good time. Nearly everything they did startled or upset the older generation.

The most influential of the early student groups was Students for a Democratic Society (SDS), founded at the University of Michigan in 1960. Inspired by the protests of the civil rights movement, members of SDS advanced the idea of "participatory democracy" and militant nonviolence. They envisioned a society shaped by a far greater range of voices in both local and national decisions. SDS advocated grassroots activism to bring economic and racial justice to the United States and desired a less confrontational approach to the Cold War. The society's organizing principles, the "Port Huron Statement," adopted in 1962, began, "We are people of this generation, bred in at least modest comfort, housed in the universities, looking uncomfortably to the world we inherit." SDS led the **New Left**, groups of young activists who intentionally distanced themselves from the ideological infighting, communism, and labor

The British Rock Invasion of the 1960s

On February 7, 1964, the Beatles landed at Kennedy International Airport in New York and were greeted by a mob of thousands of screaming teenage girls. Two days later, the band from Liverpool, England, played to a hysterical studio audience on CBS's *The Ed Sullivan Show*. Seventy-three million people—more than 60 percent of the nation's television viewers—tuned in to watch John Lennon, Paul McCartney, George Harrison, and Ringo Starr perform. Even more Americans, still reeling emotionally from John F. Kennedy's assassination, watched the Beatles' televised performance from Miami on the next week's show. Before returning to England, where they were already adored, the band also played two sold-out concerts in New York and Washington, DC. In the span of nine days, Americans bought more than 2 million Beatles records and over $2.5 million in Beatles merchandise.

"Beatlemania" erupted in the United States in early 1964. Millions of Americans, particularly teenage girls of the baby boom generation, were smitten with the band's catchy songs, romantic lyrics, fashion sense, wholesome but sexualized image, wit, and charm. Young men started growing their hair longer to copy their new idols and began wearing "Beatle boots." The Beatles seemed to represent freedom and fun to a generation of youth. For their part the Beatles had found American music—especially Elvis Presley, Chuck Berry, rhythm and blues, and rockabilly—an escape from working-class life in postwar England.

The Beatles' popularity, paving the way for many other British rock bands, opened the insular American music market and initiated the "British Invasion." Throughout the decade British bands thrived in the United States. Some drew their inspiration from Chicago blues artists such as Muddy Waters and Willie Dixon. The Rolling Stones, who took their name from a Waters song, became the most famous of these blues-based groups. Encouraged by their manager, who wanted people to think "the Stones were threatening, uncouth, and animalistic," the band adopted a rougher, more rebellious image than the Beatles. Another band, The Who, brought London's "Mod" scene to Americans, and The Animals had a number one hit in the United States and Great Britain with a reworked version of an American folk song, "The House of the Rising Sun."

British and American musical artists fueled each other's creativity. American folk-singer Bob Dylan decided to "go electric" after hearing the Beatles. Dylan introduced the Beatles to marijuana and encouraged them to branch out musically and

The Beatles on *The Ed Sullivan Show*, February 1964. The global appeal of the Beatles demonstrated the transnational transfer of music and culture. The Beatles interpreted American blues for British audiences and then brought this newly British style back to the United States.

write more introspective lyrics. The result was the album *Rubber Soul* (1965), which inspired Brian Wilson of the Beach Boys to create the musically experimental *Pet Sounds* (1966). That album, a departure from the Beach Boys' earlier, more innocent songs, in turn pushed the Beatles to produce their psychedelic *Sgt. Pepper's Lonely Hearts Club Band* in 1967. It was popular worldwide. A journalist reported that "In every city in Europe and America the stereo systems and the radio played ["Lucy in the Sky with Diamonds" from the album]. For a brief while the irreparably fragmented consciousness of the West was unified, at least in the minds of the young." *Sgt Pepper's* became part of the soundtrack for the so-called Summer of Love of the counterculture in San Francisco.

This artistic competition, as well as the growing influence of older blues and rock-and-roll musicians, created an international music scene that deeply affected popular culture on both sides of the Atlantic and around the globe. The historian Terry H. Anderson has noted that the British Invasion "demonstrated that rock and roll—although a uniquely American invention—was becoming the music of the international postwar baby boom: The sixties would not just be an American phenomenon."

organizing of the Old Left. International in its scope, the American New Left was heavily influenced by socialist thinkers in Britain, France, and West Germany, and by the Cuban revolution.

After the Free Speech Movement at Berkeley in the fall of 1964, more students began to echo the same complaints toward their own universities. In addition to free speech, free political activity, curriculum reform, and opposition to the "military-industrial complex," students took on *in loco parentis*, the idea that colleges and universities acted in the place of one's parents. In particular, students rallied for changes—with moderate success—in old-fashioned rules regarding curfews, visiting hours, and housing organized by gender, to moderate success.

In the second half of the 1960s young people unnerved mainstream society outside politics as well. Some rejected establishment values by advocating personal freedom above the older generation's emphasis on collective responsibility and materialism. Inspired by the Beats of the 1950s, its vanguard rejected the security and boredom of middle-class life to pursue a liberated, often hedonistic, lifestyle. These diverse counterculturalists launched a significant resettlement of the rural West. Communes and settlements sprung up in and around towns like Bolinas, California, and Taos, New Mexico. Local economies and cultural traditions were strained by the new frontiers people, but coalitions and economic opportunities resulted as well. In cities, counterculturalists moved into blighted urban areas, setting the stage for historic preservation efforts and gentrification in the coming decades.

Mind-altering drugs played a significant role in the countercultural awakening. Timothy Leary, a former professor of psychology at Harvard, promoted the use of the hallucinogenic drug LSD to help people "turn on, tune in, and drop out." The drug had first been tested by the U.S. military as a way to expand the minds of soldiers. Members of the counterculture, labeled "hippies" by the mainstream media, smoked

TIMELINE 1960–1968

1960

May 11 FDA approves oral contraceptive pill *Enovid* for use as birth control

February 1 Sit-in at Woolworth lunch counter, Greensboro, NC

November 8 John F. Kennedy elected president over Richard M. Nixon

1961

May 4 First Freedom Rider buses leave Washington, DC, heading across the South

April 12 Soviet cosmonaut Yuri Gagarin orbits the Earth

April 17 Bay of Pigs invasion fails

August 17 Construction of the Berlin Wall begins

1962

February 20 U.S. astronaut John Glenn orbits the earth

June 15 Publication of the Students for a Democratic Society's *Port Huron Statement*

June 25 Supreme Court decides *Engel v. Vitale* banning prayer in public schools

September 27 Publication of Rachel Carson's *Silent Spring*

October 1 James Meredith successfully integrates the University of Mississippi

October 14–26 Cuban Missile Crisis

1963

February 17 Publication of Betty Friedan's *The Feminine Mystique*

March 18 Supreme Court decides *Gideon v. Wainwright*

August 28 March on Washington

September 15 16th Street Baptist Church bombed in Birmingham, Alabama

November 22 Assassination of John F. Kennedy

1964

January 11 Surgeon General says smoking causes lung cancer,

beginning a decades-long antismoking movement

March 9 Supreme Court decides *New York Times v. Sullivan*

June–August Mississippi Freedom Summer

July 2 Civil Rights Act bans racial discrimination on public accommodations

October–December Free Speech Movement at University of California, Berkeley

November 3 Lyndon Johnson elected president over Barry Goldwater

1965

February–March Civil rights demonstration at Selma, AL

marijuana and experimented with a wide range of drugs new and old. They ushered in a "sexual revolution," celebrating casual sex and rejecting traditional Protestant prudishness, a development facilitated by the availability of the birth control pill in 1960. They sometimes grew their hair long and dressed flamboyantly in colorful clothes and beads. But many dressed traditionally while embracing the values. There was no typical "hippie," and the movement was far more complicated and diverse than the popular media or conservative critics presumed.

Although countercultural communities developed in many cities and college towns, the Haight-Ashbury district of San Francisco served as the epicenter of the movement. In 1967, during the "Summer of Love," young men and women flocked to the Haight for free drugs, free music, and free love. By the end of the summer, however, serious problems developed. The streets became overcrowded with drunk or wasted hippies, enterprising drug dealers, prostitutes, young runaways, and panhandlers. There were rapes, muggings and chaos. The dark side of the counterculture was immortalized in films like Dennis Hopper's *Easy Rider* (1969), which showed both the hope and the despair of utopian escape in all its forms.

As the utopianism of the early counterculture faded, a generation of inventive, counterculture veterans turned their energies to creating the framework of the new economy of the information age of the 1980s and 1990s. Computer pioneers like **Steve Jobs** used the creative energy of the counterculture to devise new products and business models. Others worked on sustainable energy technologies and ecological design.

The majority of teenagers and college students in the late 1960s, however, stayed away from radical politics and never committed to the most extreme countercultural rejections of mainstream society. Hollywood and savvy marketers catered to the youth market, and cashed in on the popularity of countercultural ideas and imagery to sell their products.

February 21 Murder of Malcolm X

April 28 U.S. invasion and occupation of the Dominican Republic

June 7 Supreme Court decides *Griswold v. Connecticut*

July 30 Passage of Medicare

August 6 Passage of Voting Rights Act

August 11–17 Watts racial uprising

1966

June 13 Supreme Court decides *Miranda v. Arizona*

June 6 Robert F. Kennedy visits South Africa

June 28–30 Founding of NOW

October 15 Creation of the Black Panthers

October 29 SNCC leader Stokely Carmichael calls for Black Power

1967

June 1 Release of the Beatles' *Sgt. Pepper's Lonely Hearts Club Band*

June–August Summer of Love in San Francisco

June 5 Reies Lopez Tijerina leads raid on federal courthouse in Rio Arriba County, New Mexico

June 5–10 Six day war between Israel, Egypt, Jordan, and Syria

July 14–17 Detroit racial uprising increases racial divide

August 30 Thurgood Marshall becomes the first African American Justice of the Supreme Court

September Formation of the Brown Berets 1967

October Publication of Jean Jacques Servan-Schreiber's *The American Challenge*

1968

April 11 Passage of Fair Housing Act

August 15–17 Woodstock Music Festival

August 21 Soviet invasion of Czechoslovakia

November 20 Indian activists begin occupation of Alcatraz

The remarkable rise of rock music demonstrated the power of the youth market. Fans could read about their favorite artists in *Rolling Stone*, begun in 1967. Like the *Whole Earth Catalog*, *Rolling Stone* moved quickly from the underground to the mainstream without losing its edgy coverage that led stores in conservative areas to ban the publication. Rock music, too, evolved with the decade, becoming more experimental, more drug influenced, and more provocative over time. By the early 1970s rock records made up 80 percent of all music sales. In rock and roll young people found a cultural medium that allowed them to rebel against traditional values—without having to change their lifestyle too dramatically. This hardly reassured the millions who saw in the hippies and the counterculture a serious threat to their traditional way of life. Love and change were in the air across America in the 1960s, but so were fear, hatred, and anxiety.

STUDY QUESTIONS FOR RACE, GENDER, YOUTH, AND THE CHALLENGE TO THE ESTABLISHMENT

1. How did changes in the movement for rights for African Americans affect other groups' struggles to advance their status in U.S. society?
2. Why did the counterculture appeal to millions of Americans?
3. Who opposed the increasing assertiveness of people of color, women, and youth?

Summary

- The 1960s began with great optimism that a prosperous country would solve long-standing problems of racial injustice and end poverty.
- The Kennedy and Johnson administrations continued early administrations' confrontation with the Communist world in the Cold War.
- President Lyndon B. Johnson's administration enacted an ambitious program of social reform.
- Science and technological innovation sparked a widespread economic boom.
- People of color, women, youth, and students created a robust counterculture as they challenged traditional authority.
- Public enthusiasm for social reform dissipated toward the end of the decade as more conservative Americans became alarmed at the culture of protest and rejected many of its aspects.

Key Terms and People

Alliance for Progress *1059*
American Indian Movement (AIM) 1077
Bay of Pigs invasion *1060*
Black Panther Party *1074*

Brezhnev, Leonid *1067*
Carmichael, Stokely *1074*
Carson, Rachel *1079*
Castro, Fidel *1059*
Chavez, Cesar *1076*

counterculture 1071
Cuban missile crisis 1060
Friedan, Betty 1077
Glenn, John 1070
Goldwater, Barry 1062
Great Society 1061
Huerta, Delores 1076
Jobs, Steve 1083
Johnson, Lyndon B. 1055
Kennedy, John F. 1055
Kennedy, Robert F. 1057
King, Martin Luther, Jr. 1058
Kosygin, Alexei 1067
Lewis, John 1062
Limited Test Ban Treaty 1060
Malcolm X 1074

Marshall, Thurgood 1066
Medicaid 1064
Medicare 1063
Meredith, James 1058
Miranda v. Arizona 1066
Model Cities 1064
National Association for the
  Advancement of Colored People
  (NAACP) 1072
National Organization for
  Women 1077
New Frontier 1055
New Left 1079
Reagan, Ronald 1054
Savio, Mario 1051
Schlafly, Phyllis 1078

Reviewing Chapter 27

1. Why were many Americans hopeful about the possibility of reforming their society in the 1960s?
2. What actions did Americans take to reform society in the 1960s?
3. Explain why and how millions of Americans opposed the challenges to traditional authority posed by the social change movements of the 1960s.

Further Reading

Branch, Taylor. *Parting the Waters: America in the King Years, 1954–65.* New York: Simon & Schuster, 1999. Multivolume history of the civil rights movement.

Braunstein, Peter, and Michael William Doyle. *Imagine Nation: The American Counterculture of the 1960s and 1970s.* New York: Routledge, 2002. Insightful essays on counterculture in all its varied forms.

Dallek, Robert. *An Unfinished Life: John F. Kennedy and His Times, 1917–1963.* New York: Little, Brown and Company, 2003. A respected biography of the president that helped define the times.

Farber, David, and Beth Bailey, eds. *The Columbia Guide to America in the 1960s.* New York: Columbia University Press, 2001. Comprehensive collection of essays on the decade.

Lassiter, Matthew D. *The Silent Majority: Suburban Politics in the Sunbelt South.* Princeton: Princeton University Press, 2006. Insightful study of the shifting power base for politics in the 1960s.

Visual Review

JFK's New Frontier

Kennedy inspires Americans to improve the country.

The Challenge of Racial Justice

A mass movement develops to obtain civil rights for African Americans.

Cold War Tensions

Kennedy focuses attention toward winning the Cold War.

Kennedy Assassination

Kennedy is assassinated, making Lyndon B. Johnson the new president.

The New Frontier

THE OPTIMISM AND THE ANGUISH OF THE 1960S

The Great Society

Civil Rights Laws

Johnson makes racial justice a priority for his administration.

Great Society Programs

From 1965 to 1967, Congress enacted the most far reaching economic and social laws since the New Deal.

The Supreme Court and Rights and Liberties

The Supreme Court plays a major role in expanding civil rights and liberties.

The United States and the World beyond Vietnam

Johnson tries to project American power around the globe, while reducing tensions with the Soviet Union.

A Robust Economy

Technological Change, Science, and Space Exploration

Technological innovations transform American life.

The Rise of the Sunbelt

The shift in political and economic strength leads to the rise of the South and West

Race, Gender, Youth, and the Challenge to the Establishment

Urban Uprisings and Black Power

Advocates for civil rights alter tactics.

Latinos and Indians Struggle for Rights

Other ethnic groups fight for racial equality.

The New Feminism

Women also demand equality in both public and private life.

The New Environmentalism

Activists create a new awareness of problems with the environment.

Youth and the Counterculture

Young people play a larger role in political, cultural, and social life.

The Vietnam Era

1961–1975

O n June 8, 1972, a plane from the South Vietnamese Air Force dropped napalm (jellied burning gasoline) on a group of Vietnamese fleeing from a North Vietnamese attack on the village of Trang Bang, in Southeast Vietnam. Several villagers were killed. Kim Phuc, a nine-year-old girl, had her clothes burned off and was photographed running naked down the road. She screamed "nong qua, nong qua [too hot, too hot]."

Associate Press cameraman Nick Ut won the Pulitzer Prize for the picture, which became an iconic image of the brutality of the war.

Ut took Phuc and other burned children to a Saigon hospital. Doctors thought she would not survive, but after 17 operations over 14 months she returned to her village. Following the Communist victory in 1975, North Vietnamese government officials publicized Phuc's suffering to demonstrate the barbarity of the defeated South Vietnamese and their American patrons. She became angry that officials took her from her studies to become a propaganda symbol against the anticommunist regime. In 1986 she left Vietnam for medical school in Cuba. There she met Bui Huy Tuan, another Vietnamese student. The couple married, and asked for and received asylum in Canada.

Phuc practiced medicine in Ontario and became an international advocate for reconciliation. On Veterans Day 1996, one year after the United States and Vietnam restored diplomatic relations broken in 1975, she spoke at the Vietnam Veterans Memorial in Washington, DC. She said, "We cannot change history, but we should try to do good things for

American troops in action, Vietnam 1968–1969

CHAPTER OUTLINE

BACKGROUND TO A WAR, 1945–1963
> Vietnam and the Cold War
> American Commitments to South Vietnam
> The 1963 Turning Point

AN AMERICAN WAR, 1964–1967
> Decisions for Escalation, 1964–1965
> Ground and Air War, 1966–1967
> The War at Home

1968: TURMOIL AND TURNING POINTS
> The Tet Offensive
> The Agony of 1968

NIXON AND THE WORLD
> From Vietnamization to Paris
> The End of the Vietnam War
> Reduction of Cold War Tensions

DOMESTIC POLICY AND THE ABUSE OF POWER
> Curtailing the Great Society
> Watergate

America in the World

The Watergate scandal resulted in public distrust of its own government (1974).

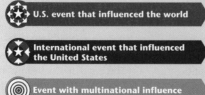

Congress adopted the Gulf of Tonkin resolution, allowing increased U.S. military presence in Vietnam (1964).

U.S. event that influenced the world

International event that influenced the United States

Event with multinational influence

Conflict

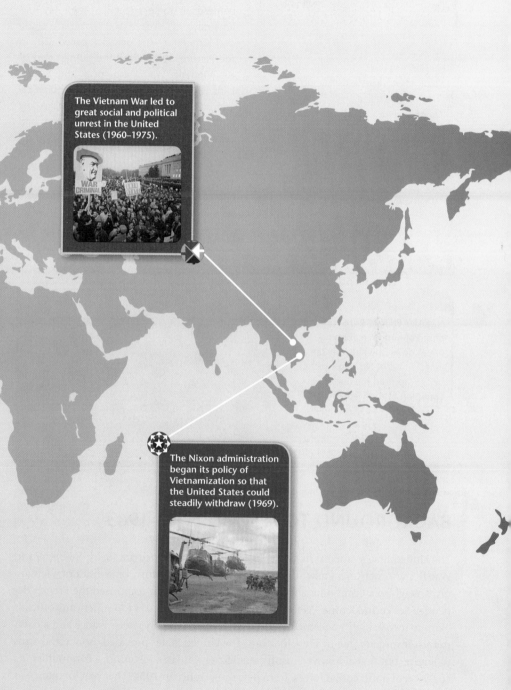

The Vietnam War led to great social and political unrest in the United States (1960–1975).

The Nixon administration began its policy of Vietnamization so that the United States could steadily withdraw (1969).

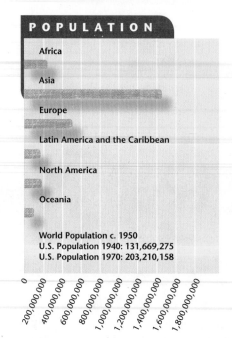

POPULATION

Africa

Asia

Europe

Latin America and the Caribbean

North America

Oceania

World Population c. 1950
U.S. Population 1940: 131,669,275
U.S. Population 1970: 203,210,158

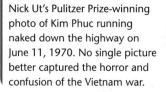

0
200,000,000
400,000,000
600,000,000
800,000,000
1,000,000,000
1,200,000,000
1,400,000,000
1,600,000,000
1,800,000,000

the present and for the future to promote peace." She forgave an American veteran who believed he had helped the South Vietnamese air force select its target on that June day.

Kim Phuc, for decades called Girl in the Picture, symbolized the human cost of the Vietnam War. Vietnamese and Americans suffered physical and psychological wounds that took decades to heal. A key battleground of the Cold War, Vietnam had repercussions around the globe.

Nick Ut's Pulitzer Prize-winning photo of Kim Phuc running naked down the highway on June 11, 1970. No single picture better captured the horror and confusion of the Vietnam war.

BACKGROUND TO A WAR, 1945–1963

The United States' interest in events in Indochina developed gradually. Before World War II few Americans knew much about the culture, history, or politics of Vietnam or its neighbors Cambodia and Laos, the three states that comprised the French dependencies of Indochina. As the Cold War developed in Asia top Americans officials became increasingly concerned with the growing conflict between France and a communist insurgency led by **Ho Chi Minh**. The United States provided money and arms to France, but that aid proved insufficient to prevent Ho's Vietminh, a communist-led coalition of anticolonial forces, from defeating France in 1954. That year Vietnam was divided into two states, a communist Vietnam and non-communist South.

For the next several years the United States helped the government of South Vietnam establish itself as a legitimate force worthy of the allegiance of its people. Beginning in 1960 a revived communist insurgency challenged the authority of an unpopular and often corrupt South Vietnamese government. The administrations of Dwight D. Eisenhower and John F. Kennedy considered Vietnam to be an important bulwark against the spread of communist-led governments in the rest of Southeast Asia. They sent millions of dollars in military and civilian aid and thousands of uniformed military advisers to help South Vietnam, but the American support could not stop the communist gains. By the time Kennedy was assassinated in 1963, the communist forces were winning the war against South Vietnam.

Ho Chi Minh declaring the independence of Democratic Republic of Vietnam, September 2, 1945. The United States steadfastly opposed efforts to establish an independent Vietnam, supporting France's fight against Ho Chi Minh that began the year after Ho Chi Minh's declaration.

Vietnam and the Cold War

From the earliest days of the Cold War the United States had backed alternatives to the Democratic Republic of Vietnam (DRV) proclaimed by Ho Chi Minh on September 2, 1945. In late 1946 war broke out between the Vietminh and France, which sought to reestablish its control over Indochina. During the war the United States backed France to encourage that country to be a strong ally in the struggle against communism.

By 1954 the United States was paying 70 percent of France's war costs against the Vietminh, yet France was unable to defeat the communists. In the spring of 1954 Vietminh fighters, supported by troops from the People's Republic of China, surrounded a French outpost at Dien Bien Phu, in northwest Vietnam. President Dwight D. Eisenhower viewed Vietnam as an important arena of the Cold War. He likened it to the first of a row of dominoes stretching throughout Southeast Asia to Australia and Japan. This domino theory later became a vivid fear of communist expansion, in which the last domino to fall would be the United States itself. But the Korean War had ended in July 1953, and the president did not want to send U.S. troops to fight in another war in Asia. He rejected advice to relieve the siege with U.S. bombing raids.

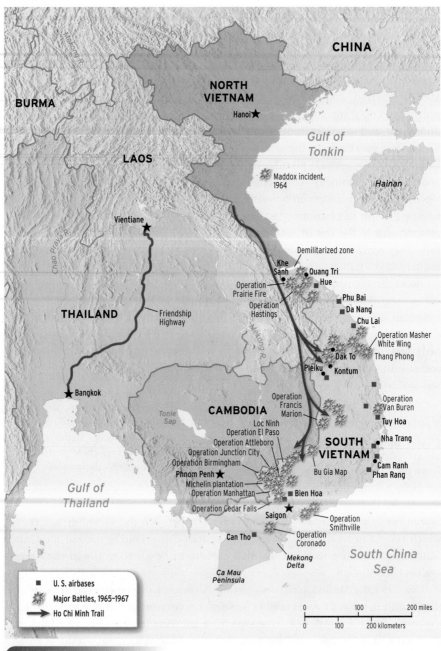

CHINA

NORTH
VIETNAM
Hanoi ★

BURMA

Gulf of
Tonkin

LAOS

Maddox incident,
1964

Hainan

Vientiane ★

Demilitarized zone

Khe
Sanh   Quang Tri
Operation   Hue
Prairie Fire
Operation   Phu Bai
Hastings   Da Nang
                    Chu Lai

THAILAND   Friendship
           Highway

Operation Masher
White Wing
Dak To   Thang Phong
Pleiku   Kontum

Bangkok ★

Operation
Francis
Marion

CAMBODIA

Operation
Van Buren
Tuy Hoa

Tonle
Sap

Loc Ninh
Operation El Paso
Operation Attleboro
Operation Junction City
Operation Birmingham
Phnom Penh ★
Michelin plantation
Operation Manhattan
Operation Cedar Falls

SOUTH
VIETNAM

Nha Trang

Cam Ranh
Phan Rang

Bu Gia Map

Bien Hoa

Saigon ★

Gulf of
Thailand

Operation
Smithville

Can Tho

Operation
Coronado

Mekong
Delta

South China
Sea

Ca Mau
Peninsula

■ U. S. airbases

✺ Major Battles, 1965–1967

➤ Ho Chi Minh Trail

0   100   200 miles

0   100   200 kilometers

▲ Map 28.1

Divided Vietnam This map of Indochina shows the division of North and South Vietnam
after the Geneva Conference. Maps of Vietnam distributed to soldiers and printing by the
American media oversimplified the political and military situation of Vietnam where a line on
the map meant little to troops on the ground.

The Vietminh captured Dien Bien Phu and 10,000 French and anticommunist Vietnamese soldiers on May 7, 1954.

An international peace conference on Indochina convened in Geneva, Switzerland, the day Dien Bien Phu fell to Ho Chi Minh's troops. On July 20 France and the DRV signed the Geneva Accords in which they agreed to a temporary, two-year partition of Vietnam at the 17th parallel. The Vietminh would control the North; a noncommunist State of Vietnam would rule the South. The accords stipulated a countrywide referendum to unify the country, to take place in 1956.

American Commitments to South Vietnam

The United States attended the Geneva conference as an observer, but it did not sign the agreements. Instead, it supplanted France as the principal backer of the noncommunist south. Washington helped Ngo Dinh Diem, a Vietnamese nationalist, become prime minister of the State of Vietnam. U.S. officials hoped his Roman Catholic faith and his American experience would make him a reliable ally. In 1955 Diem deposed the emperor Bao Dai, established the Republic of (South) Vietnam, and seized the position of president. The United States supported his decision not to allow the 1956 nationwide unification elections promised by the Geneva accords. Despite the trappings of democracy in South Vietnam, Diem ruled as a virtual dictator. His domestic support came from a minority of upper class Catholics, landlords, and businesses. The United States helped Diem build the Army of the Republic of Vietnam (ARVN) and a national police force. The South's military and police forces arrested 20,000 and killed over 1,000 former members of the Vietminh who remained in the South after 1954. Yet Diem's forces could not eliminate all of the former Vietminh fighters, who regrouped with supplies from the North.

Full-scale civil war erupted in South Vietnam in late 1960. Diem's government, which relied heavily on the support of the small Catholic minority in South Vietnam, had grown increasingly unpopular with the Buddhist majority, who made up over 80 percent of the population. On December 20, 1960, Le Duan, the leader of the Vietminh in the south, established the National Front for the Liberation of Vietnam (NLF), a communist-led coalition that included Buddhists, students, and nationalists opposed to Diem. NLF fighters, derisively called the Viet Cong, or Vietnamese communists, by the ARVN, attacked government positions across the South, and by mid 1961 the NLF controlled about 58 percent of South Vietnamese territory.

The new Kennedy administration feared that the deteriorating situation in Vietnam put the United States at a disadvantage in the global fight against communism. American officials considered Soviet Communist Party Chairman Nikita Khrushchev's promise to support wars of national liberation around the world as a direct challenge to the United States. Consequently, Kennedy increased military aid to South Vietnam. He dispatched 400 Army Special Forces, known as Green Berets for their distinctive headgear, to help 9,000 mountain tribesmen stop the infiltration of pro-NLF fighters from North Vietnam to help the NLF. Thus, in 1962 over 9,000 American military personnel were in Vietnam.

The Americans helped the ARVN move hundreds of thousands of Vietnamese peasants from their traditional villages into larger strategic hamlets—small villages protected by fences and guard towers. Once the hamlets were created, the ARVN bombed the countryside to crush the NLF and killed thousands of civilians. The hamlets proved to be a catastrophe for the ARVN. The NLF won adherents to their cause by denouncing the government for forcibly removing farmers from their beloved land and also because they killed innocent civilians.

The 1963 Turning Point

Diem's government became increasingly unpopular in early 1963. Peasants hated being moved to strategic hamlets, and they resented Diem's ties to landowners who demanded increasing rents. Buddhist monks objected to Diem's reliance on a few Catholic advisers and insisted that he resign. In May and June Buddhists led antigovernment demonstrations in the streets on major South Vietnamese cities. On June 11, 73-year-old monk **Thich Quang Duc** poured gasoline on himself in the midst of a busy Saigon intersection and set himself on fire. Pictures of his ritual suicide appeared on the front pages of newspapers around the world. When Kennedy saw the picture, he said "no news picture in history has generated so much emotion around the world as that one." The People's Republic of China distributed millions of copies of the picture in Asia and Africa to highlight what they called the crimes of American imperialism. Madame Ngo Dinh Nhu, Diem's sister-in-law who acted as South Vietnam's First Lady, muddied her family's reputation more when she said she would happily "clap hands at seeing another monk barbecue show."

The Kennedy administration lost faith in Diem over the summer of 1963. A new U.S. ambassador, **Henry Cabot Lodge**, the Republican vice-presidential candidate in 1960, arrived in Saigon in August. He immediately encouraged some senior ARVN officers to oust Diem and his brother, Ngo Dinh Nhu, the head of the state police and a hated figure for the Buddhists. The ARVN generals, fearful that Diem had discovered the plot, aborted their plans. U.S. officials pressured Diem and Nhu to leave Vietnam. Instead, they turned on their American patrons and hinted that they might reach an agreement with Ho Chi Minh that would leave their family in charge of a neutral Vietnam. American officials in Washington and Saigon then helped the ARVN generals restart the coup. On November 1, 1963, ARVN commanders led by Gen. Duong Van Minh seized the presidential palace and captured Diem and Nhu. The next morning the plotters murdered them.

Kennedy's plans for Vietnam remained in flux during the three weeks between Diem's murder and his own assassination. He worried that South Vietnam was too weak to defeat the communist-led insurgency. He feared the cost of a fully American war to save Vietnam, and he speculated about reducing the American commitment after he won reelection in 1964. Some of Kennedy's trusted advisors later said he would not have committed the United States to fight in Vietnam as his successor, Lyndon B. Johnson, did. Although Kennedy believed a successful South Vietnam was necessary to counter the Soviet Union, he also had grown increasingly hopeful of reducing tensions with the Soviets in the year since the Cuban missile crisis, and he was beginning to believe that Vietnam mattered less to the United States than it had before the crisis.

STUDY QUESTIONS FOR BACKGROUND TO A WAR, 1945–1963

1. What effect did the Cold War have in shaping U.S. policy toward the conflict in Vietnam?
2. What did the Vietnamese think of the governments in North and South Vietnam?
3. Why did the administration of John F. Kennedy increase America's commitment to the government of South Vietnam?

AN AMERICAN WAR, 1964–1967

As the new president, Lyndon Johnson vowed to continue Kennedy's policies in Vietnam, just after Kennedy had expressed misgivings about fighting there. Johnson anguished over Americanizing the war, but he decided to do so to avoid appearing weak. He feared that communist success in Vietnam would be as costly to him and the Democratic Party as the communist victory in China's civil war had been to President Harry Truman in the 1940s and early 1950s. He worried that an angry debate over "who lost Vietnam" would drain public support for the Great Society, his cherished program of domestic economic and social reform. From 1964 to 1967 the United States gradually sent more than 500,000 troops to fight against the insurgency in the South. After 1964 the Americans continuously bombed North Vietnam in a futile effort to stop Ho Chi Minh from sending supplies and troops to the South. The war devastated the land and people of both North and South Vietnam. Hundreds of thousands of civilians died and millions became refugees. The war strained U.S. relations with traditional allies, and it halted progress in dampening Cold War tensions.

Decisions for Escalation, 1964–1965

Ill at ease in dealing with international issues, President Johnson relied on a corps of advisers inherited from John F. Kennedy, most of whom were committed to South Vietnam despite Kennedy's concerns. In late November 1963, the new president told an American diplomat in Saigon, "Lyndon Johnson is not going down as the president who lost Vietnam." He demanded that his advisers reach consensus on a strategy to prevent a communist victory before the American election of 1964.

The United States slowly increased its military commitments to Vietnam in 1964. In January the CIA helped General **Nguyen Khanh** oust General Minh, who was preparing to negotiate with North Vietnam. Khanh wanted American help in invading

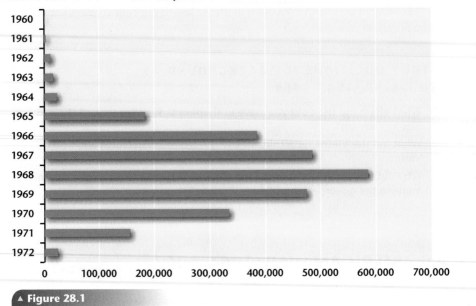

▲ **Figure 28.1**

Troop escalation This graph shows U.S. troops levels in Vietnam from 1961 to 1972.

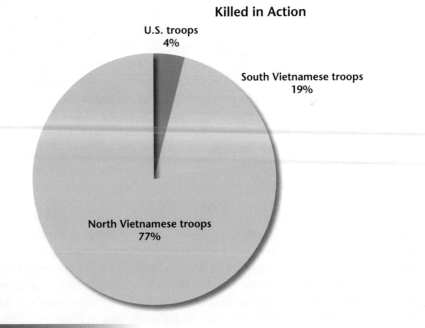

▲ **Figure 28.2**

Vietnam death toll This graph includes figures for U.S., North Vietnamese, and South Vietnamese deaths in Vietnam, 1961–1975.

the North, a move Johnson resisted. He feared provoking Chinese intervention in the war, as had occurred in Korea. But Goldwater also goaded Johnson by suggesting that American field commanders in Vietnam had the right to use tactical nuclear weapons.

In the summer of 1964 U.S. naval vessels escorted South Vietnamese ships inside North Vietnam's declared 12-mile coastal limit to attack northern ports. On the night of August 2, North Vietnamese patrol boats attacked the *Maddox*, a U.S. electronic surveillance ship in the Gulf of Tonkin. Two nights later, the commander of another destroyer, the *C. Turner Joy*, believed the North Vietnamese had attacked his ship. The *C. Turner Joy* fired its guns into the night but hit nothing, because, in fact, no North Vietnamese boats were attacking. Nevertheless, Johnson ordered U.S. Navy planes to attack North Vietnamese radars and ports. He also asked Congress for authorization "to take all necessary steps, including the use of armed force, to assist" Southeast Asian countries requesting military aid from the United States. On August 7, Congress passed the **Gulf of Tonkin Resolution** with little debate and minimal opposition.

A few years after the Tonkin Gulf Resolution passed Congress it became clear that the North Vietnamese attacks either had not occurred or they had been provoked by the U.S. Navy. The resolution, however, justified Americanizing the fighting. Support by the Republican presidential candidate Barry Goldwater removed Vietnam as an issue in the 1964 election. Johnson appeared as the more moderate candidate. He said that "only as a last resort" would he "start dropping bombs around that are likely to involve American boys in a war in Asia with 700 million Chinese."

Safely reelected, Johnson proceeded to make Vietnam an American war. They continued to suffer losses against the NLF, and the South Vietnamese government grew ever more desperate and pleaded for Americans to send ground troops and attack the North. On February 7, 1965, NLF fighters attacked the American air base at Pleiku. They killed eight American airmen and destroyed 10 planes. In retaliation Johnson authorized Operation Rolling Thunder, the sustained bombing of North Vietnamese military installations, roads, rail lines, bridges, power plants, and fuel depots. Rolling Thunder disappointed advocates of air power, because the North Vietnamese quickly rebuilt. The thick cloud cover and heavy foliage helped them hide the thousands of tons of supplies, arms, and soldiers they had infiltrated from the North to the South through Laos and Cambodia on a complex system of hundreds of miles of hidden roads, bridges, tunnels, camps, and paths called the Ho Chi Minh Trail.

From March to July Johnson made the final decisions to escalate the war. In March American marines waded ashore at Da Nang to provide added protection to the American forces in Vietnam. In April General William Westmoreland, the U.S. commander in Vietnam, wrote the president that the United States had to "put our own finger in the dike" or the South would lose the war. In April the general asked for another 150,000 American troops in addition to the 90,000 already there to fight a ground war throughout South Vietnam.

In July Johnson settled on sending another 100,000 American troops by the end of 1965. This policy of gradual escalation prevented a quick communist victory. But neither did it lead to an American and South Vietnamese triumph. The war went on

▶ **Map 28.2**

Ho Chi Minh Trail The Ho Chi Minh Trail linked the North and the South while circumnavigating American defenses. The ability of the Vietcong to resupply via the trail despite massive bombing campaigns vexed American military leaders and contributed to the sense at home that the war was unwinnable.

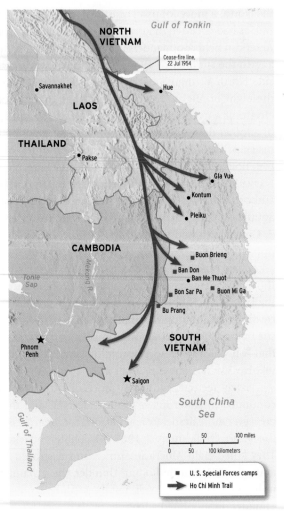

inconclusively for the remainder of Johnson's term. Meanwhile, the public was growing disillusioned with the war, with the president, and with Johnson's Great Society.

Ground and Air War, 1966–1967

In 1966 and 1967 the United States escalated the number of troops in Vietnam from 190,000 to 535,000. They took over the bulk of fighting from their South Vietnamese allies. The Americans tried to use the modern technology of warfare—withering firepower, tank and heavy artillery attacks, bombing from the air—to defeat a more numerous, less well-equipped enemy. But this reliance on technology grossly misjudged the abilities of North Vietnamese and NLF forces to outlast the Americans. The communists avoided fighting the U.S. forces in large battles where superior American fire power could overwhelm them. Instead, the communist forces chose their battles carefully.

General Westmoreland advocated a strategy of attrition to wear down the number of NLF and North Vietnamese fighters until they were no longer capable of continuing the fight. Americans used helicopters to ferry soldiers into the field on search-and-destroy missions designed to kill as many enemy fighters as possible. The body count of dead NLF or North Vietnamese served as a measure of military success for the American public at home. Reliance on these numbers rather than territory captured encouraged inflated reports about the number of enemy killed and the inclusion of dead civilians in the body count. The NLF did not wear uniforms and American soldiers could not distinguish them from the South Vietnamese peasants whom the Americans presumably were helping. Atrocities occur in all wars, but the emphasis on the body count enhanced brutality. Some soldiers, including Americans, even dismembered the bodies of enemy fighters and kept their ears for trophies.

Giant B-52s bombed the battlefield before American troops descended from their helicopters on search-and-destroy operations. The United States dropped more bombs on South Vietnam in a single month of the war than fell on Europe during all of World War II. Initially bombing terrified the NLF and North Vietnamese. But they soon realized that the Americans bombed at the same time each day, and they retreated into deep tunnels. They used unexploded bombs to improvise booby traps that killed more than 1,000 U.S. troops in 1966 alone.

Americans and the South Vietnamese allies continued to conduct huge search-and-destroy operations in late 1966 and 1967. They warned peasants to leave their villages for the cities and declared vast stretches of Vietnam free fire zones. Anyone who remained in them would be considered an enemy fighter and would be shot and

U.S. helicopters lift off as they go out on a search-and-destroy mission, September 1967. "Search and Destroy" became a metaphor for the unclear mission in Vietnam. Military leaders hoped the nimble craft would turn the tide but the slow-moving copters were easy targets. Between 1962 and 1972, the United States lost over 4,800 helicopters.

killed. The U.S. army also dropped over one million pounds of defoliants, often called Agent Orange, on the forests of Vietnam to deny the enemy the invisibility provided by the leaves. The defoliants destroyed over half of South Vietnam's trees, killed peasants' livestock, and caused birth defects among their children, all of which turned more Vietnamese into supporters of the NLF. The horrific environmental and health effects of the defoliation campaign lasted for decades.

The sustained bombing of the Ho Chi Minh Trail achieved minimal results. North Vietnamese trucks carrying supplies hid under camouflage and the jungle cover during the day and traveled at night to avoid firepower. Thousands of mostly female Vietnamese peasants helped maintain the trail by staying at campsites along the route every nine miles. Russian and Chinese engineers also helped repair the trail.

North Vietnam faced the most devastating air attacks of the war. Bombing destroyed homes and schools, and it damaged a number of small cities. Health care, food supplies, and education suffered. Between 1965 and 1967 the United States dropped almost 650,000 tons of bombs. The bombing infuriated the Vietnamese. One North Vietnamese soldier recalled that after assaults "the people got very mad and cursed the Americans."

The United States looked for ways to increase faltering public support for its war efforts. American officials tried to reassemble the multinational coalition that had joined the UN forces in repelling the North Korean attack in 1950. Yet none of the European allies agreed to send troops. Relations between the United States, France, Great Britain, and West Germany, where antiwar sentiment ran high, grew tense. Australia and New Zealand did send about 10,000 troops to fight alongside the Americans. The largest contingent of troops from other nations fighting alongside the ARVN came from the Republic of (South) Korea. About 50,000 South Korean forces, paid for by the United States, joined the fighting.

With no victory in sight, the Johnson administration explored negotiations with North Vietnam. In late summer and early fall Harvard professor **Henry Kissinger**, a private citizen acting on behalf of the U.S. government, secretly informed unofficial North Vietnamese representatives that the Johnson administration would temporarily suspend bombing North Vietnam if the North would agree to hold talks with the United States about ending the war. The United States would not insist, as it had earlier, that the North remove its troops from the South before talks could begin. Johnson directly addressed Ho Chi Minh in a widely publicized speech on September 28. He proclaimed, "I am ready to send a trusted representative of America to any spot on this earth to talk in public or private with a spokesman of Hanoi." But these overtures failed. The United States did not suspend the bombing as it promised, and the North Vietnamese continued to denounce the war as illegal.

The War at Home

After 1965 the Vietnam War grew increasingly unpopular in the United States. Protests against the war combined with the movements for civil rights, the empowerment of youth, and Second Wave feminism opened deep divisions in American society. Opposition to the war mounted in Congress, and hundreds of thousands of Americans took to the streets in unprecedented protests of the war's physical, financial, and moral costs. Television showed gritty examples of the war, often at odds with the optimistic government declarations of progress toward creating a stable, legitimate, and self-reliant government of South Vietnam. Journalists in Vietnam spoke contemptuously of a credibility gap between what government officials from President Johnson on down was saying about the war and what actually was taking place in Vietnam.

Domestic opposition to the war grew steadily. In February 1966 the Senate Committee on Foreign Relations held televised hearings on Vietnam. George F. Kennan, the father of the containment doctrine, opposed deeper American involvement in Vietnam because, he said, "unbalanced concentration of resources and attention" on the war diverted American resources from more important foreign policy concerns in Europe. Senator J. William Fulbright, the committee's chair, emerged as one of the Senate's most prominent doves, people who sought a quick, peaceful end to the war. He rejected assertions by hawks, advocates of a military victory in Vietnam such as Secretary of State Dean Rusk, that Vietnam "is a clear case of international Communist aggression." Instead, Fulbright considered Vietnam to be "a civil war in which outside parties have become involved."

A peace movement made up of liberals, pacifists, and radicals emerged to oppose the war. It organized antiwar marches that drew thousands at first. In 1965 opponents of the war held the first of hundreds of teach-ins at college campuses across the country. In October 1967 over 100,000 antiwar demonstrators converged on Washington, DC, to demand an end to the fighting and an American withdrawal from Vietnam. Some publicly burned their draft cards in open defiance of the law.

The draft galvanized opposition to the war. All men aged 18–26 faced the possibility of conscription. But the government applied the draft haphazardly. Fewer than half of draft-age men served in the military during the Vietnam era. Fewer still went to

Peace demonstrators display a huge sign referring to the president as a war criminal during March on the Pentagon, October 1967.

Vietnam. An array of draft deferments, exemptions, and military alternatives to Vietnam was available, especially to more educated and wealthier young men who managed to avoid military service altogether or service in Vietnam. Many Americans came to see Selective Service or the draft as unfair. The inequities of the draft heightened popular distrust for the government and intensified opposition to the war.

Large demonstrations and the coverage of the fighting changed Americans' perceptions of the war. Scenes of battles appeared on the evening news within 24 hours. The sight of American soldiers burning villages proved deeply troubling to many. In 1967 the proportion of Americans who believed American involvement was a mistake rose from 33 percent in January to 46 percent in October. That fall only 28 percent of the public approved of Johnson's handling of the war.

STUDY QUESTIONS FOR AN AMERICAN WAR, 1964–1967

1. Why did President Lyndon B. Johnson decide to Americanize the Vietnam War?
2. What were American tactics in Vietnam? What were the consequences of these tactics?
3. Why did opposition grow to the war in Vietnam?

1968: TURMOIL AND TURNING POINTS

The war in Vietnam reached its climax and American society came close to a breaking point in 1968. Public unhappiness with the course of the Vietnam War combined with other 1960s social movements to make 1968 one of the most tumultuous in American history. Two political assassinations, the bloodiest urban uprisings of the 1960s, and a tumultuous president election campaign shook American self-confidence. Protests against the war in Vietnam and against other government policies erupted around the world. These protests sparked resistance from people opposed to radical change and from authorities. Conservatives eventually prevailed at home and internationally.

The Tet Offensive

In October 1967 North Vietnam leaders decided to launch a nationwide offensive throughout South Vietnam during the annual ceasefire for the lunar new year celebration of Tet. U.S. and South Vietnamese intelligence saw signs of a massive increase in North Vietnamese forces in the South in December 1967, but neither foresaw a coordinated attack. Instead, the Americans worried that North Vietnamese forces would assault Khe Sanh, a Marine base in northwest South Vietnam. President Johnson believed the North Vietnamese wanted to reenact the defeat of the French at Dien Bien Phu by capturing Khe Sanh, and he ordered that the base be held at all costs.

With American attention distracted at Khe Sanh, in the early morning hours of January 31, 1968, the North Vietnamese and NLF attacked throughout South Vietnam. The Tet Offensive began when 19 NLF fighters blasted through the thick wall surrounding the U.S. embassy in Saigon and fought with Marine guards for the next six hours. The daring raid coincided with attacks on the South Vietnamese presidential palace, Saigon's airport, radio stations, and 36 of 40 district capitals.

Bloody battles occurred for the next six weeks. **Nguyen Ngoc Loan,** chief of the National Police Force, publicly executed a captured NLF fighter on a Saigon street on February 1. Pictures of blood spurting from the prisoner's head sickened the American public. The ARVN and U.S. forces, applying massive firepower, killed about 40,000 NLF and North Vietnamese troops, while they lost 3,400 of their own. As many as one million South Vietnamese were forced to flee their homes. The bitterest fighting took place in the old imperial capital of Hue, which the NLF controlled for three weeks in February. American and ARVN bombs and artillery leveled much of the city's core; they left it, as one U.S. solider recalled, "a shattered, stinking hulk, its street choked with rubble and rotting bodies." After the battle ARVN soldiers discovered a mass grave of 2,800 South Vietnamese officials murdered by the NLF.

On March 16 American troops committed their grossest atrocity of the war in the village of My Lai. Company C of the American division entered the village at dawn after being told that it was a major sanctuary for the NLF. Instead of enemy fighters, the Americans found only old men, women, and children. In the words of an eyewitness, the American soldiers "went berserk, gunning down unarmed men, women, children and babies. . . . Those who emerged with hands held high were murdered." The Americans raped women and mutilated dead bodies. All told, soldiers killed 504 Vietnamese. The carnage stopped only when one heroic U.S. army helicopter pilot threatened to turn his chopper's guns on the rampaging soldiers. The **My Lai massacre** remained a secret in the United States for over a year. When knowledge of it leaked in late 1969, opposition to the war intensified.

American public opinion turned sharply against President Johnson and his handling of the war in the wake of Tet; 78 percent of the public said the United States was not making progress, and only 2 percent approved of Johnson's handling of the war. As Tet revealed the vulnerabilities of the South, Westmoreland requested an additional 206,000 United States troops. Johnson asked the new secretary of defense Clark Clifford to review Westmoreland's request. The president reluctantly accepted Clifford's advice to begin deescalating the war. On March 31, hoping to begin peace negotiations with Hanoi, he announced a halt to the bombing of North Vietnam north of the 19th parallel. He also shocked the nation by announcing that he would not seek reelection in November.

The Agony of 1968

Johnson's withdrawal from the presidential race shook up an already turbulent contest for the Democratic Party's presidential nomination. In the fall of 1967 antiwar Democrats encouraged Minnesota senator **Eugene "Gene" McCarthy** to challenge

GLOBAL PASSAGES

The Growth of the Global Antiwar Movement

Students, politicians, radicals, and typical citizens around the world condemned American involvement in Vietnam. Antiwar rallies took place in several European capitals during the International Days of Protest in October 1965 and March 1966. At other times they protested outside U.S. embassies or military bases. Protests by Japanese students dissuaded the government from providing financial support to the American war effort. Frequently, the protests, taking their own form, targeted issues within the respective countries' cultural, social, and political structures in addition to the more narrow antiwar and anti-American critiques. American and European activists looked to one another for encouragement. Antiwar protests played a significant part in what one historian has called the "global disruption" of 1968. The mass student movement that arose in France in the spring had its roots in a protest of the Vietnam War. Protesters in West Germany, moreover, stressed the need for Germany to come to terms with its guilt for the Holocaust and to prevent what they viewed as another genocide in Vietnam from continuing.

The Nazi analogy went far beyond actual American behavior in Vietnam, but it resonated with other radical critics of the war overseas. In May 1967 British philosopher **Bertrand Russell** and French intellectual Jean-Paul Sartre organized an International War Crimes Tribunal held in Stockholm, Sweden, to judge America's conduct in the war. Sartre suggested that, like the Nazis' ethnic cleansing, the "armed forces of the United States torture and kill men, women and children in Vietnam *because they are Vietnamese*." The tribunal found the United States guilty and provided

Johnson for the nomination. McCarthy's campaign attracted little interest until the Tet Offensive undermined support for the war. In February thousands of college-age volunteers cut their long hair, shaved their beards, and wore shirts and ties or skirts and sweaters, to become "clean for Gene" as they campaigned for him in the New Hampshire primary against Johnson. The Minnesotan had come within a few hundred votes of defeating Johnson before he withdrew.

The next few months were among the most turbulent in the 20th century in both the United States and around the world. On April 4, Martin Luther King, Jr., was murdered in Memphis, where he had gone to support the nearly all black garbage workers in a strike. King's assassination set off waves of black rage across the country. Uprisings occurred in more than 100 cities across the country. The police, the National Guard, and the regular army called in to quell the violence killed 37 people. Later in

those resisting military service with a rationale based on the Nuremberg Principles. In 1972 Olaf Palme, the fiercely antiwar prime minister of Sweden, also compared the Christmas bombings to Nazi atrocities.

The Eastern bloc countries supported the cause of the North Vietnamese. So did third-world revolutionaries, who looked toward the NLF's struggle for inspiration. **Che Guevara**, the Cuban revolutionary hero, called for "one, two . . . many Vietnams." American radical activists themselves raised the ire of most Americans when they traveled to conferences in these countries to meet with North Vietnamese and NLF officials. They failed to gain any wider sympathy with the larger public with their provocative statements of solidarity at such events.

Beginning in 1966 the Great Cultural Revolution, directed by Mao Zedong, convulsed China. Millions of young Chinese Red Guards took to the streets to denounce and assault thousands of teachers, village leaders, and Communist Party officials who had incurred Mao's displeasure. Opposition to the U.S. role in Vietnam played only a minor role in the Cultural Revolution. But the international publicity given to the world's most populated nation upended by millions of young revolutionaries aroused protesters worldwide. At the same time scenes of the Cultural Revolution also fortified the resolve of the Johnson administration to prevail in Vietnam.

The global antiwar movement elevated anti-Americanism to new levels in many parts of the world. It also subsequently eroded the prestige that the United States had held on the world stage after World War II.

- How did opponents of U.S. policies in Vietnam express their dissent?

- In what ways did international protests of the Vietnam War contribute to the global disruptions of the 1960s?

April student uprisings erupted. Members of the Students for a Democratic Society at Columbia University, occupying several classroom buildings, demanded that the university stop construction of a gymnasium in Morningside Park, which separated the mostly white Ivy League university from largely African American Harlem. University administrators called in the police who cleared the buildings by swinging their clubs and fists. Pictures of bloodied student demonstrators invoked some sympathy, but many Americans were frightened by the protests.

French students had grievances of their own against a paternalistic university system where they were forced to stand or sit in the aisles of overcrowded lecture halls. The rigid curriculum allowed almost no opportunity to explore contemporary issues. Thousands walked out of classes across Paris. The government sent police with clubs against the protesting students, who then set up barricades. In May the students joined

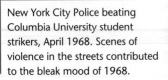

New York City Police beating Columbia University student strikers, April 1968. Scenes of violence in the streets contributed to the bleak mood of 1968.

a general strike of workers throughout France. Marching through the capital, over one million demonstrators demanded the resignation of President Charles de Gaulle. Some supporters thought that the country was experiencing a new revolution. Public opinion turned against the strikers, however, and de Gaulle won a resounding victory in special parliamentary elections.

Student demonstrations and strikes also shook authorities elsewhere in Europe and in Latin America. In West Germany New Left students occupied university buildings in sympathy with their fellow students in France. Uprisings were especially dramatic in communist-ruled Eastern Europe. Polish students briefly took to the streets against the communist government. The deepest challenge to communist rule in Eastern Europe occurred in Czechoslovakia. There the Prague Spring began in April with student protests against authoritarian university rules. The experiment with a nonrepressive style of socialism, called "socialism with a human face," by the new Czech leader **Alexander Dubcek**, lasted until the Soviet Union invaded Czechoslovakia in August. However, the most brutal suppression of student protests occurred in Mexico City in October. Students closed the university with demands for reforms similar to the student demands in France. They also protested the government's flattening of poor neighborhoods to make way for the Olympic Games. The government, unwilling to have protests anywhere near the site of the Games, cracked down with brute force. The Mexican army shot and killed over 1,000 demonstrators the week before the Games began.

Other shocking events further unnerved Americans. A few days after the New Hampshire primary, Senator Robert Kennedy entered the race to challenge Johnson.

After Johnson withdrew, a three-way battle ensued among senators McCarthy and Kennedy and Vice President **Hubert Humphrey**. Kennedy pulled ahead of McCarthy by winning the California primary on June 5. In the early morning hours of June 6, as Kennedy declared his victory, Sirhan Sirhan, a Palestinian angered by the senator's support for Israel, shot and killed him. The country, hardly recovered from the grief of King's murder, was stunned and depressed. Even for his detractors, the killing of RFK so soon after King added to the sense of chaos and disorder that seemed to be escalating.

McCarthy now was the sole hope of most antiwar Democrats, who desperately wanted to deny the nomination to Humphrey. The vice president had the support of the pro-war faction of the Democratic Party, scheduled to hold its convention in Chicago in late August. Some antiwar protesters vowed to come to the Chicago convention to undermine what they called the "party of death."

Chicago's Democratic mayor Richard J. Daley vowed that the demonstrators would not interrupt the convention. He ordered his 12,000-member police force to work 12-hour shifts and had the governor send 6,000 National Guard troops to the city. President Johnson sent 7,500 regular army soldiers to patrol the African American community. On the night of August 28, when the convention nominated Humphrey, police and national guardsman clubbed and tear-gassed a crowd of demonstrators outside the Hilton hotel in downtown Chicago. Certain that the country would sympathize with them against the brutal and unnecessary police tactics, the protesters shouted "the whole world is watching." According to opinion surveys, however, the American public sided with the police by a margin of two to one.

Humphrey's nomination originally seemed worthless. He left the convention trailing former vice president **Richard M. Nixon**, the Republican nominee, by more than 20 points. A third candidate, Alabama democratic governor **George C. Wallace**, also polled strongly with about 20 percent in early September. Wallace appealed to white working-class voters, mostly but not exclusively in the South, who had left the Democratic Party over its support for civil rights for African Americans.

Nixon and Wallace both opposed Johnson's handling of the war. The Republican nominee had been a hawk on Vietnam. During the campaign he avoided specifics, while calling for "peace with honor," a formulation that appealed both to those who wanted the war to end soon and to those who craved an American victory. Wallace implied he would end the war more quickly than either Humphrey or Nixon by adopting the toughest tactics.

Nixon also campaigned against civil rights activists and antiwar and youth protesters. He adopted a Southern Strategy designed to transform the traditionally Democratic South into a Republican stronghold. He campaigned against "crime in the streets," code for the African American urban uprisings after the assassination of Martin Luther King, Jr., and for the antiwar protests at the Democratic convention.

Humphrey's campaign picked up support after he distanced himself from Johnson on September 30 and offered a total halt to the bombing of North Vietnam as "an acceptable risk for peace." Progress in the peace talks between the United States and North Vietnam in Paris also helped Humphrey. For months the North Vietnamese refused to engage directly in talks with representatives of South Vietnam. But the pace of negotiations quickened in late October. The North Vietnamese indicated that they would hold meaningful talks if the United States halted the bombing. The weekend before the election Johnson announced a total bombing halt. Serious negotiations would begin on Thursday, November 7, two days after the election.

The announcement of the bombing halt was not quite enough to turn the election to Humphrey. Members of Nixon's campaign, including Henry Kissinger, alerted representatives of South Vietnam's President **Nguyen Van Thieu** about the proposed bombing halt. Thieu denounced it and said his government would not attend the talks. Humphrey's surge stalled, and Nixon won a close election by 512,000 votes (Nixon: 31,783,000 votes, 43.6 percent, 301 electoral votes; Humphrey: 31,271,000 votes, 42.9 percent, 191 electoral votes; Wallace: 9,901,000 votes, 13.5 percent, 46 electoral votes). The narrow difference between Nixon and Humphrey masked the extent of the public's turn against Johnson, the Great Society, the Vietnam War, and political liberalism. Together Nixon and Wallace, the two conservative candidates, received over 56 percent of the popular vote. The Democratic Party's share of the vote fell from 60.5 percent in the landslide election of 1964 to under 43 percent. Nixon's victory began more than two decades of nearly uninterrupted success for Republican presidential candidates.

STUDY QUESTIONS FOR 1968: TURMOIL AND TURNING POINTS

1. How did the Tet Offensive change the course of the War in Vietnam?
2. How did opponents of the U.S. involvement in the war in Vietnam express their dissent, both at home and abroad?
3. Why was the presidential election of 1968 so tumultuous? Why did Richard Nixon win it?

NIXON AND THE WORLD

Richard Nixon came to the presidency vowing to restore America's badly damaged credibility in world affairs. Together with Henry Kissinger, his national security adviser and later secretary of state, Nixon engineered some of the most dramatic diplomatic changes in the 20th century. From 1969 to 1973 the United States reduced its forces in Vietnam and in 1973 signed a ceasefire agreement with Hanoi. Although the Paris Peace Accords were hailed at the time, they did not last, and in 1975 the communist side won the Vietnam War.

Nixon, pursuing **détente**, or the relaxation of tension with the Soviet Union, had more success in calming the Cold War. Nixon also visited the People's Republic of China (PRC), and thus ended a more than two-decades-long estrangement between the two countries. Nixon and Kissinger conducted foreign affairs in secret, however, and often expressed contempt for the public, Congress, and other government officials. Their maneuverings cost them widespread support for their foreign policies.

From Vietnamization to Paris

The Nixon administration managed to divert public attention from the Vietnam War, beginning a process of Vietnamization of the war in 1969. The United States gradually reduced its ground forces in Vietnam and provided more arms and training for the ARVN. Nixon met South Vietnam's President Thieu in June 1969 and informed him that he planned to remove 25,000 U.S. forces from Vietnam. Nixon also promised that after the war ended the United States would continue to aid Asian countries to resist communist revolutions, but it would expect them to assume the "primary responsibility of providing the manpower for [their] own defense." As U.S. troop levels fell, monthly draft calls declined; as a result, draft protests lessened but tensions remained high.

At the same time the United States increased the pace of bombing in South Vietnam and in neighboring Cambodia. Nixon hoped to keep the bombing of Cambodia a secret to preserve a fiction that it was a neutral country. Despite removing an additional 150,000 troops from Vietnam in 1970, the United States expanded the ground war into neighboring Cambodia. On April 30, U.S. and South Vietnamese troops entered Cambodia to bolster the fortunes of a new anticommunist government and to destroy the headquarters of the NLF they believed were located near the Cambodian and South Vietnamese border. The invasion was a disaster. The South Vietnamese were unprepared and outmatched and never found the rumored headquarters.

The expansion of the war into Cambodia ignited some of the largest antiwar demonstrations of the Vietnam era. On college campuses and in high schools across the country students rallied against the Cambodian invasion. The protests turned deadly at Kent State University in northern Ohio when National Guardsmen, called in by the governor to stop the demonstrations, shot and killed four demonstrators. After the violence at Kent State student strikes shut down hundreds of universities and colleges. Over 100,000 young people descended on Washington to petition Congress to end the war. Congress repealed the Gulf of Tonkin Resolution and tried unsuccessfully to cut off funds for fighting in Cambodia.

After the killings at Kent State, mass antiwar demonstrations declined because they were dangerous and because fewer Americans were dying in the war. Another 150,000 American troops left Vietnam in 1970 and the U.S. death toll fell below 100 a week. Consequently, public attention drifted away from Vietnam until February 1971 when the American military led 36,000 ARVN troops into neighboring Laos. Once more the ARVN fought poorly and left in disarray after six weeks without achieving its goal of disrupting the NLF.

Public confidence in the government's handling of the war was shaken further in June 1971 when the *New York Times* published excerpts from the **Pentagon Papers**, a collection of government documents outlining U.S. decision making in Vietnam occurring as early as World War II. Daniel Ellsberg, a once hawkish former Defense

Department adviser who now opposed the war, leaked copies to the newspaper. He hoped that the documents' record of successive administrations' misstatements and outright lies about the war would persuade more Americans to demand a quick end to the fighting. The Nixon administration reacted furiously to the leak and obtained an injunction forbidding the *New York Times* from further publication of the papers. The Supreme Court, overturning the restraining order, ruled that the Nixon administration had not proved that publication would harm national security.

John Ehrlichman, Nixon's chief domestic policy adviser, responded to the Court's rebuff by assembling a team of White House Plumbers, so named because they plugged leaks, to embarrass Ellsberg. A year later veterans of the Plumbers' operation broke into the offices of the Democratic National Committee at the **Watergate** office complex in Washington in an attempt to steal campaign secrets. Their actions set in motion the scandal that forced Nixon's resignation in 1974.

For the next eight months Henry Kissinger conducted secret talks in Paris with North Vietnam's **Le Duc Tho**. Kissinger and Nixon publicly supported South Vietnam's president Thieu. Privately, however, they favored an end to the war and the withdrawal of U.S. forces, followed by a decent interval before the communists took over. They wanted to give South Vietnam a chance to succeed, but if it lost the war the failure would be Saigon's, not Washington's.

North Vietnam launched a major offensive across the border into South Vietnam in April 1972. The United States responded by resuming bombing over all of North Vietnam and by mining the harbor of the port of Haiphong. Still, Kissinger continued to negotiate with Le Duc Tho. In October 1972, less than two weeks before the U.S. presidential election, Kissinger, announcing that he and Tho had reached a breakthrough, declared that "peace is at hand." President Thieu, furious at the deal, refused to accept it. The announcement of an impending peace helped Nixon coast to a landslide victory over Democratic presidential candidate **George McGovern**. Nixon won 47.1 million votes, 60.7 percent, and 520 electoral votes; McGovern received 29.1 million votes, 37.5 percent, and 17 electoral votes.

The United States initiated the heaviest bombing campaign of the war over North Vietnam in December 1972 to persuade President Thieu to accept a settlement and to convince him that the United States would come to his assistance if the war resumed. The agreements signed at Paris on January 27, 1973, were almost the same as the deal hammered out in October. The United States agreed to withdraw all of its troops from Vietnam. North Vietnam would keep a force of 200,000 in the South, but Thieu agreed not to increase this. Prisoners of war would be returned within 60 days. North Vietnam dropped its key demand that Thieu and his administration resign. Thieu remained in power, but the accords called for the eventual creation of a government of national reconciliation.

The End of the Vietnam War

The ceasefire promised by the Paris Accords never held. President Thieu ordered the ARVN to attack in March 1973. He hoped renewed fighting would encourage Washington to honor its pledge for increased military support. But he badly misjudged

American public opinion, which was heartily sick of the war. Once 591 American prisoners of war returned home in March, Americans shifted their attention to the growing Watergate scandal.

Nixon resigned in August 1974, and Vice President **Gerald R. Ford**, who succeeded Nixon as president, had little desire to reengage in Vietnam (more below). A Democratic Party sweep in the 1974 congressional elections further weakened Ford's standing.

In early 1975 North Vietnam launched a final offensive to defeat Thieu. After North Vietnamese forces captured the coastal city of Da Nang in March, ARVN troops retreated in terror. Many threw down their weapons and shed their uniforms. Hundreds of them fought with thousands of desperate refugees for places on helicopters, planes, trucks, and buses to flee the communist advances. On April 29 the last Americans departed from Saigon on a helicopter that lifted off from the roof of a building near the embassy. Although the Americans helped about 150,000 Vietnamese who had worked for the Americans or supported the South Vietnamese government escape, they left hundreds of thousands behind. On April 30, 1975, the government of South Vietnam surrendered to the NLF, and the capital city of Saigon was renamed Ho Chi Minh City.

The Vietnam War ended at enormous cost. Over two million Vietnamese and 58,000 Americans died. The war wrecked the Vietnamese countryside and created over three million Vietnamese refugees. Vietnam also exacted a heavy price on American outlook and optimism. The attitude of most Americans changed from trust to skepticism to eventual outright disbelief as the credibility gap widened throughout the Johnson and Nixon administrations.

Reduction of Cold War Tensions

Richard Nixon gained prominence in the early Cold War years as an ardent anticommunist and foe of the Soviet Union, but as president he eased tensions. He and Kissinger concluded agreements dampening the nuclear arms race and increasing trade between East and West. Nixon and Kissinger did not succeed, however, in gaining Moscow's cooperation in persuading North Vietnam to agree to American terms for ending the Vietnam War.

In 1969 Kissinger opened secret backchannel negotiations with the Soviet ambassador to the United States. The United States and the Soviet Union conducted arduous secret negotiations for three years. In May 1972 Nixon traveled to Moscow for a summit meeting with Soviet Communist Party secretary **Leonid Brezhnev**. The two leaders signed three important agreements: an Anti-Ballistic Missile (ABM) treaty limiting each country to only two missile sites; an Interim Agreement on Limitations of Strategic Armaments (SALT-I), which limited the number of each side's nuclear missiles and promised a treaty with greater limitations within five years; and The Basic Principles of United States-Soviet Cooperation, a document promising that each nation would deal with the other on "the principle of equality."

Nixon and Kissinger came back from the Moscow summit lauded as masters of foreign policy. Détente with the Soviet Union won praise from old adversaries astonished that Nixon, the veteran Cold Warrior, had succeeded in reducing the conflict

Henry Kissinger and Soviet Ambassador Anatoly Dobrynin, 1974.

with the Soviets after his predecessors had failed. Brezhnev returned Nixon's visit with one of his own to Washington and California in June 1973, and Nixon went back to Moscow in June 1974. By that time, however, Nixon's presidency was nearing its end, as his reputation became destroyed by the Watergate scandal. By 1974 détente had also lost much of its early allure. Many officials in the Department of Defense and their supporters in Congress and the press claimed that arms control agreements gave the Soviet Union a military advantage. Advocates for human rights complained that Nixon and Kissinger ignored the Soviet Union's mistreatment of its own people.

Nixon's most astonishing foreign policy reversal was opening the frozen relations between the United States and the People's Republic of China. The president believed that forging a working relationship with the PRC far outweighed whatever happened in Vietnam. Chinese Communist Party Chairman Mao Zedong sought better relations with the United States to counterbalance the power of the Soviet Union, its former patron that was now a bitter rival.

In July 1971 Kissinger secretly traveled to Beijing to met China's Premier Zhou Enlai, whom he called "one of the two or three most impressive men I have ever met." The two agreed that Nixon would visit China in 1972 and spoke of the threat of Soviet domination of Europe and Asia. Nixon made a celebrated five-day visit to China in February 1972. He toasted Chairman Mao, and he and his wife Pat visited the Great Wall. He ended his visit in Shanghai, where the two nations issued a carefully crafted declaration of what they had accomplished. The Shanghai Communiqué announced that each country would open "interests sections," embassies in all but name, in each other's capitals. The United States would maintain its embassy on the island of Taiwan, the Republic of China. The communiqué stated that all Chinese on both sides of the Straits of Taiwan must formally affirm that China was a single country, a key issue for the PRC. Nixon's visit to China and his 1972 summit in Moscow indicated that the Vietnam War no longer paralyzed U.S. foreign policy as it had in 1968.

Crises in Latin America and the Middle East, however, eroded Nixon's and Kissinger's reputation for foreign policy success. In September 1973 Kissinger became secretary of state and retained the position of national security adviser. Days before Kissinger was sworn in, the commander of Chile's army, General **Augusto Pinochet**, overthrew the democratically elected government of Socialist president **Salvador Allende**. The United States had tried to thwart Allende for years. In 1970, before Allende was elected in the last of his four tries for the presidency, Kissinger told an interagency intelligence group, "I don't see why we have to let a country go Marxist just because its people are irresponsible."

After Allende's inauguration the United States cut off economic aid to Chile and the CIA spent $20 million supporting his political opponents. In August 1973 the economy plunged and strikes paralyzed the country. After Pinochet seized power the military murdered Allende, although they claimed he committed suicide. The military government killed hundreds and forced thousands to flee into exile. The thousands of presumed dead militants became known as the "disappeared." The "Madres of the Plaza de Mayo" protested steadfastly in the streets for decades demanding an end to the violence and information on the locations of the bodies of their murdered children. The Nixon administration ignored the human rights abuses and restored economic and military aid to Chile. Pinochet ruled a police state for the next 17 years.

On the afternoon of October 6, 1973, the Jewish Holy Day of Yom Kippur, the Yom Kippur War broke out in the Middle East. Egypt and Syria launched coordinated attacks on Israeli military positions. The Egyptian and Syrian forces made major gains. Egypt's army captured hundreds of Israeli soldiers in the Sinai Peninsula and Syria recovered much of the Golan Heights. Shaken by the success of the attackers, Israel's prime minister **Golda Meir** begged the United States to resupply tanks, arms, planes, and ammunition lost in the first days of the war. The United States responded with an airlift of military equipment that enabled Israel to counterattack. Egypt's President **Anwar Sadat**, who had evicted Soviet advisers from his country in 1972, now called on Moscow for military aid. Nixon and Kissinger worried that Soviet intervention threatened superpower détente, so Kissinger traveled to Moscow to arrange an end to the fighting. He and Soviet foreign minister **Andrei Gromyko** jointly called on the UN Security Council to sponsor a cease-fire.

Kissinger achieved his highest level of international celebrity after the Yom Kippur War. He traveled back and forth between Israel's capital of Jerusalem and Cairo and Damascus, the capitals of Egypt and Syria, respectively. This shuttle diplomacy resulted in the disengagement of the nations' military forces. Israel moved its forces east of the Suez Canal and thus enabled Egypt to open the important waterway. Israel also withdrew from some, but not all, of Syrian territory on the Golan Heights. Shuttle diplomacy diminished the threat of the resumption of the war and it began a peace process that led eventually to direct talks and a treaty between Israel and Egypt. It did not, however, address the complex issue of a Palestinian demand for an independent state.

During the Yom Kippur War members of the **Organization of Petroleum Exporting Countries** (OPEC), the oil cartel formed in 1960, supported Egypt and Syria. Angered at the West's backing of Israel, OPEC boycotted the sale of oil to the United States, Western Europe, and Japan. Because the United States imported less of its oil from the Middle East than did Europe or Japan, it agreed to make up some of its allies' shortfall by reducing its own oil supplies to 80 percent of their customary levels. After the price of a barrel of oil shot up by 400 percent, the industrial world sank into the gravest economic recession since the Great Depression. The next year unemployment in the United States rose from 5 percent to 7 percent in the next year, and the price of a gallon of gasoline more than doubled from 45 cents to one dollar.

STUDY QUESTIONS FOR NIXON AND THE WORLD

1. How did the Nixon administration reduce the public's interest in the Vietnam War?
2. Why did the communists prevail in the Vietnam War?
3. What were the successes and the failures of the Nixon administration's foreign policy? Explain why some policies succeeded and others did not.

DOMESTIC POLICY AND THE ABUSE OF POWER

An enormous gulf separated the Nixon administration's rhetoric from the reality of its actions. It cut back but did not eliminate Great Society programs of social reform. Nixon appointed conservative justices to the Supreme Court, but they too did not alter the Court's expansion of individual rights and liberties. His Southern Strategy encouraged the movement of whites in the Old Confederacy and border states toward the Republican Party, especially as regarded the presidential elections. In 1972 he won one of the most lopsided electoral victories in U.S. history, yet his suspicious nature proved to be his undoing. From 1971 to 1973 numerous White House operatives committed a series of illegal acts known as Watergate, a scandal that forced Nixon to resign from the presidency in August 1974.

Curtailing the Great Society

When Nixon campaigned for the presidency in 1968, he endorsed the Great Society's goals of eliminating poverty and racial discrimination. However, he criticized the Johnson administration's conduct of the War on Poverty as inept and inefficient.

Congress, controlled by Democrats, reluctantly accepted Nixon's plan to transfer control over antipoverty programs to the states.

Democrats in Congress, however, prevailed on the Nixon administration to enact laws protecting the environment, workers, and consumers. In 1971, responding to the growing environmental movement, Congress created the Environmental Protection Agency. The EPA brought hundreds of law suits against polluters and set emissions standards for cars and power plants. Congress also addressed issues of worker and consumer protection by creating the Occupational Health and Safety Administration (OSHA) and the Consumer Products Safety Council (CPSC). OSHA leaders wrote rules for workplace safety and sent inspectors into factories, stores, and offices. Their actions reduced workplace accidents and injuries, but business groups complained that the regulations raised costs and made them uncompetitive. The CPSC's reports on toys and on children's clothing safety were highly popular with parents. Manufacturers, however, resented the regulations; they argued that the additional costs of compliance made their products unaffordable.

International pressures forced Nixon to break with conservative economic orthodoxy. From 1969 to 1971 the economy nearly stagnated while inflation increased. This combination defined the expectations of economists, who called it **stagflation**. Nixon believed the hard economic times endangered his chances for reelection in 1972. In the summer of 1971 European governments that owned U.S. dollars threatened to redeem their greenbacks for gold. On August 15, Nixon announced a New Economic Policy, the wording of which he borrowed from Democratic Party liberals. He imposed a three-month freeze on wages and prices and announced that the United States would no longer redeem its dollars for gold. The New Economic Policy began a process under which governments around the world no longer fixed the value of their currency to the value of the dollar. The more cohesive exchange rates that followed helped create a unified global market for goods to flow more freely across national boundaries.

During the election campaign of 1968 Nixon promised to appoint conservative justices to the Supreme Court. When Nixon became president he appointed **Warren Burger**, a moderately conservative Minnesota Federal judge, as Chief Justice. As part of Nixon's Southern Strategy of encouraging Democrats in the states of the Old Confederacy to cross over to the Republican Party, he tried to make good on a promise to appoint a Southerner to the Court. This effort failed, however, when the Senate defeated the confirmation of Clement Haynsworth and G. Harrold Carswell on the grounds that each had supported racial segregation in the past. Harry Blackmun and **William Rehnquist** joined the Court instead.

Despite liberals' fears and conservatives' hopes, the Burger Court did not sharply reverse the Warren Court's expansion of civil rights and liberties. In some notable cases it even went beyond its predecessor. In *Swann v. Charlotte-Mecklenburg Board of Education* (1971) and *Keyes v. Denver School District No. 1* (1973), the Court upheld the use of buses to transport students throughout a school district to achieve racial balance. The decisions provoked angry outbursts. Whites burned school buses in Southern states but also generally more moderate cities like Denver, Colorado, and Pontiac,

Michigan. In Boston white mobs attacked black school children who under Court order attended previously all white schools. In 1974 Congress stipulated that busing should be used only as a last resort.

The Court also advanced women's rights. In 1971 it held in *Phillips v. Martin Marietta* that companies could not discriminate against women with small children in their hiring practices. In *Frontiero v. Richardson*, (1973), the Court required the military to provide women the same pension rights as men. In *Roe v. Wade* (1973) the Court decided that the right to privacy extended to "a woman's decision whether or not to terminate her pregnancy." It therefore concluded that states could not limit the right to an abortion during the first trimester, about 13 weeks of a pregnancy. States could regulate, but not outlaw, abortion in the second 13 weeks. Only in the last trimester could states ban abortion.

Watergate

Richard Nixon constantly felt he was being unfairly attacked by the media, intellectuals, and Democratic Party officials. He treated his domestic political opponents as not merely rivals but as enemies. As he prepared for his reelection campaign he authorized an illegal plot against the Democratic Party designed to undermine their presidential candidates and assure his reelection. Nixon relied on a team of operatives called the "White House Plumbers."

At 1:40 AM on June 17, 1972, seven men working for G. Gordon Liddy, an employee of the Committee to Reelect the President, broke into the headquarters of the Democratic National Committee to repair an illegal bug, or listening device, they had installed in May. A night watchman called the police, who arrested the burglars. When Liddy heard of the arrest, he telephoned John Ehrlichman at the White House.

TIMELINE 1945–1975

1945

September 2 Ho Chi Minh declares the independence of the Democratic Republic of Vietnam

1946

December 19 War begins between France and the Vietminh

1954

April President Eisenhower decides against American military operation to relieve French at Dien Bien Phu

May 7 Vietminh capture Dien Bien Phu

July 21 Geneva Accords on Vietnam signed

1960

December 20 Creation of the National Front for the Liberation of Vietnam (the Viet Cong)

1963

May–June Buddhist crisis in South Vietnam

November 1–2 Military coup deposes President Ngo Dinh Diem

1964

August 7 Congress adopts Gulf of Tonkin resolution

1965

March 24–25 First anti-Vietnam teach-in at the University of Michigan

July 28 President Johnson makes final decision to Americanize the War

1966

May 6 Great Proletarian Cultural Revolution begins in China

1967

October 21 Over 100,000 people join an antiwar march on Washington

1968

January–August Prague Spring in Czechoslovakia

January 31 Tet Offensive begins

March 16 My Lai massacre

March 31 Johnson announces he will not seek the Democratic Party presidential nomination

April 4 Martin Luther King assassinated

April 23–30 Student demonstrations at Columbia University

May 13 Student uprising in Paris leads to a crippling nationwide general strike

June 6 Robert F. Kennedy assassinated

August 26–29 Demonstrations at the Democratic National Convention in Chicago

October 2 Mexican troops kill hundreds of young people protesting before the Olympic Games in Mexico City

Senator Sam Ervin speaks at the Senate Watergate Committee in May 1973. Senator Howard Baker (R) covers the microphone with his hand.

Ehrlichman relayed the message to Nixon's chief of staff **H. R. Haldeman**. The president and his chief of staff immediately began a cover-up of White House involvement in bugging the Democrats' headquarters. Nixon put his legal counsel **John Dean** in charge of the cover-up.

November 5 Richard Nixon defeats Hubert Humphrey and George Wallace for the presidency

1969

March Vietnamization begins

1970

April 30 U.S. and South Vietnamese invasion of Cambodia

May 4 National Guard kills four protesters at Kent State University

1971

January–April U.S. and South Vietnamese invasion of Laos ends

in failure

February 21–27 Nixon visits the PRC

June 13 Publication of the Pentagon Papers

July Henry Kissinger secretly visits the People's Republic of China

1972

May 22 Nixon visits Soviet Union, furthering détente between the world's two nuclear superpowers

June 17 Watergate break-in that eventually leads to Nixon's resignation

November 7 Nixon reelected in landslide

1973

May 9 Senate Watergate hearings begin

October 17 to March 17 Mideast Arab oil embargo against the United States and other supporters of Israel; a sharp international economic recession follows.

October 10 Spiro Agnew resigns as vice president

December 6 Gerald R. Ford becomes vice president

1974

July 27 House Judiciary Committee votes three

articles of impeachment against Richard Nixon

August 8 Nixon resigns as president

1975

March 30 North Vietnamese and NLF forces capture Da Nang

April 30 Communist forces win the Vietnam War

Dean's efforts were successful for nearly 6 months. Few Americans paid attention to articles by *Washington Post* reporters **Bob Woodward** and **Carl Bernstein** which sought to expose the money trail leading from the Watergate burglars to the White House. Democratic Presidential candidate George McGovern made little headway with voters when he characterized Nixon as leading "the most corrupt administration in history." In November 1972 Nixon easily defeated McGovern in a landslide election in which he won all but Massachusetts and the District of Columbia. Early in 1973, however, the Watergate cover-up began to unravel. The Senate appointed a Select Committee on Campaign Finances, chaired by North Carolina democrat Sam Ervin. As the committee prepared for hearings on how Nixon had raised money for his reelection, federal judge **John Sirica** threatened the Watergate burglars with long sentences unless they revealed who had ordered the break-in. In April prosecutors began questioning Dean about his role. Dean agreed to cooperate in return for immunity, and he told Ervin committee staff members all he knew. On April 30, Nixon fired Dean and accepted the resignations of Haldeman and Ehrlichman, who had also been part of the break-in and its cover-up aftermath. Hoping to buy time, Nixon appointed Harvard law school professor **Archibald Cox** as a special independent prosecutor to investigate Watergate.

In the spring and summer of 1973 the Senate Watergate Committee held televised hearings on events surrounding the break-in and cover-up. The public watched in fascination and disgust as witnesses outlined the millions raised in cash, the administration's dirty tricks against political adversaries, and the extent of the cover-up. The climax came in July when White House aide **Alexander Butterfield** revealed that Nixon had secretly taped his conversations since 1970.

Meanwhile, another scandal hit the White House in August when the *Wall Street Journal* reported that Vice President **Spiro T. Agnew** was being investigated for taking bribes when he served as governor of Maryland. Agnew made a deal with prosecutors to avoid jail time and resigned in October. Nixon then appointed House Minority Leader Gerald R. Ford, untainted by Watergate, to replace Agnew.

In October special prosecutor Cox asked Judge Sirica to order Nixon to provide him with the tapes. Instead, Nixon fired Cox and closed the office of the independent counsel. The public responded with a deluge of outraged telegrams and phone calls to Congress demanding that the House of Representatives begin impeachment proceedings against Nixon. In the first six months of 1974 the Judiciary Committee built a case against Nixon. In July the committee voted three articles of impeachment against him for obstruction of justice, abuse of power, and an illegal disregard of congressional subpoenas. Nixon continued to deny wrongdoing until the Supreme Court unanimously ordered him to release the tapes of 64 conversations. One of them contained the "smoking gun" conversation in which he and Haldeman conspired to use the CIA to cover up the burglary at the Watergate. With the release of that tape Nixon lost all of his remaining Republican congressional support, and he resigned on August 9, 1974.

Nixon's resignation temporarily unified the country. Americans were outraged by the abuses of power, but they felt relieved that Congress, the court system, and the press had worked together to reveal the extent of the misconduct. Most agreed with President Ford, who exclaimed after he took the oath of office, "our long national nightmare is over."

STUDY QUESTIONS FOR DOMESTIC POLICY AND THE ABUSE OF POWER

1. What domestic goals did the Nixon administration pursue?
2. Where was the Nixon administration successful and where did it fail in changing the direction and scope of the Great Society programs of the Johnson administration?
3. What threats to constitutional government did the Watergate scandal represent?

Summary

- From 1945 to 1963 the United States supported anticommunist forces in Vietnam as part of the Cold War competition with the Soviet Union and Communist China.
- From 1964 to 1967 the administration of President Lyndon B. Johnson Americanized the Vietnam War. By 1968 approximately 500,000 U.S. forces were fighting in Vietnam.
- After 1965 opposition to the war grew at home and abroad.
- 1968 was the climatic year in the war. Assassinations, urban uprisings, and protests shocked Americans and led to the election of Richard M. Nixon as president.
- President Nixon and National Security Adviser Henry Kissinger engineered dramatic reversals in American foreign policy toward the Soviet Union and China.
- The Paris Peace Accords of 1973 ended U.S. involvement in the Vietnam War. The communist North won the war in 1975.
- The Nixon administration curtailed but did not eliminate the Great Society programs of the Johnson administration.
- The Watergate scandal was the gravest constitutional crisis of the 20th century for the United States. It led to the resignation of President Nixon in 1974.

Key Terms and People

Agnew, Spiro T. *1120*

Allende, Salvador *1115*

Bernstein, Carl *1120*

Brezhnev, Leonid *1113*

Burger, Warren *1117*

Butterfield, Alexander *1120*

Cox, Archibald *1120*

Dean, John *1119*

détente *1110*

Dubcek, Alexander *1108*

Duc, Thich Quang *1096*

Ford, Gerald R. *1113*

Gromyko, Andrei *1115*

Guevara, Che *1107*

Gulf of Tonkin Resolution *1099*

Haldeman, H. R. *1119*

Humphrey, Hubert *1109*

Khanh, Nguyen, *1097*

Kissinger, Henry *1102*

Loan, Nguyen Ngoc *1105*

Lodge, Henry Cabot *1096*

McCarthy, Eugene "Gene" *1105*

McGovern, George *1112*

Meir, Golda *1115*

Minh, Ho Chi *1092*

My Lai massacre *1105*

Nixon, Richard M. *1109*

Organization of Petroleum Exporting Countries (OPEC) *1116*

Pentagon Papers *1111*

Pinochet, Augusto *1115*

Rehnquist, William *1117*

Russell, Bertrand *1106*

Sadat, Anwar *1115*

Sirica, John *1120*

stagflation *1117*

Thieu, Nguyen Van *1110*

Tho, Le Duc *1112*

Wallace, George C. *1109*

Watergate *1112*

Woodward, Bob *1120*

Reviewing Chapter 28
1. How did the war in Vietnam affect U.S. foreign policies?
2. How did growing dissatisfaction with the war in Vietnam contribute to wider disillusionment with public institutions and officials?
3. How did the actions of the Nixon administration, at home and abroad, affect public attitudes toward government and public institutions?

Further Reading
Farber, David R. *Chicago '68*. Chicago: The University of Chicago Press, 1988. An innovative study of a critical turning point in history.

Herring, George C. *America's Longest War: The United States and Vietnam, 1950–1975*. New York: McGraw-Hill, 2002. A detailed yet readable account of the uncertain U.S. entry, often perplexing escalation of involvement, and painful exit from Vietnam.

O'Brien, Tim. *The Things They Carried*. New York: Houghton Mifflin, 1990. An award-winning collection of stories based on the author's actual experience in Vietnam. A captivating study of the tension between memory and history.

Schulzinger, Robert D. *A Time for War: The United States and Vietnam, 1941–1975*. New York: Oxford University Press, 1997. Insightful analysis of the war from the perspective of a leading diplomatic historian.

Small, Melvin. *Antiwarriors: The Vietnam War and the Battle for America's Hearts and Minds*. New York: Rowman & Littlefield, 2002. A critical analysis of the antiwar movement in politics and culture.

Visual Review

Vietnam and the Cold War

The United States backs several alternatives to a Vietnamese government led by Ho Chi Minh.

American Commitments to South Vietnam

The United States supplants France as the principal supporter of the noncommunist South.

The 1963 Turning Point

The United States plans remain in flux after dropping support for President Ngo Dinh Diem.

Background to a War, 1945–1963

THE VIETNAM ERA, 1961–1975

An American War, 1964–1967

Decisions for Escalation, 1964–1965

The United States increases its military commitments to Vietnam.

Ground and Air War, 1966–1967

The U.S. strategy focuses on attrition of the enemy.

The War at Home

The Vietnam War grows increasingly unpopular in the United States.

1968: Turmoil and Turning Points

The Tet Offensive
North Vietnam launches a massive offensive into South Vietnam.

The Agony of 1968
1968 is among the most turbulent years in U.S. history, filled with assassinations, protests, and riots.

Nixon and the World

From Vietnamization to Paris
The Nixon administration adjusts strategy while seeking a peace plan.

The End of the Vietnam War
Peace never takes hold and the North Vietnamese take over control of the south while the United States disengages.

Reduction of Cold War Tensions
Nixon eases tensions with the Soviet Union.

Domestic Policy and the Abuse of Power

Curtailing the Great Society
The Nixon administration curtails Great Society programs, but enacts new laws protecting the environment, workers, and consumers.

Watergate
Nixon resigns due to the Watergate scandal.

W SAMO POŁUDNIE
4 CZERWCA 1989

Conservatism Resurgent

1974–1989

R ace, religion, and taxes produce a volatile mix in American politics. Although the Supreme Court outlawed school segregation in 1954, large-scale integration did not begin until the early 1970s when federal courts ordered school busing and other measures to break down color barriers. As African American students entered previously all-white public schools, many white parents, especially in the South, moved their children to newly opened "Christian academies." In 1978, however, President **Jimmy Carter** ordered the IRS to eliminate the tax breaks enjoyed by these private schools because they practiced racial discrimination. Outraged parents condemned Carter while IRS Commissioner Jerome Kurtz received so many death threats he was placed under full-time protection. Richard Viguerie, a fundraiser for conservative causes, described this event as a "spark" that transformed many politically inactive evangelical Christians into the politically engaged "Religious Right."

Jerry Falwell, a Baptist minister in Lynchburg, Virginia, who had built a regional following through his televised Old Time Gospel Hour, channeled the parents' anger. Like many of them, he resented what he perceived as a liberal assault on traditional religious values and a growing "culture of permissiveness." Among the other faults they attributed to "big government" were high taxes, onerous business regulation, court-ordered integration, legal abortion, gay rights, and military weakness in the face of communist threats. The minister then cofounded the **Moral Majority**, a

CHAPTER OUTLINE

BACKLASH
> An Accidental President
> The Politics of Limits and Malaise
> A Dangerous World, 1974–1980
> America Held Hostage

THE RISING TIDE ON THE RIGHT
> Economic Limits
> The Religious Right and Neoconservatism
> The Collapse of the Political Center

IT'S MORNING AGAIN IN AMERICA
> The Rise of Reagan
> A New Administration
> Economic Realities
> Conservative Justice
> Sexuality, Families, and Health

CHALLENGING THE "EVIL EMPIRE"
> A New Arms Race
> Interventions
> Iran Contra
> Cold War Thaw

Solidarity Movement poster, Warsaw, Poland, 1989

America in the World

The Iran-Contra scandal resulted in an illegal arms for hostages exchange by the Reagan administration (1985–1986).

President Reagan unveiled the Strategic Defense Initiative, ramping up U.S. development of missile defenses (1983).

U.S. event that influenced the world

International event that influenced the United States

Event with multinational influence

Conflict

Gorbachev signed INF
treaty and withdrew
Soviets from Afghanistan
(1987–1988).

HIV identified as the
virus causing AIDS,
resulting in an intense
worldwide search for a
cure (1981–1984).

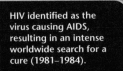

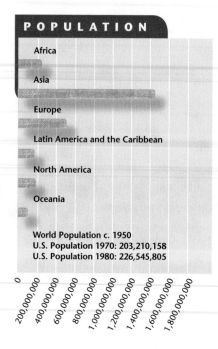

POPULATION

Africa

Asia

Europe

Latin America and the Caribbean

North America

Oceania

World Population c. 1950
U.S. Population 1970: 203,210,158
U.S. Population 1980: 226,545,805

0 200,000,000 400,000,000 600,000,000 800,000,000 1,000,000,000 1,200,000,000 1,400,000,000 1,600,000,000 1,800,000,000

political lobbying group designed to mobilize evangelicals and "get them saved, baptized and registered" to vote.

Religious-inspired resistance to entrenched political regimes took many forms during the 1970s and 1980s. In Poland Catholic lay activists and labor organizers opposed to communist rule created Solidarity, a movement encouraged by the new Polish Pope, Jean Paul II. In parts of the Muslim world so-called Islamists pushed back violently against modernization by demanding a return to orthodoxy. In Iran and Afghanistan, for example, they condemned gender equality and secular education and called for jihad (struggle) against both the atheistic Soviet Union and the "great Satan," as they dubbed the United States.

In assessing what both ailed and motivated Americans during the 1970s, novelist Tom Wolfe dubbed this era as the "Me Decade." He poked fun at self-indulgent Americans who abandoned the social and political protest movements of the 1960s to focus, instead, on self-improvement. All problems, it seemed, could be solved by some form of group therapy.

For most Americans, however, the economic and social strains of the 1970s reflected worrisome trends that undermined their faith in a secure future. Jimmy Carter's admonition to adjust to a future of limits only made them feel worse. Carter's opponent in 1980, Ronald Reagan, recognized the public's concerns but addressed them in a wholly different manner. He rallied Americans fed up with gasoline lines, rising prices, and a sense of powerlessness by demonizing government and pointing to patriotism, free markets, and faith as solutions. Actively appealing to the religious right, he called the Biblical account of creation a better explanation than Darwin's theory of evolution. He promised that if elected he would confront with greater force "godless Communism." And he assured angry parents that, as president, he would restore tax breaks to Christian academies. By electing Reagan, Americans signaled frustration with the previous six years of economic decline and political drift. They appeared to reject the era of social liberalism and big government that stretched back to the New Deal. But what they intended to replace it with was less certain.

BACKLASH

The political upheaval of 1980—signified by a resurgent conservative movement under the banner of the Republican Party—was the culmination of a decade-long erosion of public faith in government at all levels. The chaotic end of the war in Vietnam; Nixon's lawbreaking; rising rates of crime, welfare, and divorce; slow economic growth; high inflation; and gasoline shortages seemed proof that misguided government policies either caused major problems or could not alleviate them. Conservatives charged that while Nixon and his successors promoted détente with the Soviets, the Kremlin increased its strength and meddled in Central America, Africa, and the Middle East. Most humiliating of all, in Iran in November 1979 Islamic radicals seized 54 American diplomats and Marine guards and defied all efforts to free them.

Nixon's resignation in August 1974 relieved the acute pain of the Watergate crisis, but his exit left unresolved problems. The economy continued to slow in the face of foreign competition and rising energy prices. Racial polarization increased. The nation seemed afflicted by rising rates of crime, drug use, and family collapse. Americans appeared more divided than ever over the right of women to have an abortion, the acceptance of gays and lesbians as full citizens, and the proper role of religion in public life.

An Accidental President

Nixon's two successors, the appointed Gerald Ford and elected Jimmy Carter, did little to restore faith in national leadership. Both began with the good wishes of the electorate but soon squandered that trust. Ford struck a healing tone as he entered the Oval Office in August 1974 after Nixon resigned. Personally untainted by Nixon's crimes he assured the nation that the "long national nightmare" of Watergate had ended. But after his decision a few weeks later to pardon Nixon, a majority of Americans lost confidence in his judgment.

As Ford groped to find his footing, it became apparent that the political alignments established during the 1930s had come apart. The Democratic coalition in the North—comprised of unionized labor, blacks, Jews, and Catholics of Irish and Eastern European origin—fragmented. As the nation's population moved West and South, many northern cities lost population as well as their tax base to more affluent and less racially diverse suburbs. In Boston, as in parts of the South, many Irish Catholic residents deeply resented efforts by the federal courts in 1974 and 1975 to integrate South Boston schools by busing in children from a mostly black neighborhood. Racial antipathy and fear of crime committed by blacks pushed many blue-collar ethnic voters into the Republican Party, which called itself the defender of law and order. Labor unions, whose members comprised another pillar of Democratic support, shrank rapidly as imported steel, automobiles, electronics, and textiles, produced by low-cost foreign manufacturers, flooded the U.S. market. To survive, many domestic industries relocated to the South where "right-to-work-laws" kept unions weak and labor costs low. Other industries simply closed down and moved factories to cheap labor markets abroad.

In the South, the Democratic Party continued to divide along racial lines. The Voting Rights Act of 1965 opened up politics to millions of blacks, but as they entered civic life, a large number of whites migrated into the Republican Party. In 1968 many Southern whites, voting for the third-party candidate George Wallace, indirectly helped Nixon. After 1968 President Nixon's criticism of school busing, his talk of a "war on crime," and his appointment of more conservative judges to the Supreme

Court—policies his aides characterized as the "Southern Strategy"—won support among conservative Democrats, North and South.

Despite his twin presidential victories, Nixon never won the hearts of many so-called Sunbelt conservatives in the South or West because of his continued support for many big government programs, efforts to improve ties with China and the Soviet Union, and endorsement of Keynesian economic policies.

Ford's decision to pardon Nixon without requiring the disgraced ex-president to come clean about his role in Watergate undermined his administration from its first days. The pardon, intended by Ford as an act of mercy, looked to most moderate and liberal Americans like an unsavory sweetheart deal. The new president's approval rating plummeted from 72 percent to 49 percent. Ford then angered conservatives by appointing former New York governor **Nelson Rockefeller**, a Republican moderate, as vice president.

The lingering shadow of Watergate, the weak economy, and Republican disarray produced big Democratic gains in the 1974 midterm election. The GOP lost 48 seats in the House and 4 in the Senate. Many Democratic leaders misinterpreted this outcome as proof of growing public support for an activist agenda rather than as an echo of disgust with Nixon's crimes and Ford's pardon. In the wake of the election Democrats passed several campaign reform bills and investigated misdeeds by the executive branch. House and Senate committees mounted several inquiries into CIA abuses going back to the 1950s, including attempts to assassinate foreign leaders, destabilize governments, and overthrow Chilean president Salvador Allende in 1973.

But while Democrats scrutinized past misdeeds, job losses mounted and inflation ate away at the value of paychecks. Since the October 1973 Arab-Israeli War, the Arab oil boycott of sales to pro-Israeli nations, along with effective marketing controls by the Organization of Petroleum Exporting Counties (OPEC), pushed oil prices up from about $3 per barrel to $15, on their way to $30 by the end of the decade. By 1975 hourly wages earned by Americans fell for the first time in 25 years. But neither President Ford nor his Democratic critics offered credible proposals to solve these problems.

Ford also had the misfortune to deal with the collapse of South Vietnam. In April 1975, after a quick military offensive, North Vietnamese troops overran the South. The Vietnam debacle left Americans confused about their nation's role in the world. Nixon and Kissinger, who stayed on as Ford's national security adviser and secretary of state, had attempted to manage the Cold War by negotiating arms control deals with the Soviet Union and restoring ties to China. But by the mid-1970s a chorus of critics from both parties complained that détente with the Soviets had failed. Democrats who criticized détente—later known as neoconservatives or **"Neocons"**—like Senator Henry Jackson of Washington, charged the Soviets with cheating on arms control and continuing to oppress political and religious dissidents.

Ford attempted to improve Soviet-American ties when he met with Brezhnev in Finland in 1975. Although the two leaders made little progress on arms control, they signed the so-called **Helsinki Accords**, a set of principles that accepted the post-1945 division of Europe into East–West spheres. The accords recognized the right of all

Europeans to seek peaceful change, and the Soviets agreed in a general way to respect human rights in their sphere. Although American conservatives attacked the results as a cave-in, dissidents in the Soviet Union and Eastern Europe celebrated the accords as a useful tool in their efforts to reform the communist system.

To deflect growing criticism from the GOP conservatives, Ford reduced the role played by Henry Kissinger and made it clear that Vice President Rockefeller would not be on his ticket when he ran for election in November. Nevertheless, former California governor Ronald Reagan challenged Ford's renomination. Reagan complained that Ford was too cozy with Democrats and too weak on defense. To improve the economy he proposed sharp tax cuts and aggressive business deregulation. Reagan also called for strict limits on abortion, restoration of school prayer, and a more militant foreign policy. These attacks and his appealing campaign style led Reagan to win nearly as many primary votes as Ford.

To win over wavering delegates at the Republican nominating convention in the summer of 1976, Ford adopted many of his rival's positions. He replaced Rockefeller with the sharp-tongued conservative senator from Kansas, **Robert Dole**, suspended talks with Panama on a canal treaty, promised to reduce taxes and government spending, and endorsed constitutional amendments to ban abortion and permit school prayer. Even so, Ford barely edged out Reagan for the nomination.

Democrats selected as their nominee Jimmy Carter, a former governor of Georgia. Carter graduated from the Naval Academy at Annapolis and served on a nuclear submarine before returning home to manage his family's peanut farm near Plains, Georgia. He was elected governor as a segregationist sympathizer, but upon taking office he pledged to end discrimination.

Carter's campaign stressed his evangelical religious beliefs and status as a Washington "outsider." He told small audiences around the country, "I'm not a lawyer, I'm not a member of Congress, and I've never served in Washington." He took centrist stands on controversial issues such as abortion and school busing for racial balance. To reassure Democratic liberals that he could be trusted, Carter selected Minnesota senator **Walter Mondale**, a traditional liberal, as his running mate.

Ford and Carter both ran lackluster campaigns that failed to energize the public. Just over half of eligible voters went to the polls in November, the lowest number in any presidential election since World War II. Carter won by a narrow margin and took office without a clear mandate to lead in any direction.

The Politics of Limits and Malaise

Some of the very characteristics that helped Carter get elected, such as his lack of Washington experience, his disdain for many politicians, and his focus on technical expertise, made it hard for him to govern or build alliances in Congress. For example, he angered powerful members of Congress by abruptly canceling 19 dam and irrigation projects in the South and West, on the mostly accurate grounds that they were both costly and bad for the environment. He seemed indifferent to the fact that they had promoted these projects as ways of assuring political support.

As president, Carter attempted to tackle "big" issues, including energy shortages and the Middle East peace process, but stumbled when trying to explain these policies to ordinary people or to get Congress to act. By frequently saying there were "no easy answers," he made it sound as if he had no answers. Many politicians agreed with Speaker of the House Thomas "Tip" O'Neill that although Carter was extremely smart he was completely inept at passing legislation.

Despite signs of public restiveness, Carter believed that his commitment to principles of "good government" would win wide backing. The president demonstrated his own commitment to racial equality by appointing a record three African Americans to cabinet-level positions. However, the administration had difficulty dealing with the contentious racial issues of affirmative action and minority set-asides. Race-preference policies, begun under Nixon, aimed to redress past discrimination by giving minorities and women preferential treatment in hiring, school admission, or receiving government contracts. Although the numbers who benefited from these preferences were modest, the policy struck many Americans as conflicting with the ideal of equality for all, regardless of race. When the Voting Rights Act of 1965 was extended in 1975, a new provision included Latinos and Asians, many of whom arrived after passage of the initial law. In a nod to the influx of these new immigrants, the law stipulated that in districts with high concentrations of nonnative English speakers, voting materials be made available in languages such as Spanish and Chinese. This provision provoked an "English-only" movement that criticized "special privileges" for minorities and gathered strength over next decade

The Supreme Court ruled on race-based preferences in 1978 in the case of *University of California Board of Regents v. Bakke*. Allan Bakke, a white male, had been denied admission to medical school. He argued that California's affirmative action program was a form of reverse discrimination because it led to the admission of less-qualified black applicants. A five-justice majority of the Court ruled that Bakke should be admitted to medical school and that rigid racial quotas were forbidden. However, the majority also stated that that race could be used as a factor in admission and hiring decisions so long as it was not the only factor. Carter ordered federal agencies to implement affirmative action programs that did not require specific set-asides or quotas.

Carter also tried, without much success, to solve America's chronic energy dilemma. By the late 1970s the United States imported over 40 percent of the 17 million barrels of oil it consumed daily. Prices had already increased from $3 per barrel in 1973 to about $18 and were likely to rise higher. Carter persuaded Congress to create a new Department of Energy (as well as a Department of Education) along with programs to boost energy conservation, expand domestic drilling, and promote new energy sources, such as synthetic fuels from coal and shale, wind, solar, and nuclear energy. But when Congress finally passed an energy bill in 1978, it rejected imposing any substantial increases in energy taxes, the one thing most likely to spur conservation and encourage investment in nonfossil fuels.

The new law did little to promote nuclear energy, which the public had soured on. The events of March 1979 enhanced that aversion when a nuclear reactor at Three Mile Island in Pennsylvania malfunctioned and nearly caused a meltdown. No new

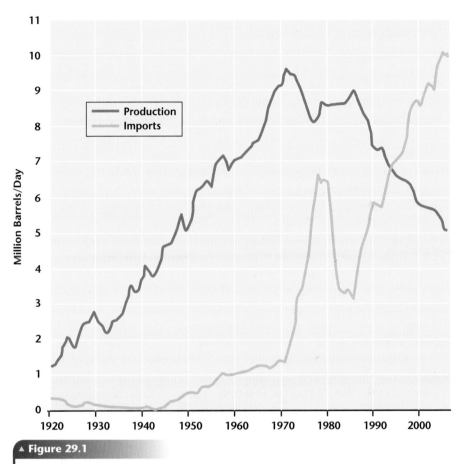

▲ **Figure 29.1**

America's energy use and sources Petroleum production in the United States peaked in the early 1970s, even as demand increased. For the past 40 years, the United States has imported half or more of its oil requirements. Most of the imports come from Canada, Mexico, Saudi Arabia, Venezuela, Colombia, and Nigeria. Aside from Saudi oil, the United States imports relatively little petroleum from the Middle East.

nuclear plants had been built in the United States as of 2011. But even short-term benefits from the energy bill were undermined in 1979 by the Iranian Revolution, which disrupted oil markets and drove up the price of gasoline to the then historic high of $30 per barrel. As domestic production declined and the price of imported petroleum surged, the annual cost of oil imports during the 1970s rose from $4 billion to around $90 billion. At the pump this increase translated into nearly a tripling of the price of gasoline, from just over 30 cents per gallon to nearly one dollar.

Spiking energy prices, along with a growing foreign trade deficit and a dollar falling in value, further weakened the American economy and caused inflation to rise to crisis levels. At the time of Carter's inauguration, annual inflation hit 6 percent. By 1978 the rate hit 9 percent per year, and a year later reached 11.3 percent. During the same period the unemployment rate remained stubbornly high, between 6 and 7.5

percent. Carter's approval rating moved in an inverse direction to the rates of inflation and unemployment. By July 1979 only 29 percent of Americans approved of Carter's performance.

Voter frustration with the failure of politicians to solve economic problems had already surfaced dramatically in California. In June 1978 residents overwhelmingly approved Proposition 13, a plan to roll back the state's high property tax and require a two-thirds vote of the legislature to raise future taxes. This so-called tax revolt followed repeated failure by the state legislature to remedy the impact of California's rapidly rising property values by lowering tax rates. Proponents of "Prop 13" claimed the Democratic legislature kept taxes high to pay for social services for the poor. A leading pollster described this as a "revolution against government," and former governor Reagan—who had actually raised taxes—compared the event to the Boston Tea Party in 1773.

In July 1979, responding to dismal poll numbers, Carter delivered a speech urging Americans to work harder, not to despair, to overcome their "crisis of confidence" through self-sacrifice, and to find alternatives to dependence on oil. Although he did not utter the word, one of his aides referred to this as Carter's "malaise speech" and the term stuck. At first the public seemed impressed by Carter's appeal for sacrifice. But they became more cynical two days later when his firing of five Cabinet members seemed to blame them for the country's troubles.

To tackle inflation Carter appointed **Paul Volcker** to head the Federal Reserve. Volcker quickly hiked interest rates above 15 percent to slow business activity by raising the cost of borrowing. Over the next three years these high rates reduced inflation dramatically, but not soon enough to help Carter. In 1979–1980 high interest rates made jobs and mortgages harder to come by and made Carter even less popular.

A Dangerous World, 1974–1980

In spite of his domestic troubles and later failures in foreign affairs, Carter initially achieved several foreign policy breakthroughs in the Middle East and Latin America. Early in his presidency Carter declared that "we are now free of the inordinate fear of communism which once led us to embrace any dictator." Respect for human rights, he promised, would be a foundation, not an afterthought, of foreign policy. Carter became the first president to visit sub-Saharan Africa and voiced support for peaceful efforts to replace the white-ruled regimes in Rhodesia and South Africa. This emphasis on human rights inspired hope among many opponents of dictatorship, but it became a target for conservatives who considered communism still the major threat.

Carter pursued a Middle Eastern peace plan after Egyptian president **Anwar Sadat** flew to Jerusalem in November 1977 to address Israel's parliament. In 1978 the president mediated between Sadat and Israeli prime minister **Menachem Begin** during negotiations at Camp David, the presidential retreat in Maryland. Begin agreed to end occupation of the Sinai Peninsula in return for Egypt's recognizing the existence of the Jewish state. They signed a formal treaty in March 1979. Carter hoped that this would prompt other Arab nations to join the process.

President Jimmy Carter achieved a breakthrough in the Middle East when he brokered a peace between Egypt and Israel. The Camp David agreement is signed by Egpyt's Anwar Sadat and Israel's Menachim Begin.

The president showed considerable skill in breaking two diplomatic log jams. In March 1978 he convinced the Senate to ratify the long-stalled treaty with Panama and gradually transfer control of the canal as long as Panama signed a treaty guaranteeing the permanent neutrality of the canal. In early 1979 he formally ended the long estrangement from China by severing formal ties with Taiwan and extending full diplomatic recognition to the People's Republic of China.

In December 1979 Soviet forces invaded neighboring Afghanistan in an attempt to shore up a teetering pro-communist government. Like many Americans Carter feared that the Soviets really intended the incursion as a way to dominate the oil-rich Persian Gulf. In response, Carter suspended consideration of the SALT II arms-control treaty with the Soviets, pulled U.S. athletes from the upcoming Moscow Olympics, suspended grain sales to the Soviets, resumed draft registration, and sharply increased military spending. The president pledged to resist any Soviet encroachment into the Middle East and authorized the CIA to secretly aid the **Mujahideen**, Islamic guerrillas fighting the Soviets in Afghanistan.

Many Americans considered the Afghan crisis part of a wider Soviet offensive. During the 1970s Brezhnev had cracked down on internal dissent and expanded nuclear and conventional forces. The Soviets deployed new missiles in Eastern Europe capable of hitting any country in Western Europe and subsidized Fidel Castro's dispatch of Cuban military advisers to Angola and Ethiopia. In Central America in 1979 the leftist Sandinista guerrillas toppled the pro-American dictator of Nicaragua, Anastasio Somoza. Their new regime allied itself with Cuba and the Soviet Union. A chorus of Republican and conservative Democratic politicians accused Carter of doing little or nothing to counter these threats.

In hindsight it is apparent that Soviet motives in Afghanistan were limited and that Moscow genuinely feared that radical Islam might spread to Soviet central Asia, a region in which Muslims predominated. Also, by 1980, the world later learned, the Soviet Union had begun a spiral of economic and social decline from which it never recovered. Its past efforts to match American military power badly strained the inefficient Soviet economy. Social problems, such as alcoholism, low birth rates, and declining longevity took a growing toll among the population. Most U.S. intelligence reports overestimated Soviet strength and overlooked the regime's many weaknesses.

America Held Hostage

The seizure of the U.S. embassy in Tehran, Iran, and the taking of 54 diplomats and Marine guards as hostages on November 4, 1979, soon dominated national politics. Tensions with Iran went back to1953 when the CIA helped depose the government of reformer **Mohammed Mossadeq** and restored to power the pro-American Shah **Mohammed Reza Pahlavi**. As oil revenues mounted during the 1960s and 1970s, the Shah built up Iran's military power and embarked on what he called a "revolution from above." He attempted to modernize schools and the agricultural system and to limit the influence of Islamic clerics. Presidents Nixon and Carter praised the Shah, but many Iranians detested the corruption around him and the lack of political freedom. An exiled, elderly ayatollah, or religious leader, **Ruholla Khomeini**, who called the United States the "Great Satan" and hoped to create a society based on the Qur'an, or Koran, emerged as the symbol of opposition. In February 1979, after months of street protests, the shah fled and the ayatollah returned as Iran's leader. Although Khomeini despised the United States, he did not sever diplomatic ties or halt oil sales.

Relations soured in October 1979 when Carter allowed the deposed shah to enter the United States to receive treatment for an ultimately fatal cancer. The Iranian government demanded that the United States send the shah and his "stolen wealth" home. When Carter balked, radical students seized the U.S. embassy in Tehran and took the hostages. The president condemned this violation of international law and pledged to free the captives. At first the U.S. public rallied behind Carter, but as the crisis dragged on he appeared weak.

In April 1980, when hope for a negotiated hostage release ended, Carter approved a daring and complex raid to rescue the captives. But sandstorms damaged several of the helicopters as they flew toward their target and Carter aborted the mission. During a refueling stop in the Iranian desert, two of the aircraft collided on the ground and killed eight crew members. Carter attributed the fiasco to "mechanical difficulties." But as details of the botched rescue came to light many Americans wondered if the Three Stooges had planned the operation.

Iranian student radicals burn an American flag as they celebrate the seizure of the U.S. embassy in Tehran and the taking of hostages in November 1979.

Bad luck also undermined Carter's attempt to support human rights in Cuba. In March 1980, when thousands of Cuban dissidents sought refuge in foreign embassies in Havana, he offered them asylum in the United States. Fidel Castro announced that for a limited time any Cuban who wanted to leave could do so by departing from the small fishing port of Mariel. The U.S. government organized a flotilla of private boats to transport the so-called Marielitos, whose numbers totaled 130,000 by the time the boatlift ended in October.

Public support for the effort faded when Castro opened jails and mental institutions and told inmates to join the exodus. Although they comprised only a few thousand of the total, the media highlighted problems caused by these undesirables. Critics claimed that a gullible Carter had allowed Castro to dump his problems on America.

In the midst of these difficulties Massachusetts senator **Edward "Ted" Kennedy**, whose reputation had partially recovered since the fatal car crash he had caused at Chappaquiddick in 1969, challenged Carter for the Democratic nomination. He faulted the incumbent for deserting the party's core liberal tenets and especially disliked the president for opposing Kennedy's bid to enact a national health plan that went beyond Carter's more modest approach. Kennedy announced his candidacy just a few days after the hostage seizure began and berated Carter for "lurching from crisis to crisis." Despite the senator's appeal most of the public instinctively rallied around

Tens of thousands of Cuban "Marielitos" fled on fishing boats toward the United States from the small port of Mariel during the spring and summer of 1980. A small number of the refugees were criminals or mentally ill.

the president in time of crisis. Carter beat Kennedy in most of the state primaries held between February and April 1980, before the failure of the hostage rescue mission.

Ronald Reagan, then gearing up for a second run at the White House, echoed Kennedy's criticism. He ridiculed Carter as a "wooly-headed idealist" who had no plan to improve the economy or reverse the nation's slide. Carter, Reagan charged, "deserted" the shah, and did nothing while the Soviets surged forward and as Cuban agents took over Nicaragua and extended their reach in Africa.

Although Carter had won enough primary votes to beat Kennedy at the Democratic convention in the summer of 1980, he ran for reelection as a badly impaired candidate. Even after the shah died in July, Iran continued to demand the return of his money and other funds frozen in Western banks by the United States before releasing the captive Americans.

A solution to the hostage crisis came from an unlikely source. In September 1980 Iraqi dictator Saddam Hussein ordered his army to invade neighboring Iran to seize oil, water, and territory. Saddam, a secular Sunni Muslim, feared and despised the Shia Muslims who controlled Iran. Iraqi and Iranian armies proceeded to fight bloody battles larger than any since World War II. The carnage lasted eight years and claimed one million lives on both sides.

The huge cost of the war even in its early phase made Iran receptive to trading the hostages for billions of Iranian dollars frozen in Western banks. Nevertheless, talks between Iranians and Carter aides dragged on for months. The Iranians purposely stalled until after the election and freed the hostages on January 20, 1981, just as Reagan took the presidential oath.

STUDY QUESTIONS FOR BACKLASH

1. Why did the public quickly lose faith in President Gerald Ford?
2. What economic problems undermined the Carter administration?
3. How did the Iran hostage crisis doom the Carter presidency?

THE RISING TIDE ON THE RIGHT

Public anger at and mistrust of government were widespread and diverse in 1980. Many Americans felt that both Jimmy Carter and Democrats in Congress debated issues and passed laws unconnected to the problems of everyday life. Some believed that government only looked after the very wealthy and the chronic poor and ignored everyone in between. Conservative Republicans seized on this anger to propose what sounded to many Americans like practical solutions to economic and social problems.

Voices on the right formed a choir that blended strands of conservative thought that formerly had pulled in separate directions. By the late 1970s politically energized evangelical Protestants, conservative Catholics, gun rights groups, antiabortion activists, business lobbyists, and tax reformers organized a variety of lobbying groups that effectively challenged liberal ideas and Democratic control of national politics.

Economic Limits

Between the end of World War II and the early 1970s, steady economic growth had been a tide that lifted nearly all boats. Three decades of high employment, increasing productivity, and annual GNP growth of about 4 percent made taxes and government regulation easy to live with. For example, living standards for a unionized blue collar automobile or steel worker rose nearly every year. A family with one spouse working for General Motors or U.S. Steel achieved middle-class status in a job he or she likely held until retirement.

Starting in 1973 the erosion in the value of the dollar, the surge in industrial imports, a gradual decline in unionized manufacturing jobs, and the steep rise in the cost of oil cut in half annual GNP growth over the next decade. By 1980 annual inflation rose above 13 percent and unemployment remained stuck at 7.4 percent. In the quarter century before 1973, real median family income had doubled. During the next 20 years, income surged for the top 3 percent of Americans, remained flat for others, and declined for many.

The traditional liberal economic tools of deficit spending to stimulate the economy did not solve the current problem of stagflation—a slowly growing economy

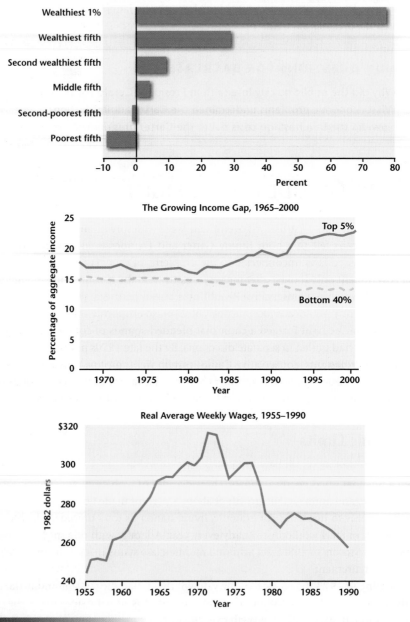

▲ Figure 29.2

Middle-Class Squeeze: The New Wealth Distribution During the 1970s through 2000, the richest 40 percent of Americans—and especially the top 5 percent—got much richer. The bottom 40 percent of households fell increasingly behind as income equality declined. Meanwhile, annual budget deficits and the cumulative national debt grew rapidly during the presidencies of Ronald Reagan and George H. W. Bush. The budget achieved first a balance, then a surplus during the Clinton presidency.

with high rates of unemployment and inflation. The problem lay partly with surging energy costs, which affected the global economy, and the bulge of late-baby boomers that entered the job market for the first time just as growth slowed. To make matters worse, income tax brackets were not adjusted for inflation. Thus many working and middle-class families paid higher taxes on incomes that, in real terms, had declined. By 1980 two-thirds of Americans described themselves economically "worse off" than they had been before 1973, and many blamed "big government" liberalism for their problems. Corporate profits, also falling steeply, declined from an average of 10 percent during the 1960s to 5 or 6 percent during the 1970s and early 1980s. To boost profit margins manufacturers shifted production and jobs to cheaper foreign locations or low-wage, nonunion regions in the Sunbelt.

New ideas for changing tax and spending policies came from conservative economists. So-called **monetarists**, led by University of Chicago economist Milton Friedman, insisted that prosperity and freedom required reduced government spending along with more stringent control of the money supply.

An even more radical group of economists, called supply siders, rejected completely the dominant Keynesian idea that the government could stimulate growth and regulate economic cycles through deficit spending. Supply siders such as economist Arthur Laffer argued that to restore growth the government must slash taxes paid by the wealthy and by business. Rich individuals and corporations would then invest the money productively and benefit both themselves and the larger economy. As the economy grew, government would collect all it needed, even at lower rates. The unstated flip side of the equation was that if revenues declined—as many economists privately suspected it would—government would be forced to reduce spending on discretionary programs.

Ronald Reagan had long complained that high tax rates and overregulation by government discouraged entrepreneurship. Supply side economics provided a theory, however dubious, to bolster his belief. Reagan made deep tax cuts, along with deregulation, major themes of his 1980 presidential campaign.

The Religious Right and Neoconservatism

Voters of faith became more politically active during the 1970s and 1980s. Evangelicals are a part of several Protestant denominations. They believe that salvation requires a personal, life-altering experience that culminates in a decision to follow Jesus, sometimes called being "born again," and passing on this faith to others. Fundamentalist Christians, who may or may not be evangelicals, stress the literal truth of the Bible.

Some of these beliefs clashed with Catholic dogma, which emphasized the centrality of the organized church in achieving salvation, and with the church's supportive view of government services for the poor. Before the 1970s most Catholics opposed organized prayer in public schools because the devotions were typically Protestant. Protestants generally opposed giving tax dollars to parochial schools because nearly all were Catholic.

The 1973 Supreme Court decision in *Roe v. Wade*, affirming a woman's right to terminate a pregnancy, created a new interfaith coalition among Protestants and

Catholics opposed to abortion. They soon discovered other areas of agreement, such as opposition to sex education in public schools and granting legal equality to gays and lesbians. As more Protestants in the South opened all-white Christian academies, they joined Catholics—whose schools were racially integrated—in seeking public funds or more generous tax benefits for these institutions.

Total rates of church membership did not change much between 1975 and 2000, but evangelical denominations grew while others lost adherents. Religious activists also became more involved in politics by the mid-1970s. **Phyllis Schlafley**, an Illinois homemaker, lawyer, Catholic, and Republican activist, organized the Eagle Forum, an association of conservative religious women. Their immediate goal was to block state ratification of the **Equal Rights Amendment** (ERA) that Congress had passed in 1972 and sent to the states for ratification. Schlafley charged that the ERA would lead to unisex bathrooms, compulsory military service for women, and same-sex marriage. In 1979 **Beverley LaHaye**, wife of Moral Majority cofounder **Tim LaHaye**, organized Concerned Women of America (CWA) to oppose laws that eased divorce and abortion or decriminalized homosexuality. CWA attracted 500,000 members, far more than its liberal counterpart, the **National Organization for Women** (NOW). James Dobson, an evangelical child psychologist, founded Focus on the Family in 1977, initially to stop school sex education programs.

To reach a wider audience, some ministers formed "mega-churches" while others began "electronic ministries." Critics dubbed them televangelists. Among the most popular religious shows during the 1970s and 1980s were the 700 Club, The PTL Club, and the Old Time Gospel Hour. Jerry Falwell, **Pat Robertson**, Jim and Tammy Faye Bakker, and Jimmy Swaggart became religious celebrities. The Reverend **Billy Graham**, who had preached on the airwaves since the 1940s, retained a huge following; he kept his distance, however, from the more flamboyant newcomers and avoided the financial and sex scandals that later beset them.

Traditionally, white evangelicals either voted in low numbers or supported Democrats. In 1976, for example, Jimmy Carter, a born-again Southern Baptist who proudly proclaimed his faith, received 56 percent of the white evangelical vote. By

Televangelists Tammy Faye and Jim Bakker captivated large numbers of viewers before their fall from grace and conviction for fraud.

1980 so-called wedge issues such as abortion, school prayer, and gay rights had dramatically altered the voting pattern among white evangelicals, especially in the South, and white Catholics in the North. Reagan received 61 percent of their votes. By 1988, 80 percent of evangelicals voted Republican, and the South had been transformed from a Democratic to a Republican stronghold.

The Collapse of the Political Center

Just as the Republican Party broadened its base and appeal, the Democratic Party fractured. By 1980, except for Jews and African Americans, much of the old New Deal coalition had peeled away. Most white southern Protestants now voted Republican. In northern cities, many Polish, Irish , and Italian Americans blamed Democratic social and economic policies for urban decay, rising rates of crime and welfare, and the availability of abortion. Republican candidates wooed these previously faithful Democrats into the GOP with appeals for law and order, patriotism, traditional religious values, and tax relief.

A growing number of working and middle-class Americans saw the Democratic Party as a tax collector for the welfare state; 69 percent of Americans polled in 1980 claimed that elected Democrats cared mostly about minorities. Around two-thirds of whites said they opposed "special help" for minorities, such as affirmative action programs. Democratic members of Congress often added to this perception by describing themselves as pro-consumer, pro-environment, pro-feminist, pro-labor, and so forth. This emphasis on what is sometimes called "identity politics" left Democrats without a cohesive framework to compete with the simple mantras such as tax cuts, defense, and opposition to abortion posed by Republicans.

Labor unions, a pillar of Democratic strength, atrophied as manufacturing jobs moved abroad or to the antiunion South. In 1960 one-third of nonfarm workers belonged to unions. By 1978 less than a quarter of these workers were union members, and in the 1990s the proportion sank to around 14 percent. Labor leaders had often been promoters of broad-based social reform proposals, such as Social Security and Medicare. Now, unions and their political allies focused mainly on preserving the declining number of manufacturing jobs by opposing imports.

Crime emerged as another wedge issue that pushed Democratic voters rightward. Between 1960 and 1980 the number of reported crimes quadrupled. African Americans comprised 11 percent of the population in 1980 but perpetrated about 30 percent of assaults and 62 percent of robberies. Although most of these crimes were within, rather than across, racial boundaries, they fueled white fears of black violence. Criminologists attributed the spike in reported crime to many factors, including better reporting, job losses in cities, the large number of single-parent households in minority communities, and the bulging cohort in the 1970s of teenagers and young adults who committed most crimes. Conservatives pointed the finger directly at "permissive judges" appointed by Democrats who were more concerned about the rights of criminals than the rights of victims. By 1980, 83 percent of the public agreed that courts were "too lenient" and failed to deter crime.

Corporate funding helped spread these criticisms of liberalism and big govern-ment. Between 1945 and the middle 1970s big business contributed money to both major political parties and their candidates even if it favored Republicans. By the end of the 1970s corporations and their allies lined up strongly behind Republican groups and candidates who promised to slash business taxes, reduce regulations, and curb union power. Corporations and wealthy donors provided a substantial amount of money to **Political Action Committees** (PACs), which could bundle donations from many sources and use the cash to assist sympathetic candidates. Among the most suc-cessful was the National Conservative Political Action Committee. By 1980 conserva-tive pro-business PACs outnumbered and outspent liberal and pro-union PACs 4 to 1.

Ronald Reagan proved the ideal candidate to both articulate and benefit from these trends and ideas. On the stump in 1980 he ridiculed Carter's efforts to deal with surging gasoline prices and shortages by asserting that the country did not have too little oil, but "too much government regulation." He blamed deficits on expensive welfare programs that aided minorities and the poor. Food stamps, Reagan claimed, "allowed some fellow ahead of you to buy T-bone steak" while you "stood in the checkout line with your package of hamburger." He ridiculed "welfare queens" with "eighty names, thirty addresses, and twelve Social Security Cards" whose "tax-free in-come alone is over $150,000." Even if most of these were fake targets and accounted for a tiny part of government spending, his attack resonated among economically stressed white working and middle-class voters.

Reagan defeated Carter by a popular vote margin of 51 to 41 percent. Independent John Anderson took the rest. Republicans won 33 new seats in the House and 12 in the Senate. This gave the GOP a 53 to 47 majority in the upper chamber. Democrats retained nominal control of the House, but enough conservative Democrats voted with the president to give Republicans a working majority.

STUDY QUESTIONS FOR THE RISING TIDE ON THE RIGHT

1. What factors drove down U.S. incomes and living standards during the 1970s?
2. What social problems emerged during the 1970s that liberalism failed to solve?
3. How did issues like abortion rights and aid to parochial schools unify and energize religious conservatives during the 1970s?

IT'S MORNING AGAIN IN AMERICA

On January 20, 1981, Ronald Reagan stood tall and poised for action as he took the presidential oath. Beside him Jimmy Carter, stooped, with hooded eyes, seemed al-most ghostlike. He had not slept for days while he negotiated details for the release of the hostages in Iran. Americans, Reagan declared in his inaugural speech, did not accept limits or dream "small dreams." Invoking past heroes, he asserted that, "In our present crisis government is not the solution to our problem, government is the problem."

Reagan hoped to restore an era of small government, traditional cultural values, and an economy controlled by market forces. During the next eight years he worked to roll back or restrain many New Deal and Great Society programs. Reagan pledged to shrink the social welfare system, limit the role of federal courts in promoting civil rights, reduce regulation of business and the environment, slash income taxes, and promote a conservative social ethic on issues of sex, drug use, and the role of religion in public life. His connection to a majority of Americans transcended specific policies and tapped a popular will to restore a sense of community, real or imagined, that had been lost since the 1960s.

The Rise of Reagan

Reagan's election capped a long journey for the 69-year-old ex-movie actor. Born in 1911, he grew up in small Illinois towns along the Mississippi River. His alcoholic father had difficulty holding a job, but his religiously devout mother helped Reagan make the most of his life. He attended a small church college and after graduating in the midst of the Great Depression found work as a sports announcer at an Iowa radio station. During a visit to Hollywood in 1937, Reagan took a screen test and won a contract from the Warner Brothers film studio. For more than a decade he had a successful career as a second tier movie actor. Reagan was an enthusiastic and very liberal Democrat until the end of the 1940s.

As Reagan's film career waned in the late 1940s, he became active in union affairs and served as head of the Screen Actors Guild. With the onset of the Cold War, Reagan's politics became more conservative. He warned of a "communist plot to take over the motion picture business" and cooperated with studio executives and the FBI to identify and fire left-wing writers, actors, and directors.

As a TV host and a corporate spokesman for the General Electric Company during the 1950s, Reagan developed a speech he delivered countless times, alerting his audience to the threat of high taxes, government regulation, and communism. He coupled his warnings with self-deprecating humor that gave his presentations a hopeful tone. Reagan formally became a Republican in 1962 and achieved national exposure by giving a spirited television speech in support of Barry Goldwater's doomed 1964 presidential bid. Two years later he ran for governor of California as "an ordinary citizen" fed up with big government that stifled business and raised taxes while "coddling criminals," supporting "welfare cheats," and tolerating "sexual perversion" at the University of California. Suburban middle-class voters gave Reagan a victory margin of a million votes over incumbent Pat Brown, a moderate Democrat.

As governor of California from 1967 to 1975, Reagan "talked Right" but generally governed from the center. He condemned Democrats for spending and taxing too much, but over the years he doubled the state budget and raised taxes. Despite his having been divorced before he married his second wife Nancy, and having frosty

GLOBAL PASSAGES

The Changing Face of America

The Immigration and Naturalization Reform Act of 1965 altered the profile of those immigrants coming to America. In place of quotas dating back to 1924 that favored Western Europeans and barred Asians, the 1965 law treated most people equally. It gave close blood relatives of earlier immigrants and people with certain job skills a priority. Immigration had declined so much in the previous two decades that the Census Bureau had stopped asking people where their parents had been born. Nearly 5 million immigrants arrived during the 1970s, about 7.5 million more came in the 1980s, and another 10 million came in the 1990s—the highest number recorded in any decade. About half of all immigrants came from Latin America and the Caribbean, 40 percent from Asia, and the rest from Europe, Africa, and the Middle East. Nearly as many people arrived in the 35 years after 1965 as during the "great migration" of the 1880s to early 1920s. For those arriving by air, Los Angeles—displacing New York as the chief port of entry—became the new "Ellis Island." Most Mexicans and Central Americans entered by land, along the borders of California, Arizona, and Texas.

During the 1980s and 1990s, about 300,000 undocumented entrants also arrived each year. These so-called illegals worked in the United States for varying periods of time before returning home. Others planted roots in the United States. Because of its proximity, Mexico was the source for about half the undocumented migrants. In 1986 the Simpson-Rodino Bill provided a path to citizenship for many of the undocumented.

At the start of the 21st century, the percentage of foreign born in the United States neared a historic high. One-quarter of the residents of the United States under 18 now were either immigrants or the children of recent immigrants. Those who study immigration patterns characterize it as a third wave of globalization that follows the movement of goods and money that accelerated in the late 20th century.

Immigration and high birth rates increased the Latino portion of the U.S. population to nearly 13 percent by 2000, and they surpassed African Americans as the largest minority group. The arrival of 3.5 million Asians to the United States doubled their numbers by 1990. By 1990 a fourth of Los Angeles's 9 million residents were recent arrivals; Latinos comprised 25 percent and Asians, a tenth of California's population. Miami, with its large number of Cuban and other Latino immigrants, was sometimes called the Latin American capital of the United States. Although immigration slowed somewhat after the attacks of September 2001 and the economic downturn after 2008 the trend of Latino and Asian migration continued.

Immigrants settled primarily in the cities of California, New York, Florida, Texas, New Jersey, and Illinois. The 2011 census revealed that several old industrial towns in northern New Jersey attracted waves of Koreans and Indians who made up half their population, with recently arrived Latinos comprising much of the rest. Many Latinos populated small towns in the Great Plains states, reversing years of white population decline. In the 1980s and 1990s, 30,000 Hmong from Laos found homes in Minneapolis, where voluntary organizations help resettle them. Villagers from Central America often moved as a group to small cities in the South where they labored in textile, furniture, and food processing plants.

Immigrants worked in all sectors of the economy, from unskilled farm labor to retail shops, to hospitals, and to computer software development. They filled cities and small towns with new languages and diverse religious life, as Muslims, Hindus, Buddhists, and Sikhs joined the traditional mix of Protestants, Catholics, and Jews. Money sent home to relatives was a major source of income in Latin America and parts of Asia such as the Philippines.

The rapid rise in the number of non-European, especially Latin American, immigrants became a heated topic in the 1980s and after. As in the Gilded Age and 1920s some Americans feared this influx threatened traditional culture. Voters in Florida, Colorado, and Arizona passed laws declaring English the official language. Several states, including California in 1994, tried to deny drivers licenses, public education, and other services to non-English speakers and the undocumented. Federal courts overturned these measures. In 2010 and 2011, several states, including Arizona, Georgia, South Carolina, and Alabama took the legal restraints even further, as they made it a state crime to be or to hire an undocumented immigrant and empowered local police to take illegals into custody. Arizona legislators, like those in several states, considered enacting laws denying citizenship to children born to a noncitizen mother, even though this would contradict the Fourteenth Amendment.

In 1980 Congress enacted a Refugee Act that offered asylum to anyone facing a "well-founded fear" of persecution for religious, political, or ethnic reasons. But the Reagan administration continued the long-standing policy of giving preferential treatment to those fleeing Cuba or other communist countries. Refusing entry to people streaming out of Haiti and Central America, it classified them as economic migrants even if they were fleeing civil war and repression.

- What major change did the 1965 immigration law make in government policy?

- Where did new immigrants settle, and how did some Americans react against them?

relations with his children, he spoke reverently of "traditional family values." He also signed into law a pioneering no-fault divorce statute and, in 1967, a bill that effectively legalized most abortions in California.

A New Administration

Reagan had tapped his chief rival, George H. W. Bush, as his vice president and once elected chose Bush's friend, **James A. Baker III**, as his chief of staff. The talented Baker convinced Reagan to focus on getting Congress to lower taxes and boost defense spending. On March 30, 1981, just six weeks into his presidency, a crazed gunman severely wounded Reagan. The good humor he displayed before going into surgery led to a surge of support for him. Congress approved Reagan's call to cut federal income taxes by about 25 percent over three years. At the same time, the lawmakers voted to substantially increase military spending while leaving expenditures on large social programs such as Social Security and Medicare intact.

The tax cuts proved no magic bullet and the economy continued to slide during 1981–1982. Democrats recaptured a large number of congressional seats in 1982 and predicted that Reagan would be a one-term president. But a variety of factors, discussed below, restored economic growth by 1983. The improving economy boosted Reagan's popularity as he faced re-election in 1984. Democrats nominated former vice president Walter Mondale to challenge Reagan. He selected New York representative **Geraldine Ferraro** as his running mate, the first woman to run for this office on the ticket of a major party. Despite an initial wave of excitement, Mondale failed to give voters a convincing reason to turn away from the Reagan-Bush team. Reagan ran on a slogan borrowed from a popular ad campaign for Chrysler automobiles: "It's Morning Again in America." Most voters agreed, giving him a sweep of 49 states in November 1984 and nearly 59 percent of the vote to Mondale's 40 percent. In spite of this reelection landslide, Republicans won few additional congressional seats and in 1986 lost control of the Senate.

Reagan's second term disappointed those who saw it as an opportunity to enact many of his conservative positions. Several of his most effective aides left the White House staff. Their successors proved far less successful in managing either Congress or the president's image. Only two major bills identified with Reagan passed Congress in his second administration. These included a tax reform passed in 1986, written partly by Democrats, that Reagan liked because it reduced the number tax brackets. But, more significantly, it closed so many loopholes and tax shelters that it actually raised taxes on the rich and corporations who had benefited from tax cuts just a few years earlier. The immigration reform that passed in 1986 not only expanded quotas for legal entrants but offered amnesty to many undocumented aliens living in the United States.

Economic Realities

"Reaganomics," as journalists called the president's economic policy, is often credited with restoring economic growth and expanding prosperity to the United States. Reagan condemned "big spenders" in Congress for "mortgaging our future" and pledged to halt the practice of "living beyond our means." After the steep economic slide that lasted until the end of 1982, the American economy did resume growth, although historians and economists disagree over whether Reagan's policies had much to do with this development or if the nation paid too high a price for modest results.

A key event proved to be the taming of inflation that had reached 13 percent when Reagan took office. Credit for this lay mostly with Federal Reserve Chairman Paul Volcker who, near the end of the Carter administration, had imposed high interest rates that gradually reduced inflation to just over 4 percent. After peaking in 1981, global oil prices declined sharply and further spurred economic recovery. Although it was natural for the president to take credit for these successes, Reaganomics had little to do with either.

Reagan is remembered for his strong advocacy of lower taxes, smaller government, and reduced spending and debt. He spoke forcefully about these policies but seldom followed his own advice. For example, he never submitted a balanced budget proposal to Congress. Federal spending as a percentage of the GDP remained steady at about 22 percent throughout the 1980s. When Reagan endorsed a constitutional amendment to bar deficit spending, he stipulated it should only apply to future presidents.

After the large tax cut of 1981, the ballooning deficit forced Reagan to raise taxes, which he preferred to call "revenue enhancements," several times after 1982. As a result, taxes accounted for just about the same 19 percent of GDP in 1989 as in 1981. Because payroll taxes that funded Social Security and Medicare increased during the 1980s, the total tax bite barely changed for most Americans. However, the distribution of the tax burden changed dramatically. The bulk of income tax cuts went to the wealthiest 2 or 3 percent of taxpayers.

Wealthy Americans fared best of all. A typical chief executive officer (CEO) made about 40 times the salary of a worker in 1980. By 1989 the CEO made 93 times as much. The share of national income going to the wealthiest 1 percent of Americans practically doubled in these years, from 8.1 percent to about 15 percent; 60 percent of income growth during the 1980s went to this richest 1 percent. These trends continued for most of the next 30 years.

Between 1982 and 1988 the economy produced around 16 million new jobs, a big improvement as compared to the dismal years from 1979 to 1982. However, the number was less impressive when compared to long-term trends. Employment grew at a faster rate during the 1960s, most of the 1970s, and again in the 1990s. Also, many of the new jobs, which were in the service sector, paid less than the manufacturing jobs that had been lost. Real wages—that is, the value of earnings adjusted for inflation—barely held steady or slightly declined for most Americans during the 1980s. Total household income rose slightly during the 1980s, usually because most wives and young mothers joined the workforce to make ends meet.

Reagan spoke forcefully and frequently about eliminating annual budget shortfalls and paying down the accumulated national debt of $1 trillion that he had inherited. Partly because of increased spending for the military and partly because tax cuts did not produce sufficient revenue, the annual federal budget deficits under Reagan grew to record levels of over $200 billion per year, three times larger than the deficit in Carter's final year. By 1989 the cumulative national debt had tripled to nearly $3 trillion. In less than 10 years, the United States went from the world's biggest lender to the world's biggest borrower.

The Justice Department adopted a relaxed attitude toward monopoly, dropping many antitrust suits against corporate giants and permitting more mergers. The Interior Department, led by James Watt, a lawyer who had worked with Western developers to speed the privatization of federal lands, a movement called the Sagebrush Rebellion, lifted many restrictions on oil drilling, logging, and mining in national forests and coastal areas. A combination of regulatory and legislative changes, begun in the 1970s but accelerated under Reagan, permitted savings and loan institutions to expand their lending practices from housing to commercial real estate. To help automobile makers save money, federal regulators approved a reduction in the safety margins of items such as bumpers.

Reagan described all these policies as an effort to "unleash market forces" and grow the economy. He believed that market forces could also do a better job than government programs in reducing poverty. America, he quipped, had fought a war against poverty for 20 years, and "poverty won." Government inefficiency and criminal scams, he claimed, hurt the taxpayer and did nothing for the poor. Programs like food stamps for the poor, he suggested, simply rewarded laziness.

As Reagan pointed out, the poverty rate of about 13 percent had not budged since Lyndon Johnson declared "war on poverty." But the demography of poverty had changed dramatically. Before 1965, the poor were mostly elderly and sick Americans. Their ranks fell after the passage of Medicare, Medicaid, and the expansion of Social Security. During the 1970s and 1980s the typical poor American was a single mother and her children, a phenomenon referred to as the "feminization of poverty."

The big winners in the Reagan era were the wealthiest 1 percent of Americans whose share of national income nearly doubled, from 8.1 to 15 percent. Wall Street traders and real estate moguls such as Carl Ichan, T. Boone Pickens, Ivan Boesky, and Donald Trump made hundreds of millions of dollars annually in dubious deals that relied on borrowed money often secured by risky "junk bonds." Boesky spoke for many in this group when he told to business majors at a graduation ceremony at the University of California, Berkeley, in 1986 that "greed is healthy." Greed certainly worked for Boesky—until he went to jail for insider stock trading.

Conservative Justice

Since the 1950s many conservatives had accused "judicial activists" on the Supreme Court of legislating from the bench. Critics of the Court often used the language of equality to attack rulings that advanced civil rights for minorities and equal rights for women. Neither Reagan nor most conservatives were racist in the narrow meaning of the term, but they insisted that laws should ignore the impact of historical inequality faced by women and minorities. Accordingly, Reagan opposed the 1964 Civil Rights Act as infringing on property and states rights, the 1965 Voting Rights Act as "insulting to Southerners," and affirmative action as "reverse discrimination." He opposed school busing and a federal holiday honoring Dr. Martin Luther King, Jr., called for a restoration of "states' rights, and urged restoring tax breaks to segregated Christian academies.

As president, Reagan appointed nearly 400 federal judges—a majority of the total number of judges—as well as a chief justice of the Supreme Court. These included **William Rehnquist**, promoted from associate justice to chief justice; and three associate justices, Sandra Day O'Connor, who was the first woman on the high court, **Antonin Scalia**, and **Anthony Kennedy**. All these justices were more conservative than their predecessors. Reagan's reshaping of the judiciary in a more conservative direction proved to be one of his most lasting impacts on public policy. Rulings by the Supreme Court in the late 1980s limited protections for criminal defendants; upheld state death penalty laws; and made it harder for women, minorities, the elderly, and the disabled to sue employers for job discrimination. The Court also restricted but did not eliminate access to abortions.

During the 1980s Reagan as well as many members of Congress and state legislatures adopted a much harsher attitude toward crime and drug use. This included stiff mandatory sentencing laws, especially for repeat felons and drug users. In 1980 state prisons held about 300,000 inmates and federal prisons about 25,000. By 1990 the combined total of more than 800,000 made the United States the leader among industrialized nations in rates of incarceration. A disproportionate number of these new prisoners were black and Latino. By the time Reagan left office, federal and state authorities were spending about $10 billion annually on the drug war, mostly for police and prisons. Between 1970 and 2010, the government spent an estimated $1 trillion on the drug war.

Sexuality, Families, and Health

During the 1970s and 1980s popular culture was embracing more inclusive notions of family, ethnicity, and sexuality even while government promoted a more restrictive view. Public policy and rhetoric seemed to move in the opposite direction of private behavior.

Television more than ever became the center of family entertainment. Many programs, such as *Dallas*, *Dynasty*, and *Life Styles of the Rich and Famous*, celebrated wealth, consumption, and material achievements. But among the era's most popular miniseries were two serious efforts to deal with some of the most dismal events in human history—slavery and the Holocaust. *Roots*, based on the book of the same name by Alex Haley, attracted a huge audience when it aired in 1977. The series chronicled an African American family from its African beginnings to enslavement to the present. The next year another award-winning miniseries, *Holocaust*, introduced almost as many Americans to the horrors of Nazi persecution.

In 1986 the Supreme Court upheld a Georgia law similar to those in 29 states that criminalized sexual acts between consenting same-sex adults. The ruling stood for nearly 20 years. Nevertheless, during the 1970s and 1980s, gays and lesbians increasingly came "out of the closet" to bravely assert their orientation and demand equal rights.

During the 1980s the Reagan administration and many in Congress promoted a conservative sexual agenda. At the president's urging lawmakers reduced funding for international health and population control agencies that promoted birth control or even mentioned abortion. Congress funded teen "chastity clinics" that stressed abstinence before marriage as the only permissible form of birth control. Reagan promoted, without success, a constitutional amendment banning abortion.

By 1983 a majority of both single and married women worked outside the home in a growing variety of professions. Cultural conservatives, however, often lumped together gay rights, pornography, abortion, working mothers, and the Equal Rights Amendment, which failed to win state ratification, as related moral lapses. Conservatives spoke reverently of the "traditional family" composed of a working husband, a homemaker wife, and the proverbial 2.2 children. But this tradition resembled a 1950s television sitcom rather than any reality. For example, the highest rate of births to teenagers since World War II occurred during the mid- to late 1950s, not the "swinging Sixties" or self-indulgent 1970s. By the 1980s, about one-third of children were born to single mothers, mostly over age 19, and an even greater number to single African American and Latino women. With divorce rates at 40 percent or more, with women outliving men, and with more unmarried couples living together and postponing having children, less than one-third of households consisted of two parents and one or more minor children.

The appearance of acquired immune deficiency syndrome (AIDS) early in the 1980s created a health crisis that made Americans more cautious about sexual relations. The result of the human immunodeficiency virus (HIV) identified in 1984, AIDS destroyed the immune system and left patients vulnerable to many infections. HIV was transmitted through the exchange of bodily fluids, typically semen or blood. Transmission was common among gay men, intravenous drug users, and their partners. Most likely, the virus originated in isolated parts of Africa decades earlier and broke out as a by-product of economic development.

The spread of the illness coincided with the growth of the gay consciousness and rights movements. This prompted some conservatives such as **Patrick Buchanan** to dub AIDS the "Gay Plague," a sort of divine retribution for immoral behavior. By the late 1980s about 50,000 Americans had died of AIDS, and as many as 1 million Americans carried the HIV virus. AIDS also struck other parts of the world, especially countries in sub-Saharan Africa, especially hard.

Until 1985, when actor Rock Hudson, a closeted gay man and friend of Reagan's, died of AIDS, the president kept silent about the epidemic. He then appointed an advisory panel that joined Surgeon General **C. Everett Koop** in calling for more funds for research and a campaign to encourage sexually active Americans to use condoms, a simple way to avoid infection. Reagan expressed compassion for AIDS victims but refused to endorse condom use.

At the same time that AIDS became a major concern, a broader health and wellness movement gained popularity. Even as the nation as a whole became more obese, many Americans shunned high-fat diets, sugar, and salt, and quit smoking in growing numbers. Exercise became a national obsession. Some Americans joined trendy health clubs while others jogged and bicycled. New groups such as Mothers Against Drunk Driving campaigned to stiffen penalties for driving intoxicated while more established public health organizations such as the American Cancer Society pressed public officials to adopt restrictions on public smoking. Confessionals about drug and alcohol addiction became a staple of television and radio talk shows.

Surgeon General Koop, who took the lead on publicizing the danger of AIDS, also played a leading role in reenergizing the national campaign against tobacco, which the federal government had begun in the 1960s. Ignoring Reagan's call for less regulation of business Koop issued a series of high-profile reports during the 1980s that called smoking the nation's "chief preventable cause of death," compared nicotine addiction to heroin and cocaine use, and lobbied for state and federal regulations to create a "smoke-free society" by the year 2000.

STUDY QUESTIONS FOR IT'S MORNING AGAIN IN AMERICA

1. What happened to taxes, deficits, and the size of government during the 1980s?
2. In what ways did policies toward justice and crime change under Ronald Reagan?
3. How did the Reagan administration respond to the AIDS crisis?

CHALLENGING THE "EVIL EMPIRE"

Reagan has often been credited for "winning the Cold War without firing a shot." As a candidate he complained that the United States suffered from a "Vietnam Syndrome," shorthand for an unwillingness to counter Soviet threats by defending allies and opposing enemies. In what was sometimes called the "Reagan Doctrine" he pledged to restore American military superiority and to support anticommunist movements around the globe. The Soviet Union, he asserted in 1981, "underlies all the unrest that is going on" in the world. In 1983 Reagan called the Soviet Union the "focus of evil in the modern world" and promised, as he later put it, to consign it to the "ash heap of history." In 1987, addressing a crowd in Berlin, he called on the Soviet leadership to "tear down this wall." After the Berlin Wall crumbled two years later, many people attributed it to his resolve. But how and why the Cold War ended is still debated and some historians believe that Reagan's hard line may have delayed rather than accelerated changes in Soviet behavior.

A New Arms Race

Reagan argued that the United States had virtually disarmed itself in the previous decade even as the Soviet Union and its proxies became stronger. To restore superiority over America's enemies, the president pushed through Congress the largest ever

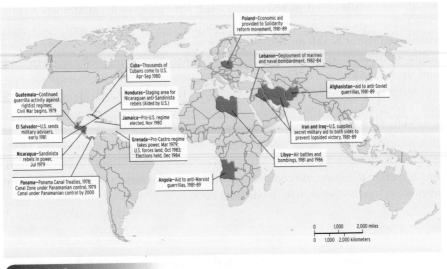

Poland—Economic aid provided to Solidarity reform movement, 1981-89

Cuba—Thousands of Cubans come to U.S. Apr-Sep 1980

Lebanon—Deployment of marines and naval bombardment, 1982-84

Guatemala—Continued guerrilla activity against rightist regimes; Civil War begins, 1979

Honduras—Staging area for Nicaraguan anti-Sandinista rebels (Aided by U.S.)

Afghanistan—aid to anti-Soviet guerrillas, 1981-89

El Salvador—U.S. sends military advisers, early 1981

Jamaica—Pro-U.S. regime elected, Nov 1980

Iran and Iraq—U.S. supplies secret military aid to both sides to prevent lopsided victory, 1981-89

Nicaragua—Sandinista rebels in power, Jul 1979

Grenada—Pro-Castro regime takes power, Mar 1979; U.S. forces land, Oct 1983; Elections held, Dec 1984

Libya—Air battles and bombings, 1981 and 1986

Panama—Panama Canal Treaties, 1978; Canal Zone under Panamanian control, 1979 Canal under Panamanian control by 2000

Angola—Aid to anti-Marxist guerrillas, 1981-89

0   1,000   2,000 miles

0 1,000 2,000 kilometers

▲ **Map 29.1**

Reagan-Era Military Interventions The Reagan administration intervened with overt and covert military force throughout Central America as well as in Angola, Libya, Lebanon, Iran, and Afghanistan. Aid to anti-Soviet Afghans helped to drive out the invaders, but sewed the seeds of Islamist radicalism. The most successful intervention occurred in Poland where the United States provided economic support to the anticommunist, pro-democratic Solidarity movement.

---

peacetime increase in military spending. Between 1981 and 1989 the defense budget rose from about $157 billion to over $304 billion per year.

The public shared Reagan's mistrust of the Soviets and generally supported re-armament. At the same time, many citizens, religious leaders, and members of Congress continued to fear the consequences of atomic war. In 1982–1983, a grass-roots "nuclear freeze movement" urged Reagan to cap the U.S. arsenal at current levels. Although he did not say so until the end of his first term, Reagan had developed a genuine terror of nuclear weapons and hoped, somehow, to eventually reduce their numbers. Nevertheless, he worried that growing public support for the nuclear freeze movement might undercut his big arms buildup before it succeeded in forcing a change in Soviet behavior.

In March 1983 Reagan revealed a program to build a "space shield" designed to render Soviet missiles "impotent and obsolete." Better, he explained, to protect than avenge American lives. The president described a space-based, nuclear-powered laser whose energy beams could destroy Soviet missiles before they reached U.S. targets. Reagan called this the Strategic Defense Initiative (SDI), while critics dubbed it "Star Wars" after the recently released popular science fiction film.

Opinions vary over whether SDI was intended mainly as a bargaining chip, an effort to ease public fears about nuclear war, a scheme to drag the Soviet Union into an arms race it could not win, or a boondoggle for defense contractors. Despite a $20 billion investment in the 1980s, none of the designs worked and the project was eventually abandoned. At first the Soviets denounced SDI as a violation of the 1972 Anti-Ballistic Missile Treaty that banned space-based weapons. Even if the SDI were only partially effective, they feared, it might be good enough to destroy a handful of Soviet missiles that survived a first strike by the United States. But by 1987 Soviet scientists concluded—as had others—that Star Wars would not work and they dropped formal objections. Nevertheless, some Americans continue to believe that that SDI intimidated the Soviets into virtual surrender.

The Reagan administration imposed a variety of economic sanctions on the Soviet Union, barring loans and the sales of certain high technology products. This ban mostly affected Western European and Japanese exporters. The major item sold by Americans to the Soviets was grain and other agricultural products. President Carter had suspended these sales when Soviet forces intervened in Afghanistan. Despite tough talk, soon after taking office Reagan resumed agricultural exports to Moscow. Many of the export bans were also lifted by 1985, before the Soviet Union changed its behavior.

Even with their misgivings about Reagan's tough approach, most Americans and Western Europeans were deeply troubled by Soviet behavior. The frail Leonid Brezhnev, in power since 1964, presided over a corrupt and lethargic administration. Upon his death in 1982, communist oligarchs selected **Yuri Andropov**, head of the secret police, to lead the nation. Although something of a reformer, Andropov suffered from kidney disease and spent his brief time in power on a dialysis machine. In 1984 party elders tapped **Konstantin Chernenko**, a plodding bureaucrat, to become head of the regime. He suffered from emphysema and died after a year.

Soviet actions such as the invasion of Afghanistan had alienated public opinion in Western Europe, Japan, and the Middle East. Soviet stature eroded further in December 1981 when Brezhnev ordered the communist Polish government to impose martial law to prevent the democratic labor movement Solidarity from taking power. Reagan denounced these "forces of tyranny" and authorized the CIA to work with the Catholic Church in Poland to provide secret funding for Solidarity.

Interventions

In addition to the arms buildup and economic sanctions, the Reagan administration planned to undermine Soviet power and spread democracy through open and covert use of force in the Middle East, South Asia, Africa, and Latin America. These interventions proved costly in lives and money while achieving dubious results.

In 1983 Reagan sent warships and a few thousand Marines to Lebanon, a nation engaged in a bloody civil war between several Christian and Muslim factions. U.S. forces bolstered Christian elements considered pro-Western and more accepting of Israel. Muslim fighters responded by blowing up the U.S. Embassy in Beirut in April 1983, killing 63 people, and the Marine barracks in October, killing 241 servicemen. Reagan offered a stirring tribute to the fallen Marines and then pulled out all remaining forces.

The ongoing war between Iraq and Iran continued to destabilize the region. Fearful of a victory by either Iraq's Saddam Hussein or Iran's Ayatollah Khomeini, the Reagan administration secretly provided aid to both nations to preserve a rough balance.

The mixed signals sent to Iraq and Iran complicated their relations with the United States during the 1980s and beyond.

Terrorist airline hijackings, bombings, and kidnappings became a weapon of choice for many frustrated groups, especially in the Middle East. But terrorist acts had more shock than military value. On average in the 1980s, more Americans were killed each year by lightning while playing golf than by terrorists. Yet Reagan portrayed terrorism as a major threat, declaring, "let terrorist beware . . . our policy will be one of swift and effective retribution."

Reagan especially detested the antics of Libya's demagogic strongman, **Muammar Qaddafi**. Qaddafi used oil profits to buy weapons from the Soviets and fund violent groups in the Middle East. In response the United States deployed naval vessels off the Libyan coast and fought several aerial battles against Libyan planes, incidents fictionalized in the 1986 Tom Cruise film *Top Gun*. In April 1986, when Libyan agents were implicated in the bombing of a Berlin night club frequented by Americans, Reagan called Qaddafi a "mad dog" and sent planes to bomb his residence. Qaddafi survived, but the attack killed his infant daughter. In December 1988, taking revenge, Libyan agents planted a bomb that destroyed a U.S. airliner flying over Lockerbie, Scotland, and killed several hundred passengers and 11 people on the ground.

As noted earlier, in December 1979 Soviet forces invaded Afghanistan to prop up a communist regime on the verge of collapse. Russian troops became mired in a brutal war against Mujahideen, Islamic-inspired Afghan and foreign guerrillas, who counted among their ranks Saudi fundamentalist Osama bin Laden. Carter began and Reagan expanded aid to these insurgents. U.S. weapons went through Pakistan, a military dictatorship that in return received tacit U.S. approval to develop an atomic bomb. The U.S.-backed guerrillas forced a Soviet pullout in the late 1980s. By then Pakistan had sold nuclear weapons technology to rogue states such as North Korea and Libya. After the Soviet departure, Islamic radicals called Taliban took power in Afghanistan and eventually played host to bin Laden, who used the skills he honed fighting the Soviets to plan a series of strikes against the United States, culminating in the attacks of September 11, 2001.

The CIA assisted anticommunist forces in several conflicts, such as those in Angola, Mozambique, and Cambodia, without achieving much success. A more decisive result came in October 1983 when U.S. military forces invaded the tiny Caribbean island of Grenada. Reagan worried that the Marxist leaders of the island might turn it into a Soviet base or make hostages of some 500 American students enrolled in a local medical school. The invasion lasted a few hours and allowed Reagan to proclaim victory over a "brutal gang of thugs."

Iran Contra

Reagan and his aides spoke frequently of a Soviet-Cuban threat to the Western Hemisphere. The administration sent military advisers, weapons, and billions of dollars to support brutal right-wing regimes in El Salvador, Honduras, and Guatemala, which were engaged in civil wars with leftwing guerrillas. Tens of thousands of unarmed

CIA-assisted Mujahideen guerrillas pose on a captured Soviet truck in the mid-1980s. Many of the Islamist fighters turned against their American patron after 1989.

civilians died, most killed by soldiers who considered them guerrilla allies. The violence pushed several million Central American immigrants toward the United States.

Nicaragua grabbed most of Reagan's attention. He had criticized Carter for abandoning the Somoza regime in 1979 when it fell to Marxist guerrillas known as Sandinistas, after a martyr who resisted Marine occupation in the 1920s. In 1981 Reagan authorized the CIA to support an existing rebel force, known as contrarevolucionarios, or Contras, to topple the Sandinistas. In 1982 Congress learned that the Contras had killed thousands of Nicaraguan civilians. In response Congress adopted a law called the Boland Amendment that cut off most aid to the rebels.

Balking at these restrictions, Reagan told key members of his national security council staff, including **Robert McFarlane** and Lieutenant Colonel **Oliver North**, "to do whatever you have to do" to help the Contras. They solicited money from wealthy conservatives such as brewer Joseph Coors, and from friendly governments such as Saudi Arabia and Taiwan. When donations dried up in 1985, North devised what he called a "neat idea." The NSC would sell U.S. weapons—at an inflated price—to "moderates" in Iran, who needed them to fight Iraq. In return the Iranians promised to persuade Islamist militias in Lebanon to release several kidnapped Americans. Finally, the CIA would use profits from the weapons sales to Iran to buy weapons for the Contras. Although the convoluted scheme violated U.S. law as well as Reagan's pledge never to negotiate or do business with terrorists, he approved it.

Lieutenant Colonel Oliver North, a central figure in the Iran-Contra Scandal, defended his role during Congressional testimony in 1987 and falsely denied President Reagan's involvement.

Several arms sales to Iran took place during 1986. Three hostages in Beirut were released, but others were promptly seized. The plan imploded in October 1986 when Sandinistas shot down a CIA-chartered plane carrying weapons to the Contras and an American survivor revealed the secret aid program. In November, Iran disclosed that

TIMELINE 1973–1988

1973

January The *Roe v. Wade* decision by Supreme Court upholds abortion rights

October The Arab-Israeli War and oil embargo occur, and stagflation begins

1974

August Nixon resigns and Gerald Ford becomes president

September Ford pardons Nixon

1975

April North Vietnam defeats South Vietnam; Americans are evacuated from Saigon

1976

November Jimmy Carter is elected president

1977

January President Jimmy Carter offers pardon to Vietnam draft resisters

1978

March Senate approves the Panama Canal Treaty

June *Bakke v. University of California* Supreme Court decision upholds affirmative action

June Proposition 13 tax cut is passed in California

September Camp David Accords signed between Israel and Egypt

1979

January The shah flees Iran

March A major accident occurs with the Three Mile Island nuclear reactor

June Moral Majority is formed

July Somoza regime is overthrown in Nicaragua

November Iranian radicals seize U.S. hostages while gasoline shortages worsen

December Soviet forces invade Afghanistan and the United States begins covert aid to Afghan guerrillas

1980

April An attempt to rescue the Iranian U.S. hostages fails

April–October Controversial Mariel boat lift from Cuba takes place

September Iraq-Iran war begins and lasts until 1988

November Ronald Reagan is elected president

1981

January Reagan is inaugurated; the Iran hostages are released. AIDS is identified for the first time in the United States; covert aid

the United States had actually sold weapons to regime hardliners only pretending to be moderates.

As Congress and the media probed what was now called the Iran-Contra Scandal, Reagan rushed for cover. NSC staff shredded documents, lied to investigators, and misled the public about the operation. Reagan denied knowing of an arms-for-hostages deal. But a special panel of inquiry, the Tower Commission, refuted his account, calling the Iranian arms sales part of a sordid ransom scheme designed to illegally fund the Contras. The panel portrayed Reagan as disengaged, uninformed, befuddled, and easily manipulated. Several of the other players were convicted for their actions. Later probes by a special prosecutor tied Reagan directly to key decisions.

Cold War Thaw

The U.S.-Soviet relationship changed dramatically after March 1985 when the relatively young, well-educated, and widely traveled **Mikhail Gorbachev** was chosen by the Communist hierarchy to lead the Soviet Union. Gorbachev impressed foreign leaders, such as Reagan's friend, British prime minister **Margaret Thatcher**, as a dynamic reformer determined to radically alter the Soviet political and economic system. He was, she told the president, "someone with whom we can do business."

Almost certainly, internal problems, not Reagan's hard line, motivated Gorbachev to radically alter Soviet policies at home and abroad. With its stagnant economy, backward technology, and chronic social problems, the Soviet Union seemed more like a developing country than a world power. Even with its nuclear arsenal, Gorbachev realized that the Soviet system was unsustainable. Gorbachev recognized the "interdependence of the world" and the fact that Soviet security could not be achieved by making its neighbors insecure. The Soviets did not so much "lose" the Cold War as simply call it off.

---

is increased to Afghan guerrillas and Contras

August–October Congress approves Reagan tax cuts and defense increase

1982

October Garn-St. Germain bill deregulates Savings and Loans

November Democrats regain some House seats

December Boland amendment bars aid to Contras

1983

March Reagan unveils SDI

October Marine barracks are bombed in Lebanon. The United States invades Grenada

1984

April HIV virus is identified as the cause of AIDS

November Reagan is reelected

1985

March Mikhail Gorbachev becomes Soviet leader

August Reagan authorizes the first secret arms sales to Iran

November Reagan and Gorbachev meet in Geneva

1986

January Space Shuttle *Challenger* explodes

October Iran-Contra scandal erupts

November Democrats regain control of Senate

1987

February Reagan is condemned by the Tower Commission for his role in the Iran-Contra scandal

November United States and Soviets agree to a treaty limiting intermediate range missiles

December Gorbachev visits United States to sign the INF treaty

1988

February Gorbachev announces the pullout of Soviet forces from Afghanistan

May Reagan visits the Soviet Union

November George H. W. Bush is elected president

December Gorbachev again visits the United States

As the Cold War began to recede during 1988, President Ronald Reagan enjoyed a stroll through the Kremlin with Soviet Premier Mikhail Gorbachev.

Reagan had the good fortune—and sense—to respond positively to these changes even if his tough policies played only a small part in causing them. Reagan cooperated with Gorbachev partly because of his own need to demonstrate an ability to govern in the wake of the Iran-Contra scandal. Also, during 1987 Reagan replaced nearly all his "hard line" anti-Soviet advisers with moderates who favored negotiating with Gorbachev.

Between 1986 and 1988, Gorbachev attempted to save the Soviet Union through radical reform. He released political prisoners, allowed freer emigration, and lifted press restrictions. To revive the dormant economy he introduced market mechanisms and courted foreign capital and technology. In 1987, after two inconclusive meetings with Reagan, Gorbachev visited Washington and agreed to a treaty, largely on American terms, eliminating all intermediate range nuclear missiles held by both sides.

During 1988 Gorbachev proposed that as the Soviets pulled out of Afghanistan, Washington and Moscow organize a unity government to prevent the rise of extremist groups like the Taliban. He endorsed a peace plan for Central America and urged deeper cuts in nuclear arsenals. But Reagan appeared increasingly detached from events. He had also been stung by criticism from some of his conservative friends that he had gone soft on communism. In June he visited Moscow for something of a victory lap and posed with Gorbachev on top of Lenin's Tomb in Red Square. When a reporter asked about the "evil empire," Reagan said that was "another time, another era." Gorbachev appealed again for joint efforts to resolve disputes in the developing world and to speed nuclear disarmament, but Reagan did little more than smile for the cameras as he coasted toward the end of his presidency. With the mellowing of the Red Menace, and the possible onset of the dementia he later suffered, Reagan's interest in foreign and domestic affairs lapsed.

STUDY QUESTIONS FOR CHALLENGING THE "EVIL EMPIRE"

1. Why did Reagan believe the Soviet Union was "winning" the Cold War in 1980 and what policies did he adopt to reverse the trend?
2. What was the purpose behind the covert programs in Iran and Nicaragua and how did they undermine Reagan?
3. Why were Reagan and Gorbachev able to find common ground and areas for international cooperation after 1985?

Summary

- In the 1970s a host of social, economic, and military problems, and two "failed presidencies," left Americans mistrustful of "big government."
- Conservative religious and political groups came to dominate the Republican Party and offered appealing alternatives to liberal ideas.
- Reagan became the vehicle for conservatism and won the presidential election by promising to restore American pride, power, and prosperity.
- Actual economic performance during the 1980s was highly selective, with a small number of Americans doing very well and most merely treading water.
- Reagan's strident anticommunism and foreign interventions achieved little success through 1986. After the Iran-Contra scandal the president's need to compromise coincided with Gorbachev's effort to reform the Soviet Union and led to a major thaw in the Cold War.

Key Terms and People

Andropov, Yuri *1157*

Baker, James A., III *1150*

Begin, Menachem *1136*

Buchanan, Patrick *1154*

Carter, Jimmy *1127*

Chernenko, Konstantin *1157*

Dole, Robert *1133*

Equal Rights Amendment (ERA) *1144*

Falwell, Jerry *1127*

Ferraro, Geraldine *1150*

Gorbachev, Mikhail *1161*

Graham, Billy *1144*

Helsinki Accords *1132*

Kennedy, Edward "Ted" *1139*

Kennedy, Anthony *1153*

Khomeini, Ruholla *1138*

Koop, C. Everett *1154*

LaHaye, Beverley *1144*

LaHaye, Tim *1144*

McFarlane, Robert *1159*

Mondale, Walter *1133*

monetarists *1143*

Moral Majority *1127*

Mossadeq, Mohammed *1138*

Mujahideen *1137*

National Organization for Women (NOW) *1144*

Neocons *1132*

North, Oliver *1159*

Pahlavi, Mohammed Reza *1138*

Political Action Committees (PACs) **1146**

Qaddafi, Muammar *1158*

Rehnquist, William *1153*

Robertson, Pat *1144*

Rockefeller, Nelson *1132*

Roe v. Wade *1143*

Sadat, Anwar *1136*

Scalia, Antonin *1153*

Schlafley, Phyllis *1144*

Thatcher, Margaret *1161*

Volcker, Paul *1136*

Reviewing Chapter 29

1. What domestic and foreign problems overwhelmed the Carter administration?
2. What was Sunbelt conservatism?
3. What was Ronald Reagan's criticism of liberal economic and social programs and how did he propose to alter course?
4. In what ways were Reagan's domestic policies successful? In what ways did they fail?
5. Why did Reagan charge that the Soviets were "winning" the Cold War?
6. Did Reagan's foreign policies alter Soviet behavior or were other factors responsible for winding down the Cold War?

Further Reading

Edsall, Thomas, and Mary Edsall. *Chain Reaction: The Impact of Race, Politics, and Taxes on American Politics.* New York: W.W. Norton, 1992. The authors examine how racial tensions, economic frustrations, and posturing by politicians shattered the liberal consensus in post-1945 America.

McGirr, Lisa. *Suburban Warriors: The Origins of the New American Right.* Princeton, N.J.: Princeton University Press, 2001. The rise of the Sunbelt and politics in Southern California, the author argues, produced a new kind of American conservatism during the 1950s and 1960s.

Mickelthwait, John, and Adrian Wooldridge. *Right Nation: Conservative Power in America.* New York: Penguin Books, 2004. The authors examine how the religious, economic, intellectual, and political strains of conservatism merged into a powerful force in American society.

Oberdorfer, Don. *From the Cold War to a New Era: The United States and the Soviet Union, 1983–1991.* Baltimore: The Johns Hopkins University Press, 1998. This well-sourced account by an accomplished journalist traces the ups and downs of the Cold War during the Reagan-Bush era.

Schulman, Bruce. *The Seventies: The Great Shift in American Culture, Society, and Politics.* New York: The Free Press, 2001. A reinterpretation of the "me decade" that examines the crisis of liberalism and the events which made conservative ideas appear so attractive.

Willentz, Sean. *The Age of Reagan: A History, 1974–2008.* New York: Harper, 2008. Partly a biography and partly a policy study, Willentz traces the sources of Reagan's ideas and their impact on America in the two decades after his presidency.

Visual Review

The Rise of Reagan

Ronald Reagan is elected president.

A New Administration

Reagan's presidency makes strides toward conservatism, but fails to fulfill some of the conservatives' agenda.

An Accidental President

Ford does little to restore faith in national leadership.

The Politics of Limits and Malaise

Carter is unable to rally Congress to help solve the major crises facing the nation.

A Dangerous World, 1974–1980

Carter achieves some diplomatic successes in the Middle East and in Latin America.

America Held Hostage

American hostages are taken from the U.S. Embassy in Iran.

Backlash

CONSERVATISM RESURGENT, 1974–1989

The Rising Tide on the Right

Economic Limits

A new conservative economic theory is proposed to lift the U.S. economy.

The Collapse of the Political Center

Fracturing of the Democratic Party causes some voters to begin voting for Republican candidates.

The Religious Right and Neoconservatism

Religious people become more politically active.

It's Morning Again in America

Economic Realities
While the economy did grow under Reagan, the gains are limited and targeted.

Conservative Justice
Reagan's judicial appointments move federal courts in new directions.

Sexuality, Families, and Health
Popular culture embraces more inclusive notions of family, ethnicity, and sexuality.

Challenging the "Evil Empire"

A New Arms Race
Reagan drastically increases military spending.

Interventions
The United States actively confronts communism with interventions in the Middle East and Latin America.

Iran Contra
The Reagan administration illegally aids Nicaraguan guerrillas, sells arms to Iran, and negotiates with hostage takers.

Cold War Thaw
Mikhail Gorbachev changes the U.S.-Soviet Union relations.

30

After the Cold War

1988–2000

In 1983, 29-year-old computer designer **Steven Jobs** persuaded John Scully, an executive at Pepsi, to leave the soft-drink maker to become the CEO of Apple Computer, a company Jobs had helped create in 1976. Jobs asked Scully, "Do you want to spend the rest of your life selling sugared water to children, or do you want a chance to change the world?" Jobs and other rebellious innovators in Silicon Valley were about to transform the way people around the world communicated and lived their lives. Apple produced a stunning commercial entitled "1984," broadcast during that year's Super Bowl. It informed consumers that it was shaking up the stodgy corporate world ruled by IBM, the manufacturer of the Personal Computer, with the introduction of its Macintosh.

Jobs, eager to promote the "next big thing" and uncomfortable with Apple's new corporate structure, moved on in the mid-1980s to found NeXT Computer, which appealed to graphic designers and scientists. Jobs called his machines "interpersonal computers," because users could communicate easily with others. The machines allowed easy access to the emerging Internet and possessed other advanced features. In 1996, with California's Silicon Valley in the midst of an Internet-inspired boom, Apple bought NeXT Computer, and Jobs returned as Apple's interim CEO. The company continued to introduce innovative products for graphic designers and scientists. Jobs developed an almost cult-like following with his enthusiastic speeches, called "SteveNotes," that launched new advances to the Mac at the company's annual Mac-World Expos.

Trading floor of the New York Stock Exchange

CHAPTER OUTLINE

GEORGE H. W. BUSH AND THE END OF THE COLD WAR
> The Election of 1988
> The Bush Presidency at Home
> The New World Order
> The Election of 1992

THE GOOD TIMES
> Innovation and New Technology
> Work, Science, and Discontent
> Migrants

BILL CLINTON AND THE NEW DEMOCRATS
> An Awkward Start
> Clinton's Recovery
> Clinton's Second Term

A POST-COLD WAR FOREIGN POLICY
> Intervention and Mediation
> International Terrorism

THE DISPUTED ELECTION OF 2000
> Bush versus Gore
> The Election in Florida and a Supreme Court Decision

1169

America in the World

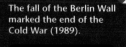

The fall of the Berlin Wall marked the end of the Cold War (1989).

Congress ratified the North American Free Trade Agreement to broaden commerce (1993).

⊕ **U.S. event that influenced the world**

⊕ **International event that influenced the United States**

◎ **Event with multinational influence**

✴ **Conflict**

The dissolution of the Soviet Union created independent Eastern European states (1988).

The Persian Gulf War established a stronger U.S. military presence in the Middle East (1991).

The Oslo Accords outlined framework for peace between Palestine and Israel (1993).

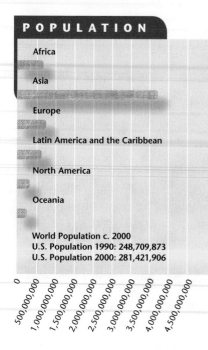

POPULATION

Africa

Asia

Europe

Latin America and the Caribbean

North America

Oceania

World Population c. 2000
U.S. Population 1990: 248,709,873
U.S. Population 2000: 281,421,906

0
500,000,000
1,000,000,000
1,500,000,000
2,000,000,000
2,500,000,000
3,000,000,000
3,500,000,000
4,000,000,000
4,500,000,000

Apple's headquarters, like many in Silicon Valley, were loose and informal places. Software designers and hardware engineers in their 20s and 30s wore sandals and T-shirts. There were no fixed hours, but workers came in early and stayed late, seven days a week.

The Personal Computer and the Mac (along with other nearly forgotten machines such as the Commodore and Amiga) made computers into household appliances as common as toasters and TVs and helped spread information technology around the globe. Computer software, along with agricultural products, films, and weapons, has comprised America's major exports since the 1980s. The end of the Cold War in the early 1990s hastened the process. Instantaneous communication and access to vast amounts of information made the world seem smaller and, for a while, richer and more peaceful.

GEORGE H. W. BUSH AND THE END OF THE COLD WAR

The Cold War ended between 1989 and 1991. With the exception of Romania, non-violent popular uprisings swept aside communist governments of Eastern Europe in 1989, and the Soviet Union disintegrated in late 1991. President **George H. W. Bush** peacefully navigated the fall of European communism. He proclaimed the dawn of a **New World Order**, in which the United States, the world's surviving superpower, would lead multinational coalitions to enforce its standards of international behavior. Many people who watched the Berlin Wall fall and communism disintegrate in Eastern Europe and the Soviet Union believed that the world had entered on an unprecedented era of personal freedom, democracy, and economic prosperity. Some believed that the end of communism actually marked "the end of history," in which people everywhere would adopt U.S. and Western European values of free market capitalism, representative government, free civil institutions, and the rule of law.

In spite of these expectations, the collapse of communism in Eastern Europe did not usher in an age of world peace and prosperity. The United States intervened militarily in the Western Hemisphere and fought a major war against Iraq. Long suppressed ethnic rivalries ripped apart the former Yugoslavia and Somalia and Rwanda in Africa. After the Cold War, as the economy soured, Americans turned inward. In 1992 voters defeated Bush for reelection in part because his foreign policy expertise seemed less valuable in the post-Cold War era when ordinary Americans worried more about their economic livelihood. They replaced him with Democrat **Bill Clinton**, the 46-year-old governor of Arkansas, who promised to revive the fortunes of the middle class.

The Election of 1988

At the end of the Reagan presidency conditions looked promising for the Democratic Party to win the presidential election in 1988. Both the personality and the philosophy of Vice President George H. W. Bush seemed unclear to most Americans. Conservative rivals for the nomination, including television preacher Pat Robertson, Kansas senator Robert Dole, and former secretary of state Alexander Haig, attacked him as an inauthentic conservative in light of his pre-1981 criticism of Reagan's tax proposals as "voodoo economics" and his vigorous support while a member of Congress of government-funded contraception. Former Texas governor John Connolly ridiculed Bush's eastern background and shallow roots in Texas: he was "all hat and no boots." Bush pointed to his loyal service under Reagan and, by selecting 39-year-old, first-term Indiana senator **Dan Quayle** as his own vice-presidential nominee, placated enough party conservatives to secure the nomination. Quayle's major qualifications for the job were his youth, good looks, and conservative voting record. Bush received the loudest cheers from conservatives at the Republican National Convention when he promised to tell congressional Democrats "read my lips, no new taxes."

The Democrats selected Massachusetts governor **Michael Dukakis** from among eight candidates. Dukakis ran as a pragmatic problem solver, responsible for the "Massachusetts miracle" of booming economic growth in the 1980s. To enhance the ticket's appeal among Southerners, Dukakis chose Texas senator Lloyd Bentsen as his running mate. Bentsen had defeated Bush for the Senate in 1970.

Bush found himself dogged by a wishy-washy image. Dukakis began the campaign in the summer of 1988 with a 17-point lead over Bush in public opinion polls. Following the advice of his campaign manager Lee Atwater to avoid discussing substantive economic and social policy issues, Bush ran a slashing series of negative ads against the Massachusetts governor, denouncing him as an unpatriotic "unrepentant liberal" and a "high tax, high spending, pro-abortion, card-carrying member of the American Civil Liberties Union." He criticized Dukakis for vetoing a law requiring school teachers to lead students in reciting the pledge of allegiance. He also blamed Dukakis for granting a prison furlough to Willie Horton, an African American convicted murderer, who raped a woman while on release. Bush justified his attacks by declaring, "I don't understand the type of thinking that lets first degree murderers . . . out on parole so they can rape and plunder again, and then isn't willing to let teachers lead the kids in the Pledge of Allegiance." Dukakis responded ineptly to these charges, citing legal precedent for the flag law veto and noting that a Republican governor had initiated the furlough program. He seemed cold and detached when he told a debate moderator he would not drop his opposition to the death penalty even if his wife were raped and murdered because vengeance was not justice.

The "slash and burn" tactics used by Bush established a style of personal attack that became standard in subsequent political campaigns. News reports in 1988 also introduced the public to terms like "sound bite" and "spin," which described how candidate's images could be manipulated through skillful media management. Ultimately, Bush coasted to an easy victory against the wooden Dukakis because times were good, the Cold War was ending, and he seemed to be the candidate most likely to likely to continue on Reagan's path. Bush carried 40 of the 50 states. He won 48.9 million votes, 54 percent, and 426 electoral votes to Dukakis' 41.8 million votes, 46 percent, and 111 electoral votes. Democrats, however, retained control of Congress.

The Bush Presidency at Home

Despite Bush's brutal electoral tactics, he tried to govern from the center. But the new president's efforts to fulfill his campaign promise of promoting a "kinder, gentler America" infuriated conservative Republicans—who wondered kinder and gentler than whom?—and failed to gain support from Democrats angry at his negative campaigning during the election.

More concerned than Reagan with the actual business of governing, President Bush supported and signed laws expanding civil rights and protecting the environment. In 1991 a new civil rights law allowed the establishment of racial and gender goals—but not quotas—in hiring. The **Americans with Disabilities Act** (ADA) of 1990 represented the culmination of years of activism on behalf of people with disabilities. As many as 45 million Americans (one-sixth of the population) were permanently or temporarily disabled. More than half of them were unemployed, and they were among the poorest people in the country. The ADA required that government, business, and educational institutions make "reasonable accommodations" so that people with mental or physical disabilities could work and have the same access as fully abled people. The law required new or remodeled public buildings to be wheelchair accessible. Within a few years sidewalk curb cuts for mobility-impaired people became standard across the country.

In March 1989 a huge oil tanker, the *Exxon Valdez*, ran aground in Alaska's Prince William Sound. Ten million gallons of oil leaked from the ship and spoiled over 800 miles of pristine coastline. Public outrage over the environmental damage led Congress to update the Clean Air and Water Acts. The new laws enhanced sewage systems and set emissions standards for vehicles. By enacting the Radiation Exposure Compensation Act of 1990, Congress provided assistance to miners, millworkers, and soldiers who had been injured by uranium processing or atomic testing since the onset of the Cold War. The Native American Graves Protection and Repatriation Act also passed in 1990 compelled museums and other institutions to return certain bones and cultural artifacts taken from tribes.

Conservatives criticized all these measures as extensions of the welfare state. They erupted in outright fury when Bush retreated from his pledge not to raise taxes. Government spending soared in 1989 as the Bush administration created the Resolution Trust Corporation to buy $129 billion in defaulted properties from Savings and Loans, banks which had made massive, risky commercial loans during the 1980s that had failed in the last year of the Reagan presidency. The federal budget deficit approached

$300 billion in 1990, and the Treasury Department feared that international owners of U.S. bonds might refuse to buy more. The Democratic congressional leadership reached a deal with Bush to raise taxes modestly and make small cuts in defense and social programs. Opposition from a coalition of conservative Republicans and liberal Democrats blocked the compromise. When Bush vetoed a stopgap budget, the government shut down for three days in October. The public flooded the White House with angry phone calls denouncing the president. Congress then adopted another bill with tax increases for the wealthy and small spending cuts. In the aftermath congressional Republicans condemned Bush for abandoning Ronald Reagan's legacy while Democrats saw him as weak and ineffectual.

The Supreme Court also became a focal point of resentments and controversy in the Bush administration. Abortion was a flashpoint. Early in his political career Bush had defended a woman's right to choose an abortion, but in the 1988 election campaign he declared that "abortion is murder." In *Webster v. Reproductive Services of Missouri* (1989) and *Planned Parenthood v. Casey* (1992), the Court decided by 5-to-4 majorities that states could restrict but not totally eliminate access to abortion. The retirement of two liberal justices, William Brennan and Thurgood Marshall, raised conservative hopes that new justices would turn the court further to the right. In 1990 Bush nominated federal judge **David Souter** to replace Brennan. He easily won Senate confirmation, and he soon astounded both Democrats and Republicans by voting with the Court's liberal minority.

Bush scrutinized his next nominee more carefully. To replace Marshall, the only African American justice, he selected 43-year-old federal judge **Clarence Thomas**. Thomas, an outspoken black conservative, had directed the office of Equal Employment Opportunity Commission (EEOC) during the Reagan years. In that position he often denied discrimination claims brought by people of color and women. Bush had appointed Thomas to the federal court of appeals in 1990. Thomas frequently criticized Court decisions legalizing abortion, banning school prayer, and restricting

Law professor Anita Hill, a former colleague of Clarence Thomas, accused the Supreme Court nominee of sexual harassment during Senate testimony in October 1991. Thomas denied the charge and most Senators dismissed Hill's accusations as fantasy, even though several coworkers were prepared to verify her story.

the death penalty. Bush, denying that he chose him because he was African American or a reliable conservative, declared instead that he was the "most qualified American" for the Court. His confirmation initially seemed assured when civil rights groups and liberal Democrats stifled their misgivings over his conservative views and endorsed him as the only African American Bush was likely to nominate. Then reports surfaced that **Anita Hill**, an African American law professor, had accused him of sexual harassment when she worked for him at the EEOC. The Senate Judiciary committee reopened its confirmation hearings. In televised testimony Hill calmly described how Thomas had harassed her and other female workers, talked incessantly about viewing pornographic movies, and boasted of his sexual prowess. Republican senators on the committee accused Hill of making up her story. Thomas accused his opponents of conducting "a high-tech lynching for uppity blacks."

The Senate confirmed Thomas, who became one of the Court's most conservative members. Bush emerged from the confirmation battle weaker than ever. Many women considered the dismissive tone taken toward Hill by both senators and the administration unforgivable—especially when it later emerged that other women who had worked with Thomas were prepared to confirm Hill's allegations but were never summoned to testify.

The New World Order

From 1989 to 1991, with revolutions sweeping through Eastern Europe and the Soviet Union, the United States and other NATO countries provided billions of dollars to promote reform in the former Soviet Empire. Bush assembled a talented team to direct foreign affairs. National Security Adviser Brent Scowcroft, Secretary of Defense Dick Cheney, Secretary of State James A. Baker III, and Chairman of the Joint Chiefs of Staff Colin Powell had held high positions in the Ford and Reagan administrations. Together they helped manage the peaceful end of the Cold War, one of the most dramatic and far reaching set of events in the 20th century.

In July 1989 Soviet president **Mikhail Gorbachev** stunned the world when he announced that his country would no longer intervene in the internal affairs of the communist states of East Europe. In a dramatic reversal of 50 years of policy, the Soviet leader made clear that his country would no longer base its security on the weakness or domination of its neighbors. No more would Eastern Europeans have to fear the arrival of Soviet tanks in their countries if they sought alternatives to communism—as had happened in Hungary in 1956 and Czechoslovakia in 1968. Huge peaceful demonstrations soon toppled the communist regimes of Czechoslovakia, Hungary, and Poland. On November 9, 1989, the Berlin Wall, perhaps the most visible symbol of the Cold War, came down after months of street demonstrations had rocked East Germany. Exuberant crowds used hammers, crowbars, and their bare hands to tear down the wall that divided Germans. Less than a year later, on October 2, 1990, East Germany ceased to exist and its territory became part of the Federal Republic of Germany.

The rapid collapse of communist regimes that followed caught both American and Soviet leaders by surprise. Bush had urged Eastern Europeans to move slowly, and

Exuberant Germans celebrate the crumbling of the hated Berlin Wall in November 1989. The iconic Cold War symbol had divided the city since 1961.

he endorsed gradual rather than rapid change. Nevertheless, communist regimes in Poland, Hungary, Czechoslovakia, and Bulgaria soon went the way of East Germany. Only the Romanian communist leadership used force in a vain effort to suppress the democratic tide. The political upheavals spread to the Soviet Union as well. In 1990 the Baltic republics of Latvia, Lithuania, and Estonia declared independence from the Soviet Union. Other Soviet Republics also wanted their own independent governments. After an initial reluctance to engage with the Soviet leader, Bush met six times with Gorbachev in 1989 and 1990, and in November of 1990 the two men declared the end of the Cold War.

Just as Bush fully embraced Gorbachev, the Soviet leader's power waned. Orthodox communists accused him of letting loose forces that had destroyed the Soviet empire. Reformers, such as **Boris Yeltsin**, a former communist and mayor of Moscow who was elected president of the Russian Federation in June 1991, complained that Gorbachev moved too slowly toward democratic and market reforms. In August 1991 communist hardliners staged a coup against Gorbachev. With Yeltsin's help he regained power after a few days, but his authority had evaporated. In the final months of 1991 power shifted to Yeltsin in Russia, and the remaining Soviet republics such as Ukraine, Belarus, Latvia, Lithuania, and Estonia declared their independence. On December 25, 1991, Gorbachev proclaimed the end of the Soviet Union and peacefully handed power to Yeltsin.

Although the Cold War and the threat of instant nuclear annihilation were over, regional conflicts persisted, and in some places, such as Yugoslavia and a number of

▲ Map 30.1

After the Fall: Russia and Eastern Europe Since 1991 Between 1989 and 1991, the Soviet empire collapsed, starting in Eastern Europe and culminating in the dissolution of the Soviet Union. To Russia's west, Ukraine, Belarus, Estonia, Latvia, and Lithuania gained independence. In what had been Soviet Central Asia, a half-dozen predominantly Muslim republics emerged.

countries in Africa, they grew worse. In Latin America, however, the hostilities between U.S.-backed regimes and leftist guerrillas in El Salvador and Honduras abated. A peace settlement in Nicaragua led to elections and the replacement of the Sandinista regime. Bush used force to oust Manuel Noriega, Panama's dictator since 1983. For some time, Reagan had ignored his drug running and money laundering because Noriega permitted the CIA to use his territory to funnel aid to the anticommunist Nicaraguan Contras. By the time Bush became president, however, the civil wars in Central America were over, and Noriega's drug activities collided with Washington's renewed stress on the so-called war on drugs. An infuriated Noriega cancelled an election in 1989 and sent club-wielding thugs to terrorize his opponents. Economic sanctions failed to drive Noriega from power, and Bush, stung by critics who said he "coddled" the dictator, turned to force. In December 1989 the United States sent 12,000 troops to arrest Noriega and install the winner of the disputed May elections. After a few days of fighting, Noriega was captured and flown to Florida where he was tried and convicted of drug smuggling.

The United States fought yet another war with far greater consequences after Iraqi leader **Saddam Hussein** invaded and annexed the oil-rich sheikdom of Kuwait on August 2, 1990. During the 1980s the United States had sometimes sided with Iraq in its eight-year war with Iran, and it had not objected to Saddam's drive to acquire chemical, biological, and nuclear weapons. Reagan and Bush had considered Iraq a useful counterweight to Iran and provided it with economic assistance.

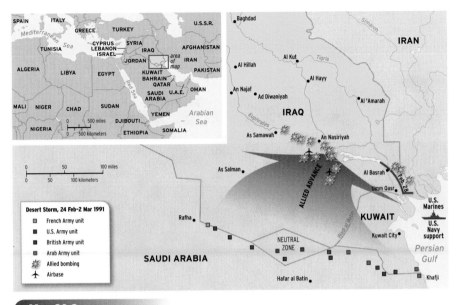

▲ **Map 30.2**

War in the Persian Gulf, 1991–1992 In 1991, President George H. W. Bush organized a broad international coalition that opposed Iraq's seizure of Kuwait and its threat to Saudi Arabia. In a short but effective air and ground war, coalition forces drove the Iraqis out of Kuwait but allowed Saddam Hussein to remain in power. Many Americans came to regret this decision.

The conquest of Kuwait, however, alarmed the richest oil kingdom, Saudi Arabia, which feared that Iraq would turn on it next. No one wanted the mercurial dictator to control a major part of the world's petroleum reserve. In addition, Iraq's seizure of Kuwait clearly violated the United Nations Charter. Bush obtained 12 UN Security Council resolutions demanding that Iraq quit Kuwait. He sent 500,000 U.S. troops to protect Saudi Arabia and prevailed on 27 other countries to contribute an additional 200,000 troops to drive Iraq out of Kuwait.

The enormous size of the coalition forces arrayed against Saddam Hussein represented the lessons learned by generals Powell and **H. Norman Schwarzkopf, Jr.**, the American commander in chief of the operation. They had concluded that the United States had failed in Vietnam partly because it had increased its forces gradually rather than employing overwhelming numbers of troops and firepower at the beginning of the war. In addition, this Powell Doctrine affirmed that the military objectives must be clear and obtainable, public support for any war must be sustainable, and there must be a clear "exit strategy" or way and timetable to end the fighting and bring the troops home.

In January 1991 it became clear that Iraq would not leave Kuwait. Congress approved a resolution authorizing the use of force, and on January 17 the United States began bombing Iraq. When he announced the beginning of Operation Desert Storm, Bush spoke words first uttered by President Wilson during World War I. "We have before us," Bush declared, "the opportunity to forge for ourselves a new world order."

Saddam Hussein speaking to Iraqi troops around 1987 during the long war he fought with Iran from 1980–1988. Nearly one million soldiers died by the time both sides stopped fighting. Saddam soon turned his attention toward Kuwait, a small, rich neighbor that had loaned Iraq money to fight the war.

U.S. and allied planes bombed Iraq and Kuwait for five weeks before Schwarzkopf launched a bold ground assault on February 23. During the fighting the Pentagon applied another lesson from the Vietnam War: to control the flow of information, they severely restricted the access of reporters to the battlefield. After only four days of fighting, Iraqi forces fled from Kuwait and the United States accepted Saddam's call for a cease-fire. During the brief conflict 227 allied troops lost their lives while between 50,000 and 80,000 Iraqis died. The low number of American casualties became an unrealistic standard by which the public and news media would evaluate later wars.

Saddam Hussein remained in power in Iraq. General Powell and Secretary of Defense Cheney advised Bush not to invade Iraq to topple the dictator. They believed that a prolonged occupation of Iraq would be deadly to Americans troops and provide an opportunity for Iran to expand its influence. However, U.S. radio broadcasts urged Kurds in the north and Shi`ites in the south to rebel against Saddam, whose power base lay with Sunni Muslims in central Iraq. When the uprisings failed, Saddam's forces slaughtered thousands of Kurds and Shi`ites.

These terrible events inside Iraq received little press coverage at the time. The public celebrated the low-cost victory in Kuwait and the apparent invincibility of American arms. In the aftermath of this triumph, Bush's approval reached an unprecedented 90 percent in public opinion polls.

The Election of 1992

Bush's soaring public approval discouraged prominent Democrats from seeking their party's presidential nomination in 1992. Bill Clinton, the 46-year-old governor of Arkansas, eventually prevailed in a crowded primary field. Clinton called himself a New Democrat, someone who believed in government as a positive force but turned away from large Great Society-like programs. A reporter wrote that he "stressed economic mobility rather than wealth transfers, took a tough-minded line on crime, welfare dependency and international security issues, and called for a new ethic of personal responsibility to temper demands for entitlements." He was chair of the Democratic Leadership Council, a group of centrist office holders, mostly from the South and West, who wanted to reverse their party's decades-long history of presidential electoral defeats. He chose as his vice president another centrist Southerner, 44-year-old Tennessee senator **Al Gore**.

By 1992 Bush had grown increasingly unpopular. Two of his famous phrases, "read my lips, no new taxes," and "the new world order" became terms of derision. Conservatives resented his agreement with congressional Democrats to raise taxes to stem growing deficits. Saddam Hussein's continuation in power in Iraq—and evidence of what befell Iraqis who acted on Bush's call to overthrow the tyrant—dampened the initial enthusiasm over the war's outcome. A sharp economic downturn arising from the Savings and Loan crisis further eroded Bush's support. As S & Ls closed across the country, construction stopped on shopping malls, apartment complexes, and commercial buildings. Also, the so-called peace dividend of reduced military spending at the end of the Cold War initially hurt the economy. California, home to many defense-related businesses, was especially hard hit as contractors laid off well-paid engineers and skilled machinists. By February 1992, Bush's approval rating had fallen from 90 percent the previous March to 44 percent; 80 percent of the public said the country was on the wrong track.

President Bush's lethargic response to a major riot in Los Angeles in April 1992 further eroded his stature. The city erupted in flames following the acquittal of several police officers tried for the videotaped beating the year before of black motorist Rodney King. Thousands of African Americans and some Latinos went on a rampage to vent their anger at the verdict and long-term economic problems especially against Asian-owned retail stores in minority neighborhoods. Over 50 people died in six days of violence, and the city sustained over a half-billion dollars in damages before National Guard troops restored calm. Bush said nothing about these events for several days, then waited a week before visiting the ravaged city. His rapid response to aggression in Kuwait contrasted dramatically to his lassitude toward Los Angeles.

Bush defeated a renomination challenge from former Reagan speechwriter **Pat Buchanan**, who led a revolt of angry conservatives who called for a "culture war" against feminists, homosexuals, and illegal immigrants. Their harsh rhetoric did nothing to broaden the Republicans appeal. By the summer of 1992 Bush ran third in national polls behind Clinton and **Ross Perot**, an extremely wealthy and quirky Texan business executive who ran as an independent promising to reduce the federal budget deficit. Although Perot's campaign ignited fervent followers in the spring and early summer, his support faded as he became increasingly erratic. Claiming that assassins had threatened his family, he dropped out of the race in the summer, only to resume his campaign several weeks later.

Clinton declared he would "focus like a laser" on repairing the economy. He promised tax cuts for the middle class; reconstruction of the nation's bridges, roads, and airports; and an ambitious plan to provide health insurance for everyone in the country. His campaign aides taped the slogan "it's the economy, stupid" to the wall of their headquarters. Bush stressed his successes in international affairs. Referring to Clinton and Gore he said, "My dog Millie knows more about foreign policy than those two Bozos." Republican attacks on Clinton for avoiding the draft during the Vietnam War gained little traction. Bush also derided Gore for his commitment to the environment. In a Clinton and Gore administration, he warned, "we'll be up to our neck in owls and out of work for every American."

Clinton, appearing knowledgeable and empathetic to the needs of ordinary American, did well in three presidential debates. Bush, by contrast, appeared remote and inarticulate. Perot was folksy and funny but no longer seemed a serious candidate. On election day, Clinton prevailed with 43 percent of the vote. Bush's share was 37 percent, the lowest Republican total since 1912. Perot received 19 percent, the highest share for a third party since 1912. Clinton won 44.9 million popular and 370 electoral votes; Bush captured 37 million popular and 178 electoral votes; and Perot obtained 19 million popular but no electoral votes. Bush lacked Ronald Reagan's charm and sunny optimism. He lost the support of militant conservatives but found little favor with centrists or liberals. Voters admired Clinton's knowledge, curiosity, and empathy, and thought he deserved a chance to put in practice his New Democratic plans.

STUDY QUESTIONS FOR GEORGE H. W. BUSH AND THE END OF THE COLD WAR

1. How did the George H. W. Bush administration respond to the end of the Cold War? In what ways were its responses successful? Where did they fall short?
2. Why did the Bush administration lose public support in 1991 and 1992?
3. Why did Bill Clinton win the 1992 presidential election?

THE GOOD TIMES

The end of the Cold War and remarkable technological changes propelled the United States to unexpected prosperity. Between December 1991 and March 2000, the U.S. economy experienced the longest period of uninterrupted growth since the economic expansion of the 1960s. The end of communism in Europe hastened the pace of **globalization**, the knitting together of the world's economies through new information technology and the end of the artificial political barriers of the Cold War. Worldwide growth quickened. Asian and some Latin American economies boomed. They exported manufactured products to the United States, while the United States supplied the world with technical innovations, food, weapons, and cultural exports such as films and software.

The new prosperity was all the more welcome because few analysts expected it. A surge in worker productivity ignited the new growth, with the information technology industry leading the way. Workplaces led by young entrepreneurs became more informal. Millions of Americans invested heavily in the stock of new companies. Thousands of them grew rich in a stock-market boom that resembled the explosive and unsustainable growth of the 1920s. As had been the case in the 1920s, many Americans believed a new era of permanent abundance had begun. Prosperity did not flow evenly, however, and the income gap between the rich and the poor continued to grow, with the fault lines reflecting differences in education as well as in race and gender.

Innovation and New Technology

Many technological advances in the 1990s changed the way Americans conducted business, communicated with one another, and spent their leisure time. As personal computers became more affordable and more common in homes and offices across the country, innovations in computing created new, radically faster ways to send information. The introduction of the Internet into daily life marked the most significant technological development for commerce and society in years.

The Internet began when the **Defense Advanced Research Projects Agency** (DARPA), founded in 1958 in response to the Soviet launch of *Sputnik*, experimented with ways to link networks of computers. In the 1960s and 1970s government agencies, mostly related to the Department of Defense, along with university scientific researchers, began sharing information on their local computers over the ARPAnet. In 1991 Tim Berners-Lee, a British computer scientist, developed the World Wide Web, making the Internet more accessible. Businesses, organizations, governmental departments, and universities built Web sites that anyone could visit. Internet users could send messages via electronic mail addresses that delivered information instantaneously.

Businesses eagerly embraced the new advancements in information technology. The Internet sped up the exchange of data and ideas within companies and connected them to new, previously inaccessible global markets. The telecommunications improvements also enabled U.S. corporations to reduce labor costs by outsourcing parts of their business, particularly customer service divisions, to developing countries with a pool of English-speaking workers. For example, when calling the phone company or a credit card company with a question or complaint, callers from, say, Chicago would be routed to a call center in Manila or New Delhi. The globalized economy drew criticism from those concerned with keeping jobs in the United States. Manufacturing jobs continued their decades-long decline. "There's nothing made here anymore," a former employee of Eastman Kodak lamented as he looked at the empty buildings in

Rochester, New York, where thousands had previously made photographic film and equipment.

But there were also many winners in this new economy. The Internet provided an entirely new opportunity for e-commerce by Web sites that sold goods or services. Two of the most successful online businesses proved to be on-line bookstore Amazon.com, founded in 1994, and eBay, a sort of electronic garage sale founded in 1995. Pornographic sites also proliferated, challenging print publications like *Playboy* that had dominated the adult entertainment market since the 1950s.

By 2001, more than 60 million of the 107 million American households had a personal computer, and 51 million of them had Internet access. Millions of people spent their spare time reading Web sites and surfing the Internet. Some played games on their computers, often as simple as Solitaire. Others connected to the Internet to play more complex games as part of online communities that connected gamers at home (or work) or at Internet cafes throughout the world. Fans of the Internet celebrated its ability to reconnect people and provide new, electronic communities for those with like-minded interests. Critics lambasted it as another way that technology drew people away from traditional social spaces and increased the isolation of modern society.

During the 1990s the new information technology industries fueled a boom on Wall Street, where stock prices more than quadrupled as the Dow Jones Industrial Average index rose from a low of 2,588 points in January 1991 to a high of 11,722 points in January 2000. The decade saw rapid growth, low unemployment, low inflation, and an increase in investment in real estate. The new communications technology and global business market at the very least helped make companies more efficient and productive, even if not entirely responsible for shaping the economy as a whole.

In 1999 economic growth received a further boost from the repeal of parts of the Glass-Steagall Act of 1933, which had barred many banks from undertaking risky investments with depositors' money.. The law was enacted originally to prevent the kind of wild speculation that had contributed to the Great Depression. Congressional Republicans who passed the repeal argued that deregulation would encourage new forms of lending and investment without increasing risk. Their prediction worked—for a while.

Widespread enthusiasm for Internet-based companies promoted the dot-com boom of the mid- and late 1990s. Indeed, more people than ever invested in the stock market, as by 2001 over 50 percent of American families owned stock, up from 32 percent in 1989 and from only 13 percent in 1980. Investment clubs sprung up throughout the country to take part in what the *New York Times* called a new era of "shareholder democracy." One study indicated that 11 percent of the population, or roughly 20 million people, belonged to an investment club in the 1990s. Pensions also became linked to the stock market as a growing number of companies dropped traditional retirement plans that offered a predictable payout in favor of so-called 401(k) plans (named for a provision in the tax code) that promoted investments.

Day trading, or buying and selling on the financial market on the same day, flourished during the peak years of the dot-com boom—from 1997 to 2000. The NASDAQ index, which included many high-tech stocks and attracted much of the day trading,

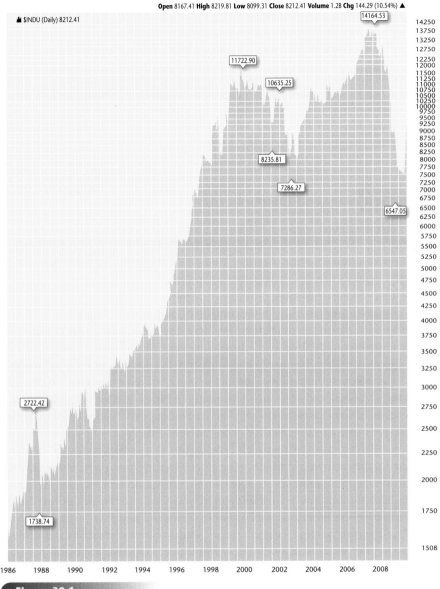

Open 8167.41 **High** 8219.81 **Low** 8099.31 **Close** 8212.41 **Volume** 1.2B **Chg** 144.29 (10.54%) ▲

▲ Figure 30.1

Stock market boom and bust The value of stocks on major exchanges surged between the 1980s and 2008. The pensions of a growing number of American workers depended on stock prices. The steep decline that began in 2008 affected spending patterns and undermined the sense of security in the future.

increased 86 percent in 1999 alone. Federal Reserve chairman **Alan Greenspan** warned against "irrational exuberance" toward the tech market in December 1996, but investment kept pouring in, stocks continued to rise, and tech stocks in particular reached unsustainable values. In 2000 the merger of relative newcomer America Online and media heavyweight Time Warner, with its huge assets of *Time, Sports Illustrated*, CNN, and Warner Bros. movie studio, illustrated the influence of the tech craze on the financial market. That said, extreme wealth still rested in the hands of a few; the richest 1 percent of stockholders owned roughly 50 percent of all stock, and less than one-third of the population invested more than $5,000. Moreover, the gap between the income of the CEO and that of the average worker widened drastically. The average CEO made nearly 110 times more than the typical worker, double the ratio from just 1989 and five times the difference from 1962. When the bubble burst in March 2000, many of the dot-coms went under. Entrepreneurs lost their quickly made fortunes, and many day traders on the NASDAQ also lost heavily.

Work, Science, and Discontent

Before the bubble burst, working at a dot-com seemed lucrative and fun. Salaries were good, but the great fortunes to be made from heady days of the dot-com craze came from the widely available stock options. Thousands of twentysomethings became instant millionaires when their companies' shares hit the markets in initial public offerings. Tens of thousands more thought, erroneously, that they, too, would strike it rich. Young executives ran many of the companies, and they frequently shunned standard office etiquette and organization. Like Steve Jobs at Apple, who flew a pirate flag outside the company headquarters, these entrepreneurs preferred a workplace that fostered creativity. They dismissed time cards and dress codes but expected workers to put in long hours. During their time at the office, however, employees could play ping-pong or pinball, work out in the recreation facilities, do their laundry, get a spa treatment, or, in some cases, take a nap. The search engine company Google, founded in 1996, even had an executive chef who provided free gourmet organic meals to employees. The rationale behind such benefits was that employees would be more productive if they enjoyed their time at the office. Google's motto was "Don't be evil."

The Internet revolution also enabled another adaptation for workers—telecommuting. Telecommuting allowed employees to work from their home through the Internet. It allowed employees to save on gasoline costs, and lowered companies' energy bills. Employees could put in eight hours of work without ever getting out of their pajamas. By 2001, more than four million people telecommuted, and many more ran their own Internet businesses.

Telecommuting also allowed some mothers to work part-time at home. Still, most women had to juggle outside employment and family responsibilities. By the beginning of the 1990s, barely one-in-four families fit the model of the traditional family, a breadwinner husband and homemaker wife. Many families struggled to find affordable, reliable child care. As noted previously, between a fourth and a half of families—varying by race, class, and education level—included children who lived with one parent or whose parents never married. The 1993 Family and Medical Leave Act, passed during the first Clinton administration, provided some relief, as it guaranteed up to 12 weeks of unpaid leave for workers needing time off. In 2002 women working full-time still earned only about 77.5 percent of what men did working in

Employees of a Silicon Valley start-up company around 2000. They combined technical talent, boundless energy, and an often chaotic lifestyle in an effort to create the next Microsoft or its equivalent.

similar positions. Few found a place in top positions at major corporations. In 1996 only 1 percent of the top five jobs at the 1,000 largest firms in the country were held by women. Still, they could find inspiration from the growth of women in national politics. Between 1991 and 2001, the number of women in the House of Representatives grew from 28 to 62, and the number in the Senate grew from 3 to 13.

During the 1990w breakthroughs occurred as well in science and biotechnology, sometimes with the help of new computer and communications technology. The single most significant advancement came in June 2000 when scientists working on the Human Genome Project successfully charted the complete structure of human DNA. This promised to open the way for advances in research on cancer and other diseases. It also raised ethical concerns among many outside the scientific community, who worried about issues such as cloning. Despite the potential of stem cell research to lead to medical cures for cancer and other diseases, opponents harbored moral qualms about it, because the cells most adaptable to study came from human embryos that would then be destroyed. DNA testing gained greater acceptance and usage in the criminal justice community, as it began to exonerate innocent citizens of crimes for which many had already been serving long sentences. The launch of the Hubble Space Telescope in 1990 represented a major advance in astronomy, and the military improved its Global Positioning System (GPS), which, like the Internet, would soon find its way into civilian life to change the way average Americans navigated in their automobiles.

The technological and scientific advances, however, left many Americans behind, and less educated young people were especially vulnerable to the fast pace of change. In 1991 Douglas Coupland's novel, *Generation X: Tales for an Accelerated Culture*, characterized young people born after the baby boom ended in 1964. Generation Xers, as they were often called, found their prospects bleak. Many were caught in "McJobs," shorthand for low-paying work in service industries like McDonald's. As one of the novel's characters put it, "We're sick of stupid labels, we're sick of being marginalized in lousy jobs, and we're tired of hearing about ourselves from others." Indeed, studies indicated that someone coming of age in the 1990s was likely to earn 12 percent less over the course of a career than someone who entered the workforce in the 1960s. Grunge and Hip Hop music became widely popular expressions of alienation among this generation. Grunge emerged from the punk and alternative rock music scene in the Pacific Northwest in the 1980s. The music had a heavy beat with lyrics that spoke of apathy, hopelessness, and a sense that the world was closing in.

Migrants

The promising economy of the 1990s attracted a large influx of immigrants from around the globe. Since the 1965 Immigration and Nationality Act, which ended the national quota system in favor of hemispheric caps and family reunification, immigrants began arriving in large numbers from Latin America, Africa, Asia, and the Middle East. A large number of Arabs, for example, settled in Dearborn, Michigan, not far from where Henry Ford had recruited Syrian and Lebanese factory workers to his auto plants early in the 20th century. Orange County in southern California became home to hundreds of thousands of Vietnamese and Laotian immigrants. By 2000, 10.4 percent of Americans were foreign born. The 1990s saw the sharpest jump in the nonwhite population of the 20th century. Over nine million legal immigrants arrived in the United States during the decade.

Between 1980 and 2000 nearly six million immigrants came from Asia. By 2002 13 million Asian Americans lived in the United States, or 4 percent of the U.S. population. Many Asian immigrants came from Southeast Asia, especially Vietnam, Cambodia, and Laos, after the United States offered them refuge following the Vietnam War. By the 1990s about one million people with Vietnamese roots lived in the United States. In the last two decades of the 20th century another eight million people came from Mexico, Central America, the Caribbean, and South America.

California attracted the largest proportion of the new arrivals; 27 percent of its population was foreign born by 2000. Over 50 percent of its population was Asian, Hispanic, or African American. Because of this influx the total population grew by 1.5 million during the second half of the 1990s—even though nearly one million, primarily white, residents moved out at the same time. Aside from California, new immigrants resided mostly in five other states: New York, Florida, Texas, New Jersey, and Illinois. Overall, the foreign born of the U.S. population was the highest since 1900.

Immigrants worked in both unskilled service positions and well-paying jobs in engineering, computers, medicine, and education. In 1995, 23 percent of science

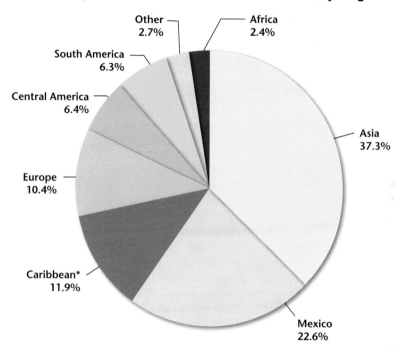

Immigrants to the United States, 1981–1990, by Origin

Other 2.7%
Africa 2.4%
South America 6.3%
Central America 6.4%
Asia 37.3%
Europe 10.4%
Caribbean* 11.9%
Mexico 22.6%

*Antigua-Barbuda, the Bahamas, Barbados, Cuba, Dominica, Dominican Republic, Grenada, Haiti, Jamaica, St. Kitts and Nevis, St. Lucia, St. Vincent and Grenadines, and Trinidad and Tobago.

▲ **Figure 30.2**

The developing world comes to America Since the 1980s, around three-quarters of immigrants to the United States came from Mexico, other parts of Latin America, and the Caribbean, or from East Asia. This represented a dramatic change from earlier periods of mass migration, such as during the late 19th century through 1924.

and engineering PhDs and 12 percent of all other PhD holders living in the United States were foreign born. Like earlier periods of sustained immigration, fierce debates emerged about how to deal with the immigration's consequences. Many Americans wondered how this new, global immigration would influence the social, cultural, economic, and political complexion of the country. Anti-immigration supporters charged that immigrants took jobs away from hard-working Americans. They generalized and cast all immigrants, especially Latinos, as illegals who swindled the American taxpayer by abusing public services. During his run for the presidency in 1992 Pat Buchanan cried, "Our country is undergoing the greatest invasion in its history, a migration of millions of 'illegal' or 'undocumented' aliens yearly from Mexico . . . A nation that cannot control its own borders can scarcely call itself a state any longer." In 1994, 60 percent of California voters favored Proposition 187, a ballot measure that planned to cut off access to public education and health care to undocumented immigrants. Supporters of immigrants, however, recoiled at the harsh nativist attacks. Some churches,

GLOBAL PASSAGE

America's Global Cities

The arrival of so many nonwhite immigrants during the final decades of the 20th century had its greatest impact on a few cities, most notably Los Angeles, New York City, and Miami. Over 20 percent of the people who immigrated in 1998, for example, intended to live in either Los Angeles or New York. Chicago; Orange County, California; Houston; and Atlanta were also especially attractive to new immigrants. They headed to these urban areas to reunite with their family sponsors, as required by Immigration and Naturalization Service (INS) rules, and to find support and security within the established ethnic communities there.

The growing Latino population throughout the United States sparked urban multiculturalism. Los Angeles had a Mexican population second in the world only to Mexico City, and a Salvadorian population at least as large as that of San Salvador. New York City had as many Puerto Ricans (American citizens at birth) and Dominicans as lived in their respective capitals. Miami had had an enormous Cuban American population in its "Little Havana" since exiles fled Cuba after Fidel Castro's rise to power in 1959. As an example of the shifting composition of the United States, 7 of its 10 largest cities had more Hispanics than African Americans in the late 1990s. In 1998, Los Angeles County's Latino population was over one million larger than its non-Hispanic white population, and comprised almost half of the total population.

The large Hispanic population in Los Angeles led efforts to revive inner city neighborhoods. In New York a large influx of Dominicans in the 1980s and Mexicans in the 1990s fostered increased interaction both with other Hispanic ethnicities and

providing sanctuary to undocumented immigrants, dared federal enforcement agents to enter and arrest poor families with children.

Both new immigrants and native-born citizens continued the earlier geographic trend of moving away from the Northeast and Midwest to the Sunbelt. While immigrants continued to move into cities, far more Americans left the cities for the suburbs.

The West grew the fastest: 6 of the 10 largest cities in 1990 were west of the Mississippi River. The 2000 census revealed that Nevada, Arizona, Colorado, Utah, and Idaho were the fastest growing states. The warm climate, affordable land, and low taxes of much of the West continued to draw people away from the heavily industrialized Rustbelt and rural areas of the heartland. Silicon Valley offered jobs for well-educated engineers and scientists and ambitious entrepreneurs. New retirees found the region especially hospitable. A larger population also meant greater political power in the

with the city's African American communities. One sympathetic writer described the result as "a rich, constantly evolving *sabor tropical* in food, music, fashion and language—always freshly spiced by the latest arrivals from Latin America."

In New York, Los Angeles, and elsewhere immigrants from other parts of the world, notably the Middle East, Africa, and Asia, contributed to a new, diverse culture. Children born in every country in the world attended New York City public schools. In Houston, Korean, Thai, Vietnamese, and Chinese businesses leased mall space and put up bilingual and trilingual roadside signs. Other immigrants there created a huge grocery store that stocked food and newspapers from around the world. They also set up a market in the parking lot in which consumers bartered in five different languages. Ethnic restaurants continued to pop up on street corners in these cities and their metropolitan areas. Salsa replaced ketchup as the most popular condiment sold in the United States.

Even more so than other cities with large immigrant populations, New York City, Los Angeles, and Miami served as true "global cities" for their significant roles as capitals of international finance, commerce, trade, and artistic culture. New York and Los Angeles are, respectively, the second and third largest metropolitan economies in the world, behind only Tokyo. Miami became the business capital for the Caribbean and Latin America. These cities, as international tourist destinations, represented the country's diversified and rapidly changing demographics at the beginning of the 21st century.

• How did increased rates of immigration transform many American cities?

• What was the specific impact of Hispanic immigration on several cities?

House of Representatives for the West and the Sunbelt states. California became even more influential, as it gained seven seats in the House of Representatives after the 1992 election.

STUDY QUESTIONS FOR THE GOOD TIMES

1. Why did the U.S. economy expand in the 1990s?
2. Who benefitted and who was left behind in the economic expansion of the 1990s?
3. In what ways did international migration and immigration alter life in the United States in the 1990s?

BILL CLINTON AND THE NEW DEMOCRATS

Bill Clinton's eight-year presidency from 1993 through 2001 raised enormous hopes of meeting domestic needs unfilled for decades. Some of these were realized, but many went unmet. As a New Democrat, Clinton tried to steer a middle course between the conservatism of the Reagan era and the liberalism of the Great Society. He ardently supported globalization. Like most economists, business executives, and financiers of the time the president expected globalization to increase wealth as it sped the flow of information and goods.

Clinton was a highly accomplished politician who remained popular for much of his term. Intelligent, curious, and articulate, he sought advice widely. He was also impulsive, and his presidency nearly ended in disgrace because of a sexual scandal. Although many Americans admired Clinton's commitment to solving problems of ordinary people, a sizeable share of the population hated him. He became a focal point of clashes between conservatives, many of whom defended traditional religious values, and liberals, who liked his embrace of new economic and cultural trends. Some conservatives considered his presidency illegitimate for somehow interrupting the Reagan legacy, and they tried to drive him from office.

An Awkward Start

Clinton outlined a bold agenda in his inaugural address: "We must do what no generation has had to do before. We must invest more in our own people, in their jobs, in their future, and at the same time cut our massive debt." But circumstances interrupted his plans.

Clinton scaled back plans to permit gays and lesbians to serve openly in the military in the face of stiff opposition from the Joint Chiefs of Staff. Instead, Clinton fashioned a compromise in which the military would not inquire about its members' sexual preferences and gays and lesbians could serve if they did not reveal their sexual identity. This policy, labeled "Don't Ask, Don't Tell," disappointed advocates for full equality between gays and straights and offended conservatives who opposed any relaxation on restrictions of gays serving in the military.

Robert Rubin, the chairman of the president's National Economic Council and a successful Wall Street bond trader, persuaded Clinton to attack the budget deficit of $300 billion. Once Wall Street believed the government was going to borrow less in the future, Rubin argued, interest rates would fall, and the economy would receive the boost it needed. In February 1993 Clinton presented Congress a program of tax increases and spending cuts to reduce the federal budget deficit. "Over the long run," he said, "this will bring us a higher rate of economic growth, improved productivity, more high-quality jobs, and an improved economic competitive position in the world."

Congress responded by defeating Clinton's program to invest in infrastructure and then began a four-month debate on the tax increases and spending cuts. Georgia representative **Newt Gingrich**, the Republican House minority whip and a rising star among conservatives, insisted that Clinton's tax increases would "lead to recession . . . and will actually increase the deficit." Democrats stood by the plan, which passed the House in August by the narrowest margin of 218 to 216. In the Senate, Vice President Al Gore cast the deciding vote to break a 50-50 tie in favor of the plan. No Republicans voted for the plan in either house. The dire predictions of economic calamity made by the law's mostly Republican opponents proved to be completely wrong. With passage of the economic plan the federal budget deficit began a sharp decline while business and employment grew.

After the passage of his economic plan Clinton's public standing improved. He persuaded enough Democrats to join Republicans in voting to approve the **North American Free Trade Agreement** (NAFTA) at the close of 1993. President George H. W. Bush had negotiated this free-trade pact with Canada and Mexico, the country's two largest trading partners, but Congress had not voted on it before he left office. NAFTA was popular with business leaders, and nearly all conventional economists believed it, like any agreement reducing barriers to trade, would lift living standards. Organized labor and its allies in the Democratic Party strongly opposed it, however; they feared that it would accelerate the loss of jobs to lower waged plants in Mexico. Environmentalists also opposed NAFTA because of Mexico's poor record of environmental protection.

Clinton advocated free trade and promoted the benefits of globalization throughout his eight years in the White House. By the late 1990s, however, a worldwide movement arose against globalization. Critics charged that it made the rich richer and the poor poorer, while destroying traditional cultures. Tens of thousands of antiglobalization demonstrators came to Seattle in December 1999 to oppose Clinton's support for the World Trade Organization that had been created in 1995 to supervise world trade.

In September 1993, in the midst of the debate over NAFTA, Clinton returned to the subject of reforming the nation's health care system. He delivered a well-received speech favoring a continuation of the current system of private health insurance, but expanding coverage to most Americans. Private employers would be mandated to provide coverage for their workers while other government programs would insure the unemployed. As a sign of the importance he assigned to this reform, Clinton asked his wife, First Lady Hillary Rodham Clinton, to develop and steer the proposal through Congress.

Although nearly every American had complaints about the costs and quality of health care, the reform plan encountered stiff opposition in Congress and among the public. The health insurance industry and some medical groups strongly opposed Clinton's proposals for mandating types of coverage and controlling costs. Their trade group, the Health Insurance Association of America, spent $30 million on a series of clever television ads featuring actors portraying Harry and Louise, a fictional middle-aged, middle-class couple, sitting at their kitchen table expressing bewilderment at the complexities of the new plan and worrying that their relationship with their doctors would be compromised by federal bureaucrats. Speaking to the electronic audience, the couple lamented, "they choose, we lose."

In August and September 1994 the Senate debated but failed to reach a consensus in favor of any of several alternative health-reform measures. Many Americans who already had medical insurance feared that extending coverage to the uninsured would come at their expense. These doubts, and others cultivated by the insurance industry's disinformation campaign, effectively killed the Clinton proposal. In the wake of this failure many employers tried to control rapidly rising medical costs by forcing workers to enroll in health maintenance organizations, or HMOs. HMOs, often run by large insurers, earned big profits by imposing many of the restrictions on treatment and coverage that the antireform campaign had warned would come with federal oversight. Ironically, Congress's failure to pass some form of health insurance program hurt everyone. Those with health insurance experienced a decline in the quality of their coverage as well as increased costs. Millions of other American remained uninsured.

The defeat of health reform made Republicans jubilant at the prospect of major gains in the November election. Several hundred Republican candidates, both incumbents and challengers, stood on the steps of the Capitol and signed their names to the **Contract with America**, a document conceived by Representative Newt Gingrich that promised to make Congress more accountable, balance the federal budget, reverse the tax increases passed in 1993, and reduce the capital gains tax. On election day, many Democrats who voted for Clinton in 1992 stayed home; Republicans captured both houses of Congress for the first time in 40 years. They also governed 9 of the 10 most populous states.

Clinton's Recovery

The Republican Congress came to power in January 1995 convinced they could make Clinton irrelevant and recapture the White House in 1996. Newt Gingrich, the new Speaker of the House, was the most prominent political figure in the early months of 1995. He denounced Clinton and promoted the agenda offered in the Contract with America. To the speaker's amazement, Clinton began a slow recovery. The president's fortunes began to rise in April after **Timothy McVeigh** and **Terry Nichols**, two angry army veterans who belonged to antigovernment white supremacist militia groups,

Newt Gingrich, the Republican firebrand from Georgia, proclaims his "Contract with America." The campaign document helped Republicans capture control of the House of Representatives in November 1994.

bombed the Federal Building in Oklahoma City. The blast killed 169 people, including federal workers, visitors, and children at a day care facility. At a memorial service Clinton spoke movingly of the victims, and he asked Americans to reflect on whether the strident antigovernment rhetoric of conservative radio talk show hosts—along with some members of Congress—had poisoned political conversation and legitimized violence.

Clinton recovered his confidence and his popularity after the Oklahoma City bombing. He adapted a strategy of "triangulation" in which he navigated positions between conservative Republicans and liberal Democrats in Congress. In the fall of 1995 Gingrich guessed that he could undermine public confidence in Clinton—as congressional Democrats had with Bush—by refusing to compromise with the White House on adoption of the federal budget. As a result of the House's failure to approve a new budget, the government shut down twice, first in November and then in December. But instead of focusing public resentment against the president, the shutdown backfired against Gingrich and other Republicans whose demeanor came across as petty and who seemed indifferent to the safety of the nation.

During 1996 Clinton undercut more of the Republicans' agenda. In his State of the Union message he said "the era of big government is over." He proposed a federal budget that would be in balance within a year and register a surplus in 1998. He compromised with Republicans on one of their perennial complaints, the cost and provisions of welfare. The Welfare Reform bill signed in July 1996 limited recipients to two years of lifetime cash benefits and required them to look for work while on assistance. Some of Clinton's liberal supporters considered the bill punitive and feared it would drive millions into grinding poverty. But the booming economy and the expansion of low-skilled service jobs in the late 1990s softened the blow. Public assistance rolls fell by 25 percent by 2001 and most welfare recipients did find jobs.

The Clinton administration continued federal efforts to discourage tobacco use. The president joined with those who called nicotine an addictive drug and in 1996 approved regulations that labeled cigarettes as "drug delivery devices." Seeking to recover the health costs of treating sick smokers, nearly every state attorney general joined in a law suit against the tobacco industry. In 1998 the industry reached a settlement that provided payments of several hundred billion dollars to be paid over 30 years. In 1999 the U.S. Department of Justice brought a criminal suit against cigarette manufacturers for selling a dangerous product. By the end of the decade major cigarette companies acknowledged what the public health community and most Americans had long recognized—cigarettes were a major cause of lung cancer and other diseases. In a massive change in public behavior, smoking rates, which hovered around 50 percent in the 1960s, fell to around 20 percent in the early 21st century.

Clinton easily won reelection in 1996. He seemed far more in touch with the concerns of suburban families, the largest voting bloc, than either of his rivals, Republican senator **Bob Dole** and independent candidate Ross Perot. Dole, a 73-year-old World War II veteran, was popular with the press for his endless stream of acerbic remarks, but voters considered him a figure of an earlier era. Perot's signature issue of reducing the federal budget deficit faded after Clinton proposed a realistic balanced budget. Clinton won 47.4 million votes, 49.2 percent of the total. He captured 379 electoral votes. Dole received 39.1 million votes, 40.7 percent, of those cast, and 159 electoral votes. Perot came in a distant third, with 8.08 million votes, or 8.4 percent.

Clinton's Second Term

Bitter partisan divisions continued during Clinton's second term. Despite Clinton's reelection Republicans retained control of Congress after 1996, and they spent much of 1997 investigating the president's fundraising. The public, enjoying the economic good times, took little notice of these hearings. Then in January 1998 news of Clinton's sexual involvement with Monica Lewinsky, a 21-year-old White House intern when the liaison began in 1995, came to dominate the headlines for a year, especially on cable television, which became a major source of news and entertainment around this time. Unrestrained by standards of accuracy that characterized most print journalism, cable news broadcasts and commentators treated politics like a contact sport and sensationalized personal scandals.

Previously the domain of trashy supermarket tabloids like the *National Enquirer*, the hair styles, marriages, divorces, sexual prowess, and crimes of the famous now became a focus of these mass audience shows. Details hardly mattered, whether it was the trial in 1995–1996 of former football star O. J. Simpson for the alleged murder of his ex-wife or the impeachment of President Clinton in 1998–1999 for lying about an affair with a young intern.

Clinton, who had a reputation for womanizing and extramarital sex going back to his days as Arkansas governor, made an easy target for what his staff called "bimbo eruptions." His relationship with Lewinsky came to light through the investigations of **Kenneth Starr**, a special prosecutor authorized by the Justice Department in 1994 to look into Bill and Hillary Clinton's involvement in a minor real estate transaction in Arkansas, known as Whitewater, 15 years earlier. After several years of probing Starr found no illegalities in the Clintons' business deals, but he was convinced they were lying about something. As Starr prepared to close his inquiries in 1998, lawyers for **Paula Jones**, a woman who accused Clinton of sexual harassment when he was governor, learned that the president had had an affair with Lewinsky. Jones' lawyers, who had ties to conservative fund-raisers, were convinced that Clinton lied to them when he denied having had sex with Lewinsky. They told Starr about the affair. Even though this transgression had nothing to do with the Whitewater investigation, Starr forced Lewinsky to divulge details of her relationship with Clinton. News quickly spread about the liaison and reporters demanded that the president tell what he knew. During a news conference Clinton wagged his finger at a questioner and said "I did not have sexual relations with that woman, Monica Lewinsky." The denial fell flat as additional details emerged that Clinton and Lewinsky had engaged in sexual play on several occasions in 1995 and 1996.

In August, after Starr forced Clinton to testify under oath, the prosecutor decided he had lied about the affair. In September, Starr sent Congress a 500-page report detailing Clinton's sexual misconduct, but presented nothing about any official wrongdoing. Republicans prepared to impeach the president, convinced he would either resign or be removed from office by votes in the House and Senate.

Once again, Gingrich and House Republicans badly misread public opinion. Clinton's behavior disappointed ordinary Americans who saw it as childish and degrading. But they were even angrier at Special Prosecutor Starr and Gingrich for making a public spectacle out of what essentially were smutty details of a private affair. During the fall of 1998, Clinton's positive approval rating among the public actually improved, to 60 percent. Democrats also gained seats in the November midterm congressional election. Stunned by these developments, Gingrich belatedly admitted that he, too, had conducted an affair with a young, female staff member and resigned from Congress.

Instead of ending the crisis, Clinton's Republican opponents renewed their effort to drive him from office. In December the House voted along party lines to impeach Clinton, making him only the second president to be impeached, as Nixon had resigned before a vote was taken. A Senate trial opened in January 1999. By then two-thirds of the public told pollsters they did not want Clinton removed from office. In February, the Senate acquitted Clinton, tacitly acknowledging how unpopular the impeachment effort had become.

STUDY QUESTIONS FOR BILL CLINTON AND THE NEW DEMOCRATS

1. What were the characteristics of the "New Democrats?"
2. How did President Clinton regain popularity after the Republicans won the 1994 Congressional elections?
3. Why did the House of Representatives impeach President Clinton? Why did the Senate acquit him?

A POST-COLD WAR FOREIGN POLICY

The United States stood as the world's only superpower after the Cold War. Secretary of State **Madeleine Albright** said in 1998 that the United States was the "indispensable nation" because it alone had to power to reduce world conflicts. The Clinton administration embraced knitting together the world's economy through globalization. It engaged in several humanitarian interventions, some of which involved the use of military force, and it sought to mediate some ancient regional disputes. Clinton formed a partnership with Russian president Boris Yeltsin to manage Russia's integration into the post-Cold War world. At the end of 1990s, the United States became more alert to the danger posed by Al Qaeda and Islamic terrorism.

Intervention and Mediation

In December 1992 the defeated Bush administration sent 28,000 U.S. troops to the East African country of Somalia to distribute food to millions who faced starvation in the face of a civil war. Clinton continued this operation since television pictures of American soldiers preventing gangs controlled by warlords from stealing relief supplies made the intervention popular. In May 1993 the United Nations took over the relief mission, and the United States was able to reduce its force to 4,000 in June. In October the remaining U.S. forces tried to help UN troops arrest one of the most powerful warlords. Eighteen U.S. Army Rangers lost their lives in a bloody firefight in which over 900 Somali fighters were also killed. Television showed Somalis dragging the corpse of one of the Americans through the streets. These graphic images—not sanitized as pictures from the Gulf War were—turned American opinion against the Somalia relief effort, and Clinton withdrew the remaining forces. The incident became the basis for a best-selling book and popular film, *Black Hawk Down*.

Public resistance to additional commitments in Africa kept the Clinton administration from intervening to stop genocide in the East Africa country of Rwanda in 1994. In a brief 100 days that spring the Hutu majority murdered 700,000 minority Tutsis. The U.S. and European governments declined urgent requests from a few hundred UN observers to send forces to stop the carnage. Six years later Clinton stopped briefly in Rwanda and apologized for Western inaction during the catastrophe of 1994.

The United States intervened most forcefully in the former Yugoslavia. During the 1992 election campaign Clinton criticized the Bush administration for doing little to stop Serbs in the former Yugoslav republic of Bosnia from their brutal ethnic cleansing of their Muslim neighbors. Once in office, however, Clinton concluded that the divisions between the Orthodox Christian Serbs, Roman Catholic Croats, and Muslim Bosnians were so deep and ancient that outside intervention could not contain them. The fighting got worse in the summer of 1995 when Serb forces massacred 4,000 Muslim men and boys in the village of Srebrenica. Serbs also raped thousands of Muslim women and girls.

The United States, Britain, and France responded by bombing Serb armaments and supplies. Yugoslav president **Slobodan Milosevic**, who promoted ethnic violence as a way to build support among Serbs, now feared that he might be driven from power, and he consented to attend a peace conference at Wright Patterson Air Force base in Dayton, Ohio. In November the warring sides agreed to share power in an independent state of Bosnia. The United States contributed 2,000 troops to a 6,000-member International Implementation Force (IFOR) to maintain peace and security in Bosnia.

In 1999 the United States and its NATO allies again used force against Yugoslavia to compel it to withdraw its troops from the province of Kosovo. Muslims made up 90 percent of Kosovo's population, and they suffered gross discrimination at the hands of the small Serb minority. A 60,000-member peacekeeping force from the United States and European countries entered Kosovo to supervise the refugees' return and maintain the peace.

The Clinton administration also came poignantly close to successfully mediating the half- century-long conflict between Israelis and Palestinians. In September 1993 Clinton brought Israeli prime minister **Yitzhak Rabin** and Palestine Liberation Organization chairman **Yasser Arafat** together to sign a peace agreement on the White House lawn. The PLO recognized Israel in exchange for a withdrawal of Israeli forces from the Gaza Strip and a large part of the West Bank over the next five years. Arafat would control the evacuated territory for a new Palestine National Authority. The two sides promised to reach a final peace within five years.

Hope for a settlement quickly faded. A Jewish extremist opposed to any peace with the PLO murdered Rabin in 1995. Israelis elected a nationalist government, reluctant to continue peace efforts with Arafat. When the more moderate Israeli Labor Party returned to power in 1999, Clinton hosted a meeting between Israeli Prime Minister Ehud Barak and Chairman Arafat in July 2000, but the sides could not agree on what land Israel would turn over to the PLO. Two months later a Palestinian uprising erupted across the West Bank against Israeli rule. Hundreds of Palestinians and dozens of Israelis were killed in the fighting. Clinton's diplomatic efforts failed, and the conflict became bloodier and a resolution seemed farther away.

International Terrorism

Fear of international terrorism sponsored by Islamic radicals was a significant but not a preeminent concern of American policy makers in the 1990s. On February 26, 1993, a little more than a month after Bill Clinton became president, several supporters of **Osama bin Laden**, the Muslim extremist leader of Al Qaeda whom the Reagan administration had supported when he fought the Soviets in Afghanistan during the 1980s, drove an explosives-laden Ryder rental truck into the parking garage of the World Trade Center in lower Manhattan. Although the bomb failed to bring down the Twin Towers as the plotters hoped, the blast killed six people and injured over 1,000.

In 1996 bin Laden moved his headquarters from Sudan to Afghanistan, where he continued to plan attacks. In 1998 he declared it was the duty of every Muslim to kill Americans anywhere in the world. His anger against the United States had been kindled by the presence of American troops in his homeland of Saudi Arabia during and after the Gulf War of 1991, U.S. support for Israel, and a sense that the United States and the West expressed contempt for Muslim civilization.

In August 1998 Al Qaeda teams detonated truck bombs outside the U.S. embassies in Nairobi, Kenya, and Dar es Salaam, Tanzania; 12 Americans and more than 200 embassy workers and visitors of other nationalities were killed, and more than 5,000

Forensic experts uncover the remains of thousands of Bosnian Muslims killed in ethnic slaughter during the 1990s.

people were injured. Clinton ordered air strikes against bin Laden's Afghanistan head-quarters and a Sudanese factory the CIA believed was producing nerve gas. The attacks killed dozens but did not disrupt Al Qaeda. Clinton's opponents suspected that he had ordered the air strikes to distract public attention from the Lewinsky scandal. The public remained far more interested in the Lewinsky affair and the generally good economic times than the whereabouts of Osama bin Laden. In October 2000, in the midst of the presidential election campaign, Al Qaeda commandos blew a hole in the hull of the navy destroyer *Cole* in a harbor off the coast of Yemen and killed 17 sailors. Clinton pressured the Taliban-led government of Afghanistan to expel bin Laden, but Afghanistan continued to provide him sanctuary.

STUDY QUESTIONS FOR A POST-COLD WAR FOREIGN POLICY

1. What international objectives did the Clinton administration pursue?
2. Where did the Clinton administration's humanitarian interventions, peace initiatives, and antiterrorism efforts succeed? Where did they fail?

THE DISPUTED ELECTION OF 2000

The 21st century began with one of the most disputed presidential contests in U.S. history. The prosperity and peace of the Clinton years favored the prospects of Democratic vice president Al Gore. But the good times also made American voters believe that politics was not that important in their daily lives. Some Democrats and independents wanted to punish Clinton for his misconduct with Monica Lewinsky by voting for the Republican candidate, Texas governor **George W. Bush**, the son of President George H. W. Bush. Others, who believed that Gore and Bush were nearly identical centrists, voted for consumer activist **Ralph Nader**. The November election ended with Gore receiving 500,000 more popular votes than Bush, but the virtually tied vote in Florida created an electoral stalemate. On December 12, 2000, the Supreme Court finally decided Florida's votes for Bush in a highly controversial 5-to-4 decision.

Bush Versus Gore

Having served as vice president for eight years and with no ties to the Lewinsky scandal, Al Gore easily secured the Democratic presidential nomination in 2000. The Republican candidate, George W. Bush, also locked up his party's nomination by winning a string of primaries. Bush, the son of President George H. W. Bush and the governor of Texas since 1995, defeated his chief rival, John McCain, by spreading rumors about McCain's mental health and about his fathering an illegitimate black child during the primary season.

Both Gore and Bush portrayed themselves as moderates. Consumer advocate Ralph Nader and Republican dissident Pat Buchanan also ran as presidential candidates.

Nader railed against corporate greed and supported progressive causes as the nominee for the Green Party. Buchanan ran on an anti-immigrant, anti-interventionist platform for the Reform Party. Although Gore had worked closely with Clinton and shared most of his policy views, the vice president felt personally betrayed by Clinton's behavior in the Lewinsky affair. During the fall campaign he kept Clinton at arm's length. Gore's campaign also failed to stress how the administration's policies had promoted both economic growth and debt reduction. He even sidestepped his long commitment to environmental protection.

Although Bush had degrees from both Yale and Harvard universities, the Republican candidate stressed his ties to Texas along with a down home, plainspoken style. To most Americans Bush came across as an average Joe to whom they could relate. He promised tax cuts, regulatory reform, and fewer foreign commitments. Clinton and Gore, he charged, had foolishly engaged in "nation building," the effort to construct functioning societies in places such as Haiti, Somalia, and Yugoslavia. Neither Gore nor Bush inspired much enthusiasm.

The Election in Florida and a Supreme Court Decision

The election's outcome hinged on Florida. On election night, TV networks first declared Gore the winner; then retracted that claim and awarded the state to Bush; and finally, in the early hours of Wednesday, November 8, said it was "too close to call." For the next 36 days, the state remained hotly contested. Officials recounted votes in select counties and debated how to resolve ballots that were misprinted, mangled by voting machines, or mailed in after the election. Besides raising the obvious question of who actually won, the Florida debacle shed light on the shoddy practices and procedures of how states counted votes.

The initial tally had given Bush the state by fewer than 800 votes out of almost 6 million cast. More than 3,000 voters in heavily Democratic Palm Beach County accidentally marked ballots for Pat Buchanan instead of Gore, whom they intended to vote for, because of difficulty in reading a confusing "butterfly" ballot that jumbled names together. Because of faulty instruction in some precincts, many people voted twice, or "overvoted," which negated their ballot. In other counties that used punch-card systems, thousands of ballots ended up only partial punched; the result was hanging or dimpled "chads" (quickly a buzzword in the media) and "undervotes" that went unrecorded. Approximately 175,000 votes fell into the category of an overvote or undervote. In addition to these problems more than 20,000 African Americans, more likely to vote for Gore, found themselves falsely named on an ex-felon list apparently prepared by Republican officials that banned them from voting.

Shortly after election day a machine recount and tally of late overseas ballots cut Bush's lead. Angry Republican and Democratic demonstrators hurled insults at each other outside Florida court houses. The most violent outburst occurred in Miami, where a crowd of several hundred Republican congressional staff members, their expenses paid by party officials, pushed their way into election headquarters shouting and disrupting election officials' recount. This "Brooks Brothers riot," so called because of the upscale clothing worn by the activists, terrified poll workers, who stopped their recount. Florida's governor, Jeb Bush, the Republican candidate's brother, and other Republican officials in the state government, tried to stop any recount. The Democrats requested manual recounts in four largely Democratic counties whose ballots seemed in question and suggested that Florida law would not allow a statewide recount. Republicans called this an arbitrary and blatantly partisan move.

On November 21 the Florida Supreme Court ruled in favor of Gore. It allowed the four-county recount to continue until November 26 and told election officials that they should try to determine the intention of voters in deciding how to count ballots with "dimpled" or "hanging chads." In other words, if the voter had attempted to punch the card but the device failed to completely penetrate the card, it could be counted as a vote. Fearful that the recount would favor Gore, irate Republicans appealed to the U.S. Supreme Court to halt the Florida recount.

The High Court surprised most observers by intervening in the state process. It first temporarily halted the recount. Then, on December 12, it ruled in *Bush v. Gore* that the recount stop entirely, effectively giving Florida's electoral votes, and hence the election, to Bush. The five more conservative justices formed the majority and the four liberals dissented. The majority opinion stated that a partial recount of Florida's votes—as requested by Gore—violated the rights of voters in counties where no recount took place. How an accurate count deprived anyone of their rights seemed an odd decision. But even if this were true, startled Democrats noted, the problem could be remedied easily by ordering a statewide recount. But rather than doing so, the High

TIMELINE 1988–2001

1988

November Vice President George H. W. Bush defeats Michael Dukakis for the presidency. His victory reflects a continuation of Republican rule

December Mikhail Gorbachev addresses the United Nations in New York; signaling a thaw in the Cold War, he meets President Ronald Reagan and President-elect Bush

1989

June Chinese troops crush pro-democracy demonstrators in Tiananmen Square, Beijing

June Mikhail Gorbachev declares that Eastern European communist nations are free to choose their own form of government without fear of Soviet intervention; the announcement hastens

the peaceful end of communist rule

November Fall of the Berlin Wall marks the end of the Cold War

December The United States invades and occupies Panama, a sign of U.S. dominance in international affairs

1990

June David Souter is confirmed as Justice of the Supreme Court

July Congress passes the Americans with Disabilities Act, recognizing the right of many people previously excluded from full participation in society

August Iraq invades and occupies Kuwait

1991

January–March The United States leads a UN coalition in the Gulf

War to force Iraq out of Kuwait

October Clarence Thomas is confirmed as Justice of the Supreme Court; his confirmation hearings spark anger among many women and their supporters, who are convinced he engaged in sexual harassment during the 1980s

1992

April Riots take place in Los Angeles

November Bill Clinton defeats George H. W. Bush and H. Ross Perot to win the presidency, a triumph for New Democrats

1993

February Al Qaeda operatives bomb New York's World Trade Center

June Ruth Bader Ginsberg is confirmed as Justice of the Supreme Court

September Raising unfulfilled hopes for the end of a century-long conflict, President Clinton hosts White House signing ceremony of a peace agreement between Israel and the Palestine Liberation Organization

September Congress ratifies the North American Free Trade Agreement

1994

June Stephen Breyer is confirmed as Justice of the Supreme Court

September United States forces oust military government in Haiti; President Jean Bertrand Aristide is restored to power

September Congress fails to enact health care reform

Dueling Democrats and Republicans rally in an effort to influence the counting of disputed ballots in the Florida presidential election, November and December, 2000.

Court simply ordered that the counting cease. Florida's Republican Secretary of State then certified Bush's victory.

Republicans and many in the middle of the political spectrum applauded the Court for resolving the dispute and deciding the winner. But Justice **John Paul Stevens**, one of the four dissenters, lamented that the real loser of the election was "the Nation's confidence in the judge as an impartial guardian of the rule of law." Gore conceded the election to Bush instead of fighting in the courts any longer. Many Democrats were bitter and believed the election had been stolen by the Supreme Court. Bush received Florida's votes for a 271 to 266 electoral vote victory (Bush: 50.4 million

November Republicans win control of House and Senate and severely constrain Bill Clinton's presidency

November California adopts Proposition 187, denying state benefits to undocumented foreign residents

1995

April Domestic terrorists bomb federal building in Oklahoma City

July Serb forces massacre 4,000 Muslims in Srebrenica, Bosnia, and provoke a NATO bombing campaign against Serbia

July–August U.S., British, and French planes bomb Serb forces

November Dayton peace accords for Bosnia are signed

November–December Congressional Republicans force

shutdown of federal government

1996

July Congress enacts welfare reform

November Bill Clinton is reelected president over Bob Dole and H. Ross Perot

December Federal Reserve Chairman Alan Greenspan warns that "irrational exuberance" could lead to an unsustainable stock market bubble

1997

October Federal government reports surplus

1998

April United States mediates peace agreement between Catholics and Protestants in Northern Ireland

August Al Qaeda bombs U.S. embassies in East Africa; United States launches airstrikes against Al Qaeda in Sudan and Afghanistan

December House of Representatives impeaches President Clinton

1999

February Senate acquits Clinton of impeachment charges

March–June U.S. and NATO forces bomb Serbia to force it to remove troops from Kosovo

December Showing limits of the appeal of globalization, antiglobalization demonstrators protest meeting of the World Trade Organization in Seattle

2000

July President Clinton hosts Camp David meeting of Israeli and Palestinian leaders in an unsuccessful effort to resolve their conflict

November Close presidential election takes place; Results are contested

December Supreme Court declares George W. Bush the winner of the presidential election over Al Gore

2001

January Bush is takes office, but many Gore voters believe his presidency is illegitimate

votes, 47.9 percent, 271 electoral votes; Gore: 51 million votes, 48.4 percent, 266 electoral votes; Nader: 2 million votes, 2.7 percent; Buchanan: 448,895 votes, 0.4 percent). Many legal analysts agreed with law scholar Jeffrey Toobin that it was "a crime against democracy that [Gore] did not win the state and thus the presidency. It isn't that the Republicans 'stole' the election or that Bush [was] an 'illegitimate' president. But. . . . the wrong man was inaugurated on January 20, 2001."

STUDY QUESTIONS FOR THE DISPUTED ELECTION OF 2000

1. What were the principal issues in the presidential election of 2000?
2. Why was the election result in doubt?
3. Why were efforts to decide the winner so controversial?

Summary

- The Cold War ended suddenly between 1989 and 1991, as—one by one—the communist regimes in Eastern Europe and ultimately the Soviet Union abandoned communism.
- The administration of President George H. W. Bush sought to create a new world order.
- The United States experienced a technology-driven economic boom in the 1990s.
- The good times of the 1990s generated the largest wave of immigration in more than a century.
- The administration of President Bill Clinton pursued a centrist, New Democratic course.
- Clinton was a popular president, but a sizeable minority fiercely opposed him. He was impeached by the House of Representatives, but acquitted by the Senate.
- The United States engaged in a number of international humanitarian interventions in the 1990s, including those in Somalia, Yugoslavia, and Haiti.
- The disputed election of 2000 was decided by a controversial vote of the U.S. Supreme Court in favor of Republican George W. Bush.

Key Terms and People

Albright, Madeleine *1197*
Americans with Disabilities Act (ADA) **1174**
Arafat, Yasser *1198*
Bin Laden, Osama *1199*
Buchanan, Pat *1181*
Bush v. Gore *1202*
Bush, George H. W. *1172*

Bush, George W. *1200*
Clinton, Bill *1173*
Contract with America *1194*
Defense Advanced Research Projects Agency (DARPA) *1183*
Dole, Bob *1195*
Dukakis, Michael *1173*
Gingrich, Newt *1193*

globalization *1182*
Gorbachev, Mikhail *1176*
Gore, Al *1181*
Greenspan, Alan *1185*
Hill, Anita *1176*
Hussein, Saddam *1178*
Jobs, Steven *1169*
Jones, Paula *1196*
McVeigh, Timothy *1194*
Milosevic, Slobodan *1198*
Nader, Ralph *1200*
New World Order *1172*
Nichols, Terry *1194*

North American Free Trade
    Agreement (NAFTA) *1193*
Perot, Ross *1181*
Quayle, Dan *1173*
Rabin, Yitzhak *1198*
Rubin, Robert *1192*
Schwarzkopf, H. Norman, Jr. *1179*
Souter, David *1175*
Starr, Kenneth *1196*
Stevens, John Paul *1203*
Thomas, Clarence *1175*
Yeltsin, Boris *1177*

Reviewing Chapter 30

1. How did the end of the Cold War affect life in the United States from 1988 to 2000?
2. What changes in the United States and the world economy affected American life in the 1990s?
3. How did scientific and technological advances alter American life in the 1990s?

Further Reading

Atkinson, Rick. *Crusade: The Untold Story of the Gulf War*. Boston: Houghton Mifflin, 1993. An account of the politics and strategy of the successful U.S.-led war that unintentionally set the stage for later regional conflicts.

Beschloss, Michael R., and Strobe Talbot. *At the Highest Levels: The Inside Story of the End of the Cold War*. Boston: Little Brown, 1993. A historian and diplomat collaborate on detailing the events surrounding the Soviet collapse and transition to the post-Cold War era.

Johnson, Haynes. *The Best of Times: America in the Clinton Years*. New York: Harcourt, 2001. An entertaining but insightful overview of the 1990s, examining the decade's highs and lows.

Schulzinger, Robert D. *A Time for Peace: The Legacy of the Vietnam War*. New York: Oxford University Press, 2006. As the author shows, the political and cultural legacies of the Vietnam War lasted much longer than the conflict and affected Americans for a generation after the end of combat.

Toobin, Jeffrey. *Too Close to Call: The Thirty-Six–Day Battle to Decide the 2000 Election*. New York: Random House, 2001. A lawyer-journalist examines the legal and political dimensions of the disputed presidential election and how it revealed the politicization of the Supreme Court.

Eckes, Alfred E., Jr., and Thomas W. Zeiler. *Globalization and the American Century*. New York: Cambridge University Press, 2003. The authors examine how the emergence of an economically integrated world altered the American economy in positive and negative ways.

Visual Review

The Election of 1988

George H. W. Bush is elected president.

The Bush Presidency at Home

Bush angers conservatives by governing from the center.

The New World Order

Bush has an active foreign policy toward former Soviet Empire nations.

The Election of 1992

Bill Clinton is elected president due to Bush's unpopularity with domestic issues.

George H. W. Bush and the End of the Cold War

AFTER THE COLD WAR, 1988–2000

The Good Times

Innovation and New Technology

Technological advances change the way Americans work, communicate, and spend their leisure time.

Migrants

The promising economy attracts a large influx of immigrants.

Work, Science, and Discontent

The Internet revolution impacts American life at work and at home.

Bill Clinton and the New Democrats

An Awkward Start
Partisanship curtails Clinton's bold agenda for change.

Clinton's Recovery
Clinton achieves some successes after altering his political strategy.

Clinton's Second Term
The Lewinsky scandal leads to Clinton's impeachment.

A Post-Cold War Foreign Policy

Intervention and Mediation
The United States intervenes militarily to avert humanitarian crises in Africa and Europe.

International Terrorism
Terrorism by Islamic radicals is an increasing concern for American policy makers.

The Disputed Election of 2000

Bush versus Gore
Al Gore and George W. Bush campaign as moderates in the 2000 election.

The Election in Florida and a Supreme Court Decision
The Supreme Court decides the election in Bush's favor.

31

21st-Century Dangers and Promises

2000–Present

n August 2001, Sherron Watkins, a vice president of Enron, a Houston-based energy trading company, e-mailed a long list of concerns about the firm's accounting practices to Kenneth Lay, the company's founder and chairman of the board. As his company prospered, Lay lavished money on Texas politicians and philanthropies. Watkins was "incredibly nervous that we will implode in a wave of accounting scandals." As she predicted, over the next several months Enron went from being what *Fortune* magazine had called "America's most innovative company" to disgrace and bankruptcy. Lay and other top executives were convicted of perpetrating massive frauds that cost banks and investors around the world billions of dollars. Thousands of Enron employees lost their jobs, their pensions, and their life's savings.

In the 1990s, as governments around the world deregulated energy prices, Lay transformed Enron from a modest natural gas pipeline company into a firm which traded gas, electricity, and water power in the United States and around the globe. In theory, competition would help consumers by reducing utility costs. But energy traders like Enron devised schemes to manipulate the market, driving up prices and company profits. For example, in early 2001, Enron traders withheld electricity from California, creating frequent power outages and a fourfold spike in the cost of electricity. At the same time, Enron executives engaged in accounting frauds to conceal huge losses in other parts of the company operations. Fake profits boosted the price of the company's stock and enriched those who bought it early.

Nevertheless, Lay and his top aides boasted they had created a brilliant new business model that enriched investors while making power cheap for consumers.

Barack Obama at his Election Night Rally in Grant Park, Chicago, Illinois, November 4, 2008

CHAPTER OUTLINE

THE AGE OF SACRED TERROR
> The United States and Terrorism before September 11, 2001
> September 11 and Al Qaeda
> The Iraq War

CONSERVATISM IN THE BUSH YEARS
> Culture Wars
> Justice in the 21st Century
> Compassionate Conservatism
> Hurricane Katrina
> Immigration
> The Election of 2006

ECONOMIC TURMOIL
> The Dot-Com Bust and the Middle Class Squeeze
> Collapse

THE OBAMA YEARS
> The Election of 2008
> The Obama Presidency

America in the World

Hurricane Katrina devastated Florida, Louisiana, and the Gulf Coast, revealing serious emergency infrastructure failures (2005).

Al Qaeda terrorists attacked the World Trade Center and Pentagon, shocking the world (2001).

U.S. event that influenced the world

International event that influenced the United States

Event with multinational influence

Conflict

U.S. troops attacked Iraq and Saddam Hussein's government fell (2003–2011).

Osama bin Laden was killed (2011).

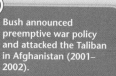

Bush announced preemptive war policy and attacked the Taliban in Afghanistan (2001–2002).

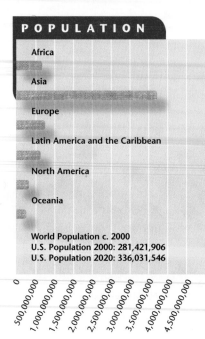

POPULATION

Africa

Asia

Europe

Latin America and the Caribbean

North America

Oceania

World Population c. 2000
U.S. Population 2000: 281,421,906
U.S. Population 2020: 336,031,546

0
500,000,000
1,000,000,000
1,500,000,000
2,000,000,000
2,500,000,000
3,000,000,000
3,500,000,000
4,000,000,000
4,500,000,000

The scheme, and Enron's stock price, unraveled during the fall of 2001. After ignoring past rumors, the slow-moving Securities and Exchange Commission launched an investigation. Enron and its accounting firm, Arthur Andersen, soon declared bankruptcy in the largest corporate collapse ever up to that time.

The Enron scandal was just one of several multibillion dollar swindles revealed early in the 21st century that involved new technologies or creative finance. But after a flurry of attention, the public and regulators lost interest in the problem, especially in the wake of the terrorist attacks of 2001. When, after a brief slump, economic growth resumed, the Enron episode faded from memory. But the frauds of 2001 were a foretaste of even greater economic catastrophes that began in 2008, many caused by the same process of market deregulation and lax oversight that caused Enron's rise and fall.

THE AGE OF SACRED TERROR

Al Qaeda, a network of loosely affiliated Islamist terrorists led by Osama bin Laden, a wealthy Saudi Arabian businessman who adopted increasingly fundamentalist views in the 1980s, began opposing American influence in the Middle East after the Cold War ended. The Reagan administration had supported bin Laden when he joined the fight against Soviet troops in Afghanistan during the 1980s. But after the Soviet retreat, he turned his fury against his former patron. Al Qaeda operatives attacked U.S. and Western targets around the globe in the 1990s. Al Qaeda catapulted to the top of the international agenda on September 11, 2001, with its spectacular assaults on New York's World Trade Center and the Pentagon. The new administration of President **George W. Bush** responded with a "global war on terror" to destroy Al Qaeda and its supporters. After toppling the Taliban regime in Afghanistan, which had given sanctuary to bin Laden, the Bush administration went to war in Iraq to drive its leader, **Saddam Hussein**, from power.

The United States and Terrorism
Before September 11, 2001

In August 1998 Al Qaeda operatives attacked the U.S. embassies in the capital cities of Kenya and Tanzania, killing hundreds of mostly local employees and people doing business with the American officials. In response President Bill Clinton ordered air strikes against bin Laden's Afghanistan headquarters and a Sudanese factory the CIA believed was producing nerve gas. The attacks killed dozens of fighters and civilians but failed to disrupt Al Qaeda.

The CIA continued to track bin Laden but failed to kill or capture him. In October 2000, in the midst of the presidential election campaign, Al Qaeda suicide bombers attacked the USS *Cole*, a U.S. Navy destroyer anchored in the port of Aden in Yemen on the southern coast of the Arabian Peninsula, killing 17 navy sailors. The Clinton administration unsuccessfully pressed the government of Afghanistan, ruled by Taliban, a radical Islamist group, to expel bin Laden into American custody.

Once the Supreme Court decided the election in favor of George W. Bush in December 2000, departing Clinton administration officials warned their successors about the growing terrorist threat. Clinton himself told Bush that he regretted not killing or capturing bin Laden and predicted that "by far your greatest threat is bin Laden and Al Qaeda." But the new president and his aides dismissed these warnings.

Still, throughout 2001, U.S. intelligence agencies intercepted increasing "chatter" from Al Qaeda operatives around the world hinting at a major strike against the United States. CIA Director George Tenet warned that "the system was flashing red" by mid-summer. On August 6, the CIA delivered to Bush a report entitled "Bin Laden determined to strike in U.S." It described the Al Qaeda leader's extensive plans to attack U.S. targets. But instead of ordering stricter security measures, Bush left Washington for an extended vacation on his Texas ranch.

September 11 and Al Qaeda

Catastrophe struck on the brilliantly clear late summer morning of September 11, 2001, when 19 Al Qaeda hijackers seized four commercial airliners. They crashed two of them into the two towers of the World Trade Center in New York's Lower Manhattan, bringing both buildings down in flame and killing over 2,750 people. A third hijacked plane slammed into the Pentagon, killing 184 people. Hijackers on a fourth jet, seized after taking off from Newark International Airport, hoped to crash the plane into the U.S. Capitol building or the White House. But when passengers stormed the cockpit, the hijackers crashed the airliner into a field southeast of Pittsburgh, killing all on board.

Demonstrations of support for the United States took place in cities across Europe, Canada, Australia, and Japan. The French newspaper *Le Monde*, often highly critical of United States culture, politics, and foreign policy, ran a front page editorial under the headline, in French, "We Are All Americans." In the days and weeks following the attacks, Americans of all political persuasion flew American flags in front of their homes and wore flag pins on their clothing.

President Bush's initial response to the attacks appeared confused, but he soon recovered his balance. Within four days he visited the smoldering remains of the World Trade Center, now labeled "Ground Zero," grabbed a bullhorn and shouted to the firefighters and rescue workers, "I can hear you, and soon the whole world will hear you." The Bush administration turned away from the rhetoric of the 2000 campaign in which he promised that the United States would pursue a "humble foreign policy." Bush now declared a full-scale war on terror, a seemingly open-ended and global

Stunned New Yorkers flee the collapsing Twin Towers of the World Trade Center after the attack of September 11, 2001.

battle. He adopted the foreign policy prescriptions of prominent conservatives, such as Vice President **Dick Cheney**, Defense Secretary **Donald Rumsfeld**, and Defense Department advisers Richard Perle and Paul Wolfowitz, who called for the use of force to sweep away dictatorial regimes around the globe, replacing them with democratic governments committed to free markets and friendly to the United States.

On September 20 the president promised that "whether we bring our enemies to justice, or bring justice to our enemies, justice will be done." He demanded that the Taliban in Afghanistan arrest bin Laden and turn him over to the United States or face an American attack. He proclaimed war on terrorism, but he denied that the United States was at war with Islam. Directly addressing the world's 1 billion Muslims, he said, "We respect your faith. . . . Its teachings are good and peaceful, and those who commit evil in the name of Allah blaspheme the name of Allah."

The American people rallied around their president, pushing his popularity above 90 percent. With little debate, Congress passed the **USA PATRIOT Act**, which expanded the Justice Department's powers to conduct surveillance on terrorist suspects at home and abroad. With just one dissenting vote, Congress also authorized an American attack against the Taliban, a policy endorsed by the NATO allies. Air strikes in Afghanistan began in early October while the Pentagon dispatched a small number of highly skilled Special Forces and Army Rangers to bolster Afghan rebels who had been fighting the Taliban for years. In December these Afghans captured Kabul, the capital of the country, and most other major cities. The Taliban government melted away with few American losses. Ominously, however, the United States failed to capture or kill Osama bin Laden—who found a safe haven in Pakistan—primarily because it lacked troops on the ground.

The United States installed a new government in Afghanistan led by **Hamid Karzai**, a pro-Western former exile. American emissaries encouraged the Afghans to draft a democratic constitution, promising free elections and equality for women and the country's many tribal and ethnic groups. Karzai won election to the presidency in October 2004, and Washington poured billions of dollars into reconstruction and the building of schools and hospitals. But the Karzai government had little sway over most of the country and was mired in corruption. Nor were the Taliban completely eliminated. Thousands of fighters who had taken haven in Pakistan began regrouping after 2005 and soon challenged the Karzai government. By 2008 the resurgent Taliban once again controlled large parts of rural Afghanistan. During the presidential election campaigns of 2004 and 2008, Democratic candidates lambasted the Bush administration for stinting the military operations in Afghanistan because of the costly involvement in Iraq. In 2009 President **Barack Obama** ordered an additional 47,000 troops to Afghanistan as a way to provide security throughout the country and train an effective Afghan armed force.

The Iraq War

Part of the reason the administration dropped the ball on Afghanistan was its obsessive concern with Iraq. Within 24 hours after the attacks of September 11, the Bush administration put in motion a plan to attack Iraq and drive Saddam Hussein from power. The president instructed his top aides to look for evidence to confirm his belief that the Iraqi strongman had been behind the attacks on that day. Over the next few months, Bush's senior foreign policy advisers prodded the CIA to confirm Iraq's link to 9/11 and the Pentagon to draw plans for an American attack on Iraq.

Although Saddam Hussein was guilty of many barbarous acts against his own people, he had little use for religious fundamentalists like bin Laden. He considered Al Qaeda's goal of imposing Islamic purity throughout the Middle East a threat to his own dictatorship. Despite the lack of evidence linking Iraq to terrorist acts, nearly all of the nation's main print and broadcast media outlets joined the Bush administration's call for bringing down the "butcher of Baghdad."

In January 2002, addressing Congress and the nation, Bush identified Iraq, Iran, and North Korea as an "axis of evil arming to threaten the peace of the world." He warned ominously that "time is not on our side," and that "the United States of America will not permit the world's most dangerous regimes to threaten us with the world's most dangerous weapons." In June Bush announced a new American strategy at a speech at West Point. He said that "we must take the battle to the enemy, disrupt his plans, and confront the worst threats before they emerge." Commentators quickly labeled this call for preemptive war the **Bush Doctrine** and predicted the president would soon take action against one or more of the nations comprising the axis of evil.

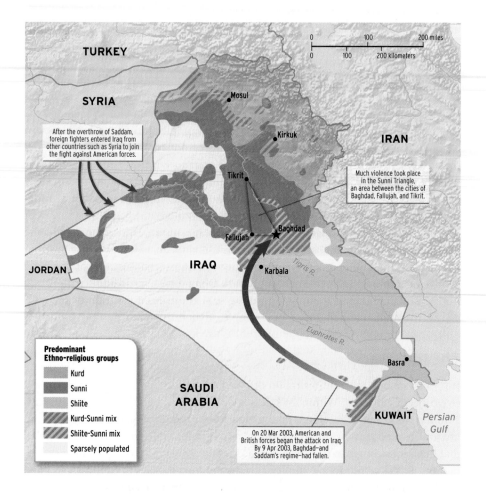

Bush told the United Nations on September 12, 2002, that the world body was in danger of sinking into irrelevance if it did not authorize military action to enforce its past resolutions demanding that Saddam Hussein abandon his weapons of mass destruction. In October Congress voted by two-thirds majorities to authorize the president to attack Iraq to compel its disarmament.

Throughout the winter of 2002–2003 the Bush administration built a case for attacking Iraq and tried to assemble allies for the war. Vice President Cheney and Defense Secretary Rumsfeld pressured the CIA for concrete examples that the United States could use to persuade the world. In February 2003, Secretary of State **Colin Powell** went before the UN Security Council with pictures and transcripts of intercepted telephone calls, which, he claimed, proved that Saddam was hiding weapons of mass destruction (WMD) that included biological, chemical, and even nuclear weapons. Although Powell may not have known it when he spoke, much of the evidence he presented about WMD had been faked or manipulated, some by Iraqi exiles who hoped to come to power through an American invasion.

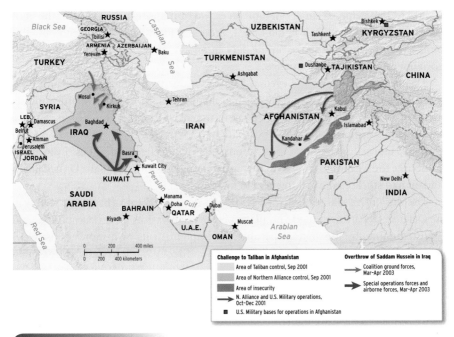

Maps 31.1 and 31.2

War in Iraq and Afghanistan Since 2003 After the devastating 9/11 attacks on the United States, the Bush administration invaded Afghanistan and drove from power the Taliban government, which had backed Osama bin Laden's Al Qaeda movement. President George W. Bush also began planning a war to drive Iraqi tyrant Saddam Hussein from power, even though he had no connection to the attacks of 9/11. U.S. forces invaded Iraq in March 2003.

In spite of his forceful presentation, Powell failed to persuade the UN to adopt a resolution authorizing force, and found it difficult to recruit many allies. Britain, Italy, and Spain, along with several former communist states in Eastern Europe and some mini-nations like the island of Tonga in the Pacific, joined the United States in what became known as "the coalition of the willing." But several of America's closest allies, such as Germany and France, balked at attacking Iraq. Kenneth Adelman, a prominent neo-conservative advocate of attacking Iraq, wrote that he believed "demolishing Hussein's military power and liberating Iraq would be a cakewalk." Vice President Cheney predicted the American forces would be "greeted as liberators in the streets of Baghdad." Deputy Defense Secretary Wolfowitz predicted that the war would be cheap, paid for by Iraq's oil revenue. Supporters of war argued forcefully that an Iraq rid of WMD and free of Hussein's tyranny would become a beacon of hope in the Middle East.

On March 17 Bush delivered an ultimatum to Saddam Hussein to leave Iraq or face war. Two days later, on March 19, the United States attacked by air and on land. The first Gulf War of 1991 lasted six weeks, and it appeared that the second war to oust Saddam would end even faster and with fewer American casualties. On April 9 American forces completed their race to Baghdad, occupied the capital, and, as TV cameras rolled, helped a small but jubilant crowd of Iraqis tear down one of the hundreds of statues of the dictator. On May 1, President Bush declared the end of major combat in Iraq when he spoke on the deck of an aircraft carrier under a banner that proclaimed "Mission Accomplished."

Disturbing signs appeared even as Baghdad residents fired guns in the air to celebrate Saddam's end. The United States had made no plans to preserve order and restore Iraq's economy. Mobs poured into government offices, electrical power stations, schools, and hospitals, stripping them bare of everything valuable. Looters attacked the Iraqi National Museum stealing thousands of priceless antiquities. Even more ominously, the weapons of mass destruction that Iraqi exiles assured the United States Saddam had stockpiled were nowhere to be found.

Despite Bush's claim of victory, Iraq soon descended into chaos and civil war. The Defense Department made no plans before the invasion for an occupation, and it resisted efforts by the State Department to implement its own more robust blueprint. Between 2003 and 2004 the United States directly ran Iraq's affairs through a Coalition Provisional Authority (CPA). CPA administrator Paul "Jerry" Bremer never seemed up to the job. He had a utopian vision of a free market Iraq modeled on Western democracies, but like most Americans had only the dimmest understanding of the sectarian rivalries dividing Iraqis. Eager to rid the country of the influence of Saddam Hussein's Ba'ath Party, Bremer disbanded the 500,000-strong Iraqi army. These armed and resentful ex-soldiers joined the nearly 50 percent of Iraqis who lacked any jobs.

By the summer of 2003, hope had faded among Iraqis that the United States would bring them a better life. An insurgency against the Americans and Iraqis who cooperated with them began and gained in ferocity over the next three years. When a reporter asked Bush about the rising number of American deaths in July 2003, the president snapped "There are some who feel . . . that they can attack us. My answer is 'Bring 'em on.'"

Bush's bravado proved badly misguided and the attacks worsened. In 2006 Bush, who was loath to admit having made mistakes, acknowledged that "' bring it on' kind of tough talk . . . sent the wrong signal to people. I learned some lessons about expressing myself maybe in a little more sophisticated manner." The Pentagon could

U.S. troops fighting Taliban guerrillas in the bleak terrain of Afghanistan, 2010.

not reduce the size of the U.S. force as it had expected. As the insurgency continued, the American death toll mounted. It passed 1,000 in 2004, climbed beyond 2,750 in 2006, and reached 4,200 in 2008. Approximately 25,000 American forces suffered severe wounds. The death toll among Iraqis was far higher, with estimates ranging from 50,000 to 900,000 in the three and one-half years after the war began.

The idealistic goals of the war were compromised further during 2004 when reports surfaced that U.S. military personnel and CIA operatives had tortured and degraded Iraqi prisoners at the **Abu Ghraib** prison near Baghdad. The story came with pictures of naked Iraqi prisoners, some with bags over their head, being led to mock executions, threatened with snarling dogs, or forced to wear women's underwear over their faces.

Other stories surfaced over the next two years about the mistreatment of more than 500 Al Qaeda prisoners being held at a prison on the Navy base at Guantanamo Bay, Cuba. Bush had authorized the CIA to use "enhanced interrogation techniques"— which critics called torture—to obtain information. One common technique, called waterboarding, simulated drowning and had been previously classified by the U.S. military as a war crime. The CIA also flew terror suspects—a practice called rendition—to other countries that tortured prisoners. After dodging the issue for several years, in 2006 the Supreme Court ruled in *Hamdan v. Rumsfeld* that the military tribunals the Bush administration established to try prisoners held in Guantanamo were unconstitutional and that prisoners retained the right to appeal to federal courts.

By late 2005, 57 percent of the American public believed that the Iraq War had been a mistake. The cost of the war passed $300 billion and kept rising, a figure that administration officials had insisted was ludicrously high in 2003. As the war went on in 2006 with the situation in Iraq deteriorating into sectarian violence that claimed the lives of 100 people a day, and 100 American service members dying each month, a plurality of Americans thought the United States should leave Iraq. Bush's approval also declined in 2006 to below 40 percent.

Public disillusionment with the war contributed to Democratic victories in both houses of congress in the 2006 election. Immediately after the election, Bush replaced

In 2004, gruesome pictures surfaced revealing that U.S. guards at Abu Ghraib prison physically and psychologically abused detained Iraqi insurgents. Here, Army Specialist Lynndie England drags a prisoner on a leash. The photographs undermined support for the war at home and abroad.

the abrasive Rumsfeld with Robert Gates as secretary of defense. Gates, a veteran foreign policy, defense, and intelligence specialist, served on the bi-partisan Iraq Study Group (ISG), created by Congress to recommend new strategies in the war. In December 2006 the ISG advised Bush to reduce the number of U.S. troops in Iraq to force the Iraqi government to take more control of the country's affairs.

Bush ignored this recommendation and instead ordered a "surge" of 30,000 additional U.S. troops to Iraq. The new forces brought the total number of Americans to 160,000 by the summer of 2007. U.S. casualties mounted for the first six months of the year as the United States adopted more active tactics to clear and hold territory. Perhaps as important as the surge, the U.S. military paid millions of dollars to tribal leaders and some insurgents to induce them to stop fighting. By the beginning of 2008, the surge and the new tactics appeared to bear fruit. Violence against Americans subsided in Iraq, although it remained an extremely dangerous and unstable place.

In addition to the lives of about 6,000 American troops lost in Iraq and Afghanistan between 2001 and 2011, the two wars cost a staggering amount of money. Congress appropriated approximately $1.2 trillion for the fighting over these 10 years. But that did not include additional billions that came from other parts of the Pentagon, CIA, and other agency budgets. The ripple effects of the wars, counting veterans' pensions and other payments, might total well over $ 3 trillion. To minimize criticism of these costs, the Bush administration and Congress declined to raise taxes but fought the war on borrowed money. This comprised a large part of the debt load handed off to the Obama administration in 2009.

STUDY QUESTIONS FOR THE AGE OF SACRED TERROR

1. How did the U.S. government and the American people respond to the terrorist attacks of September 11, 2001?
2. How did the George W. Bush administration justify the decision to go to war against the government of Iraq in 2003?
3. Why did public opinion in the United States and around the world turn against the United States presence in Iraq after 2003?

CONSERVATISM IN THE BUSH YEARS

Conservatives returned to power in 2001 after a brief interruption in the Clinton years. Bush modeled himself more closely on President Reagan than his own father, President George H. W. Bush. Reagan, in fact, often moderated his conservative principles with practical compromises. Although he described himself as a pragmatic or "compassionate conservative," Bush and Congressional Republicans actually pursued a more strident agenda of cultural and economic conservatism than had Reagan. In Bush's second term, however, growing public uneasiness with the Iraq war eroded the appeal of cultural conservatism. Increasing numbers of Americans became alarmed at the incompetence and cronyism they witnessed in government, and they favored a truce in the culture wars. In 2006 voters returned control of Congress to the Democratic Party.

Culture Wars

Between 1968 and 1992 Republicans won every presidential election except for Jimmy Carter's 1976 post-Watergate victory by stressing "wedge" or "hot button" issues. Their attacks on school busing for racial balance, crime, restrictions on school prayer, gun control, welfare abuses, abortion and gay rights, pornography, and judicial activism had stripped away large numbers of voters from traditional Democratic constituencies, including Catholics and Protestant evangelicals, who were uncomfortable with their party's positions on these social and cultural issues.

However, the recession of 1992 and the letdown many Americans felt following the inconclusive Gulf War undermined confidence in President George H. W. Bush and permitted Democrats to rediscover their voice. Bill Clinton campaigned under the banner "It's the economy, stupid." Clinton won reelection in 1996; yet, the culture wars only partially abated, and many on the Right never accepted Clinton as a legitimate president. When Texas governor George W. Bush campaigned for president in 2000, he stressed that even though the economy might be booming, the budget in surplus, and the nation at peace, Clinton's moral lapses tainted Al Gore, the Democratic candidate.

Early in his first administration, Bush implemented several policies advocated by culture warriors. These included a ban on using federal funds for most research on stem cell lines derived from human fetuses, reimposing a "gag" rule begun by Ronald Reagan that blocked federal aid to any family planning agencies that even mentioned abortion as an option, and creating a White House Office of Faith Based and Community Initiatives designed to steer federal money to religious charities. Bush and his appointees also disputed evidence that human activities had caused climate change.

These words and actions comforted many conservatives and outraged many liberals and scientists. The stem cell ban severely restricted medical research that promised cures for ailments including multiple sclerosis, Alzheimer's, and Parkinson's diseases. Many social service providers complained that the faith-based initiative violated the separation of church and state. Religious groups such as Catholic Family Services already received federal and state contracts to provide vital aid to the homeless, the elderly, and substance abusers. However, they could not use public funds to proselytize or to refuse to hire, say, social workers, who were not Catholics. The Bush initiative blurred the lines, permitting religious groups, often evangelical Christian congregations, to discriminate in who they hired and to require those receiving services to participate in religious worship.

Nearly all mainstream scientists expressed disdain for Bush's endorsement of intelligent design as a scientific theory and for his refusal to acknowledge evidence of climate change. To prepare students for the modern world, they considered it vital that schools distinguish between faith, which asked "why" life evolved, and science, which examined "how" it did so. In a series of federal court decisions that mirrored the Scopes trial of the 1920s, efforts to mandate the teaching of intelligent design were overturned as religious intrusion into public education.

Gay rights advocates took heart from a U.S. Supreme Court decision in 2003 (*Lawrence v. Texas*) that overturned most state antisodomy laws used to criminalize homosexual behavior, and from a ruling by the Massachusetts Supreme Judicial Court that same year that found no legal basis for prohibiting same-sex marriage. In February 2004, the Massachusetts court explicitly ruled that gay men and women had the right to marry in the state. Almost a decade before, congressional Republicans had pushed through a national **Defense of Marriage Act**. That 1996 law decreed that no state would be compelled to recognize a same-sex marriage performed in another state, nor would the federal government recognize the existence of such a marriage even if it were performed legally in a state.

Few people disagreed that marriage was a troubled institution and that families labored under great stress. Nearly half of all marriages ended in divorce, creating serious problems for children and sometimes for ex-spouses. At least a third of children were born to unmarried mothers. Lack of affordable child care proved a constant problem for millions of families. None of this, however, had anything to do with same sex marriage. Nevertheless, in the wake of the court ruling in Massachusetts, **Patrick Buchanan** and President Bush described traditional marriage as an endangered species under siege by homosexual and judicial "activists." Bush suggested he might support a constitutional amendment to prohibit same-sex unions.

As gay Americans pressed for the right to marry, the public showed a range of strong beliefs about same-sex marriage. By a substantial margin, younger Americans favored the right of gays to wed.

The president's tone reflected his personal beliefs as well as a political calculus designed to assist his reelection in 2004 by highlighting so-called values issues. Pollsters reported that voters had qualms about the ongoing war in Iraq and Bush's handling of the economy. However, Republicans enjoyed a strong advantage over Democrats when people were queried about subjects such as gay marriage.

Democrats had problems confronting Bush effectively in 2004. Most of the candidates running for the Democratic nomination were senators who had voted in favor of authorizing war against Iraq in 2002. In the fall of 2003 they faced Democratic primary voters who had distanced themselves from the war. The eventual Democratic Party nominee was Massachusetts senator **John Kerry**, a decorated Vietnam War veteran who had first come to national prominence at the age of 26 when he spoke out against the Vietnam War. Throughout the campaign Kerry criticized the Bush administration's poor diplomacy and lack of planning for postwar Iraq. He never disavowed his vote for the war, however, and Bush portrayed him as a waffler on Iraq specifically and the war on terror more generally. Bush defeated Kerry by approximately three million votes. The electoral vote total was tight, Bush 286, Kerry 251, the closest victory by an incumbent since 1916.

Following his reelection, Bush declared that he had accumulated "political capital" that he now intended to spend. He spoke of launching a crusade aimed at "ending tyranny in our world." But these large aspirations quickly became mired in an unpopular plan to reform Social Security, an effort to prevent a husband from allowing his brain-dead wife to die, a botched federal response to a hurricane, and an increasingly unpopular war in Iraq.

Conservatives had long condemned Social Security, a pillar of the New Deal, as an emblem of the problems with big government. Social Security faced funding challenges in the early 21st century because people lived longer after retiring than they had in the 1930s, the large "baby boom" generation nearing retirement would quickly draw down reserves, and the number of young workers whose contributions helped fund the system was declining. But these were not insoluble problems. Public policy specialists proposed several ways to solve the problems, including raising the retirement age, reducing benefits for those with other income sources, and increasing payroll taxes that funded the system.

Bush instead proposed partially privatizing Social Security by converting it to a system in which individuals managed their own stock accounts. The president's advisers pointed to a similar program adopted in Chile at the urging of U.S. economists. As critics pointed out, this might provide higher returns in boom times, but left individuals at the mercy of speculative forces. Bush dropped the idea when most Democrats, some Republicans, and groups representing the elderly ridiculed privatization.

Early in 2005, the president and Congressional Republicans spent additional capital on a "right-to-die" case that they thought might boost their standing among "right-to-life" activists. It involved **Terri Schiavo**, a young Florida woman who suffered cardiac arrest from unknown causes in 1990. After several months in a coma, she partially awoke but sustained profound brain injury. Kept alive by a feeding tube and with no hope of recovery, she lived in a "persistent vegetative state." In 1998, eight years after her collapse, her husband and caregiver, Michael Schiavo, petitioned a Florida court to permit him to disconnect the feeding tube, an act he believed his wife would have approved of.

Terri's parents filed numerous lawsuits in Florida alleging Michael had abused his wife and that they should be named her guardians. When the suits were dismissed and Michael authorized the removal of the feeding tube, the Florida legislature intervened. It passed "Terri's Law," a special act giving Governor Jeb Bush—the president's brother—power to seize and protect Terri. The governor ordered Terri placed under state protection and ordered her feeding tube replaced. Early in 2005, however, Florida's Supreme Court declared Terri's Law unconstitutional. The involvement of Jeb Bush and several prominent conservative theologians and media pundits transformed the case into a national obsession.

Congress, with President Bush's enthusiastic support, enacted a law on March 21, 2005, that transferred jurisdiction in the Schiavo case from state to federal courts, but no federal court agreed to intervene. Governor Bush considered ordering Florida state police to place Terri Schiavo in "protective custody" so he could restore the feeding tube Michael Schiavo had again removed. However, Terri died on March 31, before he acted. The episode tarnished conservative activists. The prospect of grandstanding politicians intervening in personal end-of-life decisions appalled most Americans.

Justice in the 21st Century

Bush had greater success in making judicial appointments that moved federal courts, especially the Supreme Court, to the right. High court membership had not changed since 1994. For the next decade the court often divided between distinctly liberal and conservative blocs. Justice **Sandra Day O'Connor** provided a swing vote, giving one bloc or the other a five-vote majority. The court's overall conservative tilt showed in its decision in 2000 to give the disputed Florida vote, and hence the presidency, to George W. Bush. In July 2005, O'Connor announced her plan to retire as soon as the President nominated and the Senate confirmed a replacement.

Bush nominated **John Roberts**, a federal appeals court judge, to replace O'Connor. Roberts had begun government service as a young lawyer in the Reagan Justice Department and moved into private practice before Bush appointed him as an appeals court judge. Roberts considered himself a disciple of Chief Justice William Rehnquist and impressed people as affable and well informed.

But on September 3, 2005, before the Senate voted to confirm the nominee, Chief Justice Rehnquist died. Bush then nominated Roberts to fill the chief justice's vacant seat and the Senate quickly approved him. Bush nominated Federal Appeals Court justice **Samuel Alito**, who also served in the Reagan Justice Department, to fill O'Connor's place. The Senate approved both appointments.

Roberts and Alito were far more congenial than the often abrasive justices Antonin Scalia and Clarence Thomas. Nevertheless, during their first years on the Court they nearly always voted with the most conservative members of the court on issues such as free speech, abortion rights, criminal rights, and the president's power in the war on terror. Justice Anthony Kennedy frequently joined the four conservative judges in a five-to-four majority. On several occasions, Kennedy voted with the liberal bloc in imposing some limits on the President's right to hold foreign nationals indefinitely in military detention. He provided a decisive fifth vote in the June 2006 decision in *Hamdan v. Rumsfeld.*

However, Kennedy's vote pushed the court sharply right in a 2010 decision know as Citizens United. The five-vote conservative block struck down as a violation of the First Amendment the 2002 McCain-Feingold Act that limited the amount of money corporations could provide to independent groups campaigning for or against a political candidate or cause. The ruling decreed that corporations had the same free speech rights as individuals and opened a potential floodgate of money from corporations to favorite causes or candidates. It also overturned some campaign finance restrictions passed by progressives over a century before.

Compassionate Conservatism

During the campaign of 2000 George W. Bush expressed concern for the struggles of poor and non-white Americans. During his first term as president, Bush's domestic program based on what he called "compassionate conservatism" included tax cuts and a pair of educational and health reforms. The 2001 and 2003 tax reductions tilted heavily in favor of higher income Americans. Democrats had questioned the size and nature of the tax cuts, but were more supportive of the Bush education and health programs. Senator Edward Kennedy, for example, lent his prestige to both the president's **No Child Left Behind Act** (NCLB) of 2001 and the Medicare drug reform act of 2003.

Bush described NCLB as especially important to improve educational outcomes for poor and minority children. It renewed federal funding for several existing school programs and provided some additional money for reading and math instruction. In return, all states had to implement "standards based educational reform," a term that in practice meant standardized testing of students in reading and math. Proponents cited the so-called Texas miracle, a school reform Bush promoted while governor, for making educators accountable for results and allowing officials to identify failing schools and teachers. Critics raised several concerns. Pressure to "teach to the test," they warned, would encourage schools to neglect subjects such as art, music, literature, etc. Failed schools would have to be reorganized, perhaps as privately run charter schools, a favorite idea of conservatives.

A decade after NCLB enactment, the program yielded only modest results. Schools in well-to-do neighborhoods continued to perform well while those populated by poorer students lagged behind. As for the Texas miracle, subsequent reviews revealed that the celebrated gains had been wildly overstated.

The Medicare program begun in 1965 had dramatically improved the health and financial condition of the elderly. But its failure to pay for prescription drugs had become a major burden. By the start of the 21st century, aging patients took a regimen of pills for ailments such as high blood pressure, heart conditions, depression, diabetes, and sexual dysfunction. The cost of medications sometimes exceeded doctor and hospital bills. In December 2003, Congress, again with heavy Democratic support, passed the Bush-designed Medicare Modernization Act to take effect in 2006. The program subsidized the cost of some, but not all, medication taken by seniors. The law proved a bonanza to pharmaceutical companies since it helped seniors buy more medication but did nothing to limit prescription costs.

Hurricane Katrina

When Hurricane Katrina smashed ashore in southeast Louisiana early on August 29, 2005, the storm caused one of the deadliest and costliest natural disasters in U.S. history. The botched federal response to the flooding of New Orleans exposed serious flaws in the Bush administration's competence and accelerated the process of disillusionment with compassionate conservatism.

During the last days of August, the National Weather Service had accurately tracked the meandering course of Katrina over Florida and the Gulf of Mexico. By August 27, meteorologists predicted the storm would head toward New Orleans, a city that lay below sea level and depended on a massive, but archaic, system of levees and pumps to remain dry. Although celebrated for its party image and boastful of its nickname, the "Big Easy," New Orleans was actually one of the nation's poorest and most dysfunctional cities. Mostly poor African Americans lived in the urban core while surrounding suburbs were mostly affluent and white. To make matters worse, city, state,

In the chaos surrounding Hurricane Katrina in August 2005, and the botched federal response, desperate residents of New Orleans appeal to authorities for rescue.

and federal officials failed to coordinate evacuation orders or to make adequate provisions for tens of thousands of poor urban residents without cars or other means of transportation. As a result, although one million Gulf residents fled inland by car to safety in advance of Katrina's landfall, around 60,000 people from New Orleans were left to fend for themselves when the levees broke and 80 percent of the city flooded. About half of these gathered in public buildings like the Louisiana Superdome, and the rest headed for rooftops.

The Federal Emergency Management Agency (FEMA) had responsibility for coordinating emergency relief efforts. For many years, FEMA was a highly regarded agency. But its head since 2003, lawyer and Bush acquaintance Michael Brown, had no experience in disaster relief. Under Brown's stewardship, many highly qualified career civil servants left FEMA and were replaced by political cronies.

Federal officials appeared oblivious to the tragedy unfolding in New Orleans. Bush arranged a "fly by" of the city by Air Force One on August 31, as he returned to Washington from a vacation in Texas. On September 1, TV news crews aired footage of tens of thousands of refugees clustered in the Superdome without food or water, others clinging to rooftops, and dead bodies floating in flooded streets. Around the world people watched in disbelief as the rich and powerful United States seemed incapable of providing for the basic needs of its people. On September 2, the president told the FEMA director "Brownie, you're doing a heck of a job."

Over the next several days, the scope of the disaster in New Orleans became apparent to everyone. By then, the death toll in and around New Orleans reached nearly 1,600 and that in Mississippi around 238. Property damage surpassed $80 billion. President Bush visited New Orleans on September 15. He assured the nation that adequate federal assistance was on the way, but his promises fell flat. This record haunted the Bush administration for the next three years.

Immigration

During the first decade of the 21st century, people from around the world continued to flock to the United States. Immigrants settled predominantly in New York, Florida, California, Texas, Pennsylvania, New Jersey, and Illinois. Some migrants had few job skills but worked hard in the service economy, in construction, and in agriculture. Others had advanced degrees. By 2006, 40 percent of PhDs in America had been born abroad and many taught in universities or worked for companies like Microsoft and Intel. As a group, immigrants tended to be younger than the average American, were more likely to be married, and were almost equally divided between males and females. As had been true since the immigration law reform of 1965, nearly 60 percent of those coming to the United States had been born in Latin America and the Caribbean, while almost 25 percent originated in East and South Asia. Despite popular fears, immigrants did not raise crime rates and half paid income and social security taxes—even though they generally received few benefits.

The attacks of September 11, 2001, heavily influenced public attitudes toward immigration. About half of Americans queried by pollsters supported tougher

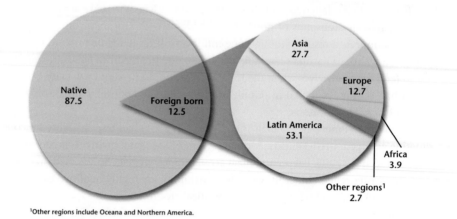

¹Other regions include Oceana and Northern America.

▲ **Figure 31.1**

The surge in immigration from Latin America and Asia to the United States The trend of Latin American and East Asian immigration accelerated during the 1990s and early 2000s. Many American cities took on an international flavor that affected their language, cuisine, and popular culture.

immigration restrictions in order to enhance national security. Nevertheless, half the public continued to think that a relatively high rate of immigration—close to 1 million annually after 2001—was good for the country. An estimated one million illegal or undocumented migrants, 80 percent from Mexico and Central America and about 10 percent from Asia, entered the country annually between 2001 and 2008. As of 2010, an estimated 12 million undocumented migrants lived in America.

The question of illegal immigration along with the demography of population growth emerged as new "wedge" issues between 2000 and 2010. In that period, the Hispanic population increased by over 30 percent. Many, but not all, congressional Republicans, along with several TV and radio personalities such as Lou Dobbs, Pat Buchanan, Glenn Beck, and Rush Limbaugh, warned of a silent invasion across the Mexican border. The millions of undocumented Hispanics, along with legal immigrants, were portrayed as a stealth army, spreading leprosy and crime while taking jobs from citizens and driving down wages. Anti-immigration crusaders demanded that the undocumented be arrested and deported, that the children born in the U.S. of undocumented mothers be denied citizenship, and that a secure fence be built along the U.S.-Mexican border.

Congress debated these questions during the run-up to the 2006 election. President Bush along with two senators, Republican **John McCain** of Arizona and Democrat Edward Kennedy of Massachusetts, proposed a broad compromise. This would combine enhanced border security, a guest worker program, and a path toward citizenship for most of the undocumented. However, conservative Republicans in the House and Senate criticized any talk of "rewarding" lawbreakers by allowing them to become citizens. Convinced that a hard line approach would rally their base, most

Sharp-tongued conservative "pundits" such as Sean Hannity dominated cable television, especially on the Fox network, by the late 1990s. Their no-holds-barred attacks on Democrats and liberals coarsened political discourse.

Republicans voted for a bill ordering construction of 700 miles of border fencing along with measures to speed the arrest and expulsion of undocumented immigrants.

But as with the botched handling of the Schiavo case and Katrina relief, a majority of Americans—and especially Hispanic voters—believed that the Bush administration had engaged in another case of "bait and switch." The president had endorsed comprehensive immigration reform but then abandoned the fight and signed a repressive law. These misgivings contributed to a surge of support for Democrats among Hispanics and helped Democrats recapture control of Congress in 2006.

Politics aside, the profile of Americans, caused partially by immigration, changed dramatically during the first decade of the 21st century. The 2010 census revealed that among those 18 years old and younger, nearly half were members of racial or ethnic minority groups. Higher birth rates among Hispanics partially explained this number. In contrast, among Americans 65 or older, 80 percent were white. This disparity meant that in coming years white "seniors," who tended to be more conservative on issues of taxes and government programs (aside from Medicare and Social Security), would be pitted as a voting bloc against a growing number of people of color who favored increased government spending on education, job creation, and other social services.

The Election of 2006

As the 2006 Congressional elections approached, the public voiced growing frustration with Republican policies and behavior. Late night comedians joked that Republicans were the party that believed government did not work and their performance

An immigrant family in California rallies in 2006 against efforts by state and federal authorities to restrict immigration and punish the undocumented.

since 2004 proved them right. A series of scandals that erupted after 2005 further eroded the standing of Bush and the GOP.

By November 2006, the Bush administration and its Congressional majority had squandered much of the public's good will. A party that stressed the primacy of safeguarding national security was shown to have used bogus intelligence to justify an unnecessary and costly war; a party devoted to fiscal responsibility had turned a healthy budget surplus into the largest string of deficits in the nation's history; a party focused on moral rectitude had used aid to religious charities as a recruiting tool and the tragedy of Terri Schiavo to rally its base; the incompetent response to Katrina revealed Bush's appointment of a crony to manage the nation's response to disaster. Meanwhile, several corruption and sex scandals involving Republican members of Congress showed party leaders who looked the other way while key lawmakers abused public trust.

Angry voters expressed their disgust by returning control of Congress to the Democrats for the first time in 12 years. On November 7, 2006, Democrats gained 31 seats in the House of Representatives, giving them a majority of 233 to 202. Senate Democrats picked up five new seats. With the votes of two independents, they had an edge over Republicans of 51 to 49.

STUDY QUESTIONS FOR CONSERVATISM IN THE BUSH YEARS

1. What were the essential elements of cultural conservatism in the early 21st century?
2. Why did President George W. Bush lose popularity in the years after he won reelection in 2004?
3. How did the question of immigration set off such an angry debate in the Bush years?

ECONOMIC TURMOIL

The economy entered the 21st century with unemployment at a historic low of 3.5 percent, worker productivity soaring, and the stock market advancing. Clinton bequeathed a balanced budget to the incoming President Bush, and most economic forecasts predicted a sharp reduction in the national debt over the next decade. Within months, however, the stock market bubble based on the high-tech sector burst and helped initiate a brief worldwide recession. The overall economy bounced back, but benefited some, particularly the wealthy, more than others. The middle class in the United States thought they had been abandoned and left to deal with a variety of increasing costs. Globalization intensified with new wealth coexisting with even more crushing deprivation. Many economies in East and South Asia boomed while large areas of Latin America fell behind. The former communist countries of Eastern Europe and the Soviet Union had mixed success in the transformation to the free market. By 2008 the American and global economy suffered from a crisis in the financial markets that stemmed from overconfidence in risky investments in the housing sector and resulted in massive government intervention to prevent even greater damage.

The Dot-Com Bust and the Middle-Class Squeeze

The 1990s had seen major advancements in computing, the Internet, and information technology. These innovations also produced dozens of high-tech start-up companies looking to become the next Microsoft or Intel. Just as importantly, these companies looked to find investors who had the same hopes for them. The dot-com business model that emerged, however, emphasized seizing a large market share instead of earning a profit. Many companies operated at a loss with the goal that good press from advertisements or an endorsement from a prominent stock analyst would allure overzealous investors to their initial public offering (IPO) on the stock market.

The enthusiasm for the high-tech sector and its seemingly boundless economic possibilities eventually caught up with itself. In addition to a general growing sense of economic insecurity, over speculation in the dot-com market by the new companies

GLOBAL PASSAGES

Globalization on Trial

International protests against globalization intensified in the 21st century. Large multinational corporations such as Coca-Cola, Starbucks, and McDonald's faced criticism for their ubiquity, and companies such as Nike remained under scrutiny for their labor practices, such as running sweatshops in developing countries to produce their upscale products. On the heels of the World Trade Organization protests in Seattle in 1999, demonstrators gathered in Washington, DC, in the spring of 2000 and Prague in the fall to confront the meeting of the World Bank and International Monetary Fund (IMF). The protesters believed the World Bank, IMF, and other international organizations favored big business and enforced rigid economic policies on developing nations that were insensitive to local conditions, human and labor rights, and environmental issues. The international antiglobalization movement also targeted the annual summits of the Group of Eight (G-8) as another venue to air their criticisms. At the July 2001 meeting in Genoa, Italy, as many as 200,000 protesters took to the streets. Some clashed with the police, and one protester was shot and killed. In 2005 hundreds of thousands assembled in Edinburgh, Scotland, to protest the G-8 summit at the nearby Gleneagles resort. The activist group "Make Poverty History" coordinated its efforts with concerts held in several European cities and in the United States, dubbed "Live 8," to pressure the meeting's participants to adopt debt relief for African countries and to seriously address increased aid to the continent. Some antiglobalization activists broke windows and firebombed Starbucks and McDonald's. These companies' thousands of stores around the world became prominent symbols of the international dominance of American culture.

Opposition to globalization came from disillusioned voices from within the U.S. government as well. In 2002, Joseph Stiglitz, a former top Clinton administration

caused the stock bubble, which burst in March 2000. The NASDAQ stock exchange average, which traded many of the high-tech stocks, reached 5,000 in March and then began to plummet, falling to as low as 1,100 during the next three years. Stocks on the whole lost an average of 40 percent of their value between the summers of 2000 and 2002. Although **Alan Greenspan**, the chairman of the Federal Reserve, had warned against "irrational exuberance" as early as 1996, he took no action to reign in the bubble until after it popped. Companies other than new dot-coms engaged in accounting and financial fraud to inflate their numbers. These included Qwest Communications, WorldCom, and Enron, the highly profitable Texas energy trading company with close ties to the Bush administration. Both the dot-com bust and accounting

economic adviser and a vice president at the World Bank, published a scathing critique of his experience working with the IMF during the 1990s. It seemed to confirm many of its opponents' grievances. In *Globalization and Its Discontents*, Stiglitz expressed concern over inadequate discussion of poverty eradication at the IMF and a lack of transparency and flexibility depending on the circumstances. He wrote, "Decisions were made on the basis of what seemed a curious blend of ideology and bad economics, dogma that sometimes seemed to be thinly veiling special interests." Not everyone viewed globalization negatively. *New York Times* columnist Thomas Friedman gained a wide audience by extolling the equalizing effect that technological advances and globalization created for innovators in his 2005 work *The World Is Flat.*

In the wake of the economic collapse of 2008, anger at the bankers, financiers, investors, and government officials thought responsible for the calamity erupted worldwide. Huge crowds assembled in the capitals of Iceland, Ireland, Latvia, the Czech Republic, and Moldova to demand that their governments resign. In the United Kingdom and the United States members of Parliament and Congress joined the public in expressing their fury over news that executives of some of the banks and insurance companies had received rich bonus payments after their companies had been taken over by the government. Some foreign leaders blamed the United States for increasing suffering around the world, while American voters punished politicians who had voted for bank bailouts. But no consensus emerged about how to better manage international economic affairs.

• Why were so many ordinary people opposed to globalization?

• How did globalization contribute to the worldwide economic crisis that began in 2008?

scandals helped usher in a recession for much of 2001 as some of the tainted companies laid off workers or went bankrupt.

Even before the Bush tax cuts disproportionately rewarded the country's richest citizens, the gap between the extremely wealthy and the rest of the country was growing. In 2000 the average CEO's salary was 42 times greater than that of the average industrial worker. Since the 1980s, real income stagnated or declined for many workers. During the 1990s, families faced increasing costs for health care and tuition for higher education for their children, as well as high gasoline prices for much of the decade. Due to these burdens and spending on homes and consumer goods, they also saved less. Household debt grew even faster. Indeed, by the end of the Bush administration, the net worth of the average American household, adjusted for inflation, was lower than when he took office. Some middle-class families blamed outsourcing and globalization for taking away jobs and for their declining standard of living.

Collapse

One sector of the American and world economy surged in the early 21st century. The housing market in the United States and much of Europe soared from the late 1990s until mid-2005. President Bush boasted that home ownership had reached record levels under his watch. The chairman of the President's Council of Economic Advisers, **Ben Bernanke**, reported in late 2005 that house prices had risen 25 percent in just the last two years, which he believed was mainly due to a fundamentally sound economy and not overspeculation. The housing boom in several "hot markets" such as Las Vegas, Phoenix, and south Florida resembled a feeding frenzy as individual purchases and speculators outbid one another, often for homes still under construction.

At the same time, lenders offered unprecedented numbers of "subprime mortgages," home loans to borrowers with poor credit and low income. Subprime mortgages often offered small down payments and low introductory interest rates but significantly higher rates down the road. This put more families into homes, including some who could not afford the higher monthly installments, but also opened up the complex financial trading services involving home mortgages to serious risk if higher numbers of borrowers began defaulting on their loans. During the boom period, banks took this gamble due to low interest rates, faith that housing prices would continue rising, and high capital availability. Borrowers deluded themselves—or were encouraged by mortgage brokers—into thinking that since home prices would always increase, they could soon refinance their new home and meet the rising mortgage payments.

The bubble, however, inevitably burst. Home prices peaked in 2006. By early 2007 house prices dropped 3 percent and fell an additional 15 percent over the next year. During 2007 several subprime mortgages lenders declared bankruptcy or found themselves purchased by larger banks. By the summer of 2007, the collapse in home prices became a national problem. As prices dropped, credit tightened, and foreclosures rose. The "toxic assets" stemming from bad mortgage payments began to infect investment banks and other parts of the financial sector at home and around the world.

Washington helped fuel the speculation by its embrace of free markets and its passion for deregulation. In 1999 Congress tore down the wall, in place since the New Deal, separating relatively safe and conservative commercial banks from risk-taking investment banks. Under Bush, government agencies that were designed to assure that markets were transparent and honest were chronically understaffed or led by officials who opposed regulation. Freed of regulation, both investment and commercial banks purchased hundreds of thousands of mortgages during the housing boom and bundled them into high-risk securities to sell off as investments. Banks and governments in Europe and Asia, also proponents of deregulation, purchased securities backed by American home mortgages; and banks in Ireland,

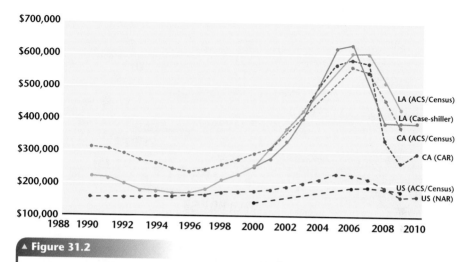

▲ **Figure 31.2**

The housing bubble Home values, along with stock prices, shot upward from the late 1980s through 2008. Banks encouraged marginal borrowers to take out mortgages on homes they could not afford, in hope that rising prices would allow them to refinance. They bundled the so-called subprime mortgages and sold them to investors around the world. When housing defaults rose, it triggered a global recession.

Iceland, Spain, and the United Kingdom aggressively sold their own versions of subprime mortgages.

For years, stock prices had risen along with the housing bubble, but in the winter of 2008 the subprime crisis hit Wall Street at full speed. In March rumors circulated that one of the smallest of these banks, Bear Stearns, was running out of cash. The rumors gained momentum, confidence in the bank was lost, and its stock dropped. Since Bear Stearns's finances were connected to the other investment banks on Wall Street, Ben Bernanke, the new Chairman of the Federal Reserve, believed it was too risky for the entire financial system to let it go bankrupt. Bernanke arranged for a loan from the Fed to save Bear Stearns and fight off the larger risk to the banking system.

The financial sector continued to suffer because of its connections to the housing market. By summer Fannie Mae (originally the Federal National Mortgage Association) and Freddie Mac (originally the Federal Home Loan Mortgage Corporation), two huge mortgage lenders, faced rapidly eroding confidence from their investors. Treasury Secretary **Henry Paulson** and Bernanke effectively nationalized them in early September to avoid too great a risk to the economy. Almost immediately after the nationalization, Lehman Brothers became the next investment bank to be haunted by its overly aggressive investment in real estate mortgages. When Lehman Brothers was unable to find a purchaser, it went bankrupt on September 15.

Lehman's bankruptcy triggered the international economic collapse of 2008, soon labeled the **Great Recession**. Credit markets around the world froze, and banks stopped lending to one another. Business activity, dependent on lending, went into

After the housing bubble burst in 2008, the economy went into freefall. Millions of homes were foreclosed on by banks. Sunbelt states such as Florida, California, Arizona, and Nevada suffered most.

a downward spiral. In the last quarter of 2008, the U.S. economy contracted at an annual rate of over 6 percent. The meltdown affected financial institutions and governments throughout the world. In the United States, the world's largest insurance company, AIG, which had also invested hundreds of billions of dollars in housing-related trading, soon faced bankruptcy itself and needed cash. Despite their past claim that government should not intervene in the free market, the Bush administration loaned AIG $85 billion to survive, aid that grew in 2009 to $180 billion.

Bernanke and Paulson turned to Congress with the request to buy toxic mortgage securities from banks in the form of a $700 billion bailout bill. Congress passed the **Emergency Economic Stabilization Act** in late September. It included a provision giving the treasury secretary the power to oversee capital injection into the banks should he see fit. The Troubled Asset Relief Program (TARP) began to purchase toxic assets.

More bad news emerged in December. The nation's three largest domestic automakers appealed to Congress to receive emergency aid to hold off bankruptcy and prevent a ripple effect in the economy of the Midwest. General Motors (GM) and Chrysler eventually received $13.4 billion in funding. Also in December the FBI, after years of oblivion by the Security and Exchange Commission (SEC), accused **Bernard Madoff** of executing the largest Ponzi scheme in American history. He cheated his clients, including dozens of celebrities and philanthropic organizations, out of tens of billions of dollars. Decisions by the Bush administration to reduce oversight of financial markets contributed to this and other investment scams. Madoff pleaded guilty to these crimes, but the billions of dollars he had managed for his clients was long gone.

The economy continued to suffer even after the massive investments by the government. It remained in a recession until early 2010. By February 2009 the annualized rate of return on the U.S. government's investment in the country's largest banks was minus 109 percent. The downturn now affected nearly all segments of the economy. In the fourth quarter of 2008, the Gross Domestic Product (GDP) shrank at a rate of 6.2 percent, the steepest quarterly decrease in 25 years. It contracted at a 5.7 percent rate in the first quarter of 2009. The national unemployment rate passed 10 percent by the end of the year.

Other countries fared even worse. Japan's economy, heavily dependent on exports, shrank at an astonishing 13 percent in the final quarter of 2008. Iceland and Ireland, two countries whose banks had been especially reckless in overseas lending, faced bankruptcy. In March the Dow Jones Industrial Average reached a 12-year low, dropping below 6,500, a full 50 percent less than it had been in October 2007. With so many private pensions pegged to stock prices, the decline affected the retirement prospects of millions of Americans.

STUDY QUESTIONS FOR ECONOMIC TURMOIL

1. Why did the economy expand after 2001?
2. What caused the economic crisis of 2008–2009?
3. What did the United States government do in 2008–2009 to reverse the economic downturn?

THE OBAMA YEARS

The economy, the subprime crisis, and the financial collapse played a large role in the election of 2008: 47-year-old Illinois Democratic Senator Barack Obama faced 71-year-old Arizona Republican Senator John McCain in the fall election. Obama rode to victory on a wave of new voters who thrilled to his promise of hope and change. He promised to end the incessant partisan bickering of the Clinton and Bush years, end the war in Iraq, restore America's battered international reputation, and pass major economic and social reform laws.

In the first years of Obama's presidency the country grappled with some of the most severe challenges in nearly a century. The Great Recession proved to be deeper and more prolonged than any since the Great Depression of the 1930s. The war in Iraq wound down, but the one in Afghanistan expanded. Obama promoted a more ambitious agenda of social and economic reform than any Democratic president since Lyndon B. Johnson persuaded Congress to enact the Great Society in the 1960s. The Democratic Congress passed significant legislation, but these successes carried a cost.

The angry political divisions of the previous decades subsided for only a few months in the aftermath of Obama's election. From the middle of 2009 public frustrations mounted as the Great Recession continued and jobs remained scarce.

The Election of 2008

Both Obama and McCain were surprising choices for their party's nomination. Obama was the son of a Kenyan father and a white Kansas-born mother. He was born in Hawaii and lived for a few years as a child in Indonesia. He graduated from Columbia University and Harvard Law School, and settled in Chicago where he worked as a community organizer and taught at the University of Chicago Law School. He identified himself as an African American. He rose to national prominence by delivering the keynote address to the 2004 Democratic National Convention. He decried the culture wars that had led to a sense that the country was more divided than it actually was. "There is not a red America and a blue America," he said "but a United States of America."

Obama stood out as soon as he entered the Senate in 2005. He began his quest for the Democratic nomination in February 2007 with calls for change and an end to the petty partisan bickering that had bedeviled politics for 20 years. Polls showed him running far behind New York senator **Hillary Clinton**, wife of the former president. But Obama ran a more focused campaign than his rivals. His steadfast opposition to the war in Iraq contrasted with her waffling on the subject. African Americans were cool to his candidacy at first, but they embraced him with wild enthusiasm after he won an initial victory in the January Iowa caucuses. His eloquence and idealism reminded many of John F. Kennedy nearly a half century before. He appealed strongly to young people and well-educated voters. After a long primary campaign, he secured the nomination over Clinton in June.

McCain was a generation older than Obama. A navy veteran who served for five and one-half years in a North Vietnamese prison camp during the Vietnam War, McCain was elected to Congress in 1982. He ran unsuccessfully for the Republican presidential nomination in 2000. Although he lost to George W. Bush, many journalists appreciated his easy accessibility, wise cracks, and willingness to criticize conservative Republicans and leaders of the Religious Right. McCain enjoyed the media adulation, but in 2008 decided that to win he must mend fences with the right wing. McCain secured the Republican nomination with a strong defense of the Bush administration's surge in the Iraq war. He expected that his national security credentials would help him defeat the less experienced Obama.

Iraq faded as an issue in the fall election campaign as voters attention turned to the slumping economy. McCain's international experience seemed less relevant in economic hard times, and he added to the problem by admitting that "economics is not my strong suit." As the financial crisis mounted in mid-September, McCain appeared out of touch.

Obama reassured voters by tapping Delaware senator **Joseph Biden**, a respected veteran lawmaker with over three decades of service, as his running mate. McCain, in contrast, selected as his running mate the nearly unknown **Sarah Palin**, who had been governor of Alaska for less than two years. The youthful, attractive, and self-described hockey mom Palin generated some initial excitement, especially among the conservative Republican base. But her near-complete lack of experience and policy knowledge became a major concern to voters.

Obama drew enormous crowds of people to campaign rallies longing for a new direction in American politics and policy. He spoke to over 200,000 people in Berlin during a tour of the Middle East and Europe in the summer. People outside the United States saw him as welcome relief to the combative and closed-minded Bush. They hoped that as a well-traveled and highly educated American who had an international upbringing, Obama appreciated the importance of understanding and cooperating with foreign countries and cultures. At a series of rallies around the United States during the weeks before the fall election, 100,000 people or more turned out in places like Denver; Columbus, Ohio; and suburban Virginia to hear him speak.

On November 4, 2008, Obama became the first African American to be elected president. He received 52 percent of the popular vote, the first Democratic candidate since Jimmy Carter in 1976 to surpass 50 percent. He also carried several traditionally Republican states such as Colorado, Indiana, North Carolina, Florida, and Virginia, some of which had not voted for a Democratic presidential candidate since 1964. Obama garnered 69.4 million popular votes and 365 electoral votes to McCain's 59.9

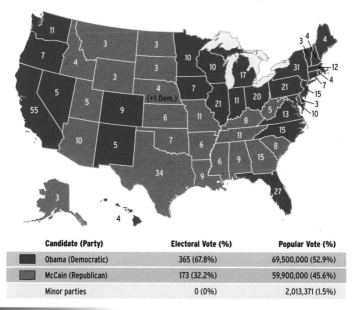

Candidate (Party)		Electoral Vote (%)	Popular Vote (%)
	Obama (Democratic)	365 (67.8%)	69,500,000 (52.9%)
	McCain (Republican)	173 (32.2%)	59,900,000 (45.6%)
	Minor parties	0 (0%)	2,013,371 (1.5%)

▲ **Map 31.3**

2008 Election: Obama's Victory After the housing bubble burst in 2008, followed by rising unemployment and falling stock prices, many Americans placed their hope in Democratic presidential candidate Barack Obama. The Illinois senator won majorities in several states—such as North Carolina, Colorado, and Virginia—that had not voted for a Democrat presidential candidate in decades.

million popular votes and 173 electoral votes. Democrats emerged with majorities of 257 to 178 in the House of Representatives and 60 to 40 in the Senate.

The Obama Presidency

Obama moved quickly to assemble his top advisers, dubbed a "team of rivals." He asked Bush's defense secretary Robert Gates to remain at the Pentagon. He appointed Hillary Clinton as secretary of state. He chose several veterans of the Clinton administration for top economic positions.

In his first months in office Obama pressed change. In February Congress passed the **American Recovery and Reinvestment Act**, a $787 billion economic stimulus bill. The package combined government spending on infrastructure, unemployment benefits, and food stamps, with tax cuts. Although Republicans favored the tax cuts that were included to gain their support, only three Republican Senators voted for the bill. No Republican voted for it in the House. Some commentators considered the lack of Republican support for the stimulus bill a sign that Obama had failed in his effort to make the tone of Washington more civil and end the partisan bickering of the recent past. As the unemployment rate surpassed 8 percent, some observers thought that the program was insufficient to return the economy to growth.

The $787 billion economic stimulus law stopped the sickening slide into another depression, and stock prices rebounded sharply after hitting lows in March. But the economy continued to hemorrhage jobs each month in 2009. By the end of the year 9.8 percent of the workforce was idle; 16 million were either totally without work or worked fewer hours than they wanted. The economy began to grow again in 2010, but fewer jobs were created than had been lost during the depth of the recession. Surprising skeptics, most banks repaid the shares owned by the government, and GM and Chrysler quickly emerged from bankruptcy. But the continuing slump in housing prices made many of those with jobs feel worse off than they had been a few years before. Millions of homeowners defaulted on their mortgages, while others found themselves "under water," owning homes worth less than the amount they owed on their loans.

Obama addressed the other parts of his agenda too. He said that science policy would be based on science, not ideology or religious beliefs. He rescinded the Bush administration's ban on research using stem cells. He ended the special military tribunals at Guantanamo Bay, but the prison remained there into 2011 despite his promise to close it within a year of becoming president. He announced that U.S. combat forces would leave Iraq by August 2010. A residual force of up to 50,000 might remain to train Iraq's armed forces. The last U.S. combat forces left Iraq in August 2010, after about 4,500 U.S. service members lost their lives in the war. A year later, 45,000 uniformed Americans remained in Iraq as "trainers." After failing to reach an agreement at the end of 2011 over the future status of these trainers, the Pentagon decided to pull out nearly all American troops. With Iraqi politicians squabbling over the makeup of their government and as insurgent attacks continued, the Bush administration's tarnished dream of Iraq becoming a force for democracy and prosperity in the Arab world appeared dimmer than ever.

Soon after Obama took office he dispatched 17,000 additional troops to Afghanistan, but the insurgency only worsened. In the fall he conducted a full-scale review of

U.S. policy toward Afghanistan and announced that another 30,000 troops would go there during 2010. The aim was to bolster the Afghan government's ability to confront the Taliban. The commitment had a tentative expiration date of July 2011, when, he said, the United States would begin to withdraw its troops.

Congress enacted significant parts of Obama's ambitious legislative program. For nearly a year it debated a major overhaul of the nation's health care system designed to increase coverage to more than 95 percent of legal residents and contain the growth of costs. The proposal provoked an angry backlash from people who feared it was a form of "socialized medicine" that would increase costs and reduce benefits to seniors already covered by Medicare. In the summer of 2009 demonstrators affiliated with the Tea Party movement, a loosely organized group of people angry at government, shouted insults at members of congress who supported health care reform. The Patient Protection and Affordable Care Act finally passed, over the unanimous opposition of Republicans, and was signed into law in March 2010. Congress also passed the Financial Regulatory Reform Act, the largest overhaul of the nation's financial system since the New Deal. It imposed tighter regulations on banks' trading practices, which had led to the financial collapse of 2008. It also created a new Bureau of Consumer Financial Protection designed to prevent many of the abuses of borrowers and bank customers that had also contributed to the crash.

Congress failed, however, to pass legislation addressing the potential dangers of climate change. In 2008, a majority of Americans told pollsters that they believed that the earth's climate was changing, that the results of a hotter planet would be bad, and that the cause was man-made. They supported Obama's plans to reduce reliance on energy obtained from the burning of oil, natural gas, and coal and switch to renewable energy sources. But enthusiasm for "green," energy faded as people became more concerned about finding or keeping jobs.

Even a major environmental disaster in the Gulf of Mexico did not revive the push to move away from petroleum. In April 2010 a rig owned by BP, one of the world's largest oil companies, exploded in the Gulf. It was drilling for oil two miles beneath the surface of the ocean in water more than one-mile deep. The burst well began spilling oil into the Gulf, fouling beaches and marshes from Louisiana to Florida. By the time BP capped the well in July, nearly five million barrels, leaked into the ocean. The spill was eight times larger than the Exxon Valdez disaster that had fouled Alaskan shores in 1989. Tens of thousands of people whose livelihood depended on fishing, catering to tourists, or the oil industry were without work in Louisiana, Mississippi, Alabama, and Florida. The Obama administration insisted that BP pay for the cleanup and create a fund of $20 billion to compensate people hurt by the spill.

Obama also appointed two women to the Supreme Court in his first two years. In 2009 the Senate confirmed Sonia Sotomayor as the first Hispanic justice. In 2010 Elena Kagan joined the Court. They replaced justices who voted with the liberal minority, so the ideological balance of the Court remained unchanged. The confirmation hearings for the two new justices were less acrimonious than expected, and a few Republican senators voted in favor of the nominees. Nevertheless, Republicans blocked votes on dozens of other judges Obama nominated for federal court posts.

In his second year in office Obama remained personally popular, although his approval had declined from about 67 percent to around 45 to 50 percent, about where Presidents Reagan and Clinton stood at the same point in their presidencies. People admired his intelligence, knowledge, and eloquence, and international opinion had turned sharply in favor of the United States, a reversal from the global disapproval of the Bush years. The hopes he inspired in other countries in a new spirit of American cooperation won him the Nobel Peace Prize. Yet Obama enjoyed less support for some of his specific policy proposals. He lost sympathy among independent voters, who complained that the bitter tone of Washington politics had not improved. Some of his enthusiastic, youthful, educated backers in 2008 also were disillusioned at the slow pace of change. The Republican opposition was emboldened by an upsurge of populist anger against rescuing the banks, health care reform, and soaring federal budget deficits. Senate Republicans used the filibuster procedure to block key legislation and appointments. So-called Birthers, with their suspiciously racist sentiments, spread rumors that Obama had been born in Kenya, not Hawaii, and was not a legitimate president. His "African roots" and supposedly secret Muslim faith, they claimed, made Obama anti-American.

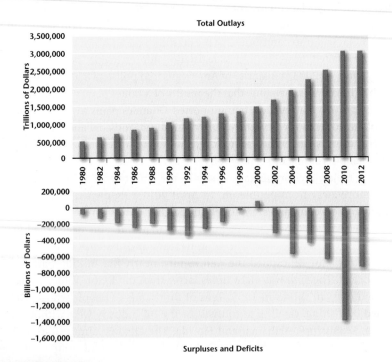

▲ **Figure 31.3**

Worrisome trends: the federal budget Annual deficits and the national debt grew rapidly after 2001. It increased by around $5 trillion during the George W. Bush administration due to tax cuts, unfunded wars in Afghanistan and Iraq, and the unfunded expansion of Medicare drug benefits. During the first three years of the Obama presidency, the debt increased by about $4 trillion, largely a product of high unemployment and low tax collections due to slow economic growth.

Perhaps more than anything, the nation's bleak economic outlook during 2010–2011, especially the high unemployment rate of around 9 percent, eroded Obama's support, emboldened his Republican critics, and made Democrats politically vulnerable. People wanted the government to grow the economy faster, even if they had widely different views on how this should be done. Some critics called for more stimulus spending while others demanded sharp cuts in the federal budget. Liberals called for raising taxes on the wealthy, while conservatives insisted that the Bush-era tax cuts be made permanent.

Voters took their revenge on incumbents in the 2010 congressional elections. With a drop in Democratic turnout and a swing by independents to the right, Republicans picked up over 60 House seats, restoring their majority. The Senate added 5 new Republicans, giving the Democrats only a 3-vote edge. Republicans also made major gains in midwestern states. Faced with this new reality, President Obama reached a budget compromise in December 2010 with the new Republican congressional majority that kept the Bush tax cuts—which favored the wealthy—in place for two more years.

At the state level, Republicans won control of several more governorships and legislatures. In states such as Wisconsin and Ohio, the governors pushed through laws stripping unionized state workers of collective bargaining rights that had been in place since the 1930s. There, as in other states, conservatives often blamed public employees—including teachers, police, and firefighters—for budget problems. In Ohio, voters rebelled against this antiunion measure by approving a November 2011 referendum that repealed it.

By the summer of 2011, Republicans forced a showdown with President Obama when they balked at raising the debt ceiling (something routinely approved by Congress over 70 times since 1962) unless he agreed to steep spending cuts. Pushed by Tea Party activists among recently elected representatives, GOP House Speaker John Boehner demanded that Obama agree to slash spending on social programs rather than raise taxes if he wanted Congress to raise the debt ceiling and avoid a default on government bonds—something that had never happened before.

The national debt had increased from about $5 trillion to $10 trillion during President George W. Bush's two terms. The unfunded costs of the wars in Afghanistan and Iraq, the unfunded Medicare drug program, large tax cuts, and slow economic growth all contributed to this increase. Nevertheless, Republican legislators voted several times between 2001 and 2008 to raise the debt ceiling and extend the federal government's borrowing authority. But in mid-2011 they balked, refusing to raise the debt ceiling until the administration agreed to deep spending cuts that would have to come from programs such as Medicare and Social Security. Republicans refused to consider any revenue increases, arguing that taxes were already too high and new taxes would stifle growth and "kill jobs." In fact, Americans were paying the lowest rate of federal taxes in 50 years and the decade of Bush tax cuts had neither boosted growth nor employment.

Beyond the immediate financial turmoil, economists recognized several disturbing long-term trends that threatened the "American dream" of upward mobility. Data released in 2011 showed that millions of working-class Americans had fallen back into poverty. The number of Americans living below the poverty level topped 46 million, the highest amount since 1993. From the end of World War II through 1979, the largest share of economic growth went to the bottom 80 percent of earners. But since 1980, the wealthiest 20 percent of Americans gained most from economic growth. The top 1 percent did best of all, doubling their share of national income to nearly 24 percent, the highest level since 1928. Looked at another way, the wealthiest 1 percent saw their inflation adjusted after-tax income rise 275 percent between 1980 and 2010, while the top 20 percent enjoyed a 65 percent income growth. During these same three decades, the middle three-fifths of earners enjoyed only a 40 percent rise in income while those in the lowest fifth had income growth of just 18 percent. In 2010 median household income (the midway point among all households) fell to the 1996 level.

This data showed both a rising rate of inequality as well as a loss of purchasing power among most wage earners. A protest movement dubbed "Occupy Wall Street" reacted during the fall of 2011 by staging demonstrations in many cities and condemning tax and other federal policies which they saw as unfairly benefitting the top 1 percent as compared to the remaining 99 percent of Americans.

Nearly all economists agreed that given the wave of aging baby boomers, Congress must find ways to restrain the growth of Medicare and to recalibrate the Social Security pension system. But most favored doing this gradually while making changes to the tax code that increased, not diminished, government revenues. After all, the cause of the $4 trillion in additional debt racked up since 2009 was not current spending on entitlements such as Medicare and Social Security, but the ongoing costs of two wars and, especially, the weak economy with its stubbornly high 9 percent unemployment rate. Nevertheless, Obama's political opponents hoped to embarrass the president and motivate their conservative supporters by manufacturing a debt crisis

TIMELINE 2001–2011

2001

June Congress reduces income and estate tax rates

July Congress passes No Child Left Behind Act

September 11 Al Qaeda terrorists attack the World Trade Center and the Pentagon

September Congress passes USA Patriot Act

October The United States attacks Afghanistan to capture or kill Osama bin Laden

November Enron declares bankruptcy

December United States overthrows Taliban government in Afghanistan

2002

Joseph Stiglitz publishes *Globalization and Its Discontents*

June President George W. Bush announces policy of preemptive war

October Congress authorizes military force against Iraq

2003

March The United States attacks Iraq

April Saddam Hussein's government falls

June Supreme Court overturns state antisodomy laws in *Lawrence v. Texas*

June Insurgency against Americans begins in Iraq

July 9/11 Commission publishes its report

December Congress passes Medicare Modernization Act

2004

February Massachusetts Supreme Court rules that gays and lesbians have the right to marry

May U.S. abuse of prisoners in Iraq revealed

November President Bush wins reelection over John F. Kerry

2005

Thomas Friedman publishes *The World Is Flat*

January–April Terri Schiavo case dominates news

August Hurricane Katrina floods New Orleans

September John Roberts named Chief Justice of the United States

2006

June Supreme Court rules in *Hamdan v. Rumsfeld* that prisoners at Guantanamo Bay have right to hearings in federal courts

November Democrats win majorities in the House and Senate in congressional elections

December Iraq Study Group issues report critical of Bush Administration policy

2007

January The United States begins a troop surge in Iraq

and possibly forcing Democrats to cut popular programs. Barely averting a default, in August 2011, Obama and Congressional Republicans forged a short-term deal that combined a rise in the debt ceiling with vague plans to cut future spending.

Congress reached an impasse at the close of 2011. Republicans balked at tax increases to reduce deficits, insisting on cuts in social programs. Democrats demanded that in return for reducing social expenditures, the wealthy should pay higher taxes. Each side hoped that its stand would motivate its base and boost the chance for victory in the upcoming 2012 election.

The sparring over the debt revealed a deeper split between the two parties and their agendas. Tea Party activists and other conservatives saw an opportunity to reverse the liberal course followed by the federal government since the New Deal. Ronald Reagan had challenged the welfare state but left it largely intact. George W. Bush mostly failed in his efforts to privatize big programs such as Social Security and had actually expanded Medicare. Even though polling revealed that most Americans continued to favor programs like Social Security and Medicare—and were willing to see taxes raised to fund them as well as to balance the budget—conservatives saw public unease over the troubled economy as cover to mount a broad attack. They argued that numerous federal programs, from Medicare and Social Security, to environmental regulation, to banking and finance oversight, to limits on corporate political activities stifled private initiative and hurt business. Major Republican figures questioned the legitimacy of the progressive income tax, the Federal Reserve System, and even the constitutional right of the government to borrow money. The attack on liberalism and big government included calls to privatize public services, to return regulatory powers to state government, to curtail the reach of federal courts, to seal off the nation's borders, and to assert the country's "Christian roots."

June Congress fails to adopt immigration reform

October Dow Jones and Standard and Poor's stock averages hit peak

2008

March Investment firm Bear Stearns nearly collapses

July Federal government takes over Fannie Mae and Freddie Mac

September Investment firm Lehman Brothers declares bankruptcy

October U.S. treasury creates Troubled Assets Relief Program (TARP)

November Democrat Barack Obama

elected president over Republican John McCain

2009

January Barack Obama inaugurated president

February Congress enacts the American Recovery and Reinvestment Act to stimulate the economy

February Crowds in Dublin, Ireland, demand resignation of the government for its mishandling of the banking crisis

February President Obama announces that U.S. combat troops will depart Iraq by the end of 2010

June President Obama addresses the Muslim

world in a speech in Cairo

2010

January Supreme Court in its *Citizens United* ruling overturns most limits on corporate political contributions

March Congress overrides Republican opposition and enacts the Patient Protection and Affordable Care Act, a sweeping overhaul of the nation's health care system

July Most U.S. combat troops leave Iraq, but over 40,000 American soldiers remain

November Republicans regain control

of the House of Representatives

December President Obama announces the United States will add 30,000 troops to its force in Afghanistan

2011

May U.S. Navy Seals kill Osama bin Laden in Pakistan

June–August President Obama and Congressional Republicans spar over raising debt ceiling and averting default

In many ways, the political and cultural conflict between liberals and conservatives resembled the debates of the Progressive Era. Then, as now, Americans questioned the role and scope of government in their daily lives, whether free markets and corporations served the common good or selfish ends, how open the country should be to immigrants, and the meanings of freedom in a complex society. Just as the choices made at that time influenced the nation's course for over a century, the actions taken by this generation will define the contours of the future.

STUDY QUESTIONS FOR THE OBAMA YEARS

1. To what extent did the Democrats' electoral successes in 2006 and 2008 represent a significant change in U.S. political attitudes?
2. Why did Barack Obama win the presidential election of 2008?
3. Explain the successes and failures of the first years of the Obama presidency.

Summary

- Al Qaeda, an international terrorist network, attacked the United States in the late 20th and early 21st centuries.
- In 2003 the United States attacked Iraq to overthrow the government of Saddam Hussein and to demonstrate its military power in the Middle East.
- The Bush administration restricted civil liberties in the midst of its war on terror.
- Cultural conservatives enhanced their influence early in the 21st century.
- Lax financial regulation, a housing bubble, and bad bank lending practices led to the Great Recession of 2008–2009.
- Barack Obama was elected the nation's first African American president in 2008.
- After Republicans regained control of the House of Representatives in 2010, they and President Obama engaged in a series of policy fights that nearly paralyzed government.

Key Terms and People

Abu Ghraib *1219*

Al Qaeda *1212*

Alito, Samuel *1224*

American Recovery and Reinvestment Act *1240*

Bernanke, Ben *1234*

Biden, Joseph *1238*

Buchanan, Patrick *1222*

Bush Doctrine *1215*

Bush, George W. *1212*

Cheney, Dick *1214*

Clinton, Hillary *1238*

Defense of Marriage Act *1222*

Emergency Economic Stabilization Act *1236*

Great Recession *1236*

Greenspan, Alan *1232*

Hussein, Saddam *1212*

Karzai, Hamid *1215*

Kerry, John *1223*

Lawrence v. Texas *1222*

Madoff, Bernard *1236*

McCain, John *1228*

No Child Left Behind Act
  (NCLB) *1225*

O'Connor, Sandra Day *1224*

Obama, Barack *1215*

Palin, Sarah *1239*

Paulson, Henry *1236*

Powell, Colin *1247*

Roberts, John *1224*

Rumsfeld, Donald *1214*

Schiavo, Terri *1223*

USA PATRIOT Act *1214*

Reviewing Chapter 31

1. What were the consequences of the U.S.'s war on terror after September 11, 2001?
2. Who benefitted and who fell behind because of 21st-century globalization?
3. How did Americans respond to the Great Recession?

Further Reading

Bergen, Peter L. *The Longest War: The Enduring Conflict Between America and Al Qaeda.* New York: Free Press, 2011. An overview of the politics and strategies of the wars on terror and the fighting in Iraq and Afghanistan.

Brinkley, Douglas. *The Great Deluge: Hurricane Katrina, New Orleans, and the Mississippi Gulf Coast.* New York: Harper Collins, 2006. The incompetence of the government response to this act of nature proved terribly hard for its victims and undercut the Bush administration's appeal.

Chandrasekaran, Rajiv. *Imperial Life in the Emerald City: Inside Iraq's Green Zone.* New York: Bloomsbury Publishing, 2006. A factual but nearly unbelievable portrait of American officials who botched the occupation of Iraq.

Frank, Thomas. *What's the Matter with Kansas? How Conservatives Won the Heart of America.* New York: Metropolitan Books, 2004. Why, the author asks, do so many Americans apparently vote against their economic interests and support a conservative social agenda?

Heilemann, John, and Mark Halperin, *Game Change: Obama and the Clintons, McCain and Palin, and the Race of a Lifetime.* New York: Harper, 2010. A detailed account of how a skilled political outsider mobilized public support for his candidacy and won the presidency.

Morgenson, Gretchen, and Joshua Rosner. *Reckless Endangerment: How Outsized Ambition, Greed, and Corruption Led to Economic Armageddon.* New York: Times Books, 2011. An examination of how private greed and government deregulation contributed to the economic collapse that began in 2008.

Moore, James, and Wayne Slater. *Bush's Brain: How Karl Rove Made George W. Bush Presidential.* Hoboken, NJ: John Wiley & Sons, 2004. An irreverent but insightful examination of how Republican strategists "packaged" and "sold" George W. Bush.

Visual Review

The United States and Terrorism before September 11, 2001

The U.S. military is a frequent target or terrorism by Islamic radicals.

September 11 and Al Qaeda

The U.S. homeland is the target of terrorist attacks.

The Iraq War

The Bush administration attacks Iraq as a response to 9/11.

The Age of Sacred Terror

21ST-CENTURY DANGERS AND PROMISES

Conservatism in the Bush Years

Culture Wars

Bush implements several policies advocated by social and cultural conservatives.

Justice in the 21st Century

Bush appoints more conservative federal judges.

Compassionate Conservatism

Bush's domestic agenda focuses on tax cuts and educational and health reforms.

Hurricane Katrina

The botched federal response to the flooding of New Orleans exposes serious flaws in the Bush administration's competence.

Immigration

The question of immigration and illegal immigration resurfaces in the wake of 9/11.

The Election of 2006

Angry with the Bush administration, voters return Congressional control back to the Democrats.

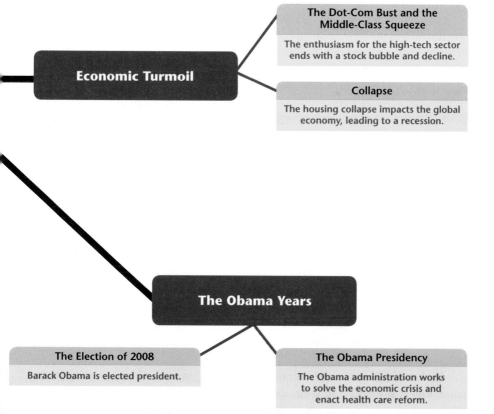

Economic Turmoil

The Dot-Com Bust and the Middle-Class Squeeze

The enthusiasm for the high-tech sector ends with a stock bubble and decline.

Collapse

The housing collapse impacts the global economy, leading to a recession.

The Obama Years

The Election of 2008

Barack Obama is elected president.

The Obama Presidency

The Obama administration works to solve the economic crisis and enact health care reform.

Appendix A

HISTORICAL DOCUMENTS

The Declaration of Independence

When in the course of human events, it becomes necessary for one people to dissolve the political bands which have connected them with another, and to assume, among the powers of the earth, the separate and equal station to which the Laws of Nature and of Nature's God entitle them, a decent respect to the opinions of mankind requires that they should declare the causes which impel them to the separation.

We hold these truths to be self-evident, that all men are created equal, that they are endowed by their Creator with certain unalienable Rights, that among these are life, liberty and the pursuit of happiness. That to secure these rights, governments are instituted among men, deriving their just powers from the consent of the governed; that whenever any form of government becomes destructive of these ends, it is the right of the people to alter or to abolish it, and to institute new Government, laying its foundation on such principles and organizing its powers in such form, as to them shall seem most likely to effect their safety and happiness. Prudence, indeed, will dictate that Governments long established should not be changed for light and transient causes; and, accordingly, all experience hath shown, that mankind are more disposed to suffer, while evils are sufferable, than to right themselves by abolishing the forms to which they are accustomed. But when a long train of abuses and usurpations, pursuing invariably the same object evinces a design to reduce them under absolute despotism, it is their right, it is their duty, to throw off such government, and to provide new guards for their future security. Such has been the patient sufferance of these colonies; and such is now the necessity which constrains them to alter their former systems of government. The history of the present King of Great Britain is a history of repeated injuries and usurpations, all having in direct object the establishment of an absolute tyranny over these States. To prove this, let facts be submitted to a candid world:

He has refused his assent to laws, the most wholesome and necessary for the public good.

He has forbidden his governors to pass laws of immediate and pressing importance, unless suspended in their operation till his assent should be obtained; and, when so suspended, he has utterly neglected to attend to them.

He has refused to pass other laws for the accommodation of large districts of people, unless those people would relinquish the right of representation in the legislature, a right inestimable to them and formidable to tyrants only.

He has called together legislative bodies at places unusual, uncomfortable, and distant from the depository of their public records, for the sole purpose of fatiguing them into compliance with his measures.

He has dissolved representative houses repeatedly, for opposing with manly firmness his invasions on the rights of the people.

He has refused for a long time, after such dissolutions, to cause others to be elected; whereby the legislative powers, incapable of annihilation, have returned to the People at large for their exercise; the State remaining in the mean time exposed to all the dangers of invasion from without, and convulsions within.

He has endeavored to prevent the population of these States; for that purpose obstructing the laws for naturalization of foreigners; refusing to pass others to encourage their migrations hither, and raising the conditions of new appropriations of lands.

He has obstructed the administration of justice, by refusing his assent to laws for establishing judiciary powers.

He has made judges dependent on his will alone, for the tenure of their offices, and the amount and payment of their salaries.

He has erected a multitude of new offices, and sent hither swarms of officers to harass our people, and eat out their substance.

He has kept among us, in times of peace, standing armies without the consent of our legislatures.

He has affected to render the Military independent of, and superior to, the civil power.

He has combined with others to subject us to a jurisdiction foreign to our constitution and unacknowledged by our laws; giving his assent to their acts of pretended legislation:

For quartering large bodies of armed troops among us;

For protecting them, by a mock trial, from punishment for any murders which they should commit on the inhabitants of these States;

For cutting off our trade with all parts of the world;

For imposing taxes on us without our Consent;

For depriving us, in many cases, of the benefits of Trial by Jury;

For transporting us beyond Seas to be tried for pretended offences;

For abolishing the free System of English Laws in a neighbouring Province, establishing therein an Arbitrary government, and enlarging its Boundaries so as to render it at once an example and fit instrument for introducing the same absolute rule into these colonies;

For taking away our charters, abolishing our most valuable laws, and altering fundamentally the forms of our governments;

For suspending our own legislatures, and declaring themselves invested with power to legislate for us in all cases whatsoever.

He has abdicated government here, by declaring us out of his protection and waging war against us.

He has plundered our seas, ravaged our coasts, burnt our towns, and destroyed the lives of our people.

He is at this time transporting large armies of foreign mercenaries to complete the works of death, desolation and tyranny, already begun with circumstances of cruelty and perfidy scarcely paralleled in the most barbarous ages, and totally unworthy the head of a civilized nation.

He has constrained our fellow citizens taken captive on the high seas to bear arms against their country, to become the executioners of their friends and brethren, or to fall themselves by their hands.

He has excited domestic insurrections amongst us, and has endeavored to bring on the inhabitants of our frontiers, the merciless Indian savages, whose known rule of warfare, is an undistinguished destruction of all ages, sexes and conditions.

In every stage of these oppressions we have petitioned for redress in the most humble terms; our repeated petitions have been answered only by repeated injury. A prince whose character is thus marked by every act which may define a tyrant, is unfit to be the ruler of a free people.

Nor have we been wanting in attentions to our British brethren. We have warned them from time to time of attempts by their legislature to extend an unwarrantable jurisdiction over us. We have reminded them of the circumstances of our emigration and settlement here. We have appealed to their native justice and magnanimity, and we have conjured them by the ties of our common kindred to disavow these usurpations, which, would inevitably interrupt our connections and correspondence. They, too, have been deaf to the voice of justice and of consanguinity. We must, therefore, acquiesce in the necessity, which denounces our separation, and hold them, as we hold the rest of mankind, enemies in war, in peace friends.

We, therefore, the representatives of the United States of America, in general Congress, assembled, appealing to the Supreme Judge of the world for the rectitude of our intentions, do, in the name, and by the authority of the good people of these colonies, solemnly publish and declare, that these united colonies are, and of right ought to be free and independent states; that they are absolved from all allegiance to the British Crown, and that all political connection between them and the state of Great Britain, is and ought to be totally dissolved; and that, as free and independent states, they have full power to levy war, conclude peace, contract alliances, establish commerce, and to do all other acts and things which independent states may of right do. And for the support of this declaration, with a firm reliance on the protection of Divine Providence, we mutually pledge to each other our lives, our fortunes and our sacred honor.

The Constitution of the United States of America

We the People of the United States, in Order to form a more perfect Union, establish Justice, insure domestic Tranquility, provide for the common defence, promote the general Welfare, and secure the Blessings of Liberty to ourselves and our Posterity, do ordain and establish this Constitution for the United States of America.

ARTICLE I

Section 1.
All legislative Powers herein granted shall be vested in a Congress of the United States, which shall consist of a Senate and House of Representatives.

Section 2.

The House of Representatives shall be composed of Members chosen every second Year by the People of the several States, and the Electors in each State shall have the Qualifications requisite for Electors of the most numerous Branch of the State Legislature.

No Person shall be a Representative who shall not have attained to the Age of twenty five Years, and been seven Years a Citizen of the United States, and who shall not, when elected, be an Inhabitant of that State in which he shall be chosen.

Representatives and direct Taxes shall be apportioned among the several States which may be included within this Union, according to their respective Numbers, which shall be determined by adding to the whole Number of free Persons, including those bound to Service for a Term of Years, and excluding Indians not taxed, three fifths of all other Persons. The actual Enumeration shall be made within three Years after the first Meeting of the Congress of the United States, and within every subsequent Term of ten Years, in such Manner as they shall by Law direct. The Number of Representatives shall not exceed one for every thirty Thousand, but each State shall have at Least one Representative; and until such enumeration shall be made, the State of New Hampshire shall be entitled to choose three, Massachusetts eight, Rhode-Island and Providence Plantations one, Connecticut five, New York six, New Jersey four, Pennsylvania eight, Delaware one, Maryland six, Virginia ten, North Carolina five, South Carolina five, and Georgia three.

When vacancies happen in the Representation from any State, the Executive Authority thereof shall issue Writs of Election to fill such Vacancies.

The House of Representatives shall choose their Speaker and other Officers; and shall have the sole Power of Impeachment.

Section 3.

The Senate of the United States shall be composed of two Senators from each State, chosen by the Legislature thereof for six Years; and each Senator shall have one Vote.

Immediately after they shall be assembled in Consequence of the first Election, they shall be divided as equally as may be into three Classes. The Seats of the Senators of the first Class shall be vacated at the Expiration of the second Year, of the second Class at the Expiration of the fourth Year, and of the third Class at the Expiration of the sixth Year, so that one third may be chosen every second Year; and if Vacancies happen by Resignation, or otherwise, during the Recess of the Legislature of any State, the Executive thereof may make temporary Appointments until the next Meeting of the Legislature, which shall then fill such Vacancies.

No Person shall be a Senator who shall not have attained to the Age of thirty Years, and been nine Years a Citizen of the United States, and who shall not, when elected, be an Inhabitant of that State for which he shall be chosen.

The Vice President of the United States shall be President of the Senate, but shall have no Vote, unless they be equally divided.

The Senate shall choose their other Officers, and also a President pro tempore, in the Absence of the Vice President, or when he shall exercise the Office of President of the United States.

The Senate shall have the sole Power to try all Impeachments. When sitting for that Purpose, they shall be on Oath or Affirmation. When the President of the United States is tried, the Chief Justice shall preside: And no Person shall be convicted without the Concurrence of two thirds of the Members present.

Judgment in Cases of Impeachment shall not extend further than to removal from Office, and disqualification to hold and enjoy any Office of honor, Trust or Profit under the United States: but the Party convicted shall nevertheless be liable and subject to Indictment, Trial, Judgment and Punishment, according to Law.

Section 4.

The Times, Places and Manner of holding Elections for Senators and Representatives, shall be prescribed in each State by the Legislature thereof; but the Congress may at any time by Law make or alter such Regulations, except as to the Places of chusing Senators.

The Congress shall assemble at least once in every Year, and such Meeting shall be on the first Monday in December, unless they shall by Law appoint a different Day.

Section 5.

Each House shall be the Judge of the Elections, Returns and Qualifications of its own Members, and a Majority of each shall constitute a Quorum to do Business; but a smaller Number may adjourn from day to day, and may be authorized to compel the Attendance of absent Members, in such Manner, and under such Penalties as each House may provide.

Each House may determine the Rules of its Proceedings, punish its Members for disorderly Behaviour, and, with the Concurrence of two thirds, expel a Member.

Each House shall keep a Journal of its Proceedings, and from time to time publish the same, excepting such Parts as may in their Judgment require Secrecy; and the Yeas and Nays of the Members of either House on any question shall, at the Desire of one fifth of those Present, be entered on the Journal.

Neither House, during the Session of Congress, shall, without the Consent of the other, adjourn for more than three days, nor to any other Place than that in which the two Houses shall be sitting.

Section 6.

The Senators and Representatives shall receive a Compensation for their Services, to be ascertained by Law, and paid out of the Treasury of the United States. They shall in all Cases, except Treason, Felony and Breach of the Peace, be privileged from Arrest during their Attendance at the Session of their respective Houses, and in going to and returning from the same; and for any Speech or Debate in either House, they shall not be questioned in any other Place.

No Senator or Representative shall, during the Time for which he was elected, be appointed to any civil Office under the Authority of the United States, which shall have been created, or the Emoluments whereof shall have been increased during such time; and no Person holding any Office under the United States, shall be a Member of either House during his Continuance in Office.

Section 7.

All Bills for raising Revenue shall originate in the House of Representatives; but the Senate may propose or concur with Amendments as on other Bills.

Every Bill which shall have passed the House of Representatives and the Senate, shall, before it become a Law, be presented to the President of the United States: If he approve he shall sign it, but if not he shall return it, with his Objections to that House in which it shall have originated, who shall enter the Objections at large on their Journal, and proceed to reconsider it. If after such Reconsideration two thirds of that House shall agree to pass the Bill, it shall be sent, together with the Objections, to the other House, by which it shall likewise be reconsidered, and if approved by two thirds of that House, it shall become a Law. But in all such Cases the Votes of both Houses shall be determined by yeas and Nays, and the Names of the Persons voting for and against the Bill shall be entered on the Journal of each House respectively. If any Bill shall not be returned by the President within ten Days (Sundays excepted) after it shall have been presented to him, the Same shall be a Law, in like Manner as if he had signed it, unless the Congress by their Adjournment prevent its Return, in which Case it shall not be a Law.

Every Order, Resolution, or Vote to which the Concurrence of the Senate and House of Representatives may be necessary (except on a question of Adjournment) shall be presented to the President of the United States; and before the Same shall take Effect, shall be approved by him, or being disapproved by him, shall be repassed by two thirds of the Senate and House of Representatives, according to the Rules and Limitations prescribed in the Case of a Bill.

Section 8.

The Congress shall have Power

To lay and collect Taxes, Duties, Imposts and Excises, to pay the Debts and provide for the common Defence and general Welfare of the United States; but all Duties, Imposts and Excises shall be uniform throughout the United States;

To borrow Money on the credit of the United States;

To regulate Commerce with foreign Nations, and among the several States, and with the Indian Tribes;

To establish an uniform Rule of Naturalization, and uniform Laws on the subject of Bankruptcies throughout the United States;

To coin Money, regulate the Value thereof, and of foreign Coin, and fix the Standard of Weights and Measures;

To provide for the Punishment of counterfeiting the Securities and current Coin of the United States;

To establish Post Offices and post Roads;

To promote the Progress of Science and useful Arts, by securing for limited Times to Authors and Inventors the exclusive Right to their respective Writings and Discoveries;

To constitute Tribunals inferior to the supreme Court;

To define and punish Piracies and Felonies committed on the high Seas, and Offences against the Law of Nations;

To declare War, grant Letters of Marque and Reprisal, and make Rules concerning Captures on Land and Water;

To raise and support Armies, but no Appropriation of Money to that Use shall be for a longer Term than two Years;

To provide and maintain a Navy;

To make Rules for the Government and Regulation of the land and naval Forces;

To provide for calling forth the Militia to execute the Laws of the Union, suppress Insurrections and repel Invasions;

To provide for organizing, arming, and disciplining the Militia, and for governing such Part of them as may be employed in the Service of the United States, reserving to the States respectively, the Appointment of the Officers, and the Authority of training the Militia according to the discipline prescribed by Congress;

To exercise exclusive Legislation in all Cases whatsoever, over such District (not exceeding ten Miles square) as may, by Cession of particular States, and the Acceptance of Congress, become the Seat of the Government of the United States, and to exercise like Authority over all Places purchased by the Consent of the Legislature of the State in which the Same shall be, for the Erection of Forts, Magazines, Arsenals, dock-Yards, and other needful Buildings;—And

To make all Laws which shall be necessary and proper for carrying into Execution the foregoing Powers, and all other Powers vested by this Constitution in the Government of the United States, or in any Department or Officer thereof.

Section 9.

The Migration or Importation of such Persons as any of the States now existing shall think proper to admit, shall not be prohibited by the Congress prior to the Year one thousand eight hundred and eight, but a Tax or duty may be imposed on such Importation, not exceeding ten dollars for each Person.

The Privilege of the Writ of Habeas Corpus shall not be suspended, unless when in Cases of Rebellion or Invasion the public Safety may require it.

No Bill of Attainder or ex post facto Law shall be passed.

No Capitation, or other direct, Tax shall be laid, unless in Proportion to the Census or enumeration herein before directed to be taken.

No Tax or Duty shall be laid on Articles exported from any State.

No Preference shall be given by any Regulation of Commerce or Revenue to the Ports of one State over those of another; nor shall Vessels bound to, or from, one State, be obliged to enter, clear, or pay Duties in another.

No Money shall be drawn from the Treasury, but in Consequence of Appropriations made by Law; and a regular Statement and Account of the Receipts and Expenditures of all public Money shall be published from time to time.

No Title of Nobility shall be granted by the United States: And no Person holding any Office of Profit or Trust under them, shall, without the Consent of the Congress, accept of any present, Emolument, Office, or Title, of any kind whatever, from any King, Prince, or foreign State.

Section 10.

No State shall enter into any Treaty, Alliance, or Confederation; grant Letters of Marque and Reprisal; coin Money; emit Bills of Credit; make any Thing but gold and silver Coin a Tender in Payment of Debts; pass any Bill of Attainder, ex post facto Law, or Law impairing the Obligation of Contracts, or grant any Title of Nobility.

No State shall, without the Consent of the Congress, lay any Imposts or Duties on Imports or Exports, except what may be absolutely necessary for executing it's inspection Laws: and the net Produce of all Duties and Imposts, laid by any State on Imports or Exports, shall be for the Use of the Treasury of the United States; and all such Laws shall be subject to the Revision and Control of the Congress.

No State shall, without the Consent of Congress, lay any Duty of Tonnage, keep Troops, or Ships of War in time of Peace, enter into any Agreement or Compact with another State, or with a foreign Power, or engage in War, unless actually invaded, or in such imminent Danger as will not admit of delay.

ARTICLE II

Section 1.

The executive Power shall be vested in a President of the United States of America. He shall hold his Office during the Term of four Years, and, together with the Vice President, chosen for the same Term, be elected, as follows:

Each State shall appoint, in such Manner as the Legislature thereof may direct, a Number of Electors, equal to the whole Number of Senators and Representatives to which the State may be entitled in the Congress: but no Senator or Representative, or Person holding an Office of Trust or Profit under the United States, shall be appointed an Elector.

The Electors shall meet in their respective States, and vote by Ballot for two Persons, of whom one at least shall not be an Inhabitant of the same State with themselves. And they shall make a List of all the Persons voted for, and of the Number of Votes for each; which List they shall sign and certify, and transmit sealed to the Seat of the Government of the United States, directed to the President of the Senate. The President of the Senate shall, in the Presence of the Senate and House of Representatives, open all the Certificates, and the Votes shall then be counted. The Person having the greatest Number of Votes shall be the President, if such Number be a Majority of the whole Number of Electors appointed; and if there be more than one who have such Majority, and have an equal Number of Votes, then the House of Representatives shall immediately choose by Ballot one of them for President; and if no Person have a Majority, then from the five highest on the List the said House shall in like Manner choose the President. But in choosing the President, the Votes shall be taken by States, the Representation from each State having one Vote; A quorum for this purpose shall consist of a Member or Members from two thirds of the States, and a Majority of all the States shall be necessary to a Choice. In every Case, after the Choice of the President, the Person having the greatest Number of Votes of the Electors shall be the Vice President. But if there should remain two or more who have equal Votes, the Senate shall choose from them by Ballot the Vice President.

The Congress may determine the Time of choosing the Electors, and the Day on which they shall give their Votes; which Day shall be the same throughout the United States.

No Person except a natural born Citizen, or a Citizen of the United States, at the time of the Adoption of this Constitution, shall be eligible to the Office of President; neither shall any Person be eligible to that Office who shall not have attained to the Age of thirty five Years, and been fourteen Years a Resident within the United States.

In Case of the Removal of the President from Office, or of his Death, Resignation, or Inability to discharge the Powers and Duties of the said Office, the Same shall devolve on the Vice President, and the Congress may by Law provide for the Case of Removal, Death, Resignation or Inability, both of the President and Vice President, declaring what Officer shall then act as President, and such Officer shall act accordingly, until the Disability be removed, or a President shall be elected.

The President shall, at stated Times, receive for his Services, a Compensation, which shall neither be increased nor diminished during the Period for which he shall have been elected, and he shall not receive within that Period any other Emolument from the United States, or any of them.

Before he enter on the Execution of his Office, he shall take the following Oath or Affirmation:—"I do solemnly swear (or affirm) that I will faithfully execute the Office of President of the United States, and will to the best of my Ability, preserve, protect and defend the Constitution of the United States."

Section 2.

The President shall be Commander in Chief of the Army and Navy of the United States, and of the Militia of the several States, when called into the actual Service of the United States; he may require the Opinion, in writing, of the principal Officer in each of the executive Departments, upon any Subject relating to the Duties of their respective Offices, and he shall have Power to grant Reprieves and Pardons for Offences against the United States, except in Cases of Impeachment.

He shall have Power, by and with the Advice and Consent of the Senate, to make Treaties, provided two thirds of the Senators present concur; and he shall nominate, and by and with the Advice and Consent of the Senate, shall appoint Ambassadors, other public Ministers and Consuls, Judges of the supreme Court, and all other Officers of the United States, whose Appointments are not herein otherwise provided for, and which shall be established by Law: but the Congress may by Law vest the Appointment of such inferior Officers, as they think proper, in the President alone, in the Courts of Law, or in the Heads of Departments.

The President shall have Power to fill up all Vacancies that may happen during the Recess of the Senate, by granting Commissions which shall expire at the End of their next Session.

Section 3.

He shall from time to time give to the Congress Information of the State of the Union, and recommend to their Consideration such Measures as he shall judge necessary and expedient; he may, on extraordinary Occasions, convene both Houses, or either of them, and in Case of Disagreement between them, with Respect to the Time of Adjournment, he may adjourn them to such Time as he shall think proper; he shall receive Ambassadors and other public Ministers; he shall take Care that the Laws be faithfully executed, and shall Commission all the Officers of the United States.

Section 4

The President, Vice President and all civil Officers of the United States, shall be removed from Office on Impeachment for, and Conviction of, Treason, Bribery, or other high Crimes and Misdemeanors.

ARTICLE III

Section 1.

The judicial Power of the United States shall be vested in one supreme Court, and in such inferior Courts as the Congress may from time to time ordain and establish. The Judges, both of the supreme and inferior Courts, shall hold their Offices during good Behaviour, and shall, at stated Times, receive for their Services a Compensation, which shall not be diminished during their Continuance in Office.

Section 2.

The judicial Power shall extend to all Cases, in Law and Equity, arising under this Constitution, the Laws of the United States, and Treaties made, or which shall be made, under their Authority;—to all Cases affecting Ambassadors, other public Ministers and Consuls;—to all Cases of admiralty and maritime Jurisdiction;—to Controversies to which the United States shall be a Party;—to Controversies between two or more States;—between a State and Citizens of another State;—between Citizens of different States;—between Citizens of the same State claiming Lands under Grants of different States, and between a State, or the Citizens thereof, and foreign States, Citizens or Subjects.

In all Cases affecting Ambassadors, other public Ministers and Consuls, and those in which a State shall be Party, the supreme Court shall have original Jurisdiction. In all the other Cases before mentioned, the supreme Court shall have appellate Jurisdiction, both as to Law and Fact, with such Exceptions, and under such Regulations as the Congress shall make.

The Trial of all Crimes, except in Cases of Impeachment, shall be by Jury; and such Trial shall be held in the State where the said Crimes shall have been committed; but when not committed within any State, the Trial shall be at such Place or Places as the Congress may by Law have directed.

Section 3.

Treason against the United States, shall consist only in levying War against them, or in adhering to their Enemies, giving them Aid and Comfort. No Person shall be convicted of Treason unless on the Testimony of two Witnesses to the same overt Act, or on Confession in open Court.

The Congress shall have Power to declare the Punishment of Treason, but no Attainder of Treason shall work Corruption of Blood, or Forfeiture except during the Life of the Person attainted.

ARTICLE IV

Section 1.

Full Faith and Credit shall be given in each State to the public Acts, Records, and judicial Proceedings of every other State. And the Congress may by general Laws prescribe the Manner in which such Acts, Records and Proceedings shall be proved, and the Effect thereof.

Section 2.

The Citizens of each State shall be entitled to all Privileges and Immunities of Citizens in the several States.

A Person charged in any State with Treason, Felony, or other Crime, who shall flee from Justice, and be found in another State, shall on Demand of the executive Authority of the State from which he fled, be delivered up, to be removed to the State having Jurisdiction of the Crime.

No Person held to Service or Labour in one State, under the Laws thereof, escaping into another, shall, in Consequence of any Law or Regulation therein, be discharged from such Service or Labour, but shall be delivered up on Claim of the Party to whom such Service or Labour may be due.

Section 3.

New States may be admitted by the Congress into this Union; but no new State shall be formed or erected within the Jurisdiction of any other State; nor any State be formed by the Junction of two or more States, or Parts of States, without the Consent of the Legislatures of the States concerned as well as of the Congress.

The Congress shall have Power to dispose of and make all needful Rules and Regulations respecting the Territory or other Property belonging to the United States; and nothing in this Constitution shall be so construed as to Prejudice any Claims of the United States, or of any particular State.

Section 4.

The United States shall guarantee to every State in this Union a Republican Form of Government, and shall protect each of them against Invasion; and on Application of the Legislature, or of the Executive (when the Legislature cannot be convened), against domestic Violence.

ARTICLE V

The Congress, whenever two thirds of both Houses shall deem it necessary, shall propose Amendments to this Constitution, or, on the Application of the Legislatures of two thirds of the several States, shall call a Convention for proposing Amendments, which, in either Case, shall be valid to all Intents and Purposes, as Part of this Constitution, when ratified by the Legislatures of three fourths of the several States, or by Conventions in three fourths thereof, as the one or the other Mode of Ratification may be proposed by the Congress; Provided that no Amendment which may be made prior to the Year One thousand eight hundred and eight shall in any Manner affect the first and fourth Clauses in the Ninth Section of the first Article; and that no State, without its Consent, shall be deprived of its equal Suffrage in the Senate.

ARTICLE VI

All Debts contracted and Engagements entered into, before the Adoption of this Constitution, shall be as valid against the United States under this Constitution, as under the Confederation.

This Constitution, and the Laws of the United States which shall be made in Pursuance thereof; and all Treaties made, or which shall be made, under the Authority of the United States, shall be the supreme Law of the Land; and the Judges in every State shall be bound thereby, any Thing in the Constitution or Laws of any State to the Contrary notwithstanding.

The Senators and Representatives before mentioned, and the Members of the several State Legislatures, and all executive and judicial Officers, both of the United States and of the several States, shall be bound by Oath or Affirmation, to support this Constitution; but no religious Test shall ever be required as a Qualification to any Office or public Trust under the United States.

ARTICLE VII

The Ratification of the Conventions of nine States, shall be sufficient for the Establishment of this Constitution between the States so ratifying the Same.

The Word, "the," being interlined between the seventh and eighth Lines of the first Page, the Word "Thirty" being partly written on an Erazure in the fifteenth Line of the first Page, The Words "is tried" being interlined between the thirty second and thirty third Lines of the first Page and the Word "the" being interlined between the forty third and forty fourth Lines of the second Page.

Attest William Jackson Secretary

Done in Convention by the Unanimous Consent of the States present the Seventeenth Day of September in the Year of our Lord one thousand seven hundred and Eighty seven and of the Independence of the United States of America the Twelfth In witness whereof We have hereunto subscribed our Names,

G°. Washington
Presidt and deputy from Virginia

Delaware
Geo: Read
Gunning Bedford jun
John Dickinson
Richard Bassett
Jaco: Broom

Maryland
James McHenry
Dan of St Thos. Jenifer
Danl. Carroll

Virginia
John Blair
James Madison Jr.

North Carolina
Wm. Blount
Richd. Dobbs Spaight
Hu Williamson

South Carolina
J. Rutledge
Charles Cotesworth
Pinckney
Charles Pinckney
Pierce Butler

Georgia
William Few
Abr Baldwin

New Hampshire
John Langdon
Nicholas Gilman

Massachusetts
Nathaniel Gorham
Rufus King

Connecticut
Wm. Saml. Johnson
Roger Sherman

New York
Alexander Hamilton

New Jersey
Wil: Livingston
David Brearley
Wm. Paterson
Jona: Dayton

Pennsylvania
B Franklin
Thomas Mifflin
Robt. Morris
Geo. Clymer
Thos. FitzSimons
Jared Ingersoll
James Wilson
Gouv Morris

Articles

In addition to, and Amendment of the Constitution of the United States of America, proposed by Congress, and ratified by the Legislatures of the several States, pursuant to the fifth Article of the original Constitution.

(The first ten amendments to the U.S. Constitution were ratified December 15, 1791, and form what is known as the "Bill of Rights.")

AMENDMENT I

Congress shall make no law respecting an establishment of religion, or prohibiting the free exercise thereof; or abridging the freedom of speech, or of the press; or the right of the people peaceably to assemble, and to petition the Government for a redress of grievances.

AMENDMENT II

A well regulated Militia, being necessary to the security of a free State, the right of the people to keep and bear Arms, shall not be infringed.

AMENDMENT III

No Soldier shall, in time of peace be quartered in any house, without the consent of the Owner, nor in time of war, but in a manner to be prescribed by law.

AMENDMENT IV

The right of the people to be secure in their persons, houses, papers, and effects, against unreasonable searches and seizures, shall not be violated, and no Warrants shall issue, but upon probable cause, supported by Oath or affirmation, and particularly describing the place to be searched, and the persons or things to be seized.

AMENDMENT V

No person shall be held to answer for a capital, or otherwise infamous crime, unless on a presentment or indictment of a Grand Jury, except in cases arising in the land or naval forces, or in the Militia, when in actual service in time of War or public danger; nor shall any person be subject for the same offence to be twice put in jeopardy of life or limb; nor shall be compelled in any criminal case to be a witness against himself, nor be deprived of life, liberty, or property, without due process of law; nor shall private property be taken for public use, without just compensation.

AMENDMENT VI

In all criminal prosecutions, the accused shall enjoy the right to a speedy and public trial, by an impartial jury of the State and district wherein the crime shall have been committed, which district shall have been previously ascertained by law, and to be informed of the nature and cause of the accusation; to be confronted with the witnesses against him; to have compulsory process for obtaining witnesses in his favor, and to have the Assistance of Counsel for his defence.

AMENDMENT VII

In Suits at common law, where the value in controversy shall exceed twenty dollars, the right of trial by jury shall be preserved, and no fact tried by a jury, shall be otherwise re-examined in any Court of the United States, than according to the rules of the common law.

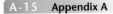

AMENDMENT VIII

Excessive bail shall not be required, nor excessive fines imposed, nor cruel and unusual punishments inflicted.

AMENDMENT IX

The enumeration in the Constitution, of certain rights, shall not be construed to deny or disparage others retained by the people.

AMENDMENT X

The powers not delegated to the United States by the Constitution, nor prohibited by it to the States, are reserved to the States respectively, or to the people.

AMENDMENT XI

Passed by Congress March 4, 1794. Ratified February 7, 1795.

Note: Article III, Section 2, of the Constitution was modified by Amendment XI.

The Judicial power of the United States shall not be construed to extend to any suit in law or equity, commenced or prosecuted against one of the United States by Citizens of another State, or by Citizens or Subjects of any Foreign State.

AMENDMENT XII

Passed by Congress December 9, 1803. Ratified June 15, 1804.

Note: A portion of Article II, Section 1, of the Constitution was superceded by the Twelfth Amendment.

The Electors shall meet in their respective states and vote by ballot for President and Vice-President, one of whom, at least, shall not be an inhabitant of the same state with themselves; they shall name in their ballots the person voted for as President, and in distinct ballots the person voted for as Vice-President, and they shall make distinct lists of all persons voted for as President, and of all persons voted for as Vice-President, and of the number of votes for each, which lists they shall sign and certify, and transmit sealed to the seat of the government of the United States, directed to the President of the Senate;—the President of the Senate shall, in the presence of the Senate and House of Representatives, open all the certificates and the votes shall then be counted;—The person having the greatest number of votes for President, shall be the President, if such number be a majority of the whole number of Electors appointed; and if no person have such majority, then from the persons having the highest numbers not exceeding three on the list of those voted for as President, the House of Representatives shall choose immediately, by ballot, the President. But in choosing the President, the votes shall be taken by states, the representation from each state having one vote; a quorum for this purpose shall consist of a member or members from two-thirds of the states, and a majority of all the states shall be necessary to a choice. [And if the House of Representatives shall not choose a President whenever the right of choice shall devolve upon them, before the fourth day of March next following, then the Vice-President shall act as President, as in case of the death or other constitutional disability of the President.—]* The person having the greatest number of votes as Vice-President, shall be the Vice-President, if such number be a majority of the whole number of Electors appointed, and if no person have a majority, then from the two highest numbers on the list, the Senate shall choose the Vice-President; a quorum for the purpose shall consist of two-thirds of the whole number of Senators, and a majority of the whole number shall be necessary to a choice. But no person constitutionally ineligible to the office of President shall be eligible to that of Vice-President of the United States.

*Superceded by Section 3 of the Twentieth Amendment.

AMENDMENT XIII

Passed by Congress January 31, 1865. Ratified December 6, 1865.

Note: A portion of Article IV, Section 2, of the Constitution was superceded by the Thirteenth Amendment.

Section 1.

Neither slavery nor involuntary servitude, except as a punishment for crime whereof the party shall have been duly convicted, shall exist within the United States, or any place subject to their jurisdiction.

Section 2.

Congress shall have power to enforce this article by appropriate legislation.

AMENDMENT XIV

Passed by Congress June 13, 1866. Ratified July 9, 1868.

Note: Article I, Section 2, of the Constitution was modified by Section 2 of the Fourteenth Amendment.

Section 1.

All persons born or naturalized in the United States, and subject to the jurisdiction thereof, are citizens of the United States and of the State wherein they reside. No State shall make or enforce any law which shall abridge the privileges or immunities of citizens of the United States; nor shall any State deprive any person of life, liberty, or property, without due process of law; nor deny to any person within its jurisdiction the equal protection of the laws.

Section 2.

Representatives shall be apportioned among the several States according to their respective numbers, counting the whole number of persons in each State, excluding Indians not taxed. But when the right to vote at any election for the choice of electors for President and Vice-President of the United States, Representatives in Congress, the Executive and Judicial officers of a State, or the members of the Legislature thereof, is denied to any of the male inhabitants of such State, being twenty-one years of age,* and citizens of the United States, or in any way abridged, except for participation in rebellion, or other crime, the basis of representation therein shall be reduced in the proportion which the number of such male citizens shall bear to the whole number of male citizens twenty-one years of age in such State.

Section 3.

No person shall be a Senator or Representative in Congress, or elector of President and Vice-President, or hold any office, civil or military, under the United States, or under any State, who, having previously taken an oath, as a member of Congress, or as an officer of the United States, or as a member of any State legislature, or as an executive or judicial officer of any State, to support the Constitution of the United States, shall have engaged in insurrection or rebellion against the same, or given aid or comfort to the enemies thereof. But Congress may by a vote of two-thirds of each House, remove such disability.

Section 4.

The validity of the public debt of the United States, authorized by law, including debts incurred for payment of pensions and bounties for services in suppressing insurrection or rebellion, shall not be questioned. But neither the United States nor any State shall assume or pay any debt or obligation incurred in aid of insurrection or rebellion against the United States, or any claim for the loss or emancipation of any slave; but all such debts, obligations and claims shall be held illegal and void.

Section 5.

The Congress shall have the power to enforce, by appropriate legislation, the provisions of this article.

    *Changed by Section 1 of the Twenty-sixth Amendment.

AMENDMENT XV

Passed by Congress February 26, 1869. Ratified February 3, 1870.

Section 1.

The right of citizens of the United States to vote shall not be denied or abridged by the United States or by any State on account of race, color, or previous condition of servitude.

Section 2.
The Congress shall have the power to enforce this article by appropriate legislation.

AMENDMENT XVI

Passed by Congress July 2, 1909. Ratified February 3, 1913.

Note: Article I, Section 9, of the Constitution was modified by Amendment XVI.

The Congress shall have power to lay and collect taxes on incomes, from whatever source derived, without apportionment among the several States, and without regard to any census or enumeration.

AMENDMENT XVII

Passed by Congress May 13, 1912. Ratified April 8, 1913.

Note: Article I, Section 3, of the Constitution was modified by the Seventeenth Amendment.

The Senate of the United States shall be composed of two Senators from each State, elected by the people thereof, for six years; and each Senator shall have one vote. The electors in each State shall have the qualifications requisite for electors of the most numerous branch of the State legislatures.

When vacancies happen in the representation of any State in the Senate, the executive authority of such State shall issue writs of election to fill such vacancies: *Provided,* That the legislature of any State may empower the executive thereof to make temporary appointments until the people fill the vacancies by election as the legislature may direct.

This amendment shall not be so construed as to affect the election or term of any Senator chosen before it becomes valid as part of the Constitution.

AMENDMENT XVIII

Passed by Congress December 18, 1917. Ratified January 16, 1919. Repealed by Amendment XXI.

Section 1.
After one year from the ratification of this article the manufacture, sale, or transportation of intoxicating liquors within, the importation thereof into, or the exportation thereof from the United States and all territory subject to the jurisdiction thereof for beverage purposes is hereby prohibited.

Section 2.
The Congress and the several States shall have concurrent power to enforce this article by appropriate legislation.

Section 3.

This article shall be inoperative unless it shall have been ratified as an amendment to the Constitution by the legislatures of the several States, as provided in the Constitution, within seven years from the date of the submission hereof to the States by the Congress.

AMENDMENT XIX

Passed by Congress June 4, 1919. Ratified August 18, 1920.

The right of citizens of the United States to vote shall not be denied or abridged by the United States or by any State on account of sex.

Congress shall have power to enforce this article by appropriate legislation.

AMENDMENT XX

Passed by Congress March 2, 1932. Ratified January 23, 1933.

Note: Article I, Section 4, of the Constitution was modified by Section 2 of this amendment. In addition, a portion of the Twelfth Amendment was superceded by Section 3.

Section 1.

The terms of the President and the Vice President shall end at noon on the 20th day of January, and the terms of Senators and Representatives at noon on the 3d day of January, of the years in which such terms would have ended if this article had not been ratified; and the terms of their successors shall then begin.

Section 2.

The Congress shall assemble at least once in every year, and such meeting shall begin at noon on the 3d day of January, unless they shall by law appoint a different day.

Section 3.

If, at the time fixed for the beginning of the term of the President, the President elect shall have died, the Vice President elect shall become President. If a President shall not have been chosen before the time fixed for the beginning of his term, or if the President elect shall have failed to qualify, then the Vice President elect shall act as President until a President shall have qualified; and the Congress may by law provide for the case wherein neither a President elect nor a Vice President shall have qualified, declaring who shall then act as President, or the manner in which one who is to act shall be selected, and such person shall act accordingly until a President or Vice President shall have qualified.

Section 4.

The Congress may by law provide for the case of the death of any of the persons from whom the House of Representatives may choose a President whenever the right of choice shall have devolved upon them, and for the case of the death of any of the persons from whom the Senate may choose a Vice President whenever the right of choice shall have devolved upon them.

Section 5.
Sections 1 and 2 shall take effect on the 15th day of October following the ratification of this article.

Section 6.
This article shall be inoperative unless it shall have been ratified as an amendment to the Constitution by the legislatures of three-fourths of the several States within seven years from the date of its submission.

AMENDMENT XXI

Passed by Congress February 20, 1933. Ratified December 5, 1933.

Section 1.
The eighteenth article of amendment to the Constitution of the United States is hereby repealed.

Section 2.
The transportation or importation into any State, Territory, or Possession of the United States for delivery or use therein of intoxicating liquors, in violation of the laws thereof, is hereby prohibited.

Section 3.
This article shall be inoperative unless it shall have been ratified as an amendment to the Constitution by conventions in the several States, as provided in the Constitution, within seven years from the date of the submission hereof to the States by the Congress.

AMENDMENT XXII

Passed by Congress March 21, 1947. Ratified February 27, 1951.

Section 1.
No person shall be elected to the office of the President more than twice, and no person who has held the office of President, or acted as President, for more than two years of a term to which some other person was elected President shall be elected to the office of President more than once. But this Article shall not apply to any person holding the office of President when this Article was proposed by Congress, and shall not prevent any person who may be holding the office of President, or acting as President, during the term within which this Article becomes operative from holding the office of President or acting as President during the remainder of such term.

Section 2.

This article shall be inoperative unless it shall have been ratified as an amendment to the Constitution by the legislatures of three-fourths of the several States within seven years from the date of its submission to the States by the Congress.

AMENDMENT XXIII

Passed by Congress June 16, 1960. Ratified March 29, 1961.

Section 1.

The District constituting the seat of Government of the United States shall appoint in such manner as Congress may direct:

A number of electors of President and Vice President equal to the whole number of Senators and Representatives in Congress to which the District would be entitled if it were a State, but in no event more than the least populous State; they shall be in addition to those appointed by the States, but they shall be considered, for the purposes of the election of President and Vice President, to be electors appointed by a State; and they shall meet in the District and perform such duties as provided by the twelfth article of amendment.

Section 2.

The Congress shall have power to enforce this article by appropriate legislation.

AMENDMENT XXIV

Passed by Congress August 27, 1962. Ratified January 23, 1964.

Section 1.

The right of citizens of the United States to vote in any primary or other election for President or Vice President, for electors for President or Vice President, or for Senator or Representative in Congress, shall not be denied or abridged by the United States or any State by reason of failure to pay poll tax or other tax.

Section 2.

The Congress shall have power to enforce this article by appropriate legislation.

AMENDMENT XXV

Passed by Congress July 6, 1965. Ratified February 10, 1967.

Note: Article II, Section 1, of the Constitution was affected by the Twenty-fifth Amendment.

Section 1.

In case of the removal of the President from office or of his death or resignation, the Vice President shall become President.

Section 2.

Whenever there is a vacancy in the office of the Vice President, the President shall nominate a Vice President who shall take office upon confirmation by a majority vote of both Houses of Congress.

Section 3.

Whenever the President transmits to the President pro tempore of the Senate and the Speaker of the House of Representatives his written declaration that he is unable to discharge the powers and duties of his office, and until he transmits to them a written declaration to the contrary, such powers and duties shall be discharged by the Vice President as Acting President.

Section 4.

Whenever the Vice President and a majority of either the principal officers of the executive departments or of such other body as Congress may by law provide, transmit to the President pro tempore of the Senate and the Speaker of the House of Representatives their written declaration that the President is unable to discharge the powers and duties of his office, the Vice President shall immediately assume the powers and duties of the office as Acting President.

Thereafter, when the President transmits to the President pro tempore of the Senate and the Speaker of the House of Representatives his written declaration that no inability exists, he shall resume the powers and duties of his office unless the Vice President and a majority of either the principal officers of the executive department or of such other body as Congress may by law provide, transmit within four days to the President pro tempore of the Senate and the Speaker of the House of Representatives their written declaration that the President is unable to discharge the powers and duties of his office. Thereupon Congress shall decide the issue, assembling within forty-eight hours for that purpose if not in session. If the Congress, within twenty-one days after receipt of the latter written declaration, or, if Congress is not in session, within twenty-one days after Congress is required to assemble, determines by two-thirds vote of both Houses that the President is unable to discharge the powers and duties of his office, the Vice President shall continue to discharge the same as Acting President; otherwise, the President shall resume the powers and duties of his office.

AMENDMENT XXVI

Passed by Congress March 23, 1971. Ratified July 1, 1971.

Note: Amendment XIV, Section 2, of the Constitution was modified by Section 1 of the Twenty-sixth Amendment.

Section 1.

The right of citizens of the United States, who are eighteen years of age or older, to vote shall not be denied or abridged by the United States or by any State on account of age.

Section 2.

The Congress shall have power to enforce this article by appropriate legislation.

AMENDMENT XXVII

Originally proposed Sept. 25, 1789. Ratified May 7, 1992.

No law, varying the compensation for the services of the Senators and Representatives, shall take effect, until an election of representatives shall have intervened.

Lincoln's Gettysburg Address

Four score and seven years ago our fathers brought forth on this continent, a new nation, conceived in Liberty, and dedicated to the proposition that all men are created equal.

Now we are engaged in a great civil war, testing whether that nation, or any nation so conceived and so dedicated, can long endure. We are met on a great battle-field of that war. We have come to dedicate a portion of that field, as a final resting place for those who here gave their lives that that nation might live. It is altogether fitting and proper that we should do this.

But, in a larger sense, we can not dedicate—we can not consecrate—we can not hallow—this ground. The brave men, living and dead, who struggled here, have consecrated it, far above our poor power to add or detract. The world will little note, nor long remember what we say here, but it can never forget what they did here. It is for us the living, rather, to be dedicated here to the unfinished work which they who fought here have thus far so nobly advanced. It is rather for us to be here dedicated to the great task remaining before us—that from these honored dead we take increased devotion to that cause for which they gave the last full measure of devotion—that we here highly resolve that these dead shall not have died in vain—that this nation, under God, shall have a new birth of freedom—and that government of the people, by the people, for the people, shall not perish from the earth.

Appendix B

HISTORICAL FACTS AND DATA

U.S. Presidents and Vice Presidents

	PRESIDENT	VICE-PRESIDENT	POLITICAL PARTY	TERM
1	George Washington	John Adams	No Party Designation	1789–1797
2	John Adams	Thomas Jefferson	Federalist	1797–1801
3	Thomas Jefferson	Aaron Burr George Clinton	Democratic-Republican	1801–1809
4	James Madison	George Clinton Elbridge Gerry	Democratic-Republican	1809–1817
5	James Monroe	Daniel D Tompkins	Democratic-Republican	1817–1825
6	John Quincy Adams	John C Calhoun	Democratic-Republican	1825–1829
7	Andrew Jackson	John C Calhoun Martin Van Buren	Democratic	1829–1837
8	Martin Van Buren	Richard M. Johnson	Democratic	1837–1841
9	William Henry Harrison	John Tyler	Whig	1841
10	John Tyler	None	Whig	1841–1845
11	James Knox Polk	George M Dallas	Democratic	1845–1849
12	Zachary Taylor	Millard Fillmore	Whig	1849–1850
13	Millard Fillmore	None	Whig	1850–1853
14	Franklin Pierce	William R King	Democratic	1853–1857
15	James Buchanan	John C Breckinridge	Democratic	1857–1861
16	Abraham Lincoln	Hannibel Hamlin Andrew Johnson	Union	1861–1865
17	Andrew Johnson	None	Union	1865–1869
18	Ulysses Simpson Grant	Schuyler Colfax Henry Wilson	Republican	1869–1877
19	Rutherford Birchard Hayes	William A Wheeler	Republican	1877–1881
20	James Abram Garfield	Chester Alan Arthur	Republican	1881

(continued)

	PRESIDENT	VICE-PRESIDENT	POLITICAL PARTY	TERM
21	Chester Alan Arthur	None	Republican	1881–1885
22	Stephen Grover Cleveland	Thomas Hendricks	Democratic	1885–1889
23	Benjamin Harrison	Levi P Morton	Republican	1889–1893
24	Chester Alan Arthur	Adlai E Stevenson	Democratic	1893–1897
25	William McKinley	Garret A. Hobart Theodore Roosevelt	Republican	1897–1901
26	Theodore Roosevelt	Charles W Fairbanks	Republican	1901–1909
27	William Howard Taft	James S Sherman	Republican	1909–1913
28	Woodrow Wilson	Thomas R Marshall	Democratic	1913–1921
29	Warren Gamaliel Harding	Calvin Coolidge	Republican	1921–1923
30	Calvin Coolidge	Charles G Dawes	Republican	1923–1929
31	Herbert Clark Hoover	Charles Curtis	Republican	1929–1933
32	Franklin Delano Roosevelt	John Nance Garner Henry A. Wallace Harry S. Truman	Democratic	1933–1945
33	Harry S. Truman	Alben W Barkley	Democratic	1945–1953
34	Dwight David Eisenhower	Richard Milhous Nixon	Republican	1953–1961
35	John Fitzgerald Kennedy	Lyndon Baines Johnson	Democratic	1961–1963
36	Lyndon Baines Johnson	Hubert Horatio Humphrey	Democratic	1963–1969
37	Richard Milhous Nixon	Spiro T. Agnew Gerald Rudolph Ford	Republican	1969–1974
38	Gerald Rudolph Ford	Nelson Rockefeller	Republican	1974–1977
39	James Earl Carter, Jr.	Walter Mondale	Democratic	1977–1981
40	Ronald Wilson Reagan	George Herbert Walker Bush	Republican	1981–1989
41	George Herbert Walker Bush	J. Danforth Quayle	Republican	1989–1993
42	William Jefferson Clinton	Albert Gore, Jr.	Democratic	1993–2001
43	George Walker Bush	Richard Cheney	Republican	2001–2008
44	Barack Hussein Obama	Joseph Biden	Democratic	2008–

Admission of States into the Union

	STATE	DATE OF ADMISSION			STATE	DATE OF ADMISSION
1	Delaware	December 7, 1787		27	Florida	March 3, 1845
2	Pennsylvania	December 12, 1787		28	Texas	December 29, 1845
3	New Jersey	December 18, 1787		29	Iowa	December 28, 1846
4	Georgia	January 2, 1788		30	Wisconsin	May 29, 1848
5	Connecticut	January 9, 1788		31	California	September 9, 1850
6	Massachusetts	February 6, 1788		32	Minnesota	May 11, 1858
7	Maryland	April 28, 1788		33	Oregon	February 14, 1859
8	South Carolina	May 23, 1788		34	Kansas	January 29, 1861
9	New Hampshire	June 21, 1788		35	West Virginia	June 20, 1863
10	Virginia	June 25, 1788		36	Nevada	October 31, 1864
11	New York	July 26, 1788		37	Nebraska	March 1, 1867
12	North Carolina	November 21, 1789		38	Colorado	August 1, 1876
13	Rhode Island	May 29, 1790		39	North Dakota	November 2, 1889
14	Vermont	March 4, 1791		40	South Dakota	November 2, 1889
15	Kentucky	June 1, 1792		41	Montana	November 11, 1889
16	Tennessee	June 1, 1796		43	Idaho	July 3, 1890
17	Ohio	March 1, 1803		44	Wyoming	July 10, 1890
18	Louisiana	April 30, 1812		45	Utah	January 4, 1896
19	Indiana	December 11, 1816		46	Oklahoma	November 16, 1907
20	Mississippi	December 10, 1817		47	New Mexico	January 6, 1912
21	Illinois	December 3, 1818		48	Arizona	February 14, 1912
22	Alabama	December 14, 1819		49	Alaska	January 3, 1959
23	Maine	March 15, 1820		50	Hawaii	August 21, 1959
24	Missouri	August 10, 1821				
25	Arkansas	June 15, 1836				

Glossary

Abolition A pre-Civil War social movement devoted to the emancipation of slaves and their inclusion in American society as citizens with equal rights.

Abu Ghraib Iraqi correctional facility near Baghdad that was widely publicized in 2004 for abuses of Iraqi prisoners of war by the U.S. military and CIA operatives.

Act of Supremacy (1534) English parliamentary act that abolished papal authority over England, making King Henry VIII the head of the Church of England.

Acts of Union (1707) Parliamentary acts that created the United Kingdom by merging the kingdoms and parliaments of England and Scotland.

Adamson Act (1916) Congressional act that granted railroad workers an eight-hour workday and overtime pay.

Agricultural Adjustment Administration (AAA, 1933) U.S. government agency created by the Agricultural Adjustment Act to provide credit, loans, and other subsidies to farmers.

Alamo A mission outpost in San Antonio, Texas, that was defended down to the last man by American and Mexican separatists in the Texas War for Independence of 1836.

Albany Congress (1754) A conference of representatives of seven British North American colonies, held in Albany, New York, to consider strategies for diplomacy with the Indians and dissuade the Iroquois from becoming French allies.

Alien and Sedition Acts (1798) Four congressional acts that severely restricted immigration into the United States and gave the president power to deport anyone thought to be dangerous—even for spreading radical political ideas.

Alliance for Progress (1961) A multibillion-dollar aid program for Latin America aimed at establishing economic cooperation between the United States and South America.

American Antislavery Society An abolitionist society organized by William Lloyd Garrison in 1833 with immediate abolition as its core objective.

American Colonization Society (ACS) A society of antislavery whites, founded in 1817, that advocated the return of freed slaves to Africa.

American Expeditionary Forces American armed forces, commanded by General John J. Pershing, sent to Europe during World War I to fight alongside British and French allied units.

American Federation of Labor A collective of craft unions, founded in 1881, comprised of highly skilled, mostly white, carpenters, plumbers, and electricians. The organization largely ignored the plight of lower paid industrial workers, excluded minority laborers, and often supported Republican candidates.

American Indian Movement Formed in Minneapolis in 1968, an activist organization devoted to protecting Indian rights and to upholding established treaties, particularly over land, with federal, state, and local governments.

American Philosophical Society Scholarly organization founded in Philadelphia in 1743 to promote the dissemination of knowledge in the science and humanities.

American Protective Association (APA) An anti-Catholic nativist organization founded in 1887. The APA advocated strict immigration laws and spread conspiracy theories about Roman Catholics.

American Railway Union (ARU) Founded in 1893, the ARU was one of the first industrial unions in the United States and the largest labor union of its time. ARU was founded on the belief that railway workers would increase their power if they would organize one industry-wide union.

American Recovery and Reinvestment Act (2009) Congressional act allocating $787 billion in economic stimulus funds. The package combined government spending on infrastructure, unemployment benefits, and food stamps, with tax cuts.

American System Senator Henry Clay's proposal of 1824 intended to spur domestic economic development as well as tariffs and currency regulation.

American Temperance Society Organization established in 1826 to advocate abstinence from distilled beverages. The movement did not end the consumption of alcohol in America, but it did help convince millions of people to rethink their relationship with drinking.

Americans with Disabilities Act (ADA) Congressional act of 1990 that provided equal rights for people with disabilities.

Anarchism A term meaning without rulers or without government.

Anti-Imperial League American organization formed in 1898 by those who opposed American colonization of the Philippines.

Articles of Capitulation (1664) English policies regarding Dutch residents of New Amsterdam, which granted them religious liberty, freedom from military conscription, property rights, the ability to leave New York within 18 months, and free trade and freedom of movement within the English Empire.

Articles of Confederation The first written framework for a government of the United States, drafted by Congress and in effect from 1781 to 1788.

Astrolabe A navigation instrument used to pinpoint and predict the location of the stars, Sun, Moon, and planets for determining longitude and latitude while sailing at sea.

Atlantic Charter (1941) A joint policy statement issued by the United States and Great Britain that defined the goals and objectives of their alliance at the beginning of World War II. The charter called for disarming defeated aggressors and establishing a permanent system of general security.

Atlantic slave trade The enslaving, trade, and transport of African people to Europe and the Americas, begun by the Portuguese in the early 1440s.

Atlantic world Name given to the area of exploration bordering the Atlantic Ocean and including the five continents of North America, South America, Antarctica, Africa, and Europe.

Baby boom The temporary but noteworthy increase in birth rate in the United States, Great Britain, and Europe in the years immediately following World War II.

Balance of powers A model of governance in which authority is distributed to several different branches of government, providing checks and balances against one another. Also known as the separation of powers.

Bank of the United States (BUS) The first federal bank, founded in 1791, that operated until 1811 and provided for the issuance of a national currency and centralization of federal tax collection.

Barbados slave code (1661) English America's first slave code; it prescribed different treatment and contrasting levels of legal protection for enslaved Africans and white servants.

Battle of the Bulge The last major offensive by Axis powers in World War II, fought in Belgium in 1944.

Bay of Pigs Invasion Failed operation approved by President Kennedy to invade Cuba with a small CIA-led military force of political Cuban exiles with hopes of liberating the country and removing Fidel Castro from power.

Bill of Rights The first 10 amendments to the United States Constitution, ratified by the states in 1791.

Black Codes (1865–1866) Congressional acts that granted rights to former slaves. These included the right to marry, to own property, and to participate in the judicial process.

Black Legend Politically motivated, factually exploitative conviction that the Spaniards indiscriminately slaughtered Indians, tyrannized them, and imposed Catholicism on them during their 16th-century conquests in the Americas.

Black Panther Party A radical civil rights organization founded in Oakland in 1966 by Huey Newton and Bobby Seale. Members of Black Panthers advocated black self-determination and armed self-defense against police brutality.

Black Tuesday (October 29, 1929) The day that marked the start of the Great Depression, precipitated by a calamitous crash of the stock market.

Board of Trade (1696) An advisory council created by King William III of England that was charged to oversee colonial matters. The act testified to the colonies' growing significance to England's economy.

Boston Massacre (1770) An altercation between occupying British troops and a Boston mob, resulting in the death of five colonists. This was a significant incident in the buildup of tensions between Britain and the colonies in the years leading up to the American Revolution.

Boston Tea Party (1773) An act of defiance on the part of Boston colonists to protest the British Tea Act of 1773, a new tax on imported tea; 30 to 60 men disguised as Mohawk Indians stormed British tea ships and dumped 90,000 pounds of tea into Boston Harbor.

***Bracero* Program (1942)** Agreement between the governments of Mexico and the United States that granted annual entry to hundreds of thousands of seasonal agricultural workers. Control of the border was generally loosened and hundreds of thousands of other Mexicans were drawn north by growing opportunities in the greatly expanding U.S. economy.

Bretton Woods agreements (1944) Multinational agreements that established a system for international trade and monetary values to promote economic recovery following World War II.

***Brown v. Board of Education* of Topeka Kansas** U.S. Supreme Court decision that outlawed racial segregation in public schools.

Bunker Hill, Battle of The first significant battle of the American Revolution. It actually took place on Breed's Hill, where colonial forces claimed victory and demonstrated that they could resist larger British forces.

Bush Doctrine Foreign policy principles of President George W. Bush, the centerpiece of which was a policy wherein the United States had the right to engage in preemptive war to secure itself against terrorist groups and countries that harbored them.

Bush v. Gore U.S. Supreme Court decision that determined the winner of the 2000 presidential race between Al Gore and George W. Bush.

Calvinism A Protestant religion that followed the teachings of theologian John Calvin that was practiced by European and American Puritans.

Central Powers Name given during World War II to the alliance of Germany, Austria-Hungary, and Ottoman Turkey.

Charter of Freedoms and Exemptions (1640) A Dutch West India Company policy that granted 200 acres to whoever brought five adults to New Netherland and promised prospective colonists religious freedom and local self-governance; these offers attracted English Puritans from Massachusetts to eastern Long Island.

Chinese Exclusion Act (1882) Congressional Act that barred the immigration of Chinese laborers. This law all but ended Chinese immigration and remained in effect until 1943.

Church of England (Anglican Church) English Christian church established by King Henry VIII after his break from papal authority in 1534.

Civil Rights Act of 1964 Congressional act that prohibited discrimination in employment or the use of public places on the basis of race, sex, religion, or national origin.

Code Noir (1685) Slave code mandated by imperial France governing the rights and treatment of African slaves in their colonial territories from the French West Indies to Louisiana.

Coercive Acts/Intolerable Acts (1774) Four British parliamentary decrees enacted in response to unrest and protests in Boston. The acts reorganized the Massachusetts government and placed more authority in the hands of royal appointees. The acts also imposed royal control over local courts and authorized troops to be forcibly housed in private homes and buildings.

Coinage Act of 1883 Congressional act that made gold the nation's monetary standard and halted the making of silver dollars.

Cold War Term given to the political, economic, and military tensions that existed between the United States and its allies and the Soviet Union between 1945 and the dissolution of the Soviet Union in 1989.

Columbian exchange The historic movement of people, plants, animals, culture, and pathogens between the Americas and the rest of the world that began during the time of Columbus.

Common law Law based on decisions previously made by judges and courts, as opposed to statutory, or written laws and statutes; the common law system was rooted in English legal practices.

Commons Lands open to all residents.

Compromise of 1850 Congressional measures created to resolve a series of regional tensions in the United States. The measures admitted California as a free state, organized the remainder of the New Mexico Territory, banned the slave trade in the District of Columbia, empowered the Treasury to assume Texas's debts from its independence struggle with Mexico, and gave the South a much stronger federal Fugitive Slave Law.

Congress of Industrial Organizations (CIO) Umbrella group of labor unions, formed in 1935, to represent semiskilled workers in major industrial sectors. Unions within the Congress accepted black and other minority workers.

Containment Name given to the foundation of U.S. foreign policy during the Cold War. George F. Kennan argued that Soviet communism was "impervious to the logic of reason," inherently expansionist, and only controllable through "long-term, patient but firm and vigilant containment."

Contract with America A document conceived by Republican Congressman

Newt Gingrich in 1993 that promised to make Congress more accountable, balance the federal budget, reverse the tax increases passed in 1993, and reduce the capital gains tax.

Conversion test An exercise developed by Massachusetts Bay Puritans to test prospective church members for membership in their congregation; prospects had to testify to their relationship with God and offer proof that God had saved them.

Counterculture In the 1960s and early 1970s, the name given to the subculture of college-age young Americans who developed distinctively liberal beliefs and practices regarding sexuality, race, gender, politics, and culture; these values stood in contrast to those of the dominant culture of their parents.

Covenant As practiced by New England Puritans, an agreement with God that required them to translate their faith into actions that obeyed God's will as revealed in the Bible.

Covenant Chain (1677) An alliance between the Iroquois and English colonies from New England south to Maryland that joined their forces against the French.

Coverture A principle of British and American law wherein a married woman lost her legal identity as an individual and in which her economic resources would be controlled by her husband. This law prevented married women from owning property.

Creoles People born in the United States, particularly in Louisiana, who were direct descendants of French and Spanish colonial settlers.

Crop lien system A credit system widely used by Southern farmers from the 1860s to the 1920s. This was a way for farmers to get credit before the planting season by borrowing against the value for anticipated harvests.

Cuban missile crisis A tense standoff between the United States and Soviet Union in October 1962 when the United States discovered that the Soviets had begun installing nuclear missiles in Cuba. The incident was the most dramatic nuclear standoff of the Cold War.

Dawes Act (1877) Congressional act that divided two-thirds of Indian tribal lands to be sold off or confiscated. Many Indians who had lived on reservations became essentially landless.

Declaration of Independence (1776) American revolutionary document that declared that the United States was free and independent of the British Empire.

Defense Advanced Research Projects Agency (DARPA) U.S. defense agency that created the Internet, originally founded in 1958 to counter Soviet advances in space science.

Defense of Marriage Act (1996) Congressional act that decreed that no state would be compelled to recognize a same-sex marriage conducted in another state, nor would the federal government recognize the existence of such a marriage even if it were performed legally in a state.

Desert Lands Act (1877) Congressional act, applicable in 11 Western states, that allowed for homesteading on 640-acre parcels of arid land at 25 cents per acre and provided title within three years for a dollar an acre for settled, irrigated land.

Détente Term given to the U.S. relaxation of tension with the Soviets during the 1970s.

Dominion of New England (1686–1689) A union of English colonies imposed by the English monarchy; it comprised eight contiguous colonies, from New England to New Jersey, under one governor, Edmond Andros, who dissolved representative assemblies, jailed dissidents, and imposed taxes on lands already owned outright.

Dred Scott v. Sandford **(1857)** U.S. Supreme Court ruling that slaves were not citizens of the United States and were therefore unable to sue in a federal court of law. As a consequence, the federal government had no authority to outlaw slavery in the territories, leaving that choice up to the states.

Dust Bowl Locations in the Great Plains, including Kansas, Colorado, Oklahoma, and Texas, afflicted by a severe drought that destroyed farmland during the 1930s, leading to the mass relocation of farm families.

Dutch West India Company (DWIC) Dutch trading company whose merchants were granted trade monopolies in parts of the New World, and whose activities included the acquisition of territories in the Hudson River Valley in New York.

Edict of Nantes (1598) Proclamation by King Henry IV of France granting rights to Huguenots (French Calvinist Protestants).

Eighteenth Amendment (1919) Constitutional amendment that barred the manufacture and sale of alcohol in the United States.

Emancipation Proclamation (1863) Proclamation by Abraham Lincoln that freed the slaves living in Confederate states.

Emergency Banking Relief Act (1933) Congressional act that followed the market crash of 1929; it reopened banks and restored bank solvency under Treasury Department supervision. The act also removed U.S. currency from the gold standard.

Emergency Economic Stabilization Act (2008) Congressional act that authorized the U.S. Treasury to budget up to $700 billion to bail out banks and other financial institutions affected by a crisis in subprime mortgage values.

Emergency Immigration Act of 1921 Congressional act that created specific immigration limitations based on national origin. The act banned all immigration from Asia, but it allowed free immigration from the Western Hemisphere, as the Southwest depended on Mexican and Central American labor.

Encomienda System whereby the Spanish government granted land, villages, and indigenous people to its military leaders who conquered land in the Americas.

Epic of Deganawidah Iroquois legend that explained the establishment of the Great League of Peace between Indian nations.

Equal Rights Amendment (ERA) Proposed amendment to the U.S. Constitution that banned the denial or abridgment of rights on the basis of gender.

Espionage Act (1917) Congressional act passed on the eve of America's entrance into World War I that expanded the definition of treason and defined a variety of acts deemed to comprise espionage. The Act was enacted to fight sabotage, spying, or interference with the war effort.

Executive Order 9981 (1948) Order by President Truman that established equality in the armed services on the basis of race, color, religion, and national origin.

Fair Deal Domestic programs for social reform proposed by the Truman administration. The 21-point program called for an increase in the minimum wage, comprehensive housing legislation for returning veterans, full employment and expanded unemployment benefits, permanent federal farm subsidies, expanded public works projects, and expanded environmental conservation programs.

Farmers' Alliance An umbrella movement of agricultural organizations, founded in Texas in 1876, that encouraged men and women to cooperate in running their households and their farms. The Alliance provided the foundation for what would become the Populist Party.

Federal Reserve Act (1913) Congressional act implemented to create a central banking system that significantly strengthened the nation's monetary policy and provided regulation of banks.

Federalism A system of government that divides powers between a centralized national administration and state governments.

Federalist Papers A series of anonymously authored essays, published in newspapers, supporting ratification of the U.S. Constitution of 1787 by Madison, Hamilton, and Jay.

Feitoria Portuguese name for a fortified trading post, early examples of which were first established in Africa in the 15th century during the early years of the Atlantic slave trade.

Fifteenth Amendment (1870) Constitutional amendment that prohibited the denial of voting rights on the basis of race.

Fireside Chats Weekly radio addresses by President Franklin Roosevelt in which he explained his proposals, policies, and actions to the American people.

First Continental Congress Representatives of the colonies who met in Philadelphia for the first time in 1774 to articulate their positions and form policies against grievous British laws and regulations. The group charged committees in each colony to vigorously enforce boycotts; endorsed a declaration of rights and grievances on October 14, 1774; and then adjourned, hoping that the King would change the course of imperial policy.

First hundred days President Franklin Roosevelt's first days in office, during which he prevailed on Congress to pass 14 major pieces of legislation including bills to raise agricultural prices, put the unemployed to work, regulate the stock market, reform banking practices, and assist home owners and farmers in paying mortgages.

Fourteenth Amendment (1868) Constitutional amendment that guaranteed national citizenship and equality to former slaves, detailed changes related to the former Confederate states, but offered no specific protection of freed people's voting rights.

Franciscans A Roman Catholic religious order, active in establishing Spanish missions in Southwestern North America in the 18th and 19th centuries.

Fugitive Slave Act (1850) Congressional act that nationalized the process of slave capture and return by requiring federal judges to appoint "commissioners" to hear cases of accused fugitives and by requiring the active complicity of state officers.

Fur trade The trading of furs, primarily through the St. Lawrence River region, that served as the primary gateway for European goods into North America into the 1600s.

Gag rule Rule adopted by Congress in 1836 to block the discussion of slavery at the national as well as the state level. The rule was repealed in 1844.

Gang system One of two general types of division of labor of plantation slaves, the other being the task system. The gang system involved the work of coordinated groups, supervised by a driver, to maintain an even level of productivity during the work day.

General Allotment Act (1887) Congressional act that divided Indian reservation land into smaller parcels of property.

Gentlemen's Agreement (1907) Agreement reached by President Theodore Roosevelt and the Japanese government that stated that the United States would no longer exclude Japanese immigrants if the Japanese promised to voluntarily limit the number of its immigrants to the United States, primarily adult male laborers.

Glass-Steagall Banking Act (1933) Congressional act that established strict guidelines for banking operations and expanded the power of the Federal Reserve System. The act also founded the Federal Deposit Insurance Corporation. Some regulations associated with the original act were repealed in 1999, leading to mismanagement and scandals in the banking and finance industries, and the recession beginning around 2009.

Globalization A term that was popularized in the 1990s to refer to the knitting together of the world's economies through new information technology and the end of the artificial political barrier of the Cold War.

Glorious Revolution (1688) Uprising of the English Parliament against King James II that transformed the English system of government from an absolute monarchy to a constitutional monarchy and the rule of Parliament.

Grand Settlement of 1701 A pair of treaties between the Iroquois and the French that stabilized relations between the two in the Great Lakes and Northeast parts of North America.

Grandfather clause Allowance created by southern state legislatures in the 1890s permitting any person who had voted before 1867, or had a father or grandfather who had voted, to be exempt from the literacy test or other restrictions. The unspoken aim of this law was to increase the number of eligible white male voters.

Great Depression America's worst economic downturn to date. Beginning at the end of 1929 and lasting for 10 years; the catastrophe spread to every corner of the country, wrecking lives and leaving people homeless, hungry, and desperate for work.

Great Migration The large scale movement of African Americans from the South to the North during and after World War I, where jobs were more plentiful.

Great Recession An international economic collapse of 2008, where credit markets around the world froze and banks stopped lending to one another. Businesses dependent on lending began to downsize and fail. The meltdown affected financial institutions and governments throughout the world.

Great Society President Lyndon Johnson's name for a series of social and economic reforms, begun in 1965, to end racial discrimination, expand educational opportunities, end hunger and poverty, and make health care available for all.

Gulf of Tonkin Resolution Congressional authorization requested by President Lyndon Johnson in 1964 that gave him the power to escalate military action in Vietnam without additional congressional approval.

Half-freedom Conditional freedom given to former African slaves and residents of New Amsterdam by the Dutch West India Company in 1644, allowing them to work for themselves and live where they wished, as long as they paid the DWIC and bound themselves and their children to serve the company.

Half-way covenant A plan by New England Puritans, whose church was losing members by the 1660s, to offer partial church membership to the children of parents who were not church members, thus bypassing established conversion practices.

Harlem Renaissance An African American cultural and arts movement of the 1920s centered in the Harlem neighborhood of New York City.

Harpers Ferry Raid (1859) Failed raid led by abolitionist John Brown on the U.S. arsenal in Harper's Ferry, Virginia. Brown's capture and execution led to greater regional tensions leading up to the Civil War.

Helsinki Accords A set of principles that accepted the post-1945 division of Europe into East–West spheres. The accords recognized the right of all Europeans to seek peaceful change, and the Soviets agreed in a general way to respect human rights in their sphere.

Homestead Act (1862) Congressional act that allowed families to claim 160 acres of land if they improved it over five years of residence. The act opened the Western United States to settlement.

House of Burgesses The first representative government assembly and ruling body established in the English settlements in America; founded by the Virginia Company in 1619, this assembly replaced martial law with English common law, setting in motion the development of the county court system.

House Committee on Un-American Activities Congressional committee formed in 1938 to search for communists and conspiracies within the United States including penetration into the labor movement and federal agencies. Although discredited during the 1950s for its investigations of entertainment and media figures, the committee was not abandoned until 1975.

Huguenots Name given to the French followers of Calvinism, a Protestant religion founded by theologian John Calvin.

Huron Confederacy A union of several tribes of Huron people, formed to established peaceful relations and trade.

Immigration Restriction League An anti-immigration organization founded in Boston in 1894 that promoted legislation to restrict the immigration of Southern and Eastern Europeans.

Indentured servitude An arrangement offered by various English enterprises to attract English people to the colonies, exchanging free passage by ship to America for up to seven years labor.

Indian Removal Act (1830) Federal law that nullified 50 years' worth of treaties between the United States and many tribes. The law resulted in the relocation of more than 45,000 Indians living east of the Mississippi to points further west, opening up lands for white settlers. The law committed the federal government to creating an Indian Territory west of the Mississippi.

Indian Reorganization Act (1934) Congressional act that slowed the division of reservation land into small plots, encouraged tribal self-government, and established Indian-run corporations to control communal land and resources.

Industrious revolution Preindustrialization period associated with 18th century British North America during which there was a diversification of labor, development of a market-oriented society, and a labor shift from services to marketable goods.

iinitiative, referendum, recall First proposed by Populists in the 1890s, the initiative and referendum, adopted originally in Oregon, made it possible for voters to place legislation directly before the electorate for a vote in general elections; the referendum allowed voters to repeal state legislation with which they disagreed; the recall gave voters the power to remove any public official who did not, in their view, act for the public good.

Insular Cases (1901–1904) A series of U.S. Supreme Court cases that would be applied to all of the new territories added to the United States in which it was ruled that American constitutional rights and liberties did not extend to all lands under U.S. control.

Interstate and Defense Highways Act (1956) The largest public works program in American history, approved by President Dwight Eisenhower, that facilitated the growth of suburban America and the businesses and industries that sustained them.

Iroquois League Also known as the Great League of Peace. A confederation formed c. 1400 and originally composed of five Iroquoian-speaking peoples of today's Upstate New York: the Seneca, Cayuga, Onondaga, Oneida, and Mohawk.

Jamestown The first permanent English settlement in America, founded in 1607 and located in what is today coastal Virginia.

Jay's Treaty (1794) Treaty with Britain granting the United States trade rights on the Mississippi, in the British East Indies, and removing remaining British forts on American territory.

Jesuits (Society of Jesus) A Catholic male religious order, founded in Spain in 1534, that was active in winning converts overseas.

Jim Crow laws State and local laws that originated in the South in the mid 1880s and legally separated people according to race. These laws spread to many public facilities and established a policy of racial segregation that favored white citizens.

Johnson–O'Malley Act (1934) Congressional act that provided federal aid to improve health care and education to Indian tribes.

joint-stock company An early form of shareholding company that was used by the British to finance development of the colonies.

kachinas In Pueblo culture, ancestral beings believed to bring rain and communal harmony.

Kansas-Nebraska Act (1854) Congressional act that repealed the Missouri Compromise. The bill's new policy of "popular sovereignty," intended to allow settlers in a territory to decide the status of slavery, initiated a strenuous debate about the future of slavery in the Western territories.

Keating–Owen Child Labor Law (1916) Law that banned interstate commerce in goods produced by child labor.

Kellogg–Briand Pact (1928) Also known as the "Pact of Paris," an agreement signed by 62 nations that agreed not to use war as an instrument of national policy. The pact was initiated by the United States and France.

Kiva An underground chamber used by Pueblo Indians for religious ceremonies.

Knights of Labor The first national labor union, founded in Baltimore, in 1869. The Knights aimed to organize all laboring people into one large, national union. The union offered membership regardless of race, gender, or national origin, excluding only "social parasites" such as lawyers, bankers, and liquor salesmen. African Americans and Mexican Americans belonged to the Knights and the organization's emphasis on equal rights for all workers and equal pay for equal work attracted many women as well.

Know-Nothing Party Antiforeign, anti-Catholic political organization established in 1854 and consisting of a network of secret fraternal associations, largely a nativist reaction against large-scale European immigration. The organization's name stemmed from its secrecy; if asked about the organization, members would essentially deny any knowledge of it, saying that they "knew nothing."

Ku Klux Klan An organization associated with the bitterest and most violent opponents of Reconstruction and black freedom. Formed in Pulaski, Tennessee, in late 1865, Klan members devoted themselves to denying African Americans any legitimate role in the public sphere, stressing the superiority of white, Protestant, Anglo-Saxon citizens.

Laissez-faire economics An economic doctrine that insisted that government should not interfere with businesses or the market. The term is from the French meaning, "leave it alone."

Lawrence v. Texas (2003) U.S. Supreme Court decision that overturned most state antisodomy laws used to criminalize homosexual behavior.

League of Nations Organization proposed by President Woodrow Wilson in 1918, following World War I, the purpose of which was to guarantee the sovereignty of individual nations, large and small, and provide a forum for mediating disputes.

Limited Test Ban Treaty (1963) An agreement between the United States and the Soviet Union that ended above-ground atomic weapon testing but permitted continued testing underground.

Linen Act of 1705 British parliamentary act that encouraged the export of Irish linen to North America. In turn, the act increased the demand in Northern Ireland for colonial flaxseed, the source of linen.

Literacy Act (1917) Clause of the U.S. Immigration Act of 1917 that barred the entry of any persons unable to read in their own language on the grounds that this lack demonstrated their ignorance.

Lochner v. New York (1905) U.S. Supreme Court decision that struck down a New York Law limiting the hours that male bakers could work because, in the court's opinion, the state had no right to regulate their hours.

Lowell Mill Girls Female workers associated with the textile mills in Lowell, Massachusetts. The mills had a large labor force of young women, who ranged between the ages of 15 and 35 and worked in one of the first large-scale, steam-powered industries in the United States.

Ludlow Massacre (1914) An attack by local deputies and state militia on striking United Mine Workers in Ludlow, Colorado. At the request of mine owners, the militia attacked a camp of striking miners who had been evicted from company-owned housing. Drenching the miner's tents with kerosene and setting them on fire, they shot up the encampment with machine guns and killed 14 people, included 11 children. Soon labeled the Ludlow Massacre, the gruesome deaths of the victims sparked violent retaliation by the miners.

Lusitania British passenger liner torpedoed by a German submarine in 1915 while sailing between New York and England. The attack killed 1,200 of the 2,000 passengers and crew, including 128 Americans.

lynching The murder of African American individuals by a mob, often by hanging, shooting, or burning. Lynchings were most prevalent in the southern United States between the 1880s and 1960s.

Maine (battleship) A U.S. battleship that exploded on February 15, 1898, killing 260 American sailors. Americans blamed Spain for the explosion, drawing the United States closer to war with Spain, which was declared two months later.

Malintzín A native Nahua woman from the Gulf Coast of Mexico who figured importantly in the Spanish conquest of Mexico by acting as the translator and advisor to Hernán Cortés, leader of a Spanish expedition.

Manhattan Project Secret U.S. scientific and military program during World War II dedicated to the development of an atomic bomb. The project was led by J. Robert Oppenheimer and employed 150,000 people at a top secret location in New Mexico.

Mann Act (1910) Congressional act that outlawed the transport of women across state lines for "immoral purposes."

Manumission The freeing of slaves by their owners.

Marbury v. Madison (1803) U.S. Supreme Court decision that firmly established the principle of "judicial review," the right of the U.S. Supreme Court to rule on the constitutionality of legislation and executive actions.

March on Washington for Jobs and Freedom Historic civil rights march on August 28, 1963, during which over 200,000 black and white demonstrators marched from the Washington Monument to the Lincoln Memorial where Martin Luther King, Jr., delivered his "I Have a Dream" speech.

Marshall Plan (European Recovery Plan) (1948) A massive foreign aid program approved following World War II, it called for aid packages to help Western Europe, including West Germany, and Japan rapidly rebuild their devastated economies, restore industries and trade, and rejoin the free world.

Massachusetts Bay Company A business enterprise founded by English Puritans and merchants in 1629 that founded the Massachusetts Bay Colony, resulting in a swell of English emigration to the colonies.

Matrilineal A society in which social identity is based on kinship and descendency from the mother.

McCarran International Security Act (1950) Congressional act requiring the registration of American Communist Party members; the act reinforced perceptions of immigrants as a source of radicalism during the Cold War and set the tone for a contentious debate about immigration in the coming decade.

McCarthyism A national communist witch hunt in post-World War II America led by Senator Joseph McCarthy.

McKinley Tariff (1890) Congressional act that ended the practice of allowing Hawaiian sugar to enter the United States duty free, ending Hawaii's favored status and threatening its sugar industry.

McNary–Haughen Acts (1927–1928) Congressional acts that required the government to support crop prices by buying basic farm commodities.

Meat Inspection Act (1906) Congressional act that required federal inspectors from the U.S. Department of Agriculture to inspect livestock in slaughterhouses and to guarantee sanitary standards.

Medicaid A health care plan that originated with President Lyndon Johnson's Great Society program in which the federal government provided states matching grants to pay for medical costs of poor people of all ages.

Medicare A health plan that originated with President Lyndon Johnson's

Great Society programs that provided universal hospital insurance for Americans over 65.

Medicare Modernization Act (2003) Congressional act that subsidized the cost of some, but not all, medication taken by seniors.

Mercantilism An economic philosophy of English and French governments founded on the belief that control of foreign trade—including the acquisition of raw materials from their colonies—was key to securing the kingdom that ruled them.

Methodists A Protestant evangelical sect, rooted in the 18th century Anglican revival movement, that accepted slaves and freed blacks and opposed government intervention in religion.

Minute men In Revolutionary War times, local militias in Massachusetts and Connecticut that went on alert in response to pending British military action.

Miranda v. Arizona U.S. Supreme Court decision that expanded the Fifth Amendment's prohibition on self-incrimination.

Mission to the slaves The responsibility of evangelical slaveholders to provide religious teaching and ministering to their slaves.

Mississippi Bubble Name given the financial collapse in 1720 of the Company of the Indies, an investment scheme intended to finance the French colonization of Louisiana.

Mississippian societies Name given to Indian societies of the Mississippi Valley, formed around 700 CE and peaking between 1100 and 1300.

Model Cities Program Federal urban aid program created by President Lyndon Johnson to encourage physical and economic revitalization of the nation's poorest urban areas.

Modernists Religious leaders, influenced by the Social Gospel movement of the late 19th century, as well as Darwin's theory of evolution and archaeological discoveries, who believed Christianity should respond positively to new knowledge and social conditions.

Monetarists Proponents of a conservative economic movement that favored a change to tax and spending policies. Led by Milton Friedman, these economists insisted that prosperity and freedom required reduced government spending along with more stringent control of the money supply.

Monopoly A business enterprise that is the only supplier of a particular service or commodity.

Monroe Doctrine (1823) Policy introduced by President James Monroe who declared that the United States shared common interest with other states in the Western Hemisphere and that the political system in Europe was "essentially different" from that of the democratic republics in North and South America.

Monroe–Pinckney Treaty (1806) An agreement that established new trade relations between Great Britain and the United States.

Montgomery Improvement Association An organization of black clergy and community leaders, formed in 1955, and led by Martin Luther King, Jr., who refined a philosophy of nonviolent protest for boycotters.

Moral Majority A political lobbying group designed to mobilize evangelical Christian voters and "get them saved, baptized and registered" to vote.

Morant Bay Rebellion (1865) A revolt of black farm workers in Jamaica. It consumed the eastern half of the island and left hundreds of black laborers dead and hundreds more beaten by state militia forces.

Moravians (United Brethren) A Protestant religious sect, revived in Germany in 1727 and brought to Georgia in 1735, that sought to create closed, economically autonomous, sex-segregated communities in which Christian liturgical rituals and piety infused daily life.

Mormons A Protestant religious sect, founded by Joseph Smith, who preached a conservative theology of patriarchal authority.

Mourning wars Skirmishes associated with Eastern North American Indians to avenge the death of relatives by capturing or killing members of neighboring tribes.

Muckraking An early form of investigative journalism in America. Believing that exposing facts could rouse the American public to demand change, "muckraking" helped bring about major reforms in the late 19th and early 20th centuries.

Mudsill theory A sociological theory first proposed by South Carolina Senator James Henry Hammond in 1858 who stated that a division of upper and lower classes was the natural order of society, a view that was interpreted by many as a thinly veiled excuse for exploiting slavery.

Mujahideen Islamic-inspired Afghan and foreign guerrillas who fought the occupying Soviets in Afghanistan during the 1980s. They counted among their ranks Saudi fundamentalist Osama Bin Laden.

Mulatto Mixed race people in the United States.

Muller v. Oregon (1908) U.S. Supreme Court decision that upheld an Oregon law limiting the work day of female laundry workers to 10 hours per day.

My Lai massacre (1968) Massacre by American troops of 504 unarmed Vietnamese villagers during the Vietnam War.

National American Woman Suffrage Association Organization of women founded in 1890 whose leaders sought a constitutional amendment to give women the right to vote.

National Association for the Advancement of Colored People (NAACP) Civil Rights organization founded in 1910 that was innovative in establishing legal action as a powerful basis in the fight for African American rights.

National Municipal League A national organization, founded in 1894, made up progressives from both parties committed to reforming government in U.S. cities.

National Organization for Women Founded in 1966, this organization advocated an end to laws that discriminated against women, opportunity to work at any job, and equal pay for equal work.

National Origins Act (1924) Congressional act that defined strict quotas regulating the flow and character of U.S. immigration.

National Parks Act (1916) Congressional act that created the National Park Service and aimed, in part, to preserve national park lands and "leave them unimpaired for the enjoyment of future generations."

National Recovery Administration (NRA) World War I programs that brought together industry leaders and labor groups to boost production. The NRA wrote "production codes" for each industry that encouraged cooperation among competing businesses to set stable prices and wages.

National Security Act (1947) This act consolidated the U.S. military command; a representative from each military branch would advise a newly created Secretary of Defense and the president through the Joint Chiefs of Staff Office.

Nativism Name given to a strong anti-immigration, anti-Catholic activist movement that flourished in America from the 1830s to the 1850s. The term "nativists" was giving to those who strongly opposed the influx of immigrants into American society.

Navigation Act of 1696 One of a series of English regulations and taxes on colonial trade dating from 1650 to 1775.

Neo-cons "Neo-conservatives," a small but influential group of conservative Democrats who bolstered Republican ranks during the presidency of George W. Bush.

New Deal Name collectively given to President Franklin Roosevelt's programs to fight the Great Depression, first articulated during his 1932 presidential campaign. He pledged to use federal power to ensure a more equitable distribution of income and rebuild the economy from the bottom up.

New Freedom Phrase used by President Woodrow Wilson who attacked all "bigness," whether in government or business, and advocated small business and fair competition enforced by only minimal government interference.

New Frontier Name given to President John F. Kennedy's phrase for a collection of programs to expand economic and social opportunities in the United States.

New Left Counterculture protest movement of the 1960s whose young activists intentionally distanced themselves from the ideological infighting, Marxist leanings, and labor organizing of the Old Left of the 1930s and 1940s.

New Look President Dwight Eisenhower's military reorganization of 1954 that established the central philosophy of the doctrine of "massive retaliation" as more economically feasible than containment alone.

New Nationalism Name given to President Theodore Roosevelt's platform in 1912 that advocated expansive government activism and regulation for the public interest.

New World Order George H. W. Bush proclaimed the dawn of a New World Order in 1989, in which the United States, the world's preeminent superpower, would lead multinational coalitions to enforce its standards of international behavior.

Nineteenth Amendment (1920) Constitutional amendment granting women the right to vote.

No Child Left Behind Act (NCLB) Program proposed by President George W. Bush in 2001 to improve educational outcomes for poor and minority children. It renewed federal funding for several existing school programs and provided some additional money for reading and math instruction. In return, all states had to implement "standards based educational reform," a term that in practice meant standardized testing of students in reading and math.

Non-Intercourse Act (1809) Congressional act that reopened trade with countries other than Britain and France.

North American Free Trade Agreement (NAFTA) Trade agreement approved by Democrats and Republicans in 1993 during the administration of President Bill Clinton. This agreement lifted barriers to trade between the United States, Mexico, and Canada, and nearly all conventional economists believed that it would lift living standards in these countries.

Olive Branch Petition (1775) Petition sent by the Continental Congress to King George III of England seeking his intervention to avoid the Revolutionary War.

Open Door Policy Principles drafted in 1899 by Secretary of State John Hay requesting that European powers put an end to the further partitioning of China and open up areas of China claimed by each power to allow them to compete fairly for Chinese trade. These policies asked for unhindered access to markets where they could compete successfully against economic rivals.

Orders in Council (1807) British policies during the Napoleonic wars that required U.S. ships to stop in British ports for licensing and inspection before they could trade with France or French colonies.

Organization of Petroleum Exporting Countries The oil cartel formed in 1960 that supported Egypt and Syria.

PAC—see Political Action Committee

Panama Canal Opened in 1914, the canal, linking the Atlantic and Pacific Oceans, enhanced access to U.S. colonies in the Pacific as well as trade with Asia, but poisoned U.S. relations with Latin American countries because of the questionable way that the United States gained rights to build the canal.

Parliament Legislative body of the British government.

Paternalism In pre-Civil War America, the belief by white slave owners that it was their duty to protect and care for members of Southern society they viewed as inferior to them, including slaves and their families but also white women.

Peace Policy Organized by General Ely Samuel Parker, the Indian commissioners and leaders of various Christian denominations provided Indians with food and clothing in exchange for promises to abandon cultural traditions and to assimilate into American society.

Pendleton Civil Service Act (1883) Congressional act that established the modern Civil Service and initiated an examination for a classified list of federal jobs, including most government departments, custom house jobs, and post office positions.

Pentagon Papers Popular name given to a collection of classified government documents that were illegally made public in 1971. The documents outlined decision making by the U.S. Defense Department during the period from World War II to the Vietnam War.

People's (Populist) Party A third party, made up largely of rural people frustrated with the unresponsiveness of the Republican and Democratic parties to their pressing needs. The People's Party ran candidates for president in 1892 and 1896 on a platform demanding major reforms, including the government ownership of railroads, a graduated income tax, and the free coinage of silver.

Pietism A Protestant religious movement that linked North America, Britain, the Netherlands, and central Europe. Pietists promoted the personal piety of believers and the evangelization of all, including American Indians and enslaved Africans.

Pinckney's Treaty (1795) A treaty with Spain that fully opened Mississippi River trade to the United States, provided tax-free markets in New Orleans, settled Florida border issues, and guaranteed Spanish help against southwest Indians who moved to block U.S. settlers from expanding west.

Plantation Act of 1740 British parliamentary act that allowed non-Catholic aliens who resided for at least seven years in British North America, received communion in a Protestant church, swore allegiance to George II, and paid two shillings, to become citizens.

Platt Amendment (1901) Amendment to the new Cuban constitution that gave the United States broad authority to intervene to preserve Cuban independence and required Cuba to sell or lease land for U.S. naval stations and coaling bases.

Plessy v. Ferguson (1896) U.S. Supreme Court decision that upheld the legality of Jim Crow laws. This led to the establishment of the NAACP and vigorous legal battles to overturn such laws.

Political Action Committees (PACs) A private group dedicated to the election of a given political candidate or to influence a policy decision in government.

Polygamy A marriage custom of having more than one partner at the same time, such as a man with more than one wife.

Popular sovereignty A policy established in the mid-19th century that permitted settlers in newly established Western territories to decide on the policy of slavery for themselves.

Prigg v. Pennsylvania (1842) U.S. Supreme Court decision that established federal protection to Southerners seeking to reclaim fugitive slaves who escaped to the North.

Privateer A government contracted but privately owned warship used to attack foreign ships and disrupt trade.

Proclamation of 1763 An order issued by King George III of England that prohibited settlements west of the Appalachians.

Protestantism A Christian reform movement that arose in Europe during the 1500s and denied the authority of the Catholic Church.

Pullman Strike Led by Eugene V. Debs and the American Railway Union in 1894 in response to massive wage cuts at the Pullman Palace Car Company, the strike and boycott of trains pulling Pullman cars froze rail service in the Midwest and slowed it elsewhere until federal troops helped crush the strike.

Pure Food and Drug Act (1906) Congressional act that outlawed adulterated or mislabeled food and drugs and gave the federal government the right to seize illegal products and fine

and jail those who manufactured and sold them.

Puritans Europeans who followed the Christian teachings of theologian John Calvin, defied the Catholic Church, and sought to place the governance of church affairs in the hands of local officials, ministers, and elders.

Quitrent A land tax or rent imposed on colonists by their European governing body.

Reconquista Expansion of western European Christian nations during the 1400s into Muslim settlements on the Iberian peninsula.

Reconstruction Finance Corporation (1932) Federal program of President Herbert Hoover to loan money to struggling banks, railroads, manufacturers, and mortgage companies during the Great Depression.

Redemptioners In the 18th century, indentured servants who paid for their passage across the Atlantic by selling their services when they landed.

Rerum novarum A papal encyclical from Pope Leo XIII, issued in 1891, condemning the exploitation of laborers and supporting state intervention to promote social justice.

Revivalists Leaders and advocates of various evangelical Protestant campaigns of the First Great Awakening (18th century). Revivalists sought to rekindle widespread religious enthusiasm in the American colonies.

Roe v. Wade U.S. Supreme Court decision affirming a woman's right to terminate a pregnancy.

Roosevelt Corollary Articulated by President Theodore Roosevelt in 1904, this corollary to the Monroe Doctrine declared that the United States had the right to intervene in the affairs of Latin American nations to ensure order.

Rough Riders Colonel Theodore Roosevelt and his First Volunteer Cavalry

Regiment, known as "The Rough Riders," became national heroes for their daring exploits during the Spanish-American War (1898).

Royal Orders for New Discoveries (1573) Decree by King Philip II of Spain that missionaries should play the principal role in exploring, pacifying, and colonizing new territories and mandated that baptized Indians should live on missions, learn to speak Spanish, keep livestock, cultivate European crops, and use European tools to master European crafts.

Russo-Japanese War Rival imperial claims in Asia sparked this war between Russia and Japan in 1904. President Theodore Roosevelt brokered a peace treaty between the two countries in 1905, earning him the Nobel Peace Prize.

Saint Augustine, Florida First Spanish settlement in America, founded in 1565.

Salutary neglect Name given to the practice of colonists to defy or ignore British laws that they found onerous, often with the complicity of those charged to enforce them.

Second Bill of Rights List of "economic bill of rights," proposed by President Franklin D. Roosevelt in 1944, that guaranteed every citizen a job, a living wage, decent housing, adequate medical care, educational opportunity, and protection against unemployment in postwar America.

Second Great Awakening Religious revivalist movement of the early 19th century that echoed the Great Awakening of the 1730s. The movement linked evangelical Christians on both sides of the Atlantic to exchange ideas and strategies that inspired a broad set of social, cultural, and intellectual changes.

Securities Act of 1933 Congressional act that required companies selling stock to the public to register with a federal agency and provide accurate information on what was being sold.

Securities Exchange Act of 1934 Congressional act that created the Securities Exchange Commission to regulate stock markets and activities by brokers.

Sedition Act (1918) Amendments to the Espionage Act of 1917 that added a variety of offenses to the list of prohibited acts, including the use of "disloyal, profane, scurrilous, or abusive language about the form of government of the United States, or the Constitution of the United States."

Separation of powers Political concept as articulated by French Enlightenment philosopher the Baron de Montesquieu that each state establish a balance between executive, legislative, and judicial powers.

Seven Years' War (1756–1763) Also known as the French and Indian War, a conflict between Britain and France and their respective Indian allies in colonial America. This was largely a conflict between empires for territorial and economic control of the colonies and related trade routes.

Seventeenth Amendment Ratified in 1913, the Seventeenth Amendment to the U.S. Constitution mandated the direct election of U.S. senators.

Sharecroppers Farmers who rented land or farmed on shares, splitting the proceeds from the yearly crop with the landlord.

Shays' Rebellion (1797) An attempt by indebted Massachusetts farmers, led by Daniel Shays, to prevent the state government from seizing their property.

Sherman Antitrust Act (1890) Congressional act aimed at dismantling "combination in the form of trust" that restrained trade. It was the first American law to restrict business monopolies.

Sixteenth Amendment (1913) Constitutional amendment that authorized a federal income tax on both personal and corporate income.

Smoot-Hawley Tariff Passed in 1930 at the onset of the Great Depression, the tariff made it especially difficult for international manufacturers to sell their products in the United States, resulting in retaliatory tariffs that worsened the international economy.

Social Darwinism A theory, popularized by Herbert Spencer, which purported that Charles Darwin's theory of evolution could be applied to human society as well. This belief that society evolved and improved through survival of the fittest was supported by many business leaders of the 19th century as a rationalization for exploiting the working class.

Social Gospel A broad, multidimensional and international movement among liberal Protestant theologians in the late 19th and early 20th centuries that insisted that Christian principles needed to be applied to social problems.

Social Security Act (1935) Congressional act that established a government administered system funded primarily by contributions—payroll taxes—from workers and employers, not general tax revenues.

Society for Promoting Christian Knowledge (SPCK) English organization formed in 1699 to further the mission of Anglican reformers by publishing and disseminating Bibles and religious tracts to the colonies.

Society for the Propagation of the Gospel in Foreign Parts (SPG) Anglican reform organization founded in 1701 for the purpose of sending missionaries to North America and the West Indies.

Society of Friends ("Quakers") A Christian religious sect that broke from the Church of England and established itself in America during the 17th century.

Sons of Liberty Stamp Act protestors who spread awareness of colonial protests between colonies.

Stagflation A slowly growing economy with high rates of unemployment and inflation.

Stamp Act (1765) British parliamentary act that required many forms of printed materials and products be affixed with revenue stamps, or taxes, to the British.

Tariff A tax on imported goods.

Task system One of two general types of division of labor of plantation slaves, the other being the gang system. The task system assigned individuals with specific tasks. Rather than being part of a group that worked continuously to the day's end, the task system allowed individuals to end their work day when their task was done and thus granted them more autonomy.

Teapot Dome Scandal In 1924, investigations revealed that Secretary of the Interior Albert Fall, a member of President Harding's cabinet, took bribes in return for lucrative leases to drill for oil on government-owned land.

Tennessee Valley Authority Federal agency created in 1933 to construct a network of dams and hydroelectric projects to control floods, generate power, and promote growth in a chronically poor area of the South.

Thirteenth Amendment (1865) Constitutional amendment that outlawed slavery in the United States.

Townshend Acts (1767) British parliamentary acts that taxed commons goods in the colonies such as tea and other commodities. The acts represented Britain's resolve to control and regulate the colonies.

Trail of Tears Cherokee name for the United States' forced removal of their people from the Southeast to other lands. In early 1838, few Cherokee had prepared for the trip; contaminated water, inadequate food, and disease killed many of those restricted in stockades, and many more perished on the 800-mile journey west.

Transcontinental Railroad Completed in 1869, the first continuous train line connecting the Midwest to the West coast of America. It ran between Omaha, Nebraska, to Sacramento, California, and reduced travel time across the nation from weeks to days.

Transportation Act (1718) British parliamentary act that mandated the exile of convicted criminals to North America, mostly those who had committed property crimes such as theft.

Treaty of Paris (1763) The treaty ending the Seven Years' War. The terms of the treaty transformed eastern North America's political geography. France surrendered North America, swapping Canada for the return of Guadeloupe. France ceded Louisiana to Spain, and Spain traded Florida to the British to regain control of Havana. The British Empire claimed almost all of North America east of the Mississippi.

Treaty of Tordesillas (1494) Treaty signed by Spain and Portugal that divided newly discovered lands between them, specifically those in Africa (to Portugal) and those associated with Columbus (to Spain).

Treaty of Versailles The treaty that ended World War I and created independent Poland, Czechoslovakia, Yugoslavia, Hungary, Finland, and the Baltic states of Latvia, Lithuania, and Estonia.

Triangle fire In March 1911, a raging fire swept through the Triangle Waist Company in New York City, killing 146 workers, mostly young women, leading to a series of workplace reforms.

U.S. Colored Troops Black troops consisting of freed black men and former slaves, enlisted for the Union Army after the Emancipation Proclamation of January 1, 1863.

United Colonies of New England (1643) Union of the Massachusetts Bay, Plymouth, Connecticut, and New Haven colonies to bolster their mutual defenses and negotiations with Indians.

United Fruit Company A Boston-based company originally established for importing bananas to the United States from Latin America, it was known as "The Octopus" for its involvement and influence in the affairs of Honduras and Costa Rica.

United Nations Organization An organization open to all nations, established in 1945, for the purpose of maintaining world peace. It is headquartered in New York.

Universal Negro Improvement Association Civil rights organization led by black Nationalist leader Marcus Garvey; the association was active from 1916 to 1923.

USA Patriot Act (2001) Congressional act that expanded the Justice Department's powers to conduct surveillance on terrorist suspects at and home and abroad.

Vice-admiralty courts Colonial courts established by the English Board of Trade to enforce the Navigation Act of 1696.

Virginia Company of London English joint-stock company established in 1606 by a royal charter that gave it exclusive rights to colonize from New England south to Virginia.

Voting Rights Act (1965) Congressional act that outlawed literacy tests to vote and gave the Justice Department the power directly to register voters in districts where discrimination existed.

Watergate Washington office building in which White House operatives committed a series of illegal surveillance acts against political rivals from 1971 to 1973, resulting in a scandal that forced President Richard Nixon to resign in August 1974.

Whig Party American political party formed in 1834 that supported government investments in infrastructure to stimulate business, and, in some parts of the North, endorsed moderate antislavery politics.

Whiskey Rebellion (1794) Violent uprising in western Pennsylvania by farmers who refused to pay a federal tax on liquor.

Williams v. Mississippi The U.S. Supreme Court ruled in 1898 that Mississippi's voting laws, put into effect in 1890 to disfranchise black voters, did not discriminate on the basis of race.

Women's Christian Temperance Union (WCTU) Formed in 1874, the nation's largest female reform organization of the 19th century, specifically dedicated to the banning of intoxicating beverages.

Yellow journalism Name given to sensationalist newspaper journalism of the late 19th century. This type of journalism provoked widespread public support for the Cuban rebels.

Credits

MAP, FIGURE, AND TABLE SOURCES

America in the World (Population) Source(s): United States Population Division; United Nations, Department of Economic and Social Affairs, Population Division (2011). *World Population Prospects: The 2010 Revision*; Massimo Livi Bacci, *A Concise History of World Population* (Wiley-Blackwell, 2001).

Chapter 1

Map 1.1   Source(s): Helen Hornbeck Tanner, ed., *The Settling of North America: The Atlas of the Great Migrations into North America from the Ice Age to the Present* (New York: MacMillan, 1995), 29; Mark C. Carnes, ed., *Historical Atlas of the United States* (New York: Routledge, 2003), 20–21.

Map 1.2   Source(s): Michael Coe et al., *Atlas of Ancient North America* (New York: Facts on File, 1986), 44–45.

Map 1.3   Source(s): Mark Kishlansky et al., *Societies and Culture in World History* (New York: Harper Collins, 1995), 414; *The Oxford Atlas of Exploration*, 2nd edition (New York: Oxford University Press, 2008), 34; Patrick K. O'Brien, gen. ed., *The Oxford Atlas of World History*, concise ed. (New York: Oxford University Press, 2002), 116–17.

Map 1.4   Source(s): D. W. Meinig, *The Shaping of America: A Geographic Perspective on 500 Years of History: Volume 1: Atlantic America, 1492–1800* (New Haven and London: Yale University Press, 1986), 5; Alfred W. Crosby, *Ecological Imperialism: The Biological Expansion of Europe, 900–1900* (New York: Cambridge University Press, 1985), 110; Albert C. Jensen, *The Cod* (New York: Thomas Y. Crowell, 1972), 3; Patrick K. O'Brien, gen. ed., *The Oxford Atlas of World History*, concise ed. (New York: Oxford University Press, 2002), 116–17.

Map 1.6   Source(s): Peter Bakewell, *A History of Latin America*, 2nd edition (Malden, Mass.: Blackwell, 2004), xxii.

Map 1.7   Source(s): *The Oxford Atlas of Exploration*, 2nd edition (New York: Oxford University Press, 2008), 34, 124; Patrick K. O'Brien, gen. ed., *The Oxford Atlas of World History*, concise ed. (New York: Oxford University Press, 2002), 120.

Chapter 2

Map 2.1   Source(s): *The Cambridge History of the Native Peoples of the Americas: Volume 1: North America: Part I*, ed. Bruce G. Trigger and Wilcomb E. Washburn (New York: Cambridge University Press, 1996), 345 and 346; *The Oxford Atlas of Exploration*, 2nd edition (New York: Oxford University Press, 2008), 124.

Map 2.2   Source(s): *The Cambridge History of the Native Peoples of the Americas: Volume 1: North America: Part I*, ed. Bruce G. Trigger and Wilcomb E. Washburn (New York:

Cambridge University Press, 1996), 341.

Map 2.3   Source(s): *The Cambridge History of the Native Peoples of the Americas: Volume 1: North America: Part I*, ed. Bruce G. Trigger and Wilcomb E. Washburn (New York: Cambridge University Press, 1996), 405; *The Settling of North America: the Atlas of the Great Migration into North America from the Ice Age to the Present*, ed. Helen Hornbeck Tanner (New York: MacMillan, 1995), 42; James Oakes et al., *Of the People: A History of the United States* (New York, Oxford: Oxford University Press, 2010), 77.

Map 2.4   Source(s): Jenny Hale Pulsipher, *Subjects unto the Same King: Indians, English, and the Contest for Authority in Colonial New England* (Philadelphia: University of Pennsylvania Press, 2005), 78.

Chapter 3

Map 3.1   Source(s): *The Historical Atlas of Canada*, ed. R. Cole Harris (Toronto: University of Toronto Press, 1987), Volume 1, Plate 35.

Map 3.2   Source(s): David Eltis and David Richardson, *Atlas of the Transatlantic Slave Trade* (New Haven and London: Yale University Press, 2010), 18–19; Assessing the Slave Trade. 2009. *Voyages: The Trans-Atlantic Slave Trade Database.* http://www.slavevoyages.org (accessed November 29, 2011); Gregory O'Malley, "Beyond the Middle Passage: Slave Migration from the Caribbean to North America, 1619–1807," *The William and Mary Quarterly*, 3rd Series, 66 (January 2009), 141–42, 146, 160–61, 163.

Map 3.3   Source(s): Mark C. Carnes, ed., *Historical Atlas of the United States* (New York: Routledge, 2003), 48.

Map 3.4   Source(s): *The Cambridge History of the Native Peoples of the Americas: Volume 1: North America: Part I*, ed. Bruce G. Trigger and Wilcomb E. Washburn (New York: Cambridge University Press, 1996), 416, 426; Andrew K. Frank, ed., *The Routledge Historical Atlas of the American South* (New York and London: Routledge, 1999), 20.

Figure 3.1   Source(s): Assessing the Slave Trade. 2009. *Voyages: The Trans-Atlantic Slave Trade Database.* http://www.slavevoyages.org (accessed November 29, 2011).

Figure 3.2   Source(s): David Eltis, *The Rise of African Slavery in the Americas* (New York: Cambridge University Press, 2000), 9.

Figure 3.3   Source(s): David W. Galenson, *White Servitude in Colonial America: An Economic Analysis* (New York: Cambridge University Press, 1981), 83, 84.

Table 3.1   Source(s): Assessing the Slave Trade. 2009. *Voyages: The Trans-Atlantic Slave Trade Database.* http://www.slavevoyages.org (accessed November 29, 2011).

Table 3.2   Source(s): Richard Middleton, *Colonial America: A History*, 3rd edition (Oxford: Blackwell, 2002); Charles M. Andrews, *The Colonial Period of American History, Volume 4: England's Commercial and Colonial Policy* (New Haven: Yale University Press, 1938).

Chapter 4

Map 4.1   Source(s): Carl Waldman, *Atlas of the North American Indian*, 3rd edition (New York: Facts on File, 2009), 79; Colin G. Calloway, *First Peoples: A Documentary Survey of American Indian History*, 3rd edition (Boston and New York: Bedford/St. Martin's, 2008), 295.

Map 4.2   Source(s): Paul Kelton, *Epidemics and Enslavement: Biological Catastrophe in the Native Southeast, 1492–1715* (Lincoln and London: University of Nebraska Press, 2007), 201.

Map 4.3   Source(s): David Eltis and David Richardson, *Atlas of the Transatlantic Slave Trade* (New Haven and London: Yale University Press, 2010), 18–19; Assessing the Slave Trade. 2009. *Voyages: The Trans-Atlantic Slave Trade Database.* http://www.slavevoyages.org (accessed November 29, 2011).

Map 4.4   Source(s): Mark C. Carnes, ed., *Historical Atlas of the United States* (New York: Routledge, 2003), 73.

Figure 4.1   Source(s): Assessing the Slave Trade. 2009. *Voyages: The Trans-Atlantic Slave Trade Database.* http://www.slavevoyages.org (accessed November 29, 2011).

Table 4.1   Source(s): Assessing the Slave Trade. 2009. *Voyages: The Trans-Atlantic Slave Trade Database.* http://www.slavevoyages.org (accessed November 29, 2011).

Table 4.2   Source(s): Assessing the Slave Trade. 2009. *Voyages: The Trans-Atlantic Slave Trade Database.* http://www.slavevoyages.org (accessed November 29, 2011).

Table 4.3   Source(s): Aaron S. Fogleman, "Migrations to the Thirteen British North American Colonies, 1700–1775: New Estimates," *Journal of Interdisciplinary History* 22 (1992), 691–709; Assessing the Slave Trade. 2009. *Voyages: The Trans-Atlantic Slave Trade Database.* http://www.slavevoyages.org (accessed November 29, 2011).

Chapter 5

Map 5.1   Source(s): David Eltis and David Richardson, *Atlas of the Transatlantic Slave Trade* (New Haven and London: Yale University Press, 2010), 18–19; Assessing the Slave Trade. 2009. *Voyages: The Trans-Atlantic Slave Trade Database.* http://www.slavevoyages.org (accessed November 29, 2011).

Map 5.2   Source(s): Mark C. Carnes, ed., *Historical Atlas of the United States* (New York: Routledge, 2003), 59.

Map 5.3   Source(s): Mark C. Carnes, ed., *Historical Atlas of the United States* (New York: Routledge, 2003), 58; Andrew K. Frank, ed., *The Routledge Historical Atlas of the American South* (New York and London: Routledge, 1999), 20.

Map 5.4   Source(s): Robert H. Ferrell and Richard Natkiel, *Atlas of American History* (New York: Facts on File, 1987, 1993), 30; Mark C. Carnes, ed., *Historical Atlas of the United States* (New York: Routledge, 2003), 58.

Map 5.6   Source(s): Robert H. Ferrell and Richard Natkiel, *Atlas of American History* (New York: Facts on File, 1987, 1993), 16; *Historical Atlas of Canada*, ed. R. Cole Harris (Toronto: University of Toronto Press, 1987), Volume 1, Plate 30.

Map 5.7   Source(s): *Historical Atlas of Canada*, ed. R. Cole Harris (Toronto: University of Toronto Press, 1987), Volume 1, Plate 30.

Figure 5.1   Source(s): Assessing the Slave Trade. 2009. *Voyages: The Trans-Atlantic Slave Trade Database.* http://www.slavevoyages.org (accessed November 29, 2011).

Figure 5.2   Source(s): Jay Coughtry, *The Notorious Triangle: Rhode Island and the African Slave Trade, 1700–1807* (Philadelphia: Temple University Press, 1981), 34.

Figure 5.3   Source(s): Jacob Cooke, ed., *Encyclopedia of North American Colonies* (New York: Scribner's, 1993), 1, 470.

Table 5.1   Source(s): Assessing the Slave Trade. 2009. *Voyages: The Trans-Atlantic Slave Trade Database.* http://www.slavevoyages.org (accessed November 29, 2011).

Table 5.2   Source(s): Aaron S. Fogleman, "Migrations to the Thirteen British North American Colonies, 1700–1775: New Estimates," *Journal of Interdisciplinary History* 22 (1992), 691–709; Assessing the Slave Trade. 2009. *Voyages: The Trans-Atlantic Slave Trade Database.* http://www.slavevoyages .org (accessed November 29, 2011).

Table 5.3   Source(s): Richard Middleton, *Colonial America: A History,* 3rd edition (Oxford: Blackwell, 2002); Jack P. Greene, ed., *Settlements to Society: A Documentary History of Colonial America* (New York: W.W. Norton, 1975).

Chapter 8

Figure 8.1   Source(s): Historical Statistics of the United States Millennial Edition Online, ed. Susan B. Carter, Scott Sigmund Gartner, Michael R. Haines, Alan L. Olmstead, Richard Sutch and Gavin Wright (Cambridge University Press, 2011). http://hsus.cambridge. org/HSUSWeb/ (accessed November 29, 2011).

Chapter 10

Map 10.2   Source(s): Steven Dutch, University of Wisconsin–Green Bay; C.O. Paullin, *Atlas of the Historical Geography of the United States,* (Carnegie Institute, 1932, reproduced in facsimile by Greenwood Press, 1975).

Chapter 11

Map 11.3   Source(s): Nathanial Philbrick, *Sea of Glory: America's Voyage of Discovery, the U.S. Exploring Ex-* *pedition, 1838–1842* (New York: Viking, 2003).

Figure 11.1   Source(s): *Historical Statistics of the United States, 1789–1945.* Dept. of the Census, 1949. Series B 304–330 – Immigration – Immigrants by Country: 1820 to 1945.

Figure 11.2   Source(s): *Historical Statistics of the United States, 1789–1945.* Dept. of the Census, 1949. Series B 13–23: Population, Decennial Summary—Sex, Urban-Rural Residence, and Race: 1790 to 1940.

Chapter 12

Map 12.1   Source(s): John H. Thompson, *Geography of New York State* (New York: Syracuse University Press, 1966).

Map 12.1   Source(s): Kenneth Greenberg, *The Confessions of Nat Turner* (Bedford/St. Martins, 1996).

Figure 12.1   Source(s): Eighth U.S. Census. Schedule 1.

Figure 12.3   Source(s): Lyn Ragsdale, *Vital Statistics on the Presidency* (Washington, D.C.: Congressional Quarterly Press, 1998), 132–38.

Chapter 13

Figure 13.1   Source(s): Campbell J. Gibson and Emily Lennon, "Historical Census Statistics on the Foreign-Born Population of the United States: 1850–1990." Population Division, U.S. Bureau of the Census, Washington, D.C. 20233–8800 February 1999 POPULATION DIVISION WORKING PAPER NO. 29, Table 4. Region and Country or Area of Birth of the Foreign-Born Population.

Chapter 14

Map 14.1   Source(s): Aaron Sheehan-Dean, *Concise Historical Atlas of the U.S. Civil War* (New York, Oxford: Oxford University Press, 2008).

Map 14.2   Source(s): Aaron Sheehan-Dean, *Concise Historical Atlas of the U.S. Civil War* (New York, Oxford: Oxford University Press, 2008).

Map 14.3   Source(s): Aaron Sheehan-Dean, *Concise Historical Atlas of the U.S. Civil War* (New York, Oxford: Oxford University Press, 2008).

Map 14.4   Source(s): Aaron Sheehan-Dean, *Concise Historical Atlas of the U.S. Civil War* (New York, Oxford: Oxford University Press, 2008).

Figure 14.2 Source(s): Douglas B. Ball, *Financial Failure and Confederate Defeat* (Urbana: University of Illinois Press, 1991); Randall, J.G. *The Civil War and Reconstruction.* Boston: D.C. Heath, 1937; Richard Cecil Todd, *Confederate Finance* (Athens: University of Georgia Press, 1954).

Chapter 15

Map 15.1   Source(s): Aaron Sheehan-Dean, *Concise Historical Atlas of the U.S. Civil War* (New York, Oxford: Oxford University Press, 2008).

Map 15.2   Source(s): Aaron Sheehan-Dean, *Concise Historical Atlas of the U.S. Civil War* (New York, Oxford: Oxford University Press, 2008).

Map 15.2   Source(s): Aaron Sheehan-Dean, *Concise Historical Atlas of the U.S. Civil War* (New York, Oxford: Oxford University Press, 2008).

Figure 15.1 Source(s): James L. Watkins, *King Cotton: A Historical and Statistical Review, 1790–1908* (New York: James L. Wakins and Sons, 1908).

Chapter 16

Map 16.1   Source(s): Steven Dutch, University of Wisconsin–Green Bay.

Map 16.2   Source(s): Samuel Truett, *Fugitive Landscapes: The Forgotten History of the U.S.-Mexico Borderlands* (New Haven, London: Yale University Press, 2006).

Chapter 17

Map 17.2   Source(s): Mona Domosh, *American Commodities in an Age of Empire* (Routledge, 2006), 33.

Figure 17.1 Source(s): O.P. Austin, "The United States: Her Industries," *National Geographic* (August 1903): 313.

Chapter 18

Map 18.1   Source(s): *London Times Atlas.*

Map 18.2   Source(s): *Historical Atlas of the United States*, Centennial Edition, ed. Wilbur E. Garrett (National Geographic, 1988).

Table 18.1 Sources(s): Eighth and Twelfth U.S. Censuses.

Chapter 20

Map 20.1   Sources(s): Thomas Paterson et al., *American Foreign Relations* (D.C. Health, 1995), vol. 2, 55, 40.

Map 20.2   Source(s): Patrick K. O'Brien, gen. ed., *The Oxford Atlas of World History*, (New York: Oxford University Press, 1999, 2007), 270.

Chapter 21

Table 21.1 Source(s): Michael Howard, *The First World War: A Very Short Introduction* (New York, Oxford: Oxford University Press, 2007), 122.

Chapter 22

Map 22.1   Source(s): *Historical Atlas of the United States*, Centennial Edition, ed. Wilbur E. Garrett (National Geographic, 1988).

Map 22.2   Source(s): James A. Henretta, David Brody and Lynn Dumenil, *America's History*, Sixth Edition (New York: Bedford/St. Martin's, 2007).

Chapter 23

Figure 23.1 Sources(s): United States Department of Commerce, *Historical Statistics of the United States* (1960), 70.

Chapter 24

Table 24.1 Source(s): Hans Dollinger, *The Decline and Fall of Nazi Germany and Imperial Japan: A Pictorial History of the Final Days of World War II* (New York, NY: Bonanza Books, 1965, 1967), 422.

Chapter 29

Figure 29.2 Source(s): U.S. Bureau of the Census, Current Population Reports, "Money Income in the United States: 2000."

Chapter 30

Map 30.2 Source(s): Mark C. Carnes et al., *Mapping America's Past* (New York: Henry Holt and Co., 1996), 267; *Hammond Atlas of the Twentieth Century* (New York: Times Books, 1996), 166.

Figure 30.1 Source(s): $INDU (Dow Jones Industrial Average) INDX, May 1, 2009. Chart courtesy of StockCharts.com.

Figure 30.2 Source(s): Center for Immigration Studies, 1990 Immigration and Naturalization Service Yearbook.

Chapter 31

Table 31.1 Source(s): U.S. Census Bureau, American Community Survey, 2009.

Figure 31.1 Sources(s): U.S. Census Bureau, American Community Survey, California Association of Realtors, Case-Shiller, National Bureau of Economic Research.

PHOTO CREDITS

Chapter 1 Page 2: *Monumenta Cartographia,* 1502 by © Royal Geographical Society, London, UK/ The Bridgeman Art Library; p. 4: (left) The Art Archive / National Anthropological Museum Mexico / Gianni Dagli Orti; (right) From *Brevis Narratio. . .* published by Theodore de Bry, 1591 / Service Historique de la Marine, Vincennes, France / Giraudon / The Bridgeman Art Library International; p. 5: (bottom) From The Discovery of America, 1878, Spanish School, (19th century) / Private Collection / Index / The Bridgeman Art Library International; (top) De Soto Discovering the Mississippi, 1541, Berninghaus, Oscar (1874–1952) / Private Collection / The Bridgeman Art Library International; (right) From *Newe Welt und Americanische Historien* by Johann Ludwig Gottfried, published by Mattaeus Merian, Frankfurt, 1631, Bry, Theodore de (1528–98) / Private Collection / The Stapleton Collection / The Bridgeman Art Library International; p. 8: Courtesy of The Bancroft Library, University of California, Berkeley; p. 10: Ira Block/ National Geographic/ Getty Images; p. 12: *Novae franciae accurata delineatio* 1657, Library and Archives Canada; p. 18: The Stapleton Collection / The Bridgeman Art Library; p. 21: © The Trustees of the British Museum; p. 24: Museo de America, Madrid, Spain / The Bridgeman Art Library; p. 27: Courtesy of Library and Archives Canada; p. 30:

Courtesy of the Peabody Museum of Archaeology and Ethnology, Harvard University, 2004.24.29636; p. 33: ©The Trustees of the British Museum / Art Resource, NY.

Chapter 2 Page 44: © The Trustees of the British Museum; p. 46: (top) The Signing of the Mayflower Compact, c.1900 (oil on canvas), Moran, Edward Percy (1862–1935) / Pilgrim Hall Museum, Plymouth, Massachusetts / The Bridgeman Art Library International; (bottom) The Granger Collection, NYC; p. 47: (all) The Granger Collection, NYC; p. 50: Private Collection / Archives Charmet / The Bridgeman Art Library; p. 51: ©Cindy Miller Hopkins / DanitaDelimont.com; p. 55: Lahontan, Louis Armand de Lom d'Arce, baron de. *New voyages to North-America: containing an account of the several nations* [. . .]. Vol. 2. London: H. Bomwicke et al., 1703. FC71 L313 1703. p. 59 [a]; p. 60: Indentured servant agreement between Richard Lowther and Edward Lyurd, 31st July 1627/ Virginia Historical Society, Richmond, Virginia, USA/ The Bridgeman Art Library; p. 63: Art Resource, NY; p. 67: Library and Archives Canada / C21404; p. 75: Machotick medal, observe (silver) by English School / Virginia Historical Society, Richmond, Virginia, USA/ The Bridgeman Art Library.

Chapter 3 Page 84: Portrait of Elsie (Rutgers) Schuyler Vas, 1723. Albany Institute of History & Art,

1957.104; p. 86: (left) The Granger Collection, NYC; (right) American School, (19th century) / Private Collection / Peter Newark American Pictures / The Bridgeman Art Library International; p. 87: (bottom left) Title page of the Navigation Act of 1651 (print), American School, (17th century) / Private Collection / Peter Newark American Pictures / The Bridgeman Art Library International; (top right) National Maritime Museum, Greenwich, UK, Caird Collection; (bottom right) Private Collection / Peter Newark American Pictures / The Bridgeman Art Library International; p. 89: Center Historique des Archives Nationales, Paris, France / Giraudon / The Bridgeman Art Library; p. 92: © The Huntington Library, Art Collections & Botanical Gardens / The Bridgeman Art Library; p. 93: British Library, London, UK / © British Library Board. All Rights Reserved / The Bridgeman Art Library; p. 99: © The British Library Board; p. 104: Danita Delimont / Alamy; p. 114: Courtesy, National Museum of the American Indian, Smithsonian Institution [23/9269]; p. 120: New York State Archives.

Chapter 4 Page 128: Library and Archives Canada, acc. no. 1977–35–4. Acquired with a special grant from the Canadian Government in 1977; p. 130: (bottom left) © Library and Archives Canada; (top right) © Historical Picture Archive/ CORBIS; p. 131: (left)

p. 267: Library of Congress Prints and Photographs Division; p. 272: Private Collection / Peter Newark American Pictures / The Bridgeman Art Library; p. 276: Art Resource, NY; p. 277: New York Public Library, USA/ The Bridgeman Art Library; p. 281: Mrs. James Warren (Mercy Otis) by John Singleton Copley, American 1738–1815. Photograph © Museum of Fine Arts, Boston.

Chapter 8 Page 288: Schomburg Center for Research in Black Culture / New York Public Library; p. 290: (left) Courtesy of the artist, Rear Admiral John W. Schmidt, USN (Retired). Official U.S. Navy Photograph; (right) National Archives and Record Administration; p. 291: (top) Bibliotheque Nationale, Paris, France / Archives Charmet / The Bridgeman Art Library International; (bottom right) Courtesy Library and Archives Canada/C-115678; (bottom left) U.S. Naval Historical Center Photograph; p. 299: Gift of Mrs. Henry Nagle, 1894 / Philadelphia Museum of Art; p. 300: (left) ©Massachusetts Historical Society, Boston, MA, USA / The Bridgeman Art Library; (right) © Massachusetts Historical Society, Boston, MA, USA / The Bridgeman Art Library; p. 301: Dallas Museum of Art, The Faith P. and Charles L. Bybee Collection, anonymous gift; p. 302: Library of Congress; p. 307: Copyright © 2000–2011 The Metropolitan Museum of Art. All rights reserved. Source: Two dresses [French] (1983.6.1,07.146.5)

| Heilbrunn Timeline of Art History | The Metropolitan Museum of Art; p. 316: Library of Congress; p. 319: Mid-Manhattan Library Picture Collection / New York Public Library.

Chapter 9 Page 324: Image copyright © The Metropolitan Museum of Art / Art Resource, NY; p. 326: (top) The Granger Collection, NYC; (left) Library of Congress; (right) Copyright © North Wind / North Wind Picture Archives; 327 (top) Courtesy of Historical Society of Pennsylvania Collection / The Bridgeman Art Library; (bottom) The Granger Collection; p. 330: Library of Congress; p. 333: Library of Congress; p. 340: Library of Congress; p. 342: Whitman Sampler Collection, gift of Pet, Incorporated, 1969 / Philadelphia Museum of Art; p. 343: Schlesinger Library, Radcliffe Institute, Harvard University; p. 347: Historic American Buildings Survey / Library of Congress; p. 348: The White House Historical Association.

Chapter 10 Page 360: Smithsonian American Art Museum, Washington, DC / Art Resource, NY; p. 362: (top) Artes e Historia México; (bottom) Copyright © North Wind / North Wind Picture Archives; p. 363: (both) The Granger Collection, NYC; p. 366: The Granger Collection, NYC; p. 368: Stephen A. Schwarzman Building / Manuscripts and Archives Division / New York Public Library; p. 372: Private Collection / Photo © Christie's Images / The Bridgeman Art Library; p. 373: Private

Collection / Ken Welsh / The Bridgeman Art Library; p. 374: The Granger Collection, NYC; p. 379: © Philadelphia History Museum at the Atwater Kent, Courtesy of Historical Society of Pennsylvania Collection / Bridgeman Art Library; p. 385: Wisconsin Historical Society, image ID: 4522; p. 387: Dangers of the whale fishery, illustration from 'Penny Magazine', 1833 (engraving) by American School (19th century), New York Public Library, USA/ The Bridgeman Art Library.

Chapter 11 Page 396: "Emigrants Crossing the Plains" 1867, Albert Bierstadt, artist. Permanent Art Collection, National Cowboy & Western Heritage Museum; p. 398: (top) Defending the Alamo, English School, (20th century) / Private Collection / © Look and Learn / The Bridgeman Art Library International; (center) The Granger Collection, NYC; (bottom) The Granger Collection, NYC; p. 399: (top) The Granger Collection, NYC; (bottom) "Morning Tears–winter, 1838–39." Copyright (c) John Guthrie, Guthrie Studios, www.guthriestudios .com p. 403: Morning Tears- winter, 1838–39. Copyright © John Guthrie, Guthrie Studios, www. guthriestudios.com; p. 411: The Granger Collection, NYC; p. 416: The Granger Collection, NYC; p. 418: © Stapleton Collection/Corbis; p. 422: © Francis G. Mayer/ CORBIS; p. 423: The Granger Collection, NYC; p. 424: The Granger Collection, NYC; p. 430: The County Election (oil on canvas), Bingham,

George Caleb (1811–79) / St. Louis Art Museum, Missouri, USA / The Bridgeman Art Library International; p. 431: De Bow's Review, April 1857.

Chapter 12 Page 440: The Granger Collection, NYC; p. 442: (left) The Granger Collection, NYC; (right) Photograph courtesy of Oberlin College Archives; p. 443: (top right) bpk, Berlin / Knud Petersen / Art Resource, NY; (center) National Maritime Museum, Greenwich, UK, Michael Graham-Stewart Slavery Collection. Acquired with the assistance of the Heritage Lottery Fund; (bottom) Library of Congress; p. 447: The Granger Collection, NYC; p. 453: Courtesy of Mississippi Department of Archives and History; p. 455: The Granger Collection, NYC; p. 456: Library of Congress; p. 462: The Granger Collection, NYC; p. 467: © CORBIS; p. 468: The Granger Collection, NYC; p. 470: Library of Congress.

Chapter 13 Page 478: Art Resource, NY; p. 480: (top) After the Battle of Monterrey, Mexican General Pedro de Ampudia surrenders the city to American General Zachary Taylor during the Mexican-American War of 1846–48 (colour litho), English School, (19th century) / Private Collection / Ken Welsh / The Bridgeman Art Library International; (bottom left) The Occupation of the Capital of Mexico by the American Army, 1846–48 (colour litho), American School, (19th century) / American Antiquarian Society, Worcester, Massachusetts, USA / The Bridgeman Art Library International;

(bottom right) Library of Congress; p. 481: (right) National Maritime Museum, Greenwich, UK; (left) The Anti-Slavery Society Convention, 1840 by Benjamin Robert Haydon, 1841. Copyright © National Portrait Gallery, London 2011; p. 482: SSPL/Science Museum / Art Resource, NY; p. 488: Courtesy of UC Berkeley, Bancroft Library; p. 492: © Everett Collection / SuperStock; p. 499: The Granger Collection, NYC; p. 502: Copyright © North Wind / Nancy Carter\North Wind Picture Archives; p. 509: The Granger Collection, NYC; p. 511: The Granger Collection, NYC.

Chapter 14 Page 518: The Granger Collection, NYC; p. 520: (both) Library of Congress; p. 521: Library of Congress; p. 526: Harper's Weekly, (1862) / Library of Congress; p. 527: Ohio Historical Society; p. 532: Andrew J. Russell, photographer / Library of Congress; p. 542: Gardner, Alexander, 1821–1882, photographer / Library of Congress; p. 543: A Ride for Liberty, or The Fugitive Slaves, c.1862 (oil on board) by Eastman Johnson (1824–1906) Brooklyn Museum of Art, New York, USA/ The Bridgeman Art Library; p. 545: The Historical Society of Pennsylvania; p. 548: Gibson, James F., b. 1828, photographer / Library of Congress; p. 555: Barnard, George N., 1819–1902, photographer / Library of Congress.

Chapter 15 Page 562: The Granger Collection, NYC; p. 564: (left) © Bettmann / CORBIS; (right) Library of

Congress; p. 565: (center) Library of Congress; (bottom) Beard, James Carter, 1837–1913 , artist / Library of Congress; (top) The Granger Collection, NYC; p. 567: Library of Congress; p. 579: Private Collection / Peter Newark American Pictures / The Bridgeman Art Library; p. 581: The Granger Collection, NYC; p. 583: Detroit Publishing Co. Photography Collection, no. 08148 / Library of Congress; p. 587: University of Washington Libraries, Special Collections Division, Captain S.E. Lancaster photograph collection. PH Coll 168; p. 589: © Bettmann / CORBIS; p. 591: The Granger Collection, NYC; p. 594: © Francis G. Mayer/CORBIS.

Chapter 16 Page 600: Courtesy of The Forgotten Gateway Exhibit; p. 602: (top) South Castle Creek, a Temple of the Hills, Black Hills, South Dakota (oil on canvas), De Haven, Franklin (1856–1934) / Private Collection / Phillips, Fine Art Auctioneers, New York, USA / The Bridgeman Art Library International; (bottom) De Bow's Review, April 1857; p. 603: (left) Library of Congress; (right) James E. Hunt / McCracken Collection / Buffalo Bill Historical Center, Cody, Wyoming; P.69.1310c; p. 605: "The Heart of the Continent." Booster brochure of imagined West, Denver Public Library, Western History Collection / The Bridgeman Art Library; p. 614: James E. Hunt / McCracken Collection / Buffalo Bill Historical Center, Cody, Wyoming; P.69.1310c; p. 615: Courtesy of Nebraska State Historical

Society; p. 618: Courtesy of the Nevada Historical Society; p. 620: Atchison, Topeka, and Santa Fe Railway Company / Kansas Historical Society; p. 626: The Granger Collection, NYC; p. 628: Courtesy of the Burton Historical Collection, Detroit Public Library. ©1999; p. 634: The Grand Canyon of the Yellowstone, 1872 (oil on canvas), Moran, Thomas (1837–1926) / National Museum of American Art, Smithsonian Institute, USA / Lent by U.S. Dept. of the Interior, National Park Service / The Bridgeman Art Library.

Chapter 17 Page 640: The Granger Collection, NYC; p. 642 (both) The Granger Collection, NYC; p. 643: (top) Library of Congress; (left) ©Illustrated London News Ltd/Mary Evans Picture Library; (right) Mary Evans Picture Library; p. 645: The Granger Collection, NYC; p. 650: © Bettmann/CORBIS; p. 656: The Granger Collection, NYC; p. 658: Early Office Museum Archives; p. 662: Library of Congress; p. 664: The Granger Collection, NYC; p. 666: © Bettmann / CORBIS; p. 673: The Granger Collection, NYC.

Chapter 18 Page 680: Library of Congress; p. 682: (left) The Granger Collection, NYC; (right) Library of Congress; p. 683: (top) © Bettmann/CORBIS; (bottom left) Rue des Archives / The Granger Collection, NYC; (bottom right) The Granger Collection, NYC; p. 690: Rue des Archives / The Granger Collection, NYC; p. 692: The Granger Collection, NYC; p. 699: The Granger Collection, NYC; p. 703:

Reproduced from an original postcard published by J. Valentine & Sons, New York; p. 704: Leopold Morse Goulston baseball collection in memory of Leo J. Bondy / New York Public Library; p. 706: Courtesy of Andrew Dolkart Collection; p. 709: © Moffett / Library of Congress; p. 710: The Granger Collection, NYC.

Chapter 19 Page 722: The Granger Collection, NYC; p. 724: (left) Copyright © North Wind / North Wind Picture Archives; (right) View of one of the locks on the Panama canal (b/w photo), / Private Collection / Roger-Viollet, Paris / The Bridgeman Art Library International; p. 725: (top left) NHHC Collection; (bottom left) Detroit Publishing Company Photograph Collection / Library of Congress; (bottom right) Cover of Life magazine, Vol. 39, #1021 first published on May 22, 1902; p. 727: © CORBIS; p. 734: Rau Studios, Inc., Philadelphia / New York Public Library; p. 735: Courtesy Frederic Remington Art Museum, Ogdensburg, New York (Public Library Collection); p. 737: New York Public Library; p. 738: Fotosearch / Getty Images; p. 741: J.S. Pughe, *Harper's Weekly*, September 5, 1900; p. 743: Rau Studios, Inc., Philadelphia / New York Public Library; p. 748: Library of Congress.

Chapter 20 Page 758: George Grantham Bain Collection / Library or Congress; p. 760: (left) The Granger Collection, NYC; (right) New York World-Telegram and the Sun Newspaper Photograph Collection (Library of Congress); p. 761: (right)

Harris & Ewing Collection (Library of Congress); (top) New York Public Library; (bottom left) Library of Congress; p. 770: Library of Congress, LC-USZ62-31911; p. 771: New York Public Library; p. 772: Oscar B. Willis / New York Public Library; p. 778: The Granger Collection, NYC; p. 782: The Granger Collection, NYC; p. 783: Library of Congress; p. 789: War Department General and Special Staff / US National Archives and Records Administration (533769); p. 791: The Granger Collection, NYC.

Chapter 21 Page 798: © Pictorial Press Ltd / Alamy; p. 800: (right) © Bettmann/ CORBIS; (left) Library of Congress; p. 801: (top) Rue des Archives / The Granger Collection, NYC; (bottom left) © Bettmann/CORBIS; (right) Mary Evans/Robert Hunt Collection; p. 802: New York Public Library; p. 807: Mary Evans/Robert Hunt Collection; p. 814: Library of Congress; p. 817: U.S. Signal Corps and Navy / Library of Congress; p. 820: Library of Congress; p. 824: U.S. Army Signal Corps / Library of Congress.

Chapter 22 Page 840: The Jacob and Gwendolyn Lawrence Foundation / Art Resource, NY and © 2011 The Jacob and Gwendolyn Lawrence Foundation, Seattle/Artists Rights Society (ARS), New York; p. 842: (top) Lebrecht Photo Library; (center) The Granger Collection, NYC; (bottom) Del Rio Historical Photo Gallery / US Department of Homeland Security; p. 843: (top) Library of Congress; (bottom) Library of Congress; (center)

Scene of panic in Wall Street, New York, 24th October 1929 (b/w photo), American Photographer, (20th century) / Private Collection / Peter Newark American Pictures / The Bridgeman Art Library International; p. 844: Famous Players/Paramount / The Kobal Collection; p. 849: Mary Evans Picture Library; p. 850: The Granger Collection, NYC; p. 854: © David J. & Janice L. Frent Collection/Corbis; p. 855: Lebrecht Photo Library; p. 860: The Granger Collection, NYC; p. 863: © Bettmann/ CORBIS.

Chapter 23 Page 878 © Associated Press; p. 880: ©Associated Press; p. 881: (left) Portrait of Hitler, 1933 (b/w photo), German Photographer (20th Century) / Private Collection / Peter Newark Military Pictures / The Bridgeman Art Library International; (right) Japanese tanks crossing a river in China, during the Second World War (b/w photo), German Photographer (20th Century) / © SZ Photo / The Bridgeman Art Library International; p. 886: ullstein bild / The Granger Collection, NYC; p. 891: Bureau of Reclamation, U.S. Dept of the Interior, 2006; p. 894: United Press International / New York World-Telegram & Sun Collection / Library of Congress; p. 896: Dorothea Lang / FSA/OWI Collection / Library of Congress; p. 908: © CORBIS.

Chapter 24 Page 920: Library of Congress; p. 922: (top) Library of Congress; (bottom left) FSA/OWI

Collection / Library of Congress; (bottom right) U.S. Signal Corps / Library of Congress; p. 923: (left) MCT / Landov; (right) Mary Evans / Sueddeutsche Zeitung Photo; p. 933: FSA/ OWI Collection / Library of Congress; p. 938: © Bettman/CORBIS; p. 941: © CORBIS; p. 947: Toni Frissell Collection / Library of Congress; p. 951: © National Archives/CORBIS; p. 954: Clem Albers / Farm Security Administration and Office of War Information Collection / Library of Congress; p. 960: U.S. Signal Corps / Library of Congress.

Chapter 25 Page 966: H. Armstrong Roberts / ClassicStock.com; p. 968: (left) Central Intelligence Agency; (right) dpa /Landov; p. 969: (top) National Archives and Records Administration (NARA), 541959; (bottom left) Library of Congress; (bottom right) H. Armstrong Roberts / ClassicStock.com; p. 972: © Hulton-Deutsch Collection/ CORBIS; p. 975: *No Place to Hide* by David Bradley. Copyright © 1948 by David Bradley. Boston: Little, Brown & Company; p. 985: © Ann Ronan Picture Library / Heritage-Images / The Image Works; p. 986: What's Become of Rosie the Riveter? by FRIEDA S. MILLER, Director, Women's Bureau, United States Department of Labor *New York Times*, May 5, 1946. ProQuest Historical Newspapers The New York Times (1851–2003) pg. SM11; p. 987: © Bettmann/ CORBIS; p. 991: Courtesy of Bracero History Archive, item # 3020; p. 994: © Bettmann/ CORBIS; p. 998: New York World-Telegram and the

Sun Newspaper Photograph Collection (Library of Congress).

Chapter 26 Page 1004: Guy Gillette/Time & Life Pictures/ Getty Images; p. 1006: (top) © Bob Campbell/San Francisco Chronicle/Corbis; (center) © March of Dimes; (bottom) AP Photo; p. 1007: (top) © National Air and Space Museum; (bottom left) The G. Eric and Edith Matson Photograph Collection/ Library of Congress; (bottom right) © Bettmann/CORBIS; p. 1011: © Bettmann/CORBIS; p. 1012: From *Dark Sun: The Making of the Hydrogen Bomb* by Richard Rhodes. Simon & Schuster, 1995. Image reproduced by permission of Molecular Biophysics & Biochemistry Department, Yale University; p. 1017: CBS / Landov; p. 1023: Lin Shi Khan and Tony Perez, *Scottsboro, Alabama: A Story in Linoleum Cuts* (New York: New York University Press, 2001 [1935]; p. 1030: Domingos Alegres, Jaudi Dudi, No. 138, 18 de Noviembre de 1956, Sociedad Editora America, S.A.; p. 1031: © Bettmann/ CORBIS; p. 1034: The Granger Collection, NYC; p. 1036: ALLIED ARTISTS / The Kobal Collection.

Chapter 27 Page 1050: © Flip Schulke/Corbis; p. 1052: (top) Courtesy of NASA; (center) Copyright © 2002 Robert Altman; (bottom) Library of Congress; p. 1053: (right) VONDERHEID/ dpa / Landov; (left) Library of Congress; p. 1054: Helen Nestor / Oakland Museum of California; p. 1056: Associated Press; p. 1073: The Granger Collection, NYC; p. 1074: Rue des Archives / The Granger Collection, NYC;

Index

AAA. *See* Agricultural Adjustment Administration

AASS. *See* American Anti-Slavery Society

Abernathy, Ralph, 1041

ABM. *See* Anti-Ballistic Missile

abolition, 412, 425, 436, 452–455

Aboriginals, 632. *See also* Native Americans

abortion: Bush, G.H.W., and, 1175; CWA and, 1144; Reagan, R., and, 1154; Republican Party and, 1221; *Roe v. Wade* and, 1118, 1143–1144, 1160; Thomas, C., and, 1175; as wedge issue, 1145

Abrams v. U.S., 819

Abu Ghraib, 1219, *1219*, 1244

Acadians (tribe), 149

Acheson, Dean, 975, 1009, 1015

acquired immune deficiency syndrome (AIDS), 1129, 1154–1155, 1160

ACS. *See* American Colonization Society

Act of Supremacy, 36, 40

Act of Union, 149, 167

ADA. *See* Americans with Disabilities Act

Adams, Abigail, 240, 248, 300

Adams, John, 240, 243, 248, 253, 257, 273, 356

Adams, John Quincy, 349, 354–355, 379–380, 433, 436

Adams, Samuel, 231, 234, 248

Adamson Act, 813

Addams, Jane, 682, 709, *709*, 715, 764, 868; Anti-Imperial League and, 741; Progressivism and, 759, 762; race and, 770; World War I and, 786, *791*

Adelman, Kenneth, 1217

Adet, Pierre, 297

ad men, 849–850

Administration of Justice Act, 226*t*

advertising, 613; with celebrities, 849; in Cold War, 992; dot-coms and, 1231; in 1920s, 849–850, 861; in 1950s, 1024, 1029; for tobacco, 850; to youth, 1036–1037

AEF. *See* American Expeditionary Force

affirmative action, 1134, 1145, 1160

Afghanistan: bin Laden in, 1199–1200; Obama and, 1215, 1241; Soviet Union in, 1129, 1137–1138, 1158, 1160; Taliban in, 1213, 1214–1215, *1218*, 1244

AFL. *See* American Federation of Labor

African Americans: in agriculture, 656; Baptists, 203, 463; in baseball, 704, *994*, 994–995, 998; at Battle of San Juan Hill, 745; beliefs and practices of, 146–147; black laboring class, 571; churches, 344, 580; churches of, 344, 580; crime by, 1145; culture of, 343–344; Democratic Party and, 775; families, 567–569; as farmers, 669; folk traditions of, 503; Ford Motor Company and, 856; in Gilded Age, 669, 704; in Great Depression, 856, 884; imperialism and, 744–745; jazz and, 855; lynchings of, 744, 769, *770*, 772–773, 856; Methodists, 203, 463, 502; in middle class, 686; migration of, 337–339, 787–788, 821; New Deal and, 908–909; newspapers and, 744; in 1920s, 854–857; in 1960s, 1072–1075; positive images of, 502; in postwar South, 580–583; in prison, 1153; Progressivism and, 767; Protestantism and, 202–204; rock 'n roll and, 1037; Roosevelt, T., and, 770–771, 792; sharecropping and, *896*; Social Security and, 898; as soldiers, 547–549; in South, 984–985, 993; suburbanization and, 1021; unemployment of, 988; urbanization and, 686; voting by,

378, 576–577, 744, 760, 775, 1063, 1072*t*; war and, 272–273; Wilson, W., and, 771; women, 767; in World War I, 787–788, 820–821; in World War II, *947*, 948–949, 952–953; in WPA, 908; YMCA and, 769. *See also* slavery

Africanization, of North America, 142–147

African Methodist Episcopal Church (AME), 502

Afro-Christianity, 462–464, 503

Agassiz, Louis, 405, 434, 436

Agent Orange, 1102

Agnew, Spiro T., 1120

agrarianism, 334–335

Agricultural Adjustment Administration (AAA), 892, 912

agriculture, 9, 334, 389; in Gilded Age, 656, 690–691; in Latin America, 900; mechanization in, 685; plantation, 29, 586–587; sheep, 136; in Soviet Union, 926; tariffs for, 712; technology and, 621. *See also* farmers/ farming; ranching

Aguinaldo, Emilio, 742, *743*, 750, 751

AIDS. *See* acquired immune deficiency syndrome

Aids to Success and Happiness, 672

AIM. *See* American Indian Movement

Aims and Aids to Success and Happiness, 674

airplanes, 806, 904, 945–946; B-17 bombers,

945; B-24 bombers, 945; B-52 bombers, *1011*, 1101; RAF, 930

Alamo, 407, 436

Albany Congress, 205, 214

Albright, Madeleine, 1197

Alcatraz, Native Americans at, *1076*, 1083

alcohol/alcoholism, 451–452, 460; crime and, 705; in Gilded Age, 711; Mothers Against Drunk Drivers and, 1155; Progressivism and, 768; Prohibition and, 760, 768, 793, 833, 864, 872, 890; in World War I, 823. *See also* Prohibition

Aleuts (tribe), 7

Alexander, Edward Porter, 570, 596

Alexander, James, 191

Alexander II (czar), 539, 620, 683, 692, 714

Alexander VI (pope), 23, 35

Alger, Horatio, 672, 673, 674

Algerian War for Independence, 1044

Algiers, 311

Algonquians (tribe), 45, 57, 65–66, 76–79, 112–115

Alianza Hispano Americana, 699

Alien Act, 301–303, 320, 787

Alien Enemies Act, 787

Alito, Samuel, 1224

Allen, Ethan, 242, 248

Allen, Gracie, 905

Allen, Richard, 339, 344, 356

Allende, Salvador, 1115, 1132

Alliance for Progress, 1059

Alpha tests, 818

Amazon.com, 1184

AME. *See* African Methodist Episcopal Church

America fever, 692–693

America First Committee, 930

The American (Frank), 1038

American Anti-Slavery Society (AASS), 454, 474

American Bible Society, 343, 458

American Board of Customs, 233

American Cancer Society, 1155

The American Challenge (Servan-Schreiber), 1068, 1083

American Civil Liberties Union, 819

American Colonization Society (ACS), 338, 356, 455, 474, 495

American Communist Party, 982

American Education Society, 458

American Enterprise Association, 1026

American Expeditionary Force (AEF), 822

American Express, 1024

American Federation of Labor (AFL), 665–666, 674, 778, 895, 899, 1026

American Fur Company, 332

American Indian Defense Association, 910

"The American Indian Gets in the War Game" (movie), 817

American Indian Movement (AIM), 1077

American Indians. *See* Native Americans

American Individualism
(Hoover, H.), 867
Americanism, 495–496
Americanization: of
immigrants, 694, 701;
in World War I, 811
American League, of
baseball, 715
American Medical
Association, 898
American Mercury
(Mencken), 859, 872
American-Philippine War,
742–744
American Philosophical
Society, 193, 214, 229
American Protective
Association (APA),
693, 714
American Protective
League (APL), 819
*American Protestant
Vindicator and Defender
of Civil Religious Liberty
against the Inroads of
Papacy*, 495–496
American Railway Union
(ARU), 667, 675
American Recovery and
Reinvestment Act,
1240
American Sugar Refining
Company, 650–651
Americans with
Disabilities Act (ADA),
1174
American System, 364,
369, 379, 381, 391
American Temperance
Society (ATS), 451, 474
American Tract Society,
343, 458
American Union Against
Militarism, 812
America Online, 1185
Ames, Adelbert, 592
Amherst, Jeffrey, 226
Amos 'n' Andy, 905
amusement parks, in
Gilded Age, 703
anarchism, 664, 833,
851–852

Anasazi (urban society),
9–10
Anderson, Joseph, 498
Anderson, Jourdan, 569
Anderson, Robert, 526
Anderson, Terry H., 1081
Andropov, Yuri, 1157
Andros, Edmund, 102, 121
Angela (African servant),
62–63
Angell, Norman, 803–804
Anglican Church, 459
Anglo-French Wars, 309
Angola, 1138, 1158
Der Anschluss, 928
Anson, "Cap," 704
antebellum era, 420–427
Anthony, Joanna, 200
Anthony, Susan B., 421,
436, 444, 577, 596
Anti-Ballistic Missile
(ABM), 1113
anti-Chinese sentiments,
609
Anti-Comintern Pact, 927,
958
Antietam, Battle of, 542
Antifederalists, 281
Anti-Imperial League,
740–741, 745, 750
Antin, Mary, 701
Anti-Saloon League, 768,
792
antisodomy laws, 1222,
1244
anti-syndicalism laws, 778
Anza, Juan Bautista de, 245
APA. *See* American
Protective Association
Apalachee, 98
APL. *See* American
Protective League
Apollo program, 1070
"The Appeal of the
Independent
Democrats," 509
*An Appeal to the Christian
Women of the South*
(Grimkè, A.), 465
*An Appeal to the Coloured
Citizens of the World*
(Walker, D.), 465, 503

An Appeal to the World (Du
Bois), 995, 999
appeasement, in World
War II, 928–929
Apple Computer, 1169,
1172, 1186
Appleton, Nathaniel, 372,
391
apprenticeship laws, 573
Arafat, Yasser, 1198–1199
Arawak (Taíno language),
22
Argentina, 690
Aristide, Jean Bertand,
1202
Arkwright, Richard, 367,
391
Armstrong, John, 314
Armstrong, Samuel, 627
Army Air Service, 798
Army of the Potomac, 533,
535, 551
Arnold, Benedict, 219,
242, 248
ARPAnet, 1183
arquebus, 18, 64
Articles of Capitulation,
102, 124
Articles of Confederation,
261, 262, 274, 278,
280, 284
artisans, 196, 410
ARU. *See* American
Railway Union
Asbury, Francis, 452, 474
Asia/Asian Americans,
1188; literature of,
470; trade of, 332–
334; Voting Rights Act
of 1965 and, 1134. *See
also specific countries;
specific countries and
national origins*
assassinations: of
Alexander II, 683,
692, 714; of Franz
Ferdinand, 805, 832;
of Garfield, 713, 714;
of Kennedy, John,
1060–1061, 1082; of
Kennedy, R., 1109; of
King, M., 1106, 1118;

of Lincoln, A., 569; of McKinley, 747, 751
Assembly Party, 184
Astaire, Fred, 905
Astor, John Jacob, 331–332, 347, 356
astrolabes, 16, 40
Atahualpa, 33
Atlanta, in Gilded Age, 687
Atlanta Compromise, 772
Atlantic Charter, 932
Atlantic slave trade, 19–20, 40, 181*f*
atomic bomb. *See* nuclear weapons
ATS. *See* American Temperance Society
Attucks, Crispus, 236
Austin, Jonathan Loring, 391
Austin, Moses, 382
Austin, Stephen, 351, 382, 391
Australia, 491, 632, 690, 1019; Chinese and, 694, 715; literacy test in, 715; Progressivism in, 762; in Vietnam War, 1102; in World War I, 806
Austria-Hungary, 805
automobiles. *See* cars
Autry, Gene, 1029, 1042
Avery, Sewell, 894
Axis Alliance, 927, 958
axis of evil, 1215
Ayllón, Nicolás Vázquez de, 35
Aztlán (tribe), 14

B-17 bombers, 945
B-24 bombers, 945
B-52 bombers, *1011*, 1101
Babbitt (Lewis), 859, 872
Babes in Arms (movie), 905
baby boom, 950, *1019*, 1019–1020, 1036–1038, 1081
Bache, Sarah Franklin, 276, 284
Bacon, Nathaniel, 110, 124

Bacon's Rebellion, 107, 111, 124
Bad Axe River, Battle of, 385
Baker, Howard, *1119*
Baker, James A., III, 1150, 1176
Bakke, Allan, 1134
Bakker, Jim, 1144, *1144*
Bakker, Tammy Faye, 1144, *1144*
balance of power, 280, 284, 804–805
Balkans, 805, 1198, *1199*, 1203. *See also* Yugoslavia
Baltimore, *686t*
Baltimore and Ohio Company, 370, 512
banks, 346–348, 381; Emergency Banking Relief Act, 889; FDIC and, 890; Glass-Steagall Banking Act, 889–890; in Great Depression, 883, 888, 914; housing bubble and, 1234–1237, *1235*, *1236*; in 1920s, 869; World Bank, 1232
bank holidays, 888
Bank of the United States (BUS), 347, 356
Bank War, 381
Bao Dai, 1095
baptism, 63, 68, 104
Baptists, 200, 203, 446, 463
Barak, Ehud, 1199
Barbados, 95–96, 97, 111–112, 124
Barbary Wars, 310–311
Barker, Ma, 904
Barnett, Samuel, 709, 714
Barnette v. West Virginia, 955
Barrow, Bennett, 501
Barton, Clara, 738
Bartram, John, 193
baseball, 682, *704*, 714, 715; African Americans

in, 704, *994*, 994–995, 998; in Gilded Age, 704, 715; in Great Depression, 906; in 1920s, 858
Basic Magnesium Facility, 990
Basic Principles of United States-Soviet Cooperation, 1113
basketball, 705, 715
Bataan Death March, 936–937
Battle of Antietam, 542
Battle of Bad Axe River, 385
Battle of Bull Run, 530
Battle of Bunker Hill, 242
Battle of Dien Bien Phu, 1044, 1118
Battle of Fallen Timbers, 336
Battle of Fort McHenry, 317
Battle of Guadalcanal, 937
Battle of Horseshoe Bend, 316
Battle of Iwo Jima, 938, 959, 973, 998
Battle of Lake Erie, 317
Battle of Little Big Horn, 624
Battle of Midway, 937
Battle of Okinawa, 973, 998
Battle of Oriskany, 272
Battle of Princeton, 258
Battle of San Juan Hill, 736, *737*, 745
Battle of Saratoga, 260
Battle of Sullivan's Island, 258
Battle of the Bulge, 940, 959
Battle of the Coral Sea, 937
Battle of the Marne, 806
Battle of Tippecanoe, 312
Battle of Trafalgar, 310
Battle of Trenton, 258
Battle of Yorktown, *272*

battleships, 725, 735–736, 750, 934
Bay of Pigs, 1059, 1060, 1082
Beach Boys, 1081
Bear Flag Republic, 486
Bear Stearns, 1235, 1245
Beatles, 1080, 1081, *1081*, 1083
beatniks, 1037
Beaumarchais, Caron de, 260
beaver hunting, *55*
Beaver Wars, 89–90, 124
Beck, Glenn, 1228
Becknell, William, 383, 391
Beecher, Catherine, 454, 457
Beecher, Lyman, 346, 356, 451, 508
Beecher's Bibles, 508
beef trust, 780, 781
Beethoven, Ludwig van, 819
Begin, Menachem, 1136, *1137*
Belgium, 670, 805, 807, 812, 826, 940
Bell, John, 523, 559
Bellamy, Edward, 674, 675–676
Bellamy Clubs, 676
Bellomont, Earl of, 155
Benavides, Alonso de, 69, 79
Benezet, Anthony, 199, 210, 214
Bennett, James Gordon, 468, 474
Benny, Jack, 905
Benton, Thomas Hart, 380, 391
Berg, Gertrude, 905
Berkeley, John, 118
Berkeley, William, 91, 110–111, 124
Berle, Adolph, 887
Berlin, 905, 971, 998
Berlin Airlift, 978
Berlin Wall, 1058–1059; building of, 1052,

1082; destruction of, 1155, 1170, 1176, *1177*, 1202
Bernanke, Ben, 1234, 1235
Bernays, Edward, 849
Berners-Lee, Tim, 1183
Bernstein, Carl, 1120
Berry, Chuck, 1037, 1080
Berthe, 945
Beta tests, 818
Bethe, Hans, 942
Bethel Church, 344
Bethlehem Steel, 658–659
Bethune, Mary MacLeod, *908*
Beveridge, Albert, 741
BIA. *See* Bureau of Indian Affairs
bicycles, 704, 1155
Biddle, Nicholas, 267, 284, 381, 391
Biden, Joseph, 1238–1239
Bierstadt, Albert, 631
big business. *See* Gilded Age
Big Stick, 746–750
Bill of Rights, 295, 320
Billy the Kid, 614
bin Laden, Osama, 1158, 1199–1200, 1211, 1212, 1213, 1215, 1244, 1245. *See also* 9/11
biracial churches, 463, 580
birth control, 860, 1066, 1082, 1083, 1154. *See also* abortion
Birthers, Obama and, 1242
The Birth of a Nation (Griffith), 771, 853
bison. *See* buffalo
Black, Hugo, 913
Blackbeard. *See* Teach, Edward
Blackboard Jungle (movie), 1037
black codes, 573, 596
Blackfeet (tribe), 133–134
Black Hawk (chief), 384, 391
Black Hawk Down (movie), 1198

Black Hawk War, 383–385
black laboring class, 571
Black Legend, 54, 79
black lung disease, 660
Blackmun, Harry, 1117
Black Muslims, 1074
Black Panthers, *1050*, 1074, 1083
Black Power, 1072, 1074–1075, 1083
Black Ships, 479
Black Tuesday, 872, 873
Blaine, James G., 732
Blair, James, 153
Bleibtreu, Karl, 551
Blitzkrieg, 929, 958
block printing, 17
Bloody Act, 237
Bloody Shirt, 575
blue collar workers: in Gilded Age, 656–658; in 1950s, 1026; Republican Party and, 1131
Blue Cross and Blue Shield, 946
Blue Mondays, 659
Board of Trade, 156, 167
Body of Liberties of 1641, 78
Boehner, John, 1243
Boesky, Ivan, 1152
Bohr, Aage, 967
Bohr, Niels, 967
Boland Amendment, 1161
Bolívar, Simón, 353, 522, 559
Bolshevik Revolution. *See* Russian Revolution
bomb shelters, 1031–1032
bonanza wheat farms, 619
Bonaparte, Napoleon, 301, 308
Bond, Phineas, Jr., 367
bonded labor, 427
Bon Homme Richard, USS, *267*
Bonnet, Stede, 156
Bonus Bill, 347, 369
Bonus Marchers, 885, 914
Book of Common Prayer, 503

The Book of Mormon, 448
books, 192
boosters, 613
Booth, John Wilkes, 569, 596
Booth, William, 681
BOR. *See* Bureau of Reclamation
Borah, William, 834
borderlands, 608
Border Patrol, 842, 872
Border War, 271
Bosch, Juan, 1066–1067
Bosnia. *See* Balkans
Boston, 686*t*, 688, 693, 703, 715; police strike in, 832, 866; segregation in, 1118
Boston Associates, 372–373
The Boston Gazette, 163
Boston Massacre, 235–238, 248
The Boston News-letter, 149, 163
Boston Port Bill, 226*t*
Boston Tea Party, 239–240, 248
Boston Town Meeting, 234
Boston Whig, 505
Bourbon Reforms, 228, 244
Bow, Clara, 860
Bowery Theater, 469
Boxer Rebellion, 746, 750
boxing, 604, 636, 703, 858, 905
Boyer, Jean-Pierre, 339
Boys' Club, 767
Boy Scouts, 767
BP oil spill, 1241
Bracero Program, 950–951, *951*, 990–991, *991*
Brackenridge, Hugh Henry, 342, 356
Braddock, Edward, 206
Bradley, David, 975, 999
Brady, Matthew, 542
brain trusts, 896
brainworkers. *See* white collar workers
Brandeis, Louis, 674

Brando, Marlon, 1037
Brant, Joseph, 271, 284
Brazil, 500, 584, 585
Breckinridge, John, 523, 559
Bremer, Paul "Jerry," 1218
Brennan, William, 1175
Brent, Margaret, 91
Brest-Litovsk Treaty, 833
Bretton Woods Agreements, 922, 948–949, 959
Breyer, Stephen, 1202
Brezhnev, Leonid, 1087, 1113, 1132
Briand, Aristide, 868–869
Britain: baby boom in, 1019; empire of, 100–102; imperialism of, 728; industrialization in, 647, 648*f*; labor systems of, 60; mainland colonies of, 177*f*; nationalism of, 809; navy of, 809–810; North America and, 53–55; pensions in, 779; rock 'n roll from, 1080–1081; Spain and, 190; Suez Canal and, 1015; textile manufacturing, 371; urbanization in, 685; Venezuela and, 733, 750; War of 1812 and, 317; World War I and, 804–805; World War II and, 930
British Guiana, 733
Brock, Isaac, 314
Broderick, David, 489, 514
Brooklyn, 686*t*
Brooks, Preston, 510
Brooks Brothers riot, 1201–1202
Brotherhood of Locomotive Firemen, 667
Brotherhood of Sleeping Car Porters, 856, 952
Brown, Edmund G. "Pat," 1054

Brown, H. Rap, *1074*
Brown, John, 509, 512–513, 514, 524
Brown, Michael, 1227
Brown, Morris, 464
Brown, Moses, 372, 391
Brownlow, William G. "Parson," 536, 559
Brown v. Board of Education of Topeka Kansas, 1039–1040, 1044, 1058
Bryan, William Cullen, 408, 436
Bryan, William Jennings, 715, 716, 741, 810, 862–864
Bryce, James, 711
Buchanan, James, 496, 510, 514, 525, 559
Buchanan, Patrick, 1154, 1181, 1228; immigration/immigrants and, 1189; on marriage, 1222; as presidential candidate, 1200–1201
Buckley, William F., 1031
Bucktail Democrats, 378
buffalo, 488, 628–630
Buffalo Bill. *See* Cody, William
Buffalo Soldiers, 744
Bulge, Battle of the, 940, 959
Bull Moose Party, 774
Bull Run, Battle of, 530
bully pulpit, 781
Bummers, 550, 563
Bunau-Varilla, Philippe, 748
Bunker Hill, Battle of, 242
Bureau of Consumer Financial Protection, 1241
Bureau of Indian Affairs (BIA), 909–910, 1077
Bureau of Land Management, 989
Bureau of Reclamation (BOR), 612

Bureau of Refugees, Freedmen, and Abandoned Land, 569
Burger, Warren, 1117
Burgoyne, John, 260
Burke, Edmund, 239
Burke, Thomas, 262
"Burned Over" district, 445
Burnett, John G., 350
Burns, Anthony, 507, 514
Burns, George, 905
Burnside, Ambrose, 546, 559
Burr, Aaron, 304, 311
Burroughs, William S., 1037
BUS. *See* Bank of the United States
Bush, George H.W., 1202; abortion and, 1175; Cold War and, 1172–1182; conservatism and, 1174–1175; deficit spending and, 1174–1175; environment and, 1174; gender and, 1174; Iraq and, 1178–1180; NAFTA and, 1193; Persian Gulf War and, 1221; as Vice President, 1150
Bush, George W., 1244; conservatism and, 1220–1230; deficit spending and, 1242*f*, 1243; Democratic Party and, 1223; disputed election of 2000 and, 1200–1204, *1203*; federal budget and, 1242*f*; Hurricane Katrina and, 1226–1227; immigration/ immigrants and, 1227–1229; Iraq War and, 1215–1220; judicial appointments by, 1224–1225; Medicare and,

1225–1226; 9/11 and, 1213–1215; Al Qaeda and, 1213–1215; social Security and, 1223; terrorism and, 1212–1213; values issues by, 1223
Bush, Jeb, 1202, 1224
Bush Doctrine, 1215
Bush v. Gore, 1202–1204
business mergers. *See* mergers
business travelers, 618–619
busing, school, 1117–1118, 1131, 1153, 1221
Butler, Benjamin, 534, 539, 547, 559
butter, 365–366
Butterfield, Alexander, 1120
butterfly ballot, 1201
Byrd, William II, 162–163, 167
Byrnes, James F., 913, 945, 972

C. *Turner Joy*, USS, 1099
Cabeza de Vaca, Álvar Nuñez, 34–35, 40
Caboto, Giovanni, 23, 26, 40
Cabrillo, Juan Rodríguez, 34
caciques (chiefs), 22
Caddo (tribe), 135
Cadore, duc de, 313
Cahokia (Mississippian society), 11
Cain, James, 906
Cajuns, 493
Calhoun, John C., 313, 347, 356, 391, 432, 499, 514
California: agriculture in, 690–691; immigration/ immigrants in, 1188, *1230*; Proposition 13 in, 1136; Proposition 187 in, 1189, 1203; San Francisco, 1083;

taxes in, 1136. *See also* Los Angeles
Californios, 487–490
Calles, Pltarco, 870
Calloway, Cab, *855*
Calvert, Leonard, 91
Calvin, John, 37, 40
Calvinism, 37, 40, 72, 346
Cambodia, 1111, 1119
campaign contributions, by corporations, 1225, 1245
Campbell, John, 163
Camp David Accords, 1136, *1137*, 1160
"Camptown Races" (Foster, S.), 469
Canada, 35, 314, 670, 806, 864; French Canadians, 655, 686, 691; Nova Scotia, 212; Quebec, 208. *See also* North American Free Trade Agreement
Canadian Pacific Railroad, 694
Canal Bank, 364
canals, 369–370
Canary Islands, 20
Cane Ridge Revival, 445
Canning, George, 354, 356
Cantor, Eddie, 905
Cão, Diogo, 20
capitalism, 389; in Great Depression, 888–895; legal structures of, 385–388; New Deal and, 888–895; Progressivism and, 777–778; Reed and, 802; unions and, 665
capitalist market economy, 371, 374
Capone, Al, 864
caravels, 16
Carey, Matthew, 342, 356
Caribbean, 188–191; Atlantic world and, 24–30; slaves of, 95–97; trade, 309–310. *See also specific countries*

Caribs (tribe), 22

Carmichael, Stokely, *1074*, 1074–1075, 1083

Carnegie, Andrew, 641, 651, 675; Anti-Imperial League and, 741; philanthropy of, 672–673; Social Darwinism and, 672

Carnegie Endowment for International Peace, 982

Carnegie Steel, 641, *645*, 649, *656*, 666–667, 675

Carranza, Venustiano, 814

cars: in Cold War, 992; GPS for, 1187; in 1920s, 847–849; in 1950s, *1004*, 1027–1028. *See also* highways; United Automobile Workers

Carson, Rachel, 1035, 1079, 1082

Carswell, G. Harrold, 1117

cartels, in Gilded Age, 649

Carter, Jimmy, 1127, 1133–1141, *1137*; China and, 1137; Cuba and, 1139; foreign policy of, 1136; inflation and, 1135–1136; IRS and, 1127; nuclear energy and, 1134–1135; oil and, 1134; Olympics and, 1137; Panama Canal and, 1137, 1160; Reagan, R., and, 1140, 1146

Carteret, George, 118

Cartier, Jacques, 35, 40

Casas, Bartolomé de las, 28, 40, 54

cash and carry, 958

Cass, Lewis, 384, 391

Castro, Fidel, 1060, 1137–1138

Catcher in the Rye (Salinger), 1037

Catherine the Great, 266, 284

Catholic Church, 36, 339, 494; Franciscans, 32–33, 40, 49; immigration/immigrants and, 448, 693; Ireland and, 494; Irish Catholics, 494; Jesuits, 36, 40, 49, 67–68; KKK and, 853; Mexico and, 405; in Northern Ireland, 1203; in Poland, 1130, 1157; reform and, 707; Salvation Army and, 684, 708; Smith, A., and, 867

Catholic Family Services, 1221

Cato's Letters, 165

Catt, Carrie Chapman, 813, 817

cattle, 617, 623

Caughey, James, 458

CBS. *See* Columbia Broadcasting System

CCC. *See* Civilian Conservation Corps

celebrities: advertising with, 849; IRS and, 944–945; in 1920s, 841, 849, 858–859; in religion, 1144

Central America, 801, 1149, 1158–1159, 1162, 1178. *See also specific countries*

Central Intelligence Agency (CIA), 969, 975, 998; Bay of Pigs and, 1060; bin Laden and, 1213; in Chile, 1115; Cuba and, 1060; Eisenhower and, 1012; Iraq War and, 1215; jazz and, 1043; Mujahideen and, 1137; in Panama, 1178; Reagan, R., and, 1157, 1158; rendition by, 1219; rock 'n roll and, 1043; Solidarity and, 1157; USIA and, 1043; in Vietnam, 1097; Watergate and, 1120

Central Powers, 787, 793, 805

Ceuta, conquest of, 19

Chaco Canyon, 10

chads, 1201, 1202

Challenger accident, 1161

Chamberlain, Neville, 929

Chambers, Whitaker, 982, 999

Champlain, Samuel de, 61, 64, 79

Chanal, François de, 550

Chandler, Raymond, 906

Charbonneau, Toussaint, 329

charity: in Gilded Age, 708, 714; in Great Depression, 885. *See also* philanthropy

Charles I (king), 71, 79

Charles II (king), 91, 100, 111, 124

Charles III (king), 222, 228, 245

Charles River Bridge v. Warren Bridge, 388

Charles V (king), 35

Charlotte, in Gilded Age, 687

Charlotte Temple (Rowson), 343

Charter of Freedoms and Exemptions, 70, 79

Chartist movement, 510

Chase, Samuel, 523, 559

chastity clinics, 1154

Chateau Thierry, 826

Chauchetière, Claude, 104–105

Chaumont, Comte de, 253

Chauncy, Charles, 202

Chavez, Cesar, *1075*, 1076

chemical weapons, in World War I, 806, 823–824

Cheney, Dick, 1176, 1180, 1214
Chernenko, Konstantin, 1157
Cherokees (tribe), 341, 401–402
Chesapeake Bay, slavery in, 107, 146
Chiang Kai-shek, 932, 934, 939, 978
Chicago, 686t; baseball in, 704; in Gilded Age, 687, 707, 715; Haymarket Square bombing in, 665, 674; protests in, 1109, 1118; skyscrapers in, 688–689, 714; stockyards in, 651
Chicago Defender, 821
chiefs, hereditary, 10
Child, Lydia Maria, 455, 474
child labor: Fair Labor Standards Act and, 914; in Gilded Age, 661–662, *662*, 697; Knights of Labor and, 665; piecework by, 659; Progressivism and, *758*, 767, 780
Chile, 1115, 1132
China/Chinese, 332, 334, 414–415, 483, 489; in agriculture, 656; anti-Chinese sentiments, 609; Australia and, 715; Carter and, 1137; communism in, 978, 999; Communist Party in, 932; discrimination against, 694; exclusion of, 609–610; in Gilded Age, 685–686; Great Cultural Revolution in, 1107, 1118; immigration and, 492, 609, 690–691, 694; imperialism in, 745–746; influenza in, 827; Japan and, 927–928,

958; Kissinger and, 1114–1115, 1119; Korean War and, 981, 999, 1044; Nixon, R., and, 1110, 1114–1115, 1119; open door policies in, 746, 750; Progressivism in, 762; Roosevelt, T., and, 749; Tiananmen Square, 1202; Vietnam War and, 1107; in World War II, 939
Chinese Exclusion Act, 610, 636, 694, 714
Choctaw (tribe), 137
choir system, 200
Cholenec, Pierre, 104
Christianity: abortion and, 1143–1144; Addams and, 764; Afro-Christianity, 462–464, 503; baptism in, 63, 68, 104; Evangelical, 197–202, 425–426, 1144–1145; imperialism and, 727–730; IRS and, 1127; masculinity and, 425–426; Narragansett, 203; Native Americans and, 910; in 1920s, 861–864; Progressivism and, 763–764. *See also specific denominations*
Christope, Henri, 307, 320
Chrysler, 1027–1028, 1240
churches: of African Americans, 344, 580; biracial, 463, 580; in Gilded Age, 659; for immigrants, 700–701; mega-churches, 1144; membership of, 448*f*; separation of church and state, 74, 202. *See also specific churches*
Churchill, Randolph, 652–653, 674

Churchill, Winston, 928, 930, 931–932, 939, 960, 971–973
Church of Christ, 346
Church of England, 36, 40, 65, 79
CIA. *See* Central Intelligence Agency
cigarettes. *See* tobacco
CIO. *See* Congress of Industrial Organization
The Cisco Kid (television program), 1029
cities, 376, 424, 493, 592, 606, 687–688; 1860-1890, 686t; in Gilded Age, 702–707; global, 1190–1191; Progressivism and, 764–773. *See also* suburbanization; urbanization; *specific cities*
Citizens' Committee to Test the Constitutionality of the Separate Car Law, 769
citizenship, 575–577; contested, 490–497
Citizens United, 1225, 1245
city manager system, 765
"Civil Disobedience" (Thoreau), 1042
Civilian Conservation Corps (CCC), 890–891, 910
Civil Liberties Bureau, 819
civil rights: Bush, G.H.W., and, 1174; in Cold War, 993–999, 1038–1039; Great Society and, 1061–1063; of Hispanics, 1075–1077; of Native Americans, 1075–1077; in 1950s, 1038–1045; in 1960s, 1072–1077; Nixon, R., and, 1109

Civil Rights Act of 1866, 575
Civil Rights Act of 1964, 776, 1062, 1082, 1152
civil service reform, in Gilded Age, 712–713
Civil War: African American soldiers, 547–549; amendments, 575–577; 1862-1863, 531–539; 1863-1864, 546–552; environmental and economic scars of, 555–556; European support of, 537–539; financing, 544f; government centralization and, 543–546; industrialization after, 647; mobilization for, 527–529; victory and defeat, 552–558
Cixi (Empress Dowager), 746
Clark, Jim, 1063
Clark, William, 329, 356
class, 410–412; black laboring, 571; consumerism and, 375–376; working, 375. See also middle class
Clay, Henry, 313, 336, 347, 356, 364, 369, 378, 455, 474, 483, 514
Clayton Antitrust Act, 783, 793
Clayton-Bulwer Treaty, 748
Clean Air Act, 1079, 1174
Clean Water Act, 1174
Clemenceau, Georges, 577, 583, 584, 828
clerks, in Gilded Age, 657
Clermont, 369
Cleveland, Grover, 510, 713–714, 715; Anti-Imperial League and,

741; Immigration Restriction Bill and, 694; Monroe Doctrine and, 733; Pullman Palace Car strike and, 667, 675
Clifford, Clark, 1105
climate change, Bush, G.W., and, 1221
Clinton, Bill, 1173, 1181–1182; bin Laden and, 1213; impeachment of, 1196–1197, 1203; national health insurance and, 1193–1194; New Democrats and, 1192–1197; Al Qaeda and, 1213; Yugoslavia and, 1198
Clinton, Cornelia, 292
Clinton, DeWitt, 388, 391
Clinton, Henry, 258, 269, 284
Clinton, Hillary Rodham, 1193, 1238, 1240
CNN, 1186
CO. See conscientious objectors
coal, 646, 648, 660. See also United Mine Workers
coalition of the willing, in Iraq War, 1217
Coalition Provisional Authority (CPA), 1218
Cobb, Freeman, 616, 618
Code Noir, 148, 167
code of honor, 425
Cody, William (Buffalo Bill), 613–614, 629, 636
Coercive Acts (Intolerable Acts), 226t, 239–240, 241, 248
The Coffeehouse Mob (Ward), 165
coffeehouses, 165–166
coffle, 337
Cohen, Ben, 904
Coinage Act, 712, 714
Coke, Thomas, 452

Colbert, Jean-Baptiste, 103, 106, 124
Colden, Cadwallader, 193
Cold War: advertising in, 992; Berlin and, 971, 998; Berlin Wall and, 1058–1059; Bush, G.H.W., and, 1172–1182; cars in, 992; civil rights in, 993–999, 1038–1039; communism in, 975, 977–983; consumerism and, 1024–1025; Cuba and, 1060; decolonization and, 1012–1014; Eisenhower and, 1009–1010; end of, 1172–1182; immigration in, 987–993; international markets and, 975; Kissinger and, 1132; KKK in, 996; Korean War and, 969, 978–981; leisure in, 992–993; media in, 1042–1043; military industrial complex in, 988–990; in 1960s, 1058–1060; Nixon, R., and, 1113–1116; nuclear weapons and, 967–1003; propaganda in, 986; Reagan, R., and, 1155–1163; segregation in, 988; thawing of, 1161–1163, 1202; Vietnam and, 1093–1095; women in, 985–986, 986. See also post-Cold War
Cole, USS, 1200, 1213
Colfax Massacre, 590–591
Coligny, Gaspard de, 37
collective violence, 614–617
colleges, 191, 447. See also specific colleges

collegia pietatis ("gatherings for piety"), 153
Colleton, John, 111
Collier, John, 910
Colombia, 748
colonial identity, 228–229
colonial resistance, 155–158
colonist-Algonquian wars, 76–79
colonization: of Philippines, 740; of Texas, 382–383; World War I and, 804; World War II and, 957. *See also* decolonization; imperialism
Colorado River, 611
Colored Farmers' Alliance, 669
Columbia Broadcasting System (CBS), 846
Columbian exchange, 25, 28, 40
Columbus, Christopher, 21–23, 40
Comanchería, 488
Comanches (tribe), 136, 187, 487–490
Comandancia General of the Interior Provinces, 245
Commerce Clause, 349
Committee of Congestion of Population in New York, 766
Committee on Public Information (CPI), 816–817
commodities, global, 616–623
common law, 61, 79
communism: in China, 978, 999; in Cold War, 975, 977–983; Containment Policy for, 981, 998; Domino Theory and, 1015; in Gilded Age, 643, 663–664; *Invasion of the Body Snatchers* and,

1036; McCarthyism and, 999, 1008, 1016–1018; Paris Commune and, 643, 663, 674; Reagan, R., and, 1130; in Vietnam, 1093; World War I and, 828–833. *See also specific communist countries*
Communist Party, 893, 982; in China, 932; in Soviet Union, 925
Company of New France, 64
Company of the Indies, 129, 132
compassionate conservatism, 1225–1226
Compromise of 1850, 506, 514
computers, personal, 1169, 1172
Comstock Lode, 617
concentration of wealth, 649–651, 1151, 1186, 1233–1234, 1243
Concerned Women of America (CWA), 1144
Conestogas, 232, 487–490
Coney Island, 703
Confederate States of America, 431, 528, 545
Confederation Congress, 504
conformity, in 1950s, 1025, 1030–1038
Congressional Reconstruction, 577–580, 589
Congress of Industrial Organization (CIO), 895, 899, 1026
Congress of Racial Equality (CORE), 1056, 1072
Conkling, Roscoe, 554
conscientious objectors (CO), 822, 947

conservation movement, 623
conservatism, 591–594, 1127–1167; after World War II, 955–956; Bush, G.H.W., and, 1174–1175; Bush, G.W., and, 1220–1230; Clinton, B., and, 1192; culture war and, 1181, 1221–1224; First Amendment and, 1225; Republican Party and, 1130–1133
Constitution, 281–283, 283; First Amendment, 982, 1066, 1225; Fifth Amendment, 982, 1066; Twelfth Amendment, 299, 378, 592; Thirteenth Amendment, 573, 597; Fourteenth Amendment, 575–576, 595, 597, 775, 1149; Fifteenth Amendment, 577, 595, 597, 775; Sixteenth Amendment, 783, 793, 813; Seventeenth Amendment, 774, 793; Eighteenth Amendment (Prohibition), 760, 768, 793, 833, 864, 872, 890; Nineteenth Amendment, 761, 789, 793, 821, 833; Twenty-second Amendment, 1044; Commerce Clause of, 349; ERA, 1078, 1144; Insular Cases and, 740
Constitutional Convention, 192, 279–281
Constitutional Union Party, 523
consumerism, 193–197, 233–238, 375–376; Cold War and,

1024–1025; in Gilded Age, 651–654; in 1920s, 849–850; in 1950s, 1024–1025
Consumer Products Safety Council (CPSC), 1117
consumer protection, Progressivism and, 780–784
Containment Policy, 981, 998, 1103
contested citizenship, 490–497
Continental Army, 262, 273
Continental Congress, 219, 241, 242, 261
Contraband camps, 541
contraceptives. *See* birth control
Contract with America, 1194
conucos, 22
Convention of 1818, 352
conversion test, 72, 79
Cook, James, 408, 436
Coolidge, Calvin, 866–867, 872
coolie trade, 609
Cooper, James Fenimore, 343, 507
Coors, Joseph, 1159
copper borderlands, 608
Copperheads, 537
Coral Sea, Battle of the, 937
Corcoran, Thomas, 904
CORE. *See* Congress of Racial Equality
Corn Laws, 428, 436
Cornwallis (lord), 258, 269, 273, 284
Coronado, Francisco de, 31, 34, 40
corporations, 348–349; bailouts for, 1235–1237; campaign contributions by, 1225, 1245; First Amendment and, 1225; in Gilded Age,

647; globalization and, 1232–1233; in 1950s, 1025–1026, 1035–1036; in 1970s, 1146; political parties and, 1146; Reagan, R., and, 1152
Corps of Discovery, 329
Corregidor, 936
Corte-Real, Gaspar, 26
Cortés, Hernán, 30, 40
Cortés, Martín, 31
Costa Rica, 752
cost-plus clause, 943
cotton, 364, 374, 582–583, 586–588, 586*f*, 656, 668
Cotton, John, 75
Cotton Club, 855, *855*
Coughlin, Charles, 893–894, *894*
Council for National Defense, 813
counterculture, of 1960s, 1079–1084
Coupland, Douglas, 1188
Covenant Chain, 106, 124
coverture laws, 277, 284, 342, 356, 421, 436
cowboys, 621, 622–623
cowpox, 9
Cox, Archibald, 1120
Cox, James C., 886
Cox, James M., 865
CPA. *See* Coalition Provisional Authority
CPI. *See* Committee on Public Information
CPSC. *See* Consumer Products Safety Council
The Cradle Will Rock, 906
craft unions, 664–666, 670, 674, 899
Craig v. Missouri, 388
Crater Lake National Park, 785
Crawford, William H., 352, 378, 391
Crazy Horse, 624

creationism, 862–864, 1130, 1221–1222
credit cards, 1024
Cree (tribe), 133–134
Creel, George, 816–817
Creoles, 202, 214, 493, 514
crime, 152; in Gilded Age, 705; in 1920s, 864; in 1950s, 1021; in 1960s, 1066; in 1970s, 1145; Republican Party and, 1221
"The Crime Against Kansas," 510
criminal justice system, 152; for juveniles, 767–768
Crisis (magazine), 818
The Crisis (Paine), 258
Croatia. *See* Balkans
Crockett, Davy, 402, 407, 436
Croix, Teodoro de, 245
Cromwell, Oliver, 90, 94, 124
crop liens, 587, 596, 656, 668
Cruikshank v. U.S., 592
Cruise, Tom, 1158
Cuba, 585, 588, 722, 735, 1030; Carter and, 1139; Cold War and, 1060; colonization of, 724; Guantanamo Bay in, 1219, 1240, 1244; Marielitos from, 1139, 1160; Refugee Act and, 1149; Soviet Union and, 1137–1138; Spain and, 734–736; Spanish-American War and, 736–740
Cuban Missile Crisis, 1052, 1060, 1082, 1097
Cuffee, Paul, 338
Cultural Revolution, in China, 1107, 1118
culture, 340–346, 416, 633; African American, 343–344; in Great

Depression, 904–911; mass, 468–469; in New Deal, 904–911; in 1920s, 857–864; of permissiveness, 1127. *See also* popular culture

culture war, conservatism and, 1181, 1221–1224

Cumberland Road, 369

Cummings, Homer S., 904

Curly Top (movie), 905

currency, in Gilded Age, 712

Currency Act, 197t, 226

currency regulation, 369

CWA. *See* Concerned Women of America

Czechoslovakia, 831, 1108, 1118, 1176; Soviet Union and, 1067, 1083, 1108; in World War II, 928–929, 958

Daily Missouri Republican, 405

Dakota Territory, 692

Daladier, Edouard, 929

Dale, Thomas, 60

Daley, Richard J., 1109

Dallas (television program), 1153

Da Nang, Vietnam, 1099, 1113, 1119

dancing, 767, 859, 906, 1037

Dar es Salaam, Tanzania, 1199–1200

DARPA. *See* Defense Advanced Research Projects Agency

Darrow, Clarence, 863–864

Dartmouth College, 203

Dartmouth College v. Woodward, 349

Darwin, Charles, 861, 1130; Social Darwinism, 627, 636, 651, 672, 693, 728

Daugherty, Harry, 866

Daughters of Liberty, 235

Daughters of the American Revolution, 909, 991

Davenport, James, 203

Davies, Thomas, 210

Davis, Jefferson, 384, 391, 525, 544, 559, 569, 596

Davis, John W., 867, 894

Davis, Lucy, 373

Davis, Miles, 1038

Davis gimlets, 556

Dawes, Charles, 869

Dawes, William, 242

Dawes Act, 630–631

Dawes Plan, 869, 872, 910

Dayton Peace Accords, 1203

day trading, 1184–1185

D-Day, 923, 940, 959

Dean, James, 1037

Dean, John, 1119–1120

Dearborn, Henry, 314

The Death of General Wolfe (West), *209*

death penalty, 1153, 1176

death rituals, 146–147, 462

DeBow, James D. B., *431*

DeBow's Review, *431*

Debs, Eugene V., 667, 774, 787, 793, 818, 865

Decatur, Stephen, 311, 320

Declaration of Causes, 524

Declaration of Independence, 243–244, 248, 256, 261, 293

Declaration of Rights, 277

"Declaration of Sentiments," 457

Declaration of the Rights of Man and of the Citizen, 293

Declaratory Act, 226t, 232

decolonization, 830, 1012–1014

Defense Advanced Research Projects Agency (DARPA), 1183

Defense of Marriage Act, 1222

deficit spending: Bush, G.H.W., and, 1174–1175; Bush, G.W., and, 1242f, 1243; Clinton, B., and, 1192; in Great Depression, 903f, 915; in 1970s, 1143; Obama and, 1242f; Reagan, R., and, 1151–1152

Defoe, Daniel, 192

de Gama, Vasco, 21

Deganawidah, epic of, 14–15, 40

de Gaulle, Charles, 929, 1108

de Kalb, Johan, 265

Delaney, Martin, 502, 514, 582, 596

Delano, Warren, 414

Delawares (tribe), 118, 186–187

de Lôme, Enrique du Puy, 735

demilitarized zone (DMZ), 981, 1010, 1044

demobilization, 274

Democratic Party, 361, 537; African Americans and, 775; Bush, G.W., and, 1223; civil rights and, 1061–1063; farmers/farming and, 669; in Gilded Age, 669, 711–714; middle class and, 1145; New Deal and, 914–915; in 1970s, 1145; protests and, 1109, 1118; in South, 1131–1132. *See also* Tammany Hall; *specific Democratic politicians*

Democratic-Republican Party, 295t, 305, 312, 335, 379

Democratic Review, 428

Dempsey, Jack, 858

Denmark, 697

Dennis v. United States, 982, 999

Denver, in Gilded Age, 687

Department of Defense, 1214, 1218
Department of Education, 1134
Department of Energy, 1134
Department of Housing and Urban Development, 1064
Department of Indian Affairs, 625
Department of Justice, 590
Department of Transportation, 1064
department stores, 702, *703*
depression, 348, 685; 1873 to 1878, 642, 660, 674; 1893 to 1897, 643, 675, 713–714, 730–731; in 1950s, 1032. *See also* Great Depression
DePriest, Oscar, 776
Desert Lands Act, 612, 624, 636
Deslondes, Charles, 307, 320
Dessalines, Jean-Jacques, 307, 308, 320
d'Estaing, Comte, 260, 268, 284
détente, 1110, 1113–1114
Detroit, *1073. See also* cars
Developing World, 975, 978, 1012–1014, 1038
Dewey, George, 736, 750
Dewey, John, 812, 817
Dewey, Thomas E., 956
DeWitt, John, 953
Dewson, Molly, 907
Dexter, Harry, 948–949
The Dial (magazine), 441
Dias, Bartolemeu, 21
Diaz, Adolfo, 753
Díaz, Bernal, 31
Diaz, Porfirio, 813
Dickinson, Emily, 469, 470–471
Dickinson, John, 232, 234
Dien Ben Phu, Battle of, 1044

Die Neuner, 534
Dillinger, John, 905
DiMaggio, Joe, 905
Diné (tribe), 7, 69
Diners Club, 1024
diplomacy, 264–266
Dirksen, Everett, 1062
A Discourse Concerning Faith and Fervency (Mather, C.), 152
discrimination, 536, 548, 694; reverse, 1152. *See also* race/racism
disease. *See* illnesses
disfranchisement, 775–776, 792
Displaced Persons Act, 991
displacement, 185–188
diversity, 450, 469, 471
Division of Forestry, U.S., 635
divorce: conservatism and, 1130; CWA and, 1144; feminism and, 1077; 2000 to present, 1222
Dixon, Willie, 1080
Dixwell, George, 414
DMZ. *See* demilitarized zone
DNA testing, 1187
Dobbs, Lou, 1228
Dobrynin, Anatoly, *1114*
Dobson, James, 1144
doctrine of nullification, 432
Doegs (tribe), 110
dole (cash payments to unemployed), 896
Dole, Bob, 1133, 1195–1196, 1203
Dole, Sanford B., 733, 750
Dollar Diplomacy, of Taft, 750–753
Dominican Republic, 832, 1066–1067, 1083
Dominion of New England, 120, 124
Domino, Fats, 1037
Domino Theory, 1015, 1044, 1093
Doniphan, A. W., 484

"Don't Ask, Don't Tell," 1192
Doolittle, James H., 937, 1012
Dorsey, George, 993
dot-coms, 1184–1185, 1186; bust of, 1231–1234
Double V campaign, of NAACP, 953, 993, 996
doughfaces, 510
Douglas, Stephen, 455, 474, 508, 514, 523
Douglas, William O., 913
Douglass, Frederick, 454–455, 474, 502, 528, 548, 595
Douglass, William, 163
Douglass's Monthly, 528
draft: Clinton, B., and, 1182; Progressivism and, 812; in Vietnam War, 1103–1104, 1111; in World War I, 818; in World War II, 947–949, 958
Draft Riots, of New York City, 548
Drake, Francis, 54
Dred Scott, 510–511, 514
droughts, 10, 339, 613, 621
drugs, 414–415; miracle drugs, 1020. *See also* LSD; marijuana; *specific medicinal drugs*
drummers, 657
Dubcek, Alexander, 1108
Du Bois, W.E.B., 771, 995, 999; Anti-Imperial League and, 741, 745; Second Pan-African Congress and, 856; Washington, B., and, 772; World War I and, 818, 821
Dukakis, Michael, 1173–1174, 1202
Dulany, Daniel, 229
Dulles, John Foster, 1011
dumb-bell tenements, 705–706

Dunkirk, 929
Duong Van Minh, 1096
du Picq, Ardant, 551
DuPont, 1028
Duportail, Louis, 264, 284
Dust Bowl, 887, 911
Dutch West India
    Company (DWIC), 64,
    70, 80, 95
Dwight, Timothy, 346, 356
Dyer, Mary, 94
Dylan, Bob, 1080–1081
Dynasty (television
    program), 1153

Eagle Forum, 1144
Earle, George, 926
Earth Day, 1079
East India Act, 155
East India Company (EIC),
    155, 162, 167, 333
Eastman, Thomas, 543
Easy Rider (movie), 1083
Eaton, William, 320
eBay, 1184
economics: change, 275–
    276, 420–423; Civil
    War and, 555–556;
    laissez-faire, 651
economy: autonomous
    slave economy, 196;
    capitalist market,
    371, 374; Civil War
    and, 555–556;
    commercial, 444;
    commercialization of,
    159; extractive, 616–
    623; of New England,
    94–95. *See also*
    extractive economies
Edict of Nantes, 53, 80,
    120
The Ed Sullivan Show, 1081
education, 495, 580–581;
    for African Americans,
    984–985; for
    assimilation, 625–627;
    *Brown v. Board of
    Education of Topeka
    Kansas*, 1039–1040,
    1044, 1058; colleges,

191, 447; English-
    only movement and,
    1149; for immigrants,
    694, 701; intelligent
    design in, 1222; NCLB
    and, 1225, 1244;
    nondenominational
    schools, 495–496;
    parochial schools,
    496; public schools,
    495, 580–581. *See also*
    GI Bill; No Child Left
    Behind Act; school
    busing; school prayer;
    *specific colleges and
    universities*
Education Society, 461
Edwards, Jonathan, 200,
    214
Edwards, Morgan, 202
EEOC. *See* Equal
    Employment
    Opportunity
    Commission
Egypt: Camp David
    Accords and, 1136;
    cotton in, 668; Sadat
    and, 1115, 1136, *1137*;
    Soviet Union and,
    1007; in World War II,
    939. *See also* Six-Day
    War; Suez Canal
Ehrlichman, John, 1112,
    1118
EIC. *See* East India
    Company
Eighteenth Amendment.
    See Prohibition
Einstein, Albert, 907, 942
Eisenhower, Dwight D.,
    1008–1018; civil rights
    and, 1040; D-Day
    and, 940; Developing
    World and, 1012–1014;
    Hungary and, 1014–
    1015; Korean War
    and, 1010; McCarthy,
    J., and, 1018; Native
    Americans and,
    1077; Nixon, R., and,
    1009; Red Scare and,

1016–1017; Soviet
    Union and, 1005; Suez
    Canal and, 1014–1015;
    Vietnam and, 1044,
    1093
El Camino Real, 609
electoral reform,
    Progressivism and,
    774–776
Eliot, John, 92, 124
Eliot, T.S., 1031
elites, 427
Elizabeth I (queen), 36,
    40, 53
Ellington, Duke, *855*
Ellis Island, *690*
Ellsberg, Daniel, 1111–1112
El Salvador, 1158
El Turco, 34
emancipation, 453;
    in comparative
    perspective, 571–572;
    contraband camps
    and, 541; hemispheric,
    584; Jamaican, 571;
    pride of, 554; as war
    policy, 542
Emancipation Day, 581
"Emancipation
    Manifesto," 539
Emancipation
    Proclamation, 538,
    559
Embargo Act, 312
Emergency Banking Relief
    Act, 889
Emergency Economic
    Stabilization Act, 1236
Emergency Farm Labor
    Program, 951, 990
Emergency Immigration
    Act of 1921, 850
Emergency Relief
    Appropriation Act, 896
Emerson, Ralph Waldo,
    441, 466–468
emigration. *See*
    immigration/
    immigrants
emotionalism, 446
empresarios, 382

The Empress of China, 332
encomiendas (grants of
    land), 18, 40
energy, 619; Enron and,
    1209, 1212; nuclear,
    1134–1135; Obama
    and, 1241; steam, 367–
    369, 654, 689, 803; use
    and sources of, 1135f.
    See also coal; oil
Enforcement Acts, 590
Engels, Frederick, 412
Engel v. Vitale, 1066
England. *See* Britain
English-Algonquian war,
    66
English Civil War, 90–94,
    124
English-only movement,
    1134, 1149
Enigma machine, 930
Enlightenment, 191–193,
    214, 228–229
Enron, 1209, 1212, 1244
enslaved labor, 161
entertainment: in Gilded
    Age, 702–704; in Great
    Depression, 904–906;
    Internet pornography
    and, 1184; in New
    Deal, 904–906; in
    1920s, 858–859; from
    television, 1028–1029.
    See also leisure;
    movies; sports
enumerated goods,
    101
environment: BP oil spill,
    1241; Bush, G.H.W.,
    and, 1174; changes
    of, 7; Civil War and,
    555–556; conservation
    movement, 623;
    Democratic Party
    and, 1145; *Exxon
    Valdez*, 1174; human
    impact on, 631;
    New Deal and,
    910–911; in 1960s,
    1079; preservation
    movements, 634–635;

Progressivism and,
    784–786; Reagan,
    R., and, 1152;
    Roosevelt, T., and,
    784–785; science and
    technology and, 1069;
    suburbanization and,
    1024; Truman and,
    984; of Vietnam, 1102
Environmental Protection
    Agency (EPA), 1079,
    1117
epic of Deganawidah,
    14–15, 40
epidemics, 68
Episcopalians, 446
Equal Employment
    Opportunity
    Commission (EEOC),
    1175
Equal Rights Amendment
    (ERA), 1078, 1144
Erie Canal, 388–389
Eries (tribe), 90
Ervin, Sam, *1119*, 1120
Española. *See* Quisqueya
Espionage Act, 787, 818,
    832
*Essay on Slavery and
    Abolitionism, with
    Reference to the Duty
    of American Females*
    (Beecher, C.), 457
Esteban (slave), 34
ethnicity, 495–496,
    713–714; violence and,
    616
eugenics, 850
Eurasian diseases, 65
Europe: Civil War and,
    537–539; goods of,
    432; immigration
    and, 103f, 149–152;
    manufacturing and,
    365; Romanticism,
    467; wars of, 312–313;
    Western, 16–19. *See
    also specific countries*
European Recovery Plan
    (ERP). *See* Marshall
    Plan

European theater, of World
    War II, 939–940
Evangelical Christianity,
    197–202, 425–426,
    458–459, 1144–1145
Evans, George Henry, 412,
    436
Evans, Oliver, 367, 368,
    391
Evans, Walker, 897
Everett, Edward, 496
Evers, Charles, 996
Evers, Medgar, 996, *998*
Executive Order 9066, 953
Executive Order 9835,
    982, 998
Executive Order 9981, 994,
    999
exiles, 212–213
exit strategy, 1179
Exodusters, 606
expansionism, 483–
    490; Conestogas,
    Comanche, and
    Californios, 487–490;
    financial, 346–349;
    imperial, 149–152;
    Mexican invasion and
    conquest, 484–485;
    politics of, 507–510;
    of Portugal, 19–20;
    race, ethnicity, and
    Americanism,
    495–496; of slavery,
    418–420; by Spain,
    247, 339; warfare
    technologies and, 17–
    18; Western geography
    and ecology, 486–487.
    See also imperialism
*The Exploration of the
    Colorado River*
    (Powell, J.), 611
exports, 310f
extended family, 376
external markets, 365–366
extractive economies,
    616–623; business
    travelers, 618–619;
    cowboys and,
    622–623; industrial

ranching, 621–622; mining and labor, 617–618; railroads and, 619–621

Exxon Valdez (ship), 1174

factionalism, 299
factory system, 371–374
Fair Deal, 983–984
Fair Employment Practices Commission (FEPC), 952
Fair Housing Act, 1083
Fair Labor Standards Act, 914, 915
faith-based initiatives, 1221
Fall, Albert, 866
Fallen Timbers, Battle of, 336
Falwell, Jerry, 1127, 1144
family: African American, 567–569; extended, 376; language families, 12–13; Reagan, R., and, 1153–1155; slavery and, 148; traditional/nuclear, 1033. *See also* marriage
Family and Medical Leave Act, 1186
famine, of Ireland, 413
Fannie Mae, 1235, 1245
"Farewell Address" (Washington), 299
A Farewell to Arms (Hemingway), 859, 873
Farley, James, 904
farmers/farming, 8–9, 334; African Americans as, 669; Coolidge and, 867; depression and, 685; Emergency Farm Labor Program, 951, 990; in Gilded Age, 668–669; in Great Depression, 887–888; NFWA and, 1075–1076; in South, 669; technologies, 621;

unions and, 668–669; wheat, 619; wheat farms, 619. *See also* sharecropping
Farmers' Alliance, 570, 596, 669, 674; *Looking Backward* and, 675; National People's Party and, 715
Farm Security Administration (FSA), 897
Farnsworth, Philo, 1028–1029
fascism, 882, 893, 901, 927
Father Knows Best (television program), 1035
Fauquier, Frances, 230
FBI. *See* Federal Bureau of Investigation
FCC. *See* Federal Communications Commission
FDIC. *See* Federal Deposit Insurance Corporation
Federal Arts, Music, Dance, Theater and Writers Project, 906
federal authority, 556
Federal Bureau of Investigation (FBI), 904–905, 1147, 1236
Federal Commission on Civil Disorders, 1065
Federal Communications Commission (FCC), 1029
Federal Deposit Insurance Corporation (FDIC), 890
Federal Emergency Management Agency (FEMA), 1227
Federal Emergency Relief Administration (FERA), 891
Federal Employee Loyalty Program, 982, 998
federal government funds, 364

Federal Highway Act, 1045
Federal Housing Administration (FHA), 1020, 1023
federalism, 278, 284, 544
Federalists, 281, 295, 295*t*, 300, 314, 335, 346, 377
Federalist Papers, 282
Federal Reserve, 882–883; Bernanke at, 1234, 1235; Greenspan at, 1185, 1203; inflation and, 1151; Republican Party and, 1245; Volcker at, 1136, 1151
Federal Reserve Act, 783, 793
Federal Theater Project, 904, 906
Federal Trade Commission (FTC), 783, 793
feitoria, 19, 24, 40
FEMA. *See* Federal Emergency Management Agency
The Feminine Mystique (Friedan), 1035, 1077, 1082
feminism: Buchanan and, 1181; Democratic Party and, 1145; in 1920s, 859; in 1960s, 1077–1078
Fenians, 576
FEPC. *See* Fair Employment Practices Commission
Ferdinand of Aragon, 18, 22, 40
Fermi, Enrico, 907, 942, 945, 967
Ferraro, Geraldine, 1150
Fessenden, William Pitt, 576, 597
feudalism, 427
FHA. *See* Federal Housing Administration
fiction, 469; serialized, 468. *See also* literature; novels; *specific works*

Field and Stream, 992
Fields, W.C., 905
Fifteenth Amendment, 577, 595, 597, 775
Fifth Amendment, 982, 1066
Fighting Irish, 534
filibustering, 350–351, 406–407
Fillmore, Millard, 496, 514
films. *See* movies
Final Solution, 941
Finland, Versailles Treaty and, 831
Finley, Robert, 338
Finney, Charles Grandison, 445–446, 447, 449, 458, 474
firearms. *See* guns
fire-eaters, 523, 525
"Fireside Chats," 889, 914, 931
First Amendment, 982, 1066, 1225
First Anglo-Dutch War, 101, 124
First Confiscation Act, 541
First Continental Congress, 241, 248
first hundred days, of New Deal, 890, 890*t*, 914
first Industrial Revolution, 645–646
First Nations, 627
First Opium War of 1839-1842, 479
First Seminole War, 350–352
fishing, 8–9, 26–27
Fitch, John, 368, 391
"Fit to Fight," 817
Fitzgerald, F. Scott, 859, 872
Five Civilized Tribes, 622
flappers, 860, *860*
flaxseed, 149
Fletcher, Benjamin, 154
Florida: Apalachee and, 98; founding of, 37–39; Spain and,

49–50; St. Augustine, 38–39, 40
Flying Down to Rio (movie), 905
Focus on the Family, 1144
folk traditions, African, 503
Food Administration, 819
Food Stamps, 1064, 1146, 1152
A Fool's Errand (Tourgee), 582
football, 705, 858, 906
Foraker Act, 751
Force Acts, 433, 591
Ford, Gerald R.: as President, 1120–1121, 1131–1133, 1160; as Vice President, 1113, 1119, 1120
Ford, Henry, 811, 812, 847, *849*
Fordlandia, 848
Ford Motor Company: African Americans and, 856; in Great Depression, 883; in 1950s, 1027–1028; in World War II, 943, 946
Fordney-McCumber Tariff, 872
foreclosures. *See* housing bubble
foreign-born population, 494*f*
foreign-born workers, 412–416
foreign policy, 328, 349, 352; of Carter, 1136; in 1920s, 865–870; in post-Cold War, 1197–1200. *See also specific policies*
foreign trade, 275, 312, 367
forests, 631–635
Forest Service, 785, 786
Forman, Martha Ogle, 366
Forrest, Nathan Bedford, 549, 559
Forten, James, 339
Fort Laramie Treaty, 625

Fort McHenry, Battle of, 317
Fort Pillow Massacre, 549
Fort Sumter, 525–526
42nd Street (movie), 905
For Whom the Bell Tolls (Hemingway), 927
Foster, George, 469
Foster, Stephen, 474
Four Essential Human Freedoms, 931, 958
Four Indian Kings, 141, 149, 153
Fourteen Points, by Wilson, W., 827, 829, 832
Fourteenth Amendment, 575–576, 592, 595, 597, 775, 1149
Fox Wars, 141, 167
France, 137–138; alliance with, 260; baby boom in, 1019; industrialization in, 648*f*; jazz in, 855–856; New France, 61–65, 67–69; pensions in, 779; protests in, 1107–1108, 1118; Quasi-War with, 300–301; work/workers in, 670; in World War II, 929, 958
Franciscans, 32–33, 40, 49, 80
"Francisco de Chicora," 35
Francke, August Hermann, 153
Franco, Francisco, 927
Frank, Robert, 1038
Frankfurter, Felix, 904, 913
Franklin, Benjamin, 181, 184, 214, 232, 248, 253, 256, 282
Franklin, James, 163–164
Franz Ferdinand (Archduke), assassination of, 805, 832
Freddie Mac, 1235, 1245
Freedmen's Bureau, 569, 574, 575, 580, 597

Freedom Riders, *1056*, 1056–1057, 1082
Free Soil Party, 471, 505
Free Speech (newspaper), 772–773
free speech, World War I and, 787
Free Speech Movement, 1051, 1054, *1054*, 1082
Frémont, John, 486, 514
Fremont, John C., 540, 559, 611
French and Indian War, 205
French Artillery Corps, 550
French Canadians, 655, 686, 691
French Revolution, 292–293
French Vietnam War, 1015–1016, 1044, 1093–1095, 1118; Ho Chi Minh and, 1092; Truman and, 1015
Frick, Henry Clay, 666–667
Friedan, Betty, 1035, 1077, *1078*, 1082
Friedman, Milton, 1025, 1143, 1244
Friedman, Thomas, 1233
Frontiero v. Richardson, 1118
FSA. *See* Farm Security Administration
FTC. *See* Federal Trade Commission
Fuchs, Klaus, 1017, 1044
Fuel Administration, 819
Fugitive Slave Act, 338, 452, 506, 507, 514
Fulbright, J. William, 1103
Fuller, Margaret, 441, 444, 466
Fulton, Robert, 368, 391
Fundamental Constitutions, 111
Fundamentalism: neocons and, 1143; in 1920s, 861–864; Al Qaeda and, 1212
fur trade, 56, 80, 331–332

G-8. *See* Group of Eight
Gabriel (Virginia slave), 303, 320
Gabriel Over the White House (movie), 882
Gabriel's Rebellion, 308
Gagarin, Yuri, 1070, 1082
Gage, Thomas, 232, 239, 241, 248
gag rule, 433, 436, 464, 1221
Gains, Edmund, 350
Gallatin, Albert, 369, 391
Galveston, Texas, 601, 622, 765, 792
Gálvez, Bernardo de, 265, 284
Gálvez, José de, 228, 244
Gandhi, Mohandas, 831, 936
gangsters, 864, 904–905
gang system, 196, 214, 419
Gannett, Deborah Sampson, 276, 284
Garfield, James A.: assassination of, 713, 714; Latin America and, 732–733
Garn-St. Germain bill, 1161
Garrison, William Lloyd, 454, 474
Garvey, Marcus, 856–857, 873
Gates, Bill, 647
Gates, Horatio, 260, 269, 284
Gates, Robert, 1220, 1240
Gates, Thomas, 58
gathering, 8–9
The Gay Divorcee (movie), 905
Gay Plague, 1154
gays. *See* homosexuals
GDP. *See* Gross Domestic Product
GE. *See* General Electric
Gehrig, Lou, 905
gender, 341–342; Bush, G.H.W., and, 1174; economic change and, 420–423; lines, 422;

norms, 200; politics and, 713–714; roles of, 341; Southwest and, 426–427. *See also* feminism; homosexuals; women
The Gene Autry Show (television program), 1029
General Allotment Act, 630, 636
General Appropriations Act, 635
General Electric (GE), 845–846; in 1950s, 1025; Reagan, R., and, 1147; in World War II, 943
General Federation of Women's Clubs, 766, 792
General Motors (GM), 847; emergency aid for, 1236, 1240; in 1950s, 1027–1028, 1045; in World War II, 943
The General Theory of Employment, Interest, and Money (Keynes), 913, 915
General Trades Union (GTU), 411
Generation X: Tales for an Accelerated Culture (Coupland), 1188
Genet, Edmund Charles, 289, 292, 320
Geneva Accords, 1095, 1118
Geneva Conference, Vietnam and, 1007, 1016, 1044
gentility, 162–163, 168
gentlemen's agreement, Roosevelt, T., and, 725, 750, 751
Geography (Ptolemy), 17, 21
Geological Survey, U.S., 554
George, Lloyd, 828
George I (king), 152, 168

George III (king), 227, 232, 234, 243
George Washington Greek-American Association, 697
Georgia, 401
Germain, George, 268, 284
Germantown Meeting, 119
Germany: Austria and, 958; Belgium and, 805; in Great Depression, 900–901, 925; immigration and, 150, 181–185, 414–416; imperialism of, 728; industrialization in, 647, 648f; inflation in, 872; League of Nations and, 958; pensions in, 779; reformers of, 522; Soviet Union and, 929, 931, 959; U-boats of, 810, 815, 832; in World War I, 804–805, 806, 815–816, 825–826; in World War II, 921, 928–929, 939–940. *See also* Berlin Wall; World War I; World War II
germ warfare, 827
Gerry, Elbridge, 301
Ghost Dance religion, 630
Gibbons v. Ogden, 349, 388
GI Bill, 952, 956, 959, 983, 984–985, 992; baby boom and, 1020; corporations and, 1025–1026
Gibraltar, conquest of, 16
Gideon v. Wainwright, 1066, 1082
Gilded Age (1877-1900): African Americans in, 669, 704; agriculture in, 656, 690–691; alcohol/alcoholism in, 711; America fever in, 692–693; amusement parks in,

703; baseball in, 704, 715; bicycles in, 704; blue collar workers in, 656–658; boxing in, 703; business mergers in, 651; cartels in, 649; charity in, 708, 714; Chicago in, 687, 707, 715; child labor in, 661–662, 662, 697; Chinese in, 685–686; churches in, 659; cities in, 702–707; civil service reform in, 712–713; communications in, 651; communism in, 643, 663–664; competition in, 645, 649; concentration of wealth in, 649–651; consumerism in, 651–654; corporations in, 646; crime in, 705; currency in, 712; defense of, 671–673; Democratic Party in, 669, 711, 713–714; entertainment in, 702–704; farmers/farming in, 668–669; football in, 703; gold and, 695–701; gold in, 712; horizontal integration in, 649; horse racing in, 703; housing in, 689, 705; immigration in, 655–656, 685–686, 689–695; industrialization in, 641–679; international markets for, 651–654; Japanese in, 685–686; labor movement in, 662–671; leisure in, 686; Los Angeles in, 687; mail-order catalogs in, 652–653; markets in, 651–654; marriage in, 643, 652–653; mass production in, 652; mechanization in,

656–657; Mexicans in, 685–686, 691; middle class in, 657, 704–705; mining in, 667–668; monopoly in, 650; nationalism in, 675; National People's Party in, 669, 714–716; New York City in, 714; patronage in, 707; Philadelphia in, 715; philanthropy in, 672–673; piecework in, 659; political machines in, 707; politics in, 711–718; railroads in, 647; reform in, 661–662, 707–711; Republican Party in, 669, 711, 713–714; salespeople in, 657; scientific management in, 658–659; self-help in, 672; settlement houses in, 709–710; south in, 656; sports in, 703–704; suburbanization in, 688; tariffs in, 712; technology in, 651, 689; textile industry in, 655–656; theaters in, 703; transportation in, 651, 688; unions in, 662–671; urbanization in, 684–689; vertical integration in, 649; wages in, 644, 655, 657, 659–661; white collar workers in, 656–658, 658; women in, 657, 661–662, 705, 711; work/workers in, 655–662. *See also* Progressivism
Gingrich, Newt, 1193, 1194, *1194*, 1195, 1197
Ginsberg, Allen, 1037–1038, 1045
Ginsberg, Ruth Bader, 1202
Girard, Stephen, 347, 356

"A Girl's a Man for A' That" (movie), 817
Girls' Club, 767
Girl Scouts, 767
Girondins, 289, 292
Gladstone, William, 538, 559
Glasgow, Scotland, 766
Glass-Steagall Banking Act, 889–890
Glenelg (lord), 576
Glenn, John, 1052, 1070, 1082
global cities, 1190–1191
global commodities, 616–623; business travelers, 618–619; cowboys and, 622–623; industrial ranching, 621–622; mining and labor, 617–618; railroads and, 619–621
globalization, 1182–1183; Clinton, B., and, 1192, 1193, 1203; corporations and, 1232–1233
Globalization and Its Discontents (Stiglitz), 1233, 1244
Global Positioning System (GPS), 1187
Glorious Revolution, 120–121, 124
GM. See General Motors
G-men (movie), 905
GNP. See gross national product
Godzilla (movie), 1027
gold, 19, 401, 490–491; Bretton Woods Agreements and, 926; Coinage Act and, 712, 714; discovery of, 486–487; in Gilded Age, 695–701, 712; Great Depression and, 883; production, 142
The Goldbergs, 905
Golden Rule, 674
Gold Mountain, 489, 514, 690

Goldstein, Robert, 818–819
Goldwater, Barry, 1062, 1082, 1099, 1147
golf, 858
Gomes, Estevão, 26
Gompers, Samuel, 665–666, 671, 674, 778; Anti-Imperial League and, 741; immigration and, 812
Gooch, William, 147
good government movement, 765–766
Good Neighbor Policy, 895
goods: enumerated, 101; European, 432; exchange of, 15; luxury, 16; stoneware, 194
Goodyear TV Playhouse (television program), 1029
Google, 1186
Gorbachev, Mikhail, 1129, 1176–1177, 1202; Reagan, R., and, 1161, 1162, 1162–1163
Gordon, Thomas, 229
Gore, Al, 1181, 1182, 1193; disputed election of 2000 and, 1200–1204, 1203
"The Gospel of Wealth" (Carnegie), 672, 673, 675
GPS. See Global Positioning System
Gracia Real de Santa Teresa de Mose, 173, 189, 214
Graham, Billy, 1030–1031, 1031, 1033, 1144
Graham, Sylvester, 452, 474
Grand Alliance, 922, 934–942, 959
Grand Canyon National Park, 785, 793
"The Grand Canyon of the Yellowstone, 1872" (Moran), 634
Grand Coulee Dam, 891
grandfather clause, 775

Grand Settlement of 1701, 140, 168
Grand Tour, 418
Grange (farmers' organization), 669
Grange, Harold "Red," 858
Grant, Ulysses S., 531, 546, 559, 579, 597; campaign of, 549–552; reelection of, 586
The Grapes of Wrath (Steinbeck), 910
Grasse, Comte de, 268, 284
Great American Desert, 486
Great Awakening, 344, 356
Great Britain. See Britain
"The Great Compromise," 280
Great Cultural Revolution, in China, 1107, 1118
Great Depression, 843, 878, 878–919; African Americans in, 856, 884; banks in, 883, 888, 914; beginning of, 871–873, 958; capitalism in, 888–895; charity in, 885; culture in, 904–911; deficit spending in, 903f, 915; entertainment in, 904–96; farmers/farming in, 887–888; fascism and, 882, 893; Germany in, 900–901, 925; gold and, 883; Italy in, 901; Japan in, 900; labor movement in, 899; Latin America in, 900; sharecropping in, 896; unemployment in, 880, 884, 902f, 914
Greater Antilles, 28–29
Greater Caribbean, 188–191
"The Greater Compromise," 280
Greater East Asia Co-Prosperity Sphere, 927–928

The Great Gatsby
(Fitzgerald), 859, 872
Great Hunger, 413
The Great Illusion (Angell),
803
Great Lakes, 89–90, 314
Great League of Peace, 14
Great Migration, 787–788,
821
Great Northern Railway,
619
Great Patriotic War, 940
Great Plains, 331
Great Railroad Strike of
1877, 663–664, 674
Great Recession, 1235,
1237
Great Society: civil rights
and, 1061–1063; Food
Stamps and, 1064;
Johnson, L., and,
1061–1067; Nixon,
R., and, 1116–1118;
Palestine and, 1067;
programs of, 1063–
1065; race riots and,
1073; Reagan, R., and,
1147; War on Poverty
and, 1061–1064
Great Wagon Road, 182
Great War. *See* World War I
Great White Fleet, 750, 751
Greece, 697
Greeley, Horace, 441, 539,
559, 684
Green, John, 332
Greene, Nathanael, 269,
273
Greene, William Cornell,
608
Green Party, 1201
Greenspan, Alan, 1185,
1203
Grenada, 1158, 1161
Grenville, George, 224,
229
Grey, Edward, 812
Griffith, D.W., 771, 853
Grimkè, Angelina, 421,
436, 454, 457, 465
Grimkè, Sarah, 421, 436,
454, 465

Griswold v. Connecticut,
1066, 1083
Gromyko, Andrei, 1115
Gross Domestic Product
(GDP): in Great
Depression, 892; in
1980s, 1151
gross national product
(GNP): in 1950s,
1021f; in 1970s, 1141;
World War II and, 973
Group of Eight (G-8),
1232
Grunge music, 1188
GTU. *See* General Trades
Union
Guadalcanal, Battle of, 937
Guam, 724, 737
Guanahaní (island), 22
Guanche (tribe), 20
Guantanamo Bay, 1219,
1240, 1244
Guatemala, 1158
Guerriere, HMS, 317
guerrilla conflict, 533
Guevara, Che, 1107
Guiteau, Charles, 713, 714
Gulf of Tonkin Resolution,
1090, 1099, 1111, 1118
Gulf War. *See* Persian Gulf
War
Gum Shan (Gold
Mountain), 489, 514
gunpowder, 17
guns, 187; control of,
1221; machine guns,
777, 806
Gurteen, S. Humphreys,
708, 714
Guthrie, Woody, 910
Guy, Buddy, 1043
Guzman, Pierre, 550

Haig, Alexander, 1173
Haiphong, Vietnam, 1112
Haiti, 539, 869–870,
1202; National Guard
in, 869; Refugee Act
and, 1149; Revolution
of, 305–308, 412, 584;
during World War I,

801, 813, 832. *See also*
Saint Domingue
Hakluyt, Richard, 54
Haldeman, H.R., 1119,
1120
Hale, Stephen, 526
Haley, Alex, 1153
half-freedom, 71, 80
Half-Way Covenant, 113,
124
"The Hallelujah Seven"
(Booth, W.), 681
Hamdan v. Rumsfeld, 1219,
1225, 1244
Hamilton, Alexander, 279,
295, 296, 299, 335,
347
Hammett, Dashiell, 906
Hammond, James Henry,
433–435, 464
Hancock, John, 242
hanging chads, 1202
Hannity, Sean, *1229*
Hanson, Alexander,
313
Hapsburgs, 428
Harding, Warren G., 833,
865–866, 872
hard rock mines, 489
hard war policy, 543
Hargraves, Edward,
490–491
Harlem Renaissance,
854–855, *855*
Harmar, Josiah, 298, 320
Harpers Ferry, 512, 514
Harper's Weekly, 660, 664
Harriman, E.F., 811
Harriman, W. Averell,
971
Harriot, Thomas, 54, 80
Harrison, Benjamin, 732
Harrison, George, 1080
Harrison, William Henry,
312, 315, 320, 458,
474, 483, 514
Hartford Convention, 314,
320
Harvard College, 73
Hasinai Confederacy, 135
Hat Act, 197t
Hatfield-McCoy feud, 533

Hawaii, 386, 724, 733–744, 750, 1045. *See also* Pearl Harbor attack
Hawkins, John, 53–54
Hawthorne, Nathanial, 469, 474
Hay, John, 737, 746, 750
Hay-Bunau-Varilla treaty, 751
Hayden, Ferdinand V., 613
Hayes, George E.C., 1039
Hayes, Rutherford B., 592, 664
Haymarket Square bombing, in Chicago, 665, 674
Haynsworth, Clement, 1117
Hays, Will, 858
Haytian Emigration Society of Coloured People, 339
Haywood, "Big" Bill, 617, 636
Haywood, William D. "Big Bill," 778, 818
HCUA. *See* House Committee on Un-American Activities
health insurance, 946. *See also* national health insurance
Health Insurance Association of America, 1193
health maintenance organizations (HMOs), 1194
health reform movements, 452
Heard, Augustine, 414–415
Heard, John, 415
Hearst, William Randolph, 735
Hearts of Oak, 237
Hearts of Steel, 237
Heaton, Hannah, 197–198
Heinz, 644, 654
helicopters: in Iran, 1138; in Vietnam War, *1101*, 1113

Helper, Hinton, 495, 499, 514
Helsinki Accords, 1132–1133
Hemingway, Ernest, 859, 873, 927
Henry (prince), 19
Henry, Patrick, 230, 248, 281, 303
Henry VIII (king), 36, 40
Henson, Josiah, 344
hereditary chiefs, 10
Hernandez v. Texas, 1044
Hersey, John, 998
Hessians, 258
Hetch Hetchy, 785–786, 793
Hickock, Lorena, 907
Higginson, Thomas Wentworth, 581, 597
highways, 369; Federal Highway Act, 1045; Interstate and Defense Highways Act, 1020; in 1920s, 848; suburbanization and, 1020–1021
Hill, Anita, *1175*, 1176
Hill, James J. "Empire Builder," 619
Hine, Lewis, *662*
Hip Hop, 1188
hippies, 1082–1084
Hiroshima, 969, 998
"Hiroshima" (Hersey), 998
Hispanics: civil rights of, 1075–1077; immigration and, 990–991, 1148–1149; in Los Angeles, 1190–1191; nationalism of, 1014; New Deal and, 909; in 1920s, 852; in 1960s, 1075–1077; in prison, 1153; Voting Rights Act of 1965 and, 1134; in WPA, 908. *See also* Latin America; Mexicans; Mexico; Spain

Hispaniola, 303
Hiss, Alger, 982–983
Hitler, Adolf: appointment as chancellor, 879, 881, 914, 958; *Lebensraum* and, 928; race and, 921; suicide of, 959; Versailles Treaty and, 928
HIV. *See* human immunodeficiency virus
HMOs. *See* health maintenance organizations
Hoar, George Frisbie, 741
Hobby, Richard, 273
hobos, 884
Ho Chi Minh, 936, 1118; French Vietnam War and, 1015–1016, 1092; World War I and, 830–831
Ho Chi Minh City, 1113
Ho Chi Minh Trail, 1099, 1100, 1102
Hodgson, Godfrey, 1023
Hohokam (urban society), 9–10
Holden v. Hardy, 779, 792
Hollywood: communism and, 982–983. *See also* movies
Holmes, Oliver Wendell, Jr., 819
Holocaust, 940–943, *941*
Holocaust (television miniseries), 1153
Holt Street Baptist Church, 1041
Homage to Catalonia (Orwell), 927
home fronts, 536–537
Home Insurance Building, 689, 714
Home Missionary Society, 458
homes, layout of, *418*
Homestead Act of 1862, 592, 597, 612, 624, 636

Homestead Works, 641, *645*, *656*, 666–667, 675

homosexuals: Buchanan and, 1181; Bush, G.W., and, 1222; Clinton, B., and, 1192; conservatism and, 1222; CWA and, 1144; marriage for, 1222, *1222*, 1244; in 1970s and 1980s, 1153; Reagan, R., and, 1153; Republican Party and, 1221; as wedge issue, 1145

Honduras, 752, 1158

honor, 425–426, 460–461

Hoover, Herbert, 619, 636, 867, 873; Bonus Marchers and, 885; communism and, 833; Prohibition and, 864; rugged individualism and, 865

Hoover, J. Edgar, 833, 904

Hoovervilles, 885

Hop Alley, 616

Hopalong Cassidy (television program), 1029

Hopkins, Harry, 887, 897, 904, 907, 956

Hopper, Dennis, 1083

horizontal integration, in Gilded Age, 649

Hornet, USS, 937

horse racing, in Gilded Age, 703

horses, 69, 133–135, 187

Horseshoe Bend, Battle of, 316

Hortalez & Cie, 260

hostage crisis, in Iran, 1138–1141, *1139*, 1160

hourglasses, 16

House, Edward M., 812, 828

House Committee on Un-American Activities (HCUA), 981, 982–983, 999

House-Grey Memorandum, 812

House of Burgesses, 61, 80, 230

House of Representatives, 304, 348

House Ways and Means Committee, 301

housing: for African Americans, 984–985; Department of Housing and Urban Development and, 1064; dumb-bell tenements, 705–706; Fair Housing Act, 1083; FHA, 1020, 1023; in Gilded Age, 689, 705; mass production of, *987*, 1022–1023; in New York City, 705–706; Progressivism and, 766; segregation of, 376; Veterans Emergency Housing Act, 984. *See also* suburbanization

housing bubble, 1234–1237, *1235*, *1236*

Houston, Charles Hamilton, 1039

Houston, Sam, 397, 436

Howard, Oliver Otis, 569, 597, 624

Howdy Doody Show (television program), 1029, 1030

Howe, Frederick C., 764

Howe, Richard, 284

Howe, William, 242, 243, 258, 269, 284

"Howl" (Ginsberg, A.), 1037, 1045

How the Other Half Lives: Studies Among the Tenements of New York (Riis), *710*, 711, 715

Huage Sih Chuen, 616

Hubbard, E. C., 541

Hubble Space Telescope, 1187

Hudson, Henry, 64

Hudson, Rock, 1154

Hudson Bay Company, 106, 124, 332

Huerta, Delores, 1076

Huerta, Victoriano, 813–814

Hughes, Charles Evans, 812, 866, 868

Hughes, Langston, 855

Huguenots, 37, 40

Huitzilopochtli (diety), 14

Hull, Isaac, 317

Hull, William, 314

Hull House, 682, 709–710, 715, 764, 770

Human Genome Project, 1187

human immunodeficiency virus (HIV), 1129, 1154

Humphrey, Hubert, 1109

Hundred Years' War, 121–123

Hungary, 697, 1176; Eisenhower and, 1014–1015; Soviet Union and, 1045; Versailles Treaty and, 831

Hunter, David, 540, 559

hunting, 8–9; of beaver, *55*

Huron Confederacy, 14, 40, 57, 64, 90

Hurricane Katrina, 1210, *1226*, 1226–1227, 1244

Hussein, Saddam, 1157, 1178, 1180, *1180*; Bush, G.W., and, 1215–1220; Iran hostage crisis and, 1140; Al Qaeda and, 1215

Hutchinson, Anne, 75, 80

Hutchinson, Thomas, 231, 239

Huxley, Aldous, 1031

Hyde, Edward, 158

hydrogen bomb, 1010, *1012*, 1044

Iberians, 16, 19–21
IBRD. *See* International Bank for Reconstruction and Development
Ice Age, 6–7; Little Ice Age, 26
Ichan, Carl, 1152
Ickes, Harold, 907, 956
ICW. *See* International Council of Women
ICWPP. *See* International Committee of Women for Permanent Peace
identity politics, 1145
ideology: racial, 277–278; resistance and, 246–247; transatlantic politics and, 257
idolatry, 115
IFOR. *See* International Implementation Force
"I Have a Dream" (King, Martin), 1052, 1058
ILGWU. *See* International Ladies Garment Workers' Union
Illinois State Register, 405
illnesses, 9, 65. *See also* *specific illnesses*
I Love Lucy (television program), 1029
IMF. *See* International Monetary Fund
immigration/immigrants, 70–72, 182, 184, 698–701; of African Americans, 337–339; Americanization of, 701; backlash against, 693–694; Buchanan and, 1181; Bush, G.W., and, 1227–1229; in California, 1188, *1230*; Catholic Church and, 448, 693; Chinese as, 492, 609, 690–691,

694; churches for, 700–701; in Cold War, 987–993; by country or region, 413*f*; to Dakota Territory, 692; diversity of, 13; education for, 694, 701; European, 100*f*, 103*f*, 149–152; German, 150, 181–185, 414–416; in Gilded Age, 655–656, 685–686, 689–695; Gompers and, 812; Great Migration, 787–788, 821; Hispanics and, 990–991, 1148–1149; of indentured servants, 109*f*; Irish, 181–185, 413–414, 493; Japanese as, 690–691, 725; Jews as, 691–692, 693, 1065; labor movement and, 670–671; from Latin America, 1228*f*; literacy test for, 818; in Los Angeles, 1190–1191; mechanization and, 696–697; Mexicans and, 691, 852–853, 990–991; in Miami, 1190–1191; by nationality, 494*f*; New Deal and, 907–908; in New York City, 1190–1191; in 1920s, 850–853, 852*f*; in 1960s, 1064–1065, 1064*f*; 1970s to 1990s, 1148–1149; patterns of, 491–493, 604–607; in post-Cold War, 1188–1191, 1189*f*; quotas on, 991, 1064–1065; religion and, 691–692; resistance and, 271; return migration of, 694–697; revolutionary, 306–307; Social Darwinism

and, 693; steel and, *656*; 2000 to present, 1227–1229, 1228*f*; unions and, 778; urbanization and, 685; as wedge issue, 1228; women as, 697, 701; World War I and, 818
the "immigrant problem," 693–694
Immigration and Naturalization Act, 991, 999
Immigration and Naturalization Reform Act of 1965, 1148–1149
Immigration and Naturalization Service (INS), 1044, 1190
Immigration Restriction Bill, 693, 715
Immigration Restriction League, 683, 693, 715
impeachment: of Clinton, B., 1196–1197, 1203; of Johnson, A., 579; of Nixon, R., 1119
The Impending Crisis (Helper), 499
imperial authority, 155–158
Imperial Colonization Law, 382
imperialism, 33–36, 149–152, 722–757; in China, 745–746; debate over, 740–742; in Latin America, 732–733, 752–753; Roosevelt, T., and, 730, 746–750; Taft and, 750–753
imperial rivalries, 36–37
imperial taxes, 226*t*
imports, 55–57, 195, 310*f*
impressment, 545
income tax, 793, 1147, 1244, 1245

indentured servants, 60, 80, 88, 109f, 182
India, 333–334, 668, 827, 1014
Indian Appropriations Act, 625
Indian National Congress, 830
Indian Ocean piracy, 154–155
Indian Removal Act of 1830, 401, 436
Indian Reorganization Act, 910, 914
Indians. *See* Native Americans
Indian Training School, 627
Indian Wars, 624
indigo, 190
individualism, 228, 466, 618, 865
industrial capitalism. *See* Gilded Age
industrialization, 161, 410; in Gilded Age, 641–679; in 1950s, 1018–1026; in World War I, 809; in World War II, 942–949, 943t. *See also* mass production; mechanization; military industrial complex
industrial ranching, 621–622
Industrial Revolution, 389–390, 645–646; in World War II, 945–946
Industrial Workers of the World (IWW), 787, 792, 818, 820
industrious revolution, 159–162, 168
inflation, 275, 872, 1135–1136, 1151
influenza, 25; pandemic, 827–828, 833
INF treaty, 1129, 1161
"In God We Trust," 1045

initial public offering (IPO), 1231
initiative, 774
in loco parentis, 1082
INS. *See* Immigration and Naturalization Service
Insular Cases, 740
Insurgent Mexico (Reed, J.), 799
intelligent design, 1221–1222
Interim Agreement on Limitations of Strategic Armaments (SALT-I), 1113
International Bank for Reconstruction and Development (IBRD), 948
International Brigades, 927
International Committee of Women for Permanent Peace (ICWPP), 790–791, 793
International Congress of Women, 790
International Council of Women (ICW), 759, 790, 792, 986
international finance, 264–266
International Harvester, 665
International Implementation Force (IFOR), 1198
International Ladies Garment Workers' Union (ILGWU), 780
international markets: cities and, 687; Cold War and, 975; for Gilded Age, 651–654. *See also* globalization
International Monetary Fund (IMF), 948, 996, 1232

International War Crimes tribunal, 1106
International Workingmen's Association, 519, 522
Internet, 1184–1187
interracial marriage, 149
Interstate and Defense Highways Act, 1020, 1028, 1045
Interstate Commerce Commission, 1057
Intolerable Acts. *See* Coercive Acts
Inuit (tribe), 7
Invasion of the Body Snatchers (movie), 1036
IPO. *See* initial public offering
IQ tests, 818
Iran: hostage crisis in, 1138–1141, *1139*, 1160; oil and, 1135; Reagan, R., and, 1157–1158
Iran-Contra scandal, 1128, 1158–1161, *1160*
Iraq: Bush, G.H.W., and, 1178–1180; Muslims in, 1140, 1180; 9/11 and, 1215; Reagan, R., and, 1157–1158
Iraq Study Group (ISG), 1220, 1244
Iraq War, 1211, 1215–1220, 1244; coalition of the willing in, 1217; deaths in, 1220; end of, 1245; "Mission Accomplished" in, 1218; Obama and, 1240–1241; public disillusionment with, 1219–1220. *See also* Persian Gulf War
Ireland, 181–185, 413–414, 493, 690; Catholic Church and, 494; Northern, 1203
Irish Rifles, 534

Iron Act, 197, 197t
iron ore, 648
Iroquois (tribe), 57, 140–141
Iroquois League, 14–15
irrigation, 612
IRS: Carter and, 1127; celebrities and, 944–945; Christianity and, 1127
Irving, Washington, 343, 356
Isabela of Castile, 18, 22, 40
ISG. See Iraq Study Group
Islam. See Muslims
Israel: Camp David Accords and, 1136; Clinton, B., and, 1198–1199, 1202; Oslo Accords and, 1171; Six-Day War, 1067; Yom Kippur War, 1115–1116
issue-specific parties, 504t
Italy: fascism in, 901; in Great Depression, 901; in World War II, 921, 926–927, 939. See also World War II
It Can't Happen Here (Lewis, S.), 906
Iturbide, Augustín de, 351, 353–354
Itzcoatl, 14
Iwo Jima, Battle of, 938, 959, 973, 998
IWW. See Industrial Workers of the World

Jackson, Andrew, 316, 318, 320, 361, 380, 472, 474; Trail of Tears and, 401–403
Jackson, Jonathan "Stonewall," 534, 559
Jackson, Robert H., 913
Jacobins, 292
Jacobite Rebellion, 152, 168
Jamaica, 178, 571, 576
James, Duke of York, 102
James, William, 803

James I (king), 48, 80
James II (king), 120
Jamestown, 45, 80
Japan/Japanese, 386, 479, 482; in agriculture, 656; China and, 927–928, 958; defeat of, 973, 998; in Gilded Age, 685–686; in Great Depression, 900; Hiroshima, 969, 998; immigration and, 690–691, 725; League of Nations and, 958; Nagasaki, 969, 998; oil and, 932; in Philippines, 933–934; Progressivism in, 762; Roosevelt, T., and, 749–750; Russo-Japanese War, 751; Tokyo, 937, 938, 939, 959, 998; in World War II, 932–939, 973. See also World War II
Japanese-American internment, in World War II, 953–955, 954, 959
Japanese-Mexican Labor Association (JMLA), 666
Java, HMS, 317
Jay, John, 266, 273, 275, 279, 284, 296
Jay's Treaty, 296–297, 320, 332
jazz, 842; African Americans and, 1038; CIA and, 1043; in 1920s, 855–856; in 1950s, 1038
The Jazz Singer (movie), 858, 873
Jean Paul II (pope), 1130
Jefferson, Thomas, 202, 240, 248, 295, 304, 328, 334–335
Jenkins, Robert, 190
jeremiads, 113, 124
Jerome, Jennie, 643, 652–653, 674

Jerry, Elbridge, 281
Jesuits, 36, 40, 49, 67–68, 80
Jesuit Relations, 68
Jews: Coughlin and, 894; Hitler and, 879; as immigrants, 691–692, 693, 1065; KKK and, 853; landsmanshaftn of, 699; mutual aid societies and, 699; nuclear weapons and, 967; Rankin, John, and, 981; suburbanization and, 1021, 1022. See also Holocaust; Israel
Jiang Jieshi, 932, 934, 939, 978
jihad, 1130
Jim Crow laws, 769, 787
JMLA. See Japanese-Mexican Labor Association
Job Corps, 1064
Jobs, Steve, 1169, 1186
Jogues, Isaac, 70
John Paul II (pope), 104
Johnson, Andrew, 572–574; impeachment of, 579
Johnson, Jack, 604, 636
Johnson, Lyndon B., 1082; Great Society and, 1061–1067; Latin America and, 1066–1067; Soviet Union and, 1067; Vietnam War and, 1067, 1097–1100
Johnson, Richard Mentor, 315, 320
Johnson, Tommy Burns, 604
Johnson, William, 206
Johnson-O'Malley Act of 1934, 910
Johnston, Joseph, 554
Joint Chiefs of Staff Office, 935, 976
joint-stock companies, 53, 80

Joinville, Prince de, 550
Jones, Absalom, 344, 356
Jones, Bobby, 858
Jones, John Paul, 264, 267, 284
Jones, Paula, 1196
Jordan. See Six-Day War
Jordan Marsh department store, in Boston, 703
Joseph (chief), 623, 632
Joseph II (emperor of Austria), 184
journeymen, 371, 376
Jubilee, 566–572; African American families and, 567–569; emancipation in comparative perspective, 571–572; southern whites and, 569–571
judicial activism, 1152; Republican Party and, 1221
judicial reform: conservatism and, 1221; New Deal and, 912–913
judicial review, 305
Judiciary Reorganization Act, 912, 915
Juneteenth, 581
The Jungle (Sinclair), 783–784, 792
junk bonds, 1152
Junto, 192
just wars, 112
juvenile court system, Progressivism and, 767–768

kachinas, 10, 40
Kagan, Elena, 1241
Kaiser, Henry J., 1023
Kaiser Permanente, 946
kamikaze, 938
Kansas-Nebraska Act, 452, 496, 497, 508–509, 514
Karzai, Hamid, 1215
Kateri Circles, 105
katsinas, 117, 124

KDKA, 845, 846, 872
Kearny, Stephen, 484, 514
Keating-Owen Child Labor Act, 767, 780, 793
Kelley, Florence, 767, 779
Kellogg, Frank, 868–869
Kellogg, William, 590, 597
Kellogg-Briand Pact, 869
Kelly, Machine Gun, 904
Kendall, John, 85
Kennan, George F., 975, 998, 1103
Kennedy, Anthony, 1153, 1225
Kennedy, Edward "Ted," 1139–1140, 1228
Kennedy, John F., 1082; assassination of, 1060–1061, 1082; Khrushchev and, 1058–1059; New Frontier of, 1055–1056; space exploration and, 1070; Vietnam and, 1093, 1095, 1096–1097
Kennedy, Joseph, 894
Kennedy, Robert F., 1057–1058, 1083, 1108–1109; assassination of, 1109
Kent State University, 1111, 1119
Kenya, 1199–1200
Keokuk, 384, 391
Keppler, Udo, 723
Kerouac, Jack, 1037, 1045
Kerr, Clark, 1051
Kerry, John, 1223, 1244
Key, Francis Scott, 317
Keyes v. Denver School District No. 1, 1117
Keynes, John Maynard, 901, 913–914, 915, 1132, 1143
Khe Sanh, Vietnam, 1104–1105
Khomeini, Ruholla, 1138, 1157
Khooscalchund, Kessressung, 415

Khrushchev, Nikita: Kennedy, John, and, 1058–1059; Nixon, R., and, 1005, 1006, 1008, 1024, 1045; Vietnam and, 1095
Kieft, William, 70, 76, 80
Kim Il-sung, 980
Kim Phuc, 1089, 1092, 1092
Kind of Blue (Davis, M.), 1038
King, Ernest, J., 935
King, Martin Luther, Jr., 1038, 1052; assassination of, 1106, 1118; nonviolence and, 1041–1045; Reagan, R., and, 1153; SCLC and, 1058
King, Rodney, 1181
King George's War, 190
King Philip's War, 110, 114, 124
King William's War, 121–123, 124, 154
Kipling, Rudyard, 729
Kissinger, Henry, 1102, 1110–1111, 1114; China and, 1114–1115, 1119; Cold War and, 1132; Ford, G., and, 1132–1133; Latin America and, 1115; Soviet Union and, 1113–1114; Vietnam War and, 1112; Yom Kippur War and, 1115–1116
Kitchen Debate, 1006, 1008, 1024
kivas, 69, 80
KKK. See Ku Klux Klan
Knights of Labor, 588, 597, 664–665, 674; immigration and, 670; Looking Backward and, 675; women in, 666
Know Nothing Party, 491, 496–497, 514, 523
Knox, Frank, 931
Knox, Philander C., 751
Kodak, 654

Koht, Halvan, 791
Koop, C. Everett,
    1154–1155
Korean War, 999, 1044;
    China and, 999, 1044;
    Cold War and, 969,
    978–981; Eisenhower
    and, 1010; Truman,
    Harry S. and, 1009. *See
    also* demilitarized zone
Korematsu, Fred, 954
Kosciuszko, Tadeusz, 264,
    265, 284
Kosovo. *See* Balkans
Kossuth, Louis, 428, 436
Kosygin, Alexei, 1067
Ku Klux Klan (KKK),
    589–591, 597, 771,
    872; *Brown v. Board
    of Education* and,
    1040; in Cold War,
    996; Jews and, 853;
    Little Rock Nine and,
    1040; in 1920s, 853;
    Prohibition and, 864
Kurtz, Jerome, 1127

labor, 617–618; black
    laboring class,
    571; bonded, 427;
    diversifying of, 159;
    enslaved, 161; free,
    504–505; nonmanual,
    416; systems, 60;
    unskilled, 410; wage
    laborers, 410. *See also*
    work/workers
labor movement: in
    Gilded Age, 662–671;
    in Great Depression,
    899; immigration
    and, 670–671; in
    1950s, 1025–1026;
    Progressivism and,
    776–780. *See also*
    Solidarity; unions
ladder of consumption,
    1027
ladies, 424, 461
Ladies' Association of
    Philadelphia, 276

Ladies' Benevolent Society,
    461
Lafayette, Marie-Joseph-
    Paul-Yves-Roch-Gilbert
    du Motier (Marquis
    de), 265, 284, 293
Laffer, Arthur, 1143
Laffite, Jean, 350, 356
La Follette, Robert
    "Fighting Bob," 774,
    786–787, 816
LaHaye, Beverley, 1144
LaHaye, Tim, 1144
laissez-faire economics,
    651
Lajoie, Napoleon "Nap,"
    704
Lake Erie, Battle of, 317
La Linea, 609
Lamson, Carl, 960
land, 334–335; commons,
    53, 79; of Confederacy,
    528; *encomiendas*,
    18, 40; free, 409;
    ownership, 53, 61;
    public, 612; *Terra
    Nullius*, 632
Landon, Alfred M., 882,
    899–900
landsmanshaftn, 699
Lane Theological Institute,
    447, 454
Lange, Dorothea, 897
language: Arawak,
    22; English-only
    movement, 1134,
    1149; families, 12–13;
    Lincoln, A., and, 537;
    of slavery, 240–241
Lansing, Robert, 828, 830
Laos, 1119
La Salle, Robert Cavalier
    de, 106
Lathrop, Julia, 759
Latin America: agriculture
    in, 900; filibustering,
    406–407; in Great
    Depression, 900;
    immigration and,
    1228f; imperialism in,
    732–733, 752–753;

Johnson, L., and,
    1066–1067; Kissinger
    and, 1115; in 1920s,
    870; Nixon, R., and,
    1115; Progressivism in,
    762; revolutions of,
    352–354; Roosevelt, F.,
    and, 895; Wilson, W.,
    and, 813–815; World
    War I and, 813–815.
    *See also specific
    countries*
Latinos. *See* Hispanics
Latrobe, Benjamin Henry,
    300
Latvia, 697
Laudonnière, Renè de, 37
Laurens, Henry, 273, 284
Law, John, 129
Lawrence, Jacob, 840
Lawrence v. Texas, 1222,
    1244
laws: apprenticeship, 573;
    common, 61, 79;
    Corn Laws, 428, 436;
    coverture, 277, 284,
    342, 356, 421, 436;
    Personal Liberty Laws,
    507. *See also specific
    laws and acts*
Lay, Kenneth, 1209
League of Armed
    Neutrality, 266
League of Nations, 827,
    829–830, 834–835,
    926; Germany and,
    958; ICWPP and,
    790–791; Japan and,
    958
League of United Latin
    American Citizens
    (LULAC), 952
League of Women Voters
    (LWV), 1035
Lease, Mary Elizabeth, 621,
    636, 716
Lebanon, 1157, 1161
Lebensraum (living space),
    928
Le Cap Français, 308
LeConte, Emma, 551–552

Lectures on Revivals of Religion (Finney), 458
Le Duan, 1095
Le Duc Tho, 1112
Lee, Ann, 448, 474
Lee, Charles, 269
Lee, Richard Henry, 243, 281
Lee, Robert E., 512, 514, 533, 538, 559, 569, 597
Lehman Brothers, 1236, 1245
Leisler, Jacob, 121, 124
leisure: in Cold War, 992–993; in Gilded Age, 686; Progressivism and, 767. *See also* entertainment
Le Jau, Francis, 153
Le Jeune, Paul, *67*
Le Moyne, Jacques, 37
Lend-Lease, 931, 958, 959
L'Enfant, Pierre, 300
Lenin, Vladimir, 824–825
Lennon, John, 1080
Leo XIII (pope), 764
lesbians. *See* homosexuals
Lesinsky, Henry, 607
Letters from a Farmer in Pennsylvania (Dickinson), 234
Levant Company, 53
Levitt, William, *987*, 1022–1023
Levittown, *987*, 1022–1023
Lewinsky, Monica, 1196
Lewis, Jerry Lee, 1037
Lewis, John (of SNCC), 1062
Lewis, John L. (union leader), 895, 946
Lewis, Meriwether, 328–329, 356
Lewis, Sinclair, 859, 872, 906
Lewis, Sybil, 946
libel, 982, 1066
Liberal Party, 870
The Liberator, 454, 464
Liberty League, 894

liberty loan bonds, 818
Liberty Party, 471, 505
Liberty Ships, 946
liberty tree, 231
libraries, 192
Library Company of Philadelphia, 192
Libya, 1158
Liddy, G. Gordon, 1118
lien, 586–588
Life (magazine), 906
"The Life of Pancho Villa" (movie), 799
Life of Washington (Carey), 342
Life Styles of the Rich and Famous (television program), 1153
Liliukalani (Hawaiian queen), 734, 750
Limbaugh, Rush, 1228
Limited Test Ban Treaty, 1060
Lincoln, Abraham, 279, 284, 384, 391, 485, 514, 523, 530, 559, 597; assassination of, 569; inauguration of, 525; language usage by, 537; Second Inaugural Address of, 553
Lincoln, Benjamin, 269
Lindbergh, Charles, 843, 858–859, 873, 930
Linen Act of 1705, 149, 168
Lingan, James, 314
Lippmann, Walter, 763, 817
literacy, 581, 597
Literacy Act, 818
literacy tests: in Australia, 715; for immigrants, 818
literature, 342–343; Asian, 470. *See also specific works*
Little Big Horn, Battle of, 624
Little Caesar (movie), 905
Little Ice Age, 26

Little Richard, 1037
Little Rock Nine, 1040, 1045
Littlest Rebel (movie), 905
Little Turtle, 298, 320
Little Warrior, 316
Live 8, 1232
Livermore National Laboratory, 989
Living Newspaper, 906
Livingston, Robert, 308, 368, 391
Lloyd, Henry Demarest, 650, 673–675, 763
lobbying, transatlantic, 158
Lochner v. New York, 779, 792
Locke, Alain, 856
Locke, John, 111, 124, 229, 244, 248
Lockerbie, Scotland, 1158
Lodge, Henry Cabot, 828, 834, 1096
Logan, James, 150
The London Gazette, 163
The London Journal, 165
London Society for Organized Charitable Relief and Mendicity, 708
The Lonely Crowd (Reisman), 1035
The Lone Ranger (television program), 1029
Long, Huey, 893, 894
Long, James, 350–351
Long, Jane, 351
Longfellow, Henry Wadsworth, 425, 436
Longfellow Copper Mining Company, 607
longhouses, 12
Long Telegram, 976, 998
Looking Backward 2000-1887 (Bellamy), 674, 675–676
Los Angeles: in Gilded Age, 687; Hispanics in, 1190–1191; immigration/

immigrants in, 1190–1191; race riots in, 1072–1073, 1083, 1202

Louis, Joe, 905

Louisiana, 129, 137–138, 178, 329; Hurricane Katrina in, 1210, *1226*, 1226–1227, 1244; New Orleans, 132–133, 493–494

Louisiana Purchase, 308, 330, 723

Louis XIV (king), 103, 124

Louis XV (king), 133, 138, 168

Louis XVI (king), 293

Louverture, Toussaint, *288*, 303, 305, 308, 320

Lovejoy, Elijah, 454, 474

Lowell, Samuel Cabot, 372, 391

Lowell Mill Girls, 423, 436

Lower East Side, in New York City, *699*, 766, 780

Lower South, secession of, 523–525

loyalists, 271

Loyola, Ignatius, 36

LSD, 1012, 1082

Luce, Henry, 925

Lucky Strike, 850

Ludlow Massacre, 777, *793*

Lukens, Rebecca, 342, 356

LULAC. *See* League of United Latin American Citizens

Lusitania (ship), 810, 832

Luther, Martin, 36, 40

Lux, Charles, 622

Luxmichund, Kavaldass, 415

luxury goods, 16

LWV. *See* League of Women Voters

lynchings: of African Americans, 744, 769, *770*, 772–773, 856; of Wobblies, 787

MacArthur, Douglas, 885, 937–938, 980–981, 999

Macbeth, 906

machine guns, 777, 806

machine production, 410

MacIntosh, Ebenezer, 231, 248

Macon's Bill No. 2, 312

Macy's department store, 702

Madagascar, 154–155

Maddox, USS, 1099

Madeira, 20

Madero, Francisco, 813

Madison, Dolley, 317, 321

Madison, James, 192, 202, 257, 279, 296, 347

Mad Magazine, 1031

Madoff, Bernard, 1236–1237

Maffit, John Newland, 458

magazines: in Great Depression, 904, 906; in 1920s, 849, 860, 861; in 1930s, 904; Progressivism and, 764. *See also specific magazines*

Magellan, Ferdinand, 34

MAGIC, 932, 933

Mahan, Alfred Thayer, 731

mail, 166, 370–371

mail-order catalogs, in Gilded Age, 652–653

Maine, 364

Maine, USS, 725, 735–736, 750

Main Street (Lewis), 859

majority parties, 504t

Makeba, Miriam, 1075

Make Poverty History, 1232

Malcolm X, 1074, 1083

male abolitionists, 425

Malintzín, 30–31, 40

"The Man" (Evans, G. H.), 412

mandatory sentencing laws, 1153

Manhattan Project, 945, 967, 973

Manifesto of the Communist Party (Marx and Engels), 412

The Man in the Grey Flannel Suit (Wilson, S.), 1035

Manly, Basil, 462

Mann Act, 768, 793

Manoel (king), 21

mansions, 162

Manteo, 54, 80

manufacturing, 371–374; European, 365; growth of, 159; regulating, 197, 197t; textile, 371, 655–656, 691

manumissions, 148, 168

Mao Zedong, 936, 978, 999, 1107, 1114–1115

Mapp v. Ohio, 1066

Marbury v. Madison, 305, 321

The March of Time, 905–906

Marestier, Jean Baptiste, 369

Marielitos, 1139, 1160

marijuana, in 1960s, 1083

market system, 364; class and consumerism, 375–376; factory system and, 373–374; internal and external markets, 365–366; technology and, 367; transportation and communication, 369–371; urban and rural life, 376–377; water and steam power, 367–369. *See also* international markets

Marlborough, Duke of, 653

Marne, Battle of the, 806

Maroons, 168, 189, 214

Marquis de Montcalm, 206–207, 214

marriage, 73; in Gilded Age, 643, 652–653; for homosexuals, 1222, *1222*, 1244; interracial, 149; in 1920s, 861; polygamy, 153, 168. *See also* divorce

Married Ladies' Missionary Society, 461

Marshall, George C., 935, 948, 978, 996–997, 998, 1017

Marshall, John, 281, 284, 301, 349, 385, 388, 401, 436

Marshall, Thurgood, 1039, 1066, 1083

Marshall Plan, 996–997, 998

Martin, Luther, 281, 284

Marx, Karl, 412

Marxism, Chile and, 1115

Mascot, José, 351, 356

masculinity, 425–426

Mason, George, 280, 281

Mason-Dixon Line, 554

Massachusetts Bay Company, 71, 80

Massachusetts Government Act, 226t

Massasoit, 66

mass culture, 468–469

The Masses (magazine), 799

Massey, Felix, 574, 597

massive retaliation doctrine, 1011

mass media, 613

mass mind, 849

mass production: department stores and, 702; in Gilded Age, 652; of housing, *987*, 1022–1023; of weapons, 945–946

Mather, Cotton, 123, 150, 168

matrilineal societies, 69, 80, 135, 168

Maury, Henry, 406

May, Karl, 614, 921

Mayflower Compact, 65

Maysville Road Bill, 381, 391

McAdoo, William Gibbs, 866–867

McCain, John, 1200, 1228, 1238–1240

McCain-Feingold Act, 1225

McCarran, Pat, 991

McCarran Act, 991, 999

McCarthy, Eugene "Gene," 1105–1106, 1109

McCarthy, Joseph/ McCarthyism, 999, 1008, 1016–1018, *1017*, 1044

McCartney, Paul, 1080

McClellan, George B., 533, 559

McClure's Magazine, 764, 781

McCormick, Cyrus, 367, 391

McCormick farm equipment, 654

McCormick Harvesting Machine, 621

McCulloch v. Maryland, 349

McDuffie, George, 432

McFarlane, Robert, 1159

McGovern, George, 1112, 1120

McJobs, 1188

McKinley, William, 680, 715, 717, 735, 745–746; assassination of, 747, 751; Philippines and, 740

McKinley Tariff, 733, 750

McNary-Haugen Acts, 867

McPherson, Aimee Semple, 861–862, *863*, 1033

McVeigh, Timothy, 1194–1195

Meadows, George, *770*

Meat Inspection Act, 784, 792

mechanization: in agriculture, 685; in

Gilded Age, 656–657; immigration and, 696–697. *See also* mass production

Me Decade, 1130

media: in Cold War, 1042–1043; mass media, 613. *See also* magazines; movies; newspapers; radio; television

Medicaid, 1064

Medicare, 1063–1064, 1225–1226, 1243, 1244, 1245

Medicare Modernization Act, 1226, 1244

Mediterranean trade, 310–311

mega-churches, 1144

Meir, Golda, 1115

Meitner, Lise, 942

Melgares, Facundo, 331

Mellon, Andrew, 866, 885

Melville, Herman, 386–387, 469, 474

Mencken, H.L., 859, 864, 872

Mendizábal, Bernardo López de, 100

Menéndez, Francisco "Don Blass," 173, 176, 189, 213

Menéndez, Lucas, 98

Menéndez, Pedro de Avilés, 38, 49

mercantilism, 103, 124

Mercer, Lucy, 886

Mercury program, 1070

Meredith, James, 1058, 1082

mergers, 651, 1152

Mesabi Range, in Minnesota, 648

mestizos, 25

Metacom "Philip," 112–113

metal, 18, 31, 648. *See also* gold; steel

Metcalfe, Jim, 607

Metcalfe, Robert, 607

Methodists, 198–199, 203, 214, 463, 502
Methodist Episcopal Church of America, 452
Metropolitan Magazine, 799
Mexica (tribe), 14, 30–33
Mexicans: civil rights of, 1044; in Gilded Age, 685–686, 691; immigration and, 691, 852–853, 990–991; mutual aid societies and, 699; New Deal and, 909; in World War II, 950–952
Mexican-American War, 607
Mexican Revolution, 799, 802, 813–815
Mexicans, wages and, 691
Mexico, 607–609; Catholic Church and, 405; invasion and conquest of, 484–485; in 1920, 870; oil in, 814, 926; Prohibition and, 864; protests in, 1108, 1118. *See also* North American Free Trade Agreement
MIA. *See* Montgomery Improvement Association
Miami, immigration/ immigrants in, 1190–1191
Miantonomi, 78–79, 80
microbes, 90
middle class, 376, 416–418, 665, 1078, 1145; African Americans in, 686; in Gilded Age, 657, 704–705; Progressivism and, 764–765; Reagan, R., and, 1147; squeeze of, 1141–1143, 1142f, 1231–1234; women in, 705, 711
Middle Colonies, 450

Midway, Battle of, 937
migration. *See* immigration/ immigrants
The Mikado, 906
Milan Decree, 312
military industrial complex, 988–990, 1082
millennialism, 449
Miller, Henry, 622
Mill Girls, 373
Milosevic, Slobodan, 1198
minimum wage, 913, 942, 984
mining, 489, 617–618, 667–668. *See also* coal; United Mine Workers
Minnesota, Mesabi Range in, 648
minstrelsy, 468–469
minute men, 241, 248
miracle drugs, 1020
Miranda v. Arizona, 1066, 1083
Miss America beauty contest, 861
"Mission Accomplished," in Iraq War, 1218
missionaries, 20–21, 67–69
Mission Dolores, 247
Mission to the Slaves, 461, 474
Mississippian societies, 10–12, 40
Mississippi Bubble, 132, 168
Mississippi Freedom Summer, 1051
Missouri Compromise, 336–337, 496, 504
Misstutin ("big dogs"), 133
Mitchell, John, 777
mob violence, 236
Moby Dick (Melville), 386, 469
Moctezuma, Isabel Tolosa Cortés, 51
Moctezuma I (ruler), 14
Model Cities, 1064

Modern Chivalry (Brackenridge), 342
modern corporations. *See* corporations
Modernists, 861
modernity, 498–499
Mohawks (tribe), 121–122
Molasses Act, 197t, 224, 248
Moley, Raymond, 887
Molotov, Vyachslav, 972
Mondale, Walter, 1133, 1150
monetarists, 1143
money: Coinage Act and, 712, 714; paper, 159, 161, 275
mongeralization, 981
monopoly, 675, 1152; in Gilded Age, 650; with sugar, 780; unions as, 651. *See also* Standard Oil; trusts
Monroe, James, 308, 337, 347, 356
Monroe Doctrine, 354–355, 356, 731, 732, 733, 870, 873
Monroe-Pinckney Treaty of 1806, 312, 321
Montesinos, Antonio de, 28
Montesquieu, 229, 261
Montgomery, Richard, 219, 222, 242, 248, 264
Montgomery Bus Boycott, 1045
Montgomery Improvement Association (MIA), 1041
Moral Majority, 1127–1128, 1144, 1160
Moran, Thomas, 631, 634
Morant Bay Rebellion, 571, 597
Moravians (United Brethren), 198–199, 202, 214
Morgan, Daniel, 269, 284

Morgan, J.P., 781
Morgenthau, Henry, 913, 948
Morley, John, 558
Mormons, 448–449, 474
Morris, Robert, 243, 275, 332
Morrow, Dwight, 870
Mossadeq, Mohammed, 1138
Mothers Against Drunk Drivers, 1155
Mott, Lucretia, 421, 436
mourning wars, 15, 40, 90
movies: in Great Depression, 904–905; in 1920s, 858–859; Reagan, R., in, 1147; for World War I, 817. *See also specific movies and actors*
muckraking, 674, 781, 802, 907
mudsill, 434, 436
Muir, John, 594–595, 597, 635, 636, 784–786
Mujahideen, 1137, 1158, 1159
mulatto, 424, 436
Muller v. Oregon, 780, 793
Munich Agreement, 958
Muniz, Felipa, 21
Murphy, Edgar Gardner, 769
Murphy, Frank, 899, 913, 954
Murray, Judith Sargent, 341, 356
Murrow, Edward R., 930, 1018, 1044
Muscovy Company, 53
Muslims, 20, 463, 1130, 1198; Black Muslims, 1074; in Iraq, 1140, 1180; Soviet Union and, 1138; in Yugoslavia, 1198
Muslim League, 830
Mussolini, Benito, 921, 926
mustard gas, 823–824

mutual aid societies, 699–700
"My Day" (Hickock), 907
My Lai massacre, 1105, 1118

NAACP. *See* National Association for the Advancement of Colored People
Nabrit, James, Jr., 1039
Na-Dene (tribe), 7, 13
Nader, Ralph, 1200
NAFTA. *See* North American Free Trade Agreement
Nagasaki, 969, 998
Nahuas, 30–31
Nairobi, Kenya, 1199–1200
Naismith, James, 715
Naked Lunch (Burroughs), 1037
Nanking, Rape of, 928
Napoleon. *See* Bonaparte, Napoleon
Napoleonic Wars, 273, 309, 332
Narragansett Christians, 203
narrowcasting, 1029
Narváez, Pánfilo de, 3, 31, 34, 40
NASA. *See* National Aeronautics and Space Administration
NASDAQ, 1184–1185
Nashville, 687
Nasser, Gamal Abdel, 1014, 1067
Natchez (tribe), 137–138
Natchez War, 138, 168
The Nation, 674
Nation, Carry A., 768
National Aeronautics and Space Administration (NASA), 1069–1070
National Americanization Committee, 811
National American Woman Suffrage

Association (NAWSA), 820
National Anti-Cigarette League, 768
National Association for the Advancement of Colored People (NAACP), 761, 772, 793, 1039, 1072; Double V campaign of, 953, 993, 996; Niagara Movement and, 771
National Association of Colored Women, 767, 792
National Broadcasting Corporation (NBC), 846, 873
National Child Labor Committee, 767, 792
National Consumers' League (NCL), 779
National Council, 341
National Defense Act of 1916, 812–813
National Economic Council, 1192
National Enquirer, 1196
National Farm Workers Association (NFWA), 1075–1076
National Forest Commission, 635
National Front for the Liberation of Vietnam (NLF), 1095, 1118
National Guard: after M.L. King's murder, 1106–1107; at Great Railroad Strike of 1877, 664; in Haiti, 869; at Homestead Works, 667; at Kent State University, 1111, 1119; at Los Angeles race riots, 1072–1073; at Palmer Raids, 832–833; at race riots, 856; at UMW strikes, 668

national health insurance: Clinton, B., and, 1193–1194; Great Society and, 1063–1064; Obama and, 1241; Truman and, 1063. *See also* Medicaid; Medicare

National Housing Association, 766

nationalism, 552–554, 557, 675, 790; in Balkans, 805; of Britain, 809; in Gilded Age, 675; of Hispanics, 1014; in India, 1014; New Nationalism, 782; World War II and, 925

Nationalist Clubs, 676

National Labor Relations Act, 777, 912, 998

National Labor Relations Board (NLRB), 899

National League, of baseball, 682, 714

National Municipal League, 765

National Organization for Women (NOW), 1077, *1078*, 1083, 1144

National Origins Act of 1924, 850–851, 872, 907, 991

national parks, 785, 891. *See also specific parks*

National Parks Act of 1916, 786

National Park Service, 633, 793

National People's Party, 669, 714–716

National Recovery Administration (NRA), 892, 912

National Republicans, 379

National Security Act of 1947, 975, 998

National Security Council (NSC), 969, 975, 998, 999, 1161; "124/2" of, 1015

National Security League, 811

National Trails Act, 1079

National Union for Social Justice, 894

National Urban League, 1072

National War Labor Policies Board, 819–820

National War Labor Relations Board (NWLRB), 946

National Wild and Scenic Rivers Act, 1079

National Wildlife Refuge System, 1079

National Woman's Party (NWP), 788, 793, 821

Nation of Islam, 1074

Native Americans, 7–9, 56, 203–204, 271–272, 297–298, 331, 340–341, 625, 627, 628–630; at Alcatraz, *1076*, 1083; civil rights of, 1075–1077; displacement of, 185–188; Eisenhower and, 1077; Indian Removal Act of 1830, 401, 436; New Deal and, 909–910; in 1960s, 1075–1077; in World War II, 950–952; in WPA, 908. *See also specific tribes*

Native American Graves Protection and Repatriation Act, 1174

nativism, 496, 693, 850

NATO. *See* North Atlantic Treaty Organization

natural resources, 616, 646, 648. *See also specific resources*

Navajo (tribe), 7, 136

Navigation Acts, 100–101, 101*t*, 107, 124, 156, 168, 224, 248

navy, 266–268, 316–317, 408; of Britain, 809–810; New Navy, 731; in World War I, 809–810; in World War II, 929, 937. *See also* U-boats; *specific ships*

NAWSA. *See* National American Woman Suffrage Association

Nazism, 881, 907–908

NBC. *See* National Broadcasting Corporation

NCL. *See* National Consumers' League

NCLB. *See* No Child Left Behind Act

NEASS. *See* New England Antislavery Society

Neau, Elias, 153

The Negro Christianized, 153

Negro Longshoremen's Association, 604

Nehru, Jawaharlal, 1014

Nelson, Baby Face, 904

neocons, 1132, 1143–1145

Neolin, 204, 214, 226, 248

neutrality, 296–297, 812–813

Neutrality Acts, 406, 926–927, 958

Neutrality Declaration, 832

Neutrals (tribe), 90

Nevada Test Site, 989–990, 999, 1044

New Deal, 878–919; African Americans and, 908–909; after World War II, 983; capitalism and, 888–895; Communist Party and, 893; Democratic Party and, 914–915; European ethics and, 907–908; first hundred days of, 890, 890*t*, 914; Hispanics and, 909; judicial reform and, 912–913; minimum wage and, 913; Native Americans and,

909–910; Nazism and, 907–908; Reagan, R., and, 1147; Roosevelt, E., and, 906–907; second hundred days of, 895–901, 896t, 914; women and, 906–907. *See also specific New Deal programs*
New Democrats, Clinton, B., and, 1192–1197
New Economic Policy, 1117
New England, 78, 80, 94–95, 112–115, 120, 124. *See also specific states*
New England Antislavery Society (NEASS), 453–454
New England Company, 92, 124, 154
The New-England Courant, 163–164
New England Emigrant Aid Society, 508
New England's Prospect, 73
New France, 61–65, 67–69
New Freedom, 782
New Frontier, 1055–1056
New Haven Colony, 76
New Jersey, 118
Newlands Reclamation Act, 785, 792
New Left, 1079–1080
New Lights, 200
New Look, 1010–1012
New Mexico, 67–69, 383
New Model Army, 91–92
New Nationalism, 782
New Navy, 731
New Netherland, 61–65, 70, 100–102
New Orleans, Louisiana, 132–133, 493–494; Hurricane Katrina in, 1210, *1226*, 1226–1227, 1244
New School for Social Research, 907
New Side, 200
New Spain, 32, 50–53

newspapers, 163, 191, 195, 374, 662, 703–704; African Americans and, 744; Cuba and, 735; in Great Depression, 904, 906; in 1920s, 849; in Soviet Union, 1067. *See also New York Times; specific newspapers*
Newsweek (magazine), Graham and, 1033
Newton, Huey, 1074
New World Order, 1172, 1176–1180
New York City, 102, 417, 686t, 710–711; Draft Riots, 548; in Gilded Age, 714; in Great Depression, 884–885; housing in, 705–706; immigration/ immigrants in, 1190–1191; Lower East Side in, *699*, 766, 780; New School for Social Research in, 907; race riots in, 953; Tammany Hall in, 707, 765; Triangle Waist Company in, 780, 793; Vietnam War protests in, *1108*. *See also* 9/11
New Yorker, 907
New York Herald, 468
New York Journal, 735
New York Stock Exchange, 883, *1169*
New York Times, 660, 715–716, 723, 1044, 1111–1112
New York Times v. Sullivan, 1065–1066, 1082
New York Weekly Journal, 191
New Zealand, 633, 690, 762, 806, 1019, 1102
NeXT Computer, 1169
NFWA. *See* National Farm Workers Association
Ngo Dinh Diem, 1095, 1118

Ngo Dinh Nhu, 1096
NGOs. *See* Non-Governmental Organizations
Nguyen Khanh, 1097
Nguyen Ngoc Loan, 1105
Nguyen Tat Than. *See* Ho Chi Minh
Nguyen Van Thieu, 1110
Niagara Movement, *771*, 773
Nicaragua, 753, 870, 873, 1138, 1160; Iran-Contra scandal and, 1128, 1158–1161, *1160*
Nicholas (Czar), 832
Nichols, Terry, 1194–1195
Nicolls, Richard, 102
Niles, Samuel, 203
Nimitz, Chester, 937
9/11, 1212, 1244; Bush, G.W., and, 1213–1215; immigration and, 1227–1228
1910s. *See* Progressivism; World War I
1920s, 840–877; African Americans in, 854–857; Christianity in, 861–864; consumerism in, 849–850; culture in, 857–864; feminism in, 859; Fundamentalists in, 861–864; highways in, 848; Hispanics in, 852; immigration/ immigrants in, 850–853, 852*f*; jazz in, 855–856; Latin America in, 870; marriage in, 861; popular culture in, 846–847; Protestantism in, 861–864; race in, 849–857; religion in, 861–864; sex/sexuality in, 860; women in, 859–861. *See also* Prohibition

1930s. *See* Great
Depression; New Deal;
World War II
1940s. *See* nuclear
weapons; World War II
1950s, 1005–1049; cars
in, *1004*, 1027–1028;
conformity in,
1025, 1030–1038;
consumerism in, 1024–
1025; corporations in,
1025–1026, 1035–
1036; Eisenhower and,
1008–1018; GE in,
1025; GNP in, 1021*f*;
industrialization
in, 1018–1026; jazz
in, 1038; popular
culture in, 1036–1038;
religion in, 1032–1033;
suburbanization in,
1020–1024; tobacco
in, 1020; white collar
workers in, 1035–1036;
women in, 1033–1035;
youth in, 1036–1038.
See also Cold War;
nuclear weapons
1960s, 1051–1087; birth
control in, 1082,
1083; civil rights in,
1072–1077; Cold
War in, 1058–1060;
counterculture
in, 1079–1084;
environment in,
1079; feminism in,
1077–1078; Hispanics
in, 1075–1077;
immigration/
immigrants in,
1064–1065, 1064*f*;
sex/sexuality in, 1083;
space exploration in,
1068–1071; tobacco
in, 1082. *See also* Cold
War; Vietnam War
1970s. *See* conservatism;
Vietnam War
1980s. *See* conservatism

Nineteenth Amendment,
761, 789, 793, 821, 833
Ninety-five Theses (Luther),
36
Nixon, E.D., 1041
Nixon, Pat, 1114
Nixon, Richard M., 1109,
1110–1121; civil
rights and, 1109;
Eisenhower and, 1009;
environment and,
1079; Great Society
and, 1116–1118;
HCUA and, 982;
impeachment of,
1119; Khrushchev
and, 1005, 1006,
1008, 1024, 1045;
Latin America and,
1115; Mao Zedong
and, 1114–1115; *New
York Times* and, 1044;
pardon of, 1132, 1160;
resignation of, 1113,
1119, 1120, 1131, 1160;
Soviet Union and,
1119; Vietnam War
and, 1091, 1110–1113
Nkruma, Kwame, 1075
NLF. *See* National Front
for the Liberation of
Vietnam
NLRB. *See* National Labor
Relations Board
No Child Left Behind Act
(NCLB), 1225, 1244
Non-Aggression Pact, 929,
958
nondenominational
schools, 495–496
Non-Governmental
Organizations
(NGOs), 983
non-importation
movement, 234
Non-Intercourse Act, 312
nonmanual labor, 416
nonviolence: by Chavez,
1076; King, M., and,
1041–1045

No Place to Hide (Bradley),
975, 999
Nordic theory, 697
Noriega, Manuel, 1178
North, Oliver, 1159, *1160*
North America, 33–36;
Africanization of, 142–
147; Atlantic world
in, 30–39; Britain
and, 53–55; to 1500,
6–15. *See also* Canada;
Mexico
North America Fur
Company, 331
North American Free Trade
Agreement (NAFTA),
1170, 1193, 1202
North Atlantic Treaty
Organization (NATO),
969, 977, 999
Northeast, 55–57,
140–141
Northern Flint (corn), 8
Northern Ireland, 1203
Northern Plains, 133–135
North Korea, nuclear
weapons in, 1158. *See
also* Korean War
North River Steamboat, 369
North West Company, 332
Northwest Ordinance,
336, 338, 504
Northwest Territory, 311,
336
Norway, immigrants from,
670
Nott, Josiah, 433, 436,
574, 597
Nova Reperta, 18
Nova Scotia, 212
novels, 192, 342. *See also
specific works*
NOW. *See* National
Organization for
Women
NRA. *See* National
Recovery
Administration
NSC. *See* National Security
Council

NSC-68, 999
nuclear energy, Carter and, 1134–1135
nuclear families, 1033
nuclear freeze movement, 1156
nuclear weapons, 907, *966*; ABM, 1113; Cold War and, 967–1003; Eisenhower and, 1011; Gorbachev and, 1163; Korean War and, 1010; Limited Test Ban Treaty and, 1060; Manhattan Project and, 945, 967, 973; Nevada Test Site for, 989–990, 999, 1044; in North Korea, 1158; Pakistan and, 1158; Reagan, R., and, 1156; SALT-I, 1113; SALT-II, 1137; SDI and, 1128, 1156–1157, 1161; in Vietnam, 1099; in World War II, 959, 960, 973. *See also* hydrogen bomb
nullification, doctrine of, 432
NWLRB. *See* National War Labor Relations Board
NWP. *See* National Woman's Party
Nzinga a Nkuwu (king), 21

Oakley, Annie, 613
Obama, Barack, *1208*, 1237–1246; Afghanistan and, 1215, 1241; deficit spending and, 1242*f*; Iraq War and, 1240–1241; McCain and, 1238–1240
Oberlin College, 447
Obregon, Alvaro, 853
Occom, Samson, 203

Occupational Safety and Health Administration (OSHA), 1079, 1117
Occupy Wall Street, 1244
O'Connor, Sandra Day, 1153, 1224
Office of Economic Opportunity, 1064
Office of Faith Based and Community Initiatives, 1221
Office of Indian Affairs, 630
Office of Price Administration (OPA), 946
Office of Scientific Research and Development (OSRD), 945
Office of War Information (OWI), 950
Office of War Mobilization (OWM), 945
Oglethorpe, James, 188, 214
O'Hara, Charles, 273
Ohio Company of Virginia, 205, 214
Ohio Valley, 204
"Oh! Susanna" (Foster, S.), 469
oil: Carter and, 1134; *Exxon Valdez*, 1174; Iran and, 1135; Japan and, 932; in Mexico, 814, 926; in 1950s, 1028; OPEC and, 1116, 1132. *See also* BP oil spill; Standard Oil
Okinawa, Battle of, 973, 998
Oklahoma City bombing, 1194–1195, 1203
Old Age Revolving Pensions Limited, 893
Old Lights, 200
Old Side, 200

Old Time Gospel Hour (television program), 1127, 1144
Olive Branch Petition, 243, 248
Olympics, 905, 1137
Omaha Platform, of National People's Party, 715
Omoo (Melville), 469
Oñate, Juan de, 51–53, 80
O'Neill, Thomas "Tip," 1134
One World (Willkie), 957
Onís, Luis de, 351–352
On the Road (Kerouac), 1037, 1045
O'Odham (tribe), 9
OPA. *See* Office of Price Administration
OPEC. *See* Organization of Petroleum Exporting Countries
Opechancanough (chief), 77
open door policies, 728, 746, 750
Operation Desert Storm, 1179
Operation MONGOOSE, 1060
Operation Wetback, 1044
opium, 414–415
Oppenheimer, J. Robert, 945, 967
Orders in Council, 312, 321
Ordinance of 1785, 612
Oregon Territory, 486
O'Reilly, Alexandre, 236
Organization for Afro-American Unity, 1074
The Organization Man (Whyte), 1035
Organization of Petroleum Exporting Countries (OPEC), 1116, 1132
Oriskany, Battle of, 272
Orlando, Vittorio, 828
Orthwood, Anne, 85, 88, 110

Ortiz, Juan, 3, 6, 34
Orwell, George, 927
Osage (tribe), 187
Osceola, 403
OSHA. *See* Occupational Safety and Health Administration
Oslo Accords, 1171
OSRD. *See* Office of Scientific Research and Development
Oswald, Lee Harvey, 1060
Ottoman Empire, in World War I, 808
Our Country (Strong), 714
Outlook (magazine), 685, 764
outsourcing, 1183–1184
Owasco (tribe), 12
Owen, Robert Dale, 412, 436
Owens, Jesse, 905
OWI. *See* Office of War Information
OWM. *See* Office of War Mobilization
Oxford Iron Works, 424

Pacific explorations, 407–409
Pacific Fur Company, 332
Pacific Northwest, 8, 617
Pacific theater, of World War II, 935–939
pacifists: in 1920s, 868–869; in Vietnam War, 1103; World War I and, 790–793, *791*; World War II and, 926
Packenham, Edward, 318
PACs. *See* Political Action Committees
Pahlevi, Mohammed Reza, 1138
Paine, Thomas, 258, 306
Pakistan, 1158, 1215
Palatinate, 184
Palatine Boors, 184
Palestine, 1067, 1171, 1198–1199

Palestine Liberation Organization (PLO), 1198–1199
Palin, Sarah, 1238–1239
Palme, Olaf, 1107
Palmer, Mitchell, 832–833
Palmer Raids, 801, 832–833
Palmerston (prime minister), 538
Pamela: Or, Virtue Rewarded (Richardson), 192
Pan-Africanism, 856–857
Panama, 1178, 1202
Panama Canal, 725, 748–749, 751, 813, 832, 1137, 1160
Pan-American Conference, 926
pandemic, influenza, 827–828, 833
Panic of 1873, 642, 660, 674
Panic of 1893, 643, 675, 713–714, 730–731
Papago (tribe), 9
paper making, 17
Pareja, Francisco de, 50
Paris Commune, 643, 663, 674
Paris Peace Accords, 1110, 1112
Paris Peace Conference, 833
Parker, Ely Samuel, 625
Parker, John, 242
parks, 631–635; amusement, 703; national parks, 631, 633, 785–786, 793, 891
Parks, Rosa, 1041, 1045
Parliament, 90, 124, 230
parochial schools, 496
Parris, Samuel, 121
PAS. *See* Pennsylvania Abolition Society
Patent Act of 1790, 367
paternalism, 570, 597
Paterson, William, 280
Patrick Henry (ship), 946

PATRIOT Act, 1214, 1244
Patriot Uprisings, 397
patronage, 707, 712–713. *See also* political machines
Paul, Alice, 788–789, 793, 821
Paulson, Henry, 1235
Paxton Boys, 232
Peace Corps, 1059
Peace of Amiens, 309
Peace Policy, 625, 636
Peale, Norman Vincent, 1033
Pearl Harbor attack, 922, 932–934, *933*, 959
Pedro (king), 142
Pendleton Civil Service Act, 713, 714
penicillin, 1020
Peninsula Campaign, 534
Penn, Thomas, 124
Penn, William, 118–119, 150, 184
Pennsylvania, 118, 648, 660
Pennsylvania Abolition Society (PAS), 453
The Pennsylvania Gazette, 181
Pennsylvanische Berichte, 184
penny presses, 468
pensions, 779, 893. *See also* Social Security
Pentagon Papers, 1111–1112, 1119
People's Party. *See* National People's Party
Pequot War, 78, 80
Perestrello, Bartolomeu, 21
Perkins, Frances, 886, 898, 904, 907
Perle, Richard, 1214
Perot, Ross, 1181–1182, 1195, 1203
Perry, Matthew C., 479, 483
Perry, Oliver Hazard, 317, 320, 321

Pershing, John J. "Black Jack," 814, 822, 823, 832

"Pershing's Crusaders" (movie), 817

Persian Gulf War, 1171, 1179–1181, 1202, 1221

personal computers, 1169, 1172

Personal Liberty Laws, 507

Pet Sounds (Beach Boys), 1081

Phelps Dodge Company, 608

Philadelphia, 118–119, 210, 686t, 704, 715, 884

philanthropy, in Gilded Age, 672–673

Philip II (king), 38, 40

Philippe, Louis, 306

Philippines, 724, 740; American-Philippine War, 742–744; Japan in, 933–934. *See also* Spanish-American War

Philippines Reservation, at St. Louis World's Fair, 723–724, 727, 751

Phillips, David Graham, 792

Phillips v. Martin Marietta, 1118

Pickens, T. Boone, 1152

piecework, 659, 661

Pierce, Franklin, 510, 514

Pierce, William, 62

Pietism, 152–154, 168

Pike, Zebulon, 314, 330–331

Pilgrims, 65–66

Pima (tribe), 9

Pinchot, Gifford, 635, 636, 785

Pinckney, Charles Cotesworth, 301

Pinckney's Treaty, 298, 321

Pinkertons, 667, 671

Pinochet, Augusto, 1115

pioneer societies, 613

piracy, 154–157, 311

Pitcairn, John, 242

Pitt, William, 207, 214, 232, 248

Pittsburgh, 641, 687, 704

Pizarro, Francisco, 33

Planned Parenthood v. Casey, 1175

plantation, 29, 88, 107, 586–587

Plantation Act of 1740, 184, 214

plastics, 1028

Platt Amendment, 739

Playground Association of America, 767, 792

Pledge of Allegiance, 1045, 1173

Plenty Kill, 627, 636

Plessy, Homer, 769

Plessy v. Ferguson, 760, 769, 792, 1039

PLO. *See* Palestine Liberation Organization

Plymouth, 65–66

Pocahontas, 45, 48, 58, 80

Poe, Edgar Allen, 469, 470, 474

poetry, 469. *See also specific works*

Poindexter, George, 352

Poitier, Sidney, 1037

Poland, 633, 697; Catholic Church in, 1130, 1157; Solidarity in, 1126, 1157; Soviet Union and, 957, 973; Versailles Treaty and, 831; in World War II, 929, 972

polio vaccine, 1006, 1020, 1044

polite society, 162

Political Action Committees (PACs), 1146

political machines, 707, 765–766. *See also* Tammany Hall

political parties, 294–296, 295t, 299–303, 504t;

corporations and, 1146; issue-specific, 504t; Progressivism and, 774–776. *See also specific parties*

politics, 471–474, 507–513; in Gilded Age, 711–718; of slave catching, 505–507; of South, 537; transatlantic, 257; voting and, 377–378. *See also specific parties and politicians*

Polk, James K., 380, 391, 483–484, 486, 514

poll taxes, 775, 776

polygamy, 153, 168

Ponce de León, Juan, 30

Pontiac, 204, 214, 226–228, 248

Popé (medicine man), 115, 117, 124

Pope, John, 542

Pope's Day, 156, 168

popular culture, 342–343; conservatism and, 1153; in 1920s, 846–847; in 1950s, 1036–1038; in 1960s, 1079; rock 'n roll and, 1081; USIA and, 1042–1043

popular sovereignty, 278, 284, 496, 508, 514

Populist Movement, 621

Populists. *See* National People's Party

pornography, 1184, 1221

"Port Huron Statement," 1079, 1082

Portland, Maine, 361, 364

Portland, Oregon, 687

portoan charts, 16

Portolá, Gaspar de, 244

Portugal, expansion of, 19–20

Postal System, U.S., 370

post-Cold War (1988–2000), 1167–1207; Clinton, B., and,

1192–1197; disputed election of 2000, 1200–1204, *1203*; foreign policy in, 1197–1200; immigration/immigrants in, 1188–1191, 1189*f*

post-traumatic stress disorder (PTSD), 824

Potsdam Conference, 969, 971–973, 998

Powderly, Terrence V., 665

Powell, Colin, 1176, 1180, 1216–1217

Powell, John Wesley, 554, 559, 611, 636

Powell Doctrine, 1179

Powhatan, 45, 48, 58

Prague Spring, 1108, 1118

Pratt, Richard Henry, 627, 636

Pravda, 1067

prayer, in schools, 1145, 1175, 1221

praying towns, 92

preemptive war policy, 1211, 1215, 1244

Prescott, William, 485

preservation movements, 634–635

President's Committee on Civil Rights, 993, 998

Presley, Elvis, 1037, 1080

Prester John, 19

Pretender, 156, 168

Prigg, Edward, 506

Prigg v. Pennsylvania, 500, 506, 514

primary opposition parties, 504*t*

Princeton, Battle of, 258

printers, 17, 468

Pritchard, "Gullah" Jack, 464, 474

privateers, 37, 40, 54

Proclamation of 1763, 227, 248

Proclamation of Neutrality, 289, 296

procreation ethic, 1020

Proctor, Henry, 314, 315

Proctor, H.H., 744

Progressivism (1890-1920): African Americans and, 767; capitalism and, 777–778; child labor and, *758*, 767; cities and, 764–773; consumer protection and, 780–784; dancing and, 767; draft and, 812; environment and, 784–786; as global movement, 762–764; good government movement and, 765–766; housing and, 766; in international context, 789–793; labor movement and, 776–780; leisure and, 767; middle class and, 764–765; nationalism and, 790; political machines and, 765–766; political parties and, 774–776; principles of, 763; public motherhood and, 766–768; public services and, 765–766; race and, 768–773; segregation and, 768–773; socialism and, 780–781; at state and national levels, 773–786; strikes and, 776–778; trusts and, 780–784; unions and, 776–780; voting and, 774–776, 776*f*; women in, 766–768, 780, 788–789; World War I and, 786–793

Prohibition, 760, 768, 793, 833, 864, 872, 890

propaganda, 817, 986

"Property Protected ála Françoise," *302*

Proposition 13, in California, 1136

Proposition 187, in California, 1189, 1203

prostitution, 236, 424, 768, 823. *See also* Mann Act

Protestant Associators, 121

Protestantism, 36, 40, 152–154, 681, 708; African Americans and, 202–204; in 1920s, 861–864; in Northern Ireland, 1203. *See also specific denominations*

protests, 411; in Chicago, 1109, 1118; in Czechoslovakia, 1108; Democratic Party and, 1109, 1118; in France, 1107–1108, 1118; at Kent State University, 1111, 1119; in Mexico, 1108, 1118; against New Deal, 893–895; against Vietnam War, 1102–1104, *1103*, 1106–1107, *1108*, 1111. *See also* counterculture; race riots; riots

PTL Club (television program), 1144

Ptolemy, 17, 21

PTSD. *See* post-traumatic stress disorder

Public Credit, 296

public education. *See* education

The Public Enemy (movie), 905

public land, 612

Public Works Administration (PWA), 891

Public Works of Arts Project, 906

Pueblo War for Independence, 115–118

Puerto Rico/Puerto Ricans, 730, 737, 739–740, 750, 751, 1076–1077
Pulaski, Casimir, 265, 285
Pulitzer, Joseph, 735
Pullman, George, 667
Pullman Palace Cars, strike at, 667, 675
pulsars, 1068
Pumpkin Papers, 982–983
Pure Food and Drug Act, 784, 792
Puritans, 36–37, 65, 73–75
PWA. *See* Public Works Administration

Qaddafi, Muammar, 1158
Al Qaeda, 1199, 1202, 1203, 1244; Bush, G.W., and, 1213–1215; Clinton, B., and, 1213; Hussein and, 1215; 9/11 and, 1212. *See also* 9/11
Qaramanli, Yusuf, 311, 321
Quakers, 93–94, 112, 119, 124, 210
quarks, 1068
Quartering Act, 226t, 232, 233–234, 235
quasars, 1068
Quasi-War, with France, 300–301
Quayle, Dan, 1173
Quebec, 103, 106, 208
Quebec Act, 226t, 239
Queen Anne's War, 140, 157, 168
Quincy, Josiah, Jr., 237, 248
Quisqueya (island), 22–25, 28
Quitman, John A., 397, 406
quitrents, 118, 124
Qwest Communications, 1232

RA. *See* Resettlement Administration

Rabin, Yitzhak, 1198
race/racism, 495–496; egalitarianism of, 454; in Haiti, 869–870; Hitler and, 921; ideology and, 277–278; imperialism and, 728–730, 742; market logic and, 374; naturalization of, 147–149; new challenge of, 554–555; in 1920s, 849–857; Progressivism and, 768–773; Rankin, John, and, 981; riots, 604; school busing and, 1117–1118, 1131; violence and, 616. *See also* African Americans; Asia/Asian Americans; civil rights; ethnicity; Hispanics; Native Americans
race riots, 770, 787–788, 792, 793; in Detroit, *1073*; Great Society and, 1065, 1073; King, R., and, 1181; in Los Angeles, 1072–1073, 1083, 1202; in 1920s, 856; during World War I, 800; during World War II, 951–952, 953
RADAR. *See* radio detection and ranging
Radiation Exposure Compensation Act of 1990, 1174
radio, 845–847, 904
Radio Corporation of America (RCA), 846
radio detection and ranging (RADAR), 931
Radio Free Dixie, 1043
RAF. *See* Royal Air Force
Ragged Dick (Alger), 674
raids, slaving, 138
railroads, 370, 619–621, 703, 769; in Gilded Age, 647; Great

Railroad Strike of 1877, 663–664, 674; Transcontinental Railroad, 687
Railroad Administration, 819
Raleigh, Walter, 54–55, 80
ranching, 617, 621–622, 623
Randolph, A. Philip, 856, 952, 993
Randolph, Edmund, 280, 293, 297
Rankin, Jeanette, 816
Rankin, John, 981, 982
Rankin, Thomas, 199
Rape of Nanking, 928
ratification, 281–283
Raysor, Michael, 536
RCA. *See* Radio Corporation of America
REA. *See* Rural Electrification Administration
Reader's Digest, 906
Reagan, Nancy, 1147
Reagan, Ronald, 1146–1163; as California governor, 1054, 1147–1148; Cold War and, 1155–1163; communism and, 1130; GE and, 1147; Gorbachev and, 1161, *1162*, 1162–1163; HCUA and, 982; military interventions of, 1156, 1157–1158; in movies, 1147; Religious Right and, 1130; taxes and, 1143, 1161
Reagan Doctrine, 1155
Reaganomics, 1150–1152
Rebel Without a Cause (movie), 1037
Rebolledo, Diego de, 99
recall, 774
recession, 913–914, 1236, 1237

Reclamation Service, 612
reconcentration, 734
reconquista (reconquest), 18, 40
Reconstruction, 580–588; Congressional, 577–580, 589; fight over, 574–575; Johnson, A., and, 572–574
Reconstruction Acts, 578
Reconstruction Finance Corporation (RFC), 885
Red Cross, 738, 823, 885, 947
redemptioners, 184, 214
Redjacket (Melville), 469
Red Scare, 977–983, 1016–1017
Red Sticks, 316, 350
Reed, David A., 802, *802*, 882
Reed, Esther DeBerdt, 276, 285
Reed, John, 799
Reed, Stanley F., 913
referendum, 774
reform, 522; abolition and, 412, 436, 452–455; Bourbon Reforms, 228, 244; Catholic Church and, 707; in Gilded Age, 661–662, 707–711; health, 452; Northern, 450–460; of patronage, 712–713; religious, 36–37; slavery and, 461–462, 464–466; Southern, 460–466; unions and, 1145. *See also* Progressivism
Reform Act, 519
Reform Party, 1201
refrigeration, 654
Refugee Act, 1149
refugees, 212–213
Regents of the University of California v. Bakke, 1134, 1160
Regulators, 237
regulators, 232

Rehnquist, William, 1117, 1153, 1224
Reisman, David, 1035
religion, 36–37, 447, 449*f*; celebrities in, 1144; faith-based initiatives by, 1221; First Amendment and, 1066; Ghost Dance, 630; immigration and, 691–692; Native Americans and, 203–204; in 1920s, 861–864; in 1950s, 1032–1033; Progressivism and, 763–764; Rankin, John, and, 981; Second Great Awakening, 444–450. *See also* churches; school prayer; *specific religions and denominations*
Religious Herald, 426
Religious Right, 1127, 1130, 1143–1145
rendition, by CIA, 1219
Report on the Lands of the Arid Region (Powell, J.), 611
Republican Party, 497, 503–513; blue collar workers and, 1131; Clinton, B., and, 1194–1195; conservatism and, 1130–1133; farmers/farming and, 669; Federal Reserve and, 1245; free soil and free labor, 504–505; in Gilded Age, 669, 711, 713–714; gold and, 712; income tax and, 1245; National Republicans, 379; in postwar South, 583–586; radical Republicans, 572; Southern Strategy of, 1117, 1132; wedge

issues and, 1221. *See also* conservatism; Democratic-Republican Party; *specific Republican politicians*
Rerum novarum (Of New Things), 764
Resettlement Administration (RA), 896–897
return migration, 694–697
Reuther, Victor, 899
Reuther, Walter, 899
revenue enhancements, 1151
Revere, Paul, 237, 242, 249
reverse discrimination, 1152
revivalists, 199–200, 214
Revolutionary War, 242, 243, 256, 258, 273, 276–277
Reynolds, John, 384, 391
RFC. *See* Reconstruction Finance Corporation
Rhode Island, Atlantic slave trade and, 181*f*
Rhodesia, 1136
Ribault, Jean, 37
rice cultivation, 145
Richardson, Samuel, 192
Rickey, Branch, 994–995
rifle clubs, 590
right-to-die, 1223–1224
right-to-life, 1223–1224
right-to-work-laws, 1131
Riis, Jacob, *710*, 710–711, 715
Riordon, William L., 705
Riot Act, 237
riots: Brooks Brothers riot, 1201–1202; New York City Draft Riots, 548. *See also* race riots
Risen from the Ranks (Alger), 672
Ritz Brothers, 905
Rivera y Moncada, Fernando de, 245

Rivington Street Settlement House, 906
road building. *See* highways
Robber Barons, 619
Roberts, John, 1224, 1244
Robertson, Pat, 1144
Robinson, Jack Roosevelt "Jackie," *994*, 994–995, 998
Rochambeau, Comte de, 273
Rochester Woolen Mills, 459
Rockefeller, John D., 647, 649, 651, 672, 717, 781
Rockefeller, Nelson, 1132
Rockingham, Marquis of, 232
rock 'n roll, 1006, 1037–1038; from Britain, 1080–1081; CIA and, 1043; popular culture and, 1081. *See also specific artists*
Rodgers, Elizabeth, *666*
Roe v. Wade, 1118, 1143–1144, 1160
Rogers, Ginger, 905
Rogers, Roy, 1029
Rolfe, John, 48, 58, 60, 80
Rolfe, Thomas, 77
Rolled Stockings (movie), 873
Roller Derbies, 906
Rolling Stone (magazine), 1084
Rolling Stones (rock 'n roll band), 1080
Romanticism, 467
Rome-Berlin Axis, 927
Rommel, Erwin, 939
Roosevelt, Eleanor, 882, 885–886, *908*, 956; Liberty League and, 894; New Deal and, 906–907; race and, 951–952
Roosevelt, Franklin D., 879, *886*, *960*; as Assistant Secretary

of the Navy, 886; Churchill, W., and, 931–932; death of, 959, 960, 998; Prohibition and, 864; World War II and, 925–926, 939. *See also* New Deal
Roosevelt, Theodore, *737*; African Americans and, 770–771, 792; Big Stick of, 746–750; Bull Moose Party and, 773–774; China and, 749; Cuba and, 736–737; environment and, 784–785; gentlemen's agreement and, 725, 750, 751; imperialism and, 730, 746–750; Japanese and, 749–750; *Maine* and, 736; Panama Canal and, 748–749; Progressivism and, 763, 764; Rough Riders and, 736–737; Standard Oil and, 781–782, 792; strenuosity and, 705; trusts and, 781–782, 792; UMW and, 668, 777
Roosevelt Corollary, 749, 751, 873
Roots (television series), 1153
Rosas, Luis de, 69
Rosenberg, Ethel, 1017
Rosenberg, Julius, 1017
Rosenman, Sam, 904
rosewater strategy, 530
Rosie the Riveter, *986*, 1033
Rothstein, Arthur, 897
Rough Riders, 736–737
Rowlandson, Mary, 115, 124
Rowson, Susannah, 343, 356
Royal African Company, 96, 107, 124

Royal Air Force (RAF), 930
Royall, Anne, 325, 328, 341
Royal Navy, 157, 207
Royal Order for New Discoveries, 49, 80
Royal Path of Life, 672, 674
Royal Society of London for the Promotion of Natural Knowledge, 113, 124, 193
The Roy Rogers Show (television program), 1029
Rubber Soul (Beatles), 1081
Rubin, Robert, 1192
Ruby, Jack, 1060
rugged, 865
rugged individualism, 865
Rumsfeld, Donald, 1214, 1220
Rural Electrification Administration (REA), 897
Rush, Richard, 352, 356
Rush-Bagot Agreement, 352
Rusk, Dean, 1103
Russell, Bertrand, 1106
Russell, William Howard, 526, 538, 559
Russia, in World War I, 808, 824–825
Russian Revolution, 802, 830, 832, 926
Russo-Japanese War, 751
Rustin, Bayard, 1041
Ruth, Babe, 858, 905
Rutledge, Wiley, 913
Rwanda, 1172, 1198

Sacagawea, 329, 356
Sacco, Nicola, 850–851
Sack of Lawrence, 510
Sadat, Anwar, 1115, 1136, *1137*
Saffin, John, 147, 168
Sagebrush Rebellion, 1152
Saigon, Vietnam, 1113
Saint Domingue, 303, 306

Salem witch trials, 121–122

salespeople, in Gilded Age, 657

Salinger, J.D., 1037

Salk, Jonas, 1006, 1020, 1044

SALT-I. *See* Interim Agreement on Limitations of Strategic Armaments

SALT-II, 1137

salutary neglect, 157, 168, 224

salvation, 460–461

Salvation Army, 681, 684, 707, 708, 714

San Agustín de la Nueva Florida, 173

San Antonio de Béjar, 136

Sand Creek massacre, 614

Sandia National Labs, 988

Sandino, Cesar Augusto, 870

San Francisco, in 1960s, 1083

San Juan Hill, Battle of, 736, 737, 745

San Martín, José, 354

San Miguel de Gualdape, 35, 40

Santa Anna, Antonio Lopez de, 407, 436

Santa Fe Trail, 383

Saratoga, Battle of, 260

Sartre, Jean-Paul, 1106

Saturday Evening Post, 906

Saturiwa (tribe), 37–38

Saudi Arabia, 1159. *See also* bin Laden, Osama

Saukamappee, 133

Saur, Christopher, 184

Savannah (steamboat), 369

Savings and Loans, 1181

Savio, Mario, 1051

Scalia, Antonin, 1153

Scarface (movie), 905

The Scarlet Letter (Hawthorne), 469

Scheibert, Justus, 550, 551, 559

schematic surveys, 611

Schenck v. U.S., 819

Schiavo, Michael, 1224

Schiavo, Terri, 1223–1224, 1244

Schlafly, Phyllis, 1078, 1144

Schmeling, Max, 905

school busing, 1117–1118, 1131, 1153, 1221

school prayer, 1145, 1175, 1221

Schurz, Carl, 573, 741

Schuyler, Philip, 242, 249

Schuyler Vas, Elsje (Rutgers), *84*

Schwarzkopf, H. Norman, Jr., 1179

science, 193; in 1960s, 1068–1071; in post–Cold War, 1186–1188. *See also* technology

science fiction, 1026–1027, 1036

scientific management, in Gilded Age, 658–659

SCLC. *See* Southern Christian Leadership Conference

Scopes, John, 862–864, 872

Scott, Winfield, 400, 485, 514, 530, 559

Scully, John, 1169

SDI. *See* Strategic Defense Initiative

SDS. *See* Students for a Democratic Society

The Sea Around Us (Carson), 1035

Seale, Bobby, 1074

Search and Destroy, *1101*

Sears, Roebuck and Co. Catalog, *640*, 653

Seattle, 687, 1232

SEC. *See* Securities and Exchange Commission

secession, 522–531; of Lower South, 523–525; in Upper South, 525–526

Second Anglo-Dutch War, 102

Second Bank of the United States, 347, 381

Second Bill of Rights, 956

Second Continental Congress, 242

Second Great Awakening, 344–346, 356, 444–450, 474

second hundred days, of New Deal, 895–901, 896*t*, 914

second Industrial Revolution, 645

Second Middle Passage, 419

Second Pan-African Congress, 856

second party system, 429–430

Second Seminole War, 402

Second Sino-Japanese War, 881

secretaries: in Gilded Age, 657; in 1920s, 861

sectionalism, 460, 510–513, 554

Securities Act of 1933, 890

Securities and Exchange Commission (SEC), 890, 914, 1212, 1236

Securities Exchange Act of 1934, 890

Sedition Act, 301–303, 320, 787, 818

See It Now (television program), 1018, 1044

segregation: in Cold War, 988; in Gilded Age, 744; of housing, 376; KKK and, 853; in 1960s, 1056–1057, 1072; Progressivism and, 768–773; Roosevelt, F., and, 909; in World War I, 822; in World War II, 952

Seider, Christopher, 235

Selective Service Act, 787. *See also* draft

self-help, in Gilded Age, 672

self-made men, 651, 673

self-reconstruction, 572

"Self Reliance" (Emerson), 466

Selma, Alabama, 1062–1063, 1082

Seminole (tribe), 350–351

Semmes, Raphael, 485, 514

Seneca Falls Conference, 457

separation of church and state, 74, 202

separation of powers, 261, 285

Separatists, 65

Sequoyah, 341, 356

Serbia, 1198, 1203

serialized fiction, 468

Serra, Junípero, 245

Servan-Schreiber, Jean Jacques, 1068, 1083

Serviceman's Readjustment Act of 1944. *See* GI Bill

settlement houses, in Gilded Age, 709–710

Settler Societies, 607, 631–632

Seven Days (campaign), 534

700 Club (television program), 1144

Seventeen Magazine, 1036

Seventeenth Amendment, 774, 793

Seven Years' War, 205, 209, 214, 224, 267

Sewall, Samuel, 122, 147, 168

Seward, William Henry, 523, 559, 569, 597

sexism, 1078

sex/sexuality: in 1920s, 860; in 1960s, 1083; pornography, 1184, 1221; Reagan, R., and, 1153–1155. *See also* homosexuals; prostitution

sexual exchange, 25

Sgt. Pepper's Lonely Hearts Band (Beatles), 1081, 1083

Shadwell, Arthur, 641, 655

Shah of Iran, 1138

Shakers, 448

The Shame of the Cities (Steffens), 765

Shanghai Communiqué, 1115

sharecropping, 582, 587, 588, 597; African Americans and, 896; in Great Depression, 896; during World War I, 809

shareholder democracy, 1184

Share Our Wealth Society, 893

Sharp, Granville, 452, 474

Shays, Daniel, 279

Shays' Rebellion, 279, 285

Sheen, Fulton, 1033

sheep, 136

The Sheik (movie), 841, 844, 872

shell shock, 824

Shelly v. Kraemer, 1021

Shepard, Alan B., 1070

Sheridan, Philip, 546, 559

Sherman, William T., 546, 549–552, 553, 559, 578, 597, 629

Sherman Antitrust Act, 650–651, 667, 675, 781, 783

Sherman neckties, 556

Sherman's March, 550

Shiloh Church, 531

shipbuilding industry, 94, 159

Short, Jack, 956

Shoshone (tribe), 134–135

Shotwell, James T., 868

Shriver, Sargent, 1064

Sibley, John, 350

Sidney, Algernon, 229, 249

Siege of Savannah, 307

Sierra Club, 635, 784

Sierra Leone, 338

"The Significance of the Frontier in American History" (Turner), 731

silent sentinels, 788

Silent Spring (Carson), 1035, 1079, 1082

Simkhovitch, Mary, 699

Simpson, O.J., 1196

Simpson-Rodino Bill, 1148

sin, 460–461

Sinclair, Upton, 783–784, 792

Singer Sewing Machine Company, 644, 654

Sioux (tribe), 187, 331

Sirhan, Sirhan, 1109

Sirica, John, 1120

sister republics, 296

Sitting Bull, 624, 630

Six-Day War, 1067

Sixteenth Amendment, 783, 793, 813

Sixteenth Street Baptist Church, 1058, 1082

skyscrapers, 688–689, 714

Slater, Samuel, 367, 372, 391

slave catching, 505–507

slave rebellions, 303

slavery: autonomous economy of, 196; Caribbean, 95–97; conflicts over, 433–435; as domestic institution, 543; expansion of, 418–420; family and, 148; future of, 500; key legal developments concerning, 108t; language of, 240–241; markets and, 374–375; modernity and, 498–499; naturalization of, 147–149; northern, 178–179; outlawing of, 278, 310; plantation, 88, 107; rebellions,

303; reform and, 461–462, 464–466; regional origin and, 144f, 145t; rental market and, 419–420; resistance to, 147, 188–191; by sending region, 180t; tobacco cultivation and, 143–145; urban, 498; women and, 424. *See also* abolition; Atlantic slave trade; emancipation
slaving raids, 138
Sloan, Alfred P., 847, 894, 1027
smallpox, 25, 68, 89–90
Smith, Alfred E., 864, 867, 894
Smith, Jacob H., 742
Smith, James McCune, 455, 474
Smith, John, 45, 48, 58, 80
Smith, Joseph, 448, 474
Smith Act, 982, 999
smoking. *See* tobacco
Smoot-Hawley Tariff, 843, 873, 883–884
SNCC. *See* Student Nonviolent Coordinating Committee
soap operas, 1029
A Social Celebrity (movie), 873
social class, 375
Social Darwinism, 627, 636, 651; Carnegie and, 672; immigration and, 693
Social Gospel, 708; Hull House and, 709–710; Progressivism and, 763–764
socialism: Czechoslovakia and, 1108; Progressivism and, 780–781. *See also* communism; Marxism; national health insurance

social isolation, 146
Socialist Party, 667; in World War I, 818
"The Social Problem," 762
Social Security, 894, 898, 912, 914, 1244, 1245; Bush, G.W., and, 1223; Truman and, 984. *See also* Medicare
social shifts, 340–346
Society for Promoting Christian Knowledge (SPCK), 153, 168
Society for the Propagation of the Gospel in Foreign Parts (SPG), 153, 168, 198
Society of Friends, 93, 124
Society of Jesus, 36, 40
Society of Negroes, 153
Solidarity, 1126, 1157
Somalia, 1172, 1197–1198
Somme, 806
Somoza, Anastasio, 870
"Song of Myself" (Whitman), 470
Sons of Liberty, 231, 234, 239, 247, 249
Soto, Hernando de, 3, 6, 34–35, 40
Sotomayor, Sonia, 1241
soul liberty, 74
sound bites, 1174
Souter, David, 1175, 1202
South: African Americans in, 984–985, 993; cities in, 687–688; Coolidge and, 866–867; democracy and, 430–433; Democratic Party in, 1131–1132; farmers/farming in, 669; in Gilded Age, 656; Jim Crow laws in, 769, 787; military industrial complex in, 988–990; nationalism of, 552–554; nuclear weapons and, 988; political landscape of,

537; postwar, 580–586; Reconstruction in, 580–588; reform and, 460–466; suburbanization in, 1022; TVA in, 891; war in, 268–271. *See also* Confederate States of America
South Africa, 1136
South Carolina, 111–112, 138–139
Southeast, 138–140, 188–191
Southern Christian Leadership Conference (SCLC), 1041–1042, 1045, 1058
Southern Farmers' Alliance, 669
Southern Negro Leaders Conference on Transportation and Nonviolent Integration, 1041–1042
Southern Strategy, of Republican Party, 1117, 1132
South Korea: in Vietnam War, 1102. *See also* Korean War
South Seas Exploring Expedition, 414
Southwest, 135–136, 336; gender and, 426–427; New Spain and, 50–53
Soviet Union: in Afghanistan, 1129, 1137–1138, 1158, 1160; agriculture in, 926; Communist Party in, 925; Cuba and, 1137–1138; Czechoslovakia and, 1067, 1083, 1108; dissolution of, 1171, 1176–1177, 1202; Egypt and, 1007; Eisenhower and, 1005; Germany and, 929, 931, 959; Hungary and, 1045; Johnson, L., and,

1067; Kissinger and, 1113–1114; Korean War and, 980; Muslims and, 1138; newspapers in, 1067; Nixon, R., and, 1119; nuclear weapons and, 999; Poland and, 957, 973; *Sputnik*, 1007, 1045, 1069–1070; in World War II, 924, 939–940. *See also* Cold War; Russia

space exploration: *Challenger* accident, 1161; in 1960s, 1068–1071; *Sputnik*, 1007, 1045, 1069–1070

Spain, 353; Britain and, 190; Cuba and, 734–736; expansion by, 247, 339; fascism in, 927; Florida and, 49–50; New Spain, 32, 50–53

Spanish-American War, 723, 736–740; poisoned beef in, 780; Treaty of Paris for, 750

Spanish Civil War, 927, 958

Spanish-Timucuan catechism, 50

SPCK. *See* Society for Promoting Christian Knowledge

The Spectator, 164

Spellman, Francis, 1032–1033

Spencer, Herbert, 651

Spener, Philipp Jakob, 153, 168

Spengler, Oswald, 1031

SPG. *See* Society for the Propagation of the Gospel in Foreign Parts

spin, 1174

"Spirit of 76" (movie), 819

Spirit of the Laws (Montesquieu), 229

Spooner Amendment, 751

sports: in Gilded Age, 703–704; in Great Depression, 905; in 1920s, 858–859. *See also specific sports and players*

Sports Illustrated (magazine), 1186

Sports Outdoors, 992

Spot Resolutions, 485

Squanto. *See* Tisquantum

St. Augustine (city), 38–39, 40

St. Clair, Arthur, 298, 321

St. George's Field Massacre, 237

St. Louis, 686t

St. Louis World's Fair, Philippines Reservation at, 723–724, 727, 751

stagflation, 1117, 1160

Stalin, Josef, 924, 925, 939, 957, 960; death of, 1010, 1044; Eisenhower and, 1008–1009; Potsdam Conference and, 971–973; Truman and, 971

Stamp Act, 226t, 229–232, 249

Standard Oil, 649, 650, 674, 780; McKinley and, 717; Roosevelt, T., and, 781–782, 792

Stanton, Edwin, 569, 597

Stanton, Elizabeth Cady, 421, 436, 457, 577

Starr, Ellen, 682, 709, 715, 1197

Starr, Kenneth, 1196

Starr, Ringo, 1080

"The Star Spangled Banner," 317

Star Wars. *See* Strategic Defense Initiative

steamboats, 368–369

steam power, 367–369

steamships, 654, 689, 803

steel: Bethlehem Steel, 658–659; Carnegie Steel, 641, 645, 649, 656, 666–667, 675; immigrants and, 656; in Pennsylvania, 660; tariffs on, 712; U.S. Steel, 642, 675, 792, 883, 943

Steffens, Lincoln, 765

Steinbeck, John, 910

stem cell research, 1187, 1221

Stephens, Alexander, 528, 559, 573, 597

Stevens, John Paul, 1203

Stevens, Thaddeus, 577–578, 597

Stevenson, Adlai, 1009

Stiglitz, Joseph, 1232–1233, 1244

Stimson, Henry L., 927, 931, 943

stimulants, 452

stockyards, in Chicago, 651

stone artifacts, 7

stoneware goods, 194

Stono Rebellion, 189, 214

Story, Joseph, 500, 514

"The Story of a Great Monopoly (Demarest), 674

Stowe, Harriet Beecher, 507

Strategic Defense Initiative (SDI), 1128, 1156–1157, 1161

Strauss, Levi, 491

Strawbridge, Robert, 199

streetcars, 715, 766

Street Life (Alger), 674

strenuosity, 705

strikes, 373, 832, 866; Great Railroad Strike of 1877, 663–664, 674; Progressivism and, 776–778; at Pullman Palace Cars, 667, 675; by UMW,

777; during World War I, 820

Strong, George Templeton, 527, 559

Strong, Josiah, 714, 729

Stuart, J. E. B., 550

Student Nonviolent Coordinating Committee (SNCC), 1056, 1072

Students for a Democratic Society (SDS), 1079–1080, 1082, 1107

subprime mortgages, 1234–1237

suburbanization: environment and, 1024; FHA and, 1020, 1023; in Gilded Age, 688; highways and, 1020–1021; in 1950s, 1020–1024; in South, 1022; VA and, 1023

subways, 715

Suez Canal, 1045; in 1950s, 1007, 1014–1015; oil and, 1028; in World War II, 939

suffrage, white male, 377

suffragists, 788–789, 789, 820, 820–821

sugar, 20, 95–96, 587; in Cuba, 734; monopoly with, 650–651, 780; production, 29

Sugar Act, 197t, 224, 226t

suicide bombers, 1213

Sullivan, John, 272, 428, 436

Sullivan's Island, Battle of, 258

Summer of Love, 1052, 1081, 1083

Sumner, Charles, 425, 436, 510, 513, 514, 571, 597

Sumner, Edward V., 546

Sunbelt, 950, 1069; in 1960s, 1070–1071; population in, 1070f. See also South; West

sundown towns, 1022

Sun Records, 1037

supply siders, 1143

Supreme Court, 348–349

surveys, schematic, 611

Susquehannocks (tribe), 56, 110–111

Swaggart, Jimmy, 1144

Swann v. Charlotte-Mecklenburg Board of Education, 1117

Swift, Gustavus, 651

Swing, Joseph, 1044

Swing Time (movie), 905

Sydney Herald, 490

Syngman Rhee, 980

Syria. See Six-Day War

Szilard, Leo, 907, 942

tabloids, 1196

Taft, William H., 743, 750–753, 773–774, 782

Taft-Hartley Act, 998

Taínos (tribe), 22–25, 29

Taliban, 1213, 1214–1215, 1218, 1244

Tallmadge, James, Jr., 336, 356

Tammany Hall, 707, 765

Tampa, Florida, 687

Tanaghrisson, 206

Taney, Roger B., 380, 381, 388, 391, 511, 514

Tanzania, 1199–1200

Tappan, Arthur, 458

Tappan, Lewis, 458

Tarbell, Ida, 781, 792

tariffs, 369, 391, 431, 712; Fordney-McCumber Tariff, 872; McKinley Tariff, 733, 750; Smoot-Hawley Tariff, 843, 873, 883–884

tariff of abominations, 379, 432

Tarleton, Banastre, 269, 285

TARP. See Troubled Asset Relief Program

task system, 195, 214, 419

taxes, 1143, 1161, 1192–1193, 1243, 1245; in California, 1136; imperial, 226t; poll tax, 775, 776; Social Security and, 898. See also income tax; IRS; tariffs

Tax Act of 1916, 813

tax-in-kind, 545

Taylor, Frederick Winslow, 658

Taylor, Nathaniel, 346, 356

Taylor, Zachary, 384, 391, 484, 514

Taylor Grazing Act, 911

Tea Act, 226t, 239

Teach, Edward (Blackbeard), 157

tea drinking, 162, 193–194, 234, 239

Tea Party, 1245

Teapot Dome scandal, 872

technology, 367; agriculture and, 621; in Gilded Age, 651, 689; in 1960s, 1068–1071; in post-Cold War, 1183–1186; of warfare, 17–18, 31. See also Industrial Revolution; mechanization

Tecumseh, 312, 314–316, 321, 340, 356

teenagers. See youth

Tejanos, 407

Tekakwitha, Catherine/Kateri, 104–105, 124

telecommuting, 1186–1187

telegraph, 651, 703

television, 1028–1030; Christianity on, 1144; civil rights and, 1040; Eisenhower and, 1009; Iraq War on, 1217–1218; in 1950s, 1028–1030; religion on, 1033, 1144. See also specific programs

Teller, Edward, 907, 942, 945, 967
Teller, Henry, 736
Teller Amendment, 739
temperance, 451–452
Temple, Shirley, 905
Ten Days that Shook the World (Reed, D.), 802
Tenet, George, 1213
Tennessee Valley Authority (TVA), 891
tennis, 858
Tenochtitlán, 14, 31
Tenskwatawa "The Prophet," 312, 321, 340
Tenure of Office Act, 579
Ternay, Marquis de, 268, 285
Terra Nullius (empty land), 632
Terri's Law, 1224
"The Terror," 293
terrorism, 1158, 1199– 1200, 1212–1213; anarchism and, 833; *Lusitania* and, 810; in 2000 to present, 1212–1220. *See also* 9/11; Oklahoma City bombing
Terry, David, 489, 514
Tet Offensive, 1104–1105, 1118
Tevis, Julia Hieronymous, 341
Texaco Star Theater (television program), 1029
Texas, 350–351, 382–383, 406–407; Galveston, 601, 622, 765, 792
Texas Rangers, 607
Texians, 407
textile industry, 371, 655–656, 691
Thatcher, Margaret, 1161
Thayer, Webster, 850–851
theater, 468; Federal Theater Project, 904, 906; in Gilded Age, 703

Them! (movie), 1026–1026
Thich Quang Duc, 1096
Third World. *See* Developing World
Thirteenth Amendment, 573, 597
Thirty Years' War, 64, 80
Thomas, Clarence, 1175– 1176, 1202, 1224
Thomas, Jesse B., 337
Thompson, Sarah Montgomery, 299
Thoreau, Henry David, 441, 466–468, 475, 488, 513, 635, 1042
Thornton, William, 300
3/5 compromise, 280
Three Mile Island, 1134– 1135, 1160
Thurmond, Strom, 977
Tiananmen Square, 1202
Tijerina, Reies Lopez, 1083
Tilden, William, 858
Till, Emmett, 1045
Time (magazine), 1033, 1186
Time Warner, 1186
time zones, 619–620
Timucua revolt, 99, 124
Tippecanoe, Battle of, 312
Tisquantum, 65, 80
Tituba, 121
Tlaloc (god), 14
tlatoani (emperors), 14
Tlaxcalans (tribe), 30–31
tobacco, 60, 143–145, 161, 498; advertising for, 850; Clinton, B., and, 1195; Koop and, 1155; in 1920s, 849; in 1950s, 1020; in 1960s, 1082; in 1980s, 1155; Progressivism and, 768; in World War I, 823
Tocqueville, Alexis de, 421, 473
Tojo Hideki, 932
Tokoi, Oskari, 697

Tokyo, in World War II, 937, *938*, 939, 959, 998
Tompkins, Daniel D., 352
Toobin, Jeffrey, 1204
Top Gun (movie), 1158
Top Hat (movie), 905
Topographical Engineers, U.S., 486
Tories, 271, 519
Torrijos-Carter Treaty, 749
Toscanelli, Paolo del Pazzo, 22
Toure, Kwame, 1075
Toure, Sekou, 1075
Tourgee, Albion, 582
tourism, 631–635
Tower Commission, 1161
Townsend, Frances, 893
Townsend National Weekly, 893
Townshend, Charles, 233, 249
Townshend Acts, 233
Townshend Duties, 233–234
Townshend Revenue Acts, 226t
Toynbee Hall, 709, 714
Tract Distribution Society, 461
trade, 9, 223–224; Asian, 332–334; coolie, 609; drug trade, 414–415; foreign, 275, 312, 367; fur trade, 56, 80, 331– 332; Mediterranean, 310–311; NAFTA, 1170, 1193; wampum, 77; World Trade Organization, 1193, 1232. *See also* Atlantic slave trade; World Trade Center
traditional families, 1033
Trafalgar, Battle of, 310
Trail of Tears, 401–403, 436
Transactions (journal), 193
transatlantic lobbying, 158
transatlantic politics, 257

transatlantic trade, 223–224, 309–310

Transcendentalists, 444, 467

Transcontinental Railroad, 505, 508, 514, 593, 609, 687

Transcontinental Treaty, 350, 352

transportation, 369–371; in Gilded Age, 651, 688. *See also* airplanes; cars; railroads

Transportation Act of 1718, 152, 168

"The Treason of the Senate" (Phillips), 792

Treaty of Alliance, 260

Treaty of Amity and Commerce, 260

Treaty of Brest, 824–825

Treaty of Detroit, 1026

Treaty of Easton, 207

Treaty of Ghent, 318

Treaty of Greenville, 298, 311

Treaty of Guadalupe Hidalgo, 486

Treaty of Kanagawa, 479

Treaty of Lancaster, 205

Treaty of Paris, 208, 209, 214, 273–274, 333, 750

Treaty of San Ildefonso, 308

Treaty of San Lorenzo, 298

Treaty of Tordesillas, 23, 40

Treaty of Versailles. *See* Versailles Treaty

Tredegar Iron Works, 498

Trenchard, John, 229

trench warfare, 552, 805, 807, 823–824

Trenton, Battle of, 258

Trespalacios, José Félix, 350–351

triad system, 1011

Triangle Waist Company, 780, 793

triangulation, 1195

trinitite, 970

Trinity, 967, 988

Tripartite Pact, 958

Trollope, Anthony, 469

Troubled Asset Relief Program (TARP), 1236, 1245

Truax, Susanna, *194*

Truman, Harry S., 956, 959, 970; civil rights and, 993–994; communism and, 975; Fair Deal and, 983–984; French Vietnam War and, 1015; Korean War and, 1009; national health insurance and, 1063; Potsdam Conference and, 971–973. *See also* Korean War

Truman Doctrine, 975, 977, 998

Trumball, Lyman, 575, 597

Trumbull, John, 219

Trump, Donald, 1152

trusts: Brandeis and, 674; Progressivism and, 780–784; Rockefeller, J., and, 649; Roosevelt, T., and, 781–782, 792. *See also* Sherman Antitrust Act

Tsenacommacah, 58–61

Tugwell, Rexford, 887, 896–897

Tuner, Henry, 542

Tupperware, 1034, *1034*

Turner, Frederick Jackson, 604, 731

Turner, Henry, 577

Turner, Nat, 462–464, 475, 503

turnpikes, 369

Tuscarora War, 138, 150, 168

Tuskegee Airmen, *947*, 948

TVA. *See* Tennessee Valley Authority

Twain, Mark, 487, 631, 644

Twelfth Amendment, 299, 378

"The Twelve," 32

Twenty-second Amendment, 1044

2000 to present, 1209–1249; concentration of wealth in, 1233–1234; conservatism in, 1220–1230; economic turmoil of, 1231–1237; housing bubble in, 1234–1237; immigration/ immigrants in, 1227–1229, *1228f*; Iraq War, 1215–1220; Obama and, 1237–1246; terrorism in, 1212–1220

Two Treatises on Government (Locke), 229

Tydings-McDuffie Act, 926

Tyler, John, 483, 514

Typee (Melville), 469

UAW. *See* United Automobile Workers

U-boats, 810, 815, 832, 930–931

Ulloa, Antonio de, 236

Ulmanis, Karlis, 697

ULTRA, 930–931

UMW. *See* United Mine Workers

UN. *See* United Nations Organization

Uncas, 78, 80

Uncle Tom's Cabin (Stowe), 507, 675

"Under God," in Pledge of Allegiance, 1045

unemployment: of African Americans, 988; in Great Depression, 880, 884, *902f*, 914

UNIA. *See* Universal Negro Improvement Association
unions, 410–412; Coolidge and, 867; craft unions, 664–666, 670, 674, 899; Democratic Party and, 1145; farmers/farming and, 668–669; in Gilded Age, 662–671; immigration and, 778; in 1950s, 1025–1026; in 1970s, 1145; Progressivism and, 776–780; Reagan, R., and, 1147; Sherman Antitrust Act and, 651; white collar workers and, 657; World War I and, 819–820; World War II and, 946. *See also specific unions*
Union Leagues, 582
United Automobile Workers (UAW), 895, 899, 1026
United Brethren. *See* Moravians
United Colonies of New England, 78, 80
United Fruit Company, 752
United Kingdom. *See* Britain
United Mine Workers (UMW), 667–668, 670, 675, 777
United Nations Organization (UN), 957–958, 959
United Nations Security Council, 980, 1067
United Service Organization (USO), 947
United States, USS, 317
United States Club, 697
United States Information Agency (USIA), 1042–1043

universal manhood suffrage, 522
Universal Negro Improvement Association (UNIA), 842, 856–857, 872
University of Halle, 153
unskilled labor, 410
Upper South, secession in, 525–526
urbanization, 417*f*; African Americans and, 686; in Britain, 685; in Gilded Age, 684–689; Jews and, 1021, 1022; population and, 1032*f*. *See also* suburbanization
urban life, 376–377
urban slavery, 498
urban trade, 224
U.S. Border Patrol, 842, 872
U.S. Colored Troops (USCT), 547, 559
U.S. Forest Service, 785, 786
U.S.-Mexican War, 607
U.S. Steel, 642, 675, 792, 883, 943
U.S. v. E.C. Knight Co., 650, 675
USA PATRIOT Act, 1214, 1244
USCT. *See* U.S. Colored Troops
USIA. *See* United States Information Agency
USO. *See* United Service Organization
Ut, Nick, 1089
Uttamatomakkin, 48

VA. *See* Veterans Administration
Valentino, Rudolph, 841, 844, 872, 873
values issues, by Bush, G.W., 1223

value systems, 460
Van Buren, Martin, 378, 380, 391, 400
Vandenberg, Arthur, 975
Vanderbilt, Consuelo, 653
Vanderbilt, Cornelius, 647
Van Rennselaer, Rennselaer, 400, 406
Van Rennselaer, Stephen, 314
Vanzetti, Bartolomeo, 850–851
Vargas, Diego de, 117–118
Vaudreuil, Pierre de Rigaud, 206
vegetarianism, 452
Venezuela, Britain and, 733, 750
Vergennes, Comte de, 260, 285
Verrazzano, Giovanni da, 26
Versailles Treaty, 788, 831, 833, 834–835, 928
vertical integration, in Gilded Age, 649
Vesey, Denmark, 344, 464
Vespucci, Amerigo, 25
Vetch, Samuel, 149
Veterans Administration (VA), 1023
Veterans Emergency Housing Act, 984
Veterans of Future Wars, 926
veto, 380–381
Vial, Pedro, 330
vice-admiralty courts, 156, 168, 233
Victoria (queen), 457
Vietnam, 1089–1125; Domino Theory and, 1093; Eisenhower and, 1044, 1093; environment of, 1102; Geneva Conference and, 1007, 1016, 1044; Kennedy, John, and, 1093, 1095; Khrushchev and, 1095;

nuclear weapons in, 1099

Vietnam War, *1088*; background for, 1092–1097; Cambodia and, 1111, 1119; China and, 1107; Containment Policy and, 1103; deaths in, 1098*f*, 1101, 1111; draft in, 1103–1104, 1111; end of, 1112–1113, 1119, 1160; Goldwater and, 1099; helicopters in, *1101*, 1113; Johnson, L., and, 1067, 1097–1100; Kissinger and, 1112; 1964-1967, 1097–1104; in 1968, 1104–1110; Nixon, R., and, 1091, 1110–1113; pacifists and, 1103; protests against, 1102–1104, *1103*, 1106–1107, *1108*, 1111; science and technology and, 1069; Tet Offensive in, 1104–1105, 1118; troop levels in, 1098*f*. *See also* French Vietnam War

View of the Plundering and Burning of the City of Grymross (Davies), *210*

vigilance leagues, 615

Viguerie, Richard, 1127

Villa, Francisco "Pancho," 799, 800, *814*, 814–815, 832

Village Quartet (Lawrence), 840

A Vindication of the Rights of Women (Wollstonecraft), 456

violence: abolition and, 454; collective, 614–617; ethnic, 616; mob, 236; in Northern Plains, 133–135; racial, 616; Reconstruction and,

589–591. *See also* crime; nonviolence; riots; war

Virginia, 58–61, 303

Virginia Company of London, 45, 48, 58–61, 80

Virginia Plan, 280

VISTA. *See* Volunteers in Service to America

Vizcaíno, Sebastián, 52

Voice of America, 1042

Volcker, Paul, 1136, 1151

Volstead Act, 890

Voltaire, 229, 253

Volunteers in Service to America (VISTA), 1064

volunteer state militia, 263

von Borcke, Heros, 550

von Clausewitz, Carl, 547

von Moltke, Helmuth, 551, 559

von Neumann, Jon, 967

von Ribbentrop, Joachim, 921

von Steuben, Friedrich Wilhelm, 264, 269, 285

voting, 377–378; by African Americans, 378, 576–577, 744, 760, 775, 1063, 1072*t*; Progressivism and, 774–776, 776*f*; turnout, 471*f*; for women, 577, 761, 788–789, *789*, 793, 820–821, 833

Voting Rights Act of 1965, 1063, 1083, 1134, 1152

WACS. *See* Women's Army Corps

wages: conservatism and, 1132; in Gilded Age, 644, 655, 657, 659–661; Mexicans and, 691; New Deal and, 883; Nixon, R., and, 1117; in textile

industry, 691; for women, 698; in World War II, 944. *See also* minimum wage

Wagner, Honus, 704, *704*

Wagner, Robert, 895

Wagner Act. *See* National Labor Relations Act

Wake Forest, 447

Walden (Thoreau), 467

Walker, David, 465–466, 475, 503, 514

Walker, William, 406, 436

Walking Purchase, 187

Wallace, George C., 1109, 1131

Wallace, Henry A., 892, 955

wampum, 66, 77

war: African Americans and, 272–273; debts, 275; European, 312–313; just, 112; mourning, 15, 40, 90; Native Americans and, 271–272, 297–298; naval, 266–268, 316–317; in South, 268–271; technology of, 17–18, 31. *See also specific wars*

Ward, Aaron Montgomery, 652–653, 674

Ward, Edward, 165

war guilt clause, 828

War Industries Board, 819

Warmoth, Henry, 590, 597

Warner, Charles Dudley, 644

Warner Bros., 1186

War of 1812, 313–320

War of Jenkins' Ear, 190, 214

War on Poverty, 1061–1064, 1116–1117, 1152

War Production Board (WPB), 943

War Relocation Authority, 954

Warren, Earl, 1039

Warren, Mercy Otis, 281, 281
Warsaw, 972
Washington, Booker T., 742, 771, 771–772
Washington, George, 205, 214, 241, 249, 262, 297, 299
Washington Naval Conference, 872
Washington Post, 1120
WASPS. See Women's Air Force Service Pilots
Watergate, 1090, 1112, 1118–1121, 1147
water power, 367–369
Water Quality Act, 1079
Waters, Muddy, 1080
Watkins, Sherron, 1209
Watt, James, 368, 391, 1152
WAVES. See Women Accepted for Voluntary Emergency Naval Service
Wayne, "Mad" Anthony, 298, 321
WCTU. See Women's Christian Temperance Union
wealth, concentration of: in Gilded Age, 649–651; in 1980s, 1151, 1186; 2000 to present, 1233–1234, 1244
Wealth Against Commonwealth (Lloyd), 674, 675
weapons, 57; chemical weapons, in World War I, 806, 823–824; germ warfare, 827; mass production of, 945–946. See also guns; nuclear weapons
weapons of mass destruction (WMD), 1216, 1218
Weaver, James B., 715
Weber, Max, 1035

Webster, Daniel, 455, 475
Webster, Ebenezer, 361
Webster v. Reproductive Services of Missouri, 1175
wedge issues, 1145, 1221, 1228
Weems, Mason Locke, 342
Weinberg, Jack, 1051
Weld, Theodore Dwight, 454, 475
welfare capitalism, 777
Welfare Reform bill, 1195, 1203
Welles, Gideon, 549, 559
Wells, H.G., 661, 702
Wells, Ida B., 745, 772, 772–773
Wesley, John, 198–199, 214, 452, 475
West, 486–487, 606, 611–616; military industrial complex in, 988–990; in post-Cold War, 1190
West, Benjamin, 219
Western Europe, in fifteenth century, 16–19
Western Federation of Miners (WFM), 617, 777–778
westerns (genre), 614, 1029
West Indies, 275, 500
Westmoreland, William, 1099, 1101
Westo, 112
West Side Story, 1037
wetbacks, 991
Weyler, Valeriano, 734–735, 750
WFM. See Western Federation of Miners
whaling, 386–387
wheat farms, 619
Wheatley, Phyllis, 202, 214
Wheelock, Eleazar, 203

Whig Party, 158, 232, 249, 429–430, 436, 471–472
Whiplash (television program), 616
Whipple (prince), 277
Whiskey Rebellion, 297, 321
White, George H., 776
White, Harry Dexter, 948
White, Henry, 828
White, John, 54, 80
White, Walter, 953
White, William Allen, 621, 636, 716, 762
white backlash: to Black Power, 1072; to Great Society, 1065
white collar workers, 416, 656–658, 658, 1035–1036
Whitefield, George, 198, 200, 202, 214
white flight, 1021
White House Plumbers, 1112, 1118
white male suffrage, 377
white supremacy, 107, 571
Whitewater, 1196
Whitman, Walt, 469, 470, 475
Whitney, Eli, 336, 367
The Who (rock 'n roll band), 1080
Whole Earth Catalog, 1069, 1084
Whyte, William H., Jr., 1035
WIDF. See Women's International Democratic Federation
Wieland (Brown, C. B.), 343
Wieland, Christoph, 265
Wigner, Eugene, 942
Wilber, Charles Dana, 613
The Wild Ones (movie), 1037
Wilhelm (Kaiser), 809, 815, 827

Wilhelm, Kaiser, 613
Wilkes, Charles, 247, 408–409, 414, 436, 538, 559
Wilkes, John, 236–237
Wilkinson, James, 311, 330, 356
Willard, Emma, 341, 356
Willard, Frances, 711, 714
William of Orange (prince), 120
Williams, Robert, 1043
Williams, Roger, 73, 80
Williams v. Mississippi, 760, 775, 792
William V (prince), 266
Willkie, Wendell, 931, 957
Wilmot, David, 504
Wilson, Brian, 1081
Wilson, Edith, 834
Wilson, Richard, 1077
Wilson, Sloan, 1035
Wilson, Woodrow, 612, 832; African Americans and, 771; Fourteen Points by, 827, 829, 832; Latin America and, 813–815; trusts and, 782; Versailles Treaty and, 834–835; World War I and, 761, 787, 793, 809
Winston-Salem, 687
Winthrop, John, 72–73, 80
Winthrop, John, Jr., 113
Wise, Henry, 512, 514
witch hunts, 93, 121–122
WMD. See weapons of mass destruction
Wobblies, 617, 778, 787
Wolfe, James, 208, 214, 219
Wolfe, Tom, 1130
Wolfowitz, Paul, 1214
wolf packs, of U-boats, 930–931
Wollstonecraft, Mary, 341, 356, 456, 475

Woman in the Nineteenth Century (Fuller, M.), 441
Woman's Land Army, 819
women, 341–342, 423–425; African Americans, 767; in Cold War, 985–986, 986; enslaved, 424; in Gilded Age, 657, 661–662, 705, 711; as immigrants, 697, 701; KKK and, 853; in Knights of Labor, 666; ladies, 424, 461; in middle class, 705, 711; migration and, 606–607; New Deal and, 906–907; in 1920s, 859–861; in 1950s, 1033–1035; in 1980s, 1186–1187; as pacifists, 790–793, 791; piecework by, 659, 661; pro-Confederate, 531; in Progressivism, 766–768, 780, 788–789; revivalism and, 200–201; Revolutionary War and, 276–277; rights of, 451, 455–458; Social Security and, 898; voting for, 577, 761, 788–789, 789, 793, 820–821, 833; wages for, 698; work/workers and, 657, 661–662; in World War I, 820–821; in World War II, 920, 947, 950. See also feminism; specific women's organizations
Women Accepted for Voluntary Emergency Naval Service (WAVES), 947
Women's Air Force Service Pilots (WASPS), 947

Women's Army Corps (WACS), 947
Women's Christian Temperance Union (WCTU), 683, 711, 714, 715, 768
Women's International Democratic Federation (WIDF), 986
Women's International League for Peace and Freedom, 791, 868, 926
women's liberation, 1078
Women's Peace Party, 790
Women's Political Council (WPC), 1041
Wood, Jethro, 367
Wood, Leonard, 739
Wood, William, 73
Woodstock Music Festival, 1083
Woodward, Bob, 1120
Woolman, John, 210, 214
Worcester v. Georgia, 401
work/workers, 410–412; Coolidge and, 867; enslaved, 498; foreign-born, 412–416; in France, 670; in Gilded Age, 655–662; in 1950s, 1025–1026; in post-Cold War, 1186–1188; white collar, 416; women and, 657, 661–662; in World War II, 943. See also labor movement; slavery; unions
workers' compensation, 779
Workers of the World (IWW), 778
working class, 375
"Workingman's Advocate" (Evans, G. H.), 412
Workingman's Party, 412, 694
Works Progress Administration (WPA),

897–898, 897t, 908, 914

World Bank, 1232

World Christian Fundamentals Association, 862–863

World Columbian Exposition, 631

WorldCom, 1232

The World is Flat (Friedman, T.), 1233, 1244

World Trade Center: bombing of, 1199, 1202. *See also* 9/11

World Trade Organization, 1193, 1232

World War I, 798–839; African Americans in, 787–788, 820–821; chemical weapons in, 806, 823–824; communism and, 828–833; deaths in, 803, 806–807, 807t; Germany in, 804–805, 806, 815–816, 825–826; immigration/immigrants and, 818; influenza pandemic during, 827–828, 833; IWW and, 818, 820; Latin America and, 813–815; movies for, 817; national security in, 811–812; neutrality in, 812–813; origins of, 803–805; pacifists in, 790–793, *791*; Progressivism and, 786–793; Russia in, 824–825; Socialist Party in, 818; trench warfare in, 805, *807*, 823–824; U.S. response to, 809–810; Versailles Treaty and, 788, 831, 833, 834–835; Wilson, W., and,

761, 787, 793, 809; women in, 820–821

World War II, 920–965; African Americans in, 947, 948–949, 952–953; conservatism after, 955–956; deaths in, 924t; draft in, 947–949, 958; European theater of, 939–940; France in, 929, 958; Germany in, 921, 928–929, 939–940; Holocaust and, 940–943, *941*; industrialization in, 942–949, 943t; isolationism and, 925–926; Italy in, 921, 926–927, 939; Japanese-American internment in, 953–955, *954*, 959; Japan in, 932–934, 935–939, 973; military production in, 943t; Native Americans in, 950–952; nuclear weapons in, 959, 960, 973; Pacific theater of, 935–939; pacifists in, 926; Poland in, 929, *972*; Roosevelt, F., and, 925–926; Soviet Union in, 924, 939–940; Suez Canal in, 939; women in, *920*, 947, 950

World Wide Web, 1183

Wounded Knee, 614, 1077

Wovoka (prophet), 630

WPA. *See* Works Progress Administration

WPB. *See* War Production Board

WPC. *See* Women's Political Council

Wright, Carrol D., 661

Wright, Fanny, 412, 472, 475

Wright, Frances, 436

XYZ Affair, 301

Yalta Summit Conference, 959, *960*, 971

Yamamoto Isoroku, 933

Yamasee War, 140, 168

Yamato (ship), 945

Yellow Bird, 631

yellow journalism, 735

Yellowstone National Park, 631

Yeltsin, Boris, 1177, 1197

Yeomen, 335, 356

Yerkes, Robert M., 818

YMCA, 769, 789, 822–823

Yom Kippur War, 1115–1116

Yorktown, Battle of, *272*

Yosemite National Park, 785–786, 793

Yosemite Valley, 631, 633

Young, Brigham, 449, 475

Young Democrats, 428

Young Ladies' Missionary Society, 461

Young Lords, 1077

Young Plan, 873

youth: in 1950s, 1036–1038; in 1960s, 1079–1084; Progressivism and, 767–768. *See also* child labor

Yugoslavia, 831, 1172, 1177–1178, 1198

Zaghlul, Sa'd, 831

Zavala, Lorenzo de, 397, 407, 436

zemis (carved idols), 22

Zenger, John Peter, 191

Zhou Enlai, 1114

Zimmerman, Arthur, 815, 832

Zuni (tribe), 10